ESSENTIAL MATHEMATICS FOR
ECONOMIC ANALYSIS

Visit the *Essential Mathematics for Economic Analysis, second edition* Companion Website at
www.pearsoned.co.uk/sydsaeter to find valuable student learning material including:

- Multiple choice questions to test your learning
- Excel supplement with exercises

PEARSON
Education

We work with leading authors to develop the
strongest educational materials in economics,
bringing cutting-edge thinking and best learning
practice to a global market.

Under a range of well-known imprints, including
Financial Times Prentice Hall, we craft high quality print
and electronic publications which help readers to
understand and apply their content,
whether studying or at work.

To find out more about the complete range of our
publishing, please visit us on the World Wide Web at:
www.pearsoned.co.uk

ESSENTIAL MATHEMATICS FOR
ECONOMIC ANALYSIS

SECOND EDITION

KNUT SYDSÆTER

AND

PETER HAMMOND

FT Prentice Hall
FINANCIAL TIMES

An imprint of **Pearson Education**
Harlow, England • London • New York • Boston • San Francisco • Toronto • Sydney • Singapore • Hong Kong
Tokyo • Seoul • Taipei • New Delhi • Cape Town • Madrid • Mexico City • Amsterdam • Munich • Paris • Milan

Pearson Education Limited
Edinburgh Gate
Harlow
Essex CM20 2JE
England

and Associated Companies throughout the world

Visit us on the World Wide Web at:
www.pearsoned.co.uk

First published by Prentice-Hall, Inc., 1995
This edition 2006

© Prentice-Hall, Inc. 1995
© Knut Sydsæter and Peter Hammond 2002, 2006

ISBN 0 273 68180 X

British Library Cataloguing-in-Publication Data
A catalogue record for this book is available from the British Library

Library of Congress Cataloging-in-Publication Data
A catalog record for this book is available from the Library of Congress

10 9 8 7 6 5 4 3 2 1
09 08 07 06 05

Typeset by Matematisk Sats, Norway, and Arne Strøm in Times Roman 10/13
Printed and bound by Ashford Colour Press Ltd., Gosport

The publisher's policy is to use paper manufactured from sustainable forests.

CONTENTS

Supporting resources

Visit www.pearsoned.co.uk/sydsaeter to find valuable online resources

Companion Website for students
- Multiple choice questions to test your learning
- Excel supplement with exercises

For instructors
- Complete, downloadable Instructor's Manual, including answers to even numbered problems
- Excel supplement with answers to exercises in Excel spreadsheets
- Additional exam style problems (with answers) which can be set as student assignments

Also: The Companion Website provides the following features:
- Search tool to help locate specific items of content
- E-mail results and profile tools to send results of quizzes to instructors
- Online help and support to assist with website usage and troubleshooting

For more information please contact your local Pearson Education sales representative or visit www.pearsoned.co.uk/sydsaeter

PREFACE

Purpose

Modern students of economics need several important mathematical tools. These include calculus for functions of one and several variables, as well as a basic understanding of multivariable optimization problems with or without constraints. Linear algebra is also used to some extent in economic theory, and even more in econometrics. Such tools are helpful, even essential, for upper-level undergraduate courses not only in economic theory, but also in many branches of applied economics, including public finance, industrial organization, and labour economics.

Experience suggests that teachers in these different areas of economics would like to assign students recently published articles to read. They find, however, that the mathematical preparation of the students is inadequate for even some of the less technical "applied" literature. Students who may well have completed courses in intermediate micro- and macroeconomics quite successfully will often not have seen the use of much or even any calculus in economic analysis. Moreover, many students' knowledge of calculus may barely extend beyond functions of a single variable, and they are often unused to seeing calculus applied to economic problems.

The purpose of *Essential Mathematics for Economic Analysis* is, therefore, to help students acquire the mathematical skills they need in order to read the less technical literature, at least. As the title suggests, this is a mathematics book with the material arranged to allow progressive learning of mathematical topics. If the student acquires some economic insights and intuitions at the same time, so much the better. At times, we do emphasize economics not only to motivate a mathematical topic, but also to help acquire mathematical intuition. Obviously, understanding our economic discussions will be easier with a certain very rudimentary understanding of economics and of what economics should be about. It should be possible, nevertheless, to study the material even before embarking on a course in elementary economics.

In particular, this is not a book about economics or even about mathematical economics. We expect students to learn economic theory systematically in other courses, based on other books. We will have succeeded if they can concentrate on the economics in these courses, having mastered beforehand the relevant mathematical tools we present.

Special Features

This is by no means the first textbook written with the foregoing aims in mind. But it benefits, we believe, from the way it has been put together. One author (Sydsæter) has a rather rare position as a Professor of Mathematics in a Department of Economics. He has many years experience in teaching material of this kind to students in Norway and in Zimbabwe. In fact, much of the material in this book originally appeared in and has been translated from textbooks in Norwegian that have been widely used throughout Scandinavia. The other author (Hammond) has taught and done research in economic theory on both sides of the Atlantic, and has long experience in seeing the different ways in which mathematical tools are used in actual economic analysis. For several years he also taught courses in mathematics for economists, primarily in the Department of Economics at Stanford University.

Over the course of these years of teaching, we have accumulated numerous worked examples as well as problems for the student to solve. A large selection of these is included in the book. We are well aware that we ourselves learned much of the material we want to teach here from numerous problems and examples. Most of the examples in the book are formulated as problems based on the previous theory, and subsequently answers are supplied. Students are strongly advised to attempt to solve these examples themselves, before looking at the solutions we suggest.

All sections of the book conclude with problems, often quite numerous. There are also many review problems at the end of each chapter. Such a large number of problems is standard in mathematics textbooks at this level, though apparently not in books on mathematics for economists. Answers to all odd numbered problems (and to all problems in Chapters 1 and 2) are provided at the end of the book, sometimes with many steps of the solution laid out. The remaining answers are available in a separate *Instructor's Manual*, which instructors who adopt the book for their course may request from the publishers.

One more feature of the problems is worth discussing. This concerns the apparently excessive notation that appears in some of them—for example, where an expression such as $An_0^\alpha a^b$ could be replaced by a single constant. The whole point of such problems is to help the student learn to see when such replacements are possible and useful. (Often, the notation in these problems is taken directly from standard economic textbooks, or from published economic research.)

Topics Covered

It will be apparent that we have included a lot of rather elementary material in the earlier chapters of this book. In fact, experience suggests that it is quite difficult to start a book like this at a level that is really too elementary. These days, in many parts of the world, students who enter college or university and specialize in economics have an enormous range of mathematical backgrounds and aptitudes. These range from, at the low end, an at best shaky command of elementary algebra, up to real facility in the calculus of functions of one variable. Furthermore, for all too many economics students, it may be some years since their last formal mathematics course. Accordingly, as we move toward mathematics being essential for specialist studies in economics, we feel the need to provide as much quite elementary material as is reasonably possible. Our aim here is to give those with weaker mathematical backgrounds the chance to get started, and even to acquire a little confidence with some easy problems they can really solve on their own.

In the accompanying *Instructor's Manual*, we have provided some diagnostic test material that teachers may wish to use so that they and the students can assess together what has already been mastered at the start of the course. Although the teacher will obviously want to adjust the starting point and pace of a course to the students' abilities, it is perhaps even more important that each individual student appreciates his or her own strengths and weaknesses, and receives some help and guidance in overcoming the latter. Thus, it is likely that weaker students will appreciate the opportunity to work through the early more elementary chapters.

The book is a revised and somewhat shorter version of our earlier text, *Mathematics for Economic Analysis*, published by Prentice Hall in 1995. It has also benefited from many changes prepared for a special edition of that earlier book for use in Zimbabwe. We have omitted much of the more advanced material, preferring to defer it to a successor volume to be entitled *Further Mathematics for Economic Analysis*. We have also tried to present the remaining material in a more accessible way, and have added numerous new problems.

After the introductory material in Chapters 1 to 3, a fairly leisurely treatment of single-variable differential calculus is contained in Chapters 4 to 8. This is followed by integration in Chapter 9, and by the application to interest rates and present values in Chapter 10. This may be as far as some elementary courses will go. However, we have already suggested the importance for budding economists of multivariable calculus (Chapters 11 and 12), optimization theory with and without constraints (Chapters 13 and 14), and the algebra of matrices and determinants (Chapters 15 and 16). In some sense Chapters 11 to 16, starting with multivariable calculus, represent the heart of the book. Students with a thorough grounding in single variable calculus can probably afford to concentrate on these chapters. From the first 10 chapters of the book, they may only need to go fairly quickly over some special topics such as elasticity and conditions for global optimization that are often not thoroughly covered in standard calculus courses.

The ordering of the chapters is fairly logical, we believe, with each chapter building on material in previous chapters. The main exception concerns Chapters 15 and 16 on linear algebra, most of which could be fitted in almost anywhere after Chapter 3. Indeed, in our earlier text, *Mathematics for Economic Analysis*, linear algebra did precede multivariate calculus, thus suggesting that Chapters 15 and 16 could be taught immediately after Chapter 10.

Key Concepts and Techniques

The less ambitious student can concentrate on learning the key concepts and techniques of each chapter. Often, these appear boxed and/or in colour, in order to emphasize their importance. Problems are essential to the learning process, and the easier ones should definitely be attempted. Students who are more ambitious, or are led on by more demanding teachers, can try the more difficult problems. They can also study the material in smaller print. The latter often provides an explanation of why certain techniques are appropriate, or offer proofs of results. Indeed, wherever possible, we encourage students to ask why results are true, and why problems should be tackled in certain ways, and so we have tried to offer explanations at an appropriate level. We admit that whereas only a minority of students can be expected to understand this material fully, some others may also be interested in gaining at least a little additional insight into the mathematics they are studying, and this is an interest we feel should certainly be encouraged.

Another reason for including such material is that it may make the book more suitable for teachers in mathematics departments who would like to arrange special courses, or sections of courses, for students who definitely intend to apply mathematics to economics rather than to the engineering or physical sciences. In fact, in comparison with many contemporary calculus textbooks used for courses in mathematics departments, it seems that we actually provide somewhat more explanation and proofs.

The most able students, especially those intending to undertake postgraduate study in economics, will benefit from a fuller explanation of some topics than we have been able to provide in this volume. On a few occasions, therefore, we take the liberty of referring to our forthcoming volume, *Further Mathematics for Economic Analysis* (usually referred to simply as FMEA). In particular, FMEA will offer a proper treatment of topics like second-order conditions for optimization, and the concavity or convexity of functions of more than two variables—topics that we think go rather beyond what is really "essential" for all economics students.

Acknowledgements

Over the years we have received help from so many colleagues, lecturers at other institutions, and also students, that it is impractical to mention them all. Naturally, all the acknowledgements we made in our earlier book apply to this new one. We concentrate here on those who have been particularly helpful as we have prepared this new book.

Arne Strøm, also at the Department of Economics of the University of Oslo, remains an indispensable member of our production team. His exceptional ability to spot errors and inaccuracies has been of enormous help. Several sections of Chapter 10 have benefited from material written for a Swedish edition by Håkan Lyckeborg.

For arranging production and publication, apart from our very helpful editors, we should particularly like to thank Arve Michaelsen at PrePress Oslo and copy editor Jennifer Dunford at Pearson Education for their exceptional diligence.

To all the many unnamed persons and institutions who have helped us in making this text possible, including some whose comments on our earlier book were forwarded to us by the publisher, we would like to express our deep appreciation and gratitude, combined with the hope that they may find the resulting product reasonably satisfactory, and even of benefit to their students. That, we can all agree, is what really matters in the end.

Knut Sydsæter and Peter Hammond

Oslo and Stanford, June 2001

Preface to the Second Edition

We are gratified by the number of students and their instructors in many countries who appear to have found the first edition useful. Given the opportunity and encouragement to produce a revised edition, we have gone through the text thoroughly once again. This has resulted in numerous improvements, many of which may not be immediately obvious.

Following requests from several adopters, the main change is the inclusion of an extra last chapter (17) on Linear Programming. This is a minor revision of a chapter that had appeared in our earlier text, *Mathematics for Economic Analysis*. Indeed, with the recent publication of *Further Mathematics for Economic Analysis* (FMEA) and now the addition of this extra chapter, virtually all the topics covered in that earlier text appear in either this new edition, or as parts of FMEA.

Most of the earlier 16 chapters are largely unchanged, except for a few extra problems, as well as some rearrangement and improvements to existing problems. We mention a few more significant changes below.

In Chapter 7, the old Section 7.1 has been split into two, with Section 7.1 dealing with the mathematical theory and Section 7.2 with economic applications. Some new problems are supplied. In the subsection on Newton's method (in Section 7.10) there is a brief statement of two convergence results.

In Chapter 8, Example 8.3.3 is new and deals with a typical comparative static exercise where the first-order conditions are differentiated w.r.t. a parameter. Two new problems ask students to use the same technique.

In Chapter 12, the old Section 12.3 has been split into two, and 12.4.2 is a new comparative static example.

In Chapter 13, the old Section 13.1 has been split into two. The new Section 13.1 limits itself to necessary condition for extreme points, with a new economic Example 13.1.5. Section 13.2 considers sufficient conditions. Several new economic problems are included in this chapter.

Chapter 14 has a few new problems in nonlinear programming.

Finally, it is our pleasant duty to acknowledge helpful input from many sources enabling us to improve the first edition. We start by thanking Fred Böker at the University of Göttingen, who not only translated the first edition into German, but showed exceptional diligence in paying close attention to the mathematical details of what he was translating. We appreciate the resulting large number of valuable suggestions for improvements and corrections that he has provided. We are also grateful to Reinhard John at Bonn University for several useful comments. Barry van der Leur and other Dutch adopters have also been particularly helpful in pointing out errors and misprints. Some of the new economic examples have been inspired by Vidar Christiansen at the Department of Economics at the University of Oslo.

Last but not least, our colleague and friend Arne Strøm has once again provided indispensable assistance in preparing the TeX and graphics computer files used to typeset the book (building on the excellent work done by Arve Michaelsen for the first edition). At the same time, he has also had numerous useful suggestions for improving the text.

Knut Sydsæter and Peter Hammond

Oslo and Stanford, June 2005

1

INTRODUCTORY TOPICS I:
ALGEBRA

Is it right I ask;
is it even prudence;
to bore thyself and bore the students?
—Mephistopheles to Faust *(From Goethe's Faust.)*

This introductory chapter basically deals with elementary algebra, but we also briefly consider a few other topics that you might need to review.

Tests reveal that even students with a good background in mathematics often benefit from a brief review of what they learned in the past. These students should browse through the material and do some of the less simple problems. Those with a weaker background in mathematics, or who have been away from mathematics for a long time, should read the text carefully and then do most of the problems. Those who have considerable difficulties with this chapter should turn to a more elementary book on algebra.

Answers to all problems in this chapter are given in the answer section.

1.1 The Real Numbers

We start by reviewing some important facts and concepts concerning numbers. The basic numbers are

$$1, \ 2, \ 3, \ 4, \ \ldots \qquad \textbf{(natural numbers)}$$

also called positive integers. Here 2, 4, 6, 8, ... are the **even numbers**, and 1, 3, 5, 7, ... are the **odd numbers**. The positive integers, together with 0 and the negative integers -1, $-2, -3, -4, \ldots$, make up the integers, which are

$$0, \ \pm 1, \ \pm 2, \ \pm 3, \ \pm 4, \ \ldots \qquad \textbf{(integers)}$$

They can be represented on a **number line** like the one shown in Fig. 1 (where the arrow gives the direction in which the numbers increase).

Figure 1 The number line

The **rational numbers** are those like 3/5 that can be written in the form a/b, where a and b are both integers. An integer n is also a rational number, because $n = n/1$. Other examples of rational numbers are

$$\frac{1}{2}, \quad \frac{11}{70}, \quad \frac{125}{7}, \quad -\frac{10}{11}, \quad 0 = \frac{0}{1}, \quad -19, \quad -1.26 = -\frac{126}{100}.$$

The rational numbers can also be represented on the number line. Imagine that we first mark 1/2 and all the multiples of 1/2. Then we mark 1/3 and all the multiples of 1/3, and so forth. You can be excused for thinking that "finally" there will be no more places left for putting more points on the line. But in fact this is quite wrong. The ancient Greeks already understood that "holes" would remain in the number line even after all the rational numbers had been marked off. For instance, there are no integers p and q such that $\sqrt{2} = p/q$. Hence, $\sqrt{2}$ is not a rational number. (Euclid proved this fact in about 300 B.C.)

The rational numbers are therefore insufficient for measuring all possible lengths, let alone areas and volumes. This deficiency can be remedied by extending the concept of numbers to allow for the so-called **irrational numbers**. This extension can be carried out rather naturally by using decimal notation for numbers, as explained below.

The way most people write numbers today is called the **decimal system**, or the **base 10 system**. It is a positional system with 10 as the base number. Every natural number can be written using only the symbols, 0, 1, 2, ..., 9, that are called **digits**. You will note that "digit" also means "finger," or "thumb," and that most humans have 10 digits. The positional system defines each combination of digits as a sum of exponents of 10. For example,

$$1984 = 1 \cdot 10^3 + 9 \cdot 10^2 + 8 \cdot 10^1 + 4 \cdot 10^0$$

Each natural number can be uniquely expressed in this manner. With the use of the signs + and −, all integers, positive or negative, can be written in the same way. Decimal points also enable us to express rational numbers other than natural numbers. For example,

$$3.1415 = 3 + 1/10^1 + 4/10^2 + 1/10^3 + 5/10^4$$

Rational numbers that can be written exactly using only a finite number of decimal places are called **finite decimal fractions**.

Each finite decimal fraction is a rational number, but not every rational number can be written as a finite decimal fraction. We also need to allow for **infinite decimal fractions** such as

$$100/3 = 33.333\ldots$$

where the three dots indicate that the decimal 3 recurs indefinitely.

If the decimal fraction is a rational number, then it will always be **recurring** or **periodic**—that is, after a certain place in the decimal expansion, it either stops or continues to repeat a finite sequence of digits. For example, $11/70 = 0.1\,\underbrace{571428}\,\underbrace{571428}\,5\ldots$ with the sequence of six digits 571428 repeated infinitely often.

The definition of a real number follows from the previous discussion. We define a **real number** as an arbitrary infinite decimal fraction. Hence, a real number is of the form $x = \pm m.\alpha_1\alpha_2\alpha_3\ldots$, where m is an integer, and α_n ($n = 1, 2\ldots$) is an infinite series of digits, each in the range 0 to 9. We have already identified the periodic decimal fractions with the rational numbers. In addition, there are infinitely many new numbers given by the nonperiodic decimal fractions. These are called **irrational numbers.** Examples include

$$\sqrt{2}, \quad -\sqrt{5}, \quad \pi, \quad 2^{\sqrt{2}}, \quad \text{and} \quad 0.12112111211112\ldots .$$

We mentioned earlier that each rational number can be represented by a point on the number line. But not all points on the number line represent rational numbers. It is as if the irrational numbers "close up" the remaining holes on the number line after all the rational numbers have been positioned. Hence, an unbroken and endless straight line with an origin and a positive unit of length is a satisfactory model for the real numbers. We frequently state that there is a *one-to-one correspondence* between the real numbers and the points on a number line. Often, too, one speaks of the "real line" rather than the "number line'.

The set of rational numbers as well as the set of irrational numbers are said to be "dense" on the number line. This means that between any two different real numbers, irrespective of how close they are to each other, we can always find both a rational and an irrational number—in fact, we can always find infinitely many of each.

When applied to the real numbers, the four basic arithmetic operations always result in a real number. The only exception is that we cannot divide by 0.[1]

$$\frac{p}{0} \text{ is not defined for any real number } p$$

This is very important and should not be confused with $0/a = 0$, for all $a \neq 0$. Notice especially that $0/0$ is not defined as any real number. For example, if a car requires 60 litres of fuel to go 600 kilometres, then its fuel consumption is $60/600 = 10$ litres per 100 kilometres. However, if told that a car uses 0 litres of fuel to go 0 kilometres, we know nothing about its fuel consumption; $0/0$ is completely undefined.

---

[1] "Black holes are where God divided by zero." (Steven Wright)

1. Which of the following statements are true?

    (a) 1984 is a natural number.   (b) −5 is to the right of −3 on the number line.

    (c) −13 is a natural number.   (d) There is no natural number that is not rational.

    (e) 3.1415 is not rational.   (f) The sum of two irrational numbers is irrational.

    (g) −3/4 is rational.   (h) All rational numbers are real.

2. Explain why the infinite decimal expansion 1.01001000100001000001 . . . is not a rational number.

1.2 Integer Powers

You should recall that we often write 3^4 instead of the product $3 \cdot 3 \cdot 3 \cdot 3$, that $\frac{1}{2} \cdot \frac{1}{2} \cdot \frac{1}{2} \cdot \frac{1}{2} \cdot \frac{1}{2}$ can be written as $\left(\frac{1}{2}\right)^5$, and that $(-10)^3 = (-10)(-10)(-10) = -1000$. If a is any number and n is any natural number, then a^n is defined by

$$a^n = \underbrace{a \cdot a \cdot \ldots \cdot a}_{n \text{ factors}}$$

In fact, a^n is called the **nth** power of **a** ; here a is the **base**, and n is the **exponent**. We have, for example, $a^1 = a$, $a^2 = a \cdot a$, $x^4 = x \cdot x \cdot x \cdot x$, and

$$\left(\frac{p}{q}\right)^5 = \frac{p}{q} \cdot \frac{p}{q} \cdot \frac{p}{q} \cdot \frac{p}{q} \cdot \frac{p}{q}$$

where $a = p/q$, and $n = 5$.

We usually drop the multiplication sign if this is unlikely to create misunderstanding. For example, we write abc instead of $a \cdot b \cdot c$, but it is safest to keep the multiplication sign in $1.05^3 = 1.05 \cdot 1.05 \cdot 1.05$. Of course, $a^1 = a$.

We define further

$$a^0 = 1 \qquad \text{for } a \neq 0$$

Thus, $5^0 = 1$, $(-16.2)^0 = 1$, and $(x \cdot y)^0 = 1$ (if $x \cdot y \neq 0$). But if $a = 0$, we do not assign a numerical value to a^0; the expression 0^0 is *undefined*.

We also need to define powers with negative exponents. What do we mean by 3^{-2}? It turns out that the sensible definition is to set 3^{-2} equal to $1/3^2 = 1/9$. In general,

$$a^{-n} = \frac{1}{a^n}$$

whenever n is a natural number and $a \neq 0$. In particular, $a^{-1} = 1/a$. In this way we have defined a^x for all integers x.

Calculators usually have a power key, denoted by $\boxed{y^x}$ or $\boxed{a^x}$, which can be used to compute powers. Make sure you know how to use it by computing 2^3 (which is 8), 3^2 (which is 9), and 25^{-3} (which is 0.000064).

PROBLEMS FOR SECTION 1.2

1. Compute:

   (a) 10^3 (b) $(-0.3)^2$ (c) 4^{-2} (d) $(0.1)^{-1}$

2. Write as powers of 2:

   (a) 4   (b) 1   (c) 64   (d) 1/16

3. Write as powers:

   (a) $15 \cdot 15 \cdot 15$ (b) $\left(-\frac{1}{3}\right)\left(-\frac{1}{3}\right)\left(-\frac{1}{3}\right)$ (c) $\frac{1}{10}$ (d) 0.0000001

   (e) $t\,t\,t\,t\,t\,t$ (f) $(a-b)(a-b)(a-b)$ (g) $a\,a\,b\,b\,b\,b$ (h) $(-a)(-a)(-a)$

Properties of Powers

For powers there are some rules that you have to know by heart and you also have to understand why they are true. The most important are these two:

$$\text{(i) } a^r \cdot a^s = a^{r+s} \qquad \text{(ii) } (a^r)^s = a^{rs}$$

Note carefully what these rules say. According to rule (i), powers with the same base are multiplied by *adding* the exponents. For example,

$$a^3 \cdot a^5 = \underbrace{a \cdot a \cdot a}_{3 \text{ factors}} \cdot \underbrace{a \cdot a \cdot a \cdot a \cdot a}_{5 \text{ factors}} = \underbrace{a \cdot a \cdot a \cdot a \cdot a \cdot a \cdot a \cdot a}_{3+5=8 \text{ factors}} = a^{3+5} = a^8$$

Here is an example of rule (ii):

$$(a^2)^4 = \underbrace{a \cdot a}_{2 \text{ factors}} \cdot \underbrace{a \cdot a}_{2 \text{ factors}} \cdot \underbrace{a \cdot a}_{2 \text{ factors}} \cdot \underbrace{a \cdot a}_{2 \text{ factors}} = \underbrace{a \cdot a \cdot a \cdot a \cdot a \cdot a \cdot a \cdot a}_{2 \cdot 4 = 8 \text{ factors}} = a^{2 \cdot 4} = a^8$$

Division of two powers with the same base goes like this:

$$a^r \div a^s = \frac{a^r}{a^s} = a^r \frac{1}{a^s} = a^r \cdot a^{-s} = a^{r-s}$$

Thus we divide two powers with the same base by *subtracting* the exponent in the denominator from that in the numerator. For example, $a^3 \div a^5 = a^{3-5} = a^{-2}$.

Finally, note that

$$(ab)^r = \underbrace{ab \cdot ab \cdot \ldots \cdot ab}_{r \text{ factors}} = \underbrace{a \cdot a \cdot \ldots \cdot a}_{r \text{ factors}} \cdot \underbrace{b \cdot b \cdot \ldots \cdot b}_{r \text{ factors}} = a^r b^r$$

and

$$\left(\frac{a}{b}\right)^r = \underbrace{\frac{a}{b} \cdot \frac{a}{b} \cdot \ldots \cdot \frac{a}{b}}_{r \text{ factors}} = \frac{\overbrace{a \cdot a \cdot \ldots \cdot a}^{r \text{ factors}}}{\underbrace{b \cdot b \cdot \ldots \cdot b}_{r \text{ factors}}} = \frac{a^r}{b^r} = a^r b^{-r}$$

These rules can be extended to cases where there are several factors. For instance,

$$(abcde)^r = a^r b^r c^r d^r e^r$$

We saw that $(ab)^r = a^r b^r$. What about $(a + b)^r$? One of the most common errors committed in elementary algebra is to think that it is equal to $a^r + b^r$. But, for example, $(2 + 3)^3 = 5^3 = 125$, but $2^3 + 3^3 = 8 + 27 = 35$. Thus,

$$(a + b)^r \neq a^r + b^r \qquad \text{(in general)}$$

EXAMPLE 1   Simplify[2]   (a) $x^p x^{2p}$ (b) $t^s \div t^{s-1}$ (c) $a^2 b^3 a^{-1} b^5$ (d) $\dfrac{t^p t^{q-1}}{t^r t^{s-1}}$.

Solution:

(a) $x^p x^{2p} = x^{p+2p} = x^{3p}$

(b) $t^s \div t^{s-1} = t^{s-(s-1)} = t^{s-s+1} = t^1 = t$

(c) $a^2 b^3 a^{-1} b^5 = a^2 a^{-1} b^3 b^5 = a^{2-1} b^{3+5} = a^1 b^8 = a b^8$

(d) $\dfrac{t^p \cdot t^{q-1}}{t^r \cdot t^{s-1}} = \dfrac{t^{p+q-1}}{t^{r+s-1}} = t^{p+q-1-(r+s-1)} = t^{p+q-1-r-s+1} = t^{p+q-r-s}$

EXAMPLE 2   If $x^{-2} y^3 = 5$, compute $x^{-4} y^6$, $x^6 y^{-9}$, and $x^2 y^{-3} + 2x^{-10} y^{15}$.

Solution: In computing $x^{-4} y^6$, how can we make use of the assumption that $x^{-2} y^3 = 5$? A moment's reflection might lead you to see that $(x^{-2} y^3)^2 = x^{-4} y^6$, and hence $x^{-4} y^6 = 5^2 = 25$. Similarly,

$$x^6 y^{-9} = (x^{-2} y^3)^{-3} = 5^{-3} = \frac{1}{125}$$

$$x^2 y^{-3} + 2x^{-10} y^{15} = (x^{-2} y^3)^{-1} + 2(x^{-2} y^3)^5 = 5^{-1} + 2 \cdot 5^5 = 6250.2$$

---

[2] Here and throughout the book we strongly suggest that when you attempt to solve the problem, you cover the solution and then gradually reveal the proposed answer to see if you are right.

NOTE 1 An important motivation for introducing the definitions $a^0 = 1$ and $a^{-n} = 1/a^n$ is that we want the rules for powers to be valid for negative and zero exponents as well as for positive ones. For example, we want $a^r \cdot a^s = a^{r+s}$ to be valid when $r = 5$ and $s = 0$. This requires that $a^5 \cdot a^0 = a^{5+0} = a^5$, so we must choose $a^0 = 1$. If $a^n \cdot a^m = a^{n+m}$ is to be valid when $m = -n$, we must have $a^n \cdot a^{-n} = a^{n+(-n)} = a^0 = 1$. Because $a^n \cdot (1/a^n) = 1$, we *must* define a^{-n} to be $1/a^n$.

NOTE 2 It is easy to make mistakes when dealing with powers. The following examples highlight some common sources of confusion.

(a) There is an important difference between $(-10)^2 = (-10)(-10) = 100$, and $-10^2 = -(10 \cdot 10) = -100$. The square of minus 10 is not equal to minus the square of 10.

(b) Note that $(2x)^{-1} = 1/(2x)$. Here the product $2x$ is raised to the power of -1. On the other hand, in the expression $2x^{-1}$ only x is raised to the power -1, so $2x^{-1} = 2 \cdot (1/x) = 2/x$.

(c) The volume of a ball with radius r is $\frac{4}{3}\pi r^3$. What is the volume if the radius is doubled? Solution: The new volume is $\frac{4}{3}\pi(2r)^3 = \frac{4}{3}\pi(2r)(2r)(2r) = \frac{4}{3}\pi 8r^3 = 8(\frac{4}{3}\pi r^3)$, so the volume is 8 times bigger than the initial one. (If we made the mistake of "simplifying" $(2r)^3$ to $2r^3$, the result would imply only a doubling of the volume; this should be contrary to common sense.)

FURTHER PROBLEMS FOR SECTION 1.2

In Problems 4–6 expand and simplify.

4. (a) $2^5 \cdot 2^5$ (b) $3^8 \cdot 3^{-2} \cdot 3^{-3}$ (c) $(2x)^3$ (d) $(-3xy^2)^3$

5. (a) $\dfrac{p^{24}p^3}{p^4 p}$ (b) $\dfrac{a^4 b^{-3}}{(a^2 b^{-3})^2}$ (c) $\dfrac{3^4(3^2)^6}{(-3)^{15}3^7}$ (d) $\dfrac{p^\gamma (pq)^\sigma}{p^{2\gamma + \sigma} q^{\sigma - 2}}$

6. (a) $2^0 \cdot 2^1 \cdot 2^2 \cdot 2^3$ (b) $\left(\dfrac{4}{3}\right)^3$ (c) $\dfrac{4^2 \cdot 6^2}{3^3 \cdot 2^3}$

(d) $x^5 x^4$ (e) $y^5 y^4 y^3$ (f) $(2xy)^3$

(g) $\dfrac{10^2 \cdot 10^{-4} \cdot 10^3}{10^0 \cdot 10^{-2} \cdot 10^5}$ (h) $\dfrac{(k^2)^3 k^4}{(k^3)^2}$ (i) $\dfrac{(x+1)^3 (x+1)^{-2}}{(x+1)^2 (x+1)^{-3}}$

7. The surface area of a sphere with radius r is $4\pi r^2$. By what factor will the surface area increase if the radius is tripled?

8. Which of the following equalities are true and which are false? Justify your answers. (Note: a and b are positive, m and n are integers.)

(a) $a^0 = 0$ (b) $(a+b)^{-n} = 1/(a+b)^n$ (c) $a^m \cdot a^m = a^{2m}$

(d) $a^m \cdot b^m = (ab)^{2m}$ (e) $(a+b)^m = a^m + b^m$ (f) $a^n \cdot b^m = (ab)^{n+m}$

9. Complete the following:

(a) $xy = 3$ implies $x^3 y^3 = \ldots$ (b) $ab = -2$ implies $(ab)^4 = \ldots$

(c) $a^2 = 4$ implies $(a^8)^0 = \ldots$ (d) n integer implies $(-1)^{2n} = \ldots$

Compound Interest

Powers are used in practically every branch of applied mathematics, including economics. To illustrate their use, recall how they are needed to calculate compound interest.

Suppose you deposit $1000 in a bank account paying 8% interest at the end of each year.[3] After one year you will have earned $1000 \cdot 0.08 = $80 in interest, so the amount in your bank account will be $1080. This can be rewritten as

$$1000 + \frac{1000 \cdot 8}{100} = 1000 \left(1 + \frac{8}{100} \right) = 1000 \cdot 1.08$$

Suppose this new amount of $1000 \cdot 1.08 is left in the bank for another year at an interest rate of 8%. After a second year, the extra interest will be $1000 \cdot 1.08 \cdot 0.08. So the total amount will have grown to

$$1000 \cdot 1.08 + (1000 \cdot 1.08) \cdot 0.08 = 1000 \cdot 1.08(1 + 0.08) = 1000 \cdot (1.08)^2$$

Each year the amount will increase by the factor 1.08, and we see that at the end of t years it will have grown to $1000 \cdot (1.08)^t$.

If the original amount is K and the interest rate is p% per year, by the end of the first year, the amount will be $K + K \cdot p/100 = K(1 + p/100)$ dollars. The growth factor per year is thus $1 + p/100$. In general, after t (whole) years, the original investment of K will have grown to an amount

$$K \left(1 + \frac{p}{100} \right)^t$$

when the interest rate is p% per year (and interest is added to the capital every year—that is, there is compound interest).

This example illustrates a general principle:

A quantity K which increases by p% per year will have increased after t years to

$$K \left(1 + \frac{p}{100} \right)^t$$

Here $1 + \dfrac{p}{100}$ *is called the* **growth factor** *for a growth of* p%.

---

[3] Remember that 1% means one in a hundred, or 0.01. So 23%, for example, is $23 \cdot 0.01 = 0.23$. To calculate 23% of $4000, we write

$$4000 \cdot \frac{23}{100} = 920 \qquad \text{or} \qquad 4000 \cdot 0.23 = 920$$

If you see an expression like $(1.08)^t$ you should immediately be able to recognize it as the amount to which \$1 has grown after t years when the interest rate is 8% per year. How should you interpret $(1.08)^0$? You deposit \$1 at 8% per year, and leave the amount for 0 years. Then you still have only \$1, because there has been no time to accumulate any interest, so that $(1.08)^0$ *must* equal 1.

NOTE 3 $1000 \cdot (1.08)^5$ is the amount you will have in your account after 5 years if you invest \$1000 at 8% interest per year. Using a calculator, you quickly find that you will have approximately \$1469.33. A rather common mistake is to put $1000 \cdot (1.08)^5 = (1000 \cdot 1.08)^5 = (1080)^5$. This is 10^{12} (or a trillion) times the right answer.

EXAMPLE 3   A new car was bought for \$15 000 and is assumed to decrease in value (depreciate) by 15% per year over a six year period. What is its value after 6 years?

Solution: After one year its value is down to

$$15\,000 - \frac{15\,000 \cdot 15}{100} = 15\,000\left(1 - \frac{15}{100}\right) = 15\,000 \cdot 0.85 = 12\,750$$

After two years its value is $15\,000 \cdot (0.85)^2 = 10\,837.50$, and so on. After six years we realize that its value must be $15\,000 \cdot (0.85)^6 \approx 5\,657$. ∎

This example illustrates a general principle:

A quantity K which decreases by $p\%$ per year, will after t years have decreased to

$$K\left(1 - \frac{p}{100}\right)^t$$

Here $1 - \dfrac{p}{100}$ *is called the* **growth factor** *for a decline of $p\%$.*

Do We Really Need Negative Exponents?

How much money should you have deposited in a bank 5 years ago in order to have \$1000 today, given that the interest rate has been 8% per year over this period? If we call this amount x, the requirement is that $x \cdot (1.08)^5$ must equal \$1000, or that $x \cdot (1.08)^5 = 1000$. Dividing by 1.08^5 on both sides yields

$$x = \frac{1000}{(1.08)^5} = 1000 \cdot (1.08)^{-5}$$

(which is approximately \$681). Thus, $\$(1.08)^{-5}$ is what you should have deposited 5 years ago in order to have \$1 today, given the constant interest rate of 8%.

In general, $\$P(1 + p/100)^{-t}$ *is what you should have deposited t years ago in order to have $\$P$ today, if the interest rate has been $p\%$ every year.*

10. Compute the following: (a) 13% of 150   (b) 6% of 2400   (c) 5.5% of 200

11. A box containing 5 balls costs $8.50. If the balls are bought individually, they cost $2.00 each. How much cheaper is it, in percentage terms, to buy the box as opposed to buying 5 individual balls?

12. Give economic interpretations to each of the following expressions and then use a calculator to find the approximate values:

 (a) $50 \cdot (1.11)^8$ (b) $10\,000 \cdot (1.12)^{20}$ (c) $5000 \cdot (1.07)^{-10}$

13. (a) $12 000 is deposited in an account earning 4% interest per year. What is the amount after 15 years?

 (b) If the interest rate is 6% each year, how much money should you have deposited in a bank 5 years ago to have $50 000 today?

14. A quantity increases by 25% each year for 3 years. How much is the combined percentage growth p over the three year period?

15. (a) A firm's profit increased from 1990 to 1991 by 20%, but it decreased by 17% from 1991 to 1992. Which of the years 1990 and 1992 had the higher profit?

 (b) What percentage decrease in profits from 1991 to 1992 would imply that profits were equal in 1990 and 1992?

1.3 Rules of Algebra

You are certainly already familiar with the most common rules of algebra. We have already used some in this chapter. Nevertheless, it may be useful to recall those that are most important. If a, b, and c are arbitrary numbers, then:

(a) $a + b = b + a$	(g) $1 \cdot a = a$
(b) $(a + b) + c = a + (b + c)$	(h) $aa^{-1} = 1$ for $a \neq 0$
(c) $a + 0 = a$	(i) $(-a)b = a(-b) = -ab$
(d) $a + (-a) = 0$	(j) $(-a)(-b) = ab$
(e) $ab = ba$	(k) $a(b + c) = ab + ac$
(f) $(ab)c = a(bc)$	(l) $(a + b)c = ac + bc$

These rules are used in the following examples:

$$5 + x^2 = x^2 + 5 \qquad\qquad (a + 2b) + 3b = a + (2b + 3b) = a + 5b$$

$$x\tfrac{1}{3} = \tfrac{1}{3}x \qquad\qquad (xy)y^{-1} = x(yy^{-1}) = x$$

$$(-3)5 = 3(-5) = -(3 \cdot 5) = -15 \qquad (-6)(-20) = 120$$

$$3x(y + 2z) = 3xy + 6xz \qquad (t^2 + 2t)4t^3 = t^2 4t^3 + 2t4t^3 = 4t^5 + 8t^4$$

The algebraic rules can be combined in several ways to give:

$$a(b - c) = a[b + (-c)] = ab + a(-c) = ab - ac$$
$$x(a + b - c + d) = xa + xb - xc + xd$$
$$(a + b)(c + d) = ac + ad + bc + bd$$

Figure 1 provides a geometric argument for the last of these algebraic rules for the case in which the numbers a, b, c, and d are all positive. The area $(a + b)(c + d)$ of the large rectangle is the sum of the areas of the four small rectangles.

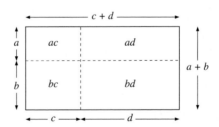

Figure 1

Important Identities

Recall the following three "quadratic identities" which are so important that you should definitely memorize them.

$$(a + b)^2 = a^2 + 2ab + b^2$$
$$(a - b)^2 = a^2 - 2ab + b^2$$
$$(a + b)(a - b) = a^2 - b^2$$

The last of these is called the *difference-of-squares formula*. The proofs are very easy. For example, $(a + b)^2$ means $(a + b)(a + b)$, which equals $aa + ab + ba + bb = a^2 + 2ab + b^2$.

EXAMPLE 1   Expand each of the following:

(a) $(3x + 2y)^2$ (b) $(1 - 2z)^2$ (c) $(4p + 5q)(4p - 5q)$

Solution:

(a) $(3x + 2y)^2 = (3x)^2 + 2(3x)(2y) + (2y)^2 = 9x^2 + 12xy + 4y^2$

(b) $(1 - 2z)^2 = 1 - 2 \cdot 1 \cdot 2 \cdot z + (2z)^2 = 1 - 4z + 4z^2$

(c) $(4p + 5q)(4p - 5q) = (4p)^2 - (5q)^2 = 16p^2 - 25q^2$ ▮

We often encounter parentheses with a minus sign in front. Because $(-1)x = -x$,

$$-(a + b - c + d) = -a - b + c - d$$

In words: *When removing a pair of parentheses with a minus in front, change the signs of* **all** *the terms within the parentheses—do not leave any out.*

We saw how to multiply two factors, $(a+b)$ and $(c+d)$. How do we compute such products when there are several factors? Here is an example:

$$(a + b)(c + d)(e + f) = \big[(a + b)(c + d)\big](e + f) = \big(ac + ad + bc + bd\big)(e + f)$$
$$= (ac + ad + bc + bd)e + (ac + ad + bc + bd)f$$
$$= ace + ade + bce + bde + acf + adf + bcf + bdf$$

Alternatively, write $(a + b)(c + d)(e + f) = (a + b)\big[(c + d)(e + f)\big]$, then expand and show that you get the same answer.

EXAMPLE 2   Expand $(r + 1)^3$.

Solution:

$$(r + 1)^3 = \big[(r + 1)(r + 1)\big](r + 1) = (r^2 + 2r + 1)(r + 1) = r^3 + 3r^2 + 3r + 1$$

Illustration: A ball with radius r metres has a volume of $\frac{4}{3}\pi r^3$ cubic metres. By how much does the volume expand if the radius increases by 1 metre? The solution is

$$\frac{4}{3}\pi(r + 1)^3 - \frac{4}{3}\pi r^3 = \frac{4}{3}\pi(r^3 + 3r^2 + 3r + 1) - \frac{4}{3}\pi r^3 = \frac{4}{3}\pi(3r^2 + 3r + 1)$$ ▮

PROBLEMS FOR SECTION 1.3

1. Expand each of the following:

(a) $(x + 2y)^2$ (b) $\left(\dfrac{1}{x} - x\right)^2$ (c) $(3u - 5v)^2$ (d) $(2z - 5w)(2z + 5w)$

2. (a) $201^2 - 199^2 =$ (b) If $u^2 - 4u + 4 = 1$, then $u =$

3. Compute $1000^2/(252^2 - 248^2)$ without using a calculator.

4. Verify the following cubic identities, which are occasionally useful:

(a) $(a + b)^3 = a^3 + 3a^2b + 3ab^2 + b^3$ (b) $(a - b)^3 = a^3 - 3a^2b + 3ab^2 - b^3$

(c) $a^3 - b^3 = (a - b)(a^2 + ab + b^2)$ (d) $a^3 + b^3 = (a + b)(a^2 - ab + b^2)$

Algebraic Expressions

Expressions involving letters such as $3xy - 5x^2y^3 + 2xy + 6y^3x^2 - 3x + 5yx + 8$ are called *algebraic expressions*. We call $3xy$, $-5x^2y^3$, $2xy$, $6y^3x^2$, $-3x$, $5yx$, and 8 the *terms* in the expression that is formed by adding all the terms together. The numbers 3, -5, 2, 6, -3, and 5 are the *numerical coefficients*. Two terms where only the numerical coefficients are different, such as $-5x^2y^3$ and $6y^3x^2$, are called *terms of the same type*. In order to simplify expressions, we collect terms of the same type. Then within each term, we put numerical coefficients first and place the letters in alphabetical order. Thus,

$$3xy - 5x^2y^3 + 2xy + 6y^3x^2 - 3x + 5yx + 8$$
$$= 3xy + 2xy + 5yx - 5x^2y^3 + 6y^3x^2 - 3x + 8$$
$$= x^2y^3 + 10xy - 3x + 8$$

EXAMPLE 3   Expand and simplify: $(2pq - 3p^2)(p + 2q) - (q^2 - 2pq)(2p - q)$.

Solution:

$$(2pq - 3p^2)(p + 2q) - (q^2 - 2pq)(2p - q)$$
$$= 2pqp + 2pq2q - 3p^3 - 6p^2q - (q^2 2p - q^3 - 4pqp + 2pq^2)$$
$$= 2p^2q + 4pq^2 - 3p^3 - 6p^2q - 2pq^2 + q^3 + 4p^2q - 2pq^2$$
$$= -3p^3 + q^3$$

In Problems 5–9, expand and simplify.

5. (a) $-3 + (-4) - (-8)$ (b) $(-3)(2 - 4)$ (c) $(-3)(-12)(-\frac{1}{2})$

(d) $-3[4 - (-2)]$ (e) $-3(-x - 4)$ (f) $(5x - 3y)9$

(g) $2x\left(\dfrac{3}{2x}\right)$ (h) $0 \cdot (1 - x)$ (i) $-7x\dfrac{2}{14x}$

6. (a) $5a^2 - 3b - (-a^2 - b) - 3(a^2 + b)$ (b) $-x(2x - y) + y(1 - x) + 3(x + y)$

(c) $12t^2 - 3t + 16 - 2(6t^2 - 2t + 8)$ (d) $r^3 - 3r^2s + s^3 - (-s^3 - r^3 + 3r^2s)$

7. (a) $-3(n^2 - 2n + 3)$ (b) $x^2(1 + x^3)$ (c) $(4n - 3)(n - 2)$

(d) $6a^2b(5ab - 3ab^2)$ (e) $(a^2b - ab^2)(a + b)$ (f) $(x - y)(x - 2y)(x - 3y)$

8. (a) $(ax + b)(cx + d)$ (b) $(2 - t^2)(2 + t^2)$ (c) $(u - v)^2(u + v)^2$

9. (a) $(2t - 1)(t^2 - 2t + 1)$ (b) $(a + 1)^2 + (a - 1)^2 - 2(a + 1)(a - 1)$

(c) $(x + y + z)^2$ (d) $(x + y + z)^2 - (x - y - z)^2$

Factoring

When we write $49 = 7 \cdot 7$ and $672 = 2 \cdot 2 \cdot 2 \cdot 2 \cdot 2 \cdot 3 \cdot 7$, we have *factored* these numbers. Algebraic expressions can often be factored in a similar way. For example, $6x^2y = 2 \cdot 3 \cdot x \cdot x \cdot y$ and $5x^2y^3 - 15xy^2 = 5 \cdot x \cdot y \cdot y(xy - 3)$.

EXAMPLE 4   Factor each of the following:

(a) $5x^2 + 15x$ (b) $-18b^2 + 9ab$ (c) $K(1 + r) + K(1 + r)r$ (d) $\delta L^{-3} + (1 - \delta)L^{-2}$

Solution:

(a) $5x^2 + 15x = 5x(x + 3)$

(b) $-18b^2 + 9ab = 9ab - 18b^2 = 3 \cdot 3b(a - 2b)$

(c) $K(1 + r) + K(1 + r)r = K(1 + r)(1 + r) = K(1 + r)^2$

(d) $\delta L^{-3} + (1 - \delta)L^{-2} = L^{-3}[\delta + (1 - \delta)L]$

The "quadratic identities" can often be used in reverse for factoring. They sometimes enable us to factor expressions that otherwise appear to have no factors.

EXAMPLE 5   Factor each of the following:

(a) $16a^2 - 1$ (b) $x^2y^2 - 25z^2$ (c) $4u^2 + 8u + 4$ (d) $x^2 - x + \frac{1}{4}$

Solution:

(a) $16a^2 - 1 = (4a + 1)(4a - 1)$

(b) $x^2y^2 - 25z^2 = (xy + 5z)(xy - 5z)$

(c) $4u^2 + 8u + 4 = (2u + 2)^2 = 4(u + 1)^2$

(d) $x^2 - x + \frac{1}{4} = (x - \frac{1}{2})^2$

NOTE 1 To factor an expression means to express it as a *product* of simpler factors. Note that $9x^2 - 25y^2 = 3 \cdot 3 \cdot x \cdot x - 5 \cdot 5 \cdot y \cdot y$ does *not* factor $9x^2 - 25y^2$. A correct factoring is $9x^2 - 25y^2 = (3x - 5y)(3x + 5y)$.

Sometimes one has to show a measure of inventiveness to find a factoring:

$$\begin{aligned} 4x^2 - y^2 + 6x^2 + 3xy &= (4x^2 - y^2) + 3x(2x + y) \\ &= (2x + y)(2x - y) + 3x(2x + y) \\ &= (2x + y)(2x - y + 3x) \\ &= (2x + y)(5x - y) \end{aligned}$$

Although it might be difficult, or impossible, to find a factoring, it is very easy to verify that an algebraic expression has been factored correctly by simply multiplying the factors. For example, we check that

$$x^2 - (a + b)x + ab = (x - a)(x - b)$$

by expanding $(x - a)(x - b)$.

Most algebraic expressions *cannot* be factored. For example, there is no way to write $x^2 + 10x + 50$ as a product of simpler factors.[4]

FURTHER PROBLEMS FOR SECTION 1.3

In Problems 10 to 15, factor the given expressions.

10. (a) $21x^2y^3$ (b) $3x - 9y + 27z$ (c) $a^3 - a^2b$ (d) $8x^2y^2 - 16xy$

11. (a) $28a^2b^3$ (b) $4x + 8y - 24z$ (c) $2x^2 - 6xy$ (d) $4a^2b^3 + 6a^3b^2$

(e) $7x^2 - 49xy$ (f) $5xy^2 - 45x^3y^2$ (g) $16 - b^2$ (h) $3x^2 - 12$

12. (a) $x^2 - 4x + 4$ (b) $4t^2s - 8ts^2$ (c) $16a^2 + 16ab + 4b^2$ (d) $5x^3 - 10xy^2$

13. (a) $a^2 + 4ab + 4b^2$ (b) $K^2L - L^2K$ (c) $K^{-4} - LK^{-5}$

(d) $9z^2 - 16w^2$ (e) $-\frac{1}{5}x^2 + 2xy - 5y^2$ (f) $a^4 - b^4$

14. (a) $5x + 5y + ax + ay$ (b) $u^2 - v^2 + 3v + 3u$ (c) $P^3 + Q^3 + Q^2P + P^2Q$

15. (a) $K^3 - K^2L$ (b) $KL^3 + KL$ (c) $L^2 - K^2$

(d) $K^2 - 2KL + L^2$ (e) $K^3L - 4K^2L^2 + 4KL^3$ (f) $K^{-3} - K^{-6}$

[4] If we introduce complex numbers, however, then $x^2 + 10x + 50$ *can* be factored.

1.4 Fractions

Recall that

$$a \div b = \frac{a}{b} \quad \begin{array}{l} \leftarrow \text{numerator} \\ \leftarrow \text{denominator} \end{array}$$

For example, $5 \div 8 = \frac{5}{8}$. For typographical reasons we often write 5/8 instead of $\frac{5}{8}$. Of course, $5 \div 8 = 0.625$, and $5/8 = 0.625$. In this case, we have written the fraction as a decimal number. The fraction 5/8 is called a *proper fraction* because 5 is less than 8. The fraction 19/8 is an *improper fraction* because the numerator is larger than (or equal to) the denominator. An improper fraction can be written as a *mixed number*:

$$\frac{19}{8} = 2 + \frac{3}{8} = 2\frac{3}{8}$$

$2\frac{3}{8}$ means 2 *plus* 3/8. On the other hand, $2 \cdot \frac{3}{8} = \frac{2 \cdot 3}{8} = \frac{3}{4}$ (by the rules reviewed in what follows). Note, however, that $2\frac{x}{8}$ means $2 \cdot \frac{x}{8}$; the notation $\frac{2x}{8}$ or $2x/8$ is obviously preferable in this case. Indeed, $\frac{19}{8}$ or 19/8 is probably better than $2\frac{3}{8}$ because it also helps avoid ambiguity.

The most important properties of fractions are listed below, with simple numerical examples. It is absolutely essential for you to master these rules, so you should carefully check that you know each of them.

Rule:

(1) $\dfrac{a \cdot \cancel{c}}{b \cdot \cancel{c}} = \dfrac{a}{b} \quad (b \neq 0 \text{ and } c \neq 0)$

(2) $\dfrac{-a}{-b} = \dfrac{(-a) \cdot (-1)}{(-b) \cdot (-1)} = \dfrac{a}{b}$

(3) $-\dfrac{a}{b} = (-1)\dfrac{a}{b} = \dfrac{(-1)a}{b} = \dfrac{-a}{b}$

(4) $\dfrac{a}{c} + \dfrac{b}{c} = \dfrac{a+b}{c}$

(5) $\dfrac{a}{b} + \dfrac{c}{d} = \dfrac{a \cdot d + b \cdot c}{b \cdot d}$

(6) $a + \dfrac{b}{c} = \dfrac{a \cdot c + b}{c}$

(7) $a \cdot \dfrac{b}{c} = \dfrac{a \cdot b}{c}$

(8) $\dfrac{a}{b} \cdot \dfrac{c}{d} = \dfrac{a \cdot c}{b \cdot d}$

(9) $\dfrac{a}{b} \div \dfrac{c}{d} = \dfrac{a}{b} \cdot \dfrac{d}{c} = \dfrac{a \cdot d}{b \cdot c}$

Example:

$\dfrac{21}{15} = \dfrac{7 \cdot \cancel{3}}{5 \cdot \cancel{3}} = \dfrac{7}{5}$

$\dfrac{-5}{-6} = \dfrac{5}{6}$

$-\dfrac{13}{15} = (-1)\dfrac{13}{15} = \dfrac{(-1)13}{15} = \dfrac{-13}{15}$

$\dfrac{5}{3} + \dfrac{13}{3} = \dfrac{18}{3} = 6$

$\dfrac{3}{5} + \dfrac{1}{6} = \dfrac{3 \cdot 6 + 5 \cdot 1}{5 \cdot 6} = \dfrac{23}{30}$

$5 + \dfrac{3}{5} = \dfrac{5 \cdot 5 + 3}{5} = \dfrac{28}{5}$

$7 \cdot \dfrac{3}{5} = \dfrac{21}{5}$

$\dfrac{4}{7} \cdot \dfrac{5}{8} = \dfrac{4 \cdot 5}{7 \cdot 8} = \dfrac{\cancel{4} \cdot 5}{7 \cdot 2 \cdot \cancel{4}} = \dfrac{5}{14}$

$\dfrac{3}{8} \div \dfrac{6}{14} = \dfrac{3}{8} \cdot \dfrac{14}{6} = \dfrac{\cancel{3} \cdot \cancel{2} \cdot 7}{\cancel{2} \cdot 2 \cdot 2 \cdot \cancel{2} \cdot \cancel{3}} = \dfrac{7}{8}$

Rule (1) is very important. It is the rule used to reduce fractions by factoring the numerator and the denominator, then cancelling *common factors* (that is, dividing both the numerator and denominator by the same nonzero quantity).

EXAMPLE 1   Simplify: (a) $\dfrac{5x^2yz^3}{25xy^2z}$ (b) $\dfrac{x^2+xy}{x^2-y^2}$ (c) $\dfrac{4-4a+a^2}{a^2-4}$

Solution:

(a) $\dfrac{5x^2yz^3}{25xy^2z} = \dfrac{5\cdot x \cdot x \cdot x \cdot x \cdot z \cdot z \cdot z}{5\cdot 5 \cdot x \cdot x \cdot y \cdot x} = \dfrac{xz^2}{5y}$

(b) $\dfrac{x^2+xy}{x^2-y^2} = \dfrac{x(x+y)}{(x-y)(x+y)} = \dfrac{x}{x-y}$

(c) $\dfrac{4-4a+a^2}{a^2-4} = \dfrac{(a-2)(a-2)}{(a-2)(a+2)} = \dfrac{a-2}{a+2}$

When we use rule (1) in reverse, we are *expanding* the fraction. For example, $5/8 = 5\cdot 125/8\cdot 125 = 625/1000 = 0.625$.

When we simplify fractions, only *common* factors can be removed. A frequently occurring error is illustrated in the following example.

$$\textbf{Wrong!} \quad \rightarrow \quad \frac{2x+3y}{xy} = \frac{2+3x}{x} = \frac{2+3}{1} = 5$$

In fact, the fraction $(2x+3y)/xy$ cannot be simplified at all, because the numerator and the denominator do not have any common factors.

Another error is shown in the next example.

$$\textbf{Wrong!} \quad \rightarrow \quad \frac{x}{x^2+2x} = \frac{x}{x^2} + \frac{x}{2x} = \frac{1}{x} + \frac{1}{2}$$

A correct way of simplifying the fraction is to cancel the common factor x, which yields $1/(x+2)$.

PROBLEMS FOR SECTION 1.4

In Problems 1 and 2, simplify the various expressions.

1. (a) $\dfrac{3}{7}+\dfrac{4}{7}-\dfrac{5}{7}$ (b) $\dfrac{3}{4}+\dfrac{4}{3}-1$ (c) $\dfrac{3}{12}-\dfrac{1}{24}$ (d) $\dfrac{1}{5}-\dfrac{2}{25}-\dfrac{3}{75}$

   (e) $3\dfrac{3}{5}-1\dfrac{4}{5}$ (f) $\dfrac{3}{5}\cdot\dfrac{5}{6}$ (g) $\left(\dfrac{3}{5}\div\dfrac{2}{15}\right)\cdot\dfrac{1}{9}$ (h) $\dfrac{\frac{2}{3}+\frac{1}{4}}{\frac{3}{4}+\frac{3}{2}}$

2. (a) $\dfrac{x}{10}-\dfrac{3x}{10}+\dfrac{17x}{10}$ (b) $\dfrac{9a}{10}-\dfrac{a}{2}+\dfrac{a}{5}$ (c) $\dfrac{b+2}{10}-\dfrac{3b}{15}+\dfrac{b}{10}$

   (d) $\dfrac{x+2}{3}+\dfrac{1-3x}{4}$ (e) $\dfrac{3}{2b}-\dfrac{5}{3b}$ (f) $\dfrac{3a-2}{3a}-\dfrac{2b-1}{2b}+\dfrac{4b+3a}{6ab}$

3. Cancel common factors:

(a) $\dfrac{325}{625}$ (b) $\dfrac{8a^2b^3c}{64abc^3}$ (c) $\dfrac{2a^2 - 2b^2}{3a + 3b}$ (d) $\dfrac{P^3 - PQ^2}{(P + Q)^2}$

Rules (4)–(6) are those used to add fractions. Note that (5) follows from (1) and (4):

$$\frac{a}{b} + \frac{c}{d} = \frac{a \cdot d}{b \cdot d} + \frac{c \cdot b}{d \cdot b} = \frac{a \cdot d + b \cdot c}{b \cdot d}$$

and we see easily that, for example,

$$\frac{a}{b} - \frac{c}{d} + \frac{e}{f} = \frac{adf}{bdf} - \frac{cbf}{bdf} + \frac{ebd}{bdf} = \frac{adf - cbf + ebd}{bdf} \qquad (*)$$

If the numbers b, d, and f have common factors, the computation carried out in $(*)$ involves unnecessarily large numbers. We can simplify the process by first finding the least common denominator (LCD) of the fractions. To do so, factor each denominator completely; the LCD is the product of all the distinct factors that appear in any denominator, each raised to the highest power to which it gets raised in any denominator. The use of the LCD is demonstrated in the following example.

EXAMPLE 2   Simplify the following:

(a) $\dfrac{1}{2} - \dfrac{1}{3} + \dfrac{1}{6}$ (b) $\dfrac{2+a}{a^2b} + \dfrac{1-b}{ab^2} - \dfrac{2b}{a^2b^2}$ (c) $\dfrac{x-y}{x+y} - \dfrac{x}{x-y} + \dfrac{3xy}{x^2 - y^2}$

Solution:

(a) The LCD is 6 and so $\dfrac{1}{2} - \dfrac{1}{3} + \dfrac{1}{6} = \dfrac{1 \cdot 3}{2 \cdot 3} - \dfrac{1 \cdot 2}{2 \cdot 3} + \dfrac{1}{2 \cdot 3} = \dfrac{3 - 2 + 1}{6} = \dfrac{2}{6} = \dfrac{1}{3}$

(b) The LCD is a^2b^2 and so

$$\frac{2+a}{a^2b} + \frac{1-b}{ab^2} - \frac{2b}{a^2b^2} = \frac{(2+a)b}{a^2b^2} + \frac{(1-b)a}{a^2b^2} - \frac{2b}{a^2b^2}$$

$$= \frac{2b + ab + a - ba - 2b}{a^2b^2} = \frac{a}{a^2b^2} = \frac{1}{ab^2}$$

(c) The LCD is $(x + y)(x - y)$ and so

$$\frac{x-y}{x+y} - \frac{x}{x-y} + \frac{3xy}{x^2 - y^2} = \frac{(x-y)(x-y)}{(x-y)(x+y)} - \frac{(x+y)x}{(x+y)(x-y)} + \frac{3xy}{(x-y)(x+y)}$$

$$= \frac{x^2 - 2xy + y^2 - x^2 - xy + 3xy}{(x-y)(x+y)} = \frac{y^2}{x^2 - y^2}$$

An Important Note

What do we mean by $1 - \frac{5-3}{2}$? It means that from the number 1, we subtract the number $\frac{5-3}{2} = \frac{2}{2} = 1$. Therefore, $1 - \frac{5-3}{2} = 0$. Alternatively,

$$1 - \frac{5-3}{2} = \frac{2}{2} - \frac{(5-3)}{2} = \frac{2-(5-3)}{2} = \frac{2-5+3}{2} = \frac{0}{2} = 0$$

In the same way,

$$\frac{2+b}{ab^2} - \frac{a-2}{a^2b}$$

means that we subtract $(a-2)/a^2b$ from $(2+b)/ab^2$:

$$\frac{2+b}{ab^2} - \frac{a-2}{a^2b} = \frac{(2+b)a}{a^2b^2} - \frac{(a-2)b}{a^2b^2} = \frac{(2+b)a - (a-2)b}{a^2b^2} = \frac{2(a+b)}{a^2b^2}$$

It is a good idea first to enclose in parentheses the numerators of the fractions that are being subtracted, as in the next example.

EXAMPLE 3   Simplify the expression $\dfrac{x-1}{x+1} - \dfrac{1-x}{x-1} - \dfrac{-1+4x}{2(x+1)}$.

Solution:

$$\frac{x-1}{x+1} - \frac{1-x}{x-1} - \frac{-1+4x}{2(x+1)} = \frac{(x-1)}{x+1} - \frac{(1-x)}{x-1} - \frac{(-1+4x)}{2(x+1)}$$

$$= \frac{2(x-1)^2 - 2(1-x)(x+1) - (-1+4x)(x-1)}{2(x+1)(x-1)}$$

$$= \frac{2(x^2 - 2x + 1) - 2(1 - x^2) - (4x^2 - 5x + 1)}{2(x+1)(x-1)}$$

$$= \frac{(x-1)}{2(x+1)(x-1)} = \frac{1}{2(x+1)}$$

We prove (9) by writing $(a/b) \div (c/d)$ as a ratio of fractions:

$$\frac{a}{b} \div \frac{c}{d} = \frac{\frac{a}{b}}{\frac{c}{d}} = \frac{b \cdot d \cdot \frac{a}{b}}{b \cdot d \cdot \frac{c}{d}} = \frac{\cancel{b} \cdot d \cdot a}{b \cdot \cancel{d} \cdot c} = \frac{d \cdot a}{b \cdot c} = \frac{a \cdot d}{b \cdot c} = \frac{a}{b} \cdot \frac{d}{c}$$

When we deal with fractions of fractions, we should be sure to emphasize which is the fraction line of the dominant fraction. For example,

$$\frac{a}{\dfrac{b}{c}} \quad \text{means} \quad a \div \frac{b}{c} = \frac{ac}{b} \qquad \text{whereas} \qquad \frac{\dfrac{a}{b}}{c} \quad \text{means} \quad \frac{a}{b} \div c = \frac{a}{bc} \qquad (*)$$

Of course, it is safer to write $\dfrac{a}{b/c}$ or $a/(b/c)$ in the first case, and $\dfrac{a/b}{c}$ or $(a/b)/c$ in the second case. As a numerical example of $(*)$,

$$\frac{1}{\dfrac{3}{5}} = \frac{5}{3} \qquad \text{whereas} \qquad \frac{\dfrac{1}{3}}{5} = \frac{1}{15}$$

FURTHER PROBLEMS FOR SECTION 1.4

4. If $x = 3/7$ and $y = 1/14$, find the simplest forms of these fractions:

   (a) $x + y$ (b) $\dfrac{x}{y}$ (c) $\dfrac{x - y}{x + y}$ (d) $\dfrac{13(2x - 3y)}{2x + 1}$

5. Simplify:

   (a) $\dfrac{1}{x - 2} - \dfrac{1}{x + 2}$
        (b) $\dfrac{6x + 25}{4x + 2} - \dfrac{6x^2 + x - 2}{4x^2 - 1}$

   (c) $\dfrac{18b^2}{a^2 - 9b^2} - \dfrac{a}{a + 3b} + 2$
        (d) $\dfrac{1}{8ab} - \dfrac{1}{8b(a + 2)} + \dfrac{1}{b(a^2 - 4)}$

   (e) $\dfrac{2t - t^2}{t + 2} \cdot \left(\dfrac{5t}{t - 2} - \dfrac{2t}{t - 2} \right)$
        (f) $2 - \dfrac{a\left(1 - \frac{1}{2a}\right)}{0.25}$

6. Simplify the following:

   (a) $\dfrac{2}{x} + \dfrac{1}{x + 1} - 3$
        (b) $\dfrac{t}{2t + 1} - \dfrac{t}{2t - 1}$
        (c) $\dfrac{3x}{x + 2} - \dfrac{4x}{2 - x} - \dfrac{2x - 1}{x^2 - 4}$

   (d) $\dfrac{\dfrac{1}{x} + \dfrac{1}{y}}{\dfrac{1}{xy}}$
        (e) $\dfrac{\dfrac{1}{x^2} - \dfrac{1}{y^2}}{\dfrac{1}{x^2} + \dfrac{1}{y^2}}$
        (f) $\dfrac{\dfrac{a}{x} - \dfrac{a}{y}}{\dfrac{a}{x} + \dfrac{a}{y}}$

7. Verify that $x^2 + 2xy - 3y^2 = (x + 3y)(x - y)$, and then simplify the expression

$$\frac{x - y}{x^2 + 2xy - 3y^2} - \frac{2}{x - y} - \frac{7}{x + 3y}$$

8. Simplify:

   (a) $\left(\dfrac{1}{4} - \dfrac{1}{5} \right)^{-2}$
        (b) $n - \dfrac{n}{1 - \dfrac{1}{n}}$
        (c) $\dfrac{1}{1 + x^{p-q}} + \dfrac{1}{1 + x^{q-p}}$

   (d) $\dfrac{\dfrac{1}{x - 1} + \dfrac{1}{x^2 - 1}}{x - \dfrac{2}{x + 1}}$
        (e) $\dfrac{\dfrac{1}{(x + h)^2} - \dfrac{1}{x^2}}{h}$
        (f) $\dfrac{\dfrac{10x^2}{x^2 - 1}}{\dfrac{5x}{x + 1}}$

1.5 Fractional Powers

In economic textbooks and research articles we constantly see powers with fractional exponents such as $K^{1/4}L^{3/4}$ and $Ar^{2.08}p^{-1.5}$. How do we define a^x when x is a rational number? Of course, we would like the usual rules for powers still to apply.

Square Roots

We already know the meaning of a^x if $x = 1/2$. In fact, if $a \geq 0$ and $x = 1/2$, then we define $a^x = a^{1/2}$ as equal to $\sqrt{a}$, the **square root** of a. Thus, $a^{1/2} = \sqrt{a}$ is defined as the nonnegative number that when multiplied by itself gives a. This definition makes sense because $a^{1/2} \cdot a^{1/2} = a^{1/2+1/2} = a^1 = a$. Note that a real number multiplied by itself must always be ≥ 0, whether that number is positive, negative, or zero. Hence,

$$a^{1/2} = \sqrt{a} \qquad \text{(valid if } a \geq 0\text{)}$$

For example, $\sqrt{16} = 16^{1/2} = 4$ because $4^2 = 16$ and $\sqrt{\frac{1}{25}} = \frac{1}{5}$ because $\frac{1}{5} \cdot \frac{1}{5} = \frac{1}{25}$.

If a and b are nonnegative numbers (with $b \neq 0$ in (ii)), then

$$\text{(i)} \quad \sqrt{ab} = \sqrt{a}\sqrt{b} \qquad \text{(ii)} \quad \sqrt{\frac{a}{b}} = \frac{\sqrt{a}}{\sqrt{b}}$$

which can also be written $(ab)^{1/2} = a^{1/2}b^{1/2}$ and $(a/b)^{1/2} = a^{1/2}/b^{1/2}$. For example, $\sqrt{16 \cdot 25} = \sqrt{16} \cdot \sqrt{25} = 4 \cdot 5 = 20$, and $\sqrt{9/4} = \sqrt{9}/\sqrt{4} = 3/2$.

Note that formulas (i) and (ii) are not valid if a or b or both are negative. For example, $\sqrt{(-1)(-1)} = \sqrt{1} = 1$, whereas $\sqrt{-1} \cdot \sqrt{-1}$ is not defined (unless one uses complex numbers).

NOTE 1 Recall that, in general, $(a + b)^r \neq a^r + b^r$. For $r = 1/2$, this says that we have

$$\sqrt{a + b} \neq \sqrt{a} + \sqrt{b} \qquad \text{(in general)}$$

The following observation illustrates just how frequently this fact is overlooked. During an examination in a basic course in mathematics for economists, 22% of 190 students simplified $\sqrt{1/16 + 1/25}$ incorrectly and claimed that it was equal to $1/4 + 1/5 = 9/20$. (The correct answer is $\sqrt{41/400} = \sqrt{41}/20$.) In a test for another group of 138 students, 40% made the same mistake.

NOTE 2 $(-2)^2 = 4$ and $2^2 = 4$. Thus $x = -2$ and $x = 2$ are both solutions of the equation $x^2 = 4$. Therefore we have $x^2 = 4 \iff x = \pm\sqrt{4} = \pm 2$. Note, however, that the symbol $\sqrt{4}$ means *only* 2, not -2.

By using a calculator, we find that $\sqrt{2} \div \sqrt{3} \approx 0.816$. Without a calculator, the division $\sqrt{2} \div \sqrt{3} \approx 1.414 \div 1.732$ would be tedious. But if we expand the fraction by rationalizing the denominator—that is, if we multiply both numerator and denominator by the same term in order to remove expressions with roots in the denominator, it becomes easier:

$$\frac{\sqrt{2}}{\sqrt{3}} = \frac{\sqrt{2} \cdot \sqrt{3}}{\sqrt{3} \cdot \sqrt{3}} = \frac{\sqrt{2 \cdot 3}}{3} = \frac{\sqrt{6}}{3} \approx \frac{2.448}{3} = 0.816$$

Sometimes the difference-of-squares formula of Section 1.3 can be used to eliminate square roots from the denominator:

$$\frac{1}{\sqrt{5}+\sqrt{3}} = \frac{\sqrt{5}-\sqrt{3}}{(\sqrt{5}+\sqrt{3})(\sqrt{5}-\sqrt{3})} = \frac{\sqrt{5}-\sqrt{3}}{5-3} = \frac{1}{2}(\sqrt{5}-\sqrt{3})$$

PROBLEMS FOR SECTION 1.5

1. Compute:

   (a) $\sqrt{9}$ (b) $\sqrt{1600}$ (c) $(100)^{1/2}$ (d) $\sqrt{9+16}$

   (e) $(36)^{-1/2}$ (f) $(0.49)^{1/2}$ (g) $\sqrt{0.01}$ (h) $\sqrt{\dfrac{1}{25}}$

2. Decide whether each "?" should be replaced by $=$ or $\neq$. Justify your answer. (Assume that a and b are positive.)

   (a) $\sqrt{25 \cdot 16}$? $\sqrt{25} \cdot \sqrt{16}$ (b) $\sqrt{25+16}$? $\sqrt{25}+\sqrt{16}$
   (c) $(a+b)^{1/2}$? $a^{1/2}+b^{1/2}$ (d) $(a+b)^{-1/2}$? $(\sqrt{a+b})^{-1}$

3. Solve for x:

   (a) $\sqrt{x} = 9$ (b) $\sqrt{x} \cdot \sqrt{4} = 4$ (c) $\sqrt{x+2} = 25$
   (d) $\sqrt{3} \cdot \sqrt{5} = \sqrt{x}$ (e) $2^{2-x} = 8$ (f) $2^x - 2^{x-1} = 4$

4. Rationalize the denominator and simplify:

   (a) $\dfrac{6}{\sqrt{7}}$ (b) $\dfrac{\sqrt{32}}{\sqrt{2}}$ (c) $\dfrac{\sqrt{3}}{4\sqrt{2}}$ (d) $\dfrac{\sqrt{54}-\sqrt{24}}{\sqrt{6}}$

   (e) $\dfrac{2}{\sqrt{3}\sqrt{8}}$ (f) $\dfrac{4}{\sqrt{2y}}$ (g) $\dfrac{x}{\sqrt{2x}}$ (h) $\dfrac{x(\sqrt{x}+1)}{\sqrt{x}}$

5. Simplify the following expressions by making the denominators rational:

   (a) $\dfrac{1}{\sqrt{7}+\sqrt{5}}$ (b) $\dfrac{\sqrt{5}-\sqrt{3}}{\sqrt{5}+\sqrt{3}}$ (c) $\dfrac{x}{\sqrt{3}-2}$

   (d) $\dfrac{x\sqrt{y}-y\sqrt{x}}{x\sqrt{y}+y\sqrt{x}}$ (e) $\dfrac{h}{\sqrt{x+h}-\sqrt{x}}$ (f) $\dfrac{1-\sqrt{x+1}}{1+\sqrt{x+1}}$

Nth Roots

What do we mean by $a^{1/n}$, where n is a natural number, and a is positive? For example, what does $5^{1/3}$ mean? If the rule $(a^r)^s = a^{rs}$ is still to apply in this case, we must have $(5^{1/3})^3 = 5^1 = 5$. This implies that $5^{1/3}$ must be a solution of the equation $x^3 = 5$. This equation can be shown to have a unique positive solution, denoted by $\sqrt[3]{5}$, the *cube root* of 5. Therefore, we must define $5^{1/3}$ as $\sqrt[3]{5}$.

In general, $(a^{1/n})^n = a^1 = a$. Thus, $a^{1/n}$ is a solution of the equation $x^n = a$. This equation can be shown to have a unique positive solution denoted by $\sqrt[n]{a}$, the **nth root** of a:

$$a^{1/n} = \sqrt[n]{a}$$

In words: *if a is positive and n is a natural number, then $a^{1/n}$ is the unique positive number that, raised to the nth power, gives a—that is, $(a^{1/n})^n = a$.*

EXAMPLE 1   Compute   (a) $\sqrt[3]{27}$ (b) $\left(\dfrac{1}{32}\right)^{1/5}$ (c) $(0.0001)^{0.25} = (0.0001)^{1/4}$

Solution:

(a) $\sqrt[3]{27} = 3$, because $3^3 = 27$.

(b) $\left(\dfrac{1}{32}\right)^{1/5} = \dfrac{1}{2}$ because $\left(\dfrac{1}{2}\right)^5 = \dfrac{1}{32}$.

(c) $(0.0001)^{1/4} = 0.1$ because $(0.1)^4 = 0.0001$. Alternatively,

$$\left(\dfrac{1}{10\,000}\right)^{1/4} = \dfrac{1}{10} \qquad \text{because} \qquad \left(\dfrac{1}{10}\right)^4 = \dfrac{1}{10\,000}$$

EXAMPLE 2   An amount \$5000 in an account has increased to \$10 000 in 15 years. What (constant) yearly interest rate p has been used?

Solution: After 15 years the amount of \$5000 has grown to $5000\,(1 + p/100)^{15}$. So we have the equation:

$$5000\left(1 + \dfrac{p}{100}\right)^{15} = 10\,000$$

Dividing by 5000 yields

$$\left(1 + \dfrac{p}{100}\right)^{15} = 2$$

In general, $(a^t)^{1/t} = a^1 = a$ for $t \neq 0$. Raising each side to the power of 1/15 yields

$$1 + \dfrac{p}{100} = 2^{1/15} \quad \text{or} \quad p = 100(2^{1/15} - 1)$$

With a calculator we find $p \approx 4.73$.

FURTHER PROBLEMS FOR SECTION 1.5

6. Compute without using a calculator:

   (a) $\sqrt[3]{125}$ (b) $(243)^{1/5}$ (c) $(-8)^{1/3}$ (d) $\sqrt[3]{0.008}$

7. Using a calculator, find approximations to:

   (a) $\sqrt[3]{55}$ (b) $(160)^{1/4}$ (c) $(2.71828)^{1/5}$ (d) $(1 + 0.0001)^{10000}$

8. A population increased from 40 million to 60 million in 12 years. What yearly percentage growth rate p achieves this increase?

We proceed to define $a^{p/q}$ whenever p is an integer, q is a natural number, and $a > 0$. Consider first $5^{2/3}$. We have already defined $5^{1/3}$. For rule $(a^r)^s = a^{rs}$ to apply, we must have $5^{2/3} = (5^{1/3})^2$. So we must define $5^{2/3}$ as $\left(\sqrt[3]{5}\right)^2$. In general, for $a > 0$, we define

$$a^{p/q} = \left(a^{1/q}\right)^p = \left(\sqrt[q]{a}\right)^p \qquad (p \text{ an integer, } q \text{ a natural number})$$

From the properties of exponents,

$$a^{p/q} = \left(a^{1/q}\right)^p = \left(a^p\right)^{1/q} = \sqrt[q]{a^p}$$

Thus, to compute $a^{p/q}$, we could either first take the qth root of a and raise the result to p, or first raise a to the power p and then take the qth root of the result. We obtain the same answer either way. For example,

$$4^{7/2} = (4^7)^{1/2} = 16384^{1/2} = 128 = 2^7 = (4^{1/2})^7$$

EXAMPLE 3   Compute:

   (a) $16^{3/2}$ (b) $16^{-1.25}$ (c) $\left(\dfrac{1}{27}\right)^{-2/3}$

   Solution:

   (a) $16^{3/2} = (16^{1/2})^3 = 4^3 = 64$

   (b) $16^{-1.25} = 16^{-5/4} = \dfrac{1}{16^{5/4}} = \dfrac{1}{\left(\sqrt[4]{16}\right)^5} = \dfrac{1}{2^5} = \dfrac{1}{32}$

   (c) $\left(\dfrac{1}{27}\right)^{-2/3} = 27^{2/3} = \left(\sqrt[3]{27}\right)^2 = 3^2 = 9$

EXAMPLE 4   Simplify the following expressions so that the answers contain only positive exponents:

(a) $\dfrac{a^{3/8}}{a^{1/8}}$ (b) $(x^{1/2}x^{3/2}x^{-2/3})^{3/4}$ (c) $\left(\dfrac{10p^{-1}q^{2/3}}{80p^2q^{-7/3}}\right)^{-2/3}$

Solution:

(a) $\dfrac{a^{3/8}}{a^{1/8}} = a^{3/8-1/8} = a^{2/8} = a^{1/4} = \sqrt[4]{a}$

(b) $(x^{1/2}x^{3/2}x^{-2/3})^{3/4} = (x^{1/2+3/2-2/3})^{3/4} = (x^{4/3})^{3/4} = x$

(c) $\left(\dfrac{10p^{-1}q^{2/3}}{80p^2q^{-7/3}}\right)^{-2/3} = (8^{-1}p^{-1-2}q^{2/3-(-7/3)})^{-2/3} = 8^{2/3}p^2q^{-2} = 4\dfrac{p^2}{q^2}$

NOTE 3 Tests reveal that many students, while they are able to handle quadratic identities, nevertheless make mistakes when dealing with more complicated powers. Here are examples taken from recent tests:

(i) $(1+r)^{20}$ is *not* equal to $1^{20} + r^{20}$.

(ii) If $u = 9 + x^{1/2}$, it does *not* follow that $u^2 = 81 + x$; instead $u^2 = 81 + 18\sqrt{x} + x$.

(iii) $(e^x - e^{-x})^p$ is *not* equal to $e^{xp} - e^{-xp}$ (unless $p = 1$).

NOTE 4 If q is an odd number and p is an integer, $a^{p/q}$ can be defined even when $a < 0$. For example, $(-8)^{1/3} = \sqrt[3]{-8} = -2$, because $(-2)^3 = -8$. However, in defining $a^{p/q}$ when $a < 0$, the fraction p/q must be reduced to its lowest terms. If not, we could get contradictions such as "$-2 = (-8)^{1/3} = (-8)^{2/6} = \sqrt[6]{(-8)^2} = \sqrt[6]{64} = 2$."

FURTHER PROBLEMS FOR SECTION 1.5

9. Compute the following without using a calculator:

   (a) $81^{1/2}$ (b) $64^{-1/3}$ (c) $16^{-2.25}$ (d) $\left(\dfrac{1}{3^{-2}}\right)^{-2}$

10. Simplify:

   (a) $\left(27x^{3p}y^{6q}z^{12r}\right)^{1/3}$ (b) $\dfrac{(x+15)^{4/3}}{(x+15)^{5/6}}$ (c) $\dfrac{8\sqrt[3]{x^2}\sqrt[4]{y}\sqrt{1/z}}{-2\sqrt[3]{x}\sqrt{y^5}\sqrt{z}}$

11. Simplify the following expressions so that each contains only a single exponent of a.

   (a) $(((a^{1/2})^{2/3})^{3/4})^{4/5}$ (b) $a^{1/2}a^{2/3}a^{3/4}a^{4/5}$

   (c) $(((3a)^{-1})^{-2}(2a^{-2})^{-1})/a^{-3}$ (d) $\dfrac{\sqrt[3]{a}\,a^{1/12}\sqrt[4]{a^3}}{a^{5/12}\sqrt{a}}$

12. Which of the following equations are valid for all x and y?

(a) $(2^x)^2 = 2^{x^2}$

(b) $3^{x-3y} = \dfrac{3^x}{3^{3y}}$

(c) $3^{-1/x} = \dfrac{1}{3^{1/x}}$ $(x \neq 0)$

(d) $5^{1/x} = \dfrac{1}{5^x}$ $(x \neq 0)$

(e) $a^{x+y} = a^x + a^y$

(f) $2^{\sqrt{x}} \cdot 2^{\sqrt{y}} = 2^{\sqrt{xy}}$ (x and y positive)

13. A firm using x units of input produces $32x^{3/2}$ units of its output by using process A, or $4x^3$ units by using process B. For what levels of input does process A produce more than process B?

1.6 Inequalities

The real numbers consist of the positive numbers, 0, and the negative numbers. If a is a positive number, we write $a > 0$ (or $0 < a$), and we say that a is greater than zero. A fundamental property of the positive numbers is:

$$a > 0 \text{ and } b > 0 \quad \text{imply} \quad a + b > 0 \text{ and } a \cdot b > 0 \tag{1}$$

If the number c is negative, we write $c < 0$ (or $0 > c$).

In general, we say that *the number a is greater than the number b*, and we write $a > b$ (or $b < a$), if $a - b$ is positive:

$$a > b \quad \text{means that} \quad a - b > 0$$

Thus, $4.11 > 3.12$ because $4.11 - 3.12 = 0.99 > 0$, and $-3 > -5$ because $-3 - (-5) = 2 > 0$. On the number line (see Fig. 1) $a > b$ means that a lies to the right of b.

When $a > b$, we often say that a *is strictly greater than* b in order to emphasize that $a = b$ is ruled out. If $a > b$ or $a = b$, then we write $a \geq b$ (or $b \leq a$) and say that a is *greater than or equal to b.*

$$a \geq b \quad \text{means that} \quad a - b \geq 0$$

For example, $4 \geq 4$ and $4 \geq 2$. Note in particular that it *is* correct to write $4 \geq 2$, because $4 - 2$ *is* positive or 0.

We call $>$ and $<$ *strict* inequalities, whereas $\geq$ and $\leq$ are *weak* inequalities. The difference is often very important in economic analysis.

One can prove a number of important properties of $>$ and $\geq$. For example,

$$\text{If } a > b, \quad \text{then} \quad a + c > b + c \text{ for all } c \tag{2}$$

The argument is simple: For all numbers a, b, and c, $(a+c)-(b+c) = a+c-b-c = a-b$. Hence, if $a - b > 0$, then $a + c - (b + c) > 0$, and the conclusion follows. On the number line, this implication is self-evident (here c is chosen to be negative):

Figure 1

At the risk of being trivial, here is an interpretation of this rule. If one day the temperature in New York is higher than that in London, and the temperature at both places then increases (or decreases) by the same number of degrees, then the ensuing New York temperature is still higher than that in London.

To deal with more complicated inequalities involves using the following further properties:

$$a > b \text{ and } b > c \;\Rightarrow\; a > c \tag{3}$$

$$a > b \text{ and } c > 0 \;\Rightarrow\; ac > bc \tag{4}$$

$$a > b \text{ and } c < 0 \;\Rightarrow\; ac < bc \tag{5}$$

$$a > b \text{ and } c > d \;\Rightarrow\; a + c > b + d \tag{6}$$

The corresponding properties are valid when each $>$ is replaced by $\geq$. These four properties all follow easily from (1). For example, (5) is proved as follows. Suppose $a > b$ and $c < 0$. Then $a - b > 0$ and $-c > 0$, so according to (1), $(a - b)(-c) > 0$. Hence $-ac + bc > 0$, implying that $ac < bc$.

According to (4) and (5):

(a) If the two sides of an inequality are multiplied by a positive number, the direction of the inequality is preserved.

(b) If the two sides of an inequality are multiplied by a negative number, the direction of the inequality is reversed.

It is important that you understand these rules, and realize that they correspond to everyday experience. For instance, (4) can be interpreted this way: given two rectangles with the same base, the one with the larger height has the larger area.

EXAMPLE 1   Find what values of x satisfy
$$3x - 5 > x - 3$$

Solution: Adding 5 to both sides of the inequality yields

$$3x - 5 + 5 > x - 3 + 5 \quad \text{or} \quad 3x > x + 2$$

Adding $(-x)$ to both sides yields

$$3x - x > x - x + 2,$$

so $2x > 2$, and after dividing by the positive number 2, the solution is $x > 1$.

1. Decide which of the following inequalities are true:

    (a) $-6.15 > -7.16$ (b) $6 \geq 6$ (c) $(-5)^2 \leq 0$ (d) $-\frac{1}{2}\pi < -\frac{1}{3}\pi$

    (e) $\dfrac{4}{5} > \dfrac{6}{7}$ (f) $2^3 < 3^2$ (g) $2^{-3} < 3^{-2}$ (h) $\dfrac{1}{2} - \dfrac{2}{3} < \dfrac{1}{4} - \dfrac{1}{3}$

2. Find what values of x satisfy:

    (a) $-x - 3 \leq 5$ (b) $3x + 5 < x - 13$ (c) $3x - (x - 1) \geq x - (1 - x)$

    (d) $\dfrac{2x - 4}{3} \leq 7$ (e) $\frac{1}{3}(1 - x) \geq 2(x - 3)$ (f) $\dfrac{t}{24} - (t + 1) + \dfrac{3t}{8} < \dfrac{5}{12}(t + 1)$

Sign Diagrams

EXAMPLE 2   Check whether the inequality $(x - 1)(3 - x) > 0$ is satisfied for $x = -3$, $x = 2$, and $x = 5$. Then find all the values x that satisfy the same inequality.

Solution: For $x = -3$, we have $(x - 1)(3 - x) = (-4) \cdot 6 = -24 < 0$; for $x = 2$, we have $(x - 1)(3 - x) = 1 \cdot 1 = 1 > 0$; and for $x = 5$, we have $(x - 1)(3 - x) = 4 \cdot (-2) = -8 < 0$. Hence, the inequality is satisfied for $x = 2$, but not for $x = -3$ or $x = 5$.

To find the entire solution set, we use a *sign diagram*. The sign variation for each factor in the product is determined. For example, the factor $x - 1$ is negative when $x < 1$, is 0 when $x = 1$, and is positive when $x > 1$. This sign variation is represented in the diagram below. The dashed line to the left of the vertical line $x = 1$ indicates that $x - 1 < 0$ if $x < 1$; the small circle indicates that $x - 1 = 0$ when $x = 1$; and the solid line to the right of $x = 1$ indicates that $x - 1 > 0$ if $x > 1$. In a similar way, we represent the sign variation for $3 - x$. The sign variation of the product is obtained as follows. When $x < 1$, then $x - 1$ is negative and $3 - x$ is positive, so the product is negative. When $1 < x < 3$, both factors are positive, so the product is positive. When $x > 3$, then $x - 1$ is positive and $3 - x$ is negative, so the product is negative. Conclusion: The solution set consists of those x that are greater than 1, but less than 3. So

$$(x - 1)(3 - x) > 0 \quad \text{if and only if} \quad 1 < x < 3$$

EXAMPLE 3   Find all values of p that satisfy

$$\frac{2p-3}{p-1} > 3 - p$$

Solution: It is tempting to begin by multiplying each side of the inequality by $p-1$. However, then we must distinguish between the two cases, $p-1 > 0$ and $p-1 < 0$, because if we multiply through by $p-1$ when $p-1 < 0$, we have to reverse the inequality sign. There is an alternative method, which makes it unnecessary to distinguish between two different cases. We begin by adding $p-3$ to both sides. This yields

$$\frac{2p-3}{p-1} + p - 3 > 0$$

Making $p-1$ the common denominator gives

$$\frac{2p-3+(p-3)(p-1)}{p-1} > 0 \qquad \text{or} \qquad \frac{p(p-2)}{p-1} > 0$$

because $2p-3+(p-3)(p-1) = 2p-3+p^2-4p+3 = p^2-2p = p(p-2)$. To find the solution set of this inequality, we again use a sign diagram. On the basis of the sign variations for p, $p-2$, and $p-1$, the sign variation for $p(p-2)/(p-1)$ is determined. For example, if $0 < p < 1$, then p is positive and $(p-2)$ is negative, so $p(p-2)$ is negative. But $p-1$ is also negative on this interval, so $p(p-2)/(p-1)$ is positive. Arguing this way for all the relevant intervals leads to the following sign diagram. (The original inequality has no meaning when $p = 1$. This is symbolized by a diagonal cross in the sign diagram.)

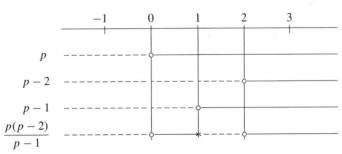

So the original inequality is satisfied if and only if $0 < p < 1$ or $p > 2$.   ▌

WARNING 1   The most common error committed in solving inequalities is precisely that indicated in Example 3: If we multiply by $p-1$, the inequality is *only* preserved if $p-1$ is positive—that is, if $p > 1$.

WARNING 2   It is vital that you really understand the method of sign diagrams. A standard error is illustrated by the following example. Find the solution set for

$$\frac{(x-2)+3(x+1)}{x+3} \leq 0$$

"Solution": We construct the sign diagram:

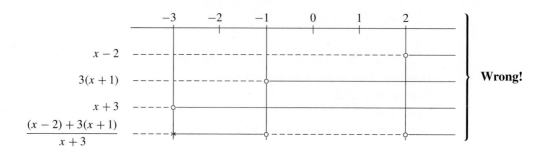

According to this diagram, the inequality should be satisfied for $x < -3$ and for $-1 \leq x \leq 2$. However, for $x = -4 \ (< -3)$, the fraction reduces to 15, which is positive. What went wrong? Suppose $x < -3$. Then $x - 2 < 0$ and $3(x + 1) < 0$ and, therefore, the numerator $(x - 2) + 3(x + 1)$ is negative. Because the denominator $x + 3$ is also negative for $x < -3$, the fraction is positive. The sign variation for the fraction in the diagram is, therefore, completely wrong. The product of two negative numbers is positive, but their sum is negative, and not positive as the wrong sign diagram suggests. We obtain a correct solution to the given problem by first collecting terms in the numerator so that the inequality becomes $(4x + 1)/(x + 3) \leq 0$. A sign diagram for this inequality reveals the correct answer, which is $-3 < x \leq -1/4$.

Double Inequalities

Two inequalities that are valid simultaneously are often written as a *double inequality*. If, for example, $a \leq z$ and moreover $z < b$, it is natural to write $a \leq z < b$. (On the other hand, if $a \leq z$ and $z > b$, but we do not know which is the larger of a and b, then we cannot write $a \leq b < z$ or $b \leq a \leq z$, and we do *not* write $a \leq z > b$.)

EXAMPLE 4   One day, the lowest temperature in Buenos Aires was 50°F, and the highest was 77°F. What is the corresponding temperature variation in degrees Celsius? (If F denotes degrees Fahrenheit and C denotes degrees Celsius, then $F = \frac{9}{5}C + 32$.)

Solution:

$$50 \leq \tfrac{9}{5}C + 32 \leq 77$$

$$50 - 32 \leq \tfrac{9}{5}C \leq 77 - 32$$

$$18 \leq \tfrac{9}{5}C \leq 45$$

$$90 \leq 9C \leq 225$$

$$10 \leq C \leq 25$$

The temperature varied between 10 and 25°C.

FURTHER PROBLEMS FOR SECTION 1.6

In Problems 3–6, solve the inequalities.

3. (a) $\dfrac{x+2}{x-1} < 0$ (b) $\dfrac{2x+1}{x-3} > 1$ (c) $5a^2 \le 125$

4. (a) $2 < \dfrac{3x+1}{2x+4}$ (b) $\dfrac{120}{n} + 1.1 \le 1.85$ (c) $g^2 - 2g \le 0$

   (d) $\dfrac{1}{p-2} + \dfrac{3}{p^2-4p+4} \ge 0$ (e) $\dfrac{-n-2}{n+4} > 2$ (f) $x^4 < x^2$

5. (a) $(x-1)(x+4) > 0$ (b) $(x-1)^2(x+4) > 0$ (c) $(x-1)^3(x-2) \le 0$

   (d) $(5x-1)^{10}(x-1) < 0$ (e) $(5x-1)^{11}(x-1) < 0$ (f) $\dfrac{3x-1}{x} > x+3$

   (g) $\dfrac{x-3}{x+3} < 2x-1$ (h) $x^2+4x-5 \le 0$ (i) $-\frac{1}{3}x^3 - x^2 + 6x \le 0$

6. (a) $1 \le \frac{1}{3}(2x-1) + \frac{8}{3}(1-x) < 16$ (b) $-5 < \dfrac{1}{x} < 0$ (c) $\dfrac{(1/x)-1}{(1/x)+1} \ge 1$

7. Decide whether the following inequalities are valid for all x and y:

   (a) $x+1 > x$ (b) $x^2 > x$ (c) $x+x > x$ (d) $x^2+y^2 \ge 2xy$

8. (a) The temperature for storing potatoes should be between 4 and 6°C. What are the corresponding temperatures in degrees Fahrenheit? (See Example 4.)

   (b) The freshness of a bottle of milk is guaranteed for 7 days if it is kept at between 36 and 40°F. Find the corresponding temperature variation in degrees Celsius.

HARDER PROBLEMS

9. The **arithmetic**, **geometric**, and **harmonic mean** of two positive numbers a and b are defined by

$$m_A = \frac{1}{2}(a+b), \qquad m_G = \sqrt{ab}, \qquad \text{and} \qquad \frac{1}{m_H} = \frac{1}{2}\left(\frac{1}{a} + \frac{1}{b}\right)$$

Prove that

$$m_A \ge m_G \ge m_H$$

with strict inequalities unless $a = b$. (*Hint:* You should first test these inequalities by choosing some specific numbers, using a calculator if you wish. To show that $m_A \ge m_G$, start with the obvious inequality, $(\sqrt{a} - \sqrt{b})^2 \ge 0$, and then expand. To show that $m_G \ge m_H$, start by showing that $\sqrt{xy} \le \frac{1}{2}(x+y)$. Then let $x = 1/a$, $y = 1/b$.)

1.7 Intervals and Absolute Values

Let a and b be any two numbers on the real line. Then we call the set of all numbers that lie between a and b an **interval**. In many situations, it is important to distinguish between the intervals that include their endpoints and the intervals that do not. When $a < b$, there are four different intervals that all have a and b as endpoints, as shown in Table 1.

Table 1

Notation	Name	The interval consists of all x satisfying:
(a, b)	The **open** interval from a to b.	$a < x < b$
$[a, b]$	The **closed** interval from a to b.	$a \leq x \leq b$
$(a, b]$	The **half-open** interval from a to b.	$a < x \leq b$
$[a, b)$	The **half-open** interval from a to b.	$a \leq x < b$

Note that an open interval includes neither of its endpoints, but a closed interval includes both of its endpoints. All four intervals, however, have the same length, $b - a$.

We usually illustrate intervals on the number line as in Fig. 1, with included endpoints represented by dots, and excluded endpoints at the tips of arrows.

Figure 1 $A = [-4, -2]$, $B = [0, 1)$, and $C = (2, 5)$

The intervals mentioned so far are all *bounded intervals*. We also use the word "interval" to signify certain unbounded sets of numbers. For example, we have

$$[a, \infty) = \text{all numbers } x \text{ with } x \geq a$$

$$(-\infty, b) = \text{all numbers } x \text{ with } x < b$$

with "∞" as the common symbol for infinity. The symbol ∞ is not a number at all, and therefore the usual rules of arithmetic do not apply to it. In the notation $[a, \infty)$, the symbol ∞ is only intended to indicate that we are considering the collection of *all* numbers larger than or equal to a, without any upper bound on the size of the number. Similarly, $(-\infty, b)$ has no lower bound. From the preceding, it should be apparent what we mean by (a, ∞) and $(-\infty, b]$. The collection of all real numbers is also denoted by the symbol $(-\infty, \infty)$.

Absolute Value

Let a be a real number and imagine its position on the real line. The distance between a and 0 is called the *absolute value* of a. If a is positive or 0, then the absolute value is the number a itself; if a is negative, then because distance must be positive, the absolute value is equal to the positive number $-a$.

The **absolute value** of a is denoted by $|a|$, and

$$|a| = \begin{cases} a & \text{if } a \geq 0 \\ -a & \text{if } a < 0 \end{cases} \tag{1}$$

For example, $|13| = 13, |-5| = -(-5) = 5, |-1/2| = 1/2$, and $|0| = 0$. Note in particular that $|-a| = |a|$.

NOTE 1 It is a common fallacy to assume that a must denote a positive number, even if this is not explicitly stated. Similarly, on seeing $-a$, many students are led to believe that this expression is always negative. Observe, however, that the number $-a$ is positive when a itself is negative. For example, if $a = -5$, then $-a = -(-5) = 5$. Nevertheless, it is often a useful convention in economics to define variables so that, as far as possible, their values are positive rather than negative.

EXAMPLE 1

(a) Compute $|x - 2|$ for $x = -3, x = 0$, and $x = 4$.

(b) Rewrite $|x - 2|$ using the definition of absolute value.

Solution:

(a) For $x = -3, |x - 2| = |-3 - 2| = |-5| = 5$. For $x = 0, |x - 2| = |0 - 2| = |-2| = 2$. For $x = 4, |x - 2| = |4 - 2| = |2| = 2$.

(b) According to the definition (1), $|x - 2| = x - 2$ if $x - 2 \geq 0$, that is, $x \geq 2$. However, $|x - 2| = -(x - 2) = 2 - x$ if $x - 2 < 0$, that is, $x < 2$. Hence,

$$|x - 2| = \begin{cases} x - 2, & \text{if } x \geq 2 \\ 2 - x, & \text{if } x < 2 \end{cases}$$

Let x_1 and x_2 be two arbitrary numbers. The *distance* between x_1 and x_2 on the number line is equal to $x_1 - x_2$ if $x_1 \geq x_2$, and equal to $-(x_1 - x_2)$ if $x_1 < x_2$. Therefore, we have

$$|x_1 - x_2| = |x_2 - x_1| = \textbf{distance} \text{ between } x_1 \text{ and } x_2 \text{ on the number line} \tag{2}$$

In Fig. 2 we have indicated geometrically that the distance between 7 and 2 is 5, whereas the distance between -3 and -5 is equal to 2, because $|-3 - (-5)| = |-3 + 5| = |2| = 2$.

Figure 2 The distance between 7 and 2, and between -3 and -5.

Suppose $|x| = 5$. What values can x have? There are only two possibilities: either $x = 5$ or $x = -5$, because no other numbers have absolute values equal to 5. Generally, if a is greater than or equal to 0, then $|x| = a$ means that $x = a$ or $x = -a$. Because $|x| \geq 0$ for all x, the equation $|x| = a$ has no solution when $a < 0$.

If a is a positive number and $|x| < a$, then the distance from x to 0 is less than a. Furthermore, when a is nonnegative, and $|x| \leq a$, the distance from x to 0 is less than or equal to a. In symbols:

$$|x| < a \quad \text{means that} \quad -a < x < a \tag{3}$$

$$|x| \leq a \quad \text{means that} \quad -a \leq x \leq a \tag{4}$$

EXAMPLE 2   Find all the x such that

$$|3x - 2| \leq 5$$

Check first to see if this inequality holds for $x = -3$, $x = 0$, $x = 7/3$, and $x = 10$.

Solution: For $x = -3$, $|3x - 2| = |-9 - 2| = 11$; for $x = 0$, $|3x - 2| = |-2| = 2$; for $x = 7/3$, $|3x - 2| = |7 - 2| = 5$; and for $x = 10$, $|3x - 2| = |30 - 2| = 28$. Hence, the given inequality is satisfied for $x = 0$ and $x = 7/3$, but not for $x = -3$ and $x = 10$.

From (4) the inequality $|3x - 2| \leq 5$ means that $-5 \leq 3x - 2 \leq 5$. Adding 2 to all three expressions gives

$$-5 + 2 \leq 3x - 2 + 2 \leq 5 + 2$$

or $-3 \leq 3x \leq 7$. Dividing by 3 gives $-1 \leq x \leq 7/3$.   ∎

PROBLEMS FOR SECTION 1.7

1. Calculate $|2x - 3|$, for $x = 0$, $1/2$, and $7/2$.

2. (a) Calculate $|5 - 3x|$, for $x = -1$, 2, and 4.

   (b) Solve the equation $|5 - 3x| = 0$.

   (c) Rewrite $|5 - 3x|$ by using the definition of absolute value.

3. Determine x such that

   (a) $|3 - 2x| = 5$ (b) $|x| \leq 2$ (c) $|x - 2| \leq 1$

   (d) $|3 - 8x| \leq 5$ (e) $|x| > \sqrt{2}$ (f) $|x^2 - 2| \leq 1$

4. A 5-metre iron bar is to be produced. The bar may not deviate by more than 1 mm from its stated length. Write a specification for the bar's length x in metres: (a) by using a double inequality; and (b) with the aid of an absolute-value sign.

1. Compute/simplify:

   (a) 5^3 (b) 10^{-3} (c) $\dfrac{1}{3^{-3}}$ (d) $\dfrac{-1}{10^{-3}}$

   (e) $3^{-2}3^3$ (f) $(3^{-2})^{-3}$ (g) $-\left(\dfrac{5}{3}\right)^0$ (h) $\left(-\dfrac{1}{2}\right)^{-3}$

2. Which of the following expressions are defined, and what are their values?

   (a) $(0+2)^0$ (b) 0^{-2} (c) $\dfrac{(10)^0}{(0+1)^0}$ (d) $\dfrac{(0+1)^0}{(0+2)^0}$

3. Simplify:

   (a) $(2^3 2^{-5})^3$ (b) $\left(\dfrac{2}{3}\right)^{-1} - \left(\dfrac{4}{3}\right)^{-1}$ (c) $(3^{-2} - 5^{-1})^{-1}$ (d) $(1.12)^{-3}(1.12)^3$

4. Expand/simplify:

   (a) $(2x)^4$ (b) $(2^{-1} - 4^{-1})^{-1}$ (c) $\dfrac{24x^3 y^2 z^3}{4x^2 yz^2}$

   (d) $\left[-(-ab^3)^{-3}(a^6 b^6)^2\right]^3$ (e) $\dfrac{a^5 \cdot a^3 \cdot a^{-2}}{a^{-3} \cdot a^6}$ (f) $\left[\left(\dfrac{x}{2}\right)^3 \cdot \dfrac{8}{x^{-2}}\right]^{-3}$

5. Compute: (a) 12% of 300 (b) 5% of 2000 (c) 6.5% of 1500

6. Give economic interpretations to each of the following expressions and then use a calculator to find the approximate values:

   (a) $100 \cdot (1.01)^8$ (b) $50\,000 \cdot (1.15)^{10}$ (c) $6000 \cdot (1.03)^{-8}$

7. (a) \$100 000 is deposited into an account earning 8% interest per year. What is the amount after 10 years?

   (b) If the interest rate is 8% each year, how much money should you have deposited in a bank 6 years ago to have \$25 000 today?

8. Expand and simplify:

   (a) $a(a-1)$ (b) $(x-3)(x+7)$ (c) $-\sqrt{3}\left(\sqrt{3} - \sqrt{6}\right)$ (d) $\left(1-\sqrt{2}\right)^2$

   (e) $(x-1)^3$ (f) $(1-b^2)(1+b^2)$ (g) $(1+x+x^2+x^3)(1-x)$ (h) $(1+x)^4$

9. Complete the following:

   (a) $x^{-1} y^{-1} = 3$ implies $x^3 y^3 = \cdots$ (b) $x^7 = 2$ implies $(x^{-3})^6 (x^2)^2 = \cdots$

   (c) $\left(\dfrac{xy}{z}\right)^{-2} = 3$ implies $\left(\dfrac{z}{xy}\right)^6 = \cdots$ (d) $a^{-1} b^{-1} c^{-1} = 1/4$ implies $(abc)^4 = \cdots$

In Problems 10 and 11 factor the expressions:

10. (a) $25x - 5$ (b) $3x^2 - x^3 y$ (c) $50 - x^2$ (d) $a^3 - 4a^2 b + 4ab^2$

11. (a) $5(x + 2y) + a(x + 2y)$ (b) $(a + b)c - d(a + b)$ (c) $ax + ay + 2x + 2y$
    (d) $2x^2 - 5yz + 10xz - xy$ (e) $p^2 - q^2 + p - q$ (f) $u^3 + v^3 - u^2 v - v^2 u$

12. Compute the following without using a calculator:
    (a) $16^{1/4}$ (b) $243^{-1/5}$ (c) $5^{1/7} \cdot 5^{6/7}$ (d) $(4^8)^{-3/16}$

13. Solve the following equations for x:
    (a) $2^{2x} = 8$ (b) $3^{3x+1} = 1/81$ (c) $10^{x^2 - 2x + 2} = 100$

14. Find the unknown x in each of the following equations:
    (a) $25^5 \cdot 25^x = 25^3$ (b) $3^x - 3^{x-2} = 24$ (c) $3^x \cdot 3^{x-1} = 81$

    (d) $3^5 + 3^5 + 3^5 = 3^x$ (e) $4^{-6} + 4^{-6} + 4^{-6} + 4^{-6} = 4^x$ (f) $\dfrac{2^{26} - 2^{23}}{2^{26} + 2^{23}} = \dfrac{x}{9}$

15. Simplify the following:

    (a) $\dfrac{t}{2t+1} - \dfrac{t}{2t-1}$ (b) $\dfrac{3x}{x+2} - \dfrac{4x}{2-x} - \dfrac{2x-1}{x^2-4}$ (c) $\dfrac{\dfrac{1}{x} + \dfrac{1}{y}}{\dfrac{1}{xy}}$

16. Reduce the following fractions:
    (a) $\dfrac{25a^3 b^2}{125ab}$ (b) $\dfrac{x^2 - y^2}{x + y}$ (c) $\dfrac{4a^2 - 12ab + 9b^2}{4a^2 - 9b^2}$ (d) $\dfrac{4x - x^3}{4 - 4x + x^2}$

17. Solve the following inequalities:
    (a) $2(x - 4) < 5$ (b) $\dfrac{1}{3}(y - 3) + 4 \geq 2$ (c) $8 - 0.2x \leq \dfrac{4 - 0.1x}{0.5}$

    (d) $\dfrac{x - 1}{-3} > \dfrac{-3x + 8}{-5}$ (e) $|5 - 3x| \leq 8$ (f) $|x^2 - 4| \leq 2$

18. Using a mobile phone costs $30 per month, and an additional $0.16 per minute.
    (a) What is the cost for one month if the phone is used for a total of x minutes?
    (b) What are the smallest and largest numbers of *hours* you can use the phone in a month if the monthly telephone bill is to be between $102 and $126?

2 INTRODUCTORY TOPICS II:

EQUATIONS

...and mathematics is nourished by dreamers
—as it nourishes them.
—D'Arcy W. Thompson (1940)

Virtually all applications of mathematics involve equations that need to be solved. Economics is no exception. This chapter considers some types of equation that appear frequently in economic models.

Many students are used to dealing with algebraic expressions and equations involving only *one* variable (usually *x*). Often they have difficulties at first in dealing with expressions involving several variables with a wide variety of names, and denoted by different letters. For economists, however, it is very important to be able to handle with ease such algebraic expressions and equations.

Answers to all problems in this chapter are given in the answer section.

2.1 How to Solve Simple Equations

Consider the following simple examples,

(a) $3x + 10 = x + 4$ (b) $\dfrac{z}{z-5} + \dfrac{1}{3} = \dfrac{-5}{5-z}$ (c) $Y = C + I$

Equation (a) contains the *variable x*, (b) has the variable z, and equation (c) has the three variables Y, C, and I.

To *solve* an equation means to find all values of the variables for which the equation is satisfied. For equation (a) this is easy. In order to isolate the unknown x on one side of the equation, we add $-x$ to both sides. This gives $2x + 10 = 4$. Adding -10 to both sides of this equation yields $2x = 4 - 10 = -6$. Dividing by 2 we get the solution $x = -3$.

If any value of a variable makes an expression in an equation undefined, that value is not allowed. Thus, the choice $z = 5$ is not allowed in (b) because it makes the expressions $z/(z-5)$ and $-5/(5-z)$ undefined, because they are 5/0 and $-5/0$, respectively. As we shall show in Example 3 below, equation (b) has no solutions.

Equation (c) has many solutions, one of which is $Y = 1000$, $C = 700$, and $I = 300$.

For problem (a) the solution procedure was probably well known. The method we used is summed up in the following frame, noting that two equations which have exactly the same solutions are called *equivalent*.

To get equivalent equations, do the following to both sides of the equality sign:

(A) add (or subtract) the same number

(B) multiply (or divide) by the same number $\neq 0$

When faced with more complicated equations involving parentheses and fractions, we usually begin by multiplying out the parentheses, and then we multiply both sides of the equation by the lowest common denominator for all the fractions. Here is an example.

EXAMPLE 1   Solve the equation $6p - \frac{1}{2}(2p - 3) = 3(1 - p) - \frac{7}{6}(p + 2)$.

Solution:

$$6p - p + \tfrac{3}{2} = 3 - 3p - \tfrac{7}{6}p - \tfrac{7}{3}$$

$$36p - 6p + 9 = 18 - 18p - 7p - 14$$

$$36p - 6p + 18p + 7p = 18 - 14 - 9$$

$$55p = -5$$

$$p = -\tfrac{5}{55} = -\tfrac{1}{11}$$

The next two examples show that sometimes a surprising degree of care is needed to find the right solutions.

EXAMPLE 2   Solve the equation $\dfrac{x+2}{x-2} - \dfrac{8}{x^2 - 2x} = \dfrac{2}{x}$.

Solution: Since $x^2 - 2x = x(x - 2)$, the common denominator is $x(x - 2)$: We see that $x = 2$ and $x = 0$ both make the equation absurd, because then at least one of the denominators becomes 0. If $x \neq 0$ and $x \neq 2$, we can multiply both sides of the equation by the common denominator $x(x - 2)$ to obtain

$$\frac{x+2}{x-2} \cdot x(x-2) - \frac{8}{x(x-2)} \cdot x(x-2) = \frac{2}{x} \cdot x(x-2)$$

$$(x+2)x - 8 = 2(x-2)$$

$$x^2 + 2x - 8 = 2x - 4$$

$$x^2 = 4$$

Equations of the form $x^2 = a$, where $a > 0$, have two solutions $x = \sqrt{a}$ and $x = -\sqrt{a}$. In our case, $x^2 = 4$ has solutions $x = 2$ and $x = -2$. But $x = 2$ makes the original equation absurd, so *only $x = -2$ is a solution.*

EXAMPLE 3   Solve the equation $\dfrac{z}{z-5} + \dfrac{1}{3} = \dfrac{-5}{5-z}$.

Solution: We see that z cannot be 5. Remembering this restriction, multiply both sides by $3(z-5)$. This gives

$$3z + z - 5 = 15$$

which has the unique solution $z = 5$. Because we had to assume $z \neq 5$, we must conclude that no solution exists for the original equation.   ▌

Often, solving a problem in economic analysis requires formulating an appropriate algebraic equation.

EXAMPLE 4   A firm manufactures a commodity that costs $20 per unit to produce. In addition, the firm has fixed costs of $2000. Each unit is sold for $75. How many units must be sold if the firm is to meet a profit target of $14 500?

Solution: If the number of units produced and sold is denoted by Q, then the revenue of the firm is $75Q$ and the total cost of production is $20Q + 2000$. Because profit is the difference between total revenue and total cost, it can be written as $75Q - (20Q + 2000)$. Because the profit target is 14 500, the equation

$$75Q - (20Q + 2000) = 14\,500$$

must be satisfied. It is easy to find the solution $Q = 16\,500/55 = 300$ units.   ▌

PROBLEMS FOR SECTION 2.1

In Problems 1–3, solve each of the equations.

1. (a) $5x - 10 = 15$
   (b) $2x - (5 + x) = 16 - (3x + 9)$
   (c) $-5(3x - 2) = 16(1 - x)$
   (d) $4x + 2(x - 4) - 3 = 2(3x - 5) - 1$
   (e) $\frac{2}{3}x = -8$
   (f) $(8x - 7)5 - 3(6x - 4) + 5x^2 = x(5x - 1)$
   (g) $x^2 + 10x + 25 = 0$
   (h) $(3x - 1)^2 + (4x + 1)^2 = (5x - 1)(5x + 1) + 1$

2. (a) $3x + 2 = 11$
   (b) $-3x = 21$
   (c) $3x = \frac{1}{4}x - 7$
   (d) $\dfrac{x - 3}{4} + 2 = 3x$
   (e) $\dfrac{1}{2x + 1} = \dfrac{1}{x + 2}$
   (f) $\sqrt{2x + 14} = 16$

3. (a) $\dfrac{x - 3}{x + 3} = \dfrac{x - 4}{x + 4}$
   (b) $\dfrac{3}{x - 3} - \dfrac{2}{x + 3} = \dfrac{9}{x^2 - 9}$
   (c) $\dfrac{6x}{5} - \dfrac{5}{x} = \dfrac{2x - 3}{3} + \dfrac{8x}{15}$

4. Solve the following problems by first formulating an equation in each case:

(a) The sum of twice a number and 5 is equal to the difference between the number and 3. Find the number.

(b) The sum of three successive natural numbers is 10 more than twice the smallest of them. Find the numbers.

(c) Jane receives double pay for every hour she works over and above 38 hours per week. Last week, she worked 48 hours and earned a total of $812. What is Jane's regular hourly wage?

(d) James has invested $15 000 at an annual interest rate of 10%. How much additional money should he invest at the interest rate of 12% if he wants the total interest income earned by the end of the year to equal $2100?

(e) When Mr. Barnes passed away, 2/3 of his estate was left to his wife, 1/4 was shared by his children, and the remainder, $100 000, was donated to a charity. How big was Mr. Barnes's estate?

5. Solve the following equations:

(a) $\dfrac{3y-1}{4} - \dfrac{1-y}{3} + 2 = 3y$ (b) $\dfrac{4}{x} + \dfrac{3}{x+2} = \dfrac{2x+2}{x^2+2x} + \dfrac{7}{2x+4}$

(c) $\dfrac{2 - \dfrac{z}{1-z}}{1+z} = \dfrac{6}{2z+1}$ (d) $\dfrac{1}{2}\left(\dfrac{p}{2} - \dfrac{3}{4}\right) - \dfrac{1}{4}\left(1 - \dfrac{p}{3}\right) - \dfrac{1}{3}(1-p) = -\dfrac{1}{3}$

6. A swimming pool can be filled by any one of three different hosepipes in 20, 30, and 60 minutes, respectively. How long will it take to fill the pool if all three hosepipes are used at the same time, without reducing the water pressure?

2.2 Equations with Parameters

Economists often use mathematical models to describe observed phenomena. These models enable them to explain the interdependence of different economic variables. In macroeconomic models, which are designed to explain the broad outlines of a country's economy, examples of such variables include the gross domestic product (GDP), total consumption, and total investment.

Simple relationships between two variables can often be described by a linear equation. Examples of such linear equations in two variables x and y are

(a) $y = 10x$ (b) $y = 3x + 4$ (c) $y = -\dfrac{8}{3}x - \dfrac{7}{2}$

These equations have a common structure which makes it possible to write down a general equation covering all the special cases:

$$y = ax + b \tag{1}$$

where a and b are real numbers. For example, letting $a = 3$ and $b = 4$ yields equation (b).

The general equation (1) describes a whole class of linear equations where x and y are the variables. The letters a and b are called **parameters**, and they take on different values. Linear equations are studied in more detail in Section 4.4.

We often need to solve equations with "strange" letters denoting the variables. In addition, there might be several parameters involved. Here are two typical examples:

EXAMPLE 1   Consider the basic macroeconomic model

$$Y = C + \bar{I}$$
$$C = a + bY \tag{$*$}$$

where Y is the gross domestic product (GDP), C is consumption, and $\bar{I}$ is total investment, which is treated as fixed.[1] Here a and b are positive parameters of the model, with $b < 1$.

The first equation in ($*$) says that GDP, by definition, is the sum of consumption and total investment. The second equation says that consumption is a linear function of GDP.

Special cases of the model are obtained by choosing particular numerical values for the parameters, such as (i) $\bar{I} = 100$, $a = 500$, $b = 0.8$, or (ii) $\bar{I} = 150$, $a = 600$, $b = 0.9$. Thus

(i)
$$Y = C + 100$$
$$C = 500 + 0.8Y$$

(ii)
$$Y = C + 150$$
$$C = 600 + 0.9Y$$

Solve model ($*$) for Y in terms of $\bar{I}$ and the parameters.

Solution: Substituting $C = a + bY$ into the first equation in ($*$) gives

$$Y = a + bY + \bar{I}$$

Now rearrange this equation so that all the terms containing Y are on the left-hand side. This can be done by adding $-bY$ to both sides, thus cancelling the bY term on the right-hand side to give

$$Y - bY = a + \bar{I}$$

Notice that the left-hand side is equal to $(1 - b)Y$, so $(1 - b)Y = a + \bar{I}$. Dividing both sides by $1 - b$, so that the coefficient of Y becomes 1, then gives the answer, which is

$$Y = \frac{a}{1 - b} + \frac{1}{1 - b}\bar{I} \tag{$**$}$$

---

[1] In economics, we often use a bar over a symbol to indicate that it is fixed. An alternative notation is to use the superscript 0, e.g. $Y = C + I^0$, or the subscript 0, e.g. $Y = C + I_0$.

This solution is a formula expressing Y in terms of $\bar{I}$ and the parameters a and b. The formula can be applied to particular values of the constants, such as $\bar{I} = 100$, $a = 500$, $b = 0.8$, to give the right answer in every case. Note the power of this approach: The model is solved only once, and then numerical answers are found simply by substituting appropriate numerical values for the parameters of the model.

Economists usually call the equations in (∗) the **structural form** of the model, whereas (∗∗) is called the **reduced form**.

EXAMPLE 2   Suppose the total demand for money in the economy is given by the formula

$$M = \alpha Y + \beta(r - \gamma)^{-\delta}$$

where M is the quantity of money in circulation, Y is national income, r is the interest rate, while $\alpha, \beta, \gamma,$ and δ are positive parameters.

(a) Solve the equation for r.

(b) For the USA during the period 1929–1952, the parameters have been estimated as $\alpha = 0.14$, $\beta = 76.03$, $\gamma = 2$, and $\delta = 0.84$. Show that r is given by

$$r = 2 + \left(\frac{76.03}{M - 0.14Y}\right)^{25/21}$$

Solution:

(a) It follows easily from the given equation that $(r - \gamma)^{-\delta} = (M - \alpha Y)/\beta$. Then raising each side to the power $-1/\delta$ yields

$$r - \gamma = \left(\frac{M - \alpha Y}{\beta}\right)^{-1/\delta}$$

Now, in general, $(a/b)^{-p} = (b/a)^p$, so

$$r = \gamma + \left(\frac{\beta}{M - \alpha Y}\right)^{1/\delta} \tag{∗}$$

(b) In this case $1/\delta = 1/0.84 = 100/84 = 25/21$. Hence, (∗) becomes

$$r = 2 + \left(\frac{76.03}{M - 0.14Y}\right)^{25/21}$$

PROBLEMS FOR SECTION 2.2

1. Find the value of Y in the models (i) and (ii) in Example 1. Verify that formula (∗∗) gives the same result.

2. Solve the following equations for x:

(a) $\dfrac{1}{ax} + \dfrac{1}{bx} = 2$

(b) $\dfrac{ax + b}{cx + d} = A$

(c) $\dfrac{1}{2}px^{-1/2} - w = 0$

(d) $\sqrt{1+x} + \dfrac{ax}{\sqrt{1+x}} = 0$

(e) $a^2x^2 - b^2 = 0$

(f) $(3 + a^2)^x = 1$

3. Solve each equation for the variable suggested:

   (a) $q = 0.15p + 0.14$ for p (supply of rice in India)

   (b) $S = \alpha + \beta P$ for P (supply function)

   (c) $A = \frac{1}{2}gh$ for g (the area of a triangle)

   (d) $V = \frac{1}{3}\pi r^3$ for r (the volume of a ball)

   (e) $AK^\alpha L^\beta = Y_0$ for L (production function)

4. Solve the following equations for the indicated variables:

   (a) $\alpha x - a = \beta x - b$ for x $\qquad\qquad$ (b) $\sqrt{pq} - 3q = 5$ for p

   (c) $Y = 94 + 0.2(Y - (20 + 0.5Y))$ for Y $\quad$ (d) $K^{1/2}\left(\frac{1}{2}\frac{r}{w}K\right)^{1/4} = Q$ for K

   (e) $\dfrac{\frac{1}{2}K^{-1/2}L^{1/4}}{\frac{1}{4}L^{-3/4}K^{1/2}} = \dfrac{r}{w}$ for L $\qquad$ (f) $\frac{1}{2}pK^{-1/4}\left(\frac{1}{2}\frac{r}{w}\right)^{1/4} = r$ for K

5. Solve for the indicated variable:

   (a) $\dfrac{1}{s} + \dfrac{1}{T} = \dfrac{1}{t}$ for s $\qquad\qquad$ (b) $\sqrt{KLM} - \alpha L = B$ for M

   (c) $\dfrac{x - 2y + xz}{x - z} = 4y$ for z $\qquad$ (d) $V = C\left(1 - \dfrac{T}{N}\right)$ for T

2.3 Quadratic Equations

This section reviews the method for solving quadratic (also called second-degree) equations. The general quadratic equation has the form

$$ax^2 + bx + c = 0 \qquad (a \neq 0) \tag{1}$$

where a, b, and c are given constants, and x is the unknown.

Two special cases are easy to handle. If $c = 0$ (there is no constant term), the equation reduces to $ax^2 + bx = 0$. This is equivalent to $x(ax + b) = 0$. Since the product of two numbers can only be 0 if at least one of the numbers is 0, we conclude that $x = 0$ or $ax + b = 0$. Because $a \neq 0$, the latter equation has the solution $x = -b/a$. So

$$ax^2 + bx = 0 \iff x = 0 \quad \text{or} \quad x = -b/a$$

If $b = 0$ (there is no term involving x), the general quadratic equation reduces to $ax^2 + c = 0$. Then $x^2 = -c/a$, and there are two possibilities. If $c/a > 0$, then the equation has no solutions. In the contrary case when $c/a \leq 0$, one has

$$ax^2 + c = 0 \iff x = \pm\sqrt{-\frac{c}{a}} \qquad \left(\frac{c}{a} \leq 0\right)$$

EXAMPLE 1   Solve the equations:

(a) $5x^2 - 8x = 0$ (b) $x^2 - 4 = 0$ (c) $x^2 + 3 = 0$

Solution:

(a) $5x^2 - 8x = x(5x - 8) = 0$, so $x = 0$ or $5x - 8 = 0$, that is $x = 0$ or $x = 8/5$.

(b) The equation yields $x^2 = 4$, and hence, $x = \pm\sqrt{4} = \pm 2$, which means that x is either 2 or -2. (Alternatively: $x^2 - 4 = (x + 2)(x - 2) = 0$, so $x = 2$ or $x = -2$.)

(c) Because x^2 is always ≥ 0, the left-hand side of the equation $x^2 + 3 = 0$ is always strictly positive and the equation has no solution.

PROBLEMS FOR SECTION 2.3

1. Solve the following quadratic equations (if they have solutions):

(a) $15x - x^2 = 0$ (b) $p^2 - 16 = 0$ (c) $(q - 3)(q + 4) = 0$

(d) $2x^2 + 9 = 0$ (e) $x(x + 1) = 2x(x - 1)$ (f) $x^2 - 4x + 4 = 0$

Harder Cases

If equation (1) has all three coefficients different from 0, solving it becomes harder. Consider, for example, $12x^2 - 16x - 3 = 0$. We could, of course, try to find the values of x that satisfy the equation by trial and error. However, it is not easy that way to find the only two solutions, which are $x = 3/2$ and $x = -1/6$.

NOTE 1 Here are two attempts to solve the equation that fail:

(a) The first is the following: $12x^2 - 16x - 3 = 0$, so $12x^2 - 16x = 3$, and $2x(6x - 8) = 3$. Thus, the product of $2x$ and $6x - 8$ must be 3. But there are infinitely many pairs of numbers whose product is 3, so this is of very little help in finding x.

(b) A second attempt is to divide each term by x to get $12x - 16 = 3/x$. Because the unknown x now occurs on both sides of the equation, we are stuck.

Evidently, we need a completely new idea in order to find the solution of a general second-degree equation. If you are only interested in a formula which always gives you the solutions to (1) (provided it has solutions), proceed directly to the boxed quadratic formula that comes two pages later. If you are interested in understanding why the formula works, read on.

EXAMPLE 2   Solve the equation $x^2 + 8x - 9 = 0$.

Solution: It is natural to begin by moving 9 to the right-hand side:

$$x^2 + 8x = 9 \qquad (*)$$

However, because x occurs in two terms, it is not obvious how to proceed. A method called *completing the square*, one of the oldest tricks in mathematics, turns out to work. In the present case this method involves adding 16 to each side of the equation to get

$$x^2 + 8x + 16 = 9 + 16 \qquad (**)$$

The point of adding 16 is that the left-hand side is then a complete square: $x^2 + 8x + 16 = (x + 4)^2$. Thus, equation ($**$) takes the form

$$(x + 4)^2 = 25 \qquad (***)$$

The equation $z^2 = 25$ has two solutions, $z = \pm\sqrt{25} = \pm 5$. Thus, either $x + 4 = 5$ or $x + 4 = -5$. The solutions to the given equation are, therefore, $x = 1$ and $x = -9$.
    Alternatively, equation ($***$) can be written as

$$(x + 4)^2 - 5^2 = 0$$

Using the difference-of-squares formula yields

$$(x + 4 - 5)(x + 4 + 5) = 0 \qquad \text{or} \qquad (x - 1)(x + 9) = 0$$

So we have the following *factoring*

$$x^2 + 8x - 9 = (x - 1)(x + 9)$$

Note that $(x - 1)(x + 9)$ is 0 precisely when $x = 1$ or $x = -9$. ▮

EXAMPLE 3   Solve $12x^2 - 16x - 3 = 0$ and factor the left-hand side.

Solution: The given equation is equivalent to $12\left(x^2 - \frac{4}{3}x - \frac{1}{4}\right) = 0$, so it has clearly the same solutions as the equation

$$x^2 - \frac{4}{3}x = \frac{1}{4}$$

Completing the square on the left-hand side yields

$$x^2 - \frac{4}{3}x + \left(-\frac{2}{3}\right)^2 = \frac{1}{4} + \left(-\frac{2}{3}\right)^2 = \frac{1}{4} + \frac{4}{9} \qquad \text{or} \qquad \left(x - \frac{2}{3}\right)^2 = \frac{25}{36}$$

Hence, $x - \frac{2}{3} = \sqrt{\frac{25}{36}} = \frac{5}{6}$ or $x - \frac{2}{3} = -\sqrt{\frac{25}{36}} = -\frac{5}{6}$. The two solutions are, therefore, $x = \frac{2}{3} + \frac{5}{6} = \frac{9}{6} = \frac{3}{2}$ and $x = \frac{2}{3} - \frac{5}{6} = -\frac{1}{6}$.

As in Example 2, we obtain the factoring

$$12\left(x^2 - \tfrac{4}{3}x - \tfrac{1}{4}\right) = 12\left(x - \tfrac{3}{2}\right)\left(x + \tfrac{1}{6}\right) = (2x - 3)(6x + 1)$$

Check that this is correct by expanding the right-hand side.

FURTHER PROBLEMS FOR SECTION 2.3

2. Solve the following quadratic equations by using the method of completing the square, and factor (if possible) the left-hand side:

(a) $x^2 - 5x + 6 = 0$ (b) $y^2 - y - 12 = 0$ (c) $2x^2 + 60x + 800 = 0$

(d) $-\tfrac{1}{4}x^2 + \tfrac{1}{2}x + \tfrac{1}{2} = 0$ (e) $m(m - 5) - 3 = 0$ (f) $0.1p^2 + p - 2.4 = 0$

The General Case

We now apply the method of completing the squares to the general quadratic equation (1). We begin by taking the nonzero coefficient of x^2 outside the parentheses so that the equation reduces to

$$a\left(x^2 + \frac{b}{a}x + \frac{c}{a}\right) = 0$$

Because $a \neq 0$ this equation has the same solutions as

$$x^2 + \frac{b}{a}x = -\frac{c}{a}$$

One half of the coefficient of x is $b/2a$. Adding the square of this number to each side of the equation yields

$$x^2 + \frac{b}{a}x + \left(\frac{b}{2a}\right)^2 = -\frac{c}{a} + \left(\frac{b}{2a}\right)^2$$

The left-hand side is now a complete square. After simplifying the right-hand side, we have

$$\left(x + \frac{b}{2a}\right)^2 = \frac{b^2 - 4ac}{4a^2} \qquad\qquad (*)$$

Note that $a^2 > 0$ and, if $b^2 - 4ac < 0$, then the right-hand side is negative. Because $(x + b/2a)^2$ is nonnegative for all choices of x, we conclude that if $b^2 - 4ac < 0$, then equation $(*)$ has no solutions. On the other hand, if $b^2 - 4ac > 0$, then $(*)$ yields two possibilities:

$$x + \frac{b}{2a} = \frac{\sqrt{b^2 - 4ac}}{2a} \qquad \text{and} \qquad x + \frac{b}{2a} = -\frac{\sqrt{b^2 - 4ac}}{2a}$$

Then the values of x are easily found. These formulas are correct even if $b^2 - 4ac = 0$, though then they give just one solution twice over. In conclusion:

QUADRATIC FORMULA

For $b^2 - 4ac \geq 0$ and $a \neq 0$,

$$ax^2 + bx + c = 0 \qquad \text{if and only if} \qquad x = \frac{-b \pm \sqrt{b^2 - 4ac}}{2a}$$

(2)

It is probably a good idea to spend a few minutes of your life to memorize this formula thoroughly. Once you have done so, you can immediately write down the solutions of any quadratic equation. Only if $b^2 - 4ac \geq 0$ are the solutions real numbers. If we use the formula when $b^2 - 4ac < 0$, the square root of a negative number appears and no real solution exists. The solutions are often called the **roots** of the equation.

EXAMPLE 4   Use the quadratic formula to find the solutions (or roots) of $2x^2 - 2x - 40 = 0$.

Solution: Write the equation as $2x^2 + (-2)x + (-40) = 0$. Because $a = 2$, $b = -2$, and $c = -40$, the quadratic formula (2) yields

$$x = \frac{-(-2) \pm \sqrt{(-2)^2 - 4 \cdot 2 \cdot (-40)}}{2 \cdot 2} = \frac{2 \pm \sqrt{4 + 320}}{4}$$

$$= \frac{2 \pm \sqrt{324}}{4} = \frac{2 \pm 18}{4} = \frac{1}{2} \pm \frac{9}{2}$$

The solutions are, therefore, $x = \frac{1}{2} + \frac{9}{2} = 5$ and $x = \frac{1}{2} - \frac{9}{2} = -4$. ∎

Suppose $b^2 - 4ac \geq 0$. By using the difference-of-squares formula as we did to obtain the factorings in Examples 2 and 3, it follows that $(*)$ is equivalent to

$$\left[x - \left(-\frac{b}{2a} + \frac{\sqrt{b^2 - 4ac}}{2a}\right)\right]\left[x - \left(-\frac{b}{2a} - \frac{\sqrt{b^2 - 4ac}}{2a}\right)\right] = 0 \qquad (**)$$

Denote by x_1 and x_2 the two solutions of equation $(**)$, which are the expressions in parentheses. Then its left-hand side can be written as the product $(x - x_1)(x - x_2) = 0$. Therefore, $x^2 + (b/a)x + c/a = (x - x_1)(x - x_2)$. Hence:

If x_1 and x_2 are the solutions of $ax^2 + bx + c = 0$, then

$$ax^2 + bx + c = a(x - x_1)(x - x_2)$$

(3)

This is a very important result, because it shows how to factor a general quadratic function. If $b^2 - 4ac < 0$, there is no factorization of $ax^2 + bx + c$. If $b^2 - 4ac = 0$, then $x_1 = x_2$ and $ax^2 + bx + c = a(x - x_1)^2 = a(x - x_2)^2$.

Expanding the right-hand side of the identity $x^2 + (b/a)x + c/a = (x - x_1)(x - x_2)$ yields $x^2 + (b/a)x + c/a = x^2 - (x_1 + x_2)x + x_1 x_2$. Equating like powers of x gives $x_1 + x_2 = -b/a$ and $x_1 x_2 = c/a$. (The same formulas are obtained by adding and multiplying the two solutions found in (2).) Thus:

If x_1 and x_2 are the roots of $ax^2 + bx + c = 0$, then

$$x_1 + x_2 = -\frac{b}{a} \qquad \text{and} \qquad x_1 x_2 = \frac{c}{a} \tag{4}$$

EXAMPLE 5   Factor (if possible) the following second-degree polynomials:

(a) $\dfrac{1}{3}x^2 + \dfrac{2}{3}x - \dfrac{14}{3}$ (b) $-2x^2 + 40x - 600$

Solution:

(a) For $\frac{1}{3}x^2 + \frac{2}{3}x - \frac{14}{3} = 0$, we have $a = \frac{1}{3}$, $b = \frac{2}{3}$, and $c = -\frac{14}{3}$, so (2) gives

$$x = \frac{-2/3 \pm \sqrt{(2/3)^2 - 4 \cdot (1/3) \cdot (-14/3)}}{2 \cdot (1/3)} = \frac{-2/3 \pm \sqrt{4/9 + 56/9}}{2/3}$$

$$= \frac{-2/3 \pm \sqrt{60}/3}{2/3} = \frac{-2 \pm \sqrt{60}}{2} = \frac{-2 \pm 2\sqrt{15}}{2} = -1 \pm \sqrt{15}$$

Thus the solutions of the equation are $x_1 = -1 + \sqrt{15}$ and $x_2 = -1 - \sqrt{15}$. The factoring in (3) becomes

$$\tfrac{1}{3}x^2 + \tfrac{2}{3}x - \tfrac{14}{3} = \tfrac{1}{3}\big(x - (-1 + \sqrt{15})\big)\big(x - (-1 - \sqrt{15})\big) = \tfrac{1}{3}(x + 1 - \sqrt{15})(x + 1 + \sqrt{15})$$

(b) For $-2x^2 + 40x - 600 = 0$, $a = -2$, $b = 40$, and $c = -600$, so $b^2 - 4ac = 1600 - 4800 = -3200$. Therefore, no factoring exists in this case. ∎

NOTE 2 The quadratic formula is very useful, since it gives the solutions to any quadratic equation. But you should not be a "quadratic formula fanatic" and use it always. If $b = 0$ or $c = 0$, we explained at the beginning of this section how the equation can be solved very easily. During a recent exam, one extreme "quadratic formula fanatic", when faced with solving the equation $(x - 4)^2 = 0$, expanded the parentheses to obtain $x^2 - 8x + 16 = 0$, and then used the quadratic formula to get the (correct) answer eventually, $x = 4$. What would you have done?

Solve the equations in 3–4 by using the quadratic formula:

3. (a) $r^2 + 11r - 26 = 0$ (b) $3p^2 + 45p = 48$ (c) $20\,000 = 300K - K^2$

   (d) $r^2 + (\sqrt{3} - \sqrt{2})r = \sqrt{6}$ (e) $0.3x^2 - 0.09x = 0.12$ (f) $\dfrac{1}{24} = p^2 - \dfrac{1}{12}p$

4. (a) $x^2 - 3x + 2 = 0$ (b) $5t^2 - t = 3$ (c) $6x = 4x^2 - 1$

   (d) $9x^2 + 42x + 44 = 0$ (e) $30\,000 = x(x + 200)$ (f) $3x^2 = 5x - 1$

5. (a) Find the lengths of the sides of a rectangle whose perimeter is 40 cm and whose area is 75 cm^2.

   (b) Find two successive natural numbers whose sum of squares is 13.

   (c) In a right-angled triangle, the hypotenuse is 34 cm. One of the short sides is 14 cm longer than the other. Find the lengths of the two short sides.

   (d) A motorist drove 80 km. In order to save 16 minutes, he had to drive 10 km/h faster than usual. What was his usual driving speed?

6. Solve the following equations:

   (a) $x^3 - 4x = 0$ (b) $x^4 - 5x^2 + 4 = 0$ (c) $z^{-2} - 2z^{-1} - 15 = 0$

2.4 Linear Equations in Two Unknowns

This section reviews some methods for solving two linear equations with two unknowns.

EXAMPLE 1   Find the values of x and y that satisfy both the equations

$$2x + 3y = 18$$
$$3x - 4y = -7$$
(∗)

We need to find the values of x and y that satisfy *both* equations. Suppose we start by trying $x = 0$ in the first equation; this implies $y = 6$. Given $x = 0$ and $y = 6$, $2x + 3y = 18$ and $3x - 4y = -24$. Thus, the first equation *is* satisfied, but not the second. Hence, $x = 0$ and $y = 6$ is *not* a solution. Only if we are very lucky will we find the solution to (∗) by such trial and error.

Fortunately, there exist more systematic methods for solving (∗).

METHOD 1   First, solve one of the equations for one of the variables in terms of the other; then substitute the result into the other equation. This leaves only one equation in one unknown, which is easily solved.

To apply this method to system ($*$), we can solve the first equation for y in terms of x. In fact, $2x + 3y = 18$ implies that $3y = 18 - 2x$ and, hence, $y = 6 - \frac{2}{3}x$. Substituting this expression for y into the second equation in ($*$) gives

$$3x - 4\left(6 - \tfrac{2}{3}x\right) = -7$$

$$3x - 24 + \tfrac{8}{3}x = -7$$

$$9x - 72 + 8x = -21$$

$$17x = 51$$

Hence, $x = 3$. Then we find y by using $y = 6 - \frac{2}{3}x$ once again to obtain $y = 6 - \frac{2}{3} \cdot 3 = 4$. The solution of ($*$) is therefore $x = 3$ and $y = 4$.

Such a solution should always be checked by direct substitution. Indeed, substituting $x = 3$ and $y = 4$ in ($*$) gives $2 \cdot 3 + 3 \cdot 4 = 18$ and $3 \cdot 3 - 4 \cdot 4 = -7$, so the check works.

METHOD 2   This method is based on eliminating one of the variables by adding or subtracting a multiple of one equation from the other. For system ($*$), suppose we want to eliminate y. If we multiply the first equation in ($*$) by 4 and the second by 3, then the coefficients of the y terms in both equations will be the same except for the sign. If we then add the transformed equations together, the term in y disappears and we obtain

$$
\begin{array}{rr}
8x + 12y = & 72 \\
9x - 12y = & -21 \\
\hline
17x = & 51
\end{array}
$$

Hence, $x = 3$. To find the value for y, substitute 3 for x in either of the original equations and solve for y. This gives $y = 4$, which agrees with the earlier result.

Some prefer to find both x and y by using the following setup:

$$
\begin{array}{ll}
2x + 3y = 18 \\
3x - 4y = -7
\end{array}
\quad \left|\ \begin{array}{c} 4 \\ 3 \end{array}\ \right|\ \begin{array}{c} 3 \\ -2 \end{array}\ \Bigg|
$$

The first column on the right-hand side suggests that we multiply the first equation by 4 and the second by 3. This leads to the previous arrangement. The second column on the right-hand side suggests that we multiply the first equation by 3 and the second by -2. Doing this eliminates x and yields

$$
\begin{array}{rr}
6x + 9y = & 54 \\
-6x + 8y = & 14 \\
\hline
17y = & 68 \\
y = & 4
\end{array}
$$

We end this section by using Method 2 to solve a general linear system of equations with two equations and two unknowns:

$$
\begin{aligned}
ax + by &= c \\
dx + ey &= f
\end{aligned}
\tag{1}
$$

Here a, b, c, d, e, and f are arbitrary given numbers, whereas x and y are the unknowns.

If we let $a = 2$, $b = 3$, $c = 18$, $d = 3$, $e = -4$, and $f = -7$, then this reduces to system (*). Using Method 2, we obtain

$$ax + by = c \qquad \begin{vmatrix} e & d \\ -b & -a \end{vmatrix}$$
$$dx + ey = f$$

$$\begin{array}{ll} aex + bey = ce & adx + bdy = cd \\ \underline{-bdx - bey = -bf} & \underline{-adx - aey = -af} \\ (ae - bd)x \quad = ce - bf & (bd - ae)y = cd - af \end{array}$$

which gives

$$x = \frac{ce - bf}{ae - bd} \qquad\qquad y = \frac{cd - af}{bd - ae} = \frac{af - cd}{ae - bd} \tag{2}$$

We have found expressions for both x and y.

These formulas break down if the denominator $ae - bd$ in both fractions is equal to 0. This case requires special attention.

PROBLEMS FOR SECTION 2.4

Solve the systems of equations in 1–3:

1. (a) $\begin{aligned} x - y &= 5 \\ x + y &= 11 \end{aligned}$
   (b) $\begin{aligned} 4x - 3y &= 1 \\ 2x + 9y &= 4 \end{aligned}$
   (c) $\begin{aligned} 3x + 4y &= 2.1 \\ 5x - 6y &= 7.3 \end{aligned}$

2. (a) $\begin{aligned} 5x + 2y &= 3 \\ 2x + 3y &= -1 \end{aligned}$
   (b) $\begin{aligned} x - 3y &= -25 \\ 4x + 5y &= 19 \end{aligned}$
   (c) $\begin{aligned} 2x + 3y &= 3 \\ 6x + 6y &= -1 \end{aligned}$

3. (a) $\begin{aligned} 2K + L &= 11.35 \\ K + 4L &= 25.8 \end{aligned}$
   (b) $\begin{aligned} 23p + 45q &= 181 \\ 10p + 15q &= 65 \end{aligned}$
   (c) $\begin{aligned} 0.01r + 0.21s &= 0.042 \\ -0.25r + 0.55s &= -0.47 \end{aligned}$

4. (a) Find two numbers whose sum is 52 and whose difference is 26.

   (b) Five tables and 20 chairs cost \$1800, whereas 2 tables and 3 chairs cost \$420. What is the price of each table and each chair?

   (c) A firm produces a good in two qualities, A and B. For the coming year, the estimated output of A is 50% higher than that of B. The profit per unit sold of the two qualities is \$300 for A and \$200 for B. If the profit target is \$13 000 over the next year, how much of each of the two qualities must be produced?

   (d) At the beginning of the year a person had a total of \$10 000 in two accounts. The interest rates were 5% and 7.2% per year, respectively. If the person has made no transfers during the year, and has earned a total of \$676 interest, what was the initial balance in each of the two accounts?

2.5 Nonlinear Equations

This chapter has already considered some types of equation frequently occurring in economic models. In this section we consider some additional types that are often encountered later in the book, particularly in connection with optimization problems.

Recall that a product of two or more factors can only be 0 if at least one of the factors is 0. This fact is used again and again. Consider the following examples.

EXAMPLE 1   Solve each of the following three separate equations:

(a) $x^3\sqrt{x+2} = 0$ (b) $x(y+3)(z^2+1)\sqrt{w-3} = 0$ (c) $x^2 - 3x^3 = 0$

Solution:

(a) If $x^3\sqrt{x+2} = 0$, then either $x^3 = 0$ or $\sqrt{x+2} = 0$. The equation $x^3 = 0$ has only the solution $x = 0$, while $\sqrt{x+2} = 0$ gives $x = -2$. The solutions of the equation are therefore $x = 0$ and $x = -2$.

(b) There are four factors in the product. One of the factors, $z^2 + 1$, is never 0. Hence, the solutions are: $x = 0$, or $y = -3$, or $w = 3$.

(c) Start by factoring: $x^2 - 3x^3 = x^2(1 - 3x)$. The product $x^2(1 - 3x)$ is 0 if and only if $x^2 = 0$ or $1 - 3x = 0$. Hence, the solutions are $x = 0$ and $x = 1/3$.   ∎

NOTE 1 When trying to solve an equation, an easy way to make a serious mistake is to cancel a factor which might be zero. It is important to check that the factor being cancelled really is not zero. For instance, suppose one cancels the common factor x^2 in the equation

$$x^2 = 3x^3$$

The result is $1 = 3x$, implying that $x = 1/3$. The solution $x = 0$ has been lost.

In general,
$$ab = ac \quad \text{is equivalent to} \quad a = 0 \quad \text{or} \quad b = c \tag{1}$$

because the equation $ab = ac$ is equivalent to $ab - ac = 0$, or $a(b - c) = 0$. This product is 0 when either $a = 0$ or when $b = c$.

If $ab = ac$ and $a \neq 0$, we conclude from (1) that $b = c$.

EXAMPLE 2   What conclusions about the variables can we draw if

(a) $x(x+a) = x(2x+b)$ (b) $\lambda y = \lambda z^2$ (c) $xy^2(1-y) - 2\lambda(y-1) = 0$

Solution:

(a) Either $x = 0$ or $x + a = 2x + b$. The last equation gives $x = a - b$. The solutions are therefore $x = 0$ and $x = a - b$.

(b) Either $\lambda = 0$ or $y = z^2$. (It is easy to "forget" the possibility $\lambda = 0$.)

(c) The equation is equivalent to

$$xy^2(1 - y) + 2\lambda(1 - y) = 0, \quad \text{that is} \quad (1 - y)(xy^2 + 2\lambda) = 0$$

We conclude from the last equation that $1 - y = 0$ or $xy^2 + 2\lambda = 0$, that is $y = 1$ or $\lambda = -\frac{1}{2}xy^2$.   ∎

Consider also some equations involving fractions. Recall that the fraction a/b is not defined if $b = 0$. If $b \neq 0$, then $a/b = 0$ is equivalent to $a = 0$.

EXAMPLE 3   Solve the following equations:

(a) $\dfrac{1 - K^2}{\sqrt{1 + K^2}} = 0$ (b) $\dfrac{45 + 6r - 3r^2}{(r^4 + 2)^{3/2}} = 0$ (c) $\dfrac{x^2 - 5x}{\sqrt{x^2 - 25}} = 0$

Solution:

(a) The denominator is never 0, so the fraction is 0 when $1 - K^2 = 0$, that is when $K = \pm 1$.

(b) Again the denominator is never 0. The fraction is 0 when $45 + 6r - 3r^2 = 0$, that is $3r^2 - 6r - 45 = 0$. Solving this quadratic equation, we find that $r = -3$ or $r = 5$.

(c) The numerator is equal to $x(x - 5)$, which is 0 if $x = 0$ or $x = 5$. At $x = 0$ the denominator is $\sqrt{-25}$, which is not defined, and at $x = 5$ the denominator is 0. We conclude that the equation has no solutions.   ∎

PROBLEMS FOR SECTION 2.5

Solve the equations in Problems 1–2:

1. (a) $x(x + 3) = 0$ (b) $x^3(1 + x^2)(1 - 2x) = 0$ (c) $x(x - 3) = x - 3$

 (d) $\sqrt{2x + 5} = 0$ (e) $\dfrac{x^2 + 1}{x(x + 1)} = 0$ (f) $\dfrac{x(x + 1)}{x^2 + 1} = 0$

2. (a) $\dfrac{5 + x^2}{(x - 1)(x + 2)} = 0$ (b) $1 + \dfrac{2x}{x^2 + 1} = 0$

 (c) $\dfrac{(x + 1)^{1/3} - \frac{1}{3}x(x + 1)^{-2/3}}{(x + 1)^{2/3}} = 0$ (d) $\dfrac{x}{x - 1} + 2x = 0$

3. Examine what conclusions can be drawn about the variables if:

 (a) $z^2(z - a) = z^3(a + b)$, $a \neq 0$ (b) $(1 + \lambda)\mu x = (1 + \lambda)y\mu$

 (c) $\dfrac{\lambda}{1 + \mu} = \dfrac{-\lambda}{1 - \mu^2}$ (d) $ab - 2b - \lambda b(2 - a) = 0$

In Problems 1–2, solve each of the equations.

1. (a) $3x - 20 = 16$ (b) $-5x + 8 + 2x = -(4-x)$ (c) $-6(x - 5) = 6(2 - 3x)$

   (d) $\dfrac{4 - 2x}{3} = -5 - x$ (e) $\dfrac{5}{2x - 1} = \dfrac{1}{2 - x}$ (f) $\sqrt{x - 3} = 6$

2. (a) $\dfrac{x - 3}{x + 3} = \dfrac{x - 4}{x + 4}$ (b) $\dfrac{3}{x - 3} - \dfrac{2}{x + 3} = \dfrac{9}{x^2 - 9}$ (c) $\dfrac{6x}{5} - \dfrac{5}{x} = \dfrac{2x - 3}{3} + \dfrac{8x}{15}$

3. Solve the following equations for the variables specified:

   (a) $x = \frac{2}{3}(y - 3) + y$ for y (b) $ax - b = cx + d$ for x

   (c) $AK\sqrt{L} = Y_0$ for L (d) $px + qy = m$ for y

   (e) $\dfrac{\dfrac{1}{1 + r} - a}{\dfrac{1}{1 + r} + b} = c$ for r (f) $Px(Px + Q)^{-1/3} + (Px + Q)^{2/3} = 0$ for x

4. Consider the macro model (see Example 2.2.1)

   $$Y = C + \bar{I} + G, \qquad C = b(Y - T), \qquad T = tY$$

   where $b \in (0, 1)$, and $t \in (0, 1)$ are parameters, T denotes taxes, and G is government expenditure.

   (a) Express Y and C in terms of $\bar{I}$, G, and the parameters.

   (b) What happens to Y and C as t increases?

5. Solve the following equations for the variables indicated:

   (a) $3K^{-1/2}L^{1/3} = 1/5$ for K (b) $(1 + r/100)^t = 2$ for r

   (c) $p - abx_0^{b-1} = 0$ for x_0 (d) $\left[(1 - \lambda)a^{-\rho} + \lambda b^{-\rho}\right]^{-1/\rho} = c$ for b

6. Solve the following second-degree equations:

   (a) $z^2 = 8z$ (b) $x^2 + 2x - 35 = 0$ (c) $p^2 + 5p - 14 = 0$

   (d) $12p^2 - 7p + 1 = 0$ (e) $y^2 - 15 = 8y$ (f) $42 = x^2 + x$

7. Solve the following equations:

   (a) $(x^2 - 4)\sqrt{5 - x} = 0$ (b) $(x^4 + 1)(4 + x) = 0$ (c) $(1 - \lambda)x = (1 - \lambda)y$

3
INTRODUCTORY TOPICS III:
MISCELLANEOUS

Everything should be made as simple as possible, but not simpler.
—Albert Einstein

This chapter starts with sums and summation notation. Most economic students will need these for their statistics and econometrics courses in particular.

Arguments in mathematics require tight logical reasoning; arguments in economic analysis are no exception to this rule. We therefore present some basic concepts from logic. A brief section on mathematical proofs might be useful for more ambitious students.

A short introduction to set theory comes next. The chapter winds up with a discussion of mathematical induction. Very occasionally, this is used directly in economic arguments. More often, it is needed to understand mathematical results which economists often use.

3.1 Summation Notation

Economists often make use of census data. Suppose a country is divided into six regions. Let N_i denote the population in region i. Then the total population is given by

$$N_1 + N_2 + N_3 + N_4 + N_5 + N_6$$

It is convenient to have an abbreviated notation for such lengthy sums. The capital Greek letter sigma Σ is conventionally used as a **summation symbol**, and the sum is written as

$$\sum_{i=1}^{6} N_i$$

This reads "the sum from $i = 1$ to $i = 6$ of N_i." If there are n regions, then

$$N_1 + N_2 + \cdots + N_n \qquad (*)$$

is one possible notation for the total population. Here $\cdots$ indicates that the obvious previous pattern continues, but comes to an end just before the last term N_n.

In summation notation, we write

$$\sum_{i=1}^{n} N_i$$

This notation tells us to form the sum of all the terms that result when we substitute successive integers for i, starting with $i = 1$ and ending with $i = n$. The symbol i is called the **index of summation**. It is a "dummy variable" that can be replaced by any other letter (which has not already been used for something else). Thus, both $\sum_{j=1}^{n} N_j$ and $\sum_{k=1}^{n} N_k$ represent the same sum as (*).

The upper and lower limits of summation can both vary. For example,

$$\sum_{i=30}^{35} N_i = N_{30} + N_{31} + N_{32} + N_{33} + N_{34} + N_{35}$$

is the total population in the six regions numbered from 30 to 35.

More generally, suppose p and q are integers with $q \geq p$. Then

$$\sum_{i=p}^{q} a_i = a_p + a_{p+1} + \cdots + a_q$$

denotes the sum that results when we substitute successive integers for i, starting with $i = p$ and ending with $i = q$. If the upper and lower limits of summation are the same, then the "sum" reduces to one term. And if the upper limit is less than the lower limit, then there are no terms at all, so the usual convention is that the "sum" reduces to zero.

EXAMPLE 1   Compute: (a) $\sum_{i=1}^{5} i^2$ (b) $\sum_{k=3}^{6}(5k - 3)$ (c) $\sum_{j=0}^{2} \frac{1}{(j + 1)(j + 3)}$.

Solution:

(a) $\sum_{i=1}^{5} i^2 = 1^2 + 2^2 + 3^2 + 4^2 + 5^2 = 1 + 4 + 9 + 16 + 25 = 55$

(b) $\sum_{k=3}^{6}(5k - 3) = (5 \cdot 3 - 3) + (5 \cdot 4 - 3) + (5 \cdot 5 - 3) + (5 \cdot 6 - 3) = 78$

(c) $\sum_{j=0}^{2} \frac{1}{(j + 1)(j + 3)} = \frac{1}{1 \cdot 3} + \frac{1}{2 \cdot 4} + \frac{1}{3 \cdot 5} = \frac{40 + 15 + 8}{120} = \frac{63}{120} = \frac{21}{40}$

Sums and the summation notation occur frequently in economics. Often, there are several variables or parameters in addition to the summation index. It is important to be able to interpret such sums. In each case, the summation symbol tells you that there is a sum of terms. The sum results from substituting successive integers for the summation index, starting with the lower limit and ending with the upper limit.

EXAMPLE 2   Expand   (a) $\sum_{i=1}^{n} p_t^{(i)} q^{(i)}$ (b) $\sum_{j=-3}^{1} x^{5-j} y^j$ (c) $\sum_{i=1}^{N} (x_{ij} - \bar{x}_j)^2$

Solution:

(a) $\sum_{i=1}^{n} p_t^{(i)} q^{(i)} = p_t^{(1)} q^{(1)} + p_t^{(2)} q^{(2)} + \cdots + p_t^{(n)} q^{(n)}$

(b) $\sum_{j=-3}^{1} x^{5-j} y^j = x^{5-(-3)} y^{-3} + x^{5-(-2)} y^{-2} + x^{5-(-1)} y^{-1} + x^{5-0} y^0 + x^{5-1} y^1$

$$= x^8 y^{-3} + x^7 y^{-2} + x^6 y^{-1} + x^5 + x^4 y$$

(c) $\sum_{i=1}^{N} (x_{ij} - \bar{x}_j)^2 = (x_{1j} - \bar{x}_j)^2 + (x_{2j} - \bar{x}_j)^2 + \cdots + (x_{Nj} - \bar{x}_j)^2$

Note that t is *not* an index of summation in (a), and j is *not* an index of summation in (c). ▌

EXAMPLE 3   Write the following sums using summation notation:

(a) $1 + 3 + 3^2 + 3^3 + \cdots + 3^{81}$ (b) $a_i^6 + a_i^5 b_j + a_i^4 b_j^2 + a_i^3 b_j^3 + a_i^2 b_j^4 + a_i b_j^5 + b_j^6$

Solution:

(a) This is easy if we note that $1 = 3^0$ and $3 = 3^1$, so that the sum can be written as $3^0 + 3^1 + 3^2 + 3^3 + \cdots + 3^{81}$. The general term is 3^i, and we have

$$1 + 3 + 3^2 + 3^3 + \cdots + 3^{81} = \sum_{i=0}^{81} 3^i$$

(b) This is more difficult. Note, however, that the indices i and j never change. Also the exponent for a_i decreases step by step from 6 to 0, whereas that for b_j increases from 0 to 6. The general term has the form $a_i^{6-k} b_j^k$, where k varies from 0 to 6. Thus,

$$a_i^6 + a_i^5 b_j + a_i^4 b_j^2 + a_i^3 b_j^3 + a_i^2 b_j^4 + a_i b_j^5 + b_j^6 = \sum_{k=0}^{6} a_i^{6-k} b_j^k \qquad ▌$$

EXAMPLE 4   **(Price indices)** In order to summarize how much the prices of different goods within a country have risen or fallen, a number of different *price indices* have been suggested. Consider a "basket" of n commodities. For $i = 1, \ldots, n$, define

$$q^{(i)} = \text{number of units of good } i \text{ in the basket}$$
$$p_0^{(i)} = \text{price per unit of good } i \text{ in year 0}$$
$$p_t^{(i)} = \text{price per unit of good } i \text{ in year } t$$

Then

$$\sum_{i=1}^{n} p_0^{(i)} q^{(i)} = p_0^{(1)} q^{(1)} + p_0^{(2)} q^{(2)} + \cdots + p_0^{(n)} q^{(n)}$$

is the cost of the basket in year 0, whereas

$$\sum_{i=1}^{n} p_t^{(i)} q^{(i)} = p_t^{(1)} q^{(1)} + p_t^{(2)} q^{(2)} + \cdots + p_t^{(n)} q^{(n)}$$

is the cost of the basket in year t. A price index for year t, with year 0 as the base year, is defined as

$$\frac{\sum_{i=1}^{n} p_t^{(i)} q^{(i)}}{\sum_{i=1}^{n} p_0^{(i)} q^{(i)}} \cdot 100 \qquad \text{(Price Index)} \qquad (1)$$

If the cost of the basket is 1032 in year 0 and the cost of the same basket in year t is 1548, then the price index is $(1548/1032) \cdot 100 = 150$.

In the case where the quantities $q^{(i)}$ are levels of consumption in the base year 0, this index is called the **Laspeyres price index**. But if the quantities $q^{(i)}$ are levels of consumption in the year t, this index is called the **Paasche price index**.

PROBLEMS FOR SECTION 3.1

1. Evaluate the following sums:

(a) $\sum_{i=1}^{10} i$ (b) $\sum_{k=2}^{6} (5 \cdot 3^{k-2} - k)$ (c) $\sum_{m=0}^{5} (2m + 1)$

(d) $\sum_{l=0}^{2} 2^{2^l}$ (e) $\sum_{i=1}^{10} 2$ (f) $\sum_{j=1}^{4} \frac{j+1}{j}$

2. Expand the following sums:

(a) $\sum_{k=-2}^{2} 2\sqrt{k+2}$ (b) $\sum_{i=0}^{3} (x+2i)^2$ (c) $\sum_{k=1}^{n} a_{ki} b^{k+1}$ (d) $\sum_{j=0}^{m} f(x_j) \Delta x_j$

3. Express these sums in summation notation:

(a) $4 + 8 + 12 + 16 + \cdots + 4n$ (b) $1^3 + 2^3 + 3^3 + 4^3 + \cdots + n^3$

(c) $1 - \frac{1}{3} + \frac{1}{5} - \frac{1}{7} + \cdots + (-1)^n \frac{1}{2n+1}$ (d) $a_{i1}b_{1j} + a_{i2}b_{2j} + \cdots + a_{in}b_{nj}$

(e) $3x + 9x^2 + 27x^3 + 81x^4 + 243x^5$ (f) $a_i^3 b_{i+3} + a_i^4 b_{i+4} + \cdots + a_i^p b_{i+p}$

(g) $a_i^3 b_{i+3} + a_{i+1}^4 b_{i+4} + \cdots + a_{i+p}^{p+3} b_{i+p+3}$ (h) $81297 + 81495 + 81693 + 81891$

4. Compute the price index (1) if $n = 3$, $p_0^{(1)} = 1$, $p_0^{(2)} = 2$, $p_0^{(3)} = 3$, $p_t^{(1)} = 2$, $p_t^{(2)} = 3$, $p_t^{(3)} = 4$, $q^{(1)} = 3$, $q^{(2)} = 5$, and $q^{(3)} = 7$.

5. Insert the approriate limits of summation in the sums on the right hand side.

(a) $\displaystyle\sum_{k=1}^{10}(k-2)t^k = \sum_{m=} mt^{m+2}$ (b) $\displaystyle\sum_{n=0}^{N} 2^{n+5} = \sum_{j=} 32 \cdot 2^{j-1}$

6. Consider a country divided into 100 regions. For a certain year, let c_{ij} be the number of persons who move from region i to region j, $i \neq j$. If, say, $i = 25$ and $j = 10$, then we write $c_{25,10}$ for c_{ij}. Explain the meaning of the sums: (a) $\sum_{j=1}^{100} c_{ij}$, (b) $\sum_{i=1}^{100} c_{ij}$.

7. Decide which of the following equalities are generally valid. (Note in particular the correct answer to (b).)

(a) $\displaystyle\sum_{k=1}^{n} ck^2 = c\sum_{k=1}^{n} k^2$ (b) $\displaystyle\left(\sum_{i=1}^{n} a_i\right)^2 = \sum_{i=1}^{n} a_i^2$ (c) $\displaystyle\sum_{j=1}^{n} b_j + \sum_{j=n+1}^{N} b_j = \sum_{j=1}^{N} b_j$

(d) $\displaystyle\sum_{k=3}^{7} 5^{k-2} = \sum_{k=0}^{4} 5^{k+1}$ (e) $\displaystyle\sum_{i=0}^{n-1} a_{i,j}^2 = \sum_{k=1}^{n} a_{k-1,j}^2$ (f) $\displaystyle\sum_{k=1}^{n} \frac{a_k}{k} = \frac{1}{k}\sum_{k=1}^{n} a_k$

3.2 Rules for Sums. Newton's Binomial Formula

The following properties of the sigma notation are helpful when manipulating sums:

$$\sum_{i=1}^{n}(a_i + b_i) = \sum_{i=1}^{n} a_i + \sum_{i=1}^{n} b_i \qquad \textbf{(additivity property)} \qquad (1)$$

$$\sum_{i=1}^{n} ca_i = c\sum_{i=1}^{n} a_i \qquad \textbf{(homogeneity property)} \qquad (2)$$

The proofs are straightforward. For example, (2) is proved by noting that

$$\sum_{i=1}^{n} ca_i = ca_1 + ca_2 + \cdots + ca_n = c(a_1 + a_2 + \cdots + a_n) = c\sum_{i=1}^{n} a_i$$

The homogeneity property (2) states that a constant factor can be moved outside the summation sign. In particular, if $a_i = 1$ for all i, then

$$\sum_{i=1}^{n} c = nc \qquad (3)$$

which just states that a constant c summed n times is equal to n times c.

The summation rules can be applied in combination to give formulas like

$$\sum_{i=1}^{n}(a_i + b_i - c_i + d) = \sum_{i=1}^{n}a_i + \sum_{i=1}^{n}b_i - \sum_{i=1}^{n}c_i + nd$$

EXAMPLE 1   Evaluate the sum

$$\sum_{m=2}^{n}\frac{1}{(m-1)m} = \frac{1}{1\cdot 2} + \frac{1}{2\cdot 3} + \cdots + \frac{1}{(n-1)n}$$

by using the identity $\dfrac{1}{(m-1)m} = \dfrac{1}{m-1} - \dfrac{1}{m}$.

Solution:

$$\sum_{m=2}^{n}\frac{1}{m(m-1)} = \sum_{m=2}^{n}\left(\frac{1}{m-1} - \frac{1}{m}\right) = \sum_{m=2}^{n}\frac{1}{m-1} - \sum_{m=2}^{n}\frac{1}{m}$$

$$= \left(\frac{1}{1} + \frac{1}{2} + \frac{1}{3} + \cdots + \frac{1}{n-1}\right) - \left(\frac{1}{2} + \frac{1}{3} + \cdots + \frac{1}{n-1} + \frac{1}{n}\right) = 1 - \frac{1}{n}$$

To derive the last equality, note that most of the terms cancel pairwise. The only exceptions are the first term within the first parentheses and the last term within the last parentheses. This powerful trick is commonly used to calculate some special sums of this kind.   ∎

EXAMPLE 2   The **arithmetic mean** (or **mean**) μ_x of T numbers $x_1, x_2, \ldots, x_T$ is their average, defined as the sum of all the numbers divided by the number of terms, T. That is, $\mu_x = \frac{1}{T}\sum_{i=1}^{T}x_i$. Prove that $\sum_{i=1}^{T}(x_i - \mu_x) = 0$ and $\sum_{i=1}^{T}(x_i - \mu_x)^2 = \sum_{i=1}^{T}x_i^2 - T\mu_x^2$.

Solution: The difference $x_i - \mu_x$ is the deviation between x_i and the mean. We prove first that the sum of these deviations is 0, using the foregoing definition of μ_x:

$$\sum_{i=1}^{T}(x_i - \mu_x) = \sum_{i=1}^{T}x_i - \sum_{i=1}^{T}\mu_x = \sum_{i=1}^{T}x_i - T\mu_x = T\mu_x - T\mu_x = 0$$

Furthermore, the sum of the squares of the deviations is

$$\sum_{i=1}^{T}(x_i - \mu_x)^2 = \sum_{i=1}^{T}(x_i^2 - 2\mu_x x_i + \mu_x^2) = \sum_{i=1}^{T}x_i^2 - 2\mu_x\sum_{i=1}^{T}x_i + \sum_{i=1}^{T}\mu_x^2$$

$$= \sum_{i=1}^{T}x_i^2 - 2\mu_x T\mu_x + T\mu_x^2 = \sum_{i=1}^{T}x_i^2 - T\mu_x^2$$

Dividing by T, the mean square deviation, $(1/T)\sum_{i=1}^{T}(x_i - \mu_x)^2$, is therefore equal to the mean square, $(1/T)\sum_{i=1}^{T}x_i^2$, minus the square of the mean, μ_x^2.   ∎

Useful Formulas

A (very) demanding teacher once asked his students to sum $81\,297 + 81\,495 + 81\,693 + \cdots + 100\,899$. There are 100 terms and the difference between successive terms is constant and equal to 198. Gauss, later one of the world's leading mathematicians, was in the class (at age 9), and is reputed to have given the right answer in only a few minutes. Problem 5 asks you match Gauss, but we will provide some help first.

Applied to the easier problem of finding the sum $x = 1 + 2 + \cdots + n$, Gauss' argument was probably as follows: First, write the sum x in two ways

$$x = 1 + 2 + \cdots + (n - 1) + n$$
$$x = n + (n - 1) + \cdots + 2 + 1$$

Summing vertically term by term gives

$$2x = (1 + n) + \left[2 + (n - 1)\right] + \cdots + \left[(n - 1) + 2\right] + (n + 1)$$
$$= (1 + n) + (1 + n) + \cdots + (1 + n) + (1 + n) = n(1 + n)$$

Thus, solving for x gives the result:

$$\sum_{i=1}^{n} i = 1 + 2 + \cdots + n = \tfrac{1}{2}n(n + 1) \tag{4}$$

The following two summation formulas are occasionally useful in economics. Check to see if they are true for $n = 1, 2$, and 3. For proofs, see Problem 3.7.2.

$$\sum_{i=1}^{n} i^2 = 1^2 + 2^2 + 3^2 + \cdots + n^2 = \tfrac{1}{6}n(n + 1)(2n + 1) \tag{5}$$

$$\sum_{i=1}^{n} i^3 = 1^3 + 2^3 + 3^3 + \cdots + n^3 = \left[\tfrac{1}{2}n(n + 1)\right]^2 = \left[\sum_{i=1}^{n} i\right]^2 \tag{6}$$

Newton's Binomial Formula

We all know that $(a + b)^1 = a + b$ and $(a + b)^2 = a^2 + 2ab + b^2$. Using the latter equality and writing $(a + b)^3 = (a + b)(a + b)^2$ and $(a + b)^4 = (a + b)(a + b)^3$, we find that

$$(a + b)^1 = a + b$$
$$(a + b)^2 = a^2 + 2ab + b^2$$
$$(a + b)^3 = a^3 + 3a^2b + 3ab^2 + b^3$$
$$(a + b)^4 = a^4 + 4a^3b + 6a^2b^2 + 4ab^3 + b^4$$

The corresponding formula for $(a + b)^m$, where m is any natural number is the following:[1]

NEWTON'S BINOMIAL FORMULA

$$(a + b)^m = a^m + \binom{m}{1}a^{m-1}b + \cdots + \binom{m}{m-1}ab^{m-1} + \binom{m}{m}b^m \qquad (7)$$

The **binomial coefficients** $\binom{m}{k}$ are defined, for $m = 1, 2, \ldots$ and for $k = 0, 1, 2, \ldots, m$, by

$$\binom{m}{k} = \frac{m(m-1)\cdots(m-k+1)}{k!}, \qquad \binom{m}{0} = 1$$

In general, $\binom{m}{1} = m$ and $\binom{m}{m} = 1$. When $m = 5$, for example, we have

$$\binom{5}{2} = \frac{5 \cdot 4}{1 \cdot 2} = 10, \qquad \binom{5}{3} = \frac{5 \cdot 4 \cdot 3}{1 \cdot 2 \cdot 3} = 10, \qquad \binom{5}{4} = \frac{5 \cdot 4 \cdot 3 \cdot 2}{1 \cdot 2 \cdot 3 \cdot 4} = 5$$

Then (7) gives $(a + b)^5 = a^5 + 5a^4b + 10a^3b^2 + 10a^2b^3 + 5ab^4 + b^5$.

The coefficients occurring in the expansions for successive powers of $(a + b)$ form the following pattern, called **Pascal's triangle** (though it was actually known in China by about the year 1100, long before Blaise Pascal was born):

$$
\begin{array}{ccccccccccccccccccc}
& & & & & & & & & 1 \\
& & & & & & & & 1 & & 1 \\
& & & & & & & 1 & & 2 & & 1 \\
& & & & & & 1 & & 3 & & 3 & & 1 \\
& & & & & 1 & & 4 & & 6 & & 4 & & 1 \\
& & & & 1 & & 5 & & 10 & & 10 & & 5 & & 1 \\
& & & 1 & & 6 & & 15 & & 20 & & 15 & & 6 & & 1 \\
& & 1 & & 7 & & 21 & & 35 & & 35 & & 21 & & 7 & & 1 \\
& 1 & & 8 & & 28 & & 56 & & 70 & & 56 & & 28 & & 8 & & 1 \\
1 & & 9 & & 36 & & 84 & & 126 & & 126 & & 84 & & 36 & & 9 & & 1
\end{array}
$$

This table can be continued indefinitely. The numbers in this triangle are indeed the binomial coefficients. For instance, the numbers in row 6 (when the first row is numbered 0) are

$$\binom{6}{0} \quad \binom{6}{1} \quad \binom{6}{2} \quad \binom{6}{3} \quad \binom{6}{4} \quad \binom{6}{5} \quad \binom{6}{6}$$

---

[1] If n is a natural number, let $n!$ (read as "n factorial") be defined as $n! = 1 \cdot 2 \cdot 3 \cdot \ldots \cdot (n-1) \cdot n$. For example, $5! = 1 \cdot 2 \cdot 3 \cdot 4 \cdot 5 = 120$. Also, the usual convention is that $0! = 1$.

Note first that the numbers are symmetric about the middle line. This symmetry can be expressed as

$$\binom{m}{k} = \binom{m}{m-k} \tag{8}$$

For example, $\binom{6}{2} = 15 = \binom{6}{4}$. Second, apart from the 1 at both ends of each row, each number is the sum of the two adjacent numbers in the row above. For instance, 56 in the eighth row is equal to the sum of 21 and 35 in the seventh row. In symbols,

$$\binom{m+1}{k+1} = \binom{m}{k} + \binom{m}{k+1} \tag{9}$$

In Problem 4 you are asked to prove these two properties.

PROBLEMS FOR SECTION 3.2

1. Use the results in (4) and (5) to find $\sum_{k=1}^{n}(k^2 + 3k + 2)$.

2. Use Newton's binomial formula to find $(a + b)^6$.

3. (a) Prove that $\sum_{k=1}^{8}(a_{k+1} - a_k) = a_9 - a_1$, and, generally, that $\sum_{k=1}^{n}(a_{k+1} - a_k) = a_{n+1} - a_1$.

   (b) Use the result in (a) to compute the following:

   (i) $\displaystyle\sum_{k=1}^{50}\left(\frac{1}{k} - \frac{1}{k+1}\right)$ (ii) $\displaystyle\sum_{k=1}^{12}\left(3^{k+1} - 3^k\right)$ (iii) $\displaystyle\sum_{k=1}^{n}\left(ar^{k+1} - ar^k\right)$

4. (a) Prove that $\binom{5}{3} = \dfrac{5!}{2!\,3!}$, and in general that

   $$\binom{m}{k} = \frac{m!}{(m-k)!\,k!} \tag{10}$$

   (b) Verify by direct computation that

   $$\binom{8}{3} = \binom{8}{8-3} \quad \text{and} \quad \binom{8+1}{3+1} = \binom{8}{3} + \binom{8}{3+1}$$

   (c) Use (10) to verify (8) and (9).

5. Prove the summation formula for an **arithmetic series**,

   $$\sum_{i=0}^{n-1}(a + id) = na + \frac{n(n-1)d}{2}$$

   Apply the result to find the sum Gauss is supposed to have found at school.

3.3 Double Sums

Often one has to combine several summation signs. Consider, for example, the following rectangular array of numbers:

$$
\begin{array}{cccc}
a_{11} & a_{12} & \cdots & a_{1n} \\
a_{21} & a_{22} & \cdots & a_{2n} \\
\vdots & \vdots & & \vdots \\
a_{m1} & a_{m2} & \cdots & a_{mn}
\end{array}
\tag{1}
$$

The array can be regarded as a *spreadsheet*. A typical number in the array is of the form a_{ij}, where $1 \leq i \leq m$ and $1 \leq j \leq n$. (For example, a_{ij} may indicate the total revenue of a firm from its sales in region i in month j.) There are $n \cdot m$ numbers in all. Let us find the sum of all the numbers in the array by first finding the sum of the numbers in each of the m rows and then adding all these row sums. The m different row sums can be written in the form $\sum_{j=1}^{n} a_{1j}$, $\sum_{j=1}^{n} a_{2j}$, $\ldots$, $\sum_{j=1}^{n} a_{mj}$. (In our example, these row sums are the total revenues in each region summed over all the n months.) The sum of these m sums is equal to $\sum_{j=1}^{n} a_{1j} + \sum_{j=1}^{n} a_{2j} + \cdots + \sum_{j=1}^{n} a_{mj}$, which can be written as $\sum_{i=1}^{m} \left(\sum_{j=1}^{n} a_{ij} \right)$. If instead we add the numbers in each of the n columns first and then add these sums, we get

$$
\sum_{i=1}^{m} a_{i1} + \sum_{i=1}^{m} a_{i2} + \cdots + \sum_{i=1}^{m} a_{in} = \sum_{j=1}^{n} \left(\sum_{i=1}^{m} a_{ij} \right)
$$

(How do you interpret this sum in our economic example?) In both these cases, we have calculated the sum of all the numbers in the array. For this reason, we must have

$$
\sum_{i=1}^{m} \sum_{j=1}^{n} a_{ij} = \sum_{j=1}^{n} \sum_{i=1}^{m} a_{ij}
$$

where, according to usual practice, we have deleted the parentheses. This formula says that *in a (finite) double sum, the order of summation is immaterial.* It is important to note that the summation limits for i and j are independent of each other.

EXAMPLE 1   Compute $\sum_{i=1}^{3} \sum_{j=1}^{4} (i + 2j)$.

Solution:

$$
\sum_{i=1}^{3} \sum_{j=1}^{4} (i + 2j) = \sum_{i=1}^{3} \left[(i + 2) + (i + 4) + (i + 6) + (i + 8) \right]
$$

$$
= \sum_{i=1}^{3} (4i + 20) = 24 + 28 + 32 = 84
$$

You should check that the result is the same by summing first over i instead.

PROBLEMS FOR SECTION 3.3

1. Expand the following:

   (a) $\displaystyle\sum_{i=1}^{3}\sum_{j=1}^{4} i \cdot 3^j$ (b) $\displaystyle\sum_{s=0}^{2}\sum_{r=2}^{4}\left(\frac{rs}{r+s}\right)^2$ (c) $\displaystyle\sum_{i=1}^{m}\sum_{j=1}^{n} i \cdot j^2$

2. Consider a group of individuals each having a certain number of units of m different goods. Let a_{ij} denote the number of units of good i owned by person j ($i = 1, \ldots, m;\ j = 1, \ldots, n$). Explain in words the meaning of the following sums:

   (a) $\displaystyle\sum_{j=1}^{n} a_{ij}$ (b) $\displaystyle\sum_{i=1}^{m} a_{ij}$ (c) $\displaystyle\sum_{j=1}^{n}\sum_{i=1}^{m} a_{ij}$

3. Prove that the sum of all the numbers in the triangular table

$$
\begin{array}{ccccc}
a_{11} & & & & \\
a_{21} & a_{22} & & & \\
a_{31} & a_{32} & a_{33} & & \\
\vdots & \vdots & \vdots & \ddots & \\
a_{m1} & a_{m2} & a_{m3} & \cdots & a_{mm}
\end{array}
$$

can be written as $\displaystyle\sum_{i=1}^{m}\left(\sum_{j=1}^{i} a_{ij}\right)$ or as $\displaystyle\sum_{j=1}^{m}\left(\sum_{i=j}^{m} a_{ij}\right)$.

HARDER PROBLEMS

4. Consider the $m \cdot n$ numbers a_{ij} in the rectangular array (1). Denote the arithmetic mean of them all by $\bar{a}$, and the mean of all the numbers in the jth column by $\bar{a}_j$, so that

$$
\bar{a} = \frac{1}{mn}\sum_{r=1}^{m}\sum_{s=1}^{n} a_{rs}, \qquad \bar{a}_j = \frac{1}{m}\sum_{r=1}^{m} a_{rj}
$$

Prove that

$$
\sum_{r=1}^{m}\sum_{s=1}^{m}(a_{rj} - \bar{a})(a_{sj} - \bar{a}) = m^2(\bar{a}_j - \bar{a})^2 \tag{$*$}
$$

3.4 A Few Aspects of Logic

We have emphasized the role of mathematical models in the empirical sciences, especially in economics. The more complicated the phenomena to be described, the more important it is to be exact. Errors in models applied to practical situations can have catastrophic consequences. For example, in the early stages of the U.S. space program, a rocket costing millions of dollars to develop had to be destroyed only seconds after launch because a semicolon was missing in the computer program controlling its guidance system. A more recent example is the Mars lander which burned up early in the year 2000 because of a confusion between metric and U.S. units of measurement.

Although the consequences may be less dramatic, errors in mathematical reasoning also occur easily. Here is a typical example of how a student (or even a professor) might use faulty logic and thus end up with an incorrect answer to a problem.

EXAMPLE 1   Find a possible solution for the equation

$$x + 2 = \sqrt{4 - x}$$

"Solution": Squaring each side of the equation gives $(x + 2)^2 = (\sqrt{4 - x})^2$, and thus $x^2 + 4x + 4 = 4 - x$. Rearranging this last equation gives $x^2 + 5x = 0$. Cancelling x results in $x + 5 = 0$, and therefore $x = -5$.

According to this reasoning, the answer should be $x = -5$. Let us check this. For $x = -5$, we have $x + 2 = -3$. Yet $\sqrt{4 - x} = \sqrt{9} = 3$, so this answer is incorrect. In Example 4 we explain how the error arose. (Note the wisdom of checking your answer whenever you think you have solved an equation.)   ▌

This example highlights the dangers of routine calculation without adequate thought. It may be easier to avoid similar mistakes after studying more closely the structure of logical reasoning.

Propositions

Assertions that are either true or false are called statements, or **propositions.** Most of the propositions in this book are mathematical ones, but other kinds may arise in daily life. "All individuals who breathe are alive" is an example of a true proposition, whereas the assertion "all individuals who breathe are healthy" is a false proposition. Note that if the words used to express such an assertion lack precise meaning, it will often be difficult to tell whether it is true or false. For example, the assertion "67 is a big number" is neither true nor false without a precise definition of "big number".

Suppose an assertion, such as "$x^2 - 1 = 0$," includes one or more variables. By substituting various real numbers for the variable x, we can generate many different propositions, some true and some false. For this reason we say that the assertion is an **open proposition.** In fact, the proposition $x^2 - 1 = 0$ happens to be true if $x = 1$ or -1, but not otherwise.

Thus, an open proposition is not simply true or false. It is neither true nor false until we choose a particular value for the variable.

Implications

In order to keep track of each step in a chain of logical reasoning, it often helps to use implication arrows.

Suppose P and Q are two propositions such that whenever P is true, then Q is necessarily true. In this case, we usually write

$$P \implies Q \tag{$*$}$$

This is read as "P implies Q," or "if P, then Q," or "Q is a consequence of P." Other ways of expressing the same implication include "Q if P", "P only if Q", and "Q is an implication of P". The symbol $\implies$ is an **implication arrow,** and it points in the direction of the logical implication. Here are some examples of correct implications.

EXAMPLE 2   (a) $x > 2 \implies x^2 > 4$

(b) $xy = 0 \implies x = 0$ or $y = 0$

(c) x is a square $\implies x$ is a rectangle

(d) x is a healthy person $\implies x$ is breathing easily

Notice that the word "or" in mathematics means the "inclusive or," signifying that "P or Q" includes the case when P and Q are both true.

All the propositions before and after each implication arrow in Example 2 are open propositions, just as are most propositions encountered in mathematics. An implication $P \implies Q$ means that for each value of some variable for which P is true, Q is also true.

In certain cases where the implication ($*$) is valid, it may also be possible to draw a logical conclusion in the other direction:

$$Q \implies P$$

In such cases, we can write both implications together in a single **logical equivalence**:

$$P \iff Q$$

We then say that "P is equivalent to Q". Because we have both "P if Q" and "P only if Q", we also say that "P if and only if Q", which is often written "P iff Q" for short. The symbol $\iff$ is an **equivalence arrow.**

In Example 2, we see that the implication arrow in (b) could be replaced with the equivalence arrow, because it is also true that $x = 0$ or $y = 0$ implies $xy = 0$. Note, however, that no other implication in Example 2 can be replaced by the equivalence arrow. For even if x^2 is larger than 4, it is not necessarily true that x is larger than 2 (for instance, x might be -3); also, a rectangle is not necessarily a square; and, finally, just because person x is breathing easily does not mean that x is healthy.

Necessary and Sufficient Conditions

There are other commonly used ways of expressing that proposition P implies proposition Q, or that P is equivalent to Q. Thus, if proposition P implies proposition Q, we state that P is a "sufficient condition" for Q. After all, for Q to be true, it is sufficient that P is true. Accordingly, we know that if P is satisfied, then it is certain that Q is also satisfied. In this case, we say that Q is a "necessary condition" for P, for Q must necessarily be true if P is true. Hence,

---

P is a **sufficient condition** for Q means: $P \implies Q$

Q is a **necessary condition** for P means: $P \implies Q$

If we formulate the implication in Example 2 (c) in this way, it would read:

A sufficient condition for x to be a rectangle is that x be a square.

or

A necessary condition for x to be a square is that x be a rectangle.

The corresponding verbal expression for $P \iff Q$ is simply: *P is a necessary and sufficient condition for Q*.

It is evident from this that it is very important to distinguish between the propositions "P is a necessary condition for Q" (meaning $Q \implies P$) and "P is a sufficient condition for Q" (meaning $P \implies Q$). To emphasize the point, consider two propositions:

Breathing is a necessary condition for a person to be healthy.

Breathing is a sufficient condition for a person to be healthy.

The first proposition is clearly true. But the second is false, because sick people are still breathing.

In the following pages, we shall repeatedly refer to necessary and sufficient conditions. Understanding them and the difference between them is a necessary condition for understanding much of economic analysis. It is not a sufficient condition, alas!

Solving Equations

Implication and equivalence arrows are very useful in helping to avoid mistakes in solving equations. Consider first the following example.

EXAMPLE 3   Find all x such that $(2x - 1)^2 - 3x^2 = 2\left(\frac{1}{2} - 4x\right)$.

Solution: By expanding $(2x - 1)^2$ and also multiplying out the right-hand side, we obtain a new equation that obviously has the same solutions as the original one:

$$(2x - 1)^2 - 3x^2 = 2\left(\tfrac{1}{2} - 4x\right) \iff 4x^2 - 4x + 1 - 3x^2 = 1 - 8x$$

Adding $8x - 1$ to each side of the second equality and then gathering terms gives the equivalent expression

$$4x^2 - 4x + 1 - 3x^2 = 1 - 8x \iff x^2 + 4x = 0$$

Now $x^2 + 4x = x(x + 4)$, and the latter expression is 0 if and only if $x = 0$ or $x = -4$. That is,

$$x^2 + 4x = 0 \iff x(x + 4) = 0 \iff x = 0 \quad \text{or} \quad x = -4$$

Putting everything together, we have derived a chain of equivalence arrows showing that the given equation is fulfilled for the two values $x = 0$ and $x = -4$, and for no other values of x. ▮

EXAMPLE 4   Find all x such that $x + 2 = \sqrt{4 - x}$. (Recall Example 1.)

Solution: Squaring both sides of the given equation yields

$$\left(x + 2\right)^2 = \left(\sqrt{4 - x}\right)^2$$

Consequently, $x^2 + 4x + 4 = 4 - x$, that is, $x^2 + 5x = 0$. From the latter equation it follows that

$$x(x + 5) = 0 \quad \text{which yields} \quad x = 0 \text{ or } x = -5$$

Thus, a necessary condition for x to solve $x + 2 = \sqrt{4 - x}$ is that $x = 0$ or $x = -5$. Inserting these two possible values of x into the original equation shows that only $x = 0$ satisfies the equation. The unique solution to the equation is, therefore, $x = 0$. ▮

In finding the solution to Example 1, why was it necessary to test whether the values we found were actually solutions, whereas this step was unnecessary in Example 3? To answer this, we must analyse the logical structure of our solution to Example 1. Using implication arrows marked by letters, we can express the solution as follows:

$$x + 2 = \sqrt{4 - x} \overset{(a)}{\Longrightarrow} (x + 2)^2 = 4 - x \overset{(b)}{\Longrightarrow} x^2 + 4x + 4 = 4 - x$$

$$\overset{(c)}{\Longrightarrow} x^2 + 5x = 0 \overset{(d)}{\Longrightarrow} x(x + 5) = 0 \overset{(e)}{\Longrightarrow} x = 0 \text{ or } x = -5$$

Implication (a) is true (because $a = b \implies a^2 = b^2$ and $\left(\sqrt{a}\right)^2 = a$). *It is important to note, however, that the implication cannot be replaced by an equivalence.* If $a^2 = b^2$, then either $a = b$ or $a = -b$; it need not be true that $a = b$. Implications (b), (c), (d), and (e) are also all true; moreover, all could have been written as equivalences, though this is not necessary in order to find the solution. Therefore, a chain of implications has been obtained that leads from the equation $x + 2 = \sqrt{4 - x}$ to the proposition "$x = 0$ or $x = -5$." Because the implication (a) cannot be reversed, there is no corresponding chain of implications going in the opposite direction. We have verified that if the number x satisfies $x + 2 = \sqrt{4 - x}$, then x must be either 0 or -5; no other value can satisfy the given equation. However, we have not yet shown that either 0 or -5 really satisfies the equation. Only after we try inserting 0 and -5 into the equation do we see that $x = 0$ is the only solution. *Note that in this case, the test we have suggested not only serves to check our calculations, but is also a logical necessity.*

Looking back at Example 1, we now realize that two errors were committed. Firstly, the implication $x^2 + 5x = 0 \Rightarrow x + 5 = 0$ is wrong, because $x = 0$ is also a solution of $x^2 + 5x = 0$. Secondly, it is logically necessary to check if 0 or -5 really satisfies the equation.

The method used in solving Example 4 is the most common. It involves setting up a chain of implications that starts from the given equation and ends with all the possible solutions. By testing each of these trial solutions in turn, we find which of them really do satisfy the equation. Even if the chain of implications is also a chain of equivalences, such a test is always a useful check of both logic and calculations.

PROBLEMS FOR SECTION 3.4

1. There are many other ways to express implications and equivalences, apart from those already mentioned. Use appropriate implication or equivalence arrows to represent the following propositions:

   (a) The equation $2x - 4 = 2$ is fulfilled only when $x = 3$.

   (b) If $x = 3$, then $2x - 4 = 2$.

   (c) The equation $x^2 - 2x + 1 = 0$ is satisfied if $x = 1$.

   (d) If $x^2 > 4$, then $|x| > 2$, and conversely.

2. Solve the equation $\dfrac{(x + 1)^2}{x(x - 1)} + \dfrac{(x - 1)^2}{x(x + 1)} - 2\dfrac{3x + 1}{x^2 - 1} = 0$.

3. Consider the following six implications and decide in each case: (i) if the implication is true, and (ii) if the converse implication is true. (x, y, and z are real numbers.)

   (a) $x = 2$ and $y = 5 \Longrightarrow x + y = 7$ (b) $(x - 1)(x - 2)(x - 3) = 0 \Longrightarrow x = 1$

   (c) $x^2 + y^2 = 0 \Longrightarrow x = 0$ or $y = 0$ (d) $x = 0$ and $y = 0 \Longrightarrow x^2 + y^2 = 0$

   (e) $xy = xz \Longrightarrow y = z$ (f) $x > y^2 \Longrightarrow x > 0$

4. Consider the proposition $2x + 5 \geq 13$.

   (a) Is the condition $x \geq 0$ necessary, sufficient, or both necessary and sufficient for the inequality to be satisfied?

(b) Answer the same question when $x \geq 0$ is replaced by $x \geq 50$.

(c) Answer the same question when $x \geq 0$ is replaced by $x \geq 4$.

5. Solve the following equations:

   (a) $x + 2 = \sqrt{4x + 13}$ (b) $|x + 2| = \sqrt{4 - x}$ (c) $x^2 - 2|x| - 3 = 0$

6. Solve the following equations:

   (a) $\sqrt{x - 4} = \sqrt{x + 5} - 9$ (b) $\sqrt{x - 4} = 9 - \sqrt{x + 5}$

7. Fill in the blank rectangles with "iff" (if and only if) when this results in a true statement, or alternatively with "if" or "only if."

   (a) $x = \sqrt{4}$ ⬚ $x = 2$ (b) $x(x + 3) < 0$ ⬚ $x > -3$

   (c) $x^2 < 9$ ⬚ $x < 3$ (d) $x(x^2 + 1) = 0$ ⬚ $x = 0$

   (e) $x^2 > 0$ ⬚ $x > 0$ (f) $x^4 + y^4 = 0$ ⬚ $x = 0$ or $y = 0$

8. Consider the following attempt to solve the equation $x + \sqrt{x + 4} = 2$:

   "From the given equation, it follows that $\sqrt{x + 4} = 2 - x$. Squaring both sides gives $x + 4 = 4 - 4x + x^2$. After rearranging the terms, it is seen that this equation implies $x^2 - 5x = 0$. Cancelling x, we obtain $x - 5 = 0$ and this equation is satisfied when $x = 5$."

   (a) Mark with arrows the implications or equivalences expressed in the text. Which ones are correct?

   (b) Solve the equation correctly.

HARDER PROBLEMS

9. If P is a statement, the *negation* of P is denoted by $\neg P$. If P is true, then $\neg P$ is false, and vice versa. For example, the negation of the statement $2x + 3y \leq 8$ is $2x + 3y > 8$. For each of the following 6 propositions, state the negation as simply as possible.

   (a) $x \geq 0$ and $y \geq 0$.   (b) All x satisfy $x \geq a$.

   (c) Neither x nor y is less than 5.   (d) For each $\varepsilon > 0$, there exists a $\delta > 0$ such that B is satisfied.

   (e) No one can help liking cats.   (f) Everyone loves somebody some of the time.

3.5 Mathematical Proofs

In every branch of mathematics, the most important results are called **theorems.** Constructing logically valid proofs for these results often can be very complicated. For example, the "four-colour theorem" states that any map in the plane needs at most four colours in order that all contiguous regions can be given different colours. Proving this involved checking hundreds of thousands of different cases, a task that was impossible without a sophisticated computer program.

In this book, we often omit formal proofs of theorems. Instead, the emphasis is on providing a good intuitive grasp of what the theorems tell us. However, although proofs do not form a major part of this book, it is still useful to understand something about the different types of proof that are used in mathematics.

Every mathematical theorem can be formulated as an implication

$$P \implies Q \tag{$*$}$$

where P represents a proposition or a series of propositions called *premises* ("what we know"), and Q represents a proposition or a series of propositions that are called the *conclusions* ("what we want to know").

Usually, it is most natural to prove a result of the type $(*)$ by starting with the premises P and successively working forward to the conclusions Q; we call this a **direct proof.** Sometimes, however, it is more convenient to prove the implication $P \implies Q$ by an **indirect proof.** In this case, we begin by supposing that Q is not true, and on that basis demonstrate that P cannot be true either. This is completely legitimate, because we have the following equivalence:

$$P \implies Q \qquad \text{is equivalent to} \qquad not \; Q \implies not \; P$$

It is helpful to consider how this rule of logic applies to a concrete example:

If it is raining, the grass is getting wet.

asserts precisely the same thing as

If the grass is not getting wet, then it is not raining.

EXAMPLE 1   Use the two methods of proof to prove that $-x^2 + 5x - 4 > 0 \implies x > 0$.

Solution:

(a) *Direct proof:* Suppose $-x^2 + 5x - 4 > 0$. Adding $x^2 + 4$ to each side of the inequality gives $5x > x^2 + 4$. Because $x^2 + 4 \geq 4$, for all x, we have $5x > 4$, and so $x > 4/5$. In particular, $x > 0$.

(b) *Indirect proof:* Suppose $x \leq 0$. Then $5x \leq 0$ and so $-x^2 + 5x - 4$, as a sum of three nonpositive terms, is ≤ 0.   ∎

Deductive vs. Inductive Reasoning

The two methods of proof just outlined are all examples of *deductive reasoning*, that is, reasoning based on consistent rules of logic. In contrast, many branches of science use *inductive reasoning*. This process draws general conclusions based only on a few (or even many) observations. For example, the statement that "the price level has increased every year for the last n years; therefore, it will surely increase next year too," demonstrates inductive reasoning. This inductive approach is nevertheless of fundamental importance in the experimental and empirical sciences, despite the fact that conclusions based upon it never can be absolutely certain. Indeed, in economics, such examples of inductive reasoning (or the implied predictions) often turn out to be false, with hindsight.

In mathematics, inductive reasoning is not recognized as a form of proof. Suppose, for instance, that students in a geometry course are asked to show that the sum of the angles of a triangle is always 180 degrees. If they painstakingly measure as accurately as possible 1000 different triangles, demonstrating that in each case the sum of the angles is 180, it would not serve as proof for the assertion. It would represent a very good indication that the proposition is true, but it is not a mathematical proof. Similarly, in business economics, the fact that a particular company's profits have risen for each of the past 20 years is no guarantee that they will rise once again this year.

PROBLEMS FOR SECTION 3.5

1. Consider the following (dubious) statement: "If inflation increases, then unemployment decreases." Which of the following statements are equivalent to the given one?

   (a) For unemployment to decrease, inflation must increase.

   (b) A sufficient condition for unemployment to decrease is that inflation increases.

   (c) Unemployment can only decrease if inflation increases.

   (d) If unemployment does not decrease, then inflation does not increase.

   (e) A necessary condition for inflation to increase is that unemployment decreases.

2. Analyse the following epitaph: (a) using logic; (b) from a poetic viewpoint.

   > Those who knew him, loved him.
   > Those who loved him not, knew him not.

3. Show by an indirect proof: If x and y are integers and xy is an odd number, then x and y are both odd.

3.6 Essentials of Set Theory

In daily life, we constantly group together objects of the same kind. For instance, we refer to the faculty of a university to signify all the members of the academic staff. A garden refers to all the plants that are growing in it. We talk about all Scottish firms with more than 300 employees, all taxpayers in Germany who earned between 50 000 and 100 000 euros in 2004. In all these cases, we have a collection of objects viewed as a whole. In mathematics, such a collection is called a **set**, and its objects are called its **elements**, or its **members**.

How is a set specified? The simplest method is to list its members, in any order, between the two braces { and }. An example is the set $S = \{a, b, c\}$ whose members are the first three letters in the English alphabet. Or it might be a set consisting of three members represented by the letters a, b, and c. For example, if $a = 0$, $b = 1$, and $c = 2$, then $S = \{0, 1, 2\}$. Also, S denotes the set of roots of the cubic equation $(x - a)(x - b)(x - c) = 0$ in the unknown x, where a, b, and c are any three real numbers.

Two sets A and B are considered **equal** if each element of A is an element of B and each element of B is an element of A. In this case, we write $A = B$. This means that the two sets consist of exactly the same elements. Consequently, $\{1, 2, 3\} = \{3, 2, 1\}$, because the order in which the elements are listed has no significance; and $\{1, 1, 2, 3\} = \{1, 2, 3\}$, because a set is not changed if some elements are listed more than once.

Alternatively, suppose that you are to eat a meal at a restaurant that offers a choice of several main dishes. Four choices might be feasible—fish, pasta, omelette, and chicken. Then the *feasible set F* has these four members, and is fully specified as

$$F = \{\text{fish, pasta, omelette, chicken}\}$$

Notice that the order in which the dishes are listed does not matter. The feasible set remains the same even if the order of the items on the menu is changed.

Specifying a Property

Not every set can be defined by listing all its members, however. For one thing, some sets are infinite—that is, they contain infinitely many members.

Actually, such infinite sets are rather common in economics. Take, for instance, the *budget set* that arises in consumer theory. Suppose there are two goods with quantities denoted by x and y. Suppose one unit of these goods can be bought at prices p and q, respectively. A consumption bundle (x, y) is a pair of quantities of the two goods. Its value at prices p and q is $px + qy$. Suppose that a consumer has an amount m to spend on the two goods. Then the *budget constraint* is $px + qy \leq m$ (assuming that the consumer is free to underspend). If one also accepts that the quantity consumed of each good must be nonnegative, then the *budget set*, that will be denoted by B, consists of those consumption bundles (x, y) satisfying the three inequalities $px + qy \leq m$, $x \geq 0$, and $y \geq 0$. (The set B is shown in Fig. 4.4.12.) Standard notation for such a set is

$$B = \{(x, y) : px + qy \leq m, \ x \geq 0, \ y \geq 0\} \tag{1}$$

The braces { } are still used to denote "the set consisting of." However, instead of listing all the members, which is impossible for the infinite set of points in the triangular budget set B, the set is specified in two parts. To the left of the colon, (x, y) is used to denote the form of the typical member of B, here a consumption bundle that is specified by listing the respective quantities of the two goods. To the right of the colon, the three properties that these typical members must satisfy are all listed, and the set thereby specified. This is an example of the general specification:

$$S = \{\text{typical member} : \text{defining properties}\}$$

Note that it is not just infinite sets that can be specified by properties—finite sets can also be specified in this way. Indeed, even some finite sets almost *have* to be specified in this way, such as the set of all human beings currently alive.

Set Membership

As we stated earlier, sets contain members or elements. There is some convenient standard notation that denotes the relation between a set and its members. First,

$$x \in S$$

indicates that x *is an element of* S. Note the special symbol $\in$ (which is a variant of the Greek letter ϵ, or "epsilon").

To express the fact that x is *not* a member of S, we write $x \notin S$. For example, $d \notin \{a, b, c\}$ says that d is not an element of the set $\{a, b, c\}$.

For additional illustrations of set membership notation, let us return to the main dish example. Confronted with the choice from the set $F = \{\text{fish, pasta, omelette, chicken}\}$, let s denote your actual selection. Then, of course, $s \in F$. This is what we mean by "feasible set"—it is possible only to choose some member of that set but nothing outside it.

Let A and B be any two sets. Then A is a **subset** of B if it is true that every member of A is also a member of B. Then we write $A \subseteq B$. In particular, $A \subseteq A$. From the definitions we see that $A = B$ if and only if $A \subseteq B$ and $B \subseteq A$.

Set Operations

Sets can be combined in many different ways. Especially important are three operations: union, intersection, and the difference of sets, as shown in Table 1.

Table 1

Notation	Name	The set consists of:
$A \cup B$	A **union** B	The elements that belong to at least one of the sets A and B
$A \cap B$	A **intersection** B	The elements that belong to both A and B
$A \setminus B$	A **minus** B	The elements that belong to A, but not to B

Thus,

$$A \cup B = \{x : x \in A \text{ or } x \in B\}$$
$$A \cap B = \{x : x \in A \text{ and } x \in B\}$$
$$A \setminus B = \{x : x \in A \text{ and } x \notin B\}$$

EXAMPLE 1   Let $A = \{1, 2, 3, 4, 5\}$ and $B = \{3, 6\}$. Find $A \cup B, A \cap B, A \setminus B$, and $B \setminus A$.

Solution: $A \cup B = \{1, 2, 3, 4, 5, 6\}, A \cap B = \{3\}, A \setminus B = \{1, 2, 4, 5\}, B \setminus A = \{6\}.$ ∎

An economic example can be obtained by considering taxpayers in Utopia in 2001. Let A be the set of all those taxpayers who had an income of at least 15 000 and let B be the set of all who had a net worth of at least 150 000. Then $A \cup B$ would be those taxpayers who earned at least 15 000 or who had a net worth of at least 150 000, whereas $A \cap B$ are those taxpayers who earned at least 15 000 and who also had a net worth of at least 150 000. Finally, $A \setminus B$ would be those who earned at least 15 000 but who had less than 150 000 in net worth.

If two sets A and B have no elements in common, they are said to be **disjoint**. The symbol "∅" denotes the set that has no elements. It is called the **empty set**. Thus, the sets A and B are disjoint if and only if $A \cap B = \emptyset$.

A collection of sets is often referred to as a **family** of sets. When considering a certain family of sets, it is usually natural to think of each set in the family as a subset of one particular fixed set Ω, hereafter called the **universal set.** In the previous example, the set of all Utopian taxpayers in 2001 would be an obvious choice for a universal set.

If A is a subset of the universal set Ω, then according to the definition of difference, $\Omega \setminus A$ is the set of elements of Ω that are not in A. This set is called the **complement** of A in Ω and is sometimes denoted by $\mathcal{C}A$, so that $\mathcal{C}A = \Omega \setminus A$. Other ways of denoting the complement of A include A^c and $\tilde{A}$.

When using the notation $\mathcal{C}A$ or some equivalent, it is important to be clear about which universal set Ω is used to construct the complement.

EXAMPLE 2   Let the universal set Ω be the set of all students at a particular university. Moreover, let F denote the set of female students, M the set of all mathematics students, C the set of students in the university choir, B the set of all biology students, and T the set of all tennis players. Describe the members of the following sets: $\Omega \setminus M, M \cup C, F \cap T, M \setminus (B \cap T)$, and $(M \setminus B) \cup (M \setminus T)$.

Solution: $\Omega \setminus M$ consists of those students who are not studying mathematics, $M \cup C$ of those students who study mathematics and/or are in the choir. The set $F \cap T$ consists of those female students who play tennis. The set $M \setminus (B \cap T)$ has those mathematics students who do not both study biology and play tennis. Finally, the last set $(M \setminus B) \cup (M \setminus T)$ has those students who either are mathematics students not studying biology or mathematics students who do not play tennis. Do you see that the last two sets are equal? (For arbitrary sets M, B, and T, it is true that $(M \setminus B) \cup (M \setminus T) = M \setminus (B \cap T)$. It will be easier to verify this equality after you have read the following discussion of Venn diagrams.) ∎

Venn Diagrams

When considering the relationships between several sets, it is instructive and extremely helpful to represent each set by a region in a plane. The region is drawn so that all the elements belonging to a certain set are contained within some closed region of the plane. Diagrams constructed in this manner are called **Venn diagrams.** The definitions discussed in the previous section can be illustrated as in Fig. 1.

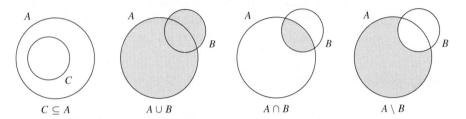

Figure 1 Venn diagrams

By using the definitions directly, or by illustrating sets with Venn diagrams, one can derive formulas that are universally valid regardless of which sets are being considered. For example, the formula $A \cap B = B \cap A$ follows immediately from the definition of the intersection between two sets. It is somewhat more difficult to verify directly from the definitions that the following relationship is valid for all sets A, B, and C:

$$A \cap (B \cup C) = (A \cap B) \cup (A \cap C) \qquad (*)$$

With the use of a Venn diagram, however, we easily see that the sets on the right- and left-hand sides of the equality sign both represent the shaded set in Fig. 2. The equality in $(*)$ is therefore valid.

Figure 2

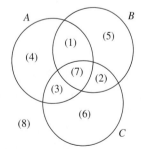

Figure 3

It is important that the three sets A, B, and C in a Venn diagram be drawn in such a way that all possible relations between an element and each of the three sets are represented. In other words, as in Fig. 3, the following eight different sets all should be nonempty:

(1) $(A \cap B) \setminus C$ (2) $(B \cap C) \setminus A$ (3) $(C \cap A) \setminus B$ (4) $A \setminus (B \cup C)$

(5) $B \setminus (C \cup A)$ (6) $C \setminus (A \cup B)$ (7) $A \cap B \cap C$ (8) $\complement(A \cup B \cup C)$

Notice, however, that this way of representing sets in the plane becomes unmanageable if four or more sets are involved, because then there would have to be at least $16 (= 2^4)$ regions in any such Venn diagram.

From the definition of intersection and union (or by the use of Venn diagrams), it easily follows that $A \cup (B \cup C) = (A \cup B) \cup C$ and that $A \cap (B \cap C) = (A \cap B) \cap C$. Consequently, it does not matter where the parentheses are placed. In such cases, the parentheses can be dropped and the expressions written as $A \cup B \cup C$ and $A \cap B \cap C$. Note, however, that the parentheses cannot generally be moved in the expression $A \cap (B \cup C)$, because this set is not always equal to $(A \cap B) \cup C$. Prove this fact by considering the case where $A = \{1, 2, 3\}$, $B = \{2, 3\}$, and $C = \{4, 5\}$, or by using a Venn diagram.

PROBLEMS FOR SECTION 3.6

1. Let $A = \{2, 3, 4\}$, $B = \{2, 5, 6\}$, $C = \{5, 6, 2\}$, and $D = \{6\}$.

   (a) Determine which of the following statements are true: $4 \in C$; $5 \in C$; $A \subseteq B$; $D \subseteq C$; $B = C$; and $A = B$.

   (b) Find $A \cap B$; $A \cup B$; $A \setminus B$; $B \setminus A$; $(A \cup B) \setminus (A \cap B)$; $A \cup B \cup C \cup D$; $A \cap B \cap C$; and $A \cap B \cap C \cap D$.

2. Let F, M, C, B, and T be the sets in Example 2. Describe the following sets: $F \cap B \cap C$, $M \cap F$, and $((M \cap B) \setminus C) \setminus T$.

3. A survey revealed that 50 people liked coffee and 40 liked tea. Both these figures include 35 who liked both coffee and tea. Finally, 10 did not like either coffee or tea. How many people in all responded to the survey?

4. With reference to Example 2, write the following statements in set terminology:

   (a) All biology students are mathematics students.

   (b) There are female biology students in the university choir.

   (c) No tennis player studies biology.

   (d) Those female students who neither play tennis nor belong to the university choir all study biology.

5. Make a complete list of all the different subsets of the set $\{a, b, c\}$. How many are there if the empty set and the set itself are included? Do the same for the set $\{a, b, c, d\}$.

6. Determine which of the following formulas are true. If any formula is false, find a counterexample to demonstrate this, using a Venn diagram if you find it helpful.

   (a) $A \setminus B = B \setminus A$ (b) $A \subseteq B \iff A \cup B = B$

   (c) $A \subseteq B \iff A \cap B = A$ (d) $A \cap B = A \cap C \implies B = C$

   (e) $A \cup B = A \cup C \implies B = C$ (f) $A \setminus (B \setminus C) = (A \setminus B) \setminus C$

7. If A is a set with a finite number of elements, let $n(A)$ denote the number of elements in A. If A and B are arbitrary finite sets, prove the following:

   (a) $n(A \cup B) = n(A) + n(B) - n(A \cap B)$

   (b) $n(A \setminus B) = n(A) - n(A \cap B)$

8. (a) A thousand people took part in a survey to reveal which newspaper, A, B, or C, they had read on a certain day. The responses showed that 420 had read A, 316 had read B, and 160 had read C. These figures include 116 who had read both A and B, 100 who had read A and C, and 30 who had read B and C. Finally, all these figures include 16 who had read all three papers.

   (i) How many had read A, but not B?

   (ii) How many had read C, but neither A nor B?

   (iii) How many had read neither A, B, nor C?

   (b) Denote the complete set of all 1000 persons in the survey by Ω (the universal set). Applying the notation in Problem 7, we have $n(A) = 420$ and $n(A \cap B \cap C) = 16$, for example. Describe the numbers given in (i), (ii), and (iii) of part (a) using the same notation. Why is $n(\Omega \setminus (A \cup B \cup C)) = n(\Omega) - n(A \cup B \cup C)$?

3.7 Mathematical Induction

Proof by induction is an important technique for verifying formulas involving natural numbers. For instance, consider the sum of the first n odd numbers. We observe that

$$
\begin{aligned}
1 &= 1 &&= 1^2 \\
1 + 3 &= 4 &&= 2^2 \\
1 + 3 + 5 &= 9 &&= 3^2 \\
1 + 3 + 5 + 7 &= 16 &&= 4^2 \\
1 + 3 + 5 + 7 + 9 &= 25 &&= 5^2
\end{aligned}
$$

This suggests a general pattern, with the sum of the first n odd numbers equal to n^2:

$$ 1 + 3 + 5 + \cdots + (2n - 1) = n^2 \qquad (*) $$

To prove that this is generally valid, we can proceed as follows. Suppose that the formula in $(*)$ is correct for a certain natural number $n = k$, so that

$$ 1 + 3 + 5 + \cdots + (2k - 1) = k^2 $$

By adding the next odd number $2k + 1$ to each side, we get

$$1 + 3 + 5 + \cdots + (2k - 1) + (2k + 1) = k^2 + (2k + 1) = (k + 1)^2$$

But this is the formula $(*)$ with $n = k + 1$. Hence, we have proved that if the sum of the first k odd numbers is k^2, then the sum of the first $k + 1$ odd numbers equals $(k + 1)^2$. This implication, together with the fact that $(*)$ *is* valid for $n = 1$, implies that $(*)$ is generally valid. For we have just shown that if $(*)$ is true for $n = 1$, then it is true for $n = 2$; that if it is true for $n = 2$, then it is true for $n = 3$; ...; that if it is true for $n = k$, then it is true for $n = k + 1$; and so on.

A proof of this type is called a *proof by induction*. It requires showing that the formula is indeed valid for $n = 1$, and second that, *if* the formula is valid for $n = k$, then it is also valid for $n = k + 1$. It follows by induction that the formula is valid for all natural numbers n.

EXAMPLE 1   Prove by induction that, for all positive integers n,

$$3 + 3^2 + 3^3 + 3^4 + \cdots + 3^n = \tfrac{1}{2}(3^{n+1} - 3)$$

Solution: For $n = 1$, both sides are 3. Suppose $(*)$ is true for $n = k$. Then

$$3 + 3^2 + 3^3 + 3^4 + \cdots + 3^k + 3^{k+1} = \tfrac{1}{2}(3^{k+1} - 3) + 3^{k+1} = \tfrac{1}{2}(3^{k+2} - 3)$$

which is $(*)$ for $n = k + 1$. Thus, by induction, $(*)$ is true for all n.   ∎

On the basis of these examples, the general structure of an induction proof can be explained as follows: We want to prove that a mathematical formula $A(n)$ that depends on n is valid for all natural numbers n. In the two previous examples, the respective statements $A(n)$ were

$$A(n) : 1 + 3 + 5 + \cdots + (2n - 1) = n^2$$
$$A(n) : 3 + 3^2 + 3^3 + 3^4 + \cdots + 3^n = \tfrac{1}{2}(3^{n+1} - 3)$$

The steps required in each proof are as follows: First, verify that $A(1)$ is valid, which means that the formula is correct for $n = 1$. Then prove that for each natural number k, if $A(k)$ is true, it follows that $A(k + 1)$ must be true. Here $A(k)$ is called *the induction hypothesis*, and the step from $A(k)$ to $A(k + 1)$ is called *the induction step* in the proof. When the induction step is proved for an arbitrary natural number k, then, by induction, statement $A(n)$ is true for all n. The general principle can now be formulated:

THE PRINCIPLE OF MATHEMATICAL INDUCTION

Suppose that $A(n)$ is a statement for all natural numbers n and that

(a) $A(1)$ is true

(b) if the induction hypothesis $A(k)$ is true, then $A(k + 1)$ is true for each natural number k

Then $A(n)$ is true for all natural numbers n.

(1)

The principle of induction seems intuitively evident. If the truth of $A(k)$ for each k implies the truth of $A(k+1)$, then because $A(1)$ is true, $A(2)$ must be true, which, in turn, means that $A(3)$ is true, and so on. (An analogy: Consider a ladder with an infinite number of steps. Suppose you can climb the first step and suppose, moreover, that after each step, you can always climb the next. Then you are able to climb up to any step.)

The principle of mathematical induction can easily be generalized to the case in which we have a statement $A(n)$ for each integer greater than or equal to an arbitrary integer n_0. Suppose we can prove that $A(n_0)$ is valid and moreover that, for each $k \geq n_0$, if $A(k)$ is true, then $A(k+1)$ is true. If follows that $A(n)$ is true for all $n \geq n_0$.

PROBLEMS FOR SECTION 3.7

1. Prove by induction statement (4) in Section 3.2:

$$1 + 2 + 3 + \cdots + n = \tfrac{1}{2}n(n+1) \qquad (*)$$

2. Prove formulas (3.2.5) and (3.2.6) by induction.

3. Prove the following by induction:

$$\frac{1}{1 \cdot 2} + \frac{1}{2 \cdot 3} + \frac{1}{3 \cdot 4} + \cdots + \frac{1}{n(n+1)} = \frac{n}{n+1} \qquad (*)$$

4. $1^3 + 2^3 + 3^3 = 36$ is divisible by 9. Prove by induction that the sum $n^3 + (n+1)^3 + (n+2)^3$ of three consecutive cubes is always divisible by 9.

REVIEW PROBLEMS FOR CHAPTER 3

1. Evaluate the following sums:

(a) $\displaystyle\sum_{i=1}^{4} \frac{1}{i(i+2)}$ 　　　　(b) $\displaystyle\sum_{j=5}^{9}(2j-8)^2$ 　　　　(c) $\displaystyle\sum_{k=1}^{5} \frac{k-1}{k+1}$

2. Evaluate the following sums:

(a) $\displaystyle\sum_{n=2}^{5}(n-1)^2(n+2)$ 　　(b) $\displaystyle\sum_{k=1}^{5}\left(\frac{1}{k} - \frac{1}{k+1}\right)$ 　　(c) $\displaystyle\sum_{i=-2}^{3}(i+3)^i$

3. Express these sums in summation notation:

(a) $3 + 5 + 7 + \cdots + 199 + 201$ 　　　　(b) $\dfrac{2}{1} + \dfrac{3}{2} + \dfrac{4}{3} + \ldots + \dfrac{97}{96}$

4. Express these sums in summation notation:

(a) $4 \cdot 6 + 5 \cdot 7 + 6 \cdot 8 + \cdots + 38 \cdot 40$
(b) $\dfrac{1}{x} + \dfrac{1}{x^2} + \cdots + \dfrac{1}{x^n}$

(c) $1 + \dfrac{x^2}{3} + \dfrac{x^4}{5} + \dfrac{x^6}{7} + \cdots + \dfrac{x^{32}}{33}$
(d) $1 - \dfrac{1}{2} + \dfrac{1}{3} - \dfrac{1}{4} + \cdots - \dfrac{1}{80} + \dfrac{1}{81}$

5. Which of these equalities are always right and which of them are sometimes wrong?

(a) $\displaystyle\sum_{i=1}^{n} a_i = \sum_{j=3}^{n+2} a_{j-2}$
(b) $\displaystyle\sum_{i=1}^{n} (a_i + b_i)^2 = \sum_{i=1}^{n} a_i^2 + \sum_{i=1}^{n} b_i^2$

(c) $\displaystyle\sum_{k=0}^{n} 5 a_{k+1,j} = 5 \sum_{k=1}^{n+1} a_{k,j}$
(d) $\displaystyle\sum_{i=1}^{3} \left(\dfrac{a_i}{b_i} \right) = \dfrac{\sum_{i=1}^{3} a_i}{\sum_{i=1}^{3} b_i}$

6. Consider the following implications and decide in each case: (i) if the implication is true; (ii) if the converse implication is true. (x and y are real numbers.)

(a) $x = 5$ and $y = -3 \implies x + y = 2$
(b) $x^2 = 16 \implies x = 4$

(c) $(x - 3)^2 (y + 2) > 0 \implies y > -2$
(d) $x^3 = 8 \implies x = 2$

7. Let $A = \{1, 3, 4\}$, $B = \{1, 4, 6\}$, $C = \{2, 4, 3\}$, and $D = \{1, 5\}$. Find $A \cap B$; $A \cup B$; $A \setminus B$; $B \setminus A$; $(A \cup B) \setminus (A \cap B)$; $A \cup B \cup C \cup D$; $A \cap B \cap C$; and $A \cap B \cap C \cap D$.

8. Let the universal set be $\Omega = \{1, 2, 3, 4, \ldots, 11, 12\}$ and define $A = \{1, 4, 6\}$ and $B = \{2, 11, 12\}$. Find $A \cap B$; $A \cup B$; $\Omega \setminus B$; $\complement A = \Omega \setminus A$.

9. A liberal arts college has 1000 students. The numbers studying various languages are: English (E) 780; French (F) 220; and Spanish (S) 52. These figures include 110 who study English and French, 32 who study English and Spanish, 15 who study French and Spanish. Finally, all these figures include 10 students taking all three languages.

(a) How many study English and French, but not Spanish?

(b) How many study English, but not French?

(c) How many are studying no languages?

10. (**Bernoulli's inequality**) Prove by induction that for all natural numbers n and all $x \geq -1$,

$$(1 + x)^n \geq 1 + nx$$

4 FUNCTIONS OF ONE VARIABLE

—mathematics is not so much a subject
as a way of studying any subject,
not so much a science as a way of life.
—G. Temple (1981)

Functions are important in practically every area of pure and applied mathematics, including mathematics applied to economics. The language of economic analysis is full of terms like demand and supply functions, cost functions, production functions, consumption functions, etc. In this chapter we present a discussion of functions of one real variable, illustrated by some very important economic examples.

4.1 Introduction

One variable is a function of another if the first variable *depends* upon the second. For instance, the area of a circle is a function of its radius. If the radius r is given, then the area A is determined. In fact $A = \pi r^2$, where π is the numerical constant $3.14159\ldots$.

One does not need a mathematical formula to convey the idea that one variable is a function of another: A table can also show the relationship. For instance, Table 1 shows the growth of annual total personal consumption expenditure, measured in current dollars, without allowing for inflation, in the United States for the period 1998–2004.

Table 1 Personal consumption expenditure in the U.S., 1998–2004 (in billions of dollars)

Year	1998	1999	2000	2001	2002	2003	2004
Personal consumption	5 879.5	6 282.5	6 739.4	7 055.0	7 376.1	7 760.9	8 231.1

This table defines consumption expenditure as a function of the calendar year.

In ordinary conversation we sometimes use the word "function" in a similar way. For example, we might say that the infant mortality rate of a country is a function of the quality of its health care, or that a country's national product is a function of the level of investment.

The dependence between two variables can also be illustrated by means of a graph. In Fig. 1 we have drawn a curve that allegedly played an important role some years ago in the discussion of "supply side economics". It shows the presumed relationship between a country's income tax rate and its total income tax revenue. Obviously, if the tax rate is 0%, then tax revenue is 0. However, if the tax rate is 100%, then tax revenue will also be (about) 0, since nobody is willing to work if their entire income is going to be confiscated. This curve, which has generated considerable controversy, is supposed to have been drawn on the back of a restaurant napkin by an American economist Arthur Laffer, who then later popularized its message with the public.

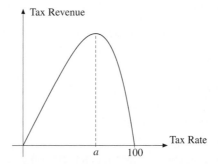

Figure 1 The "Laffer curve", which relates tax revenue to tax rates

In some instances a graph is preferable to a formula. A case in point is an electrocardiogram (ECG) showing the heartbeat pattern of a patient. Here the doctor studies the pattern of repetitions directly from the graphs and a formula approximating the ECG picture would usually be of little interest.

All of the relationships discussed above have one characteristic in common: A definite rule relates each value of one variable to a definite value of another variable. In the ECG example the function is the rule showing electrical activity as a function of time.

In all of our examples it is implicitly assumed that the variables are subject to certain constraints. For instance, in Table 1 only the years between 1998 and 2004 are relevant.

4.2 Basic Definitions

The examples in the preceding section lead to the following general definition:

A **function** of a real variable x with **domain** D is a rule that assigns a unique real number to each number x in D. As x varies over the whole domain, the set of all possible resulting values $f(x)$ is called the **range** of f.

The word "rule" is used in a very broad sense. *Every* rule with the properties described is called a function, whether that rule is given by a formula, described in words, defined by a table, illustrated by a curve, or expressed by any other means.

Functions are given letter names, such as f, g, F, or φ. If f is a function and x is a number in its domain D, then $f(x)$ denotes the number that the function f assigns to x. The symbol $f(x)$ is pronounced "f of x", or often just "f x". It is important to note the difference between f, which is a symbol for the function (the rule), and $f(x)$, which denotes the value of f at x.

If f is a function, we sometimes let y denote the value of f at x, so

$$y = f(x)$$

Then we call x the **independent variable**, or the **argument** of f, whereas y is called the **dependent variable**, because the value y (in general) depends on the value of x. The domain of the function f is then the set of all possible values of the independent variable, whereas the range is the set of corresponding values of the dependent variable. In economics, x is often called the *exogenous* variable, whereas y is the *endogenous* variable.

A function is often defined by a formula such as $y = 8x^2 + 3x + 2$. The function is then the rule that assigns the number $8x^2 + 3x + 2$ to each value of x.

Functional Notation

To become familiar with the relevant notation, it helps to look at some examples of functions that are defined by formulas.

EXAMPLE 1   A function is defined for all numbers by the following rule:

Assign to any number its third power

This function will assign $0^3 = 0$ to 0, $3^3 = 27$ to 3, $(-2)^3 = (-2)(-2)(-2) = -8$ to -2, and $(1/4)^3 = 1/64$ to 1/4. In general, it assigns the number x^3 to the number x. If we denote this third power function by f, then

$$f(x) = x^3$$

So $f(0) = 0^3 = 0$, $f(3) = 3^3 = 27$, $f(-2) = (-2)^3 = -8$, $f(1/4) = (1/4)^3 = 1/64$.

Substituting a for x in the formula for f gives $f(a) = a^3$, whereas

$$f(a + 1) = (a + 1)^3 = (a + 1)(a + 1)(a + 1) = a^3 + 3a^2 + 3a + 1 \qquad \blacksquare$$

NOTE 1 A common error is to presume that $f(a) = a^3$ implies $f(a + 1) = a^3 + 1$. The error can be illustrated by considering a simple interpretation of f. If a is the edge of a cube measured in metres, then $f(a) = a^3$ is the volume of the cube measured in cubic metres (or m^3). Suppose that each edge of the cube expands by 1 m. Then the volume of the new cube is $f(a + 1) = (a + 1)^3$ m^3. The number $a^3 + 1$ can be interpreted as the number obtained when the volume of a cube with edge a is increased by 1 m^3. In fact, $f(a + 1) = (a + 1)^3$ is quite different from $a^3 + 1$, as illustrated in Figs. 1 and 2.

Figure 1 Volume $f(a+1) = (a+1)^3$ **Figure 2** Volume $a^3 + 1$

EXAMPLE 2   The total dollar cost of producing x units of a product is given by

$$C(x) = 100x\sqrt{x} + 500$$

Find the cost of producing: (i) 16 units, (ii) a units. Suppose the firm produces a units; find the *increase* in the cost from producing one additional unit.

Solution: The cost of producing 16 units is found by substituting 16 for x in the formula for $C(x)$:

$$C(16) = 100 \cdot 16\sqrt{16} + 500 = 100 \cdot 16 \cdot 4 + 500 = 6900$$

Similarly, the cost of producing a units is

$$C(a) = 100a\sqrt{a} + 500$$

The cost of producing $a + 1$ units is $C(a + 1)$, so that the increase in cost is

$$C(a + 1) - C(a) = 100(a + 1)\sqrt{a + 1} + 500 - 100a\sqrt{a} - 500$$
$$= 100\left[(a + 1)\sqrt{a + 1} - a\sqrt{a}\right]$$

In economic theory, we often study functions that depend on a number of parameters in addition to the independent variable. A typical example follows.

EXAMPLE 3   Suppose that the cost of producing x units of a commodity is

$$C(x) = Ax\sqrt{x} + B \qquad (A \text{ and } B \text{ are constants})$$

Find the cost of producing 0, 10, and $x + h$ units.

Solution: The cost of producing 0 units is $C(0) = A \cdot 0 \cdot \sqrt{0} + B = 0 + B = B$ (Parameter B simply represents fixed costs. These are the costs that must be paid whether or not anything is actually produced, such as a taxi driver's annual licence fee.) Similarly, $C(10) = A10\sqrt{10} + B$. Finally, substituting $x + h$ for x in the given formula gives

$$C(x+h) = A(x+h)\sqrt{x+h} + B$$

So far we have used x to denote the independent variable, but we could just as well have used almost any other symbol. For example, all of the following formulas define exactly the same function (and hence we can set $f = g = \varphi$):

$$f(x) = x^4, \qquad g(t) = t^4, \qquad \varphi(\xi) = \xi^4$$

For that matter, we could also express this function as follows:

$$f(\cdot) = (\cdot)^4$$

Here it is understood that the dot between the parentheses can be replaced by an arbitrary number, or an arbitrary letter, or even another function (like $1/y$). Thus,

$$f(1) = (1)^4 = 1, \qquad f(k) = k^4, \qquad \text{and} \qquad f(1/y) = (1/y)^4$$

Domain and Range

The definition of a function is incomplete unless its domain is specified. The natural domain of the function f defined by $f(x) = x^3$ is the set of all real numbers. In Example 2, where $C(x) = 100x\sqrt{x} + 500$ denotes the cost of producing x units of a product, the domain was not specified, but the natural domain is the set of numbers 0, 1, 2, ..., x_0, where x_0 is the maximum number of items the firm can produce. If output x is a continuous variable, the natural domain is the closed interval $[0, x_0]$.

We shall adopt the convention that *if a function is defined using an algebraic formula, the domain consists of all values of the independent variable for which the formula gives a unique value (unless another domain is explicitly mentioned).*

EXAMPLE 4   Find the domains of (a) $f(x) = \dfrac{1}{x+3}$ and (b) $g(x) = \sqrt{2x+4}$.

Solution:
(a) For $x = -3$, the formula reduces to the meaningless expression "1/0." For all other values of x, the formula makes $f(x)$ a well-defined number. Thus, the domain consists of all numbers $x \neq -3$.
(b) The expression $\sqrt{2x+4}$ is defined for all x such that $2x+4$ is nonnegative. Solving the inequality $2x+4 \geq 0$ for x gives $x \geq -2$. Hence, the domain of g is the interval $[-2, \infty)$.

Let f be a function with domain D. The set of all values $f(x)$ that the function assumes is called the *range* of f. Often, we denote the domain of f by D_f, and the range by R_f. These concepts are illustrated in Fig. 3, using the idea of the graph of a function. (Graphs are discussed in the next section.)

Alternatively, we can think of any function f as an engine operating so that if x in the domain is an input, the output is $f(x)$. (See Fig. 4.) The range of f is then all the numbers we get as output using all numbers in the domain as inputs. If we try to use as an input a number not in the domain, the engine does not work, and there is no output.

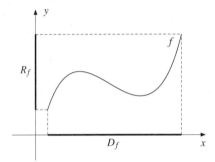

Figure 3 The domain and range of f **Figure 4** Function engine

EXAMPLE 5   Show that the number 4 belongs to the range of the function defined by $g(x) = \sqrt{2x + 4}$. Find the entire range of g.

Solution: To show that 4 is in the range of g, we must find a number x such that $g(x) = 4$. That is, we must solve the equation $\sqrt{2x + 4} = 4$ for x. By squaring both sides of the equation, we get $2x + 4 = 4^2 = 16$, that is, $x = 6$. Because $g(6) = 4$, the number 4 does belong to the range R_g.

In order to determine the whole range of g, we must answer the question: As x runs through the whole of the interval $[-2, \infty)$, what are all the possible values of $\sqrt{2x + 4}$? For $x = -2$, $\sqrt{2x + 4} = 0$, and $\sqrt{2x + 4}$ can never be negative. We claim that whatever number $y_0 \geq 0$ is chosen, there exists a number x_0 such that $\sqrt{2x_0 + 4} = y_0$. Indeed, squaring each side of this last equation gives $2x_0 + 4 = y_0^2$. Hence, $2x_0 = y_0^2 - 4$, which implies that $x_0 = \frac{1}{2}(y_0^2 - 4)$. Because $y_0^2 \geq 0$, we have $x_0 = \frac{1}{2}\left(y_0^2 - 4\right) \geq \frac{1}{2}(-4) = -2$. Hence, for every number $y_0 \geq 0$, we have found a number $x_0 \geq -2$ such that $g(x_0) = y_0$. The range of g is, therefore, $[0, \infty)$. ∎

Even if a function is completely specified by a formula, including a specific domain, it is not always easy to find the range of the function. For example, without using the methods of differential calculus, it is not easy to find R_f exactly when $f(x) = 3x^3 - 2x^2 - 12x - 3$ and $D_f = [-2, 3]$.

A function f is called **increasing** if $x_1 \leq x_2$ implies $f(x_1) \leq f(x_2)$, and **strictly increasing** if $x_1 < x_2$ implies $f(x_1) < f(x_2)$. *Decreasing* and *strictly decreasing* functions are defined in the obvious way. (See Section 6.3.) The function g in Example 5 is strictly increasing in $[-2, \infty)$.

Calculators (including calculator programs on personal computers) often have many special functions built into them. For example, most of them would have the $\sqrt{\ }$-function that, given a number x, assigns the square-root of the number, $\sqrt{x}$. If we enter a nonnegative number such as 25, and press the square-root key, then the number 5 appears. If we enter -3, then "Error", or "Not a number" is shown, which is the way the calculator tells us that $\sqrt{-3}$ is not defined (within the real number system).

PROBLEMS FOR SECTION 4.2

1. Let $f(x) = x^2 + 1$.

   (a) Compute $f(0)$, $f(-1)$, $f(1/2)$, and $f(\sqrt{2})$.

   (b) For what values of x is it true that

   (i) $f(x) = f(-x)$?   (ii) $f(x+1) = f(x) + f(1)$?   (iii) $f(2x) = 2f(x)$?

2. Suppose $F(x) = 10$, for all x. Find $F(0)$, $F(-3)$, and $F(a+h) - F(a)$.

3. Let $f(t) = a^2 - (t-a)^2$ (a is a constant).

   (a) Compute $f(0)$, $f(a)$, $f(-a)$, and $f(2a)$.   (b) Compute $3f(a) + f(-2a)$.

4. Let f be defined for all x by $f(x) = \dfrac{x}{1+x^2}$.

   (a) Compute $f(-1/10)$, $f(0)$, $f(1/\sqrt{2})$, $f(\sqrt{\pi})$, and $f(2)$.

   (b) Show that $f(-x) = -f(x)$ for all x, and that $f(1/x) = f(x)$ for $x \neq 0$.

5. Let $F(t) = \sqrt{t^2 - 2t + 4}$. Compute $F(0)$, $F(-3)$, and $F(t+1)$.

6. The cost of producing x units of a commodity is given by

$$C(x) = 1000 + 300x + x^2$$

   (a) Compute $C(0)$, $C(100)$, and $C(101) - C(100)$.

   (b) Compute $C(x+1) - C(x)$, and explain in words the meaning of the difference.

7. H. Schultz has estimated the demand for cotton in the U.S. for the period 1915–1919 to be $D(P) = 6.4 - 0.3P$ (with appropriate units for the price P and the quantity $D(P)$).

   (a) Find the demand in each case if the price is 8, 10, and 10.22.

   (b) If the demand is 3.13, what is the price?

8. (a) If $f(x) = 100x^2$, show that for all t, $f(tx) = t^2 f(x)$.

   (b) If $P(x) = x^{1/2}$, show that for all $t \geq 0$, $P(tx) = t^{1/2} P(x)$.

9. The cost of removing $p\%$ of the impurities in a lake is given by $b(p) = \dfrac{10p}{105 - p}$.

   (a) Find $b(0)$, $b(50)$, and $b(100)$.

   (b) What does $b(50 + h) - b(50)$ mean? $(h \geq 0)$

10. Only for very special "additive" functions is it true that $f(a + b) = f(a) + f(b)$ for all a and b. Determine whether $f(2 + 1) = f(2) + f(1)$ for the following:

    (a) $f(x) = 2x^2$ 　 (b) $f(x) = -3x$ 　 (c) $f(x) = \sqrt{x}$

11. (a) If $f(x) = Ax$, show that $f(a + b) = f(a) + f(b)$ for all a and b.

    (b) If $f(x) = 10^x$, show that $f(a + b) = f(a) \cdot f(b)$ for all natural numbers a and b.

12. A student claims that $(x + 1)^2 = x^2 + 1$. Can you use a geometric argument to show that this is wrong?

13. Find the domains of the functions defined by the following formulas:

    (a) $y = \sqrt{5 - x}$ 　 (b) $y = \dfrac{2x - 1}{x^2 - x}$ 　 (c) $y = \sqrt{\dfrac{x - 1}{(x - 2)(x + 3)}}$

14. Consider the function f defined by the formula $f(x) = \dfrac{3x + 6}{x - 2}$.

    (a) Find the domain of f.

    (b) Show that the number 5 is in the range of f by finding a number x such that $(3x + 6)/(x - 2) = 5$.

    (c) Show that the number 3 is not in the range of f.

15. Find the domain and the range of $g(x) = 1 - \sqrt{x + 2}$.

4.3 Graphs of Functions

Recall that a **rectangular** (or a **Cartesian**) coordinate system is obtained by first drawing two perpendicular lines, called coordinate axes. The two axes are respectively the *x-axis* (or the *horizontal axis*) and the *y-axis* (or the *vertical axis*). The intersection point O is called the *origin*. We measure the real numbers along each of these lines, as shown in Fig. 1. The unit distance on the *x*-axis is not necessarily the same as on the *y*-axis, although this is the case in Fig. 1.

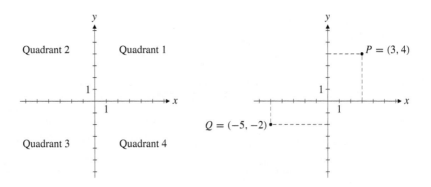

Figure 1 A coordinate system   **Figure 2** Points $(3, 4)$ and $(-5, -2)$

The rectangular coordinate system in Fig. 1 is also called the **xy-plane**. The coordinate axes separate the plane into four quadrants, which traditionally are numbered as in Fig. 1. Any point P in the plane can be represented by a pair (a, b) of real numbers. These can be found by dropping perpendiculars onto the axes. The point which can be represented by (a, b), lies at the intersection of the vertical straight line $x = a$ with the horizontal straight line $y = b$. Conversely, any pair of real numbers represents a unique point in the plane. For example, in Fig. 2, if the ordered pair $(3, 4)$ is given, the corresponding point P lies at the intersection of $x = 3$ with $y = 4$. Thus, P lies 3 units to the right of the y-axis and 4 units above the x-axis. We call $(3, 4)$ the **coordinates** of P. Similarly, Q lies 5 units to the left of the y-axis and 2 units below the x-axis, so the coordinates of Q are $(-5, -2)$.

Note that we call (a, b) an **ordered pair**, because the order of the two numbers in the pair is important. For instance, $(3, 4)$ and $(4, 3)$ represent two different points.

As you surely know, each function of one variable can be represented by a graph in such a rectangular coordinate system. Such a representation helps us visualize the function. This is because the shape of the graph reflects the properties of the function.

The **graph** of a function f is simply the set of all points $(x, f(x))$, where x belongs to the domain of f. Consider the following simple example.

EXAMPLE 1   Consider the function $f(x) = x^2 - 4x + 3$. The values of $f(x)$ for some special choices of x are given in the following table.

Table 1 Values of $f(x) = x^2 - 4x + 3$

x	0	1	2	3	4
$f(x) = x^2 - 4x + 3$	3	0	-1	0	3

Plot the points $(0, 3)$, $(1, 0)$, $(2, -1)$, $(3, 0)$, and $(4, 3)$ obtained from the table in a xy-plane and draw a smooth curve through these points.

Solution: This is done in Fig. 3. The graph is called a parabola. (See Section 4.6.) ▌

Figure 3 The graph of
$f(x) = x^2 - 4x + 3$

Figure 4 The graph of
$g(x) = 2x - 1$

EXAMPLE 2   Find some of the points on the graph of $g(x) = 2x - 1$, and sketch it.

Solution: One has $g(-1) = 2 \cdot (-1) - 1 = -3$, $g(0) = 2 \cdot 0 - 1 = -1$, and
$g(1) = 2 \cdot 1 - 1 = 1$. Moreover, $g(2) = 3$. There are infinitely many points on the graph,
so we cannot write them all down. In Fig. 4 the four points $(-1, -3)$, $(0, -1)$, $(1, 1)$, and
$(2, 3)$ are marked off, and they seem to lie on a straight line. That line is the graph.

Some Important Graphs

Some special functions occur so often in applications that you should learn to recognize
their graphs. You should in each case make a table of function values to confirm the form
of these graphs.

Figure 5 $y = x$

Figure 6 $y = x^2$

Figure 7 $y = x^3$

Figure 8 $y = \sqrt{x}$

Figure 9 $y = 1/x$

Figure 10 $y = |x|$

NOTE 1 When plotting the graph of a function, we must try to find a sufficient number of points on the graph, otherwise we might miss some of its important features. Actually, by merely plotting a finite set of points, we can never be entirely sure that there are no wiggles or bumps we have missed. For more complicated functions we have to use differential calculus to decide how many bumps and wiggles there are.

PROBLEMS FOR SECTION 4.3

1. Plot the points $(2, 3)$, $(-3, 2)$, $(-3/2, -2)$, $(4, 0)$, and $(0, 4)$ in a coordinate system.

2. The graph of the function f is given in the figure.

   (a) Find $f(-5)$, $f(-3)$, $f(-2)$, $f(0)$, $f(3)$, and $f(4)$ by examining the graph.

   (b) Determine the domain and the range of f.

In problems 3–6 fill in the tables and draw the graphs of the functions.

3.

x	0	1	2	3	4
$g(x) = -2x + 5$					

4.

x	−2	−1	0	1	2	3	4
$h(x) = x^2 - 2x - 3$							

5.

x	−2	−1	0	1	2
$F(x) = 3^x$					

6.

x	−2	−1	0	1	2	3
$G(x) = 1 - 2^{-x}$						

4.4 Linear Functions

Linear functions occur very often in economics. They are defined as follows.

$$y = ax + b \qquad (a \text{ and } b \text{ are constants})$$

The graph of the equation is a straight line. If we let f denote the function that assigns y to x, then $f(x) = ax + b$, and f is called a **linear** function.

Take an arbitrary value of x. Then

$$f(x + 1) - f(x) = a(x + 1) + b - ax - b = a$$

This shows that a measures the change in the value of the function when x increases by 1 unit. For this reason, the number a is the slope of the line, and so is called the **slope** of the function. If the slope a is positive, the line slants upward to the right, and the larger the value of a, the steeper is the line. On the other hand, if a is negative, then the line slants downward to the right, and the absolute value of a measures the steepness of the line. For example, when $a = -3$, the steepness is 3. In the special case when $a = 0$, we have $y = ax + b = b$ for all x and the line is parallel to the x-axis. The three cases are illustrated in Figs. 1 to 3. If $x = 0$, then $y = ax + b = b$, and b is called the **y-intercept** (or often just the intercept).

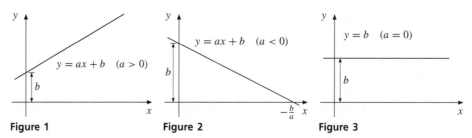

Figure 1   Figure 2   Figure 3

EXAMPLE 1   Find and interpret the slopes of the following straight lines.

(a) $C = 55.73x + 182\,100\,000$ Estimated cost function for the U.S. Steel Corp. over the period 1917–1938 (C is the total cost in dollars per year, and x is the production of steel in tons per year).

(b) $q = -0.15p + 0.14$ Estimated annual demand function for rice in India for the period 1949–1964. (p is price, q is consumption per person.)

Solution:

(a) The slope is 55.73, which means that if production increases by 1 ton, then the cost *increases* by $55.73.

(b) The slope is −0.15, which tells us that if the price increases by one unit, then the quantity demanded *decreases* by 0.15 units.

Finding the Slope

How do we compute the slope of a straight line in the plane? Here is an easy way. Pick two different points on the line $P = (x_1, y_1)$ and $Q = (x_2, y_2)$, as shown in Fig. 4.

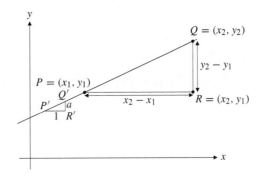

Figure 4   Slope $a = (y_2 - y_1)/(x_2 - x_1)$.

The slope of the line is the ratio $(y_2 - y_1)/(x_2 - x_1)$. If we denote the slope by a, then:

SLOPE OF A STRAIGHT LINE

The **slope** of the straight line l is

$$a = \frac{y_2 - y_1}{x_2 - x_1}, \qquad x_1 \neq x_2$$

where (x_1, y_1) and (x_2, y_2) are any two distinct points on l.

Multiplying both the numerator and the denominator of $(y_2 - y_1)/(x_2 - x_1)$ by -1, we obtain $(y_1 - y_2)/(x_1 - x_2)$. This shows that it does not make any difference which point is P and which is Q. Moreover, the properties of similar triangles imply that the ratios $Q'R'/P'R'$ and QR/PR in Fig. 4 must be equal. For this reason, the number $a = (y_2 - y_1)/(x_2 - x_1)$ is equal to the change in the value of y when x increases by 1 unit.

EXAMPLE 2   Determine the slopes of the three straight lines l, m, and n.

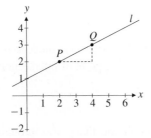

Figure 5 The line l

Figure 6 The line m

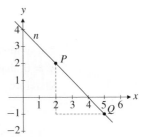

Figure 7 The line n

Solution: The lines l, m, and n all pass through $P = (2, 2)$. In Fig. 5, Q is $(4, 3)$, in Fig. 6, Q is $(1, -2)$ and in Fig. 7, Q is $(5, -1)$. Therefore, the respective slopes of the lines l, m, and n are

$$a_l = \frac{3-2}{4-2} = \frac{1}{2}, \qquad a_m = \frac{-2-2}{1-2} = 4, \qquad a_n = \frac{-1-2}{5-2} = -1$$

The Point–Slope and Point–Point Formulas

Let us find the equation of a straight line l passing through the point $P = (x_1, y_1)$ with slope a. If (x, y) is any other point on the line, the slope a is given by the formula:

$$\frac{y - y_1}{x - x_1} = a$$

Multiplying each side by $x - x_1$, we obtain $y - y_1 = a(x - x_1)$. Hence,

---

POINT—SLOPE FORMULA OF A STRAIGHT LINE

The equation of the straight line passing through (x_1, y_1) with slope a is

$$y - y_1 = a(x - x_1)$$

Note that when using this formula, x_1 and y_1 are fixed numbers giving the coordinates of the fixed point. On the other hand, x and y are variables denoting the coordinates of an arbitrary point on the line.

EXAMPLE 3   Find the equation of the line through $(-2, 3)$ with slope -4. Then find the y-intercept and the point at which this line intersects the x-axis (the x-intercept).

Solution: The point–slope formula with $(x_1, y_1) = (-2, 3)$ and $a = -4$ gives

$$y - 3 = (-4)(x - (-2)) \qquad \text{or} \qquad y - 3 = -4(x + 2) \qquad \text{or} \qquad 4x + y = -5$$

The y-intercept has $x = 0$, so $y = -5$. The line intersects the x-axis at the point where $y = 0$, that is, where $4x = -5$, so $x = -5/4$. The point of intersection with the x-axis is therefore $(-5/4, 0)$. (Draw a graph.)

Often we need to find the equation of the straight line that passes through two given distinct points. Combining the slope formula and the point–slope formula, we obtain the following:

POINT—POINT FORMULA OF A STRAIGHT LINE

The equation of the straight line passing through (x_1, y_1) and (x_2, y_2), where $x_1 \neq x_2$, is obtained as follows:

1. Compute the slope of the line, $a = \dfrac{y_2 - y_1}{x_2 - x_1}$

2. Substitute the expression for a into the point–slope formula: $y - y_1 = a(x - x_1)$. The result is

$$y - y_1 = \frac{y_2 - y_1}{x_2 - x_1}(x - x_1)$$

EXAMPLE 4   Find the equation of the line passing through $(-1, 3)$ and $(5, -2)$.

Solution: Let $(x_1, y_1) = (-1, 3)$ and $(x_2, y_2) = (5, -2)$. Then the point–point formula gives

$$y - 3 = \frac{-2 - 3}{5 - (-1)}\left[x - (-1)\right] \quad \text{or} \quad y - 3 = -\frac{5}{6}(x + 1) \quad \text{or} \quad 5x + 6y = 13 \qquad ▌$$

The General Equation for a Straight Line

Any nonvertical line in the plane has the equation $y = ax + b$. Any vertical line is parallel to the y-axis. Obviously, it must intersect the x-axis at some point $(c, 0)$. Every point on the line has the same x-coordinate c, so the equation for a straight line through $(c, 0)$ parallel to the y-axis is $x = c$.

The equations $y = ax + b$ and $x = c$ can both be written as

$$Ax + By + C = 0 \qquad (1)$$

for suitable values of the constants A, B, and C. Specifically, $y = ax + b$ corresponds to $A = a$, $B = -1$, and $C = b$, whereas $x = c$ corresponds to $A = 1$, $B = 0$, and $C = -c$. Conversely, disregarding the uninteresting case when $A = B = 0$, every equation of the form (1) represents a straight line in the plane. If $B = 0$, it follows from (1) that $Ax = -C$, or, $x = -C/A$. This is the equation for a straight line parallel to the y-axis. On the other hand, if $B \neq 0$, solving (1) for y yields

$$y = -\frac{A}{B}x - \frac{C}{B}$$

This is the equation for a straight line with slope $-A/B$. Equation (1) thus deserves to be called the *general equation for a straight line in the plane*.

Graphical Solutions of Linear Equations

Section 2.4 dealt with algebraic methods for solving a system of two linear equations in two unknowns. The equations are linear, so their graphs are straight lines. The coordinates of any point on a line satisfy the equation of that line. Thus, the coordinates of any point of intersection of these two lines will satisfy both equations. This means that any point where these lines intersect will satisfy the equation system.

EXAMPLE 5   Solve each of the following three pairs of equations graphically:

$$\text{(a)} \quad \begin{aligned} x + y &= 5 \\ x - y &= -1 \end{aligned} \qquad \text{(b)} \quad \begin{aligned} 3x + y &= -7 \\ x - 4y &= 2 \end{aligned} \qquad \text{(c)} \quad \begin{aligned} 3x + 4y &= 2 \\ 6x + 8y &= 24 \end{aligned}$$

Solution:

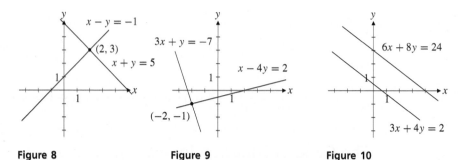

Figure 8   Figure 9   Figure 10

(a) Figure 8 shows the graphs of the straight lines $x + y = 5$ and $x - y = -1$. There is only one point of intersection, which is $(2, 3)$. The solution of the system is, therefore, $x = 2$, $y = 3$.

(b) Figure 9 shows the graphs of the straight lines $3x + y = -7$ and $x - 4y = 2$. There is only one point of intersection, which is $(-2, -1)$. The solution of the system is, therefore, $x = -2$, $y = -1$.

(c) Figure 10 shows the graphs of the straight lines $3x + 4y = 2$ and $6x + 8y = 24$. These lines are parallel and have no point of intersection. The system has no solutions.   ∎

Linear Inequalities

This section concludes by discussing how to represent linear inequalities geometrically. We present two examples.

EXAMPLE 6   Sketch in the xy-plane the set of all pairs of numbers (x, y) that satisfy the inequality $2x + y \le 4$. (Using set notation, this set is $\{(x, y) : 2x + y \le 4\}$.)

Solution: The inequality can be written as $y \le -2x + 4$. The set of points (x, y) that satisfy the equation $y = -2x + 4$ is a straight line. Therefore, the set of points (x, y) that satisfy the inequality $y \le -2x + 4$ must have y-values below those of points on the line $y = -2x + 4$. So it must consist of all points that lie on or below this line. See Fig. 11.   ∎

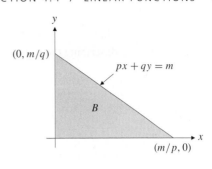

Figure 11 $\{(x, y) : 2x + y \le 4\}$

Figure 12 Budget set:
$px + qy \le m$, $x \ge 0$, and $y \ge 0$

EXAMPLE 7   A person has $m to spend on the purchase of two commodities. The prices of the two commodities are $p and $q per unit. Suppose x units of the first commodity and y units of the second commodity are bought. Assuming one cannot purchase negative units of x and y, the *budget set* is

$$B = \{(x, y) :\ px + qy \le m,\ x \ge 0,\ y \ge 0\}$$

as in (1) in Section 3.6. Sketch the budget set B in the xy-plane. Find the slope of the budget line $px + qy = m$, and its x- and y-intercepts.

Solution: The set of points (x, y) that satisfy $x \ge 0$ and $y \ge 0$ is the first (nonnegative) quadrant. If we impose the additional requirement that $px + qy \le m$, we obtain the triangular domain B shown in Fig. 12.

If $px + qy = m$, then $qy = -px + m$ and so $y = (-p/q)x + m/q$. This shows that the slope is $-p/q$. The budget line intersects the x-axis when $y = 0$. Then $px = m$, so $x = m/p$. The budget line intersects the y-axis when $x = 0$. Then $qy = m$, so $y = m/q$. So the two points of intersection are $(m/p, 0)$ and $(0, m/q)$, as shown in Fig. 12.   ∎

PROBLEMS FOR SECTION 4.4

1. Find the slopes of the lines passing through the following pairs of points:

   (a) $(2, 3)$ and $(5, 8)$ (b) $(-1, -3)$ and $(2, -5)$ (c) $\left(\frac{1}{2}, \frac{3}{2}\right)$ and $\left(\frac{1}{3}, -\frac{1}{5}\right)$

2. Draw graphs for the following straight lines:

   (a) $3x + 4y = 12$ (b) $\dfrac{x}{10} - \dfrac{y}{5} = 1$ (c) $x = 3$

3. Suppose demand D for a good is a linear function of its price per unit, P. When price is $10, demand is 200 units, and when price is $15, demand is 150 units. Find the demand function.

4. Find the slopes of the five lines L_1 to L_5 shown in the figure, and give equations describing them. (L_3 is horizontal.)

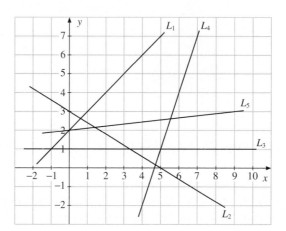

5. Decide which of the following relationships are linear:

(a) $5y + 2x = 2$ (b) $P = 10(1 - 0.3t)$ (c) $C = (0.5x + 2)(x - 3)$

(d) $p_1x_1 + p_2x_2 = R$ (p_1, p_2, and R constants)

6. A printing company quotes the price of $1400 for producing 100 copies of a report, and $3000 for 500 copies. Assuming a linear relation, what would be the price of printing 300 copies?

7. Determine the equations for the following straight lines:

(a) L_1 passes through $(1, 3)$ and has a slope of 2.

(b) L_2 passes through $(-2, 2)$ and $(3, 3)$.

(c) L_3 passes through the origin and has a slope of $-1/2$.

(d) L_4 passes through $(a, 0)$ and $(0, b)$ (suppose $a \neq 0$).

8. Sketch in the xy-plane the set of all pairs of numbers (x, y) that satisfy the following inequalities:

(a) $2x + 4y \geq 5$ (b) $x - 3y + 2 \leq 0$ (c) $100x + 200y \leq 300$

9. Solve the following three systems of equations graphically:

(a) $\begin{aligned} x - y &= 5 \\ x + y &= 1 \end{aligned}$

(b) $\begin{aligned} x + y &= 2 \\ x - 2y &= 2 \\ x - y &= 2 \end{aligned}$

(c) $\begin{aligned} 3x + 4y &= 1 \\ 6x + 8y &= 6 \end{aligned}$

10. Sketch in the xy-plane the set of all pairs of numbers (x, y) that satisfy all the following three inequalities:

$$3x + 4y \leq 12, \qquad x - y \leq 1, \qquad \text{and} \qquad 3x + y \geq 3$$

4.5 Linear Models

Linear relations occur frequently in mathematical models. The relationship between the Celsius and Fahrenheit temperature scales (F $= \frac{9}{5}$C$+32$, see Example 1.6.4), is an example of an exact (by definition) linear relation between two variables. Most of the linear models in economics are approximations to more complicated models. Two typical relations are those shown in Example 4.4.1. Statistical methods have been devised to construct linear functions that approximate the actual data as closely as possible. Let us consider a very naive attempt to construct a linear model based on some data.

EXAMPLE 1   In a United Nations report, the European population in 1960 was estimated as 641 million, and in 1970 the estimate was 705 million. Use these estimates to construct a linear function of t that approximates the population in Europe (in millions), where t is the number of years from 1960 ($t = 0$ is 1960, $t = 1$ is 1961, and so on). Then use the function to estimate the population in 1975 and in 2000. How do you estimate the population in 1930 on the basis of this linear relationship?

Solution: If P denotes the population in millions, we construct an equation of the form $P = at + b$. We know that the graph must pass through the points $(t_1, P_1) = (0, 641)$ and $(t_2, P_2) = (10, 705)$. So we use the point–point formula, replacing x and y with t and P, respectively. This gives

$$P - 641 = \frac{705 - 641}{10 - 0}(t - 0) = \frac{64}{10}t \qquad \text{or} \qquad P = 6.4t + 641 \qquad (*)$$

In Table 1, we have compared our estimates with UN forecasts. Note that because $t = 0$ corresponds to 1960, $t = -30$ will correspond to 1930.

Note that the slope of line $(*)$ is 6.4. This means that if the European population had developed according to $(*)$, then the annual increase in the population would have been constant and equal to 6.4 million.

Table 1 Population estimates for Europe

Year	1930	1975	2000
t	-30	15	40
UN estimates	573	728	854
Formula $(*)$ gives	449	737	897

Actually, Europe's population grew unusually fast during the 1960s. Of course, it grew unusually slowly when millions died during the war years 1939–1945. We see that formula ($*$) does not give very good results compared to the UN estimates. (For a better way to model population growth see Example 4.9.1.)

EXAMPLE 2   (**The Consumption Function**) In Keynesian macroeconomic theory, total consumption expenditure on goods and services, C, is assumed to be a function of national income Y, with

$$C = f(Y)$$

In many models, the consumption function is assumed to be linear, so that

$$C = a + bY$$

The slope b is called the **marginal propensity to consume**. If C and Y are measured in millions of dollars, the number b tells us by how many millions of dollars consumption increases if the national income increases by 1 million dollars. The number b will usually lie between 0 and 1.

In a study of the U.S. economy for the period 1929–1941, T. Haavelmo found the following consumption function:

$$C = 95.05 + 0.712\,Y$$

Here, the marginal propensity to consume is equal to 0.712.

EXAMPLE 3   (**Supply and Demand**) The number of units of a good that consumers demand (that is, are willing to buy) in a certain period will depend on the price of that good. Usually, as the price increases the demand will decrease.[1] Also, the number of units that the producers are willing to supply to the market during a certain period depends on the price they are able to obtain. Usually, the supply will increase as the price increases. So typical demand and supply curves are as indicated in Fig. 1.

Figure 1

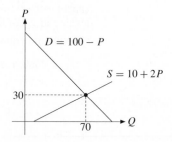

Figure 2

---

[1] For certain luxury goods like perfume, demand might increase as the price increases. For absolutely essential goods, like insulin for diabetics, demand might be almost independent of the price.

The point E in Fig. 1, at which demand is equal to supply, represents an **equilibrium**. The price P^* at which this occurs is the **equilibrium price** and the corresponding quantity Q^* is the **equilibrium quantity**. The equilibrium price is thus the price at which consumers will buy the same amount of the good as the producers wish to sell at that price.

As a very simple example, consider the following linear demand and supply functions

$$D = 100 - P$$
$$S = 10 + 2P$$

Here demand is equal to supply provided that $100 - P = 10 + 2P$, that is, $3P = 90$. So the equilibrium price is $P^* = 30$, with equilibrium quantity $Q^* = 70$. See Fig. 2.   ∎

NOTE 1 A peculiarity of Fig. 1 is that, although quantity is usually regarded as a function of price, here we measure price on the vertical axis and quantity on the horizontal axis. This has been standard practice in elementary price theory since the work of the English economist Alfred Marshall in the late 19th century.

EXAMPLE 4   (**Linear Supply and Demand Functions**) Consider the following general linear demand and supply schedules:

$$D = a - bP$$
$$S = \alpha + \beta P$$

Here a and b are positive parameters of the demand function D, while α and β are positive parameters of the supply function.

Such linear supply and demand functions play an important role in economics. It is often the case that the market for a particular commodity, such as a brand of mobile phones, can be represented approximately by linear demand and supply functions.

At the equilibrium price P^e, demand equals supply, so that $D = S$ at $P = P^e$. Thus, $a - bP^e = \alpha + \beta P^e$. Adding $bP^e - \alpha$ to each side gives

$$a - bP^e + bP^e - \alpha = \alpha + \beta P^e + bP^e - \alpha$$

Thus, $a - \alpha = (\beta + b)P^e$. The corresponding equilibrium quantity is $Q^e = a - bP^e$. Hence, equilibrium occurs when

$$P^e = \frac{a - \alpha}{\beta + b}, \qquad Q^e = a - b\frac{a - \alpha}{\beta + b} = \frac{a\beta + \alpha b}{\beta + b}$$ ∎

PROBLEMS FOR SECTION 4.5

1. The consumption function $C = 4141 + 0.78\,Y$ was estimated for the UK during the period 1949–1975. What is the marginal propensity to consume?

2. Find the equilibrium price for each of the two linear models of supply and demand:

   (a) $D = 75 - 3P$, $S = 20 + 2P$ (b) $D = 100 - 0.5P$, $S = 10 + 0.5P$

3. The total cost C of producing x units of some commodity is a linear function. Records show that on one occasion, 100 units were made at a total cost of $200, and on another occasion, 150 units were made at a total cost of $275. Express the linear equation for total cost C in terms of the number of units x produced.

4. The expenditure of a household on consumer goods, C, is related to the household's income, y, in the following way: When the household's income is $1000, the expenditure on consumer goods is $900, and whenever income is increased by $100, the expenditure on consumer goods is increased by $80. Express the expenditure on consumer goods as a function of income, assuming a linear relationship.

5. For most assets such as cars, stereo equipment, and furniture, the value decreases, or *depreciates*, each year. If the value of an asset is assumed to decrease by a fixed percentage of the original value each year, it is referred to as *straight line depreciation*.

   (a) Suppose the value of a car which initially costs $20 000 depreciates by 10% of its original value each year. Find a formula for its value $P(t)$ after t years.

   (b) If a $500 washing machine is completely depreciated after 10 years (straight line depreciation), find a formula for its value $W(t)$ after t years.

6. According to the 20th report of the International Commission on Whaling, the number N of fin whales in the Antarctic for the period 1958–1963 was estimated to be

$$N = -17\,400\,t + 151\,000, \qquad 0 \le t \le 5$$

where $t = 0$ corresponds to Jan. 1958, $t = 1$ corresponds to Jan. 1959, and so on.

   (a) According to this equation, how many fin whales would be left in April 1960?

   (b) If the decrease continued at the same rate, when would there be no fin whales left? (Actually, the 1993 estimate was approximately 21 000.)

4.6 Quadratic Functions

Economists often find that linear functions are too limited to allow some important phenomena to be described sufficiently accurately. Many economic models involve functions that either decrease down to some minimum value and then increase, or else increase up to some maximum value and then decrease. Some simple functions with this property are the general **quadratic** functions

$$f(x) = ax^2 + bx + c \qquad (a, b, \text{ and } c \text{ are constants}, a \neq 0) \tag{1}$$

(If $a = 0$, the function is linear; hence, the restriction $a \neq 0$.) In general, the graph of $f(x) = ax^2 + bx + c$ is called a **parabola**. The shape of this parabola roughly resembles

$\cap$ when $a < 0$ and $\cup$ when $a > 0$. Three typical cases are illustrated in Fig. 1. The graphs are symmetric about the **axis of symmetry**, which is the vertical dashed line in each of the three cases.

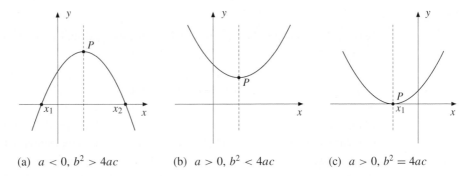

(a) $a < 0$, $b^2 > 4ac$ (b) $a > 0$, $b^2 < 4ac$ (c) $a > 0$, $b^2 = 4ac$

Figure 1 The graph of the parabola $y = ax^2 + bx + c$ for different values of a, b, and c

In order to investigate the function $f(x) = ax^2 + bx + c$ in more detail, we should find the answers to the following questions:

A. For which values of x (if any) is $ax^2 + bx + c = 0$?

B. What are the coordinates of the maximum/minimum point P, also called the **vertex** of the parabola?

EXAMPLE 1   In Example 4.3.1 we considered a special case of (1) in which $a = 1$, $b = -4$, and $c = 3$. Thus

$$f(x) = x^2 - 4x + 3$$

Both questions A and B can be answered by completing the square, as discussed in Section 2.3. In fact,

$$f(x) = x^2 - 4x + 3 = x^2 - 4x + 2^2 + 3 - 2^2 = (x - 2)^2 - 1 \qquad (*)$$

First, $f(x) = 0$ provided $(x-2)^2 - 1 = 0$, that is $(x-2)^2 = 1$. Then one has $(x-2) = \pm 1$, so $x = 2 - 1 = 1$, or $x = 2 + 1 = 3$. The roots of the equation are therefore $x = 1$ and $x = 3$. Question A is answered. (Alternatively, use the quadratic formula (3).)

In order to answer question B, look at the expression $(x - 2)^2 - 1$ in $(*)$. If $x = 2$, its value is -1. Any other value of x than 2 will make $(x - 2)^2 - 1$ larger than -1. Thus $x = 2$ is the point at which $f(x)$ has its minimum value. The line $x = 2$ is the axis of symmetry. (The graph of this function appears in Fig. 4.3.3.)

Looking at the general quadratic function (1), finding the answers to questions A and B again involves using the method of completing the square. In fact, as was shown in Section 2.3, when $a \neq 0$, we can write the formula for $f(x)$ in the following way:

$$f(x) = ax^2 + bx + c = a\left(x + \frac{b}{2a}\right)^2 - \frac{b^2 - 4ac}{4a} \qquad (2)$$

Using this expression for $f(x)$ we find that, provided $b^2 - 4ac \geq 0$ and $a \neq 0$, then

$$ax^2 + bx + c = 0 \iff x_{1,2} = \frac{-b \pm \sqrt{b^2 - 4ac}}{2a} \qquad (3)$$

Here $x_{1,2}$ has two possible values, which are the **roots** x_1 and x_2 of the quadratic equation, and the **zeros** of the quadratic function (1). Also,

$$ax^2 + bx + c = a(x - x_1)(x - x_2) \qquad (4)$$

In Fig. 1(a), the zeros are given by x_1 and x_2. By contrast, in Fig. 1(b) there are no zeros, whereas the graph in Fig. 1(c) has x_1 as its only point of intersection with the x-axis.

To answer question B, consider (2). When x varies, only the value of $a(x + b/2a)^2$ changes. This term is equal to 0 only when $x = -b/2a$, and if $a > 0$, it is never less than 0. This means that when $a > 0$, then the function $f(x)$ attains its minimum when $x = -b/2a$, and the value of $f(x)$ is then equal to $f(-b/2a) = -(b^2 - 4ac)/4a = c - b^2/4a$. If $a < 0$ on the other hand, then $a(x + b/2a)^2 \leq 0$ for all x, and the squared term is equal to 0 only when $x = -b/2a$. Hence, $f(x)$ attains its maximum when $x = -b/2a$ in this second case. To summarize, we have shown the following:

If $a > 0$, then $f(x) = ax^2 + bx + c$ has a **minimum** $c - \dfrac{b^2}{4a}$ at $x = -\dfrac{b}{2a}$

$\qquad (5)$

If $a < 0$, then $f(x) = ax^2 + bx + c$ has a **maximum** $c - \dfrac{b^2}{4a}$ at $x = -\dfrac{b}{2a}$

If you find it difficult to follow the argument leading up to this result, you should study the following special examples very carefully.

EXAMPLE 2   Complete the square for the following functions, and then find the maximum/minimum point of each:

(a) $f(x) = -2x^2 + 40x - 600$ (b) $f(x) = \frac{1}{3}x^2 + \frac{2}{3}x - \frac{8}{3}$

Solution:

(a) $\quad -2x^2 + 40x - 600 = -2(x^2 - 20x) - 600$

$$= -2(x^2 - 20x + 100) + 200 - 600$$

$$= -2(x - 10)^2 - 400$$

The expression $-2(x - 10)^2 - 400$ attains its largest value, which is -400, at $x = 10$.

(b) $\quad \dfrac{1}{3}x^2 + \dfrac{2}{3}x - \dfrac{8}{3} = \dfrac{1}{3}(x^2 + 2x) - \dfrac{8}{3}$

$$= \dfrac{1}{3}(x^2 + 2x + 1) - \dfrac{1}{3} - \dfrac{8}{3}$$

$$= \dfrac{1}{3}(x + 1)^2 - 3$$

The expression $\frac{1}{3}(x + 1)^2 - 3$ attains its smallest value, which is -3, at $x = -1$. ▮

A useful exercise is to solve the two cases in Example 2 by using the expressions set out in (5) directly, substituting appropriate values for the three parameters a, b, and c. You should then check that the same results are obtained.

The axis of symmetry for a parabola is the vertical line through its vertex. Thus, in Fig. 1, the axis of symmetry is the vertical line through P in each case.[2] This follows from formula (2), because if u is any number, then

$$f\left(-\dfrac{b}{2a} + u\right) = au^2 - \dfrac{b^2 - 4ac}{4a} = f\left(-\dfrac{b}{2a} - u\right)$$

Much of economic analysis is concerned with optimization problems. Economics, after all, is the science of choice, and optimization problems are the form in which choice is usually expressed mathematically. A general discussion of such problems must be postponed until we have developed the necessary tools from calculus. Here we show how the simple results from this section on maximizing quadratic functions can be used to illustrate some basic economic ideas.

EXAMPLE 3   The price P per unit obtained by a firm in producing and selling Q units is

$$P = 102 - 2Q$$

and the cost of producing and selling Q units is

$$C = 2Q + \tfrac{1}{2}Q^2$$

Then the profit is[3]

$$\pi(Q) = PQ - C = (102 - 2Q)Q - C = (102 - 2Q)Q - \left(2Q + \dfrac{1}{2}Q^2\right)$$

$$= 100Q - \dfrac{5}{2}Q^2$$

Find the value of Q which maximizes profits, and the corresponding maximal profit.

---

[2] The function f is symmetric about $x = a$ if $f(a + x) = f(a - x)$ for all x. See Section 5.2.
[3] In mathematics π is used to denote the constant ratio $3.1415\dots$ between the circumference of a circle and its diameter. In economics, this constant is not used very often. Also, p and P usually denote a price, so π has come to denote profit.

Solution: Using formula (5) we find that profit is maximized at

$$Q = Q^* = -\frac{100}{2(-\frac{5}{2})} = 20 \quad \text{with} \quad \pi^* = \pi(Q^*) = -\frac{100^2}{4(-\frac{5}{2})} = 1000$$

This example is a special case of the monopoly problem studied in the next example.   ▌

EXAMPLE 4   (**A Monopoly Problem**) Consider a firm that is the only seller of the commodity it produces, possibly a patented medicine, and so enjoys a monopoly. The total costs of the monopolist are assumed to be given by the quadratic function

$$C = \alpha Q + \beta Q^2, \qquad Q \geq 0$$

of its output level Q, where α and β are positive constants. For each Q, the price P at which it can sell its output is assumed to be determined from the linear "inverse" demand function

$$P = a - bQ, \qquad Q \geq 0$$

where a and b are constants with $a > 0$ and $b \geq 0$. So for any nonnegative Q, the total revenue R is given by the quadratic function

$$R = PQ = (a - bQ)Q$$

and profit by the quadratic function

$$\pi(Q) = R - C = (a - bQ)Q - \alpha Q - \beta Q^2 = (a - \alpha)Q - (b + \beta)Q^2$$

The monopolist's objective is to maximize $\pi = \pi(Q)$. By using (5), we see that there is a maximum of π (for the monopolist M) at

$$Q^M = \frac{a - \alpha}{2(b + \beta)} \quad \text{with} \quad \pi^M = \frac{(a - \alpha)^2}{4(b + \beta)} \qquad (*)$$

This is valid if $a > \alpha$; if $a \leq \alpha$, the firm will not produce, but will have $Q^M = 0$ and $\pi^M = 0$. The two cases are illustrated in Figs. 2 and 3. In Fig. 3, the part of the parabola to the left of $Q = 0$ is dashed, because it is not really relevant given the natural requirement that $Q \geq 0$. The price and cost associated with Q^M in $(*)$ can be found by routine algebra.

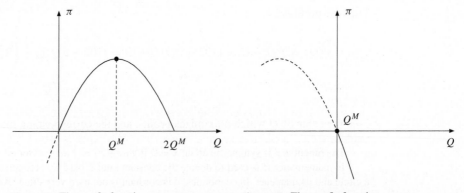

Figure 2 The profit function, $a > \alpha$ **Figure 3** The profit function, $a \leq \alpha$

If we put $b = 0$ in the price function $P = a - bQ$, then $P = a$ for all Q. In this case, the firm's choice of quantity does not influence the price at all and so the firm is said to be *perfectly competitive*. By replacing a by P in our previous expressions, we see that profit is maximized for a perfectly competitive firm at

$$Q^* = \frac{P - \alpha}{2\beta} \qquad \text{with} \qquad \pi^* = \frac{(P - \alpha)^2}{4\beta} \qquad (**)$$

provided that $P > \alpha$. If $P \leq \alpha$, then $Q^* = 0$ and $\pi^* = 0$.

Solving the first equation in $(**)$ for P yields $P = \alpha + 2\beta Q^*$. Thus,

$$P = \alpha + 2\beta Q \qquad (***)$$

represents the *supply curve* of this perfectly competitive firm for $P > \alpha$. For $P \leq \alpha$, the profit maximizing output Q^* is 0. The supply curve relating the price on the market to the firm's choice of output quantity is shown in Fig. 4; it includes all the points of the line segment between the origin and $(0, \alpha)$, where the price is too low for the firm to earn any profit by producing a positive output.

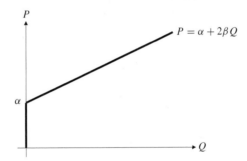

Figure 4 The supply curve of a perfectly competitive firm

Let us return to the monopoly firm (which has no supply curve). If it could somehow be made to act like a competitive firm, taking price as given, it would be on the supply curve $(***)$. Given the demand curve $P = a - bQ$, equilibrium between supply and demand occurs when $(***)$ is also satisfied, and so $P = a - bQ = \alpha + 2\beta Q$. Solving the second equation for Q, and then substituting for P and π in turn, we see that the equilibrium level of output, the corresponding price, and the profit would be

$$Q^e = \frac{a - \alpha}{b + 2\beta}, \qquad P^e = \frac{2a\beta + \alpha b}{b + 2\beta}, \qquad \pi^e = \frac{\beta(a - \alpha)^2}{(b + 2\beta)^2}$$

In order to have the monopolist mimic a competitive firm by choosing to be at (Q^e, P^e), it may be desirable to tax (or subsidize) the output of the monopolist. Suppose that the monopolist is required to pay a specific tax of t per unit of output. Because the tax payment tQ is added to the firm's costs, the new total cost function is

$$C = \alpha Q + \beta Q^2 + tQ = (\alpha + t)Q + \beta Q^2$$

Carrying out the same calculations as before, but with α replaced by $\alpha + t$, gives the monopolist's choice of output as

$$Q_t^M = \begin{cases} \dfrac{a - \alpha - t}{2(b + \beta)}, & \text{if } a \geq \alpha + t \\ 0, & \text{otherwise} \end{cases}$$

So $Q_t^M = Q^e$ when $(a - \alpha - t)/2(b + \beta) = (a - \alpha)/(b + 2\beta)$. Solving this equation for t yields $t = -(a - \alpha)b/(b + 2\beta)$. Note that t is actually negative, indicating the desirability of *subsidizing* the output of the monopolist in order to encourage additional production. (Of course, subsidizing monopolists is usually felt to be unjust, and many additional complications need to be considered carefully before formulating a desirable policy for dealing with monopolists. Still the previous analysis suggests that if it is desirable to lower a monopolist's price or its profit, this is much better done directly than by taxing its output.)

PROBLEMS FOR SECTION 4.6

1. (a) Let $f(x) = x^2 - 4x$. Complete the following table:

x	-1	0	1	2	3	4	5
$f(x)$							

   (b) Using the table in part (a), sketch the graph of f.

   (c) Using (5), determine the minimum point.

   (d) Solve the equation $f(x) = 0$.

2. (a) Let $f(x) = -\frac{1}{2}x^2 - x + \frac{3}{2}$. Complete the following table:

x	-4	-3	-2	-1	0	1	2
$f(x)$							

   (b) Use the information in part (a) to sketch the graph of f.

   (c) Using (5), determine the maximum point of $f(x)$.

   (d) Solve the equation $-\frac{1}{2}x^2 - x + \frac{3}{2} = 0$ for x.

   (e) Show that $f(x) = -\frac{1}{2}(x - 1)(x + 3)$, and use this to study how the sign of $f(x)$ varies with x. Compare the result with the graph.

3. Complete the squares as in (2) for the following quadratic functions, and then determine the maximum/minimum points:

   (a) $x^2 + 4x$ (b) $x^2 + 6x + 18$ (c) $-3x^2 + 30x - 30$

   (d) $9x^2 - 6x - 44$ (e) $-x^2 - 200x + 30\,000$ (f) $x^2 + 100x - 20\,000$

4. Find all the zeros of each quadratic function in Problem 3, and write each function in the form $a(x - x_1)(x - x_2)$ (if possible).

5. Find solutions to the following equations, where p and q are positive parameters.

   (a) $x^2 - 3px + 2p^2 = 0$ (b) $x^2 - (p+q)x + pq = 0$ (c) $x^2 + px + q = 0$

6. A model occurring in the theory of efficient loan markets involves the function

$$U(x) = 72 - (4 + x)^2 - (4 - rx)^2$$

   where r is a constant. Find the value of x for which $U(x)$ attains its largest value.

7. A farmer has 1000 metres of fence wire with which to make a rectangular enclosure, as illustrated in the figure below.

   (a) Find the areas of the three rectangles whose bases are 100, 250, and 350 metres.

   (b) Let the base have length $250 + x$. Then the height is $250 - x$ (see the figure).

What choice of x gives the maximum area?[4]

8. If a cocoa shipping firm sells Q tons of cocoa in England, the price received is given by $P = \alpha_1 - \frac{1}{3}Q$. On the other hand, if it buys Q tons from its only source in Ghana, the price it has to pay is given by $P = \alpha_2 + \frac{1}{6}Q$. In addition, it costs γ per ton to ship cocoa from its supplier in Ghana to its customers in England (its only market). The numbers α_1, α_2, and γ are all positive.

   (a) Express the cocoa shipper's profit as a function of Q, the number of tons shipped.

   (b) Assuming that $\alpha_1 - \alpha_2 - \gamma > 0$, find the profit maximizing shipment of cocoa. What happens if $\alpha_1 - \alpha_2 - \gamma \le 0$?

   (c) Suppose the government of Ghana imposes an export tax on cocoa of t per ton. Find the new expression for the shipper's profits and the new quantity shipped.

   (d) Calculate the Ghanaian government's export tax revenue T as a function of t, and advise it on how to obtain as much tax revenue as possible.

---

[4] It is reported that certain surveyors in antiquity wrote contracts with farmers to sell them rectangular pieces of land in which only the perimeter was specified. As a result, the lots were long narrow rectangles.

HARDER PROBLEMS

9. Let $a_1, a_2, \ldots, a_n$ and $b_1, b_2, \ldots, b_n$ be arbitrary real numbers. We claim that the following inequality (called the **Cauchy–Schwarz inequality**) is always valid:

$$(a_1 b_1 + a_2 b_2 + \cdots + a_n b_n)^2 \leq (a_1^2 + a_2^2 + \cdots + a_n^2)(b_1^2 + b_2^2 + \cdots + b_n^2) \qquad (6)$$

(a) Check the inequality for (i) $a_1 = 1$, $a_2 = 3$, $b_1 = 2$, and $b_2 = 5$; and for (ii) $a_1 = -3$, $a_2 = 2$, $b_1 = 5$, and $b_2 = -2$. (In both cases $n = 2$.)

(b) Prove (6) by means of the following trick: first, define f for all x by

$$f(x) = (a_1 x + b_1)^2 + \cdots + (a_n x + b_n)^2$$

It should be obvious that $f(x) \geq 0$ for all x. Write $f(x)$ as $Ax^2 + Bx + C$, where the expressions for A, B, and C are related to the terms in (6). Because $Ax^2 + Bx + C \geq 0$ for all x, we must have $B^2 - 4AC \leq 0$. Why? The conclusion follows.

4.7 Polynomials

After considering linear and quadratic functions, the logical next step is to examine **cubic functions** of the form

$$f(x) = ax^3 + bx^2 + cx + d \qquad (a, b, c, \text{ and } d \text{ are constants; } a \neq 0) \qquad (1)$$

It is relatively easy to examine the behaviour of linear and quadratic functions. Cubic functions are considerably more complicated, because the shape of their graphs changes drastically as the coefficients a, b, c, and d vary. Two examples are given in Figs. 1 and 2.

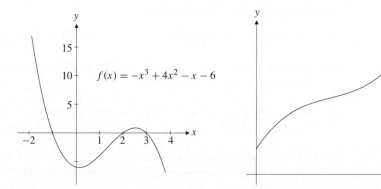

Figure 1 A cubic function   **Figure 2** A cubic cost function

Cubic functions do occasionally appear in economic models. Let us look at an example.

EXAMPLE 1   Consider a firm producing a single commodity. The total cost of producing Q units of the commodity is $C(Q)$. Cost functions often have the following properties: First, $C(0)$ is positive, because an initial fixed expenditure is involved. When production increases, costs also increase. In the beginning, costs increase rapidly, but the rate of increase slows down as production equipment is used for a higher proportion of each working week. However, at high levels of production, costs again increase at a fast rate, because of technical bottlenecks and overtime payments to workers, for example. It can be shown that the cubic cost function $C(Q) = aQ^3 + bQ^2 + cQ + d$ exhibits this type of behaviour provided that $a > 0$, $b < 0$, $c > 0$, $d > 0$, and $3ac > b^2$. Such a function is sketched in Fig. 2.

Cubic cost functions whose coefficients have a different sign pattern have also been studied. For instance, a study of a particular power plant revealed that over a certain period, the cost of fuel y as a function of output Q was given by

$$y = -Q^3 + 214.2Q^2 - 7900Q + 320700$$

(This cost function cannot be valid for all Q, however, because it suggests that fuel costs would be negative for large enough Q.) ∎

The detailed study of cubic functions is made easier by applying the differential calculus, as will be seen later.

General Polynomials

Linear, quadratic, and cubic functions are all examples of **polynomials**. The function P defined for all x by

$$P(x) = a_n x^n + a_{n-1} x^{n-1} + \cdots + a_1 x + a_0 \qquad (a\text{'s are constants}; a_n \neq 0) \qquad (2)$$

is called the **general polynomial of degree n** with **coefficients** $a_0, a_1, \ldots, a_n$. Here a_n is called the *leading* coefficient. When $n = 4$, we obtain $P(x) = a_4 x^4 + a_3 x^3 + a_2 x^2 + a_1 x + a_0$, which is the general polynomial of degree 4, with leading coefficient a_4.

EXAMPLE 2

(a) $-\frac{1}{2}x^5 + 5x^4 + x - 1$ is a polynomial of degree 5 with leading coefficient $-\frac{1}{2}$.

(b) $\dfrac{x^3 - 2x^2 + 5}{28}$ is a polynomial of degree 3 with leading coefficient $\dfrac{1}{28}$.

(c) $5x^{-3} + x^{-2} + x^{-1} + 2$ is *not* a polynomial, and neither is $\dfrac{28}{x^3 - 2x^2 + 5}$.

(But the first function is a polynomial $5u^3 + u^2 + u + 2$ in the new variable $u = x^{-1}$.) ∎

Numerous problems in mathematics and its applications involve polynomials. Often, one is particularly interested in finding the number and location of the **zeros** of $P(x)$—that is, the values of x such that $P(x) = 0$. The equation

$$a_n x^n + a_{n-1} x^{n-1} + \cdots + a_1 x + a_0 = 0 \qquad (3)$$

is called the **general nth-order equation**. It will soon be shown that this equation has *at most n* (real) solutions, also called **roots**, but it need not have any. The corresponding nth degree polynomial has a graph which has at most $n - 1$ "turning points", but there may be fewer such points. For example, the 100th-order equation

$$x^{100} + 1 = 0$$

has no solutions because $x^{100} + 1$ is always greater than or equal to 1, and its graph has only one turning point.

According to the **fundamental theorem of algebra**, every polynomial of the form (3) can be written as a product of polynomials of first or second degree. Here is a somewhat complicated case:

$$x^5 - x^4 + x - 1 = (x - 1)(x^4 + 1) = (x - 1)(x^2 - \sqrt{2}x + 1)(x^2 + \sqrt{2}x + 1)$$

Factoring Polynomials

Let $P(x)$ and $Q(x)$ be two polynomials for which the degree of $P(x)$ is greater than or equal to the degree of $Q(x)$. Then there always exist unique polynomials $q(x)$ and $r(x)$ such that

$$P(x) = q(x)Q(x) + r(x) \tag{4}$$

where the degree of $r(x)$ is less than the degree of $Q(x)$. This fact is called the **remainder theorem**. When x is such that $Q(x) \neq 0$, then (4) can be written in the form

$$\frac{P(x)}{Q(x)} = q(x) + \frac{r(x)}{Q(x)}$$

where $r(x)$ is the remainder. If $r(x) = 0$, we say that $Q(x)$ *is a factor of $P(x)$*, or that $P(x)$ *is divisible by $Q(x)$*. Then $P(x) = q(x)Q(x)$ or $P(x)/Q(x) = q(x)$.

An important special case is when $Q(x) = x - a$. Then $Q(x)$ is of degree 1, so the remainder $r(x)$ must have degree 0, and is therefore a constant. In this special case, for all x,

$$P(x) = q(x)(x - a) + r$$

For $x = a$ in particular, we get $P(a) = r$. Hence, $x - a$ *divides $P(x)$ if and only if $P(a) = 0$*. This important observation can be formulated as follows:

> The polynomial $P(x)$ has the factor $x - a \iff P(a) = 0$ $\qquad$ (5)

NOTE 1 It follows from (5) that an nth-degree polynomial $P(x)$ can have *at most n* different zeros. The reason is that each zero gives rise to a different factor of the form $x - a$. Then, as an nth degree polynomial, $P(x)$ can have at most n such factors. The result in (5) is often used when we try to factor polynomials.

NOTE 2 (**Integer Solutions**) Each integer m which satisfies the cubic equation

$$-x^3 + 4x^2 - x - 6 = 0 \qquad (*)$$

must satisfy the equation $m(-m^2 + 4m - 1) = 6$. Since $-m^2 + 4m - 1$ is also an integer, m must be a factor of the constant term 6. Thus ± 1, ± 2, ± 3, and ± 6 are the only possible integer solutions. Direct substitution into the left-hand side (LHS) of equation $(*)$ reveals that of these eight possibilities, $-1, 2,$ and 3 are roots of the equation. A third degree equation has at most three roots, so we have found all of them, and clearly then

$$-x^3 + 4x^2 - x - 6 = -(x + 1)(x - 2)(x - 3)$$

In general: *Suppose that a_n, a_{n-1}, ..., a_1, a_0 are all integers. Then all possible integer roots of the equation*

$$a_n x^n + a_{n-1} x^{n-1} + \cdots + a_1 x + a_0 = 0$$

must be factors of the constant term a_0.

EXAMPLE 3 Find all possible integer roots of the equation $\frac{1}{2} x^3 - x^2 + \frac{1}{2} x - 1 = 0$.

Solution: We multiply both sides of the equation by 2 to obtain an equation whose coefficients are all integers:
$$x^3 - 2x^2 + x - 2 = 0$$

Now, all integer solutions of the equation must be factors of 2. So only ± 1 and ± 2 can be integer solutions. A check shows that $x = 2$ is the only integer solution. In fact, because $x^3 - 2x^2 + x - 2 = (x - 2)(x^2 + 1)$, there is only one real root. ▮

EXAMPLE 4 Find possible quadratic and cubic functions which have the graphs in Figs. 3 and 4 respectively.

Figure 3

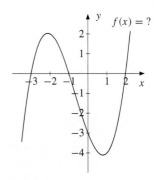

Figure 4

Solution: Figure 3: Since the graph intersects the x-axis at the two points $x = -2$ and $x = 2$, we try the quadratic function $f(x) = a(x - 2)(x + 2)$. Then $f(0) = -4a$. According to the graph, $f(0) = -2$, so $a = 1/2$, and hence

$$f(x) = \frac{1}{2}(x - 2)(x + 2) = \frac{1}{2}x^2 - 2$$

Figure 4: Because the equation $f(x) = 0$ has roots $x = -3, -1, 2$, we try the cubic function $f(x) = b(x + 3)(x + 1)(x - 2)$. Then $f(0) = -6b$. According to the graph, $f(0) = -3$. So $b = 1/2$, and hence

$$f(x) = \frac{1}{2}(x + 3)(x + 1)(x - 2)$$

Polynomial Division

One can divide polynomials in much the same way as one divides numbers. Consider first a simple numerical example:

$$
\begin{array}{rl}
2735 \div 5 & = 500 + 40 + 7 \\
\underline{2500} & \\
235 & \\
\underline{200} & \\
35 & \\
\underline{35} & \\
0 & \text{remainder}
\end{array}
$$

Hence, $2735 \div 5 = 547$. Note that the horizontal lines instruct you to subtract the numbers above the lines. (You might be more accustomed to a different way of arranging the numbers, but the idea is the same.)

Consider next

$$(-x^3 + 4x^2 - x - 6) \div (x - 2)$$

We write the following:

$$
\begin{array}{ll}
(-x^3 + 4x^2 - x - 6) \div (x - 2) = -x^2 \qquad\qquad + 2x \qquad + 3 \\
\underline{-x^3 + 2x^2} \qquad\qquad\qquad \longleftarrow \boxed{-x^2(x-2)} \\
\quad 2x^2 - x \\
\quad \underline{2x^2 - 4x} \qquad\qquad\qquad \longleftarrow \boxed{2x(x - 2)} \\
\qquad\quad 3x - 6 \\
\qquad\quad \underline{3x - 6} \qquad\qquad \longleftarrow \boxed{3(x - 2)} \\
\qquad\qquad 0 \ \text{remainder}
\end{array}
$$

(You can omit the boxes, but they should help you to see what is going on.) We conclude that $(-x^3 + 4x^2 - x - 6) \div (x - 2) = -x^2 + 2x + 3$. However, it is easy to see that $-x^2 + 2x + 3 = -(x + 1)(x - 3)$. So

$$-x^3 + 4x^2 - x - 6 = -(x + 1)(x - 3)(x - 2)$$

EXAMPLE 5   Prove that the polynomial $P(x) = -2x^3 + 2x^2 + 10x + 6$ has a zero at $x = 3$, and factor the polynomial.

Solution: Inserting $x = 3$ into the polynomial yields $P(3) = 0$. So according to (5), $P(x)$ has $x - 3$ as a factor. Performing the division $(-2x^3 + 2x^2 + 10x + 6) \div (x - 3)$, we find that the result is $-2(x^2 + 2x + 1) = -2(x + 1)^2$, and so

$$P(x) = -2(x - 3)(x + 1)^2$$

Polynomial Division with a Remainder

The division $2734 \div 5$ gives 546 and leaves the remainder 4. So $2734/5 = 546 + 4/5$. We consider a similar form of division for polynomials.

EXAMPLE 6   Perform the division: $(x^4 + 3x^2 - 4) \div (x^2 + 2x)$.

Solution:

$$
\begin{array}{l}
(x^4 \qquad\quad + 3x^2 \qquad\quad - 4) \div (x^2 + 2x) = x^2 - 2x + 7 \\
\underline{x^4 + 2x^3} \\
\quad -2x^3 + 3x^2 \qquad\quad -4 \\
\quad \underline{-2x^3 - 4x^2} \\
\qquad\quad 7x^2 \qquad\quad -4 \\
\qquad\quad \underline{7x^2 + 14x} \\
\qquad\qquad\quad -14x - 4 \qquad \text{remainder}
\end{array}
$$

(The polynomial $x^4 + 3x^2 - 4$ has no terms in x^3 and x, so we inserted some extra space between the powers of x to make room for the terms in x^3 and x that arise in the course of the calculations.) We conclude that $x^4 + 3x^2 - 4 = (x^2 - 2x + 7)(x^2 + 2x) + (-14x - 4)$. Hence,

$$\frac{x^4 + 3x^2 - 4}{x^2 + 2x} = x^2 - 2x + 7 - \frac{14x + 4}{x^2 + 2x}$$

Rational Functions

A **rational function** is a function $R(x) = P(x)/Q(x)$ that can be expressed as the ratio of two polynomials $P(x)$ and $Q(x)$. This function is defined for all x where $Q(x) \neq 0$. The rational function $R(x)$ is called **proper** if the degree of $P(x)$ is less than the degree of $Q(x)$. When the degree of $P(x)$ is greater than or equal to that of $Q(x)$, then $R(x)$ is called an **improper** rational function. By using polynomial division, any improper rational function can be written as a polynomial plus a proper rational function, as in Example 6.

EXAMPLE 7 $f(x) = \dfrac{3x}{-x^2 + 4x - 1}$ is a rational function since the numerator and the denominator are each polynomials. The fraction is not defined when $-x^2 + 4x - 1 = 0$, that is when $x = 2 \pm \sqrt{3}$. At these points the graph has vertical *asymptotes*. Its graph is shown in Fig. 5.

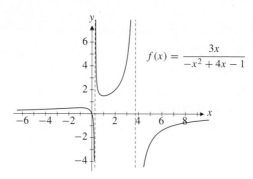

$$f(x) = \frac{3x}{-x^2 + 4x - 1}$$

Figure 5

Studying the behaviour of rational functions becomes easier once we have developed the proper tools from calculus. (See Problem 6.7.8.)

PROBLEMS FOR SECTION 4.7

1. Find all integer roots of the following equations:

   (a) $x^4 - x^3 - 7x^2 + x + 6 = 0$ (b) $2x^3 + 11x^2 - 7x - 6 = 0$

   (c) $x^4 + x^3 + 2x^2 + x + 1 = 0$ (d) $\frac{1}{4}x^3 - \frac{1}{4}x^2 - x + 1 = 0$

2. Find all integer roots of the following equations:

   (a) $x^2 + x - 2 = 0$ (b) $x^3 - x^2 - 25x + 25 = 0$ (c) $x^5 - 4x^3 - 3 = 0$

3. Perform the following divisions:

   (a) $(2x^3 + 2x - 1) \div (x - 1)$ (b) $(x^4 + x^3 + x^2 + x) \div (x^2 + x)$

   (c) $(x^5 - 3x^4 + 1) \div (x^2 + x + 1)$ (d) $(3x^8 + x^2 + 1) \div (x^3 - 2x + 1)$

4. Find possible formulas for each of the three polynomials with graphs shown in in the figures.

(a) (b) (c)

5. Perform the following divisions:

   (a) $(x^2 - x - 20) \div (x - 5)$ (b) $(x^3 - 1) \div (x - 1)$ (c) $(-3x^3 + 48x) \div (x - 4)$

6. Show that the division $(x^4 + 3x^2 + 5) \div (x - c)$ leaves a remainder for all values of c.

7. The following function has been used in demand theory

$$E = \alpha \frac{x^2 - \gamma x}{x + \beta} \qquad (\alpha, \beta, \text{ and } \gamma \text{ are constants})$$

   Perform the division $(x^2 - \gamma x) \div (x + \beta)$, and use the result to express E as a sum of a linear function and a proper fraction.

4.8 Power Functions

Consider the general **power function** f defined by the formula

$$f(x) = Ax^r \qquad (x > 0, \ r \text{ and } A \text{ are any constants}) \tag{1}$$

We saw in Section 1.5 how the number x^r can be defined for all rational numbers r (that is, for all fractional exponents). When we consider the power function, we assume that $x > 0$. This is because for many values of r, such as $r = 1/2$, the symbol x^r is not defined for negative values of x. And we exclude $x = 0$ because 0^0 is undefined.

   Here are three examples of why powers with rational exponents are needed:

A. The formula $S \approx 4.84V^{2/3}$ gives the approximate surface S of a ball as a function of its volume V. (See Problem 6.)

B. The flow of blood (in litres per second) through the heart of an individual is approximately proportional to $x^{0.7}$, where x is the body weight.

C. The formula $Y = 2.262K^{0.203}L^{0.763}(1.02)^t$ appears in a study of the growth of national product, and shows how powers with fractional exponents can arise in economics. (Here Y is the net national product, K is capital stock, L is labour, and t is time.)

So far we have defined x^r for any rational number r. We also need to consider x^r when r is irrational in order for x^r to be defined for all real numbers r. How do we define, say, 5 raised to the irrational number π, that is 5^π? Because π is close to 3.1, we should define 5^π as approximately $5^{3.1} = 5^{31/10} = \sqrt[10]{5^{31}}$, which *is* defined. An even better approximation is $5^\pi \approx 5^{3.14} = 5^{314/100} = 5^{157/50} = \sqrt[50]{5^{157}}$. We can continue by taking more decimal places in the representation of $\pi = 3.14159\,26535, \ldots$, and our approximation will be better with every additional decimal digit. Then the meaning of 5^π should be reasonably clear. In any case, most readers would be content with just using a calculator to find that $5^\pi \approx 156.993$. (Section 7.10 further discusses the definition of x^r when r is irrational.)

Graphs of Power Functions

We return to the power function $f(x) = x^r$, which is now defined for all real numbers r provided that $x > 0$. We always have $f(1) = 1^r = 1$, so the graph of the function passes through the point $(1, 1)$ in the xy-plane. The shape of the graph depends crucially on the value of r, as Figs. 1–3 indicate. If $0 < r < 1$, the graph is like that in Fig. 1, which resembles the graph of $f(x) = x^{0.5}$ shown in Fig. 4.3.8. For $r > 1$ the graph is like that shown in Fig. 2. (For $r = 2$, the graph is the half of the parabola $y = x^2$ shown in Fig. 4.3.6.) Finally, for $r < 0$, the graph is like that shown in Fig. 3. (For $r = -1$, the graph is half of the hyperbola $y = 1/x$ shown in Fig. 4.3.9.)

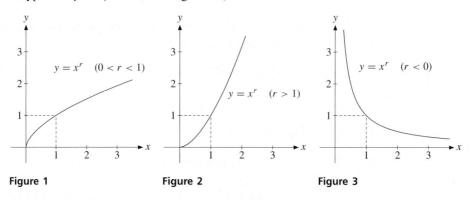

Figure 1   Figure 2   Figure 3

Figure 4 illustrates how the graph of $y = x^r$ changes with changing values of the exponent.

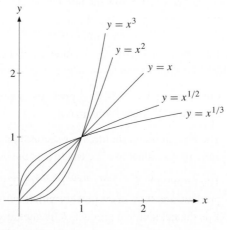

Figure 4

1. Sketch the graphs of $y = x^{-3}$, $y = x^{-1}$, $y = x^{-1/2}$, and $y = x^{-1/3}$, defined for $x > 0$.

2. Match each of the graphs A–F with one of the functions (a)–(f) in the following table. (In (f) try to find a suitable function which has the remaining graph.)

(a) $y = \frac{1}{2}x^2 - x - \frac{3}{2}$ has graph ___

(b) $y = 2\sqrt{2-x}$ has graph ___

(c) $y = -\frac{1}{2}x^2 + x + \frac{3}{2}$ has graph ___

(d) $y = \left(\frac{1}{2}\right)^x - 2$ has graph ___

(e) $y = 2\sqrt{x-2}$ has graph ___

(f) $y =$ has graph ___

A

B

C

D

E

F

3. Use a calculator to find approximate values for (a) $\sqrt{2}^{\sqrt{2}}$ (b) π^π.

4. Solve the following equations for x:

   (a) $2^{2x} = 8$ (b) $3^{3x+1} = 1/81$ (c) $10^{x^2-2x+2} = 100$

5. Find t when   (a) $3^{5t}9^t = 27$ (b) $9^t = (27)^{1/5}/3$

6. The formulas for the surface S and the volume V of a ball with radius r are $S = 4\pi r^2$ and $V = (4/3)\pi r^3$. Express S as a power function of V.

4.9 Exponential Functions

A quantity that increases (or decreases) by a fixed factor per unit of time is said to *increase* (or *decrease*) *exponentially*. If the fixed factor is a, this leads to the function

$$f(t) = Aa^t \qquad (a \text{ and } A \text{ are positive constants}) \qquad (1)$$

(It is obvious how to modify the subsequent discussion for the case when A is negative.) Note that if $f(t) = Aa^t$, then $f(t + 1) = Aa^{t+1} = Aa^t \cdot a^1 = af(t)$, so the value of f at time $t + 1$ is a times the value of f at time t. If $a > 1$, then f is increasing; if $0 < a < 1$, then f is decreasing. (See Figs. 1 and 2.) Because $f(0) = Aa^0 = A$, we can write $f(t) = f(0)a^t$.

Exponential functions appear in many important economic, social, and physical models. For instance, economic growth, population growth, continuously accumulated interest, radioactive decay, and decreasing illiteracy have all been described by exponential functions. In addition, the exponential function is one of the most important functions in statistics.

NOTE 1 Observe the fundamental difference between the two functions

$$f(x) = a^x \qquad \text{and} \qquad g(x) = x^a$$

The second of these two is the *power function* discussed in Section 4.8. For the exponential function a^x, it is the exponent that varies, while the base is constant. For the power function x^a, on the other hand, the exponent is constant, while the base varies.

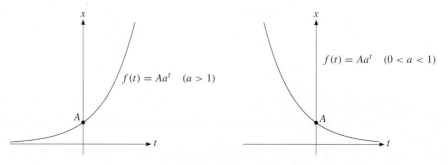

Figure 1 Graph of $f(t) = Aa^t$ $(a > 1)$ **Figure 2** Graph of $f(t) = Aa^t$ $(0 < a < 1)$

EXAMPLE 1   (**Population Growth**) Consider a growing population like that of Europe during the 20th century. In Example 4.5.1, we constructed a linear function $P = 6.4t + 641$, where P denotes the population in millions, $t = 0$ corresponds to the year 1960 when the population was 641 million, and $t = 10$ corresponds to the year 1970 when the population estimate was 705 million. According to this formula, the annual increase in population would be constant and equal to 6.4 million. This is a very unreasonable assumption. After all, populations tend to grow faster as they get bigger because there are more people to have babies, and the death rate usually decreases or stays the same. In fact, according to UN estimates, the European population was expected to grow by approximately 0.72% annually during the period 1960 to 2000. With a population of 641 million in 1960, the population in 1961 would then be $641 \cdot 1.0072$ (see Section 1.2), which is approximately 645 million. Next year, in 1962, it would have grown to $641 \cdot 1.0072^2$, which is approximately 650 million. If growth were to continue at 0.72% annually, the population figure would grow by the factor 1.0072 each year. Then, t years after 1960, the population would be given by

$$P(t) = 641 \cdot 1.0072^t$$

Thus, $P(t)$ is an exponential function of the form (1). For the year 2000, corresponding to $t = 40$, the formula yields the estimate $P(40) \approx 854$ million. (The actual figure turned out to be about 728 million, which shows the limitations of naive projections.)

Many countries, particularly in Africa, have recently had far faster population growth than Europe. For instance, during the 1970s and 1980s, the growth rate of Zimbabwe's population was close to 3.5% annually. If we let $t = 0$ correspond to the census year 1969 when the population was 5.1 million, the population t years after 1969 is $P(t) = 5.1 \cdot 1.035^t$. If we calculate $P(20)$, $P(40)$, and $P(60)$ using this formula, we get roughly 10, 20, and 40. Thus, the population of Zimbabwe roughly doubles after 20 years; during the next 20 years, it doubles again, and so on. We say that the *doubling time* of the population is approximately 20 years. Of course, extrapolating so far into the future is quite dubious, because exponential growth of population cannot go on forever. (If the growth rate continued at 3.5% annually, there was no emigration, and the Zimbabwean territory did not expand, then in the year 2296 each Zimbabwean would have only 1 square metre of land on average. See Problem 6.)

If $a > 1$ (and $A > 0$), the exponential function $f(t) = Aa^t$ is increasing. Its **doubling time** is the time it takes for it to double. Its value at $t = 0$ is A, so the doubling time t^* is given by the equation $f(t^*) = Aa^{t^*} = 2A$, or after cancelling A, by $a^{t^*} = 2$. Thus the doubling time of the exponential function $f(t) = Aa^t$ is the power to which a must be raised in order to get 2.[5] (In Problem 7 you will be asked to show that the doubling time is independent of which year you take as the base.)

EXAMPLE 2   Use your calculator to find the doubling time of

(a) a population (like that of Zimbabwe) increasing at 3.5% annually (thus confirming the earlier calculations)

(b) the population of Kenya in the 1980s (which had the world's highest annual growth rate of population, 4.2%).

Solution:

(a) The doubling time t^* is given by the equation $1.035^{t^*} = 2$. Using a calculator shows that $1.035^{15} \approx 1.68$, whereas $1.035^{25} \approx 2.36$. Thus, t^* must lie between 15 and 25. Because $1.035^{20} \approx 1.99$, t^* is close to 20. In fact, $t^* \approx 20.15$.

(b) The doubling time t^* is given by the equation $1.042^{t^*} = 2$. Using a calculator, we find that $t^* \approx 16.85$. Thus, with a growth rate of 4.2%, Kenya's population would double in less than 17 years.

EXAMPLE 3   (**Compound Interest**) A savings account of $\$K$ that increases by $p\%$ interest each year will have increased after t years to

$$K(1 + p/100)^t$$

(see Section 1.2). According to this formula, $\$1$ ($K = 1$) earning interest at 8% per year ($p = 8$) will have increased after t years to $(1 + 8/100)^t = 1.08^t$.

Table 1 How $1 of savings increases with time at 8% annual interest

t	1	2	5	10	20	30	50	100	200
$(1.08)^t$	1.08	1.17	1.47	2.16	4.66	10.06	46.90	2199.76	4 838 949.60

[5] By using natural logarithms (see Example 4.10.2) we find that $t^* = \ln 2 / \ln a$.

After 30 years, $1 of savings has increased to more than $10, and after 200 years, it has grown to more than $4.8 million! Observe that the expression 1.08^t defines an exponential function of the type (1) with $a = 1.08$. Even if a is only slightly larger than 1, $f(t)$ will increase very quickly when t is large. ∎

EXAMPLE 4　　(**Continuous Depreciation**) Each year the value of most assets such as cars, stereo equipment, or furniture decreases, or *depreciates*. If the value of an asset is assumed to decrease by a fixed percentage each year, then the depreciation is called *continuous*. (Straight line depreciation was discussed in Problem 4.5.5.)

Assume that a car, which at time $t = 0$ has the value P_0, depreciates at the rate of 20% each year over a 5 year period. What is its value $A(t)$ at time t, for $t = 1, 2, 3, 4, 5$?

Solution: After 1 year its value is $P_0 - (20P_0/100) = P_0(1 - 20/100) = P_0(0.8)^1$. Thus, each year it depreciates by the factor 0.8, so after t years, its value is

$$A(t) = P_0(0.8)^t$$

In particular, $A(5) = P_0(0.8)^5 \approx 0.32P_0$, so after 5 years its value has decreased to about 32% of its original value. ∎

The most important properties of the exponential function are summed up by the following:

THE GENERAL EXPONENTIAL FUNCTION

The **general exponential function** with base $a > 0$ is

$$f(x) = Aa^x$$

where $f(0) = A$, and a is the factor by which $f(x)$ changes when x increases by 1.

If $a = 1 + p/100$, where $p > 0$ and $A > 0$, then $f(x)$ will increase by $p\%$ for each unit increase in x.

If $a = 1 - p/100$, where $p > 0$ and $A > 0$, then $f(x)$ will decrease by $p\%$ for each unit increase in x.

The Natural Exponential Function

Each base a of $f(x) = Aa^x$ gives a different exponential function. In mathematics, one particular value of a gives an exponential function that is far more important than all others. One might guess that $a = 2$ or $a = 10$ would be this special base. Certainly, powers to the base of 2 are important in computing, and powers to the base 10 occur in our usual decimal number system. Nevertheless, once we have studied some calculus, it will turn out that the most important base for an exponential function is an irrational number a little larger than 2.7. In fact, it is so distinguished that it is denoted by the single letter e, probably because it is the first letter of the word "exponential". Its value to 15 decimals is[6]

$$e = 2.718281828459045\ldots$$

Many formulas in calculus become much simpler when e is used as the base for exponential functions. Given this base e, the corresponding exponential function

$$f(x) = e^x \tag{2}$$

is called the **natural exponential function**. We shall give an explicit way of approximating e to an arbitrary degree of accuracy. Of course, all the usual rules for powers apply also to the natural exponential function. In particular,

$$\text{(a) } e^s e^t = e^{s+t} \qquad \text{(b) } \frac{e^s}{e^t} = e^{s-t} \qquad \text{(c) } (e^s)^t = e^{st}$$

The graphs of $f(x) = e^x$ and $f(x) = e^{-x}$ are given in Fig. 3.

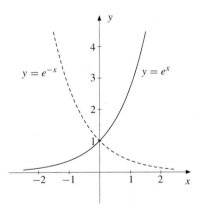

Figure 3 The graphs of the functions $y = e^x$ and $y = e^{-x}$.

Powers with e as their base, even e^1, are difficult to compute by hand. A pocket calculator with an $\boxed{e^x}$ function key can do this immediately, however. For instance, one finds that $e^{1.0} \approx 2.7183$, $e^{0.5} \approx 1.6487$, and $e^{-\pi} \approx 0.0432$.

NOTE 2 Sometimes the notation $\exp(u)$, or even $\exp u$, is used in place of e^u. If u is a complicated expression like $x^3 + x\sqrt{x - 1/x} + 5$, it is easier to read and write $\exp(x^3 + x\sqrt{x - 1/x} + 5)$ instead of $e^{x^3 + x\sqrt{x-1/x}+5}$.

---

[6] The number e was first introduced by Euler in 1731. He subsequently proved that it was irrational and calculated it to 23 decimal places.

1. If the population of Europe grew at the rate of 0.72% annually, what would be the doubling time?

2. The population of Botswana was estimated to be 1.22 million in 1989, and to be growing at the rate of 3.4% annually. If $t = 0$ denotes 1989, find a formula for the population at date t, $P(t)$. What is the doubling time?

3. A savings account with an initial deposit of $100 earns 12% interest per year. What is the amount of savings after t years? Make a table similar to Table 1. (Stop at 50 years.)

4. Fill in the following table and sketch the of graphs of $y = 2^x$ and $y = 2^{-x}$.

x	-3	-2	-1	0	1	2	3
2^x							
2^{-x}							

5. Use your calculator to fill in the following table and then sketch the graph of

$$y = \frac{1}{\sqrt{2\pi}} e^{-\frac{1}{2}x^2} \quad \text{(the \textbf{normal density function})}$$

which is one of the most important functions in statistics. (Of course, just five points are not a very reliable basis on which to draw the graph.)

x	-2	-1	0	1	2
$y = \dfrac{1}{\sqrt{2\pi}} e^{-\frac{1}{2}x^2}$					

6. The area of Zimbabwe is approximately $3.91 \cdot 10^{11}$ square metres. Referring to the text at the end of Example 1 and using a calculator, solve the equation $5.1 \cdot 10^6 \cdot 1.035^t = 3.91 \cdot 10^{11}$ for t, and interpret your answer. (Recall that $t = 0$ corresponds to 1969.)

7. With $f(t) = Aa^t$, if $f(t + t^*) = 2f(t)$, prove that $a^{t^*} = 2$. (This shows that the doubling time t^* of the general exponential function is independent of the initial time t.)

8. Which of the following equations do *not* define exponential functions of x?

(a) $y = 3^x$ (b) $y = x^{\sqrt{2}}$ (c) $y = (\sqrt{2})^x$

(d) $y = x^x$ (e) $y = (2.7)^x$ (f) $y = 1/2^x$

9. If the rate of inflation in a country is 19% per year, the equation $P(t) = P_0(1.19)^t$ yields the predicted price $P(t)$ after t years of an item that presently costs P_0. What is predicted price of:

   (a) A 20 kg bag of corn, presently costing $16, after 5 years?

   (b) A $4.40 can of coffee after 10 years?

   (c) A $250 000 house after 4 years?

10. Find possible exponential functions for the graphs in the figures.

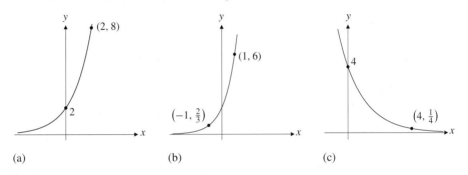

(a)   (b)   (c)

4.10 Logarithmic Functions

The doubling time of an exponential function $f(t) = Aa^t$ was defined as the time it takes for $f(t)$ to become twice as large. In order to find the doubling time t^*, we must solve the equation $a^{t^*} = 2$ for t^*. In economics, we often need to solve similar problems:

A. At the present rate of inflation, how long will it take the price level to triple?

B. If the world's population grows at 2% per year, how long does it take to double its size?

C. If $1000 is invested in a savings account bearing interest at the annual rate of 8%, how long does it take for the account to reach $10 000?

All these questions involve solving equations of the form $a^x = b$ for x. For instance, problem C reduces to the problem of finding which x solves the equation $1000(1.08)^x = 10 000$.

We begin with equations in which the base of the exponential is e, which was, as you recall, the irrational number $2.718\ldots$. Here are some examples:

$$\text{(i)} \quad e^x = 4 \qquad \text{(ii)} \quad 5e^{-3x} = 16 \qquad \text{(iii)} \quad A\alpha e^{-\alpha x} = k$$

In all these equations, the unknown x occurs as an exponent. We therefore introduce the following useful definition. If $e^u = a$, we call u the **natural logarithm** of a, and we write $u = \ln a$. Hence, we have the following definition of the symbol $\ln a$:

$$e^{\ln a} = a \qquad (a \text{ is any positive number}) \tag{1}$$

Thus, $\ln a$ is the power of e you need to get a. In particular, if $e^x = 4$, then x must be $\ln 4$.

Because e^u is a strictly increasing function of u, it follows that $\ln a$ *is* uniquely determined by the definition (1). You should memorize this definition. It is the foundation for everything in this section, and for a good part of what comes later. The following example illustrates how to use this definition.

EXAMPLE 1   Find the following:

(a) $\ln 1$ (b) $\ln e$ (c) $\ln(1/e)$ (d) $\ln 4$ (e) $\ln(-6)$

Solution:

(a) $\ln 1 = 0$, because $e^0 = 1$ and so 0 is the power of e that you need to get 1.

(b) $\ln e = 1$, because $e^1 = e$ and so 1 is the power of e that you need to get e.

(c) $\ln(1/e) = \ln e^{-1} = -1$, because -1 is the power of e that you need to get $1/e$.

(d) $\ln 4$ is the power of e you need to get 4. Because $e^1 \approx 2.7$ and $e^2 = e^1 \cdot e^1 \approx 7.3$, the number $\ln 4$ must lie between 1 and 2. By using the $\boxed{e^x}$ key on a calculator, you should be able to find a good approximation to $\ln 4$ by trial and error. However, it is easier to press 4 and the $\boxed{\ln x}$ key. Then you find that $\ln 4 \approx 1.386$. Thus, $e^{1.386} \approx 4$.

(e) $\ln(-6)$ would be the power of e you need to get -6. Because e^x is positive for all x, it is obvious that $\ln(-6)$ must be undefined.

The following box collects some useful rules for natural logarithms.

RULES FOR THE NATURAL LOGARITHMIC FUNCTION LN:

(a) $\ln(xy) = \ln x + \ln y$ (x and y positive)

(The logarithm of a *product* is the *sum* of the logarithms of the factors.)

(b) $\ln \dfrac{x}{y} = \ln x - \ln y$ (x and y positive)

(The logarithm of a *quotient* is the *difference* between the logarithms of its numerator and denominator.) $\tag{2}$

(c) $\ln x^p = p \ln x$ (x positive)

(The logarithm of a *power* is the exponent multiplied by the logarithm of the base.)

(d) $\ln 1 = 0,\quad \ln e = 1,\quad x = e^{\ln x}, \ (x > 0)\quad \text{and}\quad \ln e^x = x$

To show (a), observe first that the definition of $\ln(xy)$ implies that $e^{\ln(xy)} = xy$. Furthermore, $x = e^{\ln x}$ and $y = e^{\ln y}$, so

$$e^{\ln(xy)} = xy = e^{\ln x} e^{\ln y} = e^{\ln x + \ln y} \tag{$*$}$$

where the last step uses the rule $e^s e^t = e^{s+t}$. In general, $e^u = e^v$ implies $u = v$, so we conclude from ($*$) that $\ln(xy) = \ln x + \ln y$.

The proofs of (b) and (c) are based on the rules $e^s/e^t = e^{s-t}$ and $(e^s)^t = e^{st}$, respectively, and are left to the reader. Finally, (d) displays some important properties for convenient reference.

It *is* tempting to replace $\ln(x + y)$ by $\ln x + \ln y$, but this is quite wrong. In fact, $\ln x + \ln y$ is equal to $\ln(xy)$, not to $\ln(x + y)$.

There are no simple formulas for $\ln(x + y)$ and $\ln(x - y)$

Here are some examples that apply the previous rules.

EXAMPLE 2   Recall that the doubling time t^* of an exponential function $f(t) = Aa^t$ is given by the formula $a^{t^*} = 2$. Solve this equation for t^*.

Solution: Taking the natural logarithm of both sides of the equation yields $\ln a^{t^*} = \ln 2$. Using rule (c) we get $t^* \ln a = \ln 2$, and so $t^* = \ln 2/\ln a$.   ▌

EXAMPLE 3   Express (a) $\ln 4$, (b) $\ln \sqrt[3]{2^5}$, and (c) $\ln(1/16)$ in terms of $\ln 2$.

Solution:

(a) $\ln 4 = \ln(2 \cdot 2) = \ln 2 + \ln 2 = 2 \ln 2$. (Or: $\ln 4 = \ln 2^2 = 2 \ln 2$.)

(b) We have $\sqrt[3]{2^5} = 2^{5/3}$. Therefore, $\ln \sqrt[3]{2^5} = \ln 2^{5/3} = (5/3) \ln 2$.

(c) $\ln(1/16) = \ln 1 - \ln 16 = 0 - \ln 2^4 = -4 \ln 2$. (Or: $\ln(1/16) = \ln 2^{-4} = -4 \ln 2$.)   ▌

EXAMPLE 4   Solve the following equations for x:

(a) $5e^{-3x} = 16$ (b) $A\alpha e^{-\alpha x} = k$ (c) $(1.08)^x = 10$ (d) $e^x + 4e^{-x} = 4$

Solution:

(a) Take $\ln$ of each side of the equation to obtain $\ln(5e^{-3x}) = \ln 16$. The product rule gives $\ln(5e^{-3x}) = \ln 5 + \ln e^{-3x}$. Here $\ln e^{-3x} = -3x$, by rule (d). Hence, $\ln 5 - 3x = \ln 16$, which gives

$$x = \frac{1}{3}(\ln 5 - \ln 16) = \frac{1}{3} \ln \frac{5}{16}$$

(b) We argue as in (a) and obtain $\ln(A\alpha e^{-\alpha x}) = \ln k$, or $\ln(A\alpha) + \ln e^{-\alpha x} = \ln k$, so $\ln(A\alpha) - \alpha x = \ln k$. Finally, therefore,

$$x = \frac{1}{\alpha}[\ln(A\alpha) - \ln k] = \frac{1}{\alpha}\ln\frac{A\alpha}{k}$$

(c) Again we take the ln of each side of the equation and obtain $x \ln 1.08 = \ln 10$. So the solution is $x = \ln 10/\ln 1.08$, which is ≈ 29.9. Thus, it takes just short of 30 years for $1 to increase to $10 when the interest rate is 8%. (See Table 1 in Example 4.9.3.)

(d) It is very tempting to begin with $\ln(e^x + 4e^{-x}) = \ln 4$, but this leads nowhere, because $\ln(e^x + 4e^{-x})$ cannot be further evaluated. Instead, we argue like this: Putting $u = e^x$ gives $e^{-x} = 1/e^x = 1/u$, so the equation is $u + 4/u = 4$, or $u^2 + 4 = 4u$. Solving this quadratic equation for u yields $u = 2$ as the only solution. Hence, $e^x = 2$, and so $x = \ln 2$.

The Function g(x) = ln x

For each positive number x, the number $\ln x$ is defined by $e^{\ln x} = x$. In other words, $u = \ln x$ is the solution of the equation $e^u = x$. This definition is illustrated in Fig. 1. We call the resulting function

$$g(x) = \ln x \qquad (x > 0) \tag{3}$$

the **natural logarithm** of x. Think of x as a point moving upwards on the vertical axis from the origin. As x increases from values less than 1 to values greater than 1, so $g(x)$ increases from negative to positive values. Because e^u tends to 0 as u becomes large negative, so $g(x)$ becomes large negative as x tends to 0. Note that

(i) $\ln e^x = x$ for all x (ii) $e^{\ln y} = y$ for all $y > 0$

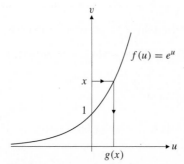

Figure 1 Illustration of the definition of $g(x) = \ln x$

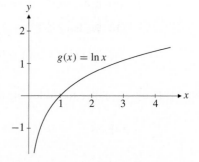

Figure 2 The graph of the logarithmic function $g(x) = \ln x$

In Fig. 2 we have drawn the graph of $g(x) = \ln x$. The shape of this graph ought to be remembered. It can be obtained by reflecting the graph of Fig. 1 about the line $v = u$ so that the u- and v-axes are interchanged, and become the y- and x-axes of Fig. 2, respectively.

According to Example 1, we have $g(1/e) = -1$, $g(1) = 0$, and $g(e) = 1$. Observe that this corresponds well with the graph.

Logarithms with Bases Other Than e

Recall that we defined $\ln x$ as the exponent to which we must raise the base e in order to obtain x. From time to time, it is useful to have logarithms based on numbers other than e. For many years, until the use of mechanical and then electronic calculators became widespread, tables of logarithms to the base 10 were frequently used to simplify complicated calculations involving multiplication, division, square roots, and so on.

Suppose that a is a fixed positive number (usually chosen > 1). If $a^u = x$, then we call u the **logarithm of x to base a** and write $u = \log_a x$. The symbol $\log_a x$ is then defined for every positive number x by the following:

$$a^{\log_a x} = x \tag{4}$$

For instance, $\log_2 32 = 5$, because $2^5 = 32$, whereas $\log_{10}(1/100) = -2$, because $10^{-2} = 1/100$. Note that $\ln x$ is $\log_e x$.

By taking the $\ln$ on each side of (4), we obtain $\log_a x \cdot \ln a = \ln x$, so that

$$\log_a x = \frac{1}{\ln a} \ln x \tag{5}$$

This reveals that the logarithm of x in the system with base a is proportional to $\ln x$, with a proportionality factor $1/\ln a$. It follows immediately that $\log_a$ obeys the same rules as $\ln$:

$$\text{(a)} \ \log_a(xy) = \log_a x + \log_a y, \quad \text{(b)} \ \log_a\left(\frac{x}{y}\right) = \log_a x - \log_a y$$

$$\text{(c)} \ \log_a x^p = p \log_a x, \quad \text{(d)} \ \log_a 1 = 0 \ \text{ and } \ \log_a a = 1 \tag{6}$$

For example, (a) follows from the corresponding rule for $\ln$:

$$\log_a(xy) = \frac{1}{\ln a}\ln(xy) = \frac{1}{\ln a}(\ln x + \ln y) = \frac{1}{\ln a}\ln x + \frac{1}{\ln a}\ln y = \log_a x + \log_a y$$

PROBLEMS FOR SECTION 4.10

1. Express the following numbers in terms of $\ln 3$:

   (a) $\ln 9$ \qquad (b) $\ln \sqrt{3}$ \qquad (c) $\ln \sqrt[5]{3^2}$ \qquad (d) $\ln \dfrac{1}{81}$

2. Solve the following equations for x:

   (a) $3^x = 8$ \qquad (b) $\ln x = 3$ \qquad (c) $\ln(x^2 - 4x + 5) = 0$

   (d) $\ln[x(x-2)] = 0$ \qquad (e) $\dfrac{x \ln(x+3)}{x^2+1} = 0$ \qquad (f) $\ln(\sqrt{x} - 5) = 0$

3. Solve the following equations for x:

   (a) $3^x 4^{x+2} = 8$ \qquad (b) $3\ln x + 2\ln x^2 = 6$ \qquad (c) $4^x - 4^{x-1} = 3^{x+1} - 3^x$

4. (a) Let $f(t) = Ae^{rt}$ and $g(t) = Be^{st}$, with $A > 0$, $B > 0$, and $r \neq s$. Solve the equation $f(t) = g(t)$ for t.

(b) In 1990 the GNP (gross national product) of China was estimated to be $1.2 \cdot 10^{12}$ US dollars, and the rate of growth was estimated to be $r = 0.09$. By comparison, the GNP for the USA was reported as $\$5.6 \cdot 10^{12}$, with an estimated rate of growth of $s = 0.02$. If the GNP of each country continued to grow exponentially at the rates $r = 0.09$ and $s = 0.02$, respectively, when would the GNP of the two nations be the same?

5. Decide whether the following formulas are always true or sometimes false (all variables are positive):

(a) $\ln \dfrac{A + B}{C} = \ln A + \ln B - \ln C$

(b) $\ln \dfrac{A + B}{C} = \ln(A + B) - \ln C$

(c) $\ln \dfrac{A}{B} + \ln \dfrac{B}{A} = 0$

(d) $p \ln(\ln A) = \ln(\ln A^p)$

(e) $p \ln(\ln A) = \ln(\ln A)^p$

(f) $\dfrac{\ln A}{\ln B + \ln C} = \ln A(BC)^{-1}$

6. Decide whether the following formulas are always true or sometimes false (all variables are positive):

(a) $(\ln A)^4 = 4 \ln A$ (b) $\ln B = 2 \ln \sqrt{B}$ (c) $\ln A^{10} - \ln A^4 = 3 \ln A^2$

7. Simplify the following expressions:

(a) $\exp\left[\ln(x)\right] - \ln\left[\exp(x)\right]$ (b) $\ln\left[x^4 \exp(-x)\right]$ (c) $\exp\left[\ln(x^2) - 2\ln y\right]$

REVIEW PROBLEMS FOR CHAPTER 4

1. Let $f(x) = 3 - 27x^3$.

(a) Compute $f(0)$, $f(-1)$, $f(1/3)$, and $f(\sqrt[3]{2})$.

(b) Show that $f(x) + f(-x) = 6$ for all x.

2. (a) Let $F(x) = 1 + \dfrac{4x}{x^2 + 4}$. Compute $F(0)$, $F(-2)$, $F(2)$, and $F(3)$.

(b) What happens to $F(x)$ when x becomes large positive or negative?

(c) Give a rough sketch of the graph of F.

3. If $f(x) = 3x - x^3$, show that $f(-x) = -f(x)$.

4. Find the domains of:

(a) $f(x) = \sqrt{x^2 - 1}$ (b) $g(x) = \dfrac{1}{\sqrt{x - 4}}$ (c) $h(x) = \sqrt{(x - 3)(5 - x)}$

5. The cost of producing x units of a commodity is given by $C(x) = 100 + 40x + 2x^2$.

   (a) Find $C(0)$, $C(100)$, and $C(101) - C(100)$.

   (b) Find $C(x + 1) - C(x)$, and explain in words the meaning of the difference.

6. Find the slopes of the following straight lines:

   (a) $y = -4x + 8$ (b) $3x + 4y = 12$ (c) $\dfrac{x}{a} + \dfrac{y}{b} = 1$

7. Determine the equations for the following straight lines:

   (a) L_1 passes through $(-2, 3)$ and has a slope of -3.

   (b) L_2 passes through $(-3, 5)$ and $(2, 7)$.

   (c) L_3 passes through (a, b) and $(2a, 3b)$ (suppose $a \neq 0$).

8. If $f(x) = ax + b$, $f(2) = 3$, and $f(-1) = -3$, then $f(-3) =$?

9. (a) Determine the relationship between the Centigrade (C) and Fahrenheit (F) temperature scales when you know that (i) the relation is linear; (ii) water freezes at $0°C$ and $32°F$; and (iii) water boils at $100°C$ and $212°F$.

   (b) Which temperature is represented by the same number in both the Centigrade and Fahrenheit scales?

10. Find the equation for the parabola $y = ax^2 + bx + c$ that passes through the three points $(1, -3)$, $(0, -6)$, and $(3, 15)$. (*Hint:* Determine a, b, and c.)

11. If a firm sells Q tons of a product, the price P received per ton is $P = 1000 - \frac{1}{3}Q$. The price it has to pay per ton is $P = 800 + \frac{1}{5}Q$. In addition, it has transportation costs of 100 per ton.

    (a) Express the firm's profit π as a function of Q, the number of tons sold, and find the profit maximizing quantity.

    (b) Suppose the government imposes a tax on the firm's product of 10 per ton. Find the new expression for the firm's profits $\hat{\pi}$ and the new profit maximizing quantity.

12. In Example 4.6.3, suppose a tax of t per unit produced is imposed. If $t < 100$, which production level now maximizes profits?

13. A firm produces a commodity and receives \$100 for each unit sold. The cost of producing and selling x units is $20x + 0.25x^2$ dollars.

    (a) Find the production level which maximizes profits.

    (b) A tax of \$10 per unit is imposed. What is now the optimal production level?

    (c) Answer the question in (b) if the sales price per unit is p, the total cost of producing and selling x units is $\alpha x + \beta x^2$, and the tax per unit is t.

14. Write the following polynomials as products of linear factors:

   (a) $p(x) = x^3 + x^2 - 12x$

   (b) $q(x) = 2x^3 + 3x^2 - 18x + 8$

15. Which of the following divisions leave no remainder? (a and b are constants; n is a natural number.)

   (a) $(x^3 - x - 1)/(x - 1)$

   (b) $(2x^3 - x - 1)/(x - 1)$

   (c) $(x^3 - ax^2 + bx - ab)/(x - a)$

   (d) $(x^{2n} - 1)/(x + 1)$

16. Find the value(s) of k which makes the second polynomial divide the first:

   (a) $x^2 - kx + 4$; $x - 2$

   (b) $k^2x^2 - kx - 6$; $x + 2$

   (c) $x^3 - 4x^2 + x + k$; $x + 2$

   (d) $k^2x^4 - 3kx^2 - 4$; $x - 1$

17. The cubic function $p(x) = \frac{1}{4}x^3 - x^2 - \frac{11}{4}x + \frac{15}{2}$ has three real zeros. Verify that $x = 2$ is one of them, and find the two others by using polynomial division.

18. In 1964 a five-year plan was introduced in Tanzania. One objective was to double the real per capita income over the next 15 years. What is the average annual rate of growth of real income per capita required to achieve this objective?

19. Fill in the following table, then make a rough sketch of the graph of $y = x^2e^x$.

x	-5	-4	-3	-2	-1	0	1
$y = x^2e^x$							

20. Solve the following equations for t:

   (a) $x = e^{at+b}$

   (b) $e^{-at} = 1/2$

   (c) $\dfrac{1}{\sqrt{2\pi}}e^{-t^2} = \dfrac{1}{8}$

21. Prove the following equalities (with appropriate restrictions on the variables):

   (a) $\ln x - 2 = \ln(x/e^2)$

   (b) $\ln x - \ln y + \ln z = \ln \dfrac{xz}{y}$

   (c) $3 + 2\ln x = \ln(e^3x^2)$

   (d) $\dfrac{1}{2}\ln x - \dfrac{3}{2}\ln\dfrac{1}{x} - \ln(x + 1) = \ln\dfrac{x^2}{x + 1}$

5

PROPERTIES
OF FUNCTIONS

*The paradox is now fully established that the
utmost abstractions are the true weapons with
which to control our thought of concrete facts.*
—A.N. Whitehead

This chapter begins by examining more closely functions of one variable and their graphs. In particular, we shall consider how changes in a function relate to shifts in its graphs, and how to construct new functions from old ones. Next we discuss when a function has an inverse, and explain how an inverse function reverses the effect of the original function, and vice versa.

Any equation in two variables can be represented by a curve (or a set of points) in the *xy*-plane. Some examples illustrate this. The chapter ends with a discussion of the general concept of a function, which is one of the most fundamental concepts in mathematics, of great importance also in economics.

5.1 Shifting Graphs

Bringing a significant new oil field into production will affect the supply curve for oil, with consequences for its equilibrium price. Adopting an improved technology in the production of a commodity will imply an upward shift in its production function. This section studies in general how the graph of a function $f(x)$ relates to the graphs of the functions

$$f(x) + c, \quad f(x + c), \quad cf(x), \quad \text{and} \quad f(-x)$$

Here c is a positive or negative constant. Before formulating any general rules, consider the following example.

EXAMPLE 1   We know the graph of $y = \sqrt{x}$. It is also drawn in Fig. 1. Sketch the graphs of $y = \sqrt{x} + 2$, $y = \sqrt{x} - 2$, $y = \sqrt{x + 2}$, $y = \sqrt{x - 2}$, $y = 2\sqrt{x}$, $y = -\sqrt{x}$, and $y = \sqrt{-x}$.

Solution: The graphs of $y = \sqrt{x} + 2$ and $y = \sqrt{x} - 2$, shown in Fig. 1, are obviously obtained by moving the graph of $y = \sqrt{x}$ upwards or downwards by two units, respectively.

The function $y = \sqrt{x+2}$ is defined for $x+2 \geq 0$, that is, for $x \geq -2$. Its graph, which is shown in Fig. 2, is obtained by moving the graph of $y = \sqrt{x}$ two units to the left. In the same way the graph of $y = \sqrt{x-2}$ is obtained by moving the graph of $y = \sqrt{x}$ two units to right, as shown in Fig. 2.

The graph of $y = 2\sqrt{x}$ is obtained by stretching the graph of f by a factor of two, as shown in Fig. 3. The graph of $y = -\sqrt{x}$ is obtained by reflecting the graph of $y = \sqrt{x}$ about the x-axis, as shown in Fig. 4.

Finally, the function $y = \sqrt{-x}$, is defined for $-x \geq 0$, that is, for $x \leq 0$, and its graph is shown in Fig. 5. It is obtained by reflecting the graph of $y = \sqrt{x}$ about the y-axis.

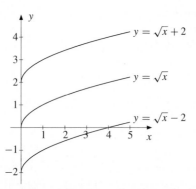

Figure 1 $y = \sqrt{x} \pm 2$

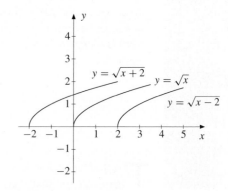

Figure 2 $y = \sqrt{x \pm 2}$

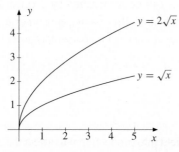

Figure 3 $y = \sqrt{x}$ and $y = 2\sqrt{x}$

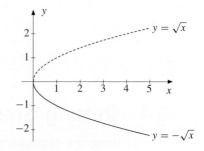

Figure 4 $y = \pm\sqrt{x}$

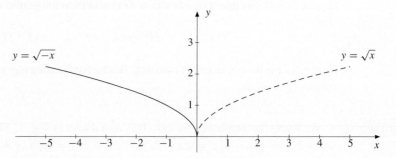

Figure 5 $y = \sqrt{\pm x}$

In general we have the following useful rules:

Shifting the graph of $y = f(x)$:

(i) If $y = f(x)$ is replaced by $y = f(x) + c$, the graph is moved upwards by c units if $c > 0$ (downwards if c is negative).

(ii) If $y = f(x)$ is replaced by $y = f(x + c)$, the graph is moved c units to the left if $c > 0$ (to the right if c is negative).

(iii) If $y = f(x)$ is replaced by $y = cf(x)$, the graph is stretched vertically if $c > 0$ (stretched vertically and reflected about the x-axis if c is negative).

(iv) If $y = f(x)$ is replaced by $y = f(-x)$, the graph is reflected about the y-axis.

NOTE 1 If the independent variable is y and $x = g(y)$, then in the recipe one should interchange the words "upwards" and "right", and "downwards" and "left".

Combining these rules with Figures 4.3.5–4.3.10, a large number of useful graphs can be sketched with ease, as the following example illustrates.

EXAMPLE 2   Sketch the graphs of   (i) $y = 2 - (x + 2)^2$ (ii) $y = \dfrac{1}{x - 2} + 3$.

Solution:

(i) First $y = x^2$ is reflected about the x-axis to obtain the graph of $y = -x^2$. This graph is then moved 2 units to the left, which results in the graph of $y = -(x + 2)^2$. Finally, this new graph is raised by 2 units, and we obtain the graph shown in Fig. 6.

(ii) The graph of $y = 1/(x - 2)$ is obtained by moving the graph of $y = 1/x$ in Fig. 4.3.9 2 units to the right. By moving the new graph 3 units up, we get the graph in Fig. 7.

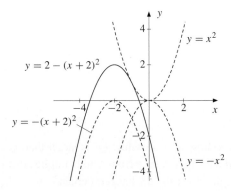

Figure 6 $y = 2 - (x + 2)^2$

Figure 7 $y = 1/(x - 2) + 3$

EXAMPLE 3   In Example 4.5.3 we studied the simple demand and supply functions

$$D = 100 - P, \qquad S = 10 + 2P \qquad\qquad (*)$$

which gave the equilibrium price $P^* = 30$ with corresponding quantity $Q^* = 70$. Suppose that there is a shift to the right in the supply function, so that the new supply at price P is $\tilde{S} = 16 + 2P$. Then the new equilibrium price $\tilde{P}^*$ is determined by the equation $100 - \tilde{P}^* = 16 + 2\tilde{P}^*$, which gives $\tilde{P}^* = 28$, with corresponding quantity $\tilde{Q}^* = 100 - 28 = 72$. Hence the new equilibrium price is lower than the old one, while the quantity is higher. The outward shift in the supply curve from S to $\tilde{S}$ implies that the equilibrium point moves down to the right along the unchanged demand curve. This is shown in Fig. 8.

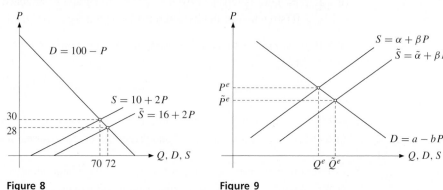

Figure 8   Figure 9

In Example 4.5.4 we studied the general linear demand and supply functions

$$D = a - bP, \qquad S = \alpha + \beta P$$

The equilibrium price P^e and corresponding equilibrium quantity Q^e were given by

$$P^e = \frac{a - \alpha}{\beta + b}, \qquad Q^e = \frac{a\beta + \alpha b}{\beta + b}$$

Suppose that there is a shift in the supply function so that the new supply at each price P is $\tilde{S} = \tilde{\alpha} + \beta P$, where $\tilde{\alpha} > \alpha$. Then the new equilibrium price $\tilde{P}^e$ is determined by the equation $a - b\tilde{P}^e = \tilde{\alpha} + \beta \tilde{P}^e$, implying that

$$\tilde{P}^e = \frac{a - \tilde{\alpha}}{\beta + b}, \qquad \text{with} \qquad \tilde{Q}^e = a - b\tilde{P}^e = \frac{a\beta + \tilde{\alpha}b}{\beta + b}$$

The difference between the new and the old equilibrium prices and quantities are

$$\tilde{P}^e - P^e = \frac{\alpha - \tilde{\alpha}}{\beta + b} \qquad \text{and} \qquad \tilde{Q}^e - Q^e = \frac{(\tilde{\alpha} - \alpha)b}{\beta + b} = -b(\tilde{P}^e - P^e)$$

We see that $\tilde{P}^e$ is less than P^e (because $\tilde{\alpha} > \alpha$), while $\tilde{Q}^e$ is larger than Q^e. This is shown in Fig. 9. The rightward shift in the supply curve from S to $\tilde{S}$ implies that the equilibrium point moves down and to the right along the unchanged demand curve. Upward shifts in the supply curve resulting from, for example, taxation or increased cost, can be analysed in the same way. So can shifts in the demand curve.

EXAMPLE 4   Suppose a person earning y (dollars) in a given year pays $f(y)$ (dollars) in income tax. The government decides to reduce taxes. One proposal is to allow every individual to deduct d dollars from their taxable income before the tax is calculated. An alternative proposal involves calculating income tax on the full amount of taxable income, and then allowing each person a "tax credit" that deducts c dollars from the total tax due. Illustrate graphically the two proposals for a "normal" tax function f, and mark off the income y^* where the two proposals yield the same tax revenue.

Solution: Figure 10 illustrates the situation for a "progressive" tax schedule in which the average tax rate, $T/y = f(y)/y$, is an increasing function of y. First draw the graph of the original tax function, $T = f(y)$. If taxable income is y and the deduction is d, then $y - d$ is the reduced taxable income, and so the tax liability is $f(y - d)$. By shifting the graph of the original tax function d units to the right, we obtain the graph of $T_1 = f(y - d)$.

The graph of $T_2 = f(y) - c$ is obtained by lowering the graph of $T = f(y)$ by c units. The income y^* which gives the same tax under the two different schemes is given by the equation

$$f(y^* - d) = f(y^*) - c$$

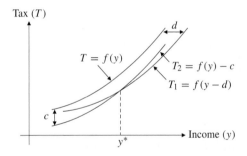

Figure 10   The graphs of $T_1 = f(y - d)$
and $T_2 = f(y) - c$

Note that $T_1 > T_2$ when $y < y^*$, but that $T_1 < T_2$ when $y > y^*$. Thus, the tax credit is worth more to those with low incomes; the deduction is worth more to those with high incomes (as one might expect).

PROBLEMS FOR SECTION 5.1

1. Use Fig. 4.3.6 and rules for shifting graphs to sketch the graphs of

(a) $y = x^2 + 1$ (b) $y = (x + 3)^2$ (c) $y = 3 - (x + 1)^2$

2. If $y = f(x)$ has the graph suggested in the figure below, sketch the graphs of

(a) $y = f(x - 2)$ (b) $y = f(x) - 2$ (c) $y = f(-x)$

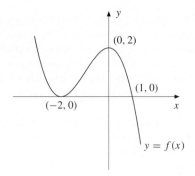

3. Suppose that in the model (∗) of Example 3, there is a positive shift in demand so that the new demand at price P is $\tilde{D} = 106 - P$. Find the new equilibrium point and illustrate.

4. Use Fig. 4.3.10 and the rules for shifting graphs to sketch the graph of $y = 2 - |x + 2|$.

5. Starting with the graph of $f(x) = 1/x^2$, sketch the graph of $g(x) = 2 - (x + 2)^{-2}$.

6. Suppose in Example 4 that $f(y) = Ay + By^2$ where A and B are positive parameters. Find y^* in this case.

5.2 New Functions from Old

Figure 1 gives a graphical representation of the number of male and female students registered at a certain university in the period 1986 to 1997.

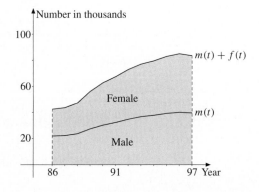

Figure 1

Let $f(t)$ and $m(t)$ denote the number of female and male students in year t, while $n(t)$ denotes the total number of students. Of course,

$$n(t) = f(t) + m(t)$$

The graph of the total number $n(t)$ is obtained by piling the graph of $f(t)$ on top of the graph of $m(t)$.

Suppose in general that f and g are functions which both are defined in a set A of real numbers. The function F defined by the formula $F(x) = f(x) + g(x)$ is called the **sum** of f and g, and we write $F = f + g$. The function G defined by $G(x) = f(x) - g(x)$ is called the **difference** between f and g, and we write $G = f - g$.

Sums and differences of functions are often seen in economic models. Consider the following typical examples.

EXAMPLE 1   The cost of producing Q units of a commodity is $C(Q)$. The cost per produced unit, $C(Q)/Q$, is called the average cost. Denoting the average cost by $A(Q)$, we have with $Q > 0$,

$$A(Q) = \frac{C(Q)}{Q} \qquad \textbf{(average cost)}$$

In particular, if $C(Q) = aQ^3 + bQ^2 + cQ + d$ is a cubic cost function of the type shown in Fig. 4.7.2, the average cost is

$$A(Q) = aQ^2 + bQ + c + \frac{d}{Q}, \qquad Q > 0$$

Thus $A(Q)$ is a sum of a quadratic function $y = aQ^2 + bQ + c$ and the hyperbola $y = d/Q$. Figure 2 shows how the graph of the average cost function $A(Q)$ is obtained by piling the graph of the hyperbola $y = d/Q$ onto the graph of the parabola $y = aQ^2 + bQ + c$.

Note that for small values of Q the graph of $A(Q)$ is close to the graph of $y = d/Q$, while for large values of Q, the graph is close to the parabola (since d/Q is small when Q is large).

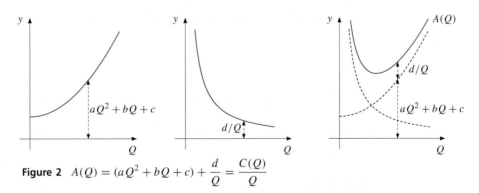

Figure 2 $A(Q) = (aQ^2 + bQ + c) + \dfrac{d}{Q} = \dfrac{C(Q)}{Q}$

Let $R(Q)$ denote the **revenue** obtained by producing (and selling) Q units. Then the **profit** $\pi(Q)$ is given by

$$\pi(Q) = R(Q) - C(Q)$$

An example showing how to construct the graph of the profit function $\pi(Q)$ is given in Fig. 3. In this case the firm gets a fixed price p per unit, so that graph of $R(Q)$ is a straight line through the origin. The graph of $-C(Q)$ must be added to that of $R(Q)$. The production level which maximizes profit is Q^*.

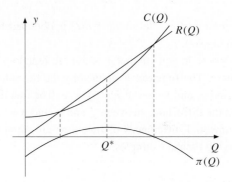

Figure 3 $\pi(Q) = R(Q) - C(Q)$

Products and Quotients

If f and g are defined in a set A, the function F defined by $F(x) = f(x) \cdot g(x)$ is called the **product** of f and g, and we put $F = f \cdot g$ (or fg). The function F defined where $g(x) \neq 0$ by $F(x) = f(x)/g(x)$ is called the **quotient** of f and g, and we write $F = f/g$. We have already seen examples of these operations. It is difficult to give useful general rules about the behaviour of the graphs of fg and f/g given the graphs of f and g.

Composite Functions

Suppose the demand for a commodity is a function x of its price p. Suppose that price p is not constant, but depends on time t. Then it is natural to regard x as a function of t.

In general, if y is a function of u, and u is a function of x, then y can be regarded as a function of x. We call y a **composite function** of x. If we denote the two functions involved by f and g, with $y = f(u)$ and $u = g(x)$, then y can be written in the form

$$y = f\big(g(x)\big)$$

Note that when computing $f\big(g(x)\big)$, we first apply g to x to obtain $g(x)$, and then we apply f to $g(x)$. The operation of first applying g to x and then f to $g(x)$ defines a **composite function**. Here $g(x)$ is called the **kernel**, or **interior function**, while f is called the **exterior function**.

NOTE 1   The function that maps x to $f\big(g(x)\big)$ is often denoted by $f \circ g$, and is read as "f of g" or "f after g", and is called the **composition** of f with g. Correspondingly, $g \circ f$ denotes the function that maps x to $g\big(f(x)\big)$. Thus, we have

$$(f \circ g)(x) = f\big(g(x)\big) \qquad \text{and} \qquad (g \circ f)(x) = g\big(f(x)\big)$$

Usually, $f \circ g$ and $g \circ f$ are quite different functions. For instance, if $g(x) = 2 - x^2$ and $f(u) = u^3$, then $(f \circ g)(x) = (2 - x^2)^3$, whereas $(g \circ f)(x) = 2 - (x^3)^2 = 2 - x^6$; the two resulting polynomials are not the same.

It is easy to confuse $f \circ g$ with $f \cdot g$, especially typographically. But these two functions are defined in entirely different ways. When we evaluate $f \circ g$ at x, we first compute $g(x)$ and then evaluate f at $g(x)$. On the other hand, the product $f \cdot g$ of f and g is the function whose value at a particular number x is simply the product of $f(x)$ and $g(x)$, so $(f \cdot g)(x) = f(x) \cdot g(x)$.

Many pocket calculators have several built-in functions. When we enter a number x_0 and strike the key for the function f, we obtain $f(x_0)$. When we compute a composite function given f and g, and try to obtain the value of $f\big(g(x)\big)$, we proceed in a similar manner: punch the number x_0, then strike the g key to get $g(x_0)$, and again strike the f key to get $f(g(x_0))$. Suppose the machine has the functions $\boxed{1/x}$ and $\boxed{\sqrt{x}}$. If we press the number 9, then strike $\boxed{1/x}$ followed by $\boxed{\sqrt{x}}$, we get $1/3 = 0.33\ldots$ The computation we have performed can be illustrated as follows:

$$\boxed{1/x} \qquad \boxed{\sqrt{x}}$$

$$9 \quad \longrightarrow \quad 1/9 \quad \longrightarrow \quad 1/3.$$

Using function notation, $f(x) = \sqrt{x}$ and $g(x) = 1/x$, so $f(g(x)) = f(1/x) = \sqrt{1/x} = 1/\sqrt{x}$. In particular, $f(g(9)) = 1/\sqrt{9} = 1/3$.

EXAMPLE 2   Write the following as composite functions:

(a) $y = (x^3 + x^2)^{50}$

(b) $y = e^{-(x-\mu)^2}$ (μ is a constant)

Solution:

(a) You should ask yourself: What is the natural way of computing the values of this function? Given a value of x, you first compute $x^3 + x^2$, which gives the interior function, $g(x) = x^3 + x^2$. Then take the fiftieth power of the result, so the exterior function is $f(u) = u^{50}$. Hence,

$$f(g(x)) = f(x^3 + x^2) = (x^3 + x^2)^{50}$$

(b) We can choose the interior function as $g(x) = -(x - \mu)^2$ and the exterior function as $f(u) = e^u$. Then

$$f(g(x)) = f(-(x - \mu)^2) = e^{-(x-\mu)^2}$$

We could also have chosen $g(x) = (x - \mu)^2$ and $f(u) = e^{-u}$.   ∎

Symmetry

If $f(-x) = f(x)$ for all x in f's domain, then f is called an **even** function, or f is said to be **symmetric about the y-axis**. An even function is shown in Fig. 4. The standard example is $f(x) = x^2$; any even power x^{2n} (with n an integer) has the same property.

If $f(-x) = -f(x)$ for all x in f's domain, then f is called an **odd** function, or f is said to be **symmetric about the origin**, as shown in Fig. 5. The standard example is $f(x) = x^3$; any odd power x^{2n+1} (with n an integer) has the same property.

Finally, f is **symmetric about the line** $x = a$ if $f(a + u) = f(a - u)$ for all u, as in Fig. 6. In Sec. 4.6 we showed that the quadratic function $f(x) = ax^2 + bx + c$ is symmetric about the line $x = -b/2a$. The function $y = e^{-(x-\mu)^2}$ from Example 2(b) is symmetric about $x = \mu$.

Figure 4 Even function

Figure 5 Odd function

Figure 6 Symmetric about $x = a$

PROBLEMS FOR SECTION 5.2

1. Show graphically how you find the graph of $y = \frac{1}{4}x^2 + \frac{1}{x}$ by adding the graph of $\frac{1}{x}$ to the graph of $y = \frac{1}{4}x^2$. Assume $x > 0$.

2. Sketch the graphs of: (a) $y = \sqrt{x} - x$ (b) $y = e^x + e^{-x}$ (c) $y = e^{-x^2} + x$

3. If $f(x) = 3x - x^3$ and $g(x) = x^3$, compute: $(f+g)(x)$, $(f-g)(x)$, $(fg)(x)$, $(f/g)(x)$, $f(g(1))$, and $g(f(1))$.

4. Let $f(x) = 3x + 7$. Compute $f(f(x))$. Find the value of x for which $f(f(x)) = 100$.

5. Compute $\ln(\ln e)$ and $(\ln e)^2$. What do you notice? (This illustrates how, if we define the function f^2 by $f^2(x) = (f(x))^2$, then, in general, $f^2(x) \neq f(f(x))$.)

5.3 Inverse Functions

Suppose that the demand quantity D for a commodity depends on the price per unit p according to

$$D = \frac{30}{p^{1/3}}$$

This formula tells us directly the demand D corresponding to a given price p. If, for example, $p = 27$, then $D = 30/27^{1/3} = 10$. So D is a function of p. That is, $D = f(p)$ with $f(p) = 30/p^{1/3}$. Note that demand decreases as the price increases.

If we look at the matter from a producer's point of view, however, it may be more natural to treat output as something he can choose and consider the resulting price. The producer wants to know the *inverse* function, in which price depends on the quantity sold. This functional relationship is obtained by solving $D = 30/p^{1/3}$ for p. First we obtain $p^{1/3} = 30/D$ and then $(p^{1/3})^3 = (30/D)^3$, so that the original equation is equivalent to

$$p = \frac{27\,000}{D^3}$$

This equation gives us directly the price p corresponding to a given output D. For example, if $D = 10$, then $p = 27\,000/10^3 = 27$. In this case, p is a function $g(D)$ of D, with $g(D) = 27\,000/D^3$.

The two variables D and p in this example are related in a way that allows each to be regarded as a function of the other. In fact, the two functions

$$f(p) = 30p^{-1/3} \qquad \text{and} \qquad g(D) = 27\,000D^{-3}$$

are *inverses* of each other. We say that f is the inverse of g, and that g is the inverse of f.

Note that the two functions f and g convey exactly the same information. For example, the fact that demand is 10 at price 27 can be expressed using either f or g:

$$f(27) = 10 \qquad \text{or} \qquad g(10) = 27$$

Suppose in general that f is a function with domain $D_f = A$, meaning that to each x in A there corresponds a unique number $f(x)$. Recall that if f has domain A, then the range of f is the set $B = R_f = \{f(x) : x \in A\}$, which is also denoted by $f(A)$. The range B consists of all numbers $f(x)$ obtained by letting x vary in A. Furthermore, f is said to be **one-to-one** in A if f never has the same value at any two different points in A. In other words, for each one y in B, there is exactly one x in A such that $y = f(x)$. Equivalently, f is one-to-one in A provided that it has the property that, whenever x_1 and x_2 both lie in A and $x_1 \neq x_2$, then $f(x_1) \neq f(x_2)$. It is evident that if a function is strictly increasing in all of A, or strictly decreasing in all of A, then it is one-to-one. A particular one-to-one function f is illustrated in Fig. 1; another function g that is not one-to-one is shown in Fig. 2.

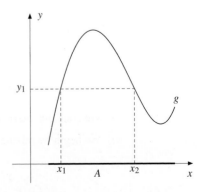

Figure 1 f is one-to-one with domain A and range B. f has an inverse

Figure 2 g is *not* one-to-one and hence has no inverse over A. Which x-value should be associated with y_1?

DEFINITION OF INVERSE FUNCTION

Let f be a function with domain A and range B. If and only if f is one-to-one, it has an **inverse function** g with domain B and range A. The function g is given by the following rule: For each $y \in B$, the value $g(y)$ is the unique number x in A such that $f(x) = y$. Then

$$g(y) = x \iff y = f(x) \qquad (x \in A, \quad y \in B)$$

(1)

A direct implication of (1) is that

$$g(f(x)) = x \quad \text{for all } x \in A \qquad \text{and} \qquad f(g(y)) = y \quad \text{for all } y \in B \qquad (2)$$

The equation $g(f(x)) = x$ shows that if we first apply f to x and then g to $f(x)$, then we get x back: *g undoes what f did to x*. Note that if g is the inverse of a function f, then f is also the inverse of g.

NOTE 1 If g is the inverse of f, it is standard to use the notation f^{-1} for g. This some-times leads to confusion. If a is a number, then a^{-1} means $1/a$. But $f^{-1}(x)$ does *not* mean $1/f(x) = (f(x))^{-1}$. For example: *The functions defined by* $y = 1/(x^2 + 2x + 3)$ *and* $y = x^2 + 2x + 3$ *are* **not** *inverses of each other, but reciprocals.*

In simple cases, we can use the same method as in the introductory example to find the inverse of a given function (and hence automatically verify that the inverse exists). Some more examples follow.

EXAMPLE 1   Solve the following equations for x and find the corresponding inverse functions:

(a) $y = 4x - 3$ (b) $y = \sqrt[5]{x + 1}$ (c) $y = \dfrac{3x - 1}{x + 4}$

Solution:

(a) Solving the equation for x, we have the following equivalences for all x and all y:

$$y = 4x - 3 \iff 4x = y + 3 \iff x = \tfrac{1}{4}y + \tfrac{3}{4}$$

We conclude that $f(x) = 4x - 3$ and $g(y) = \tfrac{1}{4}y + \tfrac{3}{4}$ are inverses of each other.

(b) We begin by raising each side to the fifth power and so obtain the equivalences

$$y = \sqrt[5]{x + 1} \iff y^5 = x + 1 \iff x = y^5 - 1$$

These are valid for all x and all y. Hence, we have shown that $f(x) = \sqrt[5]{x + 1}$ and $g(y) = y^5 - 1$ are inverses of each other.

(c) We solve the given equation for x by first multiplying both sides by $x + 4$:

$$y(x + 4) = 3x - 1$$

From this equation, we obtain $yx + 4y = 3x - 1$ or $x(3 - y) = 4y + 1$. Hence,

$$x = \frac{4y + 1}{3 - y}$$

We conclude that $f(x) = (3x - 1)/(x + 4)$ and $g(y) = (4y + 1)/(3 - y)$ are inverses of each other. Observe that f is only defined for $x \neq -4$, and g is only defined for $y \neq 3$. So the equivalence in (1) is valid only with these restrictions.

A Geometric Characterization of Inverse Functions

In our introductory example, we saw that $f(p) = 30p^{-1/3}$ and $g(D) = 27\,000D^{-3}$ were inverse functions. Because of the concrete interpretation of the symbols p and D, it was natural to describe the functions the way we did. In other circumstances, it may be convenient to use the same variable as argument in both f and g. In Example 1(a), we saw that $f(x) = 4x - 3$ and $g(y) = \frac{1}{4}y + \frac{3}{4}$ were inverses of each other. If also we use x instead of y as the variable of the function g, we find that

$$f(x) = 4x - 3 \quad \text{and} \quad g(x) = \tfrac{1}{4}x + \tfrac{3}{4} \quad \text{are inverses of each other} \quad (*)$$

In the same way, on the basis of Example 1(b) we can say that

$$f(x) = (x + 1)^{1/5} \quad \text{and} \quad g(x) = x^5 - 1 \quad \text{are inverses of each other} \quad (**)$$

There is an interesting geometric property of the graphs of inverse functions. For the pairs of inverse functions in $(*)$ and $(**)$, the graphs of f and g are mirror images of each other with respect to the line $y = x$. This is illustrated in Figs. 3 and 4.

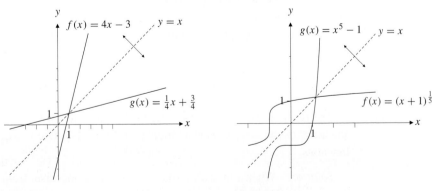

Figure 3   Figure 4

Suppose in general that f and g are inverses of each other. The fact that (a, b) lies on the graph f means that $b = f(a)$. According to (1), this implies that $g(b) = a$, so that (b, a)

lies on the graph of g. Because (a, b) and (b, a) lie symmetrically about the line $y = x$ (see Problem 8), we have the following conclusion:

When two functions f and g are inverses of each other, then the graphs of $y = f(x)$ and $y = g(x)$ are symmetric about the line $y = x$. (The units on the coordinate axes must be same.)   (3)

NOTE 2   When the functions f and g are inverses of each other, then by definition (1), the equations $y = f(x)$ and $x = g(y)$ are equivalent. The two functions actually have exactly the same graph, though in the second case we should think of x depending on y, instead of the other way around. On the other hand, the graphs of $y = f(x)$ and $y = g(x)$ are symmetric about the line $y = x$.

In all the examples examined so far, the inverse could be expressed in terms of known formulas. It turns out that even if a function has an inverse, it may be impossible to express it in terms of a function we know. *Inverse functions are actually an important source of new functions.* A typical case arises in connection with the exponential function. In Section 4.9 we showed that $y = e^x$ is strictly increasing and that it tends to 0 as x tends $-\infty$ and to ∞ as x tends to ∞. For each positive y there exists a uniquely determined x such that $e^x = y$. In Section 4.10 we called the new function the natural logarithm function, ln, and we have the equivalence $y = e^x \iff x = \ln y$. The *functions $f(x) = e^x$ and $g(y) = \ln y$ are therefore inverses of each other.* Because the ln-function appears in so many connections, it is tabulated, and moreover represented by a separate key on many pocket calculators.

If a pocket calculator has a certain function f represented by a key, then it will usually have another which represents its inverse function f^{-1}. If, for example, it has a $\boxed{e^x}$-key, it also has a $\boxed{\ln x}$-key. Since $f^{-1}(f(x)) = x$, if we feed in a number x, press the $\boxed{f}$-key and then press the $\boxed{f^{-1}}$-key, then we should get x back again. Try to press 5, use the $\boxed{e^x}$-key and then the $\boxed{\ln x}$-key. You should then get 5 back again. (One reason why you might not get exactly 5 is a rounding error.)

If f and g are inverses of each other, the domain of f is equal to the range of g, and vice versa. Consider the following examples.

EXAMPLE 2   The function $f(x) = \sqrt{3x + 9}$, defined in the interval $[-3, \infty)$, *is* strictly increasing and hence has an inverse. Find a formula for the inverse. Use x as the free variable for both functions.

   Solution: When x increases from -3 to ∞, $f(x)$ increases from 0 to ∞, so the range of f is $[0, \infty)$. Hence f has an inverse g defined on $[0, \infty)$. To find a formula for the inverse, we solve the equation $y = \sqrt{3x + 9}$ for x. Squaring gives $y^2 = 3x + 9$, which solved for x gives $x = \frac{1}{3}y^2 - 3$. Exchanging the names for the variables, we find that the inverse function of f is $g(x) = \frac{1}{3}x^2 - 3$, defined on $[0, \infty)$. See Fig. 5.

Figure 5

EXAMPLE 3   Consider the function f defined by the formula $f(x) = 4\ln(\sqrt{x+4} - 2)$.

(a) For which values of x is $f(x)$ defined? Determine the range of f.

(b) Find a formula for its inverse. Use x as the free variable.

Solution:

(a) In order for $\sqrt{x+4}$ to be defined, x must be ≥ -4. But we also have to make sure that $\sqrt{x+4} - 2 > 0$, for otherwise the logarithm is not defined. Now, $\sqrt{x+4} - 2 > 0$ means that $\sqrt{x+4} > 2$, or $x + 4 > 4$, that is, $x > 0$. The domain of f is therefore $(0, \infty)$. As x varies from near 0 to ∞, $f(x)$ increases from $-\infty$ to ∞. The range of f is therefore $(-\infty, \infty)$.

(b) If $y = 4\ln(\sqrt{x+4} - 2)$, then $\ln(\sqrt{x+4} - 2) = y/4$, so that $\sqrt{x+4} - 2 = e^{y/4}$ and then $\sqrt{x+4} = 2 + e^{y/4}$. By squaring each side we obtain $x + 4 = (2 + e^{y/4})^2 = 4 + 4e^{y/4} + e^{y/2}$, so that $x = 4e^{y/4} + e^{y/2}$. The inverse function, with x as the free variable, is therefore $y = e^{x/2} + 4e^{x/4}$. It is defined in $(-\infty, \infty)$ with range $(0, \infty)$. ∎

PROBLEMS FOR SECTION 5.3

1. Demand D as a function of price p is given by $D = \frac{32}{5} - \frac{3}{10}p$. Solve the equation for p and find the inverse function.

2. The demand D for sugar in the U.S. in the period 1915–1929, as a function of the price p, was estimated by H. Schultz as

$$D = f(p) = \frac{157.8}{p^{0.3}} \qquad (D \text{ and } p \text{ are measured in appropriate units})$$

Solve the equation for p and so find the inverse of f.

3. Find the inverses of the functions given by the formulas

(a) $y = -3x$ (b) $y = 1/x$ (c) $y = x^3$ (d) $y = \sqrt{\sqrt{x} - 2}$

4. The function f is defined by the following table:

x	-4	-3	-2	-1	0	1	2
$f(x)$	-4	-2	0	2	4	6	8

(a) Denote the inverse of f by f^{-1}. What is its domain? What is the value of $f^{-1}(2)$?

(b) Find a formula for $f(x)$ which gives this table. What is the formula for its inverse?

5. Why does $f(x) = x^2$, for $x \in (-\infty, \infty)$, have no inverse function? Show that f restricted to $[0, \infty)$ has an inverse, and find that inverse.

6. Formalize the following statements:

(a) Halving and doubling are inverse operations.

(b) The operation of multiplying a number by 3 and then subtracting 2 is the inverse of the operation of adding 2 to the number and then dividing by 3.

(c) The operation of subtracting 32 from a number and then multiplying the result by 5/9 is the inverse of the operation of multiplying a number by 9/5 and then adding 32. "Fahrenheit to Centigrade and Centigrade to Fahrenheit". (See Example 1.6.4.)

7. If f is the function that tells you how many kilograms of carrots you can buy for a specified amount of money, then what does f^{-1} tell you?

8. (a) Draw a coordinate system in the plane. Show that points $(3, 1)$ and $(1, 3)$ are symmetric about the line $y = x$, and the same for $(5, 3)$ and $(3, 5)$.

(b) Use properties of congruent triangles to prove that points (a, b) and (b, a) in the plane are symmetric about the line $y = x$.

9. Find inverses of the following functions (use x as the independent variable):

(a) $f(x) = (x^3 - 1)^{1/3}$ (b) $f(x) = \dfrac{x+1}{x-2}$ (c) $f(x) = (1 - x^3)^{1/5} + 2$

10. The functions defined by the following formulas are strictly increasing in their domains. Find the domain of each inverse function, and a formula for the corresponding inverse.

(a) $y = e^{x+4}$ (b) $y = \ln x - 4, \ x > 0$ (c) $y = \ln\left(2 + e^{x-3}\right)$

HARDER PROBLEMS

11. Find the inverse of $f(x) = \frac{1}{2}(e^x - e^{-x})$. (*Hint:* You need to solve a second-degree equation in $z = e^x$.)

5.4 Graphs of Equations

The equations

$$x\sqrt{y} = 2, \qquad x^2 + y^2 = 16, \qquad \text{and} \qquad y^3 + 3x^2y = 13$$

are three examples of equations in two variables x and y. A **solution** of such an equation is an ordered pair (a, b) such that the equation is satisfied when we replace x by a and y by b. The **solution set** of the equation is the set of all solutions. Representing all pairs in the solution set in a Cartesian coordinate system gives a set called the **graph** of the equation.

EXAMPLE 1   Find some solutions of each of the equations $x\sqrt{y} = 2$ and $x^2 + y^2 = 16$, and try to sketch their graphs.

Solution: From $x\sqrt{y} = 2$ we obtain $y = 4/x^2$. Hence it is easy to find corresponding values for x and y as given in Table 1.

Table 1 Solutions of $x\sqrt{y} = 2$

x	1	2	4	6
y	4	1	1/4	1/9

The graph is drawn in Fig. 1.

Figure 1 $x\sqrt{y} = 2$ **Figure 2** $x^2 + y^2 = 16$ **Figure 3** $y^3 + 3x^2y = 13$

For $x^2 + y^2 = 16$, if $y = 0$, $x^2 = 16$, so $x = \pm 4$. Thus $(4, 0)$ and $(-4, 0)$ are two solutions. Table 2 combines these with some other solutions.

Table 2 Solutions of $x^2 + y^2 = 16$

x	-4	-3	-1	0	1	3	4
y	0	$\pm\sqrt{7}$	$\pm\sqrt{15}$	± 4	$\pm\sqrt{15}$	$\pm\sqrt{7}$	0

In Fig. 2 we have plotted the points given in the table, and the graph seems to be a circle. (This is confirmed in the next section.)

EXAMPLE 2   What can you say about the graph of the equation $y^3 + 3x^2y = 13$?

Solution: If $x = 0$, then $y^3 = 13$, so that $y = \sqrt[3]{13} \approx 2.35$. Hence $(0, \sqrt[3]{13})$ lies on the graph. Note that if (x_0, y_0) lies on the graph, so does $(-x_0, y_0)$, since x is raised to the second power. Hence the graph is symmetric about the y-axis. You may notice that $(2, 1)$, and hence $(-2, 1)$, are solutions. (Additional points can found by solving the equation for x, to obtain $x = \pm\sqrt{(13 - y^3)/3y}$.)

If we write the equation in the form

$$y = \frac{13}{y^2 + 3x^2} \qquad (*)$$

we see that no point (x, y) on the graph can have $y \leq 0$, so that the whole graph lies above the x-axis. From $(*)$ it also follows that if x is large positive or negative, then y must be small. Figure 3 displays the graph, drawn by computer program, which accords with these findings.   ▌

Vertical-Line Test

Graphs of different functions can have innumerable different shapes. However, not all curves in the plane are graphs of functions. A function assigns to each point x in the domain only one y-value. *The graph of a function therefore has the property that a vertical line through any point on the x-axis has at most one point of intersection with the graph.* This simple *vertical-line test* is illustrated in Figs. 4 and 5.

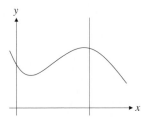

Figure 4 The graph represents a function

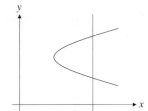

Figure 5 The graph does *not* represent a function

The graph of the circle $x^2 + y^2 = 16$, shown in Fig. 2, is a typical example of a graph that does *not* represent a function, since it does not pass the vertical-line test. A vertical line $x = a$ for any a with $-4 < a < 4$ intersects the circle at *two* points. Solving the equation $x^2 + y^2 = 16$ for y, we obtain $y = \pm\sqrt{16 - x^2}$. Note that the upper semicircle alone is the graph of the function $y = \sqrt{16 - x^2}$, and the lower semicircle is the graph of the function $y = -\sqrt{16 - x^2}$. Both these functions are defined on the interval $[-4, 4]$.

Choosing Units

A function of one variable is a rule assigning numbers in its range to numbers in its domain. When we describe an empirical relationship by means of a function, we must first choose the units of measurement. For instance we might measure time in years, days, or weeks. We might measure money in dollars, yen, or euros. The choice we make will influence the visual impression conveyed by the graph of the function.

Figure 6 illustrates a standard trick which is often used to influence people's impressions of empirical relationships. In both diagrams time is measured in years and consumption in billions of dollars. They both graph the same function. But if you were trying to impress an audience with the performance of the national economy, which one would you choose?

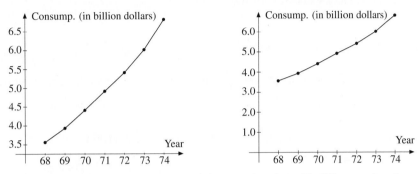

Figure 6   Graphical representations of the same function with different units of measurement

Compound Functions

Sometimes a function is defined in several pieces, by giving a separate formula for each of a number of disjoint parts of the domain. Two examples of such **compound functions** are presented next.

EXAMPLE 3   Draw the graph of the function f defined by

$$f(x) = \begin{cases} -x & \text{for } x \leq 0 \\ x^2 & \text{for } 0 < x \leq 1 \\ 1.5 & \text{for } x > 1 \end{cases}$$

Solution: The graph is drawn in Fig. 7. The arrow at $(1, 1.5)$ indicates that this point is not part of the graph of the function. The function has a *discontinuity* at $x = 1$. (See Section 7.7.)

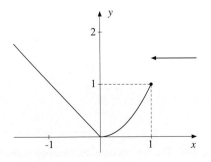

Figure 7   Graph of the function in Example 3

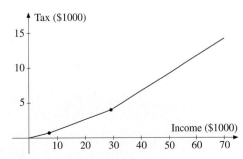

Figure 8   U.S. Federal Income Tax

EXAMPLE 4   (U.S. Federal Income Tax (2004) for Single Persons) In Fig. 8 we show a part of the graph of this income tax function.[1] Income up to \$7 150 was taxed at 10%, income between \$7 151 and \$29 050 was taxed at 15%, income between \$29 051 and \$70 350 and was taxed at 25%. For income above this level there are higher marginal rates; the highest is 35% for income above \$319 100.

PROBLEMS FOR SECTION 5.4

1. Try to sketch graphs of these equations by finding some solutions.

   (a) $x^2 + 2y^2 = 6$ (b) $y^2 - x^2 = 1$

2. (a) Sketch the graph of the function g defined for all x by

$$g(x) = \begin{cases} x^2 - 2x + 2 & \text{for } x \le 1 \\ 1 - \sqrt{x-1} & \text{for } x > 1 \end{cases}$$

   (b) Show that $a = g(g(a))$ for all values of a, and determine the inverse of g.

3. Try to sketch the graph of $\sqrt{x} + \sqrt{y} = 5$.

4. The function F is defined for all $R_N \ge 0$ by the following formulas:

$$F(R_N) = \begin{cases} 0 & \text{for } R_N \le 7500 \\ 0.044(R_N - 7500) & \text{for } R_N > 7500 \end{cases}$$

   Compute $F(100\,000)$, and sketch the graph of F.

5.5 Distance in the Plane. Circles

Let $P_1 = (x_1, y_1)$ and $P_2 = (x_2, y_2)$ be two points in the xy-plane as shown in Fig. 1. By Pythagoras' theorem, the distance d between these points satisfies the equation $d^2 = (x_2 - x_1)^2 + (y_2 - y_1)^2$. This gives the following important formula:

DISTANCE FORMULA

The distance between the points (x_1, y_1) and (x_2, y_2) is

$$d = \sqrt{(x_2 - x_1)^2 + (y_2 - y_1)^2}$$ (1)

[1] Of course, Fig. 8 is an idealization. The true income tax function is defined only for integral numbers of dollars—or, more precisely, it is a discontinuous "step function" which jumps up slightly whenever income rises by another dollar.

Figure 1

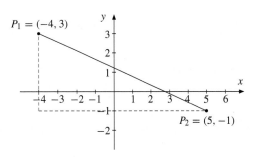

Figure 2

We considered two points in the first quadrant to prove the distance formula. It turns out that the same formula is valid irrespective of where the two points P_1 and P_2 lie. Note also that since $(x_1 - x_2)^2 = (x_2 - x_1)^2$ and $(y_1 - y_2)^2 = (y_2 - y_1)^2$, it makes no difference which point is P_1 and which is P_2.

Some find formula (1) hard to grasp. In words it tells us that we can find the distance between two points in the plane as follows:

Take the difference between the x-coordinates and square what you get. Do the same with the y-coordinates. Add the results and then take the square root.

EXAMPLE 1   Find the distance d between $P_1 = (-4, 3)$ and $P_2 = (5, -1)$. (See Fig. 2.)

Solution: Using (1) with $x_1 = -4$, $y_1 = 3$ and $x_2 = 5$, $y_2 = -1$, we have

$$d = \sqrt{(5 - (-4))^2 + (-1 - 3)^2} = \sqrt{9^2 + (-4)^2} = \sqrt{81 + 16} = \sqrt{97} \approx 9.85$$

Circles

Let (a, b) be a point in the plane. *The circle with radius r and centre at (a, b) is the set of all points (x, y) whose distance from (a, b) is equal to r.* Applying the distance formula to Fig. 3 gives

$$\sqrt{(x - a)^2 + (y - b)^2} = r$$

Squaring each side yields:

EQUATION OF A CIRCLE

The equation of a circle with centre at (a, b) and radius r is

$$(x - a)^2 + (y - b)^2 = r^2 \tag{2}$$

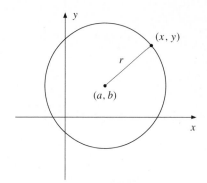

Figure 3   Circle with centre at (a, b) and radius r

Figure 4   Circle with centre at $(-4, 1)$ and radius 3

Note that if we let $a = b = 0$ and $r = 4$, then (2) reduces to $x^2 + y^2 = 16$. This is the equation of a circle with centre at $(0, 0)$ and radius 4, as shown in Fig. 5.4.2.

EXAMPLE 2   Find the equation of the circle with centre at $(-4, 1)$ and radius 3.

Solution: Here $a = -4$, $b = 1$, and $r = 3$. (See Fig. 4.) So according to (2), the equation for the circle is

$$(x + 4)^2 + (y - 1)^2 = 9 \qquad (*)$$

Thus $x^2 + 8x + 16 + y^2 - 2y + 1 = 9$, and collecting terms,

$$x^2 + y^2 + 8x - 2y + 8 = 0 \qquad (**)$$

The equation of the circle given in (**) has the disadvantage that we can not immediately read off its centre and radius. If we are given equation (**), however, we can use the method of "completing the squares" to deduce (*) from (**). See Problem 5.

Ellipses and Other Conics

A very important type of curve in physics and astronomy is the ellipse. (After all, the planets, including the Earth, move around the Sun in orbits that are approximately elliptical.) Occasionally, ellipses also appear in economics and statistics. The simplest type of ellipse has the equation

$$\frac{(x - x_0)^2}{a^2} + \frac{(y - y_0)^2}{b^2} = 1 \qquad \textbf{(ellipse)}$$

This ellipse has centre at (x_0, y_0) and the graph is shown in Fig. 5. Note that when $a = b$, the ellipse degenerates into a circle.

Figure 5 Ellipse

Figure 6 Hyperbola

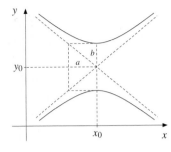

Figure 7 Hyperbola

Figures 6 and 7 show the graphs of the two **hyperbolas**

$$\frac{(x - x_0)^2}{a^2} - \frac{(y - y_0)^2}{b^2} = +1 \qquad \text{and} \qquad \frac{(x - x_0)^2}{a^2} - \frac{(y - y_0)^2}{b^2} = -1$$

respectively. The asymptotes are the dashed lines in Figs. 6 and 7. They are the same pair in each figure. Their equations are $y - y_0 = \pm\frac{b}{a}(x - x_0)$.

We end this section by noting that the graph of the general quadratic equation

$$Ax^2 + Bxy + Cy^2 + Dx + Ey + F = 0$$

where A, B, and C are not all 0, will have one of the following shapes:

- If $4AC > B^2$, either an ellipse (possibly a circle), or a single point, or empty.

- If $4AC = B^2$, either a parabola, or one line or two parallel lines, or empty.

- If $4AC < B^2$, either a hyperbola, or two lines which intersect.

PROBLEMS FOR SECTION 5.5

1. Determine the distance between the following pairs of points:

   (a) $(1, 3)$ and $(2, 4)$ (b) $(-1, 2)$ and $(-3, 3)$ (c) $(3/2, -2)$ and $(-5, 1)$

   (d) (x, y) and $(2x, y + 3)$ (e) (a, b) and $(-a, b)$ (f) $(a, 3)$ and $(2 + a, 5)$

2. The distance between $(2, 4)$ and $(5, y)$ is $\sqrt{13}$. Find y. (Explain geometrically why there must be two values of y.)

3. Find the distance between each pair of points:

   (a) $(3.998, 2.114)$ and $(1.130, -2.416)$ (b) $(\pi, 2\pi)$ and $(-\pi, 1)$

4. Find the equations of the circles with:

    (a) Centre at $(2, 3)$ and radius 4.   (b) Centre at $(2, 5)$ and one point at $(-1, 3)$.

5. We can show that the graph of $x^2 + y^2 - 10x + 14y + 58 = 0$ is a circle by arguing like this: First rearrange the equation to read $(x^2 - 10x) + (y^2 + 14y) = -58$. Completing the two squares gives: $(x^2 - 10x + 5^2) + (y^2 + 14y + 7^2) = -58 + 5^2 + 7^2 = 16$. Thus the equation becomes

$$(x - 5)^2 + (y + 7)^2 = 16$$

   whose graph is a circle with centre $(5, -7)$ and radius $\sqrt{16} = 4$. Use this method to find the centre and the radius of the two circles with equations:

    (a) $x^2 + y^2 + 10x - 6y + 30 = 0$ (b) $3x^2 + 3y^2 + 18x - 24y = -39$

6. Prove that if the distance from a point (x, y) to the point $(-2, 0)$ is twice the distance from (x, y) to $(4, 0)$, then (x, y) must lie on the circle with centre $(6, 0)$ and radius 4.

HARDER PROBLEMS

7. Show that the graph of

$$x^2 + y^2 + Ax + By + C = 0 \qquad (A, B, \text{ and } C \text{ constants}) \qquad (*)$$

   is a circle if $A^2 + B^2 > 4C$. Find its centre and radius. (See Problem 5.) What happens if $A^2 + B^2 \leq 4C$?

5.6 General Functions

So far we have studied functions of one variable. These are functions whose domain is a set of real numbers, and whose range is also a set of real numbers. Yet a realistic description of many economic phenomena requires considering a large number of variables simultaneously. For example, the demand for a good like butter is a function of several variables such as the price of the good, the prices of complements like bread, or substitutes like olive oil or margarine, as well as consumers' incomes, and so on.

Actually, you have probably already seen many special functions of several variables. For instance, the formula $V = \pi r^2 h$ for the volume V of a cylinder with base radius r and height h involves a function of two variables. (Of course, in this case $\pi \approx 3.14159$ is a mathematical constant.) A change in one of these variables will not affect the value of the other variable. For each pair of positive numbers (r, h), there is a definite value for the volume V. To emphasize that V depends on the values of both r and h, we write

$$V(r, h) = \pi r^2 h$$

For $r = 2$ and $h = 3$, we obtain $V(2, 3) = 12\pi$, whereas $r = 3$ and $h = 2$ give $V(3, 2) = 18\pi$. Also, $r = 1$ and $h = 1/\pi$ give $V(1, 1/\pi) = 1$. Note in particular that $V(2, 3) \neq V(3, 2)$.

In some abstract economic models, it may be enough to know that there is some functional relationship between variables, without specifying the dependence more closely. For instance, suppose a market sells three commodities whose prices per unit are respectively p, q, and r. Then economists generally assume that the demand for one of the commodities by an individual with income m is given by a function $f(p, q, r, m)$ of four variables, without necessarily specifying the precise form of that function.

An extensive discussion of functions of several variables begins in Chapter 11. This section introduces an even more general type of function. In fact, general functions of the kind presented here are of fundamental importance in practically every area of pure and applied mathematics, including mathematics applied to economics. Here is the general definition:

A **function** is a rule which to each element in a set A associates one and only one element in a set B. (1)

The following indicates how very wide is the concept of a function.

EXAMPLE 1 (a) The function that assigns to each triangle in a plane the area of that triangle (measured, say, in cm^2).

(b) The function that determines the social security number, or other identification number, of each taxpayer.

(c) The function that for each point P in a horizontal plane determines the point lying 3 units above P.

(d) Let A be the set of possible actions that a person can choose in a certain situation. Suppose that every action $a \in A$ produces a certain result (say, a certain profit) $\varphi(a)$. In this way, we have defined a function φ with domain A.

If we denote the function by f, the set A is called the **domain** of f, and B is called the **target**. The two sets A and B need not consist of numbers, but can be sets of arbitrary elements. The definition of a function requires three objects to be specified:

(i) A domain A

(ii) A target B

(iii) A rule that assigns a *unique* element in B to *each* element in A.

Nevertheless, in many cases, we refrain from specifying the sets A and/or B explicitly when it is obvious from the context what these sets are.

An important requirement in the definition of a function is that to each element in the domain A, there corresponds a *unique* element in the target B. While it is meaningful to talk about the function that assigns the natural mother to every child, the rule that assigns the aunt to any child does not, in general, define a function, because many children have more than one aunt. Explain why the following rule, as opposed to the one in Example 1(c), does not define a function: "to a point P in the plane assign a point that lies 3 units from P."

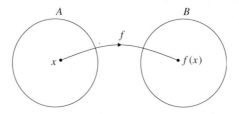

Figure 1   A function from A to B

If f is a function with domain A and target B, we often say that f is a **function from** A **to** B, and write $f : A \rightarrow B$. The functional relationship is often represented as in Fig. 1. Other words that are sometimes used instead of "function" include **transformation** and **map** or **mapping**.

The particular value $f(x)$ is often called the **image** of the element x by the function f. The set of elements in B that are images of at least one element in A is called the **range** of the function. Thus, the range is a subset of the target. If we denote the range of f by R_f, then $R_f = \{f(x) : x \in A\}$. This is also written as $f(A)$. The range of the function in Example 1(a) is the set of all positive numbers. Explain why the range of the function in (c) must be a whole plane.

The definition of a function requires that only *one* element in B be assigned to each element in A. However, different elements in A might be mapped to the same element in B. In Example 1(a), for instance, many different triangles have the same area. If each element of B is the image of at most one element in A, the function f is called **one-to-one**. Otherwise, if one or more elements of B are the images of more than one element in A, the function f is many-to-one. (If a relation is one-to-many, it is not even a function.)

The social security function in Example 1(b) is one-to-one, because two different tax-payers should always have different numbers. Can you explain why the function defined in Example 1(c) is also one-to-one, whereas the function that assigns to each child his or her mother is not?

Inverse Functions

The definition of inverse function in Sec. 5.3 can easily be extended to general functions. Suppose f is a one-to-one function from a set A to a set B, and assume that the range of f is all of B. We can then define a function g from B to A by the following obvious rule: Assign to each element v of B the one and only element $u = g(v)$ of A that f maps to

v—that is, the u satisfying $v = f(u)$. Because f is one-to-one, there can be only one u in A such that $v = f(u)$, so g is a function, its domain is B and its target and range are both equal to A. The function g is called the **inverse function** of f. For instance, the inverse of the social security function mentioned in Example 1(b) is the function that, to each social security number in its range, assigns the person carrying that number.

PROBLEMS FOR SECTION 5.6

1. Which of the following rules define functions?

   (a) The rule that assigns to each person in a classroom his or her height.

   (b) The rule that assigns to each mother her youngest child alive today.

   (c) The rule that assigns the perimeter of a rectangle to its area.

   (d) The rule that assigns the surface area of a spherical ball to its volume.

   (e) The rule that assigns the pair of numbers $(x + 3, y)$ to the pair of numbers (x, y).

2. Determine which of the functions defined in Problem 1 are one-to-one, and which then have an inverse. Determine each inverse when it exists.

REVIEW PROBLEMS FOR CHAPTER 5

1. Use Fig. 4.3.10 and the rules for shifting graphs to sketch the graphs of

   (a) $y = |x| + 1$　　　　(b) $y = |x + 3|$　　　　(c) $y = 3 - |x + 1|$

2. If $f(x) = x^3 - 2$ and $g(x) = (1 - x)x^2$, compute: $(f + g)(x)$, $(f - g)(x)$, $(fg)(x)$, $(f/g)(x)$, $f(g(1))$, and $g(f(1))$.

3. (a) Consider the demand and supply functions

$$D = 150 - \tfrac{1}{2}P, \qquad S = 20 + 2P$$

   Find the equilibrium price, and the corresponding quantity.

   (b) Suppose a tax of \$2 per unit is imposed on the producer. How will this influence the equilibrium price?

   (c) Compute the total revenue obtained by the producer before and after the tax is imposed.

4. Demand D as a function of price p is given by $D = \tfrac{32}{5} - \tfrac{3}{10}p$. (See Problem 4.2.7 for an economic interpretation.) Solve the equation for p and find the inverse function.

5. The demand D for a product as a function of the price P is given by $D = 120 - 5P$. Solve the equation for P and so find the inverse function.

6. Find the inverses of the functions given by the formulas:

   (a) $y = 100 - 2x$ (b) $y = 2x^5$ (c) $y = 5e^{3x-2}$

7. The following functions are strictly increasing in their domains. Find the domains of their inverses and formulas for the inverses. Use x as the free variable.

   (a) $f(x) = 3 + \ln(e^x - 2), \quad x > \ln 2$

   (b) $f(x) = \dfrac{a}{e^{-\lambda x} + a}, \quad a$ and λ positive, $x \in (-\infty, \infty)$

8. Determine the distance between the following pairs of points:

   (a) $(2, 3)$ and $(5, 5)$ (b) $(-4, 4)$ and $(-3, 8)$ (c) $(2a, 3b)$ and $(2 - a, 3b)$

9. Find the equations of the circles with:

   (a) Centre at $(2, -3)$ and radius 5.   (b) Centre at $(-2, 2)$ and a point at $(-10, 1)$.

10. A point P moves in the plane so that it is always equidistant from each of the points $A = (3, 2)$ and $B = (5, -4)$. Find a simple equation that the coordinates (x, y) of P must satisfy. (*Hint:* Compute the square of the distance from P to A and to B, respectively.)

11. Each person in a team is known to have red blood cells that belong to one and only one of four blood groups denoted A, B, AB, and O. Consider the function that assigns each person in the team to his or her blood group. Can this function be one-to-one if the team consists of at least five persons?

DIFFERENTIATION

To think of it [differential calculus] merely as a
more advanced technique is to miss its real content.
In it, mathematics becomes a dynamic mode of thought,
and that is a major mental step in the ascent of man.
—J. Bronowski (1973)

An important topic in many scientific disciplines, including economics, is the study of how quickly quantities change over time. In order to compute the future position of a planet, to predict the growth in population of a biological species, or to estimate the future demand for a commodity, we need information about rates of change.

The concept used to describe the rate of change of a function is the derivative, which is *the* central concept in mathematical analysis. This chapter defines the derivative of a function and presents some of the important rules for calculating it.

Isaac Newton (1642–1727) and Gottfried Leibniz (1646–1716) discovered most of these general rules independently of each other. This initiated differential calculus, which has been the foundation for the development of modern science. It has also been of central importance to the theoretical development of modern economics.

6.1 Slopes of Curves

Even though in economics we are usually interested in the derivative as a rate of change, we begin this chapter with a geometrical motivation for the concept. When we study the graph of a function, we would like to have a precise measure of the steepness of the graph at a point.

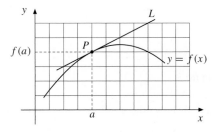

Figure 1 $f'(a) = 1/2$

We know that for the line $y = ax + b$, the number a denotes its slope. If a is large and positive, then the line rises steeply from left to right; if a is large and negative, the line falls steeply. But for an arbitrary function f, what is the steepness of its graph? A natural answer is to define the steepness of a curve *at a particular point* as the slope of the tangent to the curve at that point—that is, as the slope of the straight line that just touches the curve at that point. For the curve in Fig. 1 the steepness at point P is seen to be $1/2$, because the slope of the tangent line L is $1/2$.

In Fig. 1, point P has coordinates $(a, f(a))$. The slope of the tangent to the graph at P is called the **derivative** of f at point a, and we denote this number by $f'(a)$ (read as "f prime a"). In general, we have

$$f'(a) = \text{the slope of the tangent to the curve } y = f(x) \text{ at the point } (a, f(a))$$

Thus, in Fig. 1, we have $f'(a) = 1/2$.

EXAMPLE 1   Find $f'(1)$, $f'(4)$, and $f'(7)$ for the function whose graph is shown in Fig. 2.

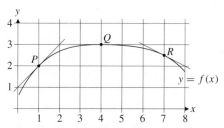

Figure 2

Solution: At $P = (1, 2)$, the tangent goes through $(0, 1)$, and so has slope 1. At $Q = (4, 3)$ the tangent is horizontal, and so has slope 0. At $R = (7, 2\frac{1}{2})$, the tangent goes through $(8, 2)$, and so has slope $-\frac{1}{2}$. Hence, $f'(1) = 1$, $f'(4) = 0$, and $f'(7) = -1/2$. ∎

PROBLEMS FOR SECTION 6.1

1. Figure 3 shows the graph of a function f. Find the values of $f(3)$ and $f'(3)$.

Figure 3

Figure 4

2. Figure 4 shows the graph of a function g. Find the values of $g(5)$ and $g'(5)$.

6.2 The Derivative. Tangents

The previous section gave a rather vague definition of the tangent to a curve at a point. All we said is that it is a straight line which just touches the curve at that point. We now give a more formal definition of the same concept.

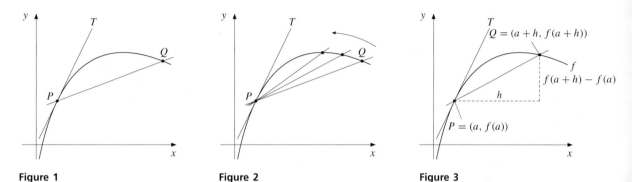

Figure 1 **Figure 2** **Figure 3**

The geometrical idea behind the definition is easy to understand. Consider a point P on a curve in the xy-plane shown in Fig. 1. Take another point Q on the curve. The straight line through P and Q is called a *secant*. If we keep P fixed, but let Q move along the curve toward P, then the secant will rotate around P, as indicated in Fig. 2. The limiting straight line PT toward which the secant tends is called the **tangent** to the curve at P.

Suppose that P is a point on the graph of the function f. The preceding considerations enable us to find the slope of the tangent at P. The method is illustrated in Fig. 3.

Point P in Fig. 3 has the coordinates $\big(a,\, f(a)\big)$. Point Q lies close to P and is also on the graph of f. Suppose that the x-coordinate of Q is $a + h$, where h is a small number $\neq 0$. Then the x-coordinate of Q is not a (because $Q \neq P$), but a number close to a. Because Q lies on the graph of f, the y-coordinate of Q is equal to $f(a+h)$. Hence, the coordinates of the points are $P = \big(a,\, f(a)\big)$ and $Q = \big(a+h,\, f(a+h)\big)$. The slope m_{PQ} of the secant PQ is

$$m_{PQ} = \frac{f(a + h) - f(a)}{h}$$

This fraction is often called a **Newton quotient** of f. Note that when $h = 0$, the fraction becomes 0/0 and so is undefined. But choosing $h = 0$ corresponds to letting $Q = P$. When Q moves toward P along the graph of f, the x-coordinate of Q, which is $a + h$, must tend to a, and so h tends to 0. Simultaneously, the secant PQ tends to the tangent to the graph at P. This suggests that we ought to *define* the slope of the tangent at P as the number that m_{PQ} approaches as h tends to 0. In the previous section we called this number $f'(a)$. So we propose the following definition of $f'(a)$:

$$f'(a) = \left\{ \begin{array}{l} \text{the limit as } h \\ \text{tends to 0 of} \end{array} \right\} \ \frac{f(a + h) - f(a)}{h}$$

It is common to use the abbreviated notation $\lim_{h \to 0}$, or $\displaystyle\lim_{h \to 0}$, for "the limit as h tends to zero" of an expression involving h. We therefore have the following definition:

The derivative of the function f at point a, denoted by $f'(a)$, is given by the formula

$$f'(a) = \lim_{h \to 0} \frac{f(a+h) - f(a)}{h}$$

(1)

The number $f'(a)$ gives the slope of the tangent to the curve $y = f(x)$ at the point $(a, f(a))$. The equation for a straight line passing through (x_1, y_1) and having a slope b is given by $y - y_1 = b(x - x_1)$. Hence, we obtain:

The equation for the tangent to the graph of $y = f(x)$ at the point $(a, f(a))$ is

$$y - f(a) = f'(a)(x - a)$$

(2)

So far the concept of a limit in the definition of $f'(a)$ is not quite clear. Section 6.5 discusses the concept of limit in more detail. Because it is relatively complicated, we rely on intuition for the time being. Consider a simple example.

EXAMPLE 1   Use (1) to compute $f'(a)$ when

$$f(x) = x^2$$

Find in particular $f'(1/2)$ and $f'(-1)$. Give geometric interpretations, and find the equation for the tangent at the point $(1/2, 1/4)$.

Solution: For $f(x) = x^2$, we have $f(a+h) = (a+h)^2 = a^2 + 2ah + h^2$, and so $f(a+h) - f(a) = (a^2 + 2ah + h^2) - a^2 = 2ah + h^2$. Hence, for all $h \neq 0$, we obtain

$$\frac{f(a+h) - f(a)}{h} = \frac{2ah + h^2}{h} = \frac{h(2a+h)}{h} = 2a + h$$

(∗)

because we can cancel h whenever $h \neq 0$. But as h tends to 0, so $2a + h$ obviously tends to $2a$. Thus, we can write

$$f'(a) = \lim_{h \to 0} \frac{f(a+h) - f(a)}{h} = \lim_{h \to 0} (2a + h) = 2a$$

This shows that when $f(x) = x^2$, then $f'(a) = 2a$. For $a = 1/2$, we obtain $f'(1/2) = 2 \cdot 1/2 = 1$. Similarly, $f'(-1) = 2 \cdot (-1) = -2$.

Figure 4 provides a geometric interpretation of (∗). In Fig. 5, we have drawn the tangents to the curve $y = x^2$ corresponding to $a = 1/2$ and $a = -1$. At $a = 1/2$, we have $f(a) = (1/2)^2 = 1/4$ and $f'(1/2) = 1$. According to (2), the equation of the tangent is

$y - 1/4 = 1 \cdot (x - 1/2)$ or $y = x - 1/4$. (Show that the other tangent drawn in Fig. 5 has the equation $y = -2x - 1$.) Note that the formula $f'(a) = 2a$ shows that $f'(a) < 0$ when $a < 0$, and $f'(a) > 0$ when $a > 0$. Does this agree with the graph?

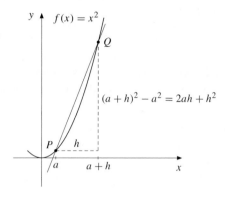

Figure 4 $f(x) = x^2$ **Figure 5** $f(x) = x^2$

If f is a relatively simple function, we can find $f'(a)$ by using the following recipe:

RECIPE FOR COMPUTING $f'(a)$

(A) Add h ($h \neq 0$) to a and compute $f(a + h)$.

(B) Compute the corresponding change in the function value: $f(a+h) - f(a)$.

(C) For $h \neq 0$, form the Newton quotient $\dfrac{f(a+h) - f(a)}{h}$.   (3)

(D) Simplify the fraction in step C as much as possible. Wherever possible, cancel h from the numerator and denominator.

(E) Then $f'(a)$ is the limit of $\dfrac{f(a+h) - f(a)}{h}$ as h tends to 0.

Let us apply this recipe to another example.

EXAMPLE 2   Compute $f'(a)$ when $f(x) = x^3$.

Solution: We follow the recipe in (3).

(A) $f(a + h) = (a + h)^3 = a^3 + 3a^2h + 3ah^2 + h^3$

(B) $f(a + h) - f(a) = (a^3 + 3a^2h + 3ah^2 + h^3) - a^3 = 3a^2h + 3ah^2 + h^3$

(C)–(D) $\dfrac{f(a+h) - f(a)}{h} = \dfrac{3a^2h + 3ah^2 + h^3}{h} = 3a^2 + 3ah + h^2$

(E) As h tends to 0, so $3ah+h^2$ will also tend to 0; hence, the entire expression $3a^2+3ah+h^2$ tends to $3a^2$. Therefore, $f'(a) = 3a^2$.

We have thus shown that the graph of the function $f(x) = x^3$ at the point $x = a$ has a tangent with slope $3a^2$. Note that $f'(a) = 3a^2 > 0$ when $a \neq 0$, and $f'(0) = 0$. The tangent points upwards to the right for all $a \neq 0$, and is horizontal at the origin. You should look at the graph of $f(x) = x^3$ in Fig. 4.3.7 to confirm this behaviour.   ∎

It is easy to use the recipe in (3) on simple functions. However, the recipe becomes very difficult if we try to use it on slightly more complicated functions such as $f(x) = \sqrt{3x^2 + x + 1}$. We shall develop rules for computing the derivative of quite complicated functions, without the need to use (3). Before presenting such rules, however, we must examine the concept of a limit a little more carefully. This is done in Section 6.5.

On Notation

We showed in Example 1 that, if $f(x) = x^2$, then for every a, we have $f'(a) = 2a$. We frequently use x as the symbol for a quantity that can take any value, so we write $f'(x) = 2x$. Using this notation, our results from the two last examples are as follows:

$$f(x) = x^2 \implies f'(x) = 2x \tag{4}$$

$$f(x) = x^3 \implies f'(x) = 3x^2 \tag{5}$$

The result in (4) is a special case of the following rule, which you are asked to show in Problem 6.

$$f(x) = ax^2 + bx + c \implies f'(x) = 2ax + b \qquad (a, b, \text{ and } c \text{ are constants}) \tag{6}$$

For $a = 1$, $b = c = 0$, this reduces to (4). Here are some other special cases of (6):

$f(x) = 3x^2 + 2x + 5 \qquad\qquad \implies f'(x) = 3 \cdot 2x + 2 = 6x + 2$

$f(x) = -16 + \dfrac{1}{2}x - \dfrac{1}{16}x^2 \qquad \implies f'(x) = -\dfrac{1}{8}x + \dfrac{1}{2}$

$f(x) = (x - p)^2 = x^2 - 2px + p^2 \implies f'(x) = 2x - 2p \qquad (p \text{ is a constant})$

If we use y to denote the value of the function $y = f(x)$, we often denote the derivative by y'. We can then write $y = x^3 \implies y' = 3x^2$.

Several other forms of notation for the derivative are often used in mathematics and its applications. One of them, originally due to Leibniz, is called the **differential notation**. If $y = f(x)$, in place of $f'(x)$, we write

$$\frac{dy}{dx} = dy/dx \qquad \text{or} \qquad \frac{df(x)}{dx} = df(x)/dx \qquad \text{or} \qquad \frac{d}{dx} f(x)$$

For instance, if $y = x^2$, then

$$\frac{dy}{dx} = 2x \qquad \text{or} \qquad \frac{d}{dx}(x^2) = 2x$$

We can think of the symbol d/dx as an instruction to differentiate what follows with respect to x. Differentiation with respect to a variable occurs so often in mathematics that it has become standard to use **w.r.t.** as an abbreviation for "with respect to." At this point, we will only think of the symbol dy/dx as meaning $f'(x)$ and will not consider it as dy divided by dx. Later chapters discuss this notation in greater detail.

When we use letters other than f, x, and y, the notation for the derivative changes accordingly. For example:

$$P(t) = t^2 \Longrightarrow P'(t) = 2t; \quad Y = K^3 \Longrightarrow Y' = 3K^2; \quad \text{and} \quad A = r^2 \Longrightarrow dA/dr = 2r$$

PROBLEMS FOR SECTION 6.2

1. Let $f(x) = 4x^2$. Show that $f(5+h) - f(5) = 40h + 4h^2$. Hence,

$$\frac{f(5+h) - f(5)}{h} = 40 + 4h$$

Using this result, find $f'(5)$. Compare the answer with (6).

2. (a) Let $f(x) = 3x^2 + 2x - 1$. Show that for $h \neq 0$,

$$\frac{f(x+h) - f(x)}{h} = 6x + 2 + 3h$$

Use this result to find $f'(x)$.

(b) Find in particular $f'(0)$, $f'(-2)$, and $f'(3)$. Find also the equation of the tangent to the graph at the point $(0, -1)$.

3. (a) The demand function for a commodity with price P is given by the formula $D(P) = a - bP$. Find $dD(P)/dP$.

(b) The cost of producing x units of a commodity is given by the formula $C(x) = p + qx^2$. Find $C'(x)$, the *marginal cost* (see Section 6.4).

4. Show that
$$f(x) = \frac{1}{x} = x^{-1} \Longrightarrow f'(x) = -\frac{1}{x^2} = -x^{-2}$$

(*Hint:* Show that $[f(x+h) - f(x)]/h = -1/x(x+h)$.)

5. Find the slope for the tangent to the graph of f at the specified points:

   (a) $f(x) = 3x + 2$ at $(0, 2)$

   (b) $f(x) = x^2 - 1$ at $(1, 0)$

   (c) $f(x) = \frac{3}{x} + 2$ at $(3, 3)$

   (d) $f(x) = x^3 - 2x$ at $(0, 0)$

   (e) $f(x) = x + \frac{1}{x}$ at $(-1, -2)$

   (f) $f(x) = x^4$ at $(1, 1)$

6. (a) If $f(x) = ax^2 + bx + c$, show that $[f(x + h) - f(x)]/h = 2ax + b + ah$. Use this to show that $f'(x) = 2ax + b$.

   (b) For what value of x is $f'(x) = 0$? Explain this result in the light of (5) in Section 4.6.

7. The figure shows the graph of a function f. Determine the sign of the derivative $f'(x)$ at the four points a, b, c, and d.

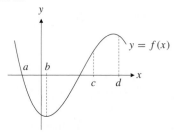

8. (a) Show that $\left(\sqrt{x + h} - \sqrt{x}\right)\left(\sqrt{x + h} + \sqrt{x}\right) = h$.

   (b) If $f(x) = \sqrt{x}$, show that $[f(x + h) - f(x)]/h = 1/\left(\sqrt{x + h} + \sqrt{x}\right)$.

   (c) Use the result in part (b) to show that for $x > 0$,

   $$f(x) = \sqrt{x} \implies f'(x) = \frac{1}{2\sqrt{x}} = \frac{1}{2}x^{-1/2}$$

9. (a) If $f(x) = ax^3 + bx^2 + cx + d$, show that

   $$\frac{f(x + h) - f(x)}{h} = 3ax^2 + 2bx + c + 3axh + ah^2 + bh$$

   and hence find $f'(x)$.

   (b) Show that the result in part (a) generalizes Example 2 and Problem 6(a).

HARDER PROBLEMS

10. Show that

    $$f(x) = x^{1/3} \implies f'(x) = \frac{1}{3}x^{-2/3}$$

    (*Hint:* Prove that $[(x + h)^{1/3} - x^{1/3}][(x + h)^{2/3} + (x + h)^{1/3}x^{1/3} + x^{2/3}] = h$. Then follow the argument used to solve Problem 8.)

6.3 Increasing and Decreasing Functions

The terms *increasing* and *decreasing* functions have been used previously to describe the behaviour of a function as we travel from *left to right* along its graph. In order to establish a definite terminology, we introduce the following definitions. We assume that f is defined in an interval I and that x_1 and x_2 are numbers from that interval.

If $f(x_2) \geq f(x_1)$ whenever $x_2 > x_1$, then f is **increasing in** I

If $f(x_2) > f(x_1)$ whenever $x_2 > x_1$, then f is **strictly increasing in** I

If $f(x_2) \leq f(x_1)$ whenever $x_2 > x_1$, then f is **decreasing in** I

If $f(x_2) < f(x_1)$ whenever $x_2 > x_1$, then f is **strictly decreasing in** I

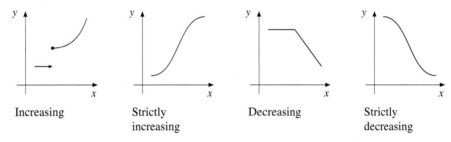

| Increasing | Strictly increasing | Decreasing | Strictly decreasing |

Figure 1

Figure 1 illustrates these definitions. Note that we allow an increasing (or decreasing) function to have sections where the graph is horizontal. This does not quite agree with common language. Few people would say that their salary increases when it stays constant! To find out on which intervals a function is (strictly) increasing or (strictly) decreasing using the definitions, we have to consider the sign of $f(x_2) - f(x_1)$ whenever $x_2 > x_1$. This is usually quite difficult to do directly by checking the values of $f(x)$ at different points x. In fact, we already know a good test of whether a differentiable function is increasing or decreasing, in terms of the sign of its derivative:

$$f'(x) \geq 0 \text{ for all } x \text{ in the interval } I \iff f \text{ is increasing in } I \qquad (1)$$

$$f'(x) \leq 0 \text{ for all } x \text{ in the interval } I \iff f \text{ is decreasing in } I \qquad (2)$$

Using the fact that the derivative of a function is the slope of the tangent to its graph, the equivalences in (1) and (2) seem almost obvious. An observation which is equally correct is the following:

$$f'(x) = 0 \text{ for all } x \text{ in the interval } I \iff f \text{ is constant in } I \qquad (3)$$

A precise proof of (1)–(3) relies on the mean-value theorem. See Note 8.4.1.

EXAMPLE 1   Examine where $f(x) = \frac{1}{2}x^2 - 2$ is increasing/decreasing. Use result (6) in the previous section.

Solution: We find that $f'(x) = x$, which is ≥ 0 for $x \geq 0$ and ≤ 0 if $x \leq 0$, and thus $f'(0) = 0$. We conclude that f is increasing in $[0, \infty)$ and decreasing in $(-\infty, 0]$. Draw the graph of f.

EXAMPLE 2   Examine where $f(x) = -\frac{1}{3}x^3 + 2x^2 - 3x + 1$ is increasing/decreasing. Use the result in Problem 9 of the previous section.

Solution: The formula in the problem can be used with $a = -1/3$, $b = 2$, $c = -3$, and $d = 1$. Thus $f'(x) = -x^2 + 4x - 3$. Solving the equation $f'(x) = -x^2 + 4x - 3 = 0$ yields $x = 1$ and $x = 3$, and thus $f'(x) = -(x - 1)(x - 3) = (x - 1)(3 - x)$. A sign diagram for $(x - 1)(3 - x)$ (see Example 1.6.2) reveals that $f'(x) = (x - 1)(3 - x)$ is ≥ 0 in the interval $[1, 3]$, and ≤ 0 in $(-\infty, 1]$ and in $[3, \infty)$. We conclude that $f(x)$ is increasing in $[1, 3]$, but decreasing in $(-\infty, 1]$ and in $[3, \infty)$. See Fig. 2.

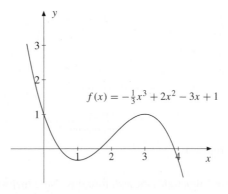

Figure 2

If $f'(x)$ is strictly positive in an interval, the function should be strictly increasing. Indeed,

$$f'(x) > 0 \text{ for all } x \text{ in the interval } I \Longrightarrow f(x) \text{ is strictly increasing in } I \qquad (4)$$

$$f'(x) < 0 \text{ for all } x \text{ in the interval } I \Longrightarrow f(x) \text{ is strictly decreasing in } I \qquad (5)$$

The implications in (4) and (5) give sufficient conditions for f to be strictly increasing or decreasing. They cannot be reversed to give necessary conditions. For example, if $f(x) = x^3$, then $f'(0) = 0$. Yet f is strictly increasing. (See Problem 3.)

NOTE 1   In student papers (and economics books), the following statement is often seen: "Suppose that f is strictly increasing—that is, $f'(x) > 0$." The example $f(x) = x^3$ shows that the statement is wrong. A function can be strictly increasing even though the derivative is 0 at certain points. In fact, suppose that $f'(x) \geq 0$ for all x in I and $f'(x) = 0$ at only a finite number of points in I. Then $f'(x) > 0$ in any subinterval between two zeros of $f'(x)$, and so f is strictly increasing on each such subinterval. It follows that f is strictly increasing on the whole interval.

1. By using (1) and (2) in this section, as well as (6) in the previous section, examine where $f(x) = x^2 - 4x + 3$ is increasing/decreasing. (Compare with Fig. 4.3.3.)

2. Examine where $f(x) = -x^3 + 4x^2 - x - 6$ is increasing/decreasing. (Use the result in Problem 9 in the previous section. Compare with Fig. 4.7.1.)

3. Show that $f(x) = x^3$ is strictly increasing. (*Hint:* Consider the sign of
$$x_2^3 - x_1^3 = (x_2 - x_1)(x_1^2 + x_1 x_2 + x_2^2) = (x_2 - x_1)\left[\left(x_1 + \tfrac{1}{2}x_2\right)^2 + \tfrac{3}{4}x_2^2\right].)$$

6.4 Rates of Change

The derivative of a function was defined as the slope of the tangent to its graph at a particular point. In economics, other interpretations are more important. Consider first how the derivative can be interpreted as a rate of change.

Suppose that a quantity y is related to a quantity x by $y = f(x)$. If x has the value a, then the value of the function is $f(a)$. Suppose that a is changed to $a + h$. The new value of y is $f(a + h)$, and the change in the value of the function when x is changed from a to $a + h$ is $f(a + h) - f(a)$. The change in y per unit change in x has a particular name, the *average rate of change of f over the interval from a to $a + h$*. It is equal to

$$\frac{f(a + h) - f(a)}{h}$$

Note that this fraction is precisely the Newton quotient of f. Taking the limit as h tends to 0 gives the derivative of f at a, and we define:

The **instantaneous rate of change** of f at a is $f'(a)$

This very important concept appears whenever we study quantities that change. When time is the independent variable, we often use the "dot notation" for differentiation with respect to time. For example, if $x(t) = t^2$, we write $\dot{x}(t) = 2t$.

Sometimes we are interested in studying the proportion $f'(a)/f(a)$:

The **relative rate of change** of f at a is $\dfrac{f'(a)}{f(a)}$

In economics, relative rates of change are often seen. Sometimes they are called **proportional rates of change**. They are usually quoted in percentages per unit of time—for example, percentages per year (or per annum, for those who think Latin is still a useful language). Often we will describe a variable as increasing at, say, 3% a year if there is a relative rate of change of 3/100 each year.

EXAMPLE 1   Let $N(t)$ be the number of individuals in a population (of, say, humans, animals, or plants) at time t. If t increases to $t + h$, then the change in population is equal to $N(t + h) - N(t)$ individuals. Hence,

$$\frac{N(t + h) - N(t)}{h}$$

is *the average rate of change*. Taking the limit as h tends to 0 gives $\dot{N}(t) = dN/dt$ for *the rate of change of population at time t.*

In Example 4.5.1 the formula $P = 6.4t + 641$ estimated (misleadingly) the number (in millions) of inhabitants in Europe t years after 1960. In this case, the rate of change is $dP/dt = 6.4$ million per year, the same for all t.

EXAMPLE 2   Consider a firm producing some commodity in a given period. Let

$$C(x) = \text{cost of producing } x \text{ units}$$

$$R(x) = \text{revenue from selling } x \text{ units}$$

$$\pi(x) = R(x) - C(x) = \text{profit from producing (and selling) } x \text{ units}$$

We call $C'(x)$ the **marginal cost** (at x), $R'(x)$ the **marginal revenue**, and $\pi'(x)$ the **marginal profit**. Economists often use the word **marginal** in this way in order to signify a derivative.

Other examples of the derivative in economics include the following. The **marginal propensity to consume** is the derivative of the consumption function with respect to income; similarly, the **marginal product** (or **productivity**) **of labour** is the derivative of the production function with respect to labour input.

According to the definition, marginal cost is equal to

$$C'(x) = \lim_{h \to 0} \frac{C(x + h) - C(x)}{h} \qquad \text{(\textbf{marginal cost})} \tag{1}$$

When h is small in absolute value, we obtain the approximation

$$C'(x) \approx \frac{C(x + h) - C(x)}{h}$$

Thus for h small, a linear approximation to $C(x + h)$ is $C(x) + hC'(x)$.

If we put $h = 1$, we get

$$C'(x) \approx C(x + 1) - C(x)$$

Marginal cost is then approximately equal to the **incremental cost** $C(x + 1) - C(x)$, that is, the *additional cost of producing one more unit of x*. In elementary economics books marginal cost is often defined as the difference $C(x + 1) - C(x)$ because more appropriate concepts from differential calculus cannot be used.

EXAMPLE 3   Let $C(x)$ denote the cost in millions of dollars for removing $x\%$ of the pollution in a lake. Give an economic interpretation to $C'(50) = 3$.

Solution: Since

$$C'(50) \approx C(50 + 1) - C(50),$$

the interpretation of $C'(50) = 3$ is that it costs about 3 million dollars extra to remove 51% instead of 50% of the pollution.

EXAMPLE 4   Let $K(t)$ be the capital stock in an economy at time t. The rate of change $\dot{K}(t)$ of $K(t)$ is called the **rate of investment**[1] at time t. It is usually denoted by $I(t)$, so

$$\dot{K}(t) = I(t) \tag{2}$$

Differentiability and Empirical Functions

The very definition of the derivative assumes that arbitrarily small increments in the independent variable are possible. In practical problems it is impossible to implement, or even measure, arbitrarily small changes in the variable. For example, economic quantities that vary with time, such as the price of a commodity or the national income of a country, are usually measured at intervals of days, weeks, or years. Further, the cost functions of the type we discussed in Example 2 are often defined only for integer values of x. In all these cases, the variables only take discrete values. The graphs of such functions, therefore, will only consist of discrete points. For functions of this type in which time and numbers both change discretely, the concept of the derivative is not defined. To remedy this, the actual function is usually replaced by a differentiable function that is a "good approximation" to the original function.

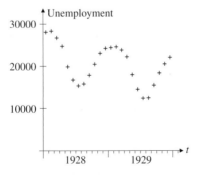

Figure 1 Unemployment in Norway (1928–1929)

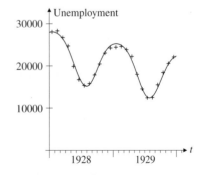

Figure 2 A smooth curve approximating the points in Fig. 1.

As an illustration, Fig. 1 graphs observations of the number of registered unemployed in Norway for each month of the years 1928–1929. This was a period in which Norway was still largely an agricultural economy, in which unemployment rose during the autumn and fell during the spring. In Fig. 2 we show the graph of a differentiable function that approximates the points plotted in Fig. 1.

[1] Actually, it is the *net* rate of investment. Some investment is needed to replace depreciated capital; including this as well gives *gross* investment.

1. Let $C(x) = x^2 + 3x + 100$ be the cost function of a firm. Show that the average rate of change when x is changed from 100 to $100 + h$ is

$$\frac{C(100 + h) - C(100)}{h} = 203 + h \qquad (h \neq 0)$$

What is the marginal cost $C'(100)$? Use (6) in Section 6.2 to find $C'(x)$ and, in particular, $C'(100)$.

2. If the cost function of a firm is $C(x) = kx + I$, give economic interpretations of the parameters k and I.

3. If the total saving of a country is a function $S(Y)$ of the national product Y, then $S'(Y)$ is called the *marginal propensity to save* (MPS). Find the MPS for the following functions:

   (a) $S(Y) = a + bY$ \qquad\qquad (b) $S(Y) = 100 + 10Y + 2Y^2$

4. If the tax a family pays is a function of its income y given by $T(y)$, then $T'(y)$ is called the *marginal tax rate*. Characterize the following tax function by determining its marginal rate:

$$T(y) = ty \qquad (t \text{ is a constant number} \in (0, 1))$$

5. Let $x(t)$ denote the number of barrels of oil left in a well at time t, where time is measured in minutes. What is the interpretation of $\dot{x}(0) = -3$?

6. The total cost of producing x units of a commodity is

$$C(x) = x^3 - 90x^2 + 7500x, \qquad x \geq 0$$

   (a) Compute the marginal cost function $C'(x)$. (Use the result in Problem 6.2.9.)

   (b) For which value of x is the marginal cost the least?

7. Refer to the definitions given in Example 2. Compute the marginal revenue, marginal cost, and marginal profit in the following two cases, and in each case find an expression for the value of x at which the marginal profit is equal to 0:

   (a) $R(x) = ax$, \qquad $C(x) = a_1 x^2 + b_1 x + c_1$

   (b) $R(x) = ax - bx^2$, \qquad $C(x) = a_1 x + b_1$

6.5 A Dash of Limits

The previous section defined the derivative of a function based on the concept of a limit. The same concept is important for many other reasons as well, so now we should take a closer look. Here we give a preliminary definition and formulate some important rules for limits. In Section 7.8, we discuss the limit concept more closely.

EXAMPLE 1   Consider the function F defined by the formula

$$F(x) = \frac{e^x - 1}{x}$$

where $e \approx 2.7$ is the base for the natural exponential function. (See Section 4.9.) Note that if $x = 0$, then $e^0 = 1$, and the fraction collapses to the absurd expression "0/0." Thus, the function F is not defined for $x = 0$, but one can still ask what happens to $F(x)$ when x is close to 0. Using a calculator (except when $x = 0$), we find the values shown in Table 1.

Table 1 Values of $F(x) = (e^x - 1)/x$ when x is close to 0

x	-1	-0.1	-0.001	-0.0001	0.0	0.0001	0.001	0.1	1
$F(x)$	0.632	0.956	0.999	1.000	*	1.000	1.001	1.052	1.718

* not defined

From the table it appears that as x gets closer and closer to 0, so the fraction $F(x)$ gets closer and closer to 1. It therefore seems reasonable to assume that $F(x)$ tends to 1 in the limit as x tends to 0. We write[2]

$$\lim_{x \to 0} \frac{e^x - 1}{x} = 1 \quad \text{or} \quad \frac{e^x - 1}{x} \to 1 \quad \text{as} \quad x \to 0$$

Figure 1 shows a portion of the graph of F. The function F is defined for all x, except at $x = 0$, and $\lim_{x \to 0} F(x) = 1$. (A small circle is used to indicate that the corresponding point $(0, 1)$ is not in the graph of F.)

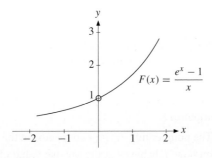

$$F(x) = \frac{e^x - 1}{x}$$

Figure 1

---

[2] Indeed, later it will be shown that the number e is defined so that this limit is 1.

Suppose, in general, that a function f is defined for all x near a, but not necessarily at $x = a$. Then we say that $f(x)$ has the number A as its limit as x tends to a, if $f(x)$ tends to A as x tends to (but is not equal to) a. We write

$$\lim_{x \to a} f(x) = A \qquad \text{or} \qquad f(x) \to A \quad \text{as} \quad x \to a$$

It is possible, however, that the value of $f(x)$ does not tend to any fixed number as x tends to a. Then we say that $\lim_{x \to a} f(x)$ *does not exist*, or that $f(x)$ *does not have a limit as x tends to a.*

EXAMPLE 2 Examine the limit $\lim\limits_{h \to 0} \dfrac{\sqrt{h+1}-1}{h}$ using a calculator.

Solution: By choosing numbers h close to 0, we find the following table:

Table 2 Values of $F(h) = (\sqrt{h+1}-1)/h$ when h is close to 0

h	−0.5	−0.2	−0.1	−0.01	0.0	0.01	0.1	0.2	0.5
$F(h)$	0.586	0.528	0.513	0.501	*	0.499	0.488	0.477	0.449

* not defined

This suggests that $\lim\limits_{h \to 0} \dfrac{\sqrt{h+1}-1}{h} = 0.5$.

The limits found previously were both based on shaky numerical foundations. For instance, in Example 2, can we really be certain that our guess is correct? Could it be that if we chose h values even closer to 0, the fraction would tend to a limit other than 0.5, or maybe not have any limit at all? Further numerical computations will support our belief that the initial guess is correct, but we can never make a table that has *all* the values of h close to 0, so numerical computation alone can never establish with certainty what the limit is. This illustrates the need to have a rigorous procedure for finding limits, based on a precise mathematical definition of the limit concept. This definition is given in Section 7.8, but we shall not elaborate here on the foundations of limits. Instead, we give a preliminary definition which will convey the right idea.

> Writing $\lim_{x \to a} f(x) = A$ means that we can make $f(x)$ as close to A as we want for all x sufficiently close to (but not equal to) a. (1)

We emphasize:

(a) The number $\lim_{x \to a} f(x)$ depends on the value of $f(x)$ for x-values close to a, but not on how f behaves at the precise value of $x = a$. When finding $\lim_{x \to a} f(x)$, we are simply not interested in the value $f(a)$, or even in whether f is defined at a.

(b) When we compute $\lim_{x \to a} f(x)$, we must take into consideration x-values on both sides of a.

Rules for Limits

Of course, one cannot really determine limits by means of numerical computations. Instead, we use some simple rules for finding limits whose validity can be shown once we have a precise definition of the limit concept. These rules are very straightforward and we have even used a few of them already in the previous section.

Suppose that f and g are defined as functions of x in a neighbourhood of a (but not necessarily at a). Then we have the following rules written down for easy reference:[3]

RULES FOR LIMITS

If $\lim\limits_{x \to a} f(x) = A$ and $\lim\limits_{x \to a} g(x) = B$, then

(a) $\lim\limits_{x \to a} \big(f(x) \pm g(x)\big) = A \pm B$

(b) $\lim\limits_{x \to a} \big(f(x) \cdot g(x)\big) = A \cdot B$ \hfill (2)

(c) $\lim\limits_{x \to a} \dfrac{f(x)}{g(x)} = \dfrac{A}{B}$ \quad (if $B \neq 0$)

(d) $\lim\limits_{x \to a} \big(f(x)\big)^r = A^r$ \quad (if A^r is defined and r is any real number)

It is easy to give intuitive explanations for these rules. Suppose that $\lim_{x \to a} f(x) = A$ and that $\lim_{x \to a} g(x) = B$. Then we know that, when x is close to a, then $f(x)$ is close to A and $g(x)$ is close to B. So intuitively the sum $f(x) + g(x)$ is close to $A + B$, the difference $f(x) - g(x)$ is close to $A - B$, the product $f(x)g(x)$ is close to $A \cdot B$, and so on.

These rules can be used repeatedly to obtain new extended rules such as

$$\lim_{x \to a} [f_1(x) + f_2(x) + \cdots + f_n(x)] = \lim_{x \to a} f_1(x) + \lim_{x \to a} f_2(x) + \cdots + \lim_{x \to a} f_n(x)$$

$$\lim_{x \to a} [f_1(x) \cdot f_2(x) \cdots f_n(x)] = \lim_{x \to a} f_1(x) \cdot \lim_{x \to a} f_2(x) \cdots \lim_{x \to a} f_n(x)$$

In words: *the limit of a sum is the sum of the limits, and the limit of a product is equal to the product of the limits.*

Suppose the function $f(x)$ is equal to the same constant value c for every x. Then

$$\lim_{x \to a} c = c \qquad \text{(at every point } a\text{)}$$

It is also evident that if $f(x) = x$, then

$$\lim_{x \to a} f(x) = \lim_{x \to a} x = a \qquad \text{(at every point } a\text{)}$$

Combining these two simple limits with the general rules allows easy computation of the limits for certain combinations of functions.

---

[3] Using the identities $f(x) - g(x) = f(x) + (-1)g(x)$, and $f(x)/g(x) = f(x)(g(x))^{-1}$, it is clear that some of these rules follow from others.

EXAMPLE 3   Compute the following limits:

(a) $\lim_{x \to -2} (x^2 + 5x)$ (b) $\lim_{x \to 4} \dfrac{2x^{3/2} - \sqrt{x}}{x^2 - 15}$ (c) $\lim_{x \to a} Ax^n$

Solution: Using the rules for limits, we get

(a) $\lim_{x \to -2} (x^2 + 5x) = \lim_{x \to -2} (x \cdot x) + \lim_{x \to -2} (5 \cdot x)$

$= \left(\lim_{x \to -2} x \right)\left(\lim_{x \to -2} x \right) + \left(\lim_{x \to -2} 5 \right)\left(\lim_{x \to -2} x \right)$

$= (-2)(-2) + 5 \cdot (-2) = -6$

(b) $\lim_{x \to 4} \dfrac{2x^{3/2} - \sqrt{x}}{x^2 - 15} = \dfrac{2 \lim_{x \to 4} x^{3/2} - \lim_{x \to 4} \sqrt{x}}{\lim_{x \to 4} x^2 - 15} = \dfrac{2 \cdot 4^{3/2} - \sqrt{4}}{4^2 - 15} = \dfrac{2 \cdot 8 - 2}{16 - 15} = 14$

(c) $\lim_{x \to a} Ax^n = \left(\lim_{x \to a} A \right)\left(\lim_{x \to a} x^n \right) = A \cdot \left(\lim_{x \to a} x \right)^n = A \cdot a^n$

It was easy to find the limits in this last example by using the rules for limits. Examples 1 and 2 are more difficult. They involve a fraction whose numerator and denominator both tend to 0. A simple observation can sometimes help us find such limits (provided that they exist). Because $\lim_{x \to a} f(x)$ can only depend on the values of f when x is close to, but not equal to a, we have the following:

If the functions f and g are equal for all x close to a (but not necessarily at $x = a$), then $\lim_{x \to a} f(x) = \lim_{x \to a} g(x)$ whenever either limit exists.   (3)

Here are some examples of how this rule works.

EXAMPLE 4   Compute the limit

$$\lim_{x \to 2} \frac{3x^2 + 3x - 18}{x - 2}$$

Solution: We see that both numerator and denominator tend to 0 as x tends to 2. Because the numerator $3x^2 + 3x - 18$ is equal to 0 for $x = 2$, it has $x - 2$ as a factor. In fact, $3x^2 + 3x - 18 = 3(x - 2)(x + 3)$. Hence,

$$f(x) = \frac{3x^2 + 3x - 18}{x - 2} = \frac{3(x - 2)(x + 3)}{x - 2}$$

For $x \neq 2$, we can cancel $x - 2$ from both numerator and denominator to obtain $3(x + 3)$. So the functions $f(x)$ and $g(x) = 3(x + 3)$ are equal for all $x \neq 2$. By (3), it follows that

$$\lim_{x \to 2} \frac{3x^2 + 3x - 18}{x - 2} = \lim_{x \to 2} 3(x + 3) = 3(2 + 3) = 15$$

EXAMPLE 5   Compute the following limits: (a) $\lim\limits_{h\to 0} \dfrac{\sqrt{h+1}-1}{h}$ (b) $\lim\limits_{x\to 4} \dfrac{x^2-16}{4\sqrt{x}-8}$.

Solution:

(a) The numerator and the denominator both tend to 0 as h tends to 0. Here we must use a little trick. We multiply both numerator and denominator by $\sqrt{h+1}+1$ to get

$$\frac{\sqrt{h+1}-1}{h} = \frac{\left(\sqrt{h+1}-1\right)\left(\sqrt{h+1}+1\right)}{h\left(\sqrt{h+1}+1\right)} = \frac{h+1-1}{h\left(\sqrt{h+1}+1\right)} = \frac{1}{\sqrt{h+1}+1}$$

where the common factor h has been cancelled. For all $h \neq 0$ (and $h \geq -1$), the given function is equal to $1/(\sqrt{h+1}+1)$, which tends to $1/2$ as h tends to 0. We conclude that the limit of our function is equal to $1/2$, which confirms the result in Example 2.

(b) We must try to simplify the fraction because $x = 4$ gives $0/0$. Again we can use a trick to factorize the fraction as follows:

$$\frac{x^2-16}{4\sqrt{x}-8} = \frac{(x+4)(x-4)}{4\left(\sqrt{x}-2\right)} = \frac{(x+4)\left(\sqrt{x}+2\right)\left(\sqrt{x}-2\right)}{4\left(\sqrt{x}-2\right)} \qquad (*)$$

Here we have used the factorization $x - 4 = \left(\sqrt{x}+2\right)\left(\sqrt{x}-2\right)$, which is correct for $x \geq 0$. In the last fraction of $(*)$, we can cancel $\sqrt{x}-2$ when $\sqrt{x}-2 \neq 0$—that is, when $x \neq 4$. Using (3) again gives

$$\lim_{x\to 4} \frac{x^2-16}{4\sqrt{x}-8} = \lim_{x\to 4} \frac{1}{4}(x+4)(\sqrt{x}+2) = \frac{1}{4}(4+4)(\sqrt{4}+2) = 8 \qquad \blacksquare$$

PROBLEMS FOR SECTION 6.5

1. Determine the following by using the rules for limits:

   (a) $\lim\limits_{x\to 0} (3+2x^2)$

   (b) $\lim\limits_{x\to -1} \dfrac{3+2x}{x-1}$

   (c) $\lim\limits_{x\to 2} (2x^2+5)^3$

   (d) $\lim\limits_{t\to 8} \left(5t + t^2 - \frac{1}{8}t^3\right)$

   (e) $\lim\limits_{y\to 0} \dfrac{(y+1)^5 - y^5}{y+1}$

   (f) $\lim\limits_{z\to -2} \dfrac{1/z+2}{z}$

2. Examine the following limits numerically by using a calculator:

   (a) $\lim\limits_{h\to 0} \dfrac{2^h - 1}{h}$

   (b) $\lim\limits_{h\to 0} \dfrac{3^h - 1}{h}$

   (c) $\lim\limits_{\lambda\to 0} \dfrac{3^\lambda - 2^\lambda}{\lambda}$

3. Consider the following limit:

$$\lim_{x\to 1} \frac{x^2 + 7x - 8}{x - 1}$$

   (a) Examine the limit numerically by making a table of values of the fraction when x is close to 1.

   (b) Find the limit precisely by using the method in Example 4.

4. Compute the following limits:

(a) $\lim\limits_{x \to 2}(x^2 + 3x - 5)$ (b) $\lim\limits_{y \to -3}\dfrac{1}{y + 8}$ (c) $\lim\limits_{x \to 0}\dfrac{x^3 - 2x - 1}{x^5 - x^2 - 1}$

(d) $\lim\limits_{x \to 0}\dfrac{x^3 + 3x^2 - 2x}{x}$ (e) $\lim\limits_{h \to 0}\dfrac{(x + h)^3 - x^3}{h}$ (f) $\lim\limits_{x \to 0}\dfrac{(x + h)^3 - x^3}{h}$ $(h \neq 0)$

5. Compute the following limits:

(a) $\lim\limits_{h \to 2}\dfrac{\frac{1}{3} - \frac{2}{3h}}{h - 2}$ (b) $\lim\limits_{x \to 0}\dfrac{x^2 - 1}{x^2}$ (c) $\lim\limits_{t \to 3}\sqrt[3]{\dfrac{32t - 96}{t^2 - 2t - 3}}$

(d) $\lim\limits_{h \to 0}\dfrac{\sqrt{h + 3} - \sqrt{3}}{h}$ (e) $\lim\limits_{t \to -2}\dfrac{t^2 - 4}{t^2 + 10t + 16}$ (f) $\lim\limits_{x \to 4}\dfrac{2 - \sqrt{x}}{4 - x}$

6. If $f(x) = x^2 + 2x$, compute the following limits:

(a) $\lim\limits_{x \to 1}\dfrac{f(x) - f(1)}{x - 1}$ (b) $\lim\limits_{x \to 2}\dfrac{f(x) - f(1)}{x - 1}$ (c) $\lim\limits_{h \to 0}\dfrac{f(2 + h) - f(2)}{h}$

(d) $\lim\limits_{x \to a}\dfrac{f(x) - f(a)}{x - a}$ (e) $\lim\limits_{h \to 0}\dfrac{f(a + h) - f(a)}{h}$ (f) $\lim\limits_{h \to 0}\dfrac{f(a + h) - f(a - h)}{h}$

HARDER PROBLEMS

7. Find the factors that allow you to compute the following limits. (*Hint:* For part (b), write the fraction as a function of $u = \sqrt[3]{27 + h}$.)

(a) $\lim\limits_{x \to 2}\dfrac{x^2 - 2x}{x^3 - 8}$ (b) $\lim\limits_{h \to 0}\dfrac{\sqrt[3]{27 + h} - 3}{h}$ (c) $\lim\limits_{x \to 1}\dfrac{x^n - 1}{x - 1}$ (*n* is a natural number)

6.6 Simple Rules for Differentiation

The derivative of a function f was defined by the formula

$$f'(x) = \lim_{h \to 0}\frac{f(x + h) - f(x)}{h} \qquad (*)$$

If this limit exists, we say that f is **differentiable** at x. The process of finding the derivative of a function is called **differentiation**. It is useful to think of this as an operation that transforms one function f into a new function f'. The function f' is then defined for the values of x where the limit in $(*)$ exists. If $y = f(x)$, we can use the symbols y' and dy/dx as alternatives to $f'(x)$.

In Section 6.2 we used formula $(*)$ to find the derivatives of some simple functions. However, it is difficult and time consuming to apply the definition directly in each separate case. We now embark on a systematic program to find general rules which ultimately will give mechanical and efficient procedures for finding the derivative of very many differentiable functions specified by a formula, even one that is complicated. We start with some simple rules.

If f is a constant function, then its derivative is 0:

$$f(x) = A \implies f'(x) = 0 \tag{1}$$

The result is easy to see geometrically. The graph of $f(x) = A$ is a straight line parallel to the x-axis. The tangent to the graph has slope 0 at each point (see Fig. 1). You should now use the definition of $f'(x)$ to get the same answer.

The next two rules are also very useful.

$$y = A + f(x) \implies y' = f'(x) \quad \text{(Additive constants disappear)} \tag{2}$$

$$y = Af(x) \implies y' = Af'(x) \quad \text{(Multiplicative constants are preserved)} \tag{3}$$

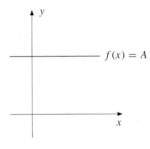

Figure 1 The derivative
of a constant is 0

Figure 2 The graphs of the functions
are parallel, and the functions have
the same derivative at each point

Rule (2) is illustrated in Fig. 2, where A is positive. The graph of $A + f(x)$ is that of $f(x)$ shifted upwards by A units in the direction of the y-axis. So the tangents to the two curves $y = f(x)$ and $y = f(x) + A$ at the same value of x must be parallel. In particular, they must have the same slope. Again you should try to use the definition of $f'(x)$ to give a formal proof of this assertion.

Let us prove rule (3) by using the definition of a derivative. If $g(x) = Af(x)$, then $g(x + h) - g(x) = Af(x + h) - Af(x) = A[f(x + h) - f(x)]$, and so

$$g'(x) = \lim_{h \to 0} \frac{g(x + h) - g(x)}{h} = A \lim_{h \to 0} \frac{f(x + h) - f(x)}{h} = Af'(x)$$

Here is a practical illustration of rule (3): If $f(t)$ denotes the sales revenue at time t of firm A, and firm B's sales revenue $g(t)$ at each time is 3 times larger than that of A, then the growth rate of B is 3 times larger than that of A. In mathematical notation: $g(t) = 3f(t) \implies g'(t) = 3f'(t)$. However, the firms *relative* growth rates $f'(t)/f(t)$ and $g'(t)/g(t)$ will be equal.

In Leibniz's notation, the three results are as follows:

$$\frac{d}{dx} A = 0, \qquad \frac{d}{dx}[A + f(x)] = \frac{d}{dx} f(x), \qquad \frac{d}{dx}[Af(x)] = A \frac{d}{dx} f(x)$$

EXAMPLE 1   Suppose we know $f'(x)$. Find the derivatives of

(a) $5 + f(x)$ (b) $f(x) - \dfrac{1}{2}$ (c) $4f(x)$ (d) $-\dfrac{f(x)}{5}$ (e) $\dfrac{Af(x) + B}{C}$

Solution: We obtain

(a) $\dfrac{d}{dx}(5 + f(x)) = f'(x)$

(b) $\dfrac{d}{dx}\left(f(x) - \dfrac{1}{2}\right) = \dfrac{d}{dx}\left(-\dfrac{1}{2} + f(x)\right) = f'(x)$

(c) $\dfrac{d}{dx}(4f(x)) = 4f'(x)$

(d) $\dfrac{d}{dx}\left(-\dfrac{f(x)}{5}\right) = \dfrac{d}{dx}\left(-\dfrac{1}{5}f(x)\right) = -\dfrac{1}{5}f'(x)$

(e) $\dfrac{d}{dx}\left(\dfrac{Af(x) + B}{C}\right) = \dfrac{d}{dx}\left(\dfrac{A}{C}f(x) + \dfrac{B}{C}\right) = \dfrac{A}{C}f'(x)$ ∎

Power Rule

Few rules of differentiation are more useful than the following:

$$f(x) = x^a \implies f'(x) = ax^{a-1} \qquad \text{(}a\text{ is an arbitrary constant)} \tag{4}$$

For $a = 2$ and $a = 3$ this rule was confirmed in Section 6.2. The method used in these two examples can be generalized to the case where a is an arbitrary natural number. Later we shall see that the rule is valid for all real numbers a.

EXAMPLE 2   Compute the derivative of: (a) $y = x^5$ (b) $y = 3x^8$ (c) $y = \dfrac{x^{100}}{100}$.

Solution:

(a) $y = x^5 \implies y' = 5x^{5-1} = 5x^4$

(b) $y = 3x^8 \implies y' = 3 \cdot 8x^{8-1} = 24x^7$

(c) $y = \dfrac{x^{100}}{100} = \dfrac{1}{100}x^{100} \implies y' = \dfrac{1}{100}100x^{100-1} = x^{99}$ ∎

EXAMPLE 3   Compute:

(a) $\dfrac{d}{dx}\left(x^{-0.33}\right)$ (b) $\dfrac{d}{dr}(-5r^{-3})$ (c) $\dfrac{d}{dp}(Ap^\alpha + B)$ (d) $\dfrac{d}{dx}\left(\dfrac{A}{\sqrt{x}}\right)$

Solution:

(a) $\dfrac{d}{dx}\left(x^{-0.33}\right) = -0.33x^{-0.33-1} = -0.33x^{-1.33}$

(b) $\dfrac{d}{dr}(-5r^{-3}) = (-5)(-3)r^{-3-1} = 15r^{-4}$

(c) $\dfrac{d}{dp}(Ap^{\alpha} + B) = A\alpha p^{\alpha-1}$

(d) $\dfrac{d}{dx}\left(\dfrac{A}{\sqrt{x}}\right) = \dfrac{d}{dx}(Ax^{-1/2}) = A\left(-\dfrac{1}{2}\right)x^{-1/2-1} = -\dfrac{A}{2}x^{-3/2} = \dfrac{-A}{2x\sqrt{x}}$

EXAMPLE 4   The so-called **Pareto income distribution** is described by the formula

$$f(r) = \frac{B}{r^{\beta}} = Br^{-\beta}, \qquad r > 0 \tag{5}$$

where B and β are positive constants and r is income measured in, say, dollars. Here $f(r)\Delta r$ is approximately the proportion of the population who earn between r and $r + \Delta r$ dollars. See Section 9.4. Empirical estimates of β have usually been in the interval $2.4 < \beta < 2.6$, and the distribution function gives a good approximation only for income above a certain level. Compute $f'(r)$ and comment on its sign.

Solution: We find that

$$f'(r) = -\beta Br^{-\beta-1} = -\frac{\beta B}{r^{\beta+1}}$$

So $f'(r) < 0$, and $f(r)$ is strictly decreasing.

PROBLEMS FOR SECTION 6.6

1. Compute the derivative of the following functions of x:

   (a) $y = 5$ (b) $y = x^4$ (c) $y = 9x^{10}$ (d) $y = \pi^7$

2. Suppose we know $g'(x)$. Find an expression for the derivative of the following:

   (a) $2g(x) + 3$ (b) $-\frac{1}{6}g(x) + 8$ (c) $\dfrac{g(x) - 5}{3}$

3. Find the derivative of the following:

   (a) x^6 (b) $3x^{11}$ (c) x^{50} (d) $-4x^{-7}$

   (e) $\dfrac{x^{12}}{12}$ (f) $-\dfrac{2}{x^2}$ (g) $\dfrac{3}{\sqrt[3]{x}}$ (h) $-\dfrac{2}{x\sqrt{x}}$

4. Compute the following: (a) $\dfrac{d}{dr}(4\pi r^2)$ (b) $\dfrac{d}{dy}\left(Ay^{b+1}\right)$ (c) $\dfrac{d}{dA}\left(\dfrac{1}{A^2\sqrt{A}}\right)$

5. Explain why

$$f'(a) = \lim_{x \to a} \frac{f(x) - f(a)}{x - a}$$

Use this to find $f'(a)$ when $f(x) = x^2$.

6. For each of the following functions, find a function $F(x)$ that has $f(x)$ as its derivative, that is $F'(x) = f(x)$. (Note that you are not asked to find $f'(x)$.)

(a) $f(x) = x^2$ (b) $f(x) = 2x + 3$ (c) $f(x) = x^a$ $(a \neq -1)$

HARDER PROBLEMS

7. The following limits are all written in the form $\lim_{h \to 0} [f(a+h) - f(a)]/h$. Use your knowledge of derivatives to find the limits.

(a) $\lim_{h \to 0} \dfrac{(5+h)^2 - 5^2}{h}$ (b) $\lim_{s \to 0} \dfrac{(s+1)^5 - 1}{s}$ (c) $\lim_{h \to 0} \dfrac{5(x+h)^2 + 10 - 5x^2 - 10}{h}$

6.7 Sums, Products, and Quotients

If we know $f'(x)$ and $g'(x)$, then what are the derivatives of $f(x) + g(x)$, $f(x) - g(x)$, $f(x) \cdot g(x)$, and $f(x)/g(x)$? You will probably guess the first two correctly, but are less likely to be right about the last two (unless you have already learned the answers).

Sums and Differences

Suppose f and g are both defined in a set A of real numbers.

DIFFERENTIATION OF SUMS AND DIFFERENCES

If both f and g are differentiable at x, then the sum $f + g$ and the difference $f - g$ is differentiable at x, and

$$F(x) = f(x) \pm g(x) \implies F'(x) = f'(x) \pm g'(x)$$

(1)

In Leibniz's notation:

$$\frac{d}{dx}\big(f(x) \pm g(x)\big) = \frac{d}{dx}f(x) \pm \frac{d}{dx}g(x)$$

Proof for the case $F(x) = f(x) + g(x)$***:*** The Newton quotient of F is

$$\frac{F(x+h) - F(x)}{h} = \frac{(f(x+h) + g(x+h)) - (f(x) + g(x))}{h}$$

$$= \frac{f(x+h) - f(x)}{h} + \frac{g(x+h) - g(x)}{h}$$

When $h \to 0$, the last two fractions tend to $f'(x)$ and $g'(x)$, respectively, and thus the sum of the fractions tends to $f'(x) + g'(x)$. Hence,

$$F'(x) = \lim_{h \to 0} \frac{F(x+h) - F(x)}{h} = f'(x) + g'(x)$$

The proof of the other case is similar—only some of the signs change in the obvious way. ∎

EXAMPLE 1   Compute $\dfrac{d}{dx}\left(3x^8 + \dfrac{x^{100}}{100}\right)$.

Solution:

$$\frac{d}{dx}\left(3x^8 + \frac{x^{100}}{100}\right) = \frac{d}{dx}(3x^8) + \frac{d}{dx}\left(\frac{x^{100}}{100}\right) = 24x^7 + x^{99}$$

where we used (1) and the results from Example 6.6.2.

EXAMPLE 2   In Example 6.4.2 we defined the profit function as the difference between the revenues and the costs, $\pi(x) = R(x) - C(x)$. According to (1), $\pi'(x) = R'(x) - C'(x)$. In particular, $\pi'(x) = 0$ when $R'(x) = C'(x)$. In words: *Marginal profit is 0 when marginal revenue is equal to marginal cost.*

Rule (1) can be extended to sums of an arbitrary number of terms. For example,

$$\frac{d}{dx}(f(x) - g(x) + h(x)) = f'(x) - g'(x) + h'(x)$$

which we see by writing $f(x) - g(x) + h(x)$ as $(f(x) - g(x)) + h(x)$, and then using (1). Using the rules above makes it easy to differentiate any polynomial.

Products

Suppose $f(x) = x$ and $g(x) = x^2$, then $(f \cdot g)(x) = x^3$. Here $f'(x) = 1$, $g'(x) = 2x$, and $(f \cdot g)'(x) = 3x^2$. Hence, the derivative of $(f \cdot g)(x)$ is *not* equal to $f'(x) \cdot g'(x) = 2x$. The correct rule for differentiating a product is a little more complicated.

THE DERIVATIVE OF A PRODUCT

If both f and g are differentiable at the point x, then so is $F = f \cdot g$, and

$$F(x) = f(x) \cdot g(x) \implies F'(x) = f'(x) \cdot g(x) + f(x) \cdot g'(x)$$

(2)

Briefly formulated: *The derivative of the product of two functions is equal to the derivative of the first times the second, plus the first times the derivative of the second.* The formula, however, is much easier to digest than these words.

In Leibniz's notation, the product rule is expressed as:

$$\frac{d}{dx}[f(x) \cdot g(x)] = \left[\frac{d}{dx}f(x)\right] \cdot g(x) + f(x) \cdot \left[\frac{d}{dx}g(x)\right]$$

Before demonstrating why (2) is valid, here are two examples:

EXAMPLE 3   Find $h'(x)$ when $h(x) = (x^3 - x) \cdot (5x^4 + x^2)$.

Solution: We see that $h(x) = f(x) \cdot g(x)$ with $f(x) = x^3 - x$ and $g(x) = 5x^4 + x^2$. Here $f'(x) = 3x^2 - 1$ and $g'(x) = 20x^3 + 2x$. Thus,

$$h'(x) = f'(x) \cdot g(x) + f(x) \cdot g'(x) = (3x^2 - 1) \cdot (5x^4 + x^2) + (x^3 - x) \cdot (20x^3 + 2x)$$

Usually we simplify the answer by expanding to obtain just one polynomial. Simple computation gives

$$h'(x) = 35x^6 - 20x^4 - 3x^2$$

Alternatively, we can begin by expanding the expression for $h(x)$. Do so and verify that you get the same expression for $h'(x)$ as before.   ∎

EXAMPLE 4   We illustrate the product rule for differentiation by considering the extraction of oil from a well. Suppose that both the amount of oil extracted per unit of time and the price per unit change with time t. We define

(i) $x(t) =$ rate of extraction in barrels per day at time t

(ii) $p(t) =$ price in dollars per barrel at time t

Then we obtain

(iii) $R(t) = p(t)x(t)$ as the revenue in dollars per day

and according to the product rule (recalling that we often use "dot notation" for differentiation with respect to time),

(iv) $\dot{R}(t) = \dot{p}(t)x(t) + p(t)\dot{x}(t)$

The right-hand side of (iv) can be interpreted as follows. Suppose that $p(t)$ and $x(t)$ both increase over time, because of inflation and because the oil company operating the well steadily expands the capacity of its extraction equipment. Then $R(t)$ increases for two reasons. First, $R(t)$ increases because of the price increase. This increase is proportional to the amount of extraction $x(t)$ and is equal to $\dot{p}(t)x(t)$. But $R(t)$ also rises because extraction increases. Its contribution to the rate of change of $R(t)$ must be proportional to the price, and is equal to $p(t)\dot{x}(t)$. Equation (iv) merely expresses the simple fact that $\dot{R}(t)$, the total rate of change of $R(t)$, is the sum of these two parts.

Note too that the relative rate of growth of revenue can be found by dividing (iv) by (iii):

$$\frac{\dot{R}}{R} = \frac{\dot{p}x + p\dot{x}}{px} = \frac{\dot{p}}{p} + \frac{\dot{x}}{x}$$

In words, the relative rate of growth of revenue is the sum of the relative rates at which the price and quantity are changing.

We have now seen how to differentiate products of two functions. What about products of more than two functions? For example, suppose that

$$y = f(x)g(x)h(x)$$

What is y'? We extend the same technique shown earlier and put $y = \left[f(x)g(x)\right]h(x)$. Then the product rule gives[4]

$$
\begin{aligned}
y' &= [f(x)g(x)]' \, h(x) + [f(x)g(x)] \, h'(x) \\
&= \left[f'(x)g(x) + f(x)g'(x)\right] h(x) + f(x)g(x)h'(x) \\
&= f'(x)g(x)h(x) + f(x)g'(x)h(x) + f(x)g(x)h'(x)
\end{aligned}
$$

If none of the three functions is equal to 0, we can write the result in the following way:

$$\frac{(fgh)'}{fgh} = \frac{f'}{f} + \frac{g'}{g} + \frac{h'}{h}$$

By analogy, it is easy to write down the corresponding result for a product of n functions.

Proof of (2): Suppose f and g are differentiable at x, so that the two Newton quotients

$$\frac{f(x+h) - f(x)}{h} \quad \text{and} \quad \frac{g(x+h) - g(x)}{h}$$

tend to the limits $f'(x)$ and $g'(x)$, respectively, as h tends to 0. We must show that the Newton quotient of F also tends to a limit, which is given by $f'(x)g(x) + f(x)g'(x)$. The Newton quotient of F is

$$\frac{F(x+h) - F(x)}{h} = \frac{f(x+h)g(x+h) - f(x)g(x)}{h} \tag{*}$$

To proceed further we must somehow transform the right-hand side (RHS) to involve the Newton quotients of f and g. We use a trick: The numerator of the RHS is unchanged if we both subtract and add the number $f(x)g(x+h)$. Hence, with suitable regrouping of the terms, we have

$$\frac{F(x+h) - F(x)}{h} = \frac{f(x+h)g(x+h) - f(x)g(x+h) + f(x)g(x+h) - f(x)g(x)}{h}$$

$$= \frac{f(x+h) - f(x)}{h}g(x+h) + f(x)\frac{g(x+h) - g(x)}{h}$$

As h tends to 0, the two Newton quotients tend to $f'(x)$ and $g'(x)$, respectively. Now we can write $g(x+h)$ for $h \neq 0$ as

$$g(x+h) = \left[\frac{g(x+h) - g(x)}{h}\right]h + g(x)$$

By definition of $g'(x)$, this tends to $g'(x) \cdot 0 + g(x) = g(x)$ as h tends to 0. It follows that the Newton quotient of F tends to $f'(x)g(x) + f(x)g'(x)$ as h tends to 0. ∎

---

[4] This result is easier to show using logarithmic differentiation. See Example 6.11.4.

Quotients

Suppose $F(x) = f(x)/g(x)$, where f and g are differentiable in x with $g(x) \neq 0$. Bearing in mind the complications in the formula for the derivative of a product, one should be somewhat reluctant to make a quick guess as to the correct formula for $F'(x)$.

In fact, it is quite easy to find the formula for $F'(x)$ if we *assume* that $F(x)$ *is* differentiable. From

$$F(x) = \frac{f(x)}{g(x)}$$

it follows that $f(x) = F(x)g(x)$. Thus, the product rule gives

$$f'(x) = F'(x) \cdot g(x) + F(x) \cdot g'(x)$$

Solving for $F'(x)$ yields $F'(x) \cdot g(x) = f'(x) - F(x) \cdot g'(x)$, and so

$$F'(x) = \frac{f'(x) - F(x)g'(x)}{g(x)} = \frac{f'(x) - \left[\dfrac{f(x)}{g(x)}\right]g'(x)}{g(x)}$$

Multiplying both numerator and denominator of the last fraction by $g(x)$ gives the following important formula.

THE DERIVATIVE OF A QUOTIENT

If f and g are differentiable at x and $g(x) \neq 0$, then $F = f/g$ is differentiable at x, and

$$F(x) = \frac{f(x)}{g(x)} \implies F'(x) = \frac{f'(x) \cdot g(x) - f(x) \cdot g'(x)}{\left(g(x)\right)^2} \tag{3}$$

In words: *The derivative of a quotient is equal to the derivative of the numerator times the denominator minus the numerator times the derivative of the denominator, this difference then being divided by the square of the denominator.* In simpler notation, we have

$$\left(\frac{f}{g}\right)' = \frac{f'g - fg'}{g^2}$$

NOTE 1 In the product rule formula, the two functions appear symmetrically, so that it is easy to remember. In the formula for the derivative of a quotient, the expressions in the numerator must be in the right order. Here is how you check that you have the order right. Write down the formula you believe is correct. Put $g \equiv 1$. Then $g' \equiv 0$, and your formula ought to reduce to f'. If you get $-f'$, then your signs are wrong.

EXAMPLE 5   Compute $F'(x)$ and $F'(4)$ when

$$F(x) = \frac{3x - 5}{x - 2}$$

Solution: We apply (3) with $f(x) = 3x - 5$, $g(x) = x - 2$. Then $f'(x) = 3$ and $g'(x) = 1$. So we obtain, for $x \neq 2$:

$$F'(x) = \frac{3 \cdot (x - 2) - (3x - 5) \cdot 1}{(x - 2)^2} = \frac{3x - 6 - 3x + 5}{(x - 2)^2} = \frac{-1}{(x - 2)^2}$$

To find $F'(4)$, we put $x = 4$ in the formula for $F'(x)$ to get $F'(4) = -1/(4 - 2)^2 = -1/4$. Note that $F'(x) < 0$ for all $x \neq 2$. Hence F is strictly decreasing both for $x < 2$ and for $x > 2$. Note that $(3x - 5)/(x - 2) = 3 + 1/(x - 2)$. The graph is shown in Fig. 5.1.7.   ∎

EXAMPLE 6   Let $C(x)$ be the total cost of producing x units of a commodity. Then $C(x)/x$ is the *average cost* of producing x units. Find an expression for $\frac{d}{dx}\big[C(x)/x\big]$.

Solution:

$$\frac{d}{dx}\left(\frac{C(x)}{x}\right) = \frac{C'(x)x - C(x)}{x^2} = \frac{1}{x}\left(C'(x) - \frac{C(x)}{x}\right)$$

Note that the marginal cost $C'(x)$ exceeds the average cost $C(x)/x$ if and only if average cost increases as output increases. (In a similar way, if a basketball team recruits a new player, the average height of the team increases if and only if the new player's height exceeds the old average height.)   ∎

The formula for the derivative of a quotient becomes more symmetric if we consider relative rates of change. By using (3), simple computation shows that

$$F(x) = \frac{f(x)}{g(x)} \quad \Longrightarrow \quad \frac{F'(x)}{F(x)} = \frac{f'(x)}{f(x)} - \frac{g'(x)}{g(x)} \qquad (4)$$

The relative rate of change of a quotient is equal to the relative rate of change of the numerator minus the relative rate of change of the denominator.

Let $W(t)$ be the nominal wage rate and $P(t)$ the price index at time t. Then $w(t) = W(t)/P(t)$ is called the **real wage rate**. According to (4),

$$\frac{\dot{w}(t)}{w(t)} = \frac{\dot{W}(t)}{W(t)} - \frac{\dot{P}(t)}{P(t)}$$

The relative rate of change of the real wage rate is equal to the difference between the relative rates of change of the nominal wage rate and the price index. Thus, if nominal wages increase at the rate of 5% per year but prices rise by 6% per year, then real wages fall by 1%. Also, if inflation leads to wages and prices increasing at the same relative rate, then the real wage rate is constant.

PROBLEMS FOR SECTION 6.7

In Problems 1–4, differentiate the functions defined by the various formulas.

1. (a) $x + 1$ (b) $x + x^2$ (c) $3x^5 + 2x^4 + 5$

    (d) $8x^4 + 2\sqrt{x}$ (e) $\frac{1}{2}x - \frac{3}{2}x^2 + 5x^3$ (f) $1 - 3x^7$

2. (a) $\frac{3}{5}x^2 - 2x^7 + \frac{1}{8} - \sqrt{x}$ (b) $(2x^2 - 1)(x^4 - 1)$ (c) $\left(x^5 + \frac{1}{x}\right)(x^5 + 1)$

3. (a) $\dfrac{1}{x^6}$ (b) $x^{-1}(x^2 + 1)\sqrt{x}$ (c) $\dfrac{1}{\sqrt{x^3}}$ (d) $\dfrac{x+1}{x-1}$

    (e) $\dfrac{x+1}{x^5}$ (f) $\dfrac{3x-5}{2x+8}$ (g) $3x^{-11}$ (h) $\dfrac{3x-1}{x^2+x+1}$

4. (a) $\dfrac{\sqrt{x}-2}{\sqrt{x}+1}$ (b) $\dfrac{(x+1)(x-1)}{(x^2+2)(x+3)}$ (c) $(3x+1)\left(\dfrac{1}{x^2} + \dfrac{1}{x}\right)$

    (d) $\dfrac{x^2-1}{x^2+1}$ (e) $\dfrac{x^2+x+1}{x^2-x+1}$ (f) $\dfrac{1}{2} + \dfrac{1}{3}\left(\dfrac{x-1}{x+1}\right)(1+x^{-2})$

5. If $D(P)$ denotes the demand for a product when the price per unit is P, then the revenue function $R(P)$ is given by $R(P) = PD(P)$. Find an expression for $R'(P)$.

6. For each of the following functions, determine the intervals where f is increasing.

    (a) $f(x) = 3x^2 - 12x + 13$ (b) $f(x) = \frac{1}{4}(x^4 - 6x^2)$

    (c) $f(x) = \dfrac{2x}{x^2+2}$ (d) $f(x) = \dfrac{x^2-x^3}{2(x+1)}$

7. Find the equations for the tangents to the graphs of the following functions at the specified points:

    (a) $y = 3 - x - x^2$ at $x = 1$ (b) $y = \dfrac{x^2-1}{x^2+1}$ at $x = 1$

    (c) $y = \left(\dfrac{1}{x^2} + 1\right)(x^2 - 1)$ at $x = 2$ (d) $y = \dfrac{x^4+1}{(x^2+1)(x+3)}$ at $x = 0$

8. Consider the function f defined by the formula

$$f(x) = \frac{3x}{-x^2 + 4x - 1}$$

Compute $f'(x)$ and determine where the function increases by using a sign diagram . (The function is not defined for $x = 2 \pm \sqrt{3}$. Now examine Fig. 4.7.5.)

9. Differentiate the following functions w.r.t. t:

(a) $\dfrac{at+b}{ct+d}$ 　　　　(b) $t^n \left(a\sqrt{t}+b \right)$ 　　　　(c) $\dfrac{1}{at^2+bt+c}$

10. If $f(x) = \sqrt{x}$, then $f(x) \cdot f(x) = x$. Use the product rule to find a formula for $f'(x)$. Compare this with the result in Problem 6.2.8.

11. Prove the power rule

$$y = x^a \;\Rightarrow\; y' = ax^{a-1}$$

for $a = -n$, where n is a natural number, by using the relation $f(x) = x^{-n} = 1/x^n$ and the quotient rule (3).

6.8 Chain Rule

Suppose that y is a function of u, and that u is a function of x. Then y is a composite function of x. Suppose that x changes. This will lead to a change in u and hence to a change in y. A change in x, therefore, causes a "chain reaction." If we know the rates of change du/dx and dy/du, then what is the rate of change dy/dx? It turns out that the relationship between these rates of change is simply:

$$\frac{dy}{dx} = \frac{dy}{du} \cdot \frac{du}{dx} \qquad \textbf{(Chain Rule)} \tag{1}$$

A slightly more detailed formulation of the rule says that *if y is a differentiable function of u, and u is a differentiable function of x, then y is a differentiable function of x*, and (1) holds. An important special case is when $y = u^a$. Then $dy/du = au^{a-1}$, and the chain rule yields the **generalized power rule**:

$$y = u^a \;\Longrightarrow\; y' = au^{a-1}u' \qquad (u = g(x)) \tag{2}$$

It is easy to remember the chain rule when using Leibniz's notation. The left-hand side of (1) is exactly what results if we "cancel" the du on the right-hand side. Of course, because dy/du and du/dx are not fractions (but merely symbols for derivatives) and du is not a number, cancelling is not defined.

The chain rule is very powerful. Facility in applying it comes from a lot of practice.

EXAMPLE 1 　(a) Find dy/dx when $y = u^5$ and $u = 1 - x^3$.

(b) Find dy/dx when $y = \dfrac{10}{(x^2+4x+5)^7}$.

Solution:

(a) Here we can use (1) directly. Since $dy/du = 5u^4$ and $du/dx = -3x^2$, we have

$$\frac{dy}{dx} = \frac{dy}{du} \cdot \frac{du}{dx} = 5u^4(-3x^2) = -15x^2 u^4 = -15x^2(1-x^3)^4$$

(b) If we write $u = x^2 + 4x + 5$, then $y = 10u^{-7}$. By the generalized power rule, one has

$$\frac{dy}{dx} = 10(-7)u^{-8}u' = -70u^{-8}(2x+4) = \frac{-140(x+2)}{(x^2+4x+5)^8} \qquad \blacksquare$$

NOTE 1 After a little training, the intermediate steps become unnecessary. For example, to differentiate

$$y = (\underbrace{1-x^3}_{u})^5$$

we can *think* of y as $y = u^5$, where $u = 1 - x^3$. We can then differentiate both u^5 and $1 - x^3$ in our heads, and immediately write down $y' = 5(1-x^3)^4(-3x^2)$.

NOTE 2 If you differentiate $y = x^5/5$ using the quotient rule, you obtain the right answer, but commit a small "mathematical crime". This is because it is much easier to write y as $y = (1/5)x^5$ to get $y' = (1/5)5x^4 = x^4$. In the same way, it is unnecessarily cumbersome to apply the quotient rule to the function given in Example 1(b). The generalized power rule is much more effective.

EXAMPLE 2   Differentiate the functions

(a) $y = (x^3 + x^2)^{50}$ (b) $y = \left(\dfrac{x-1}{x+3}\right)^{1/3}$ (c) $y = \sqrt{x^2 + 1}$

Solution:

(a) $y = (x^3 + x^2)^{50} = u^{50}$ where $u = x^3 + x^2$, so $u' = 3x^2 + 2x$. Then (2) gives

$$y' = 50u^{50-1} \cdot u' = 50(x^3 + x^2)^{49}(3x^2 + 2x)$$

(b) Again we use (2):

$$y = \left(\frac{x-1}{x+3}\right)^{1/3} = u^{1/3} \qquad \text{where} \qquad u = \frac{x-1}{x+3}$$

The quotient rule gives

$$u' = \frac{1 \cdot (x+3) - (x-1) \cdot 1}{(x+3)^2} = \frac{4}{(x+3)^2}$$

and hence

$$y' = \frac{1}{3}u^{(1/3)-1} \cdot u' = \frac{1}{3}\left(\frac{x-1}{x+3}\right)^{-2/3} \cdot \frac{4}{(x+3)^2}$$

(c) Note first that $y = \sqrt{x^2 + 1} = (x^2 + 1)^{1/2}$, so $y = u^{1/2}$ where $u = x^2 + 1$. Hence,

$$y' = \frac{1}{2}u^{(1/2)-1} \cdot u' = \frac{1}{2}(x^2 + 1)^{-1/2} \cdot 2x = \frac{x}{\sqrt{x^2 + 1}} \qquad \blacksquare$$

The formulation of the chain rule might appear abstract and difficult. However, when we interpret the derivatives involved in (1) as rates of change, the chain rule becomes rather intuitive, as the next example from economics will indicate.

EXAMPLE 3   The demand x for a commodity depends on price p. Suppose that price p is not constant, but depends on time t. Then x is a composite function of t, and according to the chain rule,

$$\frac{dx}{dt} = \frac{dx}{dp} \cdot \frac{dp}{dt} \qquad (*)$$

Suppose, for instance, that the demand for butter decreases by 5000 pounds if the price goes up by \$1 per pound. So $dx/dp \approx -5000$. Suppose further that the price per pound increases by \$0.05 per month, so $dp/dt \approx 0.05$. What is the decrease in demand in pounds per month?

Solution: Because the price per pound increases by \$0.05 per month, and the demand decreases by 5000 pounds for every dollar increase in the price, the demand *decreases* by $5000 \cdot 0.05 \approx 250$ pounds per month. This means that $dx/dt \approx -250$ (measured in pounds per month). Note how this argument roughly confirms $(*)$. $\blacksquare$

The next example uses the chain rule several times.

EXAMPLE 4   Find $x'(t)$ when $x(t) = 5\left(1 + \sqrt{t^3 + 1}\right)^{25}$.

Solution: The initial step is easy. Let $x(t) = 5u^{25}$, where $u = 1 + \sqrt{t^3 + 1}$, to obtain

$$x'(t) = 5 \cdot 25u^{24} \frac{du}{dt} = 125u^{24} \frac{du}{dt} \qquad (*)$$

The new feature in this example is that we cannot write down du/dt at once. Finding du/dt requires using the chain rule a second time. Let $u = 1 + \sqrt{v} = 1 + v^{1/2}$, where $v = t^3 + 1$. Then

$$\frac{du}{dt} = \frac{1}{2}v^{(1/2)-1} \cdot \frac{dv}{dt} = \frac{1}{2}v^{-1/2} \cdot 3t^2 = \frac{1}{2}(t^3 + 1)^{-1/2} \cdot 3t^2 \qquad (**)$$

From $(*)$ and $(**)$, we get

$$x'(t) = 125\left(1 + \sqrt{t^3 + 1}\right)^{24} \cdot \frac{1}{2}(t^3 + 1)^{-1/2} \cdot 3t^2 \qquad \blacksquare$$

Suppose, as in the last example, that x is a function of u, u is a function of v, and v is in turn a function of t. Then x is a composite function of t, and the chain rule can be used twice to obtain

$$\frac{dx}{dt} = \frac{dx}{du} \cdot \frac{du}{dv} \cdot \frac{dv}{dt}$$

This is precisely the formula used in the last example. Again the notation is suggestive because the left-hand side is exactly what results if we "cancel" both du and dv on the right-hand side.

An Alternative Formulation of the Chain Rule

Although Leibniz's notation makes it very easy to remember the chain rule, it suffers from the defect of not specifying where each derivative is evaluated. We remedy this by introducing names for the functions involved. So let $y = f(u)$ and $u = g(x)$. Then y can be written in the form

$$y = f\big(g(x)\big)$$

Here y a *composite function*, with $g(x)$ as the *kernel*, and f as the *exterior function*.

THE CHAIN RULE

If g is differentiable at x_0 and f is differentiable at $u_0 = g(x_0)$, then $F(x) = f\big(g(x)\big)$ is differentiable at x_0, and   (3)

$$F'(x_0) = f'(u_0)g'(x_0) = f'\big(g(x_0)\big)g'(x_0)$$

In words: *to differentiate a composite function, first differentiate the exterior function w.r.t. the kernel, then multiply by the derivative of the kernel.*

EXAMPLE 5   Find the derivative of $F(x) = f(g(x))$ at $x_0 = -3$ if $f(u) = u^3$ and $g(x) = 2 - x^2$.

Solution: In this case, $f'(u) = 3u^2$ and $g'(x) = -2x$. So (3) gives $F'(-3) = f'(g(-3)) g'(-3)$. Now $g(-3) = 2-(-3)^2 = 2-9 = -7$; $g'(-3) = 6$; and $f'(g(-3)) = f'(-7) = 3(-7)^2 = 3 \cdot 49 = 147$. So $F'(-3) = f'(g(-3)) g'(-3) = 147 \cdot 6 = 882$. ∎

Proof of (3): To find the derivative of $F(x) = f(g(x))$ at $x = x_0$, we must examine the limit of the following Newton quotient as h tends to 0:

$$N = \frac{F(x_0 + h) - F(x_0)}{h} = \frac{f(g(x_0 + h)) - f(g(x_0))}{h}$$

The change in x from x_0 to x_0+h causes the value of g to change by the amount $k = g(x_0+h)-g(x_0)$. As h tends to 0, so $k = \{[g(x_0 + h) - g(x_0)]/h\} \cdot h$ tends to $g'(x_0) \cdot 0 = 0$. *Suppose that $k \neq 0$*

whenever $h \neq 0$ *is small enough.* Because $g(x_0 + h) = g(x_0) + k$, we can write the Newton quotient as

$$N = \frac{f(g(x_0) + k) - f(g(x_0))}{k} \cdot \frac{k}{h} = \frac{f(g(x_0) + k) - f(g(x_0))}{k} \cdot \frac{g(x_0 + h) - g(x_0)}{h}$$

As $h \to 0$, so $k \to 0$, and the last two fractions tend to $f'(g(x_0))$ and $g'(x_0)$, respectively. This yields the desired formula.

We cannot divide by 0, so the argument fails if $g(x_0 + h) = g(x_0)$, because then $k = 0$ for arbitrary small values of h. A more complicated argument can take care of this case as well. ∎

PROBLEMS FOR SECTION 6.8

1. Use the chain rule (1) to find dy/dx for the following:

   (a) $y = 5u^4$ where $u = 1 + x^2$ (b) $y = u - u^6$ where $u = 1 + 1/x$

2. Compute the following:

   (a) dY/dt when $Y = -3(V + 1)^5$ and $V = \frac{1}{3}t^3$.

   (b) dK/dt when $K = AL^a$ and $L = bt + c$ (A, a, b, and c are positive constants).

3. Find the derivatives of the following functions, where a, p, q, and b are constants:

   (a) $y = \dfrac{1}{(x^2 + x + 1)^5}$ (b) $y = \sqrt{x + \sqrt{x + \sqrt{x}}}$ (c) $y = x^a(px + q)^b$

4. If Y is a function of K, and K is a function of t, find the formula for the derivative of Y with respect to t at $t = t_0$.

5. If $Y = F(K)$ and $K = h(t)$, find the formula for dY/dt.

6. Compute dx/dp for the demand function $x = b - \sqrt{ap - c}$, where a, b, and c are positive constants, while x is the number of units demanded, and p is the price per unit, with $p > c/a$.

7. Find a formula for $h'(x)$ when (i) $h(x) = f(x^2)$ (ii) $h(x) = f(x^n g(x))$.

8. Let $s(t)$ be the distance in kilometres a car goes in t hours. Let $B(s)$ be the number of litres of fuel the car uses to go s kilometres. Provide an interpretation of the function $b(t) = B(s(t))$, and find a formula for $b'(t)$.

9. Suppose that $C = 20q - 4q\left(25 - \frac{1}{2}x\right)^{1/2}$, where q is a constant and $x < 50$. Find dC/dx.

10. Differentiate each of the following in two different ways:

    (a) $y = (x^4)^5 = x^{20}$ (b) $y = (1 - x)^3 = 1 - 3x + 3x^2 - x^3$

11. (a) Suppose you invest 1000 euros at $p\%$ interest per year. Then after 10 years you will have $K = g(p)$ euros. What are the economic interpretations of (i) $g(5) \approx 1629$ (ii) $g'(5) \approx 155$?

    (b) To check the numbers in (a), find a formula for $g(p)$, and then compute $g(5)$ and $g'(5)$.

12. If f is differentiable at x, find expressions for the derivatives of the following functions:

    (a) $x + f(x)$ (b) $\left[f(x)\right]^2 - x$ (c) $\left[f(x)\right]^4$ (d) $x^2 f(x) + \left[f(x)\right]^3$

    (e) $x f(x)$ (f) $\sqrt{f(x)}$ (g) $\dfrac{x^2}{f(x)}$ (h) $\dfrac{\left[f(x)\right]^2}{x^3}$

6.9 Higher-Order Derivatives

The derivative of a function f is often called the **first derivative** of f. If f' is also differentiable, then we can differentiate f' in turn to get $(f')'$, the derivative of f'. In fact, we call $(f')'$ the **second derivative** of f. We write f'' instead of $(f')'$, and let $f''(x)$ denote the second derivative of f evaluated at the particular point x.

EXAMPLE 1   Find $f'(x)$ and $f''(x)$ when $f(x) = 2x^5 - 3x^3 + 2x$.

Solution: Using the rules for differentiating polynomials, we first differentiate $2x^5 - 3x^3 + 2x$ to get $f'(x) = 10x^4 - 9x^2 + 2$. Then we differentiate $10x^4 - 9x^2 + 2$ to get $f''(x) = 40x^3 - 18x$.

The different forms of notation for the second derivative are analogous to those for the first derivative. For example, we write $y'' = f''(x)$ in order to denote the second derivative of $y = f(x)$. The Leibniz notation for the second derivative is also used. In the notation dy/dx or $df(x)/dx$ for the first derivative, we interpreted the symbol d/dx as an operator indicating that what follows is to be differentiated with respect to x. The second derivative is obtained by using the operator d/dx twice: $f''(x) = (d/dx)(d/dx)f(x)$. We usually think of this as $f''(x) = (d/dx)^2 f(x)$, and so write it as follows:

$$f''(x) = \frac{d^2 f(x)}{dx^2} = d^2 f(x)/dx^2 \quad \text{or} \quad y'' = \frac{d^2 y}{dx^2} = d^2 y/dx^2$$

Pay special attention to where the superscripts 2 are placed.

Of course, the notation for the second derivative must change if the variables have other names.

EXAMPLE 2   (a) Find Y'' when $Y = AK^a$ is a function of K ($K > 0$), with A and a as constants.

(b) Find $d^2 L/dt^2$ when $L = \dfrac{t}{t+1}$, and $t \geq 0$.

Solution:

(a) Differentiating $Y = AK^a$ with respect to K gives $Y' = AaK^{a-1}$. A second differentiation with respect to K yields $Y'' = Aa(a-1)K^{a-2}$.

(b) First, we use the quotient rule to find that

$$\frac{dL}{dt} = \frac{d}{dt}\left(\frac{t}{t+1}\right) = \frac{1\cdot(t+1)-t\cdot 1}{(t+1)^2} = (t+1)^{-2}$$

Then

$$\frac{d^2L}{dt^2} = -2(t+1)^{-3} = \frac{-2}{(t+1)^3}$$

Convex and Concave Functions

Recall how the sign of the first derivative determines whether a function is increasing or decreasing on an interval I. If $f'(x) \geq 0\,(f'(x) \leq 0)$ on I, then f is increasing (decreasing) on I, and vice versa. The second derivative $f''(x)$ is the derivative of $f'(x)$. Hence:

$$f''(x) \geq 0 \text{ on } I \iff f' \text{ is increasing on } I \tag{1}$$

$$f''(x) \leq 0 \text{ on } I \iff f' \text{ is decreasing on } I \tag{2}$$

The equivalence in (1) is illustrated in Fig. 1. The slope of the tangent, $f'(x)$, is increasing as x increases. On the other hand, the slope of the tangent to the graph in Fig. 2 is decreasing as x increases. (Place a ruler as a tangent to the graph of the function. As the ruler slides along the curve from left to right, the tangent rotates counterclockwise in Fig. 1, clockwise in Fig. 2.)

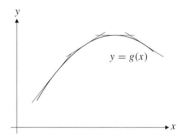

Figure 1 The slope of the tangent increases as x increases. $f'(x)$ is increasing

Figure 2 The slope of the tangent decreases as x increases. $g'(x)$ is decreasing

We introduce the following definitions, assuming that f is continuous in the interval I and twice differentiable in the interior of I:

$$f \text{ is \textbf{convex} on } I \iff f''(x) \geq 0 \text{ for all } x \text{ in } I$$

$$f \text{ is \textbf{concave} on } I \iff f''(x) \leq 0 \text{ for all } x \text{ in } I \tag{3}$$

The distinction between convexity and concavity of a function is absolutely crucial in many economic models. Study carefully the cases illustrated in Fig. 3.

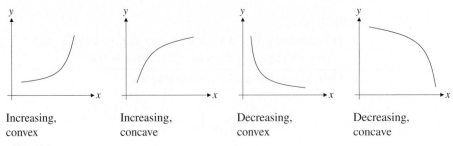

Increasing, convex   Increasing, concave   Decreasing, convex   Decreasing, concave

Figure 3

EXAMPLE 3   Check the convexity/concavity of the following functions:

$$\text{(a) } f(x) = x^2 - 2x + 2 \quad \text{and} \quad \text{(b) } f(x) = ax^2 + bx + c$$

Solution:

(a) Here $f'(x) = 2x - 2$ so $f''(x) = 2$. Because $f''(x) > 0$ for all x, f is convex.

(b) Here $f'(x) = 2ax + b$, so $f''(x) = 2a$. If $a = 0$, then f is linear and f is convex as well as concave. If $a > 0$, then $f''(x) > 0$, so f is convex. If $a < 0$, then $f''(x) < 0$, so f is concave. Compare with the graphs in Fig. 4.6.1.

We consider two typical examples of convex and concave functions.

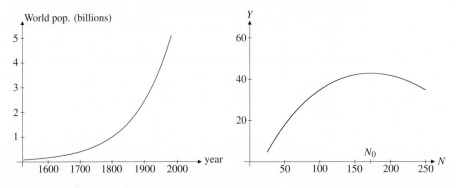

Figure 4 World population   **Figure 5** Wheat production

Figure 4 shows a rough graph of the function P, where

$$P(t) = \text{world population (in billions) in year } t$$

It appears from the figure that not only is $P(t)$ increasing, but the rate of increase increases. (Each year the *increase* becomes larger.) So $P(t)$ is convex.

The graph in Fig. 5 shows the crop of wheat $Y(N)$ when N pounds of fertilizer per acre are used, based on fertilizer experiments in Iowa during 1952. The function has a maximum at $N = N_0 \approx 172$. Increasing the amount of fertilizer beyond N_0 will cause wheat production to decline. Moreover, $Y(N)$ is concave. If $N < N_0$, increasing N by one unit will lead to less *increase* in $Y(N)$ the larger is N. On the other hand, if $N > N_0$, increasing N by one unit will lead to a larger *decrease* in $Y(N)$ the larger is N.

EXAMPLE 4   Examine the concavity/convexity of the production function

$$Y = AK^a \qquad (A > 0; \quad 0 < a < 1)$$

defined for all $K > 0$.

Solution: From Example 2(a), $Y'' = Aa(a - 1)K^{a-2}$. Because $a \in (0, 1)$, the coefficient $Aa(a - 1) < 0$, so that $Y'' < 0$ for all $K > 0$. Hence, the function is concave. The graph of $Y = AK^a$ for $0 < a < 1$, is shown in Fig. 6. If $a > 1$, then $Y'' > 0$ and Y is a convex function of K, as shown in Fig. 7.

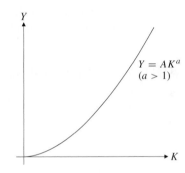

Figure 6   Concave production function

Figure 7   Convex production function

EXAMPLE 5   Suppose that the functions U and g are both increasing and concave, with $U' \geq 0$, $U'' \leq 0$, $g' \geq 0$, and $g'' \leq 0$. Prove that the composite function $f(x) = g(U(x))$ is also increasing and concave.

Solution: Using the chain rule yields

$$f'(x) = g'(U(x)) \cdot U'(x) \qquad (*)$$

Because g' and U' are both ≥ 0, so $f'(x) \geq 0$. Hence, f is increasing. (*An increasing transformation of an increasing function is increasing.*)

In order to compute $f''(x)$, we must differentiate the product of the two functions $g'(U(x))$ and $U'(x)$. According to the chain rule, the derivative of $g'(U(x))$ is equal to $g''(U(x)) \cdot U'(x)$. Hence,

$$f''(x) = g''(U(x)) \cdot (U'(x))^2 + g'(U(x)) \cdot U''(x) \qquad (**)$$

Because $g'' \leq 0$, $g' \geq 0$, and $U'' \leq 0$, it follows that $f''(x) \leq 0$. (*An increasing concave transformation of a concave function is concave.*)

Nth Order Derivatives

If $y = f(x)$, the derivative of $y'' = f''(x)$ is called the **third derivative**, and we use the notation $y''' = f'''(x)$ for this. It is notationally cumbersome to continue using more and more primes to indicate differentiation, so the **fourth derivative** is usually denoted by $y^{(4)} = f^{(4)}(x)$. (We must put the number 4 in parentheses so that it will not get confused with y^4, the fourth power of y.) The same derivative can be expressed as d^4y/dx^4. In general, let

$$y^{(n)} = f^{(n)}(x) \quad \text{or} \quad \frac{d^n y}{dx^n} \qquad \text{denote the } n\text{th derivative of } f \text{ at } x$$

The number n is called the **order** of the derivative. For example, $f^{(6)}(x_0)$ denotes the sixth derivative of f calculated at x_0, found by differentiating six times.

EXAMPLE 6   Compute all the derivatives up to and including order 4 of

$$f(x) = 3x^{-1} + 6x^3 - x^2 \qquad (x \neq 0)$$

Solution: Repeated differentiation gives

$$f'(x) = -3x^{-2} + 18x^2 - 2x, \qquad f''(x) = 6x^{-3} + 36x - 2,$$

$$f'''(x) = -18x^{-4} + 36 \qquad\qquad f^{(4)}(x) = 72x^{-5}$$

PROBLEMS FOR SECTION 6.9

1. Compute the second derivative of:

    (a) $y = x^5 - 3x^4 + 2$ 　　　　 (b) $y = \sqrt{x}$ 　　　　 (c) $y = (1 + x^2)^{10}$

2. Find d^2y/dx^2 when $y = \sqrt{1 + x^2} = (1 + x^2)^{1/2}$.

3. Compute:

    (a) y'' 　for 　$y = 3x^3 + 2x - 1$ 　　　　 (b) Y''' 　for 　$Y = 1 - 2x^2 + 6x^3$

    (c) d^3z/dt^3 　for 　$z = 120t - (1/3)t^3$ 　　　 (d) $f^{(4)}(1)$ 　for 　$f(z) = 100z^{-4}$

4. Find $g''(2)$ when $g(t) = \dfrac{t^2}{t - 1}$.

5. Find formulas for y'' and y''' when $y = f(x)g(x)$.

6. Find d^2L/dt^2 when $L = 1/\sqrt{2t - 1}$.

7. If $u(y)$ denotes an individual's utility of having income (or consumption) y, then

$$R = -yu''(y)/u'(y)$$

is the coefficient of **relative risk aversion**. ($R_A = R/y$ is the degree of **absolute risk aversion**.) Compute R for the following utility functions (where A_1, A_2, and ρ are positive constants with $\rho \neq 1$, and we assume that $y > 0$):

(a) $u(y) = \sqrt{y}$ (b) $u(y) = A_1 - A_2 y^{-2}$ (c) $u(y) = A_1 + A_2 y^{1-\rho}/(1-\rho)$

8. Let $U(x) = \sqrt{x}$ and $g(u) = u^3$. Then $f(x) = g(U(x)) = x^{3/2}$, which is not a concave function. Why does this not contradict the conclusion in Example 5?

9. The US defence secretary claimed in 1985 that Congress had reduced the defence budget. Representative Gray pointed out that the budget had not been reduced; Congress had only reduced the rate of increase. If P denotes the size of the defence budget, translate the statements into statements about the signs of P' and P''.

10. Sentence in a newspaper: "The rate of increase of bank loans is increasing at an increasing rate." If $L(t)$ denotes total bank loans at time t, translate the statement into a statement on the sign of a certain derivative.

6.10 Exponential Functions

Exponential functions were introduced in Section 4.9. They were shown to be well suited in describing certain economic phenomena such as growth and compound interest. In particular we introduced the *natural* exponential function, $f(x) = e^x$, where $e \approx 2.7$. (Recall the alternative notation, $f(x) = \exp(x)$.)

Now we explain why this particular function deserves to be called "natural". Consider the Newton quotient of $f(x) = e^x$, which is

$$\frac{f(x+h) - f(x)}{h} = \frac{e^{x+h} - e^x}{h} \tag{*}$$

If this fraction tends to a limit as h tends to 0, then $f(x) = e^x$ is differentiable and $f'(x)$ is precisely equal to this limit.

The fraction in $(*)$ can be simplified if we make use of the rule $e^{x+h} = e^x \cdot e^h$. In fact, $e^{x+h} - e^x = e^x(e^h - 1)$, so

$$\frac{f(x+h) - f(x)}{h} = e^x \cdot \frac{e^h - 1}{h}$$

When taking the limit as h tends to zero of this fraction, e^x is a constant. We have seen a fraction similar to $(e^h - 1)/h$ before. In Example 6.5.1 we argued that this fraction tends to 1 as h tends to 0. (Although in that example the variable was x and not h.) It follows that

$$f(x) = e^x \quad \Longrightarrow \quad f'(x) = e^x \tag{1}$$

Thus the **natural exponential function** $f(x) = e^x$ *has the remarkable property that its derivative is equal to the function itself.* This is the main reason why the function appears so often in mathematics and applications. Observe also that $f''(x) = e^x$. Because $e^x > 0$ for all x, both $f'(x)$ and $f''(x)$ are positive. Hence, both f and f' are strictly increasing. This confirms the shape suggested in Fig. 4.9.3.

Combining (1) with the other rules of differentiation, we can differentiate many expressions involving the exponential function e^x.

EXAMPLE 1   Find the first and second derivative of   (a) $y = x^3 + e^x$ (b) $y = x^5 e^x$ (c) $y = e^x/x$

Solution:

(a) We find that $y' = 3x^2 + e^x$ and $y'' = 6x + e^x$.

(b) We have to use the product rule: $y' = 5x^4 e^x + x^5 e^x = x^4 e^x(5+x)$. To compute y'', we differentiate $y' = 5x^4 e^x + x^5 e^x$ once more to obtain, $y'' = 20x^3 e^x + 5x^4 e^x + 5x^4 e^x + x^5 e^x = x^3 e^x(x^2 + 10x + 20)$.

(c) The quotient rule yields

$$y = \frac{e^x}{x} \implies y' = \frac{e^x x - e^x \cdot 1}{x^2} = \frac{e^x(x-1)}{x^2}$$

Differentiating $y' = \dfrac{e^x x - e^x}{x^2}$ once more w.r.t. x gives

$$y'' = \frac{(e^x x + e^x - e^x)x^2 - (e^x x - e^x)2x}{(x^2)^2} = \frac{e^x(x^2 - 2x + 2)}{x^3}$$

after some rearrangement and then cancellation of x.

By combining rule (1) with the chain rule, we can compute the derivative of very complicated functions. First note that $y = e^{g(x)} = e^u \implies y' = e^u \cdot u' = e^{g(x)} \cdot g'(x)$, so that

$$y = e^{g(x)} \implies y' = e^{g(x)} g'(x) \tag{2}$$

EXAMPLE 2   Differentiate:

(a) $y = e^{-x}$ (b) $y = x^p e^{ax}$ (*p* and *a* are constants)   (c) $y = \sqrt{e^{2x} + x}$

Solution:

(a) Direct use of (2) gives $y = e^{-x} \implies y' = e^{-x} \cdot (-1) = -e^{-x}$. This derivative is always negative, so the function is strictly decreasing. Furthermore, $y'' = e^{-x} > 0$, so the function is convex. This agrees with the graph shown in Fig. 4.9.3.

(b) The derivative of e^{ax} is ae^{ax}. Hence, using the product rule,

$$y' = px^{p-1} e^{ax} + x^p a e^{ax} = x^{p-1} e^{ax}(p + ax)$$

(c) Let $y = \sqrt{e^{2x} + x} = \sqrt{u}$, with $u = e^{2x} + x$. Then $u' = 2e^{2x} + 1$, where we used the chain rule. Using the chain rule again, we obtain

$$y = \sqrt{e^{2x} + x} = \sqrt{v} \;\Rightarrow\; y' = \frac{1}{2\sqrt{v}} \cdot v' = \frac{2e^{2x} + 1}{2\sqrt{e^{2x} + x}}$$

EXAMPLE 3   Find the intervals where the following functions are increasing:

(a) $y = \dfrac{e^x}{x}$ (b) $y = x^4 e^{-2x}$ (c) $y = xe^{-\sqrt{x}}$

Solution:

(a) According to Example 1(c), $y' = \dfrac{e^x(x-1)}{x^2}$, so $y' \geq 0$ when $x \geq 1$. Thus y is increasing in $[1, \infty)$.

(b) According to Example 2(b), with $p = 4$ and $a = -2$, $y' = x^3 e^{-2x}(4 - 2x)$. A sign diagram reveals that y is increasing in $[0, 2]$.

(c) The function is only defined for $x \geq 0$. Using the chain rule, for $x > 0$ the derivative of $e^{-\sqrt{x}}$ is $-e^{-\sqrt{x}}/2\sqrt{x}$, so by the product rule, the derivative of $y = xe^{-\sqrt{x}}$ is

$$y' = 1 \cdot e^{-\sqrt{x}} - \frac{xe^{-\sqrt{x}}}{2\sqrt{x}} = e^{-\sqrt{x}}\left(1 - \frac{1}{2}\sqrt{x}\right)$$

where we have used the fact that $x/\sqrt{x} = \sqrt{x}$. It follows that y is increasing when $x > 0$ and $1 - \frac{1}{2}\sqrt{x} \geq 0$. Because $y = 0$ when $x = 0$ and $y > 0$ when $x > 0$, it follows that y is increasing in $[0, 4]$.

NOTE 1 A common error when differentiating exponential functions is to believe that the derivative of e^x is "xe^{x-1}". This is due to confusing the exponential function with a power function.

SURVEY OF THE PROPERTIES OF EXP(X)

The natural exponential function

$$f(x) = \exp(x) = e^x \qquad (e = 2.71828\ldots)$$

is differentiable, strictly increasing and convex.

$$f(x) = e^x \;\Longrightarrow\; f'(x) = f(x) = e^x$$

The following properties hold for all exponents s and t:

(a) $e^s e^t = e^{s+t}$ (b) $e^s/e^t = e^{s-t}$ (c) $(e^s)^t = e^{st}$

Moreover,

$$e^x \to 0 \quad \text{as} \quad x \to -\infty, \qquad e^x \to \infty \quad \text{as} \quad x \to \infty$$

Differentiation of More General Exponential Functions

What is the derivative of the more general exponential function studied in Section 4.9, $y = a^x$? According to rule (1) of Section 4.10, for every positive number a one has $a = e^{\ln a}$. So, using the general property $(e^r)^s = e^{rs}$, we have the formula

$$a^x = \left(e^{\ln a}\right)^x = e^{(\ln a)x}$$

This shows that in problems where the function a^x occurs, we can just as easily work with the special exponential function e^{bx}, where b is a constant equal to $\ln a$. In particular, we can differentiate a^x by differentiating $e^{x \ln a}$. According to (2), with $g(x) = (\ln a)x$, we have

$$y = a^x \;\Rightarrow\; y' = a^x \ln a \tag{3}$$

EXAMPLE 4   Find the derivatives of (a) $f(x) = 10^{-x}$ (b) $g(x) = x2^{3x}$

Solution:

(a) $f(x) = 10^{-x} = 10^u$ where $u = -x$. Using (3) and the chain rule gives $f'(x) = -10^{-x} \ln 10$.

(b) We differentiate 2^{3x} by letting $y = 2^{3x} = 2^u$, where $u = 3x$. By the chain rule, $y' = (2^u \ln 2)u' = (2^{3x} \ln 2) \cdot 3 = 3 \cdot 2^{3x} \ln 2$, and using the product rule we obtain

$$g'(x) = 1 \cdot 2^{3x} + x \cdot 3 \cdot 2^{3x} \ln 2 = 2^{3x}(1 + 3x \ln 2)$$

PROBLEMS FOR SECTION 6.10

1. Find the first-order derivatives of:

   (a) $y = e^x + x^2$ (b) $y = 5e^x - 3x^3 + 8$ (c) $y = \dfrac{x}{e^x}$ (d) $y = \dfrac{x + x^2}{e^x + 1}$

   (e) $y = -x-5-e^x$ (f) $y = x^3 e^x$ (g) $y = e^x x^{-2}$ (h) $y = (x + e^x)^2$

2. Find the first-order derivatives w.r.t. t of the following functions, where a, b, c, p, and q are constants.

   (a) $x = (a + bt + ct^2)e^t$ (b) $x = \dfrac{p + qt^3}{te^t}$ (c) $x = \dfrac{(at + bt^2)^2}{e^t}$

3. Find the first and second-order derivatives of:

   (a) $y = e^{-3x}$ (b) $y = 2e^{x^3}$ (c) $y = e^{1/x}$ (d) $y = 5e^{2x^2 - 3x + 1}$

4. Find the intervals where the following functions are increasing:

   (a) $y = x^3 + e^{2x}$ (b) $y = 5x^2 e^{-4x}$ (c) $y = x^2 e^{-x^2}$

5. Find the intervals where the following functions are increasing:

(a) $y = x^2/e^{2x}$ (b) $y = e^x - e^{3x}$ (c) $y = \dfrac{e^{2x}}{x+2}$

6. Find:

(a) $\dfrac{d}{dx}\left(e^{(e^x)}\right)$ (b) $\dfrac{d}{dt}\left(e^{t/2} + e^{-t/2}\right)$ (c) $\dfrac{d}{dt}\left(\dfrac{1}{e^t + e^{-t}}\right)$ (d) $\dfrac{d}{dz}\left(e^{z^3} - 1\right)^{1/3}$

7. Differentiate:

(a) $y = 5^x$ (b) $y = x2^x$ (c) $y = x^2 2^{x^2}$ (d) $y = e^x 10^x$

6.11 Logarithmic Functions

In Section 4.10 we introduced the natural logarithmic function, $g(x) = \ln x$. It is defined for all $x > 0$ and has the following graph (reproduced from Fig. 4.10.2):

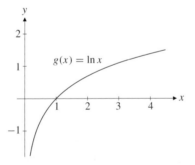

Figure 1 The graph of the logarithmic function $g(x) = \ln x$

According to Section 5.3, the function $g(x) = \ln x$ has $f(x) = e^x$ as its *inverse*. If we *assume* that $g(x) = \ln x$ has a derivative for all $x > 0$, we can easily find the derivative. We differentiate the equation defining $g(x) = \ln x$,

$$e^{g(x)} = x \tag{$*$}$$

w.r.t. x. Using the result in (2) in the previous section, we obtain[5] $e^{g(x)}g'(x) = 1$. Since $e^{g(x)} = x$, we have $xg'(x) = 1$, and thus

$$g(x) = \ln x \implies g'(x) = \frac{1}{x} \tag{1}$$

Thus, the derivative of $\ln x$ at x is simply the number $1/x$. For $x > 0$, we have $g'(x) > 0$, so that $g(x)$ is *strictly* increasing. Note moreover that $g''(x) = -1/x^2$, which is less than 0 for

---

[5] This type of implicit differentiation is explained in detail in Section 7.1.

all $x > 0$, so that $g(x)$ is concave. This confirms the shape of the graph in Fig. 1. In fact, the growth of $\ln x$ is quite slow. For example, $\ln x$ first attains the value 10 when $x > 22\,026$, because $\ln x = 10$ gives $x = e^{10} \approx 22\,026.5$.

EXAMPLE 1   Compute y' and y'' when: (a) $y = x^3 + \ln x$ (b) $y = x^2 \ln x$ (c) $y = \ln x / x$.

Solution:

(a) We find easily that $y' = 3x^2 + 1/x$. Furthermore, $y'' = 6x - 1/x^2$.

(b) The product rule gives

$$y' = 2x \ln x + x^2(1/x) = 2x \ln x + x$$

Differentiating the last expression w.r.t. x gives $y'' = 2 \ln x + 2x(1/x) + 1 = 2 \ln x + 3$.

(c) Here we use the quotient rule:

$$y' = \frac{(1/x)x - (\ln x) \cdot 1}{x^2} = \frac{1 - \ln x}{x^2}$$

Differentiating again yields

$$y'' = \frac{-(1/x)x^2 - (1 - \ln x)2x}{(x^2)^2} = \frac{2 \ln x - 3}{x^3}$$

Often, we need to consider composite functions involving natural logarithms. Because $\ln u$ is defined only when $u > 0$, a composite function of the form $y = \ln h(x)$ will only be defined for values of x satisfying $h(x) > 0$.

Combining the rule for differentiating $\ln x$ with the chain rule allows us to differentiate many different types of function. Suppose, for instance, that $y = \ln h(x)$, where $h(x)$ is differentiable and positive. By the chain rule, $y = \ln u$ with $u = h(x)$ implies that $y' = (1/u)u' = (1/h(x))h'(x)$, so:

$$y = \ln h(x) \implies y' = \frac{h'(x)}{h(x)} \tag{2}$$

NOTE 1 If $N(t)$ is a function of t, then

$$\frac{d}{dt} \ln N(t) = \frac{1}{N(t)} \frac{dN(t)}{dt}$$

is the relative rate of growth of $N(t)$.

EXAMPLE 2   Find the domains of the following functions and compute their derivatives:

(a) $y = \ln(1 - x)$ (b) $y = \ln(4 - x^2)$ (c) $y = \ln\left(\frac{x-1}{x+1}\right) - \frac{1}{4}x$

Solution:

(a) $\ln(1 - x)$ is defined if $1 - x > 0$, that is if $x < 1$. To find its derivative, we use (2) with $h(x) = 1 - x$. Then $h'(x) = -1$, so (2) gives

$$y' = \frac{-1}{1 - x} = \frac{1}{x - 1}$$

(b) $\ln(4 - x^2)$ is defined if $4 - x^2 > 0$, that is if $(2 - x)(2 + x) > 0$. This is satisfied if and only if $-2 < x < 2$. Formula (2) gives

$$y' = \frac{-2x}{4 - x^2} = \frac{2x}{x^2 - 4}$$

(c) We must require that $\dfrac{x - 1}{x + 1} > 0$. A sign diagram shows that this is satisfied if $x < -1$ or $x > 1$. We can write $f(x) = \ln u - \frac{1}{4}x$, where $u = (x - 1)/(x + 1)$. Using (2), we obtain:

$$f'(x) = \frac{u'}{u} - \frac{1}{4} \qquad \text{where} \qquad u' = \frac{1 \cdot (x + 1) - 1 \cdot (x - 1)}{(x + 1)^2} = \frac{2}{(x + 1)^2}$$

So

$$f'(x) = \frac{2(x + 1)}{(x + 1)^2 (x - 1)} - \frac{1}{4} = \frac{9 - x^2}{4(x^2 - 1)} = \frac{(3 - x)(3 + x)}{4(x - 1)(x + 1)} \qquad \blacksquare$$

EXAMPLE 3   Find the intervals where the following functions are increasing:

(a) $y = x^2 \ln x$ (b) $y = 4x - 5 \ln(x^2 + 1)$ (c) $y = 3 \ln(1 + x) + x - \frac{1}{2}x^2$

Solution:

(a) The function is defined for $x > 0$, and

$$y' = 2x \ln x + x^2(1/x) = x(2 \ln x + 1)$$

so $y' \geq 0$ when $\ln x \geq -1/2$, that is, when $x \geq e^{-1/2}$. Thus y is increasing in $[e^{-1/2}, \infty)$.

(b) We find that

$$y' = 4 - \frac{10x}{x^2 + 1} = \frac{4(x - 2)\left(x - \frac{1}{2}\right)}{x^2 + 1}$$

A sign diagram reveals that y is increasing in each of the intervals $(-\infty, \frac{1}{2}]$ and $[2, \infty)$.

(c) The function is defined for $x > -1$, and

$$y' = \frac{3}{1 + x} + 1 - x = \frac{(2 - x)(2 + x)}{x + 1}$$

A sign diagram reveals that y is increasing in $(-1, 2]$. $\qquad \blacksquare$

SURVEY OF THE PROPERTIES OF LN(X)

The natural logarithmic function

$$g(x) = \ln x$$

is differentiable, strictly increasing and concave in $(0, \infty)$. In fact,

$$g'(x) = 1/x, \qquad g''(x) = -1/x^2$$

By definition, $e^{\ln x} = x$ for all $x > 0$, and $\ln e^x = x$ for all x. The following properties hold for all $x > 0$, $y > 0$:

(a) $\ln(xy) = \ln x + \ln y$ (b) $\ln(x/y) = \ln x - \ln y$ (c) $\ln x^p = p \ln x$

Moreover,

$$\ln x \to -\infty \quad \text{as} \quad x \to 0^+, \qquad \ln x \to \infty \quad \text{as} \quad x \to \infty$$

Logarithmic Differentiation

When differentiating an expression containing products, quotients, roots, powers, and combinations of these, it is often an advantage to use **logarithmic differentiation**. The method is illustrated by two examples:

EXAMPLE 4   Find the derivative of $y = x^x$ defined for all $x > 0$.

Solution: The power rule of differentiation, $y = x^a \implies y' = ax^{a-1}$, requires the exponent a to be a constant, while the rule $y = a^x \implies y' = a^x \ln a$ requires that the base a is constant. In the expression x^x both the exponent and the base vary with x, so neither of the two rules can be used.

Begin by taking the natural logarithm of each side, $\ln y = x \ln x$. Differentiating w.r.t. x gives $y'/y = 1 \cdot \ln x + x(1/x) = \ln x + 1$. Multiplying by $y = x^x$ gives us the result:

$$y = x^x \implies y' = x^x(\ln x + 1)$$

EXAMPLE 5   Find the derivative of $y = [A(x)]^\alpha [B(x)]^\beta [C(x)]^\gamma$, where α, β, and γ are constants and A, B, and C are positive functions.

Solution: First, take the natural logarithm of each side to obtain

$$\ln y = \alpha \ln(A(x)) + \beta \ln(B(x)) + \gamma \ln(C(x))$$

Differentiation with respect to x yields

$$\frac{y'}{y} = \alpha \frac{A'(x)}{A(x)} + \beta \frac{B'(x)}{B(x)} + \gamma \frac{C'(x)}{C(x)}$$

Multiplying by y we have

$$y' = \left[\alpha \frac{A'(x)}{A(x)} + \beta \frac{B'(x)}{B(x)} + \gamma \frac{C'(x)}{C(x)} \right] [A(x)]^{\alpha} [B(x)]^{\beta} [C(x)]^{\gamma} \qquad \blacksquare$$

In Section 4.10 we showed (see equation (5)) that the logarithm of x in the system with base a is proportional to $\ln x$, with a proportionality factor $1/\ln a$: $\log_a x = \frac{1}{\ln a} \ln x$. It follows immediately that

$$y = \log_a x \implies y' = \frac{1}{\ln a} \frac{1}{x} \qquad (3)$$

A Characterization of the Number e

If $g(x) = \ln x$, then $g'(x) = 1/x$, and, in particular, $g'(1) = 1$. Using in turn the definition of $g'(1)$, the fact that $\ln 1 = 0$, together with the rule $\ln x^p = p \ln x$, we obtain

$$1 = g'(1) = \lim_{h \to 0} \frac{\ln(1+h) - \ln 1}{h} = \lim_{h \to 0} \frac{1}{h} \ln(1+h) = \lim_{h \to 0} \ln(1+h)^{1/h}$$

Because $\ln(1+h)^{1/h}$ tends to 1 as h tends to 0, it follows that $(1+h)^{1/h}$ itself must tend to e:

$$e = \lim_{h \to 0} (1+h)^{1/h} \qquad (4)$$

The following table has been computed using a pocket calculator, and it seems to confirm that the decimal expansion we gave for e starts out correctly. (Of course, this by no means proves that the limit exists.)

Table 1 Values of $(1+h)^{1/h}$ when h gets smaller and smaller

h	1	1/2	1/10	1/1000	1/100 000	1/1 000 000
$(1+h)^{1/h}$	2	2.25	2.5937...	2.7169...	2.71825...	2.718281828...

From the table we can see that a closer and closer approximation to e is obtained by choosing h smaller and smaller.

Power Functions

In Section 6.6 we claimed that, for all real numbers a,

$$f(x) = x^a \implies f'(x) = ax^{a-1} \qquad (*)$$

This important rule has only been established for certain special values of a, particularly the rational numbers. Because $x = e^{\ln x}$, we have $x^a = (e^{\ln x})^a = e^{a \ln x}$. Using the chain rule, we obtain

$$\frac{d}{dx}(x^a) = \frac{d}{dx}(e^{a \ln x}) = e^{a \ln x} \cdot \frac{a}{x} = x^a \frac{a}{x} = ax^{a-1}$$

In this way, the power rule is justified also when a is an irrational number.

1. Compute the first and second-order derivatives of:

   (a) $y = \ln x + 3x - 2$ (b) $y = x^2 - 2\ln x$ (c) $y = x^3 \ln x$ (d) $y = \dfrac{\ln x}{x}$

2. Find the derivative of:

   (a) $y = x^3(\ln x)^2$ (b) $y = \dfrac{x^2}{\ln x}$ (c) $y = (\ln x)^{10}$ (d) $y = (\ln x + 3x)^2$

3. Find the derivative of:

   (a) $\ln(\ln x)$ (b) $\ln \sqrt{1 - x^2}$ (c) $e^x \ln x$

   (d) $e^{x^3} \ln x^2$ (e) $\ln(e^x + 1)$ (f) $\ln(x^2 + 3x - 1)$

4. Determine the domains of the functions defined by:

   (a) $y = \ln(x + 1)$ (b) $y = \ln\left(\dfrac{3x - 1}{1 - x}\right)$ (c) $y = \ln |x|$

5. Determine the domains of the functions defined by:

   (a) $y = \ln(x^2 - 1)$ (b) $y = \ln(\ln x)$ (c) $y = \dfrac{1}{\ln(\ln x) - 1}$

6. Find the intervals where the following functions are increasing:

   (a) $y = \ln(4 - x^2)$ (b) $y = x^3 \ln x$ (c) $y = \dfrac{(1 - \ln x)^2}{2x}$

7. Find the equation for the tangent to the graph of

   (a) $y = \ln x$ at the points with x-coordinates   (i) 1   (ii) $\frac{1}{2}$ (iii) e

   (b) $y = xe^x$ at the points with x-coordinates   (i) 0   (ii) 1   (iii) -2

8. Use logarithmic differentiation to find $f'(x)/f(x)$ when:

   (a) $f(x) = \left(\dfrac{x + 1}{x - 1}\right)^{1/3}$ (b) $f(x) = x^{2x}$ (c) $f(x) = \sqrt{x - 2}\,(x^2 + 1)(x^4 + 6)$

HARDER PROBLEMS

9. Differentiate the following functions using logarithmic differentiation:

   (a) $y = (2x)^x$ (b) $y = x^{\sqrt{x}}$ (c) $y = \left(\sqrt{x}\right)^x$

10. Prove that if u and v are differentiable functions of x, and $u > 0$, then

$$y = u^v \;\Rightarrow\; y' = u^v\left(v' \ln u + \dfrac{vu'}{u}\right)$$

11. If $f(x) = e^x - 1 - x$, then $f'(x) = e^x - 1 > 0$ for all $x > 0$. The function $f(x)$ therefore increases when x increases. Since $f(0) = 0$, it follows that $f(x) > 0$ for all $x > 0$, and so that $e^x > 1 + x$ for all $x > 0$. Use the same method to prove the following inequalities:

(a) $e^x > 1 + x + x^2/2$ for $x > 0$

(b) $\frac{1}{2}x < \ln(1 + x) < x$ for $0 < x < 1$

(c) $\ln x < 2(\sqrt{x} - 1)$ for $x > 1$

REVIEW PROBLEMS FOR CHAPTER 6

1. Let $f(x) = x^2 - x + 2$. Show that $[f(x + h) - f(x)]/h = 2x - 1 + h$, and use this result to find $f'(x)$.

2. Let $f(x) = -2x^3 + x^2$. Compute $[f(x + h) - f(x)]/h$, and find $f'(x)$.

3. Compute the first and second-order derivatives of the following functions:

(a) $y = 2x - 5$ (b) $y = \frac{1}{3}x^9$ (c) $y = 1 - \frac{1}{10}x^{10}$ (d) $y = 3x^7 + 8$

(e) $y = \frac{x - 5}{10}$ (f) $y = x^5 - x^{-5}$ (g) $y = \frac{x^4}{4} + \frac{x^3}{3} + \frac{5^2}{2}$ (h) $y = \frac{1}{x} + \frac{1}{x^3}$

4. Let $C(Q)$ denote the cost of producing Q units per month of a commodity. What is the interpretation of $C'(1000) = 25$? Suppose the price obtained per unit is fixed at 30 and that the current output per month is 1000. Is it profitable to increase production?

5. For each of the following functions, find the equation for the tangent to the graph at the specified point:

(a) $y = -3x^2$ at $x = 1$ (b) $y = \sqrt{x} - x^2$ at $x = 4$ (c) $y = \frac{x^2 - x^3}{x + 3}$ at $x = 1$

6. Let $A(x)$ denote the dollar cost of building a house with a floor area of x square metres. What is the interpretation of $A'(100) = 250$?

7. Differentiate the following functions:

(a) $f(x) = x(x^2 + 1)$ (b) $g(w) = w^{-5}$ (c) $h(y) = y(y - 1)(y + 1)$

(d) $G(t) = \frac{2t + 1}{t^2 + 3}$ (e) $\varphi(\xi) = \frac{2\xi}{\xi^2 + 2}$ (f) $F(s) = \frac{s}{s^2 + s - 2}$

8. Find the derivatives: (a) $\frac{d}{da}(a^2t - t^2)$ (b) $\frac{d}{dt}(a^2t - t^2)$ (c) $\frac{d}{d\varphi}(x\varphi^2 - \sqrt{\varphi})$

9. Use the chain rule to find dy/dx for the following:

   (a) $y = 10u^2$ and $u = 5 - x^2$ (b) $y = \sqrt{u}$ and $u = \dfrac{1}{x} - 1$

10. Compute the following:

   (a) dZ/dt when $Z = (u^2 - 1)^3$ and $u = t^3$.

   (b) dK/dt when $K = \sqrt{L}$ and $L = 1 + 1/t$.

11. If $a(t)$ and $b(t)$ are positive valued differentiable functions of t, and if A, α, and β are constants, find expressions for $\dot{x}/x$ where:

   (a) $x = \left(a(t)\right)^2 b(t)$ (b) $x = A\left(a(t)\right)^\alpha \left(b(t)\right)^\beta$ (c) $x = A\left((a(t))^\alpha + (b(t))^\beta\right)^{\alpha+\beta}$

12. If $R = S^\alpha$, $S = 1 + \beta K^\gamma$, and $K = At^p + B$, find an expression for dR/dt.

13. Find the derivatives of the following functions, where a, b, p, and q are constants:

   (a) $h(L) = (L^a + b)^p$ (b) $C(Q) = aQ + bQ^2$ (c) $P(x) = \left(ax^{1/q} + b\right)^q$

14. Find the first-order derivatives of:

   (a) $y = -7e^x$ (b) $y = e^{-3x^2}$ (c) $y = \dfrac{x^2}{e^x}$ (d) $y = e^x \ln(x^2 + 2)$

   (e) $y = e^{5x^3}$ (f) $y = 2 - x^4 e^{-x}$ (g) $y = (e^x + x^2)^{10}$ (h) $y = \ln(\sqrt{x} + 1)$

15. Find the intervals where the following functions are increasing:

   (a) $y = (\ln x)^2 - 4$ (b) $y = \ln(e^x + e^{-x})$ (c) $y = x - \dfrac{3}{2}\ln(x^2 + 2)$

16. (a) Suppose $\pi(Q) = QP(Q) - cQ$, where P is a differentiable function and c is a constant. Find an expression for $d\pi/dQ$.

   (b) Suppose $\pi(L) = PF(L) - wL$, where F is a differentiable function and P and w are constants. Find an expression for $d\pi/dL$.

7 DERIVATIVES IN USE

Although this may seem a paradox, all science is dominated by the idea of approximation.
—Bertrand Russell

Many economic models involve functions that are defined implicitly by one or more equations. In some simple but economically relevant cases, we begin this chapter by showing how to compute derivatives of such functions, including how to differentiate the inverse. It is very important for economists to master the technique of implicit differentiation.

Next we consider linear approximations and differentials, followed by a discussion of quadratic and higher order polynomial approximations. Section 7.6 studies Taylor's formula, which makes it possible to analyse the resulting error when a function is approximated by a polynomial.

A discussion of the important economic concept of elasticity follows in Section 7.7.

The word *continuous* is common even in everyday language. We use it, in particular, to characterize changes that are gradual rather than sudden. This usage is closely related to the idea of a continuous function. In Section 7.8 we discuss this concept and explain its close relationship with the limit concept. Limits and continuity are key ideas in mathematics, and also very important in the application of mathematics to economic problems. The preliminary discussion of limits in Section 6.5 was necessarily very sketchy. In Section 7.9 we take a closer look at this concept and extend it in several directions.

Next we present the intermediate value theorem, which makes precise the idea that a continuous function has a "connected" graph. This makes it possible to prove that certain equations have solutions. A brief discussion of Newton's method for finding approximate solutions to equations is given. A short section on infinite sequences follows. Finally, Section 7.12 presents l'Hôpital's rule for indeterminate forms, which is sometimes useful for evaluating limits.

7.1 Implicit Differentiation

We know how to differentiate functions given by explicit formulas. Now we consider how to differentiate functions defined implicitly by an equation. We begin by considering a very simple case.

EXAMPLE 1   Consider the following equation in x and y,

$$xy = 5 \qquad (*)$$

If $x = 1$, then $y = 5$. Also, $x = 3$ gives $y = 5/3$. And $x = 5$ gives $y = 1$. In general, for each number $x \neq 0$, there is a unique number y such that the pair (x, y) satisfies the equation. We say that equation $(*)$ *defines y implicitly as a function of x*. The graph of equation $(*)$ for $x > 0$ is shown in Fig. 1.

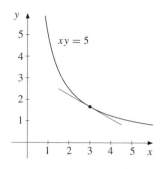

Figure 1 $xy = 5$, $x > 0$

Economists often need to know the slope of the tangent at an arbitrary point on such a graph. i.e. to know the derivative of y as a function of x.

The answer can be found by implicit differentiation of equation $(*)$, which defines y as a function of x. If we denote this function by f, then replacing y by $f(x)$ gives

$$xf(x) = 5 \qquad \text{for all} \quad x \neq 0$$

Because the left and right sides of the equation are equal for all $x > 0$, the derivative of the left-hand side w.r.t. x must be equal to the derivative of the right-hand side w.r.t. x. The derivative of the constant 5 is 0. When we differentiate $xf(x)$, we must use the product rule. Therefore, by differentiating $(*)$ w.r.t. x, we obtain

$$1 \cdot f(x) + xf'(x) = 0 \qquad (**)$$

It follows that for $x \neq 0$,

$$f'(x) = -\frac{f(x)}{x}$$

If $x = 3$, then $f(3) = 5/3$, and thus $f'(3) = -(5/3)/3 = -5/9$, which agrees with Fig. 1.

Usually, we do not introduce a name like f for y as a function of x. Instead, when we differentiate $(*)$ w.r.t. x, we recall that y is a differentiable function of x, and so we write $y + xy' = 0$. Solving for y' gives

$$y' = -\frac{y}{x} \qquad (***)$$

For this particular example, there is another way to find the answer. Solving equation $(*)$ for y gives $y = 5/x = 5x^{-1}$, and hence direct differentiation gives $y' = 5(-1)x^{-2} = -5/x^2$. Note that substituting $5/x$ for y in $(***)$ yields $y' = -5/x^2$ again.

EXAMPLE 2   The graph of

$$y^3 + 3x^2 y = 13 \tag{$*$}$$

was studied in Example 5.4.2. It passes through the point $(2, 1)$. Find the slope of the graph at that point. (The graph is shown in Fig. 2.)

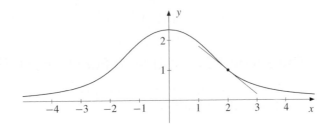

Figure 2 The graph of $y^3 + 3x^2 y = 13$

Solution: Since there is no simple way of expressing y as an explicit function of x, we use implicit differentiation. We think of replacing y with an unspecified function of x wherever y occurs. Then $y^3 + 3x^2 y$ becomes a function of x which is equal to the constant 13 for all x. So the derivative of $y^3 + 3x^2 y$ w.r.t. x must be equal to zero for all x. According to the chain rule, the derivative of y^3 w.r.t. x is equal to $3y^2 y'$. Using the product rule, the derivative of $3x^2 y$ is equal to $6xy + 3x^2 y'$. Hence, differentiating $(*)$ gives

$$3y^2 y' + 6xy + 3x^2 y' = 0 \tag{$**$}$$

Solving this equation for y' yields

$$y' = \frac{-6xy}{3x^2 + 3y^2} = \frac{-2xy}{x^2 + y^2} \tag{$***$}$$

For $x = 2$, $y = 1$ we find $y' = -4/5$, which agrees with Fig. 2.

Examples 1 and 2 illustrate the following general method.

THE METHOD OF IMPLICIT DIFFERENTIATION

If two variables x and y are related by an equation, to find y':

(a) Differentiate each side of the equation w.r.t. x, considering y as a function of x. (Usually, you will need the chain rule.)

(b) Solve the resulting equation for y'.

The next section shows several economic examples. Particularly important applications of this method are found in the next chapter where a general type of question is: What happens to the optimal solution when parameters change?

EXAMPLE 3   The equation $x^2 y^3 + (y+1)e^{-x} = x + 2$ defines y as a differentiable function of x in a neighbourhood of $(x, y) = (0, 1)$. Compute y' at this point.

Solution: Implicit differentiation w.r.t. x gives

$$2xy^3 + x^2 3y^2 y' + y'e^{-x} + (y+1)(-e^{-x}) = 1$$

Inserting $x = 0$ and $y = 1$ yields $y' + 2(-1) = 1$, implying that $y' = 3$.

The Second Derivative of Functions Defined Implicitly

The following examples suggest how to compute the second derivative of a function that is defined implicitly by an equation.

EXAMPLE 4   Compute y'' when y is given implicitly as a function of x by

$$xy = 5$$

Solution: In Example 1 we found by implicit differentiation that $y + xy' = 0$. Differentiating this equation implicitly w.r.t. x once more, taking into account that y and y' depend on x, we obtain

$$y' + y' + xy'' = 0$$

Inserting the expression $-y/x$ we already have for y' gives $-2y/x + xy'' = 0$. Solving for y'' finally yields

$$y'' = \frac{2y}{x^2}$$

We see that if $y > 0$, then $y'' > 0$, which accords with Fig. 1 since the graph is convex. Because $y = 5/x$, we also get $y'' = 10/x^3$.

In this simple case, we can check the answer directly. Since $y = 5x^{-1}$ and $y' = -5x^{-2}$, we have $y'' = 10x^{-3}$.

In order to find y'' we can also use formula (***) in Example 1 and differentiate the fraction w.r.t. x, again taking into account that y depends on x:

$$y'' = -\frac{y'x - y}{x^2} = -\frac{(-y/x)x - y}{x^2} = \frac{2y}{x^2}$$

EXAMPLE 5   For the function defined by the equation $y^3 + 3x^2 y = 13$ in Example 2, find y'' at the point $(2, 1)$.

Solution: The easiest approach is to differentiate equation (**) in Example 2 w.r.t. x. The derivative of $3y^2 y'$ w.r.t. x is $(6yy')y' + 3y^2 y'' = 6y(y')^2 + 3y^2 y''$. The two other terms are differentiated in the same way, and we obtain

$$6y(y')^2 + 3y^2 y'' + 6y + 6xy' + 6xy' + 3x^2 y'' = 0$$

Inserting $x = 2$, $y = 1$, and $y' = -4/5$ (see Example 2), then solving the resulting equation, gives $y'' = 78/125$. (An alternative method is to differentiate the fraction in (***) in Example 2 w.r.t. x.)

1. For the following equations, find dy/dx and d^2y/dx^2 by implicit differentiation:

   (a) $x^2y = 1$ (b) $x - y + 3xy = 2$ (c) $y^5 = x^6$

   Check by solving each equation for y and then differentiating.

2. A curve in the uv-plane is given by $u^2 + uv - v^3 = 0$. Compute dv/du by implicit differentiation. Find the point (u, v) on the curve where $dv/du = 0$ and $u \neq 0$.

3. Suppose that y is a differentiable function of x that satisfies the equation

$$2x^2 + 6xy + y^2 = 18$$

   Find y' and y'' at the point $(x, y) = (1, 2)$.

4. For each of the following equations, answer the question: If $y = f(x)$ is a differentiable function that satisfies the equation, what is y'? (a is a positive constant.)

   (a) $x^2 + y^2 = a^2$ (b) $\sqrt{x} + \sqrt{y} = \sqrt{a}$ (c) $x^4 - y^4 = x^2y^3$

5. In one of his papers, the Norwegian mathematician Niels Henrik Abel studied properties related to the curve shown in the figure below, known as a *lemniscate*. It is given by the equation

$$(x^2 + y^2)^2 = a^2(x^2 - y^2) \qquad \text{(a is a positive constant)}$$

   (a) Find the slope of the tangent to this curve at a point (x, y) where $y \neq 0$.

   (b) Determine those points on the curve where the tangent is parallel to the x-axis.

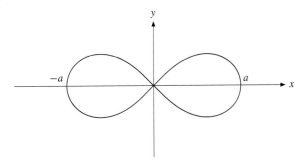

6. Suppose F is a differentiable function of one variable with $F(0) = 0$ and $F'(0) \neq -1$. Find an expression for y' at the point $(x, y) = (1, 0)$ if y is defined implicitly as a differentiable function of x by the equation

$$x^3 F(xy) + e^{xy} = x$$

7.2 Economic Examples

Few mathematical techniques are more important in economics than implicit differentiation, since so many functions in economic models are defined implicitly by an equation or a system of equations. Often the variables have other names than x and y, and one needs to practice differentiating equations with other names for the variables.

EXAMPLE 1   In a standard macroeconomic model for determining national income in a closed economy, it is assumed that

$$\text{(i) } Y = C + I \qquad \text{(ii) } C = f(Y)$$

Here (ii) is the consumption function discussed in Example 4.5.2, whereas (i) states that the national income Y is divided up between consumption C and investment I. Assume that $f'(Y)$, the *marginal propensity to consume*, is between 0 and 1.

(a) Suppose first that $C = f(Y) = 95.05 + 0.712\,Y$ (see Example 4.5.2), and use equations (i) and (ii) to find Y in terms of I.

(b) Inserting the expression for C from (ii) into (i) gives $Y = f(Y) + I$. Suppose that this equation defines Y as a differentiable function of I. Find an expression for dY/dI.

(c) Find $Y'' = d^2Y/dI^2$.

Solution:

(a) In this case, we find that $Y = 95.05 + 0.712\,Y + I$. Solving for Y yields

$$Y = (95.05 + I)/(1 - 0.712) \approx 3.47\,I + 330.03$$

In particular, $dY/dI \approx 3.47$, so if I is increased by \$1 million, then the corresponding increase in the national product is approximately 3.47 million dollars.

(b) Differentiating $Y = f(Y) + I$ w.r.t. I, and using the chain rule, we have

$$\frac{dY}{dI} = f'(Y)\frac{dY}{dI} + 1 \qquad \text{or} \qquad \frac{dY}{dI}\big[1 - f'(Y)\big] = 1 \tag{$*$}$$

Solving for dY/dI yields

$$\frac{dY}{dI} = \frac{1}{1 - f'(Y)} \tag{$**$}$$

For example, if $f'(Y) = 1/2$, then $dY/dI = 2$. If $f'(Y) = 0.712$, then $dY/dI \approx 3.47$. In general, we see that because of the assumption that $f'(Y)$ lies between 0 and 1, so $1 - f'(Y)$ also lies between 0 and 1. Hence $1/\big(1 - f'(Y)\big)$ is always larger than 1. In this model, therefore, a \$1 million increase in investment will always lead to a more than \$1 million increase in the national product. Also, the larger is $f'(Y)$, the marginal propensity to consume, the smaller is $1 - f'(Y)$, and so the larger is dY/dI.

(c) We differentiate the first equation in (∗) implicitly w.r.t. I. The derivative of $f'(Y)$ w.r.t. I is $f''(Y)(dY/dI)$. According to the product rule, the derivative of the product $f'(Y)(dY/dI)$ w.r.t. I is $f''(Y)(dY/dI)(dY/dI) + f'(Y)(dY^2/dI^2)$. Hence,

$$\frac{d^2Y}{dI^2} = f''(Y)\left(\frac{dY}{dI}\right)^2 + f'(Y)\frac{d^2Y}{dI^2}$$

Since $dY/dI = 1/(1 - f'(Y))$, easy algebra yields

$$\frac{d^2Y}{dI^2} = \frac{f''(Y)}{[1 - f'(Y)]^3}$$

EXAMPLE 2   In the linear supply and demand model of Example 4.5.4, suppose that a tax of t per unit is imposed on consumers. Then

$$D = a - b(P + t), \qquad S = \alpha + \beta P \qquad (*)$$

Here a, b, α, and β are positive constants. The equilibrium price is determined by equating supply and demand, so that

$$a - b(P + t) = \alpha + \beta P \qquad (**)$$

(a) Equation (∗∗) implicitly defines the price P as a function of the unit tax t. Compute dP/dt by implicit differentiation. What is its sign? What is the sign of $\frac{d}{dt}(P + t)$? Check the result by first solving equation (∗∗) for P and then finding dP/dt explicitly.

(b) Compute tax revenue T as a function of t. For what value of t does the quadratic function T reach its maximum?

(c) Generalize the foregoing model by assuming that

$$D = f(P + t) \qquad \text{and} \qquad S = g(P)$$

where f and g are differentiable functions with $f' < 0$ and $g' > 0$. The equilibrium condition

$$f(P + t) = g(P)$$

defines P implicitly as a differentiable function of t. Find an expression for dP/dt by implicit differentiation.

Solution:

(a) Differentiating (∗∗) w.r.t. t yields $-b(dP/dt + 1) = \beta\, dP/dt$. Solving for dP/dt gives

$$\frac{dP}{dt} = \frac{-b}{b + \beta}$$

We see that dP/dt is negative. Because P is the price received by the producer, this price will go down if the tax rate t increases. But $P + t$ is the price paid by the consumer. Because

$$\frac{d}{dt}(P + t) = \frac{dP}{dt} + 1 = \frac{-b}{b + \beta} + 1 = \frac{-b + b + \beta}{b + \beta} = \frac{\beta}{b + \beta}$$

we see that $0 < d(P+t)/dt < 1$. Thus, the consumer price increases, but by less than the increase in the tax.

If we solve (∗∗) for P, we obtain

$$P = \frac{a - \alpha - bt}{b + \beta} = \frac{a - \alpha}{b + \beta} - \frac{b}{b + \beta} t$$

This equation shows that the equilibrium price is a linear function of the tax per unit, with slope $-b/(b + \beta)$.

(b) The total tax revenue is $T = St = (\alpha + \beta P)t$, where P is the equilibrium price. Thus,

$$T = \left[\alpha + \beta \left(\frac{a - \alpha}{b + \beta} - \frac{b}{b + \beta} t \right) \right] t = \frac{-b\beta}{b + \beta} t^2 + \frac{a\beta + \alpha b}{b + \beta} t$$

This quadratic function has its maximum at $t = (\alpha b + \beta a)/2b\beta$.

(c) Differentiating the equation $f(P + t) = g(P)$ w.r.t. t yields $f'(P + t)(dP/dt + 1) = g'(P) dP/dt$. Solving for dP/dt gives

$$\frac{dP}{dt} = \frac{f'(P + t)}{g'(P) - f'(P + t)}$$

Because $f' < 0$ and $g' > 0$, we see that dP/dt is negative in this case as well. Moreover,

$$\frac{d}{dt}(P + t) = \frac{dP}{dt} + 1 = \frac{f'(P + t)}{g'(P) - f'(P + t)} + 1 = \frac{g'(P)}{g'(P) - f'(P + t)}$$

which implies that $0 < d(P + t)/dt < 1$. ▌

PROBLEMS FOR SECTION 7.2

1. According to Wold, the demand Q for butter in Stockholm during the period 1925–1937 was related to the price P by the equation $Q \cdot P^{1/2} = 38$. Find dQ/dP by implicit differentiation. Check the answer by using a different method to compute the derivative.

2. Consider a profit maximizing firm producing a single commodity. If the firm gets a fixed price P per unit sold, its profit from selling Q units is $\pi(Q) = PQ - C(Q)$, where $C(Q)$ is the cost function. Assume that $C'(Q) > 0$ and $C''(Q) > 0$. In Example 8.5.1, it will be shown that $Q = Q^* > 0$ maximizes profits provided

$$P = C'(Q^*) \tag{∗}$$

Thus, at the optimum, marginal cost must equal the price per unit.

(a) By implicit differentiation of (∗) w.r.t. P, find an expression for dQ^*/dP.

(b) Comment on the sign of dQ^*/dP.

3. Suppose the demand $D(P, r)$ for a certain commodity (like a Rolls-Royce car) depends on price per unit P and the interest rate r. What are the natural requirements on the signs of the partial derivatives of D w.r.t. P and r? Suppose the supply is constant R, so that in equilibrium, $D(P, r) = R$. By implicit differentiation find dP/dr, and comment on its sign.

4. A standard macroeconomic model for income determination in an open economy is

(i) $Y = C + I + \bar{X} - M$ (ii) $C = f(Y)$ (iii) $M = g(Y)$

where $0 < f'(Y) < 1$. Here $\bar{X}$ is an exogenous constant that denotes exports, whereas M denotes the volume of imports. The function g in (iii) is called an *import function*. By inserting (ii) and (iii) into (i), we obtain an equation that defines Y as a function of exogenous investment I.

(a) Find an expression for dY/dI by implicit differentiation. What is the likely sign of $g'(Y)$? Discuss the sign of dY/dI.

(b) Find an expression for d^2Y/dI^2.

7.3 Differentiating the Inverse

Section 5.3 dealt with inverse functions. If f is a one-to-one function defined on an interval I, it has an inverse function g defined on the range $f(I)$ of f. What is the relationship between the derivatives of f and g?

EXAMPLE 1   The two linear functions

$$f(x) = ax + b \quad \text{and} \quad g(x) = \frac{1}{a}x - \frac{b}{a} \quad (a \neq 0)$$

are inverses of each other. (Verify this.) The graphs are straight lines which are symmetric about the line $y = x$. The slopes are respectively a and $1/a$. Look back at Figure 5.3.3 and notice that this result is confirmed, since the slope of f is 4 and the slope of g is $1/4$.

In general, if f and g are inverses of each other, then

$$g(f(x)) = x \qquad \text{for all } x \text{ in } I \tag{1}$$

By implicit differentiation we can easily find the relationship between the derivatives of f and g, if we *assume* that both f and g are differentiable. Differentiating (1) w.r.t. x gives

$$g'(f(x))f'(x) = 1$$

so that if $f'(x) \neq 0$, then

$$g'\big(f(x)\big) = \frac{1}{f'(x)} \tag{2}$$

It follows from (2) that f' and g' have the same sign. If f is strictly increasing (decreasing), then g is strictly increasing (decreasing), and vice versa.

The most important facts about inverse functions are summed up in this theorem:

THEOREM 7.3.1 (INVERSE FUNCTIONS)

If f is differentiable and strictly increasing (or strictly decreasing) in an interval I, then f has an inverse function g, which is strictly increasing (strictly decreasing) in the interval $f(I)$. If x_0 is an interior point of I and $f'(x_0) \neq 0$, then g is differentiable at $y_0 = f(x_0)$ and $\qquad$ (3)

$$g'(y_0) = \frac{1}{f'(x_0)} \qquad (y_0 = f(x_0))$$

NOTE 1 Formula (3) is used as follows to find the derivative of g at a point y_0. First find, if possible, the point x_0 in I at which $f(x_0) = y_0$. Thereafter, compute $f'(x)$, and then find $f'(x_0)$. If $f'(x_0) \neq 0$, then g has a derivative at y_0 given by $g'(y_0) = 1/f'(x_0)$.

The geometric interpretation of formula (3) is shown in Fig. 1, where f and g are inverses of each other. Let the slope of the tangent at P be $a = f'(x_0)$. At the point Q, the x-coordinate is $f(x_0)$, and the slope of the tangent at that point is $g'(f(x_0))$. This number is equal to $1/a$. (In the figure, $a \approx 1/3$, and $1/a \approx 3$.)

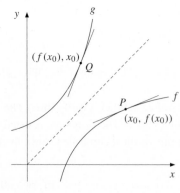

Figure 1

EXAMPLE 2   Suppose the function f is defined for all x by the following formula

$$f(x) = x^5 + 3x^3 + 6x - 3$$

Show that f has an inverse function g. Use formula (3) to find $g'(7)$. (Note that $f(1) = 7$.)

Solution: Differentiating $f(x)$ yields $f'(x) = 5x^4 + 9x^2 + 6$. Clearly, $f'(x) > 0$ for all x, so f is strictly increasing and consequently it is one-to-one. It therefore has an inverse function g.

To find $g'(7)$, we use formula (3) with $x_0 = 1$ and $y_0 = 7$. Since $f'(1) = 20$, we obtain $g'(7) = 1/f'(1) = 1/20$. Note that we have found $g'(7)$ exactly even though it is impossible to find any algebraic formula for the function g. ❙

EXAMPLE 3   Suppose that f and g are twice differentiable functions which are inverses of each other. Differentiating (2) w.r.t. x, find an expression for $g''(f(x))$.

Solution: Differentiating (2) w.r.t. x yields

$$g''(f(x))f'(x) = (-1)(f'(x))^{-2}f''(x)$$

It follows that if $f'(x) \neq 0$, then

$$g''(f(x)) = -\frac{f''(x)}{(f'(x))^3} \tag{4}$$

(If $f' > 0$, then $f''(x)$ and $g''(f(x))$ have opposite sign, but they have the same sign if $f' < 0$. In particular, if f is increasing and concave, the inverse g is increasing and convex as in Fig. 1.) ❙

PROBLEMS FOR SECTION 7.3

1. The function defined for all x by $f(x) = e^{2x-2}$ has an inverse g. Use formula (3) to find $g'(1)$. Check your result by finding a formula for g.

2. The function f is defined for $|x| \leq 2$ by the formula

$$f(x) = \tfrac{1}{3}x^3\sqrt{4 - x^2}$$

(a) Find the intervals of increase and decrease and sketch the graph of f.

(b) Explain why f has an inverse function g on $[0, \sqrt{3}\,]$, and compute $g'(\tfrac{1}{3}\sqrt{3})$. (*Hint:* $f(1) = \tfrac{1}{3}\sqrt{3}$.)

3. Let f be defined by $f(x) = \ln(2 + e^{x-3})$ for all x.

(a) Show that f is strictly increasing and find the range of f.

(b) Find an expression for the inverse function g of f. Where is g defined?

(c) Verify that $f'(3) = 1/g'(f(3))$.

7.4 Linear Approximations

To avoid working with a complicated function, we might try replacing it with a simpler function as an approximation. Linear functions are easy to work with, so it is natural to try first using a "linear approximation" to the given function.

Consider a function $f(x)$ that is differentiable at $x = a$. The tangent to the graph at $(a, f(a))$ has the equation $y = f(a) + f'(a)(x - a)$ (see (2) in Section 6.2). If we approximate the graph of f by its tangent line at $x = a$, as shown in Fig. 1, the resulting approximation has a special name.

The **linear approximation** to f about $x = a$ is

$$f(x) \approx f(a) + f'(a)(x - a) \qquad (x \text{ close to } a)$$

(1)

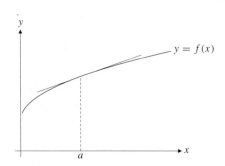

Figure 1 Approximation of a function by its tangent

Note that if $p(x)$ is the linear function $f(a) + f'(a)(x - a)$ of x, then f and p have both the same value and the same derivative at $x = a$. [1]

EXAMPLE 1   Find the linear approximation to $f(x) = \sqrt[3]{x}$ about $x = 1$.

Solution: We have $f(x) = \sqrt[3]{x} = x^{1/3}$, so $f'(x) = \frac{1}{3}x^{-2/3}$ and $f'(1) = \frac{1}{3}$. Because $f(1) = 1$, using (1) yields

$$\sqrt[3]{x} \approx f(1) + f'(1)(x - 1) = 1 + \frac{1}{3}(x - 1) \qquad (x \text{ close to } 1)$$

For example, $\sqrt[3]{1.03} \approx 1 + \frac{1}{3}(1.03 - 1) = 1 + \frac{1}{3}(0.03) = 1.01$. The correct value to 4 decimals is 1.0099. ▌

EXAMPLE 2   In a paper by economists Samuelson and Swamy, the authors were concerned with the behaviour of the following function about $\varepsilon = 0$:

$$f(\varepsilon) = \left(1 + \tfrac{3}{2}\varepsilon + \tfrac{1}{2}\varepsilon^2\right)^{1/2}$$

Find the linear approximation to $f(\varepsilon)$ about $\varepsilon = 0$.

---

[1] One can prove that if f is differentiable, then $f(x) - f(a) = f'(a)(x - a) + \varepsilon(x - a)$ where $\varepsilon \to 0$ as $x \to a$. (If $x - a$ is very small, then ε is very small, and $\varepsilon(x - a)$ is "very-very small".)

Solution: Here $f'(\varepsilon) = \frac{1}{2}\left(1 + \frac{3}{2}\varepsilon + \frac{1}{2}\varepsilon^2\right)^{-1/2} \cdot \left(\frac{3}{2} + \varepsilon\right)$ and so $f'(0) = \frac{3}{4}$. Because $f(0) = 1$, using (1) we get

$$\left(1 + \tfrac{3}{2}\varepsilon + \tfrac{1}{2}\varepsilon^2\right)^{1/2} \approx 1 + \tfrac{3}{4}\varepsilon \qquad (\varepsilon \text{ close to } 0)$$

EXAMPLE 3   Use (1) to find an approximate value for $(1.001)^{50}$.

Solution: We put $f(x) = x^{50}$. Then $f(1) = 1$ and $f'(x) = 50x^{49}$, implying that $f'(1) = 50 \cdot 1^{49} = 50$. Hence, by formula (1), with $x = 1.001$ and $a = 1$,

$$(1.001)^{50} \approx 1 + 50 \cdot 0.001 = 1.05$$

(Using a calculator, we find $(1.001)^{50} \approx 1.0512$.)

The Differential of a Function

Consider a differentiable function $f(x)$, and let dx denote an arbitrary change in the variable x. In this notation, "dx" is not a product of d and x. Rather, dx is a single symbol representing the change in the value of x. The expression $f'(x)\,dx$ is called the **differential** of $y = f(x)$, and it is denoted by dy (or df), so that

$$dy = f'(x)\,dx \qquad (2)$$

Note that dy is proportional to dx, with $f'(x)$ as the factor of proportionality.

Now, if x changes by dx, then the corresponding change in $y = f(x)$ is

$$\Delta y = f(x + dx) - f(x) \qquad (3)$$

In the approximation (1), suppose we replace x by $x + dx$ and a by x. The result is $f(x + dx) \approx f(x) + f'(x)\,dx$. Using the definitions of dy and Δy in (2) and (3) above, we get

$$\Delta y \approx dy = f'(x)\,dx$$

The error resulting from using dy rather than Δy is illustrated graphically in Fig. 2.

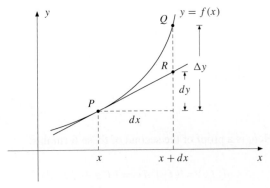

Figure 2 A geometric representation of the differential dy and $\Delta y = f(x + dx) - f(x)$

The differential dy is not the actual increment in y as x is changed to $x + dx$, but rather the change in y that would occur if y continued to change at the fixed rate $f'(x)$ as x changes to $x + dx$. Fig. 2 illustrates the difference between Δy and dy. Consider, first, the movement from P to Q along the curve $y = f(x)$: as x changes by dx, the actual change in the vertical height of the point is Δy. Suppose instead that we are only allowed to move along the tangent to the graph at P. Thus, as we move from P to R along the tangent, the change in height that corresponds to dx is dy. As in Fig. 2, the approximation $\Delta y \approx dy$ is usually better if dx is smaller in absolute value. This is because the length of line segment RQ, representing the difference between Δy and dy, tends to 0 as dx tends to 0.

Rules for Differentials

The notation $(d/dx)(\cdot)$ calls for the expression in parentheses to be differentiated with respect to x. For example, $(d/dx)(x^3) = 3x^2$. In the same way, we let $d(\cdot)$ denote the differential of whatever is inside the parentheses.

EXAMPLE 4   Compute the following differentials:

(a) $d(Ax^a + B)$ (A, B, and a are constants)

(b) $d(f(K))$ (f is a differentiable function of K)

Solution:

(a) Putting $f(x) = Ax^a + B$, we get $f'(x) = Aax^{a-1}$, so $d(Ax^a + B) = Aax^{a-1}\,dx$.

(b) $d(f(K)) = f'(K)\,dK$.   ∎

All the usual rules for differentiation can be expressed in terms of differentials. If f and g are two differentiable functions of x, then the following rules hold.

RULES FOR DIFFERENTIALS

$$d(af + bg) = a\,df + b\,dg \qquad (a \text{ and } b \text{ are constants})$$

$$d(fg) = g\,df + f\,dg$$

$$d\left(\frac{f}{g}\right) = \frac{g\,df - f\,dg}{g^2} \qquad (g \neq 0)$$

(4)

Here is a proof of the second of these formulas:

$$d(fg) = (fg)'\,dx = (f'g + fg')\,dx = gf'\,dx + fg'\,dx = g\,df + f\,dg$$

You should now prove the other rules in the same way.

Suppose that $y = f(x)$ and that $x = g(t)$ is a function of t. Then $y = h(t) = f\big(g(t)\big)$ is a function of t. The differential of $y = h(t)$ is $dy = h'(t)\, dt$. According to the chain rule, $h'(t) = f'\,(g(t))\, g'(t)$, so that $dy = f'\big(g(t)\big) g'(t)\, dt$. Because $x = g(t)$, the differential of x is equal to $dx = g'(t)\, dt$, and therefore, $dy = f'(x)\, dx$.

This shows that *if $y = f(x)$, then the differential of y is equal to $dy = f'(x)\, dx$, whether x depends on another variable or not.*

Economists often use differentials in their models. A typical example follows.

EXAMPLE 5   Consider again the model in Example 7.2.1:

$$\text{(i)}\ \ Y = C + I \qquad \text{(ii)}\ \ C = f(Y)$$

Find the differential dY expressed in terms of dI. If in addition to (i) and (ii) it is assumed that employment $N = g(Y)$ is a function of Y, find also the differential dN expressed in terms of dI.

Solution: Taking differentials in (i) and (ii), we obtain

$$\text{(iii)}\ \ dY = dC + dI \qquad \text{(iv)}\ \ dC = f'(Y)\, dY$$

Substituting dC from (iv) into (iii) and solving for dY yields

$$dY = \frac{1}{1 - f'(Y)}\, dI$$

which is the same formula found previously. From $N = g(Y)$, we get $dN = g'(Y)\, dY$, so

$$dN = \frac{g'(Y)}{1 - f'(Y)}\, dI$$

Provided that $g'(Y) > 0$ (employment increases as national income increases) and $f'(Y)$, the marginal propensity to consume, is between 0 and 1, we see from the formula for dN that if investment increases, then employment increases.   ∎

PROBLEMS FOR SECTION 7.4

1. Prove that

$$\sqrt{1 + x} \approx 1 + \frac{1}{2}x$$

   for x close to 0, and illustrate this approximation by drawing the graphs of $y = 1 + \frac{1}{2}x$ and $y = \sqrt{1 + x}$ in the same coordinate system.

2. Use (1) to find the linear approximation to $f(x) = (5x + 3)^{-2}$ about $x = 0$.

3. Find the linear approximations to the following functions about $x = 0$:

   (a) $f(x) = (1+x)^{-1}$ (b) $f(x) = (1+x)^5$ (c) $f(x) = (1-x)^{1/4}$

4. Find the linear approximation to $F(K) = AK^\alpha$ about $K = 1$.

5. Find the differentials:

   (a) $d(10x^3)$ (b) $d(5x^3 - 5x^2 + 5x + 5)$ (c) $d(1/x^3)$ (d) $d(\ln x)$

6. Find the differentials (p, q, and r are constants):

   (a) $d(x^p + x^q)$ (b) $d(x^p x^q)$ (c) $d(px + q)^r$ (d) $d(e^{px} + e^{qx})$

7. Prove that $(1+x)^m \approx 1 + mx$ for x close to 0, and use this to find approximations to the following numbers:

   (a) $\sqrt[3]{1.1} = \left(1 + \dfrac{1}{10}\right)^{1/3}$ (b) $\sqrt[5]{33} = 2\left(1 + \dfrac{1}{32}\right)^{1/5}$ (c) $\sqrt[3]{9} = \sqrt[3]{8+1}$

   (d) $(0.98)^{25}$ (e) $\sqrt{37} = \sqrt{36+1}$ (f) $(26.95)^{1/3}$

8. Compute $\Delta y = f(x+dx) - f(x)$ and the differential $dy = f'(x)\, dx$ for the following:

   (a) $f(x) = x^2 + 2x - 3$ when $x = 2$ and: (i) $dx = 1/10$; (ii) $dx = 1/100$

   (b) $f(x) = 1/x$ when $x = 3$ and: (i) $dx = -1/10$; (ii) $dx = -1/100$

   (c) $f(x) = \sqrt{x}$ when $x = 4$ and (i) $dx = 1/20$; (ii) $dx = 1/100$

9. (a) The equation
   $$3xe^{xy^2} - 2y = 3x^2 + y^2$$

   defines y as a differentiable function of x about the point $(x, y) = (1, 0)$. Find the slope of the graph at this point by implicit differentiation.

   (b) What is the linear approximation to y about $x = 1$?

HARDER PROBLEMS

10. (a) A circle with radius r has area $A(r) = \pi r^2$. Then $A'(r) = 2\pi r$, the circumference of the circle. Explain geometrically the approximation $A(r+dr) - A(r) \approx 2\pi r\, dr$.

    (b) Explain geometrically the approximation $V(r + dr) - V(r) \approx 4\pi r^2\, dr$, where $V(r) = \frac{4}{3}\pi r^3$ is the volume and $V'(r) = 4\pi r^2$ is the surface area of a sphere with radius r.

11. Find the linear approximation to the following function about the point $\mu = 0$:

    $$g(\mu) = A(1 + \mu)^{a/(1+b)} - 1 \qquad (A, a, \text{ and } b \text{ are positive constants})$$

7.5 Polynomial Approximations

The previous section discussed approximations of functions of one variable by linear functions. In particular, Example 7.4.1 established the approximation

$$\sqrt[3]{x} \approx 1 + \tfrac{1}{3}(x - 1) \qquad (x \text{ close to } 1)$$

In this case, at $x = 1$, the functions $y = \sqrt[3]{x}$ and $y = 1 + \tfrac{1}{3}(x - 1)$ both have the same value 1, and the same derivative $1/3$.

Approximation by linear functions may well be insufficiently accurate. So it is natural to try quadratic approximations, or approximations by polynomials of a higher order.

Quadratic Approximations

We begin by showing how a twice differentiable function $y = f(x)$ can be approximated near $x = a$ by a quadratic polynomial

$$f(x) \approx p(x) = A + B(x - a) + C(x - a)^2$$

There are three coefficients A, B, and C, to be determined. So we are free to impose three conditions on the polynomial. We arrange that, at $x = a$, both $f(x)$ and $p(x) = A + B(x - a) + C(x - a)^2$ have the same value, the same derivative, and the same second derivative. In symbols, we require $f(a) = p(a)$, $f'(a) = p'(a)$, and $f''(a) = p''(a)$. Now $p'(x) = B + 2C(x - a)$ and $p''(x) = 2C$, so, after inserting $x = a$ into our expressions for $p(x)$, $p'(x)$, and $p''(x)$, it follows that $A = p(a)$, $B = p'(a)$, and $C = \tfrac{1}{2}p''(a)$. This justifies the following:

The **quadratic approximation** to $f(x)$ about $x = a$ is

$$f(x) \approx f(a) + f'(a)(x - a) + \tfrac{1}{2}f''(a)(x - a)^2 \qquad (x \text{ close to } a)$$

(1)

Note that, compared with (7.4.1), we have simply added one extra term. For $a = 0$, in particular, we obtain the following:

$$f(x) \approx f(0) + f'(0)x + \tfrac{1}{2}f''(0)x^2 \qquad (x \text{ close to } 0) \tag{2}$$

EXAMPLE 1   Find the quadratic approximation to $f(x) = \sqrt[3]{x}$ about $x = 1$.

Solution: Here $f'(x) = \tfrac{1}{3}x^{-2/3}$ and $f''(x) = \tfrac{1}{3}(-\tfrac{2}{3})x^{-5/3}$. It follows that $f'(1) = \tfrac{1}{3}$ and $f''(1) = -\tfrac{2}{9}$. Because $f(1) = 1$, using (1) yields

$$\sqrt[3]{x} \approx 1 + \tfrac{1}{3}(x - 1) - \tfrac{1}{9}(x - 1)^2 \qquad (x \text{ close to } 1)$$

For example, $\sqrt[3]{1.03} \approx 1 + \tfrac{1}{3} \cdot 0.03 - \tfrac{1}{9}(0.03)^2 = 1 + 0.01 - 0.0001 = 1.0099$. This is correct to 4 decimals, and so it is better than the linear approximation derived in Example 7.4.1. ∎

EXAMPLE 2   Find the quadratic approximation to $y = y(x)$ about $x = 0$ when y is defined implicitly as a function of x near $(x, y) = (0, 1)$ by $xy^3 + 1 = y$.

Solution: Implicit differentiation w.r.t. x yields

$$y^3 + 3xy^2y' = y' \qquad\qquad (*)$$

Substituting $x = 0$ and $y = 1$ into $(*)$ gives $y' = 1$. Differentiating $(*)$ w.r.t x now yields

$$3y^2y' + (3y^2 + 6xyy')y' + 3xy^2y'' = y''$$

Substituting $x = 0$, $y = 1$, and $y' = 1$, we obtain $y'' = 6$. Hence, according to (2),

$$y(x) \approx y(0) + y'(0)x + \tfrac{1}{2}y''(0)x^2 = 1 + x + 3x^2 \qquad\qquad \blacksquare$$

Higher-Order Approximations

So far, we have considered linear and quadratic approximations. For functions with third and higher order derivatives, we can find even better approximations near one point by using polynomials of a higher degree. Suppose we want to approximate a function $f(x)$ over an interval centred at $x = a$ with an nth-degree polynomial of the form

$$p(x) = A_0 + A_1(x - a) + A_2(x - a)^2 + A_3(x - a)^3 + \cdots + A_n(x - a)^n \qquad (3)$$

Because $p(x)$ has $n + 1$ coefficients, we can impose the following $n + 1$ conditions on this polynomial:

$$f(a) = p(a), \qquad f'(a) = p'(a), \qquad \ldots, \qquad f^{(n)}(a) = p^{(n)}(a)$$

These conditions require that $p(x)$ and its first n derivatives agree with the value of $f(x)$ and its first n derivatives at $x = a$. Let us see what these conditions become when $n = 3$. In this case,

$$p(x) = A_0 + A_1(x - a) + A_2(x - a)^2 + A_3(x - a)^3$$

and we find that

$$p'(x) = A_1 + 2A_2(x - a) + 3A_3(x - a)^2$$
$$p''(x) = 2A_2 + 2 \cdot 3A_3(x - a)$$
$$p'''(x) = 2 \cdot 3A_3$$

Thus, when $x = a$, we have

$$p(a) = A_0, \qquad p'(a) = 1!\, A_1, \qquad p''(a) = 2!\, A_2, \qquad p'''(a) = 3!\, A_3$$

This implies the following approximation:

$$f(x) \approx f(a) + \frac{1}{1!}f'(a)(x - a) + \frac{1}{2!}f''(a)(x - a)^2 + \frac{1}{3!}f'''(a)(x - a)^3$$

Thus, we have added an extra term to the quadratic approximation (1).

The general case follows the same pattern, and we obtain the following approximation to $f(x)$ by an nth-degree polynomial:

Approximation to $f(x)$ about $x = a$:

$$f(x) \approx f(a) + \frac{f'(a)}{1!}(x-a) + \frac{f''(a)}{2!}(x-a)^2 + \cdots + \frac{f^{(n)}(a)}{n!}(x-a)^n$$ (4)

The polynomial on the right-hand side of (4) is called the nth-order **Taylor polynomial** (or Taylor approximation) for f about $x = a$.

The function f and its nth-order Taylor polynomial have such a high degree of contact at $x = a$ that it is reasonable to expect the approximation in (4) to be good over some (possibly small) interval centred about $x = a$. The next section analyses the error that results from using such polynomial approximations. In the case when f is itself a polynomial whose degree does not exceed n, the formula becomes exact, without any approximation error at any point.

EXAMPLE 3   Find the third-order Taylor approximation of $f(x) = \sqrt{1 + x}$ about $x = 0$.

Solution: We write $f(x) = \sqrt{1 + x} = (1 + x)^{1/2}$. Then

$$f'(x) = \tfrac{1}{2}(1 + x)^{-1/2}$$

$$f''(x) = \tfrac{1}{2}\left(-\tfrac{1}{2}\right)(1 + x)^{-3/2}$$

$$f'''(x) = \tfrac{1}{2}\left(-\tfrac{1}{2}\right)\left(-\tfrac{3}{2}\right)(1 + x)^{-5/2}$$

Putting $x = 0$ gives $f(0) = 1$, $f'(0) = 1/2$, $f''(0) = (1/2)(-1/2) = -1/4$, and finally $f'''(0) = (1/2)(-1/2)(-3/2) = 3/8$. Hence, by (4) for the case $n = 3$, we have

$$f(x) \approx 1 + \frac{1}{1!}\frac{1}{2}x + \frac{1}{2!}\left(-\frac{1}{4}\right)x^2 + \frac{1}{3!}\frac{3}{8}x^3 = 1 + \frac{1}{2}x - \frac{1}{8}x^2 + \frac{1}{16}x^3 \qquad \blacksquare$$

EXAMPLE 4   Apply the approximation (4) to $f(x) = e^x$ about $x = 0$.

Solution: This case is particularly simple, because all derivatives of f are equal to e^x, and thus $f^{(k)}(0) = 1$ for all $k = 1, 2, \ldots, n$. Hence (4) yields

$$e^x \approx 1 + \frac{x}{1!} + \frac{x^2}{2!} + \cdots + \frac{x^n}{n!}$$ (5)

which is an important result. $\blacksquare$

1. Find quadratic approximations to the following functions about the given points:

   (a) $f(x) = (1+x)^5$, $x = 0$ (b) $F(K) = AK^\alpha$, $K = 1$

   (c) $f(\varepsilon) = \left(1 + \frac{3}{2}\varepsilon + \frac{1}{2}\varepsilon^2\right)^{1/2}$, $\varepsilon = 0$ (d) $H(x) = (1-x)^{-1}$, $x = 0$

2. Find the fifth-order Taylor polynomial of $f(x) = \ln(1+x)$ about $x = 0$.

3. Find the Taylor polynomial of degree 2 about $x = 0$ for

$$f(x) = 5\left(\ln(1+x) - \sqrt{1+x}\right)$$

4. A study of attitudes to risk is based on the following approximation to a consumer's utility function. Explain how to derive this approximation.

$$U(y + M - s) \approx U(y) + U'(y)(M-s) + \tfrac{1}{2}U''(y)(M-s)^2$$

5. Find the quadratic approximation for y about $(x, y) = (0, 1)$ when y is defined implicitly as a function of x by the equation $1 + x^3 y + x = y^{1/2}$.

6. Let the function $x(t)$ be given by the conditions $x(0) = 1$ and

$$\dot{x}(t) = tx(t) + 2\big[x(t)\big]^2$$

   Determine the second-order Taylor polynomial for $x(t)$ about $t = 0$.

7. Establish the approximation

$$e^{\sigma\sqrt{t/n}} \approx 1 + \sigma\sqrt{t/n} + \sigma^2 t/2n$$

8. Establish the approximation

$$\left(1 + \frac{p}{100}\right)^n \approx 1 + n\frac{p}{100} + \frac{n(n-1)}{2}\left(\frac{p}{100}\right)^2$$

9. The function h is defined for all $x > 0$ by

$$h(x) = \frac{x^p - x^q}{x^p + x^q} \qquad (p > q > 0)$$

   Find the first-order Taylor polynomial about $x = 1$ for $h(x)$.

7.6 Taylor's Formula

The previous section presented polynomial approximations. In particular, the **nth-order Taylor polynomial** approximation of $f(x)$ about $x = 0$ is

$$f(x) \approx f(0) + \frac{1}{1!}f'(0)x + \frac{1}{2!}f''(0)x^2 + \cdots + \frac{1}{n!}f^{(n)}(0)x^n \qquad (*)$$

The usefulness of such polynomial approximations is limited unless something is known about the error that results. Taylor's formula remedies this deficiency. This formula is often used by economists, and is regarded as one of the main results in mathematical analysis.

Consider the approximation in $(*)$. Except at $x = 0$, function $f(x)$ and the Taylor polynomial on the RHS of $(*)$ are usually different. The difference between the two will depend on x as well as on n, and is called the *remainder* after n terms. We denote it by $R_{n+1}(x)$. Hence,

$$f(x) = f(0) + \frac{1}{1!}f'(0)x + \cdots + \frac{1}{n!}f^{(n)}(0)x^n + R_{n+1}(x) \qquad (1)$$

The following theorem gives an important explicit formula for the remainder.[2] (The proof will be given in Note 8.4.2.)

LAGRANGE'S FORM OF THE REMAINDER

Suppose f is $n + 1$ times differentiable in an interval including 0 and x. Then the remainder $R_{n+1}(x)$ given in (1) can be written as

$$R_{n+1}(x) = \frac{1}{(n+1)!}f^{(n+1)}(c)x^{n+1} \qquad (2)$$

for some number c between 0 and x.

Using this formula for $R_{n+1}(x)$ in (1), we obtain

TAYLOR'S FORMULA

$$f(x) = f(0) + \frac{1}{1!}f'(0)x + \cdots + \frac{1}{n!}f^{(n)}(0)x^n + \frac{1}{(n+1)!}f^{(n+1)}(c)x^{n+1} \qquad (3)$$

Note that the remainder resembles the preceding terms in the sum. The only difference is that in the formula for the remainder, $f^{(n+1)}$ is evaluated at a point c, where c is some

[2] The English mathematician Brook Taylor had already found polynomial approximations of the general form $(*)$ in 1715. Lagrange proved (2) approximately 50 years later.

unspecified number between 0 and x, whereas in all the other terms, the derivatives are evaluated at 0. The number c is not fixed because it depends, in general, on x as well as on n.

If we put $n = 1$ in formula (3), we obtain

$$f(x) = f(0) + f'(0)x + \tfrac{1}{2}f''(c)x^2 \qquad \text{for some } c \text{ between 0 and } x \qquad (4)$$

This formula tells us that $\tfrac{1}{2}f''(c)x^2$ is the error that results if we replace $f(x)$ with its linear approximation about $x = 0$.

How do we use the remainder formula? It suggests an upper limit for the error that results if we replace f with its nth Taylor polynomial. Suppose, for instance, that for all x in an interval I, the absolute value of $f^{(n+1)}(x)$ is at most M. Then we can conclude that in this interval

$$|R_{n+1}(x)| \le \frac{M}{(n+1)!}|x|^{n+1} \qquad (5)$$

Note that if n is a large number and if x is close to 0, then $|R_{n+1}(x)|$ is small for two reasons: first, if n is large, the number $(n+1)!$ in the denominator in (5) is large; second, if $|x|$ is less than 1, then $|x|^{n+1}$ is also small when n is large.

EXAMPLE 1   Find Taylor's formula for

$$f(x) = \sqrt{25+x} = (25+x)^{1/2}$$

with $n = 1$, and use it to give an estimate of $\sqrt{25.01}$.

Solution: We use the approximation in (4). Here $f(0) = 5$, and

$$f'(x) = \frac{1}{2}(25+x)^{-1/2}, \qquad f''(x) = \frac{1}{2}\left(-\frac{1}{2}\right)(25+x)^{-3/2}$$

Thus, $f'(0) = 1/2 \cdot 1/5 = 1/10$ and $f''(c) = -(1/4)(25+c)^{-3/2}$. So by (4), for some c between 0 and x, one has

$$\sqrt{25+x} = 5 + \frac{1}{10}x + \frac{1}{2}\left(-\frac{1}{4}\right)(25+c)^{-3/2}x^2 = 5 + \frac{1}{10}x - \frac{1}{8}(25+c)^{-3/2}x^2 \qquad (*)$$

In order to estimate $\sqrt{25.01}$, we write $25.01 = 25 + 0.01$ and use $(*)$. If $x = 0.01$, then c lies between 0 and 0.01, so $25 + c > 25$. Then $(25+c)^{-3/2} < (25)^{-3/2} = 1/125$, so the absolute value of the remainder is

$$|R_2(0.01)| = \left|\frac{-1}{8}(25+c)^{-3/2}\left(\frac{1}{100}\right)^2\right| \le \frac{1}{80\,000} \cdot \frac{1}{125} = 10^{-7}$$

We conclude that $\sqrt{25.01} \approx 5 + 1/10 \cdot 1/100 = 5.001$, with an error less than 10^{-7}.   ∎

EXAMPLE 2   Find Taylor's formula for $f(x) = e^x$, and estimate the error term for $n = 3$ and $x = 0.1$.

Solution: From Example 4 in the previous section, it follows that there exists a number c between 0 and x such that

$$e^x = 1 + \frac{x}{1!} + \frac{x^2}{2!} + \cdots + \frac{x^n}{n!} + \frac{x^{n+1}}{(n+1)!} e^c \tag{6}$$

One can prove that for each fixed number x the remainder term in (6) approaches 0 as n approaches infinity. Using (6) one can therefore find the value of e^x for any x to an arbitrary degree of accuracy. However, if $|x|$ is large, a large number of terms have to be used in order to obtain a good degree of accuracy, because the remainder approaches 0 very slowly as n approaches infinity.

For $n = 3$ and $x = 0.1$, we obtain for some c in the interval $(0, 0.1)$,

$$e^{0.1} = 1 + \frac{1}{10} + \frac{1}{200} + \frac{1}{6000} + \frac{(0.1)^4}{24} e^c \tag{$*$}$$

For $c < 0.1$, we have $e^c < e^{0.1}$. We claim that $e^{0.1} < 1.2$. To prove this note that $(1.2)^{10} \approx 6.2$, so $e < (1.2)^{10}$, and thus $e^{0.1} < ((1.2)^{10})^{0.1} = 1.2$. Hence

$$\left| R_4 \left(\frac{1}{10} \right) \right| = \frac{(0.1)^4}{24} e^c < \frac{1}{240\,000} 1.2 = 0.000\,005 = 5 \cdot 10^{-6}$$

The error that results from dropping the remainder from $(*)$ is therefore less than $5 \cdot 10^{-6}$. ∎

NOTE 1   Suppose we consider the Taylor formula on an interval about $x = a$ instead of $x = 0$. The new remainder is

$$R_{n+1}(x) = \frac{1}{(n+1)!} f^{(n+1)}(c)(x-a)^{n+1} \qquad (c \text{ is between } x \text{ and } a) \tag{7}$$

This term must be added to the right-hand side of (4) in the previous section in order to obtain equality.

It is easy to show that (7) follows from (1) and (2) by considering the function g defined by $g(t) = f(a+t)$ when t is close to 0.

PROBLEMS FOR SECTION 7.6

1. Write Taylor's formula (3) with $n = 2$ for $f(x) = \ln(1 + x)$.

2. Use the approximation $(1 + x)^m \approx 1 + mx + \frac{1}{2}m(m-1)x^2$ to find values of

    (a) $\sqrt[3]{25}$ (b) $\sqrt[5]{33}$

    (*Hint:* Note that $\sqrt[3]{25} = 3(1 - 2/27)^{1/3}$.) Check these approximations by using a calculator.

3. Show that $\sqrt[3]{9} = 2\,(1 + 1/8)^{1/3}$. Use formula (3) (with $n = 2$) to compute $\sqrt[3]{9}$ to the third decimal.

4. Let
$$g(x) = \sqrt[3]{1+x}$$

(a) Find the Taylor polynomial of $g(x)$ of order 2 about the origin.

(b) For $x \geq 0$ show that $|R_3(x)| \leq 5x^3/81$.

(c) Find $\sqrt[3]{1003}$ to 7 significant digits.

7.7 Why Economists Use Elasticities

Economists often study how demand for a certain commodity such as coffee reacts to price changes. We can ask by how many units such as kilograms the quantity demanded will change when the price increases by $1. In this way, we obtain a concrete number, measured in units of the commodity. There are, however, several unsatisfactory aspects to this way of measuring the sensitivity of demand to price changes. For instance, a $1 increase in the price of a kilo of coffee may be considerable, whereas a $1 increase in the price of a car is insignificant.

This problem arises because the sensitivity of demand to price changes is being measured in the same arbitrary units as those used to measure both quantity demanded and price. The difficulties are eliminated if we use relative changes instead. We ask by what percentage the quantity demanded changes when the price increases by 1%. The number we obtain in this way will be independent of the units in which both quantities and prices are measured. This number is called the **price elasticity of demand**, measured at a given price.

In 1960, the price elasticity of butter in a certain country was estimated to be -1. This means that an increase of 1% in the price would lead to a decrease of 1% in the demand, if all the other factors that influence the demand remained constant. The price elasticity for potatoes was estimated to be -0.2. What is the interpretation? Why do you think the absolute value of this elasticity is so much less than that for butter?

Assume now that the demand for a commodity can be described by the function

$$x = D(p)$$

of the price p. When the price changes from p to $p + \Delta p$, the quantity demanded, x, also changes. The absolute change in x is $\Delta x = D(p + \Delta p) - D(p)$, and the *relative* (or proportional) change is

$$\frac{\Delta x}{x} = \frac{D(p + \Delta p) - D(p)}{D(p)}$$

The ratio between the relative change in the quantity demanded and the relative change in the price is

$$\frac{\Delta x}{x} \bigg/ \frac{\Delta p}{p} = \frac{p}{x} \frac{\Delta x}{\Delta p} = \frac{p}{D(p)} \frac{D(p + \Delta p) - D(p)}{\Delta p} \qquad (*)$$

When $\Delta p = p/100$ so that p increases by 1%, then $(*)$ becomes $(\Delta x / x) \cdot 100$, which is the percentage change in the quantity demanded. We call the proportion in $(*)$ *the average elasticity of x in the interval* $[p, p + \Delta p]$. Observe that the number defined in $(*)$ depends both on the price change Δp and on the price p, but is unit-free. Thus, it makes no difference whether the quantity is measured in tons, kilograms, or pounds, or whether the price is measured in dollars, pounds, or euros.

We would like to define the elasticity of D at p so that it does not depend on the size of the increase in p. We can do this if D is a differentiable function of p. For then it is natural to define the elasticity of D w.r.t. p as the limit of the ratio in $(*)$ as Δp tends to 0. Because the Newton quotient $[D(p + \Delta p) - D(p)]/\Delta p$ tends to $D'(p)$ as Δp tends to 0, we obtain:

$$\textit{the elasticity of } D(p) \textit{ with respect to } p \textit{ is} \quad \frac{p}{D(p)} \frac{dD(p)}{dp}$$

Usually, we get a good approximation to the elasticity by letting $\Delta p / p = 1/100 = 1\%$ and computing $p \, \Delta x / (x \, \Delta p)$.

The General Definition of Elasticity

The above definition of elasticity concerned a function determining quantity demanded as a function of price. Economists, however, also consider income elasticities of demand, when demand is regarded as a function of income. They also consider elasticities of supply, elasticities of substitution, and several other kinds of elasticity. It is therefore helpful to see how elasticity can be defined for a general differentiable function. If f is differentiable at x and $f(x) \neq 0$, we define the elasticity of f w.r.t. x as

$$\text{El}_x \, f(x) = \frac{x}{f(x)} f'(x) \qquad (\textbf{elasticity} \text{ of } f \text{ w.r.t. } x) \qquad (1)$$

EXAMPLE 1   Find the elasticity of $f(x) = Ax^b$ (A and b are constants, with $A \neq 0$).

Solution: In this case, $f'(x) = Abx^{b-1}$. Hence, $\text{El}_x \, Ax^b = (x/Ax^b)Abx^{b-1} = b$, so

$$f(x) = Ax^b \implies \text{El}_x \, f(x) = b$$

The elasticity of the power function Ax^b w.r.t. x is simply the exponent b. This is an example of a function whose elasticity is constant. (In fact, it is the only type of function which has constant elasticity.)

EXAMPLE 2   Assume that the quantity demanded of a particular commodity is given by

$$D(p) = 8000p^{-1.5}$$

Compute the elasticity of $D(p)$ and find the exact percentage change in quantity demanded when the price increases by 1% from $p = 4$.

Solution: Using the result in Example 1 we find that $\text{El}_p\, D(p) = -1.5$, so that an increase in the price of 1% causes quantity demanded to decrease by about 1.5%.

In this case we can compute the decrease in demand exactly. When the price is 4, the quantity demanded is $D(4) = 8000 \cdot 4^{-1.5} = 1000$. If the price $p = 4$ is increased by 1%, the new price will be $4 + 4/100 = 4.04$, so that the *change* in demand is

$$D(4.04) - D(4) = 8000 \cdot 4.04^{-1.5} - 1000 = -14.81$$

The percentage change in demand from $D(4) = 1000$ is $-(14.81/1000) \cdot 100 = -1.481\%$.

EXAMPLE 3   Let $D(P)$ denote the demand function for a product. By selling $D(P)$ units at price P, the producer earns revenue $R(P)$ given by $R(P) = PD(P)$. The elasticity of $R(P)$ w.r.t. P is

$$\text{El}_P\, R(P) = \frac{P}{PD(P)} \frac{d}{dP}[PD(P)] = \frac{1}{D(P)}[D(P) + PD'(P)] = 1 + \text{El}_P\, D(P)$$

Observe that if $\text{El}_P\, D(P) = -1$, then $\text{El}_P\, R(P) = 0$. Thus, when the price elasticity of the demand at a point is equal to -1, a small price change will have (almost) no influence on the revenue. More generally, the marginal revenue dR/dP generated by a price change is positive if the price elasticity of demand is greater than -1, and negative if the elasticity is less than -1.

NOTE 1 Economists sometimes use the following terminology:

- If $|\text{El}_x\, f(x)| > 1$, then f is elastic at x.
- If $|\text{El}_x\, f(x)| = 1$, then f is unit elastic at x.
- If $|\text{El}_x\, f(x)| < 1$, then f is inelastic at x.
- If $|\text{El}_x\, f(x)| = 0$, then f is completely inelastic at x.

There are some rules for elasticities of sums, products, quotients, and composite functions that are occasionally useful. You might like to derive these rules by solving Problem 10.

Elasticities as Logarithmic Derivatives

Suppose that two variables x and y are related by the equation

$$y = Ax^a \qquad (x, y, \text{ and } A \text{ are positive}) \tag{2}$$

Taking the natural logarithm of each side of (2) while applying the rules for logarithms, we find that (2) is equivalent to the equation

$$\ln y = \ln A + a \ln x \tag{3}$$

From (3), we see that $\ln y$ is a linear function of $\ln x$, and so we say that (2) is a **loglinear** relation between x and y. The transformation from (2) to (3) is often seen in economic models, sometimes using logarithms to a base other than e.

For the function defined by (2), we know from Example 1 that $\text{El}_x\, y = a$. So from (3) we see that $\text{El}_x\, y$ is equal to the (double) logarithmic derivative $d \ln y / d \ln x$, which is the constant slope of this loglinear relationship.

This example illustrates the general rule that elasticities are equal to such logarithmic derivatives. In fact, whenever x and y are both positive variables, with y a differentiable function of x, one has

$$\text{El}_x\, y = \frac{x}{y}\frac{dy}{dx} = \frac{d \ln y}{d \ln x} \tag{4}$$

The first equality just repeats the definition of elasticity. To see why the second must hold, let us introduce the two new variables $u = \ln x$ and $v = \ln y$. Note that v is a differentiable function of y, whereas y is assumed to be a differentiable function of x, and $x = e^u$ is a differentiable function of u. So the chain rule can be applied twice to give

$$\frac{d \ln y}{d \ln x} = \frac{dv}{du} = \frac{dv}{dy}\frac{dy}{dx}\frac{dx}{du}$$

But

$$\frac{dv}{dy} = \frac{d \ln y}{dy} = \frac{1}{y} \quad \text{and} \quad \frac{dx}{du} = e^u = x$$

Substituting these values into the previous expression for $d \ln y / d \ln x$ implies that

$$\frac{d \ln y}{d \ln x} = \frac{1}{y}\frac{dy}{dx}x = \frac{x}{y}\frac{dy}{dx} = \text{El}_x\, y$$

PROBLEMS FOR SECTION 7.7

1. Find the elasticities of the functions given by the following formulas:

   (a) $3x^{-3}$ (b) $-100x^{100}$ (c) $\sqrt{x}$ (d) $\dfrac{A}{x\sqrt{x}}$ (A constant)

2. A study of transport economics uses the relation $T = 0.4K^{1.06}$, where K is expenditure on building roads, and T is a measure of traffic volume. Find the elasticity of T w.r.t. K. In this model, if expenditure increases by 1%, by what percentage (approximately) does traffic volume increase?

3. (a) A study of Norway's State Railways revealed that, for rides up to 60km, the price elasticity of the volume of traffic was approximately -0.4. According to this study, what is the consequence of a 10% increase in fares?

   (b) The corresponding elasticity for journeys over 300 km was calculated to be approximately -0.9. Can you think of a reason why this elasticity is larger in absolute value than the previous one ?

CHAPTER 7 / DERIVATIVES IN USE

4. Use definition (1) to find $\text{El}_x\, y$ for the following (a and p are constants):

(a) $y = e^{ax}$ (b) $y = \ln x$ (c) $y = x^p e^{ax}$ (d) $y = x^p \ln x$

5. Prove that $\text{El}_x(f(x))^p = p\,\text{El}_x f(x)$ (p is a constant).

6. The demand D for apples in the U.S. as a function of income r for the period 1927 to 1941 was estimated as $D = Ar^{1.23}$, where A is a constant. Find and interpret the elasticity of D w.r.t. r. (This elasticity is called the income elasticity of demand, or the *Engel elasticity*.)

7. Voorhees and colleagues studied the transportation systems in 37 American cities and estimated the average travel time to work, m (in minutes), as a function of the number of inhabitants, N. They found that $m = e^{-0.02} N^{0.19}$. Write the relation in loglinear form. What is the value of m when $N = 480\,000$?

8. Agronomists have studied the effect on chicken embryos of cooling their eggs. The following table shows results from an experiment where the pulse of a chicken embryo was measured at different temperatures.

Temperature T (°C)	36.3	35.0	33.9	32.4	24.7	24.2
Pulse n (heartbeats/minute)	154	133	110	94	38	36

(a) Prepare a table showing the relationship between T and $\ln n$, and plot the pairs of numbers $(T, \ln n)$ in a coordinate system with $\ln n$ on the vertical axis and T on the horizontal axis. Fit a straight line through the two extreme points.

(b) We want to find an empirical function $f(T) = ce^{aT}$ that approximates the pulse rate as a function of the temperature T. Using the line obtained in part (a), determine a and c.

(c) By how many degrees does the temperature have to fall in order to halve the pulse rate?

9. Find $\text{El}_x\, Af(x)$ and $\text{El}_x[A + f(x)]$ in terms of $\text{El}_x\, f(x)$. (A is a positive constant.)

HARDER PROBLEMS

10. Prove that if f and g are positive valued differentiable functions of x and A is a constant, then the following rules hold (where we write, for instance, $\text{El}_x f$ instead of $\text{El}_x f(x)$).

(a) $\text{El}_x\, A = 0$ (b) $\text{El}_x(fg) = \text{El}_x f + \text{El}_x g$

(c) $\text{El}_x\left(\dfrac{f}{g}\right) = \text{El}_x f - \text{El}_x g$ (d) $\text{El}_x(f + g) = \dfrac{f\,\text{El}_x f + g\,\text{El}_x g}{f + g}$

(e) $\text{El}_x(f - g) = \dfrac{f\,\text{El}_x f - g\,\text{El}_x g}{f - g}$ (f) $\text{El}_x\, f(g(x)) = \text{El}_u\, f(u)\text{El}_x u$ ($u = g(x)$)

11. Use the rules of Problem 10 to evaluate the following:

(a) $\text{El}_x(-10x^{-5})$

(b) $\text{El}_x(x+x^2)$

(c) $\text{El}_x(x^3+1)^{10}$

(d) $\text{El}_x(\text{El}_x 5x^2)$

(e) $\text{El}_x(1+x^2)$

(f) $\text{El}_x\left(\dfrac{x-1}{x^5+1}\right)$

7.8 Continuity

Roughly speaking, a function is continuous if small changes in the independent variable produce small changes in the function value. Geometrically, *a function is continuous on an interval if its graph is connected—that is, it has no breaks.* An example is indicated in Fig. 1.

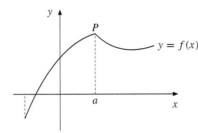

Figure 1 A continuous function

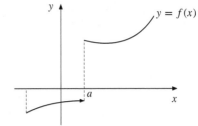

Figure 2 A discontinuous function

It is often said that a function is continuous if its graph can be drawn without lifting one's pencil off the paper. On the other hand, if the graph makes one or more jumps, we say that f is *discontinuous.* Thus, the function whose graph is shown in Fig. 2 is discontinuous at $x = a$, but continuous at all other points of the interval that constitutes its domain. The graph indicates that $f(x) < 0$ for all $x < a$, but $f(x) > 0$ for all $x \geq a$, so there is a jump at $x = a$.

Why are we interested in distinguishing between continuous and discontinuous functions? One important reason is that we must usually work with numerical approximations. For instance, if a function f is given by some formula and we wish to compute $f(\sqrt{2})$, we usually take it for granted that we can compute $f(1.4142)$ and obtain a good approximation to $f(\sqrt{2})$. In fact, this implicitly assumes that f is continuous. Then, because 1.4142 is close to $\sqrt{2}$, the value $f(1.4142)$ must be close to $f(\sqrt{2})$.

In applications of mathematics to natural sciences and economics, a function will often represent the change in some phenomenon over time. Continuity of the function will then reflect the continuity of the phenomenon, in the sense of a gradual development without sudden changes. We might, for example, think of a person's body temperature as a function of time. Here we may assume that it changes continuously and that it does not jump from one value to another without passing through the intermediate values. On the other hand, if we consider the price of a barrel of oil in a certain market, this function of time will be discontinuous. One reason is that the price (measured in dollars or some other currency) must always be a rational number. A second, more interesting, reason for occasional large jumps in the price is the sudden arrival of news or a rumour that significantly affects either the demand or supply function—for example, a sudden change in the government of a major oil exporting country.

The concept of continuity just discussed must obviously be made more precise before we can use it in mathematical arguments. We need a definition of continuity not based solely on geometric intuition.

Continuity in Terms of Limits

As discussed above, a function $y = f(x)$ is continuous at $x = a$ if small changes in x produce small changes in $f(x)$. Stated differently, if x is close to a, then $f(x)$ must be close to $f(a)$. This motivates the following definition:

$$f \text{ is } \textbf{continuous} \text{ at } x = a \text{ if } \lim_{x \to a} f(x) = f(a) \tag{1}$$

Hence, we see that in order for f to be continuous at $x = a$, the following three conditions must all be fulfilled:

 (i) The function f must be defined at $x = a$

 (ii) The limit of $f(x)$ as x tends to a must exist

(iii) This limit must be exactly equal to $f(a)$

Unless all three of these conditions are satisfied, we say that f is **discontinuous** at a.

Figure 3 below indicates two important different types of discontinuity that can occur. At $x = a$, the function is discontinuous because $f(x)$ clearly has no limit as x tends to a. Hence, condition (ii) is not satisfied. This is an "irremovable" discontinuity. On the other hand, the limit of $f(x)$ as x tends to b exists and is equal to A. But because $A \neq f(b)$, condition (iii) is not satisfied, so f is discontinuous at b. This is a "removable" discontinuity that would disappear if the function were redefined at $x = b$ to make $f(b)$ equal to A.

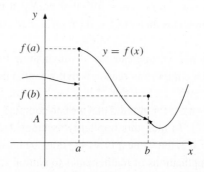

Figure 3 f has two points of discontinuity. $x = a$ is an irremovable and $x = b$ is a removable discontinuity point for f

Properties of Continuous Functions

Mathematicians have discovered many important results that are true only for continuous functions. It is therefore important to be able to determine whether or not a given function is continuous. The rules for limits given in Section 6.5 make it is easy to establish continuity of many types of function. Note that because $\lim_{x \to a} c = c$ and $\lim_{x \to a} x = a$ (at each point a), the two functions

$$f(x) = c \quad \text{and} \quad f(x) = x \text{ are continuous everywhere} \tag{2}$$

This is as it should be, because the graphs of these functions are straight lines. Now, using definition (1) and the limit rules in (6.5.2), (a)–(c) in the following theorem are immediate. The result in (d) is a little trickier to prove, but it is easy to believe because the graphs of f and its inverse f^{-1} are symmetric about the line $y = x$.

RESULTS ON CONTINUOUS FUNCTIONS

If f and g are continuous at a, then

(a) $f + g$ and $f - g$ are continuous at a

(b) fg and f/g (if $g(a) \neq 0$) are continuous at a \hfill (3)

(c) $[f(x)]^r$ is continuous at a if $[f(a)]^r$ is defined   (r any real number)

(d) If f is continuous and has an inverse on the interval I, then its inverse f^{-1} is continuous on $f(I)$.

For instance, to prove the first part of (b), if both f and g are continuous at a, then $f(x) \to f(a)$ and $g(x) \to g(a)$ as $x \to a$. But then, according to rules for limits, $f(x)g(x) \to f(a)g(a)$ as $x \to a$, and this means precisely that fg is continuous at $x = a$.

By combining (2) and (3), it follows that, say, $h(x) = x + 8$ and $k(x) = 3x^3 + x + 8$ are continuous. In general, because a polynomial is a sum of continuous functions, it is continuous everywhere. Moreover, a rational function

$$R(x) = \frac{P(x)}{Q(x)} \quad (P(x) \text{ and } Q(x) \text{ are polynomials})$$

is continuous at all x where $Q(x) \neq 0$.

Consider a composite function $f(g(x))$ where f and g are assumed to be continuous. If x is close to a, then by the continuity of g at a, $g(x)$ is close to $g(a)$. In turn, $f(g(x))$ becomes close to $f(g(a))$ because f is continuous at $g(a)$, and thus $f(g(x))$ is continuous at a. In short: *Composites of continuous functions are continuous*: If g is continuous at $x = a$, and f is continuous at $g(a)$, then $f\big(g(x)\big)$ is continuous at $x = a$. In general:

Any function that can be constructed from continuous functions by combining one or more operations of addition, subtraction, multiplication, division (except by zero), and composition, is continuous at all points where it is defined. \hfill (4)

By using the results just discussed, a mere glance at the formula defining a function will usually suffice to determine the points at which it is continuous.

EXAMPLE 1   Determine at which values of x the functions f and g are continuous:

(a) $f(x) = \dfrac{x^4 + 3x^2 - 1}{(x - 1)(x + 2)}$ (b) $g(x) = (x^2 + 2)\left(x^3 + \dfrac{1}{x}\right)^4 + \dfrac{1}{\sqrt{x + 1}}$

Solution:

(a) This is a rational function that is continuous at all x, except where the denominator $(x - 1)(x + 2)$ vanishes. Hence, f is continuous at all x different from 1 and -2.

(b) This function is defined when $x \neq 0$ and $x + 1 > 0$. Hence, g is continuous in the domain $(-1, 0) \cup (0, \infty)$.

Knowing where a function is continuous simplifies the computation of many limits. If f is continuous at $x = a$, then the limit of $f(x)$ as x tends to a is found simply by evaluating $f(a)$. For instance, since the function $f(x) = x^2 + 5x$ we studied in Example 6.5.3(a) is a continuous function of x,

$$\lim_{x \to -2} (x^2 + 5x) = (-2)^2 + 5(-2) = 4 - 10 = -6$$

Thus, we find the limit by just evaluating $f(x) = x^2 + 5x$ at $x = -2$, which is easier than using the rules for limits.

Compound functions, that is functions which are defined by different formulas on disjoint intervals, such as Example 5.4.3, are frequently discontinuous at the junction points. As another example, the amount of postage you pay for a letter is a discontinuous function of the weight. (As long as we use preprinted stamps, it would be extremely inconvenient to have the "postage function" be even approximately continuous.) On the other hand, the tax you pay as a function of your net income is (essentially) a continuous function (although many people seem to believe that it is not).

PROBLEMS FOR SECTION 7.8

1. Which of the following functions are likely to be continuous functions of time?

(a) The price in the Zürich gold market of an ounce of gold.

(b) The height of a growing child.

(c) The height of an aeroplane above sea level.

(d) The distance travelled by a car.

2. Let f and g be defined for all x by

$$f(x) = \begin{cases} x^2 - 1, & \text{for } x \leq 0 \\ -x^2, & \text{for } x > 0 \end{cases} \quad \text{and } g(x) = \begin{cases} 3x - 2, & \text{for } x \leq 2 \\ -x + 6, & \text{for } x > 2 \end{cases}$$

Draw a graph of each function. Is f continuous at $x = 0$? Is g continuous at $x = 2$?

3. Determine the values of x at which each of the functions defined by the following formulas is continuous:

(a) $x^5 + 4x$

(b) $\dfrac{x}{1-x}$

(c) $\dfrac{1}{\sqrt{2-x}}$

(d) $\dfrac{x}{x^2+1}$

(e) $\dfrac{x^8 - 3x^2 + 1}{x^2 + 2x - 2}$

(f) $\dfrac{1}{\sqrt{x}} + \dfrac{x^7}{(x+2)^{3/2}}$

4. Draw the graph of y as a function of x if y depends on x as indicated in Figure 4—that is, y is the height of the aeroplane above the point on the ground vertically below. Is y a continuous function of x?

Figure 4

5. For what value of a is the following function continuous for all x?

$$f(x) = \begin{cases} ax - 1, & \text{for } x \le 1 \\ 3x^2 + 1, & \text{for } x > 1 \end{cases}$$

6. Sketch the graph of a function f that is one-to-one on an interval, but neither strictly increasing nor strictly decreasing. (*Hint:* f cannot be continuous.)

7.9 More on Limits

Section 6.5 gave a preliminary discussion of limits. We now supplement this with some additional concepts and results, still keeping the discussion at an intuitive level. The reason for this gradual approach is that it is important and quite easy to acquire a working knowledge of limits. Experience suggests, however, that the precise definition is rather difficult to understand, as are proofs based on this definition.

Limits That Do Not Exist

Suppose f is defined for all x close to a, but not necessarily at a. According to Section 6.5, as x tends to a, the function $f(x)$ has A as its limit provided that the number $f(x)$ can be made as close to A as one pleases by making x sufficiently close to (but not equal to) a. Then we say that the limit exists. Consider a case in which the limit does not exist.

EXAMPLE 1   Examine $\lim\limits_{x \to -2} \dfrac{1}{(x+2)^2}$ using a pocket calculator.

Solution: Choosing x-values close to -2, we obtain the values in Table 1.

Table 1 Values of $1/(x+2)^2$ when x is close to -2

x	-1.8	-1.9	-1.99	-1.999	-2.0	-2.001	-2.01	-2.1	-2.2
$\dfrac{1}{(x+2)^2}$	25	100	10000	1000000	*	1000000	10000	100	25

*not defined

As x gets closer and closer to -2, we see that the value of the fraction becomes larger and larger. By extending the values in the table, we see, for example, that for $x = -2.0001$ and $x = -1.9999$, the value of the fraction is 100 million. Figure 1 shows the graph of $f(x) = 1/(x+2)^2$. The line $x = -2$ is called a *vertical asymptote* for the graph of f.

Because the fraction becomes larger and larger as x tends to -2, we say instead that it tends to infinity, and write

$$\frac{1}{(x+2)^2} \to \infty \qquad \text{as} \qquad x \to -2$$

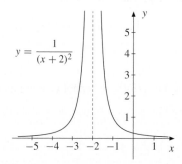

Figure 1 $f(x) \to \infty$ as $x \to -2$

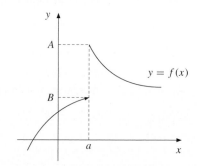

Figure 2 $\lim\limits_{x \to a} f(x)$ does not exist

(Note that ∞ is NOT a number, so ∞ is not a limit.)

One-Sided Limits

The function whose graph is shown in Fig. 2 also fails to have a limit as x tends to a. However, it seems from the figure that if x tends to a with values less than a, then $f(x)$ tends to the number B. We say, therefore, that the *limit of $f(x)$ as x tends to a from below is B*, and we write

$$\lim_{x \to a^-} f(x) = B \quad \text{or} \quad f(x) \to B \text{ as } x \to a^-$$

Analogously, also referring to Fig. 2, we say that the *limit of $f(x)$ as x tends to a from above is A*, and we write

$$\lim_{x \to a^+} f(x) = A \quad \text{or} \quad f(x) \to A \text{ as } x \to a^+$$

We call these *one-sided limits*, the first *from below* and the second *from above*. They can also be called the *left limit* and *right limit*, respectively.

A necessary and sufficient condition for the (ordinary) limit to exist is that the two one-sided limits of f at a exist and are equal:

$$\lim_{x \to a} f(x) = A \quad \Longleftrightarrow \quad \left[\lim_{x \to a^-} f(x) = A \text{ and } \lim_{x \to a^+} f(x) = A \right] \qquad (1)$$

It should now also be clear what is meant by

$$f(x) \to \pm\infty \text{ as } x \to a^- \quad \text{and} \quad f(x) \to \pm\infty \text{ as } x \to a^+$$

EXAMPLE 2   Figure 3 shows the graph of a function f defined on $[0, 9]$. Use the figure to check that the following limits seem correct:

$$\lim_{x \to 2} f(x) = 3, \quad \lim_{x \to 4^-} f(x) = 1/2, \quad \lim_{x \to 4^+} f(x) = 3, \quad \text{`` } \lim_{x \to 6} f(x) = -\infty\text{''} \qquad \blacksquare$$

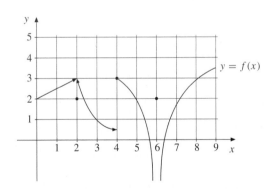

Figure 3

EXAMPLE 3   Explain the following limits:

$$\frac{1}{\sqrt{2 - x}} \to \infty \text{ as } x \to 2^-, \qquad \frac{-1}{\sqrt{x - 2}} \to -\infty \text{ as } x \to 2^+$$

Solution: If x is slightly smaller than 2, then $2 - x$ is small and positive. Hence, $\sqrt{2 - x}$ is close to 0, and $1/\sqrt{2 - x}$ is a large positive number. For example, $1/\sqrt{2 - 1.9999} = 1/\sqrt{0.0001} = 100$. As x tends to 2^-, so $1/\sqrt{2 - x}$ tends to ∞.

The other limit is similar, because if x is slightly larger than 2, then $\sqrt{x - 2}$ is positive and close to 0, and $-1/\sqrt{x - 2}$ is a large negative number. $\blacksquare$

One-Sided Continuity

The introduction of one-sided limits allows us to define one-sided continuity. Suppose f is defined on the half-open interval $(c, a]$. If $f(x)$ tends to $f(a)$ as x tends to a^-, we say that f is *left continuous* at a. Similarly, if f is defined on $[a, d)$, we say that f is *right continuous* at a if $f(x)$ tends to $f(a)$ as x tends to a^+. Because of (1), we see that a function f is continuous at a if and only if f is both left and right continuous at a.

EXAMPLE 4   Figure 3 shows that f is right continuous at $x = 4$ since $\lim_{x \to 4^+} f(x)$ exists and is equal to $f(4) = 3$. At $x = 2$,

$$\lim_{x \to 2^-} f(x) = \lim_{x \to 2^+} f(x) = 3$$

but $f(2) = 2$, so f is neither right nor left continuous at $x = 2$. ∎

If a function f is defined on a closed bounded interval $[a, b]$, we usually say that f is continuous in $[a, b]$ if it is continuous at each point of (a, b), and is in addition right continuous at a and left continuous at b. It should be obvious how to define continuity on half-open intervals. The continuity of a function at all points of an interval (including one-sided continuity at the end points) is often a minimum requirement we impose when speaking about "well-behaved" functions.

Limits at Infinity

We can also use the language of limits to describe the behaviour of a function as its argument becomes infinitely large through positive or negative values. Let f be defined for arbitrarily large positive numbers x. We say that $f(x)$ *has the limit A as x tends to infinity* if $f(x)$ can be made arbitrarily close to A by making x sufficiently large. We write

$$\lim_{x \to \infty} f(x) = A \quad \text{or} \quad f(x) \to A \text{ as } x \to \infty$$

In the same way,

$$\lim_{x \to -\infty} f(x) = B \quad \text{or} \quad f(x) \to B \text{ as } x \to -\infty$$

indicates that $f(x)$ can be made arbitrarily close to B by making x a sufficiently large negative number. The two limits are illustrated in Fig. 4. The horizontal line $y = A$ is a (horizontal) **asymptote** for the graph of f as x tends to ∞, whereas $y = B$ is a (horizontal) asymptote for the graph as x tends to $-\infty$.

Figure 4 $y = A$ and $y = B$ are horizontal asymptotes

EXAMPLE 5 Examine the following functions as $x \to \infty$ and as $x \to -\infty$:

(a) $f(x) = \dfrac{3x^2 + x - 1}{x^2 + 1}$ (b) $g(x) = \dfrac{1 - x^5}{x^4 + x + 1}$

Solution:

(a) A rough argument is as follows: If x is a large negative or a large positive number, then the term $3x^2$ "dominates" in the numerator, whereas x^2 dominates in the denominator. Thus, if $|x|$ is a large number, $f(x)$ behaves like the fraction $3x^2/x^2 = 3$. We conclude that $f(x)$ tends to 3 as $|x|$ tends to ∞.

  More formally, we argue as follows. First, divide each term in the numerator and the denominator by the highest power of x, which is x^2, to obtain

$$f(x) = \frac{3x^2 + x - 1}{x^2 + 1} = \frac{3 + (1/x) - (1/x^2)}{1 + (1/x^2)}$$

If x is large in absolute value, then both $1/x$ and $1/x^2$ are close to 0. Thus, $f(x)$ is arbitrarily close to 3 if $|x|$ is sufficiently large, and $f(x) \to 3$ both as $x \to -\infty$ and $x \to \infty$.

(b) A first rough argument is that if $|x|$ is a large number, then $g(x)$ behaves like the fraction $-x^5/x^4 = -x$. Therefore, $g(x) \to -\infty$ as $x \to \infty$, whereas $g(x) \to \infty$ as $x \to -\infty$. Alternatively,

$$g(x) = \frac{1 - x^5}{x^4 + x + 1} = \frac{(1/x^4) - x}{1 + (1/x^3) + 1/x^4}$$

You should now finish the argument yourself along the lines given in part (a). ∎

Warnings

We have extended the original definition of a limit in several different directions. For these extended limit concepts, the previous limit rules set out in Section 6.5 still apply. For example, all the usual limit rules are valid if we consider left-hand limits or right-hand limits. Also, if we replace $x \to a$ by $x \to \infty$ or $x \to -\infty$, then again the corresponding limit properties are valid.

  When $f(x)$ and $g(x)$ both tend to ∞ as x tends to a, however, we must be much more careful. Because $f(x)$ and $g(x)$ can each be made arbitrarily large if x is sufficiently close to a, both $f(x) + g(x)$ and $f(x)g(x)$ can also be made arbitrarily large. But, in general, we cannot say what are the limits of $f(x) - g(x)$ and $f(x)/g(x)$. The limits of these expressions will depend on how "fast" $f(x)$ and $g(x)$, respectively, tend to ∞ as x tends to a. Briefly formulated:

$$f(x) \to \infty \ \text{and} \ g(x) \to \infty \ \text{as} \ x \to a \Rightarrow \begin{cases} f(x) + g(x) \to \infty & \text{as } x \to a \\ f(x)g(x) \to \infty & \text{as } x \to a \\ f(x) - g(x) \to ? & \text{as } x \to a \\ f(x)/g(x) \to ? & \text{as } x \to a \end{cases}$$

The two question marks mean that we cannot determine the limits of $f(x) - g(x)$ and $f(x)/g(x)$ without more information about f and g. We do not even know if these limits exist or not. The following example illustrates some of the possibilities.

EXAMPLE 6   Let $f(x) = 1/x^2$ and $g(x) = 1/x^4$. As $x \to 0$, then $f(x) \to \infty$ and $g(x) \to \infty$. Examine the limits as $x \to 0$ of the following expressions:

$$f(x) - g(x), \qquad g(x) - f(x), \qquad \frac{f(x)}{g(x)}, \qquad \frac{g(x)}{f(x)}$$

Solution: $f(x) - g(x) = \dfrac{x^2 - 1}{x^4}$. As $x \to 0$, the numerator tends to -1 and the denominator tends to 0. The fraction therefore tends to $-\infty$. For the other three limits we have:

$$g(x) - f(x) = \frac{1 - x^2}{x^4} \to \infty, \qquad \frac{f(x)}{g(x)} = x^2 \to 0, \qquad \frac{g(x)}{f(x)} = \frac{1}{x^2} \to \infty \qquad \blacksquare$$

These examples serve to illustrate that infinite limits require extreme care. Let us consider some other tricky examples. Suppose we study the product $f(x)g(x)$ of two functions, where $g(x)$ tends to 0 as x tends to a. Will the product $f(x)g(x)$ also tend to 0 as x tends to a? Not necessarily. If $f(x)$ tends to a limit A, then we know that $f(x)g(x)$ tends to $A \cdot 0 = 0$. On the other hand, if $f(x)$ tends to $\pm\infty$, then it is easy to construct examples in which the product $f(x)g(x)$ does not tend to 0 at all. (You should try to construct some examples of your own before turning to Problem 3.)

Continuity and Differentiability

Consider the function f graphed in Fig. 5.

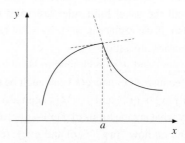

Figure 5 f is continuous, but not differentiable at $x = a$

At point $(a, f(a))$ the graph does not have (a unique) tangent. Thus f has no derivative at $x = a$, but f is continuous at $x = a$. So a function can be continuous at a point without being differentiable at that point. (For a standard example, see the graph of $f(x) = |x|$ shown in Figure 4.3.10 which is continuous, but not differentiable, at $x = 0$.) On the other hand, it is easy to see that differentiability implies continuity:

If f is differentiable at $x = a$, then f is continuous at $x = a$ $\qquad$ (2)

Proof: The function f is continuous at $x = a$ provided $f(a + h) - f(a)$ tends to 0 as $h \to 0$. Now, for $h \neq 0$,

$$f(a + h) - f(a) = \frac{f(a + h) - f(a)}{h} \cdot h \qquad (*)$$

If f is differentiable at $x = a$, the Newton quotient $[f(a + h) - f(a)]/h$ tends to the number $f'(a)$ as $h \to 0$. So the right-hand side of $(*)$ tends to $f'(a) \cdot 0 = 0$ as $h \to 0$. Thus, f is continuous at $x = a$. ∎

Suppose that f is some function whose Newton quotient $[f(a + h) - f(a)]/h$ tends to a limit as h tends to 0 through positive values. Then the limit is called the *right derivative* of f at a. The *left derivative* of f at a is defined similarly, and we use the notation

$$f'(a^+) = \lim_{h \to 0^+} \frac{f(a + h) - f(a)}{h}, \qquad f'(a^-) = \lim_{h \to 0^-} \frac{f(a + h) - f(a)}{h} \qquad (3)$$

if the one-sided limits exist. If f is continuous at a and has left and right derivatives satisfying $f'(a^+) \neq f'(a^-)$, then the graph of f is said to have a **kink** (or **corner**) at $(a, f(a))$.

EXAMPLE 7 $\quad$ (U.S. Federal income tax (2004) for single persons) This income tax function was discussed in Example 5.4.4. Figure 5.4.8 gives the graph of the tax function. If $t(x)$ denotes the tax paid at income x, its graph has corners at $x = 7150$, at $x = 29\,050$, and at $x = 70\,350$. We see, for instance, that $t'(29\,050^-) = 0.15$ because the tax is 15 cents on the last dollar earned before reaching 29 050. Also, $t'(29\,050^+) = 0.25$ because the tax is 25 cents on the first dollar earned above 29 050. Because $t'(29\,050^-) \neq t'(29\,050^+)$, the tax function t is not differentiable at $x = 29\,050$. Check that $t'(70\,350^+) = 0.28$. ∎

A Rigorous Definition of Limits

Our preliminary definition of the limit concept in Section 6.5 was as follows:

$\lim_{x \to a} f(x) = A$ means that we can make $f(x)$ as close to A as we want, for all x sufficiently close to (but not equal to) a

The closeness, or, more generally, the distance, between two numbers can be measured by the absolute value of the difference between them. Using absolute values, the definition can be reformulated in this way:

$\lim_{x \to a} f(x) = A$ means that *we can make* $|f(x) - A|$ *as small as we want for all* $x \neq a$ *with* $|x - a|$ *sufficiently small*

Towards the end of the 19th century some of the world's best mathematicians at the time gradually realized that this definition can be made precise in the following way:

We say that $f(x)$ has limit (or tends to) A as x tends to a, and write $\lim_{x \to a} f(x) = A$, if for each number $\varepsilon > 0$ there exists a number $\delta > 0$ such that $|f(x) - A| < \varepsilon$ for every x with $0 < |x - a| < \delta$. $\qquad$ (4)

This is the definition on which all rigorous work on limits is based. It is illustrated in Fig. 6. The graph of f must remain within the box, for all $x \neq a$ in $(a - \delta, a + \delta)$.

It should be regarded as a part of your general mathematical education *to have seen* this $\varepsilon\delta$ definition of the limit concept. However, in this book we rely only on an intuitive understanding of limits. From the definition (7.8.1) of continuity, an $\varepsilon\delta$ definition of continuous function is immediate, based on (4) above.

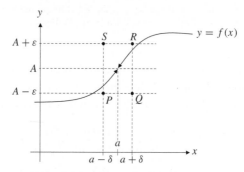

Figure 6   For every ϵ, there is a δ, so $\lim_{x \to a} f(x) = A$

1. Evaluate the following limits:

   (a) $\lim\limits_{x \to 0^+} (x^2 + 3x - 4)$

   (b) $\lim\limits_{x \to 0^-} \dfrac{x + |x|}{x}$

   (c) $\lim\limits_{x \to 0^+} \dfrac{x + |x|}{x}$

   (d) $\lim\limits_{x \to 0^+} \dfrac{-1}{\sqrt{x}}$

   (e) $\lim\limits_{x \to 3^+} \dfrac{x}{x - 3}$

   (f) $\lim\limits_{x \to 3^-} \dfrac{x}{x - 3}$

2. Evaluate the following limits:

   (a) $\lim\limits_{x \to \infty} \dfrac{x - 3}{x^2 + 1}$

   (b) $\lim\limits_{x \to -\infty} \sqrt{\dfrac{2 + 3x}{x - 1}}$

   (c) $\lim\limits_{x \to \infty} \dfrac{(ax - b)^2}{(a - x)(b - x)}$

3. Let $f_1(x) = x$, $f_2(x) = x$, $f_3(x) = x^2$, and $f_4(x) = 1/x$. Determine $\lim\limits_{x \to \infty} f_i(x)$ for $i = 1, 2, 3, 4$. Then examine the limits of the following functions as $x \to \infty$.

   (a) $f_1(x) + f_2(x)$ (b) $f_1(x) - f_2(x)$ (c) $f_1(x) - f_3(x)$ (d) $f_1(x)/f_2(x)$

   (e) $f_1(x)/f_3(x)$ (f) $f_1(x)f_2(x)$ (g) $f_1(x)f_4(x)$ (h) $f_3(x)f_4(x)$

4. The nonvertical line $y = ax + b$ is said to be an **asymptote** as $x \to \infty$ (or $x \to -\infty$) to the curve $y = f(x)$ if

$$f(x) - (ax + b) \to 0 \quad \text{as} \quad x \to \infty \ (\text{or } x \to -\infty)$$

This condition means that the vertical distance between point $(x, f(x))$ on the curve and point $(x, ax + b)$ on the line tends to 0 as $x \to \pm\infty$. (See Fig. 7.)

If $f(x) = P(x)/Q(x)$ is a rational function where the degree of the polynomial $P(x)$ is *one greater* than that of the polynomial $Q(x)$, then $f(x)$ will have an asymptote that can be found by performing the long division $P(x) \div Q(x)$ and ignoring the remainder. Use this method to find asymptotes for the graph of each of the functions defined by the following formulas:

(a) $\dfrac{x^2}{x+1}$ (b) $\dfrac{2x^3 - 3x^2 + 3x - 6}{x^2 + 1}$ (c) $\dfrac{3x^2 + 2x}{x - 1}$ (d) $\dfrac{5x^4 - 3x^2 + 1}{x^3 - 1}$

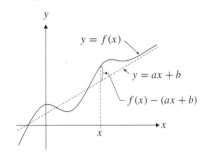

Figure 7

5. Consider the cost function defined for $x \geq 0$ by

$$C(x) = A\frac{x(x+b)}{x+c} + d$$

Here $A, b, c,$ and d are positive constants. Find the asymptotes.

6. Graph the function f defined by $f(x) = 0$ for $x \leq 0$, and $f(x) = x$ for $x > 0$. Compute $f'(0^+)$ and $f'(0^-)$.

7.10 Intermediate Value Theorem. Newton's Method

An important reason for introducing the concept of a continuous function was to make precise the idea of a connected graph—that is one which has no breaks. Using the $\varepsilon\delta$ definition one can prove the following result, which shows that the graph of a continuous function has no breaks.

THEOREM 7.10.1 (THE INTERMEDIATE VALUE THEOREM)

Let f be a function continuous in $[a, b]$ and assume that $f(a)$ and $f(b)$ have different signs. Then there is at least one c in (a, b) such that $f(c) = 0$.

(Draw a figure!) This theorem is important in assuring the existence of solutions to some equations that cannot be solved explicitly.

EXAMPLE 1   Prove that the following equation has at least one solution c between 0 and 1:

$$x^6 + 3x^2 - 2x - 1 = 0$$

Solution: Define

$$f(x) = x^6 + 3x^2 - 2x - 1$$

As a polynomial, f is continuous for all x—in particular in $[0, 1]$. Moreover, $f(0) = -1$ and $f(1) = 1$. According to Theorem 7.10.1, there exists at least one number c in $(0, 1)$ such that $f(c) = 0$.   ∎

Sometimes we need to prove that certain equations have unique solutions. Consider the following example.

EXAMPLE 2   Prove that the equation

$$2x - 5e^{-x}(1 + x^2) = 0$$

has a unique solution, which lies in the interval $(0, 2)$.

    Solution: Define $g(x) = 2x - 5e^{-x}(1 + x^2)$. Then $g(0) = -5$ and $g(2) = 4 - 25/e^2$. In fact $g(2) > 0$ because $e > 5/2$. According to the intermediate value theorem, therefore, the continuous function g must have at least one zero in $(0, 2)$. Moreover, note that $g'(x) = 2 + 5e^{-x}(1 + x^2) - 10xe^{-x} = 2 + 5e^{-x}(1 - 2x + x^2) = 2 + 5e^{-x}(x - 1)^2$. But then $g'(x) > 0$ for all x, so g is strictly increasing. It follows that g can have only one zero.   ∎

Newton's Method

The intermediate value theorem can often be used to show that an equation $f(x) = 0$ has a solution in a given interval, but it gives no additional information about the location of the zero. In this subsection we shall explain a method which usually leads to a good approximate solution in an efficient way. The method was first suggested by Newton and it has an easy geometric explanation.

    Consider the graph of the function $y = f(x)$ shown in Fig. 1. It is shown with a zero at $x = a$ (but this zero is not known). We start with an initial estimate, x_0, of a. (It is an advantage to start with an initial estimate not too far from a, if possible.) In order to find a better estimate, construct the tangent line to the graph at the point $(x_0, f(x_0))$, and find the point x_1 at which the tangent crosses the x-axis, as shown in Fig. 1.

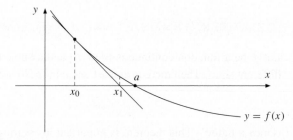

Figure 1

Usually x_1 is a significantly better estimate of a than x_0. After having found x_1, repeat the procedure by constructing the tangent line to the curve at the point $(x_1, f(x_1))$. Denote by x_2 the point where this tangent line crosses the x-axis. Continuing in this way, we obtain a sequence of points which usually converges very quickly to a.

It is easy to find formulas for x_1, x_2, ... The slope of the tangent at x_0 is $f'(x_0)$. According to the point–slope formula, the equation for the tangent line through the point $(x_0, f(x_0))$ with slope $f'(x_0)$ is given by

$$y - f(x_0) = f'(x_0)(x - x_0)$$

At the point where this tangent line crosses the x-axis, $y = 0$ and $x = x_1$. Hence $-f(x_0) = f'(x_0)(x_1 - x_0)$. Solving this equation for x_1, we get

$$x_1 = x_0 - \frac{f(x_0)}{f'(x_0)}$$

In a similar way, given x_1, we find the formula for x_2 to be

$$x_2 = x_1 - f(x_1)/f'(x_1)$$

In general, one has the following formula for the $(n+1)$-th approximation x_{n+1}, expressed in terms of the n-th approximation x_n:

NEWTON'S METHOD

As long as $f'(x_n) \neq 0$, Newton's method generates the sequence of points given by the formula

$$x_{n+1} = x_n - \frac{f(x_n)}{f'(x_n)}, \qquad n = 0, 1, \ldots$$

(1)

EXAMPLE 3   Find an approximate value for the zero of

$$f(x) = x^6 + 3x^2 - 2x - 1$$

in the interval $[0, 1]$, using Newton's method once (see Example 1).

Solution: Choose $x_0 = 1$. Then $f(x_0) = f(1) = 1$. Because $f'(x) = 6x^5 + 6x - 2$, we have $f'(1) = 10$. Hence, equation (1) for $n = 0$ yields

$$x_1 = 1 - \frac{f(1)}{f'(1)} = 1 - \frac{1}{10} = \frac{9}{10} = 0.9$$

EXAMPLE 4   Use Newton's method twice to find an approximate value for $\sqrt[15]{2}$.

Solution: We need an equation of the form $f(x) = 0$ which has $x = \sqrt[15]{2} = 2^{1/15}$ as a root. The equation $x^{15} = 2$ has this root, so we let $f(x) = x^{15} - 2$. Choose $x_0 = 1$. Then $f(x_0) = f(1) = -1$, and because $f'(x) = 15x^{14}$, we have $f'(1) = 15$. Thus (1) for $n = 0$ gives

$$x_1 = 1 - \frac{f(1)}{f'(1)} = 1 - \frac{-1}{15} = \frac{16}{15} \approx 1.0667$$

Moreover,

$$x_2 = x_1 - \frac{f(x_1)}{f'(x_1)} = \frac{16}{15} - \frac{f(16/15)}{f'(16/15)} = \frac{16}{15} - \frac{(16/15)^{15} - 2}{15(16/15)^{14}} \approx 1.04729412$$

This is actually correct to 8 decimal places.[3]

NOTE 1 In most cases Newton's method is very efficient, but it can happen that the sequence $\{x_n\}$ defined in (1) does not converge. Figure 2 is an example showing that x_1 can be a bad approximation to x_0. The formula in (1) breaks down if $f'(x_n) = 0$. Usually, Newton's method fails only if the absolute value of $f'(x_n)$ becomes too small, for some n.

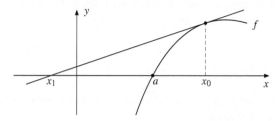

Figure 2

A Precise Estimate of Convergence

One can prove the following results on the convergence of Newton's method.

THEOREM 7.10.2 (CONVERGENCE OF NEWTON'S METHOD)

Suppose in (1) that $f(x^*) = 0$, $f'(x^*) \neq 0$, and that $f''(x^*)$ exists and is continuous for all x in a neighbourhood of x^*. Then there exists a $\delta > 0$ such that the sequence $\{x_n\}$ in (1) converges to x^* starting from any $x_0 \in (x^* - \delta, x^* + \delta)$.

---

[3] A frequently used rule of thumb says that, to obtain an approximation that is correct to n decimal places, use Newton's method until it gives the same n decimal places twice in a row.

THEOREM 7.10.3 (CONVERGENCE OF NEWTON'S METHOD)

Suppose in (1) that f is twice differentiable with $f(x^*) = 0$ and $f'(x^*) \neq 0$. Suppose further that there exist a $K > 0$ and a $\delta > 0$ such that for all x in $(x^* - \delta, x^* + \delta)$,

$$\frac{|f(x)f''(x)|}{f'(x)^2} \leq K|x - x^*| < 1$$

Then if $x_0 \in (x^* - \delta, x^* + \delta)$, the sequence $\{x_n\}$ in (1) converges to x^* and $|x_n - x^*| \leq (\delta K)^{2^n}/K$.

PROBLEMS FOR SECTION 7.10

1. Show that each of the following equations has at least one root in the given interval.

(a) $x^7 - 5x^5 + x^3 - 1 = 0$ in $(-1, 1)$ (b) $x^3 + 3x - 8 = 0$ in $(1, 3)$

(c) $\sqrt{x^2 + 1} = 3x$ in $(0, 1)$ (d) $e^{x-1} = 2x$ in $(0, 1)$

2. Explain why anybody taller than 1 metre was once exactly 1 metre tall.

3. Find a better approximation to $\sqrt[3]{17} \approx 2.5$ by using Newton's method once.

4. The equation $x^4 + 3x^3 - 3x^2 - 8x + 3 = 0$ has an integer root. Find it. The three additional roots are close to $-1.9, 0.4$, and 1.5. Find a better approximation to each of these roots by using Newton's method once.

5. The equation $(2x)^x = 15$ has a solution which is approximately an integer. Find a better approximation by using Newton's method once.

6. In Fig. 1, $f(x_0) > 0$ and $f'(x_0) < 0$. Moreover, x_1 is to the right of x_0. Verify that this agrees with the formula (1) for $n = 0$. Check the other combinations of signs for $f(x_0)$ and $f'(x_0)$ to see both geometrically and analytically on which side of x_0 the point x_1 lies.

7.11 Infinite Sequences

We often encounter functions like those in Newton's method which associate a number $s(n)$ to each natural number n. Such a function is called an **infinite sequence**, or just a sequence. Its terms $s(1), s(2), s(3), \ldots, s(n), \ldots$ are usually denoted by using subscripts: $s_1, s_2, s_3, \ldots, s_n, \ldots$. We use the notation $\{s_n\}_{n=1}^{\infty}$, or simply $\{s_n\}$, for an arbitrary infinite sequence. For example, if $s(n) = 1/n$, $n = 1, 2, 3, \ldots$, then the terms of the sequence are

$$1, \quad \frac{1}{2}, \frac{1}{3}, \frac{1}{4}, \quad \ldots, \quad \frac{1}{n}, \quad \ldots$$

If we choose n large enough, the terms of this sequence can be made as small as we like. We say that the sequence *converges* to 0. In general, we introduce the following definition:

A sequence $\{s_n\}$ is said to **converge** *to a number s if s_n can be made arbitrarily close to s by choosing n sufficiently large.* We write

$$\lim_{n \to \infty} s_n = s \quad \text{or} \quad s_n \to s \quad \text{as} \quad n \to \infty$$

This definition is just a special case of the previous definition that $f(x) \to A$ as $x \to \infty$. All the ordinary limit rules in Section 6.5 apply to limits of sequences.

A sequence that does not converge to any real number is said to **diverge**. Two typical divergent sequences are:

$$\{2^n\}_{n=0}^{\infty} \quad \text{and} \quad \{(-1)^n\}_{n=1}^{\infty}$$

Explain why these sequences diverge. Occasionally, as in the first of these sequences, the starting index is not 1, but another integer, here 0.

EXAMPLE 1   For $n \geq 3$ let A_n be the area of a regular n-polygon inscribed in a circle with radius 1. For $n = 3$, A_3 is the area of a triangle; for $n = 4$, A_4 is the area of a square; for $n = 5$, A_5 is the area of a pentagon; and so on (see Figure 1).

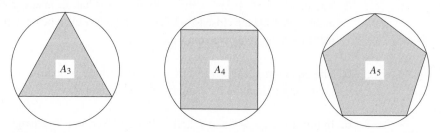

Figure 1

The larger n is, the larger is A_n, but each A_n is less than π, the area of a circle with radius 1. It seems intuitively evident that we can make the difference between A_n and π as small as we wish provided that n becomes sufficiently large, so that

$$A_n \to \pi \quad \text{as} \quad n \to \infty$$

In this example, A_1 and A_2 have no meaning, so the sequence starts with A_3.

EXAMPLE 2   In Section 6.11 we argued that $\lim_{h \to 0}(1 + h)^{1/h}$ is $e = 2.718\ldots$. If we let $h = 1/n$, where the natural number $n \to \infty$ as $h \to 0$, we obtain the following important limit:

$$e = \lim_{n \to \infty} \left(1 + \frac{1}{n}\right)^n \tag{1}$$

Irrational Numbers As Limits of Sequences

The sequence $\{A_n\}$ in Example 1 converges to the irrational number $\pi = 3.14159265\ldots$. Another sequence that converges to π starts this way: $s_1 = 3.1$, $s_2 = 3.14$, $s_3 = 3.141$, $s_4 = 3.1415$, etc. Each new number is obtained by including an additional digit in the decimal expansion for π. For this sequence, $s_n \to \pi$ as $n \to \infty$.

Consider an arbitrary irrational number r. Just as for π, the decimal expansion of r will define one particular sequence r_n of rational numbers that converges to r.

Section 1.5 defined the power a^x when x is rational, and Section 4.8 suggested how to define a^x when x is irrational, by considering the special case of 5^π.

Let r be an arbitrary irrational number. Then there exists a sequence r_n of rational numbers such that $r_n \to r$ as $n \to \infty$. The power a^{r_n} is well-defined for all n. Since r_n converges to r, it is reasonable to define a^r as the limit of a^{r_n} as n approaches infinity:

$$a^r = \lim_{n\to\infty} a^{r_n} \tag{$*$}$$

Actually, there are infinitely many sequences that converge to a given irrational number r, but one can show that the limit in $(*)$ exists and is independent of which sequence we choose.

PROBLEMS FOR SECTION 7.11

1. Let $\alpha_n = \dfrac{3-n}{2n-1}$ and $\beta_n = \dfrac{n^2+2n-1}{3n^2-2}$, $n = 1, 2, \ldots$. Find the following limits:

   (a) $\displaystyle\lim_{n\to\infty} \alpha_n$ (b) $\displaystyle\lim_{n\to\infty} \beta_n$ (c) $\displaystyle\lim_{n\to\infty} (3\alpha_n + 4\beta_n)$

   (d) $\displaystyle\lim_{n\to\infty} \alpha_n\beta_n$ (e) $\displaystyle\lim_{n\to\infty} \alpha_n/\beta_n$ (f) $\displaystyle\lim_{n\to\infty} \sqrt{\beta_n - \alpha_n}$

2. Examine the convergence of the sequences whose general terms are as follows:

   (a) $s_n = 5 - \dfrac{2}{n}$ (b) $s_n = \dfrac{n^2-1}{n}$ (c) $s_n = \dfrac{3n}{\sqrt{2n^2-1}}$

3. Prove that $e^x = \displaystyle\lim_{n\to\infty}\left(1 + \dfrac{x}{n}\right)^n$ for $x > 0$. (It is actually valid also for $x < 0$.)

7.12 L'Hôpital's Rule

We often need to examine the limit as x tends to a of a quotient in which both numerator and denominator tend to 0. Then we write

$$\lim_{x \to a} \frac{f(x)}{g(x)} = \frac{\text{``0''}}{0}$$

We call such a limit an **indeterminate form of type 0/0**. Here a may be replaced by a^+, a^-, ∞, or $-\infty$. The words "indeterminate form" indicate that the limit (or one-sided limit) cannot be found without further examination.

We start with the simple case in which we have an indeterminate form $f(x)/g(x)$ where f and g are differentiable and $f(a) = g(a) = 0$. When $x \neq a$ and $g(x) \neq g(a)$, then some routine algebra shows that

$$\frac{f(x)}{g(x)} = \frac{\big[f(x) - f(a)\big]/(x - a)}{\big[g(x) - g(a)\big]/(x - a)}$$

Letting $x \to a$, we see that provided $g'(a) \neq 0$, the fraction on the right-hand side tends to $f'(a)/g'(a)$. This gives the following result:

L'HÔPITAL'S RULE (SIMPLE VERSION)

If $f(a) = g(a) = 0$ and $g'(a) \neq 0$, then

$$\lim_{x \to a} \frac{f(x)}{g(x)} = \frac{f'(a)}{g'(a)} \tag{1}$$

According to (1), we can find the limit of an indeterminate form of type "0/0" by differentiating the numerator and the denominator separately.

EXAMPLE 1   Use (1) to confirm (see Example 6.5.1) that

$$\lim_{x \to 0} \frac{f(x)}{g(x)} = \lim_{x \to 0} \frac{e^x - 1}{x} = 1$$

Solution: In this case $f(0) = e^0 - 1 = 0$ and $g(0) = 0$. Moreover, $f'(x) = e^x$ and $g'(x) = 1$. Thus from (1)

$$\lim_{x \to 0} \frac{e^x - 1}{x} = \frac{f'(0)}{g'(0)} = \frac{1}{1} = 1$$

EXAMPLE 2   Compute $\lim_{\lambda \to 0} \dfrac{x^\lambda - y^\lambda}{\lambda}$ $(x > 0, \; y > 0)$.

Solution: In this limit x and y are kept fixed. Define $f(\lambda) = x^\lambda - y^\lambda$ and $g(\lambda) = \lambda$. Then, $f(0) = g(0) = 0$. Using the rule $(a^x)' = a^x \ln a$, we obtain $f'(\lambda) = x^\lambda \ln x - y^\lambda \ln y$, so that $f'(0) = \ln x - \ln y$. Moreover, $g'(\lambda) = 1$, so $g'(0) = 1$. Using l'Hôpital's rule,

$$\lim_{\lambda \to 0} \frac{x^\lambda - y^\lambda}{\lambda} = \ln x - \ln y = \ln \frac{x}{y}$$

In particular, if $y = 1$, then

$$\lim_{\lambda \to 0} \frac{x^\lambda - 1}{\lambda} = \ln x \tag{2}$$

which is a useful result.

Suppose we have a "0/0" form as in (1), but that $f'(a)/g'(a)$ is also of the type "0/0". Because $g'(a) = 0$, the argument for (1) breaks down. What do we do then? The answer is to differentiate once more both numerator and denominator separately. If we still obtain an expression of the type "0/0", we go on differentiating numerator and denominator repeatedly until the limit is determined (if possible). Here is an example from statistics.

EXAMPLE 3   Find $\lim_{x \to 0} \dfrac{e^{xt} - 1 - xt}{x^2}$.

Solution: The numerator and denominator are both 0 at $x = 0$. Applying l'Hôpital's rule twice, we have

$$\lim_{x \to 0} \frac{e^{xt} - 1 - xt}{x^2} = \frac{\text{``0''}}{0} = \lim_{x \to 0} \frac{te^{xt} - t}{2x} = \frac{\text{``0''}}{0} = \lim_{x \to 0} \frac{t^2 e^{xt}}{2} = \frac{1}{2}t^2$$

NOTE 1 Here are some important warnings concerning the most common errors in applying l'Hôpital's rule:

1. Check that you really do have an indeterminate form; otherwise, the method usually gives an erroneous result (see Problem 4).

2. Do not differentiate f/g as a fraction, but compute f'/g' instead.

The method explained here and used to solve Example 3 is built on the following theorem. Note that the requirements on f and g are weaker than might have appeared from the examples presented so far. For instance, f and g need not even be differentiable at $x = a$. Thus the theorem actually gives a more general version of l'Hôpital's rule.

THEOREM 7.12.1   (L'HÔPITAL'S RULE FOR "0/0" FORMS)

Suppose that f and g are differentiable in an interval (α, β) that contains a, except possibly at a, and suppose that $f(x)$ and $g(x)$ both tend to 0 as x tends to a. If $g'(x) \neq 0$ for all $x \neq a$ in (α, β), and if $\lim_{x \to a} f'(x)/g'(x) = L$, then

$$\lim_{x \to a} \frac{f(x)}{g(x)} = \lim_{x \to a} \frac{f'(x)}{g'(x)} = L$$

This is true whether L is finite, ∞, or $-\infty$.

Extensions of L'Hôpital's Rule

L'Hôpital's rule can be extended to some other cases. For instance, a can be an endpoint of the interval (α, β). Thus, $x \to a$ can be replaced by $x \to a^+$ or $x \to a^-$. Also it is easy to see that a may be replaced by ∞ or $-\infty$ (see Problem 6). The rule also applies to other indeterminate forms such as "$\pm\infty / \pm\infty$", although the proof is more complicated (see Problem 7). Here is an example:

$$\lim_{x \to \infty} \frac{1 - 3x^2}{5x^2 + x - 1} = \text{``}\frac{-\infty}{\infty}\text{''} = \lim_{x \to \infty} \frac{-6x}{10x + 1} = \text{``}\frac{-\infty}{\infty}\text{''} = \lim_{x \to \infty} \frac{-6}{10} = -\frac{3}{5}$$

Indeed, a variety of other indeterminate forms can sometimes be transformed into expressions of the type we have already mentioned by means of algebraic manipulations or substitutions.

EXAMPLE 4   Find $L = \lim_{x \to \infty} \left(\sqrt[5]{x^5 - x^4} - x \right)$.

Solution: We reduce this "$\infty - \infty$" case to a "0/0" case by some algebraic manipulation. Note first that for $x \neq 0$,

$$\sqrt[5]{x^5 - x^4} - x = \left[x^5 (1 - 1/x) \right]^{1/5} - x = x(1 - 1/x)^{1/5} - x$$

Thus,

$$\lim_{x \to \infty} \left(\sqrt[5]{x^5 - x^4} - x \right) = \lim_{x \to \infty} \frac{(1 - 1/x)^{1/5} - 1}{1/x} = \text{``}\frac{0}{0}\text{''}$$

Using l'Hôpital's rule, we have

$$L = \lim_{x \to \infty} \frac{(1/5)(1 - 1/x)^{-4/5} (1/x^2)}{-1/x^2} = \lim_{x \to \infty} \left[-\frac{1}{5} \left(1 - \frac{1}{x} \right)^{-4/5} \right] = -\frac{1}{5} \qquad \blacksquare$$

EXAMPLE 5   Consider the CES ("constant elasticity of substitution") function

$$F(K, L) = A \left(aK^{-\varrho} + (1 - a)L^{-\varrho} \right)^{-1/\varrho} \tag{$*$}$$

where $A > 0$, $K > 0$, $L > 0$, $a \in (0, 1)$, and $\varrho \neq 0$. (Functions of two variables are studied systematically in Chapter 11.) Keeping A, K, L, and a fixed, apply l'Hôpital's rule to $z = \ln[F(K, L)/A]$ as $\varrho \to 0$ to show that $F(K, L)$ converges to the Cobb–Douglas function $AK^a L^{1-a}$.

Solution: We get

$$z = \ln \left(aK^{-\varrho} + (1 - a)L^{-\varrho} \right)^{-1/\varrho} = -\ln \left(aK^{-\varrho} + (1 - a)L^{-\varrho} \right) / \varrho \to \text{``0/0''} \quad \text{as } \varrho \to 0$$

Then by l'Hôpital's rule,

$$\lim_{\varrho \to 0} z = \lim_{\varrho \to 0} - \left(\frac{aK^{-\varrho} \ln K + (1 - a)L^{-\varrho} \ln L}{aK^{-\varrho} + (1 - a)L^{-\varrho}} \right) \Big/ 1$$

$$= a \ln K + (1 - a) \ln L = \ln K^a L^{1-a}$$

Hence $e^z \to K^a L^{1-a}$, and the conclusion follows. $\qquad \blacksquare$

An Important Limit

If a is an arbitrary number greater than 1, then $a^x \to \infty$ as $x \to \infty$. For example, $(1.0001)^x \to \infty$ as $x \to \infty$. Furthermore, if p is an arbitrary positive number, then $x^p \to \infty$ as $x \to \infty$. If we compare $(1.0001)^x$ and x^{1000}, it is clear that the former increases quite slowly at first, whereas the latter increases very quickly. Nevertheless, $(1.0001)^x$ eventually "overwhelms" x^{1000}. In general, one can prove the following:

$$\lim_{x \to \infty} \frac{x^p}{a^x} = 0 \qquad (a > 1, \ p \text{ is a fixed positive number}) \tag{3}$$

For example x^2/e^x and $x^{10}/(1.1)^x$ will both tend to 0 as x tends to ∞. This result is actually quite remarkable. It can be expressed briefly by saying that, for an arbitrary base $a > 1$, *the exponential function a^x increases faster than any power x^p of x. Even more succinctly:* "Exponentials drown powers." (If $p \leq 0$, the limit is obviously 0.)

To prove (4) note first that

$$\frac{x^p}{a^x} = \frac{x^p}{e^{(\ln a)x}} = \left(\frac{x}{e^{((\ln a)/p)x}} \right)^p$$

and by l'Hôpital's rule,

$$\lim_{x \to \infty} \frac{x}{e^{((\ln a)/p)x}} = \frac{\text{``}\infty\text{''}}{\infty} = \lim_{x \to \infty} \frac{1}{((\ln a)/p)e^{((\ln a)/p)x}} = 0$$

The conclusion follows. (Note how the assumption $a > 1$ is crucial in concluding that the last limit is 0.)

PROBLEMS FOR SECTION 7.12

1. Use l'Hôpital's rule to find the following limits:

   (a) $\displaystyle\lim_{x \to 1} \frac{x - 1}{x^2 - 1}$ (b) $\displaystyle\lim_{x \to -2} \frac{x^3 + 3x^2 - 4}{x^3 + 5x^2 + 8x + 4}$ (c) $\displaystyle\lim_{x \to 2} \frac{x^4 - 4x^3 + 6x^2 - 8x + 8}{x^3 - 3x^2 + 4}$

2. Find the limits: (a) $\displaystyle\lim_{x \to a} \frac{x^2 - a^2}{x - a}$ (b) $\displaystyle\lim_{x \to 0} \frac{2\sqrt{1 + x} - 2 - x}{2\sqrt{1 + x + x^2} - 2 - x}$.

3. Find the following limits:

   (a) $\displaystyle\lim_{x \to \infty} \frac{\ln x}{x}$ (b) $\displaystyle\lim_{x \to 0^+} x \ln x$ (c) $\displaystyle\lim_{x \to 0^+} (xe^{1/x} - x)$

4. Find the error in the following:

$$\lim_{x \to 1} \frac{x^2 + 3x - 4}{2x^2 - 2x} = \lim_{x \to 1} \frac{2x + 3}{4x - 2} = \lim_{x \to 1} \frac{2}{4} = \frac{1}{2}$$

   What is the correct value of the first limit?

5. With $\beta > 0$ and $\gamma > 0$, find $\lim\limits_{v \to 0^+} \dfrac{1 - (1 + v^\beta)^{-\gamma}}{v}$. (Consider first the case $\beta = 1$.)

HARDER PROBLEMS

6. Suppose that f and g are both differentiable for all large x and that $f(x)$ and $g(x)$ both tend to 0 as $x \to \infty$. If in addition, $\lim_{x \to \infty} g'(x) \neq 0$, show that

$$\lim_{x \to \infty} \frac{f(x)}{g(x)} = \frac{\text{``0''}}{0} = \lim_{x \to \infty} \frac{f'(x)}{g'(x)}$$

by introducing $x = 1/t$ in the first fraction and then using l'Hôpital's rule as $t \to 0^+$.

7. Suppose that $\lim_{x \to a} f(x)/g(x) = $ "$\pm \infty / \pm \infty$" $= L \neq 0$. By applying l'Hôpital's rule to the equivalent limit, $\lim_{x \to a} [1/g(x)]/[1/f(x)] = $ "0/0", show that $L = \lim_{x \to a} [f'(x)/g'(x)]$ provided this limit exists. (Ignore cases where $f'(x)$ or $g'(x)$ tends to 0 as x tends to a.)

REVIEW PROBLEMS FOR CHAPTER 7

1. For the following equations, find dy/dx and d^2y/dx^2 by implicit differentiation:

   (a) $5x + y = 10$
   (b) $xy^3 = 125$
   (c) $e^{2y} = x^3$

   Check by solving each equation for y and then differentiating.

2. Compute y' when y is defined implicitly by the equation $y^5 - xy^2 = 24$. Is y' ever 0?

3. The graph of the equation $x^3 + y^3 = 3xy$ passes through the point $(3/2, 3/2)$. Find the slope of the tangent line to the curve at this point. (This equation has a nice graph which is called *Descartes' folium*. See the figure in the answer to this problem.)

4. (a) Find the slope of the tangent to the curve $x^2y + 3y^3 = 7$ at $(x, y) = (2, 1)$.

   (b) Prove that $y'' = -210/13^3$ at $(2, 1)$.

5. If $K^{1/3}L^{1/3} = 24$, compute dL/dK by implicit differentiation.

6. The equation
$$\ln y + y = 1 - 2 \ln x - 0.2(\ln x)^2$$

   defines y as a function of x for $x > 0$, $y > 0$. Compute y' and show that $y' = 0$ for $x = e^{-5}$.

7. (a) Determine the domain and the range of the function f defined by the formula

$$f(x) = \frac{1}{2} \ln \frac{1+x}{1-x}$$

(b) Prove that f has an inverse g, and find a formula for the inverse. Note that $f(\frac{1}{2}) = \frac{1}{2} \ln 3$. Find $g'(\frac{1}{2} \ln 3)$ in two different ways.

8. (a) Let $f(x)$ be defined for all $x > 0$ by

$$f(x) = (\ln x)^3 - 2(\ln x)^2 + \ln x$$

Compute $f(e^2)$ and find the zeros of $f(x)$.

(b) Prove that $f(x)$ defined on $[e, \infty)$ has an inverse function h and determine $h'(2)$.

9. Find the linear approximations to the following functions about $x = 0$:

   (a) $f(x) = \ln(2x + 4)$ (b) $g(x) = (1 + x)^{-1/2}$ (c) $h(x) = xe^{2x}$

10. Find the differentials:

   (a) $d(\sqrt{1 + x^2})$ (b) $d(4\pi r^2)$ (c) $d(100K^4 + 200)$ (d) $d(\ln(1 - x^3))$

11. Compute the differential of $f(x) = \sqrt{1 + x^3}$. What is the approximate change in $f(x)$ when x changes from $x = 2$ to $x = 2 + dx$, where $dx = 0.2$?

12. Use formula (7.6.6) with $n = 5$ to find an approximate value of $\sqrt{e}$. Show that the answer is correct to three decimal places. (*Hint:* For $0 < c < 1/2$, $e^c < e^{1/2} < 2$.)

13. Find the second-order Taylor polynomials about $x = 0$ for the functions in Problem 9.

14. Find the quadratic approximation to $y = y(x)$ about $(x, y) = (0, 1)$ when y is defined implicitly as a function of x by the equation $y + \ln y = 1 + x$.

15. Determine the values of x at which each of the functions defined by the following formulas is continuous:

   (a) $e^x + e^{1/x}$ (b) $\dfrac{\sqrt{x} + 1/x}{x^2 + 2x + 2}$ (c) $\dfrac{1}{\sqrt{x+2}} + \dfrac{1}{\sqrt{2-x}}$

16. The demands for margarine and for meals away from home in the UK during the period 1920–1937, as functions of personal income r, were estimated to be $D_{marg} = Ar^{-0.165}$ and $D_{mah} = Br^{2.39}$, respectively, for suitable constants A and B. Find and interpret the (Engel) elasticities of D_{marg} and D_{mah} w.r.t. r.

17. Find the elasticities of the functions given by the following formulas:

   (a) $50x^5$ (b) $\sqrt[3]{x}$ (c) $x^3 + x^5$ (d) $\dfrac{x-1}{x+1}$

18. The equation $x^3 - x - 5 = 0$ has a root close to 2. Find an approximation by using Newton's method once, with $x_0 = 2$.

19. Prove that $f(x) = e^{\sqrt{x}} - 3$ has a unique zero in the interval $[1, 4]$. Find an approximate value for this zero by using Newton's method once, with $x_0 = 1$.

20. Evaluate the limits:

    (a) $\lim\limits_{x \to 3^-} (x^2 - 3x + 2)$ (b) $\lim\limits_{x \to -2^+} \dfrac{x^2 - 3x + 14}{x + 2}$ (c) $\lim\limits_{x \to -1} \dfrac{3 - \sqrt{x + 17}}{x + 1}$

21. Evaluate the limits:

    (a) $\lim\limits_{x \to 0} \dfrac{(2 - x)e^x - x - 2}{x^3}$ (b) $\lim\limits_{x \to 3} \left(\dfrac{1}{x - 3} - \dfrac{5}{x^2 - x - 6} \right)$ (c) $\lim\limits_{x \to 4} \dfrac{x - 4}{2x^2 - 32}$

22. Evaluate the limits:

    (a) $\lim\limits_{x \to 2} \dfrac{x^2 - 3x + 2}{x - 2}$ (b) $\lim\limits_{x \to -1} \dfrac{4 - \sqrt{x + 17}}{2x + 2}$ (c) $\lim\limits_{x \to -1} \dfrac{2e^{x+1} - x^2 - 4x - 5}{(x + 1)^3}$

23. Evaluate the limits:

    (a) $\lim\limits_{x \to 1} \dfrac{\ln x - x + 1}{(x - 1)^2}$ (b) $\lim\limits_{x \to 1} \dfrac{1}{x - 1} \ln \left(\dfrac{7x + 1}{4x + 4} \right)$ (c) $\lim\limits_{x \to 1} \dfrac{x^x - x}{1 - x + \ln x}$

24. Examine the following limit for different values of the constants a, b, c, and d, assuming that b and d are positive:

$$\lim\limits_{x \to 0} \dfrac{\sqrt{ax + b} - \sqrt{cx + d}}{x}$$

25. Evaluate $\lim\limits_{x \to 0} \dfrac{a^x - b^x}{e^{ax} - e^{bx}}$ $(a \neq b, a$ and b positive)

26. The equation $x^{21} - 11x + 10 = 0$ has a root at $x = 1$, and another root in the interval $(0, 1)$. Starting from $x_0 = 0.9$, use Newton's method as many times as necessary to find the latter root to 3 decimal places.

8

SINGLE-VARIABLE OPTIMIZATION

If you want literal realism,
look at the world around you;
if you want understanding,
look at theories.
—R. Dorfman (1964)

Finding the best way to do a specific task involves what is called an **optimization problem**. Examples abound in almost all areas of human activity. A manager seeks those combinations of inputs (such as capital and labour) that maximize profits or minimize costs. A doctor might want to know when is the best time of day to inject a drug, so as to avoid the concentration in the bloodstream becoming dangerously high. A farmer might want to know what amount of fertilizer per square yard will maximize profits. An oil company may wish to find the optimal rate of extraction from one of its wells.

Studying an optimization problem of this sort systematically requires a mathematical model. Constructing one is usually not easy, and only in simple cases will the model lead to the problem of maximizing or minimizing a function of a single variable—the main topic of this chapter.

In general, no mathematical methods are more important in economics than those designed to solve optimization problems. Though economic optimization problems usually involve several variables, the examples of quadratic optimization in Section 4.6 indicate how useful economic insights can be gained even from simple one-variable optimization.

8.1 Introduction

Those points in the domain of a function where it reaches its largest and its smallest values are usually referred to as maximum and minimum points. If we do not need to bother about the distinction between maxima and minima, we call them **extreme points**. Thus, if $f(x)$ has domain D, then

$$c \in D \text{ is a } \textbf{maximum point} \text{ for } f \iff f(x) \leq f(c) \text{ for all } x \in D \qquad (1)$$

$$d \in D \text{ is a } \textbf{minimum point} \text{ for } f \iff f(x) \geq f(d) \text{ for all } x \in D \qquad (2)$$

In (1), we call $f(c)$ the **maximum value**, and in (2), we call $f(d)$ the **minimum value**. If the value of f at c is strictly larger than at any other point in D, then c is a **strict maximum point**. Similarly, d is a **strict minimum** point if $f(x) > f(d)$ for all $x \in D$, $x \neq d$. As collective names, we use the terms **optimal points** and **values**, or **extreme points** and **values**.

If f is any function with domain D, then the function $-f$ is defined in D by $(-f)(x) = -f(x)$. Note that $f(x) \leq f(c)$ for all x in D if and only if $-f(x) \geq -f(c)$ for all x in D. Thus, c maximizes f in D if and only if c minimizes $-f$ in D. This simple observation, which is illustrated in Fig. 1, can be used to convert maximization problems to minimization problems and vice versa.

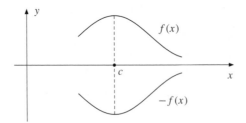

Figure 1   The point c is a maximum point for $f(x)$ and a minimum point for $-f(x)$

Sometimes we can find the maximum and minimum points of a function simply by studying the formula that defines it.

EXAMPLE 1   Find possible maximum and minimum points for:

(a) $f(x) = 3 - (x - 2)^2$ (b) $g(x) = \sqrt{x - 5} - 100, \quad x \geq 5$

Solution:

(a) Because $(x - 2)^2 \geq 0$ for all x, it follows that $f(x) \leq 3$ for all x. But $f(x) = 3$ when $(x - 2)^2 = 0$ at $x = 2$. Therefore, $x = 2$ is a maximum point for f. Because $f(x) \to -\infty$ as $x \to \infty$, f has no minimum.

(b) Since $\sqrt{x - 5}$ is ≥ 0 for all $x \geq 5$, it follows that $f(x) \geq -100$ for all $x \geq 5$. Since $f(5) = -100$, we conclude that $x = 5$ is a minimum point. Since $f(x) \to \infty$ as $x \to \infty$, f has no maximum.

Rarely can we find extreme points as simply as in the example. The main task of this chapter is to explain how to locate possible extreme points in more complicated cases. An essential observation is a result which you have already observed: If f is a differentiable function that has a maximum or minimum at an interior point c of its domain, then the tangent line to its graph must be horizontal (parallel to the x-axis) at that point. Hence, $f'(c) = 0$. Points c at which $f'(c) = 0$ are called **stationary points** for f. Precisely formulated, one has the following theorem:

THEOREM 8.1.1 NECESSARY FIRST-ORDER CONDITION

Suppose that a function f is differentiable in an interval I and that c is an interior point of I. For $x = c$ to be a maximum or minimum point for f in I, a necessary condition is that it is a stationary point for f—i.e. that $x = c$ satisfies the equation

$$f'(x) = 0 \qquad \textbf{(first-order condition)}$$

Proof: Suppose that f has a maximum at c (the proof in the case when c is a minimum point is similar). If the absolute value of h is sufficiently small, then $c + h \in I$ because c is an interior point of I. Because c is a maximum point, $f(c + h) - f(c) \leq 0$. If h is sufficiently small and positive, the Newton quotient $[f(c + h) - f(c)]/h \leq 0$. The limit of this quotient as $h \to 0^+$ is therefore ≤ 0 as well. But because $f'(c)$ exists, this limit is equal to $f'(c)$, so $f'(c) \leq 0$. For negative values of h, on the other hand, we get $[f(c + h) - f(c)]/h \geq 0$. The limit of this expression as $h \to 0^-$ is therefore ≥ 0. So $f'(c) \geq 0$. We have now proved that $f'(c) \leq 0$ and $f'(c) \geq 0$, so $f'(c) = 0$. ∎

Before starting to explore systematically other properties of maxima and minima, we provide some geometric examples. They will indicate for us the role played by the stationary points of a function in the theory of optimization.

Figure 2 shows the graph of a function f defined in an interval $[a, b]$ having two stationary points, c and d. At c, there is a maximum; at d, there is a minimum.

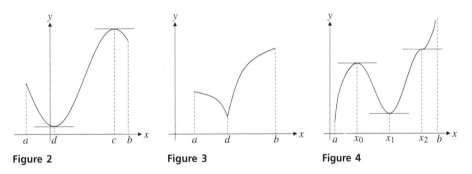

Figure 2   Figure 3   Figure 4

In Fig. 3, the function has no stationary points. There is a maximum at the end point b and a minimum at d. At d, the function is not differentiable. At b, the derivative (the left-hand derivative) is not 0.

Theorem 8.1.1 implies that $f'(x) = 0$ is a *necessary* condition for a differentiable function f to have a maximum or minimum at an interior point x in its domain. The condition is far from sufficient. This is indicated in Fig. 4 where f has three stationary points, x_0, x_1, and x_2. At the end point a there is a minimum, whereas f does not have any maximum value because it approaches ∞ as x tends to b. At the stationary point x_0 the function f has a "local maximum", in the sense that its value at that point is higher than at all neighbouring points. Similarly, at x_1 it has a local "minimum", whereas at x_2 there is a stationary point that is neither a local maximum nor a local minimum. In fact, x_2 is a special case of an *inflection point*.

The situation suggested in Fig. 2 is the most typical for problems arising in applications, since maximum and minimum points usually will be attained at stationary points. But Figs. 3 and 4 illustrate situations that *can* occur, also in economic problems.

Actually, the three figures represent important aspects of single-variable optimization problems. Because the theory is so important in economics, we must not simply rely on vague geometric insights. Instead, we must develop a firmer analytical foundation by formulating precise mathematical results.

PROBLEMS FOR SECTION 8.1

1. Use arguments similar to those in Example 1 to find the maximum or minimum points for the following functions:

   (a) $f(x) = \dfrac{8}{3x^2 + 4}$ (b) $g(x) = 5(x + 2)^4 - 3$ (c) $h(x) = \dfrac{1}{1 + x^4}$, $x \in [-1, 1]$

2. Use arguments similar to those in Example 1 to find the maximum or minimum points for the following functions:

   (a) $F(x) = \dfrac{-2}{2 + x^2}$ (b) $G(x) = 2 - \sqrt{1 - x}$ (c) $H(x) = 100 - e^{-x^2}$

8.2 Simple Tests for Extreme Points

In many important cases we can find maximum or minimum values for a function just by studying the sign of its first derivative. Suppose $f(x)$ is differentiable in an interval I and that it has only one stationary point, $x = c$. Suppose $f'(x) \geq 0$ for all x in I such that $x \leq c$, whereas $f'(x) \leq 0$ for all x in I such that $x \geq c$. Then $f(x)$ is increasing to the left of c and decreasing to the right of c. It follows that $f(x) \leq f(c)$ for all $x \leq c$, and $f(c) \geq f(x)$ for all $x \geq c$. Hence, $x = c$ is a maximum point for f in I, as illustrated in Fig. 1.

Figure 1 $x = c$ is a maximum point

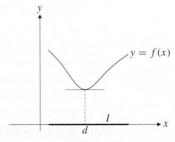

Figure 2 $x = d$ is a minimum point

With obvious modifications, a similar result holds for minimum points, as illustrated in Fig. 2. Briefly stated:[1]

THEOREM 8.2.1 (FIRST-DERIVATIVE TEST FOR MAXIMUM/MINIMUM)

If $f'(x) \geq 0$ for $x \leq c$ and $f'(x) \leq 0$ for $x \geq c$, then $x = c$ is a maximum point for f.

If $f'(x) \leq 0$ for $x \leq c$ and $f'(x) \geq 0$ for $x \geq c$, then $x = c$ is a minimum point for f.

EXAMPLE 1   Measured in milligrams per litre, the concentration of a drug in the bloodstream t hours after injection is given by the formula

$$c(t) = \frac{t}{t^2 + 4}, \qquad t \geq 0$$

Find the time of maximum concentration.

Solution: Differentiating with respect to t yields

$$c'(t) = \frac{1 \cdot (t^2 + 4) - t \cdot 2t}{(t^2 + 4)^2} = \frac{4 - t^2}{(t^2 + 4)^2} = \frac{(2 + t)(2 - t)}{(t^2 + 4)^2}$$

For $t \geq 0$, the term $2 - t$ alone determines the algebraic sign of the fraction, because the other terms are positive. In fact, if $t \leq 2$, then $c'(t) \geq 0$, whereas if $t \geq 2$, then $c'(t) \leq 0$. We conclude that $t = 2$ maximizes $c(t)$. Thus, the concentration of the drug is highest 2 hours after injection. Because $c(2) = 0.25$, the maximum concentration is 0.25 milligrams per litre.

EXAMPLE 2   Consider the function f defined for all x by

$$f(x) = e^{2x} - 5e^x + 4 = (e^x - 1)(e^x - 4)$$

(a) Find the zeros of $f(x)$ and compute $f'(x)$.

(b) Find the intervals where f increases and decreases, and determine possible extreme points and values.

(c) Examine $\lim_{x \to -\infty} f(x)$. Sketch the graph of f.

---

[1] Many books in mathematics for economists instruct students always to check so-called second-order conditions, even when this first-derivative test is much easier to use.

Solution:

(a) $f(x) = (e^x - 1)(e^x - 4) = 0$ when $e^x = 1$ and when $e^x = 4$. Hence $f(x) = 0$ for $x = 0$ and for $x = \ln 4$. By differentiating the first expression for $f(x)$, we obtain $f'(x) = 2e^{2x} - 5e^x$.

(b) $f'(x) = 2e^{2x} - 5e^x = e^x(2e^x - 5)$. Thus $f'(x) = 0$ for $e^x = 5/2 = 2.5$, that is, $x = \ln 2.5$. Furthermore, $f'(x) \leq 0$ for $x \leq \ln 2.5$, and $f'(x) \geq 0$ for $x \geq \ln 2.5$. Hence $f(x)$ is decreasing in the interval $(-\infty, \ln 2.5]$ and increasing in $[\ln 2.5, \infty)$. Hence $f(x)$ has a minimum at $x = \ln 2.5$, and $f(\ln 2.5) = (2.5 - 1)(2.5 - 4) = -2.25$. Since $f(x) \to \infty$ as $x \to \infty$, $f(x)$ has no maximum.

(c) When $x \to -\infty$, then e^x tends to 0, and $f(x)$ tends to 4. The graph is drawn in Fig. 3. ($y = 4$ is an asymptote as $x \to -\infty$.)

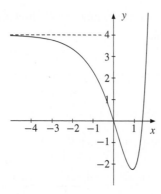

Figure 3 $f(x) = e^{2x} - 5e^x + 4$

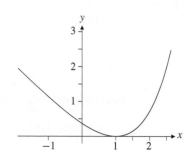

Figure 4 $f(x) = e^{x-1} - x$

Extreme Points for Concave and Convex Functions

Recall the definitions of concave and convex functions in Section 6.9. Suppose that f is concave with $f''(x) \leq 0$ for all x in an interval I. Then $f'(x)$ is decreasing in I. If $f'(c) = 0$ at an interior point c of I, then $f'(x)$ must be ≥ 0 to the left of c, while $f'(x) \leq 0$ to the right of c. This implies that the function itself is increasing to the left of c and decreasing to the right of c. We conclude that $x = c$ is a maximum point for f in I. We obviously get a corresponding result for a minimum of a convex function.

THEOREM 8.2.2 (MAXIMUM/MINIMUM FOR CONCAVE/CONVEX FUNCTIONS)

Suppose f is a concave (convex) function in an interval I. If c is a stationary point for f in the interior of I, then c is a maximum (minimum) point for f in I.

EXAMPLE 3   Consider the function f defined for all x by $f(x) = e^{x-1} - x$. Show that f is convex and find its minimum point. Sketch the graph.

Solution: $f'(x) = e^{x-1} - 1$ and $f''(x) = e^{x-1} > 0$, so f is convex. Note that $f'(x) = e^{x-1} - 1 = 0$ for $x = 1$. From Theorem 8.2.2 it follows that $x = 1$ minimizes f. See Fig. 4. ▮

PROBLEMS FOR SECTION 8.2

1. Let y denote the weekly average quantity of pigmeat produced in Chicago during 1948 (in millions of pounds) and let x be the total weekly work effort (in thousands of hours). Nichols estimated the relation

$$y = -2.05 + 1.06x - 0.04x^2$$

   Determine the value of x that maximizes y by studying the sign variation of y'.

2. Find the derivative of the function h defined for all x by the formula $h(x) = \dfrac{8x}{3x^2 + 4}$. Use the sign variation of $h'(x)$ to find the extreme points of $h(x)$.

3. The height of a flowering plant after t months is given by

$$h(t) = \sqrt{t} - \tfrac{1}{2}t, \qquad t \in [0, 3]$$

   At what time is the plant at its highest?

4. Show that

$$f(x) = \frac{2x^2}{x^4 + 1} \quad \Rightarrow \quad f'(x) = \frac{4x(1 + x^2)(1 + x)(1 - x)}{(x^4 + 1)^2}$$

   and find the maximum value of f on $[0, \infty)$.

5. Find possible extreme points for $g(x) = x^3 \ln x$, $x \in (0, \infty)$.

6. Find possible extreme points for $f(x) = e^{3x} - 6e^x$, $x \in (-\infty, \infty)$.

7. Find the maximum of $y = x^2 e^{-x}$ on $[0, 4]$.

8. Use Theorem 8.2.2 to find the values of x that maximize/minimize the functions given by the following formulas:

   (a) $y = e^x + e^{-2x}$ (b) $y = 9 - (x - a)^2 - 2(x - b)^2$ (c) $y = \ln x - 5x$, $x > 0$

9. Consider n numbers $a_1, a_2, \ldots, a_n$. Find the number $\bar{x}$ which gives the best approximation to these numbers, in the sense of minimizing

$$d(x) = (x - a_1)^2 + (x - a_2)^2 + \cdots + (x - a_n)^2$$

HARDER PROBLEMS

10. After the big flood catastrophe in Holland in 1953, a research project was initiated to determine the optimal height of the dikes. One of the (simpler) models involved finding the value of x that minimizes the function

$$f(x) = I_0 + kx + Ae^{-\alpha x} \qquad (x \geq 0)$$

Here x denotes the number of metres that should be added to the dikes, $I_0 + kx$ is the construction cost, and $Ae^{-\alpha x}$ is an estimate of the expected loss caused by flooding. The parameters I_0, k, A, and α are all positive constants.

(a) Suppose that $f(x)$ has minimum for some $x_0 > 0$. Find x_0. What condition must be put on α, A, and k for x_0 to be positive? Show that if the condition is satisfied, then x_0 solves the minimization problem.

(b) The constant A is defined as $A = p_0 V(1 + 100/\delta)$, where p_0 is the probability that the dikes will be flooded if they are not rebuilt, V is an estimate of the cost of flood damage, and δ is an interest rate. Show that x_0 may be written in the form

$$x_0 = \frac{1}{\alpha} \ln \left[\frac{\alpha p_0 V}{k} \left(1 + \frac{100}{\delta} \right) \right]$$

Examine what happens to x_0 when one of the variables p_0, V, δ, or k increases. Comment on the reasonableness of the results.[2]

8.3 Economic Examples

This section presents some interesting examples of economic optimization problems.

EXAMPLE 1   Suppose $Y(N)$ bushels of wheat are harvested per acre of land when N pounds of fertilizer per acre are used. If P is the dollar price per bushel of wheat and q is the dollar price per pound of fertilizer, then profits in dollars per acre are

$$\pi(N) = PY(N) - qN, \qquad N \geq 0$$

Suppose there exists N^* such that $\pi'(N) \geq 0$ for $N \leq N^*$, whereas $\pi'(N) \leq 0$ for $N \geq N^*$. Then N^* maximizes profits, and $\pi'(N^*) = 0$. That is, $PY'(N^*) - q = 0$, so

$$PY'(N^*) = q \qquad\qquad\qquad (*)$$

---

[2] The problem is discussed in D. van Dantzig, "Economic Decision Problems for Flood Prevention," *Econometrica*, 24 (1956): 276–287.

Let us give an economic interpretation of this condition. Suppose N^* units of fertilizer are used and we contemplate increasing N^* by one unit. What do we gain? If N^* increases by one unit, then $Y(N^*+1) - Y(N^*)$ more bushels are produced. Now $Y(N^*+1) - Y(N^*) \approx Y'(N^*)$. For each of these bushels, we get P dollars, so

$$\text{by increasing } N^* \text{ by one unit, we gain} \approx PY'(N^*) \text{ dollars}$$

On the other hand,

$$\text{by increasing } N^* \text{ by one unit, we lose } q \text{ dollars}$$

because this is the cost of one unit of fertilizer. Hence, we can interpret (∗) as follows: In order to maximize profits, you should increase the amount of fertilizer to the level N^* at which an additional pound of fertilizer equates your gains and losses.

(a) In a (constructed) example $Y(N) = \sqrt{N}$, $P = 10$, and $q = 0.5$. Find the amount of fertilizer which maximizes profits in this case.

(b) In a certain study from Iowa in 1952, the yield function $Y(N)$ was estimated as

$$Y(N) = -13.62 + 0.984N - 0.05N^{1.5}$$

If the price of wheat is \$1.40 per bushel and the price of fertilizer is \$0.18 per pound, find the amount of fertilizer that maximizes profits.

Solution:

(a) The profit function is

$$\pi(N) = PY(N) - qN = 10N^{1/2} - 0.5N, \qquad N \geq 0$$

Then $\pi'(N) = 10(1/2)N^{-1/2} - 0.5 = 5N^{-1/2} - 0.5$. We see that $\pi'(N^*) = 0$ when $(N^*)^{-1/2} = 0.1$, hence $N^* = 100$. Moreover, it follows that $\pi'(N) \geq 0$ when $N \leq 100$ and $\pi'(N) \leq 0$ when $N \geq 100$. We conclude that $N^* = 100$ maximizes profits. See Fig. 1.

(b) In this case

$$\pi(N) = 1.4(-13.62 + 0.984N - 0.05N^{1.5}) - 0.18N$$
$$= -19.068 + 1.1976N - 0.07N^{1.5}$$

so that

$$\pi'(N) = 1.1976 - 0.07 \cdot 1.5N^{0.5} = 1.1976 - 0.105\sqrt{N}$$

Hence $\pi'(N^*) = 0$ when $0.105\sqrt{N^*} = 1.1976$. This implies that

$$\sqrt{N^*} = \frac{1.1976}{0.105} \approx 11.4 \quad \text{or} \quad N^* \approx (11.4)^2 \approx 130$$

By studying the expression for $\pi'(N)$, we see that $\pi'(N)$ is positive to the left of N^* and negative to the right of N^*. Hence, $N^* \approx 130$ maximizes profits. The graph of $\pi(N)$ is shown in Fig. 2.

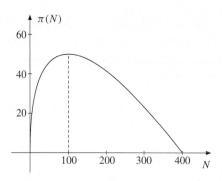

Figure 1 $\pi(N) = 10N^{1/2} - 0.5N$ **Figure 2** Iowa (1952)

EXAMPLE 2   (a) The total cost of producing Q units of a commodity is

$$C(Q) = 2Q^2 + 10Q + 32, \qquad Q > 0$$

Find the value of Q which minimizes $A(Q) = C(Q)/Q = 2Q + 10 + 32/Q$, the average cost.

(b) The total cost of producing Q units of a commodity is

$$C(Q) = aQ^2 + bQ + c, \qquad Q > 0$$

where a, b, and c are positive constants. Show that the average cost function

$$A(Q) = \frac{C(Q)}{Q} = aQ + b + \frac{c}{Q}$$

has a minimum at $Q^* = \sqrt{c/a}$. In the same coordinate system, draw the graphs of the average cost, the marginal cost, and the straight line $P = aQ + b$.

Solution:

(a) We find that $A'(Q) = 2 - 32/Q^2$ and $A''(Q) = 64/Q^3$. Since $A''(Q) > 0$ for all $Q > 0$, A is convex, and since $A'(Q) = 0$ for $Q = 4$, this is a minimum point.

(b) We find that $A'(Q) = a - c/Q^2$ and $A''(Q) = 2c/Q^3$. Since $A''(Q) > 0$ for all $Q > 0$, A is convex, and since $A'(Q) = 0$ for $Q^* = \sqrt{c/a}$, this is a minimum point. The graphs are drawn in Fig. 3. (We see that at the minimum point Q^*, marginal cost is equal to average cost. This is no coincidence because it is true in general that $A'(Q) = 0$ if and only if $C'(Q) = A(Q)$. (See Example 6.7.6.) The minimum average cost is $A(Q^*) = a\sqrt{c/a} + b + c/\sqrt{c/a} = \sqrt{ac} + b + \sqrt{ac} = 2\sqrt{ac} + b$.)

Figure 3

The following example is typical of how economists use implicit differentiation in connection with optimization problems.

EXAMPLE 3   A monopolist is faced with the demand function $P(Q)$ denoting the price when output is Q. The monopolist has a constant average cost k per unit produced.

(a) Find the profit function $\pi(Q)$, and prove that the first-order condition for maximal profit at $Q^* > 0$ is

$$P(Q^*) + Q^* P'(Q^*) = k \qquad (*)$$

(b) By implicit differentiation of $(*)$ find how the monopolist's choice of optimal production is affected by changes in k.

(c) How does the optimal profit react to a change in k?

Solution: (a) The profit function is $\pi(Q) = QP(Q) - kQ$, and $\pi'(Q) = P(Q) + QP'(Q) - k$. In order for $Q^* > 0$ to maximize $\pi(Q)$, one must have $\pi'(Q^*) = 0$, i.e. $P(Q^*) + Q^* P'(Q^*) = k$.

(b) Assuming that equation $(*)$ defines Q^* as a differentiable function of k, we obtain

$$P'(Q^*)\frac{dQ^*}{dk} + \frac{dQ^*}{dk}P'(Q^*) + Q^* P''(Q^*)\frac{dQ^*}{dk} = 1$$

Solving for dQ^*/dk gives

$$\frac{dQ^*}{dk} = \frac{1}{Q^* P''(Q^*) + 2P'(Q^*)}$$

(c) Because $\pi(Q^*) = Q^* P(Q^*) - kQ^*$, differentiating w.r.t. k gives

$$\frac{d\pi(Q^*)}{dk} = \frac{dQ^*}{dk}P(Q^*) + Q^* P'(Q^*)\frac{dQ^*}{dk} - Q^* - k\frac{dQ^*}{dk}$$

But the terms containing dQ^*/dk all cancel because of the first-order condition $(*)$. So $d\pi^*/dk = -Q^*$. Thus, if the cost increases by one unit, the optimal profit will decrease by Q^*, the optimal output level.

PROBLEMS FOR SECTION 8.3

1. (a) A firm produces $Q = 2\sqrt{L}$ units of a commodity when L units of labour are employed. If the price obtained per unit is 160 euros, and the price per unit of labour is 40 euros, what value of L maximizes profits?

   (b) A firm produces $Q = f(L)$ units of a commodity when L units of labour are employed. Assume that $f'(L) > 0$ and $f''(L) < 0$. If the price obtained per unit is 1 and price per unit of labour is w, what is the first-order condition for maximizing profits at $L = L^*$?

   (c) By implicitly differentiating the first-order condition in (b) w.r.t. w, find how L^* changes when w changes.

2. (a) The price a firm obtains from producing and selling Q units of a commodity is $P = 102 - 2Q$ per unit, whereas the costs are $C = 2Q + \frac{1}{2}Q^2$. Find the profit function and the value of Q which maximize profits.

   (b) A tax of t per unit produced is imposed. If $t < 100$, what value of Q now maximizes profits? If you put $t = 0$ in your answer, what do you get?

3. A square tin plate whose edges are 18 cm long is to be made into an open square box of depth x cm by cutting out equally sized squares of width x in each corner and then folding over the edges. Draw a figure, and show that the volume of the box is

$$V(x) = x(18 - 2x)^2 = 4x^3 - 72x^2 + 324x, \qquad x \in [0, 9]$$

Also find the maximum point of V in $[0, 9]$.

4. In an economic model, the proportion of families whose income is no more than x, and who have a home computer, is given by

$$p(x) = a + k(1 - e^{-cx}) \qquad (a, k, \text{ and } c \text{ are positive constants})$$

Determine $p'(x)$ and $p''(x)$. Does $p(x)$ have a maximum? Sketch the graph of p.

HARDER PROBLEMS

5. The tax T a person pays on gross income W is given by $T = a(bW + c)^p + kW$, where $a, b, c,$ and k are positive constants, and $p > 1$. Then the average tax rate is

$$\overline{T}(W) = \frac{T}{W} = a\frac{(bW + c)^p}{W} + k$$

Find the value of W that minimizes the average tax rate.

8.4 The Extreme-Value Theorem

The main theorems used so far in this chapter to locate extreme points require the function to be steadily increasing on one side of the point and steadily decreasing on the other side. Many functions with a derivative whose sign varies in a more complicated way may still have a maximum or minimum. This section shows how to locate possible extreme points for an important class of such functions.

Geometric examples in Section 8.1 have already indicated that not all functions have extreme points. The following theorem gives important sufficient conditions for the existence of some maximum and a minimum.

THEOREM 8.4.1 (EXTREME-VALUE THEOREM)

If f is a continuous function over a closed bounded interval $[a, b]$, then there exists a point d in $[a, b]$ where f has a minimum, and a point c in $[a, b]$ where f has a maximum, so that

$$f(d) \leq f(x) \leq f(c) \qquad \text{for all } x \text{ in } [a, b]$$

NOTE 1 One of the most common misunderstandings of the extreme-value theorem is illustrated by the following statement from a student's exam paper: "The function is continuous, but since it is not defined on a closed, bounded interval, the extreme-value theorem shows that there is no maximum." The misunderstanding here is that, although the conditions of the theorem are sufficient, they certainly are not *necessary* for the existence of an extreme point. In Problem 9, you are asked to study a function defined in an interval that is neither closed nor bounded, and moreover the function is not even continuous. Even so, it has both a maximum and a minimum.

The proof of the extreme-value theorem is surprisingly difficult. Yet the result is not hard to believe. Imagine, for example, a cyclist going for a ride on hilly roads. Since roads avoid going over cliffs, the height of the road above sea level is a continuous function of the distance travelled, as illustrated in Fig. 1. During the trip, the cyclist has to pass through some highest point P and some lowest point Q, as shown in the figure.

Figure 1

How to Search for Maxima/Minima

Suppose we know that a function f has a maximum and/or a minimum in some bounded interval I. The optimum must occur either at an interior point of I or at one of the end points. If it occurs at an interior point (inside the interval I) and if f is differentiable, then the derivative f' is zero at that point. In addition, there is the possibility that the optimum occurs at a point where f is not differentiable. Hence, every extreme point must belong to one of the following three different sets:

(a) Interior points in I where $f'(x) = 0$

(b) End points of I (if included in I)

(c) Interior points in I where f' does not exist

Points satisfying any one of these three conditions will be called *candidate extreme points*. Whether they are actual extreme points depends on a careful comparison of function values, as explained below.

A typical example showing that a minimum can occur at a point of type (c) is shown in Fig. 8.1.3. However, most functions that economists study are differentiable everywhere. The following recipe, therefore, covers most problems of interest.

Problem: Find the maximum and minimum values of a differentiable function f defined on a closed, bounded interval $[a, b]$.

Solution:

(I) Find all stationary points of f in (a, b)—that is, find all points x in (a, b) that satisfy the equation $f'(x) = 0$.   (1)

(II) Evaluate f at the end points a and b of the interval and also at all stationary points.

(III) The largest function value found in (II) is the maximum value, and the smallest function value is the minimum value of f in $[a, b]$.

A differentiable function is continuous, so the extreme-value theorem assures us that maximum and minimum points do exist. Following the procedure just given, we can, in principle, find these extreme points.

EXAMPLE 1   Find the maximum and minimum values for

$$f(x) = 3x^2 - 6x + 5, \qquad x \in [0, 3]$$

Solution: The function is differentiable everywhere, and $f'(x) = 6x - 6 = 6(x - 1)$. Hence $x = 1$ is the only stationary point. The candidate extreme points are the end points 0 and 3, as well as $x = 1$. We calculate the value of f at these three points. The results are $f(0) = 5$, $f(3) = 14$, and $f(1) = 2$. We conclude that the maximum value is 14, obtained at $x = 3$, and the minimum value is 2 at $x = 1$.

EXAMPLE 2   Find the maximum and minimum values of

$$f(x) = \tfrac{1}{4}x^4 - \tfrac{5}{6}x^3 + \tfrac{1}{2}x^2 - 1, \qquad x \in [-1, 3]$$

Solution: The function is differentiable everywhere, and

$$f'(x) = x^3 - \tfrac{5}{2}x^2 + x = x\left(x^2 - \tfrac{5}{2}x + 1\right)$$

Solving the quadratic equation $x^2 - \tfrac{5}{2}x + 1 = 0$, we get the roots $x = 1/2$ and $x = 2$. Thus $f'(x) = 0$ for $x = 0, 1/2$, and 2. These three points, together with the two end points -1 and 3 of the interval $[-1, 3]$, constitute the five candidate extreme points. We find that $f(-1) = 7/12$, $f(0) = -1$, $f(1/2) = -185/192$, $f(2) = -5/3$, and $f(3) = 5/4$. Thus the maximum value of f is $5/4$ at $x = 3$. The minimum value is $-5/3$ at $x = 2$.

Note that it is unnecessary to study the sign variation of $f'(x)$ or use other tests to verify that we have found the maximum and minimum values.   ∎

In the two previous examples we had no trouble in finding the solutions to the equation $f'(x) = 0$. However, in some cases, finding all the solutions to $f'(x) = 0$ might constitute a formidable or even insuperable problem. For instance,

$$f(x) = x^{26} - 32x^{23} - 11x^5 - 2x^3 - x + 28, \qquad x \in [-1, 5]$$

is a continuous function, so it does have a maximum and a minimum in $[-1, 5]$. Yet it is impossible to find any exact solution to the equation $f'(x) = 0$.

Difficulties of this kind are often encountered in practical optimization problems. In fact, only in very special cases can the equation $f'(x) = 0$ be solved exactly. Fortunately, there are standard numerical methods for use on a computer that in most cases will find points arbitrarily close to the actual solutions of such equations—see, for example, Newton's method discussed in Section 7.9.

The Mean-Value Theorem

This optional section deals with the mean-value theorem, which is a principal tool for the precise demonstration of results in calculus.

Consider a function f defined on an interval $[a, b]$, and suppose that the graph of f is connected and lacks corners, as illustrated in Fig. 2. Because the graph of f joins A to B by a connected curve having a tangent at each point, it is geometrically plausible that for at least one value of x between a and b, the tangent to the graph at x should be parallel to the line AB. In Fig. 2, x^* appears to be such a value of x. The line AB has slope $[f(b) - f(a)]/(b - a)$. So the condition for the tangent line at $(x^*, f(x^*))$ to be parallel to the line AB is that $f'(x^*) = [f(b) - f(a)]/(b - a)$. In fact, x^* can be chosen so that the vertical distance between the graph of f and AB is as large as possible. The proof that follows is based on this fact.

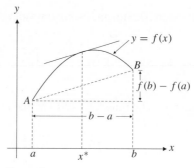

Figure 2

THEOREM 8.4.2 (THE MEAN-VALUE THEOREM)

If f is continuous in the closed bounded interval $[a, b]$, and differentiable in the open interval (a, b), then there exists at least one interior point x^* in (a, b) such that

(2)

$$f'(x^*) = \frac{f(b) - f(a)}{b - a}$$

Proof: According to the point–point formula, the line segment between A and B in Fig. 2 has the equation

$$y - f(a) = \frac{f(b) - f(a)}{b - a}(x - a)$$

The function

$$g(x) = f(x) - f(a) - \frac{f(b) - f(a)}{b - a}(x - a)$$

therefore measures the vertical distance between the graph of f and the line segment. Note that

$$g'(x) = f'(x) - \frac{f(b) - f(a)}{b - a} \qquad (*)$$

Obviously, $g(a) = g(b) = 0$. The function $g(x)$ inherits from f the properties of being continuous in $[a, b]$ and differentiable in (a, b). By the extreme-value theorem, $g(x)$ has a maximum and a minimum over $[a, b]$. Because $g(a) = g(b)$, at least one of these extreme points x^* must lie in (a, b). Theorem 8.1.1 tells us that $g'(x^*) = 0$, and the conclusion follows from $(*)$. ∎

EXAMPLE 3   Test the mean-value theorem on $f(x) = x^3 - x$ in $[0, 2]$.

Solution: We find that $[f(2) - f(0)]/(2 - 0) = 3$ and $f'(x) = 3x^2 - 1$. The equation $f'(x) = 3$ has two solutions, $x = \pm 2\sqrt{3}/3$. Because the positive root $x^* = 2\sqrt{3}/3 \in (0, 2)$, we have

$$f'(x^*) = \frac{f(2) - f(0)}{2 - 0}$$

Thus, the mean-value theorem is confirmed in this case.

NOTE 2 (**Increasing and Decreasing Functions**) If $f(x_2) \geq f(x_1)$ whenever $x_2 > x_1$ (with x_1 and x_2 in I), then we called the function f *increasing* in I (see Section 6.3). Using the definition of the derivative, we see easily that if $f(x)$ is increasing and differentiable, then $f'(x) \geq 0$. The mean-value theorem can be used to make this precise and to prove the converse. Let f be a function which is continuous in the interval I and differentiable in the interior of I (that is, at points other than the end points). Suppose $f'(x) \geq 0$ for all x in the interior of I. Let $x_2 > x_1$ be two arbitrary numbers in I. According to the mean-value theorem, there exists a number x^* in (x_1, x_2) such that

$$f(x_2) - f(x_1) = f'(x^*)(x_2 - x_1) \tag{$*$}$$

Because $x_2 > x_1$ and $f'(x^*) \geq 0$, it follows that $f(x_2) \geq f(x_1)$, so $f(x)$ is increasing. This proves (1) in Section 6.3. The equivalence in (2) is proved in the same way, and (3) follows easily by using equation $(*)$.

NOTE 3 (**Proof of Lagrange's remainder formula (2) in Section 7.5**) We start by proving that the formula is correct for $n = 1$. This means that we want to prove formula (4) in Section 7.5. For $x \neq 0$, define the function $S(x)$ implicitly by the equation

$$f(x) = f(0) + f'(0)x + \tfrac{1}{2}S(x)x^2 \tag{$*$}$$

If we can prove that there exists a number c between 0 and x such that $S(x) = f''(c)$, then (4) is established. Keep x fixed and define the function g for all t between 0 and x by

$$g(t) = f(x) - [f(t) + f'(t)(x - t) + \tfrac{1}{2}S(x)(x - t)^2] \tag{$**$}$$

Then $(*)$ and $(**)$ imply that $g(0) = f(x) - [f(0) + f'(0)x + \tfrac{1}{2}S(x)x^2] = 0$ and that $g(x) = f(x) - [f(x) + 0 + 0] = 0$. So, by the mean-value theorem, there exists a number c strictly between 0 and x such that $g'(c) = 0$. Differentiating $(**)$ with respect to t, with x fixed, we get

$$g'(t) = -f'(t) + f'(t) - f''(t)(x - t) + S(x)(x - t)$$

Thus, $g'(c) = -f''(c)(x - c) + S(x)(x - c)$. Because $g'(c) = 0$ and $c \neq x$, it follows that $S(x) = f''(c)$. Hence, we have proved (4).

The proof in the general case is based on precisely the same idea, because we define $S(x)$ and $g(t)$ by generalizing $(*)$ and $(**)$ in the obvious way. ∎

PROBLEMS FOR SECTION 8.4

1. Find the maximum and minimum and draw the graph of

$$f(x) = 4x^2 - 40x + 80, \qquad x \in [0, 8]$$

2. Find the maximum and minimum of each function over the indicated interval:

   (a) $f(x) = -2x - 1$, $[0, 3]$ (b) $f(x) = x^3 - 3x + 8$, $[-1, 2]$

   (c) $f(x) = \dfrac{x^2 + 1}{x}$, $[\tfrac{1}{2}, 2]$ (d) $f(x) = x^5 - 5x^3$, $[-1, \sqrt{5}]$

   (e) $f(x) = x^3 - 4500x^2 + 6 \cdot 10^6 x$, $[0, 3000]$

3. A sports club plans to charter a plane, and charge its members 10% commission on the price they pay to buy seats. That price is arranged by the charter company. The standard fare for each passenger is $800. For each additional person above 60, all travellers (including the first 60) get a discount of $10. The plane can take at most 80 passengers.

   (a) How much commission is earned when there are $61, 70, 80$, and $60+x$ passengers?

   (b) Find the number of passengers that maximizes the total commission earned by the sports club.

4. Suppose the function g is defined for all $x \in [-1, 2]$ by $g(x) = \frac{1}{5}(e^{x^2} + e^{2-x^2})$. Calculate $g'(x)$ and find the extreme points of g.

5. Let the function f be defined for $x \in [1, e^3]$ by

$$f(x) = (\ln x)^3 - 2(\ln x)^2 + \ln x$$

   (a) Compute $f(e^{1/3})$, $f(e^2)$, and $f(e^3)$. Find the zeros of $f(x)$.

   (b) Find the extreme points of f.

   (c) Show that f defined over $[e, e^3]$ has an inverse function g and determine $g'(2)$.

HARDER PROBLEMS

6. For the following functions determine all numbers x^* in the specified intervals such that $f'(x^*) = [f(b) - f(a)]/(b - a)$:

   (a) $f(x) = x^2$ in $[1, 2]$ (b) $f(x) = \sqrt{1 - x^2}$ in $[0, 1]$

   (c) $f(x) = 2/x$ in $[2, 6]$ (d) $f(x) = \sqrt{9 + x^2}$ in $[0, 4]$

7. You are supposed to sail from point A in a lake to point B. What does the mean-value theorem have to say about your trip?

8. Is the function f defined for all $x \in [-1, 1]$ by

$$f(x) = \begin{cases} x & \text{for } x \in (-1, 1) \\ 0 & \text{for } x = -1 \text{ and for } x = 1 \end{cases}$$

continuous? Does f attain a maximum or minimum?

9. Let f be defined for all x in $(0, \infty)$ by

$$f(x) = \begin{cases} x + 1 & \text{for } x \in (0, 1] \\ 1 & \text{for } x \in (1, \infty) \end{cases}$$

Prove that f attains maximum and minimum values. Verify that nevertheless *none* of the conditions in the extreme-value theorem is satisfied.

8.5 Further Economic Examples

EXAMPLE 1   A firm that produces a single commodity wants to maximize its profits. The total revenue generated in a certain period by producing and selling Q units is $R(Q)$ dollars, whereas $C(Q)$ denotes the associated total dollar cost. The profit obtained as a result of producing and selling Q units is then

$$\pi(Q) = R(Q) - C(Q) \qquad (*)$$

Because of technical limitations there is a maximum quantity $\bar{Q}$ that can be produced by the firm in a given period. Assume that R and C are differentiable functions of Q in the interval $[0, \bar{Q}]$. The profit function π is then differentiable, so continuous. Consequently π does have a maximum value. In special cases, that maximum might occur at $Q = 0$ or at $Q = \bar{Q}$. If not, the maximum production level Q^* satisfies $\pi'(Q^*) = 0$, and so

$$R'(Q^*) = C'(Q^*) \qquad (**)$$

Hence, *production should be adjusted to a point where the marginal revenue is equal to the marginal cost.*

Let us assume that the firm gets a fixed price P per unit sold. Then $R(Q) = PQ$, and $(**)$ takes the form

$$P = C'(Q^*) \qquad (***)$$

Thus, in the case when the firm has no control over the price, *production should be adjusted to a level at which the marginal cost is equal to the price per unit of the commodity* (assuming that π does not have a maximum at 0 or at $\bar{Q}$).

It is quite possible that the firm has functions $R(Q)$ and $C(Q)$ for which equation $(**)$ has several solutions. If so, the maximum profit occurs at that point Q^* among the solutions of $(**)$ which gives the highest value of $\pi(Q^*)$.

Equation $(**)$ has an economic interpretation rather like that for the corresponding optimality condition in Example 8.3.1. Indeed, suppose we contemplate increasing production from the level Q^* by one unit. We would increase revenue by the amount $R(Q^* + 1) - R(Q^*) \approx R'(Q^*)$. We would increase cost by the amount $C(Q^* + 1) - C(Q^*) \approx C'(Q^*)$. Equation $(**)$ equates $R'(Q^*)$ and $C'(Q^*)$, so that the marginal revenue earned by selling an extra unit is exactly offset by the marginal cost of producing that unit.

EXAMPLE 2   Suppose that the firm in the preceding example obtains a fixed price $P = 121$ per unit, and that the cost function is

$$C(Q) = 0.02Q^3 - 3Q^2 + 175Q + 500$$

The firm can produce at most $\bar{Q} = 110$ units.

(a) Make a table of the values of the functions $R(Q) = 121Q$, $C(Q)$, and $\pi(Q) = R(Q) - C(Q)$ for $Q = 0, 10, 30, 50, 70, 90,$ and 110. Draw the graphs of $R(Q)$ and $C(Q)$ in the same coordinate system.

(b) Answer the following questions (approximately) by using the graphs in (a):

    (i) How many units must be produced in order for the firm to make a profit?

    (ii) How many units must be produced for the profit to be 2000 dollars?

    (iii) Which production level maximizes profits?

(c) Answer the question in (b)(iii) by computation.

(d) What is the smallest price per unit the firm must charge in order not to lose money, if capacity is fully utilized (that is if it produces 110 units)?

Solution:

(a) We form the following table:

Table 1

Q	0	10	30	50	70	90	110
$R(Q) = 121Q$	0	1 210	3 630	6 050	8 470	10 890	13 310
$C(Q)$	500	1 970	3 590	4 250	4 910	6 530	10 070
$\pi(Q) = R(Q) - C(Q)$	−500	−760	40	1 800	3 560	4 360	3 240

The graphs of $R(Q)$ and $C(Q)$ are shown in Fig. 1.

Figure 1

(b)   (i) The firm earns a profit if $\pi(Q) > 0$, that is when $R(Q) > C(Q)$. On the figure we see that $R(Q) > C(Q)$ when Q is larger than (approximately) 30.

    (ii) We must find where the "gap" between $R(Q)$ and $C(Q)$ is 2000. This occurs when $Q \approx 52$.

    (iii) The profit is the largest when the gap between $R(Q)$ and $C(Q)$ is the largest. This seems to occur when $Q \approx 90$.

(c) When the formula for $C'(Q)$ is inserted into equation (∗∗∗) of the preceding example, because $P = 121$, the result is

$$121 = 0.06Q^2 - 6Q + 175$$

Solving this quadratic equation yields $Q = 10$ and $Q = 90$. We know that $\pi(Q)$ must have a maximum point in $[0, 110]$, and there are four candidates: $Q = 0, 10, 90$, and 110. Using Table 1, we see that

$$\pi(0) = -500, \quad \pi(10) = -760, \quad \pi(90) = 4360, \quad \pi(110) = 3240$$

The firm therefore attains maximum profit by producing 90 units.

(d) If the price per unit is P, the profit from producing 110 units is

$$\pi(110) = P \cdot 110 - C(110) = 110P - 10070$$

The smallest price P which ensures that the firm does not lose money when producing 110 units, satisfies $\pi(110) = 0$, that is $110P = 10070$ with solution $P \approx 91.55$. This is the average cost of producing 110 units. The price must be at least 91.55 dollars if revenue is going to be enough to cover the cost of producing at full capacity. ▮

EXAMPLE 3 In the model of the previous example, the firm took the price as given. Consider an example at the other extreme, where the firm has a monopoly in the sale of the commodity. Assume that the price per unit, $P(Q)$, varies with Q according to the formula

$$P(Q) = 100 - \frac{1}{3}Q, \qquad Q \in [0, 300]$$

Suppose now the cost function is

$$C(Q) = \frac{1}{600}Q^3 - \frac{1}{3}Q^2 + 50Q + \frac{1000}{3}$$

Then the profit is

$$\pi(Q) = QP(Q) - C(Q) = -\frac{1}{600}Q^3 + 50Q - \frac{1000}{3}, \qquad Q \in [0, 300]$$

Find the production level that maximizes profits, and compute the maximum profit.

Solution: The derivative of $\pi(Q)$ is $\pi'(Q) = -\frac{1}{200}Q^2 + 50$. Hence

$$\pi'(Q) = 0 \quad \text{for} \quad Q^2 = 10000, \quad \text{that is} \quad Q = 100$$

(The other possibility, $Q = -100$, is not permissible.) The values of $\pi(Q)$ at the end points of $[0, 300]$ are $\pi(0) = -1000/3$ and $\pi(300) = -91000/3$. Since $\pi(100) = 3000$, we conclude that $Q = 100$ maximizes profit, and the maximum profit is 3000. ▮

EXAMPLE 4   ("**Either a Borrower or a Lender Be**")[3] A student has current income y_1 and expects future income y_2. She plans current consumption c_1 and future consumption c_2 in order to maximize the utility function

$$U = \ln c_1 + \frac{1}{1+\delta} \ln c_2, \qquad c_1, c_2 > 0$$

where δ is her discount rate. If she borrows now, so that $c_1 > y_1$, then future consumption, after repaying the loan amount $c_1 - y_1$ with interest charged at rate r, will be

$$c_2 = y_2 - (1+r)(c_1 - y_1)$$

Alternatively, if she saves now, so that $c_1 < y_1$, then future consumption will be

$$c_2 = y_2 + (1+r)(y_1 - c_1)$$

after receiving interest at rate r on her savings. Find the optimal borrowing or saving plan.

Solution: Whether the student borrows or saves, second period consumption is

$$c_2 = y_2 - (1+r)(c_1 - y_1)$$

in either case. So the student will want to maximize

$$U = \ln c_1 + \frac{1}{1+\delta} \ln[y_2 - (1+r)(c_1 - y_1)] \tag{*}$$

We restrict attention to the interval $0 < c_1 < y_1 + (1+r)^{-1} y_2$, so that both c_1 and c_2 are positive. Differentiating (*) w.r.t. the choice variable c_1 gives

$$\frac{dU}{dc_1} = \frac{1}{c_1} - \frac{1+r}{1+\delta} \cdot \frac{1}{y_2 - (1+r)(c_1 - y_1)}$$

Rewriting the fractions so that they have a common denominator yields

$$\frac{dU}{dc_1} = \frac{(1+\delta)[y_2 - (1+r)(c_1 - y_1)] - (1+r)c_1}{c_1(1+\delta)[y_2 - (1+r)(c_1 - y_1)]}$$

Rearranging the numerator and equating the derivative to 0, we have

$$\frac{dU}{dc_1} = \frac{(1+\delta)[(1+r)y_1 + y_2] - (2+\delta)(1+r)c_1}{c_1(1+\delta)[y_2 - (1+r)(c_1 - y_1)]} = 0 \tag{**}$$

The unique solution of this equation is

$$c_1^* = \frac{(1+\delta)[(1+r)y_1 + y_2]}{(2+\delta)(1+r)} = y_1 + \frac{(1+\delta)y_2 - (1+r)y_1}{(2+\delta)(1+r)}$$

From (**), we see that for $c_1 < c_1^*$ one has $dU/dc_1 > 0$, whereas for $c_1 > c_1^*$ one has $dU/dc_1 < 0$. We conclude that c_1^* indeed maximizes U. Moreover, the student lends if and only if $(1+\delta)y_2 < (1+r)y_1$. In the more likely case when $(1+\delta)y_2 > (1+r)y_1$ because future income is considerably higher than present income, she will borrow. Only if by some chance $(1+\delta)y_2$ is exactly equal to $(1+r)y_1$ will she be neither a borrower nor a lender. However, this discussion has neglected the difference between borrowing and lending rates of interest that one always observes in reality.

---

[3] According to Shakespeare, Polonius's advice to Hamlet was: "Neither a borrower nor a lender be".

PROBLEMS FOR SECTION 8.5

1. With reference to Example 1, suppose that

$$R(Q) = 10Q - \frac{Q^2}{1000}, \quad C(Q) = 5000 + 2Q, \quad Q \in [0, 10\,000]$$

Find the value of Q that maximizes profits.

2. (a) With reference to Example 1, let

$$R(Q) = 80Q \quad \text{and} \quad C(Q) = Q^2 + 10Q + 900$$

The firm can at most produce 50 units. Draw the graphs of R and C in the same coordinate system.

(b) Answer the following questions both graphically and by computation:
   (i) How many units must be produced for the firm to make a profit?
   (ii) How many units must be produced for the firm to maximize profits?

3. A pharmaceutical firm produces penicillin. The sales price per unit is 200, while the cost of producing x units is given by

$$C(x) = 500\,000 + 80x + 0.003x^2$$

The firm can produce at most 30\,000 units. What value of x maximizes profits?

4. Consider Example 1 and find the production level which maximizes profits when

$$\begin{aligned}
&\text{(i)} && R(Q) = 1840Q, && C(Q) = 2Q^2 + 40Q + 5000 \\
&\text{(ii)} && R(Q) = 2240Q, && C(Q) = 2Q^2 + 40Q + 5000 \\
&\text{(iii)} && R(Q) = 1840Q, && C(Q) = 2Q^2 + 1940Q + 5000
\end{aligned}$$

5. The price a firm obtains for a commodity varies with demand Q according to the formula $P(Q) = 18 - 0.006Q$. Total cost is $C(Q) = 0.004Q^2 + 4Q + 4500$.

(a) Find the firm's profit $\pi(Q)$ and the value of Q which maximizes profit.

(b) Find a formula for the elasticity of $P(Q)$ w.r.t. Q, and find the particular value Q^* of Q at which the elasticity is equal to -1.

(c) Show that the marginal revenue is 0 at Q^*.

6. With reference to Example 1, let $R(Q) = PQ$ and $C(Q) = aQ^b + c$, where P, a, b, and c are positive constants, and $b > 1$. Find the value of Q which maximizes the profit $\pi(Q) = PQ - (aQ^b + c)$. Make use of Theorem 8.2.2.

8.6 Local Extreme Points

So far this chapter has discussed what are often referred to as *global* optimization problems. The reason for this terminology is that we have been seeking the largest or smallest values of a function when we compare the function values "globally"—that is, at *all* points in the domain without exception. In applied optimization problems, especially those arising in economics, it is usually these global maxima and minima that are of interest. However, sometimes one is interested in the local maxima and minima of a function. In this case, we compare the function value at the point in question only with alternative function values at nearby points.

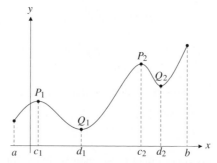

Figure 1 c_1, c_2, and b are local maximum points; a, d_1, and d_2 are local minimum points

Consider Fig. 1 and think of the graph as representing the profile of a landscape. Then the mountain tops P_1 and P_2 represent local maxima, whereas the valley bottoms Q_1 and Q_2 represent local minima. The precise definitions are as follows:

The function f has a **local maximum (minimum)** at c, if there exists an interval (α, β) about c such that $f(x) \leq (\geq) f(c)$ for all x in (α, β) which are in the domain of f. $\qquad$ (1)

NOTE 1   These definitions imply that point a in Fig. 1 is a local minimum point, while b is a local (and global) maximum point. Some authors restrict the definition of local maximum/minimum points only to *interior* points of the domain of the function. According to this definition, a global maximum point that is not an interior point of the domain is not a local maximum point. It seems desirable that a global maximum/minimum point should always to be a local maximum/minimum point as well, so we stick to definition (1).

Function values corresponding to local maximum (minimum) points are called **local maximum (minimum) values**. As collective names we use **local extreme points** and **local extreme values**.

In searching for (global) maximum and minimum points, Theorem 8.1.1 was very useful. Actually, the same result is valid for local extreme points: *At a local extreme point in the interior of the domain of a differentiable function, the derivative must be zero.* This is clear if we recall that the proof of Theorem 8.1.1 needed to consider the behaviour of the function in only a small interval about the optimal point. Consequently, in order to find possible local maxima and minima for a function f defined in an interval I, we can again search among the following types of point:

    (i) Interior points in I where $f'(x) = 0$

    (ii) End points of I (if included in I)

    (iii) Interior points in I where f' does not exist

We have thus established *necessary* conditions for a function f defined in an interval I to have a local extreme point. But how do we decide whether a point satisfying the necessary conditions is a local maximum, a local minimum, or neither? In contrast to global extreme points, it does not help to calculate the function value at the different points satisfying these necessary conditions. To see why, consider again the function whose graph is given in Fig. 1. Point P_1 is a local maximum point and Q_2 is a local minimum point, but the function value at P_1 is *smaller* than the function value at Q_2. (Point Q_2 is higher than P_1.)

The First-Derivative Test

There are two main ways of determining whether a given stationary point is a local maximum, a local minimum, or neither. One of them is based on studying the sign of the first derivative about the stationary point, and is an easy modification of Theorem 8.2.1.

THEOREM 8.6.1 (FIRST-DERIVATIVE TEST FOR LOCAL EXTREME POINTS)

Suppose c is a stationary point for $y = f(x)$.

    (a) If $f'(x) \geq 0$ throughout some interval (a, c) to the left of c and $f'(x) \leq 0$ throughout some interval (c, b) to the right of c, then $x = c$ is a local maximum point for f.

    (b) If $f'(x) \leq 0$ throughout some interval (a, c) to the left of c and $f'(x) \geq 0$ throughout some interval (c, b) to the right of c, then $x = c$ is a local minimum point for f.

    (c) If $f'(x) > 0$ both throughout some interval (a, c) to the left of c and throughout some interval (c, b) to the right of c, then $x = c$ is not a local extreme point for f. The same conclusion holds if $f'(x) < 0$ on both sides of c.

Only case (c) is not already covered by Theorem 8.2.1. In fact, if $f'(x) > 0$ in (a, c) and also in (c, b), then $f(x)$ is strictly increasing in $(a, c]$ as well as in $[c, b)$. Then $x = c$ cannot be a local extreme point.

EXAMPLE 1   Classify the stationary points of $f(x) = \frac{1}{9}x^3 - \frac{1}{6}x^2 - \frac{2}{3}x + 1$.

Solution: We get $f'(x) = \frac{1}{3}(x+1)(x-2)$, so $x = -1$ and $x = 2$ are the stationary points. The sign diagram for $f'(x)$ is:

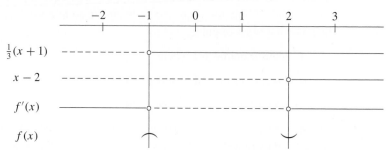

We conclude from this sign diagram that $x = -1$ is a local maximum point whereas $x = 2$ is a local minimum point.

EXAMPLE 2   Classify the stationary points of $f(x) = x^2 e^x$.

Solution: Differentiating, we get $f'(x) = 2xe^x + x^2 e^x = xe^x(2+x)$. Then $f'(x) = 0$ for $x = 0$ and for $x = -2$. A sign diagram shows that f has a local maximum point at $x = -2$ and a local (and global) minimum point at $x = 0$. (The graph of f is given in Fig. A4.R.19 in the answer section.)

The Second-Derivative Test

For most problems of practical interest in which an explicit function is specified, the first-derivative test on its own will determine whether a stationary point is a local maximum, a local minimum, or neither. Note that the theorem requires knowing the sign of $f'(x)$ at points both to the left and to the right of the given stationary point. The next test requires knowing the first two derivatives of the function, but only at the stationary point itself.

THEOREM 8.6.2 (SECOND-DERIVATIVE TEST)

Let f be a twice differentiable function in an interval I, and let c be an interior point of I. Then:

(a) $f'(c) = 0$ and $f''(c) < 0 \Longrightarrow x = c$ is a strict local maximum point.

(b) $f'(c) = 0$ and $f''(c) > 0 \Longrightarrow x = c$ is a strict local minimum point.

(c) $f'(c) = 0$ and $f''(c) = 0 \Longrightarrow$?

Proof: To prove part (a), assume $f'(c) = 0$ and $f''(c) < 0$. By definition of $f''(c)$ as the derivative of $f'(x)$ at c,

$$f''(c) = \lim_{h \to 0} \frac{f'(c+h) - f'(c)}{h} = \lim_{h \to 0} \frac{f'(c+h)}{h}$$

Because $f''(c) < 0$, it follows that $f'(c + h)/h < 0$ if $|h|$ is sufficiently small. In particular, if h is a small positive number, then $f'(c + h) < 0$, so f' is negative in an interval to the right of c. In the same way, we see that f' is positive in some interval to the left of c. But then c is a strict local maximum point for f.

Part (b) can be proved in the same way. For the inconclusive part (c), see the comments that follow.   ∎

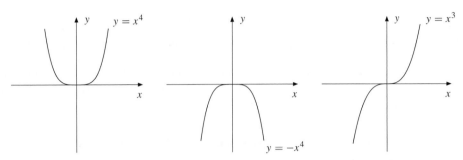

Figure 2 $f'(0) = f''(0) = 0$, and 0 is a minimum point

Figure 3 $f'(0) = f''(0) = 0$, and 0 is a maximum point

Figure 4 $f'(0) = f''(0) = 0$, and 0 is an inflection point

The theorem leaves unsettled case (c) where $f'(c) = f''(c) = 0$. Then "anything" can happen. Each of three functions $f(x) = x^4$, $f(x) = -x^4$, and $f(x) = x^3$ satisfies $f'(0) = f''(0) = 0$. At $x = 0$, they have, as shown in Figs. 2 to 4 respectively, a minimum, a maximum, and what in Section 8.7 will be called a point of inflection. Usually (as here), the first-derivative test can be used to classify stationary points at which $f'(c) = f''(c) = 0$.

EXAMPLE 3   Classify the stationary points of

$$f(x) = \tfrac{1}{9}x^3 - \tfrac{1}{6}x^2 - \tfrac{2}{3}x + 1$$

by using the second-derivative test.

Solution: We saw in Example 1 that $f'(x) = \tfrac{1}{3}x^2 - \tfrac{1}{3}x - \tfrac{2}{3} = \tfrac{1}{3}(x+1)(x-2)$, with two stationary points $x = -1$ and $x = 2$. Furthermore, $f''(x) = \tfrac{2}{3}x - \tfrac{1}{3}$, so that $f''(-1) = -1$ and $f''(2) = 1$. From Theorem 8.6.2 it follows that $x = -1$ is a local maximum point and $x = 2$ is a local minimum point. This confirms the results in Example 1.   ▌

EXAMPLE 4   Classify the stationary points of $f(x) = x^2 e^x$ by using the second-derivative test.

Solution: From Example 2, $f'(x) = 2xe^x + x^2 e^x$, with $x = 0$ and $x = -2$ as the two stationary points. The second derivative of f is

$$f''(x) = 2e^x + 2xe^x + 2xe^x + x^2 e^x = e^x(2 + 4x + x^2)$$

We find that $f''(0) = 2 > 0$ and $f''(-2) = -2e^{-2} < 0$. From Theorem 8.6.2 it follows that $x = 0$ is a local minimum point and $x = -2$ is a local maximum point. This confirms the results in Example 2.   ▌

Theorem 8.6.2 can be used to obtain a useful necessary condition for local extrema. Suppose that f is twice differentiable in the interval I and that c is an interior point of I where there is a local maximum. Then $f'(c) = 0$. Moreover, $f''(c) > 0$ is impossible, because by Theorem 8.6.2(b) this inequality would imply that c is a strict local minimum. Hence, $f''(c)$ has to be ≤ 0. In the same way, we see that $f''(c) \geq 0$ is a necessary condition for local minimum. Briefly formulated:

$$c \text{ is a local maximum for } f \implies f''(c) \leq 0 \tag{2}$$

$$c \text{ is a local minimum for } f \implies f''(c) \geq 0 \tag{3}$$

In theoretical economic models, it is more common to postulate an appropriate sign for the second derivative rather than suitable variations in the sign of the first derivative.

EXAMPLE 5   Suppose that the firm in Example 8.5.1 faces a sales tax of t dollars per unit. The firm's profit from producing and selling Q units is then

$$\pi(Q) = R(Q) - C(Q) - tQ$$

In order to maximize profits at some quantity Q^* satisfying $0 < Q^* < \bar{Q}$, one must have $\pi'(Q^*) = 0$. Hence,

$$R'(Q^*) - C'(Q^*) - t = 0 \tag{*}$$

Suppose $R''(Q^*) < 0$ and $C''(Q^*) > 0$. Equation (*) implicitly defines Q^* as a differentiable function of t. Find an expression for dQ^*/dt and discuss its sign. Also compute the derivative w.r.t. t of the optimal value $\pi(Q^*)$ of the profit function, and show that $d\pi(Q^*)/dt = -Q^*$.

Solution: Differentiating (*) with respect to t yields

$$R''(Q^*)\frac{dQ^*}{dt} - C''(Q^*)\frac{dQ^*}{dt} - 1 = 0$$

Solving for dQ^*/dt gives

$$\frac{dQ^*}{dt} = \frac{1}{R''(Q^*) - C''(Q^*)} \tag{**}$$

The sign assumptions on R'' and C'' imply that $dQ^*/dt < 0$. Thus, the optimal number of units produced will decline if the tax rate t increases.

The optimal value of the profit function is $\pi(Q^*) = R(Q^*) - C(Q^*) - tQ^*$. Taking into account the dependence of Q^* on t, we get

$$\frac{d\pi(Q^*)}{dt} = R'(Q^*)\frac{dQ^*}{dt} - C'(Q^*)\frac{dQ^*}{dt} - Q^* - t\frac{dQ^*}{dt}$$

$$= \left[R'(Q^*) - C'(Q^*) - t\right]\frac{dQ^*}{dt} - Q^* = -Q^*$$

Note how the square bracket disappears from this last expression because of the first-order condition (*). This is an instance of the "envelope theorem," which will be discussed in Section 14.6. If the sales tax increases by 1 cent, then profits decrease by approximately Q^* cents, where Q^* is the number of units produced at the optimum.

PROBLEMS FOR SECTION 8.6

1. Consider the function f defined for all x by $f(x) = x^3 - 12x$. Find the stationary points of f and classify them by using both the first- and second-derivative tests.

2. Determine possible local extreme points and values for the following functions:

   (a) $f(x) = -2x - 1$ (b) $f(x) = x^3 - 3x + 8$ (c) $f(x) = x + \dfrac{1}{x}$

   (d) $f(x) = x^5 - 5x^3$ (e) $f(x) = \frac{1}{2}x^2 - 3x + 5$ (f) $f(x) = x^3 + 3x^2 - 2$

3. A function f is given by the formula

$$f(x) = \left(1 + \frac{2}{x}\right)\sqrt{x + 6}$$

   (a) Find the domain of f and the intervals where $f(x)$ is positive.

   (b) Find possible local extreme points.

   (c) Examine $f(x)$ as $x \to 0^-$, $x \to 0^+$, and $x \to \infty$. Also determine the limit of $f'(x)$ as $x \to \infty$. Has f a maximum or a minimum in the domain?

4. Figure 5 graphs the *derivative* of a function f. Which of points a, b, c, d, and e are local maximum points for f, local minimum points for f, or neither?

Figure 5

5. What requirements must be imposed on the constants a, b, and c in order that

$$f(x) = x^3 + ax^2 + bx + c$$

   (a) will have a local minimum at $x = 0$?

   (b) will have stationary points at $x = 1$ and $x = 3$?

6. Find the local extreme points for (a) $f(x) = x^3 e^x$; (b) $g(x) = x^2 2^x$.

HARDER PROBLEMS

7. Find the local extreme points of $f(x) = x^3 + ax + b$. Use the answer to show that the equation $f(x) = 0$ has three different real roots if and only if $4a^3 + 27b^2 < 0$.

8.7 Inflection Points

Recall that in Section 6.9 we defined a twice differentiable function $f(x)$ to be concave (convex) in an interval I if $f''(x) \leq 0 \ (\geq)$ for all x in I. Points at which a function changes from being convex to being concave, or *vice versa*, are called **inflection points**. For twice differentiable functions they can be defined this way:

INFLECTION POINTS

The point c is called an **inflection point** for the function f if there exists an interval (a, b) about c such that:

(a) $f''(x) \geq 0$ in (a, c) and $f''(x) \leq 0$ in (c, b),   (1)

or

(b) $f''(x) \leq 0$ in (a, c) and $f''(x) \geq 0$ in (c, b).

Briefly, $x = c$ is an inflection point if $f''(x)$ *changes sign* at $x = c$, and we refer to the point $(c, f(c))$ as an inflection point on the graph. Figure 1 gives an example.

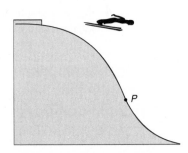

Figure 1 Point P is an inflection point on the graph ($x = c$ is an inflection point for the function)

Figure 2 The point P, where the slope is steepest, is an inflection point

Figure 2 shows the profile of a ski jump. Point P, where the slope is steepest, is an inflection point.

When looking for possible inflection points of a function, we usually use part (b) in the following theorem:

THEOREM 8.7.1 (TEST FOR INFLECTION POINTS)

Let f be a function with a continuous second derivative in an interval I, and let c be an interior point of I.

(a) If c is an inflection point for f, then $f''(c) = 0$.

(b) If $f''(c) = 0$ and f'' changes sign at c, then c is an inflection point for f.

Proof:

(a) Because $f''(x) \leq 0$ on one side of c and $f''(x) \geq 0$ on the other, and because f'' is continuous, it must be true that $f''(c) = 0$.

(b) If f'' changes sign at c, then c is an inflection point for f, according to (1). ∎

This theorem implies that $f''(c) = 0$ is a *necessary* condition for c to be an inflection point. It is not a sufficient condition, however, because $f''(c) = 0$ does not imply that f'' changes sign at $x = c$. A typical case is given in the next example.

EXAMPLE 1   Show that $f(x) = x^4$ does not have an inflection point at $x = 0$, even though $f''(0) = 0$.

Solution: Here $f'(x) = 4x^3$ and $f''(x) = 12x^2$, so that $f''(0) = 0$. But $f''(x) > 0$ for all $x \neq 0$, and so f'' does not change sign at $x = 0$. Hence, $x = 0$ is not an inflection point. (In fact, it is a global minimum, of course, as shown in Fig. 8.6.2.) ∎

EXAMPLE 2   Find possible inflection points for $f(x) = \frac{1}{9}x^3 - \frac{1}{6}x^2 - \frac{2}{3}x + 1$.

Solution: From Example 3 in the previous section we find that $f''(x) = \frac{2}{3}x - \frac{1}{3} = \frac{2}{3}\left(x - \frac{1}{2}\right)$. Hence, $f''(x) \leq 0$ for $x \leq 1/2$, whereas $f''(1/2) = 0$ and $f''(x) \geq 0$ for $x > 1/2$. According to Theorem 8.7.1(b), $x = 1/2$ is an inflection point for f. ∎

EXAMPLE 3   Find possible inflection points for $f(x) = x^6 - 10x^4$.

Solution: In this case $f'(x) = 6x^5 - 40x^3$ and

$$f''(x) = 30x^4 - 120x^2 = 30x^2(x^2 - 4) = 30x^2(x - 2)(x + 2)$$

A sign diagram for f'' is as follows:

From the sign diagram we see that f'' changes sign at $x = -2$ and at $x = 2$, so these are inflection points. Since f'' does not change sign at $x = 0$, it is not an inflection point, even though $f''(0) = 0$. ∎

Economic models often involve functions having inflection points. The cost function in Fig. 4.7.2 is a typical example. Here is another.

EXAMPLE 4   A firm produces a commodity using only one input. Let $x = f(v)$, $v \geq 0$, be the maximum output obtainable when v units of the input are used. Then f is called a **production function**. It is often assumed that the marginal product $f'(v)$ is increasing up to a certain production level v_0, and then decreasing. Such a production function is indicated in Fig. 3. If f is twice differentiable, then $f''(v)$ is ≥ 0 in $[0, v_0]$ and ≤ 0 in $[v_0, \infty)$. Hence, f is first convex and then concave, with v_0 as an inflection point.

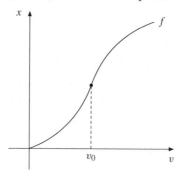

Figure 3 f is a production function. v_0 is an inflection point

More General Definitions of Concave and Convex Functions

So far the convexity and concavity properties of functions have been defined by looking at the sign of the second derivative. An alternative geometric characterization of convexity and concavity suggests a more general definition that is valid even for functions that are not differentiable.

> Function f is called **concave (convex)** if the line segment joining any two points on the graph is below (above) the graph, or on the graph. (2)

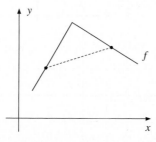

Figure 4 f is concave

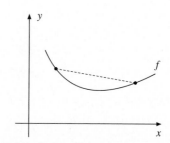

Figure 5 f is convex

These definitions are illustrated in Figs. 4 and 5. Because the graph has a "corner" in Fig. 4, this function is not even differentiable, let alone twice differentiable. For twice differentiable functions, one can prove that (2) is equivalent to the definitions in (6.9.3).

In order to use definition (2) to examine the convexity/concavity of a given function, we need an algebraic formulation. This will be discussed in FMEA.

Strictly Concave and Strictly Convex Functions

A function f is called **strictly concave (convex)** if the line segment joining any two points on the graph is strictly below (above) the graph (except at the end points of the segment). For instance, the function whose graph is shown in Fig. 4 has two linear pieces, on which line segments joining two points coincide with part of the graph. Thus this function is concave, but not strictly concave. By contrast, the function graphed in Fig. 5 is strictly convex.

Fairly obvious sufficient conditions for strict concavity/convexity are the following, which will be further discussed in FMEA:

$$f''(x) < 0 \text{ for all } x \in (a, b) \implies f(x) \text{ is strictly concave in } (a, b)$$
$$f''(x) > 0 \text{ for all } x \in (a, b) \implies f(x) \text{ is strictly convex in } (a, b)$$
(3)

The reverse implications are not correct. For instance, one can prove that $f(x) = x^4$ is strictly convex in the interval $(-\infty, \infty)$, but $f''(x)$ is not > 0 everywhere, because $f''(0) = 0$.

For twice differentiable functions, it is usually much easier to check concavity/convexity by considering the sign of the second derivative than by using the definitions in (2). However, in theoretical arguments, the definitions in (2) are often very useful, especially because they generalize easily to functions of several variables. (See FMEA.)

PROBLEMS FOR SECTION 8.7

1. Let f be defined for all x by $f(x) = x^3 + \frac{3}{2}x^2 - 6x + 10$.

   (a) Find the stationary points of f and determine the intervals where f increases.

   (b) Find the inflection point for f.

2. Decide where the following functions are convex and determine possible inflection points:

   (a) $f(x) = \dfrac{x}{1 + x^2}$ (b) $g(x) = \dfrac{1 - x}{1 + x}$ (c) $h(x) = xe^x$

3. Find local extreme points and inflection points for the functions defined by the following formulas:

   (a) $y = (x + 2)e^{-x}$ (b) $y = \ln x + 1/x$ (c) $y = x^3 e^{-x}$

   (d) $y = \dfrac{\ln x}{x^2}$ (e) $y = e^{2x} - 2e^x$ (f) $y = (x^2 + 2x)e^{-x}$

4. A competitive firm receives a price p for each unit of its output, and pays a price w for each unit of its only variable input. It also incurs set up costs of F. Its output from using x units of variable input is $f(x) = \sqrt{x}$.

(a) Determine the firm's revenue, cost, and profit functions.

(b) Write the first-order condition for profit maximization, and give it an economic interpretation. Check whether profit really is maximized at a point satisfying the first-order condition.

5. What are the extreme points and the inflection points of the function f whose graph is given in Fig. 6?

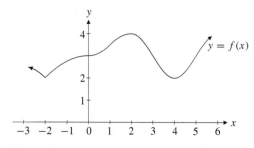

Figure 6

6. Find numbers a and b such that the graph of

$$f(x) = ax^3 + bx^2$$

passes through $(-1, 1)$ and has an inflection point at $x = 1/2$.

7. Find the intervals where the following cubic cost function, defined for $x \geq 0$, is convex and where it is concave. Find also the unique inflection point.

$$C(x) = ax^3 + bx^2 + cx + d, \qquad a > 0, \quad b < 0, \quad c > 0, \quad d > 0$$

HARDER PROBLEMS

8. Use the same coordinate system to draw the graphs of two concave functions f and g, both defined for all x. Let the function h be defined by

$$h(x) = \min\{f(x), g(x)\}$$

(For each given x, the number $h(x)$ is the smaller of $f(x)$ and $g(x)$.) Draw the graph of h and explain why it is also concave.

1. Let

$$f(x) = \frac{x^2}{x^2 + 2}$$

   (a) Compute $f'(x)$ and determine where $f(x)$ is increasing/decreasing.

   (b) Find possible inflection points.

   (c) Determine the limit of $f(x)$ as $x \to \pm\infty$, and sketch the graph of $f(x)$.

2. A firm's production function is $Q(L) = 12L^2 - \frac{1}{20}L^3$, where L denotes the number of workers, with $L \in [0, 200]$.

   (a) What size of the work force (L^*) maximizes output $Q(L)$? What size of the work force (L^{**}) maximizes output per worker, $Q(L)/L$?

   (b) Note that $Q'(L^{**}) = Q(L^{**})/L^{**}$. Is this a coincidence?

3. By producing and selling Q units of some commodity a firm earns total revenue $R(Q) = -0.0016Q^2 + 44Q$ and incurs cost $C(Q) = 0.0004Q^2 + 8Q + 64\,000$.

   (a) What production level Q^* maximizes profits?

   (b) The elasticity $\mathrm{El}_\varrho C(Q) \approx 0.12$ for $Q = 1000$. Interpret this result.

4. Let $f(x) = x^3 e^{-x}$.

   (a) Find possible extreme points and inflection points.

   (b) Determine the limit of $f(x)$ as $x \to \pm\infty$ and sketch the graph of $f(x)$.

5. Let $f(x) = \ln(x + 1) - x + \dfrac{x^2}{2} - \dfrac{x^3}{6}$.

   (a) Find the domain D_f and prove that $f'(x) = \dfrac{x^2 - x^3}{2(x + 1)}$ for $x \in D_f$.

   (b) Find possible extreme points and inflection points.

   (c) Check $f(x)$ as $x \to (-1)^+$, and sketch the graph on the interval $(-1, 2]$.

6. Let f be defined on $[-3, 3]$ by $f(x) = -x^2 + x + e^{-x}$.

   (a) Calculate $f'(x)$ and $f''(x)$. Where is $f'(x)$ increasing/decreasing?

   (b) Discuss the number of solutions of the equation $f'(x) = 0$ in $[-3, 3]$.

   (c) Find the maximum of $f(x)$ in $[-3, 3]$.

7. Consider the function h defined for all x by $h(x) = \dfrac{e^x}{2 + e^{2x}}$.

   (a) Where is h increasing/decreasing? Find possible maximum and minimum points for h.

   (b) Why does h defined on $(-\infty, 0]$ have an inverse? Find an expression for the inverse function.

8. Let $f(x) = \left(e^{2x} + 4e^{-x}\right)^2$.

   (a) Find $f'(x)$ and $f''(x)$.

   (b) Determine where f is increasing/decreasing, and show that f is convex.

   (c) Find possible global extreme points for f.

HARDER PROBLEMS

9. Classify the stationary points of $f(x) = \dfrac{6x^3}{x^4 + x^2 + 2}$ by using the first-derivative test.

10. (a) Let g be defined by the formula

$$g(x) = (a - 1)x + c^a x^{1-a} - a \quad \text{for } x > 0$$

   where a and c are constants satisfying $a > 1 > c > 0$. Compute $g'(x)$ and $g''(x)$, and examine the limit of $g(x)$ as $x \to 0^+$ and as $x \to \infty$.

   (b) Prove that g has a (global) minimum and compute the minimum value of g.

   (c) Prove that g has exactly two zeros, one in the interval $(0, c)$, and the other in $\left(1, \dfrac{a}{a-1}\right)$.

9 INTEGRATION

*The true mathematician is
not a juggler of numbers,
but of concepts.*
—I. Stewart (1975)

D ifferentiation has been the main topic in the preceding three chapters, where we have seen how it can be applied to interesting economic problems.

Some problems in mathematics require finding a function from information about its derivative. This can be regarded as the "inverse" of differentiation. The process of reconstructing a function from its derivative is generally called *integration*.

Already the ancient Babylonians were concerned with estimating the area of a plane region like a circle which may not be bounded by straight lines. The modern approach to finding such areas is intimately related to integration, as will be explained in Section 9.2, which introduces the concept of definite integral. Its further properties are the topic of Section 9.3. Apart from providing an introduction to integration, in Section 9.4 this chapter will also show that the concepts and results have many important applications in economics. Thereafter, Sections 9.5 and 9.6 present brief introductions to the commonly used techniques of integration by parts and integration by substitution. Section 9.7 deals with some difficulties that arise when integrating over an infinite interval, or when the function being integrated becomes infinite at some point of the interval of integration. Finally, a brief introduction to simple differential equations in Section 9.8 concludes the chapter.

9.1 Indefinite Integrals

Suppose we do not know the function f, but we have been told that its derivative is equal to x^2, so that $f'(x) = x^2$. What is f? Since the derivative of x^3 is $3x^2$, we see that $\frac{1}{3}x^3$ has x^2 as its derivative. But so does $\frac{1}{3}x^3 + C$ where C is an arbitrary constant, since additive constants disappear with differentiation.

In fact, let $g(x)$ denote an arbitrary function having x^2 as its derivative. Then the derivative of $g(x) - \frac{1}{3}x^3$ is equal to 0 for all x. But a function that has derivative equal to 0 for all x must be constant. (See (3) in Section 6.3.)

This shows that

$$f'(x) = x^2 \iff f(x) = \tfrac{1}{3}x^3 + C$$

with C as an arbitrary constant.

EXAMPLE 1   Assume that the marginal cost function of a firm is

$$C'(x) = 2x^2 + 2x - 5$$

and that the fixed costs are 100. Find the cost function.

Solution: Considering each term separately, we realize that the cost function must have the form $C(x) = \tfrac{2}{3}x^3 + x^2 - 5x + c$, because if we differentiate this function we obtain precisely $2x^2 + 2x - 5$. But the fixed costs are 100, which means that $C(0) = 100$. Inserting $x = 0$ into the proposed formula for $C(x)$ yields $c = 100$. Hence, the required cost function must be

$$C(x) = \tfrac{2}{3}x^3 + x^2 - 5x + 100$$

Suppose $f(x)$ and $F(x)$ are two functions of x having the property that $f(x) = F'(x)$. Of course, we pass from F to f by taking the derivative. So the reverse process of passing from f to F could appropriately be called taking the **antiderivative**. But following usual practice we prefer to call F an **indefinite integral** of f. As notation for an indefinite integral of f we use $\int f(x)\, dx$. Two functions having the same derivative throughout an interval must differ by a constant, so we write

$$\int f(x)\, dx = F(x) + C \qquad \text{when} \qquad F'(x) = f(x) \tag{1}$$

For instance, the solution to Example 1 implies that

$$\int (2x^2 + 2x - 5)\, dx = \tfrac{2}{3}x^3 + x^2 - 5x + C$$

The symbol $\int$ is the **integral sign**, and the function $f(x)$ appearing in (1) is the **integrand**. Then we write dx to indicate that x is the **variable of integration**. Finally, C is a **constant of integration**. We read (1) this way: The indefinite integral of $f(x)$ w.r.t. x is $F(x)$ plus a constant. We call it an *indefinite* integral because $F(x) + C$ is not to be regarded as one definite function, but as a whole class of functions, all having the same derivative f.

It follows directly from the above definition that the derivative of the indefinite integral is equal to the integrand:

$$\frac{d}{dx}\int f(x)\, dx = f(x) \tag{2}$$

Also

$$\int F'(x)\, dx = F(x) + C \tag{3}$$

Thus, *integration and differentiation cancel each other out.*

Some Important Integrals

There are some important integration formulas which follow immediately from the corresponding rules for differentiation.

Let a be a fixed number $\neq -1$. Because the derivative of $x^{a+1}/(a+1)$ is x^a, it follows that

$$\int x^a \, dx = \frac{1}{a+1} x^{a+1} + C \qquad (a \neq -1) \tag{4}$$

This very important result states that the indefinite integral of any power of x (except x^{-1}) is obtained by increasing the exponent of x by 1, then dividing by the new exponent, and finally adding a constant of integration. Here are some examples:

(a) $\displaystyle \int x \, dx = \int x^1 \, dx = \frac{1}{1+1} x^{1+1} + C = \frac{1}{2} x^2 + C$

(b) $\displaystyle \int \frac{1}{x^3} \, dx = \int x^{-3} \, dx = \frac{1}{-3+1} x^{-3+1} + C = -\frac{1}{2x^2} + C$

(c) $\displaystyle \int \sqrt{x} \, dx = \int x^{1/2} \, dx = \frac{1}{\frac{1}{2}+1} x^{\frac{1}{2}+1} + C = \frac{2}{3} x^{3/2} + C$

When $a = -1$, the formula in (4) is not valid, because the right-hand side involves division by zero and so becomes meaningless. The integrand is then $1/x$, and the problem is thus to find a function having $1/x$ as its derivative. Now $\ln x$ has this property, but it is only defined for $x > 0$. Note, however, that $\ln(-x)$ is defined for $x < 0$, and according to the chain rule, its derivative is $[1/(-x)](-1) = 1/x$. Recall that $|x| = x$ when $x \geq 0$ and $|x| = -x$ when $x < 0$. Thus, whether $x > 0$ or $x < 0$, we have

$$\int \frac{1}{x} \, dx = \ln |x| + C \tag{5}$$

Consider next the exponential function. The derivative of e^x is e^x. Thus $\int e^x \, dx = e^x + C$. More generally,

$$\int e^{ax} \, dx = \frac{1}{a} e^{ax} + C \qquad (a \neq 0) \tag{6}$$

because the derivative of $(1/a)e^{ax}$ is e^{ax}. For $a > 0$ we can write $a^x = e^{(\ln a)x}$. As a special case of (6), when $\ln a \neq 0$ because $a \neq 1$, we obtain

$$\int a^x \, dx = \frac{1}{\ln a} a^x + C \qquad (a > 0 \text{ and } a \neq 1) \tag{7}$$

Knowing how to differentiate a function given by a formula automatically gives us a corresponding indefinite integral. Indeed, suppose it were possible to construct a complete table with every formula that we knew how to differentiate in the first column, and the derivative in the second column. For example, corresponding to the entry $y = x^2 e^x$ in the first column, there would be $y' = 2xe^x + x^2 e^x$ in the second column. Because integration is the reverse of differentiation, we infer the corresponding integration result that $\int (2xe^x + x^2 e^x) \, dx = x^2 e^x + C$ for a constant C.

Even after this superhuman effort, you would look in vain for e^{-x^2} in the second column of this table. The reason is that there is no "elementary" function that has e^{-x^2} as its derivative. (See Section 9.3.) Indeed, the integral of e^{-x^2} is a new special "error function" that plays a prominent role in statistics because of its relationship to the "normal distribution"—see Problem 4.9.5.

By systematically using the proper rules, we can *differentiate* very complicated functions. On the other hand, finding the indefinite integral of even quite simple functions can be very difficult, or even impossible. Where it is possible, mathematicians have developed a number of *integration methods* to help in the task. Some of these methods will be explained in this chapter.

It is usually quite easy, however, to check whether a proposed indefinite integral is correct. We simply differentiate the proposed function to see if its derivative really is equal to the integrand.

EXAMPLE 2   Verify that for $x > 0$, $\int \ln x \, dx = x \ln x - x + C$.

Solution: We put $F(x) = x \ln x - x + C$. Then $F'(x) = 1 \cdot \ln x + x \cdot (1/x) - 1 = \ln x + 1 - 1 = \ln x$, which shows that the integral formula is correct. ▌

Some General Rules

The two differentiation rules $(a F(x))' = a F'(x)$ and $(F(x) + G(x))' = F'(x) + G'(x)$ immediately imply the following integration rules

$$\int af(x)\,dx = a \int f(x)\,dx \qquad (a \text{ is a constant}) \tag{8}$$

$$\int [f(x) + g(x)]\,dx = \int f(x)\,dx + \int g(x)\,dx \tag{9}$$

The first of these rules say that a constant factor can be moved outside the integral, while the other shows that the integral of a sum is the sum of the integrals.
    Repeated use of these properties yields the general rule:

$$\int [a_1 f_1(x) + \cdots + a_n f_n(x)]\,dx = a_1 \int f_1(x)\,dx + \cdots + a_n \int f_n(x)\,dx \tag{10}$$

EXAMPLE 3   Evaluate (a) $\int (3x^4 + 5x^2 + 2)\,dx$ (b) $\int \left(\dfrac{3}{x} - 8e^{-4x}\right) dx$

Solution:

(a) $\displaystyle \int (3x^4 + 5x^2 + 2)\,dx = 3 \int x^4\,dx + 5 \int x^2\,dx + 2 \int 1\,dx$

$$= 3\left(\tfrac{1}{5}x^5 + C_1\right) + 5\left(\tfrac{1}{3}x^3 + C_2\right) + 2(x + C_3)$$

$$= \tfrac{3}{5}x^5 + \tfrac{5}{3}x^3 + 2x + 3C_1 + 5C_2 + 2C_3$$

$$= \tfrac{3}{5}x^5 + \tfrac{5}{3}x^3 + 2x + C$$

Because C_1, C_2, and C_3 are arbitrary constants, $3C_1 + 5C_2 + 2C_3$ is also an arbitrary constant. So in the last line we have replaced it by just one constant C. In future examples of this kind, we will usually drop the two middle lines of the displayed equations.

(b) $\int \left(\dfrac{3}{x} - 8e^{-4x} \right) dx = 3 \int \dfrac{1}{x} dx + (-8) \int e^{-4x} dx = 3 \ln |x| + 2e^{-4x} + C$ ∎

So far, we have always used x as the variable of integration. In applications, the variables often have other labels, but this makes no difference to the rules of integration.

EXAMPLE 4   Evaluate: (a) $\displaystyle\int \dfrac{B}{r^{2.5}}\, dr$ (b) $\displaystyle\int (a + bq + cq^2)\, dq$

Solution:

(a) Writing $B/r^{2.5}$ as $Br^{-2.5}$, formula (4) can be used with r replacing x, and so

$$\int \dfrac{B}{r^{2.5}}\, dr = B \int r^{-2.5}\, dr = B \dfrac{1}{-2.5+1} r^{-2.5+1} + C = -\dfrac{B}{1.5r^{1.5}} + C$$

(b) $\displaystyle\int (a + bq + cq^2)\, dq = aq + \tfrac{1}{2}bq^2 + \tfrac{1}{3}cq^3 + C$ ∎

PROBLEMS FOR SECTION 9.1

1. Find the following integrals by using (4):

   (a) $\displaystyle\int x^{13}\, dx$ (b) $\displaystyle\int x\sqrt{x}\, dx$ (c) $\displaystyle\int \dfrac{1}{\sqrt{x}}\, dx$ (d) $\displaystyle\int \sqrt{x\sqrt{x\sqrt{x}}}\, dx$

2. Find the following integrals:

   (a) $\displaystyle\int e^{-x}\, dx$ (b) $\displaystyle\int e^{\frac{1}{4}x}\, dx$ (c) $\displaystyle\int 3e^{-2x}\, dx$ (d) $\displaystyle\int 2^x\, dx$

3. In the manufacture of a product, the marginal cost of producing x units is $C'(x)$ and fixed costs are $C(0)$. Find the total cost function $C(x)$ when:

   (a) $C'(x) = 3x + 4$, $C(0) = 40$ (b) $C'(x) = ax + b$, $C(0) = C_0$

4. Find the following integrals:

   (a) $\displaystyle\int (t^3 + 2t - 3)\, dt$ (b) $\displaystyle\int (x - 1)^2\, dx$ (c) $\displaystyle\int (x - 1)(x + 2)\, dx$

   (d) $\displaystyle\int (x + 2)^3\, dx$ (e) $\displaystyle\int (e^{3x} - e^{2x} + e^x)\, dx$ (f) $\displaystyle\int \dfrac{x^3 - 3x + 4}{x}\, dx$

5. Find the following integrals:

   (a) $\displaystyle\int \dfrac{(y - 2)^2}{\sqrt{y}}\, dy$ (b) $\displaystyle\int \dfrac{x^3}{x + 1}\, dx$ (c) $\displaystyle\int x(1 + x^2)^{15}\, dx$

(*Hint:* In part (a), first expand $(y-2)^2$, and then divide each term by $\sqrt{y}$. In part (b), do polynomial division as in Section 4.7. In part (c), what is the derivative of $(1+x^2)^{16}$?)

6. Show that

(a) $\displaystyle\int x^2 \ln x \, dx = \tfrac{1}{3}x^3 \ln x - \tfrac{1}{9}x^3 + C$

(b) $\displaystyle\int \sqrt{x^2+1} \, dx = \tfrac{1}{2}x\sqrt{x^2+1} + \tfrac{1}{2}\ln\left(x+\sqrt{x^2+1}\right) + C$

7. Suppose that $f(0) = 2$ and that the *derivative* of f has the graph given in Fig. 1. Sketch the graph of $f(x)$, and find an explicit function $f(x)$ which has this graph. (Suggest first a formula for $f'(x)$.)

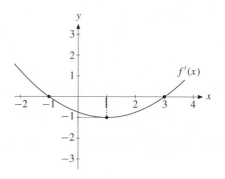

Figure 1   Figure 2

8. Suppose that $f(0) = 0$ and that the *derivative* of f has the graph given in Fig. 2. Sketch the graph of $f(x)$ and find an explicit function $f(x)$ which has this graph.

9. Prove that $\displaystyle\int 2x \ln(x^2+a^2)\, dx = (x^2+a^2)\ln(x^2+a^2) - x^2 + C$.

10. (a) Show that $\displaystyle\int (ax+b)^p \, dx = \frac{1}{a(p+1)}(ax+b)^{p+1} + C$ $(a \neq 0, \, p \neq -1)$

(b) Evaluate   (i) $\displaystyle\int (2x+1)^4 \, dx$ (ii) $\displaystyle\int \sqrt{x+2}\, dx$ (iii) $\displaystyle\int \frac{1}{\sqrt{4-x}}\, dx$.

11. (a) Find $F(x)$ if $F'(x) = \tfrac{1}{2}e^x - 2x$ and $F(0) = \tfrac{1}{2}$.

(b) Find $F(x)$ if $F'(x) = x(1-x^2)$ and $F(1) = 5/12$.

12. Find the general form of a function f whose second derivative, $f''(x)$, is x^2. If we require in addition that $f(0) = 1$ and $f'(0) = -1$, what is $f(x)$?

13. Suppose that $f''(x) = x^{-2} + x^3 + 2$ for $x > 0$, and $f(1) = 0$, $f'(1) = 1/4$. Find $f(x)$.

9.2 Area and Definite Integrals

This section will show how the concept of the integral can be used to calculate the area of many plane regions.

In ancient Babylonia and Egypt, rivers would flood and change course. Some farmers would gain new land from the river, while others would lose land. Since taxes were often assessed on land area, it became necessary to re-calculate the area of a parcel of land whose boundary might be an irregularly shaped river bank.

As early as about 360 B.C., the Greek mathematician Eudoxos developed a general method for determining the areas of irregularly shaped plane regions, known as the *method of exhaustion*. The idea was to inscribe and circumscribe the region by general polygonal regions—whose area we already know how to measure. Now, if the area of the inscribed region and the area of the circumscribed region tend to the same limit as more and more refined polygons are chosen, this limit is defined as the *area* of the region. This method of exhaustion was used by Eudoxos and Archimedes to determine quite accurate approximations to the areas of a number of specific plane regions, such as a circular disk.

However, the method of exhaustion turned out to work only in a limited number of cases, partly because of the algebraic problems encountered. Nearly 1900 years passed after Eudoxos before the problem was solved. Newton and Leibniz are the mathematicians primarily responsible for the early development of both the differential and integral calculus. Besides allowing areas to be measured much more accurately, these techniques have many other applications. Demonstrating the precise logical relationship between differentiation and integration is one of the main achievements of mathematical analysis. It has even been argued that this discovery is the single most important in all of science.

The problem to be considered and solved in this section is illustrated in Fig. 1: *How do we compute the area A under the graph of a continuous and nonnegative function f over the interval* $[a, b]$?

Figure 1

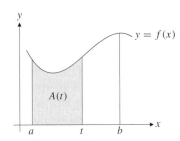

Figure 2

Let t be an arbitrary point in $[a, b]$, and let $A(t)$ denote the area under the curve $y = f(x)$ over the interval $[a, t]$, as shown in Fig. 2. Clearly, $A(a) = 0$, because there is no area from a to a. On the other hand, the area in Fig. 1 is $A = A(b)$. It is obvious from Fig. 2 that, because f is always positive, $A(t)$ increases as t increases. Suppose we increase t by a positive amount Δt. Then $A(t + \Delta t)$ is the area under the curve $y = f(x)$ over the interval $[a, t + \Delta t]$. Hence, $A(t + \Delta t) - A(t)$ is the area ΔA under the curve over the interval $[t, t + \Delta t]$, as shown in Fig. 3.

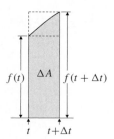

Figure 3   **Figure 4**

In Fig. 4, the area ΔA has been magnified. It cannot be larger than the area of the rectangle with edges Δt and the maximum of f on $[t, t + \Delta t]$ (which in our particular case is $f(t + \Delta t)$), nor smaller than the area of the rectangle with edges Δt and the minimum of f on $[t, t + \Delta t]$ (which is in our particular case is $f(t)$). Hence, for all $\Delta t > 0$, one has

$$f(t)\,\Delta t \le A(t + \Delta t) - A(t) \le f(t + \Delta t)\,\Delta t \tag{*}$$

Because $\Delta t > 0$, this implies

$$f(t) \le \frac{A(t + \Delta t) - A(t)}{\Delta t} \le f(t + \Delta t) \tag{**}$$

Let us consider what happens to $(**)$ as $\Delta t \to 0$. The interval $[t, t + \Delta t]$ shrinks to the single point t, and by continuity of f, the value $f(t + \Delta t)$ approaches $f(t)$. The Newton quotient $[A(t + \Delta t) - A(t)]/\Delta t$, squeezed between $f(t)$ and a quantity $f(t + \Delta t)$ that approaches $f(t)$, must therefore approach $f(t)$ as $\Delta t \to 0$. So we arrive at the remarkable conclusion that the function $A(t)$, which measures the area under the graph of f over the interval $[a, t]$, is differentiable, with derivative given by

$$A'(t) = f(t) \quad \text{for all } t \text{ in } (a, b) \tag{***}$$

This proves that *the derivative of the area function $A(t)$ is the curve's "height" function $f(t)$, and the area function is therefore one of the indefinite integrals of $f(t)$.*[1]

Let us now use x as the free variable, and suppose that $F(x)$ is an arbitrary indefinite integral of $f(x)$. Then $A(x) = F(x) + C$ for some constant C. Recall that $A(a) = 0$. Hence, $0 = A(a) = F(a) + C$, so $C = -F(a)$. Therefore,

$$A(x) = F(x) - F(a) \quad \text{where} \quad F(x) = \int f(x)\,dx \tag{1}$$

---

[1] The function f in the figures is increasing in the interval $[t, t + \Delta t]$. It is easy to see that the same conclusion is obtained whatever the behaviour of f in the interval $[t, t + \Delta t]$. On the left-hand side of $(*)$, just replace $f(t)$ by $f(c)$, where c is the minimum point of the continuous function f in the interval; and on the right-hand side, replace $f(t + \Delta t)$ by $f(d)$, where d is the maximum point of f in $[t, t + \Delta t]$. Then $f(c)$ and $f(d)$ must both tend to $f(t)$ as $\Delta t \to 0$. So $(***)$ holds also for general continuous functions f.

Suppose $G(x)$ is another function with $G'(x) = f(x)$. Then $G(x) = F(x) + C$ for some constant C, and so

$$G(x) - G(a) = F(x) + C - \left(F(a) + C\right) = F(x) - F(a)$$

This argument tells us that the area we compute using (1) is independent of which indefinite integral of f we choose.

EXAMPLE 1   Calculate the area under the parabola $f(x) = x^2$ over the interval $[0, 1]$.

Solution: The area in question is the shaded region in Fig. 5. The area is equal to $A = F(1) - F(0)$ where $F(x)$ is an indefinite integral of x^2. Now, $\int x^2\,dx = \frac{1}{3}x^3 + C$, so we choose $F(x) = \frac{1}{3}x^3$. Thus the required area is

$$A = F(1) - F(0) = \frac{1}{3} \cdot 1^3 - \frac{1}{3} \cdot 0^3 = \frac{1}{3}$$

Figure 5 suggests that this answer is reasonable, because the shaded region appears to have roughly 1/3 the area of a square whose side is of length 1. ▌

Figure 5

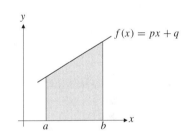

Figure 6

The argument leading to (1) is based on rather intuitive considerations. Formally, we choose to *define* the area under the graph of a continuous and nonnegative function f over the interval $[a, b]$ as the number $F(b) - F(a)$, where $F'(x) = f(x)$. The concept of area that emerges agrees with the usual concept for regions bounded by straight lines. The next example verifies this in a special case.

EXAMPLE 2   Find the area A under the straight line $f(x) = px + q$ over the interval $[a, b]$. (We assume that the constants are chosen so that $f(x) \geq 0$ in $[a, b]$.)

Solution: The area is shown shaded in Fig. 6. It is equal to $F(b) - F(a)$ where $F(x)$ is an indefinite integral of $px + q$. Now, $\int (px + q)\,dx = \frac{1}{2}px^2 + qx + C$. The obvious choice of an indefinite integral is $F(x) = \frac{1}{2}px^2 + qx$, and so

$$A = F(b) - F(a) = \frac{1}{2}pb^2 + qb - \left(\frac{1}{2}pa^2 + qa\right) = \frac{1}{2}p(b^2 - a^2) + q(b - a)$$

Evaluate the same area as the sum of a triangle and a rectangle, and check that you really get the same answer. ▌

The Definite Integral

Let f be a continuous function defined in the interval $[a, b]$. Suppose that the function F is continuous in $[a, b]$ and has a derivative with $F'(x) = f(x)$ for every x in (a, b). Then the difference $F(b) - F(a)$ is called the **definite integral** of f over $[a, b]$. We observed above that this difference does not depend on which of the indefinite integrals of f we choose as F. The definite integral of f over $[a, b]$ is therefore a *number* that depends only on the function f and the numbers a and b. We denote this number by

$$\int_a^b f(x)\,dx \tag{2}$$

This notation makes explicit the function $f(x)$ we integrate and the interval of integration $[a, b]$. The numbers a and b are called, respectively, the **lower** and **upper limit of integration**. The letter x is a *dummy variable* in the sense that the integral is independent of its label. For instance,

$$\int_a^b f(x)\,dx = \int_a^b f(y)\,dy = \int_a^b f(\xi)\,d\xi$$

The difference $F(b) - F(a)$ is denoted by $\Big|_a^b F(x)$, or by $\big[F(x)\big]_a^b$. Thus:

DEFINITION OF THE DEFINITE INTEGRAL

$$\int_a^b f(x)\,dx = \Big|_a^b F(x) = F(b) - F(a) \tag{3}$$

where F is any function satisfying $F'(x) = f(x)$ for all $x \in (a, b)$.

EXAMPLE 3   Evaluate   (a) $\displaystyle\int_2^5 e^{2x}\,dx$ (b) $\displaystyle\int_{-2}^2 (x - x^3 - x^5)\,dx$

Solution:

(a)   Because $\int e^{2x} = \frac{1}{2}e^{2x} + C$, we have

$$\int_2^5 e^{2x}\,dx = \Big|_2^5 \frac{1}{2}e^{2x} = \frac{1}{2}e^{10} - \frac{1}{2}e^4 = \frac{1}{2}e^4(e^6 - 1)$$

(b) $\displaystyle\int_{-2}^2 (x - x^3 - x^5)\,dx = \Big|_{-2}^2 \left(\frac{1}{2}x^2 - \frac{1}{4}x^4 - \frac{1}{6}x^6\right)$

$$= \left(\frac{1}{2}4 - \frac{1}{4}16 - \frac{1}{6}64\right) - \left(\frac{1}{2}4 - \frac{1}{4}16 - \frac{1}{6}64\right) = 0$$

After reading the next subsection and realizing that the graph of $f(x) = x - x^3 - x^5$ is symmetric about the origin, you should understand better why the answer must be 0.

Definition (3) does not necessarily require $a < b$. However, if $a > b$ and $f(x)$ is positive throughout the interval $[b, a]$, then $\int_a^b f(x)\,dx$ is a negative number.

Note that we have defined the definite integral without necessarily giving it a geometric interpretation as the area under a curve. In fact, depending on the context, it can have different interpretations. For instance, if $f(r)$ is an income distribution function, then $\int_a^b f(r)\,dr$ is the proportion of people with income between a and b. (See Section 9.4.)

Although the notation for definite and indefinite integrals is similar, the two integrals are entirely different. In fact, $\int_a^b f(x)\,dx$ denotes a single number, whereas $\int f(x)\,dx$ represents any one of the infinite set of functions all having $f(x)$ as their derivative.

Area when f(x) is Negative

If $f(x) \geq 0$ over $[a, b]$, then

$$\int_a^b f(x)\,dx \quad \text{is the area below the graph of } f \text{ over } [a, b] \tag{4}$$

If f is defined in $[a, b]$ and $f(x) \leq 0$ for all x in $[a, b]$, the graph of f, the x-axis and the lines $x = a$ and $x = b$ still enclose an area. This area is $-\int_a^b f(x)\,dx$, with a minus sign before the integral because the area of a region must be positive (or zero), whereas the definite integral is negative.

EXAMPLE 4   Evaluate the area A shaded in Fig. 7. It is the area between the x-axis and the graph of $f(x) = e^{x/3} - 3$ over the interval $[0, 3\ln 3]$. (Note that $f(3\ln 3) = 0$.)

Solution: Because $f(x) \leq 0$ in the interval $[0, 3\ln 3]$, we obtain

$$A = -\int_0^{3\ln 3} \left(e^{x/3} - 3\right) dx = -\Big|_0^{3\ln 3} (3e^{x/3} - 3x)$$

$$= -(3e^{\ln 3} - 3 \cdot 3\ln 3) + 3e^0 = -9 + 9\ln 3 + 3 = 9\ln 3 - 6 \approx 3.89$$

Is the answer reasonable? Yes, because the shaded set in Fig. 7 seems to be a little less than the area of the triangle enclosed by the points $(0, 0)$, $(0, -2)$ and $(4, 0)$, whose area is 4. ∎

Figure 7

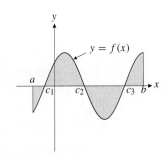

Figure 8

Suppose f is defined and continuous in $[a, b]$, and that it is positive in some subintervals, negative in others, as is the case in Fig. 8. Let c_1, c_2, c_3 denote three roots of the equation $f(x) = 0$—that is, three points where the graph crosses the x-axis. The total area bounded by the graph of f, the x-axis, and the lines $x = a$ and $x = b$ is then calculated by computing the positive areas in each subinterval $[a, c_1]$, $[c_1, c_2]$, $[c_2, c_3]$, and $[c_3, b]$ in turn according to the previous definitions, and then adding these areas. Specifically, the shaded area is

$$- \int_a^{c_1} f(x)\,dx + \int_{c_1}^{c_2} f(x)\,dx - \int_{c_2}^{c_3} f(x)\,dx + \int_{c_3}^{b} f(x)\,dx$$

The definite integral $\int_a^b f(x)\,dx$, on the other hand, is the sum of the two shaded areas above the x-axis, minus the sum of the two shaded areas below the x-axis.

PROBLEMS FOR SECTION 9.2

1. Compute the areas under the graphs of (a) $f(x) = x^3$ and (b) $f(x) = x^{10}$ over $[0, 1]$.

2. Compute the area bounded by the graph of the function over the indicated interval. In (c), sketch the graph and indicate by shading the area in question.

   (a) $f(x) = 3x^2$ in $[0, 2]$ (b) $f(x) = x^6$ in $[0, 1]$

   (c) $f(x) = e^x$ in $[-1, 1]$ (d) $f(x) = 1/x^2$ in $[1, 10]$

3. Compute the area A bounded by the graph of $f(x) = 1/x^3$, the x-axis, and the two lines $x = -2$ and $x = -1$. Make a drawing. (*Hint:* $f(x) < 0$ in $[-2, -1]$.)

4. Compute the area A bounded by the graph of $f(x) = \frac{1}{2}(e^x + e^{-x})$, the x-axis, and the lines $x = -1$ and $x = 1$.

5. Evaluate the following integrals:

   (a) $\int_0^1 x\,dx$ (b) $\int_1^2 (2x + x^2)\,dx$ (c) $\int_{-2}^{3} \left(\frac{1}{2}x^2 - \frac{1}{3}x^3\right) dx$

   (d) $\int_0^2 (t^3 - t^4)\,dt$ (e) $\int_1^2 \left(2t^5 - \frac{1}{t^2}\right) dt$ (f) $\int_2^3 \left(\frac{1}{t-1} + t\right) dt$

6. (a) Let $f(x) = x(x - 1)(x - 2)$. Calculate $f'(x)$. Where is $f(x)$ increasing?

   (b) Sketch the graph and calculate $\int_0^1 f(x)\,dx$.

7. The profit of a firm as a function of its output x is given by

   $$f(x) = 4000 - x - 3\,000\,000/x, \quad x > 0$$

   (a) Find the level of output that maximizes profit. Sketch the graph of f.

   (b) The actual output varies between 1000 and 3000 units. Compute the average profit $I = \frac{1}{2000} \int_{1000}^{3000} f(x)\,dx$.

8. Evaluate the integrals

(a) $\displaystyle\int_1^3 \frac{3x}{10}\,dx$ (b) $\displaystyle\int_{-3}^{-1} \xi^2\,d\xi$ (c) $\displaystyle\int_0^1 \alpha e^{\beta\tau}\,d\tau$ $(\beta \neq 0)$ (d) $\displaystyle\int_{-2}^{-1} \frac{1}{y}\,dy$

9.3 Properties of Definite Integrals

From the definition of the definite integral, a number of properties can be derived. If f is a continuous function in an interval that contains a, b, and c, then

$$\int_a^b f(x)\,dx = -\int_b^a f(x)\,dx \tag{1}$$

$$\int_a^a f(x)\,dx = 0 \tag{2}$$

$$\int_a^b \alpha f(x)\,dx = \alpha \int_a^b f(x)\,dx \quad (\alpha \text{ an arbitrary number}) \tag{3}$$

$$\int_a^b f(x)\,dx = \int_a^c f(x)\,dx + \int_c^b f(x)\,dx \tag{4}$$

All these rules follow easily from definition (3) in the previous section. For example, (4) can be proved as follows: Let F be continuous in $[a, b]$, and suppose that $F'(x) = f(x)$ for all x in an interval big enough to include a, b, and c. Then

$$\int_a^c f(x)\,dx + \int_c^b f(x)\,dx = \big[F(c) - F(a)\big] + \big[F(b) - F(c)\big]$$

$$= F(b) - F(a) = \int_a^b f(x)\,dx$$

When the definite integral is interpreted as an area, (4) is the additivity property of areas, as illustrated in Fig. 1. Of course, (4) easily generalizes to the case in which we partition the interval $[a, b]$ into an arbitrary finite number of subintervals.

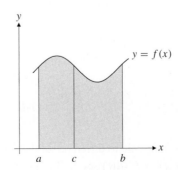

Figure 1 $\int_a^b f(x)\,dx = \int_a^c f(x)\,dx + \int_c^b f(x)\,dx$

The constant multiple property and the summation property for indefinite integrals ((8) and (9) in Section 9.1) are also valid for definite integrals. In fact, if f and g are continuous in $[a, b]$, and if α and β are real numbers, then it is easy to prove that

$$\int_a^b \left[\alpha f(x) + \beta g(x)\right] dx = \alpha \int_a^b f(x)\,dx + \beta \int_a^b g(x)\,dx \tag{5}$$

This rule can obviously be extended to more than two functions.

Differentiation w.r.t. the Limits of Integration

If $F'(x) = f(x)$, then $\int_a^t f(x)\,dx = \big|_a^t F(x) = F(t) - F(a)$, so that

$$\frac{d}{dt} \int_a^t f(x)\,dx = F'(t) = f(t) \tag{6}$$

In other words: *The derivative of the definite integral w.r.t. the upper limit of integration is equal to the integrand evaluated at that limit.*

Correspondingly, $\int_t^b f(x)\,dx = \big|_t^b F(x) = F(b) - F(t)$, so that

$$\frac{d}{dt} \int_t^b f(x)\,dx = -F'(t) = -f(t) \tag{7}$$

In other words: *The derivative of the definite integral w.r.t. the lower limit of integration is equal to minus the integrand evaluated at that limit.*

NOTE 1 Suppose that $f(x) \geq 0$ and $t \leq b$. We can interpret $\int_t^b f(x)\,dx$ as the area below the graph of f over the interval $[t, b]$. Then the interval shrinks as t increases, and the area will decrease. So the fact that the derivative in (7) is negative is not surprising.

The results in (6) and (7) can be generalized. In fact, if $a(t)$ and $b(t)$ are differentiable and $f(x)$ is continuous, then

$$\frac{d}{dt} \int_{a(t)}^{b(t)} f(x)\,dx = f(b(t))\,b'(t) - f(a(t))\,a'(t) \tag{8}$$

To prove this formula, suppose F is an indefinite integral satisfying $F'(x) = f(x)$. Then $\int_u^v f(x)\,dx = F(v) - F(u)$, so in particular,

$$\int_{a(t)}^{b(t)} f(x)\,dx = F(b(t)) - F(a(t))$$

Using the chain rule to differentiate the right-hand side of this equation w.r.t. t, we obtain $F'(b(t))b'(t) - F'(a(t))a'(t)$. But $F'(b(t)) = f(b(t))$ and $F'(a(t)) = f(a(t))$, so (8) results.

Continuous Functions Are Integrable

Suppose $f(x)$ is a continuous function in $[a, b]$. Then we defined $\int_a^b f(x)\,dx$ as the number $F(b) - F(a)$, provided that $F(x)$ is some function whose derivative is $f(x)$. In some cases, we are able to find an explicit expression for $F(x)$. For instance, we can evaluate $\int_0^1 x^5\,dx$ as $1/6$ because $(1/6)x^6$ has x^5 as its derivative. On the other hand, for the function $f(x) = (1/\sqrt{2\pi})e^{-x^2/2}$ (the standard normal density function in statistics), it turns out to be impossible to write down an explicit standard expression for a function whose derivative is $f(x)$. Here $f(x)$ *is* continuous in (say) $[0, 2]$, and there should be an area under the graph from 0 to 2. (See the graph of f in the answer to problem 4.9.5.)

In fact, one can prove that any continuous function has an antiderivative. Here are some integrals that really are impossible to "solve", except by introducing special new functions:

$$\int e^{x^2}\,dx, \quad \int e^{-x^2}\,dx, \quad \int \frac{e^x}{x}\,dx, \quad \int \frac{1}{\ln x}\,dx, \quad \int \frac{1}{\sqrt{x^4 + 1}}\,dx \qquad (9)$$

The Riemann Integral

The kind of integral discussed so far, which is based on the antiderivative, is called the *Newton–Leibniz* (N–L) *integral*. Several other kinds of integral are considered by mathematicians. For continuous functions, they all give the same result as the N–L integral. We briefly sketch the so-called *Riemann integral*. The idea behind the definition is closely related to the exhaustion method that was described in Section 9.2.

Let f be a *bounded* function in the interval $[a, b]$, and let n be a natural number. Subdivide $[a, b]$ into n parts by choosing points $a = x_0 < x_1 < x_2 < \cdots < x_{n-1} < x_n = b$. Put $\Delta x_i = x_{i+1} - x_i$, $i = 0, 1, \ldots, n - 1$, and choose an arbitrary number ξ_i in each interval $[x_i, x_{i+1}]$ (draw a figure). The sum

$$f(\xi_0)\Delta x_0 + f(\xi_1)\Delta x_1 + \cdots + f(\xi_{n-1})\Delta x_{n-1}$$

is called a *Riemann sum* associated with the function f. This sum will depend on f as well as on the subdivision and on the choice of the different ξ_i's. Suppose that, when n approaches infinity and simultaneously the largest of the numbers $\Delta x_0, \Delta x_1, \ldots, \Delta x_{n-1}$ approaches 0, the limit of the sum exists. Then f is called *Riemann integrable* (R integrable) in the interval $[a, b]$, and we put

$$\int_a^b f(x)\,dx = \lim \sum_{i=0}^{n-1} f(\xi_i)\,\Delta x_i$$

Textbooks on mathematical analysis show that the value of the integral is independent of how the ξ_i's are chosen. They also show that every continuous function is R integrable, and that the R integral in this case satisfies (3) in Section 9.2. The N-L integral and the R integral thus coincide for continuous functions.

PROBLEMS FOR SECTION 9.3

1. Evaluate the following integrals:

(a) $\int_0^5 (x + x^2)\,dx$

(b) $\int_{-2}^2 (e^x - e^{-x})\,dx$

(c) $\int_2^{10} \frac{dx}{x - 1}$

(d) $\int_0^1 2xe^{x^2}\,dx$

(e) $\int_{-4}^4 (x - 1)^3\,dx$

(f) $\int_1^2 (x^5 + x^{-5})\,dx$

2. (a) Evaluate the integral $\int_0^1 x^p(x^q + x^r)\, dx$, where p, q, and r are positive constants.

   (b) Find the function $f(x)$ if $f'(x) = ax^2 + bx$, and

   (i) $f'(1) = 6$ (ii) $f''(1) = 18$ (iii) $\int_0^2 f(x)\, dx = 18$

3. Evaluate the following integrals (in (d) all constants are positive):

   (a) $\displaystyle\int_0^3 \left(\frac{1}{3}e^{3t-2} + \frac{1}{t+2}\right) dt$ (b) $\displaystyle\int_0^1 (x^2+2)^2\, dx$

   (c) $\displaystyle\int_0^1 \frac{x^2 + x + \sqrt{x+1}}{x+1}\, dx$ (d) $\displaystyle\int_1^b \left(A\frac{x+b}{x+c} + \frac{d}{x}\right) dx$

4. (a) Put $F(x) = \displaystyle\int_0^x (t^2 + 2)\, dt$ and $G(x) = \displaystyle\int_0^{x^2} (t^2 + 2)\, dt$. Find $F'(x)$ and $G'(x)$.

   (b) Define $H(t) = \int_0^{t^2} K(\tau)e^{-\rho\tau}\, d\tau$. Find $H'(t)$. Here $K(\tau)$ is a given continuous function and ρ is a constant.

5. Find: (a) $\displaystyle\frac{d}{dt}\int_0^t x^2\, dx$ (b) $\displaystyle\frac{d}{dt}\int_t^3 e^{-x^2}\, dx$ (c) $\displaystyle\frac{d}{dt}\int_{-t}^t \frac{1}{\sqrt{x^4+1}}\, dx$

6. Find the area between the two parabolas defined by the equations $y + 1 = (x-1)^2$ and $3x = y^2$. (The points of intersection have integer coordinates.)

HARDER PROBLEMS

7. A theory of investment has used a function W defined for all $T > 0$ by

$$W(T) = \frac{K}{T}\int_0^T e^{-\varrho t}\, dt \qquad (K \text{ and } \varrho \text{ are positive constants})$$

Evaluate the integral, then prove that $W(T)$ takes values in the interval $(0, K)$ and is strictly decreasing. (*Hint:* Problem 6.11.9.)

8. Consider the function f defined for $x > 0$ by the formula $f(x) = 4\ln(\sqrt{x+4} - 2)$.

   (a) Show that f has an inverse function g, and find a formula for g.

   (b) Draw the graphs of f and g in the same coordinate system.

   (c) We wish to compute $A = \int_5^{10} 4\ln(\sqrt{x+4}-2)\, dx$. Give a geometric interpretation of A. Explain why

$$A = 10 \cdot a - \int_0^a (e^{x/2} + 4e^{x/4})\, dx, \qquad \text{where} \quad a = f(10)$$

   Use this to find A expressed in terms of a.

9.4 Economic Applications

We motivated the definite integral as a tool for computing the area under a curve. However, the integral has many other important interpretations. In statistics, many important probability distributions are expressed as integrals of continuous probability density functions. This section presents some examples showing the importance of integrals in economics.

Extraction from an Oil Well

Assume that at time $t = 0$ we start extracting oil from a well that contains K barrels of oil. Let us define

$$x(t) = \text{number of barrels of oil that is left at time } t$$

In particular, $x(0) = K$. Assuming we will never put oil back into the well, $x(t)$ is a decreasing function of t. The amount of oil that is extracted in a time interval $[t, t + \Delta t]$ (where $\Delta t > 0$) is $x(t) - x(t + \Delta t)$. Extraction per unit of time is, therefore,

$$\frac{x(t) - x(t + \Delta t)}{\Delta t} = -\frac{x(t + \Delta t) - x(t)}{\Delta t} \tag{$*$}$$

If we assume that $x(t)$ is differentiable, then the limit as Δt approaches zero of the fraction ($*$) is equal to $-\dot{x}(t)$. Letting $u(t)$ denote the **rate of extraction** at time t, we have

$$\dot{x}(t) = -u(t) \qquad \text{with} \qquad x(0) = K \tag{1}$$

The solution to equation (1) is

$$x(t) = K - \int_0^t u(\tau)\, d\tau \tag{2}$$

Indeed, we check (2) as follows. First, setting $t = 0$ gives $x(0) = K$. Moreover, differentiating (2) w.r.t. t according to rule (6) in Section 9.3 yields $\dot{x}(t) = -u(t)$.

The result (2) may be interpreted as follows: The amount of oil left at time t is equal to the initial amount K, minus the total amount that has been extracted during the time span $[0, t]$, namely $\int_0^t u(\tau)\, d\tau$.

If the rate of extraction is constant, with $u(t) = \bar{u}$, then (2) yields

$$x(t) = K - \int_0^t \bar{u}\, d\tau = K - \Big|_0^t \bar{u}\tau = K - \bar{u}t$$

In particular, we see that the well will be empty when $K - \bar{u}t = 0$, that is when $t = K/\bar{u}$. (Of course, this particular answer could have been found more directly, without recourse to integration.)

The example illustrates two concepts that are important to distinguish in many economic arguments. The quantity $x(t)$ is a *stock*, measured in barrels. On the other hand, $u(t)$ is a *flow*, measured in barrels *per unit of time*.

Income Distribution

In many countries, data from income tax authorities can be used to reveal some properties of the income distribution within a given year, as well as how the distribution changes from year to year.

Suppose we measure annual income in dollars and let $F(r)$ denote the proportion of individuals that receive no more than r dollars in a particular year. Thus, if there are n individuals in the population, $nF(r)$ is the number of individuals with income no greater than r. If r_0 is the lowest and r_1 is the highest (registered) income in the group, we are interested in the function F defined on the interval $[r_0, r_1]$. By definition, F is not continuous and therefore also not differentiable in $[r_0, r_1]$, because r has to be a multiple of \$0.01 and $F(r)$ has to be a multiple of $1/n$. However, if the population consists of a large number of individuals, then it is usually possible to find a "smooth" function that gives a good approximation to the true income distribution. Assume, therefore, that F is a function with a continuous derivative denoted by f, so that $f(r) = F'(r)$ for all r in (r_0, r_1). According to the definition of the derivative, we have

$$f(r)\,\Delta r \approx F(r + \Delta r) - F(r)$$

for all small Δr. Thus, $f(r)\,\Delta r$ is approximately equal to the proportion of individuals who have incomes between r and $r + \Delta r$. The function f is called an **income distribution function**, and F is the associated **cumulative distribution function**.[2]

Suppose that f is a continuous income distribution for a certain population with incomes in the interval $[r_0, r_1]$. If $r_0 \le a \le b \le r_1$, then the previous discussion and the definition of the definite integral imply that $\int_a^b f(r)\,dr$ is the proportion of individuals with incomes in $[a, b]$. Thus,

$$n \int_a^b f(r)\,dr = \text{the \textbf{number of individuals} with incomes in } [a, b] \tag{3}$$

We will now find an expression for the combined income of those who earn between a and b dollars. Let $M(r)$ denote the total income of those who earn no more than r dollars during the year, and consider the income interval $[r, r + \Delta r]$. There are approximately $nf(r)\,\Delta r$ individuals with incomes in this interval. Each of them has an income approximately equal to r, so that the total income of these individuals, $M(r + \Delta r) - M(r)$, is approximately equal to $nrf(r)\,\Delta r$. So we have

$$\frac{M(r + \Delta r) - M(r)}{\Delta r} \approx nrf(r)$$

The approximation improves (in general) as Δr decreases. By taking the limit as $\Delta r \to 0$, we obtain $M'(r) = nrf(r)$, so $n \int_a^b rf(r)\,dr = M(b) - M(a)$. Hence,

$$n \int_a^b rf(r)\,dr = \text{\textbf{total income} of individuals with income in } [a, b] \tag{4}$$

---

[2] Readers who know some elementary statistics will see the analogy with probability density functions and with cumulative (probability) distribution functions.

The argument that leads to (4) can be made more exact: $M(r + \Delta r) - M(r)$ is the total income of those who have income in the interval $[r, r + \Delta r]$, when $\Delta r > 0$. In this income interval, there are $n[F(r + \Delta r) - F(r)]$ individuals each of whom earns at least r and at most $r + \Delta r$. Thus,

$$nr\left[F(r + \Delta r) - F(r)\right] \leq M(r + \Delta r) - M(r) \leq n(r + \Delta r)\left[F(r + \Delta r) - F(r)\right] \quad (*)$$

If $\Delta r > 0$, division by Δr yields

$$nr\frac{F(r + \Delta r) - F(r)}{\Delta r} \leq \frac{M(r + \Delta r) - M(r)}{\Delta r} \leq n(r + \Delta r)\frac{F(r + \Delta r) - F(r)}{\Delta r} \quad (**)$$

(If $\Delta r < 0$, then the inequalities in $(*)$ are left unchanged, whereas those in $(**)$ are reversed.) Letting $\Delta r \to 0$ gives $nr F'(r) \leq M'(r) \leq nr F'(r)$, so that $M'(r) = nr F'(r) = nrf(r)$. ∎

The ratio between the total income and the number of individuals belonging to a certain income interval $[a, b]$, is called the mean income for the individuals in this income interval. We have, therefore,

$$\left.\begin{array}{r}\textbf{Mean income} \text{ of individuals with} \\ \text{incomes in the interval } [a, b]\end{array}\right\} : \quad m = \frac{\displaystyle\int_a^b rf(r)\,dr}{\displaystyle\int_a^b f(r)\,dr} \quad (5)$$

A function that approximates actual income distributions quite well, particularly for large incomes, is the **Pareto distribution**. In this case, the proportion of individuals who earn at most r dollars is given by

$$f(r) = \frac{B}{r^\beta} \quad (6)$$

Here B and β are positive constants. Empirical estimates of β are usually in the range $2.4 < \beta < 2.6$. For values of r close to 0, the formula is of no use. In fact, the integral $\int_0^a f(r)\,dr$ diverges to ∞, as will be seen using the arguments of Section 9.7.

EXAMPLE 1   In a population suppose the income distribution for those with incomes between a and b is given by $f(r) = B/r^{2.5}$. Here $b > a > 0$, and B is positive. Determine the mean income in this group.

Solution: According to (3), the total number of individuals is

$$N = n\int_a^b Br^{-2.5}\,dr = nB\left.\left(-\tfrac{2}{3}r^{-1.5}\right)\right|_a^b = \tfrac{2}{3}nB\left(a^{-1.5} - b^{-1.5}\right)$$

According to (4), the total income of these individuals is

$$M = n\int_a^b r Br^{-2.5}\,dr = nB\int_a^b r^{-1.5}\,dr = -2nB\left.r^{-0.5}\right|_a^b = 2nB\left(a^{-0.5} - b^{-0.5}\right)$$

So the mean income of the group is

$$m = \frac{M}{N} = 3\frac{a^{-0.5} - b^{-0.5}}{a^{-1.5} - b^{-1.5}}$$

Suppose that b is very large. Then $b^{-0.5}$ and $b^{-1.5}$ are both close to 0, and so $m \approx 3a$. The mean income of those who earn at least a is therefore approximately $3a$.

The Influence of Income Distribution on Demand

Assume that the individuals in a population are offered a commodity for which demand depends only on the price p and the income r of each individual. Let $D(p, r)$ be a continuous function that denotes the number of commodity units demanded by an individual with income r when the price per unit is p. If the incomes in the group vary between a and b, and the income distribution is $f(r)$, what is the total demand for the commodity when the price is p?

Let the price p be fixed, and denote by $T(r)$ the total demand for the commodity by all individuals who earn less than or equal to r. Consider the income interval $[r, r + \Delta r]$. There are approximately $nf(r) \Delta r$ individuals with incomes in this interval. Because each of them demands approximately $D(p, r)$ units of the commodity, the total demand of these individuals will be approximately $nD(p, r)f(r) \Delta r$. However, the actual total demand of individuals with incomes in the interval $[r, r + \Delta r]$ is given by $T(r + \Delta r) - T(r)$. So we must have $T(r + \Delta r) - T(r) \approx nD(p, r)f(r) \Delta r$, and thus

$$\frac{T(r + \Delta r) - T(r)}{\Delta r} \approx nD(p, r)f(r)$$

The approximation improves (in general) as Δr decreases, and by taking the limit as $\Delta r \to 0$, we obtain $T'(r) = nD(p, r)f(r)$. By definition of the definite integral, $T(b) - T(a) = n \int_a^b D(p, r)f(r)\,dr$. But $T(b) - T(a)$ is the desired measure of total demand for the commodity by all the individuals in the group. This will naturally depend on the price p. So we denote it by $x(p)$, and thus we have

$$x(p) = \int_a^b nD(p, r)f(r)\,dr \qquad \text{(total demand)} \qquad (7)$$

EXAMPLE 2   Let the income distribution function be that of Example 1, and let $D(p, r) = Ap^{-1.5}r^{2.08}$. (This function describes the demand for milk in Norway during the period 1925–1935. See Example 11.1.2.) Compute the total demand.

Solution: Using (7) gives

$$x(p) = \int_a^b nAp^{-1.5}r^{2.08}Br^{-2.5}\,dr = nABp^{-1.5}\int_a^b r^{-0.42}\,dr$$

Hence,

$$x(p) = nABp^{-1.5}\left.\frac{1}{0.58}r^{0.58}\right|_a^b = \frac{nAB}{0.58}p^{-1.5}(b^{0.58} - a^{0.58}) \qquad \blacksquare$$

Consumer and Producer Surplus

Economists are interested in studying how much consumers and producers benefit (or lose) when market conditions change. A common (but theoretically questionable) measure of these benefits used by many applied economists is the total amount of consumer and producer surplus defined below.[3]

Consider the typical demand and supply curves shown in Fig. 1. (Look back at Example 4.5.3.)

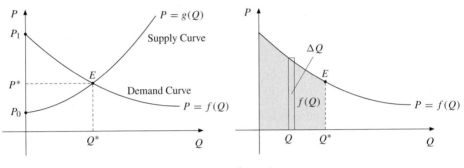

Figure 1   **Figure 2**

At the equilibrium point E in Fig. 1, demand is equal to supply. The corresponding equilibrium price P^* is the one which induces consumers to purchase (demand) precisely the same aggregate amount that producers are willing to offer (supply) at that price, as in Example 4.5.3. According to the demand curve in Fig. 1, there are consumers who are willing to pay more than P^* per unit. In fact, even if the price is almost as high as P_1, some consumers still wish to buy some units at that price. The total amount "saved" by all such consumers is called the **consumer surplus**.

Consider the rectangle suggested in Fig. 2. It has base ΔQ and height $f(Q)$, so its area is $f(Q)\,\Delta Q$. It can be interpreted as the maximum amount consumers are willing to pay for an extra ΔQ units at price $f(Q)$, if they already have bought Q units. For those willing to buy the commodity at price P^* or higher, the total amount they are willing to pay is the total area below the demand curve over the interval $[0, Q^*]$, that is $\int_0^{Q^*} f(Q)\,dQ$. This area is shaded in Fig. 2. If all consumers together buy Q^* units of the commodity, the total cost is $P^* Q^*$. This represents the area of the rectangle with base Q^* and height P^*. It can therefore be expressed in terms of the integral $\int_0^{Q^*} P^*\,dQ$. The consumer surplus is defined as

$$\text{CS} = \int_0^{Q^*} [f(Q) - P^*]\,dQ \tag{8}$$

since this is the total amount consumers are willing to pay minus what they actually pay. In Fig. 3, $\int_0^{Q^*} f(Q)\,dQ$ is the area $O P_1 E Q^*$, whereas $O P^* E Q^*$ is $P^* Q^*$. So CS is equal to the area $P^* P_1 E$ between the demand curve and the horizontal line $P = P^*$. This is also the area to the left of the demand curve—that is between the demand curve and the P-axis. So the consumer surplus CS is the weakly shaded set in Fig. 3.

---

[3] See, for example, H. Varian: *Intermediate Microeconomics*, 5th ed., Norton, 1999, Chapter 14, for a closer treatment of the concepts.

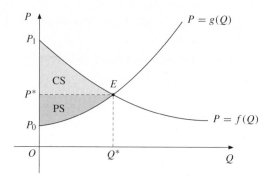

Figure 3

Most producers also derive positive benefit or "surplus" from selling at the equilibrium price because they would be willing to supply the commodity for less than the equilibrium price. In Fig. 3, even if the price is almost as low as P_0, some producers are still willing to supply the commodity. Consider the total surplus of all the producers who receive more than the price at which they are willing to sell. We call this the **producer surplus**. Geometrically it is represented by the darkly shaded set in Fig. 3. Analytically, it is defined by

$$PS = \int_0^{Q^*} [P^* - g(Q)]\, dQ \tag{9}$$

since this is the total revenue producers actually receive, minus what would make them willing to supply. In Fig. 3, the area OP^*EQ^* is again P^*Q^*, and $\int_0^{Q^*} g(Q)\, dQ$ is the area OP_0EQ^*. So PS is equal to the area P^*P_0E between the supply curve and the line $P = P^*$. This is also the area to the left of the supply curve—that is between the supply curve and the P-axis.

EXAMPLE 3   Suppose that the demand curve is $P = f(Q) = 50 - 0.1Q$ and the supply curve is $P = g(Q) = 0.2Q + 20$. Find the equilibrium price and compute the consumer and producer surplus.

Solution: The equilibrium quantity is determined by the equation $50 - 0.1Q^* = 0.2Q^* + 20$, which gives $Q^* = 100$. Then $P^* = 0.2Q^* + 20 = 40$. Hence,

$$CS = \int_0^{100} [50 - 0.1Q - 40]\, dQ = \int_0^{100} [10 - 0.1Q]\, dQ = \Big|_0^{100} (10Q - 0.05Q^2) = 500$$

and

$$PS = \int_0^{100} [40 - (0.2Q + 20)]\, dQ = \int_0^{100} [20 - 0.2Q]\, dQ = \Big|_0^{100} (20Q - 0.1Q^2) = 1000 \parallel$$

PROBLEMS FOR SECTION 9.4

1. Assume that the rate of extraction $u(t)$ from an oil well decreases exponentially over time, with

$$u(t) = \bar{u}e^{-at}$$

where $\bar{u}$ and a are positive constants. Given the initial stock $x(0) = K$, find an expression $x(t)$ for the remaining amount of oil at time t. Under what condition will the well never be exhausted?

2. (a) Follow the pattern in Example 1 and find the mean income m over the interval $[b, 2b]$ when $f(r) = Br^{-2}$.

   (b) Assume that the individuals' demand function is $D(p, r) = Ap^\gamma r^\delta$ with $A > 0$ $\gamma < 0$, $\delta > 0$, $\delta \neq 1$. Compute the total demand $x(p)$ by using formula (7), assuming that there are n individuals in the population.

3. Let $K(t)$ denote the capital stock of an economy at time t. Then **net investment** at time t, denoted by $I(t)$, is given by the rate of increase $\dot{K}(t)$ of $K(t)$.

   (a) If $I(t) = 3t^2 + 2t + 5$ $(t \geq 0)$, what is the total increase in the capital stock during the interval from $t = 0$ to $t = 5$?

   (b) If $K(t_0) = K_0$, find an expression for the total increase in the capital stock from time $t = t_0$ to $t = T$ when the investment function $I(t)$ is as in part (a).

4. An oil company is planning to extract oil from one of its fields, starting today at $t = 0$, where t is time measured in years. It has a choice between two extraction profiles f and g giving the instantaneous flow of oil per year. Both extraction profiles last for 10 years, with $f(t) = 10t^2 - t^3$ and $g(t) = t^3 - 20t^2 + 100t$ for t in $[0, 10]$.

   (a) Sketch the two profiles in the same coordinate system.

   (b) Show that $\int_0^t g(\tau)\, d\tau \geq \int_0^t f(\tau)\, d\tau$ for all t in $[0, 10]$.

   (c) The company sells its oil at a price per unit given by $p(t) = 1 + 1/(t + 1)$. Total revenue is then given by $\int_0^{10} p(t)f(t)\, dt$ and $\int_0^{10} p(t)g(t)\, dt$ respectively. Compute these integrals. Which of the two extraction profiles should be chosen?

5. Suppose that the demand and supply curves are $P = f(Q) = 200 - 0.2Q$ and $P = g(Q) = 20 + 0.1Q$, respectively. Find the equilibrium quantity and compute the consumer and producer surplus.

6. Suppose the demand and supply curves are $P = f(Q) = \dfrac{6000}{Q + 50}$, $P = g(Q) = Q + 10$. Find the equilibrium price, and compute the consumer and producer surplus.

9.5 Integration by Parts

We often need to evaluate integrals such as $\int x^3 e^{2x}\, dx$ whose integrand is a product of two functions. We know that $\frac{1}{4}x^4$ has x^3 as its derivative and that $\frac{1}{2}e^{2x}$ has e^{2x} as its derivative, but $(\frac{1}{4}x^4)(\frac{1}{2}e^{2x})$ certainly does not have $x^3 e^{2x}$ as its derivative. In general, because the derivative of a product is *not* the product of the derivatives, the integral of a product is not the product of the integrals.

The correct rule for differentiating a product allows us to derive an important and useful rule for integrating products. By the product rule for differentiation,

$$\bigl(f(x)g(x)\bigr)' = f'(x)g(x) + f(x)g'(x) \tag{$*$}$$

Taking the indefinite integral of each side and using the rule for integrating a sum gives

$$f(x)g(x) = \int f'(x)g(x)\, dx + \int f(x)g'(x)\, dx$$

where the constants of integration are implicit in the indefinite integrals on the right-hand side of this equation. Rearranging this last equation yields:

FORMULA FOR INTEGRATION BY PARTS

$$\int f(x)g'(x)\, dx \,=\, f(x)g(x) - \int f'(x)g(x)\, dx \tag{1}$$

At first sight, this formula does not look at all helpful. Yet the examples that follow show how this impression is quite wrong, once one has learned to use it properly.

Suppose we are asked to integrate a function $H(x)$ that can be written in the form $f(x)g'(x)$. By using (1), the problem can be transformed into that of integrating $f'(x)g(x)$. Usually, a function $H(x)$ can be written as $f(x)g'(x)$ in several different ways. The point is, therefore, to choose f and g so that it is easier to find $\int f'(x)g(x)\, dx$ than it is to find $\int f(x)g'(x)\, dx$.

EXAMPLE 1   Use integration by parts to evaluate $\int x e^x\, dx$.

Solution: In order to use (1), we must write the integrand in the form $f(x)g'(x)$. Let $f(x) = x$ and $g'(x) = e^x$, implying that $g(x) = e^x$. Then $f(x)g'(x) = x e^x$, and so

$$\int \underset{\substack{\downarrow\quad\downarrow \\ f(x)\ g'(x)}}{x \,\cdot\, e^x}\ dx = \underset{\substack{\downarrow\quad\downarrow \\ f(x)\ g(x)}}{x \,\cdot\, e^x} - \int \underset{\substack{\downarrow\quad\downarrow \\ f'(x)\ g(x)}}{1 \,\cdot\, e^x}\ dx = x e^x - \int e^x\, dx = x e^x - e^x + C$$

The derivative of $x e^x - e^x + C$ is indeed $e^x + x e^x - e^x = x e^x$, so the integration has been carried out correctly.

The right choice of f and g enabled us to evaluate the integral. Let us see what happens if we interchange the role of f and g, and try $f(x) = e^x$ and $g'(x) = x$ instead. Then $g(x) = \frac{1}{2}x^2$. Again $f(x)g'(x) = e^x x = xe^x$, and by (1):

$$\underbrace{\int e^x}_{f(x)} \cdot \underbrace{x}_{g'(x)} \, dx = \underbrace{e^x}_{f(x)} \cdot \underbrace{\frac{1}{2}x^2}_{g(x)} - \int \underbrace{e^x}_{f'(x)} \cdot \underbrace{\frac{1}{2}x^2}_{g(x)} \, dx$$

In this case, the integral on the right-hand side is more complicated than the original one. Thus, this second choice of f and g does not simplify the integral.

The example illustrates that we must be careful how we split the integrand. Insights into making a good choice, if there is one, come only with practice.

Sometimes integration by parts works not by producing a simpler integral, but one that is similar, as in (a) of the next example.

EXAMPLE 2   Evaluate the following: (a) $I = \int \frac{1}{x} \ln x \, dx$ (b) $J = \int e^{2x} x^3 \, dx$.

Solution:

(a) Choosing $f(x) = 1/x$ and $g'(x) = \ln x$ leads nowhere. Choosing $f(x) = \ln x$ and $g'(x) = 1/x$ works better:

$$I = \int \frac{1}{x} \ln x \, dx = \int \underbrace{\ln x}_{f(x)} \underbrace{\frac{1}{x}}_{g'(x)} \, dx = \underbrace{\ln x}_{f(x)} \underbrace{\ln x}_{g(x)} - \int \underbrace{\frac{1}{x}}_{f'(x)} \underbrace{\ln x}_{g(x)} \, dx$$

In this case, the last integral is exactly the one we started with, namely I. So it must be true that $I = (\ln x)^2 - I + C_1$ for some constant C_1. Solving for I yields $I = \frac{1}{2}(\ln x)^2 + \frac{1}{2}C_1$. We conclude that (with $C = \frac{1}{2}C_1$),

$$\int \frac{1}{x} \ln x \, dx = \frac{1}{2}(\ln x)^2 + C$$

(b) We begin by arguing rather loosely as follows. Differentiation makes x^3 simpler by reducing the power in the derivative $3x^2$ from 3 to 2. On the other hand, e^{2x} is about equally simple whether we differentiate or integrate it. Therefore, we choose $f(x) = x^3$ and $g'(x) = e^{2x}$ so that we differentiate f and integrate g'. This yields $f'(x) = 3x^2$ and we can choose $g(x) = \frac{1}{2}e^{2x}$. Therefore,

$$J = \int x^3 e^{2x} \, dx = x^3 \left(\frac{1}{2}e^{2x} \right) - \int (3x^2) \left(\frac{1}{2}e^{2x} \right) dx = \frac{1}{2}x^3 e^{2x} - \frac{3}{2} \int x^2 e^{2x} \, dx \quad \text{(i)}$$

The last integral *is* somewhat simpler than the one we started with because the power of x has been reduced. Integrating by parts once more yields

$$\int x^2 e^{2x}\, dx = x^2\left(\frac{1}{2}e^{2x}\right) - \int (2x)\left(\frac{1}{2}e^{2x}\right) dx = \frac{1}{2}x^2 e^{2x} - \int x e^{2x}\, dx \quad \text{(ii)}$$

Using integration by parts a third and final time gives

$$\int x e^{2x}\, dx = x\left(\frac{1}{2}e^{2x}\right) - \int \frac{1}{2}e^{2x}\, dx = \frac{1}{2}x e^{2x} - \frac{1}{4}e^{2x} + C \quad \text{(iii)}$$

Successively inserting the results of (iii) and (ii) into (i) yields (with $3C/2 = c$):

$$J = \frac{1}{2}x^3 e^{2x} - \frac{3}{4}x^2 e^{2x} + \frac{3}{4}x e^{2x} - \frac{3}{8}e^{2x} + c$$

It is a good idea to double-check your work by verifying that $dJ/dx = x^3 e^{2x}$. ∎

There is a corresponding result for definite integrals. From the definition of the definite integral and (∗) (the product rule for differentiation), we have

$$\int_a^b \left[f'(x)g(x) + f(x)g'(x)\right] dx = \int_a^b \frac{d}{dx}\left[f(x)g(x)\right] dx = \Big|_a^b f(x)g(x)$$

implying that

$$\int_a^b f(x)g'(x)\, dx = \Big|_a^b f(x)g(x) - \int_a^b f'(x)g(x)\, dx \quad \text{(2)}$$

EXAMPLE 3   Evaluate $\int_0^{10}(1+0.4t)e^{-0.05t}\, dt$.

Solution: Put $f(t) = 1 + 0.4t$ and $g'(t) = e^{-0.05t}$. Then we can choose

$$g(t) = -(1/0.05)e^{-0.05t} = -20e^{-0.05t}$$

Now (2) yields

$$\int_0^{10}(1+0.4t)e^{-0.05t}\, dt = \Big|_0^{10}(1+0.4t)(-20)e^{-0.05t} - \int_0^{10}(0.4)(-20)e^{-0.05t}\, dt$$

$$= -100e^{-0.5} + 20 + 8\int_0^{10} e^{-0.05t}\, dt$$

$$= -100e^{-0.5} + 20 - 160(e^{-0.5} - 1)$$

$$= -260e^{-0.5} + 180 \approx 22.3 \quad ∎$$

1. Use integration by parts to find the following:

   (a) $\displaystyle\int xe^{-x}\,dx$ (b) $\displaystyle\int 3xe^{4x}\,dx$ (c) $\displaystyle\int (1+x^2)e^{-x}\,dx$ (d) $\displaystyle\int x\ln x\,dx$

2. Evaluate the following: (a) $\displaystyle\int_{-1}^{1} x\ln(x+2)\,dx$ (b) $\displaystyle\int_{0}^{2} x2^x\,dx$ (c) $\displaystyle\int_{0}^{1} x^2 e^x\,dx$

3. Of course, $f(x) = 1 \cdot f(x)$ for any function $f(x)$. Use this fact to prove that

   $$\int f(x)\,dx = xf(x) - \int xf'(x)\,dx$$

   Apply this formula to $f(x) = \ln x$. Compare with Example 9.1.2.

4. Show that $\displaystyle\int x^{\rho} \ln x\,dx = \frac{x^{\rho+1}}{\rho+1}\ln x - \frac{x^{\rho+1}}{(\rho+1)^2} + C, \quad (\rho \neq -1).$

5. Evaluate the following integrals ($r \neq 0$):

   (a) $\displaystyle\int_{0}^{T} bte^{-rt}\,dt$ (b) $\displaystyle\int_{0}^{T} (a+bt)e^{-rt}\,dt$ (c) $\displaystyle\int_{0}^{T} (a - bt + ct^2)e^{-rt}\,dt$

9.6 Integration by Substitution

In this section we shall see how the chain rule for differentiation leads to an important method for evaluating many complicated integrals. We start with some simple examples.

EXAMPLE 1   Evaluate   (a) $\displaystyle\int (x^2 + 10)^{50} 2x\,dx$ (b) $\displaystyle\int_{0}^{a} xe^{-cx^2}\,dx \;\; (c \neq 0)$

Solution:

(a) Attempts to use integration by parts fail. Expanding $(x^2 + 10)^{50}$ to get a polynomial of degree 100, and then integrating the 51 resulting terms term by term would be extremely cumbersome. Instead, let us introduce $x^2 + 10$ as a new variable. We let dx denote the differential of x, and argue as follows: If we substitute $u = x^2 + 10$, then $du = 2x\,dx$, and inserting this into the integral in (a) yields

$$\int u^{50}\,du$$

This integral is easy, $\int u^{50}\,du = \frac{1}{51}u^{51} + C$. Because $u = x^2 + 10$, it appears that

$$\int (x^2 + 10)^{50} 2x\,dx = \frac{1}{51}(x^2 + 10)^{51} + C$$

By the chain rule, the derivative of $\frac{1}{51}(x^2 + 10)^{51} + C$ is precisely $(x^2 + 10)^{50}2x$, so the result *is* confirmed.

(b) We try the same method on $\int xe^{-cx^2}\,dx$ and substitute $u = -cx^2$. Then $du = -2cx\,dx$, and thus $x\,dx = -du/2c$. The integral is then easily evaluated:

$$\int xe^{-cx^2}\,dx = \int \frac{-1}{2c}e^u\,du = -\frac{1}{2c}e^u + C = -\frac{1}{2c}e^{-cx^2} + C$$

The definite integral is

$$\int_0^a xe^{-cx^2}\,dx = -\frac{1}{2c}\bigg|_0^a e^{-cx^2} = \frac{1}{2c}(1 - e^{-ca^2}) \qquad\qquad \blacksquare$$

In both of these examples, the integrand could be written in the form $f(u)u'$, where $u = g(x)$. In (a), we put $f(u) = u^{50}$ with $u = g(x) = x^2 + 10$. In (b), we put $f(u) = e^u$ with $u = g(x) = -cx^2$. Then the integrand is a constant $-1/(2c)$ multiplied by $f(g(x))g'(x)$.

Let us try the same method on the more general integral

$$\int f(g(x))g'(x)\,dx$$

If we put $u = g(x)$, then $du = g'(x)\,dx$, and so the integral reduces to $\int f(u)\,du$. Suppose we could find an antiderivative function $F(u)$ such that $F'(u) = f(u)$. Then we would have $\int f(u)\,du = F(u) + C$, which implies that

$$\int f(g(x))g'(x)\,dx = F(g(x)) + C$$

Does this purely formal method always give the right result? To convince you that it does, we use the chain rule to differentiate $F(g(x)) + C$ w.r.t. x. The derivative is $F'(g(x))g'(x)$, which is precisely equal to $f(g(x))g'(x)$, thus confirming the following rule:

INTEGRATION BY SUBSTITUTION (CHANGE OF VARIABLE)

$$\int f(g(x))g'(x)\,dx = \int f(u)\,du \qquad (u = g(x)) \qquad\qquad (1)$$

NOTE 1 Precise assumptions for this formula to be valid are as follows: g is continuously differentiable, and $f(u)$ is continuous at all points u belonging to the relevant range of g.

EXAMPLE 2   Evaluate $\int 8x^2(3x^3 - 1)^{16}\,dx$.

Solution: Substitute $u = 3x^3 - 1$. Then $du = 9x^2\,dx$, so that $8x^2\,dx = \frac{8}{9}\,du$. Hence

$$\int 8x^2(3x^3 - 1)^{16}\,dx = \frac{8}{9}\int u^{16}\,du = \frac{8}{9}\cdot\frac{1}{17}u^{17} + C = \frac{8}{153}(3x^3 - 1)^{17} + C \qquad \blacksquare$$

The definite integral in Example 1(b) can be evaluated more simply by "carrying over" the limits of integration. We substituted $u = -cx^2$. As x varies from 0 to a, so u varies from 0 to $-ca^2$. This allows us to write:

$$\int_0^a xe^{-cx^2}\,dx = \int_0^{-ca^2} \frac{-1}{2c}e^u\,du = \frac{-1}{2c}e^u \Big|_0^{-ca^2} = \frac{1}{2c}(1 - e^{-ca^2})$$

This method of carrying over the limits of integration can be used in general. In fact,

$$\int_a^b f\big(g(x)\big)g'(x)\,dx = \int_{g(a)}^{g(b)} f(u)\,du \qquad (u = g(x)) \tag{2}$$

The argument is simple: Provided that $F'(u) = f(u)$, we obtain

$$\int_a^b f\big(g(x)\big)g'(x)\,dx = \Big|_a^b F\big(g(x)\big) = F\big(g(b)\big) - F\big(g(a)\big) = \int_{g(a)}^{g(b)} f(u)\,du$$

EXAMPLE 3   Evaluate the integral $\displaystyle\int_1^e \frac{1 + \ln x}{x}\,dx$.

Solution: We suggest the substitution $u = 1 + \ln x$. Then $du = (1/x)\,dx$. Also, if $x = 1$ then $u = 1$, and if $x = e$ then $u = 2$. So we have

$$\int_1^e \frac{1 + \ln x}{x}\,dx = \int_1^2 u\,du = \frac{1}{2}u^2 \Big|_1^2 = \frac{1}{2}(4 - 1) = \frac{3}{2}$$

In FMEA we present more complicated examples of integration by substitution, as well as some other techniques.

PROBLEMS FOR SECTION 9.6

1. Find the following integrals by using (1):

(a) $\displaystyle\int (x^2 + 1)^8 \, 2x\,dx$ (b) $\displaystyle\int (x + 2)^{10}\,dx$ (c) $\displaystyle\int \frac{2x - 1}{x^2 - x + 8}\,dx$

2. Find the following integrals by means of an appropriate substitution:

(a) $\displaystyle\int x(2x^2 + 3)^5\,dx$ (b) $\displaystyle\int x^2 e^{x^3 + 2}\,dx$ (c) $\displaystyle\int \frac{\ln(x + 2)}{2x + 4}\,dx$

(d) $\displaystyle\int x\sqrt{1 + x}\,dx$ (e) $\displaystyle\int \frac{x^3}{(1 + x^2)^3}\,dx$ (f) $\displaystyle\int x^5\sqrt{4 - x^3}\,dx$

3. Find the following integrals:

(a) $\displaystyle\int_0^1 x\sqrt{1 + x^2}\,dx$ (b) $\displaystyle\int_1^e \frac{\ln y}{y}\,dy$ (c) $\displaystyle\int_1^3 \frac{1}{x^2}e^{2/x}\,dx$

4. Solve the equation $\int_3^x \dfrac{2t-2}{t^2-2t}\,dt = \ln\left(\dfrac{2}{3}x - 1\right)$ for values of x satisfying $x > 2$.

5. Show that $\int_{t_0}^{t_1} S'\big(x(t)\big)\dot{x}(t)\,dt = S\big(x(t_1)\big) - S\big(x(t_0)\big)$.

HARDER PROBLEMS

6. Calculate the following integrals:

(a) $\displaystyle\int_0^1 (x^4 - x^9)(x^5 - 1)^{12}\,dx$ (b) $\displaystyle\int \dfrac{\ln x}{\sqrt{x}}\,dx$ (c) $\displaystyle\int_0^4 \dfrac{dx}{\sqrt{1+\sqrt{x}}}$

7. Calculate:

(a) $\displaystyle\int_1^4 \dfrac{e^{\sqrt{x}}}{\sqrt{x}\,(1 + e^{\sqrt{x}})}\,dx$ (b) $\displaystyle\int_0^{1/3} \dfrac{dx}{e^x + 1}$ (c) $\displaystyle\int_{8.5}^{41} \dfrac{dx}{\sqrt{2x-1} - \sqrt[4]{2x-1}}$

(*Hint:* For (b), substitute $t = e^{-x}$; for (c), substitute $z^4 = 2x - 1$.)

9.7 Infinite Intervals of Integration

In Example 9.6.1(b) we proved that

$$\int_0^a xe^{-cx^2}\,dx = \frac{1}{2c}(1 - e^{-ca^2})$$

Suppose c is a positive number and let a tend to infinity. Then the right-hand expression tends to $1/(2c)$. This makes it seem natural to write

$$\int_0^\infty xe^{-cx^2}\,dx = \frac{1}{2c}$$

In statistics and economics it is common to encounter such integrals over an infinite interval of integration.

In general, suppose f is a function that is continuous for all $x \geq a$. Then $\int_a^b f(x)\,dx$ is defined for each $b \geq a$. If the limit of this integral as $b \to \infty$ exists (and is finite), then we say that f is **integrable over** $[a, \infty)$, and define

$$\int_a^\infty f(x)\,dx = \lim_{b \to \infty} \int_a^b f(x)\,dx \tag{1}$$

The **improper integral** $\int_a^\infty f(x)\,dx$ is then said to **converge**. If the limit does *not* exist, the improper integral is said to **diverge**. If $f(x) \geq 0$ in $[a, \infty)$, we interpret the integral (1) as the *area* below the graph of f over the interval $[a, \infty)$.

Analogously, we define

$$\int_{-\infty}^{b} f(x)\,dx = \lim_{a \to -\infty} \int_{a}^{b} f(x)\,dx \tag{2}$$

when f is continuous in $(-\infty, b]$. If this limit exists, the improper integral is said to converge. Otherwise, it diverges.

EXAMPLE 1   The *exponential distribution* in statistics is defined by the density function

$$f(x) = \lambda e^{-\lambda x} \qquad (x \geq 0; \ \lambda \text{ is a positive constant})$$

Show that the area below the graph of f over $[0, \infty)$ is equal to 1. (See Fig. 1.)

Solution: For $b > 0$, the area below the graph of f over $[0, b]$ is equal to

$$\int_{0}^{b} \lambda e^{-\lambda x}\,dx = \Big|_{0}^{b} \left(-e^{-\lambda x}\right) = -e^{-\lambda b} + 1$$

As $b \to \infty$, so $-e^{-\lambda b} + 1$ approaches 1. Therefore,

$$\int_{0}^{\infty} \lambda e^{-\lambda x}\,dx = \lim_{b \to \infty} \int_{0}^{b} \lambda e^{-\lambda x}\,dx = \lim_{b \to \infty} \left(-e^{-\lambda b} + 1\right) = 1 \qquad \blacksquare$$

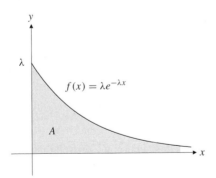

Figure 1   Area A has an unbounded base but the height decreases to 0 so rapidly that the total area is 1.

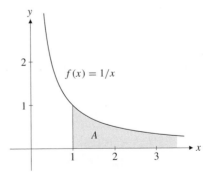

Figure 2   "$A = \int_{1}^{\infty}(1/x)\,dx = \infty$." $1/x$ does not approach 0 sufficiently fast, so the improper integral diverges.

EXAMPLE 2   For $a > 1$, show that

$$\int_{1}^{\infty} \frac{1}{x^a}\,dx = \frac{1}{a-1} \tag{$*$}$$

Then study the case $a \leq 1$.

Solution: For $a \neq 1$ and $b > 1$,

$$\int_1^b \frac{1}{x^a}\,dx = \int_1^b x^{-a}\,dx = \Big|_1^b \frac{1}{1-a}x^{1-a} = \frac{1}{1-a}(b^{1-a} - 1) \qquad (**)$$

For $a > 1$, one has $b^{1-a} = 1/b^{a-1} \to 0$ as $b \to \infty$. Hence, $(*)$ follows from $(**)$ by letting $b \to \infty$.

For $a = 1$, we have $\int_1^b (1/x)\,dx = \ln b - \ln 1 = \ln b$, which tends to ∞ as b tends to ∞, so $\int_1^\infty (1/x)\,dx$ diverges. See Fig. 2.

For $a < 1$, the last expression in $(**)$ tends to ∞ as b tends to ∞. Hence, the integral diverges in this case also.

If both limits of integration are infinite, the improper integral of a continuous function f on $(-\infty, \infty)$ is defined by

$$\int_{-\infty}^{\infty} f(x)\,dx = \int_{-\infty}^{0} f(x)\,dx + \int_0^{\infty} f(x)\,dx \qquad (3)$$

If *both* integrals on the right-hand side converge, the improper integral $\int_{-\infty}^{\infty} f(x)\,dx$ is said to *converge*; otherwise, it *diverges*. Instead of using 0 as the point of subdivision, one could use an arbitrary fixed real number c. The value assigned to the integral will always be the same, provided that the integral does converge.

It is important to note that definition (3) requires both integrals on the right-hand side to converge. Note in particular that

$$\lim_{b \to \infty} \int_{-b}^{b} f(x)\,dx \qquad (4)$$

is *not* the definition of $\int_{-\infty}^{+\infty} f(x)\,dx$. Problem 4 provides an example in which (4) exists, yet the integral in (3) diverges because $\int_{-b}^{0} f(x)\,dx \to -\infty$ as $b \to \infty$, and $\int_0^b f(x)\,dx \to \infty$ as $b \to \infty$. So (4) is not an acceptable definition, whereas (3) is.

EXAMPLE 3   For $c > 0$, prove that the following integral converges, and find its value:

$$\int_{-\infty}^{+\infty} xe^{-cx^2}\,dx$$

Solution: In the introduction to this section we proved that $\int_0^{\infty} xe^{-cx^2}\,dx = 1/2c$. In the same way we see that

$$\int_{-\infty}^{0} xe^{-cx^2}\,dx = \lim_{a \to -\infty} \int_a^0 xe^{-cx^2}\,dx = \lim_{a \to -\infty} \Big|_a^0 -\frac{1}{2c}e^{-cx^2} = -\frac{1}{2c}$$

It follows that

$$\int_{-\infty}^{\infty} xe^{-cx^2}\,dx = -\frac{1}{2c} + \frac{1}{2c} = 0 \qquad (c > 0) \qquad (**)$$

In fact, the function $f(x) = xe^{-cx^2}$ satisfies $f(-x) = -f(x)$ for all x, and so its graph is symmetric about the origin. For this reason, the integral $\int_{-\infty}^{0} xe^{-cx^2}\,dx$ must also exist and be equal to $-1/2c$. (This result is very important in statistics. See Problem 12.)

Integrals of Unbounded Functions

We turn next to improper integrals where the *integrand* is not bounded. Consider first the function $f(x) = 1/\sqrt{x}$, with $x \in (0, 2]$. (See Fig. 3.)

Figure 3 As $h \to 0$ the shaded area becomes unbounded, but the graph of f approaches the y-axis so quickly that the total area is finite.

Note that $f(x) \to \infty$ as $x \to 0^+$. The function f is continuous in the interval $[h, 2]$ for any fixed number h in $(0, 2)$. Therefore, the definite integral of f over the interval $[h, 2]$ exists, and

$$\int_h^2 \frac{1}{\sqrt{x}}\, dx = \Big|_h^2 2\sqrt{x} = 2\sqrt{2} - 2\sqrt{h}$$

The limit of this expression as $h \to 0^+$ is $2\sqrt{2}$. Then, by definition,

$$\int_0^2 \frac{1}{\sqrt{x}}\, dx = 2\sqrt{2}$$

The improper integral is said to converge in this case, and the area below the graph of f over the interval $(0, 2]$ is $2\sqrt{2}$. The area of $1/\sqrt{x}$ over the interval $(h, 2]$ is shown in Fig. 3.

More generally, suppose that f is a continuous function in the interval $(a, b]$, but $f(x)$ is not defined at $x = a$. Then we can define

$$\int_a^b f(x)\, dx = \lim_{h \to 0^+} \int_{a+h}^b f(x)\, dx \tag{5}$$

if the limit exists, and the improper integral of f is said to **converge** in this case. If $f(x) \geq 0$ in $(a, b]$, we identify the integral as the *area under the graph* of f over the interval $(a, b]$.

In the same way, if f is not defined at b, we can define

$$\int_a^b f(x)\, dx = \lim_{h \to 0^+} \int_a^{b-h} f(x)\, dx \tag{6}$$

if the limit exists, in which case the improper integral of f is said to **converge**.

Suppose f is continuous in (a, b). We may not even have f defined at a or b. For instance, suppose $f(x) \to -\infty$ as $x \to a^+$ and $f(x) \to +\infty$ as $x \to b^-$. In this case, f is said to be **integrable** in (a, b), and we can define

$$\int_a^b f(x)\,dx = \int_a^c f(x)\,dx + \int_c^b f(x)\,dx \tag{7}$$

provided that both integrals on the right-hand side of (7) converge. Here c is an arbitrary fixed number in (a, b), and neither the convergence of the integral nor its value depends on the choice of c. If either of the integrals on the right-hand side of (7) does not converge, the left-hand side is not well defined.

A Comparison Test for Convergence

The following convergence test for integrals is frequently useful because it does not require evaluation of the integral.

THEOREM 9.7.1 (A COMPARISON TEST FOR CONVERGENCE)

Suppose that f and g are continuous for all $x \geq a$ and

$$|f(x)| \leq g(x) \qquad \text{(for all } x \geq a)$$

If $\int_a^\infty g(x)\,dx$ converges, then $\int_a^\infty f(x)\,dx$ converges, and

$$\left| \int_a^\infty f(x)\,dx \right| \leq \int_a^\infty g(x)\,dx$$

Considering the case in which $f(x) \geq 0$, Theorem 9.7.1 can be interpreted as follows: If the area below the graph of g is finite, then the area below the graph of f is finite as well, because at no point in $[a, \infty)$ does the graph of f lie above the graph of g. (Draw a figure.) This result seems quite plausible and we shall not give an analytical proof. A corresponding theorem holds for the case where the lower limit of integration is $-\infty$. Also, similar comparison tests can be proved for unbounded functions defined on bounded intervals.

EXAMPLE 4   Integrals of the form

$$\int_{t_0}^\infty U\big(c(t)\big)e^{-\alpha t}\,dt \tag{*}$$

often appear in economic growth theory. Here $c(t)$ denotes consumption at time t, U is an instantaneous utility function, and α is a positive discount rate. Suppose that there exist numbers M and β, with $\beta < \alpha$, such that

$$|U\big(c(t)\big)| \leq M e^{\beta t} \tag{**}$$

for all $t \geq t_0$ and for each possible consumption level $c(t)$ at time t. Thus, the absolute value of the utility of consumption is growing at a rate less than the discount rate α. Prove that then (*) converges.

Solution: From (∗∗), we have $|U(c(t))e^{-\alpha t}| \le Me^{-(\alpha-\beta)t}$ for all $t \ge t_0$. Moreover,

$$\int_{t_0}^T Me^{-(\alpha-\beta)t}\,dt = \Big|_{t_0}^T \frac{-M}{\alpha-\beta}e^{-(\alpha-\beta)t} = \frac{M}{\alpha-\beta}\left[e^{-(\alpha-\beta)t_0} - e^{-(\alpha-\beta)T}\right]$$

Because $\alpha - \beta > 0$, the last expression tends to

$$[M/(\alpha-\beta)]\,e^{-(\alpha-\beta)t_0} \qquad \text{as} \quad T \to \infty$$

From Theorem 9.7.1 it follows that (∗) converges.

EXAMPLE 5   The function $f(x) = e^{-x^2}$ is extremely important in statistics. When multiplied by a suitable constant (actually $1/\sqrt{\pi}$) it is the density function associated with a *Gaussian*, or *normal*, distribution. We want to show that the improper integral

$$\int_{-\infty}^{+\infty} e^{-x^2}\,dx \qquad (*)$$

converges. Recall from Section 9.1 that the indefinite integral of $f(x) = e^{-x^2}$ cannot be expressed in terms of "elementary" functions. Because $f(x) = e^{-x^2}$ is symmetric about the y-axis, it suffices to prove that $\int_0^\infty e^{-x^2}\,dx$ converges. To show this, subdivide the interval of integration so that

$$\int_0^\infty e^{-x^2}\,dx = \int_0^1 e^{-x^2}\,dx + \int_1^\infty e^{-x^2}\,dx \qquad (**)$$

Of course, $\int_0^1 e^{-x^2}\,dx$ presents no problem because it is the integral of a continuous function over a bounded interval. For $x \ge 1$, one has $x^2 \ge x$ and so $0 \le e^{-x^2} \le e^{-x}$. Now $\int_1^\infty e^{-x}\,dx$ converges (to $1/e$), so according to Theorem 9.7.1, the integral $\int_1^\infty e^{-x^2}\,dx$ must also converge. From (∗∗), it follows that $\int_0^\infty e^{-x^2}\,dx$ converges. Thus, the integral (∗) does converge, but we have not found its value. In fact, more advanced techniques of integration are used in FMEA to show that

$$\int_{-\infty}^{+\infty} e^{-x^2}\,dx = \sqrt{\pi} \qquad (8)$$

PROBLEMS FOR SECTION 9.7

1. Determine the following integrals, if they converge. Indicate those that diverge.

   (a) $\displaystyle\int_1^\infty \frac{1}{x^3}\,dx$ (b) $\displaystyle\int_1^\infty \frac{1}{\sqrt{x}}\,dx$ (c) $\displaystyle\int_{-\infty}^0 e^x\,dx$ (d) $\displaystyle\int_0^a \frac{x\,dx}{\sqrt{a^2-x^2}}$ $(a > 0)$

2. Define f for all x by $f(x) = 1/(b-a)$ for $x \in [a, b]$, and $f(x) = 0$ for $x \notin [a, b]$, where $b > a$. (In statistics, f is the density function of the *uniform* (or *rectangular*) *distribution* on the interval $[a, b]$.) Find the following:

   (a) $\displaystyle\int_{-\infty}^{+\infty} f(x)\,dx$ (b) $\displaystyle\int_{-\infty}^{+\infty} xf(x)\,dx$ (c) $\displaystyle\int_{-\infty}^{+\infty} x^2 f(x)\,dx$

3. In connection with Example 1, find the following:

(a) $\displaystyle\int_0^\infty x\lambda e^{-\lambda x}\,dx$ (b) $\displaystyle\int_0^\infty (x-1/\lambda)^2 \lambda e^{-\lambda x}\,dx$ (c) $\displaystyle\int_0^\infty (x-1/\lambda)^3 \lambda e^{-\lambda x}\,dx$

(The three numbers you obtain are called respectively the *expectation*, the *variance*, and the *third central moment* of the exponential distribution.)

4. Prove that $\int_{-\infty}^{+\infty} x/(1+x^2)\,dx$ diverges, but that $\lim_{b\to\infty}\int_{-b}^{b} x/(1+x^2)\,dx$ converges.

5. The function f is defined by for $x>0$ by $f(x)=(\ln x)/x^3$.

   (a) Find the maximum and minimum points of f, if there are any.

   (b) Examine the convergence of $\int_0^1 f(x)\,dx$ and $\int_1^\infty f(x)\,dx$.

6. Use Theorem 9.7.1 to prove the convergence of $\displaystyle\int_1^\infty \frac{1}{1+x^2}\,dx$.

7. Show that $\displaystyle\int_{-2}^3 \left(\frac{1}{\sqrt{x+2}}+\frac{1}{\sqrt{3-x}}\right)dx = 4\sqrt{5}$

8. R. E. Hall and D. W. Jorgenson, in their article on "Tax Policy and Investment Behavior," use the integral

$$z = \int_0^\infty e^{-rs} D(s)\,ds$$

to represent the present discounted value, at interest rate r, of the time-dependent stream of depreciation allowances $D(s)$ $(0 \le s < \infty)$. Find z as a function of τ in the following cases:

   (a) $D(s) = 1/\tau$ for $0 \le s \le \tau$, $D(s) = 0$ for $s > \tau$. (Constant depreciation over τ years.)

   (b) $D(s) = 2(\tau - s)/\tau^2$ for $0 \le s \le \tau$, $D(s) = 0$ for $s > \tau$. (Straight-line depreciation.)

9. Suppose you evaluate $\int_{-1}^{+1}(1/x^2)\,dx$ by using the definition of the definite integral without thinking carefully. Show that you get a negative answer even though the integrand is never negative. What has gone wrong?

10. Prove that the integral $\displaystyle\int_0^1 \frac{\ln x}{\sqrt{x}}\,dx$ converges and find its value.

HARDER PROBLEMS

11. Find the integral

$$I_k = \int_1^\infty \left(\frac{k}{x} - \frac{k^2}{1+kx}\right)dx \qquad (k \text{ is a positive constant})$$

Find the limit of I_k as $k \to \infty$, if it exists.

12. In statistics, the normal, or Gaussian, density function with mean μ and variance σ^2 is defined by

$$f(x) = \frac{1}{\sigma\sqrt{2\pi}} \exp\left[-(x - \mu)^2/2\sigma^2\right]$$

in the interval $(-\infty, \infty)$.[4] Prove that

(a) $\displaystyle\int_{-\infty}^{+\infty} f(x)\,dx = 1$ (b) $\displaystyle\int_{-\infty}^{+\infty} xf(x)\,dx = \mu$ (c) $\displaystyle\int_{-\infty}^{+\infty} x^2 f(x)\,dx = \sigma^2 + \mu^2$

(*Hint:* Use the substitution $u = (x - \mu)/\sqrt{2}\sigma$, together with (8) and the result in Example 3.)

9.8 A Glimpse at Differential Equations

In economic growth theory, in studies of the extraction of natural resources, in many models in environmental economics, and in several other areas of economics, one encounters equations where the unknowns are functions, and where the derivatives of these functions also appear. One such simple equation has already been presented — see (9.4.1). Equations of this general type are called **differential equations**, and their study is one of the most fascinating fields of mathematics, with many important applications. Here we shall consider only a few simple types of such equation. We denote the independent variable by t, because most of the differential equations in economics have time as the independent variable.

We have already solved the simplest type of differential equation: Let $f(t)$ be a given function. Find all functions that have $f(t)$ as their derivative—that is, functions which solve $\dot{x}(t) = f(t)$ for $x(t)$. (Recall that $\dot{x}$ denotes the derivative of x w.r.t. time t.) We already know that the answer is an indefinite integral:

$$\dot{x}(t) = f(t) \iff x(t) = \int f(t)\,dt + C$$

We call $x(t) = \int f(t)\,dt + C$ the *general* solution of the equation $\dot{x}(t) = f(t)$.

Consider next some more interesting types of differential equation.

The Law for Natural Growth

Let $x(t)$ denote an economic quantity such as the national output of China. The ratio $\dot{x}(t)/x(t)$ has previously been called the *relative rate of change* of this quantity. Several economic models postulate that the relative rate of change is approximately a constant, r. Thus,

$$\dot{x}(t) = rx(t) \qquad \text{for all} \quad t \tag{1}$$

---

[4] This function, its bell-shaped graph, and a portrait of its inventor Carl Friedrich Gauss (1777–1855), appear on the German 10-mark bank note that circulated between 1989 and 2001.

Which functions have a constant relative rate of change? For $r = 1$ the differential equation is $\dot{x} = x$, and we know that the derivative of $x = e^t$ is again $\dot{x} = e^t$. More generally, the function $x = Ae^t$ satisfies the equation $\dot{x} = x$ for all values of the constant A. By trial and error you will probably be able to come up with $x(t) = Ae^{rt}$ as a solution of (1). In any case, it is easy to verify: If $x = Ae^{rt}$, then $\dot{x}(t) = Are^{rt} = rx(t)$. Moreover, we can prove that no other function satisfies (1): Indeed, multiply equation (1) by the positive function e^{-rt} and collect all terms on the left-hand side. This gives

$$\dot{x}(t)e^{-rt} - rx(t)e^{-rt} = 0 \qquad \text{for all} \quad t \tag{2}$$

Equation (2) must have precisely the same solutions as (1). But the left-hand side of this equation is the derivative of the product $x(t)e^{-rt}$. So equation (2) can be rewritten as $\frac{d}{dt}[x(t)e^{-rt}] = 0$. It follows that $x(t)e^{-rt}$ must equal a constant A. Hence, $x(t) = Ae^{rt}$. If the value of $x(t)$ at $t = 0$ is x_0, then $x_0 = Ae^0 = A$. We conclude that

$$\dot{x}(t) = rx(t), \ x(0) = x_0 \iff x(t) = x_0 e^{rt} \tag{3}$$

Another way to solve (1) is to take logarithms. In fact $\frac{d}{dt}(\ln x) = \dot{x}/x = r$, so $\ln x(t) = \int r \, dt = rt + C$, and so $x(t) = e^{rt+C} = e^{rt}e^C = Ae^{rt}$, where $A = e^C$.

EXAMPLE 1   Let $S(t)$ denote the sales volume of a particular commodity per unit of time, evaluated at time t. In a stable market where no sales promotion is carried out, the decrease in $S(t)$ per unit of time is proportional to $S(t)$. Thus sales decelerate at the constant proportional rate $a > 0$, implying that

$$\dot{S}(t) = -aS(t)$$

(a) Find an expression for $S(t)$ when sales at time 0 are S_0.

(b) Solve the equation $S_0 e^{-at} = \frac{1}{2} S_0$ for t. Interpret the answer.

Solution:

(a) This is an equation of type (1) with $x = S$ and $r = -a$. According to (3), the solution is $S(t) = S_0 e^{-at}$.

(b) From $S_0 e^{-at} = \frac{1}{2} S_0$, we obtain $e^{-at} = \frac{1}{2}$. Taking the natural logarithm of each side yields $-at = \ln(1/2) = -\ln 2$. Hence $t = \ln 2/a$. This is the time it takes before sales fall to half their initial level.

Equation (1) is called the **law for natural growth**, and it is probably the most important differential equation that economists have to know.

Suppose that $x(t)$ denotes the number of individuals in a population at time t. The population could be, for instance, a particular colony of bacteria, or polar bears in the Arctic. We call $\dot{x}(t)/x(t)$ the *per capita growth rate* of the population. If there is neither immigration nor emigration, then the per capita rate of increase will be equal to the difference between the per capita birth and death rates. These rates will depend on many factors such as food supply, age distribution, available living space, predators, disease, and parasites, among other things.

Equation (1) specifies a simple model of population growth, the so-called **Malthus's law**. According to (3), if the per capita growth rate is constant, then the population must grow exponentially. In reality, of course, exponential growth can go on only for a limited time. Let us consider some alternative models for population growth.

Growth Towards an Upper Limit

Suppose the population size $x(t)$ cannot exceed some carrying capacity K, and that the rate of change of population is proportional to its deviation from this carrying capacity:

$$\dot{x}(t) = a(K - x(t)) \qquad (*)$$

With a little trick, it is easy to find all the solutions to this equation. Define a new function $u(t) = K - x(t)$, which at each time measures the deviation of the population size from the carrying capacity K. Then $\dot{u}(t) = -\dot{x}(t)$. Inserting this into $(*)$ gives $-\dot{u}(t) = au(t)$, or $\dot{u}(t) = -au(t)$. This is an equation like (1). The solution is $u(t) = Ae^{-at}$, so that $K - x(t) = Ae^{-at}$, hence $x(t) = K - Ae^{-at}$. If $x(0) = x_0$, then $x_0 = K - A$, and so $A = K - x_0$. It follows that

$$\dot{x}(t) = a(K - x(t)), \ x(0) = x_0 \iff x(t) = K - (K - x_0)e^{-at} \qquad (4)$$

In Problem 4 we shall see that the same equation can describe the growth of population in countries where the indigenous population has a fixed relative rate of growth, but where there is immigration each year. The same equation results from several other phenomena, some of which are discussed in the problems section.

EXAMPLE 2   Suppose that a population has a carrying capacity of $K = 200$ (millions) and that at time $t = 0$ there are 50 (millions). Let $x(t)$ denote the population at time t. Suppose that $a = 0.05$ and find the solution of equation $(*)$ in this case. Sketch a graph of the solution.

Solution: Using (4) we find that

$$x(t) = 200 - (200 - 50)e^{-0.05t} = 200 - 150e^{-0.05t}$$

The graph is drawn in Fig. 1.

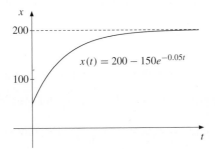

Figure 1 Growth to level 200

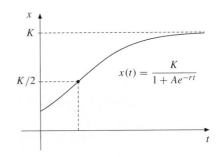

Figure 2 Logistic growth to level K

Logistic Growth

Instead of the differential equation (∗), a more realistic assumption is that the relative rate of increase is approximately constant while the population is small, but that it converges to zero as the population converges to its carrying capacity K. A special form of this assumption is expressed by the equation

$$\dot{x}(t) = rx(t)\left(1 - \frac{x(t)}{K}\right) \tag{5}$$

Indeed, when the population $x(t)$ is small in proportion to K, so that $x(t)/K$ is small, then $\dot{x}(t) \approx rx(t)$, and $x(t)$ increases (approximately) exponentially. As $x(t)$ becomes larger, however, the factor $1 - x(t)/K$ increases in significance. In general, we claim that if $x(t)$ satisfies (5) (and is not identically equal to 0), then $x(t)$ must have the form

$$x(t) = \frac{K}{1 + Ae^{-rt}} \qquad \text{for some constant } A \tag{6}$$

The function x given in (6) is called a **logistic function**.

Proof of (6): We use a little trick. Suppose that $x = x(t)$ is not 0 and introduce as a new variable $u = u(t) = -1 + K/x$. Then $\dot{u} = -K\dot{x}/x^2 = -Kr/x + r = -r(-1 + K/x) = -ru$. Hence $u = u(t) = Ae^{-rt}$ for some constant A. But then $-1 + K/x(t) = Ae^{-rt}$, and solving this equation for $x(t)$ yields (6). ∎

If there are x_0 individuals at time $t = 0$, and thus $x(0) = x_0$, then (6) gives $x_0 = K/(1+A)$, so that $A = (K - x_0)/x_0$. All in all, we have shown that

$$\dot{x}(t) = rx(t)\left(1 - \frac{x(t)}{K}\right), \quad x(0) = x_0 \iff x(t) = \frac{K}{1 + \dfrac{K - x_0}{x_0}e^{-rt}} \tag{7}$$

If $0 < x_0 < K$, it follows from (7) that $x(t)$ is strictly increasing and that $x(t) \to K$ as $t \to \infty$ (assuming $r > 0$). We say in this case that there is *logistic growth* to the level K. The graph of the solution is shown in Fig. 2. It has an inflection point at the height $K/2$ above the t-axis. We verify this by differentiating (5) w.r.t. t. Thus $\ddot{x} = r\dot{x}(1 - x/K) + rx(-\dot{x}/K) = r\dot{x}(1 - 2x/K) = 0$ when $x = K/2$, so $\ddot{x}$ changes sign at this point.

Equations of type (5), and hence logistic functions of the form (6), appear in many economic models. Some of them are discussed in the problems.

The simple differential equations studied here are so important that we present them and their general solutions in a form which makes it easier to see their structure. As is often done in the theory of differential equations, we suppress the symbol for time dependence.

$$\dot{x} = ax \quad \text{for all } t \iff x = Ae^{at} \quad \text{for some constant } A \tag{8}$$

$$\dot{x} + ax = b \quad \text{for all } t \iff x = Ae^{-at} + \frac{b}{a} \quad \text{for some constant } A \tag{9}$$

$$\dot{x} + ax = bx^2 \quad \text{for all } t \iff x = \frac{a}{b - Ae^{at}} \quad \text{for some constant } A \tag{10}$$

(In (9) we must assume that $a \neq 0$. In (10) the function $x(t) \equiv 0$ is also a solution.)

1. Which of the following functions have a constant relative rate of increase, $\dot{x}/x$?

   (a) $x = 5t + 10$ (b) $x = \ln(t + 1)$ (c) $x = 5e^t$

   (d) $x = -3 \cdot 2^t$ (e) $x = e^{t^2}$ (f) $x = e^t + e^{-t}$

2. Suppose that a firm's capital stock $K(t)$ satisfies the differential equation

$$\dot{K}(t) = I - \delta K(t)$$

   where investment I is constant, and $\delta K(t)$ denotes depreciation, with δ a positive constant.

   (a) Find the solution of the equation if the capital stock at time $t = 0$ is K_0.

   (b) Let $\delta = 0.05$ and $I = 10$. Explain what happens when (i) $K_0 = 150$ and (ii) $K_0 = 250$.

3. Let $N(t)$ denote the number of people in a country whose homes have a telephone service. Suppose that the rate at which new people get access to a telephone service is proportional to the number of people who still have no access. If the population size is P, the differential equation for $N(t)$ is then

$$\dot{N}(t) = k(P - N(t))$$

   where k is a positive constant. Find the solution of this equation if $N(0) = 0$. Then find the limit of $N(t)$ as $t \to \infty$.

4. A country's annual natural rate of population growth (births minus deaths) is 2%. In addition there is a net immigration of 40 000 persons per year. Write down a differential equation for the function $N(t)$ which denotes the number of persons in the country at time t (year). Suppose that the population at time $t = 0$ is 2 000 000. Find $N(t)$.

5. Let $P(t)$ denote Europe's population in millions t years after 1960. According to UN estimates, $P(0) = 641$ and $P(10) = 705$. Suppose that $P(t)$ grows exponentially, with $P(t) = 641e^{kt}$. Compute k and then find $P(15)$ and $P(40)$ (estimates of the population in 1975 and in 2000).

6. When a colony of bacteria is subjected to strong ultraviolet light, they die as their DNA is destroyed. In a laboratory experiment it was found that the number of living bacteria decreased approximately exponentially with the length of time they were exposed to ultraviolet light. Suppose that 70.5% of the bacteria still survive after 7 seconds of exposure. What percentage will be alive after 30 seconds? How long does it take to kill 95% of the bacteria?

7. Solve the following differential equations by using one of (8)–(10):

(a) $\dot{x} = -0.5x$ (b) $\dot{K} = 0.02K$ (c) $\dot{x} = -0.5x + 5$

(d) $\dot{K} - 0.2K = 100$ (e) $\dot{x} + 0.1x = 3x^2$ (f) $\dot{K} = K(-1 + 2K)$

8. A study of tractors in British agriculture from 1950 onwards estimated that the number y in use (measured in thousands) was a function of t (measured in years, so that $t = 0$ corresponds to 1950) given by

$$y = 250.9 + \frac{228.46}{1 + 8.11625e^{-0.340416t}}$$

(a) Find the number of tractors in 1950. How many tractors were added in the decade up to 1960?

(b) Find the limit of y as $t \to \infty$, and draw the graph.

9. The number $N(t)$ of persons who develop influenza t days after all members of a group of 1000 people have been in contact with a carrier of infection is given by

$$N(t) = \frac{1000}{1 + 999e^{-0.39t}}$$

(a) How many develop influenza after 20 days?

(b) How many days does it take until 800 are sick?

(c) Will all 1000 people eventually get influenza?

HARDER PROBLEMS

10. According to *Newton's law of cooling*, the rate at which a warm object cools is proportional to the difference between the temperature of the object and the temperature of its surroundings. If the temperature of the object at time t is equal to $T(t)$ and (the constant) temperature of the surroundings is C, then $\dot{T}(t) = k(C - T(t))$. Note that this is an equation of the type given in (4). At 12 noon, the police enter a room and discover a dead body. Immediately they measure its temperature, which is 35 degrees (Centigrade). At 1 pm they take the temperature again, which is now 32 degrees. The temperature in the room is 20 degrees. When did the person die? (*Hint:* Let the temperature be $T(t)$, where t is measured in hours and 12 noon corresponds to $t = 0$.)

REVIEW PROBLEMS FOR CHAPTER 9

1. Find the following integrals:

(a) $\int (-16)\, dx$ (b) $\int 5^5\, dx$ (c) $\int (3 - y)\, dy$ (d) $\int (r - 4r^{1/4})\, dr$

(e) $\int x^8\, dx$ (f) $\int x^2 \sqrt{x}\, dx$ (g) $\int \frac{1}{p^5}\, dp$ (h) $\int (x^3 + x)\, dx$

2. Find the following integrals:

(a) $\displaystyle\int 2e^{2x}\,dx$ (b) $\displaystyle\int (x - 5e^{\frac{2}{5}x})\,dx$ (c) $\displaystyle\int (e^{-3x} + e^{3x})\,dx$ (d) $\displaystyle\int \frac{2}{x+5}\,dx$

3. Evaluate the following integrals:

(a) $\displaystyle\int_0^{12} 50\,dx$ (b) $\displaystyle\int_0^2 (x - \frac{1}{2}x^2)\,dx$ (c) $\displaystyle\int_{-3}^3 (u + 1)^2\,du$

(d) $\displaystyle\int_1^5 \frac{2}{z}\,dz$ (e) $\displaystyle\int_2^{12} \frac{3\,dt}{t+4}\,dt$ (f) $\displaystyle\int_0^4 v\sqrt{v^2 + 9}\,dv$

4. Find the following integrals:

(a) $\displaystyle\int_1^\infty \frac{5}{x^5}\,dx$ (b) $\displaystyle\int_0^1 x^3(1 + x^4)^4\,dx$ (c) $\displaystyle\int_0^\infty \frac{-5t}{e^t}\,dt$

(d) $\displaystyle\int_1^e (\ln x)^2\,dx$ (e) $\displaystyle\int_0^2 x^2\sqrt{x^3 + 1}\,dx$ (f) $\displaystyle\int_{-\infty}^0 \frac{e^{3z}}{e^{3z} + 5}\,dz$

5. Find the following integrals:

(a) $\displaystyle\int_0^{25} \frac{1}{9 + \sqrt{x}}\,dx$ (b) $\displaystyle\int_2^7 t\sqrt{t + 2}\,dt$ (c) $\displaystyle\int_0^1 57x^2\sqrt[3]{19x^3 + 8}\,dx$

6. Find $F'(x)$ if $F(x) = \displaystyle\int_4^x \left(\sqrt{u} + \frac{x}{\sqrt{u}}\right)du$.

7. With $C(Y)$ as the consumption function, suppose the marginal propensity to consume is $C'(Y) = 0.69$, with $C(0) = 1000$. Find $C(Y)$.

8. In the manufacture of a product, the marginal cost of producing x units is $C'(x) = \alpha e^{\beta x} + \gamma$, with $\beta \neq 0$, and fixed costs are C_0. Find the total cost function $C(x)$

9. Suppose that the demand curve is $f(Q) = 100 - 0.05Q$ and the supply curve is $g(Q) = 10 + 0.1Q$. Find the equilibrium price and quantity. Then calculate the consumer and producer surplus.

10. Suppose that the demand curve is $f(Q) = 50/(Q+5)$ and the supply curve is $g(Q) = 4.5 + 0.1Q$. Find the equilibrium price and quantity. Then calculate the consumer and producer surplus.

11. (a) Define f for $t > 0$ by $f(t) = 4\dfrac{(\ln t)^2}{t}$. Find $f'(t)$ and $f''(t)$.

(b) Find possible local extreme points, and sketch the graph of f.

(c) Calculate the area below the graph of f over the interval $[1, e^2]$.

12. Solve the following differential equations:

(a) $\dot{x} = -3x$ (b) $\dot{x} + 4x = 12$ (c) $\dot{x} - 3x = 12x^2$

(d) $5\dot{x} = -x$ (e) $3\dot{x} + 6x = 10$ (f) $\dot{x} - \frac{1}{2}x = x^2$

13. (a) Let $V(x)$ denote the number of litres of fuel left in an aircraft's fuel tank if it has flown x km. Suppose that $V(x)$ satisfies the following differential equation:

$$V'(x) = -aV(x) - b$$

(The fuel consumption per km is a constant $b > 0$. The term $-aV(x)$, with $a > 0$, is due to the weight of the fuel.) Find the solution of the equation with $V(0) = V_0$.

(b) How many km, x^*, can the plane fly if it takes off with V_0 litres in its tank? What is the minimum number of litres, V_m, needed at the outset if the plane is to fly $\hat{x}$ km? Put $b = 8$, $a = 0.001$, $V_0 = 12\,000$, and $\hat{x} = 1200$. Find x^* and V_m in this case.

14. Suppose $Y = Y(t)$ is national product, $C(t)$ is consumption at time t, and $\bar{I}$ is investment, which is constant. Suppose $\dot{Y} = \alpha(C + \bar{I} - Y)$ and $C = aY + b$, where a, b, and α are constants with $0 < a < 1$.

(a) Derive a differential equation for Y.

(b) Find its solution with $Y(0) = Y_0$ is given.

15. A probability density function f is defined for all x by

$$f(x) = \frac{\lambda a e^{-\lambda x}}{(e^{-\lambda x} + a)^2} \qquad (a \text{ and } \lambda \text{ are positive constants})$$

(a) Show that $F(x) = \dfrac{a}{e^{-\lambda x} + a}$ is an indefinite integral of $f(x)$, and determine $\lim_{x \to \infty} F(x)$ and $\lim_{x \to -\infty} F(x)$.

(b) Show that $\int_{-\infty}^{x} f(t)\, dt = F(x)$, and that $F(x)$ is strictly increasing.

(c) Compute $F''(x)$ and show that F has an inflection point x_0. Compute $F(x_0)$ and sketch the graph of F.

(d) Compute $\int_{-\infty}^{\infty} f(x)\, dx$.

10

INTEREST RATES AND PRESENT VALUES

*Then you ought to have invested
my money with the bankers,
and at my coming I should have
received what was mine with interest.*
—Matthew 25:27

This chapter treats some basic topics in the mathematics of finance. The main concern is how the values of investments and loans at different times are affected by interest rates.

Sections 1.2 and 4.9 have already discussed some elementary calculations involving interest rates. This chapter goes a step further and considers different interest periods. It also discusses effective rates of interest, continuously compounded interest, present values of future claims, annuities, mortgages, and the internal rate of return on investment projects. The calculations involve the summation formula for geometric series, which we therefore derive.

10.1 Interest Periods and Effective Rates

In advertisements that offer bank loans or savings accounts, interest is usually quoted as an *annual rate*, also called a *nominal rate*, even if the actual interest period is different. This **interest period** is the time which elapses between successive dates when interest is added to the account. For some bank accounts the interest period is one year, but recently it has become increasingly common for financial institutions to offer other interest schemes. For instance, many U.S. bank accounts now add interest daily, some others at least monthly. If a bank offers 9% annual rate of interest with interest payments each month, then $(1/12)9\% = 0.75\%$ of the capital accrues at the end of each month. The annual rate must be divided by the number of interest periods to get the **periodic rate**—that is, the interest per period.

Suppose a principal (or capital) of S_0 yields interest at the rate $p\%$ per period (for example one year). As explained in Section 1.2, after t periods it will have increased to the amount

$$S_t = S_0(1 + r)^t \qquad \text{where} \quad r = p/100$$

Each period the principal increases by the factor $1 + r$. Note that $p\%$ means $p/100$, and we say that "the interest is $p\%$" or that "the interest rate is r".

The formula requires the interest to be added to the principal at the end of each period. Suppose that the annual interest is $p\%$, but that we are offered biannual interest payments at the rate $p/2\%$. Then the principal after half a year will have increased to

$$S_0 + S_0 \frac{p/2}{100} = S_0\left(1 + \frac{r}{2}\right)$$

Each half year the principal increases by the factor $1 + r/2$. After 2 periods (= one year) it will have increased to $S_0(1 + r/2)^2$, and after t years it will have increased to

$$S_0\left(1 + \frac{r}{2}\right)^{2t}$$

Note that a biannual interest payment at the rate $\frac{1}{2}r$ is better for a lender than an annual interest payment at the rate r. This follows from the fact that $(1 + r/2)^2 = 1 + r + r^2/4 > 1 + r$.

More generally, suppose that interest at the rate $p/n\%$ is added to the principal at n different times distributed more or less evenly over the year. For example, $n = 4$ if interest is added quarterly, $n = 12$ if it is added monthly, etc. Then the *principal will be multiplied by a factor* $(1 + r/n)^n$ *each year*. After t years, the principal will have increased to

$$S_0\left(1 + \frac{r}{n}\right)^{nt} \tag{1}$$

The greater is n, the faster interest accrues to the lender. (See Problem 10.2.6.)

EXAMPLE 1   A deposit of £5000 is put into an account earning interest at the annual rate of 9%, with interest paid quarterly. How much will there be in the account after 8 years?

Solution: The periodic rate r/n is $0.09/4 = 0.0225$ and the number of periods nt is $4 \cdot 8 = 32$, so formula (1) gives:

$$5000(1 + 0.0225)^{32} \approx 10\,190.52$$

EXAMPLE 2   How long will it take for the £5000 in Example 1 (with annual interest rate 9% and interest paid quarterly) to increase to £15 000?

Solution: After t quarterly periods the account will increase to $5000(1 + 0.0225)^t$. So

$$5000(1 + 0.0225)^t = 15\,000 \quad \text{or} \quad 1.0225^t = 3$$

To find t we take the natural logarithm of each side:

$$t \ln 1.0225 = \ln 3 \quad \text{(because } \ln a^p = p \ln a\text{)}$$

$$t = \frac{\ln 3}{\ln 1.0225} \approx 49.37$$

Thus it takes approximately 49.37 quarterly periods, that is approximately 12 years and four months, before the account has increased to £15 000.

Effective Rate of Interest

A consumer who needs a loan may be faced with several offers from competing financial institutions. It is therefore important to know how to compare various offers. The concept of *effective interest rate* is often used in making such comparisons.

Consider a loan which implies an annual interest rate of 9% with interest at the rate 0.75% added 12 times a year. If no interest is paid in the meantime, after one year an initial principal of S_0 will have grown to a debt of $S_0(1+0.09/12)^{12} \approx S_0 \cdot 1.094$. In fact, as long as no interest is paid, the debt will grow at a constant proportional rate that is (approximately) 9.4 % per year. For this reason, we call 9.4% the effective yearly rate. More generally:

EFFECTIVE YEARLY RATE

When interest is added n times during the year at the rate r/n per period, then the effective yearly rate R is defined as

$$R = \left(1 + \frac{r}{n}\right)^n - 1$$

(2)

The effective yearly rate is independent of the amount S_0. For a given value of $r > 0$, it is increasing in n. (See Problem 10.2.5.)

EXAMPLE 3   What is the effective yearly rate R corresponding to an annual interest rate of 9% with interest compounded: (i) each quarter; (ii) each month?

Solution:

(i) Applying formula (2) with $r = 0.09$ and $n = 4$, the effective rate is

$$R = \left(1 + 0.09/4\right)^4 - 1 = (1 + 0.0225)^4 - 1 \approx 0.0931 \quad \text{or} \quad 9.31\%$$

(ii) In this case $r = 0.09$ and $n = 12$, so the effective rate is

$$R = \left(1 + 0.09/12\right)^{12} - 1 = (1 + 0.0075)^{12} - 1 \approx 0.0938 \quad \text{or} \quad 9.38\%$$

A typical case in which we can use the effective rate of interest to compare different financial offers is the following.

EXAMPLE 4   When investing in a savings account, which of the following offers are better: 5.9% with interest paid quarterly; or 6% with interest paid twice a year?

Solution: According to (2), the effective rates for the two offers are

$$R = \left(1 + 0.059/4\right)^4 - 1 \approx 0.0603, \qquad R = \left(1 + 0.06/2\right)^2 - 1 = 0.0609$$

The second offer is therefore better for the saver.

NOTE 1 In many countries there is an official legal definition of effective interest rate which takes into account different forms of fixed or "closing" costs incurred when initiating a loan. The effective rate of interest is then defined as the rate which implies that the combined present value of all the costs is equal to the size of the loan. This is the internal rate of return, as defined in Section 10.7. (Present values are discussed in Section 10.3.)

PROBLEMS FOR SECTION 10.1

1. (a) What will be the size of an account after 5 years if $8000 is invested at an annual interest rate of 5% compounded (i) monthly; (ii) daily (with 365 days in a year)?

   (b) How long does it take for the $8000 to double with monthly compounding?

2. (a) An amount $5000 earns interest at 3% per year. What will this amount have grown to after 10 years?

   (b) How long does it take for the $5000 to triple?

3. What annual percentage rate of growth is needed for a country's GDP to become 100 times as large after 100 years? ($\sqrt[100]{100} \approx 1.047$.)

4. (a) An amount of 2000 euros is invested at 7% per year. What is the balance in the account after (i) 2 years; (ii) 10 years?

   (b) How long does it take (approximately) for the balance to reach 6000 euros?

5. Calculate the effective yearly interest if the nominal rate is 17% and interest is added (i) biannually; (ii) quarterly; (iii) monthly.

6. Which is preferable for a borrower: (i) to take out a loan with an annual interest rate of 21.5%, with interest paid yearly; or (ii) to take out a loan with an annual interest rate of 20%, with interest paid quarterly?

7. (a) The sum of $12 000 is invested at 4% annual interest. What will this amount have grown to after 15 years?

   (b) How much should you have deposited in a bank account 5 years ago in order to have $50 000 today, given that the interest rate has been 5% per year over the period?

   (c) A credit card is offered with interest on the outstanding balance charged at 2% per month. What is the effective annual rate of interest?

8. What is the nominal yearly interest rate if the effective yearly rate is 28% and interest is compounded quarterly?

10.2 Continuous Compounding

We saw in the previous section that if interest at the rate r/n is added to the principal S_0 at n different times during the year, the principal will be multiplied by a factor $(1+r/n)^n$ each year. After t years, the principal will have increased to $S_0(1+r/n)^{nt}$. In practice, there is a limit to how frequently interest can be added to an account. However, let us examine what happens to the expression as the annual frequency n tends to infinity. We put $r/n = 1/m$. Then $n = mr$ and so

$$S_0\left(1+\frac{r}{n}\right)^{nt} = S_0\left(1+\frac{1}{m}\right)^{mrt} = S_0\left[\left(1+\frac{1}{m}\right)^m\right]^{rt} \tag{1}$$

As $n \to \infty$ (with r fixed), so $m = n/r \to \infty$, and according to Example 7.10.2, we have $(1+1/m)^m \to e$. Hence, the expression in (1) approaches $S_0 e^{rt}$ as n tends to infinity, implying that interest is compounded more and more frequently. In the limit, we talk about *continuous compounding* of interest:

CONTINUOUS COMPOUNDING OF INTEREST

The formula

$$S(t) = S_0 e^{rt}$$

$$\tag{2}$$

shows how much a principal of S_0 will have increased to after t years, if the annual interest is r, and there is continuous compounding of interest.

EXAMPLE 1   Suppose the sum of 5000 euros is invested in an account earning interest at an annual rate of 9%. What is the balance after 8 years if interest is compounded continuously?

Solution: Using formula (2) with $r = 9/100 = 0.09$, we see that the balance is

$$5000e^{0.09 \cdot 8} = 5000e^{0.72} \approx 10\,272.17$$

(Compare with the result in Example 1 of the previous section.)   ▌

If $S(t) = S_0 e^{rt}$, then $S'(t) = S_0 r e^{rt} = r S(t)$ (according to formula (2) in Section 6.10), and so $S'(t)/S(t) = r$. Using the terminology introduced in Section 6.4:

With continuous compounding of interest at the rate r, the principal increases at the constant relative rate r, so that $S'(t)/S(t) = r$.

From (2), we infer that $S(1) = S_0 e^r$, so that the principal increases by the factor e^r during the first year. In general, $S(t+1) = S_0 e^{r(t+1)} = S_0 e^{rt} e^r = S(t)e^r$. Hence:

With continuous compounding of interest, the principal increases each year by a fixed factor e^r.

Comparing Different Interest Periods

Given any fixed interest rate of $p\%$ ($= 100r$) per year, continuous compounding of interest is best for the lender. (See Problem 6.) For comparatively low interest rates, however, the difference between annual and continuous compounding of interest is quite small, when the number of years of compounding is relatively small.

EXAMPLE 2   Find the amount K by which \$1 increases in the course of a year when the interest rate is 8% per year and interest is added: (a) yearly; (b) biannually; (c) continuously.

Solution: In this case $r = 8/100 = 0.08$, and we obtain

(a) $K = (1 + 0.08) = 1.08$

(b) $K = (1 + 0.08/2)^2 = 1.0816$

(c) $K = e^{0.08} \approx 1.08329$

If we increase either the interest rate or the number of years over which interest accumulates, then the difference between yearly and continuous compounding of interest increases.

In the previous section the effective yearly interest was defined by the formula $(1 + r/n)^n - 1$, when interest is compounded n times a year with rate r/n per period. Letting n approach infinity in this formula, we see that the expression approaches

$$e^r - 1 \tag{3}$$

This is called the **effective interest** rate with continuous compounding at the annual rate r.

1. (a) How much does \$8000 grow to after 5 years if the annual interest rate is 5%, with continuous compounding?

   (b) How long does it take before the \$8000 has doubled?

2. An amount \$1000 earns interest at 5% per year. What will this amount have grown to after (a) 10 years, and (b) 50 years, when interest is compounded (i) yearly, or (ii) monthly, or (iii) continuously?

3. (a) Find the effective rate corresponding to an annual rate of 10% compounded continuously.

   (b) What is the maximum amount of compound interest that can be earned at an annual rate of 10%?

4. The value v_0 of a new car depreciates continuously at the annual rate of 10%—that is, $v(t) = v_0 e^{-\delta t}$ where $\delta = 0.1$ is the *rate of depreciation*. How many years does it take for the car to lose 90% of its original value?.

5. The value of a machine depreciates continuously at the annual rate of 6%. How many years will it take for the value of the machine to halve?

HARDER PROBLEMS

6. We showed that $(1 + r/n)^n \to e^r$ as $n \to \infty$. For each fixed $r > 0$ we claim that $(1 + r/n)^n$ is strictly increasing in n. In particular, this implies that

$$(1 + r/n)^n < e^r \quad \text{for} \quad n = 1, 2, \ldots \tag{*}$$

This shows that continuous compounding at interest rate r, is more profitable for the lender than interest payments n times a year at interest rate r/n.

To confirm these results, given any $r > 0$, define the function $g(x) = (1 + r/x)^x$ for all $x > 0$. Use logarithmic differentiation to show that

$$g'(x) = g(x)\left[\ln\left(1 + \frac{r}{x}\right) - \frac{r/x}{1 + r/x}\right]$$

Next, put $h(u) = \ln(1 + u) - u/(1 + u)$. Then $h(0) = 0$. Show that $h'(u) > 0$ for $u > 0$, and hence $g'(x) > 0$ for all $x > 0$. What conclusion can you draw?

10.3 Present Value

The sum of $1000 in your hand today is worth more than $1000 to be received at some future date. One important reason is that you can invest the $1000 and hope to earn some interest or other positive return.[1] If the interest rate is 11% per year, then after 1 year the original $1000 will have grown to the amount $1000(1 + 11/100) = 1110$, and after 6 years, it will have grown to $1000(1 + 11/100)^6 = 1000 \cdot (1.11)^6 \approx 1870$. This shows that, at the interest rate 11% per year, $1000 now has the same value as $1110 next year, or $1870 in 6 years time. Accordingly, if the amount $1110 is due for payment 1 year from now and the interest rate is 11% per year, then the *present value* of this amount is $1000. Because $1000 is less than $1110, we often speak of $1000 as the *present discounted value* (or PDV) of $1110 next year. The ratio $1000/$1110 = 1/(1 + 11/100) \approx 0.9009$ is called the (annual) *discount factor*, whose reciprocal 1.11 is one plus the *discount rate*, making the discount rate equal to the interest rate of 11%.

Similarly, if the interest rate is 11% per year, then the PDV of $1870 due 6 years from now is $1000. Again, the ratio $1000/$1870 \approx 0.53$ is called the *discount factor*.

Suppose that an amount K is due for payment t years after the present date. What is the *present value* when the interest rate is $p\%$ per year? Equivalently, how much must be deposited today earning $p\%$ annual interest in order to have the amount K after t years?

---

[1] If prices are expected to increase, another reason for preferring $1000 today is inflation, because $1000 to be paid at some future date will buy less then than $1000 does today.

If interest is paid annually, an amount A will have increased to $A(1 + p/100)^t$ after t years, so that we need $A(1 + p/100)^t = K$. Thus, $A = K(1 + p/100)^{-t} = K(1+r)^{-t}$, where $r = p/100$. Here the annual discount factor is $(1+r)^{-1}$, and $(1+r)^{-t}$ is the discount factor appropriate for t years.

If interest is compounded continuously, then the amount A will have increased to Ae^{rt} after t years. Hence, $Ae^{rt} = K$, or $A = Ke^{-rt}$. Here e^{-rt} is the discount factor. To summarize:

PRESENT DISCOUNTED VALUE

If the interest or discount rate is $p\%$ per year and $r = p/100$, an amount K that is payable in t years has the present value (or present discounted value, or PDV):

$$K(1+r)^{-t}, \quad \text{with annual interest payments}$$
$$Ke^{-rt}, \quad \text{with continuous compounding of interest}$$

(1)

EXAMPLE 1   Find the present value of $100\,000$ which is due for payment after 15 years if the interest rate is 6% per year, compounded (i) annually, or (ii) continuously.

Solution:

(i) According to (1), the present value is $100\,000(1 + 0.06)^{-15} \approx 41726.51$.

(ii) According to (1), the present value is $100\,000e^{-0.06 \cdot 15} = 100\,000e^{-0.9} \approx 40656.97$. As expected, the present value with continuous compounding is the smaller, because capital increases most rapidly with continuously compounding of interest.   ∎

EXAMPLE 2   (**When to Harvest a Tree?**) Consider a tree that is planted at time $t = 0$, and let $P(t)$ be its current market value at time t, where $P(t)$ is differentiable. Assume that the interest rate is $100r\%$ per year, and assume continuous compounding of interest.

(a) When should this tree be cut down in order to maximize its present discounted value?

(b) The optimal cutting time t^* depends on the interest rate r. Find an expression for dt^*/dr.

Solution: (a) The present value is $f(t) = P(t)e^{-rt}$, whose derivative is

$$f'(t) = P'(t)e^{-rt} + P(t)(-r)e^{-rt} = e^{-rt}\left[P'(t) - rP(t)\right]$$

(∗)

A necessary condition for $t^* > 0$ to maximize $f(t)$ is that $f'(t^*) = 0$. We see that this occurs when

$$P'(t^*) = rP(t^*)$$

(∗∗)

The tree, therefore, should be cut down at a time t^* when the relative rate of increase in the value of the tree is precisely equal to the interest rate. Of course, some conditions have to be placed on f in order for t^* to be a maximum point. It suffices to have $P'(t)/P(t) \geq r$ for $t < t^*$ and $P'(t)/P(t) \leq r$ for $t > t^*$.

(b) Differentiating (∗∗) w.r.t r yields

$$P''(t^*)\frac{dt^*}{dr} = P(t^*) + rP'(t^*)\frac{dt^*}{dr}$$

Solving for dt^*/dr,

$$\frac{dt^*}{dr} = \frac{P(t^*)}{P''(t^*) - rP'(t^*)} \qquad (***)$$

NOTE 1 Differentiating (∗) w.r.t. t yields

$$f''(t) = P''(t)e^{-rt} - rP'(t)e^{-rt} - P'(t)re^{-rt} + r^2 P(t)e^{-rt}$$

Using (∗∗) we see that the second-order condition $f''(t^*) < 0$ is satisfied if and only if

$$e^{-rt}[P''(t^*) - 2rP'(t^*) + r^2 P(t^*)] = e^{-rt}[P''(t^*) - rP'(t^*)] < 0$$

in which case $dt^*/dr < 0$. Thus the optimal growing time shortens as r increases (which makes the foresters more impatient). In particular, given any $r > 0$, the optimal t^* is less than the time $\hat{t}$ that maximizes current market value $P(t)$, which is optimal only if $r = 0$.

NOTE 2 In the example, we did not consider how the ground the tree grows on may be used after cutting—for example, by planting a new tree. This generalization is studied in Problem 10.4.8.

PROBLEMS FOR SECTION 10.3

1. Find the present value of 350 000 which is due after 10 years if the interest rate is 8% per year (i) compounded annually, or (ii) compounded continuously.

2. Find the present value of 50 000 which is due after 5 years when the interest rate is 5.75% per year, paid (i) annually, or (ii) continuously.

3. With reference to the tree-cutting problem of Example 2, consider the case where

$$f(t) = (t+5)^2 e^{-0.05t} \qquad t \geq 0$$

(a) Find the value of t that maximizes $f(t)$. (Study the sign variation of $f'(t)$.)

(b) Find $\lim_{t \to \infty} f(t)$ and draw the graph of f.

10.4 Geometric Series

This section studies finite and infinite geometric series. These have many applications in economics and finance. Here we shall use them to calculate annuities and mortgage payments.

Finite Geometric Series

EXAMPLE 1   This year a firm has an annual revenue of $100 million that it expects to increase by 16% per year throughout the next decade. How large is its expected revenue in the tenth year, and what is the total revenue expected over the whole period?

Solution: The expected revenue in the second year (in millions of dollars) amounts to $100(1 + 16/100) = 100 \cdot 1.16$, and in the third year, it is $100 \cdot (1.16)^2$. In the tenth year, the expected revenue is $100 \cdot (1.16)^9$. The total revenue expected during the decade is thus

$$100 + 100 \cdot 1.16 + 100 \cdot (1.16)^2 + \cdots + 100 \cdot (1.16)^9$$

If we used a calculator to add the ten different numbers, we would find that the sum is approximately $2132 million.

Finding the sum in Example 1 by adding 10 different numbers on a calculator would be very tedious. When there are infinitely many terms, it is obviously impossible. There is an easier method, as we now explain.

Consider the n numbers $a, ak, ak^2, \ldots, ak^{n-1}$. Each term is obtained by multiplying the previous one by a constant k. We wish to find the sum

$$s_n = a + ak + ak^2 + \cdots + ak^{n-2} + ak^{n-1} \tag{1}$$

of these numbers. We call this sum a (finite) **geometric series** with **quotient** k. The sum in Example 1 occurs in the case when $a = 100$, $k = 1.16$, and $n = 10$.

To find the sum s_n of the series, we use a trick. First multiply both sides of (1) by k to obtain

$$ks_n = ak + ak^2 + ak^3 + \cdots + ak^{n-1} + ak^n$$

Subtracting this equation from (1) yields

$$s_n - ks_n = a - ak^n \tag{2}$$

because all the other terms cancel. This is the point of the trick. (If $k = 1$, then all terms in (1) are equal to a, and the sum is equal to $s_n = an$.) For $k \neq 1$, because $s_n - ks_n = (1-k)s_n$, (2) implies that

$$s_n = \frac{a - ak^n}{1 - k} = a\frac{k^n - 1}{k - 1}$$

In conclusion:

SUMMATION FORMULA FOR A FINITE GEOMETRIC SERIES

$$a + ak + ak^2 + \cdots + ak^{n-1} = a \frac{k^n - 1}{k - 1} \qquad (k \neq 1)$$

(3)

EXAMPLE 2   For the sum in Example 1 we have $a = 100$, $k = 1.16$, and $n = 10$. Hence, (3) yields

$$100 + 100 \cdot 1.16 + \cdots + 100 \cdot (1.16)^9 = 100 \frac{(1.16)^{10} - 1}{1.16 - 1}$$

Now it takes many fewer operations on the calculator than in Example 1 to show that the sum is about 2132.

Infinite Geometric Series

Consider the infinite sequence of numbers

$$1, \quad \frac{1}{2}, \quad \frac{1}{4}, \quad \frac{1}{8}, \quad \frac{1}{16}, \quad \frac{1}{32}, \quad \cdots$$

Each term in the sequence is formed by halving its predecessor, so that the nth term is $1/2^{n-1}$. The sum of the n first terms is a finite geometric series with quotient $k = 1/2$ and the first term $a = 1$. Hence, (3) gives

$$1 + \frac{1}{2} + \frac{1}{2^2} + \cdots + \frac{1}{2^{n-1}} = \frac{1 - \left(\frac{1}{2}\right)^n}{1 - \frac{1}{2}} = 2 - \frac{1}{2^{n-1}}$$

(*)

We now ask what is meant by the "infinite sum"

$$1 + \frac{1}{2} + \frac{1}{2^2} + \frac{1}{2^3} + \cdots + \frac{1}{2^{n-1}} + \cdots$$

(**)

Because all the terms are positive, and there are infinitely many terms, you might be inclined to think that the sum must be infinitely large. However, if we look at formula (*), we see that the sum of the n first terms is equal to $2 - 1/2^{n-1}$. This number is never larger than 2, irrespective of our choice of n. As n increases, the term $1/2^{n-1}$ comes closer and closer to 0, and the sum in (*) tends to 2 as limit. This makes it natural to *define* the infinite sum in (**) as the number 2.

In general, we ask what meaning can be given to the "infinite sum"

$$a + ak + ak^2 + \cdots + ak^{n-1} + \cdots$$

(4)

We use the same idea as in (∗∗), and consider the sum s_n of the n first terms in (4). According to (3),

$$s_n = a \frac{1 - k^n}{1 - k} \qquad (k \neq 1)$$

What happens to this expression as n tends to infinity? The answer evidently depends on k^n, because only this term depends on n. In fact, k^n tends to 0 if $-1 < k < 1$, whereas k^n does not tend to any limit if $k > 1$ or $k \leq -1$. (If you are not yet convinced that this claim is true, study the cases $k = -2$, $k = -1$, $k = -1/2$, $k = 1/2$, and $k = 2$.) It follows that if $|k| < 1$, then the sum s_n of the n first terms in (4) will tend to the limit $a/(1 - k)$ as n tends to infinity. In this case, we let (4) *define* the sum, and say that the infinite series in (4) **converges**. To summarize:

SUMMATION FORMULA FOR AN INFINITE GEOMETRIC SERIES

$$a + ak + ak^2 + \cdots + ak^{n-1} + \cdots = \frac{a}{1 - k} \qquad \text{if} \quad |k| < 1 \tag{5}$$

Using sigma notation for summation (see Section 3.1), (5) becomes

$$\sum_{n=1}^{\infty} ak^{n-1} = \frac{a}{1 - k} \qquad \text{if} \quad |k| < 1 \tag{6}$$

If $|k| \geq 1$, we say that the infinite series (4) **diverges**. A divergent series has no (finite) sum. Divergence is obvious if $|k| > 1$. When $k = 1$, then $s_n = na$, which tends to $+\infty$ if $a > 0$ or to $-\infty$ if $a < 0$. When $k = -1$, then s_n is a when n is odd, but 0 when n is even; again there is no limit as $n \to \infty$ (if $a \neq 0$).

EXAMPLE 3   A rough estimate of the total oil and gas reserves under the Norwegian continental shelf at the beginning of 1999 was 13 billion ($13 \cdot 10^9$) tons (of oil equivalent). Output that year was approximately 250 million ($250 \cdot 10^6$) tons.

(a) When will the reserves be exhausted if output is kept at the same constant level?

(b) Suppose that output is reduced each year by 2% per year beginning in 1999. How long will the reserves last in this case?

Solution:

(a) The number of years for which the reserves will last is given by

$$\frac{13 \cdot 10^9}{250 \cdot 10^6} = 52$$

That is, the reserves will be exhausted around the year 2051.

(b) In 1999, output was $a = 250 \cdot 10^6$. In 2000, it would be $a - 2a/100 = a \cdot 0.98$. In 2001, it becomes $a \cdot 0.98^2$, and so on. If this continues forever, the total amount extracted will be

$$a + a \cdot 0.98 + a \cdot (0.98)^2 + \cdots + a \cdot (0.98)^{n-1} + \cdots$$

This geometric series has quotient $k = 0.98$. According to (5), the sum is

$$s = \frac{a}{1 - 0.98} = 50a$$

Since $a = 250 \cdot 10^6$, $s = 50 \cdot 250 \cdot 10^6 = 12.5 \cdot 10^9$, which is less than $13 \cdot 10^9$. The extraction, therefore, may be continued indefinitely, leaving 500 million $(= 0.5 \cdot 10^9)$ tons which will never be extracted.

PROBLEMS FOR SECTION 10.4

1. Find the sum s_n of the following finite geometric series

$$1 + \frac{1}{3} + \frac{1}{3^2} + \cdots + \frac{1}{3^{n-1}}$$

When n approaches infinity, what is the limit of s_n? Find the sum $\sum_{n=1}^{\infty} \frac{1}{3^{n-1}}$.

2. Find the sums of the following geometric series:

   (a) $\frac{1}{5} + (\frac{1}{5})^2 + (\frac{1}{5})^3 + (\frac{1}{5})^4 + \cdots$

   (b) $0.1 + (0.1)^2 + (0.1)^3 + (0.1)^4 + \cdots$

   (c) $517 + 517(1.1)^{-1} + 517(1.1)^{-2} + 517(1.1)^{-3} + \cdots$

   (d) $a + a(1 + a)^{-1} + a(1 + a)^{-2} + a(1 + a)^{-3} + a(1 + a)^{-4} + \cdots, \quad (a > 0)$

   (e) $5 + \frac{5 \cdot 3}{7} + \frac{5 \cdot 3^2}{7^2} + \cdots + \frac{5 \cdot 3^{n-1}}{7^{n-1}} + \cdots$

3. Determine whether the following series are geometric, and find the sums of those geometric series that do converge.

   (a) $8 + 1 + 1/8 + 1/64 + \cdots$ (b) $-2 + 6 - 18 + 54 - \cdots$

   (c) $2^{1/3} + 1 + 2^{-1/3} + 2^{-2/3} + \cdots$ (d) $1 - 1/2 + 1/3 - 1/4 + \cdots$

4. Examine the convergence of the following geometric series, and find their sums when they exist:

   (a) $\frac{1}{p} + \frac{1}{p^2} + \frac{1}{p^3} + \cdots$ (b) $x + \sqrt{x} + 1 + \frac{1}{\sqrt{x}} + \cdots$ (c) $\sum_{n=1}^{\infty} x^{2n}$

5. Find the sum $\sum_{k=0}^{\infty} b\left(1+\dfrac{p}{100}\right)^{-k}$, $\quad p > 0$.

6. Total world consumption of iron was approximately $794 \cdot 10^6$ tons in 1971. If consumption had increased by 5% each year and the resources available for mining in 1971 were $249 \cdot 10^9$ tons, how much longer would the world's iron resources have lasted?

7. The world's total consumption of natural gas was 1824 million tons oil equivalent (mtoe) in 1994. The reserves at the end of that year were estimated to be 128 300 mtoe. If consumption had increased by 2% in each of the coming years, and no new sources were ever discovered, how much longer would these reserves have lasted?

8. Consider Example 10.3.2. Assume that immediately after one tree is felled, a new tree of the same type is planted. If we assume that a new tree is planted at times t, $2t$, $3t$, etc., then the present value of all the trees will be

$$f(t) = P(t)e^{-rt} + P(t)e^{-2rt} + \cdots$$

(a) Find the sum of this infinite geometric series.

(b) Prove that if $f(t)$ has a maximum for some $t^* > 0$, then

$$\frac{P'(t^*)}{P(t^*)} = \frac{r}{1 - e^{-rt^*}}$$

(c) Examine the limit of $P'(t^*)/P(t^*)$ as $r \to 0$.

10.5 Total Present Value

Suppose that three successive annual payments are to be made, with the amount $1000 falling due after 1 year, then $1500 after 2 years, and $2000 after 3 years. How much must be deposited in an account today in order to have enough savings to cover these three payments, given that the interest rate is 11% per year? We call this amount the *present value* of the three payments.

In order to have $1000 after 1 year, we must deposit an amount x_1 today, where

$$x_1(1+0.11) = 1000, \quad \text{so that} \quad x_1 = \frac{1000}{1+0.11} = \frac{1000}{1.11}$$

In order to have $1500 after 2 years, we must deposit an amount x_2 today, where

$$x_2(1+0.11)^2 = 1500, \quad \text{so that} \quad x_2 = \frac{1500}{(1+0.11)^2} = \frac{1500}{(1.11)^2}$$

Finally, to have \$2000 after 3 years, we must deposit an amount x_3 today, where

$$x_3(1 + 0.11)^3 = 2000, \quad \text{so that} \quad x_3 = \frac{2000}{(1 + 0.11)^3} = \frac{2000}{(1.11)^3}$$

So the total present value of the three payments, which is the total amount A that must be deposited today in order to cover all three payments, is given by

$$A = \frac{1000}{1.11} + \frac{1500}{(1.11)^2} + \frac{2000}{(1.11)^3}$$

The total is approximately $A \approx 900.90 + 1217.43 + 1462.38 = 3580.71$.

Suppose, in general, that n successive payments $a_1, \ldots, a_n$ are to be made, with a_1 being paid after 1 year, a_2 after 2 years, and so on. How much must be deposited into an account today in order to have enough savings to cover all these future payments, given that the annual interest is r? In other words, what is the *present value* of all these payments?

In order to have a_1 after 1 year, we must deposit $a_1/(1+r)$ today, to have a_2 after 2 years we must deposit $a_2/(1 + r)^2$ today, and so on. The total amount P_n that must be deposited today in order to cover all n payments is therefore

$$P_n = \frac{a_1}{1 + r} + \frac{a_2}{(1 + r)^2} + \cdots + \frac{a_n}{(1 + r)^n} \tag{1}$$

Here P_n is the **present value** of the n instalments.

An **annuity** is a sequence of equal payments made at fixed periods of time over some time span. If $a_1 = a_2 = \cdots = a_n = a$ in (1), then (1) represents the present value of an annuity. In this case the sum in (1) is a finite geometric series with n terms. The first term is $a/(1+r)$ and the quotient is $1/(1+r)$. According to the summation formula for a geometric series, (3) in the previous section, with $k = (1 + r)^{-1}$, the sum is

$$P_n = \frac{a}{(1 + r)} \frac{[1 - (1 + r)^{-n}]}{[1 - (1 + r)^{-1}]} = \frac{a}{r}\left[1 - \frac{1}{(1 + r)^n}\right]$$

(The second equality holds because the denominator of the middle expression reduces to r.) Hence, we have the following.

PRESENT VALUE OF AN ANNUITY

The present value of an annuity of a per payment period for n periods at the rate of interest r per period, where each payment is at the end of the period, is given by

$$P_n = \frac{a}{1 + r} + \cdots + \frac{a}{(1 + r)^n} = \frac{a}{r}\left[1 - \frac{1}{(1 + r)^n}\right] \quad \text{where } r = p/100 \tag{2}$$

This sum is illustrated below:

Formula (2) gives the present value of n future claims, each of a (say) dollars. If we want to find how much is accumulated in the account after n periods, immediately after the last deposit, then the **future value** F_n of the annuity is given by:

$$F_n = a + a(1+r) + a(1+r)^2 + \cdots + a(1+r)^{n-1}$$

This different sum is illustrated below:

The summation formula for a geometric series yields:

$$F_n = \frac{a[1 - (1+r)^n]}{1 - (1+r)} = \frac{a}{r}[(1+r)^n - 1]$$

We can also find the future value directly by calculating the interest earned on the present value P_n in n periods: $F_n = P_n(1+r)^n = \frac{a}{r}[(1+r)^n - 1]$. So:

FUTURE VALUE OF AN ANNUITY

An amount a is deposited in an account each period for n periods, earning interest at r per period. The future (total) value of the account, immediately after the last deposit, is

$$F_n = \frac{a}{r}[(1+r)^n - 1]$$

(3)

EXAMPLE 1   Compute the present and the future values of a deposit of $1000 in each of the coming 8 years if the annual interest rate is 6%.

Solution: To find the present value, we apply formula (2) with $a = 1000$, $n = 8$ and $r = 6/100 = 0.06$. This gives

$$P_8 = \frac{1000}{0.06}\left(1 - \frac{1}{(1.06)^8}\right) \approx 6209.79$$

The future value is found by applying formula (3), which gives

$$F_8 = \frac{1000}{0.06}\left[(1.06)^8 - 1\right] \approx 9897.47$$

Alternatively, $F_8 = P_8(1.06)^8 \approx 6209.79(1.06)^8 \approx 9897.47$. ∎

If $r > 0$ and we let n approach infinity in (2), then $(1 + r)^n$ approaches infinity and P_n approaches a/r. So in the limit,

$$\frac{a}{1+r} + \frac{a}{(1+r)^2} + \cdots = \frac{a}{r} \qquad (r > 0) \tag{4}$$

This corresponds to the case where an investment pays a per period in perpetuity when the interest rate is r.

EXAMPLE 2   Compute the present value of a series of deposits of $1000 at the end of each year in perpetuity when the annual interest rate is 14%.

Solution: According to formula (4), we obtain

$$\frac{1000}{1 + 0.14} + \frac{1000}{(1 + 0.14)^2} + \cdots = \frac{1000}{0.14} \approx 7142.86$$ ∎

Present Value of a Continuous Future Income Stream

We have discussed the present value of a series of future payments made at specific discrete moments in time. It is often more natural to consider revenue as accruing continuously, like the timber yield from a large growing forest.

Suppose that income is to be received continuously from time $t = 0$ to time $t = T$ at the rate of $f(t)$ dollars per year at time t. We assume that interest is compounded continuously at rate r per year.

Let $P(t)$ denote the present discounted value (PDV) of all payments made over the time interval $[0, t]$. This means that $P(T)$ represents the amount of money you would have to deposit at time $t = 0$ in order to match what results from (continuously) depositing the income stream $f(t)$ over the time interval $[0, T]$. If Δt is any number, the present value of the income received during the interval $[t, t + \Delta t]$ is $P(t + \Delta t) - P(t)$. If Δt is a small number, the income received during this interval is approximately $f(t)\,\Delta t$, and the PDV of this amount is approximately $f(t)e^{-rt}\,\Delta t$. Thus, $P(t + \Delta t) - P(t) \approx f(t)e^{-rt}\,\Delta t$ and so

$$[P(t + \Delta t) - P(t)]/\Delta t \approx f(t)e^{-rt}$$

This approximation gets better the smaller is Δt, and in the limit as $\Delta t \to 0$, we have $P'(t) = f(t)e^{-rt}$. By the definition of the definite integral, $P(T) - P(0) = \int_0^T f(t)e^{-rt}\,dt$. Because $P(0) = 0$, we have the following:

PRESENT VALUE OF A CONTINUOUS INCOME STREAM

The present (discounted) value (at time 0) of a continuous income stream at the rate of $f(t)$ dollars per year over the time interval $[0, T]$, with continuously compounded interest at rate r per year, is given by   (5)

$$\text{PDV} = \int_0^T f(t)e^{-rt}\,dt$$

Equation (5) gives the value at time 0 of income stream $f(t)$ received during time interval $[0, T]$. The value of this amount at time T, with continuously compounded interest at rate r, is $e^{rT}\int_0^T f(t)e^{-rt}\,dt$. Because the number e^{rT} is a constant, we can rewrite the integral as $\int_0^T f(t)e^{r(T-t)}\,dt$. This is called the future discounted value (FDV) of the income stream:

FUTURE VALUE OF A CONTINUOUS INCOME STREAM

The future (discounted) value (at time T) of a continuous income stream at the rate of $f(t)$ dollars per year over the time interval $[0, T]$, with continuously compounded interest at rate r per year, is given by   (6)

$$\text{FDV} = \int_0^T f(t)e^{r(T-t)}\,dt$$

An easy modification of (5) will give us the discounted value (DV) at any time $s \in [0, T]$ of an income stream $f(t)$ received during time interval $[s, T]$. In fact, the DV at time s of income $f(t)$ received in the small time interval $[t, t + dt]$ is $f(t)e^{-r(t-s)}\,dt$. So we have the following:

DISCOUNTED VALUE OF A CONTINUOUS INCOME STREAM

The discounted value at any time s of a continuous income stream at the rate of $f(t)$ dollars per year over the time interval $[s, T]$, with continuously compounded interest at rate r per year, is given by   (7)

$$\text{DV} = \int_{t=s}^T f(t)e^{-r(t-s)}\,dt$$

EXAMPLE 3   Find the PDV and the FDV of a constant income stream of $1000 per year over the next 10 years, assuming an interest rate of $r = 8\% = 0.08$ annually, compounded continuously.

Solution:

$$\text{PDV} = \int_0^{10} 1000 e^{-0.08t} \, dt = \left. 1000 \left(-\frac{e^{-0.08t}}{0.08} \right) \right|_0^{10} = \frac{1000}{0.08}(1 - e^{-0.8}) \approx 6883.39$$

$$\text{FDV} = e^{0.08 \cdot 10} \text{PDV} \approx e^{0.8} \cdot 6883.39 \approx 15\,319.27$$

PROBLEMS FOR SECTION 10.5

1. What is the present value of 15 annual deposits of $3500 if the first deposit is after one year and the annual interest rate is 12%?

2. (a) An account has been dormant for many years earning interest at the constant rate of 4% per year. Now the amount is $100 000. How much was in the account 10 years ago?

   (b) At the end of each year for 4 years you deposit $10 000 into an account earning interest at a rate of 6% per year. How much is in the account at the end of the fourth year?

3. Suppose you are given the following options:

   (i) $13 000 paid after 10 years, or

   (ii) $1000 paid each year for 10 years, first payment today.

   Which of these alternatives would you choose, if the annual interest rate is 6% per year for the whole period?

4. An author is to be paid a royalty for a book. Two alternative offers are made:

   (a) The author can be paid $21 000 immediately,

   (b) There can be 5 equal annual payments of $4600, the first being paid at once.

   Which of these offers will be more valuable if the interest rate is 6% per annum?

5. Compute the present value of a series of deposits of $1500 at the end of each year in perpetuity when the interest rate is 8% per year.

6. A trust fund is being set up with a single payment of K. The amount is invested at a fixed annual interest rate of r. The fund pays out a fixed annual amount. The first payment is to be made one year after the trust fund was set up. What is the largest amount which can be paid out each year if the fund is to last for ever?

7. The present discounted value of a payment D growing at a constant rate g when the discount rate is r is given by

$$\frac{D}{1+r} + \frac{D(1+g)}{(1+r)^2} + \frac{D(1+g)^2}{(1+r)^3} + \cdots$$

where r and g are positive. What is the condition for convergence? Show that if the series converges with sum P_0, then $P_0 = D/(r-g)$.

8. Find the present and future values of a constant income stream of \$500 per year over the next 15 years, assuming an interest rate of $r = 6\% = 0.06$ annually, compounded continuously.

10.6 Mortgage Repayments

When a family takes out a home mortgage at a fixed interest rate, this means that, like an annuity, equal payments are due each period — say, at the end of each month. The payments continue until the loan is paid off after, say, 20 years. Each payment goes partly to pay interest on the outstanding principal, and partly to repay principal (that is, to reduce the outstanding balance). The interest part is largest in the beginning, because interest has to be paid on the whole loan for the first period, and is smallest in the last period, because by then the outstanding balance is small. For the principal repayment, which is the difference between the fixed monthly payment and the interest, it is the other way around.

EXAMPLE 1   A person borrows \$50 000 at the beginning of a year and is supposed to pay it off in 5 equal instalments at the end of each year, with interest at 15% compounding annually. Find the annual payment.

Solution: If the five repayments are each of amount \$$a$, their present value in dollars is

$$\frac{a}{1.15} + \frac{a}{(1.15)^2} + \frac{a}{(1.15)^3} + \frac{a}{(1.15)^4} + \frac{a}{(1.15)^5} = \frac{a}{0.15}\left[1 - \frac{1}{(1.15)^5}\right]$$

according to formula (2) in the previous section. This sum must be equal to \$50 000, so

$$\frac{a}{0.15}\left[1 - \frac{1}{(1.15)^5}\right] = 50\,000 \tag{$*$}$$

This has the solution $a \approx 14\,915.78$. Alternatively, we can calculate the sum of the future values of all repayments and equate it to the future value of the original loan. This yields the equation

$$a + a(1.15) + a(1.15)^2 + a(1.15)^3 + a(1.15)^4 = 50\,000(1.15)^5$$

which is equivalent to (∗), and so also has the solution $a \approx 14915.78$.

To illustrate how the interest part and the principal repayment part of the yearly payment vary from year to year, we construct the following table:

Year	Payment	Interest	Principal Repayment	Outst. Balance
1	14 915.78	7 500.00	7 415.78	42 584.22
2	14 915.78	6 387.63	8 528.15	34 056.07
3	14 915.78	5 108.41	9 807.37	24 248.70
4	14 915.78	3 637.31	11 278.47	12 970.23
5	14 915.78	1 945.55	12 970.23	0

Note that the interest payment each year is 15% of the outstanding balance from the previous year. The remainder of each annual payment of $14 915.78 is the principal repayment that year, which is subtracted from the outstanding balance left over from the previous year.

Figure 1 is a chart showing each year's interest and principal repayments:

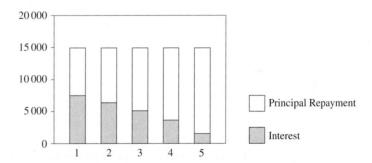

Figure 1 Interest and principal repayment in Example 1

Suppose a loan of K dollars is repaid as an annuity over n periods, at the interest rate $p\%$ per period, where the first payment a is due after one period, and the rest at equally spaced periods. According to (2) in the previous section, the payment a each period must satisfy

$$K = \frac{a}{r}\left[1 - \frac{1}{(1+r)^n}\right] = \frac{a}{r}[1 - (1-r)^{-n}] \tag{1}$$

Solving equation (1) for a yields:

$$a = \frac{rK}{1 - (1+r)^{-n}} \tag{2}$$

where $r = p/100$. We could have used this formula in Example 1. Do so.

EXAMPLE 2   Suppose that the loan in Example 1 is being repaid by monthly payments at the end of each month with interest at the nominal rate 15% per year compounding monthly. Find the monthly payment.

Solution: The interest period is 1 month and the monthly rate is $15/12 = 1.25\%$, so that $r = 1.25/100 = 0.0125$. Also, $n = 5 \cdot 12 = 60$, so formula (2) gives:

$$a = \frac{0.0125 \cdot 50\,000}{1 - 1.0125^{-60}} \approx 1189.50$$

The annuities considered so far were **ordinary** annuities where each payment is made at the *end* of the payment period. If the payment each period is made at the beginning of the period, the annuity is called an **annuity due**. This kind of annuity can be handled easily by regarding it as an ordinary annuity, except that there is an immediate initial payment.

EXAMPLE 3   A person is assuming responsibility for a $335\,000$ loan which should be repaid in 15 equal repayments of $\$a$, the first one immediately and the following after each of the coming 14 years. Find a if the annual interest rate is 14%.

Solution: The present value of the first payment is obviously a. The present value of the following 14 repayments is found by applying formula (1) with $r = 0.14$ and $n = 14$. The sum of the present values must be equal to 335 000:

$$a + \frac{a}{0.14}\left[1 - \frac{1}{(1 + 0.14)^{14}}\right] = 335\,000$$

This reduces to $a + 6.0020715a = 335\,000$, and solving for a gives $a \approx 47\,843$.

Some lenders prefer to specify a fixed payment each period, and let the loan run for however many periods it takes to pay off the debt. This way of paying off the loan functions essentially as an annuity. The difference is that there will be a final adjustment in the last payment in order for the present value of all the payments to be equal to the borrowed amount. In this case it is convenient to use the formula obtained by solving equation (1) for n. The result is

$$\frac{rK}{a} = 1 - \frac{1}{(1 + r)^n} \iff \frac{1}{(1 + r)^n} = 1 - \frac{rK}{a} = \frac{a - rK}{a} \iff (1 + r)^n = \frac{a}{a - rK}$$

Taking the natural logarithm of each side yields $n \ln(1 + r) = \ln[a/(a - rK)]$, so:

The number of periods n needed to pay off a loan of amount K at the rate a per period, when the interest rate is r per period, is given by

$$n = \frac{\ln a - \ln(a - rK)}{\ln(1 + r)}$$

(3)

EXAMPLE 4   A loan of $50 000 is to be repaid by paying $20 000, which covers both interest and the principal repayment, at the end of each of the coming years, until the loan is fully paid off. When is the loan paid off, and what is the final payment if the annual rate is 15%?

Solution: We begin by computing the number n of annual payments of $20 000 which are needed to pay off $50 000. According to (3), with $r = 0.15$, $a = 20 000$, and $K = 50 000$, we obtain:

$$n = \frac{\ln(20\,000) - \ln(20\,000 - 0.15 \cdot 50\,000)}{\ln(1 + 0.15)} \approx 3.3629$$

Thus three payments of $20 000 are needed, with an additional payment in the fourth year. Let us calculate the future value of the three payments of $20 000 three years after the loan was made. This value is:

$$20\,000 \cdot (1.15)^2 + 20\,000 \cdot 1.15 + 20\,000 = \frac{20\,000}{0.15}\left[(1.15)^3 - 1\right] \approx 69\,450$$

The future value of the $50 000 loan after the same 3 years is $50\,000 \cdot (1.15)^3 = 76\,043.75$. Thus the remaining debt after the third payment is $76\,043.75 - 69\,450 = 6593.75$. If the remaining debt and the accumulated interest are paid one year later, the amount due is $6593.75 \cdot 1.15 = 7582.81$.

Deposits within an Interest Period

Many bank accounts have an interest period of one year, or at least one month. If you deposit an amount *within* an interest period, the bank will often use simple interest, not compound interest. In this case, if you make a deposit within an interest period, then at the end of the period the amount you deposited will be multiplied by the factor $1 + rt$, where t is the remaining fraction of the interest period.

EXAMPLE 5   At the end of each quarter, beginning on March 31, 1999, a person deposits $100 in an account on which interest is paid annually at the rate 10% per year. How much is there in the account on December 31, 2001?

Solution: The deposits during 1999 are illustrated in the following figure:

31/3	30/6	30/9	31/12
100	100	100	100

These four deposits are made within the year. In order to find the balance at the end of the year (the interest period), we use simple (i.e. not compound) interest. This gives:

$$100\left(1 + 0.10 \cdot \frac{3}{4}\right) + 100\left(1 + 0.10 \cdot \frac{2}{4}\right) + 100\left(1 + 0.10 \cdot \frac{1}{4}\right) + 100 = 415$$

Doing the same for 2000 and 2001 as well, we replace the 12 original deposits by the amount 415.00 at the end of each of the years 1999, 2000, and 2001.

31/12-1999	31/12-2000	31/12-2001
415	415	415

The balance on 31/12/2001 is:

$$415 \cdot (1.10)^2 + 415 \cdot 1.10 + 415 = 1373.65$$

So on December 31, 2001 the person has $1373.65.

PROBLEMS FOR SECTION 10.6

1. A person borrows $80 000 at the beginning of one year, and is supposed to pay it off in 10 equal installments at the end of each year, with interest at 7% compounding annually. Find the annual payment.

2. Suppose that the loan in Problem 1 is being repaid in equal installments at the end of each month, with interest at the nominal rate 7% compounded monthly. Find the monthly payment.

3. (a) If you deposit $8000 in an account each year for 6 years at the rate of interest 7%, how much do you have immediately after the last deposit? How much do you have 4 years after the last deposit?

   (b) Ronald invests money in a project which triples his money in 20 years. Assuming annual compounding of interest, what is the rate of interest? What if you assume continuous compounding?

HARDER PROBLEMS

4. A construction firm wants to buy a building site and has the choice between three different payment schedules:

   (a) Pay $67 000 in cash.
   (b) Pay $12 000 per year for 8 years, where the first instalment is to be paid at once.
   (c) Pay $22 000 in cash and thereafter $7000 per year for 12 years, where the first instalment is to be paid after 1 year.

   Determine which schedule is least expensive if the interest rate is 11.5% and the firm has at least $67 000 available to spend in cash. What happens if the interest rate is 12.5%?

10.7 Internal Rate of Return

Consider $n+1$ numbers $a_0, a_1, \ldots, a_n$ which represent the returns in successive years earned by an investment project. Negative numbers represent losses, positive numbers represent profits, so each a_i is actually the *net return*. Also, we think of a_i as associated with year i, whereas a_0 is associated with the present period. In most investment projects, a_0 is a big negative number, because a large expense precedes any positive returns. If we consider an interest rate of $p\%$ per year and let $r = p/100$, then the net present value of the profits accruing from the project is given by

$$A = a_0 + \frac{a_1}{1+r} + \frac{a_2}{(1+r)^2} + \cdots + \frac{a_n}{(1+r)^n}$$

Several different criteria are used to compare alternative investment projects. One is simply this: Choose the project whose profit stream has the largest present value. The interest rate to use could be an accepted rate for capital investments.

A different criterion is based on the **internal rate of return**, defined as an interest rate that makes the present value of all payments equal to 0.

As a simple example, suppose you invest an amount a which pays back b one year later. Then the rate of return is the interest rate r that makes the present value of the investment project equal to zero. That is, r must satisfy $-a + (1+r)^{-1}b = 0$, so $r = (b/a) - 1$. For example, when $a = 1000$ and $b = 1200$, the rate of return is $r = (1200/1000) - 1 = 0.2$, or 20% per year.

For a general investment project yielding returns $a_0, a_1, \ldots, a_n$, the internal rate of return is a number r such that

$$a_0 + \frac{a_1}{1+r} + \frac{a_2}{(1+r)^2} + \cdots + \frac{a_n}{(1+r)^n} = 0 \tag{1}$$

If two investment projects both have a unique internal rate of return, then a criterion for choosing between them is to prefer the project that has the higher internal rate of return. Note that (1) is a polynomial equation of degree n in the discount factor $(1 + r)^{-1}$. In general, this equation does not have a unique positive solution r.

EXAMPLE 1   An investment project has an initial outlay of \$50 000, and at the end of the next two years has returns of \$30 000 and \$40 000, respectively. Find the associated internal rate of return.

Solution: In this case, equation (1) takes the form

$$-50\,000 + \frac{30\,000}{1+r} + \frac{40\,000}{(1+r)^2} = 0$$

Put $s = (1+r)^{-1}$. Then the equation becomes

$$40\,000s^2 + 30\,000s - 50\,000 = 0 \qquad \text{or} \qquad 4s^2 + 3s - 5 = 0$$

This has only one positive solution, $s \approx 0.804$. Then $r = 1/s - 1 \approx 0.243$. The internal rate of return is therefore 24.3%.

NOTE 1 Suppose that $a_0 < 0$ and $a_1, \ldots, a_n$ are all > 0. Then (1) has a unique solution satisfying $1 + r^* > 0$, that is a unique internal rate of return $r^* > -1$. Also, the internal rate of return is positive if $\sum_{i=0}^{n} a_i > 0$. You are asked to prove these results in Problem 3.

1. An investment project has an initial outlay of $50 000 and at the end of each of the next two years has returns of $30 000. Find the associated internal rate of return r.

2. Suppose that in (1) we have $a_0 < 0$ and $a_i = a > 0$ for $i = 1, 2, \ldots$. Find an expression for the internal rate of return in the limit as $n \to \infty$.

3. Consider an investment project with an initial loss, so that $a_0 < 0$, and thereafter no losses. Suppose also that the sum of the later profits is larger than the initial loss. Prove the two claims in Note 1. (*Hint:* Define $f(r)$ as the expression on the left side of (1). Then study the signs of $f(r)$ and $f'(r)$ on the interval $(0, \infty)$.)

4. An investment in a certain machine is expected to earn a profit of $400 000 each year. What is the maximum price that should be paid for the machine if it has a lifetime of 7 years, the interest rate is 17.5%, and the annual profit is earned at the end of each year?

HARDER PROBLEMS

5. An investment project has an initial outlay of $100 000, and at the end of each of the next 20 years has a return of $10 000. Show that there is a unique positive internal rate of return, and find its approximate value. (*Hint:* Use $s = (1 + r)^{-1}$ as a new variable. Prove that the equation you obtain for s has a unique positive solution. Verify that $s = 0.928$ is an approximate root.)

6. A is obliged to pay B $1000 yearly for 5 years, the first payment in 1 year's time. B sells this claim to C for $4340 in cash. Find an equation that determines the rate of return p that C obtains from this investment. Prove that it is a little less than 5%.

1. (a) An amount $5000 earns interest at 3% per year. What will this amount have grown to after 10 years?

   (b) How long does it take for the $5000 to double?

2. An amount of 8000 euros is invested at 5% per year.

   (a) What is the balance in the account after 3 years?

   (b) What is the balance after 13 years?

   (c) How long does it take (approximately) for the balance to reach 32 000 euros?

3. Which is preferable for a borrower: (i) to borrow at the annual interest rate of 11% with interest paid yearly; or (ii) to borrow at annual interest rate 10% with interest paid monthly?

4. Suppose the sum of £15 000 is invested in an account earning interest at an annual rate of 7%. What is the balance after 12 years if interest is compounded continuously?

5. (a) How much has $8000 increased to after 3 years if the annual interest rate is 6%, with continuous compounding?

   (b) How long does it take before the $8000 has doubled?

6. Find the sums of the following infinite series:

   (a) $44 + 44 \cdot 0.56 + 44 \cdot (0.56)^2 + \cdots$

   (b) $\sum_{n=0}^{\infty} 20 \left(\frac{1}{1.2}\right)^n$

   (c) $3 + \dfrac{3 \cdot 2}{5} + \dfrac{3 \cdot 2^2}{5^2} + \cdots + \dfrac{3 \cdot 2^{n-1}}{5^{n-1}} + \cdots$

   (d) $\sum_{j=-2}^{\infty} \dfrac{1}{20^j}$

7. (a) Find the present discounted value (PDV) of a constant income stream of a dollars per year over the next T years, assuming an interest rate of r annually, compounded continuously.

   (b) What is the limit of the PDV as $T \to \infty$? Compare this result with (10.5.4).

8. (a) At the beginning of a year $5000 is deposited in an account earning 4% annual interest. What is the balance after 4 years?

   (b) At the end of each year for four years, $5000 is deposited in an account earning 4% annual interest. What is the balance immediately after the fourth deposit?

   (c) Suppose you had $10 000 in your account on 1st January 1996. You agreed to deposit a fixed amount K each year for 8 years, the first deposit on 1st January 1999. What choice of the fixed amount K will imply that you have a balance of $70 000 immediately after the last deposit? The annual interest rate is 4%.

9. A business borrows 500 000 euros from a bank at the beginning of one year, and is supposed to pay it off in 10 equal instalments at the end of each year, with interest at 7% compounding annually.

   (a) Find the annual payment. What is the total amount paid to the bank?

   (b) What is the total amount if the business has to pay twice a year?

10. Lucy is offered the choice between the following three options:

    (a) She gets $3200 each year for 10 years. First payment due after 1 year.

    (b) She gets $7000 today, and thereafter $3000 each year for 5 years. First payment after 1 year.

    (c) She gets $4000 each year for 10 years. First payment only due after 5 years.
    The annual interest rate is 8%. Calculate the present values of the three options. What would you advise Lucy to choose?

11. The revenue produced by a new oil well is $1 million per year initially ($t = 0$), and it is assumed that it will rise uniformly to $5 million per year after 10 years. If we measure time in years and let $f(t)$ denote the revenue (in millions of dollars) per unit of time at time t, it follows that $f(t) = 1 + 0.4t$. If $F(t)$ denotes the total revenue which accumulates over the time interval $[0, t]$, then $F'(t) = f(t)$.

    (a) Calculate the total revenue earned during the 10 year period (i.e. $F(10)$).

    (b) Find the present value of the revenue stream over the time interval $[0, 10]$, if we assume continuously compounded interest at the rate $r = 0.05$ per year.

11

FUNCTIONS OF MANY VARIABLES

Mathematics is not a careful march down a well-cleared highway,
but a journey into a strange wilderness, where the explorers often
get lost.
—W.S. Anglin (1992)

So far, this book has been concerned with functions of one variable almost exclusively. Yet a realistic description of many economic phenomena requires considering a large number of variables. For example, one consumer's demand for a good like orange juice depends on its price, on the consumer's income, and on the prices of substitutes like other soft drinks, or complements like some kinds of food.

Previous chapters have presented important properties of functions of one variable. For functions of several variables, most of what economists need to know consists of relatively simple extensions of properties presented in the previous chapters for functions of one variable. Moreover, most of the difficulties already arise in the transition from one variable to two variables. To help students see how to overcome these difficulties, the first three sections of this chapter deal exclusively with functions of two variables. These have graphs in three dimensions, which it is possible to represent even in two-dimensional figures—though with some difficulty. However, as the previous example of the demand for orange juice suggests, there are many interesting economic problems that can only be represented mathematically by functions of many variables. These are discussed in the last four sections of the chapter.

11.1 Functions of Two Variables

We begin with the following definition:

FUNCTIONS OF TWO VARIABLES

A **function** f **of two variables** x **and** y with **domain** D is a rule that assigns a specified number $f(x, y)$ to each point (x, y) in D. (1)

If f is a function of two variables, we sometimes let a letter like z denote the value of f at (x, y), so $z = f(x, y)$. Then we call x and y the **independent variables**, or the **arguments** of f, whereas z is called the **dependent variable**, because the value z (in general) depends on the values of x and y. The domain of the function f is then the set of all possible pairs of the independent variables, whereas the **range** is the set of corresponding values of the dependent variable. In economics, x and y are often called the *exogenous* variables, whereas z is the *endogenous* variable.

EXAMPLE 1   Consider the function f that, to every pair of numbers (x, y), assigns the number $2x + x^2 y^3$. The function f is thus defined by

$$f(x, y) = 2x + x^2 y^3$$

What are $f(1, 0)$, $f(0, 1)$, $f(-2, 3)$, and $f(a + 1, b)$?

Solution: First, $f(1, 0)$ is the value when $x = 1$ and $y = 0$. So $f(1, 0) = 2 \cdot 1 + 1^2 \cdot 0^3 = 2$. Similarly, $f(0, 1) = 2 \cdot 0 + 0^2 \cdot 1^3 = 0$, and $f(-2, 3) = 2(-2) + (-2)^2 \cdot 3^3 = -4 + 4 \cdot 27 = 104$. Finally, we find $f(a + 1, b)$ by replacing x with $a + 1$ and y with b in the formula for $f(x, y)$, giving $f(a + 1, b) = 2(a + 1) + (a + 1)^2 b^3$. ∎

EXAMPLE 2   A study of the demand for milk by R. Frisch and T. Haavelmo found the relationship

$$x = A \frac{m^{2.08}}{p^{1.5}} \qquad (A \text{ is a positive constant})$$

where x is milk consumption, p is the relative price of milk, and m is income per family. This equation defines x as a function of p and m. Note that milk consumption goes up when income m increases, and goes down when the price of milk increases, which seems reasonable. ∎

EXAMPLE 3   A function of two variables appearing in many economic models is

$$F(x, y) = A x^a y^b \qquad (A, a, \text{ and } b \text{ are constants}) \tag{2}$$

Usually, one assumes that F is defined only for $x > 0$ and $y > 0$. Then F is generally called a **Cobb–Douglas function**.[1] Note that the function defined in the previous example is a Cobb–Douglas function, because we have $x = A p^{-1.5} m^{2.08}$.

The Cobb–Douglas function is most often used to describe certain production processes. Then x and y are called *input factors*, while $F(x, y)$ is the number of units produced, or the *output*. Also, F is called a *production function*. ∎

---

[1] The function in (2) is named after two American researchers, C. W. Cobb and P. H. Douglas, who applied it (with $a + b = 1$) in a paper that appeared in 1927 on the estimation of production functions. The function should properly be called a "Wicksell function," because the Swedish economist Knut Wicksell (1851–1926) introduced such production functions before 1900.

It is important to become thoroughly familiar with standard functional notation.

EXAMPLE 4   For the function F given in (2), find an expression for $F(2x, 2y)$ and for $F(tx, ty)$, where t is an arbitrary positive number. Find also an expression for $F(x + h, y) - F(x, y)$. Give economic interpretations.

Solution: We find that

$$F(2x, 2y) = A(2x)^a (2y)^b = A2^a x^a 2^b y^b = 2^a 2^b Ax^a y^b = 2^{a+b} F(x, y)$$

When F is a production function, this shows that if each of the input factors is doubled, then the output is 2^{a+b} times as large. For example, if $a + b = 1$, then doubling each factor of production implies doubling the output. In the general case,

$$F(tx, ty) = A(tx)^a (ty)^b = At^a x^a t^b y^b = t^a t^b Ax^a y^b = t^{a+b} F(x, y) \qquad (*)$$

Formulate this result in your own words. Because of property $(*)$, we call the function F *homogeneous of degree* $a + b$. Homogeneous functions are discussed in Sections 12.6 and 12.7.

Finally, we see that

$$F(x + h, y) - F(x, y) = A(x + h)^a y^b - Ax^a y^b = Ay^b [(x + h)^a - x^a] \qquad (**)$$

This shows the change in output when the first input factor is changed by h units while the other input factor is unchanged. For example, suppose $A = 100$, $a = 1/2$, and $b = 1/4$, in which case $F(x, y) = 100x^{1/2} y^{1/4}$. Now, if we choose $x = 16$, $y = 16$, and $h = 1$, then $(**)$ implies that

$$F(16 + 1, 16) - F(16, 16) = 100 \cdot 16^{1/4} [17^{1/2} - 16^{1/2}] = 100 \cdot 2[\sqrt{17} - 4] \approx 24.6$$

Hence, if we increase the input of the first factor from 16 to 17, while keeping the input of the second factor constant at 16 units, then we increase production by about 24.6 units.   ▌

Domains

For functions studied in economics, there are usually explicit or implicit restrictions on the domain D where the function is defined, as in (1). For instance, if $f(x, y)$ is a production function, we usually assume that the input quantities are nonnegative, so $x \geq 0$ and $y \geq 0$. In economics, it is often crucially important to be clear what are the domains of the functions being used.

As for functions of one variable, we assume, unless otherwise stated, that the domain of a function defined by a formula is the largest domain in which the formula gives a meaningful and unique value.

For functions of two variables x and y, the domain D is a set of points in the xy-plane. Sometimes it is helpful to draw a picture of the domain in the xy-plane.

EXAMPLE 5   Determine the domains of the functions given by the following formulas, then draw the sets in the xy-plane.

(a) $f(x, y) = \sqrt{x - 1} + \sqrt{y}$ (b) $g(x, y) = \dfrac{2}{(x^2 + y^2 - 4)^{1/2}} + \sqrt{9 - (x^2 + y^2)}$

Solution:

(a) We must require that $x \geq 1$ and $y \geq 0$, for only then do $\sqrt{x - 1}$ and $\sqrt{y}$ have any meaning. The (unbounded) domain is indicated in Fig. 1.

(b) $(x^2 + y^2 - 4)^{1/2} = \sqrt{x^2 + y^2 - 4}$ is only defined if $x^2 + y^2 \geq 4$. Moreover, we must have $x^2 + y^2 \neq 4$; otherwise, the denominator is equal to 0. Furthermore, we must require that $9 - (x^2 + y^2) \geq 0$, or $x^2 + y^2 \leq 9$. All in all, therefore, we must have $4 < x^2 + y^2 \leq 9$. Because the graph of $x^2 + y^2 = r^2$ consists of all the points on the circle with centre at the origin and radius r, the domain is the set of points (x, y) that lie outside (but not on) the circle $x^2 + y^2 = 4$, and inside or on the circle $x^2 + y^2 = 9$. This set is shown in Fig. 2.

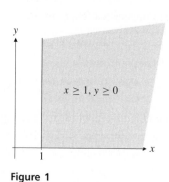

Figure 1

Figure 2

PROBLEMS FOR SECTION 11.1

1. Let $f(x, y) = x + 2y$. Find $f(0, 1)$, $f(2, -1)$, $f(a, a)$, and $f(a + h, b) - f(a, b)$.

2. Let $f(x, y) = xy^2$. Find $f(0, 1)$, $f(-1, 2)$, $f(10^4, 10^{-2})$, $f(a, a)$, $f(a + h, b)$, and $f(a, b + k) - f(a, b)$.

3. Let $f(x, y) = 3x^2 - 2xy + y^3$. Find $f(1, 1)$, $f(-2, 3)$, $f(1/x, 1/y)$, $p = \left[f(x + h, y) - f(x, y)\right]/h$, and $q = \left[f(x, y + k) - f(x, y)\right]/k$.

4. (a) Let $f(x, y) = x^2 + 2xy + y^2$. Find $f(-1, 2)$, $f(a, a)$, and $f(a + h, b) - f(a, b)$.

   (b) Prove that $f(2x, 2y) = 2^2 f(x, y)$ and that $f(tx, ty) = t^2 f(x, y)$ for all t.

5. Let $F(K, L) = 10K^{1/2}L^{1/3}$, $K \geq 0$, $L \geq 0$. Find $F(1, 1)$, $F(4, 27)$, $F(9, 1/27)$, $F(3, \sqrt{2})$, $F(100, 1000)$, and $F(2K, 2L)$.

6. Examine for which (x, y) the functions given by the following formulas are defined, then draw the domains of (b) and (c) in the xy-plane.

   (a) $\dfrac{x^2 + y^3}{y - x + 2}$ (b) $\sqrt{2 - (x^2 + y^2)}$ (c) $\sqrt{(4 - x^2 - y^2)(x^2 + y^2 - 1)}$

7. Find the domains of the functions defined by the following formulas:

   (a) $\dfrac{1}{e^{x+y} - 3}$ (b) $\ln(x - a)^2 + \ln(y - b)^2$ (c) $2\ln(x - a) + 2\ln(y - b)$

11.2 Partial Derivatives with Two Variables

For a function $y = f(x)$ of one variable, the derivative $f'(x)$ is a number which measures the function's rate of change as x changes. For functions of two variables, such as $z = f(x, y)$, we also want to examine how quickly the value of the function changes w.r.t. changes in the values of the independent variables. For example, if $f(x, y)$ is a firm's profit when it uses quantities x and y of two different inputs, we want to know whether and by how much profit can increase as x and y are varied.

Consider the function

$$z = x^3 + 2y^2 \qquad (*)$$

Suppose first that y is held constant. Then $2y^2$ is constant. Really there is only one variable now. Of course, the rate of change of z w.r.t. x is given by

$$\frac{dz}{dx} = 3x^2$$

On the other hand, we can keep x fixed in $(*)$ and examine how z varies as y varies. This involves taking the derivative of z w.r.t. y while keeping x constant. The result is

$$\frac{dz}{dy} = 4y$$

Obviously, there are many other variations we could study. For example, x and y could vary simultaneously. But in this section, we restrict our attention to variations in *either* x *or* y.

When we consider functions of two variables, mathematicians (and economists) usually write $\partial z/\partial x$ instead of dz/dx for the derivative of z w.r.t. x when y is held fixed. This slight change of notation, replacing d by ∂, is intended to remind the reader that only one independent variable is changing, with the other(s) held fixed. In the same way, we write $\partial z/\partial y$ instead of dz/dy when y varies and x is held fixed. Hence, we have

$$z = x^3 + 2y^2 \implies \frac{\partial z}{\partial x} = 3x^2 \quad \text{and} \quad \frac{\partial z}{\partial y} = 4y$$

In general, we introduce the following definitions:

PARTIAL DERIVATIVES

If $z = f(x, y)$, then $\partial z/\partial x$ denotes the derivative of $f(x, y)$ w.r.t. x when y is held constant, and $\partial z/\partial y$ denotes the derivative of $f(x, y)$ w.r.t. y when x is held constant.   (1)

When $z = f(x, y)$, we also denote the derivative $\partial z/\partial x$ by $\partial f/\partial x$, and this is called the **partial derivative** of z (or f) w.r.t. x. Often $\partial z/\partial x$ is pronounced "partial $dz\,dx$". In the same way, $\partial z/\partial y = \partial f/\partial y$ is the **partial derivative** of z (or f) w.r.t. y. Note that $\partial f/\partial x$ is the rate of change of $f(x, y)$ w.r.t. x when y is constant, and correspondingly for $\partial f/\partial y$. Of course, because there are two variables, there are two partial derivatives.

It is usually easy to find the partial derivatives of a function $z = f(x, y)$. To find $\partial f/\partial x$, just think of y as a constant and differentiate $f(x, y)$ w.r.t. x as if f were a function only of x. The rules for finding derivatives of functions of one variable can all be used when we want to compute $\partial f/\partial x$. The same is true for $\partial f/\partial y$. Let us look at some further examples.

EXAMPLE 1   Find the partial derivatives of the following functions:

(a) $f(x, y) = x^3 y + x^2 y^2 + x + y^2$ (b) $f(x, y) = \dfrac{xy}{x^2 + y^2}$

Solution:

(a) We find

$$\frac{\partial f}{\partial x} = 3x^2 y + 2xy^2 + 1 \qquad \text{(holding } y \text{ constant)}$$

$$\frac{\partial f}{\partial y} = x^3 + 2x^2 y + 2y \qquad \text{(holding } x \text{ constant)}$$

(b) For this function the quotient rule gives

$$\frac{\partial f}{\partial x} = \frac{y(x^2 + y^2) - 2xxy}{(x^2 + y^2)^2} = \frac{y^3 - x^2 y}{(x^2 + y^2)^2}, \qquad \frac{\partial f}{\partial y} = \frac{x^3 - y^2 x}{(x^2 + y^2)^2}$$

Observe that the function in (b) is symmetric in x and y, in the sense that the function value is unchanged if we interchange x and y. By interchanging x and y in the formula for $\partial f/\partial x$, therefore, we will find the correct formula for $\partial f/\partial y$. (Find $\partial f/\partial y$ in the usual way and check that the foregoing answer is correct.)   ∎

Several other forms of notation are often used to indicate the partial derivatives of $z = f(x, y)$. Some of the most common are

$$\frac{\partial f}{\partial x} = \frac{\partial z}{\partial x} = z'_x = f'_x(x, y) = f'_1(x, y) = \frac{\partial f(x, y)}{\partial x}$$

$$\frac{\partial f}{\partial y} = \frac{\partial z}{\partial y} = z'_y = f'_y(x, y) = f'_2(x, y) = \frac{\partial f(x, y)}{\partial y}$$

Among these, $f_1'(x, y)$ and $f_2'(x, y)$ are the most satisfactory. Here the numerical subscript refers to the position of the argument in the function. Thus, f_1' indicates the partial derivative w.r.t. the first variable, and f_2' w.r.t. the second variable. This notation also reminds us that the partial derivatives themselves are functions of x and y. Finally, $f_1'(a, b)$ and $f_2'(a, b)$ are suitable designations of the values of the partial derivatives at point (a, b) instead of at (x, y). For example, given the function $f(x, y) = x^3 y + x^2 y^2 + x + y^2$ in Example 1(a), one has

$$f_1'(x, y) = 3x^2 y + 2xy^2 + 1 \, , \quad f_1'(a, b) = 3a^2 b + 2ab^2 + 1, \quad \text{etc.}$$

In particular, $f_1'(0, 0) = 1$ and $f_1'(-1, 2) = 3(-1)^2 2 + 2(-1)2^2 + 1 = -1$.

The alternative notation $f_x'(x, y)$ and $f_y'(x, y)$ is often used, but especially in connection with composite functions it is sometimes too ambiguous. For instance, what is the meaning of $f_x'(x^2 y, x - y)$?

Remember that the numbers $f_1'(x, y)$ and $f_2'(x, y)$ measure the rate of change of f w.r.t. x and y, respectively. For example, if $f_1'(x, y) > 0$, then a small increase in x will lead to an increase in $f(x, y)$.

EXAMPLE 2   In Example 11.1.2 we studied the function $x = Ap^{-1.5} m^{2.08}$. Find the partial derivatives of x w.r.t. p and m, and discuss their signs.

Solution: We find that $\partial x / \partial p = -1.5 Ap^{-2.5} m^{2.08}$ and $\partial x / \partial m = 2.08 Ap^{-1.5} m^{1.08}$. Because A, p, and m are positive, $\partial x / \partial p < 0$ and $\partial x / \partial m > 0$. These signs are in accordance with the final remarks in the example.   ∎

Formal Definitions of Partial Derivatives

So far the functions have been given by explicit formulas and we have found the partial derivatives by using the ordinary rules for differentiation. If these rules cannot be used, however, we must resort directly to the formal definition of partial derivative. This is derived from the definition of derivative for functions of one variable in the following rather obvious way.

If $z = f(x, y)$, then with $g(x) = f(x, y)$ (y fixed), the partial derivative of $f(x, y)$ w.r.t. x is simply $g'(x)$. Now, the definition $g'(x)$ is $g'(x) = \lim_{h \to 0} [g(x + h) - g(x)] / h$. Because $f_1'(x, y) = g'(x)$, it follows that

$$f_1'(x, y) = \lim_{h \to 0} \frac{f(x + h, y) - f(x, y)}{h} \qquad (2)$$

In the same way,

$$f_2'(x, y) = \lim_{k \to 0} \frac{f(x, y + k) - f(x, y)}{k} \qquad (3)$$

If the limit in (2) (or (3)) does not exist, then we say that $f_1'(x, y)$ (or $f_2'(x, y)$) *does not exist*, or that z is *not differentiable* w.r.t. x or y at the point. For instance, the function $f(x, y) = |x| + |y|$ is not differentiable at the point $(x, y) = (0, 0)$.

If $h = dx$ is small in absolute value, then from (2) we obtain the approximation, $f_1'(x, y) \approx [f(x + dx, y) - f(x, y)]/dx$, so

$$f_1'(x, y)dx \approx f(x + dx, y) - f(x, y) \tag{4}$$

Similarly, if dy is small in absolute value,

$$f_2'(x, y)dy \approx f(x, y + dy) - f(x, y) \tag{5}$$

In these approximations, if we put $dx = 1$ and $dy = 1$, we can interpret them in the following way:

(A) The partial derivative $f_1'(x, y)$ is approximately equal to the change in $f(x, y)$ that results from increasing x by one unit while holding y constant.

(B) The partial derivative $f_2'(x, y)$ is approximately equal to the change in $f(x, y)$ that results from increasing y by one unit while holding x constant.

(6)

NOTE 1 The approximations in (6) must be used with caution. Roughly speaking, they will not be too inaccurate provided that the partial derivatives do not vary too much over the actual intervals.

EXAMPLE 3   Let $Y = F(K, L)$ be the number of units produced when K units of capital and L units of labour are used as inputs in a production process. What is the economic interpretation of $F_K'(100, 50) = 5$?

Solution: From (6), $F_K'(100, 50) \approx F(101, 50) - F(100, 50)$. So $F_K'(100, 50) = 5$ means that increasing capital input from 100 to 101 and keeping labour input fixed at 50, production increases by approximately 5 units.

Higher-Order Partial Derivatives

If $z = f(x, y)$, then $\partial f/\partial x$ and $\partial f/\partial y$ are called **first-order partial derivatives**. These partial derivatives are, in general, again functions of two variables. From $\partial f/\partial x$, provided this derivative is itself differentiable, we can generate two new functions by taking the partial derivatives w.r.t. x and y. In the same way, we can take the partial derivatives of $\partial f/\partial y$ w.r.t. x and y. The four functions we obtain by differentiating twice in this way are called **second-order partial derivatives** of $f(x, y)$. They are expressed as

$$\frac{\partial}{\partial x}\left(\frac{\partial f}{\partial x}\right) = \frac{\partial^2 f}{\partial x^2}, \qquad \frac{\partial}{\partial y}\left(\frac{\partial f}{\partial x}\right) = \frac{\partial^2 f}{\partial y \partial x}$$

$$\frac{\partial}{\partial x}\left(\frac{\partial f}{\partial y}\right) = \frac{\partial^2 f}{\partial x \partial y}, \qquad \frac{\partial}{\partial y}\left(\frac{\partial f}{\partial y}\right) = \frac{\partial^2 f}{\partial y^2}$$

For brevity, we sometimes refer to the first- and second-order "partials," suppressing the word "derivatives."

EXAMPLE 4   For the function in Example 1(a), we obtain

$$\frac{\partial^2 f}{\partial x^2} = 6xy + 2y^2, \qquad \frac{\partial^2 f}{\partial y \partial x} = 3x^2 + 4xy = \frac{\partial^2 f}{\partial x \partial y}, \qquad \frac{\partial^2 f}{\partial y^2} = 2x^2 + 2 \qquad \blacksquare$$

As with first-order partial derivatives, several other kinds of notation are also frequently used for second-order partial derivatives. For example, $\partial^2 f/\partial x^2$ is also denoted by $f_{11}''(x, y)$ or $f_{xx}''(x, y)$. In the same way, $\partial^2 f/\partial y \partial x$ can also be written as $f_{12}''(x, y)$ or $f_{xy}''(x, y)$. Note that $f_{12}''(x, y)$ means that we differentiate $f(x, y)$ first w.r.t. the first argument x and then w.r.t. the second argument y. To find $f_{21}''(x, y)$, we must differentiate in the reverse order. In Example 4, these two "mixed" second-order partial derivatives (or "cross-partials") are equal. For most functions $z = f(x, y)$, it will actually be the case that

$$\frac{\partial^2 f}{\partial x \partial y} = \frac{\partial^2 f}{\partial y \partial x} \tag{7}$$

Sufficient conditions for the equality in (7) are given in Theorem 11.6.1.

It is very important to note the exact meaning of the different symbols that have been introduced. If we consider (7), for example, it would be a serious mistake to believe that the two expressions are equal because $\partial x \partial y$ is the same as $\partial y \partial x$. Here the expression on the left-hand side is in fact the derivative of $\partial f/\partial y$ w.r.t. x, and the right-hand side is the derivative of $\partial f/\partial x$ w.r.t. y. It is a remarkable fact, and not a triviality, that the two are usually equal. As another example, we observe that $\partial^2 z/\partial x^2$ is quite different from $(\partial z/\partial x)^2$. For example, if $z = x^2 + y^2$, then $\partial z/\partial x = 2x$. Therefore, $\partial^2 z/\partial x^2 = 2$, whereas $(\partial z/\partial x)^2 = 4x^2$.

Analogously, we define partial derivatives of the third, fourth, and higher orders. For example, we write $\partial^4 z/\partial x \partial y^3 = z_{yyyx}''''$ when we first differentiate z three times w.r.t. y and then differentiate the result once more w.r.t. x.

Here is an additional example.

EXAMPLE 5   If $f(x, y) = x^3 e^{y^2}$, find the first- and second-order partial derivatives at $(x, y) = (1, 0)$.

Solution: To find $f_1'(x, y)$, we differentiate $x^3 e^{y^2}$ w.r.t. x while treating y as a constant. When y is a constant, so is e^{y^2}. Hence,

$$f_1'(x, y) = 3x^2 e^{y^2} \qquad \text{and so} \qquad f_1'(1, 0) = 3 \cdot 1^2 e^{0^2} = 3$$

To find $f_2'(x, y)$, we differentiate $f(x, y)$ w.r.t. y while treating x as a constant:

$$f_2'(x, y) = x^3 2y e^{y^2} = 2x^3 y e^{y^2} \qquad \text{and so} \qquad f_2'(1, 0) = 0$$

To find the second-order partial $f_{11}''(x, y)$, we must differentiate $f_1'(x, y)$ w.r.t. x once more, while treating y as a constant. Hence,

$$f_{11}''(x, y) = 6x e^{y^2} \qquad \text{and so} \qquad f_{11}''(1, 0) = 6 \cdot 1 e^{0^2} = 6$$

To find $f_{22}''(x, y)$, we must differentiate $f_2'(x, y) = 2x^3 y e^{y^2}$ w.r.t. y once more, while treating x as a constant. Because $y e^{y^2}$ is a product of two functions, each involving y, we use the product rule to obtain

$$f_{22}''(x, y) = (2x^3)(1 \cdot e^{y^2} + y 2 y e^{y^2}) = 2x^3 e^{y^2} + 4x^3 y^2 e^{y^2}$$

Evaluating this at $(1, 0)$ gives $f_{22}''(1, 0) = 2$. Moreover,

$$f_{12}''(x, y) = \frac{\partial}{\partial y}\left[f_1'(x, y) \right] = \frac{\partial}{\partial y}(3x^2 e^{y^2}) = 3x^2 2 y e^{y^2} = 6x^2 y e^{y^2}$$

and

$$f_{21}''(x, y) = \frac{\partial}{\partial x}\left[f_2'(x, y) \right] = \frac{\partial}{\partial x}(2x^3 y e^{y^2}) = 6x^2 y e^{y^2}$$

Hence, $f_{12}''(1, 0) = f_{21}''(1, 0) = 0$.

PROBLEMS FOR SECTION 11.2

1. Find $\partial z/\partial x$ and $\partial z/\partial y$ for the following:

   (a) $z = 2x + 3y$ (b) $z = x^2 + y^3$ (c) $z = x^3 y^4$ (d) $z = (x + y)^2$

2. Find $\partial z/\partial x$ and $\partial z/\partial y$ for the following:

   (a) $z = x^2 + 3y^2$ (b) $z = xy$ (c) $z = 5x^4 y^2 - 2xy^5$ (d) $z = e^{x+y}$

   (e) $z = e^{xy}$ (f) $z = e^x/y$ (g) $z = \ln(x + y)$ (h) $z = \ln(xy)$

3. Find $f_1'(x, y)$, $f_2'(x, y)$, and $f_{12}''(x, y)$ for the following:

   (a) $f(x, y) = x^7 - y^7$ (b) $f(x, y) = x^5 \ln y$ (c) $f(x, y) = (x^2 - 2y^2)^5$

4. Find all first- and second-order partial derivatives for the following:

   (a) $z = 3x + 4y$ (b) $z = x^3 y^2$ (c) $z = x^5 - 3x^2 y + y^6$

   (d) $z = x/y$ (e) $z = (x - y)/(x + y)$ (f) $z = \sqrt{x^2 + y^2}$

5. Find all the first- and second-order partial derivatives of:

   (a) $z = x^2 + e^{2y}$ (b) $z = y \ln x$ (c) $z = xy^2 - e^{xy}$ (d) $z = x^y$

6. Let $F(S, E) = 2.26 \, S^{0.44} E^{0.48}$. (This is an estimated production function for a certain lobster fishery where S denotes the stock of lobster, E the harvesting effort, and $F(S, E)$ the catch.)

   (a) Find $F_S'(S, E)$ and $F_E'(S, E)$.

   (b) Show that $SF_S' + EF_E' = kF$ for a suitable constant k.

7. Prove that if $z = (ax + by)^2$, then $xz'_x + yz'_y = 2z$.

8. Let

$$z = \frac{1}{2}\ln(x^2 + y^2)$$

Show that $\partial^2 z/\partial x^2 + \partial^2 z/\partial y^2 = 0$.

11.3 Geometric Representation

When studying functions of one variable, we saw how useful it was to represent the function by its graph in a coordinate system in the plane. This section considers how to visualize functions of two variables as having graphs which form surfaces in (three-dimensional) space. We begin by introducing a coordinate system in space.

Recall how any point in a plane can be represented by a pair of real numbers by using two mutually orthogonal coordinate lines: a rectangular coordinate system in the plane. In a similar way, points in space can be represented by triples of real numbers using three mutually orthogonal coordinate lines. In Fig. 1 we have drawn such a coordinate system. The three lines that are orthogonal to each other and intersect at the point O in Fig. 1 are called *coordinate axes*. They are usually called the x-axis, y-axis, and z-axis. We choose units to measure the length along each axis, and select a positive direction on each of them as indicated by the arrows.

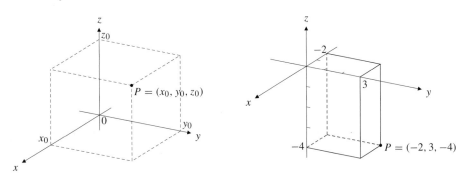

Figure 1   Figure 2

The equation $x = 0$ is satisfied by all points in a *coordinate plane* spanned by the y-axis and the z-axis. This is called the yz-plane. There are two other coordinate planes: the xy-plane on which $z = 0$; and the xz-plane on which $y = 0$. We often think of the xy-plane as horizontal, with the z-axis passing vertically through it.

Each coordinate plane divides the space into two *half-spaces*. For example, the xy-plane separates the space into the regions where $z > 0$, above the xy-plane, and $z < 0$, below the xy-plane. The three coordinate planes together divide up the space into 8 *octants*. The octant which has $x \geq 0$, $y \geq 0$, and $z \geq 0$ is called the *nonnegative octant*.

Every point P in space now has an associated triple of numbers (x_0, y_0, z_0) that describes its location, as suggested in Fig. 1. Conversely, it is clear that every triple of numbers also represents a unique point in space in this way. Note in particular that when z_0 is negative, the point (x_0, y_0, z_0) lies below the xy-plane in which $z = 0$. In Fig. 2, we have constructed the point P with coordinates $(-2, 3, -4)$. The point P in Fig. 1 lies in the positive octant.

The Graph of a Function of Two Variables

Suppose $z = f(x, y)$ is a function of two variables defined over a domain D in the xy-plane. The **graph** of the function f is the set of all points $(x, y, f(x, y))$ in the space obtained by letting (x, y) "run through" D. If f is a sufficiently "nice" function, the graph of f will be a connected surface in the space, like the graph in Fig. 3. In particular, if (x_0, y_0) is a point in the domain D, we see how the point $P = (x_0, y_0, f(x_0, y_0))$ on the surface is obtained by letting $f(x_0, y_0)$ be the "height" of f at (x_0, y_0).

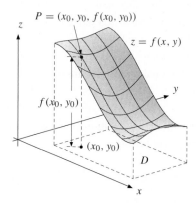

Figure 3   Graph of $y = f(x, y)$

This method of representing a function of two variables helps us to visualize its behaviour in broad outline. However, it requires considerable artistic ability to represent in only two dimensions the graph of $z = f(x, y)$, which lies in three-dimensional space. It is certainly difficult to use the resulting drawing for quantitative measurements. (Using modern computer graphics, however, complicated functions of two variables can have their graphs drawn fairly easily, and these can be rotated or transformed to display the shape of the graph better.)

We now describe a second kind of geometric representation that often does better when we are confined to two dimensions (as we are in the pages of this book).

Level Curves

Map makers can describe some topographical features of the earth's surface such as hills and valleys even in a plane map. One way of doing so is to draw a set of *level curves* or contours connecting points on the map that represent places on the earth's surface with the same elevation above sea level. For instance, there may be such contours corresponding to 100 metres above sea level, others for 200, 300, and 400 metres above sea level, and so on.

Off the coast, or in places like the valley of the River Jordan, there may be contours for 100 metres below sea level, etc. Where the contours are close together, there is a steep slope. Thus, studying a contour map carefully can give a good idea how the altitude varies on the ground.

The same idea can be used to give a geometric representation of an arbitrary function $z = f(x, y)$. The graph of the function in three-dimensional space is visualized as being cut by horizontal planes parallel to the xy-plane. The resulting intersection between each plane and the graph is then projected onto the xy-plane. If the intersecting plane is $z = c$, then the projection of the intersection onto the xy-plane is called the **level curve** at height c for f. This level curve will consist of points satisfying the equation

$$f(x, y) = c$$

Figure 4 illustrates the construction of such a level curve.

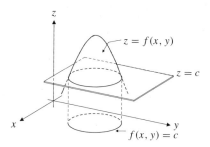

Figure 4 The graph of $z = f(x, y)$ and one of its level curves

EXAMPLE 1   Consider the function of two variables defined by the equation

$$z = x^2 + y^2 \tag{$*$}$$

What are the level curves? Draw both a set of level curves and the graph of the function.

Solution: The variable z can only assume values ≥ 0. Each level curve has the equation

$$x^2 + y^2 = c \tag{$**$}$$

for some $c \geq 0$. We see that these are circles in the xy-plane centred at the origin and with radius $\sqrt{c}$. See Fig. 5.

Concerning the graph of $(*)$, all the level curves are circles. For $y = 0$, we have $z = x^2$. This shows that the graph of $(*)$ cuts the xz-plane (where $y = 0$) in a parabola. Similarly, for $x = 0$, we have $z = y^2$, which is the graph of a parabola in the yz-plane. In fact, the graph of $(*)$ is obtained by rotating the parabola $z = x^2$ around the z-axis. The surface (of revolution) is called a **paraboloid**, and a part of it is shown in Fig. 6. Five of the level curves in the xy-plane are also indicated.

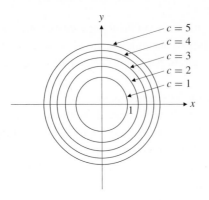

Figure 5　　　　　　　　　　　**Figure 6**

EXAMPLE 2　　Suppose $F(K, L)$ denotes a firm's output when its input of capital is K and that of labour is L. A level curve for the function is a curve in the KL-plane given by

$$F(K, L) = Y_0 \qquad (Y_0 \text{ is a constant})$$

This curve is called an **isoquant** (indicating "equal quantity"). For a Cobb–Douglas function $F(K, L) = AK^aL^b$ with $a + b < 1$ and $A > 0$, Figs. 7 and 8 respectively show a part of the graph near the origin, and three of the isoquants.

Figure 7

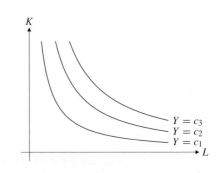

Figure 8

EXAMPLE 3　　Show that all points (x, y) satisfying $xy = 3$ lie on a level curve for the function

$$g(x, y) = \frac{3(xy + 1)^2}{x^4y^4 - 1}$$

Solution:　By substituting $xy = 3$ in the expression for g, we find

$$g(x, y) = \frac{3(xy + 1)^2}{(xy)^4 - 1} = \frac{3(3 + 1)^2}{3^4 - 1} = \frac{48}{80} = \frac{3}{5}$$

This shows that, for all (x, y) where $xy = 3$, the value of $g(x, y)$ is a constant $3/5$. Hence, any point (x, y) satisfying $xy = 3$ is on a level curve (at height $3/5$) for g. (In fact, for any value of $c \neq \pm 1$, $xy = c$ is the equation of a level curve for g because $g(x, y) = 3(c + 1)^2/(c^4 - 1)$ when $xy = c \neq \pm 1$.)

Geometric Interpretations of Partial Derivatives

Partial derivatives of the first order have an interesting geometric interpretation. Let $z = f(x, y)$ be a function of two variables, with its graph as shown in Fig. 9. Let us keep the value of y fixed at y_0. The points $(x, y, f(x, y))$ on the graph of f that have $y = y_0$ are those that lie on the curve K_y indicated in the figure. The partial derivative $f'_x(x_0, y_0)$ is the derivative of $z = f(x, y_0)$ w.r.t. x at the point $x = x_0$, and is therefore the slope of the tangent line l_y to the curve K_y at $x = x_0$. In the same way, $f'_y(x_0, y_0)$ is the slope of the tangent line l_x to the curve K_x at $y = y_0$.

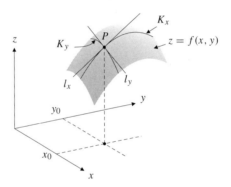

Figure 9

This geometric interpretation of the two partial derivatives can be explained another way. Imagine that the graph of f describes the surface of a mountain, and suppose that we are standing at point P with coordinates $(x_0, y_0, f(x_0, y_0))$ in three dimensions, where the height is $f(x_0, y_0)$ units above the xy-plane. The slope of the terrain at P varies as we look in different directions. In particular, suppose we look in the direction parallel to the positive x-axis. Then $f'_x(x_0, y_0)$ is a measure of the "steepness" in this direction. In the figure, $f'_x(x_0, y_0)$ is negative, because moving from P in the direction given by the positive x-axis will take us downwards. In the same way, we see that $f'_y(x_0, y_0)$ is a measure of the "steepness" in the direction parallel to the positive y-axis. We see that $f'_y(x_0, y_0)$ is positive, meaning that the slope is upward in this direction.

Let us now briefly consider the geometric interpretation of the "direct" second-order derivatives f''_{xx} and f''_{yy}. Consider the curve K_y on the graph of f in the figure. It seems that along this curve, $f''_{xx}(x, y_0)$ is negative, because $f'_x(x, y_0)$ decreases as x increases. In particular, $f''_{xx}(x_0, y_0) < 0$. In the same way, we see that moving along K_x makes $f'_y(x_0, y)$ decrease as y increases, so $f''_{yy}(x_0, y) < 0$ along K_x. In particular, $f''_{yy}(x_0, y_0) < 0$. (The mixed partials, f''_{xy} and f''_{yx}, do not have such easy geometric interpretations.)

EXAMPLE 4   Consider Fig. 10, which shows some level curves of a function $z = f(x, y)$. On the basis of this figure, answer the following questions:

(a) What are the signs of $f_x'(x, y)$ and $f_y'(x, y)$ at the points P and Q? Estimate also the *value* of $f_x'(3, 1)$.

(b) What are the solutions of the equations: (i) $f(3, y) = 4$ and (ii) $f(x, 4) = 6$?

(c) What is the largest value that $f(x, y)$ can attain when $x = 2$, and for which y value does this maximum occur?

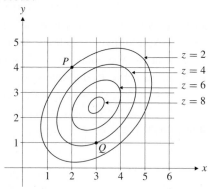

Figure 10

Solution:

(a) If you stand at P, you are on the level curve $f(x, y) = 2$. If you look in the direction of the positive x-axis (along the line $y = 4$), then you will see the terrain sloping upwards, because the (nearest) level curves will correspond to larger z values. Hence, $f_x' > 0$. If you stand at P and look in the direction of the positive y-axis (along $x = 2$), the terrain will slope downwards. Thus, at P, we must have $f_y' < 0$. At Q, we find similarly that $f_x' < 0$ and $f_y' > 0$. To estimate $f_x'(3, 1)$, we use $f_x'(3, 1) \approx f(4, 1) - f(3, 1) = 2 - 4 = -2$. (This approximation is actually far from exact. If we keep $y = 1$ and *decrease* x by one unit, then $f(2, 1) \approx 4$, which should give the estimate $f_x'(3, 1) \approx 4 - 4 = 0$. "The map" is not sufficiently finely graded around Q.)

(b) Equation (i) has the solutions $y = 1$ and $y = 4$, because the line $x = 3$ cuts the level curve $f(x, y) = 4$ at $(3, 1)$ and at $(3, 4)$. Equation (ii) has no solutions, because the line $y = 4$ does not meet the level curve $f(x, y) = 6$ at all.

(c) The highest value of c for which the level curve $f(x, y) = c$ has a point in common with the line $x = 2$ is $c = 6$. The largest value of $f(x, y)$ when $x = 2$ is therefore 6, and we see from Fig. 10 that this maximum value is attained when $y \approx 2.2$.   ∎

PROBLEMS FOR SECTION 11.3

1. Draw a three-dimensional coordinate system and mark the points

$$P = (3, 0, 0), \qquad Q = (0, 2, 0), \qquad R = (0, 0, -4), \qquad S = (3, -2, 4)$$

(For S, you should draw a box like those in Figs. 1 and 2.)

2. Describe geometrically the set of points (x, y, z) in three dimensions where

    (a) $y = 2$, $\quad z = 3$ (*x* varies freely) $\qquad$ (b) $y = x$ (*z* varies freely)

3. Show that
$$x^2 + y^2 = 6$$
   is a level curve of $f(x, y) = \sqrt{x^2 + y^2} - x^2 - y^2 + 2$.

4. Show that
$$x^2 - y^2 = c$$
   is a level curve for $f(x, y) = e^{x^2} e^{-y^2} + x^4 - 2x^2 y^2 + y^4$, for all values of the constant c.

5. Explain why two level curves of the function $z = f(x, y)$ corresponding to different values of z cannot intersect.

6. Let $f(x)$ represent a function of one variable. If we let $g(x, y) = f(x)$, then we have defined a function of two variables, but y is not present in its formula. Explain how the graph of g is obtained from the graph of f. Illustrate with $f(x) = x$ and also with $f(x) = -x^3$.

7. Draw the graphs of the following functions in three-dimensional space, and draw a set of level curves for each of them:

    (a) $z = 3 - x - y$ $\qquad\qquad$ (b) $z = \sqrt{3 - x^2 - y^2}$

8. The figure shows some level curves for the function $z = f(x, y)$.

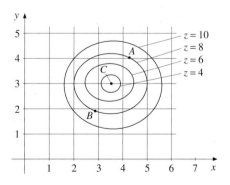

    (a) What is $f(2, 3)$? Solve the equation $f(x, 3) = 8$ for x.

    (b) Find the smallest value of $z = f(x, y)$ if $x = 2$. What is the corresponding value of y?

    (c) What are the signs of $f_1'(x, y)$ and $f_2'(x, y)$ at the points A, B, and C? Estimate the values of these two partial derivatives at A.

9. The figure shows some level curves for a function $z = f(x, y)$, together with the line $2x + 3y = 12$.

   (a) What are the signs of f_x' and f_y' at the points P and Q?

   (b) Find possible solutions of the equations (i) $f(1, y) = 2$ and (ii) $f(x, 2) = 2$.

   (c) What is the largest value of $f(x, y)$ among those (x, y) that satisfy $2x + 3y = 12$?

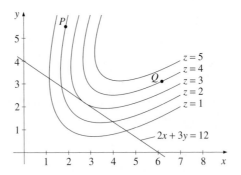

10. Suppose $F(x, y)$ is a function about which all we know is that $F(0, 0) = 0$, as well as that $F_1'(x, y) \geq 2$ for all (x, y), and $F_2'(x, y) \leq 1$ for all (x, y). What can be said about the relative sizes of $F(0, 0)$, $F(1, 0)$, $F(2, 0)$, $F(0, 1)$, and $F(1, 1)$? Write down the inequalities that have to hold between these numbers.

11.4 Surfaces and Distance

An equation such as $f(x, y) = c$ in *two* variables x and y can be represented by a point set in the plane, called the graph of the equation. (See Section 5.4.) In a similar way, an equation $g(x, y, z) = c$ in *three* variables x, y, and z can be represented by a point set in space, also called the **graph** of the equation. This graph consists of all triples (x, y, z) satisfying the equation, and will usually form what can be called a **surface** in space.

One of the simplest types of equation in three variables is

$$ax + by + cz = d \quad \textbf{(the general equation for a plane in space)} \quad (1)$$

(with a, b, and c not all 0). The graph of this equation intersects the xy-plane when $z = 0$. Then $ax + by = d$, which is a straight line in the xy-plane (assuming a and b are not both 0). In the same way we see that, provided at most one of a, b, and c is equal to zero, the graph intersects the two other coordinate planes in straight lines.

Let us rename the coefficients and consider the equation

$$px + qy + rz = m \quad \textbf{(budget plane)} \quad (2)$$

where p, q, r, m are all positive. This equation can be given an economic interpretation. Suppose a person spends an amount m on the purchase of three commodities, whose prices are respectively p, q, and r per unit. If the person buys x units of the first, y units of the second, and z units of the third commodity, then the total cost is $px + qy + rz$. Hence, (2) is the individual's *budget equation*: Only triples (x, y, z) that satisfy (2) can be bought if expenditure is m. Equation (2) represents a *plane* in space, called the **budget plane**. Because in most cases one also has $x \geq 0$, $y \geq 0$, and $z \geq 0$, the interesting part of the plane is the triangle with vertices at $P = (m/p, 0, 0)$, $Q = (0, m/q, 0)$, and $R = (0, 0, m/r)$, as shown in Fig. 1. If we allow the person to underspend, the **budget set** is defined as

$$B = \{ (x, y, z) : px + qy + rz \leq m, \ x \geq 0, \ y \geq 0, \ z \geq 0 \}$$

This represents the three-dimensional body bounded by the three coordinate planes and the budget plane. It generalizes the two-commodity budget set discussed in Example 4.4.7.

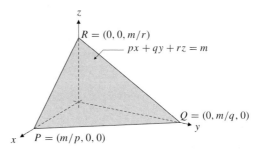

Figure 1

It is usually not at all simple to draw the graphs of equations in three variables. Yet, in recent years, a number of powerful computer programs for drawing surfaces in three-dimensional space have been developed. Two surfaces that can be drawn in this way appear in Figs. 2 and 3. Figure 2 exhibits a surface which is called an **ellipsoid**. (Some readers may recognize its shape as that of a rugby ball.)

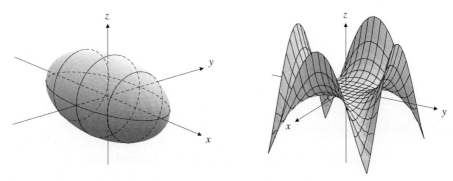

Figure 2 $x^2/a^2 + y^2/b^2 + z^2/c^2 = 1$
where $a > b = c$

Figure 3 $z = x^4 - 3x^2y^2 + y^4$

The Distance Formula

In Section 5.5 we gave the formula for the distance between two points in the plane. Now we derive the corresponding formula for the distance between two points in three-dimensional space.

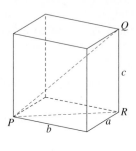

Figure 4   **Figure 5**

We begin by computing the length of the diagonal of a rectangular box with edges a, b, and c, as shown in Fig. 4. We see that, according to Pythagoras' theorem, $(PR)^2 = a^2 + b^2$, and $(PQ)^2 = (PR)^2 + (RQ)^2 = a^2 + b^2 + c^2$, so that the diagonal has length $PQ = \sqrt{a^2 + b^2 + c^2}$.

In Fig. 5 we wish to find the distance between $P = (x_1, y_1, z_1)$ and $Q = (x_2, y_2, z_2)$. These points lie precisely at the corners of a rectangular box with edges of lengths $a = |x_2 - x_1|$, $b = |y_2 - y_1|$, and $c = |z_2 - z_1|$. Hence $(PQ)^2 = a^2 + b^2 + c^2 = |x_2 - x_1|^2 + |y_2 - y_1|^2 + |z_2 - z_1|^2 = (x_2 - x_1)^2 + (y_2 - y_1)^2 + (z_2 - z_1)^2$. This motivates the following definition:

DEFINITION OF DISTANCE

The **distance** between (x_1, y_1, z_1) and (x_2, y_2, z_2) is

$$d = \sqrt{(x_2 - x_1)^2 + (y_2 - y_1)^2 + (z_2 - z_1)^2}$$

(3)

EXAMPLE 1   Calculate the distance d between the points $(1, 2, -3)$ and $(-2, 4, 5)$.

Solution: According to formula (3),

$$d = \sqrt{(-2 - 1)^2 + (4 - 2)^2 + (5 - (-3))^2} = \sqrt{(-3)^2 + 2^2 + 8^2} = \sqrt{77} \approx 8.77$$ ∎

Let (a, b, c) be a point in space. The sphere with radius r and centre at (a, b, c) is the set of all points (x, y, z) whose distance from (a, b, c) is equal to r. Using the distance formula, we obtain

$$\sqrt{(x - a)^2 + (y - b)^2 + (z - c)^2} = r$$

Squaring each side yields:

EQUATION FOR A SPHERE

The equation for a **sphere** with centre at (a, b, c) and radius r is

$$(x - a)^2 + (y - b)^2 + (z - c)^2 = r^2$$

(4)

EXAMPLE 2   Find the equation for the sphere with centre at $(-2, -2, -2)$ and radius 4.

Solution: According to formula (4), the equation is

$$(x - (-2))^2 + (y - (-2))^2 + (z - (-2))^2 = 4^2$$

or $$(x + 2)^2 + (y + 2)^2 + (z + 2)^2 = 16$$

EXAMPLE 3   How do you interpret the expression $(x + 4)^2 + (y - 3)^2 + (z + 5)^2$? As:

(i) The sphere with centre at the point $(-4, 3, -5)$.

(ii) The distance between the points (x, y, z) and $(-4, 3, -5)$.

(iii) The square of the distance between the points (x, y, z) and $(-4, 3, -5)$.

Solution: Only (iii) is correct.

PROBLEMS FOR SECTION 11.4

1. Sketch graphs of the surfaces in space described by each of the following equations:

   (a) $x = a$　　　　　　　(b) $y = b$　　　　　　　(c) $z = c$

2. Find the distance d between the points $(-1, 2, 3)$ and $(4, -2, 0)$.

3. Find the distance d between the points (a, b, c) and $(a + 1, b + 1, c + 1)$.

4. Find the equation for the sphere with centre at $(2, 1, 1)$ and radius 5.

5. What is the geometric interpretation of the equation $(x+3)^2 + (y-3)^2 + (z-4)^2 = 25$?

6. The graph of $z = x^2 + y^2$ is a paraboloid (see Fig. 11.3.6). If the point (x, y, z) lies on this paraboloid, interpret the expression $(x - 4)^2 + (y - 4)^2 + \left(z - \frac{1}{2}\right)^2$.

11.5 Functions of More Variables

Many of the most important functions we study in economics, such as the gross domestic product (GDP) of a country, depend on a very large number of variables. In some abstract models, it may be sufficient to ascertain that such a connection exists without specifying the dependence more closely. In this case, we say only that the GDP is a *function* of the different variables.

Any ordered collection of n numbers $(x_1, x_2, \ldots, x_n)$ is called an **n-vector**. To save space, n-vectors are often denoted by bold letters. For example, we write $\mathbf{x} = (x_1, x_2, \ldots, x_n)$. This is called **vector notation**.

FUNCTIONS OF N VARIABLES

> **A function f of n variables** $x_1, \ldots, x_n$ with **domain** D is a rule that assigns a specified number $f(\mathbf{x}) = f(x_1, \ldots, x_n)$ to each n-vector $\mathbf{x} = (x_1, \ldots, x_n)$ in D. $\qquad$ (1)

EXAMPLE 1 (a) The demand for sugar in the United States in the period 1929–1935 was estimated by T. W. Schultz, who found that it could be described approximately by the formula

$$x = 108.83 - 6.0294p + 0.164w - 0.4217t$$

Here the demand x for sugar is a function of three variables: p (the price of sugar), w (a production index), and t (the date, where $t = 0$ corresponds to 1929).

(b) R. Stone estimated the following formula for the demand for beer in the UK:

$$x = 1.058\, x_1^{0.136} x_2^{-0.727} x_3^{0.914} x_4^{0.816}$$

Here the quantity demanded x is a function of four variables: x_1 (the income of the individual), x_2 (the price of beer), x_3 (a general price index for all other commodities), and x_4 (the strength of the beer). $\qquad$ ▌

The simpler of the functions in Example 1 is (a). The variables p, w, and t occur here only to the first power, and they are only multiplied by constants, not by each other. Such functions are called *linear*. In general,

$$f(x_1, x_2, \ldots, x_n) = a_1 x_1 + a_2 x_2 + \cdots + a_n x_n + b \qquad (2)$$

(where $a_1, a_2, \ldots, a_n$, and b are constants) is a **linear function** in n variables.[2]
Example 1(b) is a special case of the general Cobb–Douglas function

$$F(x_1, x_2, \ldots, x_n) = A x_1^{a_1} x_2^{a_2} \cdots x_n^{a_n} \quad (A, a_1, \ldots, a_n \text{ are constants}; A > 0) \qquad (3)$$

defined for $x_1 > 0, x_2 > 0, \ldots, x_n > 0$. We use this function many times in this book.

NOTE 1 Taking the natural logarithm of each side of (3) gives

$$\ln F = \ln A + a_1 \ln x_1 + a_2 \ln x_2 + \cdots + a_n \ln x_n \qquad (4)$$

This shows that the Cobb–Douglas function is **log-linear** (or ln-linear), because $\ln F$ is a linear function of $\ln x_1, \ln x_2, \ldots, \ln x_n$.

---

[2] This is rather common terminology, although many mathematicians would insist that f should really be called *affine* if $b \neq 0$, and *linear* only if $b = 0$.

EXAMPLE 2   Suppose an economist makes n observations of a quantity such as the price of apples in different stores. Suppose the results are the n positive numbers $x_1, x_2, \ldots, x_n$. In statistics, several different measures for their average value are used. Some of the most common are:

(a)   the **arithmetic** mean: $\bar{x}_A = \dfrac{1}{n}(x_1 + x_2 + \cdots + x_n)$

(b)   the **geometric** mean: $\bar{x}_G = \sqrt[n]{x_1 x_2 \ldots x_n}$

(c)   the **harmonic** mean: $\bar{x}_H = \dfrac{1}{\dfrac{1}{n}\left(\dfrac{1}{x_1} + \dfrac{1}{x_2} + \cdots + \dfrac{1}{x_n}\right)}$

Note that $\bar{x}_A$ is a linear function of $x_1, \ldots, x_n$, whereas $\bar{x}_G$ and $\bar{x}_H$ are nonlinear functions. ($\bar{x}_G$ is log-linear.)

For example, if the results of 4 observations are $x_1 = 1$, $x_2 = 2$, $x_3 = 3$, and $x_4 = 4$, then $\bar{x}_A = (1 + 2 + 3 + 4)/4 = 2.5$, $\bar{x}_G = \sqrt[4]{1 \cdot 2 \cdot 3 \cdot 4} = \sqrt[4]{24} \approx 2.21$, and $\bar{x}_H = \left[(1/1 + 1/2 + 1/3 + 1/4)/4\right]^{-1} = 48/25 = 1.92$. In this case, $\bar{x}_H \leq \bar{x}_G \leq \bar{x}_A$, and it turns out that these inequalities are valid in general:

$$\bar{x}_H \leq \bar{x}_G \leq \bar{x}_A \tag{5}$$

For $n = 2$, you were asked to show (5) in Problem 1.6.9. The harmonic mean $\bar{x}_H$ appears in the solution to Problem 6.   ∎

EXAMPLE 3   An individual must decide what quantities of n different commodities to buy during a given time period. Consumer demand theory often assumes that the individual has a utility function $U(x_1, x_2, \ldots, x_n)$ representing preferences, and that this measures the satisfaction the individual obtains by acquiring x_1 units of good no. 1, x_2 units of good no. 2, and so on. This is an important economic example of a function of n variables, to which we return several times.

Some economic models assume that

$$U(x_1, x_2, \ldots, x_n) = a_1 \ln(x_1 - c_1) + a_2 \ln(x_2 - c_2) + \cdots + a_n \ln(x_n - c_n)$$

where the parameters or constants $c_1, c_2, \ldots, c_n$ represent the minimum "subsistence" quantities that the consumer must have of the different commodities in order to survive. (Some or even all of the constants c_i could be equal to 0.) Because $\ln z$ is only defined when $z > 0$, we see that $x_1 > c_1$, $x_2 > c_2, \ldots, x_n > c_n$ is the requirement for U to be defined. Usually one assumes that each $a_i > 0$, implying that the consumer prefers to have more of each good i.   ∎

Continuity

The concept of continuity for functions of one variable may be generalized to functions of several variables. Roughly speaking, a function of n variables is **continuous** if small changes in any or all of the independent variables induce small changes in the function value. Just as in the one-variable case, we have the following useful rule:

CONTINUITY

> Any function of n variables that can be constructed from continuous functions by combining the operations of addition, subtraction, multiplication, division, and functional composition is continuous wherever it is defined.

If a function of one variable is continuous, it will also be continuous when considered as a function of several variables. For example, $f(x, y, z) = x^2$ is a continuous function of x, y, and z. (Small changes in x, y, and z give at most small changes in x^2.)

EXAMPLE 4   Where are the functions given by the following formulas continuous?

$$\text{(a)} \ f(x, y, z) = x^2y + 8x^2y^5z - xy + 8z \qquad \text{(b)} \ g(x, y) = \frac{xy - 3}{x^2 + y^2 - 4}$$

Solution:

(a) As the sum of products of positive powers, f is defined and continuous for all x, y, and z.

(b) The function g is defined and continuous for all (x, y) except those that lie on the circle $x^2 + y^2 = 4$. There the denominator is zero, and so $g(x, y)$ is not defined. ∎

Euclidean n-Dimensional Space

No concrete geometric interpretation is possible for functions of n variables in the general case when $n \geq 3$. Yet economists still use *geometric language* when dealing with functions of n variables. It is usual to call the set of all possible n-vectors $(x_1, x_2, \ldots, x_n)$ of real numbers the **Euclidean n-dimensional space**, or **n-space**, and to denote it by $\mathbb{R}^n$. For $n = 1$, 2, and 3, we have geometric interpretations of $\mathbb{R}^n$ as a line, a plane, and a 3-dimensional space, respectively. But for $n \geq 4$, there is no geometric interpretation.

If $z = f(x_1, x_2, \ldots, x_n) = f(\mathbf{x})$ represents a function of n variables, we define the **graph** of f as the set of all points $(\mathbf{x}, f(\mathbf{x}))$ in $\mathbb{R}^{n+1}$ for which $\mathbf{x}$ belongs to the domain of f. We also call the graph a **surface** (or sometimes a **hypersurface**) in $\mathbb{R}^{n+1}$. For $z = z_0$ (constant), the set of points in $\mathbb{R}^n$ satisfying $f(\mathbf{x}) = z_0$ is called a **level surface** of f. When $f(\mathbf{x})$ is a linear function such as $a_1x_1 + a_2x_2 + \cdots + a_nx_n + b$, this surface, which would be a plane if $n = 3$, is called a **hyperplane** when $n > 3$.

In production theory, it is usual to give level surfaces a different name. If $x = f(\mathbf{v}) = f(v_1, v_2, \ldots, v_n)$ is the amount produced when the input quantities of n different factors of production are respectively $v_1, v_2, \ldots, v_n$, the level surfaces where $f(v_1, v_2, \ldots, v_n) = x_0$ (constant) are called *isoquants*, as in Example 11.3.2.

1. Let $f(x, y, z) = xy + xz + yz$.

   (a) Find $f(-1, 2, 3)$, $f(-2, 4, 6)$, and $f(a + 1, b + 1, c + 1) - f(a, b, c)$.

   (b) Show that $f(tx, ty, tz) = t^2 f(x, y, z)$ for all t.

2. Some studies in agricultural economics employ production functions of the form $Y = F(K, L, T)$, where Y is the size of the harvest, K is capital invested, L is labour, and T is the area of agricultural land used to grow the crop.

   (a) Explain the meaning of $F(K + 1, L, T) - F(K, L, T)$.

   (b) Many studies assume that F is Cobb–Douglas. What form does F then have?

   (c) If F is Cobb–Douglas, find $F(tK, tL, tT)$ expressed in terms of t and $F(K, L, T)$.

3. In a study of milk production, Hjelm and Sandquist found that

$$y = 2.90 \, x_1^{0.015} x_2^{0.250} x_3^{0.350} x_4^{0.408} x_5^{0.030}$$

   where y is the output of milk, and $x_1, \ldots, x_5$ are the quantities of five different input factors. (For instance, x_1 is work effort and x_3 is grass consumption.)

   (a) If all the factors of production were doubled, what would happen to y?

   (b) Write the relation in log-linear form.

4. On a drive to a neighbouring city centre, you spend 5 minutes stopped at traffic lights at an average speed of 0 kilometres per hour, 10 minutes driving on local roads at an average speed of 30 kph, 20 minutes on a main road at an average speed of 60 kph, and 15 minutes on a motorway driving at an average speed of 80 kph. How far do you drive, and what is your average speed for the whole journey?

HARDER PROBLEMS

5. Consider the so-called CES function defined by

$$x(v_1, v_2, \ldots, v_n) = A\left(\delta_1 v_1^{-\varrho} + \delta_2 v_2^{-\varrho} + \cdots + \delta_n v_n^{-\varrho}\right)^{-m/\varrho}$$

   where $A, \delta_1, \delta_2, \ldots, \delta_n, \varrho$, and m are constants. Find a number k such that

$$x(tv_1, tv_2, \ldots, tv_n) = t^k x(v_1, v_2, \ldots, v_n) \qquad \text{for all} \quad t > 0$$

   (In the terminology of Section 12.7, this function is homogeneous of degree k. CES stands for "constant elasticity of substitution" — see Section 12.5 for more details.)

6. It is observed that three machines A, B, and C produce, respectively, 60, 80, and 40 units of a product during one workday lasting 8 hours (or 480 minutes). The average output is then 60 units per day.

(a) We see that A, B, and C use, respectively, 8, 6, and 12 minutes to make one unit. If all machines were equally efficient and jointly produced $60 + 80 + 40 = 180$ units during a day, then how much time would be required to produce each unit? (Note that the answer is not $(8 + 6 + 12)/3$.)

(b) Suppose that n machines $A_1, A_2, \ldots, A_n$ produce the same product simultaneously during a time interval of length T. Given that the production times per unit are respectively $t_1, t_2, \ldots, t_n$, find the total output Q. Show that if all the machines were equally efficient and together had produced exactly the same total amount Q in the time span T, then the time needed for each machine to produce one unit would be precisely the harmonic mean $\bar{t}_H$ of $t_1, t_2, \ldots, t_n$.

11.6 Partial Derivatives with More Variables

The functions economists study often have many variables, so we need to extend the concept of partial derivative to functions with more than two variables.

PARTIAL DERIVATIVES IN N VARIABLES

If $z = f(\mathbf{x}) = f(x_1, x_2, \ldots, x_n)$, then $\partial f/\partial x_i$, for $i = 1, 2, \ldots, n$, means the partial derivative of $f(x_1, x_2, \ldots, x_n)$ w.r.t. x_i when all the other variables x_j $(j \neq i)$ are held constant. $\qquad$ (1)

So provided they all exist, there are n partial derivatives of first order, one for each variable x_i, $i = 1, \ldots, n$. Other notation used for the first-order partials of $z = f(x_1, x_2, \ldots, x_n)$ includes

$$\frac{\partial f}{\partial x_i} = \frac{\partial z}{\partial x_i} = \partial z/\partial x_i = z_i' = f_i'(x_1, x_2, \ldots, x_n)$$

EXAMPLE 1   Find the first-order partials of $z = 5x_1^2 + x_1 x_2^3 - x_2^2 x_3^2 + x_3^3$.

Solution: We find that

$$\frac{\partial z}{\partial x_1} = 10x_1 + x_2^3, \qquad \frac{\partial z}{\partial x_2} = 3x_1 x_2^2 - 2x_2 x_3^2, \qquad \frac{\partial z}{\partial x_3} = -2x_2^2 x_3 + 3x_3^2 \qquad \blacksquare$$

As in (6) of Section 11.2 we have the following rough approximation:

The partial derivative $\partial z / \partial x_i$ is approximately equal to the change in

$$z = f(x_1, x_2, \ldots, x_n) \qquad (2)$$

caused by an increase in x_i of one unit while all the other x_j $(j \neq i)$ are held constant.

In symbols:

$$f_i'(x_1, \ldots, x_n)$$
$$\approx f(x_1, \ldots, x_{i-1}, x_i + 1, x_{i+1}, \ldots, x_n) - f(x_1, \ldots, x_{i-1}, x_i, x_{i+1}, \ldots, x_n)$$

For each of the n first-order partials of f, we have n second-order partials:

$$\frac{\partial}{\partial x_j} \left(\frac{\partial f}{\partial x_i} \right) = \frac{\partial^2 f}{\partial x_j \partial x_i} = z_{ij}''$$

Here both i and j may take any value $1, 2, \ldots, n$, so altogether there are n^2 second-order partials. It is usual to display these second-order partials in an $n \times n$ square array as follows

$$f''(\mathbf{x}) = \begin{pmatrix} f_{11}''(\mathbf{x}) & f_{12}''(\mathbf{x}) & \cdots & f_{1n}''(\mathbf{x}) \\ f_{21}''(\mathbf{x}) & f_{22}''(\mathbf{x}) & \cdots & f_{2n}''(\mathbf{x}) \\ \vdots & \vdots & \ddots & \vdots \\ f_{n1}''(\mathbf{x}) & f_{n2}''(\mathbf{x}) & \cdots & f_{nn}''(\mathbf{x}) \end{pmatrix} \qquad \text{(The **Hessian**)} \qquad (3)$$

Such rectangular arrays of numbers (or symbols) are called **matrices**, and (3) is called the **Hessian matrix** of f at $\mathbf{x} = (x_1, x_2, \ldots, x_n)$. See Chapter 15 for more discussion of matrices in general.

The n second-order partial derivatives f_{ii}'' found by differentiating twice w.r.t. the same variable are called *direct second-order partials*; the others, f_{ij}'' where $i \neq j$, are *mixed* or *cross* partials.

EXAMPLE 2   Find the Hessian matrix of of $z = 5x_1^2 + x_1 x_2^3 - x_2^2 x_3^2 + x_3^3$. (See Example 1.)

Solution: We differentiate the first-order partials found in Example 1. The resulting Hessian is:

$$\begin{pmatrix} \dfrac{\partial^2 z}{\partial x_1^2} & \dfrac{\partial^2 z}{\partial x_2 \partial x_1} & \dfrac{\partial^2 z}{\partial x_3 \partial x_1} \\[2mm] \dfrac{\partial^2 z}{\partial x_1 \partial x_2} & \dfrac{\partial^2 z}{\partial x_2^2} & \dfrac{\partial^2 z}{\partial x_3 \partial x_2} \\[2mm] \dfrac{\partial^2 z}{\partial x_1 \partial x_3} & \dfrac{\partial^2 z}{\partial x_2 \partial x_3} & \dfrac{\partial^2 z}{\partial x_3^2} \end{pmatrix} = \begin{pmatrix} 10 & 3x_2^2 & 0 \\ 3x_2^2 & 6x_1 x_2 - 2x_3^2 & -4x_2 x_3 \\ 0 & -4x_2 x_3 & -2x_2^2 + 6x_3 \end{pmatrix}$$

Young's Theorem

If $z = f(x_1, x_2, \ldots, x_n)$, then the two second-order cross partial derivatives z''_{ij} and z''_{ji} are usually equal. That is, $\dfrac{\partial}{\partial x_i} \left(\dfrac{\partial f}{\partial x_j} \right) = \dfrac{\partial}{\partial x_j} \left(\dfrac{\partial f}{\partial x_i} \right)$. This implies that the order of differentiation does not matter. The next theorem makes precise a more general result.

THEOREM 11.6.1 (YOUNG'S THEOREM)

Suppose that all the mth-order partial derivatives of the function $f(x_1, x_2, \ldots, x_n)$ are continuous. If any two of them involve differentiating w.r.t. each of the variables the same number of times, then they are necessarily equal.

The content of this result can be explained as follows: Let $m = m_1 + \cdots + m_n$, and suppose that $f(x_1, x_2, \ldots, x_n)$ is differentiated m_1 times w.r.t. x_1, m_2 times w.r.t. x_2, $\ldots$, and m_n times w.r.t. x_n. (Some of the integers $m_1, \ldots, m_n$ can be zero, of course.) Suppose that the continuity condition is satisfied for these mth-order partial derivatives. Then we end up with the same result no matter what is the order of differentiation, because each of the final partial derivatives is equal to

$$\frac{\partial^m f}{\partial x_1^{m_1} \partial x_2^{m_2} \ldots \partial x_n^{m_n}}$$

In particular, for the case when $m = 2$,

$$\frac{\partial^2 f}{\partial x_j \partial x_i} = \frac{\partial^2 f}{\partial x_i \partial x_j} \qquad (i = 1, 2, \ldots, n; \quad j = 1, 2, \ldots, n)$$

if both these partials are continuous. A proof of Young's theorem is given in most advanced calculus books.

Formal Definitions of Partial Derivatives

In Section 11.2, we gave a formal definition of partial derivatives for functions of two variables. This was done by modifying the definition of the (ordinary) derivative for a function of one variable. The same modification works for a function of n variables.

Indeed, if $z = f(x_1, \ldots, x_n)$, then with $g(x_i) = f(x_1, \ldots, x_{i-1}, x_i, x_{i+1}, \ldots, x_n)$, we have $\partial z / \partial x_i = g'(x_i)$. (Here we think of all the variables x_j other than x_i as constants.) If we use the definition of $g'(x_i)$ (see (1) in Section 6.2), we obtain

$$\frac{\partial z}{\partial x_i} = \lim_{h \to 0} \frac{f(x_1, \ldots, x_i + h, \ldots, x_n) - f(x_1, \ldots, x_i, \ldots, x_n)}{h} \tag{4}$$

(If we consider $h = 1$ as a number close to 0, we obtain the approximation in (2).) If the limit in (4) does not exist, then we say that $\partial z / \partial x_i$ *does not exist*, or that z is not differentiable w.r.t. x_i at the point.

Virtually all the functions we consider have continuous partial derivatives everywhere in their domains. If $z = f(x_1, x_2, \ldots, x_n)$ has continuous partial derivatives of first-order in a domain D, we call f **continuously differentiable** in D. In this case, f is also called a C^1 **function** on D. If all partial derivatives up to order k exist and are continuous, f is called a C^k **function**.

PROBLEMS FOR SECTION 11.6

1. Calculate $F_1'(1, 1, 1)$, $F_2'(1, 1, 1)$, and $F_3'(1, 1, 1)$ for $F(x, y, z) = x^2 e^{xz} + y^3 e^{xy}$.

2. Calculate all first-order partials of the following functions:

   (a) $f(x, y, z) = x^2 + y^3 + z^4$ (b) $f(x, y, z) = 5x^2 - 3y^3 + 3z^4$

   (c) $f(x, y, z) = xyz$ (d) $f(x, y, z) = x^4/yz$

   (e) $f(x, y, z) = (x^2 + y^3 + z^4)^6$ (f) $f(x, y, z) = e^{xyz}$

3. Let x and y be the populations of two cities and d the distance between them. Suppose that the number of travellers T between the cities is given by

$$T = k\frac{xy}{d^n} \qquad (k \text{ and } n \text{ are positive constants})$$

   Find $\partial T/\partial x$, $\partial T/\partial y$, and $\partial T/\partial d$, and discuss their signs.

4. Find all first- and second-order partials of $w(x, y, z) = 3xyz + x^2y - xz^3$.

5. If $f(x, y, z) = p(x) + q(y) + r(z)$, what are f_1', f_2', and f_3'?

6. Find the Hessian matrices of

   (a) $f(x, y, z) = ax^2 + by^2 + cz^2$ (b) $g(x, y, z) = Ax^a y^b z^c$

7. Prove that if $w = \left(\dfrac{x - y + z}{x + y - z}\right)^h$, then

$$x\frac{\partial w}{\partial x} + y\frac{\partial w}{\partial y} + z\frac{\partial w}{\partial z} = 0$$

8. Calculate the first-order partial derivatives of the following function

$$f(x, y, z) = x^{y^z}$$

   assuming that all variables are positive. (You might find it easier first to take the natural logarithm of both sides.)

11.7 Economic Applications

This section considers a number of economic applications of partial derivatives.

EXAMPLE 1   Consider an agricultural production function $Y = F(K, L, T)$, where Y is the number of units produced, K is capital invested, L is labour input, and T is the area of agricultural land that is used. Then $\partial Y/\partial K = F'_K$ is called the **marginal product of capital**. It is the rate of change of output Y w.r.t. K when L and T are held fixed. Similarly, $\partial Y/\partial L = F'_L$ and $\partial Y/\partial T = F'_T$ are the **marginal products of labour and of land**, respectively. For example, if K is the value of capital equipment measured in dollars, and $\partial Y/\partial K = 5$, then increasing capital input by 1 dollar would increase output by approximately 5 units.

Suppose, in particular, that F is the Cobb–Douglas function

$$F(K, L, T) = AK^a L^b T^c \qquad (A, a, b, \text{ and } c \text{ are positive constants})$$

Find the marginal products, and the second-order partials. Discuss their signs.

Solution: The marginal products are

$$F'_K = AaK^{a-1}L^b T^c, \qquad F'_L = AbK^a L^{b-1}T^c, \qquad F'_T = AcK^a L^b T^{c-1}$$

Assuming K, L, and T are all positive, the marginal products are positive. Thus, an increase in capital, labour, or land will increase the number of units produced.

The mixed second-order partials (or cross partials) are

$$F''_{KL} = AabK^{a-1}L^{b-1}T^c, \quad F''_{KT} = AacK^{a-1}L^b T^{c-1}, \quad F''_{LT} = AbcK^a L^{b-1}T^{c-1}$$

Check for yourself that F''_{LK}, F''_{TK}, and F''_{TL} give, respectively, the same results. Note that these partials are positive. We call each pair of factors *complementary*, because more of one increases the marginal product of the other.

The direct second-order partials are

$$F''_{KK} = Aa(a-1)K^{a-2}L^b T^c, \ F''_{LL} = Ab(b-1)K^a L^{b-2}T^c, \ F''_{TT} = Ac(c-1)K^a L^b T^{c-2}$$

For instance, F''_{KK} is the partial derivative of the marginal product of capital (F'_K) w.r.t. K. If $a < 1$, then $F''_{KK} < 0$, and there is a diminishing marginal product of capital—that is, a small increase in the capital invested will lead to a decrease in the marginal product of capital. We can interpret this to mean that, although small increases in capital cause output to rise ($F'_K > 0$), this rise occurs at a decreasing rate ($F''_{KK} < 0$). Similarly for labour (if $b < 1$), and for land (if $c < 1$).

EXAMPLE 2   Let x be an index of the total amount of goods produced and consumed in a society, and let z be a measure of the level of pollution. If $u(x, z)$ measures the total well-being of the society (not a very easy function to estimate!), what signs do you expect $u'_x(x, z)$ and $u'_z(x, z)$ to have? Can you guess what economists usually assume about the sign of $u''_{xz}(x, z)$?

Solution: It is reasonable to expect that well-being increases as the amount of goods increases, but decreases as the level of pollution increases. Hence, we will usually have $u'_x(x, z) > 0$ and $u'_z(x, z) < 0$. According to (2) in the previous section, $u''_{xz} = (\partial/\partial z)(u'_x)$ is approximately equal to the change in u'_x when the level of pollution increases by one unit. Here $u'_x \approx$ the increase in welfare obtained by a unit increase in x. It is often assumed that $u''_{xz} < 0$. This implies that the increase in welfare obtained by an extra unit of x will decrease when the level of pollution increases. (An analogy: When a confirmed non-smoker sits in a smoke-filled room, the extra satisfaction from one more piece of cake will decrease if the concentration of smoke increases too much.) Because of Young's Theorem (11.6.1), the inequality $u''_{xz} < 0$ also implies that the increase in welfare obtained from being exposed to one unit less pollution (which is approximately $-u'_z$) increases with consumption x. This accords with the (controversial) view that, as people can afford to consume more, they also become less tolerant of pollution.

PROBLEMS FOR SECTION 11.7

1. The demand for money M in the United States for the period 1929–1952 has been estimated as
$$M = 0.14Y + 76.03(r - 2)^{-0.84} \qquad (r > 2)$$
where Y is the annual national income, and r is the interest rate measured in percent per year. Find $\partial M/\partial Y$ and $\partial M/\partial r$ and discuss their signs.

2. If a and b are constants, compute the expression $KY'_K + LY'_L$ for the following:

(a) $Y = AK^a + BL^a$ (b) $Y = AK^a L^b$ (c) $Y = \dfrac{K^2 L^2}{aL^3 + bK^3}$

3. The demand for a product depends on the price p of the product and on the price q charged by a competing producer. In fact, $D(p, q) = a - bpq^{-\alpha}$, where a, b, and α are positive constants with $\alpha < 1$. Find $D'_p(p, q)$ and $D'_q(p, q)$, and comment on the signs of the partial derivatives.

4. Let $D(p, q)$ and $E(p, q)$ be the demands for two commodities when the prices per unit are p and q, respectively. Suppose the commodities are *substitutes* in consumption, such as butter and margarine. What are the normal signs of the partial derivatives of D and E w.r.t. p and q?

5. Find $\partial U/\partial x_i$ when $U(x_1, x_2, \ldots, x_n) = 100 - e^{-x_1} - e^{-x_2} - \cdots - e^{-x_n}$.

HARDER PROBLEMS

6. Calculate the expression $KY'_K + LY'_L$ if $Y = Ae^{\lambda t}\left[aK^{-\rho} + (1 - a)L^{-\rho}\right]^{-m/\rho}$.

11.8 Partial Elasticities

Section 7.7 introduced the concept of elasticity for functions of one variable. Here we study the corresponding concept for functions of several variables. This enables us to distinguish between, for instance, the price and income elasticities of demand, as well as between own and cross price elasticities.

Two Variables

If $z = f(x, y)$, we define the partial elasticity of z w.r.t. x and y by

$$\text{El}_x\, z = \frac{x}{z}\frac{\partial z}{\partial x}, \qquad \text{El}_y\, z = \frac{y}{z}\frac{\partial z}{\partial y} \tag{1}$$

Often economists just refer to the elasticity rather than the partial elasticity. Thus, $\text{El}_x\, z$ is the elasticity of z w.r.t. x when y is held constant, and $\text{El}_y\, z$ is the elasticity of z w.r.t. y when x is held constant. The number $\text{El}_x\, z$ is (approximately) the percentage change in z caused by a 1% increase in x when y is held constant, and $\text{El}_y\, z$ has a corresponding interpretation.

As in Section 7.7, when all variables are positive, elasticities can be expressed as logarithmic derivatives. Accordingly,

$$\text{El}_x\, z = \frac{\partial \ln z}{\partial \ln x}, \qquad \text{El}_y\, z = \frac{\partial \ln z}{\partial \ln y} \tag{2}$$

EXAMPLE 1   Find the (partial) elasticity of z w.r.t. x when   (a) $z = Ax^a y^b$ (b) $z = xye^{x+y}$.

Solution:

(a) When finding the elasticity of $Ax^a y^b$ w.r.t. x, the variable y, and thus Ay^b, is held constant. From Example 7.7.1 we obtain $\text{El}_x\, z = a$. In the same way, $\text{El}_y\, z = b$.

(b) It is convenient here to use formula (2). Assuming all variables are positive, taking appropriate natural logarithms gives

$$\ln z = \ln x + \ln y + x + y = \ln x + \ln y + e^{\ln x} + y$$

Hence $\text{El}_x\, z = \partial \ln z / \partial \ln x = 1 + e^{\ln x} = 1 + x$.   ∎

EXAMPLE 2   The demand D_1 for potatoes in the United States for the period 1927 to 1941 was estimated to be $D_1 = Ap^{-0.28}m^{0.34}$, where p is the price of potatoes and m is mean income. The demand for apples was estimated to be $D_2 = Bq^{-1.27}m^{1.32}$, where q is the price of apples.

Find the price elasticities of demand, $\text{El}_p\, D_1$ and $\text{El}_q\, D_2$, as well as the income elasticities of demand $\text{El}_m\, D_1$ and $\text{El}_m\, D_2$, and comment on their signs.

Solution: According to Example 1(a), $\text{El}_p\, D_1 = -0.28$. If the price of potatoes increases by 1%, the demand decreases by 0.28%. Furthermore, $\text{El}_q\, D_2 = -1.27$, $\text{El}_m\, D_1 = 0.34$, and $\text{El}_m\, D_2 = 1.32$.

Both price elasticities $\text{El}_p\, D_1$ and $\text{El}_q\, D_2$ are negative, so demand decreases when the price increases in both cases—as seems reasonable. Both income elasticities $\text{El}_m\, D_1$ and $\text{El}_m\, D_2$ are positive, so demand increases when mean income increases—as seems reasonable. Note that the demand for apples is more sensitive to both price and income increases than is the demand for potatoes. This also seems reasonable, since at that time potatoes were a more essential commodity than apples for most consumers. ▌

n Variables

If $z = f(x_1, x_2, \ldots, x_n) = f(\mathbf{x})$, we define the **(partial) elasticity** of z (or of f) w.r.t. x_i as the elasticity of z w.r.t. x_i when all the other variables are held constant. Thus,

$$\text{El}_i\, z = \frac{x_i}{f(\mathbf{x})} \frac{\partial f(\mathbf{x})}{\partial x_i} = \frac{x_i}{z} \frac{\partial z}{\partial x_i} = \frac{\partial \ln z}{\partial \ln x_i} \tag{3}$$

(Of course, the last characterization is only valid when all variables are positive.) The number $\text{El}_i\, z$ is approximately equal to the percentage change in z caused by a 1% increase in x_i, keeping all the other x_j $(j \neq i)$ constant. Among other forms of notation commonly used instead of $\text{El}_i\, z$, we mention

$$\text{El}_i\, f(\mathbf{x}), \qquad \text{El}_{x_i}\, z, \qquad \hat{z}_i \text{ (“z hat } i\text{”)}, \qquad \varepsilon_i, \qquad \text{and} \qquad e_i$$

EXAMPLE 3 Suppose $D = Ax_1^{a_1} x_2^{a_2} \cdots x_n^{a_n}$ with $A > 0, a_1, a_2, \ldots, a_n$ constants and $x_1 > 0, x_2 > 0,$ $\ldots, x_n > 0$. Find the elasticity of D w.r.t. x_i, for $i = 1, \ldots, n$.

Solution: Take the natural logarithm of both sides to get

$$\ln D = \ln A + a_1 \ln x_1 + \cdots + a_n \ln x_n$$

Using the logarithmic derivative version (3) of the definition of elasticity, we find immediately

$$\text{El}_i\, D = \frac{\partial \ln D}{\partial \ln x_i} = a_i, \quad i = 1, 2, \ldots, n$$

As a special case of this example, suppose that $D_i = Am^\alpha p_i^{-\beta} p_j^\gamma$, where m is income, p_i is the own price, and p_j is the price of a substitute good. Then α is the income elasticity of demand, $-\beta$ is the own price elasticity, and γ is the cross price elasticity. However, because own price elasticities of demand are usually negative, one often describes β rather than $-\beta$ as being the own price elasticity of demand.

Note that the proportion of income spent on good i is

$$\frac{p_i D_i}{m} = Am^{\alpha-1} p_i^{1-\beta} p_j^\gamma$$

When the income elasticity $\alpha < 1$, this proportion is a decreasing function of income. Economists describe a good with this property as a *necessity*. On the other hand, when

$\alpha > 1$, the proportion of income spent on good i rises with income, in which case economists describe good i as a *luxury*. Referring back to Example 2, these definitions imply that during the period 1927–1941, which includes the years of the Great Depression, potatoes were a necessity, but apples a (relative) luxury.

Problem 4 below considers this distinction between necessities and luxuries for more general demand functions.

PROBLEMS FOR SECTION 11.8

1. Find the partial elasticities of z w.r.t. x and y in the following cases:

   (a) $z = xy$ (b) $z = x^2 y^5$ (c) $z = x^n e^x y^n e^y$ (d) $z = x + y$

2. Let $z = (ax_1^d + bx_2^d + cx_3^d)^g$, where a, b, c, d, and g are constants. Find $\sum_{i=1}^{3} \text{El}_i \, z$.

3. Let $z = x_1^p \cdots x_n^p \exp(a_1 x_1 + \cdots + a_n x_n)$, where $a_1, \ldots, a_n$, and p are constants. Find the partial elasticities of z w.r.t. $x_1, \ldots, x_n$.

4. Let $D(p, m)$ indicate a typical consumer's demand for a particular commodity, as a function of its price p and the consumer's own income m. Show that the proportion pD/m of income spent on the commodity increases with income if $\text{El}_m \, D > 1$ (in which case the good is a "luxury"), whereas it is a "necessity" if $\text{El}_m \, D < 1$).

REVIEW PROBLEMS FOR CHAPTER 11

1. Let $f(x, y) = 3x - 5y$. Calculate $f(0, 1)$, $f(2, -1)$, $f(a, a)$, and $f(a+h, b) - f(a, b)$.

2. Let $f(x, y) = 2x^2 - 3y^2$. Calculate $f(-1, 2)$, $f(2a, 2a)$, $f(a, b+k) - f(a, b)$, and $f(tx, ty) - t^2 f(x, y)$.

3. Let $f(x, y, z) = \sqrt{x^2 + y^2 + z^2}$. Calculate $f(3, 4, 0)$, $f(-2, 1, 3)$, and $f(tx, ty, tz)$ for $t \geq 0$.

4. The annual herring catch is given by the function $Y(K, S) = 0.06157 K^{1.356} S^{0.562}$ of the catching effort K and the herring stock S.

   (a) Find $\partial Y / \partial K$ and $\partial Y / \partial S$.

   (b) If K and S are both doubled, what happens to the catch?

5. For which pairs of numbers (x, y) are the functions given by the following formulas defined?

   (a) $3xy^3 - 45x^4 - 3y$ (b) $\sqrt{1 - xy}$ (c) $\ln(2 - (x^2 + y^2))$

6. Let $F(K, L, M) = AK^aL^bM^c$. Show that $KF'_K + LF'_L + MF'_M = (a+b+c)F$.

7. For which pairs of numbers (x, y) are the functions given by the following formulas defined?

   (a) $\dfrac{1}{\sqrt{x+y-1}}$ (b) $\sqrt{x^2 - y^2} + \sqrt{x^2 + y^2 - 1}$ (c) $\sqrt{y - x^2} - \sqrt{\sqrt{x} - y}$

8. Let g be defined for all (x, y, z) by

   $$g(x, y, z) = 2x^2 - 4xy + 10y^2 + z^2 - 4x - 28y - z + 24$$

   (a) Calculate $g(2, 1, 1)$, $g(3, -4, 2)$, and $g(1, 1, a+h) - g(1, 1, a)$.

   (b) Find all partial derivatives of the first and second order.

9. Let f be defined for all (x, y) by $f(x, y) = (x-2)^2(y+3)^2$.

   (a) Calculate $f(0, 0)$, $f(2, -3)$, and $f(a+2, b-3)$.

   (b) Find $\dfrac{\partial f}{\partial x}$ and $\dfrac{\partial f}{\partial y}$.

10. Complete the following implications:

   (a) $z = (x^2y^4 + 2)^5 \implies \dfrac{\partial z}{\partial x} =$

   (b) $F(K, L) = (\sqrt{K} + \sqrt{L})^2 \implies \sqrt{K}\dfrac{\partial F}{\partial K} =$

   (c) $F(K, L) = (K^a + L^a)^{1/a} \implies KF'_K(K, L) + LF'_L(K, L) =$

   (d) $g(t, w) = \dfrac{3t}{w} + wt^2 \implies \dfrac{\partial^2 g}{\partial w \partial t} =$

   (e) $g(t_1, t_2, t_3) = (t_1^2 + t_2^2 + t_3^2)^{1/2} \implies g'_3(t_1, t_2, t_3) =$

   (f) $f(x, y, z) = 2x^2yz - y^3 + x^2z^2 \implies f'_1(x, y, z) =$, $f''_{13}(x, y, z) =$

11. Verify that the points $(-1, 5)$ and $(1, 1)$ lie on the same level curve for the function $g(x, y) = (2x + y)^3 - 2x + 5/y$.

12. Verify that $x - y = c$ is a level curve for $F(x, y) = \ln(x^2 - 2xy + y^2) + e^{2x-2y}$.

13. (a) If $f(x, y) = x^4 + 2y^2 - 4x^2y + 4y$, find $f'_1(x, y)$ and $f'_2(x, y)$.

    (b) Find all pairs (x, y) which solve both equations $f'_1(x, y) = 0$ and $f'_2(x, y) = 0$.

14. Find the partial elasticities of z w.r.t. x and y in the following cases:

    (a) $z = x^3y^{-4}$ (b) $z = \ln(x^2 + y^2)$ (c) $z = e^{x+y}$ (d) $z = (x^2 + y^2)^{1/2}$

12

TOOLS FOR COMPARATIVE STATICS

Logic merely sanctions the
conquests of the intuition.
—J. Hadamard (1945)

One important aim of this chapter is to present properties of functions defined implicitly by one equation, or by a system of simultaneous equations. In particular, we are interested in how economic variables like demand and supply respond to changes in parameters like price. This is the subject of comparative statics, in which the general question is: What happens to an optimal solution when the parameters of the problem change? A large proportion of economic analysis relies on comparative statics, so this topic is extremely important. Simple examples will be studied in this chapter and the next two chapters, while more demanding problems are treated in FMEA.

Section 12.5 discusses the concept of elasticity of substitution, which is often used by economists to characterize the "curvature" of level curves.

Homogeneous and homothetic functions are important in economics. They are studied in Sections 12.6 and 12.7. The last sections of the chapter consider linear approximations, then differentials, and finally systems of equations, together with some properties that result from differentiating such systems.

12.1 A Simple Chain Rule

Many economic models involve composite functions. These are functions of one or several variables in which the variables are themselves functions of other basic variables. For example, many models of economic growth regard output as a function of capital and labour, both of which are functions of time. How does output vary with time? More generally, what happens to the value of a composite function as its basic variables change? This is the general problem we discuss in this and the next section.

Suppose z is a function of x and y, with

$$z = F(x, y)$$

where x and y both are functions of a variable t, with

$$x = f(t), \qquad y = g(t)$$

Substituting for x and y in $z = F(x, y)$ gives

$$z = F(f(t), g(t))$$

This reduces z to a function of t alone. A change in t will in general lead to changes in both $f(t)$ and $g(t)$, and as a result, z changes. How does z change when t changes? For example, will a small increase in t lead to an increase or a decrease in z? Such questions would become much easier to answer if we could find an expression for dz/dt, the rate of change of z w.r.t. t. This is given by the following rule:

THE CHAIN RULE

When $z = F(x, y)$ with $x = f(t)$ and $y = g(t)$, then

$$\frac{dz}{dt} = F_1'(x, y)\frac{dx}{dt} + F_2'(x, y)\frac{dy}{dt} \tag{1}$$

It is important to understand the precise content of (1). It gives the derivative of $z = F(x, y)$ w.r.t. t when x and y are both differentiable functions of t. This derivative is called the **total derivative** of z w.r.t. t. According to (1), one contribution to the total derivative occurs because the first variable in $F(x, y)$, namely x, depends on t. This contribution is $F_1'(x, y)\, dx/dt$. A second contribution arises because the second variable in $F(x, y)$, namely y, also depends on t. This contribution is $F_2'(x, y)\, dy/dt$. The total derivative dz/dt is the *sum* of the two contributions.

EXAMPLE 1   Find dz/dt when $z = F(x, y) = x^2 + y^3$ with $x = t^2$ and $y = 2t$.

Solution: In this case $F_1'(x, y) = 2x$, $F_2'(x, y) = 3y^2$, $dx/dt = 2t$, and $dy/dt = 2$. So formula (1) gives

$$\frac{dz}{dt} = 2x \cdot 2t + 3y^2 \cdot 2 = 4tx + 6y^2 = 4t^3 + 24t^2$$

where the last equality comes from substituting the appropriate functions of t for x and y respectively. In this case, we can verify the chain rule by substituting $x = t^2$ and $y = 2t$ in the formula for $F(x, y)$ and then differentiating w.r.t. t. The result is

$$z = x^2 + y^3 = (t^2)^2 + (2t)^3 = t^4 + 8t^3 \implies \frac{dz}{dt} = 4t^3 + 24t^2$$

as before.

EXAMPLE 2   Find dz/dt when $z = F(x, y) = xe^{2y}$ with $x = \sqrt{t}$ and $y = \ln t$.

Solution: Here $F_1'(x, y) = e^{2y}$, $F_2'(x, y) = 2xe^{2y}$, $dx/dt = 1/2\sqrt{t}$, and $dy/dt = 1/t$. Then formula (1) gives

$$\frac{dz}{dt} = e^{2y}\frac{1}{2\sqrt{t}} + 2xe^{2y}\frac{1}{t} = t^2\frac{1}{2\sqrt{t}} + 2\sqrt{t}\,t^2\frac{1}{t} = \frac{5}{2}t^{3/2}$$

(To derive the second equality, we used the fact that when $y = \ln t$, then $e^{2y} = e^{2\ln t} = (e^{\ln t})^2 = t^2$.) As in Example 1, we can verify the chain rule directly by substituting $x = \sqrt{t}$ and $y = \ln t$ in the formula for $F(x, y)$ and then differentiating w.r.t. t. The result is $z = xe^{2y} = \sqrt{t} \cdot t^2 = t^{5/2} \Rightarrow dz/dt = \frac{5}{2}t^{3/2}$.   ∎

Here are some rather typical examples of ways in which economists use (1).

EXAMPLE 3   Let $D = D(p, m)$ denote the demand for a commodity as a function of price p and income m. Suppose that price p and income m vary continuously with time t, so that $p = p(t)$ and $m = m(t)$. Then demand can be determined as a function $D = D(p(t), m(t))$ of t alone. Find an expression for $\dot{D}/D$, the relative rate of growth of D.

Solution: Using (1) we obtain

$$\dot{D} = \frac{\partial D(p, m)}{\partial p}\dot{p} + \frac{\partial D(p, m)}{\partial m}\dot{m}$$

where we have denoted time derivatives by "dots." The first term on the right-hand side gives the effect on demand that arises because the price p is changing, and the second term gives the effect of the change in m. Denoting the price elasticity of demand by $\varepsilon_{Dp} = \mathrm{El}_p\, D$ and the income elasticity of demand by $\varepsilon_{Dm} = \mathrm{El}_m\, D$, we can write the relative rate of growth of D as

$$\frac{\dot{D}}{D} = \frac{p}{D}\frac{\partial D(p, m)}{\partial p}\frac{\dot{p}}{p} + \frac{m}{D}\frac{\partial D(p, m)}{\partial m}\frac{\dot{m}}{m} = \varepsilon_{Dp}\frac{\dot{p}}{p} + \varepsilon_{Dm}\frac{\dot{m}}{m}$$

So the relative rate of growth is found by multiplying the relative rates of change of price and income by their respective elasticities, then adding.   ∎

EXAMPLE 4   Let $u(x, z)$ denote the "total well-being" of a society, where x is an index of the total amount of goods produced and consumed, and z is a measure of the level of pollution. Assume that $u_x'(x, z) > 0$ and $u_z'(x, z) < 0$. (See Example 11.7.2.) Suppose the level of pollution z is some increasing function $z = h(x)$ of x, with $h'(x) > 0$. Then total well-being becomes a function

$$U(x) = u(x, h(x))$$

of x alone. Find a necessary condition for $U(x)$ to have a maximum at $x = x^* > 0$, and give this condition an economic interpretation.

Solution: A necessary condition for $U(x)$ to have a maximum at $x^* > 0$ is that $U'(x^*) = 0$. In order to find $U'(x)$, we use the chain rule (1):

$$U'(x) = u'_x(x, h(x)) \cdot 1 + u'_z(x, h(x))h'(x)$$

So $U'(x^*) = 0$ requires that

$$u'_x(x^*, h(x^*)) = -u'_z(x^*, h(x^*))h'(x^*) \tag{$*$}$$

Suppose we think of increasing x^* by one unit. How much do we gain directly? Approximately $u'_x(x^*, h(x^*))$, (see (11.2.6)). On the other hand, if we increase x^* by one unit, the level of pollution increases by about $h'(x^*)$ units. For each unit increase in pollution, we lose $u'_z(x^*, h(x^*))$ in well-being, so in all we lose about $u'_z(x^*, h(x^*))h'(x^*)$ from a unit increase in x^*. Equation $(*)$ just states that what we gain directly from a unit increase in x^* equals what we lose indirectly through increased pollution.　▌

In fact, the chain rule (1) has many implications. In particular, all the general rules for differentiating functions of one variable turn out to be just special cases of this result (see Problem 5).

Higher-Order Derivatives

We sometimes need formulas for the second derivatives of composite functions. A general formula for d^2z/dt^2, based on formula (1), is suggested in Problem 7. Here we derive a special case of interest in optimization theory.

EXAMPLE 5   Suppose

$$z = F(x, y) \qquad \text{where} \quad x = x_0 + th, \quad y = y_0 + tk$$

Keeping (x_0, y_0) and (h, k) fixed, z becomes a function only of t. So we can write $z = g(t)$. Find expressions for $g'(t)$ and $g''(t)$. (The function g records what happens to F as one moves away from (x_0, y_0) in the direction (h, k) or, when $t < 0$, in the reverse direction $(-h, -k)$. See Fig. 13.2.2.)

Solution: With $x = x_0 + th$ and $y = y_0 + tk$, we have $g(t) = F(x, y)$. Using (1) we get

$$g'(t) = F'_1(x, y)\frac{dx}{dt} + F'_2(x, y)\frac{dy}{dt} = F'_1(x_0 + th, y_0 + tk)h + F'_2(x_0 + th, y_0 + tk)k$$

To find $g''(t)$, we have to differentiate the expression for $g'(t)$ w.r.t. t, which yields

$$g''(t) = \frac{d}{dt}F'_1(x, y)h + \frac{d}{dt}F'_2(x, y)k \tag{$*$}$$

To evaluate the derivatives on the right-hand side, we must use the chain rule (1) again. This gives

$$\frac{d}{dt}F'_1(x, y) = F''_{11}(x, y)\frac{dx}{dt} + F''_{12}(x, y)\frac{dy}{dt} = F''_{11}(x, y)h + F''_{12}(x, y)k$$

$$\frac{d}{dt}F'_2(x, y) = F''_{21}(x, y)\frac{dx}{dt} + F''_{22}(x, y)\frac{dy}{dt} = F''_{21}(x, y)h + F''_{22}(x, y)k$$

Assuming that $F''_{12} = F''_{21}$, inserting these expressions into $(*)$ gives

$$g''(t) = F''_{11}(x, y)h^2 + 2F''_{12}(x, y)hk + F''_{22}(x, y)k^2$$

where $x = x_0 + th$, $y = y_0 + tk$.　▌

A Rough Argument for the Chain Rule

In order to show that the chain rule is valid, none of the earlier rules for derivatives can be applied. Instead, we must go all the way back to the definition of derivative. Letting $\varphi(t)$ denote $F(f(t), g(t))$, we must examine the limit as $\Delta t \to 0$ of the Newton quotient

$$\frac{\varphi(t + \Delta t) - \varphi(t)}{\Delta t} = \frac{F(f(t + \Delta t), g(t + \Delta t)) - F(f(t), g(t))}{\Delta t} \qquad (*)$$

Because $x = f(t)$ and $y = g(t)$, we define $\Delta x = f(t + \Delta t) - f(t)$ and $\Delta y = g(t + \Delta t) - g(t)$, so that $f(t + \Delta t) = x + \Delta x$, $g(t + \Delta t) = y + \Delta y$. Substituting the last two expressions into $(*)$, then subtracting and adding $F(x, y + \Delta y)$, we obtain

$$\frac{\varphi(t + \Delta t) - \varphi(t)}{\Delta t} = \frac{F(x + \Delta x, y + \Delta y) - F(x, y + \Delta y) + F(x, y + \Delta y) - F(x, y)}{\Delta t}$$

Now assume that Δx and Δy are different from 0 for all Δt close to 0.[1] Then some simple algebraic manipulations suggest that, for all Δt close to 0, we have

$$\frac{\varphi(t + \Delta t) - \varphi(t)}{\Delta t} = \frac{F(x + \Delta x, y + \Delta y) - F(x, y + \Delta y)}{\Delta x} \frac{\Delta x}{\Delta t}$$
$$+ \frac{F(x, y + \Delta y) - F(x, y)}{\Delta y} \frac{\Delta y}{\Delta t}$$

When $\Delta t \to 0$, then $\Delta x / \Delta t \to dx/dt = f'(t)$, and $\Delta y / \Delta t \to dy/dt = g'(t)$. In particular, $\Delta x \to 0$ and $\Delta y \to 0$. From the formal definition of partial derivatives (see (2) and (3) of Section 11.2), we see that $[F(x + \Delta x, y + \Delta y) - F(x, y + \Delta y)]/\Delta x$ tends to $F_1'(x, y + \Delta y)$ as $\Delta x \to 0$, and that $[F(x, y + \Delta y) - F(x, y)]/\Delta y$ tends to $F_2'(x, y)$ as $\Delta y \to 0$. Also, as $\Delta t \to 0$, both Δx and Δy tend to 0, and so, because F_1' is a continuous function, $F_1'(x, y + \Delta y) \to F_1'(x, y)$. Finally, taking all the limits as $\Delta t \to 0$ gives

$$\varphi'(t) = \lim_{\Delta t \to 0} \frac{\varphi(t + \Delta t) - \varphi(t)}{\Delta t} = F_1'(x, y)\frac{dx}{dt} + F_2'(x, y)\frac{dy}{dt}$$

as required.

PROBLEMS FOR SECTION 12.1

1. In the following cases, find dz/dt by using the chain rule (1):

   (a) $F(x, y) = x + y^2$, $\quad x = t^2$, $\quad y = t^3$.

   (b) $F(x, y) = x^p y^q$, $\quad x = at$, $\quad y = bt$

   (c) Check the answers by first substituting the expressions for x and y and then differentiating.

2. Find dz/dt when:

   (a) $F(x, y) = x \ln y + y \ln x$, $\quad x = t + 1$, $\quad y = \ln t$

   (b) $F(x, y) = \ln x + \ln y$, $\quad x = Ae^{at}$, $\quad y = Be^{bt}$

---

[1] This is a "rough" argument because this assumption is not always valid, even when F, f, and g are all C^1 functions.

3. (a) If $z = F(t, y)$ and $y = g(t)$, find a formula for dz/dt. Consider in particular the case where $z = t^2 + ye^y$ and $y = t^2$.

   (b) If $Y = F(K, L)$ and $K = g(L)$, find a formula for dY/dL.

4. Let $Y = 10KL - \sqrt{K} - \sqrt{L}$. Suppose too that $K = 0.2t + 5$ and $L = 5e^{0.1t}$. Find dY/dt for $t = 0$.

5. What do you get if you apply the chain rule (1) when $F(x, y)$ is as follows?

   (a) $x + y$ (b) $x - y$ (c) $x \cdot y$ (d) x/y (e) $G(x)$

   Here $x = f(t)$, $y = g(t)$, and $G(x)$ are all differentiable functions.

HARDER PROBLEMS

6. Consider Example 4 and let $u(x, z) = \ln(x^\alpha + z^\alpha) - \alpha \ln z$. Let $z = h(x) = \sqrt[3]{ax^4 + b}$, with the constants α, a, and b all positive. Find the optimal x^* in this case.

7. Suppose that $z = F(x, y)$, $x = g(t)$, and $y = h(t)$. Modify the solution to Example 5 in order to prove that

$$\frac{d^2z}{dt^2} = \frac{\partial z}{\partial x}\frac{d^2x}{dt^2} + \frac{\partial z}{\partial y}\frac{d^2y}{dt^2} + \frac{\partial^2 z}{\partial x^2}\left(\frac{dx}{dt}\right)^2 + 2\frac{\partial^2 z}{\partial x \partial y}\left(\frac{dx}{dt}\right)\left(\frac{dy}{dt}\right) + \frac{\partial^2 z}{\partial y^2}\left(\frac{dy}{dt}\right)^2$$

under appropriate assumptions on F, g, and h.

12.2 Chain Rules for Many Variables

Economists often need even more general chain rules than the simple one for two variables presented in the previous section. For example, in consumer demand theory we assume that a household's utility depends on the number of units of each good it is able to consume. The number of units consumed will depend in turn on the prices of these goods and on the household's income. Thus the household's utility is related, indirectly, to all the prices and to income. How does utility respond to an increase in one of the prices, or to an increase in income? The general chain rule is the mathematical device that can be used to answer many questions of this kind.

Consider first the situation where

$$z = F(x, y), \qquad x = f(t, s), \qquad y = g(t, s)$$

(Problem 6 supplies an economic example.) In this case, z is a function of both t and s, with

$$z = F(f(t, s), g(t, s))$$

Here it makes sense to look for both partial derivatives $\partial z/\partial t$ and $\partial z/\partial s$. If we keep s fixed, then z is a function of t alone, and we can therefore use the chain rule (1) from the previous section. In the same way, by keeping t fixed, we can differentiate z w.r.t. s. The result is the following:

THE CHAIN RULE

If $z = F(x, y)$ with $x = f(t, s)$ and $y = g(t, s)$, then

(a) $\dfrac{\partial z}{\partial t} = F_1'(x, y)\dfrac{\partial x}{\partial t} + F_2'(x, y)\dfrac{\partial y}{\partial t}$ $\qquad\qquad$ (1)

(b) $\dfrac{\partial z}{\partial s} = F_1'(x, y)\dfrac{\partial x}{\partial s} + F_2'(x, y)\dfrac{\partial y}{\partial s}$

EXAMPLE 1   Find $\partial z/\partial t$ and $\partial z/\partial s$ when $z = F(x, y) = x^2 + 2y^2$, with $x = t - s^2$ and $y = ts$.

Solution: We obtain

$$F_1'(x, y) = 2x, \quad F_2'(x, y) = 4y, \quad \frac{\partial x}{\partial t} = 1, \quad \frac{\partial x}{\partial s} = -2s, \quad \frac{\partial y}{\partial t} = s, \quad \frac{\partial y}{\partial s} = t$$

Formula (1) therefore gives:

$$\frac{\partial z}{\partial t} = 2x \cdot 1 + 4y \cdot s = 2(t - s^2) + 4tss = 2t - 2s^2 + 4ts^2$$

$$\frac{\partial z}{\partial s} = 2x \cdot (-2s) + 4y \cdot t = 2(t - s^2)(-2s) + 4tst = -4ts + 4s^3 + 4t^2s$$

Check these answers by first expressing z as a function of t and s, then differentiating.   ∎

EXAMPLE 2   Find $z_t'(1, 0)$ if $z = e^{x^2} + y^2 e^{xy}$, with $x = 2t + 3s$ and $y = t^2 s^3$.

Solution: We obtain

$$\frac{\partial z}{\partial x} = 2xe^{x^2} + y^3 e^{xy}, \quad \frac{\partial z}{\partial y} = 2ye^{xy} + xy^2 e^{xy}, \quad \frac{\partial x}{\partial t} = 2, \quad \frac{\partial y}{\partial t} = 2ts^3$$

Using somewhat more concise notation, formula (1) gives

$$z_t'(t, s) = \frac{\partial z}{\partial x}\frac{\partial x}{\partial t} + \frac{\partial z}{\partial y}\frac{\partial y}{\partial t} = (2xe^{x^2} + y^3 e^{xy}) \cdot 2 + (2ye^{xy} + xy^2 e^{xy}) \cdot 2ts^3$$

When $t = 1$ and $s = 0$, then $x = 2$ and $y = 0$, so $z_t'(1, 0) = 4e^4 \cdot 2 = 8e^4$.   ∎

The General Case

Economists often need a more general version of the chain rule. Suppose that

$$z = F(x_1, \ldots, x_n) \quad \text{with} \quad x_1 = f_1(t_1, \ldots, t_m), \ldots, x_n = f_n(t_1, \ldots, t_m) \qquad (2)$$

Substituting for all the variables x_i as functions of the variables t_j into the function F expresses z as a **composite function**

$$z = F(f_1(t_1, \ldots, t_m), \ldots, f_n(t_1, \ldots, t_m))$$

of $t_1, \ldots, t_m$. In vector notation, $z = F(\mathbf{x}(\mathbf{t}))$. An obvious generalization of (1) is as follows:

THE GENERAL CHAIN RULE

When (2) is true, then

$$\frac{\partial z}{\partial t_j} = \frac{\partial z}{\partial x_1}\frac{\partial x_1}{\partial t_j} + \frac{\partial z}{\partial x_2}\frac{\partial x_2}{\partial t_j} + \cdots + \frac{\partial z}{\partial x_n}\frac{\partial x_n}{\partial t_j}, \qquad j = 1, 2, \ldots, m \tag{3}$$

This is an important formula that every economist should understand. A small change in a basic variable t_j sets off a chain reaction. First, every x_i depends on t_j in general, so it changes when t_j is changed. This affects z in turn. The contribution to the total derivative of z w.r.t. t_j that results from the change in x_i is $(\partial z/\partial x_i)(\partial x_i/\partial t_j)$. Formula (3) shows that $\partial z/\partial t_j$ is the sum of all these contributions.

EXAMPLE 3   Example 11.7.1 considered an agricultural production function $Y = F(K, L, T)$, where Y is the size of the harvest, K is capital invested, L is labour, and T is the area of agricultural land used to grow the crop. Suppose that K, L, and T are all functions of time. Then, according to (3), one has

$$\frac{dY}{dt} = \frac{\partial F}{\partial K}\frac{dK}{dt} + \frac{\partial F}{\partial L}\frac{dL}{dt} + \frac{\partial F}{\partial T}\frac{dT}{dt}$$

If F is the Cobb–Douglas function $F(K, L, T) = AK^a L^b T^c$, then

$$\frac{dY}{dt} = aAK^{a-1}L^b T^c\frac{dK}{dt} + bAK^a L^{b-1}T^c\frac{dL}{dt} + cAK^a L^b T^{c-1}\frac{dT}{dt} \tag{$*$}$$

Denoting time derivatives by "dots", and dividing each term in $(*)$ by $Y = AK^a L^b T^c$, we get

$$\frac{\dot{Y}}{Y} = a\frac{\dot{K}}{K} + b\frac{\dot{L}}{L} + c\frac{\dot{T}}{T}$$

The relative rate of change of output is, therefore, a weighted sum of the relative rates of change of capital, labour, and land. The weights are the respective powers a, b, and c. ∎

1. Use (1) to find $\partial z/\partial t$ and $\partial z/\partial s$ for the following cases:

   (a) $z = F(x, y) = x + y^2$, $x = t - s$, $y = ts$

   (b) $z = F(x, y) = 2x^2 + 3y^3$, $x = t^2 - s$, $y = t + 2s^3$

2. Using (1), find $\partial z/\partial t$ and $\partial z/\partial s$ for the following cases:

   (a) $z = xy^2$, $x = t + s^2$, $y = t^2 s$ (b) $z = \dfrac{x - y}{x + y}$, $x = e^{t+s}$, $y = e^{ts}$

3. Using (3), find $\partial w/\partial t$ for the following cases:

   (a) $w = xy^2 z^3$, $x = t^2$, $y = s$, $z = t$

   (b) $w = x^2 + y^2 + z^2$, $x = \sqrt{t + s}$, $y = e^{ts}$, $z = s^3$

4. Find expressions for $\partial z/\partial t_1$ and $\partial z/\partial t_2$ when $z = F(x)$ and $x = f(t_1, t_2)$.

5. (a) Suppose $Z = G + Y^2 + r^2$, where Y and r are both functions of G. Find an expression for $\partial Z/\partial G$.

   (b) Suppose $Z = G + I(Y, r)$, where I is a differentiable function of two variables, and Y, r are both functions of G. Find an expression for $\partial Z/\partial G$.

6. The cost C of producing Q_1 units of good 1 and Q_2 units of good 2 is given by $C = aQ_1 + bQ_2 + cQ_1^2$. The demand functions for the two goods, which are substitutes in consumption (see Problem 11.7.4), are $Q_1 = Ap_1^{-\alpha_1} p_2^{\beta_1}$ and $Q_2 = Bp_1^{\alpha_2} p_2^{-\beta_2}$, where p_1 and p_2 are the prices per unit of the two goods. All the constants are positive. Find expressions for the partial derivatives of C w.r.t. p_1 and p_2.

7. (a) If $u = \ln(x^3 + y^3 + z^3 - 3xyz)$, show that

   (i) $x\dfrac{\partial u}{\partial x} + y\dfrac{\partial u}{\partial y} + z\dfrac{\partial u}{\partial z} = 3$ (ii) $(x + y + z)\left(\dfrac{\partial u}{\partial x} + \dfrac{\partial u}{\partial y} + \dfrac{\partial u}{\partial z}\right) = 3$

   (b) If $z = f(x^2 y)$, show that $x\dfrac{\partial z}{\partial x} = 2y\dfrac{\partial z}{\partial y}$

8. (a) Find a formula for $\partial u/\partial r$ when $u = f(x, y, z, w)$ and x, y, z, and w all are functions of two variables r and s.

   (b) Suppose $u = xyzw$, where $x = r + s$, $y = r - s$, $z = rs$, $w = r/s$. Find $\partial u/\partial r$ when $(r, s) = (2, 1)$.

12.3 Implicit Differentiation along a Level Curve

Economists often need to differentiate functions that are defined implicitly by an equation. Section 7.2 considered some simple cases; it is a good idea to review those examples now. Here we study the problem from a more general point of view.

Let F be a function of two variables, and consider the equation

$$F(x, y) = c \qquad (c \text{ is a constant})$$

The equation represents a level curve for F. (See Section 11.3.) Suppose this equation defines y implicitly as a function $y = f(x)$ of x in some interval I, as illustrated in Fig. 1. This means that

$$F(x, f(x)) = c \qquad \text{for all } x \text{ in } I \tag{$*$}$$

If f is differentiable, what is the derivative of $y = f(x)$? If the graph of f looks like the one given in Fig. 1, the geometric problem is to find the slope of the graph at each point like P.

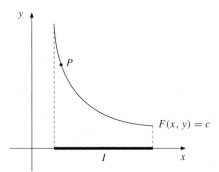

Figure 1 What is the slope at P?

To find an expression for the slope, introduce the auxiliary function u defined for all x in I by $u(x) = F(x, f(x))$. Then $u'(x) = F_1'(x, f(x)) \cdot 1 + F_2'(x, f(x)) \cdot f'(x)$ according to the chain rule. Now, $(*)$ states that $u(x) = c$ for all x in I. The derivative of a constant is 0, so we have $u'(x) = F_1'(x, f(x)) + F_2'(x, f(x)) \cdot f'(x) = 0$. If we replace $f(x)$ by y and solve for $f'(x) = y'$, we reach the conclusion:

SLOPE OF A LEVEL CURVE

$$F(x, y) = c \implies y' = -\frac{F_1'(x, y)}{F_2'(x, y)} \qquad (F_2'(x, y) \neq 0) \tag{1}$$

This is an important result. In the formula for y', be sure to note that the pair (x, y) must satisfy the equation $F(x, y) = c$. Note also that when $F(x, y) = c$ defines y implicitly as a function of x, formula (1) gives the derivative of y w.r.t. x even when it is impossible to solve the equation $F(x, y) = c$ explicitly for y.

The same argument gives an analogous result to (1), with x and y interchanged. Thus, if x is a continuously differentiable function of y which satisfies $F(x, y) = c$, then

$$F(x, y) = c \implies \frac{dx}{dy} = -\frac{\partial F/\partial y}{\partial F/\partial x} \qquad \left(\frac{\partial F}{\partial x} \neq 0\right) \tag{2}$$

EXAMPLE 1   Use (1) to find y' when $xy = 5$.

Solution: We put $F(x, y) = xy$. Then $F_1'(x, y) = y$ and $F_2'(x, y) = x$. Hence (1) gives

$$y' = -\frac{F_1'(x, y)}{F_2'(x, y)} = -\frac{y}{x}$$

This confirms the result in Example 7.1.1. ▌

EXAMPLE 2   For the curve given by
$$x^3 + x^2 y - 2y^2 - 10y = 0$$

find the slope and the equation for the tangent at the point $(x, y) = (2, 1)$.

Solution: Let $F(x, y) = x^3 + x^2 y - 2y^2 - 10y$. Then the given equation is equivalent to $F(x, y) = 0$, which is a level curve for F. First, we check that $F(2, 1) = 0$, so $(x, y) = (2, 1)$ is a point on the curve. Also, $F_1'(x, y) = 3x^2 + 2xy$ and $F_2'(x, y) = x^2 - 4y - 10$. So (1) implies that

$$y' = -\frac{3x^2 + 2xy}{x^2 - 4y - 10}$$

For $x = 2$ and $y = 1$ in particular, one has $y' = 8/5$. Then the point–slope formula for a line implies that the tangent at $(2, 1)$ must have the equation $y - 1 = (8/5)(x - 2)$, or $5y = 8x - 11$. See Fig. 2, in which the curve has been drawn by a computer program. Note that, for many values of x, there is more than one corresponding value of y such that (x, y) lies on the curve. For instance, $(2, 1)$ and $(2, -4)$ both lie on the curve. Find y' at $(2, -4)$. (Answer: $y' = 0.4$.) ▌

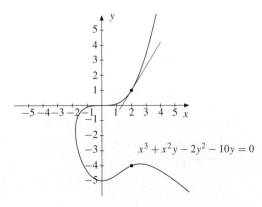

Figure 2 The graph of the equation in Example 2.

EXAMPLE 3   Assume that the equation

$$e^{xy^2} - 2x - 4y = c$$

implicitly defines y as a differentiable function $y = f(x)$ of x. Find a value of the constant c such that $f(0) = 1$, and find y' at $(x, y) = (0, 1)$.

Solution: When $x = 0$ and $y = 1$, the equation becomes $1 - 4 = c$, so $c = -3$. Let $F(x, y) = e^{xy^2} - 2x - 4y$. Then $F_1'(x, y) = y^2 e^{xy^2} - 2$, and $F_2'(x, y) = 2xye^{xy^2} - 4$. Thus, from (1) we have

$$y' = -\frac{F_1'(x, y)}{F_2'(x, y)} = -\frac{y^2 e^{xy^2} - 2}{2xye^{xy^2} - 4}$$

When $x = 0$ and $y = 1$, we find $y' = -1/4$. (Note that in this example it is impossible to solve $e^{xy^2} - 2x - 4y = -3$ explicitly for y. Even so, we have managed to find an explicit expression for the derivative of y w.r.t. x.)

Here is an important economic example using a function defined implicitly by an equation.

EXAMPLE 4   We generalize Example 7.2.2, and assume that $D = f(t, P)$ is the demand for a commodity that depends on the price P before tax, as well as on the sales tax per unit, denoted by t. Suppose that $S = g(P)$ is the supply function. At equilibrium, when supply is equal to demand, the equilibrium price $P = P(t)$ depends on t. Indeed, $P = P(t)$ must satisfy the equation

$$f(t, P) = g(P) \tag{$*$}$$

for all t in some relevant interval. Suppose that $(*)$ defines P implicitly as a differentiable function of t. Find an expression for dP/dt, then discuss its sign.

Solution: Let $F(t, P) = f(t, P) - g(P)$. Then equation $(*)$ becomes $F(t, P) = 0$, so formula (1) yields

$$\frac{dP}{dt} = -\frac{F_t'(t, P)}{F_P'(t, P)} = -\frac{f_t'(t, P)}{f_P'(t, P) - g'(P)} = \frac{f_t'(t, P)}{g'(P) - f_P'(t, P)} \tag{$**$}$$

It is reasonable to assume that $g'(P) > 0$ (meaning that supply increases if price increases) and that $f_t'(t, P)$ and $f_P'(t, P)$ are both < 0 (meaning that demand decreases if either the tax or the price increases). Then $(**)$ tells us that $dP/dt < 0$, implying that the pre-tax price faced by suppliers decreases as the tax increases. Thus the suppliers, as well as the consumers, are adversely affected if the tax on their product rises.

Of course, we can also derive formula $(**)$ by implicit differentiation of $(*)$ w.r.t. t. This procedure gives

$$f_t'(t, P) \cdot 1 + f_P'(t, P)\frac{dP}{dt} = g'(P)\frac{dP}{dt}$$

Solving this equation for dP/dt yields $(**)$ again.

A Formula for the Second Derivative

Sometimes we need to know whether a level curve $F(x, y) = c$ is the graph of a function $y = f(x)$ that is convex or concave. So we need to calculate y'', that is to find the derivative of $y' = -F_1'(x, y)/F_2'(x, y)$. Write $G(x) = F_1'(x, y)$ and $H(x) = F_2'(x, y)$, where y is a function of x. Our aim now is to differentiate the quotient $y' = -G(x)/H(x)$ w.r.t. x. According to the rule for differentiating quotients,

$$y'' = -\frac{G'(x)H(x) - G(x)H'(x)}{[H(x)]^2} \tag{$*$}$$

Keeping in mind that y is a function of x, both $G(x)$ and $H(x)$ are composite functions. So we differentiate them both by using the chain rule, thereby obtaining

$$G'(x) = F_{11}''(x, y) \cdot 1 + F_{12}''(x, y) \cdot y'$$

$$H'(x) = F_{21}''(x, y) \cdot 1 + F_{22}''(x, y) \cdot y'$$

Assuming that F is a C^2 function, Young's Theorem (Theorem 11.6.1) implies that $F_{12}'' = F_{21}''$. Replace y' in both the preceding equations by the quotient $-F_1'/F_2'$, and then insert the results into $(*)$. After some algebraic simplification, this yields the formula

$$F(x, y) = c \implies y'' = -\frac{1}{(F_2')^3}[F_{11}''(F_2')^2 - 2F_{12}''F_1'F_2' + F_{22}''(F_1')^2] \tag{3}$$

This formula is useful in some theoretical arguments, but usually it is easier to find y'' by direct differentiation, as in the examples in Section 7.1.

EXAMPLE 5   Use (3) to find y'' when

$$xy = 5$$

Solution: With $F(x, y) = xy$ we have $F_1' = y$, $F_2' = x$, $F_{11}'' = 0$, $F_{12}'' = 1$, and $F_{22}'' = 0$. According to (3), we obtain

$$y'' = -\frac{1}{x^3}(-2 \cdot 1 \cdot y \cdot x) = \frac{2y}{x^2}$$

which is the same result we found in Example 7.1.4.   ∎

For those who are familiar with 3×3 determinants, which are discussed in Section 16.2, the result in (3) can be expressed in the following more memorable form:

$$F(x, y) = c \implies y'' = \frac{d^2y}{dx^2} = \frac{1}{(F_2')^3}\begin{vmatrix} 0 & F_1' & F_2' \\ F_1' & F_{11}'' & F_{12}'' \\ F_2' & F_{21}'' & F_{22}'' \end{vmatrix} \tag{4}$$

This is valid for $F_2' \neq 0$, obviously.

1. Use formula (1) to find y' when y is defined implicitly by $2x^2 + 6xy + y^2 = 18$. Let $F(x, y) = 2x^2 + 6xy + y^2$ and $c = 18$. Compare with the result in Problem 7.1.3.

2. Use formula (1) to find y' for the following level curves. Also find y'' using (3).

   (a) $x^2 y = 1$ (b) $x - y + 3xy = 2$ (c) $y^5 - x^6 = 0$

3. A curve in the xy-plane is given by the equation $2x^2 + xy + y^2 - 8 = 0$.

   (a) Find y', y'', and the equation for the tangent at the point $(2, 0)$.

   (b) Which points on the curve have a horizontal tangent?

4. The equation $3x^2 - 3xy^2 + y^3 + 3y^2 = 4$ defines y implicitly as a function $h(x)$ of x in a neighbourhood of the point $(1, 1)$. Find $h'(1)$.

5. Let $D = f(R, P)$ denote the demand for a commodity when the price is P and R is advertising expenditure. If the supply is $S = g(P)$, equilibrium in the market requires that $f(R, P) = g(P)$. What is dP/dR? Discuss the sign.

6. Let f be a differentiable function of one variable, and let a and b be two constants. Suppose that the equation $x - az = f(y - bz)$ defines z as a differentiable function of x and y. Prove that z satisfies $az'_x + bz'_y = 1$.

12.4 More General Cases

Consider the equation $F(x, y, z) = c$, where c is a constant. In general, this equation determines a surface in three-dimensional space consisting of all the triples (x, y, z) that satisfy the equation. This is called the **graph** of the equation. Suppose that $z = f(x, y)$ defines implicitly a function that, for all (x, y) in some domain A, satisfies the equation $F(x, y, z) = c$. Then

$$F(x, y, f(x, y)) = c \qquad \text{for all } (x, y) \text{ in } A$$

Suppose F and f are differentiable. Because the function $g(x, y) = F(x, y, f(x, y))$ is equal to the constant c for all $(x, y) \in A$, the partial derivatives g'_x and g'_y must both be 0. However, $g(x, y)$ is a composite function of x and y whose partial derivatives can be found by using the general chain rule (12.2.3.) Therefore,

$$g'_x = F'_x \cdot 1 + F'_z \cdot z'_x = 0, \qquad g'_y = F'_y \cdot 1 + F'_z \cdot z'_y = 0$$

This implies the following expressions for the partial derivatives of $z = f(x, y)$:

$$F(x, y, z) = c \quad \Longrightarrow \quad z'_x = -\frac{F'_x}{F'_z}, \quad z'_y = -\frac{F'_y}{F'_z} \qquad (F'_z \neq 0) \qquad (1)$$

Using (1) allows formulas for z'_x and z'_y to be found even if it is impossible to solve the equation $F(x, y, z) = c$ explicitly for z as a function of x and y.

EXAMPLE 1   The equation $x - 2y - 3z + z^2 = -2$ defines z as a twice differentiable function of x and y about the point $(x, y, z) = (0, 0, 2)$. Find z'_x and z'_y, and then z''_{xx}, z''_{xy}, and z''_{yy}. Find also the numerical values of all these partial derivatives at $(0, 0)$.

Solution: Let $F(x, y, z) = x - 2y - 3z + z^2$ and $c = -2$. Then $F'_x = 1$, $F'_y = -2$, and $F'_z = 2z - 3$. Whenever $z \neq 3/2$, we have $F'_z \neq 0$, so formula (1) gives

$$z'_x = -\frac{1}{2z - 3}, \qquad z'_y = -\frac{-2}{2z - 3} = \frac{2}{2z - 3}$$

For $x = 0$, $y = 0$, and $z = 2$ in particular, we obtain $z'_x = -1$ and $z'_y = 2$.

We find z''_{xx} by differentiating the expression for z'_x partially w.r.t. x. Keeping in mind that z is a function of x and y, we get $z''_{xx} = (\partial/\partial x)(-(2z - 3)^{-1}) = (2z - 3)^{-2}2z'_x$. Using the expression for z'_x found above, we have

$$z''_{xx} = \frac{-2}{(2z - 3)^3}$$

Correspondingly,

$$z''_{xy} = \frac{\partial}{\partial y}z'_x = \frac{\partial}{\partial y}[-(2z - 3)^{-1}] = (2z - 3)^{-2}2z'_y = \frac{4}{(2z - 3)^3}$$

and

$$z''_{yy} = \frac{\partial}{\partial y}z'_y = \frac{\partial}{\partial y}[2(2z - 3)^{-1}] = -2(2z - 3)^{-2}2z'_y = \frac{-8}{(2z - 3)^3}$$

For $x = y = 0$ and $z = 2$, we get $z''_{xx} = -2$, $z''_{xy} = 4$, and $z''_{yy} = -8$.   ∎

EXAMPLE 2   A firm produces $Q = f(L)$ units of a commodity using L units of labour. We assume that $f'(L) > 0$ and $f''(L) < 0$, so f is strictly increasing and strictly concave. (It might be a good idea to look at Problem 3 where a special case is considered.)

(a) If the firm gets P euros per unit produced and pays w euros for a unit of labour, write down the profit function, and find the first-order condition for profit maximization at $L^* > 0$.

(b) By implicit differentiation of the first-order condition, examine how changes in P and w influence the optimal choice of L^*.

Solution: (a) The profit function is $\pi(L) = Pf(L) - wL$, so $\pi'(L) = Pf'(L) - w$. Thus an optimal L^* must satisfy

$$Pf'(L^*) - w = 0 \qquad\qquad (*)$$

(b) If we define $F(P, w, L^*) = Pf'(L^*) - w$, then $(*)$ is equivalent to $F(P, w, L^*) = 0$. According to formula (1),

$$\frac{\partial L^*}{\partial P} = -\frac{F'_P}{F'_{L^*}} = -\frac{f'(L^*)}{Pf''(L^*)}, \quad \frac{\partial L^*}{\partial w} = -\frac{F'_w}{F'_{L^*}} = -\frac{-1}{Pf''(L^*)} = \frac{1}{Pf''(L^*)}$$

The sign assumptions on f' and f'' imply that $\partial L^*/\partial P > 0$ and $\partial L^*/\partial w < 0$. Thus, the optimal labour input goes up if the price P increases, while it goes down if labour costs increase. This makes economic sense. (Actually, economists would usually prefer to use implicit differentiation rather than relying on formula (1).)

EXAMPLE 3   **(Gains from Search)**   Suppose you intend to buy x^0 units of a certain commodity which has been offered at a price today of p^0 per unit. But you expect that searching among other sellers will yield a lower price. Let $p(t)$ denote the lowest price per unit you expect to find after searching the market for t hours. It is reasonable to assume that $\dot{p}(t) < 0$. Moreover, since it is usually harder to find lower prices as the search progresses, we assume that $\ddot{p}(t) > 0$. Suppose your hourly wage is w. By searching for t hours, you save $p^0 - p(t)$ dollars for each unit you buy. Since you are buying x^0 units, total savings are $[p^0 - p(t)]x^0$. On the other hand, searching for t hours costs you wt in foregone wages. So the expected profit from searching for t hours is

$$\pi(t) = [p^0 - p(t)]x^0 - wt$$

A necessary first-order condition for $t = t^* > 0$ to maximize profit is that

$$\dot{\pi}(t^*) = -\dot{p}(t^*)x^0 - w = 0 \qquad\qquad (*)$$

This condition is also sufficient, because $\ddot{\pi}(t) = -\ddot{p}(t)x^0 < 0$ for all t. (Here is an economic interpretation of the condition $-\dot{p}(t^*)x^0 = w$: What do you gain by searching for one hour more than t^*? Answer: $[p(t^*) - p(t^* + 1)]x^0$, which is approximately $-\dot{p}(t^*)x^0$. On the other hand you lose an hour's wage, w. So the first-order condition says that you should search until the marginal gain from searching for an extra hour is just offset by the hourly wage.)

The optimal search time t^* depends on x^0 and w. Economists typically want to know how t^* changes as x^0 or w changes. We see that equation $(*)$ is similar to equation $(*)$ in Example 2 (with $x^0 = -P$, $p = f$, and $t^* = L^*$). It follows immediately that

$$\frac{\partial t^*}{\partial x^0} = -\frac{\dot{p}(t^*)}{\ddot{p}(t^*)x^0} > 0, \quad \frac{\partial t^*}{\partial w} = -\frac{1}{\ddot{p}(t^*)x^0} < 0$$

because $\dot{p}(t^*) < 0$, $\ddot{p}(t^*) > 0$, and $x^0 > 0$. Thus, the optimal search time rises as the number of units you want to buy increases, and falls as the wage rate rises.

These qualitative results can easily be obtained by a geometric argument. Figure 1 illustrates the optimal search time t^*. It is the value of t at which the tangent to the curve $R = [p^0 - p(t)]x^0$ has slope w, and so is parallel to the line $C = wt$. If x^0 increases, the R curve is magnified vertically but not horizontally, so t^* moves to the right. On the other hand, if w increases, the straight line $C = wt$ will rotate anti-clockwise about the origin, so the optimal t^* will decrease.

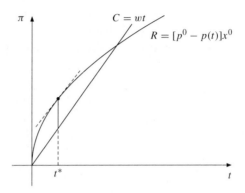

Figure 1 Optimal search

The General Case

The foregoing can be extended to any number of variables. The proof of the following result is a direct extension of the argument we gave for (1), so is left to the reader. Assuming that $\partial F / \partial z \neq 0$, we have

$$F(x_1, \ldots, x_n, z) = c \quad \Longrightarrow \quad \frac{\partial z}{\partial x_i} = -\frac{\partial F / \partial x_i}{\partial F / \partial z}, \qquad i = 1, 2, \ldots, n \qquad (2)$$

PROBLEMS FOR SECTION 12.4

1. Use (1) to find $\partial z / \partial x$ for the following:

   (a) $3x + y - z = 0$ (b) $xyz + xz^3 - xy^2z^5 = 1$ (c) $e^{xyz} = 3xyz$

2. Find z'_x, z'_y, and z''_{xy} when $x^3 + y^3 + z^3 - 3z = 0$.

3. Assume in Example 2 that $f(L) = \sqrt{L}$. Write down equation $(*)$ in this case and find an explicit expression for L^* as a function of P and w. Find the partial derivatives of L^* w.r.t. P and w. Then verify the signs obtained in Example 2.

4. The equation $x^y + y^z + z^x = k$, where k is a positive constant, defines z as a function of x and y, for $x > 0$ and $y > 0$. Find the partial derivatives of z w.r.t. x and y.

5. Replace $S = g(P)$ in the model of Problem 12.3.5 by $S = g(w, P)$, where w is an index for how favourable the weather has been. Assume $g'_w(w, P) > 0$. (We are studying the market for an agricultural product.) Equilibrium now requires $f(R, P) = g(w, P)$. Assume that this equation defines P implicitly as a differentiable function of R and w. Find an expression for P'_w, and comment on its sign.

6. (a) The function F is defined for all x and y by $F(x, y) = xe^{y-3} + xy^2 - 2y$. Show that the point $(1, 3)$ lies on the level curve $F(x, y) = 4$, and find the equation for the tangent line to the curve at the point $(1, 3)$.

   (b) The Nerlove–Ringstad production function $y = y(K, L)$ is defined implicitly by $y^{1+c \ln y} = AK^\alpha L^\beta$, where A, α, and β are positive constants. Find the marginal productivities of y w.r.t. K (capital) and L (labour)—that is, find $\partial y / \partial K$ and $\partial y / \partial L$. (*Hint:* Take the logarithm of each side and then differentiate implicitly.)

12.5 Elasticity of Substitution

Economists are often interested in the slope of the tangent to a level curve at a particular point. Often, the level curve is downwards sloping, but economists prefer a positive answer. So we change the sign of the slope defined by (12.3.1), and use a special name:

$$R_{yx} = \frac{F'_1(x, y)}{F'_2(x, y)} \quad \text{(the \textbf{marginal rate of substitution} of } y \text{ for } x) \qquad (1)$$

The marginal rate of substitution has the standard abbreviation MRS. Note that $R_{yx} = -y' \approx -\Delta y / \Delta x$ when we move along the level curve $F(x, y) = c$. If $\Delta x = -1$ in particular, then $R_{yx} \approx \Delta y$. Thus, R_{yx} is approximately the quantity of y we must substitute (add) per unit of x removed, if we are to stay on the same level curve.

EXAMPLE 1   Let $F(K, L) = 100$ be an isoquant for a production function, where K is capital input, L is labour input, and 100 is the output. Look at Fig. 1. At all the points P, Q, and R, 100 units are produced. At P a little capital and a lot of labour input is used. The slope of the isoquant at P is approximately -4, so the MRS at P is approximately 4. This means that if 4 units of labour are taken away, adding only one unit of capital will ensure that output remains at (approximately) 100 units. At P capital is more "valuable" than labour. At Q the MRS is approximately 1, so capital and labour are equally "valuable". Finally, at R, the MRS is approximately $1/5$, so at this point approximately 5 units of capital are required to compensate for the loss of one unit of labour.

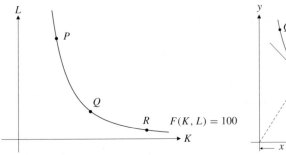

Figure 1 What is the MRS at P, Q, and R? (See Example 1.)

Figure 2

Consider a level curve $F(x, y) = c$ for a function F of two variables, as shown in Fig. 2. The marginal rate of substitution R_{yx} varies along the curve. At point Q, the MRS R_{yx} is a large positive number. At P, the number R_{yx} is about 1, and at R it is about 0.2. As we move along the level curve from left to right, R_{yx} will be strictly decreasing with values in some positive interval I. For each value of R_{yx} in I, there is a corresponding point (x, y) on the level curve $F(x, y) = c$, and thus a corresponding value of y/x. The fraction y/x is therefore a function of R_{yx}, and we define the following:

ELASTICITY OF SUBSTITUTION

When $F(x, y) = c$, the elasticity of substitution between y and x is

$$\sigma_{yx} = \text{El}_{R_{yx}}\left(\frac{y}{x}\right)$$

(2)

Thus, σ_{yx} is the elasticity of the fraction y/x w.r.t. the marginal rate of substitution. Roughly speaking, σ_{yx} is the percentage change in the fraction y/x when we move along the level curve $F(x, y) = c$ far enough so that R_{yx} increases by 1%. Note that σ_{yx} is symmetric in x and y. In fact, $R_{xy} = 1/R_{yx}$, and so the logarithmic formula for elasticities implies that $\sigma_{xy} = \sigma_{yx}$. Also, Problem 3 asks you to derive a (symmetric) expression for the elasticity of substitution in terms of the first and second order partial derivatives of F.

EXAMPLE 2   Calculate σ_{KL} for the Cobb–Douglas function $F(K, L) = AK^a L^b$.

Solution: The marginal rate of substitution of K for L is

$$R_{KL} = \frac{F'_L}{F'_K} = \frac{bAK^a L^{b-1}}{aAK^{a-1}L^b} = \frac{b}{a}\frac{K}{L}$$

Thus, $K/L = (a/b)R_{KL}$. The elasticity of the last expression w.r.t. R_{KL} is 1. Hence, $\sigma_{KL} = 1$ for the Cobb–Douglas function.

EXAMPLE 3   Find the elasticity of substitution for

$$F(K, L) = A(aK^{-\varrho} + bL^{-\varrho})^{-m/\varrho}$$

where A, a, and b are positive constants, $m \neq 0$, $\varrho > -1$, and $\varrho \neq 0$.

Solution: Here

$$F'_K = A(-m/\varrho)(aK^{-\varrho} + bL^{-\varrho})^{(-m/\varrho)-1}a(-\varrho)K^{-\varrho-1}$$

$$F'_L = A(-m/\varrho)(aK^{-\varrho} + bL^{-\varrho})^{(-m/\varrho)-1}b(-\varrho)L^{-\varrho-1}$$

Hence,

$$R_{KL} = \frac{F'_L}{F'_K} = \frac{b}{a}\frac{L^{-\varrho-1}}{K^{-\varrho-1}} = \frac{b}{a}\left(\frac{K}{L}\right)^{\varrho+1}$$

Therefore

$$\frac{K}{L} = \left(\frac{a}{b}\right)^{1/(\varrho+1)}(R_{KL})^{1/(\varrho+1)}$$

Recalling that the elasticity of Ax^b w.r.t. x is b, definition (2) implies that

$$\sigma_{KL} = \mathrm{El}_{R_{KL}}\left(\frac{K}{L}\right) = \frac{1}{\varrho+1}$$

We have thus shown that the function F has constant elasticity of substitution $1/(\varrho+1)$. For this reason, F is usually called the **CES function** (where CES stands for "constant elasticity of substitution").

Note that the elasticity of substitution for the CES function tends to 1 as $\varrho \to 0$, and this is precisely the elasticity of substitution for the Cobb–Douglas function in the previous example. This is in accordance with the result in Example 7.12.5.   ∎

PROBLEMS FOR SECTION 12.5

1. Calculate the elasticity of substitution between y and x for $F(x, y) = 10x^2 + 15y^2$.

2. (a) Find the marginal rate of substitution of y for x in

$$F(x, y) = x^a + y^a \qquad (a \text{ is a constant, } a \neq 0 \text{ and } a \neq 1)$$

   (b) Calculate the elasticity of substitution between y and x.

3. The elasticity of substitution defined in (2) can be expressed in terms of the partial derivatives of the function F:

$$\sigma_{yx} = \frac{-F'_1 F'_2 (x F'_1 + y F'_2)}{xy[(F'_2)^2 F''_{11} - 2F'_1 F'_2 F''_{12} + (F'_1)^2 F''_{22}]}, \qquad F(x, y) = c$$

   Use this formula to derive the result in Example 2.

12.6 Homogeneous Functions of Two Variables

One class of especially important functions in economics consists of the homogeneous functions. The function $\varphi(t) = t^k$ of one variable has *degree k*. Accordingly, the function f of two variables x and y defined in a domain D is said to be **homogeneous of degree k** if, for all (x, y) in D,

$$f(tx, ty) = t^k f(x, y) \qquad \text{for all } t > 0 \tag{1}$$

Multiplication of both variables by a positive factor t will thus multiply the value of the function by the factor t^k.

The degree of homogeneity of a function can be an arbitrary number—positive, zero, or negative. Earlier we determined the degree of homogeneity for several particular functions. For instance, we found in Example 11.1.4 that the Cobb–Douglas function F defined by $F(x, y) = Ax^a y^b$ is homogeneous of degree $a + b$. Here is an even simpler example:

EXAMPLE 1   Show that the following function is homogeneous of degree 3:

$$f(x, y) = 3x^2 y - y^3$$

Solution: If we replace x by tx and y by ty in the formula for $f(x, y)$, we obtain

$$f(tx, ty) = 3(tx)^2(ty) - (ty)^3 = 3t^2 x^2 ty - t^3 y^3 = t^3(3x^2 y - y^3) = t^3 f(x, y)$$

Thus f is homogeneous of degree 3. If we let $t = 2$, then

$$f(2x, 2y) = 2^3 f(x, y) = 8 f(x, y)$$

After doubling both x and y, the value of this function increases by a factor of 8.

Note that the sum of the exponents in each term of the polynomial in Example 1 is equal to 3. In general, a polynomial is homogeneous of degree k if and only if the sum of the exponents in each term is k. Other types of polynomial with different sums of exponents in different terms, such as $f(x, y) = 1 + xy$ or $g(x, y) = x^3 + xy$, are not homogeneous of any degree. (See Problem 6.)

Let us mention some important properties of homogeneous functions of two variables that are of interest in economic applications. The first is **Euler's theorem**, which says that

$$f(x, y) \text{ is homogeneous of degree } k \iff xf_1'(x, y) + yf_2'(x, y) = kf(x, y) \tag{2}$$

It is easy to demonstrate that when f is homogeneous of degree k, then the right-hand side of (2) is true. Indeed, differentiating each side of (1) w.r.t. t, using the chain rule to differentiate the left-hand side, gives

$$xf_1'(tx, ty) + yf_2'(tx, ty) = kt^{k-1} f(x, y)$$

Putting $t = 1$ gives $xf_1'(x, y) + yf_2'(x, y) = kf(x, y)$ immediately. Theorem 12.7.1 in the next section also proves the converse, and considers the case of n variables.

We note three other interesting general properties of functions $f(x, y)$ that are homogeneous of degree k:

$$f_1'(x, y) \text{ and } f_2'(x, y) \text{ are both homogeneous of degree } k - 1 \qquad (3)$$

$$f(x, y) = x^k f(1, y/x) = y^k f(x/y, 1) \qquad \text{(for } x > 0, y > 0) \qquad (4)$$

$$x^2 f_{11}''(x, y) + 2xy f_{12}''(x, y) + y^2 f_{22}''(x, y) = k(k - 1)f(x, y) \qquad (5)$$

To prove (3), keep t and y constant and differentiate equation (1) partially w.r.t. x. Then $tf_1'(tx, ty) = t^k f_1'(x, y)$, so $f_1'(tx, ty) = t^{k-1} f_1'(x, y)$, thus showing that $f_1'(x, y)$ is homogeneous of degree $k - 1$. The same argument shows that $f_2'(x, y)$ is homogeneous of degree $k - 1$.

We can prove the two equalities in (4) by replacing t in (1) first by $1/x$ and then by $1/y$, respectively.

Finally, to show (5) (assuming that $f(x, y)$ is twice continuously differentiable), we note first that because $f_1'(x, y)$ and $f_2'(x, y)$ are both homogeneous of degree $k - 1$, Euler's theorem in (2) can be applied to f_1' and f_2'. It implies that

$$
\begin{aligned}
xf_{11}''(x, y) + yf_{12}''(x, y) &= (k - 1)f_1'(x, y) \\
xf_{21}''(x, y) + yf_{22}''(x, y) &= (k - 1)f_2'(x, y)
\end{aligned}
\qquad (*)
$$

Let us now multiply the first of these equations by x, the second by y, and then add. Because f is C^2, Young's theorem implies that $f_{12}'' = f_{21}''$, so the result is

$$x^2 f_{11}''(x, y) + 2xy f_{12}''(x, y) + y^2 f_{22}''(x, y) = (k - 1)[xf_1'(x, y) + yf_2'(x, y)]$$

By Euler's theorem, however, $xf_1'(x, y) + yf_2'(x, y) = kf(x, y)$. So (5) is verified.

EXAMPLE 2   Check properties (2) to (5) for the function $f(x, y) = 3x^2 y - y^3$.

Solution: We find that $f_1'(x, y) = 6xy$ and $f_2'(x, y) = 3x^2 - 3y^2$. Hence,

$$xf_1'(x, y) + yf_2'(x, y) = 6x^2 y + 3x^2 y - 3y^3 = 3(3x^2 y - y^3) = 3f(x, y)$$

Example 1 showed that f is homogeneous of degree 3, so this confirms (2).

Obviously f_1' and f_2' are polynomials that are homogeneous of degree 2, which confirms (3). As for (4), in this case it takes the form

$$3x^2 y - y^3 = x^3[3(y/x) - (y/x)^3] = y^3[3(x/y)^2 - 1]$$

Finally, to show (5), first calculate the second-order partial derivatives, $f_{11}''(x, y) = 6y$, $f_{12}''(x, y) = 6x$, and $f_{22}''(x, y) = -6y$. Hence,

$$x^2 f_{11}''(x, y) + 2xy f_{12}''(x, y) + y^2 f_{22}''(x, y) = 6x^2 y + 12x^2 y - 6y^3 = 6(3x^2 y - y^3)$$
$$= 3 \cdot 2f(x, y)$$

which confirms (5) as well.

EXAMPLE 3   Suppose that the production function $Y = F(K, L)$ is homogeneous of degree one. Show that $Y/L = f(K/L)$, where $f(K/L) = F(K/L, 1)$. (Thus, when a production function involving capital K and labour L is homogeneous of degree 1, one can express the output–labour ratio Y/L as a function of the capital–labour ratio K/L.) Find the form of f when F is the Cobb–Douglas function $AK^a L^b$ with $a + b = 1$.

Solution: Because F is homogeneous of degree 1, $Y=F(K, L)=F(L(K/L), L \cdot 1) = LF(K/L, 1) = Lf(K/L)$. (Really, this is just a special case of (4).) When $F(K, L) = AK^a L^{1-a}$, then $f(K/L) = F(K/L, 1) = A(K/L)^a$.

Geometric Aspects of Homogeneous Functions

Homogeneous functions in two variables have some interesting geometric properties. Let $f(x, y)$ be homogeneous of degree k. Consider a ray in the xy-plane from the origin $(0, 0)$ through the point $(x_0, y_0) \neq (0, 0)$. An arbitrary point on this ray is of the form (tx_0, ty_0) for some positive number t. If we let $f(x_0, y_0) = c$, then $f(tx_0, ty_0) = t^k f(x_0, y_0) = t^k c$. Above any ray in the xy-plane through a point (x_0, y_0), the relevant portion of the graph of f therefore consists of the curve $z = t^k c$, where t measures the distance along the ray from the origin, and $c = f(x_0, y_0)$. A function that is homogeneous of degree k is therefore completely determined if its value is known at one point on each ray through the origin. (See Fig 1.)

In particular, let $k = 1$ so that $f(x, y)$ is homogeneous of degree 1. The curve $z = t^k c$ lying vertically above each relevant ray through the origin is then the straight line $z = tc$. Because of this, it is often said that *the graph of a homogeneous function of degree 1 is generated by straight lines through the origin*. Fig. 2 illustrates this.

Figure 1

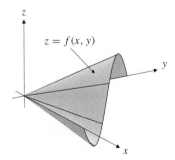

Figure 2 f is homogeneous of degree 1.

We have seen how it is often convenient to consider the level curves of a function $f(x, y)$ of two variables instead of its graph. What can we say about the level curves of a function if the function is homogeneous? It turns out that *for a homogeneous function, even if only one of its level curves is known, then so are all its other level curves.*

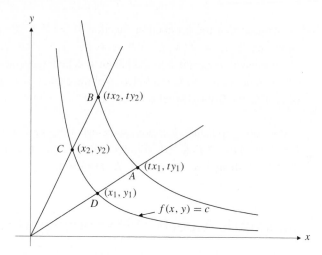

Figure 3 Level curves for a homogeneous function

To see this, consider a function $f(x, y)$ that is homogeneous of degree k, and let $f(x, y) = c$ be one of its level curves, as illustrated in Fig. 3. We now explain how to construct the level curve through an arbitrary point A not lying on $f(x, y) = c$: First, draw the ray through the origin and the point A. This ray intersects the level curve $f(x, y) = c$ at a point D with co-ordinates (x_1, y_1). The coordinates of A will then be of the form (tx_1, ty_1) for some value of t. (In the figure, $t \approx 1.7$.) In order to construct a new point on the same level curve as A, draw a new ray through the origin. This ray intersects the original level curve $f(x, y) = c$ at (x_2, y_2). Now use the value of t found earlier to determine the new point B with coordinates (tx_2, ty_2). This new point B is on the same level curve as A because $f(tx_2, ty_2) = t^k f(x_2, y_2) = t^k c = t^k f(x_1, y_1) = f(tx_1, ty_1)$. By repeating this construction for different rays through the origin that intersect the level curve $f(x, y) = c$, we can find as many points as we wish on the new level curve $f(x, y) = f(tx_1, ty_1)$.

The foregoing argument shows that if $f(x, y)$ is homogeneous, then the whole form of the function is determined by any one of its level curves and by the degree of homogeneity of the function. The shape of each level curve of a homogeneous function is often determined by specifying its elasticity of substitution, as defined in (12.5.2).

Another point worth noticing in connection with Fig. 3 is that the tangents to the level curves along each ray are parallel. We keep the assumption that f is homogeneous of degree k. If the level curve is $f(x, y) = c$, its slope is $-f_1'(x, y)/f_2'(x, y)$. At the point A in Fig. 3 the slope is

$$-\frac{f_1'(tx_1, ty_1)}{f_2'(tx_1, ty_1)} = -\frac{t^{k-1} f_1'(x_1, y_1)}{t^{k-1} f_2'(x_1, y_1)} = -\frac{f_1'(x_1, y_1)}{f_2'(x_1, y_1)} \qquad (**)$$

where we have used equation (3), expressing the fact that the partial derivatives of f are homogeneous of degree $k - 1$. The equality in $(**)$ shows that the slope of the level curve through D is the same as the slope of the level curve through A. Stated differently, after removing the minus signs, $(**)$ shows that the marginal rate of substitution of y for x is a homogeneous function of degree 0.

1. Show that $f(x, y) = x^4 + x^2 y^2$ is homogeneous of degree 4 by using (1).

2. Find the degree of homogeneity of $x(p, r) = Ap^{-1.5} r^{2.08}$.

3. Show that $f(x, y) = xy^2 + x^3$ is homogeneous of degree 3. Verify that the four properties (2) to (5) all hold.

4. See whether the function $f(x, y) = xy/(x^2 + y^2)$ is homogeneous, and check Euler's theorem if it is.

5. Let $F(K, L)$ be the homogeneous of degree one CES production function $F(K, L) = A(aK^{-\varrho} + bL^{-\varrho})^{-1/\varrho}$. Express Y/L as a function of K/L.

6. Show that $f(x, y) = x^3 + xy$ is not homogeneous of any degree. (*Hint:* Let $x = y = 1$. Apply (1) with $t = 2$ and $t = 4$ to get a contradiction.)

7. Use (∗) in the proof of (5) to show that if $f(x, y)$ is homogeneous of degree 1 for $x > 0$ and $y > 0$, then $f_{11}''(x, y) f_{22}''(x, y) - [f_{12}''(x, y)]^2 \equiv 0$.

HARDER PROBLEMS

8. Prove that if $F(x, y)$ is homogeneous of degree 1, then the elasticity of substitution can be expressed as $\sigma_{yx} = F_1' F_2'/F F_{12}''$. (*Hint:* Use Euler's theorem (2), together with (∗) in the proof of (5), and the result in Problem 12.5.3.)

12.7 General Homogeneous and Homothetic Functions

Suppose that f is a function of n variables defined in a domain D. Suppose also that whenever $(x_1, x_2, \ldots, x_n) \in D$ and $t > 0$, then $(tx_1, tx_2, \ldots, tx_n)$ also lies in D. (A set D with this property is called a **cone**.) We say that f is **homogeneous of degree** k on D if

$$f(tx_1, tx_2, \ldots, tx_n) = t^k f(x_1, x_2, \ldots, x_n) \qquad \text{for all} \quad t > 0 \qquad (1)$$

The constant k can be any number—positive, zero, or negative.

EXAMPLE 1   Test the homogeneity of $f(x_1, x_2, x_3, x_4) = \dfrac{x_1 + 2x_2 + 3x_3 + 4x_4}{x_1^2 + x_2^2 + x_3^2 + x_4^2}$.

Solution: Here f is defined on the set D of all points in four-dimensional space excluding the origin. This set is a cone. Also,

$$f(tx_1, tx_2, tx_3, tx_4) = \frac{tx_1 + 2tx_2 + 3tx_3 + 4tx_4}{(tx_1)^2 + (tx_2)^2 + (tx_3)^2 + (tx_4)^2} = \frac{t(x_1 + 2x_2 + 3x_3 + 4x_4)}{t^2(x_1^2 + x_2^2 + x_3^2 + x_4^2)}$$

$$= t^{-1} f(x_1, x_2, x_3, x_4)$$

Hence, f is homogeneous of degree -1.

Euler's theorem can be generalized to functions of n variables:

THEOREM 12.7.1 (EULER'S THEOREM)

Suppose f is a differentiable function of n variables in an open domain D, where $\mathbf{x} = (x_1, x_2, \ldots, x_n) \in D$ and $t > 0$ imply $t\mathbf{x} \in D$. Then f is homogeneous of degree k in D if and only if the following equation holds for all $\mathbf{x}$ in D:

$$\sum_{i=1}^{n} x_i f_i'(\mathbf{x}) = kf(\mathbf{x}) \qquad (2)$$

Proof: Suppose f is homogeneous of degree k, so (1) holds. Differentiating this equation w.r.t. t (with $\mathbf{x}$ fixed) yields $\sum_{i=1}^{n} x_i f_i'(t\mathbf{x}) = kt^{k-1} f(\mathbf{x})$. Setting $t = 1$ gives (2) immediately.

To prove the converse, assume that (2) is valid for all $\mathbf{x}$ in D. Keep $\mathbf{x}$ fixed and define the function g for all $t > 0$ by $g(t) = t^{-k} f(t\mathbf{x}) - f(\mathbf{x})$. Then differentiating w.r.t. t gives

$$g'(t) = -kt^{-k-1} f(t\mathbf{x}) + t^{-k} \sum_{i=1}^{n} x_i f_i'(t\mathbf{x}) \qquad (*)$$

Because $t\mathbf{x}$ lies in D, (2) must also be valid when each x_i is replaced by tx_i. Therefore, we get $\sum_{i=1}^{n} (tx_i) f_i'(t\mathbf{x}) = kf(t\mathbf{x})$. Applying this to the last term of $(*)$ implies that, for all $t > 0$, $g'(t) = -kt^{-k-1} f(t\mathbf{x}) + t^{-k-1} kf(t\mathbf{x}) = 0$. It follows that $g(t)$ must be a constant C. Obviously, $g(1) = 0$, so $C = 0$, implying that $g(t) \equiv 0$. According to the definition of g, this proves that $f(t\mathbf{x}) = t^k f(\mathbf{x})$. Thus, f is indeed homogeneous of degree k. ∎

An interesting version of the Euler equation (2) is obtained by dividing each term of the equation by $f(\mathbf{x})$, provided this number is not 0. Recalling the definition of the partial elasticity (El$_i\, f(\mathbf{x}) = (x_i/f(\mathbf{x})) f_i'(\mathbf{x})$), we have

$$\text{El}_1\, f(\mathbf{x}) + \text{El}_2\, f(\mathbf{x}) + \cdots + \text{El}_n\, f(\mathbf{x}) = k \qquad (3)$$

Thus, the sum of the partial elasticities of a function of n variables that is homogeneous of degree k must be equal to k.

The results in (3) to (5) in the previous section can also be generalized to functions of n variables. The proofs are similar, so they can be safely left to the reader. We simply state the general versions of (3) and (5):

If $f(\mathbf{x})$ is homogeneous of degree k, then:

$$f_i'(\mathbf{x}) \text{ is homogeneous of degree } k-1, \qquad i = 1, 2, \ldots, n \qquad (4)$$

$$\sum_{i=1}^{n} \sum_{j=1}^{n} x_i x_j f_{ij}''(\mathbf{x}) = k(k-1) f(\mathbf{x}) \qquad (5)$$

Economic Applications

Let us consider some typical examples of homogeneous functions in economics.

EXAMPLE 2   Let $f(\mathbf{v}) = f(v_1, \ldots, v_n)$ denote the output of a production process when the input quantities are $v_1, \ldots, v_n$. It is often assumed that if all the input quantities are scaled by a factor t, then t times as much output as before is produced, so that

$$f(t\mathbf{v}) = t f(\mathbf{v}) \qquad \text{for all} \quad t > 0 \qquad (*)$$

This implies that f is homogeneous of degree 1. Production functions with this property are said to exhibit *constant returns to scale*.

For any fixed input vector $\mathbf{v}$, consider the function $\varphi(t) = f(t\mathbf{v})/t$. This indicates the average returns to scale—i.e. the average output per unit input when all inputs are rescaled together. For example when $t = 2$, all inputs are doubled. When $t = \frac{3}{4}$, all inputs are reduced proportionally by $\frac{1}{4}$.

Now, when $(*)$ holds, then $\varphi(t) = f(\mathbf{v})$, independent of t. Also, a production function that is homogeneous of degree $k < 1$ has *decreasing returns to scale* because $\varphi(t) = t^{k-1} f(\mathbf{v})$ and so $\varphi'(t) < 0$. On the other hand, a production function has *increasing returns to scale* if $k > 1$ because then $\varphi'(t) > 0$.

EXAMPLE 3   The general Cobb–Douglas function $F(v_1, \ldots, v_n) = A v_1^{a_1} \cdots v_n^{a_n}$ is often used as an example of a production function. Prove that it is homogeneous, and examine when it has constant/decreasing/increasing returns to scale. Also show that formula (3) is confirmed.

Solution: Here

$$F(t\mathbf{v}) = A(tv_1)^{a_1} \ldots (tv_n)^{a_n} = A t^{a_1} v_1^{a_1} \ldots t^{a_n} v_n^{a_n} = t^{a_1 + \cdots + a_n} F(\mathbf{v})$$

So F is homogeneous of degree $a_1 + \cdots + a_n$. Thus it has constant, decreasing, or increasing returns to scale according as $a_1 + \cdots + a_n$ is $= 1$, < 1, or > 1.

Because $\text{El}_i\, F = a_i$, $i = 1, \ldots, n$, we get $\sum_{i=1}^{n} \text{El}_i\, F = \sum_{i=1}^{n} a_i$, which confirms (3) in this case.

EXAMPLE 4   Consider a market with three commodities with quantities denoted by x, y, and z, whose prices per unit are respectively p, q, and r. Suppose that the demand for one of the commodities by a consumer with income m is given by $x(p, q, r, m)$. Suppose that the three prices and income m are all multiplied by some $t > 0$. (Imagine, for example, that the prices of all commodities rise by 10%. Or that all prices and incomes have been converted into euros from, say, German marks.) Then the consumer's budget constraint $px + qy + rz \leq m$ becomes $tpx + tqy + trz \leq tm$, which is exactly the same constraint. The multiplicative constant t is irrelevant to the consumer. It is therefore natural to assume that the consumer's demand remains unchanged, with

$$x(tp, tq, tr, tm) = x(p, q, r, m)$$

Requiring this equation to be valid for all $t > 0$ means that the demand function x is homogeneous of degree 0. In this case, it is often said that demand is not influenced by "money illusion"; a consumer with 10% more money to spend realizes that nothing has really changed if all prices have also risen by 10%.

A concrete example of such a function that has been used in demand analysis is

$$x(p, q, r, m) = \frac{mp^b}{p^{b+1} + q^{b+1} + r^{b+1}} \qquad (b \text{ is a constant})$$

Here

$$x(tp, tq, tr, tm) = \frac{(tm)(tp)^b}{(tp)^{b+1} + (tq)^{b+1} + (tr)^{b+1}} = \frac{t^{1+b}}{t^{b+1}} x(p, q, r, m)$$

$$= x(p, q, r, m)$$

so that the function *is* homogeneous of degree 0. ∎

Sometimes we encounter nonhomogeneous functions of several variables that are, however, homogeneous when regarded as functions of some of the variables only, with the other variables fixed. For instance, the (minimum) cost of producing y units of a single output is often expressed as a function $C(\mathbf{w}, y)$ of y and the vector $\mathbf{w} = (w_1, \ldots, w_n)$ of prices of n different input factors. Then, if all input prices double, it is reasonable to expect cost to double. So economists usually assume that $C(t\mathbf{w}, y) = tC(\mathbf{w}, y)$ for all $t > 0$—i.e. that the cost function is homogeneous of degree 1 in $\mathbf{w}$ (for each fixed y). See Problem 6 for a prominent example.

Homothetic Functions

Let f be a function of n variables $\mathbf{x} = (x_1, \ldots, x_n)$ defined in a cone K. Then f is called **homothetic** provided that

$$\mathbf{x}, \mathbf{y} \in K, \quad f(\mathbf{x}) = f(\mathbf{y}), \quad t > 0 \quad \implies \quad f(t\mathbf{x}) = f(t\mathbf{y}) \tag{6}$$

For instance, if f is some consumer's utility function, (6) requires that whenever there is indifference between the two commodity bundles $\mathbf{x}$ and $\mathbf{y}$, then there is also indifference after they have both been magnified or shrunk by the same proportion. (If this consumer is indifferent between 2 litres of soda and 3 litres of juice, she is also indifferent between 4 litres of soda and 6 litres of juice.)

A homogeneous function f of any degree k is homothetic. In fact, it is easy to prove a more general result. Define the function $F(\mathbf{x})$ by

$$F(\mathbf{x}) = H(f(\mathbf{x})), \qquad \text{where} \qquad \begin{cases} H \text{ is strictly increasing and} \\ f \text{ is homogeneous of degree } k \end{cases} \qquad (7)$$

We claim that $F(\mathbf{x})$ is homothetic. To prove this, suppose that $F(\mathbf{x}) = F(\mathbf{y})$, or equivalently, that $H(f(\mathbf{x})) = H(f(\mathbf{y}))$. Because H is strictly increasing, this implies that $f(\mathbf{x}) = f(\mathbf{y})$. Because f is homogeneous of degree k, it follows that if $t > 0$, then

$$F(t\mathbf{x}) = H(f(t\mathbf{x})) = H(t^k f(\mathbf{x})) = H(t^k f(\mathbf{y})) = H(f(t\mathbf{y})) = F(t\mathbf{y})$$

This proves that $F(\mathbf{x})$ is homothetic. Hence, any strictly increasing function of a homogeneous function is homothetic. It is actually quite common to take (7) as the definition of a homothetic function, usually with $k = 1$.[2]

The next example shows that not all homothetic functions are homogeneous.

EXAMPLE 5   Show that the function $F(x, y) = xy + 1$, which is obviously not homogeneous, is nevertheless homothetic.

Solution: Define $H(u) = u + 1$. Then H is strictly increasing. The function $f(x, y) = xy$ is homogeneous of degree 2, and $F(x, y) = xy + 1 = H(f(x, y))$. According to (7), F is homothetic. (You can also use definition (6) to show that F is homothetic directly.) ∎

Suppose that $F(\mathbf{x}) = F(x_1, x_2, \ldots, x_n)$ is a differentiable production function, defined for all $(x_1, \ldots, x_n)$ satisfying $x_i \geq 0$, $i = 1, \ldots, n$. The **marginal rate of substitution** of factor j for factor i is defined by

$$h_{ji}(\mathbf{x}) = \frac{\partial F(\mathbf{x})}{\partial x_i} \bigg/ \frac{\partial F(\mathbf{x})}{\partial x_j}, \qquad i, j = 1, 2, \ldots, n \qquad (8)$$

We claim that if F is a strictly increasing transformation of a homogeneous function (as in (7)), these marginal rates of substitution are homogeneous of degree 0. To prove this, note that if $F(\mathbf{x}) = H(f(\mathbf{x}))$, where H is strictly increasing and $f(\mathbf{x})$ is homogeneous of degree k, then $\partial F(\mathbf{x})/\partial x_i = H'(f(\mathbf{x}))(\partial f(\mathbf{x})/\partial x_i)$. Hence

$$\frac{\partial F(\mathbf{x})}{\partial x_i} \bigg/ \frac{\partial F(\mathbf{x})}{\partial x_j} = \frac{\partial f(\mathbf{x})}{\partial x_i} \bigg/ \frac{\partial f(\mathbf{x})}{\partial x_j}, \qquad i, j = 1, 2, \ldots, n$$

---

[2] One can prove the following. Suppose that $F(\mathbf{x})$ is any continuous homothetic function defined on the cone K of vectors $\mathbf{x}$ satisfying $x_i \geq 0$, $i = 1, \ldots, n$. Suppose too that $F(t\mathbf{x}_0)$ is a strictly increasing function of t for each fixed $\mathbf{x}_0$ in K. Then F can be written in the form (7), with $f(\mathbf{x})$ homogeneous of degree 1.

because the factor H' can be cancelled. But f is homogeneous of degree k, so we can use (4) to show that, for all $t > 0$,

$$h_{ji}(t\mathbf{x}) = \frac{\partial f(t\mathbf{x})}{\partial x_i} \Big/ \frac{\partial f(t\mathbf{x})}{\partial x_j} = t^{k-1}\frac{\partial f(\mathbf{x})}{\partial x_i} \Big/ t^{k-1}\frac{\partial f(\mathbf{x})}{\partial x_j} = h_{ji}(\mathbf{x}), \ i, j = 1, 2, \ldots, n \quad (9)$$

Formula (9) shows precisely that the marginal rates of substitution are homogeneous of degree 0. This generalizes the result mentioned at the end of Section 12.6.

PROBLEMS FOR SECTION 12.7

1. Examine which of the following functions are homogeneous, and find, if possible, the degree of homogeneity:

   (a) $f(x, y) = 3x + 4y$

   (b) $g(x, y) = 3x + 4y - 2$

   (c) $h(x, y, z) = \dfrac{\sqrt{x} + \sqrt{y} + \sqrt{z}}{x + y + z}$

   (d) $G(x, y) = \sqrt{xy} \, \ln\dfrac{x^2 + y^2}{xy}$

   (e) $H(x, y) = \ln x + \ln y$

   (f) $p(\mathbf{x}) = \displaystyle\sum_{i=1}^{n} x_i^n$

2. Examine the homogeneity of the following functions:

   (a) $F(x_1, x_2, x_3) = \dfrac{(x_1 x_2 x_3)^2}{x_1^4 + x_2^4 + x_3^4}\left(\dfrac{1}{x_1} + \dfrac{1}{x_2} + \dfrac{1}{x_3}\right)$

   (b) $G(x_1, x_2, x_3) = \left(ax_1^d + bx_2^d + cx_3^d\right)^g$

3. Examine the homogeneity of $\bar{x}_A$, $\bar{x}_G$, and $\bar{x}_H$, as defined in Example 11.5.2.

4. D. W. Katzner has considered a utility function $u(\mathbf{x}) = u(x_1, \ldots, x_n)$ with continuous partial derivatives that for some constant a satisfy

$$\sum_{i=1}^{n} x_i \frac{\partial u}{\partial x_i} = a \qquad (\text{for all } x_1 > 0, \ldots, x_n > 0)$$

   Show that the function $v(\mathbf{x}) = u(\mathbf{x}) - a \ln(x_1 + \cdots + x_n)$ is homogeneous of degree 0. (*Hint*: Use Theorem 12.7.1.)

HARDER PROBLEMS

5. Suppose that $f(\mathbf{x})$ and $g(\mathbf{x})$ are homogeneous of degree r and s, respectively. Examine whether the following functions $h(\mathbf{x})$ are homogeneous. Determine the degree of homogeneity in each case.

   (a) $h(\mathbf{x}) = f(x_1^m, x_2^m, \ldots, x_n^m)$

   (b) $h(\mathbf{x}) = (g(\mathbf{x}))^p$

   (c) $h = f + g$

   (d) $h = fg$

   (e) $h = f/g$

6. The **translog cost function** $C(\mathbf{w}, y)$, where $\mathbf{w}$ is the vector of factor prices and y is the level of output, is defined implicitly by

$$\ln C(\mathbf{w}, y) = a_0 + c_1 \ln y + \sum_{i=1}^{n} a_i \ln w_i + \frac{1}{2} \sum_{i,j=1}^{n} a_{ij} \ln w_i \ln w_j + \ln y \sum_{i=1}^{n} b_i \ln w_i$$

Prove that this translog (short for "transcendental logarithmic") function is homogeneous of degree 1 in $\mathbf{w}$, for each fixed y, provided that all the following conditions are met: $\sum_{i=1}^{n} a_i = 1$; $\sum_{i=1}^{n} b_i = 0$; $\sum_{j=1}^{n} a_{ij} = 0$ for all i; and $\sum_{i=1}^{n} a_{ij} = 0$ for all j.

12.8 Linear Approximations

Section 7.4 discussed the linear approximation $f(x) \approx f(a) + f'(a)(x-a)$ for a function of one variable. We will find a similar approximation for functions $z = f(x, y)$ of two variables.

For fixed values of x_0, y_0, x, and y, define the function $g(t)$ by

$$g(t) = f(x_0 + t(x - x_0), y_0 + t(y - y_0))$$

We see that $g(0) = f(x_0, y_0)$ and $g(1) = f(x, y)$. Generally, $g(t)$ is the value of f at the point $(x_0 + t(x - x_0), y_0 + t(y - y_0)) = ((1-t)x_0 + tx, (1-t)y_0 + ty)$, which lies on the line joining (x_0, y_0) to (x, y). According to the chain rule,

$$g'(t) = f_1'(x_0 + t(x - x_0), y_0 + t(y - y_0))(x - x_0) + f_2'(x_0 + t(x - x_0), y_0 + t(y - y_0))(y - y_0)$$

Replacing t by 0 and making use of the approximation $g(1) \approx g(0) + g'(0)$, we obtain:

LINEAR APPROXIMATION

The linear approximation to $f(x, y)$ about (x_0, y_0) is

$$f(x, y) \approx f(x_0, y_0) + f_1'(x_0, y_0)(x - x_0) + f_2'(x_0, y_0)(y - y_0)$$

(1)

NOTE 1 The approximation in (1) is usually better the closer (x, y) is to (x_0, y_0). The usefulness of the approximation is still limited unless something is known about the error that results. Taylor's formula for n variables (discussed in FMEA) remedies this deficiency.

EXAMPLE 1   Find the linear approximation to $f(x, y) = e^{x+y}(xy - 1)$ about $(0, 0)$.

Solution: Here $f(0,0) = -1$ and

$$f_1'(x, y) = e^{x+y}(xy - 1) + e^{x+y}y, \qquad f_2'(x, y) = e^{x+y}(xy - 1) + e^{x+y}x$$

So $f_1'(0,0) = -1$ and $f_2'(0,0) = -1$. Hence, (1) gives

$$e^{x+y}(xy - 1) \approx -1 - x - y$$

For x and y close to 0, the complicated function $z = e^{x+y}(xy - 1)$ is approximated by the simple linear function $z = -1 - x - y$. ▮

Formula (1) can be used to find approximate numerical values of a function near any point where the function and its derivatives are easily evaluated. Consider the following simple example.

EXAMPLE 2   Let $f(x, y) = xy^3 - 2x^3$. Then $f(2, 3) = 38$. Using (1), find an approximate numerical value for $f(2.01, 2.98)$.

Solution: Here $f_1'(x, y) = y^3 - 6x^2$ and $f_2'(x, y) = 3xy^2$, so $f_1'(2, 3) = 3$ and $f_2'(2, 3) = 54$. Putting $x_0 = 2$, $y_0 = 3$, $x = 2 + 0.01$, and $y = 3 - 0.02$, we obtain

$$f(2.01, 2.98) \approx f(2, 3) + f_1'(2, 3) \cdot 0.01 + f_2'(2, 3) \cdot (-0.02)$$

$$= 38 + 3(0.01) + 54(-0.02) = 36.95$$

The exact value is $f(2.01, 2.98) = 36.95061792$. The error committed by the approximation is therefore roughly -0.0006. ▮

The linear approximation in (1) can be generalized to functions of several variables. (See Problem 8.)

LINEAR APPROXIMATION

The linear approximation to $z = f(\mathbf{x}) = f(x_1, \ldots, x_n)$ about $\mathbf{x}^0 = (x_1^0, \ldots, x_n^0)$ is

$$f(\mathbf{x}) \approx f(\mathbf{x}^0) + f_1'(\mathbf{x}^0)(x_1 - x_1^0) + \cdots + f_n'(\mathbf{x}^0)(x_n - x_n^0)$$

(2)

Tangent Planes

In (1) the function $f(x, y)$ is approximated by the *linear function,*

$$z = f(x_0, y_0) + f_1'(x_0, y_0)(x - x_0) + f_2'(x_0, y_0)(y - y_0)$$

The graph of this linear function is a plane which passes through the point $P = (x_0, y_0, z_0)$, with $z_0 = f(x_0, y_0)$, on the graph of $z = f(x, y)$. This plane is called the **tangent plane** to $z = f(x, y)$ at P:

TANGENT PLANE

The tangent plane to the graph of $z = f(x, y)$ at the point (x_0, y_0, z_0), with $z_0 = f(x_0, y_0)$, has the equation (3)

$$z - z_0 = f_1'(x_0, y_0)(x - x_0) + f_2'(x_0, y_0)(y - y_0)$$

The tangent plane is illustrated in Fig. 1.

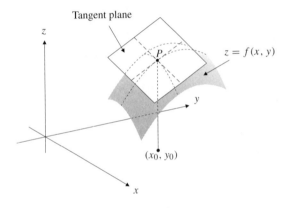

Figure 1 The graph of $z = f(x, y)$ and the tangent plane at P

Does the plane determined by (3) deserve to be called the tangent plane to $z = f(x, y)$ at the point $P = (x_0, y_0, f(x_0, y_0))$? Look back at Fig. 11.3.9, where l_x and l_y are the tangents at P to the two curves K_x and K_y that lie on the surface. Since the slope of the line l_x is $f_2'(x_0, y_0)$, the points (x, y, z) which lie on l_x are characterized by $x = x_0$ and $z - z_0 = f_2'(x_0, y_0)(y - y_0)$. But we see from (3) that these points also lie in the tangent plane. In the same way we see that the line l_y also lies in the tangent plane. Because the tangent lines l_x and l_y both lie in the plane which is the graph of (3), and because this plane is determined by these two lines, it makes good sense to use the term "tangent plane".

EXAMPLE 3   Find the tangent plane at $(x_0, y_0, z_0) = (1, 1, 5)$ to the graph of

$$f(x, y) = x^2 + 2xy + 2y^2$$

Solution: Because $f(1, 1) = 5$, the given point lies on the graph of f. We find that $f_1'(x, y) = 2x + 2y$ and $f_2'(x, y) = 2x + 4y$. Hence, $f_1'(1, 1) = 4$ and $f_2'(1, 1) = 6$. Thus, (3) yields

$$z - 5 = 4(x - 1) + 6(y - 1) \qquad \text{or} \qquad z = 4x + 6y - 5$$

1. Find the linear approximation about $(0, 0)$ for the following:

   (a) $f(x, y) = \sqrt{1 + x + y}$ (b) $f(x, y) = e^x \ln(1 + y)$

2. Find the linear approximation about (x_0, y_0) for $f(x, y) = Ax^a y^b$.

3. Suppose that $g^*(\mu, \varepsilon) = [(1 + \mu)(1 + \varepsilon)^\alpha]^{1/(1-\beta)} - 1$, with α and β as constants. Show that if μ and ε are close to 0, then

$$g^*(\mu, \varepsilon) \approx \frac{1}{1 - \beta} \mu + \frac{\alpha}{1 - \beta} \varepsilon$$

4. Let $f(x, y) = 3x^2 y + 2y^3$. Then $f(1, -1) = -5$. Use the approximation (1) to estimate the value of $f(0.98, -1.01)$. How large is the error caused by this approximation?

5. Let $f(x, y) = 3x^2 + xy - y^2$.

   (a) Compute $f(1.02, 1.99)$ exactly.

   (b) Let $f(1.02, 1.99) = f(1 + 0.02, 2 - 0.01)$ and use (1) to find an approximate numerical value for $f(1.02, 1.99)$. How large is the error?

6. Suppose you have been told that a function v of two variables satisfies $v(1, 0) = -1$, $v_1'(1, 0) = -4/3$, and $v_2'(1, 0) = 1/3$. Find an approximate value for $v(1.01, 0.02)$

7. Find the tangent planes to the following surfaces at the indicated points:

   (a) $z = x^2 + y^2$ at $(1, 2, 5)$ (b) $z = (y - x^2)(y - 2x^2)$ at $(1, 3, 2)$

HARDER PROBLEMS

8. Define
$$g(t) = f(x_1^0 + t (x_1 - x_1^0), \ldots, x_n^0 + t (x_n - x_n^0))$$
Use the approximation $g(1) \approx g(0) + g'(0)$ to derive (2).

9. Let $f(x, y)$ be any differentiable function. Prove that f is homogeneous of degree 1 iff the tangent plane to any point on its graph passes through the origin.

12.9 Differentials

Suppose that $z = f(x, y)$ is a differentiable function of two variables. Let dx and dy denote arbitrary real numbers (not necessarily small). Then we define the **differential** of $z = f(x, y)$ at (x, y), denoted by dz or df, so that

$$z = f(x, y) \implies dz = f_1'(x, y)\, dx + f_2'(x, y)\, dy \tag{1}$$

When x is changed to $x + dx$ and y is changed to $y + dy$, then the actual change in the value of the function is the **increment**

$$\Delta z = f(x + dx, y + dy) - f(x, y)$$

If dx and dy are small in absolute value, then Δz can be approximated by dz:

$$\Delta z \approx dz = f_1'(x, y)\, dx + f_2'(x, y)\, dy \qquad \text{(when } |dx| \text{ and } |dy| \text{ are small)} \tag{2}$$

The approximation in (2) follows from (1) in the previous section. We first replace $x - x_0$ by dx and $y - y_0$ by dy, and thus x by $x_0 + dx$ and y by $y_0 + dy$. Finally, in the formula which emerges, replace x_0 by x and y_0 by y. The approximation (2) can be given a geometric interpretation, as illustrated in Fig. 1. The error that arises from replacing Δz by dz results from "following the tangent plane" from P to the point S, rather than "following the graph" to the point R.

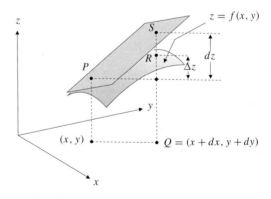

Figure 1 The geometric interpretation of Δz and the differential dz

Here is an analytical argument. Let

$$Z - f(x, y) = f_1'(x, y)(X - x) + f_2'(x, y)(Y - y)$$

be the equation for the set of points (X, Y, Z) belonging to the tangent plane at the point $P = (x, y, f(x, y))$. Letting $X = x + dx$ and $Y = y + dy$, we obtain

$$Z = f(x, y) + f_1'(x, y)\, dx + f_2'(x, y)\, dy = f(x, y) + dz$$

The length of the line segment QS in the figure is therefore $f(x, y) + dz$.

NOTE 1 In the literature on mathematics for economists, a common definition of the differential $dz = f_1'(x, y)\,dx + f_2'(x, y)\,dy$ requires that dx and dy be "infinitesimals," or "infinitely small". In this case, it is often claimed, Δz becomes equal to dz. Imprecise ideas of this sort have caused confusion over the centuries since Leibniz first introduced them, and they have largely been abandoned in mathematics. However, in nonstandard analysis, a respectable branch of modern mathematics, a modified version of Leibniz's ideas about infinitesimals can be made precise. There have even been some interesting applications of nonstandard analysis to theoretical economics.

EXAMPLE 1   Let $Y = F(K, L)$ be a production function with K and L as capital and labour inputs, respectively. Then F_K' and F_L' are the marginal products of capital and labour. If dK and dL are arbitrary increments in K and L, respectively, the *differential* of $Y = F(K, L)$ is

$$dY = F_K'\,dK + F_L'\,dL$$

The increment $\Delta Y = F(K + dK, L + dL) - F(K, L)$ in Y can be approximated by dY provided dK and dL are small in absolute value, and so

$$\Delta Y = F(K + dK, L + dL) - F(K, L) \approx F_K'\,dK + F_L'\,dL$$

NOTE 2 If $z = f(x, y)$, we can always find the differential $dz = df$ by first finding the partial derivatives $f_1'(x, y)$ and $f_2'(x, y)$, and then using the definition of dz. Conversely, once we know the differential of a function of two variables, then we have the partial derivatives: Suppose that $dz = A\,dx + B\,dy$ for all dx and dy. By definition, $dz = f_1'(x, y)\,dx + f_2'(x, y)\,dy$ for all dx and dy. Putting $dx = 1$ and $dy = 0$ yields $A = f_1'(x, y)$. In the same way, $dx = 0$ and $dy = 1$ implies $B = f_2'(x, y)$. So

$$dz = A\,dx + B\,dy \implies \frac{\partial z}{\partial x} = A \quad \text{and} \quad \frac{\partial z}{\partial y} = B \tag{3}$$

Rules for Differentials

Section 7.4 developed several rules for working with differentials of functions of one variable. The same rules apply to functions of several variables. Indeed, suppose that $f(x, y)$ and $g(x, y)$ are differentiable, with differentials $df = f_1'\,dx + f_2'\,dy$ and $dg = g_1'\,dx + g_2'\,dy$. If $d(\ )$ denotes the differential of whatever is inside the parentheses, then the following rules are exactly the same as (7.4.4):

$$d(af + bg) = a\,df + b\,dg$$

$$d(fg) = g\,df + f\,dg$$

$$d\left(\frac{f}{g}\right) = \frac{g\,df - f\,dg}{g^2}, \quad g \neq 0 \tag{4}$$

These rules are also quite easy to prove. For example, the formula for $d(fg)$ is proved as follows (keeping in mind that $(fg)(x, y) = f(x, y) \cdot g(x, y)$):

$$d(fg) = \frac{\partial}{\partial x}[f(x, y) \cdot g(x, y)] \, dx + \frac{\partial}{\partial y}[f(x, y) \cdot g(x, y)] \, dy$$

$$= (f'_x \cdot g + f \cdot g'_x) \, dx + (f'_y \cdot g + f \cdot g'_y) \, dy$$

$$= g(f'_x \, dx + f'_y \, dy) + f(g'_x \, dx + g'_y \, dy) = g \, df + f \, dg$$

There is also a chain rule for differentials. Suppose that $z = F(x, y) = g(f(x, y))$, where g is a differentiable function of one variable. Then

$$dz = F'_x \, dx + F'_y \, dy = g'(f(x, y)) f'_x \, dx + g'(f(x, y)) f'_y \, dy$$

$$= g'(f(x, y))(f'_x \, dx + f'_y \, dy) = g'(f(x, y)) \, df$$

because $F'_x = g' f'_x$, $F'_y = g' f'_y$, and $df = f'_x \, dx + f'_y \, dy$. Briefly formulated:

$$z = g(f(x, y)) \implies dz = g'(f(x, y)) \, df \tag{5}$$

EXAMPLE 2   Find an expression for dz in terms of dx and dy for the following:

(a) $z = Ax^a + By^b$ (b) $z = e^{xu}$ with $u = u(x, y)$ (c) $z = \ln(x^2 + y)$

Solution:

(a) $dz = A \, d(x^a) + B \, d(y^b) = Aax^{a-1} \, dx + Bby^{b-1} \, dy$

(b) $dz = e^{xu} \, d(xu) = e^{xu}(x \, du + u \, dx) = e^{xu}\{x[u'_1(x, y) \, dx + u'_2(x, y) \, dy] + u \, dx\}$

$$= e^{xu}\{[xu'_1(x, y) + u] \, dx + xu'_2(x, y) \, dy\}$$

(c) $dz = d \ln(x^2 + y) = \dfrac{d(x^2 + y)}{x^2 + y} = \dfrac{2x \, dx + dy}{x^2 + y}$

Invariance of the Differential

Suppose that
$$z = F(x, y), \qquad x = f(t, s), \qquad y = g(t, s)$$

where F, f, and g are all differentiable functions. Thus, z is a composite function of t and s together. Suppose that t and s are changed by dt and ds, respectively. The differential of z is then

$$dz = z'_t \, dt + z'_s \, ds$$

Using the expressions for z'_t and z'_s obtained from the chain rule (12.2.1), we find that

$$dz = [F'_1(x, y)x'_t + F'_2(x, y)y'_t] \, dt + [F'_1(x, y)x'_s + F'_2(x, y)y'_s] \, ds$$

$$= F'_1(x, y)(x'_t \, dt + x'_s \, ds) + F'_2(x, y)(y'_t \, dt + y'_s \, ds)$$

$$= F'_1(x, y) \, dx + F'_2(x, y) \, dy$$

where dx and dy denote the differentials of $x = f(t, s)$ and $y = g(t, s)$, respectively, as functions of t and s. Note that the final expression for dz is precisely the definition of the differential of $z = F(x, y)$ when x and y are changed by dx and dy, respectively. *Thus, the differential of z has the same form whether x and y are free variables, or whether they depend on other variables t and s.* This property is referred to as the **invariance** of the differential.

The Differential of a Function of n Variables

The differential of a function $z = f(x_1, x_2, \ldots, x_n)$ of n variables is defined in the obvious way as

$$dz = df = f_1' \, dx_1 + f_2' \, dx_2 + \cdots + f_n' \, dx_n \tag{6}$$

If the absolute values of $dx_1, \ldots, dx_n$ are all small, then again $\Delta z \approx dz$, where Δz is the actual increment of z when $(x_1, \ldots, x_n)$ is changed to $(x_1 + dx_1, \ldots, x_n + dx_n)$.

The rules for differentials in (4) are valid for functions of n variables, and there is also a general rule for invariance of the differential: *The differential of $z = F(x_1, \ldots, x_n)$ has the same form whether $x_1, \ldots, x_n$ are free variables, or depend on other basic variables.* The proofs are easy extensions of those for two variables.

1. Determine the differential of $z = xy^2 + x^3$ by:

   (a) computing $\partial z/\partial x$ and $\partial z/\partial y$ and then using the definition of dz.

   (b) using the rules in (4).

2. Calculate the differentials of the following:

   (a) $z = x^3 + y^3$ (b) $z = xe^{y^2}$ (c) $z = \ln(x^2 - y^2)$

3. Find dz expressed in terms of dx and dy when $u = u(x, y)$ and

   (a) $z = x^2 u$ (b) $z = u^2$ (c) $z = \ln(xy + yu)$

4. Find an approximate value for $T = [(2.01)^2 + (2.99)^2 + (6.02)^2]^{1/2}$ by using the approximation $\Delta T \approx dT$.

5. Find dU expressed in terms of dx and dy when $U = U(x, y)$ satisfies the equation

   $$Ue^U = x\sqrt{y}$$

6. (a) Differentiate the equation $X = AN^\beta e^{\varrho t}$, where A, β, and ϱ are constants.

   (b) Differentiate the equation $X_1 = BX^E N^{1-E}$, where B and E are constants.

7. Calculate the differentials of the following:

(a) $U = a_1 u_1^2 + \cdots + a_n u_n^2$

(b) $U = A(\delta_1 u_1^{-\varrho} + \cdots + \delta_n u_n^{-\varrho})^{-1/\varrho}$

where $a_1, \ldots, a_n, A, \delta_1, \ldots, \delta_n$, and ϱ are positive constants.

8. Find dz when $z = A x_1^{a_1} x_2^{a_2} \ldots x_n^{a_n}$, where $x_1 > 0, x_2 > 0, \ldots, x_n > 0$, and $A, a_1, a_2, \ldots, a_n$ are all constants with A positive. (*Hint:* First, take the natural logarithm of each side.)

HARDER PROBLEMS

9. The differential dz defined in (1) is called the *differential of first order*. If f has continuous partial derivatives of second order, we define the *differential of second order* as the differential of $dz = f_1'(x, y)dx + f_2'(x, y)dy$. This implies that

$$d^2 z = d(dz) = f_{11}''(x, y)\, (dx)^2 + 2 f_{12}''(x, y)\, dx\, dy + f_{22}''(x, y)\, (dy)^2$$

(a) Calculate $d^2 z$ for $z = xy + y^2$.

(b) Suppose that $x = t$ and $y = t^2$. Express dz and $d^2 z$ in terms of dt, for the function in part (a). Also find $d^2 z/dt^2$, then show that $d^2 z \neq (d^2 z/dt^2)(dt)^2$. (This example shows that there is no rule of invariance for the second-order differential.)

12.10 Systems of Equations

Many economic models relate a large number of variables to each other through a system of simultaneous equations. To keep track of the structure of the model, the concept of *degrees of freedom* is very useful.

Let $x_1, x_2, \ldots, x_n$ be n variables. If no restrictions are placed on them then, by definition, there are n *degrees of freedom*, because all n variables can be freely chosen. If the variables are required to satisfy *one* equation of the form $f_1(x_1, x_2, \ldots, x_n) = 0$, then the number of degrees of freedom is usually reduced by 1. Whenever one further "independent" restriction is introduced, the number of degrees of freedom is again reduced by 1. In general, introducing $m < n$ independent restrictions on the variables $x_1, x_2, \ldots, x_n$ means that they satisfy a system of m independent equations having the form

$$f_1(x_1, x_2, \ldots, x_n) = 0$$
$$f_2(x_1, x_2, \ldots, x_n) = 0$$
$$\cdots\cdots\cdots\cdots\cdots\cdots$$
$$f_m(x_1, x_2, \ldots, x_n) = 0$$

(1)

Then, provided that $m < n$, the remaining number of degrees of freedom is $n - m$. The rule that emerges from these considerations is rather vague, especially as it is hard to explain precisely what it means for equations to be "independent." Nevertheless, the following rule is much used in economics and statistics:

THE COUNTING RULE

To find the number of degrees of freedom for a system of equations, count the number of variables, n, and the number of "independent" equations, m. In general, if $n > m$, there are $n - m$ degrees of freedom in the system. If $n < m$, there is no solution to the system.

(2)

This rule of counting variables and equations is used to justify the following economic proposition: "The number of independent targets the government can pursue cannot possibly exceed the number of available policy instruments." For example, if a national government seeks simultaneous low inflation, low unemployment, and stability of its currency's exchange rate against, say, the US dollar, then it needs at least three independent policy instruments.

It should be noted that the counting rule is not generally valid. For example, if 100 variables $x_1, \ldots, x_{100}$ are restricted to satisfy one equation, the rule says that the number of degrees of freedom should be 99. However, if the equation happens to be

$$x_1^2 + x_2^2 + \cdots + x_{100}^2 = 0$$

then there is only one solution, $x_1 = x_2 = \ldots = x_{100} = 0$, and so there are no degrees of freedom at all. And if $x_1^2 + x_2^2 + \cdots + x_{100}^2 = -1$, even this one solution is lost.

It is obvious that the word "independent" cannot be dropped from the statement of the counting rule. For instance, if we just repeat an equation that has appeared before, the number of degrees of freedom will certainly not be reduced.

The concept of degrees of freedom introduced earlier needs to be generalized.

DEGREES OF FREEDOM FOR A SYSTEM OF EQUATIONS

A system of equations in n variables is said to have k **degrees of freedom** if there is a set of k variables that can be freely chosen, while the remaining $n - k$ variables are uniquely determined once the k free variables have been assigned specific values.

(3)

In order for a system to have k degrees of freedom, it suffices that *there exist* k of the variables that can be freely chosen. We do not require that *any* set of k variables can be chosen freely. If the n variables are restricted to vary within a subset A of $\mathbb{R}^n$, we say that the system has k *degrees of freedom in* A.

The counting rule claims that if the number of equations is larger than the number of variables, then the system is, in general, **inconsistent**—that is, it has no solutions. For example, the system

$$f(x, y) = 0, \qquad g(x, y) = 0, \qquad h(x, y) = 0$$

with two variables and three equations, is usually inconsistent. Each of the equations represents a curve in the plane, and any pair of curves will usually have at least one point in common. But if we add a third equation, the corresponding curve will seldom pass through any points where the first two curves intersect, so the system is usually inconsistent.

So far, we have discussed the two cases $m < n$ and $m > n$. What about the case $m = n$, in which the number of equations is equal to the number of unknowns? Even in the simplest case of one equation in one variable, $f(x) = 0$, such an equation might have any number of solutions. Consider, for instance, the following three different single equations in one variable:

$$x^2 + 1 = 0, \qquad x - 1 = 0, \qquad (x - 1)(x - 2)(x - 3)(x - 4)(x - 5) = 0$$

These have 0, 1, and 5 solutions, respectively. Those of you who know something about trigonometric functions will realize that the simple equation $\sin x = 0$ has infinitely many solutions, namely $x = n\pi$ for any integer n.

In general, a system with as many equations as unknowns is usually **consistent** (that is, has solutions), but it may have several solutions. Economists, however, ideally like their models to have a system of equations that produce a unique, economically meaningful solution, because then the model purports to predict the values of particular economic variables. Based on the earlier discussion, we can at least formulate the following rough rule: *A system of equations does not, in general, have a unique solution unless there are exactly as many equations as unknowns.*

EXAMPLE 1   Consider the macroeconomic model described by the system of equations

(i) $Y = C + I + G$ (ii) $C = f(Y - T)$ (iii) $I = h(r)$ (iv) $r = m(M)$

where f, h, and m are given functions, Y is national income, C is consumption, I is investment, G is public expenditure, T is tax revenue, r is the interest rate, and M is the money supply (or more exactly, the quantity of money in circulation). How many degrees of freedom are there?

Solution: The number of variables is 7 and the number of equations is 4, so according to the counting rule there should be $7 - 4 = 3$ degrees of freedom. Usually macroeconomists regard M, T, and G as the exogenous (free) variables. Then the system will in general determine the endogenous variables Y, C, I, and r as functions of M, T, and G. (For a further analysis of this model, see Example 12.11.3. For a discussion of exogenous and endogenous variables, see Section 12.11.)

EXAMPLE 2   Consider the alternative macroeconomic model

$$\text{(i) } Y = C + I + G \qquad \text{(ii) } C = f(Y - T) \qquad \text{(iii) } G = \overline{G}$$

whose variables have the same interpretations as in the previous example. Here the level of public expenditure is a constant, $\overline{G}$. Determine the number of degrees of freedom in the model.

Solution: There are now 5 variables (Y, C, I, G, and T) and 3 equations. Hence, there are 2 degrees of freedom. For suitable functions f, two of the variables can be freely chosen, while allowing the remaining variables to be determined once the values of these 2 are fixed. It is natural to consider I and T as the two free variables. Note that G cannot be chosen as a free variable in this case because G is completely fixed by equation (iii). ▮

PROBLEMS FOR SECTION 12.10

1. Use the counting rule to find the number of degrees of freedom for the following systems of equations:

(a) $\begin{aligned} xu^3 + v &= y^2 \\ 3uv - x &= 4 \end{aligned}$

(b) $\begin{aligned} x_2^2 - x_3^3 + 2y_1 - y_2^3 &= 1 \\ x_1^3 - x_2 + y_1^5 - y_2 &= 0 \end{aligned}$

(c) $\begin{aligned} f(y + z + w) &= x^3 \\ x^2 + y^2 + z^2 &= w^2 \\ g(x, y) - z^3 &= w^3 \end{aligned}$

(In (c) assume that f and g are specified functions.)

2. Use the counting rule to find the number of degrees of freedom in the following macroeconomic model (which is studied further in Problem 12.11.7):

$$\text{(i) } Y = C + I + G \qquad \text{(ii) } C = F(Y, T, r) \qquad \text{(iii) } I = f(Y, r)$$

(The symbols have the same interpretation as in Example 1. We assume that F and f are specified functions of their respective arguments.)

3. In the text above, many of the statements concerning degrees of freedom were modified by the phrase "in general" or "usually". Explain how each of the following systems illustrates the need for this qualifier when we drop the assumption of independence:

(a) $\begin{aligned} 3x - y &= 2 \\ 6x - 2y &= 4 \\ 9x - 3y &= 6 \end{aligned}$

(b) $\begin{aligned} x - 2y &= 3 \\ x - 2y &= 4 \end{aligned}$

(c) $\begin{aligned} x - 2y &= 3 \\ 2x - 4y &= 6 \end{aligned}$

(d) $x_1^2 + x_2^2 + \cdots + x_{100}^2 = 1$ (e) $x_1^2 + x_2^2 + \cdots + x_{100}^2 = -1$

12.11 Differentiating Systems of Equations

This section shows how using differentials can be an efficient way to find the partial derivatives of functions defined implicitly by a system of equations. We begin with three examples.

EXAMPLE 1   Consider the following system of 2 linear equations in 4 variables

$$5u + 5v = 2x - 3y$$

$$2u + 4v = 3x - 2y$$

It has 2 degrees of freedom. In fact, it defines u and v as functions of x and y. Differentiate the system and then find the differentials du and dv expressed in terms of dx and dy. Derive the partial derivatives of u and v w.r.t. x and y. Check the results by solving the system explicitly for u and v.

Solution: For both equations, take the differential of each side and use the rules in Section 12.9. The result is

$$5du + 5dv = 2dx - 3dy$$

$$2du + 4dv = 3dx - 2dy$$

(Note that in a linear system like this, the differentials satisfy the same equations as the variables.) Solving for du and dv in terms of dx and dy yields

$$du = -\frac{7}{10}dx - \frac{1}{5}dy, \qquad dv = \frac{11}{10}dx - \frac{2}{5}dy$$

We read off the following partial derivatives: $u'_x = -\frac{7}{10}, u'_y = -\frac{1}{5}, v'_x = \frac{11}{10}$, and $v'_y = -\frac{2}{5}$.
If we solve the given system for u and v, we obtain $u = -\frac{7}{10}x - \frac{1}{5}y$ and $v = \frac{11}{10}x - \frac{2}{5}y$. From these expressions we easily confirm the values found for the partial derivatives.   ∎

EXAMPLE 2   Consider the system of non-linear equations

$$u^2 + v = xy$$

$$uv = -x^2 + y^2 \qquad (*)$$

(a) What has the counting rule to say about this system? Find the differentials of u and v expressed in terms of dx and dy.
(b) Find the partial derivatives of u and v w.r.t. x and y.
(c) The point $P = (x, y, u, v) = (1, 0, 1, -1)$ satisfies system $(*)$. If $x = 1$ is increased by 0.01 and $y = 0$ is increased by 0.02, what is the new value of u, approximately?
(d) Calculate u''_{12} at the point P.

Solution: (a) There are 4 variables and 2 equations, so there should be 2 degrees of freedom. Suppose we choose fixed values for x and y. Then there are two equations for determining the two remaining variables, u and v. For example, if $x = 1$ and $y = 0$, then (*) reduces to $u^2 = -v$ and $uv = -1$, from which we find that $u^3 = 1$, so $u = 1$ and $v = -1$. For other values of x and y, it is more difficult to find solutions for u and v. However, it seems reasonable to assume that system (*) defines $u = u(x, y)$ and $v = v(x, y)$ as differentiable functions of x and y, at least if the domain of the pair (x, y) is suitably restricted.

Because u and v are functions of x and y, so is $u^2 + v$, and it is equal to xy for all x and y. Hence the differentials of $u^2 + v$ and of xy must be equal—i.e. $d(u^2 + v) = d(xy)$. In the same way, $d(uv) = d(-x^2 + y^2)$. Using the rules for differentials, we obtain

$$2u\,du + dv = y\,dx + x\,dy$$
$$v\,du + u\,dv = -2x\,dx + 2y\,dy$$

Note that by the invariance property of the differential in Section 12.9, this system is valid whichever pair of variables are independent.

We want to solve the system for du and dv. There are two equations in the two unknowns du and dv of the form

$$A\,du + B\,dv = C$$
$$D\,du + E\,dv = F$$

where, for instance, $A = 2u$, $C = y\,dx + x\,dy$, and so on. Using (2) in Section 2.4, or standard elimination, provided that $v \neq 2u^2$, we find that

$$du = \frac{2x + yu}{2u^2 - v}\,dx + \frac{xu - 2y}{2u^2 - v}\,dy, \qquad dv = \frac{-4xu - yv}{2u^2 - v}\,dx + \frac{4uy - xv}{2u^2 - v}\,dy$$

(b) From the first of these two equations, we obtain immediately that

$$u_1' = \frac{2x + yu}{2u^2 - v}, \qquad u_2' = \frac{xu - 2y}{2u^2 - v}$$

Similarly, the partial derivatives of v w.r.t. x and y are the coefficients of dx and dy in the expression for dv. So we have found all the first-order partial derivatives.

(c) We use the approximation

$$u(x + dx, y + dy) \approx u(x, y) + du$$

Letting $x = 1$, $y = 0$, $dx = 0.01$, and $dy = 0.02$, we obtain

$$u(1 + 0.01, 0 + 0.02) \approx u(1, 0) + u_1'(1, 0) \cdot 0.01 + u_2'(1, 0) \cdot 0.02$$
$$= 1 + \tfrac{2}{3} \cdot 0.01 + \tfrac{1}{3} \cdot 0.02 \approx 1 + 0.0133 = 1.0133$$

Note that in this case, it is not easy to find the exact value of $u(1.01, 0.02)$.

(d) We find u_{12}'' by using the chain rule as follows:

$$u_{12}'' = \frac{\partial}{\partial y}(u_1') = \frac{\partial}{\partial y}\left(\frac{2x + yu}{2u^2 - v}\right) = \frac{(yu_2' + u)(2u^2 - v) - (2x + yu)(4uu_2' - v_2')}{(2u^2 - v)^2}$$

At the point P where $(x, y, u, v) = (1, 0, 1, -1)$, we obtain $u_{12}'' = 1/9$.

EXAMPLE 3   Consider the following macroeconomic model:

$$\text{(i) } Y = C + I + G \qquad \text{(ii) } C = f(Y - T) \qquad \text{(iii) } I = h(r) \qquad \text{(iv) } r = m(M)$$

Here Y is national income, C consumption, I investment, G public expenditure, T tax revenue, r interest rate, and M money supply. (See Example 12.10.1.) If we assume that f, h, and m are differentiable functions with $0 < f' < 1$, $h' < 0$, and $m' < 0$, then these equations will determine Y, C, I, and r as differentiable functions of M, T, and G. Differentiate the system and express the differentials of Y, C, I, and r in terms of the differentials of M, T, and G. Find $\partial Y / \partial T$ and $\partial C / \partial T$, and comment on their signs.

Suppose $P_0 = (M_0, T_0, G_0, Y_0, C_0, I_0, r_0)$ is an initial equilibrium point for the system. If the money supply M, tax revenue T, and public expenditure G are all slightly changed as a result of government policy or central bank intervention, find the approximate changes in national income Y and in consumption C.

Solution: Differentiating the system yields

$$
\begin{aligned}
dY &= dC + dI + dG \\
dC &= f'(Y - T)(dY - dT) \\
dI &= h'(r) \, dr \\
dr &= m'(M) \, dM
\end{aligned}
\tag{v}
$$

We wish to solve this linear system for the differential changes dY, dC, dI, and dr in the (endogenous) variables Y, C, I, and r, expressing these differentials in terms of the differentials of the (exogenous) policy variables dM, dT, and dG.

From the last two equations in (v), we can find dI and dr immediately. In fact

$$dr = m'(M) \, dM, \qquad dI = h'(r)m'(M) \, dM \tag{vi}$$

Inserting the expression for dI from (vi) into the first equation in (v), while also rearranging the second equation in (v), we obtain the system

$$
\begin{aligned}
dY - dC &= h'(r)m'(M) \, dM + dG \\
f'(Y - T)dY - dC &= f'(Y - T) \, dT
\end{aligned}
$$

These are two equations to determine the two unknowns dY and dC. Solving for dY and dC, using a simplified notation, we have

$$
\begin{aligned}
dY &= \frac{h'm'}{1 - f'} \, dM - \frac{f'}{1 - f'} \, dT + \frac{1}{1 - f'} \, dG \\[2mm]
dC &= \frac{f'h'm'}{1 - f'} \, dM - \frac{f'}{1 - f'} \, dT + \frac{f'}{1 - f'} \, dG
\end{aligned}
\tag{vii}
$$

We have now expressed the differentials dY, dC, dI, and dr as linear functions of the differentials dM, dT, and dG. Moreover, the solution is valid because $f' < 1$ by assumption.

From (vii) and (vi), we can at once find the partial derivatives of Y, C, I, and r w.r.t. M, T, and G. For example, $\partial Y/\partial T = \partial C/\partial T = -f'/(1-f')$ and $\partial r/\partial T = 0$. Note that because $0 < f' < 1$, we have $\partial Y/\partial T = \partial C/\partial T = -f'/(1-f') < 0$. Thus, a small increase in the tax level (keeping M and G constant) decreases national income in this model, but not if the extra tax revenue is all spent by the government. For if $dT = dG = dx$ (and $dM = 0$), then $dY = dx$ and $dC = dI = dr = 0$.

If dM, dT, and dG are small in absolute value, then

$$\Delta Y = Y(M_0 + dM, T_0 + dT, G_0 + dG) - Y(M_0, T_0, G_0) \approx dY$$

When computing dY, the partial derivatives are evaluated at the equilibrium point P_0.   ∎

The General Case

When economists deal with systems of equations, notably in comparative static analysis, the variables are usually divided a priori into two types: **endogenous** variables, which the model is intended to determine, and **exogenous** variables, which are supposed to be determined by "forces" such as government policy, consumers' tastes, or technical progress, which are assumed to lie outside the economic model. This classification depends on the model in question. Public expenditure, for example, is often treated as exogenous in public finance theory, which seeks to understand how tax changes affect the economy. But it is often endogenous in a "political economy" model which tries to explain how political variables like public expenditure emerge from the political system.

Economic models often give rise to a general system of **structural equations** having the form

$$f_1(x_1, x_2, \ldots, x_n, y_1, y_2, \ldots, y_m) = 0$$
$$f_2(x_1, x_2, \ldots, x_n, y_1, y_2, \ldots, y_m) = 0$$
$$\cdots\cdots\cdots\cdots\cdots\cdots\cdots\cdots\cdots\cdots\cdots\cdots\cdots$$
$$f_m(x_1, x_2, \ldots, x_n, y_1, y_2, \ldots, y_m) = 0 \tag{1}$$

Here it is assumed that $x_1, \ldots, x_n$ are the exogenous variables, whereas $y_1, \ldots, y_m$ are the endogenous variables. An "initial equilibrium" or "status quo" solution $(\mathbf{x}^0, \mathbf{y}^0) = (x_1^0, \ldots, x_n^0, y_1^0, \ldots, y_m^0)$ is frequently known, or else assumed to exist. This equilibrium might, for instance, represent a state in which there is equality between current supply and demand for each good.

Note that if the counting rule applies, then system (1) with m equations in $n+m$ unknowns has $n + m - m = n$ degrees of freedom. Suppose it defines all the endogenous variables $y_1, \ldots, y_m$ as C^1 functions of $x_1, \ldots, x_n$ in a neighbourhood of $(\mathbf{x}^0, \mathbf{y}^0)$. Then the system can be solved "in principle" for $y_1, \ldots, y_m$ in terms of $x_1, \ldots, x_n$ to give

$$y_1 = \varphi_1(x_1, \ldots, x_n), \ldots, y_m = \varphi_m(x_1, \ldots, x_n) \tag{2}$$

In this case, (2) is said to be the **reduced form** of the structural equation system (1). The endogenous variables have all been expressed as functions of the exogenous variables. The form of the functions $\varphi_1, \varphi_2, \ldots, \varphi_m$ is not necessarily known.

The previous examples showed how we can often find an explicit expression for the partial derivative of any endogenous variable w.r.t. any exogenous variable. The same type of argument can be used in the general case, but a detailed discussion is left for FMEA.

1. Differentiate the system

$$au + bv = cx + dy$$
$$eu + fv = gx + hy$$

with a, b, c, d, e, f, g, and h as constants, $af \neq be$, and find the partial derivatives of u and v w.r.t. x and y.

2. Consider the system of equations:

$$xu^3 + v = y^2 \tag{$*$}$$
$$3uv - x = 4$$

(a) Differentiate the system. Solve for du and dv in terms of dx and dy.

(b) Find u'_x and v'_x by using the results in part (a).

(c) The point $(x, y, u, v) = (0, 1, 4/3, 1)$ satisfies $(*)$. Find u'_x and v'_x at this point.

3. Suppose y_1 and y_2 are implicitly defined as differentiable functions of x_1 and x_2 by

$$f_1(x_1, x_2, y_1, y_2) = 3x_1 + x_2^2 - y_1 - 3y_2^3 = 0$$
$$f_2(x_1, x_2, y_1, y_2) = x_1^3 - 2x_2 + 2y_1^3 - y_2 = 0$$

Find $\partial y_1/\partial x_1$ and $\partial y_2/\partial x_1$.

4. A version of the "IS–LM" macroeconomic model originally devised by J. R. Hicks leads to the system of equations

$$\text{(i) } I(r) = S(Y) \qquad \text{(ii) } aY + L(r) = M$$

Here a is a positive parameter, while I, S, and L are given, continuously differentiable functions.[3] Suppose that the system defines Y and r implicitly as differentiable functions of a and M. Find expressions for $\partial Y/\partial M$ and $\partial r/\partial M$.

5. Find u''_{xx} when u and v are defined as functions of x and y by the equations $xy + uv = 1$ and $xu + yv = 0$.

---

[3] The first "IS equation" involves the investment function I and savings function S. The second "LM equation" involves the liquidity preference function L (the demand for money) and the money supply M. The variable Y denotes national income and r denotes the interest rate.

6. Consider the macroeconomic model

$$\text{(i) } Y = C + I + G \qquad \text{(ii) } C = F(Y, T, r) \qquad \text{(iii) } I = f(Y, r)$$

where F and f are continuously differentiable functions, with $F_Y' > 0$, $F_T' < 0$, $F_r' < 0$, $f_Y' > 0$, $f_r' < 0$, and $F_Y' + f_Y' < 1$.

(a) Differentiate the system, and express dY in terms of dT, dG, and dr.

(b) What happens to Y if T increases? Or if T and G undergo equal increases?

7. (a) Determine the number of degrees of freedom in the macroeconomic model

$$\text{(i) } Y = C(Y, r) + I + \alpha \qquad \text{(ii) } I = F(Y, r) + \beta \qquad \text{(iii) } M = L(Y, r)$$

where Y is national income, r is the interest rate, I is total investments, α is public consumption, β is public investment, and M is the money supply. Here C, F, and L are given differentiable functions.

(b) Differentiate the system. Put $d\beta = dM = 0$ and find dY, dr, and dI expressed in terms of $d\alpha$.

8. A standard macroeconomic model consists of the system of equations

$$\text{(i) } M = lPy + L(r) \qquad \text{(ii) } S(y, r, g) = I(y, r)$$

Here M, l, and P are positive constants, whereas L, S, and I are differentiable functions.

(a) By using the counting rule, explain why it is reasonable to assume that system, in general, defines y and r as differentiable functions of g.

(b) Differentiate the system and find expressions for dy/dg and dr/dg.

9. Consider the system

$$u^2 v - u = x^3 + 2y^3$$
$$e^{ux} = vy$$

(a) The system defines u and v as differentiable functions of x and y around the point $P = (x, y, u, v) = (0, 1, 2, 1)$. Find the differentials of u and v expressed in terms of the differentials of x and y. Find $\partial u/\partial y$ and $\partial v/\partial x$ at P.

(b) If x increases by 0.1 and y decreases by 0.2 from their values at P, what are the approximate changes in u and v?

HARDER PROBLEMS

10. With two goods, consumer demand theory involves the equation system

$$\text{(i) } U_1'(x_1, x_2) = \lambda p_1 \quad \text{(ii) } U_2'(x_1, x_2) = \lambda p_2 \quad \text{(iii) } p_1 x_1 + p_2 x_2 = m$$

where $U(x_1, x_2)$ is a given utility function. Suppose that the system defines x_1, x_2, and λ as differentiable functions of p_1, p_2, and m. Find an expression for $\partial x_1/\partial p_1$.

1. In the following cases, find dz/dt by using the chain rule:

   (a) $z = F(x, y) = 6x + y^3$, $x = 2t^2$, $y = 3t^3$.

   (b) $z = F(x, y) = x^p + y^p$, $x = at$, $y = bt$

   (c) Check the answers by first substituting the expressions for x and y and then differentiating.

2. Let $z = G(u, v)$, $u = \varphi(t, s)$, and $v = \psi(s)$. Find expressions for $\partial z/\partial t$ and $\partial z/\partial s$.

3. Find expressions for $\partial w/\partial t$ and $\partial w/\partial s$ when

$$w = x^2 + y^3 + z^4,   x = t + s, \ y = t - s, \ z = st$$

4. Suppose production X depends on the number of workers N according to the formula $X = Ng(\varphi(N)/N)$, where g and φ are given differentiable functions. Find expressions for dX/dN and d^2X/dN^2.

5. Suppose that a representative household's demand for a commodity is a function $E(p, m) = Ap^{-a}m^b$ of the price p and income m (where A, a, and b are positive constants).

   (a) Suppose that p and m are both differentiable functions of time t. Then demand E is a function only of t. Find an expression for $\dot{E}/E$ in terms of $\dot{p}/p$ and $\dot{m}/m$.

   (b) Put $p = p_0(1.06)^t$, $m = m_0(1.08)^t$, where p_0 is the price and m_0 is the income at time $t = 0$. Show that in this case $\dot{E}/E = \ln Q$, where $Q = (1.08)^b/(1.06)^a$.

6. The equation

$$x^3 \ln x + y^3 \ln y = 2z^3 \ln z$$

defines z as a differentiable function of x and y in a neighbourhood of the point $(x, y, z) = (e, e, e)$. Calculate $z'_1(e, e)$ and $z''_{11}(e, e)$.

7. What is the elasticity of substitution between y and x when $F(x, y) = x^2 - 10y^2$?

8. Find the marginal rate of substitution (MRS) between y and x when:

   (a) $U(x, y) = 2x^{0.4}y^{0.6}$ (b) $U(x, y) = xy + y$ (c) $U(x, y) = 10(x^{-2} + y^{-2})^{-4}$

9. If homogeneous, find the degree of homogeneity of the functions:

   (a) $f(x, y) = 3x^3y^{-4} + 2xy^{-2}$ (b) $Y(K, L) = (K^a + L^a)^{2c}e^{K^2/L^2}$

   (c) $f(x_1, x_2) = 5x_1^4 + 6x_1x_2^3$ (d) $F(x_1, x_2, x_3) = e^{x_1+x_2+x_3}$

10. What is the elasticity of substitution between y and x for the function in Problem 8(c)?

11. Find the elasticity of y w.r.t. x when $y^2e^{x+1/y} = 3$.

12. If homogeneous, find the degree of homogeneity of the functions:

(a) $f(x, y) = xg(y/x)$, where g is an arbitrary function of one variable.

(b) $F(x, y, z) = z^k f(x/z, y/z)$, where f is an arbitrary function of two variables.

(c) $G(K, L, M, N) = K^{a-b} \cdot L^{b-c} \cdot M^{c-d} \cdot N^{d-a}$ (a, b, c, and d are constants)

13. Suppose the production function $F(K, L)$ is homogeneous of degree 1. If $F''_{KK} < 0$, so that the marginal productivity of capital is a strictly decreasing function of K, prove that $F''_{KL} > 0$, so that the marginal productivity of capital is strictly increasing as labour input increases. This is called *Wicksell's law*. (*Hint:* Use (∗) in Section 12.6.)

14. Show that no generalization of the concept of a homogeneous function emerges if one replaces t^k in definition (1) in Section 12.7 by an arbitrary function $g(t)$. (*Hint:* Differentiate the new (1) w.r.t. t, and let $t = 1$. Then use Euler's theorem.)

15. The following system of equations defines $u = u(x, y)$ and $v = v(x, y)$ as differentiable functions of x and y around the point $P = (x, y, u, v) = (1, 1, -1, 0)$:

$$u + xe^y + v = e - 1$$
$$x + e^{u+v^2} - y = e^{-1}$$

Differentiate the system and find the values of u'_x, u'_y, v'_x, and v'_y at that point.

16. (a) An equilibrium model of labour demand and output pricing leads to the following system of equations:

$$pF'(L) - w = 0$$
$$pF(L) - wL - B = 0 \qquad (*)$$

Here F is twice differentiable with $F'(L) > 0$ and $F''(L) < 0$. All the variables are positive. Regard w and B as exogenous, so that p and L are endogenous variables which are functions of w and B. Find expressions for $\partial p/\partial w$, $\partial p/\partial B$, $\partial L/\partial w$, and $\partial L/\partial B$ by implicit differentiation.

(b) What can be said about the signs of these partial derivatives? Show, in particular, that $\partial L/\partial w < 0$.

17. (a) The following system of equations defines $u = u(x, y)$ and $v = v(x, y)$ as differentiable functions of x and y around the point $P = (x, y, u, v) = (1, 1, 1, 2)$:

$$u^\alpha + v^\beta = 2^\beta x + y^3$$
$$u^\alpha v^\beta - v^\beta = x - y$$

where α and β are positive constants. Differentiate the system. Then find $\partial u/\partial x$, $\partial u/\partial y$, $\partial v/\partial x$, and $\partial v/\partial y$ at the point P.

(b) For the function $u(x, y)$ in (a), find an approximation to $u(0.99, 1.01)$.

13 MULTIVARIABLE OPTIMIZATION

At first sight it is curious that a subject as pure and passionless as mathematics can have anything useful to say about that messy, ill-structured, chancy world in which we live. —Fortunately we find that whenever we comprehend what was previously mysterious, there is at the centre of everything order, pattern and common sense.
—B. H. P. Rivett (1978)

Chapter 8 was concerned with optimization problems involving functions of one variable. Most interesting economic optimization problems require the simultaneous choice of several variables, however. For example, a profit-maximizing producer of a single commodity chooses quantities of many different inputs, as well as its output level. A consumer chooses what quantities of the many different goods to buy.

In fact, most of the difficulties already arise in the transition from one to two variables. Also, textbooks in economics often illustrate economic problems by using functions of only two variables, for which one can at least draw level curves in the plane. We therefore begin this chapter by studying the two-variable case. The first section presents the basic results, illustrated by relatively simple examples and problems. Then we give a more systematic presentation of the theory with two variables. Subsequently we consider how the theory can be generalized to functions of several variables.

Much of economic analysis involves seeing how the solution to an optimization problem responds when the situation changes—for example, if some relevant parameters change. Thus, the theory of the firm considers the effect of a change in the price of one input or output good on the optimal input and output quantities, as well as on the optimal profit. Some simple results of this kind are briefly introduced at the end of the chapter.

13.1 Two Variables: Necessary Conditions

Consider a function $z = f(x, y)$ defined on a set S in the xy-plane. Suppose that f attains its largest value (its maximum) at an interior point (x_0, y_0) of S, as indicated in Fig. 1. If we keep y fixed at y_0, then the function $g(x) = f(x, y_0)$ depends only on x and has its maximum at $x = x_0$. (Geometrically, if P is the highest point on the surface in Fig. 1, then P is certainly also the highest point on the curve through P that has $y = y_0$—i.e. on the curve which is the intersection of the surface with the plane $y = y_0$.) From Theorem 8.1.1 we know that $g'(x_0) = 0$. But for all x, the derivative $g'(x)$ is exactly the same as the partial derivative $f_1'(x, y_0)$. At $x = x_0$, therefore, one has $f_1'(x_0, y_0) = 0$. In the same way, we see that (x_0, y_0) must satisfy $f_2'(x_0, y_0) = 0$, because the function $h(y) = f(x_0, y)$ has its maximum at $y = y_0$. A point (x_0, y_0) where both the partial derivatives are 0 is called a **stationary point** of f.

If f attains its smallest value (its minimum) at an interior point (x_0, y_0) of S, a similar argument shows that the point again must be a stationary point. So we have the following important result:[1]

THEOREM 13.1.1 (NECESSARY CONDITIONS FOR INTERIOR EXTREMA)

A differentiable function $z = f(x, y)$ can only have a maximum or minimum at an interior point (x_0, y_0) of S if it is a **stationary point**—that is, if the point $(x, y) = (x_0, y_0)$ satisfies the two equations

$$f_1'(x, y) = 0, \qquad f_2'(x, y) = 0 \qquad \text{(\textbf{first-order conditions}, or FOCs)}$$

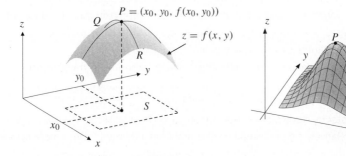

Figure 1 $f(x, y)$ has maximum at P, the highest point on the surface $z = f(x, y)$, where $f_1'(x_0, y_0) = f_2'(x_0, y_0) = 0$.

Figure 2 P is a maximum, Q is a local maximum, and R is a saddle point.

In Fig. 2, the three points P, Q, and R are all stationary points, but only P is a maximum. (Later, we shall call Q a *local maximum*, whereas R is a *saddle point*.)

In the following examples and problems only the first-order conditions are considered. The next section explains how to verify that we have found the optimum.

EXAMPLE 1   The function f is defined for all (x, y) by

$$f(x, y) = -2x^2 - 2xy - 2y^2 + 36x + 42y - 158$$

Assume that f has a maximum point. Find it.

---

[1] Interior point is defined precisely in Section 13.5.

Solution: Theorem 13.1.1 applies. So a maximum point (x, y) must be a stationary point satisfying the first-order conditions

$$f_1'(x, y) = -4x - 2y + 36 = 0$$
$$f_2'(x, y) = -2x - 4y + 42 = 0$$

These are two linear equations which determine x and y. We find that $(x, y) = (5, 8)$ is the only pair of numbers which satisfies both equations. Assuming there is a maximum point, these must be its coordinates. The maximum value is $f(5, 8) = 100$. (In Example 13.2.2 we prove that $(5, 8)$ *is* a maximum point.) ∎

EXAMPLE 2   A firm produces two different kinds A and B of a commodity. The daily cost of producing x units of A and y units of B is

$$C(x, y) = 0.04x^2 + 0.01xy + 0.01y^2 + 4x + 2y + 500$$

Suppose that the firm sells all its output at a price per unit of 15 for A and 9 for B. Find the daily production levels x and y that maximize profit per day.

Solution: Profit per day is $\pi(x, y) = 15x + 9y - C(x, y)$, so

$$\pi(x, y) = 15x + 9y - 0.04x^2 - 0.01xy - 0.01y^2 - 4x - 2y - 500$$
$$= -0.04x^2 - 0.01xy - 0.01y^2 + 11x + 7y - 500$$

If $x > 0$ and $y > 0$ maximize profit, then (x, y) must satisfy

$$\frac{\partial \pi}{\partial x} = -0.08x - 0.01y + 11 = 0, \qquad \frac{\partial \pi}{\partial y} = -0.01x - 0.02y + 7 = 0$$

These two linear equations in x and y have the unique solution $x = 100$, $y = 300$, with $\pi(100, 300) = 1100$. (We have not proved that this actually is a maximum. See Problem 13.2.1(a).) ∎

EXAMPLE 3   (**Profit maximization**)   Suppose that $Q = F(K, L)$ is a production function with K as the capital input and L as the labour input. The price per unit of output is p, the cost (or rental) per unit of capital is r, and the wage rate is w. The constants p, r, and w are all positive. The profit π from producing and selling $F(K, L)$ units is then given by the function

$$\pi(K, L) = pF(K, L) - rK - wL \tag{1}$$

If F is differentiable and π has a maximum with $K > 0$, $L > 0$, then the first-order conditions (FOCs) are

$$\pi_K'(K, L) = pF_K'(K, L) - r = 0$$
$$\pi_L'(K, L) = pF_L'(K, L) - w = 0 \tag{*}$$

Thus, a necessary condition for profit to be a maximum when $K = K^*$ and $L = L^*$ is that

$$p F_K'(K^*, L^*) = r, \qquad p F_L'(K^*, L^*) = w \qquad (**)$$

The first equation says that r, the price of capital, must equal the sales value at the price p per unit of the marginal product of capital. The second equation has a similar interpretation.

Suppose we think of increasing capital input from the level K^* by 1 unit. How much would be gained? We would increase production by approximately $F_K'(K^*, L^*)$ units. Because each of these units is priced at p, the gain in revenue is approximately $p F_K'(K^*, L^*)$. How much is lost by increasing capital input by one unit? We lose r, because this is the price for one unit of capital. These two must be equal. The second equation in $(**)$ has a similar interpretation: Increasing labour input by one unit from level L^* will lead to the approximate gain $p F_L'(K^*, L^*)$ in revenue, whereas the extra labour cost is w. The profit-maximizing pair (K^*, L^*) thus has the property that the extra revenue from increasing each input by one unit is just offset by the extra cost.

Economists often formulate the first-order conditions in the alternative form $F_K'(K, L) = r/p$, $F_L'(K, L) = w/p$. So, to obtain maximum profit, the firm must choose K and L such that the marginal productivity of capital is equal to the relative price of capital (r/p), and the marginal productivity of labour is equal to the relative price of labour (w/p).

Note that the conditions in $(*)$ are necessary, but generally not sufficient for an interior maximum. Sufficient conditions for an optimum are given in Theorem 13.2.1. ∎

EXAMPLE 4   Find the only possible solution to the following special case of Example 3.

$$\max \pi(K, L) = 12 K^{1/2} L^{1/4} - 1.2K - 0.6L$$

Solution: The first-order conditions are

$$\pi_K'(K, L) = 6 K^{-1/2} L^{1/4} - 1.2 = 0, \qquad \pi_L'(K, L) = 3 K^{1/2} L^{-3/4} - 0.6 = 0$$

These equations imply that $K^{-1/2} L^{1/4} = K^{1/2} L^{-3/4} = 0.2 = 1/5$. Multiplying each side of the first equation here by $K^{1/2} L^{3/4}$ reduces it to $L = K$. Hence $K^{-1/4} = L^{-1/4} = 1/5$. It follows that $K = L = 5^4 = 625$ is the only possible solution. (See Example 13.2.3 for a proof that this is indeed a maximum point.) ∎

EXAMPLE 5   A firm is a monopolist in the domestic market but takes as given the price of its product in the world market. The quantities sold in the two markets are denoted by x_d and x_w, respectively. The price obtained in the domestic market, as a function of its sales, is $p_d = f(x_d)$. The fixed world market price is p_w. The cost function is $c(x_d + x_w)$. (Note that c is here a function of one variable, not a constant.)

(a) Find the profit function $\pi(x_d, x_w)$ and write down the first-order conditions for maximal profit at $x_d > 0$, $x_w > 0$. Give economic interpretations of these conditions.

(b) Suppose the firm in the domestic market is faced with a demand curve whose price elasticity is a constant equal to -2. What is the relationship between the prices in the domestic and world markets?

Solution: (a) The revenue from selling x_d units in the domestic market at price $p_d = f(x_d)$ is $p_d x_d = f(x_d)x_d$. In the world market the revenue is $p_w x_w$. The profit function is $\pi = \pi(x_d, x_w) = p_d x_d + p_w x_w - c(x_d + x_w)$. Thus the first-order conditions are

(i) $\pi_1' = p_d + (dp_d/dx_d)x_d - c'(x_d + x_w) = 0$,   (ii) $\pi_2' = p_w - c'(x_d + x_w) = 0$

According to (ii), the marginal cost in the world market must equal the price, which is the marginal revenue in this case. In the domestic market the marginal cost must also equal the marginal revenue. Here is an interpretation of (i): Suppose the firm contemplates producing and selling one extra unit in the domestic market. The extra revenue is the price of one unit (p_d) minus the loss that arises because selling this extra unit lowers the price of all units sold domestically. This loss is $[f(x_d + 1) - f(x_d)]x_d \approx f'(x_d)x_d = (dp_d/dx_d)x_d$. (Note that $f'(x_d)$ is presumably negative.) Since selling one extra unit has marginal cost $c'(x_d + x_w)$, (i) expresses the fact that the gain from selling an extra unit in the domestic market is just offset by the cost.

(b) If the price elasticity of demand is -2, then $\text{El}_{p_d} x_d = (p_d/x_d)(dx_d/dp_d) = -2$. Because the rule for differentiating inverse functions implies that $dp_d/dx_d = 1/(dx_d/dp_d)$, it follows that $(dp_d/dx_d)x_d = -\frac{1}{2}p_d$. Then (i) and (ii) imply that $\frac{1}{2}p_d = c'(x_d + x_w) = p_w$, so the world market price is half the domestic market price.

PROBLEMS FOR SECTION 13.1

1. The function f defined for all (x, y) by $f(x, y) = -2x^2 - y^2 + 4x + 4y - 3$ has a maximum. Find the corresponding values of x and y.

2. (a) The function f defined for all (x, y) by $f(x, y) = x^2 + y^2 - 6x + 8y + 35$ has a minimum point. Find it.

   (b) Show that $f(x, y)$ can be written in the form $f(x, y) = (x - 3)^2 + (y + 4)^2 + 10$. Explain why this shows that you have really found the minimum in part (a).

3. In the profit maximizing problem of Example 3, let $p = 1, r = 0.65, w = 1.2$, and

$$F(K, L) = 80 - (K - 3)^2 - 2(L - 6)^2 - (K - 3)(L - 6)$$

   Find the only possible values of K and L that maximize profits.

4. Yearly profits (in millions of dollars) for a firm are given by

$$P(x, y) = -x^2 - y^2 + 22x + 18y - 102$$

   where x is the amount spent on research (in millions of dollars), and y is the amount spent on advertising (in millions of dollars).

   (a) Find the profits when $x = 10, y = 8$ and when $x = 12, y = 10$.

   (b) Find the only possible values of x and y that can maximize profits, and the corresponding profit.

13.2 Two Variables: Sufficient Conditions

Suppose f is a function of one variable which is twice differentiable in an interval I. In this case a very simple sufficient condition for a stationary point in I to be a maximum point is that $f''(x) \leq 0$ for all x in I. The function f is then called "concave". (Theorem 8.2.2.)

For functions of two variables there is a corresponding test involving the second-order *partial* derivatives. The test ensures that the function is concave. Provided the function has an interior stationary point, this test implies that its graph is a surface shaped like the one in Fig. 13.1.1. Consider any curve parallel to the xz-plane which lies in the surface, like QPR in the figure. Any such curve is concave, implying that $f_{11}''(x, y) \leq 0$. Similarly, any curve parallel to the xy-plane which lies in the surface must also be concave, implying that $f_{22}''(x, y) \leq 0$. In general, however, these two requirements alone will *not* ensure that the surface is shaped like the one in Fig. 13.1.1. This is clear from the next example.

EXAMPLE 1   The function

$$f(x, y) = 3xy - x^2 - y^2$$

has $f_{11}''(x, y) = f_{22}''(x, y) = -2$. Each curve parallel to the xz-plane that lies in the surface defined by the graph has the equation $z = 3xy_0 - x^2 - y_0^2$ for some fixed y_0. It is therefore a concave parabola. So is each curve parallel to the yz-plane that lies in the surface. But along the line $y = x$ the function reduces to $f(x, x) = x^2$, which is a convex rather than a concave parabola. It follows that f has no maximum (or minimum) at $(0, 0)$, which is the only stationary point.

What Example 1 shows is that conditions ensuring that the graph of f looks like the one in Fig. 13.1.1 cannot ignore the second-order mixed partial derivatives. The following result will be discussed in FMEA. (See the end of Section 13.3 for a proof of the local version.) To formulate the theorem we need a new concept. A set S in the xy-plane is **convex** if, for each pair of points P and Q in S, all the line segment between P and Q lies in S.

THEOREM 13.2.1 (SUFFICIENT CONDITIONS FOR A MAXIMUM AND MINIMUM)

Suppose that (x_0, y_0) is a stationary point for a C^2-function $f(x, y)$ in a convex set S.

(a) If for all (x, y) in S,

$$f_{11}''(x, y) \leq 0, \quad f_{22}''(x, y) \leq 0, \quad \text{and} \quad f_{11}''(x, y)f_{22}''(x, y) - \left(f_{12}''(x, y)\right)^2 \geq 0$$

then (x_0, y_0) is a maximum point for $f(x, y)$ in S.

(b) If for all (x, y) in S,

$$f_{11}''(x, y) \geq 0, \quad f_{22}''(x, y) \geq 0, \quad \text{and} \quad f_{11}''(x, y)f_{22}''(x, y) - \left(f_{12}''(x, y)\right)^2 \geq 0$$

then (x_0, y_0) is a minimum point for $f(x, y)$ in S.

NOTE 1 The conditions in part (a) of Theorem 13.2.1 are sufficient for a stationary point to be a maximum point. They are far from being necessary. This is clear from the function whose graph is shown in Fig. 13.1.2, which *has* a maximum at P, but where the conditions in (a) are certainly not satisfied in the whole of S.

NOTE 2 If a twice differentiable function $z = f(x, y)$ satisfies the inequalities in (a) throughout a convex set S, it is called **concave**, whereas it is called **convex** if it satisfies the inequalities in (b) throughout S. It follows from these definitions that f is concave if and only if $-f$ is convex, just as in the one-variable case.

There are more general definitions of concave and convex functions which apply to functions that are not necessarily twice differentiable. These are presented in FMEA. (The one-variable case was briefly discussed in Section 8.7.)

EXAMPLE 2   Show that
$$f(x, y) = -2x^2 - 2xy - 2y^2 + 36x + 42y - 158$$
has a maximum at the stationary point $(x_0, y_0) = (5, 8)$. (See Example 13.1.1.)

Solution: We found that $f_1'(x, y) = -4x - 2y + 36$ and $f_2'(x, y) = -2x - 4y + 42$. Furthermore, $f_{11}'' = -4$, $f_{12}'' = -2$, and $f_{22}'' = -4$. Thus

$$f_{11}''(x, y) \leq 0, \quad f_{22}''(x, y) \leq 0, \quad f_{11}''(x, y)f_{22}''(x, y) - \left(f_{12}''(x, y)\right)^2 = 16 - 4 = 12 \geq 0$$

According to (a) in Theorem 13.2.1, these inequalities guarantee that the stationary point $(5, 8)$ is a maximum point.

EXAMPLE 3   Show that we have found the maximum in Example 12.1.4.

Solution: If $K > 0$ and $L > 0$, we find that

$$\pi_{KK}'' = -3K^{-3/2}L^{1/4}, \qquad \pi_{KL}'' = \tfrac{3}{2}K^{-1/2}L^{-3/4}, \quad \text{and} \quad \pi_{LL}'' = -\tfrac{9}{4}K^{1/2}L^{-7/4}$$

Clearly, $\pi_{KK}'' < 0$, $\pi_{LL}'' < 0$, and moreover,

$$\pi_{KK}''\pi_{LL}'' - (\pi_{KL}'')^2 = \tfrac{27}{4}K^{-1}L^{-3/2} - \tfrac{9}{4}K^{-1}L^{-3/2} = \tfrac{9}{2}K^{-1}L^{-3/2} > 0$$

It follows that the stationary point $(K, L) = (625, 625)$ maximizes profit.

This section concludes with two examples that each involve a constraint. Nevertheless, a simple transformation can be used to convert the problem into the form we have been discussing, without any constraint.

EXAMPLE 4   Suppose that any production by the firm in Example 13.1.2 creates pollution, so it is legally restricted to produce a total of 320 units of the two kinds of output. The firm's problem is then:

$$\text{max } -0.04x^2 - 0.01xy - 0.01y^2 + 11x + 7y - 500 \quad \text{subject to} \quad x + y = 320$$

What now are the optimal quantities of the two kinds of output?

Solution: The firm still wants to maximize its profits. But because of the restriction $y = 320 - x$, the new profit function is

$$\hat{\pi}(x) = -0.04x^2 - 0.01x(320 - x) - 0.01(320 - x)^2 + 11x + 7(320 - x) - 500$$

We easily find $\hat{\pi}'(x) = -0.08x + 7.2$, so $\hat{\pi}'(x) = 0$ for $x = 7.2/0.08 = 90$. Since $\hat{\pi}''(x) = -0.08 < 0$ for all x, the point $x = 90$ does maximize $\hat{\pi}$. The corresponding value of y is $y = 320 - 90 = 230$. The maximum profit is 1040.   ∎

EXAMPLE 5   A firm has three factories each producing the same item. Let x, y, and z denote the respective output quantities that the three factories produce in order to fulfill an order for 2000 units in total. Hence, $x + y + z = 2000$. The cost functions for the three factories are

$$C_1(x) = 200 + \frac{1}{100}x^2, \qquad C_2(y) = 200 + y + \frac{1}{300}y^3, \qquad C_3(z) = 200 + 10z$$

The total cost of fulfilling the order is thus

$$C(x, y, z) = C_1(x) + C_2(y) + C_3(z)$$

Find the values of x, y, and z that minimize C. (*Hint:* Reduce the problem to one with only two variables by solving $x + y + z = 2000$ for z.)

Solution: Solving the equation $x + y + z = 2000$ for z yields $z = 2000 - x - y$. Substituting this expression for z in the expression for C yields, after simplifying,

$$\hat{C}(x, y) = C(x, y, 2000 - x - y) = \frac{1}{100}x^2 - 10x + \frac{1}{300}y^3 - 9y + 20\,600$$

Any stationary points of $\hat{C}$ must satisfy the two equations

$$\hat{C}_1'(x, y) = \frac{1}{50}x - 10 = 0, \qquad \hat{C}_2'(x, y) = \frac{1}{100}y^2 - 9 = 0$$

The only solution is $x = 500$ and $y = 30$, implying that $z = 1470$. The corresponding value of C is 17 920.

The second-order partial derivatives are $\hat{C}_{11}''(x, y) = \frac{1}{50}$, $\hat{C}_{12}''(x, y) = 0$, and $\hat{C}_{22}''(x, y) = \frac{1}{50}y$. It follows that for all $x \geq 0$, $y \geq 0$, one has

$$\hat{C}_{11}''(x, y) \geq 0, \ \hat{C}_{22}''(x, y) \geq 0, \quad \text{and} \quad \hat{C}_{11}''(x, y)\hat{C}_{22}''(x, y) - \left(\hat{C}_{12}''(x, y)\right)^2 = \frac{y}{2500} \geq 0$$

Part (b) of Theorem 13.2.1 implies that $(500, 30)$ is a minimum point of $\hat{C}$ within the convex domain of points (x, y) satisfying $x \geq 0$, $y \geq 0$. It follows that $(500, 30, 1470)$ is a minimum point of C within the domain of (x, y, z) satisfying $x \geq 0$, $y \geq 0$, $z \geq 0$, and $x + y + z = 2000$.   ∎

1. (a) Prove that the optimum has been found in Example 13.1.2.

   (b) Prove that the optimum has been found in Problem 13.1.1.

   (c) Prove that the optimum has been found in Problem 13.1.3.

2. (a) A firm produces two different kinds A and B of a commodity. The daily cost of producing x units of A and y units of B is

$$C(x, y) = 2x^2 - 4xy + 4y^2 - 40x - 20y + 514$$

   Suppose that the firm sells all its output at a price per unit of \$24 for A and \$12 for B. Find the daily production levels x and y that maximize profit.

   (b) The firm is required to produce exactly 54 units per day of the two kinds combined. What now is the optimal production plan?

3. If x, y, and z are positive numbers such that $x + 3y + 4z = 108$, find the only possible maximum value of the product $P = xyz$. (*Hint:* Make P a function of y and z by eliminating the variable x.) Economic interpretation: xyz is the "utility" a person derives from consuming x, y, and z units, respectively, of three commodities. The prices per unit of the three commodities are 1, 3, and 4; income is 108.

4. The demands for a monopolist's two products is determined by the equations

$$p = 25 - x, \qquad q = 24 - 2y$$

   where p and q are prices per unit of the two goods, and x and y are the corresponding quantities. Suppose that the costs of producing and selling x units of the first good and y units of the other are
$$C(x, y) = 3x^2 + 3xy + y^2$$

   (a) Find the monopolist's profit $\pi(x, y)$ from producing and selling x units of the first good and y units of the other.

   (b) Find the values of x and y that maximize $\pi(x, y)$. Verify that you have found the maximum profit.

5. A firm produces two goods. The cost of producing x units of good 1 and y units of good 2 is
$$C(x, y) = x^2 + xy + y^2 + x + y + 14$$

   Suppose that the firm sells all its output of each good at prices per unit of p and q respectively. Find the values of x and y that maximize profits.

6. The profit function of a firm is $\pi(x, y) = px + qy - \alpha x^2 - \beta y^2$, where p and q are the prices per unit and $\alpha x^2 + \beta y^2$ are the costs of producing and selling x units of the first good and y units of the other. The constants are all positive.

   (a) Find the values of x and y that maximize profits. Denote them by x^* and y^*. Verify that the second-order conditions are satisfied.

   (b) Define $\pi^*(p, q) = \pi(x^*, y^*)$. Verify that

   $$\partial \pi^*(p, q)/\partial p = x^*, \qquad \partial \pi^*(p, q)/\partial q = y^*$$

   Give these results economic interpretations.

7. Find the smallest value of $x^2 + y^2 + z^2$ when we require that $4x + 2y - z = 5$. (Geometrically, the problem is to find the point in the plane $4x + 2y - z = 5$ which is closest to the origin.)

8. Show that the Cobb–Douglas function $f(x, y) = Ax^a y^b$ (where A, a, b are positive constants) is concave for $x \geq 0$, $y \geq 0$ provided that $a + b \leq 1$. (See Note 2.)

13.3 Local Extreme Points

Sometimes one needs to consider *local* extreme points of a function. The point (x_0, y_0) is said to be a **local maximum point** of f in S if $f(x, y) \leq f(x_0, y_0)$ for all pairs (x, y) in S that lie sufficiently close to (x_0, y_0). More precisely, the definition is that there exists a positive number r such that $f(x, y) \leq f(x_0, y_0)$ for all (x, y) in S that lie inside the circle with centre (x_0, y_0) and radius r. If the inequality is strict for $(x, y) \neq (x_0, y_0)$, then (x_0, y_0) is a **strict** local maximum point.

A **(strict) local minimum** point is defined in the obvious way, and it should also be clear what we mean by *local maximum and minimum values, local extreme points*, and *local extreme values*. Note how these definitions imply that a global extreme point is also a local extreme point; the converse is not true, of course.

In searching for maximum and minimum points, the first-order conditions were very useful. The same result also applies to the local extreme points:

   At a local extreme point in the interior of the domain of a differentiable function, all first-order partial derivatives are 0.

This observation follows because in the argument for Theorem 13.1.1 it was sufficient to consider the behaviour of the function in a small neighbourhood of the optimal point.

These first-order conditions are necessary for a differentiable function to have a local extreme point. However, a stationary point does not have to be a local extreme point. A stationary point (x_0, y_0) of f which, like point R in Fig. 13.1.2, is neither a local maximum nor a local minimum point, is called a **saddle point** of f. Hence:

A saddle point (x_0, y_0) is a stationary point with the property that there exist points (x, y) arbitrarily close to (x_0, y_0) with $f(x, y) < f(x_0, y_0)$, and there also exist such points with $f(x, y) > f(x_0, y_0)$.

EXAMPLE 1   Show that $(0, 0)$ is a saddle point of $f(x, y) = x^2 - y^2$.

Solution: It is easy to check that $(0, 0)$ is a stationary point at which $f(0, 0) = 0$. Moreover, $f(x, 0) = x^2$, so $f(x, y)$ takes positive values arbitrarily close to the origin. In addition, $f(0, y) = -y^2$, so $f(x, y)$ also takes negative values arbitrarily close to the origin. Hence, $(0, 0)$ is a saddle point. The graph of the function is indicated in Fig. 1.   ∎

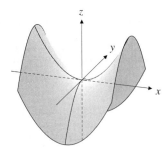

Figure 1 $f(x, y) = x^2 - y^2$. The point $(0, 0)$ is a saddle point

These concepts can be illustrated by thinking of the mountains in the Himalayas. Every summit is a local maximum, but only the highest (Mount Everest) is the (global) maximum. The deepest points of the lakes are local minima. The highest points of the mountain passes are saddle points. The stationary points of a function thus fall into three categories:

(a) Local maximum points   (b) Local minimum points   (c) Saddle points

To help decide whether a given stationary point is of type (a), (b), or (c), one can use the *second-derivative test* described below.

Consider a function $z = f(x, y)$ defined on a domain S. Let (x_0, y_0) be an interior point of S that is also a stationary point of f, so that $f_1'(x_0, y_0) = 0$ and $f_2'(x_0, y_0) = 0$. Then (x_0, y_0) is either a local maximum point, a local minimum point, or a saddle point. How do we distinguish between these three cases?

Consider first the case when $z = f(x, y)$ has a local maximum at (x_0, y_0). The functions $g(x) = f(x, y_0)$ and $h(y) = f(x_0, y)$ describe the behaviour of f along the straight lines $y = y_0$ and $x = x_0$, respectively (see Fig. 13.1.1). These functions must achieve local maxima at x_0 and y_0, respectively. Therefore, $g''(x_0) = f_{11}''(x_0, y_0) \leq 0$ and $h''(y_0) = f_{22}''(x_0, y_0) \leq 0$. On the other hand, if $g''(x_0) < 0$ and $h''(y_0) < 0$, then we know that g and h really do achieve local maxima at x_0 and y_0, respectively. Stated differently, the conditions $f_{11}''(x_0, y_0) < 0$ and $f_{22}''(x_0, y_0) < 0$ will ensure that $f(x, y)$ has a local maximum in the directions through (x_0, y_0) that are parallel to the x-axis and the y-axis.

However, note that the signs of $f_{11}''(x_0, y_0)$ and $f_{22}''(x_0, y_0)$ on their own do not reveal much about the behaviour of the graph of $z = f(x, y)$ when we move away from (x_0, y_0) in directions other than the two mentioned. Example 1 illustrated the problem.

It turns out that in order to have a correct second-derivative test for functions f of two variables, the mixed second-order partial $f_{12}''(x_0, y_0)$ must also be considered, just as it had to be in Section 13.2. The following theorem can be used to determine the nature of the stationary points in most cases. (A proof is given at the end of this section.)

THEOREM 13.3.1 (SECOND-DERIVATIVE TEST FOR LOCAL EXTREMA)

Suppose $f(x, y)$ is a function with continuous second order partial derivatives in a domain S, and let (x_0, y_0) be an interior point of S that is a stationary point for f. Write

$$A = f_{11}''(x_0, y_0), \qquad B = f_{12}''(x_0, y_0), \quad \text{and} \quad C = f_{22}''(x_0, y_0)$$

(i) If $A < 0$ and $AC - B^2 > 0$, then (x_0, y_0) is a (strict) local maximum point.

(ii) If $A > 0$ and $AC - B^2 > 0$, then (x_0, y_0) is a (strict) local minimum point.

(iii) If $AC - B^2 < 0$, then (x_0, y_0) is a saddle point.

(iv) If $AC - B^2 = 0$, then (x_0, y_0) could be a local maximum, a local minimum, or a saddle point.

Note that $AC - B^2 > 0$ in (i) implies that $AC > B^2 \geq 0$, and so $AC > 0$. Thus, if $A < 0$, then also $C < 0$. The condition $C = f_{22}''(x_0, y_0) < 0$ is thus (indirectly) included in the assumptions in (i). The corresponding observation for (ii) is also valid.

The conditions in (i), (ii), and (iii) are usually called (local) **second-order conditions**. Note that these are sufficient conditions for a stationary point to be, respectively, a *strict local* maximum point, a *strict local* minimum point, or a saddle point. None of these conditions is necessary. The result in Problem 6 will confirm (iv), because it shows that a stationary point where $AC - B^2 = 0$ can fall into any of the three categories. The second-derivative test is inconclusive in this case.

EXAMPLE 2 Find the stationary points and classify them when $f(x, y) = x^3 - x^2 - y^2 + 8$.

Solution: The stationary points must satisfy the two equations

$$f_1'(x, y) = 3x^2 - 2x = 0 \qquad \text{and} \qquad f_2'(x, y) = -2y = 0$$

Because $3x^2 - 2x = x(3x - 2)$, we see that the first equation has the solutions $x = 0$ and $x = 2/3$. The second equation has the solution $y = 0$. We conclude that $(0, 0)$ and $(2/3, 0)$ are the only stationary points.

Furthermore, $f_{11}''(x, y) = 6x - 2$, $f_{12}''(x, y) = 0$, and $f_{22}''(x, y) = -2$. A convenient way of classifying the stationary points is to make a table like the following (with A, B, and C defined in the theorem):

(x, y)	A	B	C	$AC - B^2$	Type of point
$(0, 0)$	-2	0	-2	4	Local maximum point
$(2/3, 0)$	2	0	-2	-4	Saddle point

EXAMPLE 3   Find the stationary points of $f(x, y)$ and classify them when

$$f(x, y) = \tfrac{1}{2}x^2 e^y - \tfrac{1}{3}x^3 - ye^{3y}$$

Solution: The stationary points must satisfy the two equations

$$f_1'(x, y) = xe^y - x^2 = x(e^y - x) = 0 \qquad \text{and} \qquad f_2'(x, y) = \tfrac{1}{2}x^2 e^y - e^{3y} - 3ye^{3y} = 0$$

The first equation is equivalent to $x = 0$ or $x = e^y$. When $x = 0$, the second equation reduces to $-e^{3y}(1 + 3y) = 0$, and so $y = -1/3$. When $x = e^y$, the second equation reduces to $\tfrac{1}{2}e^{2y}e^y - e^{3y} - 3ye^{3y} = 0$, so $e^{3y}(\tfrac{1}{2} - 1 - 3y) = 0$. Then $y = -1/6$, with $x = e^{-1/6}$. Hence there are two stationary points, namely $(0, -1/3)$ and $(e^{-1/6}, -1/6)$.

The second-order partial derivatives are $f_{11}''(x, y) = e^y - 2x$, $f_{12}''(x, y) = xe^y$, and $f_{22}''(x, y) = \tfrac{1}{2}x^2 e^y - 6e^{3y} - 9ye^{3y}$. We get the following classification:

(x, y)	A	B	C	$AC - B^2$	Type of point
$(0, -1/3)$	$e^{-1/3}$	0	$-3e^{-1}$	$-3e^{-4/3}$	Saddle point
$(e^{-1/6}, -1/6)$	$-e^{-1/6}$	$e^{-1/3}$	$-4e^{-1/2}$	$3e^{-2/3}$	Local maximum point

Proof of the Second-Derivative Test

Let $z = f(x, y)$ be the function graphed in Fig. 2, with (x_0, y_0) as a local maximum point. For fixed values of h and k, define the function g of one variable by

$$g(t) = f(x_0 + th, y_0 + tk)$$

This function tells us what happens to f as one moves away from (x_0, y_0) in the direction (h, k), or in the reverse direction $(-h, -k)$.

If f has a local maximum at (x_0, y_0), then $g(t)$ must certainly have a local maximum at $t = 0$. Necessary conditions for this are that $g'(0) = 0$ and $g''(0) \leq 0$. The first and second order derivatives of $g(t)$ were calculated in Example 12.1.5. At $t = 0$ the second derivative of g is

$$g''(0) = f_{11}''(x_0, y_0)h^2 + 2f_{12}''(x_0, y_0)hk + f_{22}''(x_0, y_0)k^2 \tag{1}$$

So if f has a local maximum at (x_0, y_0), the expression in (1) must be ≤ 0 for all choices of (h, k).

In this way we have obtained a *necessary* condition for (x_0, y_0) to be a local maximum point for f. We are more interested in *sufficient* conditions for local maximum. For the one variable function g we know that the conditions $g'(0) = 0$ and $g''(0) < 0$ are sufficient for g to have a local maximum at $t = 0$. It is therefore reasonable to conjecture that we have the following result:

If $f_1'(x_0, y_0) = f_2'(x_0, y_0) = 0$ and the expression in (1) is < 0 for all $(h, k) \neq (0, 0)$, then (x_0, y_0) is a (strict) local maximum point for f. (2)

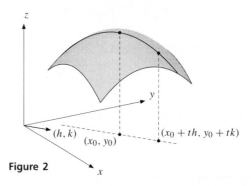

Figure 2

This turns out to be correct: If f has a strict local maximum in each direction through (x_0, y_0), then this point is a local maximum point for $f(x, y)$. This will be proved in FMEA. Problem 8 shows that if you delete the word "strict", the conclusion is wrong.

Relying on (2), we can prove (i) in Theorem 13.3.1. It suffices to verify that

$$A < 0 \quad \text{and} \quad AC - B^2 > 0 \implies Ah^2 + 2Bhk + Ck^2 < 0 \quad \text{for all} \quad (h, k) \neq (0, 0) \quad (3)$$

To this end we "complete the square":

$$Ah^2 + 2Bhk + Ck^2 = A\left[\left(h + \frac{B}{A}k\right)^2 + \frac{AC - B^2}{A^2}k^2 \right] \quad (4)$$

The square bracket is obviously ≥ 0, and $= 0$ only if both $h + Bk/A = 0$ and $k = 0$, implying that $h = k = 0$. Because $A < 0$, the whole expression in (4) is negative for all $(h, k) \neq (0, 0)$, so we have proved (2). ∎

PROBLEMS FOR SECTION 13.3

1. Consider the function f defined for all (x, y) by

$$f(x, y) = 5 - x^2 + 6x - 2y^2 + 8y$$

   (a) Find all the partial derivatives of first and second order.

   (b) Find the only stationary point and classify it by using the second-derivative test. What does Theorem 13.2.1 tell us?

2. Consider the function f defined for all (x, y) by $f(x, y) = x^2 + 2xy^2 + 2y^2$.

   (a) Find the first and second order partial derivatives of f.

   (b) Show that the stationary points are $(0, 0)$, $(-1, 1)$, $(-1, -1)$, and classify them.

3. (a) Compute the partial derivatives of the first and second order of

$$f(x, y) = x^3 + 2xy - 5x - y^2$$

(b) Find the stationary points and classify them.

4. The function f is defined for all x and y by

$$f(x, y) = 8x^3 - 12xy + y^3$$

(a) Find all stationary points and classify them.

(b) Does the function $g(x, y) = (8x^3 - 12xy + y^3)^2$ have a global minimum?

5. Find all the stationary points of the following functions and examine what the second-derivative test says about them:

(a) $f(x, y) = x^3 + y^3 - 3xy$ (b) $f(x, y) = e^{x+y} + e^{x-y} - \frac{3}{2}x - \frac{1}{2}y$

(c) $f(x, y) = \sqrt{1 - x^2 - y^2} + x^2 - 2y^2$ (d) $f(x, y) = x^4 + 2y^2 - 2xy$

6. Consider the three functions:

(a) $z = -x^4 - y^4$ (b) $z = x^4 + y^4$ (c) $z = x^3 + y^3$

Prove that the origin is a stationary point for each one of these functions, and that $AC - B^2 = 0$ at the origin in each case. By studying the functions directly, prove that the origin is respectively a maximum point for (a), a minimum point for (b), and a saddle point for (c).

7. Consider the function f defined for all (x, y) by

$$f(x, y) = \frac{1}{2}x^2 - x + ay(x - 1) - \frac{1}{3}y^3 + a^2y^2$$

where a is a constant.

(a) Find all the stationary points of f and classify them.

(b) Where in the xy-plane is f convex?

HARDER PROBLEMS

8. (a) Find the domain of the function $f(x, y) = \ln(1 + x^2y)$.

(b) Prove that the stationary points are all the points on the y-axis.

(c) Show that the second-derivative test fails. Try to classify the stationary points by looking at the formula for f. Then look at the figure in the answer section.

9. Suppose f is defined for all (x, y) by $f(x, y) = (y - x^2)(y - 2x^2)$.

   (a) The graph of $z = f(x, y)$ intersects the xy-plane $z = 0$ in two parabolas. In the xy-plane, draw the domains where f is negative, and where f is positive. Show that $(0, 0)$ is the only stationary point, and that it is a saddle point.

   (b) Suppose $(h, k) \neq (0, 0)$ is any direction vector. Let $g(t) = f(th, tk)$ and show that g has a local minimum at $t = 0$, whatever the direction (h, k) may be. (Thus, although $(0, 0)$ is a saddle point, the function has a local minimum at the origin in each direction through the origin.)

13.4 Linear Models with Quadratic Objectives

In this section we consider some other interesting economic applications of optimization theory when there are two variables. Versions of the first example have already appeared in Example 13.1.5 and Problems 13.1.4, 13.2.2, and 13.2.4–6.

EXAMPLE 1   **(Discriminating Monopolist)** Consider a firm that sells a product in two isolated geographical areas. If it wants to, it can then charge different prices in the two different areas because what is sold in one area cannot easily be resold in the other. As an example, it seems that express mail or courier services find it possible to charge much higher prices in Europe than they can in North America. Another example—pharmaceutical firms often charge much more for the same medication in the U.S.A. than they do in Europe or Canada.

Suppose that such a firm also has some monopoly power to influence the different prices it faces in the two separate markets by adjusting the quantity it sells in each. Economists generally use the term "discriminating monopolist" to describe a firm having this power.

Faced with two such isolated markets, the discriminating monopolist has two independent demand curves. Suppose that, in inverse form, these are

$$P_1 = a_1 - b_1 Q_1, \qquad P_2 = a_2 - b_2 Q_2 \qquad (*)$$

for market areas 1 and 2, respectively. Suppose, too, that the total cost is proportional to total production:[2]

$$C(Q) = \alpha(Q_1 + Q_2)$$

As a function of Q_1 and Q_2, total profits are

$$\pi(Q_1, Q_2) = P_1 Q_1 + P_2 Q_2 - \alpha(Q_1 + Q_2)$$

$$= (a_1 - b_1 Q_1)Q_1 + (a_2 - b_2 Q_2)Q_2 - \alpha(Q_1 + Q_2)$$

$$= (a_1 - \alpha)Q_1 + (a_2 - \alpha)Q_2 - b_1 Q_1^2 - b_2 Q_2^2$$

---

[2] It is true that this cost function neglects transport costs. But the point to be made is that, even though supplies to the two areas are perfect substitutes in production, the monopolist will generally charge different prices, if allowed.

We want to find the values of $Q_1 \geq 0$ and $Q_2 \geq 0$ that maximize profits. The first-order conditions are

$$\pi_1'(Q_1, Q_2) = (a_1 - \alpha) - 2b_1 Q_1 = 0, \qquad \pi_2'(Q_1, Q_2) = (a_2 - \alpha) - 2b_2 Q_2 = 0$$

with the solutions

$$Q_1^* = (a_1 - \alpha)/2b_1, \qquad Q_2^* = (a_2 - \alpha)/2b_2$$

Furthermore, $\pi_{11}''(Q_1, Q_2) = -2b_1, \pi_{12}''(Q_1, Q_2) = 0$, and $\pi_{22}''(Q_1, Q_2) = -2b_2$. Hence, for all (Q_1, Q_2)

$$\pi_{11}'' \leq 0, \qquad \pi_{22}'' \leq 0, \qquad \text{and} \qquad \pi_{11}'' \pi_{22}'' - (\pi_{12}'')^2 = 4b_1 b_2 \geq 0$$

We conclude from Theorem 13.2.1 that if Q_1^* and Q_2^* are both positive, implying that (Q_1^*, Q_2^*) is an interior point in the domain of π, then the pair (Q_1^*, Q_2^*) really does maximize profits.

The corresponding prices can be found by inserting these values in ($*$) to get

$$P_1^* = a_1 - b_1 Q_1^* = \tfrac{1}{2}(a_1 + \alpha), \qquad P_2^* = a_2 - b_2 Q_2^* = \tfrac{1}{2}(a_2 + \alpha)$$

The maximum profit is

$$\pi^* = \frac{(a_1 - \alpha)^2}{4b_1} + \frac{(a_2 - \alpha)^2}{4b_2}$$

Both demands Q_1^* and Q_2^* are positive provided $a_1 > \alpha$ and $a_2 > \alpha$. In this case, P_1^* and P_2^* are both greater than α. This implies that there is no "dumping", with the price in one market less than the cost α. Nor is there any "cross subsidy", with the losses due to dumping in one market being subsidized out of profits in the other market. It is notable that the optimal prices are independent of b_1 and b_2. More important, note that the prices are *not* the same in the two markets, except in the special case when $a_1 = a_2$. Indeed, $P_1^* > P_2^*$ if and only if $a_1 > a_2$. This says that the price is higher in the market where consumers are willing to pay a higher price for each unit when the quantity is close to zero.   ▮

EXAMPLE 2   Suppose that the monopolist in Example 1 has the demand functions

$$P_1 = 100 - Q_1, \qquad P_2 = 80 - Q_2$$

and that the cost function is $C = 6(Q_1 + Q_2)$.

(a) How much should be sold in the two markets to maximize profits? What are the corresponding prices?

(b) How much profit is lost if it becomes illegal to discriminate?

(c) The authorities in market 1 impose a tax of t per unit sold in market 1. Discuss the consequences.

Solution:

(a) Here $a_1 = 100$, $a_2 = 80$, $b_1 = b_2 = 1$, and $\alpha = 6$. Example 1 gives the answers

$$Q_1^* = (100 - 6)/2 = 47, \quad Q_2^* = 37, \quad P_1^* = \tfrac{1}{2}(100 + 6) = 53, \quad P_2^* = 43$$

The corresponding profit is $P_1^* Q_1^* + P_2^* Q_2^* - 6(Q_1^* + Q_2^*) = 3578$.

(b) If price discrimination is not permitted, then $P_1 = P_2 = P$, and $Q_1 = 100 - P$, $Q_2 = 80 - P$, with total demand $Q = Q_1 + Q_2 = 180 - 2P$. Then $P = 90 - \tfrac{1}{2}Q$, so profits are

$$\pi = \left(90 - \tfrac{1}{2}Q\right)Q - 6Q = 84Q - \tfrac{1}{2}Q^2$$

This has a maximum at $Q = 84$ when $P = 48$. The corresponding profit is now 3528, so the loss in profit is $3578 - 3528 = 50$.

(c) With the introduction of the tax, the new profit function is

$$\hat{\pi} = (100 - Q_1)Q_1 + (80 - Q_2)Q_2 - 6(Q_1 + Q_2) - tQ_1$$

We easily see that this has a maximum at $\hat{Q}_1 = 47 - \tfrac{1}{2}t$, $\hat{Q}_2 = 37$, with corresponding prices $\hat{P}_1 = 53 + \tfrac{1}{2}t$, $\hat{P}_2 = 43$. The tax therefore has no influence on the sales in market 2, while the amount sold in market 1 is lowered and the price in market 1 goes up. The optimal profit is easily worked out:

$$\pi^* = (53 + \tfrac{1}{2}t)(47 - \tfrac{1}{2}t) + 43 \cdot 37 - 6(84 - \tfrac{1}{2}t) - t(47 - \tfrac{1}{2}t) = 3578 - 47t + \tfrac{1}{4}t^2$$

So introducing the tax makes the profit fall by $47t - \tfrac{1}{4}t^2$. The authorities in market 1 obtain a tax revenue which is

$$T = t\hat{Q}_1 = t(47 - \tfrac{1}{2}t) = 47t - \tfrac{1}{2}t^2$$

Thus we see that profits fall by $\tfrac{1}{4}t^2$ more than the tax revenue. This amount $\tfrac{1}{4}t^2$ represents the so-called deadweight loss from the tax. ∎

A monopolist is a firm facing a downward-sloping demand curve. A *discriminating monopolist* such as in Example 1 faces separate downward-sloping demand curves in two or more isolated markets. A *monopsonist*, on the other hand, is a firm facing an upward-sloping supply curve for one or more of its factors of production, and a *discriminating monopsonist* faces two or more upward-sloping supply curves for different kinds of the same input—for example, workers of different race or gender. Of course, discrimination by race or gender is illegal in many countries. The following example, however, suggests one possible reason why firms might want to discriminate if they were allowed to.

EXAMPLE 3   **(Discriminating Monopsonist)**   Consider a firm using quantities L_1 and L_2 of two kinds of labour as its only inputs in order to produce output Q according to the simple production function

$$Q = L_1 + L_2$$

Thus, both output and labour supply are measured so that each unit of labour produces one unit of output. Note especially how the two kinds of labour are essentially indistinguishable, because each unit of each type makes an equal contribution to the firm's output. Suppose, however, that there are two segmented labour markets, with different inverse supply functions specifying the wage that must be paid to attract a given labour supply. Specifically, suppose that

$$w_1 = \alpha_1 + \beta_1 L_1, \qquad w_2 = \alpha_2 + \beta_2 L_2$$

Assume moreover that the firm is competitive in its output market, taking price P as fixed. Then the firm's profits are

$$\pi(L_1, L_2) = PQ - w_1 L_1 - w_2 L_2 = P(L_1 + L_2) - (\alpha_1 + \beta_1 L_1)L_1 - (\alpha_2 + \beta_2 L_2)L_2$$

$$= (P - \alpha_1)L_1 - \beta_1 L_1^2 + (P - \alpha_2)L_2 - \beta_2 L_2^2$$

The firm wants to maximize profits. The first-order conditions are

$$\pi_1'(L_1, L_2) = (P - \alpha_1) - 2\beta_1 L_1 = 0, \qquad \pi_2'(L_1, L_2) = (P - \alpha_2) - 2\beta_2 L_2 = 0$$

These have the solutions

$$L_1^* = \frac{P - \alpha_1}{2\beta_1}, \qquad L_2^* = \frac{P - \alpha_2}{2\beta_2}$$

It is easy to see that the conditions for maximum in Theorem 13.2.1 are satisfied, so that L_1^*, L_2^* really do maximize profits if $P > \alpha_1$ and $P > \alpha_2$. The maximum profit is

$$\pi^* = \frac{(P - \alpha_1)^2}{4\beta_1} + \frac{(P - \alpha_2)^2}{4\beta_2}$$

The corresponding wages are

$$w_1^* = \alpha_1 + \beta_1 L_1^* = \tfrac{1}{2}(P + \alpha_1), \qquad w_2^* = \alpha_2 + \beta_2 L_2^* = \tfrac{1}{2}(P + \alpha_2)$$

Hence, $w_1^* = w_2^*$ only if $\alpha_1 = \alpha_2$. Generally, the wage is higher for the type of labour that demands a higher wage for very low levels of labour supply—perhaps this is the type of labour with better job prospects elsewhere.

EXAMPLE 4   **(Econometrics: Linear Regression)**   Most applied economics is concerned with analysing data in order to try to discern some pattern that helps in understanding the past, and possibly in predicting the future. For example, price and quantity data for a particular commodity such as natural gas may be used in order to try to estimate a demand curve. This might then be used to predict how demand will respond to future price changes. The most common technique for estimating such a curve is *linear regression*.

Suppose it is thought that variable y—say, the quantity demanded—depends upon variable x—say, price or income. Suppose that we have observations (x_t, y_t) of both variables at times $t = 1, 2, \ldots, T$. Then the technique of linear regression seeks to fit a linear function

$$y = \alpha + \beta x$$

to the data, as indicated in Fig. 1.

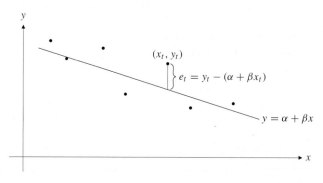

Figure 1

Of course, an exact fit is possible only if there exist numbers α and β for which $y_t = \alpha + \beta x_t$ for $t = 1, 2, \ldots, T$. This is rarely possible. Generally, however α and β may be chosen, one has instead

$$y_t = \alpha + \beta x_t + e_t, \qquad t = 1, 2, \ldots, T$$

where e_t is an *error* or *disturbance* term. Obviously, one hopes that the errors will be small, on average. So the parameters α and β are chosen to make the errors as "small as possible," somehow. One idea would be to make the sum $\sum_{t=1}^{T}(y_t - \alpha - \beta x_t)$ equal to zero. However, in this case, large positive discrepancies would cancel large negative discrepancies. Indeed, the sum of errors could be zero even though the line is very far from giving a perfect or even a good fit. We must somehow prevent large positive errors from cancelling large negative errors. Usually, this is done by minimizing the "loss" function

$$L(\alpha, \beta) = \frac{1}{T} \sum_{t=1}^{T} e_t^2 = \frac{1}{T} \sum_{t=1}^{T} (y_t - \alpha - \beta x_t)^2 \quad \textbf{(loss function)} \qquad (*)$$

which equals the mean (or average) square error. Expanding the square gives[3]

$$L(\alpha, \beta) = T^{-1} \sum_t (y_t^2 + \alpha^2 + \beta^2 x_t^2 - 2\alpha y_t - 2\beta x_t y_t + 2\alpha\beta x_t)$$

This is a quadratic function of α and β. We shall show how to derive the *ordinary least-squares* estimates of α and β. Before doing so, however, it helps to introduce some standard notation. Write

$$\mu_x = \frac{x_1 + \cdots + x_T}{T} = T^{-1} \sum_t x_t, \qquad \mu_y = \frac{y_1 + \cdots + y_T}{T} = T^{-1} \sum_t y_t$$

---

[3] From now on, we often use $\sum_t$ to denote $\sum_{t=1}^{T}$.

for the *statistical means* of x_t and y_t, respectively. And write

$$\sigma_{xx} = T^{-1} \sum_t (x_t - \mu_x)^2$$

$$\sigma_{yy} = T^{-1} \sum_t (y_t - \mu_y)^2$$

$$\sigma_{xy} = T^{-1} \sum_t (x_t - \mu_x)(y_t - \mu_y)$$

for the *statistical variances* of x_t and y_t and for the *covariance*, respectively. Using the result in Example 3.2.2, we have

$$\sigma_{xx} = T^{-1} \sum_t x_t^2 - \mu_x^2, \qquad \sigma_{yy} = T^{-1} \sum_t y_t^2 - \mu_y^2, \qquad \sigma_{xy} = T^{-1} \sum_t x_t y_t - \mu_x \mu_y$$

(You should check the last as an exercise.) Then the expression for $L(\alpha, \beta)$ becomes

$$
\begin{aligned}
L(\alpha, \beta) &= (\sigma_{yy} + \mu_y^2) + \alpha^2 + \beta^2(\sigma_{xx} + \mu_x^2) - 2\alpha\mu_y - 2\beta(\sigma_{xy} + \mu_x\mu_y) + 2\alpha\beta\mu_x \\
&= \alpha^2 + \mu_y^2 + \beta^2\mu_x^2 - 2\alpha\mu_y - 2\beta\mu_x\mu_y + 2\alpha\beta\mu_x + \beta^2\sigma_{xx} - 2\beta\sigma_{xy} + \sigma_{yy}
\end{aligned}
$$

First-order conditions for a minimum of $L(\alpha, \beta)$ take the form

$$L_1'(\alpha, \beta) = 2\alpha - 2\mu_y + 2\beta\mu_x = 0$$

$$L_2'(\alpha, \beta) = 2\beta\mu_x^2 - 2\mu_x\mu_y + 2\alpha\mu_x + 2\beta\sigma_{xx} - 2\sigma_{xy} = 0$$

Note that $L_2'(\alpha, \beta) = \mu_x L_1'(\alpha, \beta) + 2\beta\sigma_{xx} - 2\sigma_{xy}$. So the values of α and β that make L stationary are given by

$$\hat{\beta} = \sigma_{xy}/\sigma_{xx}, \qquad \hat{\alpha} = \mu_y - \hat{\beta}\mu_x = \mu_y - (\sigma_{xy}/\sigma_{xx})\mu_x \qquad (**)$$

Furthermore,

$$L_{11}'' = 2, \qquad L_{12}'' = 2\mu_x, \qquad L_{22}'' = 2\mu_x^2 + 2\sigma_{xx}$$

Thus $L_{11}'' \geq 0$, $L_{22}'' \geq 0$, and moreover,

$$L_{11}'' L_{22}'' - (L_{12}'')^2 = 2(2\mu_x^2 + 2\sigma_{xx}) - (2\mu_x)^2 = 4\sigma_{xx} = 4T^{-1} \sum_t (x_t - \mu_x)^2 \geq 0$$

We conclude that the conditions in Theorem 13.2.1(b) are satisfied, and therefore the pair $(\hat{\alpha}, \hat{\beta})$ given by $(**)$ minimizes $L(\alpha, \beta)$. Note in particular that $\hat{\alpha}$ is chosen to make the estimated straight line

$$y = \hat{\alpha} + \hat{\beta}x$$

go through the mean (μ_x, μ_y) of the observed pairs (x_t, y_t), $t = 1, \ldots, T$.

The problem is then completely solved:

The straight line $y = \hat{\alpha} + \hat{\beta}x$, with $\hat{\alpha}$ and $\hat{\beta}$ given by $(**)$, is the one which best fits the observations (x_1, y_1), (x_2, y_2), $\ldots$, (x_T, y_T), in the sense of minimizing the mean square error in $(*)$.

1. Suppose that the monopolist in Example 1 has the demand functions

$$P_1 = 200 - 2Q_1, \qquad P_2 = 180 - 4Q_2$$

and that the cost function is $C = 20(Q_1 + Q_2)$

(a) How much should be sold in the two markets to maximize profits? What are the corresponding prices?

(b) How much profit is lost if it becomes illegal to discriminate?

(c) The authorities in market 1 impose a tax of 5 per unit sold in market 1. Discuss the consequences.

2. A firm produces and sells a product in two separate markets. When the price in market A is p per ton, and the price in market B is q per ton, the demand in tons per week in the two markets are, respectively,

$$Q_A = a - bp, \qquad Q_B = c - dq$$

The cost function is $C(Q_A, Q_B) = \alpha + \beta(Q_A + Q_B)$, and all constants are positive.

(a) Find the firm's profit as a function of the prices p and q, and then find the pair (p^*, q^*) which maximizes profits.

(b) Suppose it becomes unlawful to discriminate by price, so that the firm must charge the same price in the two markets. What price $\hat{p}$ will now maximize profits?

(c) In the case $\beta = 0$, find the firm's loss of profit if it has to charge the same price in both markets. Comment?

3. In Example 1, discuss the effects of a tax imposed in market 1 of t per unit of Q_1.

4. The following table shows the Norwegian gross national product (GNP) and spending on foreign aid (FA) for the period 1970–1973 (in millions of crowns).

Year	1970	1971	1972	1973
GNP	79 835	89 112	97 339	110 156
FA	274	307	436	524

Growth of both GNP and FA was almost exponential during the period. So, approximately:

$$\text{GNP} = Ae^{a(t-t_0)}, \qquad t_0 = 1970$$

Define $x = t - t_0$ and $b = \ln A$. Then $\ln(\text{GNP}) = ax + b$. On the basis of the table above, one gets the following

Year	1970	1971	1972	1973
$y = \ln(\text{GNP})$	11.29	11.40	11.49	11.61

(a) Using the method of least squares, determine the straight line $y = ax + b$ which best fits the data in the last table.

(b) Repeat the method above to estimate c and d, where $\ln(\text{FA}) = cx + d$.

(c) The Norwegian government had a stated goal of eventually giving 1% of its GNP as foreign aid. If the time trends of the two variables had continued as they did during the years 1970–1973, when would this goal have been reached?

5. **(Duopoly)** Each of two firms A and B produces its own brand of a commodity such as mineral water in amounts denoted by x and y, and these are sold at prices p and q per unit, respectively. Each firm determines its own price and produces exactly as much as is demanded. The demands for the two brands are given by

$$x = 29 - 5p + 4q, \qquad y = 16 + 4p - 6q$$

Firm A has total costs $5 + x$, whereas firm B has total costs $3 + 2y$. (Assume that the functions to be maximized have maxima, and at positive prices.)

(a) Initially, the two firms cooperate in order to maximize their combined profit, as one monopolist would. Find the prices (p, q), the production levels (x, y), and the profits of firms A and B.

(b) Then cooperation breaks down, with each producer maximizing its own profit, taking the other's price as given.

   If q is fixed, how will A choose p? (Find p as a function $p = p_A(q)$ of q.)

   If p is fixed, how will B choose q? (Find q as a function $q = q_B(p)$ of p.)

(c) Under the assumptions in part (b), what constant equilibrium prices are possible? What are the production levels and profits in this case?

(d) Draw a diagram with p along the horizontal axis and q along the vertical axis, and draw the "reaction" curves $p_A(q)$ and $q_B(p)$. Show on the diagram how the two firms' prices change over time if A breaks the cooperation first by maximizing its profit, taking B's initial price as fixed, then B answers by maximizing its profit with A's price fixed, then A responds, and so on.

13.5   The Extreme-Value Theorem

As with functions of one variable, it is easy to find examples of functions of several variables that do not have any maximum or minimum points. For providing sufficient conditions to ensure that extreme points do exist, however, the extreme-value theorem (Theorem 8.4.1) was very useful for functions of one variable. It can be directly generalized to functions of several variables. In order to formulate the theorem, however, we need a few new concepts.

For many of the results concerning functions of one variable, it was important to distinguish between different kinds of domain for the functions. For functions of several variables, the distinction between different kinds of domain is no less important. In the one variable case, most functions were defined over intervals, and there are not many different kinds of interval. For functions of several variables, however, there are many different kinds of domain. Fortunately, the distinctions that are relevant to the extreme-value theorem can be made using only the concepts of open, closed, and bounded sets.

A point (a, b) is called an **interior point** of a set S in the plane if *there exists* a circle centred at (a, b) such that all points strictly inside the circle lie in S. (See Fig. 1.) A set is called **open** if it consists only of interior points. (See the second set illustrated in Fig. 1, where we indicate boundary points that belong to the set by a solid curve, and those that do not by a dashed curve.) The point (a, b) is called a **boundary point** of a set S if *every* circle centred at (a, b) contains points of S as well as points in its complement, as illustrated in the first figure. A boundary point of S does not necessarily lie in S. If S contains all its boundary points, then S is called **closed**. (See the third set in Fig. 1.) Note that a set that contains some but not all its boundary points, like the last of those illustrated in Fig. 1, is neither open nor closed. In fact, a set is closed if and only if its complement is open.

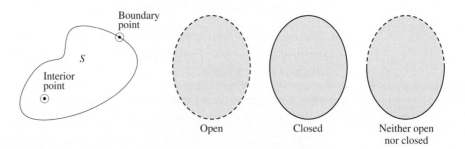

Figure 1

These illustrations give only very loose indications of what it means for a set to be either open or closed. Of course, if a set is not even precisely defined, it is impossible to decide conclusively whether it is open or closed.

In many of the optimization problems considered in economics, sets are defined by one or more inequalities, and boundary points occur where one or more of these inequalities are satisfied with equality. For instance, provided that p, q, and m are positive parameters, the (budget) set of points (x, y) that satisfy the inequalities

$$px + qy \leq m, \quad x \geq 0, \quad y \geq 0 \qquad (*)$$

is closed. This set is a triangle, as shown in Fig. 4.4.12. Its boundary consists of the three sides of the triangle. Each of the three sides corresponds to having one of the inequalities in (∗) be satisfied with equality. On the other hand, the set that results from replacing ≤ by < and ≥ by > in (∗) is open.

In general, if $g(x, y)$ is a continuous function and c is a real number, then the sets

$$\{(x, y) : g(x, y) \geq c\}, \qquad \{(x, y) : g(x, y) \leq c\}, \qquad \{(x, y) : g(x, y) = c\}$$

are all closed. If ≥ is replaced by >, or ≤ is replaced by <, or = by ≠, then the corresponding set becomes open.

A set in the plane is **bounded** if the whole set is contained within a sufficiently large circle. The sets in Fig. 1 and the budget triangle in Fig. 4.4.12 are all bounded. On the other hand, the set of all (x, y) satisfying

$$x \geq 1 \qquad \text{and} \qquad y \geq 0$$

is a closed, but unbounded set. (See Fig. 11.1.1.) The set is closed because it contains all its boundary points. How would you characterize the set in Fig. 11.1.2? (In fact, it is neither open nor closed, but it is bounded.) A set in the plane that is both closed and bounded is often called **compact**.

We are now ready to formulate the main result in this section.

THEOREM 13.5.1 (EXTREME-VALUE THEOREM)

Suppose the function $f(x, y)$ is continuous throughout a non-empty, closed and bounded set S in the plane. Then there exists both a point (a, b) in S where f has a minimum and a point (c, d) in S where f has a maximum—that is,

$$f(a, b) \leq f(x, y) \leq f(c, d) \qquad \text{for all } (x, y) \text{ in } S$$

Theorem 13.5.1 is a pure existence theorem. It tells us nothing about *how to find* the extreme points. Its proof is found in most advanced calculus books and in FMEA. Also, even though the conditions of the theorem are *sufficient* to ensure the existence of extreme points, they are far from necessary. (See Note 8.4.1.)

Finding Maxima and Minima

Sections 13.1 and 13.2 presented some simple cases where we could find the maximum and minimum points of a function of two variables by finding its stationary points. The procedure set out in the following frame covers many additional optimization problems.

FINDING MAXIMA AND MINIMA

Find the maximum and minimum values of a differentiable function $f(x, y)$ defined on a closed, bounded set S in the plane.

Solution:

(I) Find all stationary points of f in the interior of S.

(II) Find the largest value and the smallest value of f on the boundary of S, along with the associated points. (If it is convenient to subdivide the boundary into several pieces, find the largest and smallest value on each piece of the boundary.)

(III) Compute the values of the function at all the points found in (I) and (II). The largest function value is the maximum value of f in S. The smallest function value is the minimum value of f in S.

(1)

We try out this procedure on the function whose graph is depicted in Fig. 2 below. (Because the function is not specified analytically, we can only give a rough geometric argument.) The function has a rectangular domain S. The only stationary point of f it includes is (x_0, y_0), which corresponds to the point P of the graph. The boundary of S consists of four straight-line segments. The point R vertically above one corner point of S represents the maximum value of f along the boundary; similarly, Q represents the minimum value of f along the boundary. The only candidates for a maximum/minimum are, therefore, the three points P, Q, and R. By comparing the values of f at these points, we see that P represents the minimum value, whereas R represents the maximum value of f in S.

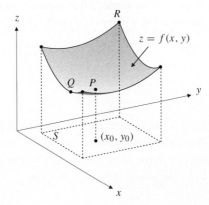

Figure 2

As an aspiring economist you will be glad to hear that most optimization problems in economics, especially those appearing in textbooks, rarely create enough difficulties to call for the full recipe. Usually there is an interior optimum that can be found by equating all the first-order partial derivatives to zero. Conditions that are sufficient for this easier approach to work are already discussed in Section 13.1. Nevertheless, we consider some examples of harder problems which illustrate how the whole recipe is sometimes needed.

EXAMPLE 1   Find the extreme values for $f(x, y)$ defined over S when

$$f(x, y) = x^2 + y^2 + y - 1, \qquad S = \{(x, y) : x^2 + y^2 \le 1\}$$

Solution: The set S consists of all the points on or inside the circle of radius 1 centred at the origin, as shown in Fig. 3. The continuous function f will attain both a maximum and a minimum over S, by the extreme-value theorem.

According to the preceding recipe, we start by finding all the stationary points in the interior of S. These stationary points satisfy the two equations

$$f_1'(x, y) = 2x = 0, \qquad f_2'(x, y) = 2y + 1 = 0$$

So $(x, y) = (0, -1/2)$ is the only stationary point, and it is in the interior of S, with $f(0, -1/2) = -5/4$.

The boundary of S consists of the circle $x^2 + y^2 = 1$. Note that if (x, y) lies on this circle, then in particular both x and y lie in the interval $[-1, 1]$. Inserting $x^2 + y^2 = 1$ into the expression for $f(x, y)$ shows that, *along the boundary of S*, the value of f is determined by the following function of one variable:

$$g(y) = 1 + y - 1 = y, \qquad y \in [-1, 1]$$

The maximum value of g is 1 for $y = 1$, and then $x = 0$. The minimum value is -1 when $y = -1$, and then again $x = 0$.

We have now found the only three possible candidates for extreme points, namely, $(0, -1/2)$, $(0, 1)$, and $(0, -1)$. But $f(0, -1/2) = -5/4$, $f(0, 1) = 1$, and $f(0, -1) = -1$. We conclude that the *maximum value* of f in S is 1, which is attained at $(0, 1)$, whereas the *minimum value* is $-5/4$, attained at $(0, -1/2)$.

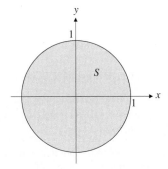

Figure 3 The domain in Example 1

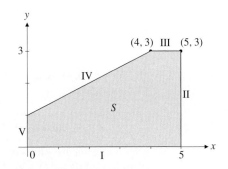

Figure 4 The domain in Example 2

EXAMPLE 2   In one study of the quantities x and y of natural gas that Western Europe should import from Norway and Siberia, respectively, it was assumed that the benefits were given by the function $f(x, y) = 9x + 8y - 6(x + y)^2$. (The term $-6(x + y)^2$ occurs because the world price of natural gas rises as total imports increase.) Because of capacity constraints, x and y must satisfy $0 \le x \le 5$ and $0 \le y \le 3$. Finally, for political reasons, it was felt that imports from Norway should not provide too small a fraction of total imports at the margin, so that $x \ge 2(y - 1)$, or equivalently $-x + 2y \le 2$. Thus, the optimization problem was cast as

$$\max \; f(x, y) = 9x + 8y - 6(x + y)^2 \quad \text{subject to } 0 \le x \le 5, \; 0 \le y \le 3, \; -x + 2y \le 2$$

In the xy-plane, draw the set S of all points satisfying the three constraints, and then solve the problem.

Solution: The set S is shown in Fig. 4. It is clearly closed and bounded, so the continuous function f has a maximum in S.

We look first for stationary points in the interior of S. Any such point must satisfy the two equations

$$\frac{\partial f}{\partial x} = 9 - 12(x + y) = 0, \qquad \frac{\partial f}{\partial y} = 8 - 12(x + y) = 0$$

Thus, $12(x + y) = 9$ and also $12(x + y) = 8$, which is a contradiction. Hence, there are no stationary points. The maximum value of f must therefore occur at the boundary, which consists of five parts. Either the maximum value occurs at one of the five corners or "extreme points" of the boundary, or else at an interior point of one of five straight "edges." The function values at the five corners are

$$f(0, 0) = 0, \quad f(5, 0) = -105, \quad f(5, 3) = -315, \quad f(4, 3) = -234, \quad f(0, 1) = 2$$

We proceed to examine the behaviour of f at interior points of each of the five edges that are labelled (I), (II), . . . , (V) in Fig. 4.

- On edge (I), $y = 0$, $x \in (0, 5)$. Here the behaviour of f is determined by the function $g_1(x) = f(x, 0) = 9x - 6x^2$ for $x \in (0, 5)$. If this function of one variable has a maximum in $(0, 5)$, it must occur at a stationary point where $g_1'(x) = 9 - 12x = 0$, and so at $x = 3/4$. We find that $g_1(3/4) = f(3/4, 0) = 27/8$.

- On edge (II), $x = 5$, $y \in (0, 3)$. Define $g_2(y) = f(5, y) = 45 + 8y - 6(5 + y)^2$ for $y \in (0, 3)$. Here $g_2'(y) = 8 - 12(5 + y) = -52 - 12y$, which is negative throughout $(0, 3)$, so there are no stationary points on this edge.

- On edge (III), $y = 3$, $x \in (4, 5)$. Define $g_3(x) = f(x, 3) = 9x + 24 - 6(x + 3)^2$ for $x \in (4, 5)$. Here $g_3'(x) = 9 - 12(x + 3) = -27 - 12x$, which is negative throughout $(4, 5)$, so there are no stationary points on this edge either.

- On edge (IV), $-x + 2y = 2$, or $y = x/2 + 1$, with $x \in (0, 4)$. Define the function

$$g_4(x) = f(x, x/2 + 1) = 9x + 8(x/2 + 1) - 6(x + x/2 + 1)^2 = -27x^2/2 - 5x + 2$$

for $x \in (0, 4)$. Here $g_4'(x) = -27x - 5$, which is negative in $(0, 4)$, so there are no stationary points here.

- On edge (V), $x = 0$, $y \in (0, 1)$. Define $g_5(y) = f(0, y) = 8y - 6y^2$. Then $g_5'(y) = 8 - 12y = 0$ at $y = 2/3$, with $g_5(2/3) = f(0, 2/3) = 8/3$.

After comparing the values of f at the five corners of the boundary and at the points found on the edges labeled (I) and (V), we conclude that the maximum value of f is $27/8$, which is achieved at $(3/4, 0)$.

PROBLEMS FOR SECTION 13.5

1. Let $f(x, y) = 4x - 2x^2 - 2y^2$, $S = \{(x, y) : x^2 + y^2 \leq 25\}$.

   (a) Compute $f_1'(x, y)$ and $f_2'(x, y)$, then find the only stationary point for f.

   (b) Find the extreme points for f over S.

2. Find the maximum and minimum points for the following:

   (a) $f(x, y) = x^3 + y^3 - 9xy + 27$ subject to $0 \leq x \leq 4$ and $0 \leq y \leq 4$.

   (b) $f(x, y) = x^2 + 2y^2 - x$ subject to $x^2 + y^2 \leq 1$.

   (c) $f(x, y) = 3 + x^3 - x^2 - y^2$ subject to $x^2 + y^2 \leq 1$ and $x \geq 0$.

   (d) $f(x, y) = (x - 2)e^{x^2 - x}(2y - 1)e^{(y-2)^2}$ subject to $0 \leq x \leq 2$ and $0 \leq y \leq 1/2$.

3. Let the domain of the function h be the set of all (x, y) satisfying both $1 \leq x \leq 2$ and $0 \leq y \leq x - 1$, and let

   $$h(x, y) = x^2 y(x - y - 1)$$

   Prove that h has global extreme points, and find them.

4. (a) Determine values of the constants a, b, and c such that

   $$f(x, y) = ax^2 y + bxy + 2xy^2 + c$$

   has a local minimum at the point $(2/3, 1/3)$ with local minimum value $-1/9$.

   (b) With the values of a, b, and c found in part (a), find the maximum and minimum values of f over the domain S in the xy-plane determined by the inequalities $x \geq 0$, $y \geq 0$, and $2x + y \leq 4$.

5. Consider the function f defined for all x, y by $f(x, y) = xe^{-x}(y^2 - 4y)$.

   (a) Find all stationary points of f and classify them by using the second-derivative test.

   (b) Show that f neither has a global maximum nor a global minimum.

   (c) Let $S = \{(x, y) : 0 \leq x \leq 5, \ 0 \leq y \leq 4\}$. Prove that f has global maximum and minimum points in S and find them.

   (d) Find the slope of the tangent to the level curve $xe^{-x}(y^2 - 4y) = e - 4$ at the point where $x = 1$ and $y = 4 - e$.

6. Which of the following sets are open, closed, bounded, or compact?

   (a) $\{(x, y) : 5x^2 + 5y^2 \leq 9\}$ (b) $\{(x, y) : x^2 + y^2 > 9\}$

   (c) $\{(x, y) : 0 \leq x^2 + y^2 \leq 9\}$ (d) $\{(x, y) : 2x + 5y \geq 6\}$

   (e) $\{(x, y) : 5x + 8y = 8\}$ (f) $\{(x, y) : 5x + 8y > 8\}$

HARDER PROBLEMS

7. Give an example of a discontinuous function g of one variable such that the set $\{x : g(x) \leq 1\}$ is not closed.

8. Suppose

$$f(x, y) = (x + y)e^{-(x+y^2)/4}$$

and let D be the domain consisting of all points (x, y) satisfying $x + y \geq 1$, $y \geq 0$.

(a) Draw the domain D in the xy-plane, and find the first-order partial derivatives of f.

(b) Take it for granted that f attains a maximum on the domain D. Find the maximum point and the maximum value.

13.6 Three or More Variables

So far this chapter has considered optimization problems for functions of two variables. In order to understand modern economic theory we definitely have to extend the analysis to an arbitrary number of variables.

The extensions of the definitions of maximum and minimum points, extreme points etc. are almost obvious. If $f(\mathbf{x}) = f(x_1, \ldots, x_n)$ is a function of n variables defined over a set S in $\mathbb{R}^n$, then $\mathbf{c} = (c_1, \ldots, c_n)$ is a (global) **maximum point** for f in S if

$$f(\mathbf{x}) \leq f(\mathbf{c}) \qquad \text{for all } \mathbf{x} \text{ in } S \tag{1}$$

Suppose that f is a function of n variables defined over a set S in $\mathbb{R}^n$ and that $f(\mathbf{x}) \leq f(\mathbf{c})$ for all $\mathbf{x}$ in S, so $\mathbf{c}$ maximizes f over S. Then $-f(\mathbf{x}) \geq -f(\mathbf{c})$ for all $\mathbf{x}$ in S. Thus, $\mathbf{c}$ maximizes f over S if and only if $\mathbf{c}$ minimizes $-f$ over S. We can use this simple observation to convert maximization problems into minimization problems and vice versa. (Recall the one variable illustration in Fig. 8.1.1.)

The concepts of interior and boundary points, and of open, closed, and bounded sets, are also easy to generalize. First, define the **distance** between the points $\mathbf{x} = (x_1, \ldots, x_n)$ and $\mathbf{y} = (y_1, \ldots, y_n)$ by

$$\|\mathbf{x} - \mathbf{y}\| = \sqrt{(x_1 - y_1)^2 + (x_2 - y_2)^2 + \cdots + (x_n - y_n)^2} \tag{2}$$

For $n = 1$, 2 and 3 this reduces to the distance concept discussed earlier. In particular, if $\mathbf{y} = \mathbf{0}$, then

$$\|\mathbf{x}\| = \sqrt{x_1^2 + x_2^2 + \cdots + x_n^2}$$

is the distance between $\mathbf{x}$ and the origin. The number $\|\mathbf{x}\|$ is also called the **norm** of the vector $\mathbf{x}$.

An **open n-ball** with centre at $\mathbf{a} = (a_1, \ldots, a_n)$ and radius r is the set of all points $\mathbf{x} = (x_1, \ldots, x_n)$ such that $\|\mathbf{x} - \mathbf{a}\| < r$. The definitions in Section 13.5 of interior point, open set, boundary point, closed set, bounded set, and compact set all become valid for sets in $\mathbb{R}^n$ provided we replace the word "circle" by "n-ball".

If $g(\mathbf{x}) = g(x_1, \ldots, x_n)$ is a continuous function, and c is a real number, then each of the three sets

$$\{\mathbf{x} : g(\mathbf{x}) \geq c\}, \qquad \{\mathbf{x} : g(\mathbf{x}) \leq c\}, \qquad \{\mathbf{x} : g(\mathbf{x}) = c\}$$

is closed. If $\geq$ is replaced by $>$, $\leq$ by $<$, or $=$ by $\neq$, the corresponding set is open.

If A is an arbitrary set in $\mathbb{R}^n$, we define the **interior** of A as the set of interior points in A. If A is open, the interior of A is equal to the set itself.

A **stationary point** for a function of n variables is a point where all the first-order derivatives are 0. We have the following important generalization of Theorem 13.1.1:

THEOREM 13.6.1 (NECESSARY FIRST-ORDER CONDITIONS)

Suppose f is defined in a set S in $\mathbb{R}^n$ and let $\mathbf{c} = (c_1, \ldots, c_n)$ be an interior point in S where f is differentiable. A necessary condition for $\mathbf{c}$ to be a maximum or minimum point for f is that $\mathbf{c}$ is a stationary point for f—that is, $\mathbf{x} = \mathbf{c}$ satisfies the n equations

$$f_i'(\mathbf{x}) = 0, \qquad i = 1, \ldots, n \qquad \textbf{(first-order conditions, or FOCs)}$$

Proof: Keep i ($1 \leq i \leq n$) fixed and define $g(x_i) = f(c_1, \ldots, c_{i-1}, x_i, c_{i+1}, \ldots, c_n)$, whose domain consists of those x_i such that $(c_1, \ldots, c_{i-1}, x_i, c_{i+1}, \ldots, c_n)$ belongs to S. If $\mathbf{c} = (c_1, \ldots, c_n)$ is a maximum (or minimum) point for f, then the function g of one variable must attain a maximum (or minimum) at $x_i = c_i$. Because $\mathbf{c}$ is an interior point of S, it follows that c_i is also an interior point in the domain of g. Hence, according to Theorem 8.1.1, we must have $g'(c_i) = 0$. But $g'(c_i) = f_i'(c_1, \ldots, c_n)$, so the conclusion follows. ∎

The extreme-value theorem is valid also for functions of n variables:

THEOREM 13.6.2 (THE EXTREME-VALUE THEOREM)

If f is a continuous function over a closed, bounded set S in $\mathbb{R}^n$, then there exists a point $\mathbf{d}$ in S where f has a minimum and a point $\mathbf{c}$ in S where f has a maximum, so that

$$f(\mathbf{d}) \leq f(\mathbf{x}) \leq f(\mathbf{c}) \qquad \text{for all } \mathbf{x} \text{ in } S$$

If $f(\mathbf{x})$ is defined over a set S in $\mathbb{R}^n$, then the maximum and minimum points (if there are any) must lie either in the interior of S or on the boundary of S. According to Theorem

13.6.1, if f is differentiable, then any maximum or minimum point in the interior must satisfy the first-order conditions. Consequently, the recipe in (13.5.1) is also valid for any function of n variables defined on a closed and bounded set in $\mathbb{R}^n$.

Both the local and the global second-order conditions for the two-variable case can be generalized to functions of n variables, though they become considerably more complicated. This will be discussed in FMEA.

A Useful Result

A simple result, which is nevertheless of considerable interest in theoretical economics, is often expressed as follows: *Maximizing a function is equivalent to maximizing a strictly increasing transformation of that function.* For instance, suppose we want to find all pairs (x, y) that maximize $f(x, y)$ over a set S in the xy-plane. Then we can just as well try to find those (x, y) that maximize over S any one of the following objective functions:

$$\text{(i) } af(x, y) + b \quad (a > 0) \quad \text{(ii) } e^{f(x,y)} \quad \text{(iii) } \ln f(x, y)$$

(In case (iii), we must assume that $f(x, y) > 0$ over S.) The maximum *points* are exactly the same. But the maximum *values* are, of course, quite different. As a concrete example, because the function $u \rightarrow e^u$ is strictly increasing, the problem

$$\text{maximize } e^{x^2 + 2xy^2 - y^3} \text{ subject to } (x, y) \in S$$

has the same solutions for x and y as the problem

$$\text{maximize } x^2 + 2xy^2 - y^3 \text{ subject to } (x, y) \in S$$

In general, it is easy to prove the following result:

THEOREM 13.6.3

Suppose $f(\mathbf{x}) = f(x_1, \ldots, x_n)$ is defined over a set S in $\mathbb{R}^n$ and let F be a function of one variable defined over the range of f. Define g over S by

$$g(\mathbf{x}) = F(f(\mathbf{x}))$$

Then:

(a) If F is increasing and $\mathbf{c}$ maximizes (minimizes) f over S, then $\mathbf{c}$ also maximizes (minimizes) g over S.

(b) If F is strictly increasing, then $\mathbf{c}$ maximizes (minimizes) f over S if and only if $\mathbf{c}$ maximizes (minimizes) g over S.

Proof: (For the maximization case—the argument in the minimization case is entirely similar.)

(a) Because **c** maximizes f over S, we have $f(\mathbf{x}) \leq f(\mathbf{c})$ for all **x** in S. But then $g(\mathbf{x}) = F(f(\mathbf{x})) \leq F(f(\mathbf{c})) = g(\mathbf{c})$ for all **x** in S, because F is increasing. It follows that **c** maximizes g over S.

(b) If F is also strictly increasing and $f(\mathbf{x}) > f(\mathbf{c})$, then it must be true that $g(\mathbf{x}) = F(f(\mathbf{x})) > F(f(\mathbf{c})) = g(\mathbf{c})$. So $g(\mathbf{x}) \leq g(\mathbf{c})$ for all **x** in S implies that $f(\mathbf{x}) \leq f(\mathbf{c})$ for all **x** in S.   ∎

NOTE 1   The proof of Theorem 13.6.3 is extremely simple. No continuity or differentiability assumptions are required. Instead, the proof is based only on the concepts of maximum/minimum, and of increasing/strictly increasing functions. Some people appear to distrust such simple, direct arguments and replace them by inefficient or even insufficient arguments based on "differentiating everything in sight" in order to use first- or second-order conditions. Such distrust merely makes matters unnecessarily complicated and risks introducing errors.

PROBLEMS FOR SECTION 13.6

1. Each of the following functions has a maximum point. Find it.

   (a) $f(x, y, z) = 2x - x^2 + 10y - y^2 + 3 - z^2$

   (b) $f(x, y, z) = 3 - x^2 - 2y^2 - 3z^2 - 2xy - 2xz$

2. (a) Suppose $f(x) = e^{-x^2}$ and $F(u) = \ln u$. Verify that $f(x)$ has maximum at $x = 0$ if and only if $g(x) = F(f(x))$ has a maximum at $x = 0$.

   (b) Suppose $f(x) = e^{-x^2}$ and $F(u) = 5$. Then $g(x) = F(f(x)) = 5$. Explain why this example shows that implication (a) in Theorem 13.6.3 cannot be reversed. (Recall that we call a constant function increasing.)

3. Suppose $g(\mathbf{x}) = F(f(\mathbf{x}))$ where $f : \mathbb{R}^n \to \mathbb{R}$ and $F : \mathbb{R} \to \mathbb{R}$ are differentiable functions, with $F' \neq 0$ everywhere. Prove that **x** is a stationary point for f if and only if it is a stationary point for g.

4. Find the first-order partial derivatives of the function of three variables given by

$$f(x, y, z) = -2x^3 + 15x^2 - 36x + 2y - 3z + \int_y^z e^{t^2}\, dt$$

   Then determine its eight stationary points.

5. Suggest how to simplify the following problems:

   (a) max $\frac{1}{2}\left(e^{x^2+y^2-2x} - e^{-(x^2+y^2-2x)}\right)$ subject to $(x, y) \in S$

   (b) max $Ax_1^{a_1} \cdots x_n^{a_n}$ subject to $x_1 + x_2 + \cdots + x_n = 1$
   Assume in (b) that $A > 0$ and $x_1 > 0, \ldots, x_n > 0$.

13.7 Comparative Statics and the Envelope Theorem

Optimization problems in economics usually involve maximizing or minimizing functions that depend not only on variables that can be chosen, but also on one or more parameters like prices, tax rates, income levels, etc. Although these parameters are held constant during the optimization, they vary according to the economic situation. For example, we may calculate a firm's profit-maximizing inputs and outputs treating the prices it faces as parameters, but then we may want to know how the optimal quantities respond to changes in those prices. So it is important to know what happens to the optimal solution when the situation changes— that is, when the parameters change.

Consider first the following simple problem. A function f depends on a single variable x as well as on a single parameter r. We wish to maximize or minimize $f(x, r)$ w.r.t. x while keeping r constant:

$$\max(\min)_x \ f(x, r)$$

The value of x that maximizes (minimizes) f will usually depend on r, so we denote it by $x^*(r)$. Inserting $x^*(r)$ into $f(x, r)$, we obtain

$$f^*(r) = f(x^*(r), r) \quad \text{(the \textbf{value function})}$$

What happens to the value function as r changes? Assuming that $f^*(r)$ is differentiable, the chain rule yields

$$\frac{df^*(r)}{dr} = f_1'(x^*(r), r)\frac{dx^*(r)}{dr} + f_2'(x^*(r), r)$$

If $f(x, r)$ has an extreme point at an interior point $x^*(r)$ in the domain of variation for x, then $f_1'(x^*(r), r) = 0$. It follows that

$$\frac{df^*(r)}{dr} = f_2'(x^*(r), r) \tag{1}$$

Note that when r is changed, then $f^*(r)$ changes for two reasons. First, a change in r changes the value of f^* directly because r is the second variable in $f(x, r)$. Second, a change in r changes the value of the function $x^*(r)$, and hence $f(x^*(r), r)$ is changed indirectly. Formula (1) shows that the total effect on the value function of a change in r is found simply by computing the partial derivative of $f(x^*(r), r)$ w.r.t. r, ignoring entirely the indirect effect of the dependence of x^* on r. At first sight, this seems very surprising. On further reflection, however, you may realize that the first-order condition for $x^*(r)$ to maximize $f(x, r)$ w.r.t. x implies that any small change in x, whether or not it is induced by a small change in r, must have a negligible effect on the value of $f(x^*, r)$.

EXAMPLE 1   Suppose that when a firm produces and sells x units of a commodity, it has revenue $R(x) = rx$, while the cost is $C(x) = x^2$, where r is a positive parameter. The profit is then

$$\pi(x, r) = R(x) - C(x) = rx - x^2$$

Find the optimal choice x^* of x, and verify (1) in this case.

Solution: The quadratic profit function has a maximum when $\pi_1' = r - 2x = 0$, that is for $x^* = r/2$. So the maximum profit as a function of r is given by $\pi^*(r) = rx^* - (x^*)^2 = r(r/2) - (r/2)^2 = r^2/4$, and then $d\pi^*/dr = r/2$. Using (1) we get the result more simply. Because $\pi_2'(x, r) = x$, (1) yields $d\pi^*/dr = \pi_2'(x^*(r), r) = x^*(r) = r/2$. ▮

EXAMPLE 2   In Example 8.6.5 we studied a firm with the profit function $\pi(Q, t) = R(Q) - C(Q) - tQ$, where t denoted a tax per unit produced. Let $Q^* = Q^*(t)$ denote the optimal choice of Q as a function of the tax rate t, and let $\pi^*(t)$ be the corresponding value function. Because $\pi_2' = -Q$, formula (1) yields

$$\frac{d\pi^*(t)}{dt} = \pi_2'(Q^*(t), t) = -Q^*(t)$$

which is the same result found earlier. ▮

It is easy to generalize (1) to the case with many choice variables and many parameters. We let $\mathbf{x} = (x_1, \ldots, x_n)$, and $\mathbf{r} = (r_1, \ldots, r_k)$. Then we can formulate the following result:

ENVELOPE THEOREM

If $f^*(\mathbf{r}) = \max_{\mathbf{x}} f(\mathbf{x}, \mathbf{r})$ and if $\mathbf{x}^*(\mathbf{r})$ is the value of $\mathbf{x}$ which maximizes $f(\mathbf{x}, \mathbf{r})$, then

$$\frac{\partial f^*(\mathbf{r})}{\partial r_j} = \left[\frac{\partial f(\mathbf{x}, \mathbf{r})}{\partial r_j} \right]_{\mathbf{x}=\mathbf{x}^*(\mathbf{r})} , \qquad j = 1, \ldots, k \tag{2}$$

provided that the partial derivative exists.

Again, $f^*(\mathbf{r})$ is the **value function** for the problem. It is easy to prove (2) by using the first-order conditions to eliminate other terms, as in the argument for (1). The same equality holds if we minimize $f(\mathbf{x}, \mathbf{r})$ w.r.t. $\mathbf{x}$ instead of maximize (or even if $\mathbf{x}^*(\mathbf{r})$ is any stationary point).

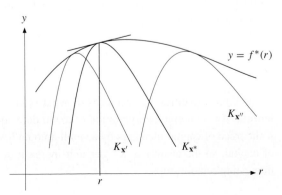

Figure 1 The curve $y = f^*(r)$ is the envelope of all the curves $y = f(\mathbf{x}, r)$

Figure 1 illustrates (2) in the case where there is only one parameter r. For each fixed value of $\mathbf{x}$ there is a curve $K_{\mathbf{x}}$ in the ry-plane, given by the equation $y = f(\mathbf{x}, r)$. Figure 1 shows some of these curves together with the graph of f^*, that is the curve $y = f^*(r)$. For all $\mathbf{x}$ and all r we have $f(\mathbf{x}, r) \leq \max_{\mathbf{x}} f(\mathbf{x}, r) = f^*(r)$. It follows that none of the $K_{\mathbf{x}}$-curves can ever lie above the curve $y = f^*(r)$. On the other hand, for each value of r there is at least one value $\mathbf{x}^*$ of $\mathbf{x}$ such that $f(\mathbf{x}^*, r) = f^*(r)$, namely the choice of $\mathbf{x}^*$ which solves the maximization problem for the given value of r. The curve $K_{\mathbf{x}^*}$ will then just touch the curve $y = f^*(r)$ at the point $(\mathbf{x}^*, f^*(r)) = (\mathbf{x}^*, f(\mathbf{x}^*, r))$, and so must have exactly the same tangent as the graph of f^* at this point. Moreover, the slope of this common tangent must be both df^*/dr, the slope of the tangent to the graph of f^*, and $\partial f(\mathbf{x}^*, r)/\partial r$, the slope of the tangent to the curve $K_{\mathbf{x}^*}$, which is the graph of $f(\mathbf{x}^*, r)$ when $\mathbf{x}^*$ is fixed. This is a geometric explanation of why $df^*/dr = (\partial/\partial r)f(\mathbf{x}^*, r)$ when there is only one parameter to consider.

As Fig. 1 suggests, the graph of $y = f^*(r)$ is the lowest curve with the property that it lies on or above all the curves $K_{\mathbf{x}}$. So its graph is like an envelope that is used to "wrap" or cover all these curves; for this reason we call the graph of f^* the **envelope** of the family of $K_{\mathbf{x}}$-curves. Also, result (2) is often called the **envelope theorem**.

EXAMPLE 3   In Example 13.1.3, $Q = F(K, L)$ denoted a production function with K as capital input and L as labour input. The price per unit of the product was p, the price per unit of capital was r, and the price per unit of labour was w. The profit obtained by using K and L units of the inputs, then producing and selling $F(K, L)$ units of the product, is given by

$$\hat{\pi}(K, L, p, r, w) = pF(K, L) - rK - wL$$

Here profit has been expressed as a new function $\hat{\pi}$ of the parameters p, r, and w, as well as of the choice variables K and L. We keep p, r, and w fixed and maximize $\hat{\pi}$ w.r.t. K and L. The optimal values of K and L are functions of p, r, and w, which we denote by $K^* = K^*(p, r, w)$ and $L^* = L^*(p, r, w)$. The value function for the problem is $\hat{\pi}^*(p, r, w) = \hat{\pi}(K^*, L^*, p, r, w)$. Usually, $\hat{\pi}^*$ is called the firm's **profit function**, though it would be more accurately described as the "maximum profit function". It is found by taking prices as given and choosing the optimal quantities of all inputs and outputs.

According to (2), one has

$$\frac{\partial \hat{\pi}^*}{\partial p} = F(K^*, L^*) = Q^*, \qquad \frac{\partial \hat{\pi}^*}{\partial r} = -K^*, \qquad \frac{\partial \hat{\pi}^*}{\partial w} = -L^* \qquad (*)$$

These three equalities are instances of what is known in producer theory as **Hotelling's lemma**. An economic interpretation of the middle equality is this: How much profit is lost if the price of capital increases by a small amount? At the optimum the firm uses K^* units of capital, so the answer is K^* per unit increase in the price. See Problem 3 for further interesting relationships.

1. A firm produces a single commodity and gets p for each unit sold. The cost of producing x units is $ax + bx^2$ and the tax per unit is t. Assume that the parameters are positive with $p > a + t$. The firm wants to maximize profits.

   (a) Find the optimal production x^* and the optimal profit π^*.

   (b) Prove that $\partial \pi^*/\partial p = x^*$, and give an economic interpretation.

2. A firm uses capital K, labour L, and land T to produce Q units of a commodity, where

$$Q = K^{2/3} + L^{1/2} + T^{1/3}$$

   (a) Suppose that the firm is paid p for each unit it produces, and that the prices it pays per unit of capital, labour, and land are r, w, and q, respectively. Find the values of K, L, and T (as functions of the four prices) that maximize the firm's profits,

$$\pi = p(K^{2/3} + L^{1/2} + T^{1/3}) - rK - wL - qT$$

   (All variables and all constants are positive, and you can assume that a maximum exists.)

   (b) Let Q^* denote the optimal number of units produced and K^* the optimal capital stock. Show that $\partial Q^*/\partial r = -\partial K^*/\partial p$.

3. With reference to Example 3, assuming that F is a C^2 function, prove the symmetry relations:

$$\frac{\partial Q^*}{\partial r} = -\frac{\partial K^*}{\partial p}, \quad \frac{\partial Q^*}{\partial w} = -\frac{\partial L^*}{\partial p}, \quad \frac{\partial L^*}{\partial r} = \frac{\partial K^*}{\partial w}$$

   (*Hint:* Using the first result in Example 3 and Young's theorem, we have the equalities $\partial Q^*/\partial r = (\partial/\partial r)(\partial \hat{\pi}^*/\partial p) = (\partial/\partial p)(\partial \hat{\pi}^*/\partial r)$. Now use the other results in Example 3.)

HARDER PROBLEMS

4. A profit-maximizing monopolist produces two commodities whose quantities are denoted by x_1 and x_2. Good 1 is subsidized at the rate of s per unit and good 2 is taxed at t per unit. The monopolist's profit function is therefore given by

$$\pi(x_1, x_2) = R(x_1, x_2) - C(x_1, x_2) + sx_1 - tx_2$$

   where R and C are the firm's revenue and cost functions, respectively. Assume that the partial derivatives of these functions have the following signs:

$$R'_1 > 0, \ R'_2 > 0, \ R''_{11} < 0, \ R''_{12} = R''_{21} < 0, \ R''_{22} < 0$$

$$C'_1 > 0, \ C'_2 > 0, \ C''_{11} > 0, \ C''_{12} = C''_{21} > 0, \ C''_{22} > 0$$

(a) Find the first-order conditions for maximum profits.

(b) Write down the local second-order conditions for maximum profits.

(c) Suppose that $x_1^* = x_1^*(s, t)$, $x_2^* = x_2^*(s, t)$ solve the problem. Find the signs of $\partial x_1^*/\partial s$, $\partial x_1^*/\partial t$, $\partial x_2^*/\partial s$, and $\partial x_2^*/\partial t$, assuming that the local second-order conditions are satisfied.

(d) Show that $\partial x_1^*/\partial t = -\partial x_2^*/\partial s$.

REVIEW PROBLEMS FOR CHAPTER 13

1. The function f defined for all (x, y) by $f(x, y) = -2x^2 + 2xy - y^2 + 18x - 14y + 4$ has a maximum. Find the corresponding values of x and y. Use Theorem 13.2.1 to prove that it is a maximum point.

2. A firm produces two different kinds A and B of a commodity. The daily cost of producing Q_1 units of A and Q_2 units of B is $C(Q_1, Q_2) = 0.1(Q_1^2 + Q_1 Q_2 + Q_2^2)$. Suppose that the firm sells all its output at a price per unit of $P_1 = 120$ for A and $P_2 = 90$ for B.

(a) Find the daily production levels that maximize profits.

(b) What price (P_1) per unit of A would imply that the optimal daily production level for A is 400 units?

3. A firms sells its output in the domestic market at a controlled price P_d, and in the world market at a price P_w which it treats as fixed. The quantities sold in the two markets are denoted by Q_d and Q_w, respectively. The cost is given by $c(Q_d + Q_w)$. (Note that c is here a function of one variable, not a constant.)

(a) Find the profit function $\pi(Q_d, Q_w)$.

(b) Write down the first-order condition for maximal profit at $Q_d^* > 0$, $Q_w^* > 0$, and give these conditions economic interpretations.

4. (a) Find all the first and second order partial derivatives of

$$f(x, y) = (x + y - 2)^2 + (x^2 + y - 2)^2$$

(b) Find the stationary points of f. Classify them by using the second-derivative test.

(c) Prove that f has two different minimum points.

5. (a) The profit obtained by a firm from producing and selling x and y units of two brands of a commodity is given by

$$P(x, y) = -0.1x^2 - 0.2xy - 0.2y^2 + 47x + 48y - 600$$

Find the production levels that maximize profits.

(b) A key raw material is rationed so that total production must be restricted to 200 units. Find the production levels that now maximize profits.

6. Find the stationary points of the following two functions:

   (a) $f(x, y) = x^3 - x^2y + y^2$

   (b) $g(x, y) = xye^{4x^2 - 5xy + y^2}$

7. (a) Find and classify (if possible) all the stationary points of

$$f(x, y) = \ln(2x + y + 2) - 2x - y$$

   (b) Sketch the domain $S = \{ (x, y) : x^2 + y^2 \leq 1, \ x + y \geq 0 \}$ and find the maximum value of the function f over this domain.

8. The function f is defined for all $x > 0$, $y > 0$ by

$$f(x, y) = \tfrac{1}{2}e^{-x-y} - e^{-x} - e^{-y}$$

   Find all the second-order partial derivatives of f, and show that $f(x, y)$ is concave. (*Hint:* $e^{-u} < 1$ for $u > 0$.)

9. Define $f(x, y)$ for all (x, y) by

$$f(x, y) = e^{x+y} + e^{x-y} - \tfrac{3}{2}x - \tfrac{1}{2}y$$

   (a) Find the first and second-order partial derivatives of f, then show that $f(x, y)$ is convex.

   (b) Find the minimum point of $f(x, y)$.

10. (a) Find and classify the stationary points of

$$f(x, y) = x^2 - y^2 - xy - x^3$$

   (b) Find the domain S where f is concave, and find the largest value f in S.

14

CONSTRAINED OPTIMIZATION

Mathematics is removed from this turmoil of human life, but its
methods and the relations are a mirror, an incredibly pure mirror,
of the relations that link facts of our existence.
—Konrad Knopp (1928)

In economic optimization problems, the variables to be chosen are often required to satisfy certain constraints. For example, the quantities of different goods demanded by a consumer must satisfy the budget constraint. This chapter introduces general constrained optimization problems.

In particular, the method of Lagrange multipliers is studied in detail. Sections 14.1–14.6 treat equality constraints, with Section 14.6 presenting some comparative static results and the envelope theorem. More general constrained optimization problems allowing inequality constraints are briefly introduced in Sections 14.7–14.8. A much fuller treatment of constrained optimization problems can be found in FMEA.

14.1 The Lagrange Multiplier Method

A typical economic example of a constrained optimization problem concerns a consumer who chooses how much of the available income m to spend on a good x whose price is p, and how much income to leave over for expenditure y on other goods. Note that the consumer then faces the budget constraint $px + y = m$. Suppose that preferences are represented by the utility function $u(x, y)$. In mathematical terms, therefore, the consumer faces the problem of choosing (x, y) in order to maximize $u(x, y)$ subject to the budget constraint $px + y = m$. This can be expressed as

$$\max u(x, y) \quad \text{subject to} \quad px + y = m$$

This is a typical *constrained maximization problem.* In this case, because $y = m - px$, the same problem can be expressed as the *unconstrained maximization* of the function $h(x) = u(x, m - px)$ w.r.t. the single variable x. Indeed, this method of reducing an optimization problem involving two variables to a one-variable problem was used in Section 13.2.

However, when the constraint is a complicated function, or when there are several equality constraints to consider, this substitution method might be difficult or impossible to carry out in practice. In such cases, other techniques should be used. In particular, economists make much use of the *Lagrange multiplier method*. Actually, the same method is often used by economists even for problems that are quite easy to express as unconstrained problems. One reason is that Lagrange multipliers have an important economic interpretation.[1] In addition, a similar method works for many more complicated optimization problems, such as those where the constraints are expressed in terms of inequalities.

Consider first the problem of maximizing (or minimizing) a function $f(x, y)$ when x and y are restricted to satisfy an equality constraint $g(x, y) = c$:

$$\max(\min) f(x, y) \quad \text{subject to} \quad g(x, y) = c \tag{1}$$

The first step of the method is to introduce a **Lagrange multiplier**, often denoted by λ, which is associated with the constraint $g(x, y) = c$. Then we define the **Lagrangian function** $\mathcal{L}$ by

$$\mathcal{L}(x, y) = f(x, y) - \lambda(g(x, y) - c) \tag{2}$$

in which the expression $g(x, y) - c$, which must be 0 when the constraint is satisfied, has been multiplied by λ. In fact, we see that $\mathcal{L}(x, y) = f(x, y)$ for all (x, y) which satisfy the constraint $g(x, y) = c$.

The Lagrange multiplier λ is a constant, so the partial derivatives of $\mathcal{L}(x, y)$ w.r.t. x and y are $\mathcal{L}_1'(x, y) = f_1'(x, y) - \lambda g_1'(x, y)$ and $\mathcal{L}_2'(x, y) = f_2'(x, y) - \lambda g_2'(x, y)$, respectively. As will be explained in the next section, a solution of problem (1) can only be a point at which, for a suitable value of λ, the first-order partial derivatives of $\mathcal{L}$ vanish. In Section 14.3 we give a geometric interpretation of the method and argue why it must lead to the right result, except in rare cases.

Here is an example of an economic application.

EXAMPLE 1   A consumer has the utility function $U(x, y) = xy$ and faces the budget constraint $2x + y = 100$. Find the only solution candidate to the consumer demand problem

$$\text{maximize } xy \quad \text{subject to} \quad 2x + y = 100$$

Solution: The Lagrangian is

$$\mathcal{L}(x, y) = xy - \lambda(2x + y - 100)$$

So the first-order conditions for the solution of the problem are

$$\mathcal{L}_1'(x, y) = y - 2\lambda = 0, \qquad \mathcal{L}_2'(x, y) = x - \lambda = 0, \qquad 2x + y = 100$$

---

[1] The method is named after its discoverer, the Italian/French mathematician J. L. Lagrange (1736–1813). The Danish economist Harald Westergaard seems to be the first who used it in economics, in 1876.

The first two equations imply that $y = 2\lambda$ and $x = \lambda$. So $y = 2x$. Inserting this into the constraint yields $2x + 2x = 100$. So $x = 25$ and $y = 50$, implying that $\lambda = x = 25$.

This solution can be confirmed by the substitution method. From $2x + y = 100$ we get $y = 100 - 2x$, so the problem is reduced to maximizing the unconstrained function $h(x) = x(100 - 2x) = -2x^2 + 100x$. Since $h'(x) = -4x + 100 = 0$ gives $x = 25$, and $h''(x) = -4 < 0$ for all x, this shows that $x = 25$ *is* a maximum point. ∎

Example 1 illustrates the following general method:[2]

THE LAGRANGE MULTIPLIER METHOD

To find the only possible solutions of the problem

$$\text{maximize (minimize)} \quad f(x, y) \quad \text{subject to} \quad g(x, y) = c$$

proceed as follows:

(I) Write down the Lagrangian function

$$\mathcal{L}(x, y) = f(x, y) - \lambda(g(x, y) - c)$$

where λ is a constant.

(II) Differentiate $\mathcal{L}$ w.r.t. x and y, and equate the partial derivatives to 0.

(III) The two equations in (II), together with the constraint, yield the following three equations:

$$\mathcal{L}_1'(x, y) = f_1'(x, y) - \lambda g_1'(x, y) = 0$$
$$\mathcal{L}_2'(x, y) = f_2'(x, y) - \lambda g_2'(x, y) = 0$$
$$g(x, y) = c$$

(IV) Solve these three equations simultaneously for the three unknowns x, y, and λ.

The conditions in (III) are called the *first-order conditions* for problem (1).

NOTE 1 Some economists prefer to consider the Lagrangian as a function $\mathcal{L}(x, y, \lambda)$ of three variables. Then the first-order condition $\partial \mathcal{L}/\partial \lambda = -[g(x, y) - c] = 0$ yields the constraint. In this way all the three necessary conditions are obtained by equating the partial derivatives of the (extended) Lagrangian to 0. However, it does seem somewhat unnatural to perform a differentiation to get an obvious necessary condition, namely the constraint equation. Also, this procedure can easily lead to trouble when treating problems with inequality constraints, so we prefer to avoid it.

---
[2] If $g_1'(x, y)$ and $g_2'(x, y)$ both vanish, the method might fail to give the right answer.

EXAMPLE 2   Solve the problem

$$\max \text{(min)} \ f(x, y) = x^2 + y^2 \quad \text{subject to} \quad g(x, y) = x^2 + xy + y^2 = 3$$

Solution: The Lagrangian in this case is

$$\mathcal{L}(x, y) = x^2 + y^2 - \lambda(x^2 + xy + y^2 - 3)$$

The three equations to consider are

$$\mathcal{L}'_1(x, y) = 2x - \lambda(2x + y) = 0 \tag{i}$$
$$\mathcal{L}'_2(x, y) = 2y - \lambda(x + 2y) = 0 \tag{ii}$$
$$x^2 + xy + y^2 - 3 = 0 \tag{iii}$$

Let us eliminate λ from (i) and (ii). From (i) we get $\lambda = 2x/(2x + y)$ provided $y \neq -2x$. Inserting this value of λ into (ii) gives

$$2y = \frac{2x}{2x + y}(x + 2y)$$

After simplification, this reduces to $y^2 = x^2$, so $y = x$ or $y = -x$.

Suppose $y = x$. Then (iii) yields $x^2 = 1$, so $x = 1$ or $x = -1$. This gives the two solution candidates $(x, y) = (1, 1)$ and $(-1, -1)$, with $\lambda = 2/3$.

Suppose $y = -x$. Then (iii) yields $x^2 = 3$, so $x = \sqrt{3}$ or $x = -\sqrt{3}$. This gives the two solution candidates $(x, y) = (\sqrt{3}, -\sqrt{3})$ and $(-\sqrt{3}, \sqrt{3})$, with $\lambda = 2$.

It remains to consider the case $y = -2x$. Then from (i), $x = 0$ and so $y = 0$. But this contradicts (iii), so this case cannot occur.

We have found the only four points (x, y) that can solve the problem. Furthermore,

$$f(1, 1) = f(-1, -1) = 2, \qquad f(\sqrt{3}, -\sqrt{3}) = f(-\sqrt{3}, \sqrt{3}) = 6$$

We conclude that if the problem has solutions, then $(1, 1)$ and $(-1, -1)$ solve the minimization problem, whereas $(\sqrt{3}, -\sqrt{3})$ and $(-\sqrt{3}, \sqrt{3})$ solve the maximization problem.

Geometrically, the constraint describes an ellipse and the problem is to find the points on the ellipse that are nearest to and furthest from the origin. See Fig. 1.

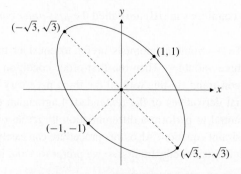

Figure 1

Here is an alternative way of proving that $(x, y) = (1, 1)$ minimizes $f(x, y) = x^2 + y^2$ subject to the constraint $x^2 + xy + y^2 = 3$. (The other points are treated in the same way.) Note, however, that this method works only in special cases.

Let $x = 1 + h$ and $y = 1 + k$. Thus h and k measure the deviation of x and y, respectively, from 1. Then $f(x, y)$ takes the form

$$f(x, y) = (1 + h)^2 + (1 + k)^2 = 2 + 2(h + k) + h^2 + k^2 \qquad (*)$$

If $(x, y) = (1 + h, 1 + k)$ satisfies the constraint, then $(1 + h)^2 + (1 + h)(1 + k) + (1 + k)^2 = 3$, so $h + k = -hk/3 - (h^2 + k^2)/3$. Inserting this expression for $h + k$ into $(*)$ yields

$$f(x, y) = 2 + 2\left[-\tfrac{1}{3}hk - \tfrac{1}{3}(h^2 + k^2)\right] + h^2 + k^2 = 2 + \tfrac{1}{3}(h - k)^2$$

Because $\tfrac{1}{3}(h - k)^2 \geq 0$ for all (h, k), it follows that $f(x, y) \geq 2$ for all values of (x, y). But because $f(1, 1) = 2$, this means that $(1, 1)$ really does minimize $f(x, y)$ subject to the constraint. ∎

EXAMPLE 3   A consumer has Cobb–Douglas utility function $U(x, y) = Ax^a y^b$ and faces the budget constraint $px + qy = m$, where A, a, b, p, q, and m are positive constants. Find the only solution candidate to the consumer demand problem

$$\max\ Ax^a y^b \quad \text{subject to} \quad px + qy = m \qquad (*)$$

Solution: The Lagrangian is

$$\mathcal{L}(x, y) = Ax^a y^b - \lambda(px + qy - m)$$

So the first-order conditions are

$$\mathcal{L}'_1(x, y) = aAx^{a-1}y^b - \lambda p = 0, \qquad \mathcal{L}'_2(x, y) = bAx^a y^{b-1} - \lambda q = 0, \qquad px + qy = m$$

Solving the first two equations for λ yields

$$\lambda = \frac{aAx^{a-1}y^b}{p} = \frac{bAx^a y^{b-1}}{q}$$

Cancelling the factor $Ax^{a-1}y^{b-1}$ from the last two fractions gives

$$\frac{ay}{p} = \frac{bx}{q}$$

Solving this equation for qy yields $qy = (b/a)px$, which inserted into the budget constraint gives $px + (b/a)px = m$. From this equation we find x and then y. The results are the following **demand functions**:

$$x = x(p, q, m) = \frac{a}{a + b}\frac{m}{p}, \qquad y = y(p, q, m) = \frac{b}{a + b}\frac{m}{q} \qquad (**)$$

(It follows from $(**)$ that for all t one has $x(tp, tq, tm) = x(p, q, m)$ and $y(tp, tq, tm) = y(p, q, m)$, so the demand functions are homogeneous of degree 0. This is as to be expected because if (p, q, m) is changed to (tp, tq, tm), then the constraint in (∗) is unchanged, and so the optimal choices of x and y are unchanged. See also Example 12.6.4.)

The solution we have found make good sense. In the utility function $Ax^a y^b$, the sizes of the coefficients a and b indicate the relative importance of x and y in the individual's preferences. For instance, if a is larger than b, then the consumer values a 1% increase in x more than a 1% increase in y. The product px is the amount spent on the first good, and (∗∗) says that the consumer should spend the fraction $a/(a+b)$ of income on this good and the fraction $b/(a+b)$ on the second good. For example, in the special case when $a = 1/2$ and $b = 1/3$, (∗∗) implies that the optimal solution satisfies

$$px = \frac{\frac{1}{2}}{\frac{1}{2} + \frac{1}{3}}m = \frac{3}{5}m, \qquad py = \frac{\frac{1}{3}}{\frac{1}{2} + \frac{1}{3}}m = \frac{2}{5}m$$

In this way you can immediately find the correct answer to thousands of exam problems in mathematical economics courses given each year all over the world! But note that the utility function has to be of the Cobb–Douglas type $Ax^a y^b$. For the problem $\max x^a + y^b$ subject to $px + qy = m$, the solution is not given by (∗∗). (See Problem 14.4.3.)

There is an underlying assumption in problem (∗) that $x \geq 0$ and $y \geq 0$. Thus, we maximize a continuous function $Ax^a y^b$ over a closed bounded set $S = \{(x, y) : px + qy = m, x \geq 0, y \geq 0\}$. According to the Extreme-Value Theorem, a maximum must exist. Since utility is 0 when $x = 0$ or when $y = 0$, and positive at the point given by (∗∗), this point indeed solves the problem.   ▌

PROBLEMS FOR SECTION 14.1

1. (a) Use the Lagrange multiplier method to find the solution to the problem:

$$\max xy \quad \text{subject to} \quad x + 3y = 24$$

(b) Check the solution by using (∗∗) in Example 3.

In Problems 2–4, find the only solution candidates to the constrained optimization problems. When there are several candidates, pick the one which gives the largest (or smallest) value to the objective function.

2. (a) min $f(x, y) = x^2 + y^2$ subject to $g(x, y) = x + 2y = 4$

   (b) min $f(x, y) = x^2 + 2y^2$ subject to $g(x, y) = x + y = 12$

3. (a) max(min) $3xy$ subject to $x^2 + y^2 = 8$

   (b) max(min) $x + y$ subject to $x^2 + 3xy + 3y^2 = 3$

4. (a) max $x^2 + y^2 - 2x + 1$ subject to $x^2 + 4y^2 = 16$

   (b) max $x^2 + 3xy + y^2$ subject to $x + y = 100$

5. Solve the following problems using (∗∗) in Example 3.

(a) max $10x^{1/2}y^{1/3}$ subject to $2x + 4y = m$

(b) max $x^{1/2}y^{1/2}$ subject to $50\,000x + 0.08y = 1\,000\,000$

(c) max $12x\sqrt{y}$ subject to $3x + 4y = 12$

HARDER PROBLEMS

6. Consider the problem max $U(x, y) = 100 - e^{-x} - e^{-y}$ subject to $px + qy = m$.

(a) Write down the first-order conditions for the problem and solve them for x, y, and λ as functions of p, q, and m.

(b) Verify that x and y are homogeneous of degree 0 as functions of p, q, and m.

14.2 Interpreting the Lagrange Multiplier

Consider again the problem

$$\max(\min) f(x, y) \quad \text{subject to} \quad g(x, y) = c$$

Suppose x^* and y^* are the values of x and y that solve this problem. In general, x^* and y^* depend on c. We *assume* that $x^* = x^*(c)$ and $y^* = y^*(c)$ are differentiable functions of c. The associated value of $f(x, y)$ is then also a function of c, with

$$f^*(c) = f(x^*(c), y^*(c)) \tag{1}$$

Here $f^*(c)$ is called the **(optimal) value function** for the problem. Of course, the associated value of the Lagrange multiplier also depends on c, in general. Provided that certain regularity conditions are satisfied, we have the remarkable result that

$$\frac{df^*(c)}{dc} = \lambda(c) \tag{2}$$

Thus, *the Lagrange multiplier $\lambda = \lambda(c)$ is the rate at which the optimal value of the objective function changes with respect to changes in the constraint constant c.*

Proof of (2) (assuming that $f^*(c)$ is differentiable): Taking the differential of (1) gives

$$df^*(c) = df(x^*, y^*) = f_1'(x^*, y^*)\,dx^* + f_2'(x^*, y^*)\,dy^* \tag{∗}$$

But from the first-order conditions we have $f_1'(x^*, y^*) = \lambda g_1'(x^*, y^*)$ and $f_2'(x^*, y^*) = \lambda g_2'(x^*, y^*)$, so (∗) can be written as

$$df^*(c) = \lambda g_1'(x^*, y^*)\,dx^* + \lambda g_2'(x^*, y^*)\,dy^* = \lambda[g_1'(x^*, y^*)\,dx^* + g_2'(x^*, y^*)\,dy^*] \tag{∗∗}$$

Moreover, taking the differential of the identity $g(x^*(c), y^*(c)) = c$ yields

$$g_1'(x^*, y^*)\,dx^* + g_2'(x^*, y^*)\,dy^* = dc$$

So (∗∗) implies that $df^*(c) = \lambda\,dc$.   ∎

In particular, if dc is a small change in c, then

$$f^*(c + dc) - f^*(c) \approx \lambda(c)\,dc \tag{3}$$

In economic applications, c often denotes the available stock of some resource, and $f(x, y)$ denotes utility or profit. Then $\lambda(c)\,dc$ measures the approximate change in utility or profit that can be obtained from dc units more (or less, when $dc < 0$) of the resource. Economists call λ a **shadow price** of the resource.

EXAMPLE 1   Suppose $Q = F(K, L)$ denotes the output of a firm when the input of capital is K and that of labour is L. Suppose the prices of capital and labour are r and w, respectively, and that the firm has m dollars to spend on the two input factors. The firm wishes to find the choice of inputs it can afford which maximizes output. So it faces the problem

$$\max F(K, L) \quad \text{subject to} \quad rK + wL = m$$

Solving this problem by using Lagrange's method, the value of the Lagrange multiplier will tells us approximately the increase in output if m is increased by 1 dollar.

Consider, for example, the specific problem

$$\max 120KL \quad \text{subject to} \quad 2K + 5L = m$$

Note that this is a special case of the problem in Example 14.1.3; only the notation is different. From (**) in Example 14.1.3 we find the solution

$$K^* = \tfrac{1}{4}m, \quad L^* = \tfrac{1}{10}m \quad \text{with} \quad \lambda = 6m$$

The optimal output is $Q^*(m) = 120K^*L^* = 120\tfrac{1}{4}m\tfrac{1}{10}m = 3m^2$, so $dQ^*/dm = 6m = \lambda$, and (2) is confirmed. In particular, if $m = 100$, then $K^* = 25$, $L^* = 10$, $\lambda = 600$, and $Q^* = 3 \cdot 100^2 = 30\,000$. If we increase m to 101, the optimal solution is $\widehat{K} = 101/4 = 25.25$, $\widehat{L} = 101/10 = 10.1$, and $\widehat{Q} = 3 \cdot 101^2 = 30\,603$. Note that $\lambda = 600$ is a good approximation to the actual increase in output allowed by increasing m from 100 to 101, which is $\widehat{Q} - Q^* = 603$.

1. Verify that equation (2) holds for the problem: max x^2y subject to $2x + 3y = m$.

2. Consider the problem max $f(x, y) = x + y$ subject to $g(x, y) = x^2 + y = 1$.

   (a) Write down the Lagrangian function for the problem and solve the necessary conditions in this case.

   (b) Explain the solution geometrically by drawing appropriate level curves for $f(x, y)$ together with the graph of the parabola $x^2 + y = 1$. Does the associated minimization problem have a solution?

(c) Replace the constraint by $x^2 + y = 1.1$, and solve the problem in this case. Find the corresponding change in the optimal value of $f(x, y) = x + y$, and check to see if this change is approximately equal to $\lambda \cdot 0.1$, as suggested by (3).

3. An individual has Cobb–Douglas utility function $U(m, l) = Am^a l^b$, where m is income and l is leisure. A, a, and b are positive constants, $a + b \leq 1$. A total of T_0 hours are allocated between work W and leisure l, so that $W + l = T_0$, If the hourly wage is w, then $m = wW$, and the individual's problem is

$$\max Am^a l^b \quad \text{subject to} \quad (m/w) + l = T_0$$

Solve the problem by using (∗∗) in Example 14.1.3.

4. (a) Solve the utility maximization problem

$$\max U(x, y) = \sqrt{x} + y \quad \text{subject to} \quad x + 4y = 100$$

using the Lagrange method, i.e. find the quantities demanded of the two goods.

(b) Suppose income increases from 100 to 101. What is the exact increase in the optimal value of $U(x, y)$? Compare with the value found in (a) for the Lagrange multiplier.

(c) Suppose we change the budget constraint to $px + qy = m$, but keep the same utility function. Derive the quantities demanded of the two goods if $m > q^2/4p$.

HARDER PROBLEMS

5. An oil producer starts extracting oil from a well at time $t = 0$. Suppose that all the oil will be extracted during the time interval $[0, y]$, and that the output per unit of time at time $t \in [0, y]$ is $xt(y - t)$ barrels. Assume that the producer can choose the size of x as well as that of y. The total amount of oil extracted in the given time span is thus given by the function $g(x, y) = \int_0^y xt(y - t)\, dt$ of x and y. Assume further that the sales price p per barrel of oil is an increasing function of time, $p = 1 + t$, and that the cost per barrel oil extracted is equal to αy^2, where α is a positive constant. The profit per unit of time is then $(1 + t - \alpha y^2)xt(y - t)$, so that the total profit earned during the time interval $[0, y]$ is a function of x and y given by $f(x, y) = \int_0^y (1 + t - \alpha y^2) xt\, (y - t)\, dt$. If the total amount of extractable oil in the field is M barrels, the producer can choose values of x and y such that $g(x, y) = M$. The producer's problem is thus

$$\max f(x, y) \quad \text{subject to} \quad g(x, y) = M \qquad (*)$$

Find explicit expressions for $f(x, y)$ and $g(x, y)$ by calculating the given integrals, and then solve problem (∗). Verify Equation (2) in this case.

14.3 Why the Lagrange Multiplier Method Works

We have explained the Lagrange multiplier method for solving the constrained optimization problem

$$\max(\min) f(x, y) \quad \text{subject to} \quad g(x, y) = c \tag{1}$$

In this section we give a geometric as well as an analytic argument for the method.

A Geometric Argument

The maximization problem in (1) can be given a geometric interpretation, as shown in Fig. 1. The graph of f is like the surface of an inverted bowl, whereas the equation $g(x, y) = c$ represents a curve in the xy-plane. The curve K on the bowl is the one that lies directly above the curve $g(x, y) = c$. (The latter curve is the projection of K onto the xy-plane.) Maximizing $f(x, y)$ without taking the constraint into account gets us to the peak A in Fig. 1. The solution to problem (1), however, is at B, which is the highest point on the curve K. If we think of the graph of f as representing a mountain, and K as a mountain path, then we seek the highest point on the path, which is B. Analytically, the problem is to find the coordinates of B.

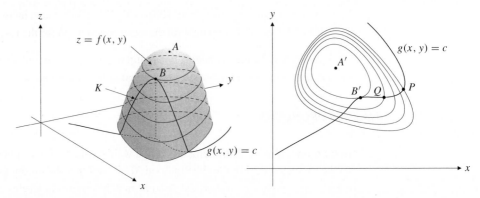

Figure 1

The right half of Fig. 1 shows some of the level curves for f, and also indicates the constraint curve $g(x, y) = c$. Now A' represents the point at which $f(x, y)$ has its unconstrained (free) maximum. The closer a level curve of f is to point A', the higher is the value of f along that level curve. We are seeking that point on the constraint curve $g(x, y) = c$ where f has its highest value. If we start at point P on the constraint curve and move along that curve toward A', we encounter level curves with higher and higher values of f. Obviously, the point Q indicated in Fig. 1 is not the point on $g(x, y) = c$ at which f has its highest value, because the constraint curve passes *through* the level curve of f at that point. Therefore, we can cross a level curve to higher values of f by proceeding further along the constraint curve. However, when we reach point B', we cannot go any higher. It is intuitively clear that B' is characterized as that point where the constraint curve touches (without intersecting) a level curve for f. This observation implies that the slope of the tangent to the curve $g(x, y) = c$ at (x, y) is equal to the slope of the tangent to the level curve of f at that point.

Recall from Section 12.3 that the slope of the level curve $F(x, y) = c$ is given by $dy/dx = -F_1'(x, y)/F_2'(x, y)$. Thus, the condition that the slope of the tangent to $g(x, y) = c$ is equal to the slope of a level curve for $f(x, y)$ can be expressed analytically as follows:[3]

$$-\frac{g_1'(x, y)}{g_2'(x, y)} = -\frac{f_1'(x, y)}{f_2'(x, y)}$$

or

$$\frac{f_1'(x, y)}{g_1'(x, y)} = \frac{f_2'(x, y)}{g_2'(x, y)} \qquad (2)$$

It follows that a necessary condition for (x, y) to solve problem (1) is that the left- and right-hand sides of (2) are equal at (x, y). Let λ denote the common value of these fractions. This is the Lagrange multiplier introduced in the previous section. Thus equation (2) can be expressed as

$$f_1'(x, y) - \lambda g_1'(x, y) = 0, \qquad f_2'(x, y) - \lambda g_2'(x, y) = 0 \qquad (3)$$

Using the Lagrangian function from the previous section, we see that (2) just tells us that the Lagrangian has a stationary point.

A corresponding argument for the problem of minimizing $f(x, y)$ subject to $g(x, y) = c$ gives the same condition.

An Analytic Argument

The geometric argument above is quite convincing. But the analytic argument we are about to offer is easier to generalize and does not rely on a geometric interpretation of the problem.

So far we have studied the problem of finding the absolute largest or smallest value of $f(x, y)$ subject to the constraint $g(x, y) = c$. Sometimes we are interested in studying the corresponding local extrema. The problem is briefly formulated:

$$\text{local max(min)} \ f(x, y) \quad \text{subject to} \quad g(x, y) = c \qquad (4)$$

Possible solutions are illustrated in Fig. 2.

Figure 2

---

[3] Disregard for the moment cases where any denominator is 0.

The point R is a local minimum point for $f(x, y)$ subject to $g(x, y) = c$, whereas Q and P are local maximum points. The global maximum of $f(x, y)$ subject to $g(x, y) = c$ is attained only at P. Each of the points P, Q, and R in Fig. 2 satisfies condition (2), so the first-order conditions are exactly as before. Let us derive them in a way which does not rely on geometric intuition. Except in some special cases, the equation $g(x, y) = c$ defines y implicitly as a differentiable function of x near any local extreme point. Denote this function by $y = h(x)$. According to formula (12.3.1), provided that $g_2'(x, y) \neq 0$, one has

$$y' = h'(x) = -g_1'(x, y)/g_2'(x, y)$$

Now, the objective function $z = f(x, y) = f(x, h(x))$ is, in effect, a function of x alone. By calculating dz/dx while taking into account how y depends on x, we obtain a necessary condition for local extreme points by equating dz/dx to 0. But

$$\frac{dz}{dx} = f_1'(x, y) + f_2'(x, y)y' \qquad \text{(with } y' = h'(x)\text{)}$$

So substituting the previous expression for $h'(x)$ gives the following necessary condition for (x, y) to solve problem (1):

$$\frac{dz}{dx} = f_1'(x, y) - f_2'(x, y)\frac{g_1'(x, y)}{g_2'(x, y)} = 0 \tag{5}$$

Assuming that $g_2'(x, y) \neq 0$, and defining $\lambda = f_2'(x, y)/g_2'(x, y)$, we deduce that the two equations $f_1'(x, y) - \lambda g_1'(x, y) = 0$ and $f_2'(x, y) - \lambda g_2'(x, y) = 0$ must both be satisfied. Hence, the Lagrangian must be stationary at (x, y). An analogous argument shows that, provided $g_1'(x, y) \neq 0$, again the Lagrangian partial derivatives must be 0. To summarize, one can prove the following precise result:

THEOREM 14.3.1 (LAGRANGE'S THEOREM)

Suppose that $f(x, y)$ and $g(x, y)$ have continuous partial derivatives in a domain A of the xy-plane, and that (x_0, y_0) is both an interior point of A and a local extreme point for $f(x, y)$ subject to the constraint $g(x, y) = c$. Suppose further that $g_1'(x_0, y_0)$ and $g_2'(x_0, y_0)$ are not both 0. Then there exists a unique number λ such that the Lagrangian function

$$\mathcal{L}(x, y) = f(x, y) - \lambda(g(x, y) - c)$$

has a stationary point at (x_0, y_0).

Problem 3 shows how trouble can result from uncritical use of the Lagrange multiplier method, disregarding the assumptions in Theorem 14.3.1. Problem 4 shows what can go wrong if $g_1'(x_0, y_0)$ and $g_2'(x_0, y_0)$ are both 0.

In constrained optimization problems in economics, it is often implicitly assumed that the variables are nonnegative. This is certainly the case in the utility maximization problem in Example 14.1.3. Because the optimal solutions were positive, nothing was lost by disregarding the nonnegativity constraints. Here is an example showing that sometimes we must take greater care.

EXAMPLE 1   Consider the utility maximization problem

$$\max xy + x + 2y \quad \text{subject to} \quad 2x + y = m, \quad x \geq 0, \ y \geq 0$$

where we explicitly have required that the amount of each good must be nonnegative. The Lagrangian is $\mathcal{L} = xy + x + 2y - \lambda(2x + y - m)$. So the first-order conditions (disregarding the nonnegativity constraints for the moment) are

$$\mathcal{L}'_1(x, y) = y + 1 - 2\lambda = 0, \quad \mathcal{L}'_2(x, y) = x + 2 - \lambda = 0$$

By eliminating λ, we find that $y = 2x + 3$. Inserting this into the budget constraint gives $2x + 2x + 3 = m$, so $x = \frac{1}{4}(m - 3)$. We easily find the corresponding value of y, and the suggested solution which emerges is

$$x^* = \tfrac{1}{4}(m - 3), \qquad y^* = \tfrac{1}{2}(m + 3)$$

Note that in the case when $m < 3$, then $x^* < 0$, so that the expressions we have found for x^* and y^* do not solve the given problem. The solution in this case is, as we shall see below, $x^* = 0$, $y^* = m$. (So when income is low, the consumer should spend everything on just one commodity.)

Let us analyse the problem by converting it so that it becomes unconstrained. From the constraint we get $y = m - 2x$. In order for both x and y to be nonnegative, one must require $0 \leq x \leq m/2$ and $0 \leq y \leq m$. Substituting $y = m - 2x$ into the utility function, we obtain utility as function $N(x)$ of x alone, where

$$N(x) = x(m - 2x) + x + 2(m - 2x) = -2x^2 + (m - 3)x + 2m, \quad x \in [0, m/2]$$

This is a quadratic function with $x = \frac{1}{4}(m - 3)$ as the stationary point. If $m > 3$, it is an interior stationary point for the concave function N, so it is a maximum point. If $m \leq 3$, then $N'(x) = -4x + (m - 3) \leq 0$ for all $x \geq 0$. Because of the constraint $x \geq 0$, it follows that $N(x)$ must have its largest value for $x = 0$.

Optimization problems with inequality constraints are generally known as *nonlinear programming problems*. Some relatively simple cases are discussed in Sections 14.7 and 14.8. A much more systematic treatment of nonlinear programming will be included in FMEA.

NOTE 1 One of the most frequently occurring errors in the economics literature concerning the Lagrange multiplier method is the claim that it transforms a constrained optimization problem into one of finding an unconstrained optimum of the Lagrangian. Problem 1 shows that this is wrong. What the method does instead is to transform a constrained optimization problem into one of finding the appropriate stationary points of the Lagrangian.

PROBLEMS FOR SECTION 14.3

1. Consider the problem max xy subject to $x + y = 2$. Using the Lagrange multiplier method, prove that $(x, y) = (1, 1)$ solves the problem with $\lambda = 1$. Prove also that $(1, 1)$ does not maximize the Lagrangian function $\mathcal{L}(x, y) = xy - 1 \cdot (x + y - 2)$.

2. The following text taken from a book on mathematics for management contains *grave* errors. Sort them out. "Consider the general problem of finding the extreme points of $z = f(x, y)$ subject to the constraint $g(x, y) = 0$. Clearly the extreme points must satisfy the pair of equations $f'_x(x, y) = 0$, $f'_y(x, y) = 0$ in addition to the constraint $g(x, y) = 0$. Thus, there are three equations that must be satisfied by the pair of unknowns x, y. Because there are more equations than unknowns, the system is said to be overdetermined and, in general, is difficult to solve. In order to facilitate computation ..." (A description of the Lagrange method follows.)

HARDER PROBLEMS

3. Consider the problem:

$$\text{max } f(x, y) = 2x + 3y \text{ subject to } g(x, y) = \sqrt{x} + \sqrt{y} = 5$$

(a) Show that the Lagrange multiplier method suggests the wrong solution $(x, y) = (9, 4)$. (Note that $f(9, 4) = 30$, and yet $f(25, 0) = 50$.)

(b) Solve the problem by studying the level curves of $f(x, y) = 2x + 3y$, and the graph of the constraint equation. (See Problem 5.4.3.)

(c) Explain why Theorem 14.3.1 cannot be used to find the solution.

4. The functions f and g are defined by

$$f(x, y) = (x + 2)^2 + y^2 \quad \text{and} \quad g(x, y) = y^2 - x(x + 1)^2$$

Find the minimum value of $f(x, y)$ subject to $g(x, y) = 0$. Show that the Lagrange multiplier method cannot locate this minimum. (*Hint:* Draw a graph of $g(x, y) = 0$. Note in particular that $(-1, 0)$ is on the graph.)

14.4 Sufficient Conditions

Under the hypotheses of Theorem 14.3.1, the Lagrange multiplier method for the problem

$$\max(\min) f(x, y) \quad \text{subject to} \quad g(x, y) = c \qquad (1)$$

gives *necessary* conditions for the solution. In order to ascertain that we have really found the solution, however, some more careful checking is needed. We have seen in examples and problems that sometimes geometric interpretations of the problem can strongly suggest that the solutions are found. If the constraint set is a closed bounded set, then the extreme value theorem will guarantee that a continuous function *will* attain both maximum and miminum values over this set. In Example 14.1.2, for example, the constraint set *is* closed and bounded (see Fig. 14.1.1), so the continuous function $f(x, y) = x^2 + y^2$ will attain a maximum and a minimum over the constraint set. Since there are 4 points satisfying the first-order conditions, it remains only to check which of them gives f its highest and lowest value. (To test your understanding of when this procedure can be used, explain why it certainly works in Problems 14.1.3(a) and 14.1.4(a), but not in Problems 14.1.1, 14.1.2(a), or 14.1.6, to mention just a few.) In some cases, ad hoc methods of the kind illustrated at the end of Example 14.1.2 can be used.

Concave/Convex Lagrangian

If (x_0, y_0) does solve problem (1), then the Lagrangian $\mathcal{L}(x, y) = f(x, y) - \lambda(g(x, y) - c)$ is stationary at (x_0, y_0), but $\mathcal{L}$ does not necessarily have a maximum (minimum) at (x_0, y_0) (see Problem 14.3.1). Suppose, however, that (x_0, y_0) happens to maximize $\mathcal{L}(x, y)$ among all (x, y). Then

$$\mathcal{L}(x_0, y_0) = f(x_0, y_0) - \lambda(g(x_0, y_0) - c) \geq \mathcal{L}(x, y) = f(x, y) - \lambda(g(x, y) - c) \quad (*)$$

for all (x, y). If (x_0, y_0) also satisfies the constraint $g(x_0, y_0) = c$, then from $(*)$ we conclude that $f(x_0, y_0) \geq f(x, y)$ for all (x, y) such that $g(x, y) = c$. Hence, (x_0, y_0) really does solve the maximization problem (1). A corresponding result is obtained for the minimization problem in (1), provided that (x_0, y_0) minimizes $\mathcal{L}(x, y)$ among all pairs (x, y). Now, recall from Theorem 13.1.2 that a stationary point for a concave (convex) function maximizes (minimizes) the function. Thus we have the following result:

THEOREM 14.4.1 (CONCAVE/CONVEX LAGRANGIAN)

Consider problem (1) and suppose (x_0, y_0) is a stationary point for the Lagrangian $\mathcal{L}(x, y)$.

(A) If the conditions in Theorem 13.1.2(a) are satisfied for $\mathcal{L}$ (that is, the Lagrangian is concave), then (x_0, y_0) solves the maximization problem.

(B) If the conditions in Theorem 13.1.2(b) are satisfied for $\mathcal{L}$ (that is, the Lagrangian is convex), then (x_0, y_0) solves the minimization problem.

EXAMPLE 1   Consider a firm that uses positive inputs K and L of capital and labour, respectively, to produce a single output Q according to the Cobb–Douglas production function $Q = F(K, L) = AK^a L^b$, where A, a, and b are positive parameters satisfying $a + b \leq 1$. Suppose that the prices of capital and labour are $r > 0$ and $w > 0$, respectively. The cost minimizing inputs of K and L must solve the problem

$$\min rK + wL \quad \text{subject to} \quad AK^a L^b = Q$$

Explain why the Lagrangian is convex, so that a stationary point of the Lagrangian must minimize costs. (*Hint:* See Problem 13.1.10.)

Solution: The Lagrangian is $\mathcal{L} = rK + wL - \lambda(AK^a L^b - Q)$. The first-order conditions are $r = \lambda A a K^{a-1} L^b$ and $w = \lambda A b K^a L^{b-1}$, and we see that $\lambda > 0$.

The second-order partial derivatives of $\mathcal{L}$ are $\mathcal{L}''_{11} = -\lambda a(a-1)AK^{a-2}L^b$, $\mathcal{L}''_{12} = \mathcal{L}''_{21} = -\lambda ab AK^{a-1}L^{b-1}$, and $\mathcal{L}''_{22} = -\lambda b(b-1)AK^a L^{b-2}$. Note that

$$\mathcal{L}''_{11}\mathcal{L}''_{22} - (\mathcal{L}''_{12})^2 = \lambda^2 ab A^2 K^{2a-2}L^{2b-2}\big[1 - (a+b)\big]$$

Since λ is positive, it follows from these expressions that the sufficient conditions for the Lagrangian to be convex are satisfied.   ∎

Local Second-Order Conditions

Sometimes we are interested in conditions which are sufficient for local extreme points of $f(x, y)$ subject to $g(x, y) = c$. We start by looking at the expression for dz/dx given by (5) in Section 14.3. The condition $dz/dx = 0$ is necessary for local optimality. If also $d^2z/dx^2 < 0$, then a stationary point of the Lagrangian must solve the local maximization problem. The derivative d^2z/dx^2 is just the total derivative of dz/dx w.r.t. x. Assuming that f and g are C^2-functions, and recalling that y is a function of x, it follows from (5) in Section 14.3 that

$$\frac{d^2z}{dx^2} = f''_{11} + f''_{12}y' - (f''_{21} + f''_{22}y')\frac{g'_1}{g'_2} - f'_2 \frac{(g''_{11} + g''_{12}y')g'_2 - (g''_{21} + g''_{22}y')g'_1}{(g'_2)^2}$$

Because f and g are C^2 functions, we have $f''_{12} = f''_{21}$ and $g''_{12} = g''_{21}$. Moreover, $y' = -g'_1/g'_2$. Also $f'_1 = \lambda g'_1$ and $f'_2 = \lambda g'_2$, because these are the first-order conditions. Using these relationships to eliminate y' and f'_2, as well as some elementary algebra, we obtain

$$\frac{d^2z}{dx^2} = \frac{1}{(g'_2)^2}\big[(f''_{11} - \lambda g''_{11})(g'_2)^2 - 2(f''_{12} - \lambda g''_{12})g'_1 g'_2 + (f''_{22} - \lambda g''_{22})(g'_1)^2\big]$$

We see that $d^2z/dx^2 < 0$ provided the expression in the square brackets is < 0. Thus we have the following result:

THEOREM 14.4.2 (LOCAL SECOND-ORDER CONDITIONS)

Consider the problem

$$\text{local max(min) } f(x, y) \quad \text{subject to} \quad g(x, y) = c$$

and suppose that (x_0, y_0) satisfies the first-order conditions

$$f_1'(x, y) = \lambda g_1'(x, y), \qquad f_2'(x, y) = \lambda g_2'(x, y)$$

Define

$$D(x, y, \lambda) = (f_{11}'' - \lambda g_{11}'')(g_2')^2 - 2(f_{12}'' - \lambda g_{12}'')g_1'g_2' + (f_{22}'' - \lambda g_{22}'')(g_1')^2$$

Now:

(A) If $D(x_0, y_0, \lambda) < 0$, then (x_0, y_0) solves the local maximization problem.

(B) If $D(x_0, y_0, \lambda) > 0$, then (x_0, y_0) solves the local minimization problem.

The conditions on the sign of $D(x_0, y_0, \lambda)$ are called the (local) *second-order conditions*.

EXAMPLE 2   Consider the problem

$$\text{local max (min) } f(x, y) = x^2 + y^2 \quad \text{subject to} \quad g(x, y) = x^2 + xy + y^2 = 3$$

In Example 14.1.2 we saw that the first-order conditions give the points $(1, 1)$ and $(-1, -1)$ with $\lambda = 2/3$, as well as $(\sqrt{3}, -\sqrt{3})$ and $(-\sqrt{3}, \sqrt{3})$ with $\lambda = 2$. Check the local second-order conditions in this case.

Solution: We find that $f_{11}'' = 2$, $f_{12}'' = 0$, $f_{22}'' = 2$, $g_{11}'' = 2$, $g_{12}'' = 1$, and $g_{22}'' = 2$. So

$$D(x, y, \lambda) = (2 - 2\lambda)(x + 2y)^2 + 2\lambda(2x + y)(x + 2y) + (2 - 2\lambda)(2x + y)^2$$

Note that $D(1, 1, \tfrac{2}{3}) = D(-1, -1, \tfrac{2}{3}) = 24$ and $D(\sqrt{3}, -\sqrt{3}, 2) = D(-\sqrt{3}, \sqrt{3}, 2) = -24$. We conclude that $(1, 1)$ and $(-1, -1)$ are local minimum points, whereas $(\sqrt{3}, -\sqrt{3})$ and $(-\sqrt{3}, \sqrt{3})$ are local maximum points. (In Example 14.1.2 we actually proved that these points were *global* extreme points.) ∎

For those who are familiar with 3×3 determinants (see Section 16.2), the rather lengthy expression $D(x, y, \lambda)$ can be written in a symmetric form that is easier to remember. In fact,

$$D(x, y, \lambda) = - \begin{vmatrix} 0 & g_1'(x, y) & g_2'(x, y) \\ g_1'(x, y) & f_{11}''(x, y) - \lambda g_{11}''(x, y) & f_{12}''(x, y) - \lambda g_{12}''(x, y) \\ g_2'(x, y) & f_{21}''(x, y) - \lambda g_{21}''(x, y) & f_{22}''(x, y) - \lambda g_{22}''(x, y) \end{vmatrix} \tag{2}$$

Note that the 2×2 matrix at the bottom right of (2) is the Hessian of the Lagrangian function (see Section 11.6). So the determinant is naturally called a **bordered Hessian**; its borders in the first row and first column, apart from from 0 on the main diagonal, are the first-order partial derivatives of g.

1. Use Theorem 14.4.1 to check that the optimal solution is found in Problem 14.1.5(a).

2. Solve the problem min $x^2 + y^2$ subject to $x + 2y = a$. Compute $D(x, y, \lambda)$ in Theorem 14.4.2 in this case. Can you give the problem a geometric interpretation?

3. Prove that $U(x, y) = x^a + y^a$, $a \in (0, 1)$, is concave when $x > 0$, $y > 0$. Solve the consumer demand problem

$$\max x^a + y^a \quad \text{subject to} \quad px + qy = m$$

14.5 More Variables and More Constraints

Constrained optimization problems in economics usually involve more than just two variables. The typical problem with n variables can be written in the form

$$\max(\min) f(x_1, \ldots, x_n) \quad \text{subject to} \quad g(x_1, \ldots, x_n) = c \tag{1}$$

The Lagrange multiplier method presented in the previous sections can be easily generalized. As before, associate a Lagrange multiplier λ with the constraint and form the Lagrangian

$$\mathcal{L}(x_1, \ldots, x_n) = f(x_1, \ldots, x_n) - \lambda\big(g(x_1, \ldots, x_n) - c\big) \tag{2}$$

Next, find all the first-order partial derivatives of $\mathcal{L}$ and equate them to zero, so that

$$\mathcal{L}'_1 = f'_1(x_1, \ldots, x_n) - \lambda g'_1(x_1, \ldots, x_n) = 0$$
$$\cdots\cdots\cdots\cdots\cdots\cdots\cdots\cdots\cdots\cdots\cdots\cdots\cdots\cdots \tag{3}$$
$$\mathcal{L}'_n = f'_n(x_1, \ldots, x_n) - \lambda g'_n(x_1, \ldots, x_n) = 0$$

These n equations, together with the constraint, form $n+1$ equations which should be solved to determine the $n + 1$ unknowns $x_1, \ldots, x_n$, and λ.

NOTE 1 This method will (in general) fail to give correct necessary conditions if all the first-order partial derivatives of $g(x_1, \ldots, x_n)$ vanish at the stationary point of the Lagrangian. Otherwise, the proof is an easy generalization of the analytic argument in Section 14.3 for the first-order conditions. If, say, $\partial g/\partial x_n \neq 0$, we "solve" $g(x_1, \ldots, x_n) = c$ for x_n and reduce the problem to an unconstrained extremum problem in $x_1, \ldots, x_{n-1}$. (See Problem 10 for the case $n = 3$.)

EXAMPLE 1   A consumer has the Cobb–Douglas utility function $U(x, y, z) = x^2 y^3 z$ defined for $x, y, z \geq 0$, and faces the budget constraint $x + y + z = 12$. Find the only solution candidates to the consumer's demand problem, which is

$$\max x^2 y^3 z \quad \text{subject to} \quad x + y + z = 12$$

Solution: The Lagrangian is

$$\mathcal{L}(x, y, z) = x^2 y^3 z - \lambda(x + y + z - 12)$$

The first-order conditions (3) become

$$\mathcal{L}'_1 = 2xy^3z - \lambda = 0, \qquad \mathcal{L}'_2 = 3x^2y^2z - \lambda = 0, \qquad \mathcal{L}'_3 = x^2y^3 - \lambda = 0 \qquad (*)$$

If *any* of the variables x, y, and z is 0, then $x^2y^3z = 0$, which is *not* the maximum value. So suppose that x, y, and z are all positive. From the two first equations in $(*)$, we have $2xy^3z = 3x^2y^2z$, so $y = 3x/2$. The first and third equations in $(*)$ likewise imply that $z = x/2$. Inserting $y = 3x/2$ and $z = x/2$ into the constraint yields $x + 3x/2 + x/2 = 12$, so $x = 4$. Then $y = 6$ and $z = 2$. Thus, the only possible solution is $(x, y, z) = (4, 6, 2)$. ∎

EXAMPLE 2   Solve the problem

$$\text{minimize} \quad f(x, y, z) = (x - 4)^2 + (y - 4)^2 + \left(z - \tfrac{1}{2}\right)^2 \quad \text{subject to} \quad x^2 + y^2 = z$$

Can you supply a geometric interpretation of the problem?

Solution: The Lagrangian is

$$\mathcal{L}(x, y, z) = (x - 4)^2 + (y - 4)^2 + \left(z - \tfrac{1}{2}\right)^2 - \lambda(x^2 + y^2 - z)$$

The first-order conditions are:

$$\mathcal{L}'_1(x, y, z) = 2(x - 4) - 2\lambda x = 0 \qquad \text{(i)}$$
$$\mathcal{L}'_2(x, y, z) = 2(y - 4) - 2\lambda y = 0 \qquad \text{(ii)}$$
$$\mathcal{L}'_3(x, y, z) = 2\left(z - \tfrac{1}{2}\right) + \lambda = 0 \qquad \text{(iii)}$$
$$x^2 + y^2 = z \qquad \text{(iv)}$$

From (i) we see that $x = 0$ is impossible. Equation (i) thus gives $\lambda = 1 - 4/x$. Inserting this into (ii) and (iii) gives $y = x$ and $z = 2/x$. Using these results, equation (iv) reduces to $2x^2 = 2/x$, that is, $x^3 = 1$, so $x = 1$.

It follows that $(x, y, z) = (1, 1, 2)$ is the only solution candidate to the problem.

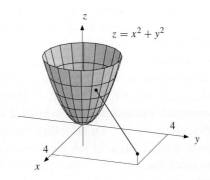

Figure 1

The expression $(x-4)^2+(y-4)^2+(z-1/2)^2$ measures the square of the distance from the point $(4, 4, 1/2)$ to the point (x, y, z). The set of points (x, y, z) which satisfy the equation $z = x^2 + y^2$ is a paraboloid, part of which is shown in Fig. 1. The minimization problem is therefore to find that point on the surface of the paraboloid which has the smallest (square) distance from $(4, 4, 1/2)$. It is geometrically "obvious" that this problem has a solution. On the other, the problem of finding the largest distance from $(4, 4, 1/2)$ to a point on the paraboloid does not have a solution, because the distance can be made as large as we want. ∎

EXAMPLE 3   The general consumer optimization problem with n goods is

$$\max_{x_1,\ldots,x_n} U(x_1, \ldots, x_n) \quad \text{subject to} \quad p_1 x_1 + \cdots + p_n x_n = m \tag{4}$$

where U is defined for $x_1 \geq 0, \ldots, x_n \geq 0$. The Lagrangian is

$$\mathcal{L}(x_1, \ldots, x_n) = U(x_1, \ldots, x_n) - \lambda(p_1 x_1 + \cdots p_n x_n - m)$$

The first-order conditions are

$$\mathcal{L}'_i(x_1, \ldots, x_n) = U'_i(x_1, \ldots, x_n) - \lambda p_i = 0, \qquad i = 1, \ldots, n$$

Writing $\mathbf{x} = (x_1, \ldots, x_n)$, we have

$$\frac{U'_1(\mathbf{x})}{p_1} = \frac{U'_2(\mathbf{x})}{p_2} = \cdots = \frac{U'_n(\mathbf{x})}{p_n} = \lambda \tag{5}$$

Apart from the last equation, which serves only to determine the Lagrange multiplier λ, we have $n - 1$ equations. (For $n = 2$, there is one equation; for $n = 3$, there are two equations; and so on.) In addition, the constraint must hold. Thus, we have n equations to determine the values of $x_1, \ldots, x_n$. From (5) it also follows that

$$\frac{U'_k(\mathbf{x})}{U'_j(\mathbf{x})} = \frac{p_k}{p_j} \qquad \text{for every pair of goods } k \text{ and } j \tag{6}$$

The left-hand side is the marginal rate of substitution (MRS) of good k for good j, whereas the right-hand side is their price ratio. So condition (6) equates the MRS for each pair of goods to the corresponding price ratio.

Consider the equations in (5), together with the budget constraint. Assume that this system is solved for $x_1, \ldots, x_n$ and λ as functions of $p_1, \ldots, p_n$ and m, giving $x_i = D_i(p_1, \ldots, p_n, m)$, for $i = 1, \ldots, n$. Then $D_i(p_1, \ldots, p_n, m)$ gives the amount of the ith commodity demanded by the individual when facing prices $p_1, \ldots, p_n$ and income m. For this reason $D_1, \ldots, D_n$ are called the **(individual) demand functions**. By the same argument as in Example 14.1.3, the demand functions must be homogeneous of degree 0. As one check that you have correctly derived the demand functions associated with a special utility function, it is a good idea to verify that the functions you find are indeed homogeneous of degree 0.

In the case when the consumer has a Cobb–Douglas utility function, the constrained maximization problem is

$$\max\ Ax_1^{a_1} \cdots x_n^{a_n} \quad \text{subject to} \quad p_1 x_1 + \cdots + p_n x_n = m$$

Then the demand functions are

$$D_i(p_1, \ldots, p_n, m) = \frac{a_i}{a_1 + \cdots + a_n} \frac{m}{p_i}, \qquad i = 1, \ldots, n$$

(see Problem 8(a)). We see how the pattern of the two variable case in Example 14.1.3 is repeated. Note also that the demand for a certain good does not depend on the prices of the other goods. This is an argument against using Cobb–Douglas utility functions, because we expect realistic demand functions to depend on prices of other goods that are either complements or substitutes. ∎

More Constraints

Occasionally economists need to consider optimization problems with more than one equality constraint (although it is much more common to have many inequality constraints—see FMEA for examples). The corresponding general Lagrangian problem is

$$\max(\min)\ f(x_1, \ldots, x_n) \quad \text{subject to} \quad \begin{cases} g_1(x_1, \ldots, x_n) = c_1 \\ \cdots\cdots\cdots\cdots\cdots \\ g_m(x_1, \ldots, x_n) = c_m \end{cases} \tag{7}$$

The Lagrange multiplier method can be extended to treat problem (7). Associate a different **Lagrange multiplier** with each of the m constraints, and define the new **Lagrangian function** by

$$\mathcal{L}(x_1, \ldots, x_n) = f(x_1, \ldots, x_n) - \sum_{j=1}^{m} \lambda_j \big(g_j(x_1, \ldots, x_n) - c_j\big) \tag{8}$$

The first-order conditions, which except in special cases must be satisfied at the optimum, require that the partial derivatives of the Lagrangian w.r.t. each x_i vanish. That is,

$$\frac{\partial \mathcal{L}}{\partial x_i} = \frac{\partial f(x_1, \ldots, x_n)}{\partial x_i} - \sum_{j=1}^{m} \lambda_j \frac{\partial g_j(x_1, \ldots, x_n)}{\partial x_i} = 0, \qquad i = 1, 2, \ldots, n \tag{9}$$

Together with the m equality constraints, these n equations form a total of $n + m$ equations in the $n + m$ unknowns $x_1, \ldots, x_n, \lambda_1, \ldots, \lambda_m$.

EXAMPLE 4　　Solve the problem

$$\max(\min)\ x^2 + y^2 + z^2 \quad \text{subject to} \quad \begin{cases} x + 2y + z = 30 & \text{(i)} \\ 2x - y - 3z = 10 & \text{(ii)} \end{cases}$$

Solution: The Lagrangian function is

$$\mathcal{L}(x, y, z) = x^2 + y^2 + z^2 - \lambda_1(x + 2y + z - 30) - \lambda_2(2x - y - 3z - 10)$$

The first-order conditions (9) require that

$$\frac{\partial \mathcal{L}}{\partial x} = 2x - \lambda_1 - 2\lambda_2 = 0 \tag{iii}$$

$$\frac{\partial \mathcal{L}}{\partial y} = 2y - 2\lambda_1 + \lambda_2 = 0 \tag{iv}$$

$$\frac{\partial \mathcal{L}}{\partial z} = 2z - \lambda_1 + 3\lambda_2 = 0 \tag{v}$$

So there are five equations, (i) to (v), to determine the five unknowns x, y, z, λ_1, and λ_2.
Solving (iii) and (iv) simultaneously for λ_1 and λ_2 gives

$$\lambda_1 = \tfrac{2}{5}x + \tfrac{4}{5}y, \qquad \lambda_2 = \tfrac{4}{5}x - \tfrac{2}{5}y$$

Inserting these expressions for λ_1 and λ_2 into (v) and rearranging yields

$$x - y + z = 0 \tag{vi}$$

This equation together with (i) and (ii) constitutes a system of three linear equations in the unknowns x, y, and z. Solving this system by elimination gives $(x, y.z) = (10, 10, 0)$. The corresponding values of the multipliers are $\lambda_1 = 12$ and $\lambda_2 = 4$.

Here is a geometric argument that might convince you that we have solved the minimization problem. Each of the two constraints represents a plane in $\mathbb{R}^3$, and the points satisfying both constraints consequently lie on the straight line where the two planes intersect. Now $x^2 + y^2 + z^2$ measures the (square of the) distance from the origin to the point (x, y, z). Therefore, our problem is to find the minimum and the maximum distances from the origin to the points on a straight line. No maximum distance can possibly exist, but it is geometrically obvious that there is a minimum distance, and it must be attained at the point we have found.

An easier alternative method to solve this particular problem is to reduce it to a one variable optimization problem by using (i) and (ii) to get $y = 20 - x$ and $z = x - 10$. Then $x^2 + y^2 + z^2 = x^2 + (20 - x)^2 + (x - 10)^2 = 3(x - 10)^2 + 200$, and this function is easily seen to have a minimum when $x = 10$. ∎

EXAMPLE 5   An economy consists of two consumers with labels $i = 1, 2$. They exchange two goods, labelled $j = 1, 2$. Suppose there is a fixed endowment e_j of each good to be distributed between the two consumers. Let c_j^i denote i's consumption of good j. Suppose that each consumer i has preferences represented by the utility function

$$U^i(c_1^i, c_2^i) = \alpha_1 \ln c_1^i + \alpha_2 \ln c_2^i$$

where the parameters α_j are positive, and independent of i, with $\alpha_1 + \alpha_2 = 1$.

Suppose the goods are to be distributed in order to maximize *social welfare* in the form of the weighted sum $W = \beta_1 U^1 + \beta_2 U^2$, where the weights β_i are positive, and $\beta_1 + \beta_2 = 1$.

(a) Formulate the welfare maximization problem with equality constraints, one for each good.

(b) Write down the Lagrangian, where λ_j denotes the Lagrange multiplier associated with the constraint for good j. Find the welfare maximizing distribution of the goods.

(c) Verify that $\lambda_j = \partial W^*/\partial e_j$, where W^* denotes the maximum value of W.

Solution: (a) The problem is to find the consumer 1's consumption of the two goods, c_1^1 and c_2^1, as well as consumer 2's consumption of the two goods, c_1^2 and c_2^2, which together solve the problem:

$$\max \left[\beta_1 \left(\alpha_1 \ln c_1^1 + \alpha_2 \ln c_2^1 \right) + \beta_2 \left(\alpha_1 \ln c_1^2 + \alpha_2 \ln c_2^2 \right) \right] \quad \text{subject to} \quad \begin{cases} c_1^1 + c_1^2 = e_1 \\ c_2^1 + c_2^2 = e_2 \end{cases}$$

(b) The Lagrangian is

$$\mathcal{L} = \beta_1 \left(\alpha_1 \ln c_1^1 + \alpha_2 \ln c_2^1 \right) + \beta_2 \left(\alpha_1 \ln c_1^2 + \alpha_2 \ln c_2^2 \right) - \lambda_1 \left(c_1^1 + c_1^2 - e_1 \right) - \lambda_2 (c_2^1 + c_2^2 - e_2)$$

The first-order conditions take the form

$$\frac{\partial \mathcal{L}}{\partial c_1^1} = \alpha_1 \beta_1 \frac{1}{c_1^1} - \lambda_1 = 0, \qquad \frac{\partial \mathcal{L}}{\partial c_2^1} = \alpha_2 \beta_1 \frac{1}{c_2^1} - \lambda_2 = 0 \qquad (*)$$

$$\frac{\partial \mathcal{L}}{\partial c_1^2} = \alpha_1 \beta_2 \frac{1}{c_1^2} - \lambda_1 = 0, \qquad \frac{\partial \mathcal{L}}{\partial c_2^2} = \alpha_2 \beta_2 \frac{1}{c_2^2} - \lambda_2 = 0 \qquad (**)$$

Here $(*)$ and $(**)$ pertain to consumers 1 and 2, respectively. From the first equality in $(*)$ we see that $c_1^1 = \alpha_1 \beta_1 (1/\lambda_1)$. The first equality in $(**)$ gives $c_1^2 = \alpha_1 \beta_2 (1/\lambda_1)$. From the first constraint, $e_1 = c_1^1 + c_1^2 = \alpha_1 \beta_1 (1/\lambda_1) + \alpha_1 \beta_2 (1/\lambda_1) = \alpha_1 (\beta_1 + \beta_2)(1/\lambda_1) = \alpha_1 (1/\lambda_1)$, because $\beta_1 + \beta_2 = 1$. So $1/\lambda_1 = e_1/\alpha_1$, and thus $c_1^1 = \alpha_1 \beta_1 e_1/\alpha_1 = \beta_1 e_1$ and $c_1^2 = \alpha_1 \beta_2 e_1/\alpha_1 = \beta_2 e_1$. In the same way, we find $c_2^1 = \beta_1 e_2$ and $c_2^2 = \beta_2 e_2$.

Thus, each individual i receives a share β_i of the total endowment of each good, which is equal to the weight given to i's utility in the welfare sum $W = \beta_1 U^1 + \beta_2 U^2$.

(c) The maximum value of W is

$$W^* = \beta_1 [\alpha_1 \ln(\beta_1 e_1) + \alpha_2 \ln(\beta_1 e_2)] + \beta_2 [\alpha_1 \ln(\beta_2 e_1) + \alpha_2 \ln(\beta_2 e_2)]$$

and we find $\partial W^*/\partial e_1 = \beta_1 \alpha_1 (1/\beta_1 e_1)\beta_1 + \beta_2 \alpha_1 (1/\beta_2 e_1)\beta_2 = (\alpha_1/e_1)(\beta_1 + \beta_2) = \alpha_1/e_1 = \lambda_1$. In the same way we see that $\partial W^*/\partial e_2 = \lambda_2$. ∎

PROBLEMS FOR SECTION 14.5

1. Consider the problem min $x^2 + y^2 + z^2$ subject to $x + y + z = 1$.

   (a) Write down the Lagrangian for this problem, and find the only point (x, y, z) that satisfies the necessary conditions.

   (b) Give a geometric argument for the existence of a solution. Does the corresponding maximization problem have any solution?

2. Solve the problem min $x + 4y + 3z$ subject to $x^2 + 2y^2 + \frac{1}{3}z^2 = b$. (Suppose that $b > 0$ and take it for granted that the problem has a solution.)

3. Each week an individual consumes quantities x and y of two goods, and works for ℓ hours. These quantities are chosen to maximize the utility function

$$U(x, y, \ell) = \alpha \ln x + \beta \ln y + (1 - \alpha - \beta) \ln(L - \ell)$$

   which is defined for $0 \le \ell < L$ and for $x, y > 0$. Here α and β are positive parameters satisfying $\alpha + \beta < 1$. The individual faces the budget constraint $px + qy = w\ell + m$, where $m \ (\ge 0)$ denotes unearned income, and w is the wage per hour.

   (a) Define $\gamma = (\alpha + \beta)/(1 - \alpha - \beta)$. Assuming that $m \le \gamma wL$, find the individual's demands x^*, y^*, and labour supply ℓ^* as functions of p, q, r, and m.

   (b) What happens if $m > \gamma wL$?

4. Consider the problem in Example 4, and let $(x, y, z) = (10 + h, 10 + k, \ell)$. Show that if (x, y, z) satisfies both constraints, then $k = -h$ and $\ell = h$. Then show that $f(x, y, z) = 200 + 3h^2$. Conclusion?

5. A statistical problem requires solving

$$\min \ a_1^2 x_1^2 + a_2^2 x_2^2 + \cdots + a_n^2 x_n^2 \quad \text{subject to} \quad x_1 + x_2 + \cdots + x_n = 1$$

   Here all the constants a_i are nonzero. Solve the problem, taking it for granted that the minimum value exists. What is the solution if one of the a_i's is zero?

6. (a) Consider Example 5 and find consumer i's demands when confronted with the budget constraint $p_1 c_1^i + p_2 c_2^i = r^i$.

   (b) Show that each consumer i will demand the optimal allocation $c_1^i = \beta_i e_1, c_2^i = \beta_i e_2$ provided that $p_1 = \lambda_1, p_2 = \lambda_2$, and $r^i = \beta_i(p_1 e_1 + p_2 e_2)$.

7. Solve the problem:

$$\max(\min) x + y \quad \text{subject to} \quad \begin{cases} x^2 + 2y^2 + z^2 = 1 \\ x + y + z = 1 \end{cases}$$

HARDER PROBLEMS

8. Consider the problem in Example 3. Find the demand functions when:

   (a) $U(x_1, \ldots, x_n) = A x_1^{a_1} \cdots x_n^{a_n}$ $\quad (A > 0, a_1 > 0, \ldots, a_n > 0)$

   (b) $U(x_1, \ldots, x_n) = x_1^a + \cdots + x_n^a$ $\quad (0 < a < 1)$

9. (a) Solve the problem (taking it for granted that there is a solution):

$$\min \ f(x, y, z) = (y + z - 3)^2 \quad \text{subject to} \quad \begin{cases} x^2 + y + z = 2 \\ x + y^2 + 2z = 2 \end{cases}$$

   (b) The necessary conditions in part (a) have two solutions. It is tempting to believe that the one which does not solve the minimization problem must solve the maximization problem. Show that this is not the case here.

10. Consider the problem max (min) $f(x_1, x_2, x_3)$ subject to $g(x_1, x_2, x_3) = c$. Suppose that the constraint equation defines x_3 as a continuously differentiable function of x_1 and x_2. Derive (3) for $n = 3$ by using the idea in the analytical proof of the first-order conditions in Section 14.3. (*Hint:* Let $\lambda = f_3' / g_3'$.)

14.6 Comparative Statics

The economic interpretation of the Lagrange multiplier from Section 14.2 can be generalized to the Lagrange problem with n variables and m constraints, which can be written in the form

$$\max(\min) \ f(\mathbf{x}) \quad \text{subject to } g_j(\mathbf{x}) = c_j, \ j = 1, \ldots, m \tag{1}$$

Let $x_1^*, \ldots, x_n^*$ be the values of $x_1, \ldots, x_n$ that satisfy the necessary conditions for the solution to (1). In general, $x_1^*, \ldots, x_n^*$ depend on the values of $c_1, \ldots, c_m$. We assume that each $x_i^* = x_i^*(c_1, \ldots, c_m)$, $i = 1, \ldots, n$ is a differentiable function of $c_1, \ldots, c_m$. The associated value $f^* = f(x_1^*, \ldots, x_n^*)$ of f is then a function of $c_1, \ldots, c_m$ as well. Indeed, if we put $\mathbf{x}^* = (x_1^*, \ldots, x_n^*)$ and $\mathbf{c} = (c_1, \ldots, c_m)$, the resulting value is

$$f^*(\mathbf{c}) = f(\mathbf{x}^*(\mathbf{c})) = f(x_1^*(\mathbf{c}), \ldots, x_n^*(\mathbf{c})) \tag{2}$$

The function f^* is called the **(optimal) value function** for problem (1). The Lagrange multipliers associated with $\mathbf{x}^*$ also depend on $c_1, \ldots, c_m$. Provided that certain regularity conditions are satisfied, we have

$$\frac{\partial f^*(\mathbf{c})}{\partial c_i} = \lambda_i(\mathbf{c}), \qquad i = 1, \ldots, m \tag{3}$$

The Lagrange multiplier $\lambda_i = \lambda_i(\mathbf{c})$ for the ith constraint is the rate at which the optimal value of the objective function changes w.r.t. changes in the constant c_i. The number λ_i is referred to as a **shadow price** *(or* **marginal value**) *imputed to a unit of resource i.*

Suppose we change $\mathbf{c} = (c_1, \ldots, c_m)$ by $d\mathbf{c} = (dc_1, \ldots, dc_m)$. According to (2) in Section 12.7, if $dc_1, \ldots, dc_m$ are small in absolute value, using (3) yields

$$f^*(\mathbf{c} + d\mathbf{c}) - f^*(\mathbf{c}) \approx \lambda_1(\mathbf{c}) \, dc_1 + \cdots + \lambda_m(\mathbf{c}) \, dc_m \tag{4}$$

EXAMPLE 1   Consider Example 14.5.4 in the previous section, and suppose we change the first constraint to $x + 2y + z = 31$ and the second constraint to $2x - y - 3z = 9$. Estimate the corresponding change in the value function by using (4). Find also the new exact value of the value function.

Solution: Using the notation introduced above and the results in Example 14.5.4, we have $c_1 = 30$, $c_2 = 10$, $dc_1 = 1$, $dc_2 = -1$, $\lambda_1(30, 10) = 12$, $\lambda_2(30, 10) = 4$, and $f^*(c_1, c_2) = f^*(30, 10) = 10^2 + 10^2 + 0^2 = 200$. Then (4) yields

$$f^*(30 + 1, 10 - 1) - f^*(30, 10) \approx \lambda_1(30, 10) \, dc_1 + \lambda_2(30, 10) \, dc_2$$
$$= 12 \cdot 1 + 4 \cdot (-1) = 8$$

Thus, $f^*(31, 9) = f^*(30 + 1, 10 - 1) \approx 200 + 8 = 208$.

To find the exact value of $f^*(31, 9)$, observe that (vi) in Example 14.5.4 is still valid. Thus, we have the three equations

$$x + 2y + z = 31, \qquad 2x - y - 3z = 9, \qquad x - y + z = 0$$

whose solutions for x, y, and z are $151/15$, $31/3$, and $4/15$, respectively. We find that $f^*(31, 9) = 15614/75 \approx 208.19$.

The Envelope Theorem

Using vector notation with $\mathbf{x} = (x_1, \ldots, x_n)$ and $\mathbf{r} = (r_1, \ldots, r_k)$, consider the problem

$$\max(\min)_{\mathbf{x}} \ f(\mathbf{x}, \mathbf{r}) \quad \text{subject to} \quad g_j(\mathbf{x}, \mathbf{r}) = 0, \qquad j = 1, \ldots, m \tag{5}$$

Suppose that $\lambda_j = \lambda_j(\mathbf{r})$, $j = 1, \ldots, m$ are the Lagrange multipliers obtained from the first-order conditions for problem (5), and let $\mathcal{L}(\mathbf{x}, \mathbf{r}) = f(\mathbf{x}, \mathbf{r}) - \sum_{j=1}^{m} \lambda_j g_j(\mathbf{x}, \mathbf{r})$ be the corresponding Lagrangian. Under certain conditions (discussed in FMEA), we have the following result:

ENVELOPE THEOREM

$$\frac{\partial f^*(\mathbf{r})}{\partial r_i} = \left[\frac{\partial \mathcal{L}(\mathbf{x}, \mathbf{r})}{\partial r_i} \right]_{\mathbf{x} = \mathbf{x}^*(\mathbf{r})}, \qquad i = 1, \ldots, k \tag{6}$$

Economists refer to this result as the general **envelope theorem**. It is a very useful result that should be studied carefully. When r_i is changed, then $f^*(\mathbf{r})$ changes for two reasons: First, a change in r_i changes the vector $\mathbf{r}$ and thus it changes $f(\mathbf{x}, \mathbf{r})$ directly. Second, a change in r_i changes, in general, all the functions $x_1^*(\mathbf{r}), \ldots, x_n^*(\mathbf{r})$, and so $f(\mathbf{x}^*(\mathbf{r}), \mathbf{r})$ is changed indirectly. The result in (6) shows that the total effect on the value function of a small change in r_i is found by computing the partial derivative of $\mathcal{L}(\mathbf{x}^*(\mathbf{r}), \mathbf{r})$ w.r.t. r_i, ignoring the indirect effect of the dependence of $\mathbf{x}^*$ on $\mathbf{r}$ altogether. The reason is that any small change in $\mathbf{x}$ has a negligible effect on the value of $f(\mathbf{x}^*, \mathbf{r})$.

EXAMPLE 2   For Example 14.5.3, let $U^*(p_1, \ldots, p_n, m)$ denote the maximum utility obtainable when prices are $p_1, \ldots, p_n$ and the income is m. This U^* is called the **indirect** utility function. Using (3), we see that

$$\lambda = \frac{\partial U^*}{\partial m} \tag{7}$$

Thus, λ is approximately the rate of increase in maximum utility as income increases. For this reason, λ is generally called the **marginal utility of income**.

Including all the parameters in the Lagrangian, it is

$$\mathcal{L}(x_1, \ldots, x_n, p_1, \ldots, p_n, m) = U(x_1, \ldots, x_n) - \lambda(p_1 x_1 + \cdots p_n x_n - m)$$

Obviously, $\partial \mathcal{L}/\partial m = \lambda$ and $\partial \mathcal{L}/\partial p_i = -\lambda x_i$. Hence, from (6) we get

$$\frac{\partial U^*(p_1, \ldots, p_n, m)}{\partial m} = \frac{\partial \mathcal{L}(x_1^*, \ldots, x_n^*, p_1, \ldots, p_n, m)}{\partial m} = \lambda$$

which is (7) again. Moreover,

$$\frac{\partial U^*(p_1, \ldots, p_n, m)}{\partial p_i} = \frac{\partial \mathcal{L}(x_1^*, \ldots, x_n^*, p_1, \ldots, p_n, m)}{\partial p_i} = -\lambda x_i^*$$

which is the so-called **Roy's identity**.[4]

This formula has a nice interpretation: the marginal disutility of a price increase is the marginal utility of income (λ) multiplied by the quantity demanded (x_i^*). Intuitively, this is because, for a small price change, the loss of real income is approximately equal to the change in price multiplied by the quantity demanded. ▎

EXAMPLE 3   A firm uses K units of capital and L units of labour to produce $F(K, L)$ units of a commodity. The prices of capital and labour are r and w, respectively. Consider the cost minimization problem

$$\text{minimize } C = rK + wL \quad \text{subject to} \quad F(K, L) = Q$$

where we want to find the values of K and L that minimize the cost of producing Q units. Let $C^* = C(r, w, Q)$ be the value function for the problem. Find

$$\frac{\partial C^*}{\partial r}, \quad \frac{\partial C^*}{\partial w}, \quad \frac{\partial C^*}{\partial Q}$$

---

[4] Named after the French economist René Roy. Thus his name should be pronounced like the French word "roi" (meaning king); a very rough English equivalent is "rwa".

Solution: The Lagrangian is $\mathcal{L} = rK + wL - \lambda(F(K, L) - Q)$, whose partial derivatives are $\partial\mathcal{L}/\partial r = K$, $\partial\mathcal{L}/\partial w = L$, and $\partial\mathcal{L}/\partial Q = \lambda$. According to the envelope theorem (6),

$$\frac{\partial C^*}{\partial r} = K^*, \qquad \frac{\partial C^*}{\partial w} = L^*, \qquad \frac{\partial C^*}{\partial Q} = \lambda \qquad (*)$$

The first two equalities are called **Shephard's lemma.** The last equation shows that λ must equal *marginal cost*, the rate at which minimum cost increases w.r.t. changes in output.   ∎

EXAMPLE 4   A family is planning its expenditure over two periods. In the first period, it is going to spend an amount h on a house, financed by its current assets y supplemented by a loan of amount b. The total present discounted value of its assets and income over two periods is w, but it can only spend $w - rb$ over two periods because the cost of borrowing exceeds the rate of discount. Assume $w > y + (1 + r)b$, where b, r, w, and y are all positive. Let c_1 and c_2 denote the present values of expenditure on goods other than housing in the two periods. Suppose the family's utility function is

$$U(h, c_1, c_2) = \alpha \ln h + \beta \ln c_1 + (1 - \alpha - \beta) \ln c_2$$

where the parameters α and β are positive with $\alpha + \beta < 1$.

(a) What are the two equality constraints the family faces if it is required to borrow the amount b? Formulate and solve the family's utility maximization problem using the Lagrange multiplier method.

(b) How does the maximum utility U^* respond to small changes in w, y, and b?

(c) What would you expect the family to do if $\partial U^*/\partial b < 0$?

Solution:

(a) Total expenditure over two periods is $h + c_1 + c_2$, which must equal $w - rb$. In addition, first period expenditure $h + c_1$ must equal $y + b$. So the family's problem is:

$$\max \ \alpha \ln h + \beta \ln c_1 + (1 - \alpha - \beta) \ln c_2 \quad \text{subject to} \quad \begin{cases} h + c_1 + c_2 = w - rb \\ h + c_1 = y + b \end{cases}$$

(Of course, from the constraints it follows that $c_2 = w - y - (1+r)b$, so we could solve the problem by reducing it to that of maximizing utility subject to $h + c_1 = y + b$. But we keep both constraints because of what can be learned from the Lagrange multipliers.)

The Lagrangian is

$$\mathcal{L} = \alpha \ln h + \beta \ln c_1 + (1 - \alpha - \beta) \ln c_2 - \lambda(h + c_1 + c_2 - w + rb) - \mu(h + c_1 - y - b)$$

The first-order conditions are

$$\frac{\partial\mathcal{L}}{\partial h} = \frac{\alpha}{h} - (\lambda + \mu) = 0, \qquad \frac{\partial\mathcal{L}}{\partial c_1} = \frac{\beta}{c_1} - (\lambda + \mu) = 0, \qquad \frac{\partial\mathcal{L}}{\partial c_2} = \frac{1 - \alpha - \beta}{c_2} - \lambda = 0$$

So $h = \alpha/(\lambda + \mu)$, $c_1 = \beta/(\lambda + \mu)$, and $c_2 = (1 - \alpha - \beta)/\lambda$. The second equality constraint then gives $y + b = h + c_1 = (\alpha + \beta)/(\lambda + \mu)$, so $1/(\lambda + \mu) = (y + b)/(\alpha + \beta)$. Moreover, $c_2 = w - y - (1 + r)b$, so[5]

$$h = \frac{\alpha(y + b)}{\alpha + \beta}, \qquad c_1 = \frac{\beta(y + b)}{\alpha + \beta}, \qquad c_2 = w - y - (1 + r)b$$

Also, $\lambda = (1 - \alpha - \beta)/c_2 = (1 - \alpha - \beta)/[w - y - (1 + r)b]$.

(b) The partial derivatives of the Lagrangian w.r.t. the parameters w, y, and b are $\partial \mathcal{L}/\partial w = \lambda$, $\partial \mathcal{L}/\partial y = \mu$, and $\partial \mathcal{L}/\partial b = \mu - \lambda r$. Denoting the maximum utility by U^*, from the envelope theorem we obtain

$$\frac{\partial U^*}{\partial w} = \lambda, \qquad \frac{\partial U^*}{\partial y} = \mu, \qquad \frac{\partial U^*}{\partial b} = \mu - \lambda r$$

Note the interpretation of $\partial U^*/\partial b = \mu - \lambda r$: Increasing b relaxes the constraint on first period expenditure $h + c_1$, conferring a marginal utility gain of μ; but it also reduces the present discounted value of wealth because of the need to pay the higher interest charges, so there is a marginal utility loss equal to λr.

(c) If $\partial U^*/\partial b < 0$, then one would expect the family not to borrow all the amount b, if allowed to borrow less. (But this requires considering inequality constraints.)

PROBLEMS FOR SECTION 14.6

1. Solve the problem $\min x + 4y + 3z$ subject to $x^2 + 2y^2 + \frac{1}{3}z^2 = b$. (Suppose that $b > 0$ and take it for granted that the problem has a solution.) Verify that (3) is valid.

2. A firm has L units of labour at its disposal. Its outputs are three different commodities. Producing x, y, and z units of these commodities requires αx^2, βy^2, and γz^2 units of labour, respectively.

   (a) Solve the problem

   $$\max (ax + by + cz) \quad \text{subject to} \quad \alpha x^2 + \beta y^2 + \gamma z^2 = L$$

   where a, b, c, α, β, and γ are positive constants.

   (b) Put $a = 4$, $b = c = 1$, $\alpha = 1$, $\beta = \frac{1}{4}$, and $\gamma = \frac{1}{5}$, and show that in this case the problem in (a) has the solution $x = \frac{4}{5}\sqrt{L}$, $y = \frac{4}{5}\sqrt{L}$, and $z = \sqrt{L}$. What happens to the maximum value of $4x + y + z$ when L increases from 100 to 101? Find both the exact change and the appropriate linear approximation based on the interpretation of the Lagrange multiplier.

---

[5] These choices of h, c_1, and c_2 do maximize utility, because the Lagrangian is concave as a sum of concave functions. See e.g. FMEA.

3. (a) Solve the problem

$$\max(\min) f(x, y, z) = x^2 + y^2 + z \text{ subject to } g(x, y, z) = x^2 + 2y^2 + 4z^2 = 1$$

(The constraint has a graph which is the surface of an ellipsoid in $\mathbb{R}^3$. This set is closed and bounded.)

(b) Suppose the constraint is changed to $x^2 + 2y^2 + 4z^2 = 1.02$. What is the approximate change in the maximum value of $f(x, y, z)$?

4. With reference to Example 3, let $F(K, L) = K^{1/2} L^{1/4}$ and solve the problem, finding explicit expressions for K^*, L^*, C^*, and λ. Verify the equalities $(*)$ in Example 3.

5. With reference to Example 3, assuming that F is a C^2 function, prove the symmetry relation $\partial K^* / \partial w = \partial L^* / \partial r$.

6. Consider the problem of maximizing $e^x + y + z$ subject to $\begin{cases} x + y + z = 1 \\ x^2 + y^2 + z^2 = 1 \end{cases}$

(a) Find the solution of the problem by using Lagrange's method.

(b) Replace the constraints by $x + y + z = 1.02$ and $x^2 + y^2 + z^2 = 0.98$. What is the approximate change in the maximum value of the objective function?

14.7 Nonlinear Programming: A Simple Case

So far this chapter has considered how to maximize or minimize a function subject to equality constraints. The final two sections concern nonlinear programming problems, which involve *inequality* constraints. Some particularly simple inequality constraints are those requiring certain variables to be nonnegative. These often have to be imposed for the solution to make economic sense. In addition, bounds on resource availability are often expressed as inequalities rather than equalities.

In this section we consider the simple **nonlinear programming problem**

$$\max f(x, y) \quad \text{subject to} \quad g(x, y) \le c \tag{1}$$

with just one inequality constraint. Thus, we seek the largest value attained by $f(x, y)$ in the **admissible** or **feasible** set S of all pairs (x, y) satisfying $g(x, y) \le c$.

Problems where one wants to minimize $f(x, y)$ subject to $(x, y) \in S$ can be handled by instead studying the problem of maximizing $-f(x, y)$ subject to $(x, y) \in S$.

Using the methods explained in Chapter 13, problem (1) can be solved by classical methods. It involves examining the stationary points of f in the interior of the feasible set S, and the behaviour of f on the boundary of S. However, since the 1950s, economists have generally tackled such problems by using an extension of the Lagrangian multiplier method due originally to H. W. Kuhn and A. W. Tucker.

In fact we begin by writing down a recipe giving all the points (x, y) that can possibly solve problem (1), except in some bizarre cases. The recipe closely resembles the one we used to solve the Lagrangian problem max $f(x, y)$ subject to $g(x, y) = c$.

RECIPE FOR SOLVING PROBLEM (1)

A. Associate a constant Lagrange multiplier λ with the constraint $g(x, y) \leq c$, and define the Lagrangian function

$$\mathcal{L}(x, y) = f(x, y) - \lambda\big(g(x, y) - c\big)$$

B. Equate the partial derivatives of $\mathcal{L}(x, y)$ to zero:

$$\mathcal{L}'_1(x, y) = f'_1(x, y) - \lambda g'_1(x, y) = 0$$
$$\mathcal{L}'_2(x, y) = f'_2(x, y) - \lambda g'_2(x, y) = 0$$

$$(2)$$

C. Introduce the **complementary slackness condition**

$$\lambda \geq 0 \ (\lambda = 0 \text{ if } g(x, y) < c) \tag{3}$$

D. Require (x, y) to satisfy the constraint

$$g(x, y) \leq c \tag{4}$$

Find all the points (x, y) which, together with associated values of λ, satisfy all the conditions B, C, and D. These are the solution candidates, at least one of which solves the problem (if it has a solution).

Note that the conditions (2) are exactly the same as those used in the Lagrange multiplier method of Section 14.1. Condition (4) obviously has to be satisfied, so the only new feature is condition (3). In fact, condition (3) is rather tricky. It requires that λ is nonnegative, and moreover that $\lambda = 0$ if $g(x, y) < c$. Thus, if $\lambda > 0$, we must have $g(x, y) = c$. An alternative formulation of this condition is that

$$\lambda \geq 0, \qquad \lambda \cdot [g(x, y) - c] = 0 \tag{5}$$

Later we shall see that even in nonlinear programming, the Lagrange multiplier λ can be interpreted as a "price" associated with increasing the right-hand side c of the "resource constraint" $g(x, y) \leq c$ by one unit. With this interpretation, prices are nonnegative, and if the resource constraint is not binding because $g(x, y) < c$ at the optimum, this means that the price associated with increasing c by one unit is 0.

It *is* possible to have *both* $\lambda = 0$ *and* $g(x, y) = c$ in (3). The two inequalities $\lambda \geq 0$ and $g(x, y) \leq c$ are **complementary** in the sense that at most one can be "slack"—that is, at most one can hold with inequality. Equivalently, at least one must be an equality.

Conditions (2) and (3) are called the **Kuhn–Tucker conditions**. Note that these are (essentially) *necessary* conditions for the solution of problem (1). In general, they are far from sufficient. Indeed, suppose one can find a point (x^0, y^0) at which f is stationary and $g(x^0, y^0) < c$. Then the Kuhn–Tucker conditions will automatically be satisfied by (x^0, y^0) together with the Lagrange multiplier $\lambda = 0$. Yet then (x_0, y_0) could be a local or global minimum or maximum, or some kind of saddle point.

NOTE 1   We say that conditions (2) and (3) are "essentially necessary" because actually the Kuhn–Tucker conditions may not hold for some rather perverse constrained optimization problems which fail to satisfy a special technical condition called the "constraint qualification." For details, see FMEA.

NOTE 2   With equality constraints, setting the partial derivative $\partial \mathcal{L}/\partial \lambda$ equal to zero just recovers the constraint $g(x, y) = c$, and so is a valid procedure for deriving a first-order condition (as was pointed out in Note 14.1.1). With an inequality constraint, however, one will have $\partial \mathcal{L}/\partial \lambda = -g(x, y) + c > 0$ at an optimum if the constraint holds with inequality at that point. For this reason, we recommend against differentiating the Lagrangian w.r.t. the multiplier λ, even though several other books advocate this procedure.

EXAMPLE 1   Solve the problem

$$\max f(x, y) = x^2 + y^2 + y - 1 \quad \text{subject to} \quad g(x, y) = x^2 + y^2 \le 1$$

Solution: The Lagrangian is $\mathcal{L}(x, y) = x^2 + y^2 + y - 1 - \lambda(x^2 + y^2 - 1)$. Here the first-order conditions are:

$$\mathcal{L}'_1(x, y) = 2x - 2\lambda x = 0 \tag{i}$$

$$\mathcal{L}'_2(x, y) = 2y + 1 - 2\lambda y = 0 \tag{ii}$$

The complementary slackness condition is

$$\lambda \ge 0 \ (\lambda = 0 \text{ if } x^2 + y^2 < 1) \tag{iii}$$

We want to find all pairs (x, y) that satisfy these conditions for some suitable value of λ.

We begin by looking at condition (i), which is $2x(1 - \lambda) = 0$. There are two possibilities: $\lambda = 1$ or $x = 0$. If $\lambda = 1$, then (ii) yields $1 = 0$, a contradiction. *Hence, $x = 0$.*

Suppose $x^2 + y^2 = 1$ and so $y = \pm 1$ because $x = 0$. Try $y = 1$ first. Then (ii) implies $\lambda = 3/2$ and so (iii) is satisfied. Thus, $(0, 1)$ *with $\lambda = 3/2$ is a candidate for optimality* (because all the conditions (i)–(iii) are satisfied). Next, try $y = -1$. Then condition (ii) yields $\lambda = 1/2$ and (iii) is again satisfied. Thus, $(0, -1)$ *with $\lambda = 1/2$ is a candidate for optimality.*

Consider, finally, the case when $x = 0$ and also $x^2 + y^2 = y^2 < 1$—that is, $-1 < y < 1$. Then (iii) implies that $\lambda = 0$, and so (ii) yields $y = -1/2$. Hence, $(0, -1/2)$ *with $\lambda = 0$ is a candidate for optimality.*

We conclude that there are three candidates for optimality. Now

$$f(0, 1) = 1, \qquad f(0, -1) = -1, \qquad f(0, -1/2) = -5/4$$

Because we want to maximize a continuous function over a closed, bounded set, by the Extreme-Value Theorem there is a solution to the problem. Because the only possible solutions are the three points already found, we conclude that $(x, y) = (0, 1)$ solves the maximization problem. (The point $(0, -1/2)$ solves the corresponding minimization problem. We solved both these problems in Example 13.4.1.)

In Theorem 14.4.1 we proved that if the Lagrangian is concave, then the first-order conditions in the problem max $f(x, y)$ subject to $g(x, y) = c$ are sufficient for optimality. The corresponding result is also valid for problem (1):

THEOREM 14.7.1 (KUHN-TUCKER SUFFICIENT CONDITIONS)

Consider problem (1) and suppose that (x_0, y_0) satisfies conditions (2)–(4).

If the Lagrangian $\mathcal{L}(x, y)$ is concave, then (x_0, y_0) solves the problem.

Proof: If (x_0, y_0) satisfies the conditions in (2), then (x_0, y_0) is a stationary point of the Lagrangian. By Theorem 13.1.2, a stationary point of the concave Lagrangian will maximize the Lagrangian. So,

$$\mathcal{L}(x_0, y_0) = f(x_0, y_0) - \lambda(g(x_0, y_0) - c) \geq \mathcal{L}(x, y) = f(x, y) - \lambda(g(x, y) - c)$$

Rearranging the terms, we obtain

$$f(x_0, y_0) - f(x, y) \geq \lambda[g(x_0, y_0) - g(x, y)] \tag{$*$}$$

If $g(x_0, y_0) < c$, then by (3), we have $\lambda = 0$, so $(*)$ implies that $f(x_0, y_0) \geq f(x, y)$ for all (x, y). On the other hand, if $g(x_0, y_0) = c$, then $\lambda[g(x_0, y_0) - g(x, y)] = \lambda[c - g(x, y)]$. Here $\lambda \geq 0$, and $c - g(x, y) \geq 0$ for all (x, y) satisfying the constraint. Hence, (x_0, y_0) solves problem (1). ∎

EXAMPLE 2   A firm has a total of L units of labour to allocate to the production of two goods. These can be sold at fixed positive prices a and b respectively. Producing x units of the first good requires αx^2 units of labour, whereas producing y units of the second good requires βy^2 units of labour, where α and β are positive constants. Find what output levels of the two goods maximize the revenue that the firm can earn by using this fixed amount of labour.

Solution: The firm's revenue maximization problem is

$$\max ax + by \quad \text{subject to} \quad \alpha x^2 + \beta y^2 \leq L$$

The Lagrangian is

$$\mathcal{L}(x, y) = ax + by - \lambda(\alpha x^2 + \beta y^2 - L)$$

The necessary conditions for (x^*, y^*) to solve the problem are

$$\frac{\partial \mathcal{L}}{\partial x} = a - 2\lambda \alpha x^* = 0$$

$$\frac{\partial \mathcal{L}}{\partial y} = b - 2\lambda \beta y^* = 0$$

$$\lambda \geq 0 \quad (\lambda = 0 \text{ if } \alpha(x^*)^2 + \beta(y^*)^2 < L)$$

Because a and b are all nonzero, it follows from these conditions that λ, x^*, and y^* are all not 0. Hence, it follows that $\lambda = a/2\alpha x^* = b/2\beta y^*$. So $y^* = (b\alpha/a\beta)x^*$. Also, because $\lambda \neq 0$, the complementary slackness condition implies that

$$\alpha(x^*)^2 + \beta(y^*)^2 = L$$

Inserting the expression found for y^*, we obtain

$$\alpha(x^*)^2 + \frac{\alpha^2}{\beta}\frac{b^2}{a^2}(x^*)^2 = L$$

Accordingly, after a little more algebra the positive solution is found to be $x^* = a\sqrt{L}/\alpha\mu$, where μ denotes the constant $\mu = \sqrt{a^2/\alpha + b^2/\beta}$. Because $y^* = (b\alpha/a\beta)x^*$, we get

$$x^* = a\sqrt{L}/\alpha\mu, \qquad y^* = b\sqrt{L}/\beta\mu$$

Because the Lagrangian is seen to be concave in (x, y), we have found the solution. ∎

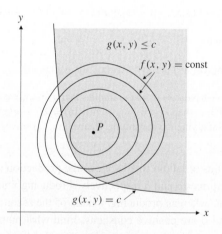

Figure 1 The point $P = (x^*, y^*)$ is an interior point of the feasible set.

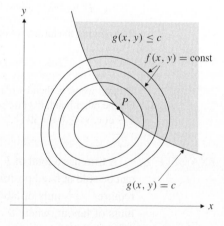

Figure 2 The constraint $g(x, y) \leq c$ is binding at $P = (x^*, y^*)$.

Why Does the Recipe Work?

Suppose (x^*, y^*) solves problem (1). Then either $g(x^*, y^*) < c$, in which case the constraint $g(x^*, y^*) \leq c$ is said to be **inactive** or **slack** at (x^*, y^*), or else $g(x^*, y^*) = c$, in which case the same inequality constraint is said to be **active** or **binding** at (x^*, y^*). The two different cases are illustrated in Figs. 1 and 2. The objective function increases as the level curves shrink. In Fig. 1, the solution (x^*, y^*) to problem (1) is an interior point of the feasible set. On the other hand, in Fig. 2, the solution (x^*, y^*) is at the boundary of the feasible set.

In case the solution (x^*, y^*) satisfies $g(x^*, y^*) < c$, as in Fig. 1, the point (x^*, y^*) is usually an interior maximum of the function f. Then it is a stationary point at which $f_1'(x^*, y^*) = f_2'(x^*, y^*) = 0$. In this case, if we set $\lambda = 0$, then conditions (2) to (4) of the recipe are all satisfied.

On the other hand, in the case when the constraint is binding at (x^*, y^*), as in Fig. 2, the point (x^*, y^*) solves the Lagrangian problem max $f(x, y)$ subject to $g(x, y) = c$ with an equality constraint. Provided that the conditions of Theorem 14.3.1 are all satisfied, there will exist a Lagrange multiplier λ such that the Lagrangian function satisfies the first-order conditions (2) at (x^*, y^*). It remains to be shown that this Lagrange multiplier λ satisfies $\lambda \geq 0$, thus ensuring that (3) is also satisfied at (x^*, y^*).

To this end, consider the two value functions

$$v(b) = \max\{f(x, y) : g(x, y) \leq b\}$$
$$f^*(b) = \max\{f(x, y) : g(x, y) = b\}$$

(6)

for the versions of problem (1) in which the constant c has been replaced by the variable parameter b, and where $f^*(b)$ arises from the problem where the inequality constraint has been replaced by the corresponding equality constraint. Recall from (2) in section 14.2 that $\lambda = df^*(c)/dc$ if f^* is differentiable at c. We shall now show that f^* is nondecreasing at $b = c$, thus implying that $\lambda \geq 0$—at least when f^* is differentiable.

Indeed, (6) implies that $f^*(b) \leq v(b)$ for all b, because the equality constraint is more stringent than the (weak) inequality constraint, and imposing a more stringent constraint never allows a higher maximum value. But also, in case $b < c$, constraint $g(x, y) \leq b$ is more stringent than $g(x, y) \leq c$, from which it follows that $v(b) \leq v(c)$. Finally, because we are discussing the case when constraint $g(x^*, y^*) = c$ binds at the solution to problem (1), we must have $v(c) = f^*(c)$. Thus, the chain $f^*(b) \leq v(b) \leq v(c) = f^*(c)$ is satisfied whenever $b < c$. From this it follows that $f^*(b) \leq f^*(c)$, so $f^*(b)$ is increasing at $b = c$, and finally $\lambda = df^*(c)/dc \geq 0$, as required.

PROBLEMS FOR SECTION 14.7

1. (a) Solve the problem max $-x^2 - y^2$ subject to $x - 3y \leq -10$.

   (b) The pair (x^*, y^*) which solve the problem in (a) also solves the minimization problem min $(x^2 + y^2)$ subject to $x - 3y \leq -10$. Sketch the admissible set S and explain the solution geometrically.

2. Consider the problem

   $$\max x^2 + 2y^2 - x \quad \text{subject to} \quad x^2 + y^2 \leq 1$$

   (a) Write down the Lagrangian function and the equations (2)–(4) for this problem.

   (b) Find all pairs (x, y) that satisfy all the necessary conditions. (There are five candidates.) Find the solution to the problem.

3. Consider the problem

$$\max f(x, y) = 2 - (x - 1)^2 - e^{y^2} \quad \text{subject to} \quad x^2 + y^2 \le a$$

where a is a positive constant.

(a) Write down the Kuhn–Tucker conditions for the solution of the problem. Find the only solution candidate. (You will need to distinguish between the cases $a \in (0, 1)$ and $a \ge 1$.) Prove optimality by using Theorem 14.7.1.

(b) The optimal value of $f(x, y)$ will depend on a. The resulting function $f^*(a)$ is called the *value function* for the problem. Verify that $df^*(a)/da = \lambda$ in both cases.

4. Check what the Kuhn–Tucker conditions have to say about the following problems:

(a) max $f(x, y)$ subject to $x \le b$

(b) max $f(x, y)$ subject to $y \ge a$

5. Suppose the firm of Example 8.5.1 earns revenue

$$R(Q) = aQ - bQ^2$$

and incurs cost

$$C(Q) = \alpha Q + \beta Q^2$$

as functions of output $Q \ge 0$, where a, b, α, and β are positive parameters. The firm maximizes profit

$$\pi(Q) = R(Q) - C(Q)$$

subject to the constraint $Q \ge 0$. Solve this one-variable problem by the Kuhn–Tucker method, and find conditions for the constraint to bind at the optimum.

14.8 More on Nonlinear Programming

A fairly general nonlinear programming problem is the following:

$$\max f(x_1, \ldots, x_n) \quad \text{subject to} \quad \begin{cases} g_1(x_1, \ldots, x_n) \le c_1 \\ \ldots\ldots\ldots\ldots\ldots\ldots \\ g_m(x_1, \ldots, x_n) \le c_m \end{cases} \tag{1}$$

The set of vectors $\mathbf{x} = (x_1, \ldots, x_n)$ that satisfy all the constraints is called the **admissible set** or the **feasible set**.

Note that minimizing $f(\mathbf{x})$ is equivalent to maximizing $-f(\mathbf{x})$. Also an inequality constraint of the form $g_j(\mathbf{x}) \ge c_j$ can be rewritten as $-g_j(\mathbf{x}) \le -c_j$, whereas an equality constraint $g_j(\mathbf{x}) = c_j$ is equivalent to the double inequality constraint $g_j(\mathbf{x}) \le c_j$ and $-g_j(\mathbf{x}) \le -c_j$. In this way, most constrained optimization problems can be expressed in the form (1).

It is now very easy to write down a recipe for solving the general nonlinear programming problem (1). (The conditions in B and C are called the *Kuhn–Tucker necessary conditions*.)

RECIPE FOR SOLVING THE GENERAL NONLINEAR PROGRAMMING PROBLEM:

$$\max \ f(\mathbf{x}) \text{ subject to } g_j(\mathbf{x}) \le c_j, \qquad j = 1, \ldots, m$$

where $\mathbf{x}$ denotes $(x_1, \ldots, x_n)$.

A. Write down the Lagrangian

$$\mathcal{L}(\mathbf{x}) = f(\mathbf{x}) - \sum_{j=1}^{m} \lambda_j(g_j(\mathbf{x}) - c_j)$$

with $\lambda_1, \ldots, \lambda_m$ as the Lagrange multipliers associated with the m constraints.

B. Equate all the first-order partial derivatives of $\mathcal{L}(\mathbf{x})$ to 0:

$$\frac{\partial \mathcal{L}(\mathbf{x})}{\partial x_i} = \frac{\partial f(\mathbf{x})}{\partial x_i} - \sum_{j=1}^{m} \lambda_j \frac{\partial g_j(\mathbf{x})}{\partial x_i} = 0, \qquad i = 1, \ldots, n$$

C. Impose the complementary slackness conditions:

$$\lambda_j \ge 0 \ (\lambda_j = 0 \text{ if } g_j(\mathbf{x}) < c_j), \qquad j = 1, \ldots, m$$

D. Require $\mathbf{x}$ to satisfy the constraints

$$g_j(\mathbf{x}) \le c_j, \qquad j = 1, \ldots, m$$

Find all the vectors $\mathbf{x}$ which, together with associated values of $\lambda_1, \ldots, \lambda_m$, satisfy conditions B, C, and D. These are the solution candidates, at least one of which solves the problem (if it has a solution).

EXAMPLE 1   Consider the problem: $\max y - e^{-x}$ subject to $e^x + e^y \le 6, \ y \ge x$.

(a) Sketch the feasible set S in the xy-plane. (First solve $e^x + e^y = 6$ for y, and draw the curve $y = \ln(6 - e^x)$.)

(b) Then solve the problem. (Verify that the Lagrangian is concave in (x, y).)

Solution: (a) See Fig. 1.   (b) The first (important) step is to write the problem in exactly the same form as (1):

$$\max y - e^{-x} \quad \text{subject to} \quad \begin{cases} e^x + e^y \le 6 & \text{(I)} \\ x - y \le 0 & \text{(II)} \end{cases}$$

The Lagrangian function is

$$\mathcal{L}(x, y) = y - e^{-x} - \lambda(e^x + e^y - 6) - \mu(x - y)$$

The Kuhn–Tucker conditions are: There exist numbers λ and μ such that

$$\mathcal{L}'_x = e^{-x} - \lambda e^x - \mu = 0 \tag{i}$$
$$\mathcal{L}'_y = 1 - \lambda e^y + \mu = 0 \tag{ii}$$
$$\lambda \geq 0 \quad (\lambda = 0 \text{ if } e^x + e^y < 6) \tag{iii}$$
$$\mu \geq 0 \quad (\mu = 0 \text{ if } x - y < 0) \tag{iv}$$

From (ii) and (iv), $\lambda e^y = 1 + \mu \geq 1$, so $\lambda > 0$, and then $e^x + e^y = 6$ because of (iii).

Suppose the constraint (II) is binding, i.e. $x = y$. Then $e^x = e^y = 3$, and equations (i) and (ii) yield

$$\tfrac{1}{3} - 3\lambda - \mu = 0$$
$$1 - 3\lambda + \mu = 0$$

It follows that $\lambda = 2/9$ and $\mu = -1/3$, which contradicts (iv).

Hence $x < y$, and (iv) gives $\mu = 0$. But with $\mu = 0$, equation (i) yields $\lambda = e^{-2x}$, and equation (ii) gives $\lambda = e^{-y}$, so $y = 2x$ and $e^y = (e^x)^2$. Hence, $(e^x)^2 + e^x = 6$. This second degree equation in e^x has the solution $e^x = 2$ (together with the impossible "solution" $e^x = -3$). We conclude that the only solution candidate is

$$x = \ln 2 \quad \text{and} \quad y = 2x = \ln 4$$

Because the Lagrangian is concave, these values of x and y solve the problem. (By studying in Fig. 1 the level curves $y - e^{-x} = c$ for the objective function, it is easy to confirm the solution.)

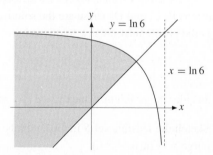

Figure 1

Nonnegativity Conditions on the Variables

Consider the general nonlinear programming problem (1) once again. Often, variables involved in economic optimization problems must be nonnegative by their very nature. It is not difficult to incorporate such constraints in the formulation of (1). If $x_1 \geq 0$, for example, this can be represented by the new constraint $h_1(x_1, \ldots, x_n) = -x_1 \leq 0$, and we introduce an additional Lagrange multiplier to go with it. But in order not to have too many Lagrange multipliers, the necessary conditions for the solution of nonlinear programming problems with nonnegativity constraints are sometimes formulated in a slightly different way.

Consider first the problem

$$\max f(x, y) \quad \text{subject to} \quad g(x, y) \leq c, \; x \geq 0, \; y \geq 0 \tag{2}$$

Here we introduce the functions $h_1(x, y) = -x$ and $h_2(x, y) = -y$, so that the constraints in problem (2) become $g(x, y) \leq c$, $h_1(x, y) \leq 0$, and $h_2(x, y) \leq 0$. Applying the recipe for solving (1), we introduce the Lagrangian

$$\mathcal{L}(x, y) = f(x, y) - \lambda(g(x, y) - c) - \mu_1(-x) - \mu_2(-y)$$

The Kuhn–Tucker conditions are

$$\frac{\partial \mathcal{L}}{\partial x} = f_1'(x, y) - \lambda g_1'(x, y) + \mu_1 = 0 \tag{i}$$

$$\frac{\partial \mathcal{L}}{\partial y} = f_2'(x, y) - \lambda g_2'(x, y) + \mu_2 = 0 \tag{ii}$$

$$\lambda \geq 0 \quad (\lambda = 0 \text{ if } g(x, y) < c) \tag{iii}$$

$$\mu_1 \geq 0 \quad (\mu_1 = 0 \text{ if } x > 0) \tag{iv}$$

$$\mu_2 \geq 0 \quad (\mu_2 = 0 \text{ if } y > 0) \tag{v}$$

From (i), we have $f_1'(x, y) - \lambda g_1'(x, y) = -\mu_1$. From (iv), we have $-\mu_1 \leq 0$ and $-\mu_1 = 0$ if $x > 0$. Thus, (i) and (iv) are together equivalent to

$$f_1'(x, y) - \lambda g_1'(x, y) \leq 0 \quad (= 0 \text{ if } x > 0) \tag{vi}$$

In the same way, (ii) and (v) are together equivalent to

$$f_2'(x, y) - \lambda g_2'(x, y) \leq 0 \quad (= 0 \text{ if } y > 0) \tag{vii}$$

So the new Kuhn–Tucker conditions are (vi), (vii), and (iii). Note that after replacing (i) and (iv) by (vi), as well as (ii) and (v) by (vii), only the multiplier λ associated with $g(x, y) \leq c$ remains.

The same idea can obviously be extended to the n-variable problem

$$\max f(\mathbf{x}) \quad \text{s.t.} \quad \begin{cases} g_1(\mathbf{x}) \leq c_1 \\ \ldots\ldots\ldots \\ g_m(\mathbf{x}) \leq c_m \end{cases}, \quad x_1 \geq 0, \ldots, x_n \geq 0 \tag{3}$$

Briefly formulated, the necessary conditions for the solution of (3) are that, for each $i = 1, \ldots, n$:

$$\frac{\partial f(\mathbf{x})}{\partial x_i} - \sum_{j=1}^{m} \lambda_j \frac{\partial g_j(\mathbf{x})}{\partial x_i} \leq 0 \quad (= 0 \text{ if } x_i > 0) \tag{4}$$

$$\lambda_j \geq 0 \quad (\lambda_j = 0 \text{ if } g_j(\mathbf{x}) < c_j), \quad j = 1, \ldots, m \tag{5}$$

EXAMPLE 2   **(Peak Load Pricing)**   Consider a producer who generates electricity by burning a fuel such as coal or natural gas. The demand for electricity varies between peak periods, during which all the generating capacity is used, and off-peak periods when there is spare capacity. We consider a certain time interval (say, a year) divided into n periods of equal length. Suppose the amounts of electric power sold in these n periods are $x_1, x_2, \ldots, x_n$. Assume that a regulatory authority fixes the corresponding prices at levels equal to $p_1, p_2, \ldots, p_n$. The total operating cost over all n periods is given by the function $C(x_1, \ldots, x_n)$, and k is the output capacity in each period. Let $D(k)$ denote the cost of maintaining output capacity k. The producer's total profit is then

$$\pi(x_1, \ldots, x_n, k) = \sum_{i=1}^{n} p_i x_i - C(\mathbf{x}) - D(k)$$

Because the producer cannot exceed capacity k in any period, it faces the constraints

$$x_1 \leq k, \ \ldots, \ x_n \leq k \tag{I}$$

We consider the problem of finding $x_1 \geq 0, \ldots, x_n \geq 0$ and $k \geq 0$ such that profit is maximized subject to the capacity constraints (I).

This is a nonlinear programming problem with $n + 1$ variables and n constraints. The Lagrangian function $\mathcal{L}$ is

$$\mathcal{L}(x_1, \ldots, x_n, k) = \sum_{i=1}^{n} p_i x_i - C(x_1, \ldots, x_n) - D(k) - \sum_{i=1}^{n} \lambda_i (x_i - k)$$

The choice $(x_1^0, \ldots, x_n^0, k^0) \geq 0$ can solve the problem only if there exist Lagrange multipliers $\lambda_1 \geq 0, \ldots, \lambda_n \geq 0$ such that

$$\frac{\partial \mathcal{L}}{\partial x_i} = p_i - C_i'(x_1^0, \ldots, x_n^0) - \lambda_i \leq 0 \quad (= 0 \text{ if } x_i^0 > 0), \qquad i = 1, \ldots, n \tag{i}$$

$$\frac{\partial \mathcal{L}}{\partial k} = -D'(k^0) + \sum_{i=1}^{n} \lambda_i \leq 0 \quad (= 0 \text{ if } k^0 > 0) \tag{ii}$$

$$\lambda_i \geq 0 \quad (\lambda_i = 0 \text{ if } x_i^0 < k), \qquad i = 1, \ldots, n \tag{iii}$$

Suppose that i is such that $x_i^0 > 0$. Then (i) implies that

$$p_i = C_i'(x_1^0, \ldots, x_n^0) + \lambda_i \tag{iv}$$

If period i is an off-peak period, then $x_i^0 < k$ and so $\lambda_i = 0$ by (iii). From (iv) it follows that $p_i = C_i'(x_1^0, \ldots, x_n^0)$. Thus, we see that *the profit-maximizing pattern of output* $(x_1^0, \ldots, x_n^0)$ *will bring about equality between the regulator's price in any off-peak period and the corresponding marginal operating cost.*

On the other hand λ_j might be positive in a peak period when $x_j^0 = k^0$. If $k^0 > 0$, it follows from (ii) that $\sum_{i=1}^{n} \lambda_i = D'(k^0)$. We conclude that the output pattern will be such that *in peak periods the price set by the regulator will exceed the marginal operating cost by an additional amount* λ_j, *which is really the "shadow price" of the capacity constraint* $x_j^0 \leq k$. *The sum of these shadow prices over all peak periods is equal to the marginal capacity cost.*

Properties of the Value Function

We return to the general nonlinear programming problem (1) without explicit nonnegativity constraints. The optimal value of the objective $f(\mathbf{x})$ obviously depends on $c_1, \ldots, c_m$. The function defined by

$$f^*(\mathbf{c}) = \max\{ f(\mathbf{x}) : g_j(\mathbf{x}) \leq c_j, \ j = 1, \ldots, m \} \tag{6}$$

assigns to each $\mathbf{c} = (c_1, \ldots, c_m)$ the optimal value $f^*(\mathbf{c})$ of f. It is called the **value function** for the problem.

The following properties of f^* are very useful:

A. $f^*(\mathbf{c})$ is nondecreasing in each variable $c_1, \ldots, c_m$.

B. If $\partial f^*(\mathbf{c})/\partial c_j$ exists, then it is equal to $\lambda_j(\mathbf{c})$, $\quad j = 1, \ldots, m$.

Here property A follows immediately because if c_j increases, and all the other variables are fixed, then the feasible set becomes larger; hence, $f^*(\mathbf{c})$ cannot decrease.

Concerning property B, each $\lambda_j(\mathbf{c})$ is a Lagrange multiplier coming from the Kuhn–Tucker conditions. However, there is a catch: The value function f^* need not be differentiable. Even if f and $g_1, \ldots, g_m$ are all differentiable, the value function can have sudden changes of slope.

The following example shows this.

EXAMPLE 3   An aircraft manufacturing firm can operate plants in either of two countries. In country A, its cost as a function of output $x \geq 0$ is $C_A(x) = \ln(1 + 3x/100)$. In country B, its cost as a function of output $y \geq 0$ is $C_B(y) = 2\ln(1 + y/100)$. The firm allocates production between the two plants in order to minimize the total cost of producing at least q units of output worldwide, where $q > 0$.

(a) Show that the firm's cost-minimizing choices of x and y must solve a particular constrained optimization problem with non-negativity constraints.

(b) Use the Lagrange multiplier method to show that there are one, two, or three solution candidates satisfying the Kuhn–Tucker conditions, depending on the value of q.

(c) Show that the firm uses only the plant in country A for levels of output below some critical level q^*, and only the plant in country B when $q > q^*$.

(d) Find the firm's minimum cost as a function of q, and show that it is not differentiable at q^*.

Solution: (a) The firm will choose (x, y) to solve the problem

$$\min C(x, y) = \ln(1 + 3x/100) + 2\ln(1 + y/100) \quad \text{s.t.} \quad x + y \geq q, \ x \geq 0, \ y \geq 0$$

(b) Because this is a minimization problem, we write the Lagrangian as

$$\mathcal{L}(x, y) = -[\ln(1 + 3x/100) + 2\ln(1 + y/100)] + \lambda(x + y - q)$$

The Kuhn–Tucker conditions from (4) and (5) are

$$-3(100 + 3x)^{-1} + \lambda \le 0 \quad (= 0 \text{ if } x > 0) \tag{i}$$

$$-2(100 + y)^{-1} + \lambda \le 0 \quad (= 0 \text{ if } y > 0) \tag{ii}$$

$$\lambda \ge 0 \quad (\lambda = 0 \text{ if } x + y > q) \tag{iii}$$

If $\lambda = 0$, then from (i) and (ii) we get $x = y = 0$, which contradicts $x + y \ge q > 0$. Thus $\lambda > 0$, and $x + y = q$.

Suppose $x > 0$ and $y > 0$. From (i) and (ii) we get $-3(100 + 3x)^{-1} = -2(100 + y)^{-1}$. So $2(100 + 3x) = 3(100 + y)$, implying that $6x - 3y = 100$. Because $x + y = q$, we have the unique solution candidate

$$(x, y) = (q/3 + 100/9, \, 2q/3 - 100/9) \text{ with } \lambda = 9(400 + 3q)^{-1} \quad (q > 50/3) \tag{$*$}$$

This interior solution candidate is valid provided that $q > 50/3$, which ensures that $y > 0$. The associated cost is $\ln[(400 + 3q)/300] + 2\ln[(400 + 3q)/450]$.

Suppose $x > 0$ and $y = 0$. The solution candidate is then $(x, y) = (q, 0)$, with $\lambda = 3(100 + 3q)^{-1}$, and an associated cost $C(q, 0) = \ln(1 + 3q/100)$. This is valid provided that (ii) is also satisfied, that is $\lambda = 3(100 + 3q)^{-1} \le 2(100 + 0)^{-1} = 2/100$. This is true for all $q \ge 50/3$.

Suppose $x = 0$ and $y > 0$. Then the solution candidate is $(x, y) = (0, q)$, with $\lambda = 2(100 + q)^{-1}$, and an associated cost $C(0, q) = 2\ln(1 + q/100)$. This is valid provided that (i) is also satisfied, that is $\lambda = 2(100 + q)^{-1} \le 3(100 + 0)^{-1} = 3/100$. This is obviously true for all $q > 0$.

Thus, for $0 < q < 50/3$ there is only one solution candidate, $(0, q)$. For $q = 50/3$, $(q, 0)$ and $(0, q)$ are both candidates. Finally, for $q > 50/3$, $(q, 0)$, $(0, q)$, and (x, y) given in ($*$) are solution candidates.

(c) Comparing these different solution candidates, note that when the interior solution candidate exists (for $q > 50/3$), it is always the worst. In fact, it is a global *maximum* of the concave function $C(x, y)$ subject to the constraints $x + y = q$ and $x \ge 0$, $y \ge 0$.

So the cost-minimizing solution is a choice between $(x, y) = (q, 0)$ with the associated cost $\ln(1 + 3q/100)$, and $(x, y) = (0, q)$ with cost $2\ln(1 + q/100)$. Note that $\ln(1 + 3q/100) > 2\ln(1 + q/100) = \ln(1 + q/100)^2$ if and only if $(1 + 3q/100) > (1 + q/100)^2$, which reduces to $q < 100$. It follows that $(q, 0)$ is cheaper when $q > q^* = 100$, but $(0, q)$ is cheaper when $q < 100$. When $q = 100$, both extreme solutions are equally good. (When $q < 50/3$, the corner solution $(q, 0)$ is actually a global maximum.)

(d) The minimum cost function is $C^*(q) = 2\ln(1 + q/100)$ if $q < 100$, and $C^*(q) = \ln(1 + 3q/100)$ if $q > 100$. Provided that $q \ne 100$, the derivative $C^{*\prime}(q) = \lambda$ (which accords with property B of the value function). But C^* is not differentiable at $q = 100$. In fact, the left-hand derivative of C^* at $q = 100$ is $1/100$, and the right-hand derivative is $3/400$.

NOTE 1 It is actually easier to solve this problem by putting $y = q - x$ and then minimizing $C(x, q - x)$ w.r.t. the single variable x over the interval $[0, q]$. Nevertheless, we have presented it as an example of the Lagrange multiplier method, which also allow us to derive a value for the Lagrange multiplier.

PROBLEMS FOR SECTION 14.8

1. Consider the problem

$$\max \tfrac{1}{2}x - y \quad \text{subject to} \quad x + e^{-x} \leq y, \ x \geq 0$$

   (a) Write down the Lagrangian function and the necessary Kuhn–Tucker conditions for this problem.

   (b) Find the only pair (x, y) that satisfies all the necessary conditions. Find the solution to the problem.

2. Consider the problem

$$\max \ x + y - e^x - e^{x+y} \quad \text{subject to} \quad x + y \geq 4, \ x \geq -1, \ y \geq 1$$

   (a) Sketch the feasible set S.

   (b) Find all pairs (x, y) that satisfy all the necessary conditions. Find the solution to the problem.

3. Consider the problem

$$\max x + ay \quad \text{subject to} \ x^2 + y^2 \leq 1, \ x + y \geq 0 \qquad (a \text{ is a constant})$$

   (a) Sketch the feasible set and write down the necessary conditions.

   (b) Find the solution for all values of the constant a.

4. Solve the following problems, assuming they have solutions:

   (a) max $y - x^2$ subject to $y \geq 0, \ y - x \geq -2, \ y^2 \leq x$

   (b) max $xe^{y-x} - 2ey$ subject to $x \geq 0, \ 0 \leq y \leq 1 + x/2$

5. Suppose that optimal capacity utilization by a firm requires that its output quantities x_1 and x_2, and its capacity level k, should be chosen to solve the problem

$$\max x_1 + 3x_2 - x_1^2 - x_2^2 - k^2 \text{ subject to } \begin{cases} x_1 \leq k \\ x_2 \leq k \end{cases}, \quad x_1 \geq 0, \ x_2 \geq 0, \ k \geq 0$$

   Show that $k = 0$ cannot be optimal, and then find the solution.

REVIEW PROBLEMS FOR CHAPTER 14

1. (a) Solve the following problem using the Lagrange multiplier method:

$$\max f(x, y) = 3x + 4y \quad \text{subject to} \quad g(x, y) = x^2 + y^2 = 225$$

   (b) Suppose 225 is changed to 224. What is the approximate change in the optimal value of f?

2. Using the result (∗∗) in Example 14.1.3, write down the solution to the problem $\max f(x, y)$ subject to $px + qy = m$ when:

   (a) $f(x, y) = 25x^2 y^3$ (b) $f(x, y) = x^{1/5} y^{2/5}$ (c) $f(x, y) = 10\sqrt{x}\,\sqrt[3]{y}$

3. (a) Solve the problem

$$\max(\min)\ x^2 + y^2 - 2x + 1 \quad \text{subject to} \quad \tfrac{1}{4}x^2 + y^2 = b$$

   where b is a constant $> \tfrac{4}{9}$. (The constraint has a graph which is an ellipse in the xy-plane. So it defines a closed, bounded set.)

   (b) If $f^*(b)$ denotes the value function for the maximization problem, verify that $df^*(b)/db = \lambda$, where λ is the corresponding Lagrange multiplier.

4. (a) A rectangular box has length x, breadth y and height z. Interpret the following problem:

$$\max F(x, y, z) = xyz \quad \text{subject to} \quad 2(xy + xz + yz) = A \qquad (*)$$

   where A is a positive constant.

   (b) Use the Lagrange multiplier method to show that (x, y, z) can only solve problem (∗) if

$$\frac{yz}{y + z} = \frac{xz}{x + z} = \frac{xy}{x + y} \quad \text{and} \quad xy + xz + yz = \frac{A}{2}$$

   (c) Assuming that (∗) has a solution, find the solution.

5. Consider the problem

$$\text{minimize } f(x, y) = x^2 - 2x + 1 + y^2 - 2y$$
$$\text{subject to} \quad g(x, y) = (x + y)\sqrt{x + y + b} = 2\sqrt{a}$$

   where a and b are positive constants, and x and y are positive.

(a) Suppose that (x, y) solves the problem. Show that x and y must then satisfy the equations

$$x = y \quad \text{and} \quad 2x^3 + bx^2 = a \qquad (*)$$

(b) The equations in $(*)$ define x and y as differentiable functions of a and b. Find expressions for $\partial x / \partial a$, $\partial^2 x / \partial a^2$, and $\partial x / \partial b$.

(c) Show that there exists exactly one point (x, y) in the first quadrant which solves the system of equations $(*)$.

6. Solve the following problem, assuming it has a solution:

$$\text{maximize} \quad -\frac{1}{x} + 4y + 4z \quad \text{subject to} \quad \begin{cases} x + y + z = 2 \\ x^2 + y^2 + z^2 = 3/2 \end{cases}$$

7. (a) Consider the consumer demand problem

$$\max_{x, y} \left[A \ln(x - a) + B \ln(y - b) \right] \quad \text{subject to} \quad px + qy = m \qquad (*)$$

where a, b, A, B, p, q, and m are positive constants with $A + B = 1$, and moreover, with $R = m - ap - bq > 0$. Show that if $x = x^*$, $y = y^*$ solve problem $(*)$, then

$$x^* = a + AR/p, \qquad y^* = b + BR/q \qquad (**)$$

(b) Suppose $U^*(p, q, m) = U(x^*, y^*)$ denotes the indirect utility function. Show that $\partial U^* / \partial m > 0$ and verify Roy's identities, $\dfrac{\partial U^*}{\partial p} = -\dfrac{\partial U^*}{\partial m} x^*$ and $\dfrac{\partial U^*}{\partial q} = -\dfrac{\partial U^*}{\partial m} y^*$.

8. (a) Suppose $f(x, y, z) = x^2 + x + y^2 + z^2$. Find the maximum and minimum of $f(x, y, z)$ subject to the constraint $x^2 + 2y^2 + 2z^2 = 16$.

(b) Find the maximum and minimum of $f(x, y, z)$ over the set

$$S = \left\{ (x, y, z) : x^2 + 2y^2 + 2z^2 \leq 16 \right\}$$

9. Suppose the firm of Example 8.5.1 earns revenue $R(Q)$ and incurs cost $C(Q)$ as functions of output $Q \geq 0$, where $R'(Q) > 0$, $C'(Q) > 0$, $R''(Q) < 0$, and $C''(Q) > 0$ for all $Q \geq 0$. The firm maximizes profit $\pi(Q) = R(Q) - C(Q)$ subject to $Q \geq 0$. Write down the first-order conditions for the solution to this problem, and find sufficient conditions for the constraint to bind at the optimum.

10. Suppose $U(x, y)$ denotes the utility enjoyed by an individual when having x hours of leisure per day (24 hours) and y units per day of other goods. The person obtains an hourly wage of w and pays an average price of p per unit of the other goods, so that

$$py = w(24 - x) \qquad (*)$$

assuming that the individual spends all earnings.

(a) Show that maximizing $U(x, y)$ subject to the constraint (∗) leads to the equation

$$pU_1'(x, y) = wU_2'(x, y) \qquad\qquad (**)$$

(b) Suppose that the equations (∗) and (∗∗) define x and y as differentiable functions of p and w, $x = x(p, w)$, $y = y(p, w)$. Show that, with appropriate requirements on $U(x, y)$,

$$\frac{\partial x}{\partial w} = \frac{(24 - x)(wU_{22}'' - pU_{12}'') + pU_2'}{p^2U_{11}'' - 2pwU_{12}'' + w^2U_{22}''}$$

(c) Find $\partial x/\partial w$ when $U(x, y) = \ln(4+x)\cdot\ln(8+y)$, $x = 14$, $y = 10$, and $p = w = 1$.

11. (a) A firm uses positive quantities K and L units of two inputs to produce $\sqrt{KL}$ units of a product. The input factor costs are r and w per unit, respectively. The firm wants to minimize the costs of producing at least Q units. Here w, p, a, and q are positive constants. Formulate the nonlinear programming problem that emerges. Reformulate the problem as a maximization problem, then write down the Kuhn–Tucker conditions for the optimum. Solve these conditions to determine K^* and L^* as functions of (r, w, Q).

(b) Define the minimum cost function as $c^*(r, w, Q) = rK^* + wL^*$. Verify that $\partial c^*/\partial r = K^*$ and $\partial c^*/\partial w = L^*$, and give these results economic interpretations.

12. (a) Sketch the feasible set for the problem

$$\max \quad 100 - \left(x + \tfrac{1}{2}\right)^2 - \tfrac{1}{2}y^2 \quad \text{subject to} \quad \begin{cases} e^{-x} - y \le 0 \\ y \le \tfrac{2}{3} \end{cases}$$

(b) Write down the Kuhn–Tucker necessary conditions for the solution of the problem, and find the solution.

MATRIX AND VECTOR ALGEBRA

Indeed, models basically play the same role in economics as in fashion. They provide an articulated frame on which to show off your material to advantage, ... a useful role, but fraught with the dangers that the designer may get carried away by his personal inclination for the model, while the customer may forget that the model is more streamlined than reality.
—J. H. Drèze (1984)

Most mathematical models used by economists ultimately involve a system of several equations. If these equations are all linear, the study of such systems belongs to an area of mathematics called **linear algebra**. Even if the equations are nonlinear, much may be learned from linear approximations around the solution we are interested in—for example, how the solution changes in response to small shocks to the exogenous variables or parameters.

Input–output analysis is one prominent area of economics that uses systems of linear equations. Models such as those based on Wassily Leontief's pioneering work *The Structure of the American Economy, 1919–1939* have systems with hundreds of equations containing hundreds of unknowns. This model, and similar ones developed in the former Soviet Union by Leonid Kantorovich, were intended to help plan the production of military equipment and other supplies during the Second World War (1939–1945).

In order to comprehend such enormous systems of equations, it is convenient to work with a number of mathematical concepts such as matrices, vectors, and determinants. These are introduced in this chapter and in the next, where we demonstrate their use in economics. Actually, the usefulness of linear algebra extends far beyond its ability to solve systems of linear equations. For instance, in the theory of differential and difference equations, in linear and nonlinear optimization theory, in statistics and econometrics, the methods of linear algebra are used extensively.

15.1 Systems of Linear Equations

Section 2.4 has already introduced systems of two simultaneous linear equations in two variables. Here is an example of such a system, where now the two unknowns are denoted by x_1 and x_2,

$$x_1 + 2x_2 = 2$$
$$2x_1 - x_2 = 4 \qquad (*)$$

A *solution* of this system is a pair of numbers (x_1, x_2) which satisfies both equations. We all know one method of finding the solution—namely, elimination. From the first equation we obtain $x_1 = -2x_2 + 2$. Inserting this expression for x_1 into the second equation gives $2(-2x_2 + 2) - x_2 = 4$. Hence we find that $x_2 = 0$, and then $x_1 = -2 \cdot 0 + 2 = 2$. *The only solution is therefore* $(x_1, x_2) = (2, 0)$.

A general notation for a system with two linear equations in two unknowns x_1 and x_2 is

$$a_{11}x_1 + a_{12}x_2 = b_1$$
$$a_{21}x_1 + a_{22}x_2 = b_2$$

Note that a_{21}, with the double subscript 2 and 1, is the coefficient in the second equation multiplying x_1, the first unknown.

Since we often need to consider a large number of equations and unknowns, we need a suitable notation for an arbitrary linear system of equations with m equations and n unknowns. We allow m to be larger than, equal to, or less than n. If the unknowns are denoted by $x_1, \ldots, x_n$, we usually write such a system in the form

$$a_{11}x_1 + a_{12}x_2 + \cdots + a_{1n}x_n = b_1$$
$$a_{21}x_1 + a_{22}x_2 + \cdots + a_{2n}x_n = b_2$$
$$\cdots\cdots\cdots\cdots\cdots\cdots\cdots\cdots\cdots\cdots \qquad (1)$$
$$a_{m1}x_1 + a_{m2}x_2 + \cdots + a_{mn}x_n = b_m$$

Here $a_{11}, a_{12}, \ldots, a_{mn}$ are called the *coefficients* of the system, and $b_1, \ldots, b_m$ are called the *right-hand sides*. All are real numbers.

Note carefully the order of the subscripts. In general, a_{ij} is the coefficient in the ith equation of the jth variable (x_j). One or more of these coefficients may be 0—indeed, a high proportion of them may be.

A **solution** of system (1) is an ordered set or list of numbers $s_1, s_2, \ldots, s_n$ that satisfies all the equations simultaneously when we put $x_1 = s_1, x_2 = s_2, \ldots, x_n = s_n$. Usually, a solution is written as $(s_1, s_2, \ldots, s_n)$. Note that the order in which we write the components is essential in the sense that if $(s_1, s_2, \ldots, s_n)$ satisfies (1), then $(s_n, s_{n-1}, \ldots, s_1)$, say, will usually *not* be a solution. For example, $(x_1, x_2) = (2, 0)$ is a solution of the system $(*)$, but $(x_1, x_2) = (0, 2)$ is not a solution.

If system (1) has at least one solution, it is said to be **consistent**. When the system has no solution, it is said to be **inconsistent**.

EXAMPLE 1   Do the following systems have solutions?

$$\text{(a)} \quad \begin{array}{l} 3x_1 + 5x_2 = 6 \\ 3x_1 + 5x_2 = 7 \end{array} \qquad \text{(b)} \quad \begin{array}{l} x_1 + x_2 - 2x_3 = 2 \\ -x_2 + 2x_3 = -1 \end{array}$$

Solution:

(a) This system is inconsistent. No matter what values values we choose for x_1 and x_2, the expression $3x_1 + 5x_2$ cannot be both 6 and 7. *The system has no solutions.*

(b) This is a system in the form (1) with 2 equations and 3 unknowns. The system is consistent and has infinitely many solutions. Choosing an arbitrary value for x_3, say $x_3 = s$, the second equation yields $x_2 = 2s + 1$, while the first gives $x_1 = 1$. *Hence for all values of s, the list $(x_1, x_2, x_3) = (1, 2s + 1, s)$ is a solution of the system.* The system has one *degree of freedom*, because one variable (s) can be changed freely. (See Section 12.9.)

There are computer programs that make it easy to check whether a system like (1) is consistent, and if it is, to find possible solutions, even if there are thousands of equations and unknowns. Still, economists need to understand the general theory of such equation systems so that they can follow theoretical arguments and conclusions related to linear models of this kind.

A Simple Leontief Model

In order to illustrate why linear systems of equations are important in economics, we briefly discuss a simple example of the Leontief model. A more general discussion of the Leontief model is given in Section 16.9.

EXAMPLE 2   An economy has three industries—fishing, forestry, and boat building.

To produce 1 ton of fish requires the services of α fishing boats.
To produce 1 ton of timber requires β tons of fish, in order to feed the foresters.
To produce 1 fishing boat requires γ tons of timber.

These are the only inputs needed for each of these three industries. Suppose there is no final (external) demand for fishing boats. Find what gross outputs each of the three industries must produce in order to meet the final demands of d_1 tons of fish and d_2 tons of timber.

Solution: Let x_1 denote the total number of tons of fish to be produced, x_2 the total number of tons of timber, and x_3 the total number of fishing boats.

Consider first the demand for fish. Because βx_2 tons of fish are needed to produce x_2 units of timber, and because the final demand for fish is d_1, we must have $x_1 = \beta x_2 + d_1$. (Producing fishing boats does not require fish as an input, so there is no term with x_3.) In the case of timber, a similar argument shows that the equation $x_2 = \gamma x_3 + d_2$ must be satisfied. Finally, for boat building, only the fishing industry needs boats; there is no final demand in this case, and so $x_3 = \alpha x_1$. Thus, the following three equations must be satisfied:

$$x_1 = \beta x_2 + d_1$$
$$x_2 = \gamma x_3 + d_2 \qquad\qquad (*)$$
$$x_3 = \alpha x_1$$

One way to solve these equations begins by inserting the third equation into the second, in order to eliminate x_3. The result is $x_2 = \gamma \alpha x_1 + d_2$. Inserting this into the first equation yields $x_1 = \alpha\beta\gamma x_1 + \beta d_2 + d_1$. Solving this last equation for x_1 gives $x_1 = (d_1 + \beta d_2)/(1 - \alpha\beta\gamma)$.

The corresponding expressions for the two other variables are easily found, and the results are:

$$x_1 = \frac{d_1 + \beta d_2}{1 - \alpha\beta\gamma}, \qquad x_2 = \frac{\alpha\gamma d_1 + d_2}{1 - \alpha\beta\gamma}, \qquad x_3 = \frac{\alpha d_1 + \alpha\beta d_2}{1 - \alpha\beta\gamma} \qquad (**)$$

Clearly, this solution for (x_1, x_2, x_3) only makes sense when $\alpha\beta\gamma < 1$. In fact, if $\alpha\beta\gamma \geq 1$, it is impossible for this economy to meet any positive final demands for fish and timber—production in the economy is too inefficient. ∎

PROBLEMS FOR SECTION 15.1

1. Decide which of the following single equations in the variables x, y, z, and w are linear and which are not. (In (f), a and b are nonnegative constants.)

   (a) $3x - y - z - w = 50$

   (b) $\sqrt{3}x + 8xy - z + w = 0$

   (c) $3(x + y - z) = 4(x - 2y + 3z)$

   (d) $3.33x - 4y + \dfrac{800}{3}z = 3$

   (e) $(x - y)^2 + 3z - w = -3$

   (f) $2a^2x - \sqrt{b}y + (2 + \sqrt{a})z = b^2$

2. Let x_1, y_1, x_2, and y_2 be given numbers and consider the following equations in the variables a, b, c, and d. (In *almost* all other cases in this book, a, b, c, and d denote constants!)

   $$ax_1^2 + bx_1 y_1 + cy_1^2 + d = 0$$
   $$ax_2^2 + bx_2 y_2 + cy_2^2 + d = 0$$

   Is this a linear system of equations in a, b, c, and d?

3. Write system (1) out in full when $n = m = 4$ and $a_{ij} = 1$ for all $i \neq j$, while $a_{ii} = 0$ for $i = 1, 2, 3, 4$. Sum the four equations to derive a simple equation for the new variable $s = \sum_{i=1}^{4} x_i$, then solve the whole system.

4. Write down the system of equations (1) when $a_{ij} = i + j$ for $i, j = 1, 2, 3$ and $b_j = j$ for $j = 1, 2, 3$.

5. In Example 2 let $\alpha = 1/2$, $\beta = 1/4$, $\gamma = 2$, $d_1 = 100$, and $d_2 = 80$. Write down system (*) in this case and find the solution of the system. Confirm the results by using the general formulas in (**).

6. Consider a collection of n individuals, each of whom owns a definite quantity of m different commodities. Let a_{ij} be the number of units of commodity i owned by individual j, where $i = 1, 2, \ldots, m$, while $j = 1, 2, \ldots, n$.

   (a) What does the list $(a_{1j}, a_{2j}, \ldots, a_{mj})$ represent?

   (b) Explain in words what $a_{11} + a_{12} + \cdots + a_{1n}$ and $a_{i1} + a_{i2} + \cdots + a_{in}$ express.

   (c) Let p_i denote the price per unit of commodity i ($i = 1, 2, \ldots, m$). What is the total value of the commodities owned by individual j?

7. T. Haavelmo devised a model of the US economy for the years 1929–1941 based on the following equations:

(i) $c = 0.712y + 95.05$ (ii) $s = 0.158(c + x) - 34.30$

(iii) $y = c + x - s$ (iv) $x = 93.53$

Here x denotes total investment, y is disposable income, s is the total saving by firms, and c is total consumption. Write the system of equations in the form (1) when the variables appear in the order x, y, s, and c. Then find the solution of the system.

15.2 Matrices and Matrix Operations

A **matrix** is simply a rectangular array of numbers considered as an entity. When there are m **rows** and n **columns** in the array, we have an m-by-n matrix (written as $m \times n$). We usually denote a matrix with bold capital letters such as **A**, **B**, and so on. In general, an $m \times n$ matrix is of the form

$$A = \begin{pmatrix} a_{11} & a_{12} & \cdots & a_{1n} \\ a_{21} & a_{22} & \cdots & a_{2n} \\ \vdots & \vdots & & \vdots \\ a_{m1} & a_{m2} & \cdots & a_{mn} \end{pmatrix} \tag{1}$$

In this book any array like (1) will be enclosed in parentheses; other mathematicians or economists may prefer to use square brackets.

The matrix **A** in (1) is said to have **order** $m \times n$. The mn numbers that constitute **A** are called its **elements** or **entries**. In particular, a_{ij} denotes the element in the ith row and the jth column. For brevity, the $m \times n$ matrix in (1) is often expressed as $(a_{ij})_{m \times n}$, or more simply as (a_{ij}), if the order $m \times n$ is either obvious or unimportant.

A matrix with only one row is also called a **row vector**, and a matrix with only one column is called a **column vector**. We refer to both types as **vectors**. It is usual to denote row or column vectors by small bold letters rather than capital letters.

EXAMPLE 1 $A = \begin{pmatrix} 3 & -2 \\ 5 & 8 \end{pmatrix}$, $B = (-1, \ 2, \ \sqrt{3}, \ 16)$, $C = \begin{pmatrix} -1 & 2 \\ 8 & 5 \\ 7 & 6 \\ 1 & 1 \end{pmatrix}$

are matrices. Of these, **A** is 2×2, **B** is 1×4 (and so a row vector), and **C** is 4×2. Also $a_{21} = 5$ and $c_{32} = 6$. Note that c_{23} is undefined because **C** only has two columns.

EXAMPLE 2 Construct the 4×3 matrix $A = (a_{ij})_{4 \times 3}$ with $a_{ij} = 2i - j$.

Solution: Matrix $\mathbf{A}$ has $4 \cdot 3 = 12$ entries. Because $a_{ij} = 2i - j$, $a_{11} = 2 \cdot 1 - 1 = 1$, $a_{12} = 2 \cdot 1 - 2 = 0$, $a_{13} = 2 \cdot 1 - 3 = -1$, and so on. The complete matrix is

$$\mathbf{A} = \begin{pmatrix} 2 \cdot 1 - 1 & 2 \cdot 1 - 2 & 2 \cdot 1 - 3 \\ 2 \cdot 2 - 1 & 2 \cdot 2 - 2 & 2 \cdot 2 - 3 \\ 2 \cdot 3 - 1 & 2 \cdot 3 - 2 & 2 \cdot 3 - 3 \\ 2 \cdot 4 - 1 & 2 \cdot 4 - 2 & 2 \cdot 4 - 3 \end{pmatrix} = \begin{pmatrix} 1 & 0 & -1 \\ 3 & 2 & 1 \\ 5 & 4 & 3 \\ 7 & 6 & 5 \end{pmatrix}$$

If $m = n$, so that the matrix has the same number of columns as rows, it is called a **square matrix** of order n. If $\mathbf{A} = (a_{ij})_{n \times n}$, then the elements $a_{11}, a_{22}, \ldots, a_{nn}$ constitute the **main diagonal** that runs from the top left (a_{11}) to the bottom right (a_{nn}). For instance, the matrix $\mathbf{A}$ in Example 1 is a square matrix of order 2. The main diagonal consists of the numbers 3 and 8. Note that only a square matrix can have such a main diagonal.

EXAMPLE 3   Consider the general linear system

$$\begin{aligned} a_{11}x_1 + a_{12}x_2 + \cdots + a_{1n}x_n &= b_1 \\ a_{21}x_1 + a_{22}x_2 + \cdots + a_{2n}x_n &= b_2 \\ & \cdots\cdots\cdots\cdots\cdots\cdots\cdots\cdots\cdots\cdots \\ a_{m1}x_1 + a_{m2}x_2 + \cdots + a_{mn}x_n &= b_m \end{aligned} \tag{2}$$

of m equations in n unknowns. It is natural to represent the coefficients of the x's in (2) by the $m \times n$ matrix $\mathbf{A}$ that is arranged as in (1). Then $\mathbf{A}$ is called the **coefficient matrix** of (1). For instance, the coefficient matrix of

$$\begin{aligned} 3x_1 - 2x_2 + 6x_3 &= 5 \\ 5x_1 + x_2 + 2x_3 &= -2 \end{aligned} \quad \text{is} \quad \begin{pmatrix} 3 & -2 & 6 \\ 5 & 1 & 2 \end{pmatrix}$$

One can also represent the b's on the right-hand side by an $m \times 1$ matrix, or column vector, often denoted by $\mathbf{b}$.

EXAMPLE 4   Consider a chain of stores with four outlets, B_1, B_2, B_3, and B_4, each selling eight different commodities, V_1, V_2, $\ldots$, V_8. Let a_{ij} denote the dollar value of the sales of commodity V_i at outlet B_j during a certain month. A suitable way of recording this data is in the 8×4 matrix or "spreadsheet"

$$\mathbf{A} = \begin{pmatrix} a_{11} & a_{12} & a_{13} & a_{14} \\ a_{21} & a_{22} & a_{23} & a_{24} \\ \vdots & \vdots & \vdots & \vdots \\ a_{81} & a_{82} & a_{83} & a_{84} \end{pmatrix}$$

The 8 rows refer to the 8 commodities, whereas the 4 columns refer to the 4 outlets. For instance, if $a_{73} = 225$, this means that the sales of commodity 7 at outlet 3 were worth \$225 for the month in question.

Matrix Operations

So far matrices have been regarded as just rectangular arrays of numbers that can be useful for storing information. The real motivation for introducing matrices, however, is that there are useful rules for manipulating them that correspond (to some extent) with the familiar rules of ordinary algebra.

First, let us agree how to define equality between matrices. If $\mathbf{A} = (a_{ij})_{m \times n}$ and $\mathbf{B} = (b_{ij})_{m \times n}$ are two $m \times n$ matrices, then $\mathbf{A}$ and $\mathbf{B}$ are said to be **equal**, and we write $\mathbf{A} = \mathbf{B}$, provided that $a_{ij} = b_{ij}$ for all $i = 1, 2, \ldots, m$, and $j = 1, 2, \ldots, n$. Thus, two matrices $\mathbf{A}$ and $\mathbf{B}$ are equal if they have the same order *and* if all their corresponding entries are equal. If $\mathbf{A}$ and $\mathbf{B}$ are *not* equal, then we write $\mathbf{A} \neq \mathbf{B}$.

EXAMPLE 5   When is $\begin{pmatrix} 3 & t-1 \\ 2t & u \end{pmatrix} = \begin{pmatrix} t & 2v \\ u+1 & t+w \end{pmatrix}$?

Solution: Both are 2×2 matrices with four elements each. So equality requires the four equations $3 = t$, $t - 1 = 2v$, $2t = u + 1$, and $u = t + w$ to be satisfied. By solving these simultaneous equations, it follows that the two matrices are equal if and only if $t = 3$, $v = 1$, $u = 5$, and $w = 2$. Then both matrices are equal to $\begin{pmatrix} 3 & 2 \\ 6 & 5 \end{pmatrix}$. ▮

Let us return to Example 4, where the 8×4 matrix $\mathbf{A}$ represents the dollar values of total sales of the 8 commodities at the 4 outlets in a certain month. Suppose that the dollar values of sales for the next month are given by a corresponding 8×4 matrix $\mathbf{B} = (b_{ij})_{8 \times 4}$. The total sales revenues from each commodity in each of the outlets in the course of these 2 months combined would then be given by a new 8×4 matrix $\mathbf{C} = (c_{ij})_{8 \times 4}$, where $c_{ij} = a_{ij} + b_{ij}$ for $i = 1, \ldots, 8$ and for $j = 1, \ldots, 4$. Matrix $\mathbf{C}$ is called the "sum" of $\mathbf{A}$ and $\mathbf{B}$, and we write $\mathbf{C} = \mathbf{A} + \mathbf{B}$.

In general, if $\mathbf{A} = (a_{ij})_{m \times n}$ and $\mathbf{B} = (b_{ij})_{m \times n}$, we define the **sum** of $\mathbf{A}$ and $\mathbf{B}$ as the $m \times n$ matrix $(a_{ij} + b_{ij})_{m \times n}$. Thus,

$$\mathbf{A} + \mathbf{B} = (a_{ij})_{m \times n} + (b_{ij})_{m \times n} = (a_{ij} + b_{ij})_{m \times n} \tag{3}$$

So we add two matrices of the same order by adding their corresponding entries.

If α is a real number, we define $\alpha \mathbf{A}$ by

$$\alpha \mathbf{A} = \alpha (a_{ij})_{m \times n} = (\alpha a_{ij})_{m \times n} \tag{4}$$

Thus, to multiply a matrix by a scalar, multiply *each* entry in the matrix by that scalar. Returning to the chain of stores, the matrix equation $\mathbf{B} = 2\mathbf{A}$ would mean that all the entries in $\mathbf{B}$ are twice the corresponding elements in $\mathbf{A}$—that is, the sales revenue for each commodity in each of the outlets has exactly doubled from one month to the next. (Of course, this is a rather unlikely event.) Equivalently, $2\mathbf{A} = \mathbf{A} + \mathbf{A}$.

EXAMPLE 6   Compute $\mathbf{A} + \mathbf{B}$, $3\mathbf{A}$, and $\left(-\frac{1}{2}\right)\mathbf{B}$, if $\mathbf{A} = \begin{pmatrix} 1 & 2 & 0 \\ 4 & -3 & -1 \end{pmatrix}$ and $\mathbf{B} = \begin{pmatrix} 0 & 1 & 2 \\ 1 & 0 & 2 \end{pmatrix}$.

Solution:

$$A + B = \begin{pmatrix} 1 & 3 & 2 \\ 5 & -3 & 1 \end{pmatrix}, \quad 3A = \begin{pmatrix} 3 & 6 & 0 \\ 12 & -9 & -3 \end{pmatrix}, \quad (-\tfrac{1}{2})B = \begin{pmatrix} 0 & -\tfrac{1}{2} & -1 \\ -\tfrac{1}{2} & 0 & -1 \end{pmatrix}$$

The matrix $(-1)A$ is usually denoted by $-A$, and the difference between the two matrices A and B of the same dimension, $A - B$, means the same as $A + (-1)B$. In our chain store example, $B - A$ denotes the (net) change in sales revenue for each commodity from each outlet between one month and the next. Positive components represent increases and negative components represent decreases.

With the definitions given earlier, it is easy to derive some useful rules. Let A, B, and C be arbitrary $m \times n$ matrices, and let α and β be real numbers. Also, let 0 denote the $m \times n$ matrix consisting only of zeros, called the **zero matrix**. Then:

RULES FOR MATRIX ADDITION AND MULTIPLICATION BY SCALARS

(a) $(A + B) + C = A + (B + C)$

(b) $A + B = B + A$

(c) $A + 0 = A$

(d) $A + (-A) = 0$ (5)

(e) $(\alpha + \beta)A = \alpha A + \beta A$

(f) $\alpha(A + B) = \alpha A + \alpha B$

Each of these rules follows directly from the definitions and the corresponding rules for ordinary numbers.

Because of rule (5)(a), there is no need to put parentheses in expressions like $A + B + C$. Note also that definitions (3) and (4) imply that $A + A + A$ is equal to $3A$.

PROBLEMS FOR SECTION 15.2

1. Construct the matrix $A = (a_{ij})_{3 \times 3}$, where $a_{ii} = 1$ for $i = 1, 2, 3$, and $a_{ij} = 0$ for $i \neq j$.

2. For what values of u and v does
$$\begin{pmatrix} (1-u)^2 & v^2 & 3 \\ v & 2u & 5 \\ 6 & u & -1 \end{pmatrix} = \begin{pmatrix} 4 & 4 & u \\ v & -3v & u-v \\ 6 & v+5 & -1 \end{pmatrix}?$$

3. Evaluate $A + B$ and $3A$ when $\quad A = \begin{pmatrix} 0 & 1 \\ 2 & 3 \end{pmatrix} \quad$ and $\quad B = \begin{pmatrix} 1 & -1 \\ 5 & 2 \end{pmatrix}.$

4. Evaluate $\mathbf{A} + \mathbf{B}$, $\mathbf{A} - \mathbf{B}$, and $5\mathbf{A} - 3\mathbf{B}$ when

$$\mathbf{A} = \begin{pmatrix} 0 & 1 & -1 \\ 2 & 3 & 7 \end{pmatrix} \quad \text{and} \quad \mathbf{B} = \begin{pmatrix} 1 & -1 & 5 \\ 0 & 1 & 9 \end{pmatrix}$$

15.3 Matrix Multiplication

The matrix operations introduced so far should seem quite natural. The way in which we define matrix multiplication is not so straightforward. An important motivation for this definition is the way it helps certain key manipulations of linear equation systems.

Consider, for example, the following two linear equation systems:

(i)
$$z_1 = a_{11}y_1 + a_{12}y_2 + a_{13}y_3$$
$$z_2 = a_{21}y_1 + a_{22}y_2 + a_{23}y_3$$

(ii)
$$y_1 = b_{11}x_1 + b_{12}x_2$$
$$y_2 = b_{21}x_1 + b_{22}x_2$$
$$y_3 = b_{31}x_1 + b_{32}x_2$$

The matrices of coefficients appearing on the right-hand sides of these two systems of equations are, respectively,

$$\mathbf{A} = \begin{pmatrix} a_{11} & a_{12} & a_{13} \\ a_{21} & a_{22} & a_{23} \end{pmatrix} \quad \text{and} \quad \mathbf{B} = \begin{pmatrix} b_{11} & b_{12} \\ b_{21} & b_{22} \\ b_{31} & b_{32} \end{pmatrix}$$

System (i) expresses the z variables in terms of the y's, whereas in (ii), the y's are expressed in terms of the x's. So the z variables must be related to the x variables. Indeed, take the expressions for y_1, y_2, and y_3 in (ii) and insert them into (i). This gives

$$z_1 = a_{11}(b_{11}x_1 + b_{12}x_2) + a_{12}(b_{21}x_1 + b_{22}x_2) + a_{13}(b_{31}x_1 + b_{32}x_2)$$
$$z_2 = a_{21}(b_{11}x_1 + b_{12}x_2) + a_{22}(b_{21}x_1 + b_{22}x_2) + a_{23}(b_{31}x_1 + b_{32}x_2)$$

Rearranging the terms yields

$$z_1 = (a_{11}b_{11} + a_{12}b_{21} + a_{13}b_{31})x_1 + (a_{11}b_{12} + a_{12}b_{22} + a_{13}b_{32})x_2$$
$$z_2 = (a_{21}b_{11} + a_{22}b_{21} + a_{23}b_{31})x_1 + (a_{21}b_{12} + a_{22}b_{22} + a_{23}b_{32})x_2$$

The coefficient matrix of this system is, therefore,

$$\mathbf{C} = \begin{pmatrix} a_{11}b_{11} + a_{12}b_{21} + a_{13}b_{31} & a_{11}b_{12} + a_{12}b_{22} + a_{13}b_{32} \\ a_{21}b_{11} + a_{22}b_{21} + a_{23}b_{31} & a_{21}b_{12} + a_{22}b_{22} + a_{23}b_{32} \end{pmatrix}$$

The matrix $\mathbf{A}$ is 2×3 and $\mathbf{B}$ is 3×2. Thus, $\mathbf{B}$ *has as many rows as* $\mathbf{A}$ *has columns*. The matrix $\mathbf{C}$ is 2×2. Note that if we let $\mathbf{C} = (c_{ij})_{2 \times 2}$, then the number

$$c_{11} = a_{11}b_{11} + a_{12}b_{21} + a_{13}b_{31}$$

is obtained by multiplying each of the three elements in the first row of **A** by the corresponding element in the first column of **B**, and then adding these three products. We call the resulting expression $a_{11}b_{11} + a_{12}b_{21} + a_{13}b_{31}$ the "inner product" of the first row in **A** with the first column in **B**. Likewise, c_{12} is the inner product of the first row in **A** and the second column in **B**, and so on. Generally, each element c_{ij} is the inner product of the ith row in **A** and the jth column in **B**.

The matrix **C** is called the **(matrix) product** of **A** and **B**, and we write **C** = **AB**. Here is a numerical example.

EXAMPLE 1

$$\begin{pmatrix} 1 & 0 & 3 \\ 2 & 1 & 5 \end{pmatrix} \begin{pmatrix} 1 & 3 \\ 2 & 5 \\ 6 & 2 \end{pmatrix} = \begin{pmatrix} 1 \cdot 1 + 0 \cdot 2 + 3 \cdot 6 & 1 \cdot 3 + 0 \cdot 5 + 3 \cdot 2 \\ 2 \cdot 1 + 1 \cdot 2 + 5 \cdot 6 & 2 \cdot 3 + 1 \cdot 5 + 5 \cdot 2 \end{pmatrix} = \begin{pmatrix} 19 & 9 \\ 34 & 21 \end{pmatrix}$$

In order to generalize the argument, assume that as in (i) the variables $z_1, \ldots, z_m$ are expressed linearly in terms of $y_1, \ldots, y_n$, and that as in (ii), the variables $y_1, \ldots, y_n$ are expressed linearly in terms of $x_1, \ldots, x_p$. Then $z_1, \ldots, z_m$ can be expressed linearly in terms of $x_1, \ldots, x_p$. The result we get leads directly to the following definition:

MATRIX MULTIPLICATION

Suppose that $\mathbf{A} = (a_{ij})_{m \times n}$ and that $\mathbf{B} = (b_{ij})_{n \times p}$. Then the product $\mathbf{C} = \mathbf{AB}$ is the $m \times p$ matrix $\mathbf{C} = (c_{ij})_{m \times p}$, whose element in the ith row and the jth column is the inner product

$$c_{ij} = \sum_{k=1}^{n} a_{ik}b_{kj} = a_{i1}b_{1j} + a_{i2}b_{2j} + \cdots + a_{ik}b_{kj} + \cdots + a_{in}b_{nj}$$

(1)

of the ith row of **A** and the jth column of **B**.

Note that to get c_{ij} we multiply each component a_{ik} in the ith row of **A** by the corresponding component b_{kj} in the jth column of **B**, then add all the products. One way of visualizing matrix multiplication is this:

$$\begin{pmatrix} a_{11} & \cdots & a_{1k} & \cdots & a_{1n} \\ \vdots & & \vdots & & \vdots \\ a_{i1} & \cdots & a_{ik} & \cdots & a_{in} \\ \vdots & & \vdots & & \vdots \\ a_{m1} & \cdots & a_{mk} & \cdots & a_{mn} \end{pmatrix} \cdot \begin{pmatrix} b_{11} & \cdots & b_{1j} & \cdots & b_{1p} \\ \vdots & & \vdots & & \vdots \\ b_{k1} & \cdots & b_{kj} & \cdots & b_{kp} \\ \vdots & & \vdots & & \vdots \\ b_{n1} & \cdots & b_{nj} & \cdots & b_{np} \end{pmatrix} = \begin{pmatrix} c_{11} & \cdots & c_{1j} & \cdots & c_{1p} \\ \vdots & & \vdots & & \vdots \\ c_{i1} & \cdots & c_{ij} & \cdots & c_{ip} \\ \vdots & & \vdots & & \vdots \\ c_{m1} & \cdots & c_{mj} & \cdots & c_{mp} \end{pmatrix}$$

It is important to note that the matrix product **AB** is defined only if the number of columns in **A** is equal to the number of rows in **B**. Also, if **A** and **B** are two matrices, then **AB** might be defined, even if **BA** is not. For instance, if **A** is 6 × 3 and **B** is 3 × 5, then **AB** is defined (and is 6 × 5), whereas **BA** is not defined.

EXAMPLE 2   Let $\mathbf{A} = \begin{pmatrix} 0 & 1 & 2 \\ 2 & 3 & 1 \\ 4 & -1 & 6 \end{pmatrix}$ and $\mathbf{B} = \begin{pmatrix} 3 & 2 \\ 1 & 0 \\ -1 & 1 \end{pmatrix}$. Compute the matrix product $\mathbf{AB}$. Is the product $\mathbf{BA}$ defined?

Solution: $\mathbf{A}$ is 3×3 and $\mathbf{B}$ is 3×2, so $\mathbf{AB}$ is a 3×2 matrix:

$$\mathbf{AB} = \begin{pmatrix} 0 & 1 & 2 \\ \boxed{2 \quad 3 \quad 1} \\ 4 & -1 & 6 \end{pmatrix} \begin{pmatrix} \boxed{3} & 2 \\ \boxed{1} & 0 \\ \boxed{-1} & 1 \end{pmatrix} = \begin{pmatrix} -1 & 2 \\ \boxed{8} & 5 \\ 5 & 14 \end{pmatrix}$$

(We have indicated how the element in the second row and first column of $\mathbf{AB}$ is found. It is the inner product of the second row in $\mathbf{A}$ and the first column in $\mathbf{B}$; this is $2 \cdot 3 + 3 \cdot 1 + 1 \cdot (-1) = 8$.) The matrix product $\mathbf{BA}$ is not defined because the number of columns in $\mathbf{B}$ ($= 2$) is not equal to the number of rows in $\mathbf{A}$ ($= 3$).

NOTE 1 In the previous example, $\mathbf{AB}$ was defined but $\mathbf{BA}$ was not. Even in cases in which $\mathbf{AB}$ and $\mathbf{BA}$ are both defined, they are usually not equal. See Problem 1 and the subsection "Errors to Avoid" in Section 15.4. When we write $\mathbf{AB}$, we say that we **premultiply B** by $\mathbf{A}$, whereas in $\mathbf{BA}$ we **postmultiply B** by $\mathbf{A}$.

EXAMPLE 3   Initially, three firms A, B, and C (numbered 1, 2, and 3) share the market for a certain commodity. Firm A has 20% of the market, B has 60%, and C has 20%. In the course of the next year, the following changes occur:

$$\begin{cases} A \text{ keeps 85\% of its customers, while losing 5\% to } B \text{ and 10\% to } C \\ B \text{ keeps 55\% of its customers, while losing 10\% to } A \text{ and 35\% to } C \\ C \text{ keeps 85\% of its customers, while losing 10\% to } A \text{ and 5\% to } B \end{cases}$$

We can represent market shares of the three firms by means of a *market share vector*, defined as a column vector $\mathbf{s}$ whose components are all nonnegative and sum to 1. Define the matrix $\mathbf{T}$ and the initial market share vector $\mathbf{s}$ by

$$\mathbf{T} = \begin{pmatrix} 0.85 & 0.10 & 0.10 \\ 0.05 & 0.55 & 0.05 \\ 0.10 & 0.35 & 0.85 \end{pmatrix} \quad \text{and} \quad \mathbf{s} = \begin{pmatrix} 0.2 \\ 0.6 \\ 0.2 \end{pmatrix}$$

Notice that t_{ij} is the percentage of j's customers who become i's customers in the next period. So $\mathbf{T}$ is called the *transition matrix*.

Compute the vector $\mathbf{Ts}$, show that it is also a market share vector, and give an interpretation. What is the interpretation of $\mathbf{T(Ts)}$, $\mathbf{T(T(Ts))}$, ...?

Solution:

$$\mathbf{Ts} = \begin{pmatrix} 0.85 & 0.10 & 0.10 \\ 0.05 & 0.55 & 0.05 \\ 0.10 & 0.35 & 0.85 \end{pmatrix} \begin{pmatrix} 0.2 \\ 0.6 \\ 0.2 \end{pmatrix} = \begin{pmatrix} 0.25 \\ 0.35 \\ 0.40 \end{pmatrix}$$

Because $0.25 + 0.35 + 0.40 = 1$, the product **Ts** is also a market share vector. The first entry in **Ts** is obtained from the calculation

$$0.85 \cdot 0.2 + 0.10 \cdot 0.6 + 0.10 \cdot 0.2 = 0.25$$

Here $0.85 \cdot 0.2$ is A's share of the market that it retains after 1 year, $0.10 \cdot 0.6$ is the share A gains from B, and $0.10 \cdot 0.2$ is the share A gains from C. The sum is therefore A's total share of the market after 1 year. The other entries in **Ts** have corresponding interpretations, so **Ts** must be the new market share vector after 1 year. Then **T(Ts)** is the market share vector after one more year—that is, after 2 years, and so on. (In Problem 6, you are asked to compute **T(Ts)**.)

Systems of Equations in Matrix Form

The definition of matrix multiplication was introduced in order to allow systems of equations to be manipulated. Indeed, it turns out that we can write linear systems of equations very compactly by means of matrix multiplication. For instance, consider the system

$$3x_1 + 4x_2 = 5$$
$$7x_1 - 2x_2 = 2$$

Now define $\mathbf{A} = \begin{pmatrix} 3 & 4 \\ 7 & -2 \end{pmatrix}$, $\mathbf{x} = \begin{pmatrix} x_1 \\ x_2 \end{pmatrix}$, and $\mathbf{b} = \begin{pmatrix} 5 \\ 2 \end{pmatrix}$. Then we see that

$$\mathbf{Ax} = \begin{pmatrix} 3 & 4 \\ 7 & -2 \end{pmatrix} \begin{pmatrix} x_1 \\ x_2 \end{pmatrix} = \begin{pmatrix} 3x_1 + 4x_2 \\ 7x_1 - 2x_2 \end{pmatrix}$$

So the original system is equivalent to the matrix equation

$$\mathbf{Ax} = \mathbf{b}$$

Consider the general linear system (1) in Section 15.1. Suppose we define

$$\mathbf{A} = \begin{pmatrix} a_{11} & a_{12} & \cdots & a_{1n} \\ a_{21} & a_{22} & \cdots & a_{2n} \\ \vdots & \vdots & & \vdots \\ a_{m1} & a_{m2} & \cdots & a_{mn} \end{pmatrix}, \quad \mathbf{x} = \begin{pmatrix} x_1 \\ x_2 \\ \vdots \\ x_n \end{pmatrix}, \quad \mathbf{b} = \begin{pmatrix} b_1 \\ b_2 \\ \vdots \\ b_m \end{pmatrix}$$

So **A** is $m \times n$ and **x** is $n \times 1$. The matrix product **Ax** is then defined and is $m \times 1$. It follows that

$$
\begin{aligned}
a_{11}x_1 + a_{12}x_2 + \cdots + a_{1n}x_n &= b_1 \\
a_{21}x_1 + a_{22}x_2 + \cdots + a_{2n}x_n &= b_2 \\
& \cdots \cdots \cdots \cdots \cdots \cdots \cdots \cdots \cdots \\
a_{m1}x_1 + a_{m2}x_2 + \cdots + a_{mn}x_n &= b_m
\end{aligned}
$$

can be written as $\mathbf{Ax} = \mathbf{b}$

This very concise notation turns out to be extremely useful.

1. Compute the products $\mathbf{AB}$ and $\mathbf{BA}$, if possible, for the following:

(a) $\mathbf{A} = \begin{pmatrix} 0 & -2 \\ 3 & 1 \end{pmatrix}$, $\mathbf{B} = \begin{pmatrix} -1 & 4 \\ 1 & 5 \end{pmatrix}$ (b) $\mathbf{A} = \begin{pmatrix} 8 & 3 & -2 \\ 1 & 0 & 4 \end{pmatrix}$, $\mathbf{B} = \begin{pmatrix} 2 & -2 \\ 4 & 3 \\ 1 & -5 \end{pmatrix}$

(c) $\mathbf{A} = \begin{pmatrix} 0 \\ -2 \\ 4 \end{pmatrix}$, $\mathbf{B} = (0, \quad -2, \quad 3)$ (d) $\mathbf{A} = \begin{pmatrix} -1 & 0 \\ 2 & 4 \end{pmatrix}$, $\mathbf{B} = \begin{pmatrix} 3 & 1 \\ -1 & 1 \\ 0 & 2 \end{pmatrix}$

2. Using the matrices

$$\mathbf{A} = \begin{pmatrix} 2 & 4 \\ 1 & 2 \end{pmatrix}, \quad \mathbf{B} = \begin{pmatrix} -2 & 4 \\ 1 & -2 \end{pmatrix}, \quad \mathbf{C} = \begin{pmatrix} 2 & 3 \\ 6 & 9 \end{pmatrix}, \quad \mathbf{D} = \begin{pmatrix} 1 & 1 \\ 1 & 3 \end{pmatrix}$$

calculate (i) $3\mathbf{A} + 2\mathbf{B} - 2\mathbf{C} + \mathbf{D}$ (ii) $\mathbf{AB}$ (iii) $\mathbf{C(AB)}$.

3. Let $\mathbf{A} = \begin{pmatrix} 1 & 2 & -3 \\ 5 & 0 & 2 \\ 1 & -1 & 1 \end{pmatrix}$, $\mathbf{B} = \begin{pmatrix} 3 & -1 & 2 \\ 4 & 2 & 5 \\ 2 & 0 & 3 \end{pmatrix}$, $\mathbf{C} = \begin{pmatrix} 4 & 1 & 2 \\ 0 & 3 & 2 \\ 1 & -2 & 3 \end{pmatrix}$.

Find the matrices $\mathbf{A} + \mathbf{B}$, $\mathbf{A} - \mathbf{B}$, $\mathbf{AB}$, $\mathbf{BA}$, $\mathbf{A(BC)}$, and $\mathbf{(AB)C}$.

4. Write the following systems as matrix equations:

(a) $\begin{aligned} x_1 + x_2 &= 3 \\ 3x_1 + 5x_2 &= 5 \end{aligned}$ (b) $\begin{aligned} x_1 + 2x_2 + x_3 &= 4 \\ x_1 - x_2 + x_3 &= 5 \\ 2x_1 + 3x_2 - x_3 &= 1 \end{aligned}$ (c) $\begin{aligned} 2x_1 - 3x_2 + x_3 &= 0 \\ x_1 + x_2 - x_3 &= 0 \end{aligned}$

5. (a) If $\mathbf{A}$ is an $m \times n$ matrix and $\mathbf{B}$ is another matrix such that both products $\mathbf{AB}$ and $\mathbf{BA}$ are defined, what must be the dimensions of $\mathbf{B}$?

   (b) Find all matrices $\mathbf{B}$ that "commute" with $\mathbf{A} = \begin{pmatrix} 1 & 2 \\ 2 & 3 \end{pmatrix}$ in the sense that $\mathbf{BA} = \mathbf{AB}$.

6. In Example 3, compute $\mathbf{T(Ts)}$.

15.4 Rules for Matrix Multiplication

The algebraic rules in Section 15.2 concerning matrix addition and multiplication by a scalar are all natural and easy to verify. Matrix multiplication is a more complicated operation and we must carefully examine what rules apply. We have already noticed that the commutative law $\mathbf{AB} = \mathbf{BA}$ does NOT hold in general. The following three important rules *are* generally valid, however.

If **A**, **B**, and **C** are matrices whose dimensions are such that the given operations are defined, then:

RULES FOR MATRIX MULTIPLICATION

$$(\mathbf{AB})\mathbf{C} = \mathbf{A}(\mathbf{BC}) \qquad \text{(associative law)} \qquad (1)$$

$$\mathbf{A}(\mathbf{B} + \mathbf{C}) = \mathbf{AB} + \mathbf{AC} \qquad \text{(left distributive law)} \qquad (2)$$

$$(\mathbf{A} + \mathbf{B})\mathbf{C} = \mathbf{AC} + \mathbf{BC} \qquad \text{(right distributive law)} \qquad (3)$$

Note that both the left and right distributive laws are stated here because, unlike for numbers, matrix multiplication is not *commutative*, and so $\mathbf{A}(\mathbf{B} + \mathbf{C}) \neq (\mathbf{B} + \mathbf{C})\mathbf{A}$ in general.

EXAMPLE 1   Verify (1), (2), and (3) for the following matrices:

$$\mathbf{A} = \begin{pmatrix} 1 & 2 \\ 0 & 1 \end{pmatrix}, \qquad \mathbf{B} = \begin{pmatrix} 0 & -1 \\ 3 & 2 \end{pmatrix}, \qquad \mathbf{C} = \begin{pmatrix} 1 & 1 \\ 2 & 1 \end{pmatrix}$$

Solution: All operations of multiplication and addition are defined, with

$$\mathbf{AB} = \begin{pmatrix} 6 & 3 \\ 3 & 2 \end{pmatrix}, \qquad (\mathbf{AB})\mathbf{C} = \begin{pmatrix} 6 & 3 \\ 3 & 2 \end{pmatrix} \begin{pmatrix} 1 & 1 \\ 2 & 1 \end{pmatrix} = \begin{pmatrix} 12 & 9 \\ 7 & 5 \end{pmatrix}$$

$$\mathbf{BC} = \begin{pmatrix} -2 & -1 \\ 7 & 5 \end{pmatrix}, \qquad \mathbf{A}(\mathbf{BC}) = \begin{pmatrix} 1 & 2 \\ 0 & 1 \end{pmatrix} \begin{pmatrix} -2 & -1 \\ 7 & 5 \end{pmatrix} = \begin{pmatrix} 12 & 9 \\ 7 & 5 \end{pmatrix}$$

Thus, $(\mathbf{AB})\mathbf{C} = \mathbf{A}(\mathbf{BC})$ in this case. Moreover,

$$\mathbf{B} + \mathbf{C} = \begin{pmatrix} 1 & 0 \\ 5 & 3 \end{pmatrix}, \qquad \mathbf{A}(\mathbf{B} + \mathbf{C}) = \begin{pmatrix} 1 & 2 \\ 0 & 1 \end{pmatrix} \begin{pmatrix} 1 & 0 \\ 5 & 3 \end{pmatrix} = \begin{pmatrix} 11 & 6 \\ 5 & 3 \end{pmatrix}$$

and

$$\mathbf{AC} = \begin{pmatrix} 5 & 3 \\ 2 & 1 \end{pmatrix}, \qquad \mathbf{AB} + \mathbf{AC} = \begin{pmatrix} 6 & 3 \\ 3 & 2 \end{pmatrix} + \begin{pmatrix} 5 & 3 \\ 2 & 1 \end{pmatrix} = \begin{pmatrix} 11 & 6 \\ 5 & 3 \end{pmatrix}$$

So $\mathbf{A}(\mathbf{B} + \mathbf{C}) = \mathbf{AB} + \mathbf{AC}$. You should now verify the right distributive law (3) for yourself.

Proof of (1): Suppose $\mathbf{A} = (a_{ij})_{m \times n}$, $\mathbf{B} = (b_{ij})_{n \times p}$, and $\mathbf{C} = (c_{ij})_{p \times q}$. It is easy to verify that these dimensions imply that $(\mathbf{AB})\mathbf{C}$ and $\mathbf{A}(\mathbf{BC})$ are both defined as $m \times q$ matrices. We have to prove that their corresponding elements are all equal.

The il-th element of $(\mathbf{AB})\mathbf{C}$ is denoted by $[(\mathbf{AB})\mathbf{C}]_{il}$, and it is the inner product of the i-th row in $\mathbf{AB}$ and the l-th column in $\mathbf{C}$. Using the notation for sums, we see that

$$[(\mathbf{AB})\mathbf{C}]_{il} = \sum_{k=1}^{p} \left(\sum_{j=1}^{n} a_{ij} b_{jk} \right) c_{kl} = \sum_{j=1}^{n} a_{ij} \left(\sum_{k=1}^{p} b_{jk} c_{kl} \right) = [\mathbf{A}(\mathbf{BC})]_{il}$$

where the two double sums are equal because they both give the sum of all the pn terms $a_{ij} b_{jk} c_{kl}$, where j runs from 1 to n and k runs from 1 to p. This proves (1). ∎

Proving rule (1) involved examining in detail all the elements of the relevant matrices, and a corresponding examination is necessary to prove rules (2) and (3). We leave the reader to prove (2). It will probably be best first to show (2) for the case when $\mathbf{A}$, $\mathbf{B}$, and $\mathbf{C}$ are all 2×2 matrices, after which it may be clearer how to treat the general case. The proof of (3) is similar.

Because of (1), parentheses are not required in a matrix product such as $\mathbf{ABC}$. Of course, a corresponding result is valid for products of more factors.

A useful technique in matrix algebra is to prove new results by using (1) to (3), rather than examining individual elements. For instance, suppose we are asked to prove that if $\mathbf{A} = (a_{ij})$ and $\mathbf{B} = (b_{ij})$ are both $n \times n$ matrices, then

$$(\mathbf{A} + \mathbf{B})(\mathbf{A} + \mathbf{B}) = \mathbf{AA} + \mathbf{AB} + \mathbf{BA} + \mathbf{BB} \qquad (*)$$

According to (2),

$$(\mathbf{A} + \mathbf{B})(\mathbf{A} + \mathbf{B}) = (\mathbf{A} + \mathbf{B})\mathbf{A} + (\mathbf{A} + \mathbf{B})\mathbf{B}$$

By (3), one has $(\mathbf{A} + \mathbf{B})\mathbf{A} = \mathbf{AA} + \mathbf{BA}$ and $(\mathbf{A} + \mathbf{B})\mathbf{B} = \mathbf{AB} + \mathbf{BB}$, from which we see that $(*)$ follows.

Powers of Matrices

If $\mathbf{A}$ is a square matrix, the associative law (1) allows us to write $\mathbf{AA}$ as $\mathbf{A}^2$, and $\mathbf{AAA}$ as $\mathbf{A}^3$, and so on. In general,

$$\mathbf{A}^n = \mathbf{AA} \cdots \mathbf{A} \qquad (\text{$\mathbf{A}$ is repeated n times})$$

EXAMPLE 2   Let $\mathbf{A} = \begin{pmatrix} 1 & -1 \\ 0 & 1 \end{pmatrix}$. Compute $\mathbf{A}^2$, $\mathbf{A}^3$, and $\mathbf{A}^4$. Then guess the general form of $\mathbf{A}^n$, and confirm your guess by induction on n. (For induction, see Section 3.7.)

Solution: We find that

$$\mathbf{A}^2 = \mathbf{AA} = \begin{pmatrix} 1 & -2 \\ 0 & 1 \end{pmatrix}, \quad \mathbf{A}^3 = \mathbf{A}^2\mathbf{A} = \begin{pmatrix} 1 & -3 \\ 0 & 1 \end{pmatrix}, \quad \mathbf{A}^4 = \mathbf{A}^3\mathbf{A} = \begin{pmatrix} 1 & -4 \\ 0 & 1 \end{pmatrix}$$

A reasonable guess, therefore, is that for all natural numbers n,

$$\mathbf{A}^n = \begin{pmatrix} 1 & -n \\ 0 & 1 \end{pmatrix} \qquad (*)$$

We confirm this by induction on n. Formula $(*)$ *is* correct for $n = 1$. *Suppose* it is correct for $n = k$ —that is,

$$\mathbf{A}^k = \begin{pmatrix} 1 & -k \\ 0 & 1 \end{pmatrix}$$

Then

$$\mathbf{A}^{k+1} = \mathbf{A}^k\mathbf{A} = \begin{pmatrix} 1 & -k \\ 0 & 1 \end{pmatrix}\begin{pmatrix} 1 & -1 \\ 0 & 1 \end{pmatrix} = \begin{pmatrix} 1 & -k-1 \\ 0 & 1 \end{pmatrix}$$

which is precisely the result we obtain in $(*)$ by putting $n = k+1$. If the induction hypothesis $(*)$ is valid for $n = k$, we have shown that it is also valid for $n = k + 1$. So $(*)$ is indeed generally valid.

EXAMPLE 3   Suppose $\mathbf{P}$ and $\mathbf{Q}$ are $n \times n$ matrices such that $\mathbf{PQ} = \mathbf{Q}^2\mathbf{P}$. Prove that $(\mathbf{PQ})^2 = \mathbf{Q}^6\mathbf{P}^2$.

Solution: The proof is simple if we use the associative law (1) and $\mathbf{PQ} = \mathbf{Q}^2\mathbf{P}$ repeatedly:

$$(\mathbf{PQ})^2 = (\mathbf{PQ})(\mathbf{PQ}) = (\mathbf{Q}^2\mathbf{P})(\mathbf{Q}^2\mathbf{P}) = (\mathbf{Q}^2\mathbf{P})\mathbf{Q}(\mathbf{QP}) = \mathbf{Q}^2(\mathbf{PQ})(\mathbf{QP})$$

$$= \mathbf{Q}^2(\mathbf{Q}^2\mathbf{P})(\mathbf{QP}) = \mathbf{Q}^2\mathbf{Q}^2(\mathbf{PQ})\mathbf{P} = \mathbf{Q}^2\mathbf{Q}^2(\mathbf{Q}^2\mathbf{P})\mathbf{P} = \mathbf{Q}^2\mathbf{Q}^2\mathbf{Q}^2\mathbf{P}^2 = \mathbf{Q}^6\mathbf{P}^2$$

It would be essentially impossible to prove this equality by looking at individual elements. Note carefully that $(\mathbf{PQ})^2$ is *not* equal to $\mathbf{P}^2\mathbf{Q}^2$.

The Identity Matrix

The **identity matrix** of order n, denoted by $\mathbf{I}_n$ (or often just by $\mathbf{I}$), is the $n \times n$ matrix having ones along the main diagonal and zeros elsewhere:

$$\mathbf{I}_n = \begin{pmatrix} 1 & 0 & \cdots & 0 \\ 0 & 1 & \cdots & 0 \\ \vdots & \vdots & \ddots & \vdots \\ 0 & 0 & \cdots & 1 \end{pmatrix}_{n \times n} \qquad \textbf{(identity matrix)}$$

If $\mathbf{A}$ is any $m \times n$ matrix, it is easy to verify that $\mathbf{AI}_n = \mathbf{A}$. Likewise, if $\mathbf{B}$ is any $n \times m$ matrix, then $\mathbf{I}_n\mathbf{B} = \mathbf{B}$. In particular,

$$\mathbf{AI}_n = \mathbf{I}_n\mathbf{A} = \mathbf{A} \qquad \text{(for every } n \times n \text{ matrix } \mathbf{A}) \tag{4}$$

Thus, $\mathbf{I}_n$ is the matrix equivalent of 1 in the real number system. In fact, it is the only matrix with this property. To prove this, suppose $\mathbf{E}$ is an arbitrary $n \times n$ matrix such that $\mathbf{AE} = \mathbf{A}$ for all $n \times n$ matrices $\mathbf{A}$. Putting $\mathbf{A} = \mathbf{I}_n$ in particular yields $\mathbf{I}_n\mathbf{E} = \mathbf{I}_n$. But $\mathbf{I}_n\mathbf{E} = \mathbf{E}$ according to (4). So $\mathbf{E} = \mathbf{I}_n$.

Errors to Avoid

The rules of matrix algebra make many arguments very easy, but one has to be extremely careful to use only valid rules when matrices are being multiplied. Look at (∗) following the proof of (1), for instance. It is tempting to simplify the expression $\mathbf{AA} + \mathbf{AB} + \mathbf{BA} + \mathbf{BB}$ on the right-hand side to $\mathbf{AA} + 2\mathbf{AB} + \mathbf{BB}$. This is wrong! Even when $\mathbf{AB}$ and $\mathbf{BA}$ are both defined, $\mathbf{AB}$ is not necessarily equal to $\mathbf{BA}$. Matrix multiplication is *not* commutative.

EXAMPLE 4   Let $\mathbf{A}$ and $\mathbf{B}$ be the matrices $\mathbf{A} = \begin{pmatrix} 2 & 0 \\ 0 & 3 \end{pmatrix}$, $\quad \mathbf{B} = \begin{pmatrix} 0 & 1 \\ 1 & 0 \end{pmatrix}$.
Show that $\mathbf{AB} \neq \mathbf{BA}$.

Solution: $\mathbf{AB} = \begin{pmatrix} 0 & 2 \\ 3 & 0 \end{pmatrix}$ and $\mathbf{BA} = \begin{pmatrix} 0 & 3 \\ 2 & 0 \end{pmatrix}$. Hence, $\mathbf{AB} \neq \mathbf{BA}$.

If a and b are real numbers, then $ab = 0$ implies that either a or b is 0. The corresponding result is not true for matrices. In fact, $\mathbf{AB}$ can be the zero matrix even if neither $\mathbf{A}$ nor $\mathbf{B}$ is the zero matrix.

EXAMPLE 5   Let $\mathbf{A} = \begin{pmatrix} 3 & 1 \\ 6 & 2 \end{pmatrix}$, $\mathbf{B} = \begin{pmatrix} 1 & 2 \\ -3 & -6 \end{pmatrix}$. Compute $\mathbf{AB}$.

Solution:

$$\mathbf{AB} = \begin{pmatrix} 3 & 1 \\ 6 & 2 \end{pmatrix}\begin{pmatrix} 1 & 2 \\ -3 & -6 \end{pmatrix} = \begin{pmatrix} 0 & 0 \\ 0 & 0 \end{pmatrix}$$

For real numbers, if $ab = ac$ and $a \neq 0$, then $b = c$, because we can cancel by multiplying each side of the equation by $1/a$. The corresponding cancellation "rule" is not valid for matrices. Example 5 illustrates this point also: There $\mathbf{AB} = \mathbf{A0}$ and $\mathbf{A} \neq \mathbf{0}$, yet $\mathbf{B} \neq \mathbf{0}$.

So we have found examples showing that in general:

$$\mathbf{AB} \neq \mathbf{BA} \tag{5}$$

$$\mathbf{AB} = \mathbf{0} \text{ does not imply that either } \mathbf{A} \text{ or } \mathbf{B} \text{ is } \mathbf{0} \tag{6}$$

$$\mathbf{AB} = \mathbf{AC} \text{ and } \mathbf{A} \neq \mathbf{0} \text{ do not imply that } \mathbf{B} = \mathbf{C} \tag{7}$$

Here (5) says that matrix multiplication is not **commutative** in general, whereas (7) shows us that the cancellation law is generally invalid for matrix multiplication. (The cancellation law *is valid* if $\mathbf{A}$ has a so-called inverse. See Section 16.6.)

The following two examples illustrate natural applications of matrix multiplication.

EXAMPLE 6   A firm uses raw materials $R_1, R_2, \ldots, R_m$ to produce the commodities $V_1, V_2, \ldots, V_n$. For $i = 1, \ldots, m$ and $j = 1, \ldots, n$, we let a_{ij} be the quantity of raw material R_i which is needed to produce each unit of commodity V_j. These quantities form the matrix

$$\mathbf{A} = (a_{ij})_{m \times n} = \begin{pmatrix} a_{11} & a_{12} & \cdots & a_{1n} \\ a_{21} & a_{22} & \cdots & a_{2n} \\ \vdots & \vdots & & \vdots \\ a_{m1} & a_{m2} & \cdots & a_{mn} \end{pmatrix}$$

Suppose that the firm plans a monthly production of u_j units of each commodity V_j, $j = 1, 2, \ldots, n$. This plan can be represented by an $n \times 1$ matrix (column vector) $\mathbf{u}$, called the firm's monthly production vector:

$$\mathbf{u} = \begin{pmatrix} u_1 \\ u_2 \\ \vdots \\ u_n \end{pmatrix}$$

Since a_{i1}, in particular, is the amount of raw material R_i which is needed to produce one unit of commodity V_1, it follows that $a_{i1}u_1$ is the amount of raw material R_i which is needed to produce u_1 units of commodity V_1. Similarly $a_{ij}u_j$ is the amount needed for u_j units of V_j $(j = 2, \ldots, n)$. The total monthly requirement of raw material R_i is therefore

$$a_{i1}u_1 + a_{i2}u_2 + \cdots + a_{in}u_n = \sum_{j=1}^{n} a_{ij}u_j$$

Note that this is the inner product of the ith row vector in $\mathbf{A}$ and the column vector $\mathbf{u}$. The firm's monthly requirement vector $\mathbf{r}$ for all raw material is therefore given by the matrix product

$$\mathbf{r} = \mathbf{Au}$$

Thus $\mathbf{r}$ is an $m \times 1$ matrix, or a column vector.

Suppose that the prices of the m raw materials are respectively $p_1, p_2, \ldots, p_m$ per unit. If we define the price vector $\mathbf{p} = (p_1, p_2, \ldots, p_m)$, then the total monthly cost K of acquiring the required raw materials to produce the vector $\mathbf{u}$ is $\sum_{i=1}^{m} p_i r_i$. This sum can also be written as the matrix product $\mathbf{pr}$. Hence,

$$K = \mathbf{pr} = \mathbf{p(Au)} = \mathbf{pAu}$$

(Since matrix multiplication is associative, it is unnecessary to use parentheses.)

EXAMPLE 7   Figure 1 indicates the number of daily international flights between major airports in three different countries A, B, and C. The number attached to each connecting line shows how many flights there are between the two airports. For instance, from airport b_3 in country B there are 4 flights to airport c_3 in country C each day, but none to airport c_2 in country C.

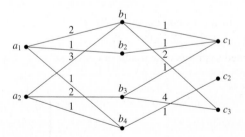

Figure 1

The relevant data can also be represented by the two matrices

$$\mathbf{P}: \begin{array}{c} \\ a_1 \\ a_2 \end{array} \begin{array}{cccc} b_1 & b_2 & b_3 & b_4 \\ \left(\begin{array}{cccc} 2 & 1 & 0 & 1 \\ 3 & 0 & 2 & 1 \end{array} \right) \end{array} \qquad \mathbf{Q}: \begin{array}{c} \\ b_1 \\ b_2 \\ b_3 \\ b_4 \end{array} \begin{array}{ccc} c_1 & c_2 & c_3 \\ \left(\begin{array}{ccc} 1 & 0 & 2 \\ 1 & 0 & 0 \\ 1 & 0 & 4 \\ 0 & 1 & 0 \end{array} \right) \end{array}$$

Each element p_{ij} of the matrix $\mathbf{P}$ represents the number of choices of flight between a_i and b_j, while each element q_{jk} of $\mathbf{Q}$ represents the number of choices of flight between b_j and c_k.

How many ways are there of getting from a_i to c_k using two flights, with one connection in country B? Between a_2 and c_3, for example, there are $3 \cdot 2 + 0 \cdot 0 + 2 \cdot 4 + 1 \cdot 0 = 14$ possibilities. This is the inner product of the second row vector in **P** and the third column vector in **Q**. The same reasoning applies for each a_i and c_k. So the total number of flight connections between the different airports in countries A and C is given by the matrix product

$$\mathbf{R} = \mathbf{PQ} = \begin{pmatrix} 2 & 1 & 0 & 1 \\ 3 & 0 & 2 & 1 \end{pmatrix} \begin{pmatrix} 1 & 0 & 2 \\ 1 & 0 & 0 \\ 1 & 0 & 4 \\ 0 & 1 & 0 \end{pmatrix} = \begin{pmatrix} 3 & 1 & 4 \\ 5 & 1 & 14 \end{pmatrix} \qquad \blacksquare$$

PROBLEMS FOR SECTION 15.4

1. Verify the distributive law $\mathbf{A}(\mathbf{B} + \mathbf{C}) = \mathbf{AB} + \mathbf{AC}$ when

$$\mathbf{A} = \begin{pmatrix} 1 & 2 \\ 3 & 4 \end{pmatrix}, \qquad \mathbf{B} = \begin{pmatrix} 2 & -1 & 1 & 0 \\ 3 & -1 & 2 & 1 \end{pmatrix}, \qquad \mathbf{C} = \begin{pmatrix} -1 & 1 & 1 & 2 \\ -2 & 2 & 0 & -1 \end{pmatrix}$$

2. Compute the matrix product $(x, \ y, \ z) \begin{pmatrix} a & d & e \\ d & b & f \\ e & f & c \end{pmatrix} \begin{pmatrix} x \\ y \\ z \end{pmatrix}$.

3. Verify by actual multiplication that $(\mathbf{AB})\mathbf{C} = \mathbf{A}(\mathbf{BC})$ if

$$\mathbf{A} = \begin{pmatrix} a_{11} & a_{12} \\ a_{21} & a_{22} \end{pmatrix}, \qquad \mathbf{B} = \begin{pmatrix} b_{11} & b_{12} \\ b_{21} & b_{22} \end{pmatrix}, \qquad \mathbf{C} = \begin{pmatrix} c_{11} & c_{12} \\ c_{21} & c_{22} \end{pmatrix}$$

4. If **A** and **B** are square matrices of order n, prove that

(a) $(\mathbf{A} + \mathbf{B})(\mathbf{A} - \mathbf{B}) \neq \mathbf{A}^2 - \mathbf{B}^2$ (b) $(\mathbf{A} - \mathbf{B})(\mathbf{A} - \mathbf{B}) \neq \mathbf{A}^2 - 2\mathbf{AB} + \mathbf{B}^2$

except in special cases. Find a necessary and sufficient condition for equality to hold in each case.

5. Compute: (a) $\begin{pmatrix} 1 & 0 & 0 \\ 0 & 1 & 0 \\ 0 & 0 & 1 \end{pmatrix} \begin{pmatrix} 5 & 3 & 1 \\ 2 & 0 & 9 \\ 1 & 3 & 3 \end{pmatrix}$ (b) $(1, \ 2, \ -3) \begin{pmatrix} 1 & 0 & 0 \\ 0 & 1 & 0 \\ 0 & 0 & 1 \end{pmatrix}$

6. A square matrix **A** is said to be **idempotent** if $\mathbf{A}^2 = \mathbf{A}$.

(a) Show that the following matrix is idempotent: $\begin{pmatrix} 2 & -2 & -4 \\ -1 & 3 & 4 \\ 1 & -2 & -3 \end{pmatrix}$.

(b) Show that if $\mathbf{AB} = \mathbf{A}$ and $\mathbf{BA} = \mathbf{B}$, then **A** and **B** are both idempotent.

(c) Show that if **A** is idempotent, then $\mathbf{A}^n = \mathbf{A}$ for all positive integers n.

HARDER PROBLEMS

7. (a) Prove that if $\mathbf{A} = \begin{pmatrix} a & b \\ c & d \end{pmatrix}$, then $\mathbf{A}^2 = (a+d)\mathbf{A} - (ad - bc)\mathbf{I}_2$.

(b) Use (a) to find an example of a matrix $\mathbf{A}$ such that $\mathbf{A}^2 = \mathbf{0}$, but $\mathbf{A} \neq \mathbf{0}$.

(c) Use part (a) to show that $\mathbf{A}^3 = \mathbf{0}$ implies $\mathbf{A}^2 = \mathbf{0}$. (*Hint:* Multiply the equality in part (a) by $\mathbf{A}$, and use the equality $\mathbf{A}^3 = \mathbf{0}$ to derive an equation, which you should then multiply by $\mathbf{A}$ once again.)

15.5 The Transpose

Consider any $m \times n$ matrix $\mathbf{A}$. The transpose of $\mathbf{A}$, denoted by $\mathbf{A}'$, is defined as the $n \times m$ matrix whose first column is the first row of $\mathbf{A}$, whose second column is the second row of $\mathbf{A}$, and so on. Thus,

$$\mathbf{A} = \begin{pmatrix} a_{11} & a_{12} & \cdots & a_{1n} \\ a_{21} & a_{22} & \cdots & a_{2n} \\ \vdots & \vdots & & \vdots \\ a_{m1} & a_{m2} & \cdots & a_{mn} \end{pmatrix} \implies \mathbf{A}' = \begin{pmatrix} a_{11} & a_{21} & \cdots & a_{m1} \\ a_{12} & a_{22} & \cdots & a_{m2} \\ \vdots & \vdots & & \vdots \\ a_{1n} & a_{2n} & \cdots & a_{mn} \end{pmatrix} \tag{1}$$

So we can write $\mathbf{A}' = (a'_{ij})$, where $a'_{ij} = a_{ji}$. The subscripts i and j have to be interchanged because the jth row of $\mathbf{A}$ becomes the jth column of $\mathbf{A}'$, whereas the ith column of $\mathbf{A}$ becomes the ith row of $\mathbf{A}'$.

EXAMPLE 1   Let $\mathbf{A} = \begin{pmatrix} -1 & 0 \\ 2 & 3 \\ 5 & -1 \end{pmatrix}$, $\mathbf{B} = \begin{pmatrix} 1 & -1 & 0 & 4 \\ 2 & 1 & 1 & 1 \end{pmatrix}$. Find $\mathbf{A}'$ and $\mathbf{B}'$.

Solution: $\mathbf{A}' = \begin{pmatrix} -1 & 2 & 5 \\ 0 & 3 & -1 \end{pmatrix}$, $\mathbf{B}' = \begin{pmatrix} 1 & 2 \\ -1 & 1 \\ 0 & 1 \\ 4 & 1 \end{pmatrix}$.

The following rules apply to matrix transposition:

RULES FOR TRANSPOSITION

(a) $(\mathbf{A}')' = \mathbf{A}$

(b) $(\mathbf{A} + \mathbf{B})' = \mathbf{A}' + \mathbf{B}'$

(c) $(\alpha \mathbf{A})' = \alpha \mathbf{A}'$

(d) $(\mathbf{AB})' = \mathbf{B}'\mathbf{A}'$

(2)

Proof: Verifying the first three rules is very easy, and you should prove them in detail, using the fact that $a'_{ij} = a_{ji}$ for each i, j. To prove rule (d), suppose that $\mathbf{A}$ is $m \times n$ and $\mathbf{B}$ is $n \times p$. Then $\mathbf{A}'$ is $n \times m$, $\mathbf{B}'$ is $p \times n$, $\mathbf{AB}$ is $m \times p$, $(\mathbf{AB})'$ is $p \times m$, and $\mathbf{B}'\mathbf{A}'$ is $p \times m$. Thus, $(\mathbf{AB})'$ and $\mathbf{B}'\mathbf{A}'$ have the same order. It remains to prove that corresponding elements in the two matrices are equal.

The rs element in $(\mathbf{AB})'$ is the sr element in $\mathbf{AB}$, which is $a_{s1}b_{1r} + a_{s2}b_{2r} + \cdots + a_{sn}b_{nr}$. On the other hand, the rs element in $\mathbf{B}'\mathbf{A}'$ is $b_{1r}a_{s1} + b_{2r}a_{s2} + \cdots + b_{nr}a_{sn}$. The two sums are clearly equal. So we have proved rule (2)(d). ∎

EXAMPLE 2   Let $\mathbf{x}$ be the column vector $(x_1, x_2, \ldots, x_n)'$. Then $\mathbf{x}'$ is a row vector of n elements. The product $\mathbf{x}'\mathbf{x}$ is $\sum_{i=1}^{n} x_i^2$. This equals $\|\mathbf{x}\|^2$, the square of the norm of $\mathbf{x}$. (See Section 13.5.) The reverse product $\mathbf{xx}'$, however, is an $n \times n$ matrix whose ij element is equal to $x_i x_j$. ∎

Symmetric Matrices

Square matrices with the property that they are symmetric about the main diagonal are called **symmetric**. For example,

$$\begin{pmatrix} -3 & 2 \\ 2 & 0 \end{pmatrix}, \quad \begin{pmatrix} 2 & -1 & 5 \\ -1 & -3 & 2 \\ 5 & 2 & 8 \end{pmatrix}, \quad \begin{pmatrix} a & b & c \\ b & d & e \\ c & e & f \end{pmatrix}$$

are all symmetric. Symmetric matrices are characterized by the fact that they are equal to their own transposes:

$$\text{The matrix } \mathbf{A} \text{ is \textbf{symmetric}} \iff \mathbf{A} = \mathbf{A}'$$

Hence, matrix $\mathbf{A} = (a_{ij})_{n \times n}$ is symmetric iff $a_{ij} = a_{ji}$ for all i, j.

EXAMPLE 3   If $\mathbf{X}$ is an arbitrary $m \times n$ matrix, show that $\mathbf{XX}'$ and $\mathbf{X}'\mathbf{X}$ are both symmetric.

Solution: First, note that $\mathbf{XX}'$ is $m \times m$, whereas $\mathbf{X}'\mathbf{X}$ is $n \times n$. Using rules (d) and (a) in (2), we find that

$$(\mathbf{XX}')' = (\mathbf{X}')'\mathbf{X}' = \mathbf{XX}'$$

This proves that $\mathbf{XX}'$ is symmetric. Prove the other equality in a similar way. ∎

PROBLEMS FOR SECTION 15.5

1. Find the transposes of $\mathbf{A} = \begin{pmatrix} 3 & 5 & 8 & 3 \\ -1 & 2 & 6 & 2 \end{pmatrix}$, $\mathbf{B} = \begin{pmatrix} 0 \\ 1 \\ -1 \\ 2 \end{pmatrix}$, $\mathbf{C} = (1, 5, 0, -1)$.

2. Let $\mathbf{A} = \begin{pmatrix} 3 & 2 \\ -1 & 5 \end{pmatrix}$, $\mathbf{B} = \begin{pmatrix} 0 & 2 \\ 2 & 2 \end{pmatrix}$, and $\alpha = -2$. Compute $\mathbf{A}'$, $\mathbf{B}'$, $(\mathbf{A} + \mathbf{B})'$, $(\alpha\mathbf{A})'$, $\mathbf{AB}$, $(\mathbf{AB})'$, $\mathbf{B}'\mathbf{A}'$, and $\mathbf{A}'\mathbf{B}'$. Then verify all the rules in (2) for these particular values of $\mathbf{A}$, $\mathbf{B}$, and α.

3. Show that $\mathbf{A} = \begin{pmatrix} 3 & 2 & 3 \\ 2 & -1 & 1 \\ 3 & 1 & 0 \end{pmatrix}$ and $\mathbf{B} = \begin{pmatrix} 0 & 4 & 8 \\ 4 & 0 & 13 \\ 8 & 13 & 0 \end{pmatrix}$ are symmetric.

4. For what values of a is $\begin{pmatrix} a & a^2 - 1 & -3 \\ a+1 & 2 & a^2 + 4 \\ -3 & 4a & -1 \end{pmatrix}$ symmetric?

5. Is the product of two symmetric matrices necessarily symmetric?

6. If $\mathbf{A}_1$, $\mathbf{A}_2$, and $\mathbf{A}_3$ are matrices for which the given products are defined, show that

$$(\mathbf{A}_1 \mathbf{A}_2 \mathbf{A}_3)' = \mathbf{A}_3' \mathbf{A}_2' \mathbf{A}_1'$$

Generalize to products of n matrices.

7. An $n \times n$ matrix $\mathbf{P}$ is said to be **orthogonal** if $\mathbf{P}'\mathbf{P} = \mathbf{I}_n$.

(a) For $\lambda = \pm 1/\sqrt{2}$, show that $\mathbf{P} = \begin{pmatrix} \lambda & 0 & \lambda \\ \lambda & 0 & -\lambda \\ 0 & 1 & 0 \end{pmatrix}$ is orthogonal.

(b) Show that the 2×2 matrix $\begin{pmatrix} p & -q \\ q & p \end{pmatrix}$ is orthogonal if and only if $p^2 + q^2 = 1$.

(c) Show that the product of two orthogonal $n \times n$ matrices is orthogonal.

15.6 Gaussian Elimination

This section explains a general method for finding possible solutions to a linear system of equations. The method involves systematic elimination of the unknowns from each equation in turn. Because it is very efficient, it is the starting point for computer programs designed to solve large systems of linear equations.

Consider first the following example.

EXAMPLE 1   Find all possible solutions of the system

$$2x_2 - x_3 = -7$$
$$x_1 + x_2 + 3x_3 = 2$$
$$-3x_1 + 2x_2 + 2x_3 = -10$$

Solution: We start by interchanging the first two equations, which certainly will not alter the set of solutions. We obtain

$$
\begin{aligned}
x_1 + x_2 + 3x_3 &= 2 \\
2x_2 - x_3 &= -7 \\
-3x_1 + 2x_2 + 2x_3 &= -10
\end{aligned}
$$

This has removed x_1 from the second equation. The next step is to use the (new) first equation to eliminate x_1 from the third equation. This is done by adding three times the first equation to the last equation. (The same result is obtained if we solve the first equation for x_1 to obtain $x_1 = -x_2 - 3x_3 + 2$, and then substitute this into the last equation.) This gives

$$
\begin{aligned}
x_1 + x_2 + 3x_3 &= 2 \\
2x_2 - x_3 &= -7 \\
5x_2 + 11x_3 &= -4
\end{aligned}
\tag{i}
$$

The last two equations now have only x_2 and x_3 as unknowns. The next step in the systematic procedure is to divide the second equation in (i) by 2, so that the coefficient of x_2 becomes 1. Thus,

$$
\begin{aligned}
x_1 + x_2 + 3x_3 &= 2 \\
x_2 - \tfrac{1}{2}x_3 &= -\tfrac{7}{2} \\
5x_2 + 11x_3 &= -4
\end{aligned}
$$

Next, eliminate x_2 from the last equation by multiplying the second equation by -5 and adding the result to the last equation. This gives:

$$
\begin{aligned}
x_1 + x_2 + 3x_2 &= 2 \\
x_2 - \tfrac{1}{2}x_3 &= -\tfrac{7}{2} \\
\tfrac{27}{2}x_3 &= \tfrac{27}{2}
\end{aligned}
$$

Finally, multiply the last equation by $\tfrac{2}{27}$ to obtain

$$
\begin{aligned}
x_1 + x_2 + 3x_3 &= 2 \\
x_2 - \tfrac{1}{2}x_3 &= -\tfrac{7}{2} \\
x_3 &= 1
\end{aligned}
\tag{ii}
$$

We see that $x_3 = 1$, and then the other unknowns can easily be found: Inserting $x_3 = 1$ into the second equation in (ii) gives $x_2 = -3$, after which the first equation in (ii) yields $x_1 = 2$. So the only solution of the given equation system is $(x_1, x_2, x_3) = (2, -3, 1)$. ∎

Our elimination procedure led to a "staircase" in system (ii), with x_1, x_2, and x_3 as *leading entries*. In matrix notation, we have

$$
\begin{pmatrix} 1 & 1 & 3 \\ 0 & 1 & -\tfrac{1}{2} \\ 0 & 0 & 1 \end{pmatrix}
\begin{pmatrix} x_1 \\ x_2 \\ x_3 \end{pmatrix} =
\begin{pmatrix} 2 \\ -\tfrac{7}{2} \\ 1 \end{pmatrix}
$$

The matrix of coefficients on the left-hand side is *upper triangular* because all entries below the main diagonal are 0. Moreover, the diagonal elements are all 1.

The solution method illustrated in this example is called **Gaussian elimination**. The operations performed on the given system of equations in order to arrive at system (ii) are called **elementary row operations**.

Sometimes we continue the elimination procedure until we also obtain zeros above the leading entries. The elementary operations required to do this are frequently represented as follows:

$$x_1 + x_2 + 3x_3 = 2$$
$$x_2 - \tfrac{1}{2}x_3 = -\tfrac{7}{2} \quad -1$$
$$x_3 = 1$$

The arrow and the number -1 are included to show that we are adding -1 times the second equation to the first. The result is

$$x_1 \qquad + \tfrac{7}{2}x_3 = \tfrac{11}{2}$$
$$x_2 - \tfrac{1}{2}x_3 = -\tfrac{7}{2}$$
$$x_3 = 1 \qquad \tfrac{1}{2} \quad -\tfrac{7}{2}$$

At the next step we add $-7/2$ times the third equation to the first, and also add $1/2$ times the third equation to the second. Note how the display indicates two operations, affecting rows 1 and 2. The result is

$$x_1 \qquad\qquad = 2$$
$$x_2 \qquad = -3$$
$$x_3 = 1$$

Let us apply this method to another example.

EXAMPLE 2   Find all possible solutions of the following system of equations:

$$x_1 + 3x_2 - x_3 = 4$$
$$2x_1 + x_2 + x_3 = 7$$
$$2x_1 - 4x_2 + 4x_3 = 6$$
$$3x_1 + 4x_2 \qquad = 11$$

Solution: We begin with three operations to remove x_1 from equations 2, 3, and 4:

$$x_1 + 3x_2 - x_3 = 4 \qquad -2 \quad -2 \quad -3$$
$$2x_1 + x_2 + x_3 = 7$$
$$2x_1 - 4x_2 + 4x_3 = 6$$
$$3x_1 + 4x_2 \qquad = 11$$

The result is

$$x_1 + 3x_2 - x_3 = 4$$
$$-5x_2 + 3x_3 = -1 \qquad -\tfrac{1}{5}$$
$$-10x_2 + 6x_3 = -2$$
$$-5x_2 + 3x_3 = -1$$

(The $-\frac{1}{5}$ witout any arrow is used to indicate that the relevant equation is multiplied by $-\frac{1}{5}$, so that the coefficient of x_2 becomes 1.) Further operations give

$$
\begin{aligned}
x_1 + 3x_2 - x_3 &= 4 \\
x_2 - \tfrac{3}{5}x_3 &= \tfrac{1}{5} \quad\quad 10 \quad 5 \\
-10x_2 + 6x_3 &= -2 \\
-5x_2 + 3x_3 &= -1
\end{aligned}
\qquad \text{and} \qquad
\begin{aligned}
x_1 + 3x_2 - x_3 &= 4 \\
x_2 - \tfrac{3}{5}x_3 &= \tfrac{1}{5} \quad\quad -3 \\
0 &= 0 \\
0 &= 0
\end{aligned}
$$

We have now constructed the staircase. The last two equations are superfluous, and we continue by creating zeros above the leading entry x_2:

$$
x_1 \quad\quad + \tfrac{4}{5}x_3 = \tfrac{17}{5}
$$
$$
x_2 - \tfrac{3}{5}x_3 = \tfrac{1}{5}
$$

From this system we conclude that the solutions of the original system can be expressed as follows:

$$
\begin{aligned}
x_1 &= -\tfrac{4}{5}x_3 + \tfrac{17}{5} \\
x_2 &= \tfrac{3}{5}x_3 + \tfrac{1}{5}
\end{aligned}
\qquad (*)
$$

Clearly, x_3 can be chosen freely, after which x_1 and x_2 are uniquely determined by $(*)$. Putting $x_3 = t$, we can represent the solution set as:

$$
(x_1, x_2, x_3) = \left(-\tfrac{4}{5}t + \tfrac{17}{5},\ \tfrac{3}{5}t + \tfrac{1}{5},\ t \right) \qquad (t \text{ is any real number})
$$

We say that the solution set of the system has *one degree of freedom*, since one of the variables can be freely chosen. (See Section 12.9.) If this variable is given a fixed value, then the other two variables are uniquely determined.

Briefly formulated, the Gaussian elimination method (often called the Gauss–Jordan method) takes the following form:

GAUSSIAN ELIMINATION METHOD

(1) Make a staircase with 1 as the coefficient for each non-zero leading entry.

(2) Produce 0's above each leading entry.

(3) The general solution is found by expressing the unknowns that occur as leading entries in terms of those unknowns that do not. The latter unknowns (if there are any) can be chosen freely. The number of unknowns that can be chosen freely (possibly 0) is the number of **degrees of freedom** for the system.

(1)

This description of the recipe assumes that the system has solutions. However, the Gaussian elimination method can also be used to show that a linear system of equations is inconsistent—that is, it has no solutions.

Before showing you an example of this, let us introduce a notation that considerably reduces the amount of notation needed. Looking back at the last two examples, we realize that we only need to know the coefficients of the system of equations and the right-hand side vector, while the variables only serve to indicate in which column the different coefficients belong. Thus, Example 2 can be represented by augmented matrices (each with an extra column) as follows:

$$
\begin{pmatrix}
1 & 3 & -1 & 4 \\
2 & 1 & 1 & 7 \\
2 & -4 & 4 & 6 \\
3 & 4 & 0 & 11
\end{pmatrix}
\begin{array}{l} -2 \;\; -2 \;\; -3 \\ \end{array}
\sim
\begin{pmatrix}
1 & 3 & -1 & 4 \\
0 & -5 & 3 & -1 \\
0 & -10 & 6 & -2 \\
0 & -5 & 3 & -1
\end{pmatrix}
\begin{array}{l} -1/5 \\ \end{array},
$$

$$
\sim
\begin{pmatrix}
1 & 3 & -1 & 4 \\
0 & 1 & -3/5 & 1/5 \\
0 & -10 & 6 & -2 \\
0 & -5 & 3 & -1
\end{pmatrix}
\begin{array}{l} 10 \;\; 5 \\ \end{array}
\sim
\begin{pmatrix}
1 & 3 & -1 & 4 \\
0 & 1 & -3/5 & 1/5 \\
0 & 0 & 0 & 0 \\
0 & 0 & 0 & 0
\end{pmatrix}
\begin{array}{l} -3 \\ \end{array}
$$

$$
\sim
\begin{pmatrix}
1 & 0 & 4/5 & 17/5 \\
0 & 1 & -3/5 & 1/5 \\
0 & 0 & 0 & 0 \\
0 & 0 & 0 & 0
\end{pmatrix}
$$

We have performed *elementary row operations* on the different 4×4 augmented matrices, and we have used the equivalence symbol $\sim$ between two matrices when the latter has been obtained by using elementary operations on the former. This is justified because such operations do always produce an equivalent system of equations. Note carefully how the system of equations in Example 2 is represented by the first matrix, and how the last matrix represents the system $x_1 + \frac{4}{5}x_3 = \frac{17}{5}$, $x_2 - \frac{3}{5}x_3 = \frac{1}{5}$.

EXAMPLE 3   For what values of the numbers a, b, and c does the following system of equations have solutions? Find the solutions when they exist.

$$
\begin{aligned}
x_1 - 2x_2 + x_3 + 2x_4 &= a \\
x_1 + x_2 - x_3 + x_4 &= b \\
x_1 + 7x_2 - 5x_3 - x_4 &= c
\end{aligned}
$$

Solution: We represent the system of equations by its augmented matrix, then perform elementary row operations as required by the Gaussian method:

$$
\begin{pmatrix}
1 & -2 & 1 & 2 & a \\
1 & 1 & -1 & 1 & b \\
1 & 7 & -5 & -1 & c
\end{pmatrix}
\begin{array}{l} -1 \;\; -1 \\ \end{array}
\sim
\begin{pmatrix}
1 & -2 & 1 & 2 & a \\
0 & 3 & -2 & -1 & b-a \\
0 & 9 & -6 & -3 & c-a
\end{pmatrix}
\begin{array}{l} -3 \\ \end{array}
$$

$$
\sim
\begin{pmatrix}
1 & -2 & 1 & 2 & a \\
0 & 3 & -2 & -1 & b-a \\
0 & 0 & 0 & 0 & 2a-3b+c
\end{pmatrix}
$$

The last row represents the equation $0 \cdot x_1 + 0 \cdot x_2 + 0 \cdot x_3 + 0 \cdot x_4 = 2a - 3b + c$. The system therefore has solutions only if $2a - 3b + c = 0$. In this case the last row has only zeros, and we continue using elementary operations till we end up with the following matrix:

$$\begin{pmatrix} 1 & 0 & -1/3 & 4/3 & \frac{1}{3}(a + 2b) \\ 0 & 1 & -2/3 & -1/3 & \frac{1}{3}(b - a) \\ 0 & 0 & 0 & 0 & 0 \end{pmatrix}$$

This means that the corresponding system of equations is:

$$x_1 \qquad - \tfrac{1}{3}x_3 + \tfrac{4}{3}x_4 = \tfrac{1}{3}(a + 2b)$$
$$x_2 - \tfrac{2}{3}x_3 - \tfrac{1}{3}x_4 = \tfrac{1}{3}(b - a)$$

Here x_3 and x_4 can be freely chosen. Once they have been chosen, however, x_1 and x_2 are uniquely determined linear functions of $s = x_3$ and $t = x_4$:

$$x_1 = \tfrac{1}{3}(a + 2b) + \tfrac{1}{3}s - \tfrac{4}{3}t$$
$$x_2 = \tfrac{1}{3}(b - a) \ + \tfrac{2}{3}s + \tfrac{1}{3}t$$

(s and t arbitrary real numbers, $2a - 3b + c = 0$)

For $2a - 3b + c \neq 0$ the given system is inconsistent, so has no solutions.

PROBLEMS FOR SECTION 15.6

1. Solve the following systems by Gaussian elimination.

(a)
$$\begin{aligned} x_1 + \ x_2 &= 3 \\ 3x_1 + 5x_2 &= 5 \end{aligned}$$

(b)
$$\begin{aligned} x_1 + 2x_2 + x_3 &= 4 \\ x_1 - \ x_2 + x_3 &= 5 \\ 2x_1 + 3x_2 - x_3 &= 1 \end{aligned}$$

(c)
$$\begin{aligned} 2x_1 - 3x_2 + x_3 &= 0 \\ x_1 + \ x_2 - x_3 &= 0 \end{aligned}$$

2. Use Gaussian elimination to discuss what are the possible solutions of the following system for different values of a and b:

$$\begin{aligned} x + \ y - \ z &= 1 \\ x - \ y + 2z &= 2 \\ x + 2y + az &= b \end{aligned}$$

3. Find the values of c for which the system

$$\begin{aligned} 2w + \ x + 4y + 3z &= 1 \\ w + 3x + 2y - \ z &= 3c \\ w + \ x + 2y + \ z &= c^2 \end{aligned}$$

has a solution, and find the complete solution for these values of c.

4. Consider the two systems of equations:

(a)
$$ax + y + (a+1)z = b_1$$
$$x + 2y + z = b_2$$
$$3x + 4y + 7z = b_3$$

(b)
$$\tfrac{3}{4}x + y + \tfrac{7}{4}z = b_1$$
$$x + 2y + z = b_2$$
$$3x + 4y + 7z = b_3$$

Find the values of a for which (a) has a unique solution, and find all solutions to system (b).

15.7 Vectors

Recall that a matrix with only one row is also called a **row vector**, and a matrix with only one column is called a **column vector**. We refer to both types as **vectors**. As remarked in Section 15.2, vectors are typically denoted by small bold letters. Thus, if **a** is a $1 \times n$ row vector, we write

$$\mathbf{a} = (a_1, a_2, \ldots, a_n)$$

Here, the numbers $a_1, a_2, \ldots, a_n$ are called the **components** (or **coordinates**) of the vector, and a_i is its ith component or ith coordinate. (Recall that when we consider **a** as a matrix, $a_1, \ldots, a_n$ are called entries or elements.) If we want to emphasize that a vector has n components, we refer to it as an **n-vector**. Alternatively, if **a** is an n-vector, then we say that it has **dimension n**.

It is clear that the row vector $(7, 13, 4)$ and the column vector $\begin{pmatrix} 7 \\ 13 \\ 4 \end{pmatrix}$ contain exactly the same information—the numbers and their order are the same, only the arrangement of the numbers is different. In fact, following the ideas presented in Chapter 11, especially Section 11.4, both the row and the column vector are represented by the same point in 3-dimensional space $\mathbb{R}^3$. And any n-vector is represented by a point in n-dimensional space $\mathbb{R}^n$.

Operations on Vectors

Since vectors are just special types of matrices, the algebraic operations introduced for matrices are equally valid for vectors. So:

(A) Two n-vectors **a** and **b** are **equal** if and only if all their corresponding components are equal; we then write $\mathbf{a} = \mathbf{b}$.

(B) If **a** and **b** are two n-vectors, their **sum**, denoted by $\mathbf{a} + \mathbf{b}$, is the n-vector obtained by adding each component of **a** to the corresponding component of **b**.[1]

(C) If **a** is an n-vector and t is a real number, we define $t\mathbf{a}$ as the n-vector whose components are t times the corresponding components in **a**.

(D) The **difference** between two n-vectors **a** and **b** is defined as $\mathbf{a} - \mathbf{b} = \mathbf{a} + (-1)\mathbf{b}$.

---

[1] If two vectors do not have the same dimension, their sum is simply not defined, nor is their difference. Nor should one add a row vector to a column vector, even if they have the same number of elements.

If $\mathbf{a}$ and $\mathbf{b}$ are two n-vectors and t and s are real numbers, the n-vector $t\mathbf{a} + s\mathbf{b}$ is said to be a **linear combination** of $\mathbf{a}$ and $\mathbf{b}$. In symbols, using column vectors,

$$t \begin{pmatrix} a_1 \\ a_2 \\ \vdots \\ a_n \end{pmatrix} + s \begin{pmatrix} b_1 \\ b_2 \\ \vdots \\ b_n \end{pmatrix} = \begin{pmatrix} ta_1 + sb_1 \\ ta_2 + sb_2 \\ \vdots \\ ta_n + sb_n \end{pmatrix}$$

Here is an interpretation: Suppose $\mathbf{a}$ and $\mathbf{b}$ are commodity vectors, whose jth components are quantities of commodity number j. Now, if t persons all buy the same commodity vector $\mathbf{a}$ and s persons all buy commodity vector $\mathbf{b}$, then the vector $t\mathbf{a} + s\mathbf{b}$ represents the total commodity vector bought by all $t + s$ persons combined.

Of course, the rules for matrix addition and multiplication by scalars in (5) in Section 15.2 apply to vectors also.

The Inner Product

Let us consider 4 different commodities—say, apples, bananas, cherries and dates. Suppose you buy the commodity vector $\mathbf{x} = (5, 3, 6, 7)$. This means, of course, that you buy 5 units— say, kilos—of the first commodity, 3 kilos of the second commodity, etc. Suppose the prices per kilo of these four different commodities are given by the price vector $\mathbf{p} = (4, 5, 3, 8)$, meaning that the price per kilo of the first good is 4, the price per kilo of the second good is 5, etc. Then the total value of the commodity vector you buy is

$$4 \cdot 5 + 5 \cdot 3 + 3 \cdot 6 + 8 \cdot 7 = 109$$

The result of this operation on the two vectors $\mathbf{p}$ and $\mathbf{x}$ is often written as $\mathbf{p} \cdot \mathbf{x}$ and is called the *inner product* or *scalar product* or *dot product* of $\mathbf{p}$ and $\mathbf{x}$. In general, we have the following definition (formulated for row vectors):

INNER PRODUCT

The inner product of the n-vectors $\mathbf{a} = (a_1, a_2, \ldots, a_n)$ and $\mathbf{b} = (b_1, b_2, \ldots, b_n)$ is defined as

$$\mathbf{a} \cdot \mathbf{b} = a_1 b_1 + a_2 b_2 + \cdots + a_n b_n = \sum_{i=1}^{n} a_i b_i \tag{1}$$

Note that the inner (scalar) product of two vectors is not a vector but a *number* (or scalar). It is obtained by simply multiplying all pairs (a_j, b_j), $j = 1, 2, \ldots, n$, of the corresponding components in the two vectors $\mathbf{a}$ and $\mathbf{b}$, and then finally adding the results. Note that $\mathbf{a} \cdot \mathbf{b}$ is *defined only if* $\mathbf{a}$ and $\mathbf{b}$ are both of the same dimension.

In the case when $\mathbf{p}$ is a price vector whose components are measured in dollars per kilo, and $\mathbf{x}$ is a commodity vector whose components are measured in kilos, then each product $p_j x_j$ is an amount of money measured in dollars, as is the inner product $\mathbf{p} \cdot \mathbf{x} = \sum_{j=1}^{n} p_j x_j$.

EXAMPLE 1   If $\mathbf{a} = (1, -2, 3)$ and $\mathbf{b} = (-3, 2, 5)$, compute $\mathbf{a} \cdot \mathbf{b}$.

Solution: We get $\mathbf{a} \cdot \mathbf{b} = 1 \cdot (-3) + (-2) \cdot 2 + 3 \cdot 5 = 8$.

Note that according to the definition of the matrix product $\mathbf{AB}$, the ijth element of the product is the inner product of the ith row vector of $\mathbf{A}$ and the jth column vector of $\mathbf{B}$.

The inner product is defined for any two n-vectors. If $\mathbf{a} = (a_1, \ldots, a_n)'$ and $\mathbf{b} = (b_1, \ldots, b_n)'$ both happen to be $n \times 1$ matrices, then the transpose $\mathbf{a}'$ of $\mathbf{a}$ is a $1 \times n$ matrix, and the matrix product $\mathbf{a}'\mathbf{b}$ is defined as a 1×1 matrix. In fact,

$$\mathbf{a}'\mathbf{b} = a_1 b_1 + a_2 b_2 + \cdots + a_n b_n$$

Because 1×1 matrices behave exactly as ordinary numbers with respect to addition and multiplication, we can regard the inner product of $\mathbf{a}$ and $\mathbf{b}$ as the matrix product $\mathbf{a}'\mathbf{b}$.

It is usual in economics to regard a typical vector $\mathbf{x}$ as a column vector, unless otherwise specified. This is especially true if it is a quantity or commodity vector. Another common convention is to regard a price vector as a row vector, often denoted by $\mathbf{p}'$ to suggest that it is the transpose of a column vector. Then $\mathbf{p}'\mathbf{x}$ is the 1×1 matrix, a scalar, that is equal to the inner product $\mathbf{p} \cdot \mathbf{x}$.

Important properties of the inner product follow:

RULES FOR THE INNER PRODUCT

If $\mathbf{a}$, $\mathbf{b}$, and $\mathbf{c}$ are n-vectors and α is a scalar, then

(a) $\mathbf{a} \cdot \mathbf{b} = \mathbf{b} \cdot \mathbf{a}$

(b) $\mathbf{a} \cdot (\mathbf{b} + \mathbf{c}) = \mathbf{a} \cdot \mathbf{b} + \mathbf{a} \cdot \mathbf{c}$ (2)

(c) $(\alpha \mathbf{a}) \cdot \mathbf{b} = \mathbf{a} \cdot (\alpha \mathbf{b}) = \alpha(\mathbf{a} \cdot \mathbf{b})$

(d) $\mathbf{a} \cdot \mathbf{a} > 0 \iff \mathbf{a} \neq \mathbf{0}$

Proof: Rules (a) and (c) are easy consequences of the definition.

To prove rule (b), apply the distributive law for matrix multiplication ((2) in Section 15.4) when $\mathbf{a}$ is $1 \times n$ whereas $\mathbf{b}$ and $\mathbf{c}$ are $n \times 1$.

To prove rule (d), it suffices to note that $\mathbf{a} \cdot \mathbf{a} = a_1^2 + a_2^2 + \cdots + a_n^2$. This is always nonnegative, and is zero only if all the a_i's are 0.   ∎

PROBLEMS FOR SECTION 15.7

1. Compute $\mathbf{a} + \mathbf{b}$, $\mathbf{a} - \mathbf{b}$, $2\mathbf{a} + 3\mathbf{b}$, and $-5\mathbf{a} + 2\mathbf{b}$ when $\mathbf{a} = \begin{pmatrix} 2 \\ -1 \end{pmatrix}$ and $\mathbf{b} = \begin{pmatrix} 3 \\ 4 \end{pmatrix}$.

2. Let $a = (1, 2, 2)$, $b = (0, 0, -3)$, and $c = (-2, 4, -3)$. Find the following:

$$a + b + c, \qquad a - 2b + 2c, \qquad 3a + 2b - 3c, \qquad -a - b - c$$

3. If $3(x, y, z) + 5(-1, 2, 3) = (4, 1, 3)$, find x, y, and z.

4. (a) If $x + 0 = 0$, what do you know about the components of x?

   (b) If $0x = 0$, what do you know about the components of x?

5. Express the vector $(4, -11)$ as a linear combination of $(2, -1)$ and $(1, 4)$.

6. Solve the vector equation $4x - 7a = 2x + 8b - a$ for x in terms of a and b.

7. If $a = \begin{pmatrix} 2 \\ -1 \end{pmatrix}$ and $b = \begin{pmatrix} 3 \\ 4 \end{pmatrix}$, compute $a \cdot a$, $a \cdot b$, and $a \cdot (a + b)$. Verify that $a \cdot a + a \cdot b = a \cdot (a + b)$.

8. For what values of x is the inner product of $(x, x - 1, 3)$ and $(x, x, 3x)$ equal to 0?

9. A construction company has an order for several houses of three different types: 5 of type A, 7 of type B, and 12 of type C. Write down a 3-dimensional vector x whose coordinates give the number of houses of each type. Suppose that each house of type A requires 20 units of timber, type B requires 18 units, and type C requires 25 units. Write down a vector u that gives the different timber quantities required for one house of each of the three different types A, B, and C. Find the total timber requirement by computing the inner product $u \cdot x$.

10. A firm produces nonnegative output quantities $z_1, z_2, \ldots, z_n$ of n different goods, using as inputs the nonnegative quantities $x_1, x_2, \ldots, x_n$ of the same n goods. For each good i ($i = 1, \ldots, n$), define $y_i = z_i - x_i$ as the net output of good i, and let p_i be the price of good i. Let $p = (p_1, \ldots, p_n)$, $x = (x_1, \ldots, x_n)$ (the **input vector**), $y = (y_1, \ldots, y_n)$ (the **net output vector**), and $z = (z_1, \ldots, z_n)$ (the **output vector**).

   (a) Calculate the firm's revenue and its costs.

   (b) Show that the firm's profit is given by the scalar product $p \cdot y$. What if $p \cdot y$ is negative?

11. A firm produces the first of two different goods as its output, using the second good as its input. Its net output vector (see Problem 10) is $\begin{pmatrix} 2 \\ -1 \end{pmatrix}$. The price vector it faces is $(1, 3)$. Find the firm's (a) input vector, (b) output vector, (c) costs, (d) revenue, (e) value of net output, and (f) profit or loss.

15.8 Geometric Interpretation of Vectors

Vectors, in contrast to general matrices, are easily interpreted geometrically. Actually, the word "vector" is originally Latin and was used to mean both "carrier" and "passenger." In particular, the word is related to the act of moving a person or object from one place to another. To this date, a biologist is likely to think of a vector as a carrier of disease, such as mosquitoes are for malaria.

In the xy-plane, any shift can be described by the distance a_1 moved in the x-direction and by the distance a_2 moved in the y-direction. A movement in the plane is therefore uniquely determined by an ordered pair or 2-vector (a_1, a_2). Geometrically, such a movement can be illustrated by an arrow from the start point P to the end point Q, as shown in Fig. 1. If we make a parallel displacement of the arrow so that it starts at P' and ends at Q', the resulting arrow will represent exactly the same shift, because the x and y components are still a_1 and a_2, respectively.

Figure 1

The vector from P to Q is denoted by $\overrightarrow{PQ}$, and we refer to it as a **geometric vector** or *directed line segment*. Two geometric vectors that have the same direction and the same length are said to be equal (in much the same way as the two fractions 2/6 and 1/3 are equal because they represent the same real number).

Suppose that the geometric vector **a** involves a movement from $P = (p_1, p_2)$ to $Q = (q_1, q_2)$. Then the pair (a_1, a_2) that describes the movement in both the x and y directions is given by $a_1 = q_1 - p_1$, $a_2 = q_2 - p_2$, or by $(a_1, a_2) = (q_1, q_2) - (p_1, p_2)$. This is illustrated in Fig. 2.

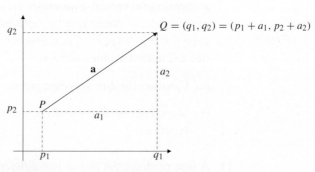

Figure 2

On the other hand, if the pair (a_1, a_2) is given, the corresponding shift is obtained by moving a_1 units in the direction of the x-axis, as well as a_2 units in the direction of the y-axis. If we start at the point $P = (p_1, p_2)$, then we arrive at the point Q with coordinates $(q_1, q_2) = (p_1 + a_1, p_2 + a_2)$, also shown in Fig. 2.

The correspondence just explained makes it merely a matter of convenience whether we think of a vector as an ordered pair of numbers (a_1, a_2), or as a directed line segment such as $\overrightarrow{PQ}$ in Fig. 2.

Vector Operations

If we represent vectors by directed line segments, the vector operations $\mathbf{a} + \mathbf{b}$, $\mathbf{a} - \mathbf{b}$, and $t\mathbf{a}$ can be given interesting geometric interpretations. Let $\mathbf{a} = (a_1, a_2)$ and $\mathbf{b} = (b_1, b_2)$ both start at the origin $(0, 0)$ of the coordinate system.

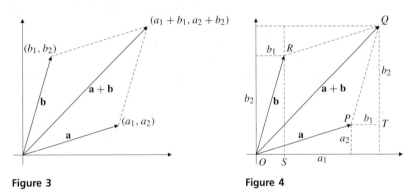

Figure 3   **Figure 4**

The sum $\mathbf{a} + \mathbf{b}$ shown in Fig. 3 is the diagonal in the parallelogram determined by the two sides $\mathbf{a}$ and $\mathbf{b}$. The geometric reason for this can be seen from Fig. 4, in which the two right-angled triangles OSR and PTQ are congruent. Thus, OR is parallel to PQ and has the same length, so $OPQR$ is a parallelogram. (This parallelogram law of adding vectors will be familiar to those who have studied physics. If $\mathbf{a}$ and $\mathbf{b}$ represent two forces acting on a particle at O, then the single combined force $\mathbf{a} + \mathbf{b}$ acting on the particle will produce the same result.) The parallelogram law of addition is also illustrated in Fig. 5. One way of interpreting this figure is that if $\mathbf{a}$ takes you from O to P and $\mathbf{b}$ takes you on from P to Q, then the combined movement $\mathbf{a} + \mathbf{b}$ takes you from O to Q. Moreover, looking at Fig. 4 again, $\mathbf{b}$ takes you from O to R, whereas $\mathbf{a}$ takes you on from R to Q. So the combined movement $\mathbf{b} + \mathbf{a}$ takes you from O to Q. Of course, this verifies that $\mathbf{a} + \mathbf{b} = \mathbf{b} + \mathbf{a}$.

Figure 6 gives a geometric interpretation to the vector $\mathbf{a} - \mathbf{b}$. Note carefully the direction of the geometric vector $\mathbf{a} - \mathbf{b}$. And note that $\mathbf{b} + (\mathbf{a} - \mathbf{b}) = \mathbf{a} = (\mathbf{a} - \mathbf{b}) + \mathbf{b}$.

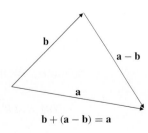

Figure 5   **Figure 6**

The geometric interpretation of $t\mathbf{a}$, where t is any real number, is also straightforward. If $t > 0$, then $t\mathbf{a}$ is the vector with the same direction as $\mathbf{a}$ and whose length is t times the length of $\mathbf{a}$. If $t < 0$, the direction is reversed and the length is multiplied by the absolute value of t. Indeed, multiplication by t is like rescaling the vector $\mathbf{a}$; that is why the number t is often called a **scalar**.

3-Space and n-Space

The plane is often also called 2-space and denoted $\mathbb{R}^2$. We represent a point or a vector in a plane by a pair of real numbers using two mutually orthogonal coordinate lines.

In a similar way, any point or vector in 3-space $\mathbb{R}^3$ can be represented by a triple of real numbers using three mutually orthogonal coordinate lines, as explained in Section 11.3. Any 3-vector (a_1, a_2, a_3) can be considered in an obvious way as a geometric vector or movement in 3-space $\mathbb{R}^3$. As with ordered pairs in the plane, there is a natural correspondence between ordered triples (a_1, a_2, a_3) and geometric vectors regarded as directed line segments. The parallelogram law of addition remains valid in $\mathbb{R}^3$, as does the geometric interpretation of the multiplication of a vector by a scalar.

The set $\mathbb{R}^n$ of all n-vectors was introduced in Section 11.5. When $n \geq 4$, it has no natural spatial interpretation. Nevertheless, geometric language is sometimes still used to discuss properties of $\mathbb{R}^n$, because many properties of $\mathbb{R}^2$ and $\mathbb{R}^3$ carry over to $\mathbb{R}^n$. In particular, the rules for addition, subtraction, and scalar multiplication of vectors remain exactly the same.

Lengths of Vectors and the Cauchy–Schwarz Inequality

If $\mathbf{a} = (a_1, a_2, \ldots, a_n)$, we define the **length** (or **norm**) of the vector $\mathbf{a}$, denoted by $\|\mathbf{a}\|$, as $\|\mathbf{a}\| = \sqrt{\mathbf{a} \cdot \mathbf{a}}$, or

$$\|\mathbf{a}\| = \sqrt{a_1^2 + a_2^2 + \cdots + a_n^2} \tag{1}$$

According to formula (2) in Section 13.5, $\|\mathbf{a}\|$ is the distance from the origin $(0, 0, \ldots, 0)$ to $(a_1, a_2, \ldots, a_n)$. In Problem 4.6.9 you were asked to prove a famous inequality. By using the notation we have just introduced, the inequality can be expressed as $(\mathbf{a} \cdot \mathbf{b})^2 \leq \|\mathbf{a}\|^2 \|\mathbf{b}\|^2$, or equivalently, as

$$|\mathbf{a} \cdot \mathbf{b}| \leq \|\mathbf{a}\| \cdot \|\mathbf{b}\| \qquad \textbf{(Cauchy–Schwarz inequality)} \tag{2}$$

EXAMPLE 1   For the two vectors $\mathbf{a} = (1, -2, 3)$ and $\mathbf{b} = (-3, 2, 5)$ check the Cauchy–Schwarz inequality.

Solution: We find that

$$\|\mathbf{a}\| = \sqrt{1^2 + (-2)^2 + 3^2} = \sqrt{14}, \qquad \|\mathbf{b}\| = \sqrt{(-3)^2 + 2^2 + 5^2} = \sqrt{38}$$

In Example 15.7.1 we found the inner product of these vectors to be 8. So inequality (2) says that $8 \leq \sqrt{14}\sqrt{38}$, which is certainly true because $\sqrt{14} > 3$ and $\sqrt{38} > 6$.   ∎

Orthogonality

Consider Fig. 7, which exhibits three vectors, **a**, **b**, and **a** − **b** in $\mathbb{R}^2$ or $\mathbb{R}^3$.

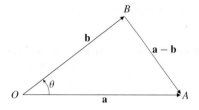

Figure 7

According to Pythagoras' theorem, the angle θ between the two vectors **a** and **b** is a right angle ($= 90°$) if and only if $(OA)^2 + (OB)^2 = (AB)^2$, or $\|\mathbf{a}\|^2 + \|\mathbf{b}\|^2 = \|\mathbf{a} - \mathbf{b}\|^2$. This implies that $\theta = 90°$ if and only if

$$\mathbf{a} \cdot \mathbf{a} + \mathbf{b} \cdot \mathbf{b} = (\mathbf{a} - \mathbf{b}) \cdot (\mathbf{a} - \mathbf{b}) = \mathbf{a} \cdot \mathbf{a} - \mathbf{a} \cdot \mathbf{b} - \mathbf{b} \cdot \mathbf{a} + \mathbf{b} \cdot \mathbf{b} \qquad (*)$$

Because $\mathbf{a} \cdot \mathbf{b} = \mathbf{b} \cdot \mathbf{a}$, equality $(*)$ requires $2\mathbf{a} \cdot \mathbf{b} = 0$, and so $\mathbf{a} \cdot \mathbf{b} = 0$. When the angle between two vectors **a** and **b** is $90°$, they are said to be **orthogonal**, and we write $\mathbf{a} \perp \mathbf{b}$. Thus, we have proved that two vectors in $\mathbb{R}^2$ or $\mathbb{R}^3$ are orthogonal if and only if their inner product is 0. In symbols:

$$\mathbf{a} \perp \mathbf{b} \quad \Longleftrightarrow \quad \mathbf{a} \cdot \mathbf{b} = 0 \qquad (3)$$

For pairs of vectors in $\mathbb{R}^n$, we *define* orthogonality between **a** and **b** by (3). The concept of orthogonality is often used in econometrics.

NOTE 1 (This relies on some elementary trigonometry) Let **a** and **b** be two non-zero vectors in $\mathbb{R}^n$. Define the *angle* θ between them by

$$\cos \theta = \frac{\mathbf{a} \cdot \mathbf{b}}{\|\mathbf{a}\| \cdot \|\mathbf{b}\|} \qquad (\theta \in [0, \pi]) \qquad (4)$$

Definition (4) makes sense because the Cauchy–Schwarz inequality implies that the right-hand side has an absolute value ≤ 1. Note also that according to (4), $\cos \theta = 0$ iff $\mathbf{a} \cdot \mathbf{b} = 0$. This agrees with (3) because for $\theta \in [0, \pi]$, we have $\cos \theta = 0$ iff $\theta = \pi/2$.

EXAMPLE 2   Suppose we repeatedly observe a commodity's price and the quantity demanded. After n observations we have n pairs $(p_1, d_1), (p_2, d_2), \ldots, (p_n, d_n)$, where p_i represents the price and d_i is the demand at observation i, $i = 1, 2, \ldots, n$. Define the statistical means

$$\bar{p} = \frac{1}{n} \sum_{i=1}^{n} p_i, \qquad \bar{d} = \frac{1}{n} \sum_{i=1}^{n} d_i$$

and

$$\mathbf{a} = (p_1 - \bar{p}, \ p_2 - \bar{p}, \ \ldots, \ p_n - \bar{p}), \qquad \mathbf{b} = (d_1 - \bar{d}, \ d_2 - \bar{d}, \ \ldots, \ d_n - \bar{d})$$

In statistics, $\cos\theta$, defined by (4), is called the **correlation coefficient**, often denoted by ρ. It is a measure of the degree of "correlation" between the data. When $\rho = 1$, there is a positive constant $\alpha > 0$ such that $d_i - \bar{d} = \alpha(p_i - \bar{p})$, implying that demand and price are *perfectly correlated*. It is more plausible, however, that $\rho = -1$ because this relationship holds for some $\alpha < 0$. Generally, if $\rho > 0$ the variables are *positively correlated*, if $\rho < 0$ the variables are *negatively correlated*, and if $\rho = 0$ they are *uncorrelated*.

EXAMPLE 3   (**Orthogonality in econometrics**) In the earlier example of linear regression (Example 13.3.4), the regression coefficients α and β were chosen to minimize the loss function

$$L(\alpha, \beta) = \frac{1}{T}\sum_{t=1}^{T} e_t^2 = \frac{1}{T}\sum_{t=1}^{T}(y_t - \alpha - \beta x_t)^2$$

This required choosing $\hat{\alpha} = \mu_y - (\sigma_{xy}/\sigma_{xx})\mu_x$ and $\hat{\beta} = \sigma_{xy}/\sigma_{xx}$, where μ_x and μ_y denote the means of x_t and y_t respectively, whereas σ_{xx} is the variance of x_t, and σ_{xy} is the covariance of x_t with y_t. The resulting errors become $\hat{e}_t = y_t - \hat{\alpha} - \hat{\beta}x_t = y_t - \mu_y - (\sigma_{xy}/\sigma_{xx})(x_t - \mu_x)$. By definition of μ_x and μ_y, one has

$$\frac{1}{T}\sum_{t=1}^{T}\hat{e}_t = 0 \qquad (*)$$

In addition,

$$\frac{1}{T}\sum_{t=1}^{T}\hat{e}_t x_t = \frac{1}{T}\sum_{t=1}^{T}x_t y_t - \mu_x\mu_y - \frac{\sigma_{xy}}{\sigma_{xx}}\left(\frac{1}{T}\sum_{t=1}^{T}x_t^2 - \mu_x^2\right) = \sigma_{xy} - \frac{\sigma_{xy}}{\sigma_{xx}}\sigma_{xx} = 0 \qquad (**)$$

Define the vectors $\mathbf{1} = (1, 1\ldots, 1)$, $\mathbf{x} = (x_1, \ldots, x_T)$, and $\hat{\mathbf{e}} = (\hat{e}_1, \ldots, \hat{e}_T)$. Then equation $(*)$ shows that the inner product of $\hat{\mathbf{e}}$ and $\mathbf{1}$ is 0. Moreover, equation $(**)$ shows that the inner product of $\hat{\mathbf{e}}$ and $\mathbf{x}$ is 0.

Note that $L(\alpha, \beta) = (1/T)\|\mathbf{y} - \alpha\mathbf{1} - \beta\mathbf{x}\|^2$. Geometrically, the scalars $\hat{\alpha}$ and $\hat{\beta}$ are chosen so that the point $\hat{\mathbf{y}} = \hat{\alpha}\mathbf{1} + \hat{\beta}\mathbf{x}$ in the hyperplane[2] containing the points $\mathbf{1}$ and $\mathbf{x}$ is as close as possible to $\mathbf{y}$ in the T-dimensional space $\mathbb{R}^T$. This involves having the vector $\mathbf{y} - \hat{\mathbf{y}} = \hat{\mathbf{e}}$ be orthogonal to $\mathbf{1}$ and $\mathbf{x}$, and to every other vector $\alpha\mathbf{1} + \beta\mathbf{x}$ in this hyperplane. Accordingly, $\hat{\mathbf{y}}$ is called the **orthogonal projection** of $\mathbf{y}$ onto this hyperplane.

PROBLEMS FOR SECTION 15.8

1. Let $\mathbf{a} = (5, -1)$ and $\mathbf{b} = (-2, 4)$. Compute $\mathbf{a} + \mathbf{b}$ and $-\frac{1}{2}\mathbf{a}$, and illustrate with geometric vectors starting at the origin.

2. Let $\mathbf{a} = (3, 1)$ and $\mathbf{b} = (-1, 2)$. Define $\mathbf{x} = (1 - \lambda)\mathbf{a} + \lambda\mathbf{b}$.

   (a) Compute $\mathbf{x}$ when $\lambda = 0, 1/4, 1/2, 3/4$, and 1. Illustrate.

   (b) As λ runs through all the real numbers between 0 and 1, what set of points does $\mathbf{x}$ trace out? Show that if λ runs through *all* the real numbers, then $\mathbf{x}$ traces out the whole straight line through $(3, 1)$ and $(-1, 2)$.

---

[2] Hyperplanes are discussed in the next section.

3. Let $\mathbf{a} = (1, 2, 2)$, $\mathbf{b} = (0, 0, -3)$, and $\mathbf{c} = (-2, 4, -3)$. Compute $\|\mathbf{a}\|$, $\|\mathbf{b}\|$, and $\|\mathbf{c}\|$, and verify that (2) holds for $\mathbf{a}$ and $\mathbf{b}$.

4. Let $\mathbf{a} = (1, 2, 1)$ and $\mathbf{b} = (-3, 0, -2)$.

   (a) Find real numbers x_1 and x_2 such that $x_1\mathbf{a} + x_2\mathbf{b} = (5, 4, 4)$.

   (b) Prove that there are no real numbers x_1 and x_2 satisfying $x_1\mathbf{a} + x_2\mathbf{b} = (-3, 6, 1)$.

5. Check which of these pairs of vectors are orthogonal:

   (a) $(1, 2)$ and $(-2, 1)$ (b) $(1, -1, 1)$ and $(-1, 1, -1)$ (c) $(a, -b, 1)$ and $(b, a, 0)$

6. For what values of x are $(x, -x - 8, x, x)$ and $(x, 1, -2, 1)$ orthogonal?

HARDER PROBLEMS

7. Show that any two different columns of an orthogonal matrix (see Problem 15.5.7) are orthogonal vectors, as are any two different rows.

8. If $\mathbf{a}$ and $\mathbf{b}$ are n-vectors, prove the *triangle inequality* $\|\mathbf{a} + \mathbf{b}\| \leq \|\mathbf{a}\| + \|\mathbf{b}\|$.
   (*Hint:* $\|\mathbf{a} + \mathbf{b}\|^2 = (\mathbf{a} + \mathbf{b}) \cdot (\mathbf{a} + \mathbf{b})$. Then use (2).)

15.9 Lines and Planes

Let $\mathbf{a} = (a_1, a_2, a_3)$ and $\mathbf{b} = (b_1, b_2, b_3)$ be two distinct vectors in $\mathbb{R}^3$. Think of them as arrows from the origin to the points with coordinates (a_1, a_2, a_3) and (b_1, b_2, b_3), respectively. The straight line L passing through these two points is shown in Fig. 1.

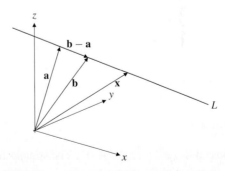

Figure 1

Let t be a real number and put $\mathbf{x} = \mathbf{a} + t(\mathbf{b} - \mathbf{a}) = (1 - t)\mathbf{a} + t\mathbf{b}$. Then $t = 0$ gives $\mathbf{x} = \mathbf{a}$ and $t = 1$ gives $\mathbf{x} = \mathbf{b}$. In general, by the geometric rule for adding vectors, we see that as t runs through all the real numbers, so $\mathbf{x}$ describes the whole straight line L.

For $\mathbb{R}^n$, we introduce the following definition:

LINE IN N-SPACE

The line L in $\mathbb{R}^n$ through two distinct points $\mathbf{a} = (a_1, \ldots, a_n)$ and $\mathbf{b} = (b_1, \ldots, b_n)$ is the set of all $\mathbf{x} = (x_1, \ldots, x_n)$ satisfying

$$\mathbf{x} = (1 - t)\mathbf{a} + t\mathbf{b} \qquad \text{for some real number } t \tag{1}$$

By using the coordinates of $\mathbf{a}$ and $\mathbf{b}$, (1) is equivalent to

$$x_1 = (1 - t)a_1 + tb_1, x_2 = (1 - t)a_2 + tb_2, \ldots, x_n = (1 - t)a_n + tb_n \tag{2}$$

EXAMPLE 1   Describe the straight line in $\mathbb{R}^3$ through the two points $(1, 2, 2)$ and $(-1, -1, 4)$. Where does it meet the x_1x_2-plane?

Solution: According to (2), the straight line is given by the equations:

$$x_1 = (1 - t) \cdot 1 + t(-1) = 1 - 2t$$
$$x_2 = (1 - t) \cdot 2 + t(-1) = 2 - 3t$$
$$x_3 = (1 - t) \cdot 2 + t \cdot 4 \;\; = 2 + 2t$$

This line intersects the x_1x_2-plane when $x_3 = 0$. Then $2 + 2t = 0$, so $t = -1$, implying that $x_1 = 3$ and $x_2 = 5$. It follows that the line meets the x_1x_2-plane at the point $(3, 5, 0)$, as shown in Fig. 2.   ∎

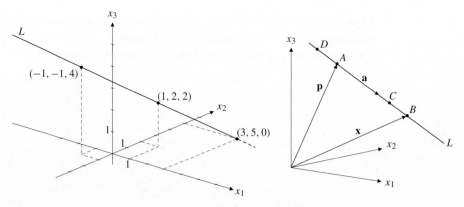

Figure 2   Figure 3

Suppose $\mathbf{p} = (p_1, \ldots, p_n) \in \mathbb{R}^n$. The straight line L passing through $(p_1, \ldots, p_n)$ in the same direction as the vector $\mathbf{a} = (a_1, \ldots, a_n)$ is given by

$$\mathbf{x} = \mathbf{p} + t\mathbf{a} \qquad (t \text{ is any real number}) \tag{3}$$

This should be apparent from Fig. 3 where A is $\mathbf{p}$, B is $\mathbf{x} = \mathbf{p} + \mathbf{a}$, C is $\mathbf{p} + \frac{3}{4}\mathbf{a}$, D is $\mathbf{p} - \frac{1}{4}\mathbf{a}$, and so on.

Hyperplanes

Consider first a plane $\mathcal{P}$ in $\mathbb{R}^3$ passing through point $\mathbf{a} = (a_1, a_2, a_3)$ and having the vector $\mathbf{p} = (p_1, p_2, p_3) \neq (0, 0, 0)$ as its normal. This is shown in Fig. 4. To say that $\mathbf{p}$ is **normal** to the plane $\mathcal{P}$ means that $\mathbf{p}$ is normal (orthogonal or perpendicular) to any line in the plane. Thus, if $\mathbf{x} = (x_1, x_2, x_3)$ is any point in $\mathcal{P}$ other than $\mathbf{a}$, then the vector $\mathbf{x} - \mathbf{a}$ is in a direction orthogonal to $\mathbf{p}$. Therefore, the inner product of $\mathbf{p}$ and $\mathbf{x} - \mathbf{a}$ must be 0, so that

$$\mathbf{p} \cdot (\mathbf{x} - \mathbf{a}) = 0 \quad \text{or} \quad (p_1, p_2, p_3) \cdot (x_1 - a_1, x_2 - a_2, x_3 - a_3) = 0 \qquad (4)$$

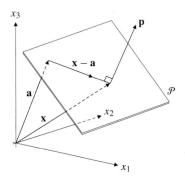

Figure 4

So (4) is the general equation of a plane in $\mathbb{R}^3$ passing through $\mathbf{a} = (a_1, a_2, a_3)$. Note that the coefficients (p_1, p_2, p_3) of x_1, x_2, x_3 represent a nonzero vector that is normal to the plane.

EXAMPLE 2   Find the equation for the plane in $\mathbb{R}^3$ through $\mathbf{a} = (2, 1, -1)$ with $\mathbf{p} = (-1, 1, 3)$ as a normal. Does the line in Example 1 intersect this plane?

Solution: Using (4), the equation is

$$-1 \cdot (x_1 - 2) + 1 \cdot (x_2 - 1) + 3(x_3 - (-1)) = 0 \quad \text{or} \quad -x_1 + x_2 + 3x_3 = -4$$

If the line given by the three equations $x_1 = 1 - 2t$, $x_2 = 2 - 3t$, and $x_3 = 2 + 2t$ meets this plane, then we must have

$$-(1 - 2t) + (2 - 3t) + 3(2 + 2t) = -4$$

Solving this equation for t yields $t = -11/5$, and so the point of intersection is given by

$$x_1 = 1 - 2(-11/5) = 27/5, \quad x_2 = 43/5, \quad x_3 = -12/5 \qquad \blacksquare$$

Motivated by this characterization of a plane in $\mathbb{R}^3$, we introduce the following general definition in $\mathbb{R}^n$.

HYPERPLANE IN N-SPACE

The hyperplane H in $\mathbb{R}^n$ through $\mathbf{a} = (a_1, \ldots, a_n)$ which is orthogonal to the non-zero vector $\mathbf{p} = (p_1, \ldots, p_n)$ is the set of all points $\mathbf{x} = (x_1, \ldots, x_n)$ satisfying

$$\mathbf{p} \cdot (\mathbf{x} - \mathbf{a}) = 0$$

(5)

Note that if the normal vector $\mathbf{p}$ is replaced by the scalar multiple $s\mathbf{p}$, where $s \neq 0$, then precisely the same set of vectors $\mathbf{x}$ will satisfy the hyperplane equation.

Using the coordinate representation of the vectors, the hyperplane has the equation

$$p_1(x_1 - a_1) + p_2(x_2 - a_2) + \cdots + p_n(x_n - a_n) = 0 \tag{6}$$

or

$$p_1 x_1 + p_2 x_2 + \cdots + p_n x_n = A, \quad \text{where} \quad A = p_1 a_1 + p_2 a_2 + \cdots + p_n a_n$$

EXAMPLE 3   A person has an amount m to spend on n different commodities, whose prices per unit are $p_1, p_2, \ldots, p_n$, respectively. This person can afford any commodity vector $\mathbf{x} = (x_1, x_2, \ldots, x_n)$ that satisfies the budget inequality

$$p_1 x_1 + p_2 x_2 + \cdots + p_n x_n \leq m \tag{7}$$

When (7) is satisfied with equality, it describes the *budget (hyper) plane* whose normal is the price vector $(p_1, p_2, \ldots, p_n)$.

Usually, it is implicitly assumed that $x_1 \geq 0, x_2 \geq 0, \ldots, x_n \geq 0$. See Fig. 11.4.1 for the case $n = 3$. Note that in this figure the vector (p, q, r) is normal to the plane.

PROBLEMS FOR SECTION 15.9

1. Find the equation for the line:

   (a) that passes through points $(3, -2, 2)$ and $(10, 2, 1)$.

   (b) that passes through point $(1, 3, 2)$ and has the same direction as $(0, -1, 1)$.

2. The line L is given by $x_1 = -t + 2$, $x_2 = 2t - 1$, and $x_3 = t + 3$.

   (a) Verify that the point $\mathbf{a} = (2, -1, 3)$ lies on L, but that $(1, 1, 1)$ does not.

   (b) Find the equation for the plane through $\mathbf{a}$ that is orthogonal to L.

   (c) Find the point where L intersects the plane $3x_1 + 5x_2 - x_3 = 6$.

3. Find the equation for the plane through the points $(3, 4, -3)$, $(5, 2, 1)$, and $(2, -1, 4)$.

4. (a) Show that $\mathbf{a} = (-2, 1, -1)$ is a point in the plane $-x + 2y + 3z = 1$.

   (b) Find the equation for the normal at $\mathbf{a}$ to the plane in part (a).

5. The price vector is $(2, 3, 5)$ and you can afford the commodity vector $(10, 5, 8)$. What is your budget constraint? (See Example 3.)

REVIEW PROBLEMS FOR CHAPTER 15

1. Construct the two matrices $\mathbf{A} = (a_{ij})_{2\times3}$, where (a) $a_{ij} = i + j$ and (b) $a_{ij} = (-1)^{i+j}$.

2. Using the matrices

$$\mathbf{A} = \begin{pmatrix} 2 & 0 \\ -1 & 1 \end{pmatrix}, \quad \mathbf{B} = \begin{pmatrix} -1 & 2 \\ 1 & -1 \end{pmatrix}, \quad \mathbf{C} = \begin{pmatrix} 2 & 3 \\ 1 & 4 \end{pmatrix}, \quad \mathbf{D} = \begin{pmatrix} 1 & 1 & 1 \\ 1 & 3 & 4 \end{pmatrix}$$

   calculate (where possible),

   (a) $\mathbf{A} - \mathbf{B}$ (b) $\mathbf{A} + \mathbf{B} - 2\mathbf{C}$ (c) $\mathbf{AB}$ (d) $\mathbf{C}(\mathbf{AB})$ (e) $\mathbf{AD}$ (f) $\mathbf{DC}$

3. Using the matrices in Problem 2, compute (where possible),

   (a) $2\mathbf{A} - 3\mathbf{B}$ (b) $(\mathbf{A} - \mathbf{B})'$ (c) $(\mathbf{C}'\mathbf{A}')\mathbf{B}'$ (d) $\mathbf{C}'(\mathbf{A}'\mathbf{B}')$ (e) $\mathbf{D}'\mathbf{D}'$ (f) $\mathbf{D}'\mathbf{D}$

4. Write the following systems of equations in matrix notation:

$$\text{(a)} \quad \begin{aligned} 2x_1 - 5x_2 &= 3 \\ 5x_1 + 8x_2 &= 5 \end{aligned}$$

$$\text{(b)} \quad \begin{aligned} x + y + z + t &= a \\ x + 3y + 2z + 4t &= b \\ x + 4y + 8z &= c \\ 2x \quad + z - t &= d \end{aligned}$$

$$\text{(c)} \quad \begin{aligned} ax + y + (a+1)z &= b_1 \\ x + 2y + \quad z &= b_2 \\ 3x + 4y + \quad 7z &= b_3 \end{aligned}$$

5. Let $\mathbf{A} = \begin{pmatrix} 0 & 1 & -2 \\ 3 & 4 & 5 \\ -6 & 7 & 15 \end{pmatrix}$, $\mathbf{B} = \begin{pmatrix} 0 & -5 & 3 \\ 5 & 2 & -1 \\ -4 & 2 & 0 \end{pmatrix}$, $\mathbf{C} = \begin{pmatrix} 6 & -2 & -3 \\ 2 & 0 & 1 \\ 0 & 5 & 7 \end{pmatrix}$.

   Find the matrices $\mathbf{A} + \mathbf{B}$, $\mathbf{A} - \mathbf{B}$, $\mathbf{AB}$, $\mathbf{BA}$, $\mathbf{A}(\mathbf{BC})$, and $(\mathbf{AB})\mathbf{C}$.

6. Define the two matrices $\mathbf{T}$ and $\mathbf{S}$ by $\mathbf{T} = \begin{pmatrix} p & q & 0 \\ \frac{1}{2}p & \frac{1}{2} & \frac{1}{2}q \\ 0 & p & q \end{pmatrix}$, $\mathbf{S} = \begin{pmatrix} p^2 & 2pq & q^2 \\ p^2 & 2pq & q^2 \\ p^2 & 2pq & q^2 \end{pmatrix}$,

   and assume that $p + q = 1$.

   (a) Prove that $\mathbf{T} \cdot \mathbf{S} = \mathbf{S}$, $\mathbf{T}^2 = \frac{1}{2}\mathbf{T} + \frac{1}{2}\mathbf{S}$, and $\mathbf{T}^3 = \frac{1}{4}\mathbf{T} + \frac{3}{4}\mathbf{S}$.

   (b) Conjecture a formula for $\mathbf{T}^n$ $(n = 2, 3, \dots)$ expressed as a linear combination of $\mathbf{T}$ and $\mathbf{S}$, then prove the formula by induction.

7. (a) Let $\mathbf{A} = \begin{pmatrix} a & b & 0 \\ -b & a & b \\ 0 & -b & a \end{pmatrix}$, where a and b are arbitrary constants. Find $\mathbf{AA} = \mathbf{A}^2$.

   (b) A square matrix $\mathbf{B}$ is called *skew-symmetric* if $\mathbf{B} = -\mathbf{B}'$, where $\mathbf{B}'$ is the transpose of $\mathbf{B}$. Show that if $\mathbf{C}$ is an arbitrary matrix such that $\mathbf{C}'\mathbf{BC}$ is defined, then $\mathbf{C}'\mathbf{BC}$ is skew-symmetric if $\mathbf{B}$ is. When is the matrix $\mathbf{A}$ defined in (a) skew-symmetric?

   (c) If $\mathbf{A}$ is any square matrix, prove that $\mathbf{A}_1 = \frac{1}{2}(\mathbf{A} + \mathbf{A}')$ is symmetric and that $\mathbf{A}_2 = \frac{1}{2}(\mathbf{A} - \mathbf{A}')$ is skew-symmetric. Verify that $\mathbf{A} = \mathbf{A}_1 + \mathbf{A}_2$, and explain in your own words what you have proved.

8. Solve the following equation systems by Gaussian elimination.

   (a) $\begin{aligned} x_1 + 4x_2 &= 1 \\ 2x_1 + 2x_2 &= 8 \end{aligned}$
   (b) $\begin{aligned} 2x_1 + 2x_2 - x_3 &= 2 \\ x_1 - 3x_2 + x_3 &= 0 \\ 3x_1 + 4x_2 - x_3 &= 1 \end{aligned}$
   (c) $\begin{aligned} x_1 + 3x_2 + 4x_3 &= 0 \\ 5x_1 + x_2 + x_3 &= 0 \end{aligned}$

9. Use Gaussian elimination to find for what values of a the following system has solutions. Then find all the possible solutions.

$$\begin{aligned} x + ay + 2z &= 0 \\ -2x - ay + z &= 4 \\ 2ax + 3a^2 y + 9z &= 4 \end{aligned}$$

10. Let $\mathbf{a} = (-1, 5, 3)$, $\mathbf{b} = (1, 1, -3)$, and $\mathbf{c} = (-1, 2, 8)$. Compute $\|\mathbf{a}\|$, $\|\mathbf{b}\|$, and $\|\mathbf{c}\|$. Verify that the Cauchy–Schwarz inequality holds for $\mathbf{a}$ and $\mathbf{b}$.

11. A firm has two plants that produce outputs of three different goods. Its total labour force is fixed. When a fraction λ of its labour force is allocated to its first plant and a fraction $1 - \lambda$ to its second plant (with $0 \le \lambda \le 1$), the total output of the three different goods are given by the vector $\lambda(8, 4, 4) + (1 - \lambda)(2, 6, 10) = (6\lambda + 2, -2\lambda + 6, -6\lambda + 10)$.

   (a) Is it possible for the firm to produce either of the two output vectors $\mathbf{a} = (5, 5, 7)$ and $\mathbf{b} = (7, 5, 5)$ if output cannot be thrown away?

   (b) How do your answers to part (a) change if output can be thrown away?

   (c) How will the revenue-maximizing choice of the fraction λ depend upon the selling prices (p_1, p_2, p_3) of the three goods? What condition must be satisfied by these prices if both plants are to remain in use?

12. If $\mathbf{P}$ and $\mathbf{Q}$ are $n \times n$-matrices with $\mathbf{PQ} - \mathbf{QP} = \mathbf{P}$, prove that $\mathbf{P}^2\mathbf{Q} - \mathbf{QP}^2 = 2\,\mathbf{P}^2$ and $\mathbf{P}^3\mathbf{Q} - \mathbf{QP}^3 = 3\,\mathbf{P}^3$.

16

DETERMINANTS AND INVERSE MATRICES

*You know we all became mathematicians
for the same reason: We were lazy.*
—Max Rosenlicht (1949)

This chapter continues the study of linear algebra. The first topic discussed is *determinants*. Though some economists have claimed that determinants are almost useless, we shall see that they do in fact play an important role in several areas of mathematics that are of interest to economists.

After introducing determinants, we consider the fundamentally important concept of the *inverse* of a square matrix and its main properties. Inverse matrices play a major role in solving systems of linear equations, and in econometrics, for deriving a linear relationship that fits a data set as well as possible. Cramer's rule for the solution of a system of n linear equations and n unknowns is discussed next. Although it is not efficient for solving systems of equations with more than 3 unknowns, Cramer's rule is often used in theoretical studies. An important theorem on homogeneous systems of equations is also discussed. The chapter concludes with a brief introduction to the Leontief model.

16.1 Determinants of Order 2

Consider the pair of linear equations with its associated coefficient matrix:

$$a_{11}x_1 + a_{12}x_2 = b_1, \qquad \mathbf{A} = \begin{pmatrix} a_{11} & a_{12} \\ a_{21} & a_{22} \end{pmatrix} \qquad (1)$$
$$a_{21}x_1 + a_{22}x_2 = b_2$$

Solving the equation system (1) in the usual way (see Section 2.4) yields

$$x_1 = \frac{b_1 a_{22} - b_2 a_{12}}{a_{11} a_{22} - a_{21} a_{12}}, \qquad x_2 = \frac{b_2 a_{11} - b_1 a_{21}}{a_{11} a_{22} - a_{21} a_{12}} \qquad (2)$$

The two fractions have a common denominator, equal to $a_{11}a_{22} - a_{21}a_{12}$. This common denominator must be non-zero for (2) to be valid, in which case system (1) has a unique solution. In this sense, the value of the denominator determines whether (1) has a unique solution. In fact, $a_{11}a_{22} - a_{21}a_{12}$ is called the **determinant** of the matrix $\mathbf{A}$. The determinant of $\mathbf{A}$ is denoted by either $\det(\mathbf{A})$ or, more usually as in this book, by $|\mathbf{A}|$. Thus,

$$|\mathbf{A}| = \begin{vmatrix} a_{11} & a_{12} \\ a_{21} & a_{22} \end{vmatrix} = a_{11}a_{22} - a_{21}a_{12} \tag{3}$$

for any 2×2 matrix $\mathbf{A}$. Such a determinant is said to have **order** 2. For the special case of order 2 determinants, the rule for calculating $|\mathbf{A}|$ is: (a) multiply the diagonal elements, (b) multiply the off-diagonal elements, and (c) subtract the product of the off-diagonal elements from the product of the diagonal elements.

EXAMPLE 1 $\begin{vmatrix} 4 & 1 \\ 3 & 2 \end{vmatrix} = 4{\cdot}2 - 3{\cdot}1 = 5, \quad \begin{vmatrix} b_1 & a_{12} \\ b_2 & a_{22} \end{vmatrix} = b_1 a_{22} - b_2 a_{12}, \quad \begin{vmatrix} a_{11} & b_1 \\ a_{21} & b_2 \end{vmatrix} = b_2 a_{11} - b_1 a_{21}$ ∎

NOTE 1 Geometrically, each of the two equations in (1) represents the graph of a straight line. If $|\mathbf{A}| \neq 0$, then the two lines intersect at a unique point (x_1, x_2) given by (2). If $|\mathbf{A}| = 0$, the expressions for x_1 and x_2 become meaningless—indeed, in this case, equation system (1) either has no solution (because the two lines are parallel), or else has infinitely many solutions (because the two lines coincide).

From Example 1, we see that the *numerators* of the expressions for x_1 and x_2 in (2) can also be written as determinants. Indeed, provided that $|\mathbf{A}| \neq 0$, one has

$$x_1 = \frac{\begin{vmatrix} b_1 & a_{12} \\ b_2 & a_{22} \end{vmatrix}}{|\mathbf{A}|}, \qquad x_2 = \frac{\begin{vmatrix} a_{11} & b_1 \\ a_{21} & b_2 \end{vmatrix}}{|\mathbf{A}|} \tag{4}$$

This is a special case of a result referred to as **Cramer's rule**.[1] It turns out that a similar rule applies to 3 equations with 3 unknowns (see the next section). Later in Section 16.8, we shall generalize the rule to n equations in n unknowns.

EXAMPLE 2   Use (4) to find the solutions of

$$2x_1 + 4x_2 = 7$$
$$2x_1 - 2x_2 = -2$$

Solution:

$$x_1 = \frac{\begin{vmatrix} 7 & 4 \\ -2 & -2 \end{vmatrix}}{\begin{vmatrix} 2 & 4 \\ 2 & -2 \end{vmatrix}} = \frac{-6}{-12} = \frac{1}{2}, \qquad x_2 = \frac{\begin{vmatrix} 2 & 7 \\ 2 & -2 \end{vmatrix}}{\begin{vmatrix} 2 & 4 \\ 2 & -2 \end{vmatrix}} = \frac{-18}{-12} = \frac{3}{2}$$

Check by substitution that $x_1 = 1/2$, $x_2 = 3/2$ really is a solution. ∎

[1] Named after the Swiss mathematician Gabriel Cramer, 1704–1752.

EXAMPLE 3   Use (4) to find Q_1^D and Q_2^D in terms of the parameters when

$$2(b + \beta_1)Q_1^D + bQ_2^D = a - \alpha_1$$

$$bQ_1^D + 2(b + \beta_2)Q_2^D = a - \alpha_2$$

Solution: The determinant of the coefficient matrix is

$$\Delta = \begin{vmatrix} 2(b + \beta_1) & b \\ b & 2(b + \beta_2) \end{vmatrix} = 4(b + \beta_1)(b + \beta_2) - b^2$$

Provided $\Delta \neq 0$, by (4) the solutions are

$$Q_1^D = \frac{\begin{vmatrix} a - \alpha_1 & b \\ a - \alpha_2 & 2(b + \beta_2) \end{vmatrix}}{\Delta} = \frac{2(b + \beta_2)(a - \alpha_1) - b(a - \alpha_2)}{\Delta}$$

$$Q_2^D = \frac{\begin{vmatrix} 2(b + \beta_1) & a - \alpha_1 \\ b & a - \alpha_2 \end{vmatrix}}{\Delta} = \frac{2(b + \beta_1)(a - \alpha_2) - b(a - \alpha_1)}{\Delta}$$

This example illustrates the convenience of Cramer's rule when several parameters are involved. In fact, experience suggests that in such cases one is less likely to make algebraic errors by using Cramer's rule instead of the elimination method.

A Geometric Interpretation

Determinants of order 2 have a nice geometric interpretation, as shown in Fig. 1. If the two vectors are situated as in Fig. 1, then the determinant is equal to the hatched area of the parallelogram. If we interchange the two row vectors in the determinant, then it becomes a negative number whose absolute value is equal to the hatched area.

Figure 2 illustrates why the result claimed in Fig. 1 is true. We want to find area T. Note that $2T_1 + 2T_2 + 2T_3 + T = (a_{11} + a_{21})(a_{12} + a_{22})$, where $T_1 = a_{12}a_{21}$, $T_2 = \frac{1}{2}a_{21}a_{22}$, and $T_3 = \frac{1}{2}a_{11}a_{12}$. Then $T = a_{11}a_{22} - a_{21}a_{12}$, by elementary algebra.

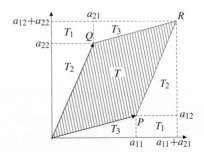

Figure 1 The area T is the absolute value of the determinant $\begin{vmatrix} a_{11} & a_{12} \\ a_{21} & a_{22} \end{vmatrix}$.

Figure 2 $2T_1 + 2T_2 + 2T_3 + T = (a_{11} + a_{21})(a_{12} + a_{22})$

1. Calculate the following determinants:

(a) $\begin{vmatrix} 3 & 0 \\ 2 & 6 \end{vmatrix}$ (b) $\begin{vmatrix} a & a \\ b & b \end{vmatrix}$ (c) $\begin{vmatrix} a+b & a-b \\ a-b & a+b \end{vmatrix}$ (d) $\begin{vmatrix} 3^t & 2^t \\ 3^{t-1} & 2^{t-1} \end{vmatrix}$

2. Illustrate the geometric interpretation in Fig. 1 for the determinant in Problem 1(a).

3. Use Cramer's rule (4) to solve the following systems of equations for x and y. Test the answers by substitution.

(a) $\begin{aligned} 3x - y &= 8 \\ x - 2y &= 5 \end{aligned}$ (b) $\begin{aligned} x + 3y &= 1 \\ 3x - 2y &= 14 \end{aligned}$ (c) $\begin{aligned} ax - by &= 1 \\ bx + ay &= 2 \end{aligned}$

4. Let $\mathbf{A} = \begin{pmatrix} a_{11} & a_{12} \\ a_{21} & a_{22} \end{pmatrix}$ and $\mathbf{B} = \begin{pmatrix} b_{11} & b_{12} \\ b_{21} & b_{22} \end{pmatrix}$. Show that $|\mathbf{AB}| = |\mathbf{A}| \cdot |\mathbf{B}|$.

5. Find two 2×2 matrices $\mathbf{A}$ and $\mathbf{B}$ such that $|\mathbf{A} + \mathbf{B}| \neq |\mathbf{A}| + |\mathbf{B}|$.

6. Use Cramer's rule to find Y and C when

$$Y = C + I_0 + G_0, \qquad C = a + bY$$

where Y is the national product and C is private consumption. The symbols I_0 (private investment), G_0 (public consumption and investment), a, and b all represent constants, with $b < 1$. (Actually, this is a typical case in which one should *not* use Cramer's rule, because Y and C can be found much more simply. How?)

HARDER PROBLEMS

7. Consider the following linked macroeconomic model of two nations, $i = 1, 2$, that trade only with each other:

$$\begin{aligned} Y_1 &= C_1 + A_1 + X_1 - M_1; & C_1 &= c_1 Y_1; & M_1 &= m_1 Y_1 \\ Y_2 &= C_2 + A_2 + X_2 - M_2; & C_2 &= c_2 Y_2; & M_2 &= m_2 Y_2 \end{aligned}$$

Here, for $i = 1, 2$, Y_i is income, C_i is consumption, A_i is (exogenous) autonomous expenditure, X_i denotes exports, and M_i denotes imports of country i.

(a) Interpret the two equations $X_1 = M_2$ and $X_2 = M_1$.

(b) Given the equations in part (a), calculate the corresponding equilibrium values of Y_1 and Y_2 as functions of the exogenous variables.

(c) How does an increase in A_1 affect Y_2? Interpret your answer.

16.2 Determinants of Order 3

Consider the system of three linear equations in three unknowns

$$a_{11}x_1 + a_{12}x_2 + a_{13}x_3 = b_1$$
$$a_{21}x_1 + a_{22}x_2 + a_{23}x_3 = b_2 \tag{1}$$
$$a_{31}x_1 + a_{32}x_2 + a_{33}x_3 = b_3$$

Here the coefficient matrix $\mathbf{A}$ is 3×3. By applying the method of elimination along with some rather heavy algebraic computation, this system can be solved eventually for x_1, x_2, and x_3. The resulting expression for x_1 is

$$x_1 = \frac{b_1 a_{22} a_{33} - b_1 a_{23} a_{32} - b_2 a_{12} a_{33} + b_2 a_{13} a_{32} + b_3 a_{12} a_{23} - b_3 a_{22} a_{13}}{a_{11} a_{22} a_{33} - a_{11} a_{23} a_{32} + a_{12} a_{23} a_{31} - a_{12} a_{21} a_{33} + a_{13} a_{21} a_{32} - a_{13} a_{22} a_{31}}$$

We shall not triple the demands on the reader's patience and eyesight by giving the corresponding expressions for x_2 and x_3. However, we do claim that these expressions share the same denominator as that given for x_1. This common denominator is called the **determinant** of $\mathbf{A}$, denoted by $\det(\mathbf{A})$ or $|\mathbf{A}|$. It is defined as

$$|\mathbf{A}| = \begin{vmatrix} a_{11} & a_{12} & a_{13} \\ a_{21} & a_{22} & a_{23} \\ a_{31} & a_{32} & a_{33} \end{vmatrix} = \left\{ \begin{array}{l} a_{11} a_{22} a_{33} - a_{11} a_{23} a_{32} + a_{12} a_{23} a_{31} \\ \qquad - a_{12} a_{21} a_{33} + a_{13} a_{21} a_{32} - a_{13} a_{22} a_{31} \end{array} \right. \tag{2}$$

Expansion by Cofactors

Consider the sum of the six terms in (2). It looks quite messy, but the method of expansion by cofactors makes it easy to write down all the terms. First, note that each of the three elements a_{11}, a_{12}, and a_{13} in the first row of $\mathbf{A}$ appears in exactly two terms of (2). In fact, $|\mathbf{A}|$ can be written as

$$|\mathbf{A}| = a_{11}(a_{22} a_{33} - a_{23} a_{32}) - a_{12}(a_{21} a_{33} - a_{23} a_{31}) + a_{13}(a_{21} a_{32} - a_{22} a_{31})$$

Applying the rule for evaluating determinants of order 2, we see that this is the same as

$$|\mathbf{A}| = a_{11} \begin{vmatrix} a_{22} & a_{23} \\ a_{32} & a_{33} \end{vmatrix} - a_{12} \begin{vmatrix} a_{21} & a_{23} \\ a_{31} & a_{33} \end{vmatrix} + a_{13} \begin{vmatrix} a_{21} & a_{22} \\ a_{31} & a_{32} \end{vmatrix} \tag{3}$$

In this way, the computation of a determinant of order 3 can be reduced to calculating three determinants of order 2. Note that a_{11} is multiplied by the second-order determinant obtained by deleting the *first* row and the *first* column of $|\mathbf{A}|$. Likewise, a_{12}, with a minus sign attached to it, is multiplied by the determinant obtained by deleting the *first* row and the *second* column of $|\mathbf{A}|$. Finally, a_{13} is multiplied by the determinant obtained by deleting the *first* row and the *third* column of $|\mathbf{A}|$.

EXAMPLE 1   Use (3) to calculate $|\mathbf{A}| = \begin{vmatrix} 3 & 0 & 2 \\ -1 & 1 & 0 \\ 5 & 2 & 3 \end{vmatrix}$.

Solution:

$$|\mathbf{A}| = 3 \cdot \begin{vmatrix} 1 & 0 \\ 2 & 3 \end{vmatrix} - 0 \cdot \begin{vmatrix} -1 & 0 \\ 5 & 3 \end{vmatrix} + 2 \cdot \begin{vmatrix} -1 & 1 \\ 5 & 2 \end{vmatrix} = 3 \cdot 3 - 0 + 2 \cdot (-2 - 5) = -5. \quad \blacksquare$$

EXAMPLE 2   Use (3) to prove that $|\mathbf{A}| = \begin{vmatrix} 1 & a & a^2 \\ 1 & b & b^2 \\ 1 & c & c^2 \end{vmatrix} = (b - a)(c - a)(c - b).$

Solution:

$$|\mathbf{A}| = 1 \cdot \begin{vmatrix} b & b^2 \\ c & c^2 \end{vmatrix} - a \cdot \begin{vmatrix} 1 & b^2 \\ 1 & c^2 \end{vmatrix} + a^2 \cdot \begin{vmatrix} 1 & b \\ 1 & c \end{vmatrix} = bc^2 - b^2c - ac^2 + ab^2 + a^2c - a^2b$$

You are not supposed to "see" that these 6 terms can be written as $(b - a)(c - a)(c - b)$. Rather, you should expand $(b - a)[(c - a)(c - b)]$ and verify the equality that way. $\quad \blacksquare$

A careful study of the numerator in the expression for x_1 in the beginning of this section reveals that it can also be written as a determinant. The same is true of the corresponding formulas for x_2 and x_3. In fact, if $|\mathbf{A}| \neq 0$, then one has

$$x_1 = \frac{\begin{vmatrix} b_1 & a_{12} & a_{13} \\ b_2 & a_{22} & a_{23} \\ b_3 & a_{32} & a_{33} \end{vmatrix}}{|\mathbf{A}|}, \quad x_2 = \frac{\begin{vmatrix} a_{11} & b_1 & a_{13} \\ a_{21} & b_2 & a_{23} \\ a_{31} & b_3 & a_{33} \end{vmatrix}}{|\mathbf{A}|}, \quad x_3 = \frac{\begin{vmatrix} a_{11} & a_{12} & b_1 \\ a_{21} & a_{22} & b_2 \\ a_{31} & a_{32} & b_3 \end{vmatrix}}{|\mathbf{A}|} \quad (4)$$

This is Cramer's rule for the solution of (1). (See Section 16.8 for a full proof of a general version of (4).)

NOTE 1   In the determinants appearing in the numerators of x_1, x_2, and x_3 of (4), observe how the right-hand column in (1),

$$\begin{pmatrix} b_1 \\ b_2 \\ b_3 \end{pmatrix}$$

shifts from the first column when solving for x_1, to the second column when solving for x_2, and then to the third column when solving for x_3. This makes it very easy to remember Cramer's rule.

EXAMPLE 3   Solve the following system of equations by using Cramer's rule:

$$2x_1 + 2x_2 - x_3 = -3$$
$$4x_1 \qquad\quad + 2x_3 = 8$$
$$6x_2 - 3x_3 = -12$$

Solution: In this case, the determinant $|\mathbf{A}|$ in (4) is seen to be

$$|\mathbf{A}| = \begin{vmatrix} 2 & 2 & -1 \\ 4 & 0 & 2 \\ 0 & 6 & -3 \end{vmatrix} = -24$$

The numerators in (4) are (verify!)

$$\begin{vmatrix} -3 & 2 & -1 \\ 8 & 0 & 2 \\ -12 & 6 & -3 \end{vmatrix} = -12, \quad \begin{vmatrix} 2 & -3 & -1 \\ 4 & 8 & 2 \\ 0 & -12 & -3 \end{vmatrix} = 12, \quad \begin{vmatrix} 2 & 2 & -3 \\ 4 & 0 & 8 \\ 0 & 6 & -12 \end{vmatrix} = -72$$

Hence, (4) yields the solution $x_1 = (-12)/(-24) = 1/2$, $x_2 = 12/(-24) = -1/2$, and $x_3 = (-72)/(-24) = 3$. Inserting this into the original system of equations verifies that this is a correct answer.   ∎

A Geometric Interpretation

Like determinants of order 2, those of order 3 also have a geometric interpretation which is shown and explained in Fig. 1.

The volume of the "box" spanned by the three vectors

$$= \pm \begin{vmatrix} a_{11} & a_{12} & a_{13} \\ a_{21} & a_{22} & a_{23} \\ a_{31} & a_{32} & a_{33} \end{vmatrix}$$

Figure 1

The rows of the determinant correspond to three different 3-vectors represented in the diagram. These vectors determine a box which is not rectangular, but has been distorted while keeping the opposite faces parallel.

Sarrus's Rule

Here is an alternative way of evaluating determinants of order 3 that many people find convenient. Write down the determinant twice, except that the last column in the second determinant should be omitted:

$$\begin{matrix} a_{11} & a_{12} & a_{13} & a_{11} & a_{12} \\ a_{21} & a_{22} & a_{23} & a_{21} & a_{22} \\ a_{31} & a_{32} & a_{33} & a_{31} & a_{32} \end{matrix} \qquad (5)$$

First, multiply along the three lines falling to the right, giving all these products a plus sign:

$$a_{11}a_{22}a_{33} + a_{12}a_{23}a_{31} + a_{13}a_{21}a_{32}$$

Then multiply along the three lines rising to the right, giving all these products a minus sign:

$$-a_{11}a_{23}a_{32} - a_{12}a_{21}a_{33} - a_{13}a_{22}a_{31}$$

The sum of all the six terms is exactly equal to $|\mathbf{A}|$. It is important to note that this rule, known as **Sarrus's rule**, *does not generalize* to determinants of order higher than 3.

1. Use (3) to calculate the following determinants:

$$\text{(a) } \begin{vmatrix} 1 & -1 & 0 \\ 1 & 3 & 2 \\ 1 & 0 & 0 \end{vmatrix} \qquad \text{(b) } \begin{vmatrix} 1 & -1 & 0 \\ 1 & 3 & 2 \\ 1 & 2 & 1 \end{vmatrix} \qquad \text{(c) } \begin{vmatrix} a & b & c \\ 0 & d & e \\ 0 & 0 & f \end{vmatrix} \qquad \text{(d) } \begin{vmatrix} a & 0 & b \\ 0 & e & 0 \\ c & 0 & d \end{vmatrix}$$

2. Let $\mathbf{A} = \begin{pmatrix} 1 & -1 & 0 \\ 1 & 3 & 2 \\ 1 & 2 & 1 \end{pmatrix}$ and $\mathbf{B} = \begin{pmatrix} 1 & 2 & 3 \\ 2 & 3 & 4 \\ 0 & 1 & -1 \end{pmatrix}$.

Calculate $\mathbf{AB}$, $|\mathbf{A}|$, $|\mathbf{B}|$, $|\mathbf{A}| \cdot |\mathbf{B}|$, and $|\mathbf{AB}|$. (Note that $|\mathbf{AB}| = |\mathbf{A}| \cdot |\mathbf{B}|$.)

3. Use Cramer's rule to solve the following systems of equations. Check your answers.

$$\text{(a)} \quad \begin{aligned} x_1 - x_2 + x_3 &= 2 \\ x_1 + x_2 - x_3 &= 0 \\ -x_1 - x_2 - x_3 &= -6 \end{aligned} \qquad \text{(b)} \quad \begin{aligned} x_1 - x_2 &= 0 \\ x_1 + 3x_2 + 2x_3 &= 0 \\ x_1 + 2x_2 + x_3 &= 0 \end{aligned} \qquad \text{(c)} \quad \begin{aligned} x + 3y - 2z &= 1 \\ 3x - 2y + 5z &= 14 \\ 2x - 5y + 3z &= 1 \end{aligned}$$

4. Show that $\begin{vmatrix} 1+a & 1 & 1 \\ 1 & 1+b & 1 \\ 1 & 1 & 1+c \end{vmatrix} = abc + ab + ac + bc.$

5. Define the matrix $\mathbf{A}_t = \begin{pmatrix} 1 & t & 0 \\ -2 & -2 & -1 \\ 0 & 1 & t \end{pmatrix}$.

(a) Calculate $|\mathbf{A}_t|$, and show that it is never 0.

(b) Show that for a certain value of t, one has $\mathbf{A}_t^3 = \mathbf{I}_3$.

6. Consider the simple macro model described by the three equations

$$Y = C + A_0, \qquad C = a + b(Y - T), \qquad T = d + tY$$

where Y is income, C is consumption, T is tax revenue, A_0 is the constant (exogenous) autonomous expenditure, and a, b, d, and t are all positive parameters. Find the equilibrium values of the endogenous variables Y, C, and T by:

(a) successive elimination or substitution;

(b) writing the equations in matrix form and applying Cramer's rule.

16.3 Determinants of Order n

This section gives a definition of determinant that is particularly useful when proving general results. If you are not so interested in these proofs, you might skip this section and rely instead on expansion by cofactors (explained in Section 16.5) in all your work on determinants.

For a 3×3 matrix

$$\mathbf{A} = (a_{ij})_{3 \times 3}$$

the determinant was defined as the sum

$$a_{11}a_{22}a_{33} - a_{11}a_{23}a_{32} + a_{12}a_{23}a_{31} - a_{12}a_{21}a_{33} + a_{13}a_{21}a_{32} - a_{13}a_{22}a_{31} \tag{1}$$

A closer examination of this sum reveals a definite pattern. Each term is the product of three different elements of the matrix. Each product contains one element from each row of $\mathbf{A}$ and one element from each column of $\mathbf{A}$. In fact, the elements in the 6 terms are chosen from the matrix $\mathbf{A}$ according to the pattern shown by the circles in Fig. 1 (disregard the lines for a moment).

Figure 1

In a 3×3 matrix, there are precisely 6 different ways of picking three elements with one element from each row and one element from each column. All the 6 corresponding products appear in (1). How do we determine the sign of each term in (1)? In Fig. 1, we have joined the three circles in each box by lines, which are solid if the line rises to the right, but dashed if the line falls to the right. Using the solid lines drawn in each of the 6 boxes, the following rule emerges:

THE SIGN RULE

To determine the sign of any term in the sum, mark in the array all the elements appearing in that term. Join all possible pairs of these elements with lines. These lines will then either fall or rise to the right. If the number of the rising lines is even, then the corresponding term is assigned a plus sign; if it is odd, it is assigned a minus sign. (2)

Let us apply this rule to the six boxes in Fig. 1. In the first box, for example, no lines rise, so $a_{11}a_{22}a_{33}$ has a plus sign. In box 4, exactly one line rises, so $a_{12}a_{21}a_{33}$ has a minus sign. And so on.

Suppose

$$\mathbf{A} = (a_{ij})_{n \times n}$$

is an arbitrary $n \times n$ matrix. Suppose we pick n elements from $\mathbf{A}$, including exactly one element from each row and exactly one element from each column. Take the product of these n elements, giving an expression of the form

$$a_{1r_1} \cdot a_{2r_2} \cdot \ldots \cdot a_{nr_n}$$

where the second subscripts $r_1, r_2, \ldots, r_n$ represent a shuffling (or permutation) of the numbers $1, 2, \ldots, n$. The numbers $1, 2, \ldots, n$ can be permuted in $n! = 1 \cdot 2 \ldots (n-1)n$ different ways: For the first element, there are n choices; for each of these first choices, there are $n - 1$ choices for the second element; and so on. So there are $n!$ different products of n factors to consider.

Now we define the determinant of $\mathbf{A}$, det($\mathbf{A}$) or $|\mathbf{A}|$, as follows:

DEFINITION OF DETERMINANT

Let $\mathbf{A}$ be an $n \times n$ matrix. Then $|\mathbf{A}|$ is a sum of $n!$ terms where:

1. Each term is the product of n elements of the matrix, with one element from each row and one element from each column. Moreover, every product of exactly n factors, in which each row and each column is represented exactly once, must appear in this sum.

2. The sign of each term is found by applying the sign rule (2).

In symbols, one has

$$|\mathbf{A}| = \begin{vmatrix} a_{11} & a_{12} & \cdots & a_{1n} \\ a_{21} & a_{22} & \cdots & a_{2n} \\ \vdots & \vdots & \ddots & \vdots \\ a_{n1} & a_{n2} & \cdots & a_{nn} \end{vmatrix} = \sum (\pm) a_{1r_1} a_{2r_2} \ldots a_{nr_n} \tag{3}$$

EXAMPLE 1   Consider the determinant of an arbitrary 4×4 matrix $\mathbf{A} = \left(a_{ij} \right)_{4 \times 4}$:

$$|\mathbf{A}| = \begin{vmatrix} a_{11} & a_{12} & a_{13} & a_{14} \\ a_{21} & a_{22} & a_{23} & a_{24} \\ a_{31} & a_{32} & a_{33} & a_{34} \\ a_{41} & a_{42} & a_{43} & a_{44} \end{vmatrix}$$

It consists of $4! = 4 \cdot 3 \cdot 2 \cdot 1 = 24$ terms. One of these terms is $a_{13}a_{21}a_{32}a_{44}$, and the corresponding factors are the boxed elements in the array. What sign should this term have? According to the sign rule, the term should have the plus sign because there are two rising lines. Check that the four indicated terms in the following sum have been given the correct sign:

$$|\mathbf{A}| = a_{11}a_{22}a_{33}a_{44} - a_{12}a_{21}a_{33}a_{44} + \cdots + a_{13}a_{21}a_{32}a_{44} - \cdots + a_{14}a_{23}a_{32}a_{41}$$

Note that there are 20 other terms which we have left out.

The determinant of an $n \times n$ matrix is called a **determinant of order n**. In general, it is difficult to evaluate determinants by using the definition directly, even if n is only 4 or 5. If $n > 5$, the work is usually enormous. For example, if $n = 6$, then $n! = 720$, and so there are 720 terms in the sum defining the determinant. Fortunately, other methods are available that reduce the work considerably. There are several standard computer programs for evaluating determinants.

In a few special cases, it is easy to evaluate a determinant even if the order is high. For instance, it is easy to see that

$$\begin{vmatrix} a_{11} & a_{12} & \cdots & a_{1n} \\ 0 & a_{22} & \cdots & a_{2n} \\ \vdots & \vdots & \ddots & \vdots \\ 0 & 0 & \cdots & a_{nn} \end{vmatrix} = a_{11}a_{22} \ldots a_{nn} \tag{4}$$

Here all the elements *below* the main diagonal are 0. The matrix whose determinant is given in (4) is called *upper triangular* because all the non-zero terms lie in the triangle on or above the main diagonal. Such a determinant can be evaluated by taking the product of all the elements on the main diagonal. To see why, note that in order to have a term that is not 0, we have to choose a_{11} from column 1. From column 2, we cannot choose a_{12}, because we have already picked the element a_{11} from the first row. Hence, from column 2, we have to pick a_{22} in order to have a term different from 0. From the third column, we have to pick a_{33}, and so on. Thus, only the term $a_{11}a_{22}\ldots a_{nn}$ can be $\neq 0$. The sign of this term is plus because no line joining any pair of elements appearing in the product rises to the right.

   If a matrix is a transpose of an upper triangular matrix, so that all elements above the diagonal are 0, then the matrix is *lower triangular*. By using essentially the same argument as for (4), we see that the determinant of a lower triangular matrix is also equal to the product of the elements on its main diagonal:

$$\begin{vmatrix} a_{11} & 0 & \cdots & 0 \\ a_{21} & a_{22} & \cdots & 0 \\ \vdots & \vdots & \ddots & \vdots \\ a_{n1} & a_{n2} & \cdots & a_{nn} \end{vmatrix} = a_{11}a_{22}\ldots a_{nn} \tag{5}$$

PROBLEMS FOR SECTION 16.3

1. Use the definition of determinant to calculate the following:

(a) $\begin{vmatrix} 1 & 0 & 0 & 0 \\ 0 & 2 & 0 & 0 \\ 0 & 0 & 3 & 0 \\ 0 & 0 & 0 & 4 \end{vmatrix}$
(b) $\begin{vmatrix} 1 & 0 & 0 & 1 \\ 0 & 1 & 0 & 0 \\ 0 & 0 & 1 & 0 \\ a & b & c & d \end{vmatrix}$
(c) $\begin{vmatrix} 1 & 0 & 0 & 2 \\ 0 & 1 & 0 & -3 \\ 0 & 0 & 1 & 4 \\ 2 & 3 & 4 & 11 \end{vmatrix}$

2. The determinant of the following 5×5 matrix consists of $5! = 120$ terms. One of them is the product of the boxed elements. Write this term with its correct sign.

$$\begin{vmatrix} a_{11} & \boxed{a_{12}} & a_{13} & a_{14} & a_{15} \\ a_{21} & a_{22} & \boxed{a_{23}} & a_{24} & a_{25} \\ a_{31} & a_{32} & a_{33} & a_{34} & \boxed{a_{35}} \\ \boxed{a_{41}} & a_{42} & a_{43} & a_{44} & a_{45} \\ a_{51} & a_{52} & a_{53} & \boxed{a_{54}} & a_{55} \end{vmatrix}$$

3. Write the term indicated by the marked boxes with its correct sign. (See the previous problem.)

$$\begin{vmatrix} a_{11} & a_{12} & a_{13} & a_{14} & \boxed{a_{15}} \\ a_{21} & a_{22} & a_{23} & \boxed{a_{24}} & a_{25} \\ a_{31} & \boxed{a_{32}} & a_{33} & a_{34} & a_{35} \\ a_{41} & a_{42} & \boxed{a_{43}} & a_{44} & a_{45} \\ \boxed{a_{51}} & a_{52} & a_{53} & a_{54} & a_{55} \end{vmatrix}$$

4. Suppose that the two $n \times n$ matrices **A** and **B** are both upper triangular. Show that $|\mathbf{AB}| = |\mathbf{A}||\mathbf{B}|$.

16.4 Basic Rules for Determinants

Based on the definition of the determinant of an $n \times n$ matrix $\mathbf{A}$, one can prove a number of important properties. All of them are of theoretical interest, but they also make it simpler to evaluate determinants.

THEOREM 16.4.1 (RULES FOR DETERMINANTS)

Let $\mathbf{A}$ be an $n \times n$ matrix. Then:

A. If all the elements in a row (or column) of $\mathbf{A}$ are 0, then $|\mathbf{A}| = 0$.

B. $|\mathbf{A}'| = |\mathbf{A}|$, where $\mathbf{A}'$ is the transpose of $\mathbf{A}$.

C. If all the elements in a single row (or column) of $\mathbf{A}$ are multiplied by a number α, the determinant is multiplied by α.

D. If two rows (or two columns) of $\mathbf{A}$ are interchanged, the determinant changes sign, but the absolute value remains unchanged.

E. If two of the rows (or columns) of $\mathbf{A}$ are proportional, then $|\mathbf{A}| = 0$.

F. The value of the determinant of $\mathbf{A}$ is unchanged if a multiple of one row (or one column) is added to a different row (or column) of $\mathbf{A}$.

G. The determinant of the product of two $n \times n$ matrices $\mathbf{A}$ and $\mathbf{B}$ is the product of the determinants of each of the factors:

$$|\mathbf{AB}| = |\mathbf{A}| \cdot |\mathbf{B}| \tag{1}$$

H. If $\mathbf{A}$ is an $n \times n$ matrix and α is a real number, then

$$|\alpha \mathbf{A}| = \alpha^n |\mathbf{A}| \tag{2}$$

NOTE 1   It should be recalled that (usually) the determinant of a sum is *not* the sum of the determinants:

$$|\mathbf{A} + \mathbf{B}| \neq |\mathbf{A}| + |\mathbf{B}| \qquad \text{(in general)} \tag{3}$$

An example of this general inequality was asked for in Problem 16.1.5.

NOTE 2   Our geometric interpretations of determinants of order 2 and 3 support several of these rules. For example, rule C with (say) $\alpha = 2$, reflects the fact that if one of the vectors in Figure 16.1.1 (16.2.1) is doubled in length, then the area (volume) is twice as big. Try to give geometric interpretations of rules A, B, D, E, and H.

Proofs for most of these properties are given at the end of this section. First, however, let us illustrate them in some special cases of 2×2 matrices.

Rule A: $\begin{vmatrix} a_{11} & a_{12} \\ 0 & 0 \end{vmatrix} = a_{11} \cdot 0 - a_{12} \cdot 0 = 0$

Rule B: $\displaystyle |\mathbf{A}| = \begin{vmatrix} a_{11} & a_{12} \\ a_{21} & a_{22} \end{vmatrix} = a_{11}a_{22} - a_{12}a_{21}, \quad |\mathbf{A}'| = \begin{vmatrix} a_{11} & a_{21} \\ a_{12} & a_{22} \end{vmatrix} = a_{11}a_{22} - a_{12}a_{21}$

We see that $|\mathbf{A}'|$ has exactly the same terms as $|\mathbf{A}|$. In particular, $|\mathbf{A}'| = |\mathbf{A}|$.

Rule C: $\displaystyle \begin{vmatrix} a_{11} & a_{12} \\ \alpha a_{21} & \alpha a_{22} \end{vmatrix} = a_{11}(\alpha a_{22}) - a_{12}(\alpha a_{21}) = \alpha(a_{11}a_{22} - a_{12}a_{21}) = \alpha \begin{vmatrix} a_{11} & a_{12} \\ a_{21} & a_{22} \end{vmatrix}$

Rule D: $\displaystyle \begin{vmatrix} a_{21} & a_{22} \\ a_{11} & a_{12} \end{vmatrix} = a_{21}a_{12} - a_{11}a_{22} = -(a_{11}a_{22} - a_{12}a_{21}) = -\begin{vmatrix} a_{11} & a_{12} \\ a_{21} & a_{22} \end{vmatrix}$

Rule E: $\displaystyle \begin{vmatrix} a_{11} & a_{12} \\ \beta a_{11} & \beta a_{12} \end{vmatrix} = a_{11}(\beta a_{12}) - a_{12}(\beta a_{11}) = \beta(a_{11}a_{12} - a_{11}a_{12}) = 0$

Let us also see how rule E helps to confirm (partly) the result in Example 16.2.2. Note that the product $(b-a)(c-a)(c-b)$ is 0 if $b = a$, $c = a$, or $c = b$, and in each of these three cases, two rows of the matrix are proportional, in fact equal.

Rule F: Multiply each entry in the first row of a determinant of order 2 by α and add it to the corresponding entry in the second row. Then the determinant does not change its value. (Note carefully the way in which we indicate this operation—see also Section 15.6.)

$$\begin{vmatrix} a_{11} & a_{12} \\ a_{21} & a_{22} \end{vmatrix} \overset{\alpha}{\longleftarrow} = \begin{vmatrix} a_{11} & a_{12} \\ a_{21} + \alpha a_{11} & a_{22} + \alpha a_{12} \end{vmatrix} = a_{11}(a_{22} + \alpha a_{12}) - a_{12}(a_{21} + \alpha a_{11})$$

$$= a_{11}a_{22} + \alpha a_{11}a_{12} - a_{12}a_{21} - \alpha a_{12}a_{11} = a_{11}a_{22} - a_{12}a_{21}$$

$$= \begin{vmatrix} a_{11} & a_{12} \\ a_{21} & a_{22} \end{vmatrix}$$

Rule G: Problem 16.1.4 has already asked for a proof of this rule for 2×2 matrices.

Rule H: $\displaystyle \begin{vmatrix} \alpha a_{11} & \alpha a_{12} \\ \alpha a_{21} & \alpha a_{22} \end{vmatrix} = \alpha a_{11}\alpha a_{22} - \alpha a_{12}\alpha a_{21} = \alpha^2(a_{11}a_{22} - a_{12}a_{21}) = \alpha^2 \begin{vmatrix} a_{11} & a_{12} \\ a_{21} & a_{22} \end{vmatrix}$

Theorem 16.4.1 exhibits some of the most important rules for determinants. Confidence in dealing with them comes only from doing many problems.

Rule F is particularly useful for evaluating large or complicated determinants. The idea is to convert the matrix into one that is (upper or lower) triangular. This is just the same procedure as that used in the Gaussian elimination method described in Section 15.6. We give two examples involving 3×3 matrices.

EXAMPLE 1

$$\begin{vmatrix} 1 & 5 & -1 \\ -1 & 1 & 3 \\ 3 & 2 & 1 \end{vmatrix} \overset{1}{\longleftarrow} = \begin{vmatrix} 1 & 5 & -1 \\ -1+1 & 1+5 & 3+(-1) \\ 3 & 2 & 1 \end{vmatrix} = \begin{vmatrix} 1 & 5 & -1 \\ 0 & 6 & 2 \\ 3 & 2 & 1 \end{vmatrix} \overset{-3}{\longleftarrow}$$

$$= \begin{vmatrix} 1 & 5 & -1 \\ 0 & 6 & 2 \\ 0 & -13 & 4 \end{vmatrix} \overset{\frac{13}{6}}{\longleftarrow} = \begin{vmatrix} 1 & 5 & -1 \\ 0 & 6 & 2 \\ 0 & 0 & 25/3 \end{vmatrix} = 1 \cdot 6 \cdot \frac{25}{3} = 50$$

Here, 1 times the first row has been added to the second row in order to obtain a zero in the first column. Then (-3) times the first row has been added to the third, which gives a second zero in the first column. Thereafter, 13/6 times the second row has been added to the third, which creates an extra zero in the second column. Note the way in which we have indicated these operations. In the end, they produce an upper triangular matrix whose determinant is easy to evaluate by means of formula (4) in Section 16.3.

In the next example, the first two steps involve more than one operation simultaneously.

EXAMPLE 2

$$\begin{vmatrix} a+b & a & a \\ a & a+b & a \\ a & a & a+b \end{vmatrix} = \begin{vmatrix} 3a+b & 3a+b & 3a+b \\ a & a+b & a \\ a & a & a+b \end{vmatrix}$$

$$= (3a+b)\begin{vmatrix} 1 & 1 & 1 \\ a & a+b & a \\ a & a & a+b \end{vmatrix} = (3a+b)\begin{vmatrix} 1 & 1 & 1 \\ 0 & b & 0 \\ 0 & 0 & b \end{vmatrix}$$

$$= (3a+b) \cdot 1 \cdot b \cdot b = b^2(3a+b)$$

Next, here is an example of rule G involving 3×3 matrices.

EXAMPLE 3   Check that $|\mathbf{AB}| = |\mathbf{A}| \cdot |\mathbf{B}|$ when $\mathbf{A} = \begin{pmatrix} 1 & 5 & -1 \\ -1 & 1 & 3 \\ 3 & 2 & 1 \end{pmatrix}$, $\mathbf{B} = \begin{pmatrix} 3 & 0 & 2 \\ -1 & 1 & 0 \\ 5 & 2 & 3 \end{pmatrix}$.

Solution: Here $|\mathbf{A}| = 50$ (as in Example 1) and you should verify that $|\mathbf{B}| = -5$. Moreover multiplication of the two matrices yields

$$\mathbf{AB} = \begin{pmatrix} -7 & 3 & -1 \\ 11 & 7 & 7 \\ 12 & 4 & 9 \end{pmatrix}$$

Using Sarrus's rule introduced at the end of Section 16.2, we find that $|\mathbf{AB}| = -250$. Thus $|\mathbf{AB}| = |\mathbf{A}| \cdot |\mathbf{B}|$.

On the proof of Theorem 16.4.1:

Rule A: Each of the $n!$ terms in the determinant must take one element from the row (or column) consisting of only zeros, so the whole determinant is 0.

Rule B: Each term in $|\mathbf{A}|$ is the product of entries chosen from $\mathbf{A}$ to include exactly one element from each row and one element from each column. Exactly the same terms, therefore, must appear in $|\mathbf{A}'|$ also. One can prove that the signs are also the same, but we skip the proof. (The proof of this property and the others we leave unproved are found in most books on linear algebra.)

Rule C: Let $\mathbf{B}$ be the matrix obtained from $\mathbf{A}$ by multiplying every element in a certain row (or column) of $\mathbf{A}$ by α. Then each term in the sum defining $|\mathbf{B}|$ is α multiplied by the corresponding term in the sum defining $|\mathbf{A}|$. Hence, $|\mathbf{B}| = \alpha|\mathbf{A}|$.

Rule D: If two rows are interchanged, or two columns, the terms involved in the definition of determinant in Section 16.3 remain the same, except that the sign of each term is reversed. Showing this, however, involves a somewhat intricate argument, so we offer only this brief explanation.

Rule E: By using rule C, the factor of proportionality can be put outside the determinant. The determinant then has two equal rows (columns). If we interchange the two rows that are equal, the determinant will be exactly the same. But according to rule D, the determinant has changed its sign. Hence, $|\mathbf{A}| = -|\mathbf{A}|$, which means that $2|\mathbf{A}| = 0$, and so $|\mathbf{A}| = 0$.

Rule F: Symbolically, the proof of this rule is as follows, for the case when the scalar multiple α of row i is added to row j:

$$\sum \pm a_{1r_1} \ldots a_{ir_i} \ldots (a_{jr_j} + \alpha a_{ir_j}) \ldots a_{nr_n}$$

$$= \sum \pm a_{1r_1} \ldots a_{ir_i} \ldots a_{jr_j} \ldots a_{nr_n} + \alpha \sum \pm a_{1r_1} \ldots a_{ir_i} \ldots a_{ir_j} \ldots a_{nr_n}$$

$$= |\mathbf{A}| + \alpha \cdot 0 = |\mathbf{A}|$$

(The last sum is zero because it is equal to a determinant with rows i and j equal.)

Rule G: The proof of this rule for the case $n = 2$ is the object of Problem 16.1.4. The case when **A** and **B** are both upper triangular is covered in Problem 16.3.4. One can prove the general case by using elementary row and column operations to convert **A** and **B** as well as **AB** to upper triangular form, but we omit the proof.

Rule H: The matrix $\alpha\mathbf{A}$ is obtained by multiplying *each* entry in **A** by α. By rule C, $|\alpha\mathbf{A}|$ is then equal to $\alpha^n|\mathbf{A}|$, because each of the n rows has α as a factor in each entry.

PROBLEMS FOR SECTION 16.4

1. Let $\mathbf{A} = \begin{pmatrix} 1 & 2 \\ 3 & 4 \end{pmatrix}$, $\mathbf{B} = \begin{pmatrix} 3 & 4 \\ 5 & 6 \end{pmatrix}$.

   (a) Calculate **AB**, **BA**, **A′B′**, and **B′A′**.

   (b) Show that $|\mathbf{A}| = |\mathbf{A}'|$ and $|\mathbf{AB}| = |\mathbf{A}| \cdot |\mathbf{B}|$. Is $|\mathbf{A}'\mathbf{B}'| = |\mathbf{A}'| \cdot |\mathbf{B}'|$?

2. Let $\mathbf{A} = \begin{pmatrix} 2 & 1 & 3 \\ 1 & 0 & 1 \\ 1 & 2 & 5 \end{pmatrix}$. Write down **A′**, then show that $|\mathbf{A}| = |\mathbf{A}'|$.

3. Evaluate the following determinants as simply as possible:

   (a) $\begin{vmatrix} 3 & 0 & 1 \\ 1 & 0 & -1 \\ 2 & 0 & 5 \end{vmatrix}$ (b) $\begin{vmatrix} 1 & 2 & 3 & 4 \\ 0 & -1 & 2 & 4 \\ 0 & 0 & 3 & -1 \\ -3 & -6 & -9 & -12 \end{vmatrix}$ (c) $\begin{vmatrix} a_1 - x & a_2 & a_3 & a_4 \\ 0 & -x & 0 & 0 \\ 0 & 1 & -x & 0 \\ 0 & 0 & 1 & -x \end{vmatrix}$

4. Let **A** and **B** be 3×3 matrices with $|\mathbf{A}| = 3$ and $|\mathbf{B}| = -4$. Where possible, find the numerical values of $|\mathbf{AB}|$, $3|\mathbf{A}|$, $|-2\mathbf{B}|$, $|4\mathbf{A}|$, $|\mathbf{A}| + |\mathbf{B}|$, and $|\mathbf{A} + \mathbf{B}|$.

5. If $\mathbf{A} = \begin{pmatrix} a & 1 & 4 \\ 2 & 1 & a^2 \\ 1 & 0 & -3 \end{pmatrix}$, calculate $\mathbf{A}^2$ and $|\mathbf{A}|$.

6. Prove that each of the following determinants is zero:

(a) $\begin{vmatrix} 1 & 2 & 3 \\ 2 & 4 & 5 \\ 3 & 6 & 8 \end{vmatrix}$ (b) $\begin{vmatrix} 1 & a & b+c \\ 1 & b & c+a \\ 1 & c & a+b \end{vmatrix}$ (c) $\begin{vmatrix} x-y & x-y & x^2-y^2 \\ 1 & 1 & x+y \\ y & 1 & x \end{vmatrix}$

7. Let $\mathbf{X} = \begin{pmatrix} 1 & 0 & 0 \\ 1 & 1 & 1 \\ 1 & 2 & 0 \\ 1 & 0 & 1 \end{pmatrix}$. Calculate $\mathbf{X}'\mathbf{X}$ and $|\mathbf{X}'\mathbf{X}|$.

8. If $\mathbf{A}_a = \begin{pmatrix} a & 2 & 2 \\ 2 & a^2+1 & 1 \\ 2 & 1 & 1 \end{pmatrix}$, calculate $|\mathbf{A}_a|$ and $|\mathbf{A}_1^6|$.

9. Show that an orthogonal matrix $\mathbf{P}$ (see Problem 15.5.7) must have determinant 1 or -1.

10. A square matrix $\mathbf{A}$ of order n is called **involutive** if $\mathbf{A}^2 = \mathbf{I}_n$.

   (a) Show that the determinant of an involutive matrix is 1 or -1.

   (b) Show that $\begin{pmatrix} -1 & 0 \\ 0 & -1 \end{pmatrix}$ and $\begin{pmatrix} a & 1-a^2 \\ 1 & -a \end{pmatrix}$ are involutive (for all a).

   (c) Show that $\mathbf{A}$ is involutive $\iff (\mathbf{I}_n - \mathbf{A})(\mathbf{I}_n + \mathbf{A}) = \mathbf{0}$.

HARDER PROBLEMS

11. Without computing the determinants, show that

$$\begin{vmatrix} b^2+c^2 & ab & ac \\ ab & a^2+c^2 & bc \\ ac & bc & a^2+b^2 \end{vmatrix} = \begin{vmatrix} 0 & c & b \\ c & 0 & a \\ b & a & 0 \end{vmatrix}^2$$

12. Prove that $D_n = \begin{vmatrix} a+b & a & \cdots & a \\ a & a+b & \cdots & a \\ \vdots & \vdots & \ddots & \vdots \\ a & a & \cdots & a+b \end{vmatrix} = b^{n-1}(na+b)$

(*Hint:* Study Example 2. This is actually a rather useful result.)

16.5 Expansion by Cofactors

According to the definition in Section 16.3, the determinant of an $n \times n$ matrix $\mathbf{A} = (a_{ij})$ is a sum of $n!$ terms. Each term contains one element from each row and one element from each column. Consider in particular row i: pick out all the terms that have a_{i1} as a factor, then all terms that have a_{i2} as a factor, and so on. Because all the terms have one and only one element from row i, in this way we get all the terms of $|\mathbf{A}|$. So we can write

$$|\mathbf{A}| = a_{i1}C_{i1} + a_{i2}C_{i2} + \cdots + a_{ij}C_{ij} + \cdots + a_{in}C_{in} \qquad (1)$$

This is called the *expansion of* $|\mathbf{A}|$ *in terms of the elements of the i th row.* The coefficients $C_{i1}, \ldots, C_{in}$ are the **cofactors** of the elements $a_{i1}, \ldots, a_{in}$.

In the same way, we can expand $|\mathbf{A}|$ in terms of the elements of the jth column:

$$|\mathbf{A}| = a_{1j}C_{1j} + a_{2j}C_{2j} + \cdots + a_{ij}C_{ij} + \cdots + a_{nj}C_{nj} \qquad (2)$$

What makes expansions (1) and (2) extremely useful is that in general each cofactor C_{ij} can be found by applying the following procedure to the determinant $|\mathbf{A}|$: First, delete row i and column j to arrive at a determinant of order $n - 1$, which is called a **minor**. Second, multiply the minor by the factor $(-1)^{i+j}$. This gives the cofactor.

In symbols, the cofactor C_{ij} is given by

$$C_{ij} = (-1)^{i+j} \begin{vmatrix} a_{11} & \cdots & a_{1,j-1} & a_{1j} & a_{1,j+1} & \cdots & a_{1n} \\ a_{21} & \cdots & a_{2,j-1} & a_{2j} & a_{2,j+1} & \cdots & a_{2n} \\ \vdots & & \vdots & & \vdots & & \vdots \\ a_{i1} & \cdots & a_{i,j-1} & \boxed{a_{ij}} & a_{i,j+1} & \cdots & a_{in} \\ \vdots & & \vdots & & \vdots & & \vdots \\ a_{n1} & \cdots & a_{n,j-1} & a_{nj} & a_{n,j+1} & \cdots & a_{nn} \end{vmatrix} \qquad (3)$$

where lines have been drawn through row i and column j, which are to be deleted from the matrix. We skip the proof. If we look back at (3) in Section 16.2, however, it confirms (3) in a special case. Indeed, put $|\mathbf{A}| = a_{11}C_{11} + a_{12}C_{12} + a_{13}C_{13}$. Then

$$C_{11} = (-1)^{1+1} \begin{vmatrix} a_{22} & a_{23} \\ a_{32} & a_{33} \end{vmatrix}, \quad C_{12} = (-1)^{1+2} \begin{vmatrix} a_{21} & a_{23} \\ a_{31} & a_{33} \end{vmatrix}, \quad C_{13} = (-1)^{1+3} \begin{vmatrix} a_{21} & a_{22} \\ a_{31} & a_{32} \end{vmatrix}$$

precisely in accordance with (3) in Section 16.2.

Generally, formula (3) is rather complicated. Test your understanding of it by studying the following example.

EXAMPLE 1   Check that the cofactor of the element c in the determinant

$$|\mathbf{A}| = \begin{vmatrix} 3 & 0 & 0 & 2 \\ 6 & 1 & \boxed{c} & 2 \\ -1 & 1 & 0 & 0 \\ 5 & 2 & 0 & 3 \end{vmatrix} \qquad \text{is} \qquad C_{23} = (-1)^{2+3} \begin{vmatrix} 3 & 0 & 2 \\ -1 & 1 & 0 \\ 5 & 2 & 3 \end{vmatrix}$$

Find the value of $|\mathbf{A}|$ by using (2) and Example 16.2.1.

Solution: Because the element c is in row 2 and column 3, its cofactor has been written correctly. To find the numerical value of $|\mathbf{A}|$ we use (2) and expand in terms of the elements of the *third column* of $|\mathbf{A}|$ (because it has so many zeros). This yields

$$|\mathbf{A}| = a_{23}C_{23} = c\,(-1)^{2+3}\begin{vmatrix} 3 & 0 & 2 \\ -1 & 1 & 0 \\ 5 & 2 & 3 \end{vmatrix} = c\,(-1)(-5) = 5c$$

Example 1 shows a case in which expansion by cofactors is particularly simple because there are many zeros in the third column. If the zeros are not there initially, we can often create them by appealing to rule F in Theorem 16.4.1. Two examples illustrate the method.[2]

EXAMPLE 2
$$\begin{vmatrix} 3 & -1 & 2 \\ 0 & -1 & -1 \\ 6 & 1 & 2 \end{vmatrix} \overset{-2}{\underset{\longleftarrow}{}} = \begin{vmatrix} 3 & -1 & 2 \\ 0 & -1 & -1 \\ 0 & 3 & -2 \end{vmatrix} \overset{(*)}{=} 3\begin{vmatrix} -1 & -1 \\ 3 & -2 \end{vmatrix} = 3(2+3) = 15$$

To derive the equality labelled $(*)$, expand by column 1.

EXAMPLE 3
$$\begin{vmatrix} 2 & 0 & 3 & -1 \\ 0 & 4 & 0 & 0 \\ 0 & 1 & -1 & 2 \\ 3 & 2 & 5 & -3 \end{vmatrix} \overset{(*)}{=} (-1)^{2+2}\cdot 4\begin{vmatrix} 2 & 3 & -1 \\ 0 & -1 & 2 \\ 3 & 5 & -3 \end{vmatrix} \overset{-3/2}{\underset{\longleftarrow}{}}$$

$$= 4\begin{vmatrix} 2 & 3 & -1 \\ 0 & -1 & 2 \\ 0 & 1/2 & -3/2 \end{vmatrix} \overset{(**)}{=} 4\cdot 2\begin{vmatrix} -1 & 2 \\ 1/2 & -3/2 \end{vmatrix} = 8\left(\tfrac{3}{2} - \tfrac{2}{2}\right) = 4$$

For equality $(*)$, expand by row 2. For equality $(**)$, expand by column 1.

Expansion by Alien Cofactors

According to (1) and (2), if the elements of any row (or column) of a determinant are multiplied by the cofactors of the elements in that row (or column) and the products are added, the result is the value of the determinant. What happens if we multiply the elements of a row by the cofactors of a different (alien) row? Or the elements of a column by the cofactors of an alien column? Consider the following example.

EXAMPLE 4   If $\mathbf{A} = (a_{ij})_{3\times3}$, then the expansion of $|\mathbf{A}|$ in terms of the elements in the second row is

$$|\mathbf{A}| = a_{21}C_{21} + a_{22}C_{22} + a_{23}C_{23}$$

---

[2] To calculate a general 10×10 determinant using the definition requires no fewer than 36,287,999 operations of addition or multiplication! Systematic use of rule F in Theorem 16.4.1 can reduce the required number of operations to about 380.

Suppose we change the elements a_{21}, a_{22}, and a_{23} to a, b, and c. Then C_{21}, C_{22}, and C_{23} are unchanged and

$$\begin{vmatrix} a_{11} & a_{12} & a_{13} \\ a & b & c \\ a_{31} & a_{32} & a_{33} \end{vmatrix} = aC_{21} + bC_{22} + cC_{23} \qquad (*)$$

In particular, if we replace a, b, and c by a_{11}, a_{12}, and a_{13}, or by a_{31}, a_{32}, and a_{33}, then the determinant in $(*)$ is 0 because two rows are equal. Hence,

$$a_{11}C_{21} + a_{12}C_{22} + a_{13}C_{23} = 0$$
$$a_{31}C_{21} + a_{32}C_{22} + a_{33}C_{23} = 0$$

That is, the sum of the products of the elements in either row 1 or row 3 multiplied by the cofactors of the elements in row 2 is zero.

Obviously, the argument used in this example can be generalized: If we multiply the elements of any row by the cofactors of a different row, and then add the products, the result is 0. Similarly if we multiply the elements of a column by the cofactors of an alien column, then add.

We summarize all the results in this section in the following theorem:

THEOREM 16.5.1 (COFACTOR EXPANSION OF A DETERMINANT)

Let $\mathbf{A} = (a_{ij})_{n \times n}$. Suppose that the cofactors C_{ij} are defined as in (3). Then:

$$a_{i1}C_{i1} + a_{i2}C_{i2} + \cdots + a_{in}C_{in} = |\mathbf{A}|$$
$$a_{i1}C_{k1} + a_{i2}C_{k2} + \cdots + a_{in}C_{kn} = 0 \qquad (k \neq i)$$

$$a_{1j}C_{1j} + a_{2j}C_{2j} + \cdots + a_{nj}C_{nj} = |\mathbf{A}|$$
$$a_{1j}C_{1k} + a_{2j}C_{2k} + \cdots + a_{nj}C_{nk} = 0 \qquad (k \neq j)$$

Theorem 16.5.1 says that an expansion of a determinant by row i in terms of the cofactors of row k vanishes when $k \neq i$, and is equal to $|\mathbf{A}|$ if $k = i$. Likewise, an expansion by column j in terms of the cofactors of column k vanishes when $k \neq j$, and is equal to $|\mathbf{A}|$ if $k = j$.

PROBLEMS FOR SECTION 16.5

1. Calculate the following determinants:

(a) $\begin{vmatrix} 1 & 2 & 4 \\ 1 & 3 & 9 \\ 1 & 4 & 16 \end{vmatrix}$
(b) $\begin{vmatrix} 1 & 2 & 3 & 4 \\ 0 & -1 & 0 & 11 \\ 2 & -1 & 0 & 3 \\ -2 & 0 & -1 & 3 \end{vmatrix}$
(c) $\begin{vmatrix} 2 & 1 & 3 & 3 \\ 3 & 2 & 1 & 6 \\ 1 & 3 & 0 & 9 \\ 2 & 4 & 1 & 12 \end{vmatrix}$

2. Calculate the following determinants:

(a) $\begin{vmatrix} 0 & 0 & a \\ 0 & b & 0 \\ c & 0 & 0 \end{vmatrix}$
(b) $\begin{vmatrix} 0 & 0 & 0 & a \\ 0 & 0 & b & 0 \\ 0 & c & 0 & 0 \\ d & 0 & 0 & 0 \end{vmatrix}$
(c) $\begin{vmatrix} 0 & 0 & 0 & 0 & 1 \\ 0 & 0 & 0 & 5 & 1 \\ 0 & 0 & 3 & 1 & 2 \\ 0 & 4 & 0 & 3 & 4 \\ 6 & 2 & 3 & 1 & 2 \end{vmatrix}$

16.6   The Inverse of a Matrix

Suppose that α is a real number different from 0. Then there is a unique number α^{-1} with the property that $\alpha\alpha^{-1} = \alpha^{-1}\alpha = 1$. We call α^{-1} the (multiplicative) inverse of α. We saw in Section 15.4 that the identity matrix $\mathbf{I}$ (with 1's along the main diagonal and 0's elsewhere) is the matrix equivalent of 1 in the real number system.[3] This makes the following terminology seem natural.

Given a matrix $\mathbf{A}$, we say that $\mathbf{X}$ is an **inverse** of $\mathbf{A}$ if there exists a matrix $\mathbf{X}$ such that

$$\mathbf{AX} = \mathbf{XA} = \mathbf{I} \tag{1}$$

Then $\mathbf{A}$ is said to be **invertible**. Because $\mathbf{XA} = \mathbf{AX} = \mathbf{I}$, the matrix $\mathbf{A}$ is also an inverse of $\mathbf{X}$—that is, $\mathbf{A}$ and $\mathbf{X}$ are inverses of each other. Note that the two matrix products $\mathbf{AX}$ and $\mathbf{XA}$ are defined and equal only if $\mathbf{A}$ and $\mathbf{X}$ are square matrices of the same order. *Thus, only square matrices can have inverses.* But not even all square matrices have inverses, as (b) in the following example shows.

EXAMPLE 1   (a) Show that $\mathbf{A} = \begin{pmatrix} 5 & 6 \\ 5 & 10 \end{pmatrix}$ and $\mathbf{X} = \begin{pmatrix} 1/2 & -3/10 \\ -1/4 & 1/4 \end{pmatrix}$ are inverses of each other.

(b) Show that $\mathbf{A} = \begin{pmatrix} 1 & 0 \\ 0 & 0 \end{pmatrix}$ has no inverse.

Solution:

(a) $\begin{pmatrix} 5 & 6 \\ 5 & 10 \end{pmatrix} \begin{pmatrix} 1/2 & -3/10 \\ -1/4 & 1/4 \end{pmatrix} = \begin{pmatrix} 5/2 - 6/4 & -15/10 + 6/4 \\ 5/2 - 10/4 & -15/10 + 10/4 \end{pmatrix} = \begin{pmatrix} 1 & 0 \\ 0 & 1 \end{pmatrix}$

and likewise we verify that $\mathbf{XA} = \mathbf{I}$.

(b) Observe that for all real numbers x, y, z, and w,

$$\begin{pmatrix} 1 & 0 \\ 0 & 0 \end{pmatrix} \begin{pmatrix} x & y \\ z & w \end{pmatrix} = \begin{pmatrix} x & y \\ 0 & 0 \end{pmatrix}$$

So there is no way of choosing x, y, z, and w to make the product of these two matrices equal to $\mathbf{I}$. Thus, $\begin{pmatrix} 1 & 0 \\ 0 & 0 \end{pmatrix}$ has no inverse.

---

[3] From now on, we write $\mathbf{I}$ instead of $\mathbf{I}_n$ whenever the order n of the identity matrix seems obvious.

The following questions arise:

A. *Which matrices have inverses?*

B. *Can a given matrix have more than one inverse?*

C. *How do we find the inverse if it exists?*

As for question A, it is easy to find a *necessary* condition for a matrix **A** to have an inverse. In fact, from (1) and rule G in Theorem 16.4.1, it follows that $|\mathbf{AX}| = |\mathbf{A}| \cdot |\mathbf{X}| = |\mathbf{I}|$. Using (4) in Section 16.3, we see that the identity matrix of any order has determinant 1. Thus, if **X** is an inverse of **A**, then $|\mathbf{A}| \cdot |\mathbf{X}| = 1$. We conclude from this equation that $|\mathbf{A}| \neq 0$ is a necessary condition for **A** to have an inverse, because $|\mathbf{A}| = 0$ would lead to a contradiction. As we shall see in the next section, the condition $|\mathbf{A}| \neq 0$ is also *sufficient* for **A** to have an inverse. Hence, for any square matrix **A**,

$$\mathbf{A} \text{ has an inverse } \iff |\mathbf{A}| \neq 0 \tag{2}$$

A square matrix **A** is said to be **singular** if $|\mathbf{A}| = 0$ and **nonsingular** if $|\mathbf{A}| \neq 0$. According to (2), a matrix has an inverse if and only if it is nonsingular.

Concerning question B, the answer is no—a matrix cannot have more than one inverse. Indeed, suppose that **X** satisfies (1) and moreover $\mathbf{AY} = \mathbf{I}$ for some other square matrix **Y**. Then

$$\mathbf{Y} = \mathbf{IY} = (\mathbf{XA})\mathbf{Y} = \mathbf{X}(\mathbf{AY}) = \mathbf{XI} = \mathbf{X}$$

A similar argument shows that if $\mathbf{YA} = \mathbf{I}$, then $\mathbf{Y} = \mathbf{X}$. Thus, *the inverse of **A** is unique if it exists*.

The inverse is usually written $\mathbf{A}^{-1}$. Whereas for numbers we can write $a^{-1} = 1/a$, the symbol $\mathbf{I}/\mathbf{A}$ has *no* meaning. *There are no rules for dividing matrices*. Note also that even if the product $\mathbf{A}^{-1}\mathbf{B}$ is defined, it is usually quite different from $\mathbf{BA}^{-1}$ because matrix multiplication does not commute, in general.

The full answer to question C is given in the next section. Here we only consider the case of 2×2 matrices.

EXAMPLE 2   Find the inverse of $\mathbf{A} = \begin{pmatrix} a & b \\ c & d \end{pmatrix}$ (when it exists).

Solution: We find a 2×2 matrix **X** such that $\mathbf{AX} = \mathbf{I}$, after which it is easy to check that $\mathbf{XA} = \mathbf{I}$. Solving $\mathbf{AX} = \mathbf{I}$ requires finding numbers x, y, z, and w such that

$$\begin{pmatrix} a & b \\ c & d \end{pmatrix} \begin{pmatrix} x & y \\ z & w \end{pmatrix} = \begin{pmatrix} 1 & 0 \\ 0 & 1 \end{pmatrix}$$

Matrix multiplication implies that

$$ax + bz = 1, \qquad ay + bw = 0$$
$$cx + dz = 0, \qquad cy + dw = 1$$

Note that we have two different systems of equations here. One is given by the two equations on the left, and the other by the two equations on the right. Both these systems have **A** as a common coefficient matrix. If $|\mathbf{A}| = ad - bc \neq 0$, solving them using Cramer's rule from Section 16.1 yields

$$x = \frac{d}{ad - bc}, \qquad z = \frac{-c}{ad - bc}, \qquad y = \frac{-b}{ad - bc}, \qquad w = \frac{a}{ad - bc}$$

Hence, we have proved the following result:

$$\mathbf{A} = \begin{pmatrix} a & b \\ c & d \end{pmatrix}, \quad |\mathbf{A}| = ad - bc \neq 0 \implies \mathbf{A}^{-1} = \frac{1}{ad - bc} \begin{pmatrix} d & -b \\ -c & a \end{pmatrix} \tag{3}$$

Note that in the inverse matrix, the diagonal elements of the original 2×2 matrix are switched, whereas the off-diagonal elements just change sign. ∎

For square matrices of order 3, one can use Cramer's rule (4) in Section 16.2 to derive a formula for the inverse. Again, the requirement for the inverse to exist is that the determinant of the coefficient matrix is not 0. Full details will be given in Section 16.7.

Some Useful Implications

If $\mathbf{A}^{-1}$ is the inverse of $\mathbf{A}$, then $\mathbf{A}^{-1}\mathbf{A} = \mathbf{I}$ and $\mathbf{A}\mathbf{A}^{-1} = \mathbf{I}$. Actually, each of these equations implies the other, in the sense that

$$\mathbf{AX} = \mathbf{I} \implies \mathbf{X} = \mathbf{A}^{-1} \tag{4}$$

$$\mathbf{YA} = \mathbf{I} \implies \mathbf{Y} = \mathbf{A}^{-1} \tag{5}$$

To prove (4), suppose $\mathbf{AX} = \mathbf{I}$. Then $|\mathbf{A}| \cdot |\mathbf{X}| = 1$, and so $|\mathbf{A}| \neq 0$. Hence, by (2), $\mathbf{A}^{-1}$ exists. Multiplying $\mathbf{AX} = \mathbf{I}$ from the left by $\mathbf{A}^{-1}$ yields $\mathbf{X} = \mathbf{A}^{-1}$. The proof of (5) is almost the same.

Implications (4) and (5) are used repeatedly in proving properties of the inverse. Here are two examples.

EXAMPLE 3   Find the inverse of the $n \times n$ matrix $\mathbf{A}$ if $\mathbf{A} - \mathbf{A}^2 = \mathbf{I}$.

Solution: The matrix equation $\mathbf{A} - \mathbf{A}^2 = \mathbf{I}$ yields $\mathbf{A}(\mathbf{I} - \mathbf{A}) = \mathbf{I}$. But then it follows from (4) that $\mathbf{A}$ has the inverse $\mathbf{A}^{-1} = \mathbf{I} - \mathbf{A}$. ∎

EXAMPLE 4   Let $\mathbf{B}$ be a $n \times n$ matrix such that $\mathbf{B}^2 = 3\mathbf{B}$. Prove that there exists a number s such that $\mathbf{I} + s\mathbf{B}$ is the inverse of $\mathbf{I} + \mathbf{B}$.

Solution: Because of (5), it suffices to find a number s such that $(\mathbf{I} + s\mathbf{B})(\mathbf{I} + \mathbf{B}) = \mathbf{I}$. Now,

$$(\mathbf{I} + s\mathbf{B})(\mathbf{I} + \mathbf{B}) = \mathbf{II} + \mathbf{IB} + s\mathbf{BI} + s\mathbf{B}^2 = \mathbf{I} + \mathbf{B} + s\mathbf{B} + 3s\mathbf{B} = \mathbf{I} + (1 + 4s)\mathbf{B}$$

which is equal to $\mathbf{I}$ provided $1 + 4s = 0$. The right choice of s is thus $s = -1/4$. ∎

Properties of the Inverse

We shall now prove some useful rules for the inverse.

THEOREM 16.6.1 (PROPERTIES OF THE INVERSE)

Let $\mathbf{A}$ and $\mathbf{B}$ be invertible $n \times n$ matrices. Then:

(a) $\mathbf{A}^{-1}$ is invertible, and $(\mathbf{A}^{-1})^{-1} = \mathbf{A}$.

(b) $\mathbf{AB}$ is invertible, and $(\mathbf{AB})^{-1} = \mathbf{B}^{-1}\mathbf{A}^{-1}$.

(c) The transpose $\mathbf{A}'$ is invertible, and $(\mathbf{A}')^{-1} = (\mathbf{A}^{-1})'$.

(d) $(c\mathbf{A})^{-1} = c^{-1}\mathbf{A}^{-1}$ whenever c is a number $\neq 0$.

Proof: In each case, we use (4):

(a) We have $\mathbf{A}^{-1}\mathbf{A} = \mathbf{I}$, so $\mathbf{A} = (\mathbf{A}^{-1})^{-1}$.

(b) To prove that $\mathbf{X} = \mathbf{B}^{-1}\mathbf{A}^{-1}$ is the inverse of $\mathbf{AB}$, we just verify that $(\mathbf{AB})\mathbf{X}$ is equal to $\mathbf{I}$. In fact, $(\mathbf{AB})\mathbf{X} = (\mathbf{AB})(\mathbf{B}^{-1}\mathbf{A}^{-1}) = \mathbf{A}(\mathbf{BB}^{-1})\mathbf{A}^{-1} = \mathbf{AIA}^{-1} = \mathbf{AA}^{-1} = \mathbf{I}$.

(c) Transposing the equation $\mathbf{A}^{-1}\mathbf{A} = \mathbf{I}$ in accordance with (15.5.2)(d) gives $(\mathbf{A}^{-1}\mathbf{A})' = \mathbf{A}'(\mathbf{A}^{-1})' = \mathbf{I}' = \mathbf{I}$. Hence, $(\mathbf{A}')^{-1} = (\mathbf{A}^{-1})'$.

(d) Here $(c\mathbf{A})(c^{-1}\mathbf{A}^{-1}) = cc^{-1}\mathbf{AA}^{-1} = 1 \cdot \mathbf{I} = \mathbf{I}$, so $c^{-1}\mathbf{A}^{-1} = (c\mathbf{A})^{-1}$. ∎

NOTE 1 It is important to think carefully through the implications of the four rules in Theorem 16.6.1 and to understand their uses. A somewhat dramatic story might help you to appreciate rule (c). Some decades ago a team of (human) calculators was working in a central bureau of statistics. After 3 weeks of hard work, they finally found the inverse $\mathbf{A}^{-1}$ of a 20×20 matrix $\mathbf{A}$. Then the boss came along and said: "Sorry, I was really interested in the inverse of the transpose of $\mathbf{A}$." Panic—until they realized that property (c) would save them from having to redo all the calculations. They simply transposed the inverse matrix that it had taken 3 weeks to find, because according to (c), the inverse of the transpose is the transpose of the inverse.

NOTE 2 Suppose that $\mathbf{A}$ is invertible and also symmetric—that is, $\mathbf{A}' = \mathbf{A}$. Then rule (c) implies that $(\mathbf{A}^{-1})' = (\mathbf{A}')^{-1} = \mathbf{A}^{-1}$, so $\mathbf{A}^{-1}$ is symmetric. *The inverse of a symmetric matrix is symmetric.*

NOTE 3 Rule (b) can be extended to products of several matrices. For instance, if $\mathbf{A}$, $\mathbf{B}$, and $\mathbf{C}$ are all invertible $n \times n$ matrices, then

$$(\mathbf{ABC})^{-1} = [(\mathbf{AB})\mathbf{C}]^{-1} = \mathbf{C}^{-1}(\mathbf{AB})^{-1} = \mathbf{C}^{-1}(\mathbf{B}^{-1}\mathbf{A}^{-1}) = \mathbf{C}^{-1}\mathbf{B}^{-1}\mathbf{A}^{-1}$$

where rule (b) has been used twice. Note the assumption in (b) that $\mathbf{A}$ and $\mathbf{B}$ are both $n \times n$ matrices. In statistics and econometrics, we often consider products of the form $\mathbf{XX}'$, where $\mathbf{X}$ is $n \times m$, with $n \neq m$. Then $\mathbf{XX}'$ is $n \times n$. If the determinant $|\mathbf{XX}'|$ is not 0, then $(\mathbf{XX}')^{-1}$ exists, but (b) does not apply because $\mathbf{X}^{-1}$ and $\mathbf{X}'^{-1}$ are only defined if $n = m$.

NOTE 4   It is a common fallacy to misinterpret (d). For instance, a correct application of (d) yields $\left(\frac{1}{2}\mathbf{A}\right)^{-1} = 2\mathbf{A}^{-1}$.

Solving Equations by Matrix Inversion

Let $\mathbf{A}$ be any $n \times n$ matrix. If $\mathbf{B}$ is an arbitrary matrix, we consider whether there are matrices $\mathbf{X}$ and $\mathbf{Y}$ of suitable order such that

$$(*)\quad \mathbf{AX} = \mathbf{B} \qquad\qquad (**)\quad \mathbf{YA} = \mathbf{B}$$

In case $(*)$, the matrix $\mathbf{B}$ must have n rows, while in case $(**)$, $\mathbf{B}$ must have n columns. Provided these conditions are satisfied, we have the following result:

THEOREM 16.6.2

If $|\mathbf{A}| \neq 0$ then:

$$\mathbf{AX} = \mathbf{B} \iff \mathbf{X} = \mathbf{A}^{-1}\mathbf{B} \tag{6}$$

$$\mathbf{YA} = \mathbf{B} \iff \mathbf{Y} = \mathbf{BA}^{-1} \tag{7}$$

Proof: Multiply each side of the equation $\mathbf{AX} = \mathbf{B}$ in (6) on the left by $\mathbf{A}^{-1}$. This yields $\mathbf{A}^{-1}(\mathbf{AX}) = \mathbf{A}^{-1}\mathbf{B}$. Because $(\mathbf{A}^{-1}\mathbf{A})\mathbf{X} = \mathbf{IX} = \mathbf{X}$, we conclude that $\mathbf{X} = \mathbf{A}^{-1}\mathbf{B}$ is the only possible solution of the equation. On the other hand, by substituting $\mathbf{X} = \mathbf{A}^{-1}\mathbf{B}$ into $\mathbf{AX} = \mathbf{B}$, we see that it really satisfies the equation.

The proof of (7) is similar—postmultiply each side of $\mathbf{YA} = \mathbf{B}$ by $\mathbf{A}^{-1}$. ∎

EXAMPLE 5   Solve the following system of equations by using Theorem 16.6.2:

$$2x + y = 3$$
$$2x + 2y = 4$$

Solution: Suppose we define

$$\mathbf{A} = \begin{pmatrix} 2 & 1 \\ 2 & 2 \end{pmatrix}, \qquad \mathbf{x} = \begin{pmatrix} x \\ y \end{pmatrix}, \qquad \mathbf{b} = \begin{pmatrix} 3 \\ 4 \end{pmatrix}$$

Then the system is equivalent to the matrix equation $\mathbf{Ax} = \mathbf{b}$. Because $|\mathbf{A}| = 2 \neq 0$, matrix $\mathbf{A}$ has an inverse, and according to Theorem 16.6.2, $\mathbf{x} = \mathbf{A}^{-1}\mathbf{b}$. The inverse of $\mathbf{A}$ is found from (3), and we obtain

$$\begin{pmatrix} x \\ y \end{pmatrix} = \mathbf{A}^{-1} \begin{pmatrix} 3 \\ 4 \end{pmatrix} = \begin{pmatrix} 1 & -1/2 \\ -1 & 1 \end{pmatrix} \begin{pmatrix} 3 \\ 4 \end{pmatrix} = \begin{pmatrix} 1 \\ 1 \end{pmatrix}$$

The solution is therefore $x = 1$, $y = 1$. (Check by substitution that this really is the correct solution.) ∎

1. Prove that the inverse of $\begin{pmatrix} 3 & 0 \\ 2 & -1 \end{pmatrix}$ is $\begin{pmatrix} 1/3 & 0 \\ 2/3 & -1 \end{pmatrix}$.

2. Prove that the inverse of $\begin{pmatrix} 1 & 1 & -3 \\ 2 & 1 & -3 \\ 2 & 2 & 1 \end{pmatrix}$ is $\begin{pmatrix} -1 & 1 & 0 \\ 8/7 & -1 & 3/7 \\ -2/7 & 0 & 1/7 \end{pmatrix}$.

3. Find numbers a and b that make $\mathbf{A}$ the inverse of $\mathbf{B}$ when

$$\mathbf{A} = \begin{pmatrix} 2 & -1 & -1 \\ a & 1/4 & b \\ 1/8 & 1/8 & -1/8 \end{pmatrix} \quad \text{and} \quad \mathbf{B} = \begin{pmatrix} 1 & 2 & 4 \\ 0 & 1 & 6 \\ 1 & 3 & 2 \end{pmatrix}$$

4. Solve the following systems of equations by using Theorem 16.6.2. (See Example 5.)

(a) $\begin{aligned} 2x - 3y &= 3 \\ 3x - 4y &= 5 \end{aligned}$
(b) $\begin{aligned} 2x - 3y &= 8 \\ 3x - 4y &= 11 \end{aligned}$
(c) $\begin{aligned} 2x - 3y &= 0 \\ 3x - 4y &= 0 \end{aligned}$

5. Let $\mathbf{A} = \dfrac{1}{2}\begin{pmatrix} -1 & -\sqrt{3} \\ \sqrt{3} & -1 \end{pmatrix}$. Show that $\mathbf{A}^3 = \mathbf{I}$. Use this to find $\mathbf{A}^{-1}$.

6. Given matrix $\mathbf{A} = \begin{pmatrix} 0 & 1 & 0 \\ 0 & 1 & 1 \\ 1 & 0 & 1 \end{pmatrix}$.

(a) Calculate $|\mathbf{A}|$, $\mathbf{A}^2$, and $\mathbf{A}^3$. Show that $\mathbf{A}^3 - 2\mathbf{A}^2 + \mathbf{A} - \mathbf{I} = \mathbf{0}$, where $\mathbf{I}$ is the identity matrix of order 3, and $\mathbf{0}$ is the zero matrix.

(b) Show that $\mathbf{A}$ has an inverse and $\mathbf{A}^{-1} = (\mathbf{A} - \mathbf{I})^2$.

(c) Find a matrix $\mathbf{P}$ such that $\mathbf{P}^2 = \mathbf{A}$. Are there other matrices with this property?

7. (a) Let $\mathbf{A} = \begin{pmatrix} 2 & 1 & 4 \\ 0 & -1 & 3 \end{pmatrix}$. Calculate $\mathbf{A}\mathbf{A}'$, $|\mathbf{A}\mathbf{A}'|$, and $(\mathbf{A}\mathbf{A}')^{-1}$.

(b) The matrices $\mathbf{A}\mathbf{A}'$ and $(\mathbf{A}\mathbf{A}')^{-1}$ in part (a) are both symmetric. Is this a coincidence?

8. Suppose that $\mathbf{A}$, $\mathbf{P}$, and $\mathbf{D}$ are square matrices such that $\mathbf{A} = \mathbf{P}\mathbf{D}\mathbf{P}^{-1}$.

(a) Show that $\mathbf{A}^2 = \mathbf{P}\mathbf{D}^2\mathbf{P}^{-1}$.

(b) Show by induction that $\mathbf{A}^m = \mathbf{P}\mathbf{D}^m\mathbf{P}^{-1}$ for any positive integer m.

9. Given $\mathbf{B} = \begin{pmatrix} -1/2 & 5 \\ 1/4 & -1/2 \end{pmatrix}$, calculate $\mathbf{B}^2 + \mathbf{B}$, $\mathbf{B}^3 - 2\mathbf{B} + \mathbf{I}$, and then find $\mathbf{B}^{-1}$.

10. (a) Let $\mathbf{C}$ be an $n \times n$ matrix that satisfies $\mathbf{C}^2 + \mathbf{C} = \mathbf{I}$. Show that $\mathbf{C}^{-1} = \mathbf{I} + \mathbf{C}$.

(b) Show that $\mathbf{C}^3 = -\mathbf{I} + 2\mathbf{C}$ and $\mathbf{C}^4 = 2\mathbf{I} - 3\mathbf{C}$.

11. (a) Suppose that $\mathbf{X}$ is an $m \times n$ matrix and that $|\mathbf{X}'\mathbf{X}| \neq 0$. Show that the matrix

$$\mathbf{A} = \mathbf{I}_m - \mathbf{X}(\mathbf{X}'\mathbf{X})^{-1}\mathbf{X}'$$

is idempotent—that is, $\mathbf{A}^2 = \mathbf{A}$. (See Problem 15.4.6.)

(b) Check the result in part (a) for the particular matrix $\mathbf{X} = \begin{pmatrix} 1 & 1 \\ 1 & 2 \\ 1 & 1 \end{pmatrix}$

12. Let $\mathbf{A} = \begin{pmatrix} 1 & 2 & 3 \\ 2 & 1 & 3 \\ 3 & 2 & 1 \end{pmatrix}$ and $\mathbf{T} = \frac{1}{12}\begin{pmatrix} s & t & 3 \\ 7 & -8 & 3 \\ 1 & t & -3 \end{pmatrix}$, where s and t are real numbers.

(a) Prove that $\mathbf{T} = \mathbf{A}^{-1}$ for suitable values of s and t.

(b) Suppose that the matrix $\mathbf{X}$ satisfies the equation $\mathbf{BX} = 2\mathbf{X} + \mathbf{C}$, where

$$\mathbf{B} = \begin{pmatrix} 3 & 2 & 3 \\ 2 & 3 & 3 \\ 3 & 2 & 3 \end{pmatrix} \quad \text{and} \quad \mathbf{C} = \begin{pmatrix} 2 & 3 & 0 & 1 \\ 1 & 0 & 3 & 1 \\ 0 & 5 & -4 & 1 \end{pmatrix}$$

Use the result in part (a) to find $\mathbf{X}$.

HARDER PROBLEMS

13. Let $\mathbf{D}$ be an $n \times n$ matrix such that $\mathbf{D}^2 = 2\mathbf{D}+3\mathbf{I}$. Prove that $\mathbf{D}^3 = a\mathbf{D}+b\mathbf{I}$ for suitable values of a and b. Find similar expressions for $\mathbf{D}^6$ and $\mathbf{D}^{-1}$ (that is, expressed in the form $\alpha\mathbf{D} + \beta\mathbf{I}$).

16.7 A General Formula for the Inverse

The previous section certainly presents the most important facts about the inverse and its properties. As such, it contains "what every economist should know." It is less important for most economists to know a lot about how to calculate the inverses of large matrices, because powerful computer programs are available.

Nevertheless, this section presents an explicit formula for the inverse of any nonsingular $n \times n$ matrix $\mathbf{A}$. Though this formula is extremely inefficient for computing inverses of large matrices, it does have theoretical interest. The key to this result is the formulas for the expansion of determinants by cofactors.

Let $C_{11}, \ldots, C_{nn}$ denote the cofactors of the elements in $\mathbf{A}$. By Theorem 16.5.1, the rules for expansion by cofactors yield n^2 equations of the form

$$a_{i1}C_{k1} + a_{i2}C_{k2} + \cdots + a_{in}C_{kn} = \begin{cases} |\mathbf{A}|, & \text{if } i = k \\ 0 & \text{if } i \neq k \end{cases} \tag{$*$}$$

for $i, k = 1, \ldots, n$. The sums on the left-hand side look very much like those appearing in matrix products. In fact, the n^2 different equations in $(*)$ reduce to the single matrix equation

$$
\begin{pmatrix}
a_{11} & a_{12} & \ldots & a_{1n} \\
\vdots & \vdots & & \vdots \\
a_{i1} & a_{i2} & \ldots & a_{in} \\
\vdots & \vdots & & \vdots \\
a_{n1} & a_{n2} & \ldots & a_{nn}
\end{pmatrix}
\begin{pmatrix}
C_{11} & \ldots & C_{k1} & \ldots & C_{n1} \\
C_{12} & \ldots & C_{k2} & \ldots & C_{n2} \\
\vdots & & \vdots & & \vdots \\
C_{1n} & \ldots & C_{kn} & \ldots & C_{nn}
\end{pmatrix}
=
\begin{pmatrix}
|A| & 0 & \ldots & 0 \\
0 & |A| & \ldots & 0 \\
\vdots & \vdots & \ddots & \vdots \\
0 & 0 & \ldots & |A|
\end{pmatrix}
$$

Here the right-hand side matrix is equal to $|A| \cdot I_n$. Let $C^+ = (C_{ij})$ denote the matrix of cofactors. Then the second matrix in the product on the left-hand side has its row and column indices interchanged. Thus, it is the *transpose* $(C^+)'$ of that matrix, which is called the **adjoint** of A, and denoted by adj (A). Thus,

$$
\text{adj} (A) = (C^+)' =
\begin{pmatrix}
C_{11} & \ldots & C_{k1} & \ldots & C_{n1} \\
C_{12} & \ldots & C_{k2} & \ldots & C_{n2} \\
\vdots & & \vdots & & \vdots \\
C_{1n} & \ldots & C_{kn} & \ldots & C_{nn}
\end{pmatrix}
\tag{1}
$$

The previous equation, therefore, can be written as $A \, \text{adj} (A) = |A| \cdot I$. In case $|A| \neq 0$, this evidently implies that $A^{-1} = (1/|A|) \cdot \text{adj} (A)$. We have proved the general formula for the inverse:

THEOREM 16.7.1 (GENERAL FORMULA FOR THE INVERSE)

Any square matrix $A = (a_{ij})_{n \times n}$ with determinant $|A| \neq 0$ has a unique inverse A^{-1} satisfying $AA^{-1} = A^{-1}A = I$. This is given by

$$
A^{-1} = \frac{1}{|A|} \cdot \text{adj} (A)
$$

If $|A| = 0$, then there is no matrix X such that $AX = XA = I$.

EXAMPLE 1   Let $A = \begin{pmatrix} 2 & 3 & 4 \\ 4 & 3 & 1 \\ 1 & 2 & 4 \end{pmatrix}$. Show that A has an inverse and find the inverse.

Solution: According to Theorem 16.7.1, A has an inverse if and only if $|A| \neq 0$. Here we find that $|A| = -5$, so the inverse exists. The cofactors are

$$
C_{11} = \begin{vmatrix} 3 & 1 \\ 2 & 4 \end{vmatrix} = 10, \quad C_{12} = - \begin{vmatrix} 4 & 1 \\ 1 & 4 \end{vmatrix} = -15, \quad C_{13} = \begin{vmatrix} 4 & 3 \\ 1 & 2 \end{vmatrix} = 5
$$

$$
C_{21} = - \begin{vmatrix} 3 & 4 \\ 2 & 4 \end{vmatrix} = -4, \quad C_{22} = \begin{vmatrix} 2 & 4 \\ 1 & 4 \end{vmatrix} = 4, \quad C_{23} = - \begin{vmatrix} 2 & 3 \\ 1 & 2 \end{vmatrix} = -1
$$

$$
C_{31} = \begin{vmatrix} 3 & 4 \\ 3 & 1 \end{vmatrix} = -9, \quad C_{32} = - \begin{vmatrix} 2 & 4 \\ 4 & 1 \end{vmatrix} = 14, \quad C_{33} = \begin{vmatrix} 2 & 3 \\ 4 & 3 \end{vmatrix} = -6
$$

Hence, the inverse of A is

$$
A^{-1} = \frac{1}{|A|} \begin{pmatrix} C_{11} & C_{21} & C_{31} \\ C_{12} & C_{22} & C_{32} \\ C_{13} & C_{23} & C_{33} \end{pmatrix} = -\frac{1}{5} \begin{pmatrix} 10 & -4 & -9 \\ -15 & 4 & 14 \\ 5 & -1 & -6 \end{pmatrix}
$$

(Check the result by showing that $AA^{-1} = I$.)

Finding Inverses by Elementary Row Operations

Theorem 16.7.1 presented a general formula for the inverse of a nonsingular matrix. Although this formula is important theoretically, it is computationally useless for matrices much larger than 2×2. An efficient way of finding the inverse of an invertible $n \times n$ matrix $\mathbf{A}$ is based on using elementary operations in a systematic way: First form the $n \times 2n$ matrix $(\mathbf{A} : \mathbf{I})$ by writing down the n columns of $\mathbf{A}$ followed by the n columns of $\mathbf{I}$. Then apply elementary row operations to this matrix in order to transform it to an $n \times 2n$ matrix $(\mathbf{I} : \mathbf{B})$ whose first n columns are all the columns of $\mathbf{I}$. It will follow that $\mathbf{B} = \mathbf{A}^{-1}$. If it is impossible to perform such row operations, then $\mathbf{A}$ has no inverse. The method is illustrated by the following example.

EXAMPLE 2   Find the inverse of $\mathbf{A} = \begin{pmatrix} 1 & 3 & 3 \\ 1 & 3 & 4 \\ 1 & 4 & 3 \end{pmatrix}$.

Solution: First, write down the 3×6 matrix whose first 3 columns are the columns of $\mathbf{A}$ and whose next 3 columns are the columns of the 3×3 identity matrix:

$$\begin{pmatrix} 1 & 3 & 3 & \vdots & 1 & 0 & 0 \\ 1 & 3 & 4 & \vdots & 0 & 1 & 0 \\ 1 & 4 & 3 & \vdots & 0 & 0 & 1 \end{pmatrix}$$

The idea is now to use elementary operations on this matrix so that, in the end, the three first columns constitute an identity matrix. Then the last three columns constitute the inverse of $\mathbf{A}$.

Now multiply the first row by -1 and add the result to the second row. This gives a zero in the second row and the first column. You should be able then to understand the other operations used and why they are chosen.

$$\begin{pmatrix} 1 & 3 & 3 & \vdots & 1 & 0 & 0 \\ 1 & 3 & 4 & \vdots & 0 & 1 & 0 \\ 1 & 4 & 3 & \vdots & 0 & 0 & 1 \end{pmatrix} \sim \begin{pmatrix} 1 & 3 & 3 & \vdots & 1 & 0 & 0 \\ 0 & 0 & 1 & \vdots & -1 & 1 & 0 \\ 1 & 4 & 3 & \vdots & 0 & 0 & 1 \end{pmatrix}$$

$$\sim \begin{pmatrix} 1 & 3 & 3 & \vdots & 1 & 0 & 0 \\ 0 & 0 & 1 & \vdots & -1 & 1 & 0 \\ 0 & 1 & 0 & \vdots & -1 & 0 & 1 \end{pmatrix} \sim \begin{pmatrix} 1 & 0 & 3 & \vdots & 4 & 0 & -3 \\ 0 & 0 & 1 & \vdots & -1 & 1 & 0 \\ 0 & 1 & 0 & \vdots & -1 & 0 & 1 \end{pmatrix}$$

$$\sim \begin{pmatrix} 1 & 0 & 0 & \vdots & 7 & -3 & -3 \\ 0 & 0 & 1 & \vdots & -1 & 1 & 0 \\ 0 & 1 & 0 & \vdots & -1 & 0 & 1 \end{pmatrix} \sim \begin{pmatrix} 1 & 0 & 0 & \vdots & 7 & -3 & -3 \\ 0 & 1 & 0 & \vdots & -1 & 0 & 1 \\ 0 & 0 & 1 & \vdots & -1 & 1 & 0 \end{pmatrix}$$

We conclude that

$$\mathbf{A}^{-1} = \begin{pmatrix} 7 & -3 & -3 \\ -1 & 0 & 1 \\ -1 & 1 & 0 \end{pmatrix}$$

(Check that $\mathbf{AA}^{-1} = \mathbf{I}$.)

1. Use Theorem 16.7.1 to calculate the inverses of the following matrices, if they exist:

(a) $\begin{pmatrix} 2 & 3 \\ 4 & 5 \end{pmatrix}$ (b) $\begin{pmatrix} 1 & 0 & 2 \\ 2 & -1 & 0 \\ 0 & 2 & -1 \end{pmatrix}$ (c) $\begin{pmatrix} 1 & 0 & 0 \\ -3 & -2 & 1 \\ 4 & -16 & 8 \end{pmatrix}$

2. Find the inverse of $\begin{pmatrix} -2 & 3 & 2 \\ 6 & 0 & 3 \\ 4 & 1 & -1 \end{pmatrix}$.

3. Let $\mathbf{A} = \begin{pmatrix} 0.2 & 0.6 & 0.2 \\ 0 & 0.2 & 0.4 \\ 0.2 & 0.2 & 0 \end{pmatrix}$. Find $(\mathbf{I} - \mathbf{A})^{-1}$.

4. Repeated observations of a phenomenon lead to p different systems of equations

$$a_{11}x_1 + \cdots + a_{1n}x_n = b_{1k}$$
$$\cdots\cdots\cdots\cdots\cdots\cdots\cdots \qquad (k = 1, \ldots, p) \qquad (*)$$
$$a_{n1}x_1 + \cdots + a_{nn}x_n = b_{nk}$$

which all share the same $n \times n$ coefficient matrix (a_{ij}). Explain how to find the the solutions $(x_{k1}, \ldots, x_{kn})$ $(k = 1, \ldots, p)$ of all the systems simultaneously by using row operations to get

$$\begin{pmatrix} a_{11} & \cdots & a_{1n} & b_{11} & \cdots & b_{1p} \\ \vdots & \ddots & \vdots & \vdots & & \vdots \\ a_{n1} & \cdots & a_{nn} & b_{n1} & \cdots & b_{np} \end{pmatrix} \sim \begin{pmatrix} 1 & \cdots & 0 & b_{11}^* & \cdots & b_{1p}^* \\ \vdots & \ddots & \vdots & \vdots & & \vdots \\ 0 & \cdots & 1 & b_{1n}^* & \cdots & b_{np}^* \end{pmatrix}$$

What then is the solution of the system of equations $(*)$ for $k = r$?

5. Use the method in Example 2 to calculate the inverses (provided they exist) of the following matrices (check each result by verifying that $\mathbf{A}\mathbf{A}^{-1} = \mathbf{I}$).

(a) $\mathbf{A} = \begin{pmatrix} 1 & 2 \\ 3 & 4 \end{pmatrix}$ (b) $\mathbf{A} = \begin{pmatrix} 1 & 2 & 3 \\ 2 & 4 & 5 \\ 3 & 5 & 6 \end{pmatrix}$ (c) $\mathbf{A} = \begin{pmatrix} 3 & 2 & -1 \\ -1 & 5 & 8 \\ -9 & -6 & 3 \end{pmatrix}$

16.8 Cramer's Rule

Cramer's rule for solving n linear equations in n unknowns is a direct generalization of the same rule for systems of equations with 2 or 3 unknowns. Consider the system

$$a_{11}x_1 + a_{12}x_2 + \cdots + a_{1n}x_n = b_1$$
$$a_{21}x_1 + a_{22}x_2 + \cdots + a_{2n}x_n = b_2$$
$$\cdots\cdots\cdots\cdots\cdots\cdots\cdots\cdots\cdots \qquad (1)$$
$$a_{n1}x_1 + a_{n2}x_2 + \cdots + a_{nn}x_n = b_n$$

Let D_j denote the determinant obtained from $|\mathbf{A}|$ by replacing the jth column vector with the column vector whose components are $b_1, b_2, \ldots, b_n$. Thus,

$$D_j = \begin{vmatrix} a_{11} & \cdots & a_{1j-1} & b_1 & a_{1j+1} & \cdots & a_{1n} \\ a_{21} & \cdots & a_{2j-1} & b_2 & a_{2j+1} & \cdots & a_{2n} \\ \vdots & & \vdots & \vdots & \vdots & & \vdots \\ a_{n1} & \cdots & a_{nj-1} & b_n & a_{nj+1} & \cdots & a_{nn} \end{vmatrix}, \qquad j = 1, \ldots, n \qquad (2)$$

Note that expanding D_j by its jth column gives

$$D_j = C_{1j}b_1 + C_{2j}b_2 + \cdots + C_{nj}b_n \qquad (3)$$

where the cofactors C_{ij} are given by (3) of Section 16.5. Now we have the following result:

THEOREM 16.8.1 (CRAMER'S RULE)

The general linear system of equations (1) with n equations and n unknowns has a unique solution if and only if $\mathbf{A}$ is nonsingular ($|\mathbf{A}| \neq 0$). The solution is

$$x_1 = \frac{D_1}{|\mathbf{A}|}, \quad x_2 = \frac{D_2}{|\mathbf{A}|}, \quad \ldots, \quad x_n = \frac{D_n}{|\mathbf{A}|} \qquad (4)$$

where $D_1, D_2, \ldots, D_n$ are defined by (2).

Proof of the "if part": Suppose $|\mathbf{A}| \neq 0$. System (1) can be written in the form

$$\begin{pmatrix} a_{11} & a_{12} & \cdots & a_{1n} \\ a_{21} & a_{22} & \cdots & a_{2n} \\ \vdots & \vdots & \ddots & \vdots \\ a_{n1} & a_{n2} & \cdots & a_{nn} \end{pmatrix} \begin{pmatrix} x_1 \\ x_2 \\ \vdots \\ x_n \end{pmatrix} = \begin{pmatrix} b_1 \\ b_2 \\ \vdots \\ b_n \end{pmatrix}$$

Using the formula for the inverse of the coefficient matrix yields

$$\begin{pmatrix} x_1 \\ x_2 \\ \vdots \\ x_n \end{pmatrix} = \frac{1}{|\mathbf{A}|} \begin{pmatrix} C_{11} & C_{21} & \cdots & C_{n1} \\ C_{12} & C_{22} & \cdots & C_{n2} \\ \vdots & \vdots & \ddots & \vdots \\ C_{1n} & C_{2n} & \cdots & C_{nn} \end{pmatrix} \begin{pmatrix} b_1 \\ b_2 \\ \vdots \\ b_n \end{pmatrix} \qquad (*)$$

where the cofactors C_{ij} are given by (3) of Section 16.5. From $(*)$, we have

$$x_j = \frac{1}{|\mathbf{A}|}[C_{1j}b_1 + C_{2j}b_2 + \cdots + C_{nj}b_n] = \frac{D_j}{|\mathbf{A}|}, \qquad j = 1, 2, \ldots, n$$

where the last equality follows from the previous equation (3). This proves (4).

The only if part will be proved in FMEA. (The basic idea of the proof is this: If $|\mathbf{A}| = 0$, then the rank of $\mathbf{A}$ is less than n, and if the system has solutions, there will be at least one degree of freedom. So for $(*)$ to have a unique solution, $|\mathbf{A}|$ has to be different from 0.) ∎

EXAMPLE 1   Find the solutions of the following system for all values of p:

$$px + y = 1$$
$$x - y + z = 0$$
$$2y - z = 3$$

Solution: The coefficient matrix has determinant

$$|\mathbf{A}| = \begin{vmatrix} p & 1 & 0 \\ 1 & -1 & 1 \\ 0 & 2 & -1 \end{vmatrix} = 1 - p$$

According to Theorem 16.8.1, the system has a unique solution if $1 - p \neq 0$—that is, if $p \neq 1$. In this case, the determinants in (2) are

$$D_1 = \begin{vmatrix} 1 & 1 & 0 \\ 0 & -1 & 1 \\ 3 & 2 & -1 \end{vmatrix}, \quad D_2 = \begin{vmatrix} p & 1 & 0 \\ 1 & 0 & 1 \\ 0 & 3 & -1 \end{vmatrix}, \quad D_3 = \begin{vmatrix} p & 1 & 1 \\ 1 & -1 & 0 \\ 0 & 2 & 3 \end{vmatrix}$$

We find that $D_1 = 2$, $D_2 = 1 - 3p$, and $D_3 = -1 - 3p$, so (4) yields for $p \neq 1$

$$x = \frac{D_1}{|\mathbf{A}|} = \frac{2}{1-p}, \qquad y = \frac{D_2}{|\mathbf{A}|} = \frac{1-3p}{1-p}, \qquad z = \frac{D_3}{|\mathbf{A}|} = \frac{-1-3p}{1-p}$$

When $p = 1$, adding the last two of the original equations implies that $x + y = 3$. This contradicts the first equation, which becomes $x + y = 1$. So there is no solution in this case.

Homogeneous Systems of Equations

Consider the special case in which the right-hand side of the system of equations (1) consists only of zeros. The system is then called **homogeneous**. A homogeneous system will always have the so-called **trivial solution** $x_1 = x_2 = \cdots = x_n = 0$. In many problems, one is interested in knowing when a homogeneous system has **nontrivial** solutions.

THEOREM 16.8.2 (NONTRIVIAL SOLUTIONS OF HOMOGENEOUS SYSTEMS)

The homogeneous linear system of equations with n equations and n unknowns

$$a_{11}x_1 + a_{12}x_2 + \cdots + a_{1n}x_n = 0$$
$$a_{21}x_1 + a_{22}x_2 + \cdots + a_{2n}x_n = 0$$
$$\cdots\cdots\cdots\cdots\cdots\cdots\cdots\cdots\cdots \tag{5}$$
$$a_{n1}x_1 + a_{n2}x_2 + \cdots + a_{nn}x_n = 0$$

has nontrivial solutions if and only if the coefficient matrix $\mathbf{A} = (a_{ij})_{n \times n}$ is singular (that is, if and only if $|\mathbf{A}| = 0$).

***Proof of the "if part"*:** Suppose that $|\mathbf{A}| \neq 0$. Then, by Cramer's rule, $x_1, \ldots, x_n$ are given by (4). But the numerator in each of these fractions is 0, because each of the determinants $D_1, \ldots, D_n$ contains a column consisting entirely of zeros. Then the system only has the trivial solution. In other words: *System (5) can only have nontrivial solutions if the determinant $|\mathbf{A}|$ vanishes.*

As for the "only if" part, concepts from FMEA can be used to show that, if $|\mathbf{A}| = 0$, then system (5) does have nontrivial solutions because then the rank of $\mathbf{A}$ is less than n, so system (5) has at least 1 degree of freedom. It follows that (5) has infinitely many solutions. ∎

EXAMPLE 2   Examine for what values of λ the following system of equations has nontrivial solutions:

$$5x + 2y + z = \lambda x$$
$$2x + \ y \qquad = \lambda y$$
$$\ x \qquad + z = \lambda z$$

Solution: The variables x, y, and z appear on both sides of the equations, so we start by putting the system into standard form:

$$(5 - \lambda)x + \qquad 2y + \qquad z = 0$$
$$2x + (1 - \lambda)y \qquad\qquad = 0$$
$$x \qquad\qquad + (1 - \lambda)z = 0$$

According to Theorem 16.8.2, this system has a nontrivial solution if and only if the coefficient matrix is singular:

$$\begin{vmatrix} 5 - \lambda & 2 & 1 \\ 2 & 1 - \lambda & 0 \\ 1 & 0 & 1 - \lambda \end{vmatrix} = 0$$

The value of the determinant is found to be

$$\lambda(1 - \lambda)(\lambda - 6)$$

Hence, system (1) has nontrivial solutions if and only if $\lambda = 0$, 1, or 6. ∎

PROBLEMS FOR SECTION 16.8

1. Use Cramer's rule to solve the following two systems of equations:

(a)
$$x + 2y - \ z = -5$$
$$2x - \ y + \ z = \ 6$$
$$x - \ y - 3z = -3$$

(b)
$$x + y \qquad\qquad = 3$$
$$x \qquad + z \qquad = 2$$
$$y + z + u = 6$$
$$y \qquad + u = 1$$

2. Use Theorem 16.8.1 to prove that the following system of equations has a unique solution for all values of b_1, b_2, b_3, and find the solution.

$$3x_1 + \ x_2 \qquad\quad = b_1$$
$$x_1 - \ x_2 + 2x_3 = b_2$$
$$2x_1 + 3x_2 - \ x_3 = b_3$$

SECTION 16.9 / THE LEONTIEF MODEL **623**

3. Prove that the homogeneous system of equations

$$ax + by + cz = 0$$
$$bx + cy + az = 0$$
$$cx + ay + bz = 0$$

has a nontrivial solution if and only if $a^3 + b^3 + c^3 - 3abc = 0$.

16.9 The Leontief Model

In Example 15.1.2 we briefly considered a simple example of the Leontief model. More generally, the Leontief model describes an economy with n interlinked industries, each of which produces a single good using only one process of production. To produce its good, each industry must use inputs from at least some other industries. For example, the steel industry needs goods from the iron mining and coal industries, as well as from many other industries. In addition to supplying its own good to other industries that need it, each industry also faces an external demand for its product from consumers, governments, foreigners, and so on. The amount needed to meet this external demand is called the *final demand*.

Let x_i denote the total number of units of good i that industry i is going to produce in a certain year. Furthermore, let

$$a_{ij} = \text{the number of units of good } i \text{ needed to produce one unit of good } j \qquad (1)$$

We assume that input requirements are directly proportional to the amount of the output produced. Then

$$a_{ij}x_j = \text{the number of units of good } i \text{ needed to produce } x_j \text{ units of good } j \qquad (2)$$

In order that x_1 units of good 1, x_2 units of good 2, ..., x_n units of good n can all be produced, industry i needs to supply a total of

$$a_{i1}x_1 + a_{i2}x_2 + \cdots + a_{in}x_n$$

units of good i. If we require industry i also to supply b_i units to meet final demand, then equilibrium between supply and demand requires that

$$x_i = a_{i1}x_1 + a_{i2}x_2 + \cdots + a_{in}x_n + b_i$$

This goes for all $i = 1, 2, \ldots, n$. So we arrive at the following system of equations:

$$
\begin{aligned}
x_1 &= a_{11}x_1 + a_{12}x_2 + \cdots + a_{1n}x_n + b_1 \\
x_2 &= a_{21}x_1 + a_{22}x_2 + \cdots + a_{2n}x_n + b_2 \\
&\cdots\cdots\cdots\cdots\cdots\cdots\cdots\cdots\cdots\cdots\cdots\cdots\cdots \\
x_n &= a_{n1}x_1 + a_{n2}x_2 + \cdots + a_{nn}x_n + b_n
\end{aligned}
\qquad (3)
$$

Note that in the first equation, x_1 appears on the left-hand side as well as in the first term on the right-hand side. In the second equation, x_2 appears on the left-hand side as well as in the second term on the right-hand side, and so on. Moving all terms involving $x_1, \ldots, x_n$ to the left-hand side and rearranging gives the system of equations

$$
\begin{aligned}
(1 - a_{11})x_1 - a_{12}x_2 - \cdots - \; &a_{1n}x_n = b_1 \\
-a_{21}x_1 + (1 - a_{22})x_2 - \cdots - \; &a_{2n}x_n = b_2 \\
&\cdots\cdots\cdots\cdots\cdots\cdots\cdots\cdots\cdots\cdots\cdots\cdots \\
-a_{n1}x_1 - a_{n2}x_2 - \cdots + (1 &- a_{nn})x_n = b_n
\end{aligned}
\tag{4}
$$

This is called the **Leontief system**. The numbers $a_{11}, a_{12}, \ldots, a_{nn}$ are called **input** (or **technical) coefficients**. Given any collection of final demand quantities $(b_1, b_2, \ldots, b_n)$, a solution $(x_1, x_2, \ldots, x_n)$ of (4) will give outputs for each industry such that the combined interindustry and final demands can just be met. Of course, only nonnegative values for x_i make sense.

It is natural to use matrix algebra to study the Leontief model. Define the following matrices:

$$
\mathbf{A} = \begin{pmatrix} a_{11} & a_{12} & \cdots & a_{1n} \\ a_{21} & a_{22} & \cdots & a_{2n} \\ \vdots & \vdots & \ddots & \vdots \\ a_{n1} & a_{n2} & \cdots & a_{nn} \end{pmatrix}, \qquad \mathbf{x} = \begin{pmatrix} x_1 \\ x_2 \\ \vdots \\ x_n \end{pmatrix}, \qquad \mathbf{b} = \begin{pmatrix} b_1 \\ b_2 \\ \vdots \\ b_n \end{pmatrix}
\tag{5}
$$

The elements of the matrix $\mathbf{A}$ are the input coefficients, so it is called the **input** or **Leontief matrix**. Recall that the element a_{ij} denotes the number of units of commodity i which is needed to produce one unit of commodity j.

With these definitions, system (3) can expressed as

$$
\mathbf{x} = \mathbf{A}\mathbf{x} + \mathbf{b}
\tag{6}
$$

This equation is evidently equivalent to the equation $\mathbf{x} - \mathbf{A}\mathbf{x} = \mathbf{b}$. If $\mathbf{I}_n$ denotes the identity matrix of order n, then $(\mathbf{I}_n - \mathbf{A})\mathbf{x} = \mathbf{I}_n\mathbf{x} - \mathbf{A}\mathbf{x} = \mathbf{x} - \mathbf{A}\mathbf{x}$, so that (3) is equivalent to

$$
(\mathbf{I}_n - \mathbf{A})\mathbf{x} = \mathbf{b}
\tag{7}
$$

which is the matrix equivalent of system (4). (Note in particular that "$\mathbf{x} - \mathbf{A}\mathbf{x} = (1 - \mathbf{A})\mathbf{x}$" is meaningless, since $1 - \mathbf{A}$ (where 1 is the number 1) is meaningless.)

Suppose now that we introduce prices into the Leontief model, and that

$$
p_i \text{ is the price of a unit of commodity } i
$$

Because a_{ij} denotes the number of units of commodity i needed to produce one unit of commodity j, the sum

$$
a_{1j}p_1 + a_{2j}p_2 + \cdots + a_{nj}p_n
$$

is the total cost of the n commodities needed to produce one unit of commodity j. The expression

$$p_j - a_{1j} p_1 - a_{2j} p_2 - \cdots - a_{nj} p_n$$

is the difference between the price of one unit of commodity j and the cost of producing that unit. This is called **unit value added** in sector j. If we denote this unit value added by v_j, then for all sectors:

$$
\begin{aligned}
p_1 - a_{11} p_1 - a_{21} p_2 - \cdots - a_{n1} p_n &= v_1 \\
p_2 - a_{12} p_1 - a_{22} p_2 - \cdots - a_{n2} p_n &= v_2 \\
&\cdots \\
p_n - a_{1n} p_1 - a_{2n} p_2 - \cdots - a_{nn} p_n &= v_n
\end{aligned}
\tag{8}
$$

Note that the input-output coefficients a_{ij} appear in transposed order. If we define the matrices

$$
\mathbf{p} = \begin{pmatrix} p_1 \\ p_2 \\ \vdots \\ p_n \end{pmatrix}
\quad \text{and} \quad
\mathbf{v} = \begin{pmatrix} v_1 \\ v_2 \\ \vdots \\ v_n \end{pmatrix}
\tag{9}
$$

we see that (8) can be written in the matrix form $\mathbf{p} - \mathbf{A}'\mathbf{p} = \mathbf{v}$, or

$$(\mathbf{I}_n - \mathbf{A}')\mathbf{p} = \mathbf{v} \tag{10}$$

By using the rules for transposing in (2) of Section 15.5, we can express (10) in an alternative way. Transposing each side of (10) gives

$$\mathbf{p}'(\mathbf{I}_n - \mathbf{A}) = \mathbf{v}' \tag{11}$$

since $\mathbf{I}'_n = \mathbf{I}_n$ and $\mathbf{A}'' = \mathbf{A}$. We see that the two systems (7) and (11) are closely related.

PROBLEMS FOR SECTION 16.9

1. Consider an economy divided into an agricultural sector (A) and an industrial sector (I). To produce one unit in sector A requires $1/6$ unit from A and $1/4$ unit from I. To produce one unit in sector I requires $1/4$ unit from A and $1/4$ unit from I. Suppose final demands in each of the two sectors are 60 units.

   (a) Write down the Leontief system for this economy.

   (b) Find the number of units that has to be produced in each sector in order to meet the final demands.

2. Consider the Leontief model (4).

   (a) What is the interpretation of the condition that $a_{ii} = 0$ for all i?

   (b) What is the interpretation of the sum $a_{i1} + a_{i2} + \cdots + a_{in}$?

   (c) What is the interpretation of the vector of input coefficients $(a_{1j}, a_{2j}, \ldots, a_{nj})$?

   (d) Can you give any interpretation to the sum $a_{1j} + a_{2j} + \cdots + a_{nj}$?

3. Write down system (4) when $n = 2$, $a_{11} = 0.2$, $a_{12} = 0.3$, $a_{21} = 0.4$, $a_{22} = 0.1$, $b_1 = 120$, and $b_2 = 90$. What is the solution to this system?

4. Consider an input–output model with 3 sectors. Sector 1 is heavy industry, sector 2 is light industry, and sector 3 is agriculture. Suppose that the input requirements are given by the following table:

	Heavy industry	Light industry	Agriculture
Units of heavy industry goods	$a_{11} = 0.1$	$a_{12} = 0.2$	$a_{13} = 0.1$
Units of light industry goods	$a_{21} = 0.3$	$a_{22} = 0.2$	$a_{23} = 0.2$
Units of agri- cultural goods	$a_{31} = 0.2$	$a_{32} = 0.2$	$a_{33} = 0.1$

Suppose the final demands for the three goods are 85, 95, and 20 units, respectively. If x_1, x_2, and x_3 denote the number of units that have to be produced in the three sectors, write down the Leontief system for the problem. Verify that $x_1 = 150$, $x_2 = 200$, and $x_3 = 100$ is a solution.

5. Write down the input matrix for the simple Leontief model of Example 15.1.2. Compare the condition for efficient production discussed in that example with the requirement that the sum of the elements of each column in the input matrix be less than 1.

6. Suppose that $\mathbf{x} = \mathbf{x}_0$ is a solution of (7) and that $\mathbf{p}' = \mathbf{p}_0'$ is a solution of (11). Prove that $\mathbf{p}_0' \mathbf{b} = \mathbf{v}' \mathbf{x}_0$.

REVIEW PROBLEMS FOR CHAPTER 16

1. Calculate the following determinants:

(a) $\begin{vmatrix} 5 & -2 \\ 3 & -2 \end{vmatrix}$ (b) $\begin{vmatrix} 1 & a \\ a & 1 \end{vmatrix}$ (c) $\begin{vmatrix} (a+b)^2 & a-b \\ (a-b)^2 & a+b \end{vmatrix}$ (d) $\begin{vmatrix} 1-\lambda & 2 \\ 2 & 4-\lambda \end{vmatrix}$

2. Calculate the determinants:

(a) $\begin{vmatrix} 2 & 2 & 3 \\ 0 & 3 & 5 \\ 0 & 4 & 6 \end{vmatrix}$ (b) $\begin{vmatrix} 4 & 5 & 6 \\ 5 & 6 & 8 \\ 6 & 7 & 9 \end{vmatrix}$ (c) $\begin{vmatrix} 31 & 32 & 33 \\ 32 & 33 & 35 \\ 33 & 34 & 36 \end{vmatrix}$

(*Hint:* In (b) and (c) you should perform suitable elementary operations.)

3. Solve the following equation for x: $\begin{vmatrix} x & a & x & b \\ b & x & a & x \\ x & b & x & a \\ a & x & b & x \end{vmatrix} = 0$.

4. Let $A_t = \begin{pmatrix} 1 & 0 & t \\ 2 & 1 & t \\ 0 & 1 & 1 \end{pmatrix}$ and $\mathbf{B} = \begin{pmatrix} 1 & 0 & 0 \\ 0 & 0 & 1 \\ 0 & 1 & 0 \end{pmatrix}$.

   (a) For what values of t does A_t have an inverse?

   (b) Find a matrix $\mathbf{X}$ such that $\mathbf{B} + \mathbf{X}\mathbf{A}_1^{-1} = \mathbf{A}_1^{-1}$.

5. Define the two 3×3 matrices $\mathbf{A} = \begin{pmatrix} q & -1 & q-2 \\ 1 & -p & 2-p \\ 2 & -1 & 0 \end{pmatrix}$, $\mathbf{E} = \begin{pmatrix} 1 & 1 & 1 \\ 1 & 1 & 1 \\ 1 & 1 & 1 \end{pmatrix}$.

   Calculate $|\mathbf{A}|$ and $|\mathbf{A} + \mathbf{E}|$. For what values of p and q does $\mathbf{A} + \mathbf{E}$ have an inverse? Why does $\mathbf{BE}$ not have an inverse for any 3×3 matrix $\mathbf{B}$?

6. For what values of t does the system of equations

$$-2x + 4y - tz = t - 4$$
$$-3x + y + tz = 3 - 4t$$
$$(t-2)x - 7y + 4z = 23$$

   have a unique solution for the three variables x, y, and z? (Use Cramer's rule.)

7. Prove that if $\mathbf{A}$ is an $n \times n$ matrix such that $\mathbf{A}^4 = \mathbf{0}$, then $(\mathbf{I} - \mathbf{A})^{-1} = \mathbf{I} + \mathbf{A} + \mathbf{A}^2 + \mathbf{A}^3$.

8. (a) Let $\mathbf{U}$ be the $n \times n$ matrix where all the elements are 1. Show that

$$(\mathbf{I}_n + a\mathbf{U})(\mathbf{I}_n + b\mathbf{U}) = \mathbf{I}_n + (a + b + nab)\mathbf{U}$$

   for all real numbers a and b.

   (b) Use the result in (a) to find the inverse of $\begin{pmatrix} 4 & 3 & 3 \\ 3 & 4 & 3 \\ 3 & 3 & 4 \end{pmatrix}$.

9. Let $\mathbf{A}, \mathbf{B}, \mathbf{C}, \mathbf{X}$, and $\mathbf{Y}$ be $n \times n$ matrices, with $|\mathbf{A}| \neq 0$, which satisfy the two equations

$$\text{(i) } \mathbf{AX} + \mathbf{Y} = \mathbf{B} \qquad \text{(ii) } \mathbf{X} + 2\mathbf{A}^{-1}\mathbf{Y} = \mathbf{C}$$

   Find $\mathbf{X}$ and $\mathbf{Y}$ expressed in terms of $\mathbf{A}$, $\mathbf{B}$, and $\mathbf{C}$.

10. Consider the matrix $\mathbf{A} = \begin{pmatrix} 11 & -6 \\ 18 & -10 \end{pmatrix}$.

    (a) Compute $|\mathbf{A}|$. Show that for a suitable number c we have $\mathbf{A}^2 + c\mathbf{A} = 2\mathbf{I}_2$, and then find the inverse of $\mathbf{A}$.

    (b) Show that there is no 2×2 matrix $\mathbf{B}$ such that $\mathbf{B}^2 = \mathbf{A}$.

11. The 3×3 matrix $\mathbf{B}$ satisfies the equation $\mathbf{B}^3 = -\mathbf{B}$. Show that $\mathbf{B}$ cannot have an inverse. (*Hint:* Use Theorem 16.4.1 (G).)

12. (a) For what values of a does the system of equations

$$ax + y + \ 4z = 2$$
$$2x + y + a^2z = 2 \qquad\qquad (*)$$
$$x \qquad - \ 3z = a$$

have one, none, or infinitely many solutions?

(b) Replace the right-hand side numbers 2, 2, and a in $(*)$ by b_1, b_2, and b_3, respectively. Find a necessary and sufficient condition for the new system of equations to have infinitely many solutions.

13. Suppose that $\mathbf{A}$ and $\mathbf{B}$ are invertible $n \times n$ matrices. Show that if $\mathbf{A}'\mathbf{A} = \mathbf{I}_n$, then $(\mathbf{A}'\mathbf{B}\mathbf{A})^{-1} = \mathbf{A}'\mathbf{B}^{-1}\mathbf{A}$.

14. Examine for what values of the constants a and b the system of equations

$$ax + y = 3$$
$$x + z = 2$$
$$y + az + bu = 6$$
$$y + u = 1$$

has a unique solution in the unknowns x, y, z, and u. Find the unique solution (expressed in terms of a and b).

17

LINEAR PROGRAMMING

*If one would take statistics about which mathematical problem is
using up most of the computer time in the world, then (not
counting database handling problems like sorting and searching)
the answer would probably be linear programming.*
—L. Lovász (1980)

Linear programming is the name used to describe problems in which the objective is to maximize or minimize a linear function subject to linear inequality constraints.

As the above quotation from Lovász indicates, linear programming is a mathematical technique of immense practical importance. Since its origins in the 1940s, there have been important theoretical and computational developments, and its methods are now used every day in many parts of the world.

Because of its extensive use in economic decision problems, all economists should have some basic knowledge of this theory. However, its importance extends even beyond its practical applications. In particular, the duality theory of linear programming is a basis for understanding more complicated optimization problems with even more interesting economic applications.

In principle, *any* linear programming problem (often called an LP problem) can be solved, if a solution exists. The *simplex method* introduced in 1947 by G. B. Dantzig is a very efficient numerical method that finds the solution in a finite number of operations. This method will not be discussed in this book. In fact, for economists, it is probably more important to understand the duality theory of LP than the details of the simplex method. After all, faced with a nontrivial LP problem, it is natural to use one of the great number of available LP computer programs to find the solution.

17.1 Preliminaries

A general linear programming problem with only two decision variables involves maximizing or minimizing a linear function

$$z = c_1x_1 + c_2x_2 \qquad \text{(objective function)}$$

subject to m constraints

$$a_{11}x_1 + a_{12}x_2 \leq b_1$$
$$a_{21}x_1 + a_{22}x_2 \leq b_2 \qquad \text{(inequality constraints)}$$
$$\dots\dots\dots\dots\dots\dots$$
$$a_{m1}x_1 + a_{m2}x_2 \leq b_m$$

Usually, we also impose explicit nonnegativity constraints on x_1 and x_2:

$$x_1 \geq 0, \ x_2 \geq 0 \qquad \text{(nonnegativity constraints)}$$

Note that having a $\leq$ sign rather than $\geq$ in each inequality constraint is merely a convention because any inequality of the alternative form $ax_1 + bx_2 \geq c$ is equivalent to the inequality $-ax_1 - bx_2 \leq -c$.

A Graphical Approach to Simple LP Problems

LP problems with only two decision variables can be solved by a simple graphical method.

EXAMPLE 1   A baker has 150 kilograms of flour, 22 kilos of sugar, and 27.5 kilos of butter with which to make two types of cake. Suppose that making one dozen A cakes requires 3 kilos of flour, 1 kilo of sugar, and 1 kilo of butter, whereas making one dozen B cakes requires 6 kilos of flour, 0.5 kilo of sugar, and 1 kilo of butter. Suppose that the profit from one dozen A cakes is 20 and from one dozen B cakes is 30. How many dozen A cakes (x_1) and how many dozen B cakes (x_2) will maximize the baker's profit?

Solution: An output of x_1 dozen A cakes and x_2 dozen B cakes would need $3x_1 + 6x_2$ kilos of flour. Because there are only 150 kilos of flour, the inequality

$$3x_1 + 6x_2 \leq 150 \qquad \text{(flour constraint)}$$

must hold. Similarily, for sugar,

$$x_1 + 0.5x_2 \leq 22 \qquad \text{(sugar constraint)}$$

and for butter,

$$x_1 + x_2 \leq 27.5 \qquad \text{(butter constraint)}$$

Of course, $x_1 \geq 0$ and $x_2 \geq 0$. The profit obtained from producing x_1 dozen A cakes and x_2 dozen B cakes is

$$z = 20x_1 + 30x_2$$

In short, the problem is to

$$\max z = 20x_1 + 30x_2 \ \text{ subject to } \begin{cases} 3x_1 + \ \ 6x_2 \ \leq \ 150 \\ \ x_1 + 0.5x_2 \ \leq \ \ \ 22 \\ \ x_1 + \ \ \ x_2 \ \leq \ 27.5 \end{cases} \quad x_1 \geq 0, \ x_2 \geq 0 \quad \text{(i)}$$

This problem will now be solved graphically.

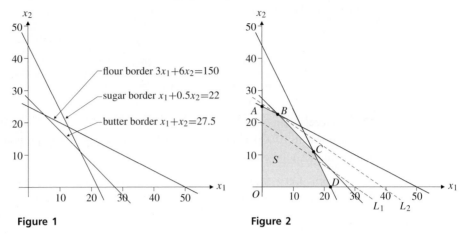

Figure 1
Figure 2

The output pair (x_1, x_2) is called *feasible* (or *admissible*) for problem (i) if all the five constraints are satisfied. Look at the flour constraint, $3x_1 + 6x_2 \leq 150$. If we use all the flour, then $3x_1 + 6x_2 = 150$, and we call this the *flour border*. We can find similar "borders" for the other two inputs. Figure 1 shows the three straight lines that represent the flour border, the sugar border, and the butter border. In order for (x_1, x_2) to be feasible, it has to be on or below (to the "southwest" of) *each* of the three borders simultaneously. Because constraints $x_1 \geq 0$ and $x_2 \geq 0$ restrict (x_1, x_2) to the nonnegative quadrant, the set of feasible pairs for problem (i), called the *feasible* (or *admissible*) *region*, is the shaded set S shown in Fig. 2. (This set S is a so-called *convex polyhedron*, and the five corner points O, A, B, C, and D are called *extreme points* of the set S.)

In principle, the baker can find the point in the feasible region that maximizes profit by calculating $20x_1 + 30x_2$ at each point of S and picking the highest value. In practice, this is impossible because there are infinitely many feasible points. Let us argue this way instead. Can the baker obtain a profit of 600? If so, the straight line $20x_1 + 30x_2 = 600$ must have points in common with S. This line is represented in Fig. 2 by dashed line L_1. It does have points in common with S. (One of them is $(x_1, x_2) = (0, 20)$, where no A cakes are produced, but 20 dozen B cakes are, and the profit *is* $20 \cdot 0 + 30 \cdot 20 = 600$.) Can the baker do better? Yes. For instance, the straight line $20x_1 + 30x_2 = 601$ also has points in common with S and the profit is 601. In fact, the straight lines

$$20x_1 + 30x_2 = c \qquad (c \text{ is a constant})$$

are all parallel to $20x_1 + 30x_2 = 600$. As c increases, the line moves out farther and farther to the northeast. It is clear that the straight line that has the highest value of c and still has a point in common with S is dashed line L_2 in the figure. It touches set S at point B. Note that B is at the intersection of the flour border and the butter border. Its coordinates, therefore, satisfy the two equations: $3x_1 + 6x_2 = 150$ and $x_1 + x_2 = 27.5$. Solving these two simultaneous equations yields $x_1 = 5$ and $x_2 = 22.5$. So the baker maximizes profit by baking 5 dozen A cakes and 22.5 dozen B cakes. This uses all the available flour and butter, but $22 - 5 - 0.5 \cdot 22.5 = 5.75$ kilos of sugar are left over. The profit earned is $20x_1 + 30x_2 = 775$.

EXAMPLE 2   A firm is producing two goods, A and B. It has two factories that jointly produce the two goods in the following quantities (per hour):

	Factory 1	Factory 2
Good A	10	20
Good B	25	25

The firm receives an order for 300 units of A and 500 units of B. The costs of operating the two factories are 10 000 and 8 000 per hour. Formulate the linear programming problem of minimizing the total cost of meeting this order.

Solution: Let u_1 and u_2 be the number of hours that the two factories operate to produce the order. Then $10u_1 + 20u_2$ units of good A are produced, and $25u_1 + 25u_2$ units of good B. Because 300 units of A and 500 units of B are required, u_1 and u_2 must satisfy

$$10u_1 + 20u_2 \geq 300 \tag{i}$$
$$25u_1 + 25u_2 \geq 500$$

In addition, of course, $u_1 \geq 0$ and $u_2 \geq 0$. The total costs of operating the two factories for u_1 and u_2 hours, respectively, are $10\,000\,u_1 + 8\,000\,u_2$. The problem is, therefore,

$$\min 10\,000\,u_1 + 8\,000\,u_2 \text{ subject to } \begin{cases} 10u_1 + 20u_2 \geq 300 \\ 25u_1 + 25u_2 \geq 500 \end{cases} \quad u_1 \geq 0, \ u_2 \geq 0$$

The feasible set S is shown in Fig. 3. Because the inequalities in (i) are of the $\geq$ type and all the coefficients of u_1 and u_2 are positive, the feasible set lies to the northeast. Figure 3 includes three of the level curves $10\,000u_1 + 8\,000u_2 = c$, marked L_1, L_2, and L_3. These three correspond to the values $100\,000$, $160\,000$, and $240\,000$ of the cost level c. As c increases, the level curve moves farther and farther to the northeast.

Figure 3

The solution to the minimization problem is clearly the level curve that touches the feasible set S at point A with coordinates $(0, 20)$. Hence, the optimal solution is to operate factory 2 for 20 hours and not to use factory 1 at all, with minimum cost $160\,000$. ∎

The graphical method of solving linear programming problems works well when there are only two decision variables. One can extend the method to the case with three decision variables. Then the feasible set is a convex polyhedron in 3-space, and the level surfaces of the objective function are planes in 3-space. However, it is not easy to visualize the solution in such cases. For more than three decision variables, no graphical method is available. (By using duality theory, however, one can solve LP problems graphically when *either* the number of unknowns *or* the number of constraints is less than or equal to 3. See Section 17.5.)

Both the previous examples had optimal solutions. If the feasible region is unbounded, however, a (finite) optimal solution might not exist, as is the case in Problem 4.

The General LP Problem

The general LP problem is that of maximizing or minimizing

$$z = c_1 x_1 + \cdots + c_n x_n \qquad \textbf{(objective function)} \qquad (1)$$

with $c_1, \ldots, c_n$ as given constants, subject to m constraints

$$
\begin{aligned}
a_{11} x_1 + \cdots + a_{1n} x_n &\leq b_1 \\
a_{21} x_1 + \cdots + a_{2n} x_n &\leq b_2 \\
\cdots\cdots\cdots\cdots\cdots\cdots\cdots\cdots\cdots \\
a_{m1} x_1 + \cdots + a_{mn} x_n &\leq b_m
\end{aligned}
\qquad \textbf{(inequality constraints)} \qquad (2)
$$

where the elements a_{ij} and b_k are given constants. Usually, we assume explicitly that

$$x_1 \geq 0, \ldots, x_n \geq 0 \qquad \textbf{(nonnegativity constraints)} \qquad (3)$$

There is no essential difference between a minimization problem and a maximization problem, because the optimal solution $(x_1^*, \ldots, x_n^*)$ that minimizes (1) subject to (2) and (3) also maximizes $-z$, and $\min z = -\max(-z)$. An n-vector $(x_1, \ldots, x_n)$ that satisfies (2) and (3) is called **feasible** or **admissible**.

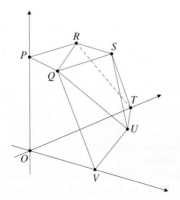

Figure 4

The set of feasible points is a so-called *convex polyhedron* in the *nonnegative orthant* of n-space. A typical example in 3-space is shown in Fig. 4. The points O, P, Q, R, S, T, U, and V are called *extreme points*. The 15 line segments OP, OT, OV, etc. joining two extreme points that are marked in Fig. 4 (including RT which is indicated with a dashed line because it is hidden behind the solid polydedron) are called *edges*. The flat portions of the boundary which are triangles or quadrilaterals lying within three or four of these edges are called *faces*. In n-space, any convex polyhedron also has extreme points, edges, and faces. If n and m are large, the number of extreme points can be astronomical.[1] If an LP problem has a solution, then it must have a solution at an extreme point. The simplex method is a procedure for moving repeatedly between adjacent extreme points of the polyhedron, along its edges, in such a way that the value of the objective function never decreases. The procedure terminates when it reaches an extreme point where no move to an adjacent extreme point will increase the value of the objective function. We have then reached the optimal solution.

PROBLEMS FOR SECTION 17.1

1. Use the graphical method to solve the following LP problems:

   (a) max $3x_1 + 4x_2$ s.t. $\begin{cases} 3x_1 + 2x_2 \leq 6 \\ x_1 + 4x_2 \leq 4 \end{cases}$ $x_1 \geq 0$, $x_2 \geq 0$

   (b) min $10u_1 + 27u_2$ s.t. $\begin{cases} u_1 + 3u_2 \geq 11 \\ 2u_1 + 5u_2 \geq 20 \end{cases}$ $u_1 \geq 0$, $u_2 \geq 0$

2. Use the graphical method to solve the following LP problems:

   (a) max $2x_1 + 5x_2$ s.t. $\begin{cases} -2x_1 + 3x_2 \leq 6 \\ 7x_1 - 2x_2 \leq 14 \\ x_1 + x_2 \leq 5 \end{cases}$ $x_1 \geq 0$, $x_2 \geq 0$

   (b) max $8x_1 + 9x_2$ s.t. $\begin{cases} x_1 + 2x_2 \leq 8 \\ 2x_1 + 3x_2 \leq 13 \\ x_1 + x_2 \leq 6 \end{cases}$ $x_1 \geq 0$, $x_2 \geq 0$

   (c) max $-2x_1 + x_2$ s.t. $0 \leq x_1 - 3x_2 \leq 3$, $x_1 \geq 2$, $x_1 \geq 0$, $x_2 \geq 0$

3. Set A consists of all (x_1, x_2) satisfying

   $$-2x_1 + x_2 \leq 2, \quad x_1 + 2x_2 \leq 8, \quad x_1 \geq 0, \ x_2 \geq 0$$

   Solve the following problems with A as the feasible set:

   (a) max x_2 (b) max x_1 (c) max $3x_1 + 2x_2$

   (d) min $2x_1 - 2x_2$ (e) max $2x_1 + 4x_2$ (f) min $-3x_1 - 2x_2$

---

[1] The typical extreme point has n of the $n + m$ inequality constraints holding with equality. Thus, there can be as many as $(n + m)!/n!m!$ extreme points. For example, if $n = 50$ and $m = 60$ (which is quite small by the standards of the problems that can be solved numerically), then there can be as many as $110!/50!60!$ or more than $6 \cdot 10^{31}$ extreme points.

4. (a) Is there a solution to the following problem?

$$\max x_1 + x_2 \ \text{s.t.} \ \begin{cases} -x_1 + \ \ x_2 \leq -1 \\ -x_1 + 3x_2 \leq \ \ 3 \end{cases} \qquad x_1 \geq 0, \ x_2 \geq 0$$

   (b) Is there a solution if the objective function is $z = -x_1 - x_2$?

5. Replace the objective function in Example 1 by $20x_1 + tx_2$. For what values of t will the maximum profit still be at $x_1 = 5$ and $x_2 = 22.5$?

6. A firm produces two types of television set, an inexpensive type (A) and an expensive type (B). The firm earns a profit of 700 from each TV of type A, and 1000 for each TV of type B. There are three stages of the production process. Stage I requires 3 units of labour on each set of type A and 5 units of labour on each set of type B. The total available quantity of labour is 3900. Stage II requires 1 unit of labour on each set of type A and 3 units on each set of type B. The total labour available is 2100 units. At stage III, 2 units of labour are needed for each type, and 2200 units of labour are available. How many TV sets of each type should the firm produce to maximize its profit?

17.2 Introduction to Duality Theory

Confronted with an optimization problem involving scarce resources, an economist will often ask: What happens to the optimal solution if the availability of the resources changes? For linear programs, answers to questions like this are intimately related to the so-called duality theory of LP. As a point of departure, let us again consider the baker's problem in Example 17.1.1.

EXAMPLE 1   Suppose the baker were to stumble across an extra kilo of flour that had been hidden away in storage. How much would this extra kilo add to his maximum profit? How much would an extra kilo of sugar contribute to profit? Or an extra kilo of butter?

Solution: If the baker finds an extra kilo of flour, the flour border would become $3x_1 + 6x_2 = 151$. It is clear from Fig. 17.1.2 that the feasible set S will expand slightly and point B will move slightly up along the butter border. The new optimal point B' will be at the intersection of the lines $3x_1 + 6x_2 = 151$ and $x_1 + x_2 = 27.5$. Solving these equations gives $x_1 = 14/3$ and $x_2 = 137/6$. The objective function attains the value $20(14/3) + 30(137/6) = 2335/3 = 775 + 10/3$. So profit rises by $10/3$.

If the baker finds an extra kilo of sugar, the feasible set will expand, but the optimal point is still at B. Recall that at the optimum in the original problem, the baker had 5.75 kilos of unused sugar. There is no extra profit.

An extra kilo of butter would give a new optimal point at the intersection of the lines $3x_1 + 6x_2 = 150$ and $x_1 + x_2 = 28.5$. Solving these equations gives $x_1 = 7$ and $x_2 = 21.5$ with $20x_1 + 30x_2 = 775 + 10$. Profit rises by 10.

These results can be summarized as follows:

(a) An extra kilo of flour would increase the optimal z by 10/3.

(b) An extra kilo of sugar would increase the optimal z by 0.

(c) An extra kilo of butter would increase the optimal z by 10.

The three numbers $u_1^* = 10/3$, $u_2^* = 0$, and $u_3^* = 10$ are related to the flour, sugar, and butter constraints, respectively. They are the *marginal* profits from an extra kilo of each ingredient. These numbers have many interesting properties we shall now explore.

Suppose (x_1, x_2) is a feasible pair in the problem, so that the three constraints in Example 17.1.1 are satisfied. Multiply the first constraint by 10/3, the second by 0, and the third by 10. Because the multipliers are all ≥ 0, the inequalities are preserved. That is,

$$(10/3)(3x_1 + 6x_2) \leq (10/3) \cdot 150$$
$$0(x_1 + 0.5x_2) \leq 0 \cdot 22$$
$$10(x_1 + x_2) \leq 10 \cdot 27.5$$

Now add all these inequalities, using the obvious fact that if $A \leq B$, $C \leq D$, and $E \leq F$, then $A+C+E \leq B+D+F$. The result is $10x_1 + 20x_2 + 10x_1 + 10x_2 \leq \frac{10}{3} \cdot 150 + 10 \cdot 27.5$, which reduces to

$$20x_1 + 30x_2 \leq 775$$

Thus, using the "magic" numbers u_1^*, u_2^*, and u_3^* defined above, we have proved that if (x_1, x_2) is any feasible pair, then the objective function has to be less than or equal to 775. Because $x_1 = 5$ and $x_2 = 22.5$ give z the value 775, we have in this way *proved algebraically* that $(5, 22.5)$ *is* the solution. ∎

The Dual Problem

The pattern revealed in the last example turns up in all linear programming problems. In fact, the numbers u_1^*, u_2^*, and u_3^* are solutions to a new LP problem called the *dual*.

Recall that the baker's problem was

$$\max 20x_1 + 30x_2 \text{ subject to } \begin{cases} 3x_1 + 6x_2 \leq 150 \\ x_1 + 0.5x_2 \leq 22 \\ x_1 + x_2 \leq 27.5 \end{cases} \quad x_1 \geq 0, x_2 \geq 0 \quad (*)$$

Suppose the baker gets tired of running the business. (After all, cakes that are this plain are unlikely to sell very fast.) Somebody else wants to take over and buy all the baker's ingredients. The baker intends to charge a price u_1 for each kilo of flour, u_2 for each kilo of sugar, and u_3 for each kilo of butter. Because one dozen A cakes requires 3 kilos of flour and 1 kilo each of sugar and butter, the baker will charge $3u_1 + u_2 + u_3$ for the ingredients needed to produce a dozen A cakes. The baker originally had a profit of 20 for each dozen A cakes, and he wants to earn at least as much from these ingredients if he quits. Hence, the baker insists that the prices (u_1, u_2, u_3) must satisfy

$$3u_1 + u_2 + u_3 \geq 20$$

Otherwise, it would be more profitable to use the ingredients himself to produce A cakes.

If the baker also wants to earn at least as much as before for the ingredients needed to produce a dozen B cakes, the requirement is

$$6u_1 + 0.5u_2 + u_3 \geq 30$$

Presumably, the entrant wants to buy the baker's resources as inexpensively as possible. The total cost of 150 kilos of flour, 22 kilos of sugar, and 27.5 kilos of butter is $150u_1 + 22u_2 + 27.5u_3$. In order to pay as little as possible while having the baker accept the offer, the entrant should suggest prices $u_1 \geq 0$, $u_2 \geq 0$, and $u_3 \geq 0$, that solve

$$\min 150u_1 + 22u_2 + 27.5u_3 \quad \text{subject to} \quad \begin{cases} 3u_1 + u_2 + u_3 \geq 20 \\ 6u_1 + 0.5u_2 + u_3 \geq 30 \end{cases} \quad (**)$$

with $u_1 \geq 0$, $u_2 \geq 0$, and $u_3 \geq 0$.

An interesting question is this: If the baker lets the entrant take over the business and solve problem (**), will the baker earn as much as before? It turns out that the answer is yes. The solution to (**) is $u_1^* = 10/3$, and $u_2^* = 0$, and $u_3^* = 10$, and the amount the baker gets for selling the resources is $150u_1^* + 22u_2^* + 27.5u_3^* = 775$, which is precisely the maximum value of the objective function in problem (*). The entrant pays for each ingredient exactly the marginal profit for that ingredient which was calculated previously. In particular, the price of sugar is zero, because the baker has more than he can use optimally.

Problem (**) is called the *dual* of problem (*). The two problems turn out to be closely related. Let us explain in general how to construct the dual of an LP problem.

The General Case

Consider the general LP problem

$$\max c_1x_1 + \cdots + c_nx_n \quad \text{subject to} \quad \begin{cases} a_{11}x_1 + \cdots + a_{1n}x_n \leq b_1 \\ \cdots\cdots\cdots\cdots\cdots\cdots \\ a_{m1}x_1 + \cdots + a_{mn}x_n \leq b_m \end{cases} \quad (1)$$

with nonnegativity constraints $x_1 \geq 0, \ldots, x_n \geq 0$.

The **dual** of (1) is the LP problem

$$\min b_1u_1 + \cdots + b_mu_m \quad \text{subject to} \quad \begin{cases} a_{11}u_1 + \cdots + a_{m1}u_m \geq c_1 \\ \cdots\cdots\cdots\cdots\cdots\cdots \\ a_{1n}u_1 + \cdots + a_{mn}u_m \geq c_n \end{cases} \quad (2)$$

with nonnegativity constraints $u_1 \geq 0, \ldots, u_m \geq 0$. Note that problem (2) is constructed using exactly the same coefficients $c_1, \ldots, c_n, a_{11}, \ldots, a_{mn}$, and $b_1, \ldots, b_m$ as in (1).

In problem (1), which we now refer to as the **primal** problem, there are n variables $x_1, \ldots, x_n$ and m constraints (disregarding the nonnegativity constraints). In the dual (2), there are m variables $u_1, \ldots, u_m$ and n constraints. Whereas the primal is a maximization problem, the dual is a minimization problem. In both problems, all variables are nonnegative.

The m constraints in the primal problem are of the "less than or equal to" type, whereas the n constraints in the dual are of the "greater than or equal to" type. The coefficients of the objective function in either problem are the right-hand side elements of the constraints in the other problem. Finally, the two matrices formed by the coefficients of the variables in the constraints in the primal and dual problems are transposes of each other, because they take the form

$$
\mathbf{A} = \begin{pmatrix} a_{11} & a_{12} & \cdots & a_{1n} \\ a_{21} & a_{22} & \cdots & a_{2n} \\ \vdots & \vdots & & \vdots \\ a_{m1} & a_{m2} & \cdots & a_{mn} \end{pmatrix} \quad \text{and} \quad \mathbf{A}' = \begin{pmatrix} a_{11} & a_{21} & \cdots & a_{m1} \\ a_{12} & a_{22} & \cdots & a_{m2} \\ \vdots & \vdots & & \vdots \\ a_{1n} & a_{2n} & \cdots & a_{mn} \end{pmatrix} \tag{3}
$$

Check carefully that problem $(**)$ is the dual of problem $(*)$ in the sense just explained. Due to the symmetry between the two problems, we call either the dual of the other.

Matrix Formulation

Let us introduce the following column vectors (matrices):

$$
\mathbf{x} = \begin{pmatrix} x_1 \\ \vdots \\ x_n \end{pmatrix}, \quad \mathbf{c} = \begin{pmatrix} c_1 \\ \vdots \\ c_n \end{pmatrix}, \quad \mathbf{b} = \begin{pmatrix} b_1 \\ \vdots \\ b_m \end{pmatrix}, \quad \mathbf{u} = \begin{pmatrix} u_1 \\ \vdots \\ u_m \end{pmatrix} \tag{4}
$$

Then the primal can be written as follows (with $\mathbf{A}$ and $\mathbf{A}'$ given by (3)):

$$
\max \mathbf{c}'\mathbf{x} \text{ subject to } \mathbf{A}\mathbf{x} \le \mathbf{b}, \ \mathbf{x} \ge \mathbf{0} \tag{5}
$$

And the dual can be written as min $\mathbf{b}'\mathbf{u}$ subject to $\mathbf{A}'\mathbf{u} \ge \mathbf{c}$, $\mathbf{u} \ge \mathbf{0}$. It is more convenient, however, to write the dual in a slightly different way. Transposing $\mathbf{A}'\mathbf{u} \ge \mathbf{c}$ using the rules in (15.5.2) yields $\mathbf{u}'\mathbf{A} \ge \mathbf{c}'$, and moreover $\mathbf{b}'\mathbf{u} = \mathbf{u}'\mathbf{b}$. So the dual can be written as

$$
\min \mathbf{u}'\mathbf{b} \text{ subject to } \mathbf{u}'\mathbf{A} \ge \mathbf{c}', \ \mathbf{u} \ge \mathbf{0} \tag{6}
$$

PROBLEMS FOR SECTION 17.2

1. Consider Problem 17.1.1(a).

    (a) Replace the constraint $3x_1 + 2x_2 \le 6$ by $3x_1 + 2x_2 \le 7$. Find the new optimal solution and compute the increase u_1^* in the objective function.

    (b) Replace the constraint $x_1 + 4x_2 \le 4$ by $x_1 + 4x_2 \le 5$. Find the new optimal solution and compute the increase u_2^* in the objective function.

    (c) By the same argument as in Example 1, prove that if (x_1, x_2) is feasible in the original problem, then the objective function can never be larger than 36/5.

2. Write down the dual to Problem 17.1.2 (b).

3. Write down the dual to Problems 17.1.1 (a) and (b).

17.3 The Duality Theorem

This section presents the main results relating the solution of an LP problem to that of its dual. We begin by considering the baker's problem yet again.

EXAMPLE 1   Consider problems (∗) and (∗∗) in Section 17.2. Suppose that (x_1, x_2) is an arbitrary feasible pair in (∗), which means that $x_1 \geq 0$, $x_2 \geq 0$, and the three $\leq$ inequalities in (∗) are satisfied. Let (u_1, u_2, u_3) be an arbitrary feasible triple in (∗∗). Multiply the $\leq$ inequalities in (∗) by the nonnegative numbers $u_1, u_2,$ and u_3, respectively, and then add the inequalities. The result is the new inequality

$$(3x_1 + 6x_2)u_1 + (x_1 + 0.5x_2)u_2 + (x_1 + x_2)u_3 \leq 150u_1 + 22u_2 + 27.5u_3$$

Rearranging the terms on the left-hand side yields

$$(3u_1 + u_2 + u_3)x_1 + (6u_1 + 0.5u_2 + u_3)x_2 \leq 150u_1 + 22u_2 + 27.5u_3 \qquad \text{(i)}$$

Similarly, we multiply the $\geq$ inequalities in (∗∗) by the nonnegative numbers x_1 and x_2, respectively, and add the results. This gives

$$(3u_1 + u_2 + u_3)x_1 + (6u_1 + 0.5u_2 + u_3)x_2 \geq 20x_1 + 30x_2 \qquad \text{(ii)}$$

From (i) and (ii) together, it follows that

$$150u_1 + 22u_2 + 27.5u_3 \geq 20x_1 + 30x_2 \qquad \text{(iii)}$$

for all feasible (x_1, x_2) in problem (∗) and for all feasible (u_1, u_2, u_3) in problem (∗∗). Thus the objective function in the dual problem is always greater than or equal to the objective function of the primal problem, whatever feasible (x_1, x_2) and (u_1, u_2, u_3) are chosen.

The inequality (iii) is valid for the feasible pair $(x_1, x_2) = (5, 22.5)$ in particular. For each feasible triple (u_1, u_2, u_3), we therefore obtain $150u_1 + 22u_2 + 27.5u_3 \geq 20 \cdot 5 + 30 \cdot 22.5 = 775$. It follows that if we can find a feasible triple (u_1^*, u_2^*, u_3^*) for problem (∗∗) such that $150u_1^* + 22u_2^* + 27.5u_3^* = 775$, then (u_1^*, u_2^*, u_3^*) must solve problem (∗∗), because no lower value of the objective function is obtainable. In Section 17.2, we saw that for $(u_1^*, u_2^*, u_3^*) = (10/3, 0, 10)$, the objective function in the dual did have the value 775. Hence, $(10/3, 0, 10)$ solves the dual problem.

The first general result we prove is the following:

THEOREM 17.3.1

If $(x_1, \ldots, x_n)$ is feasible in the primal problem (17.2.1) and $(u_1, \ldots, u_m)$ is feasible in the dual problem (17.2.2), then

$$b_1u_1 + \cdots + b_mu_m \geq c_1x_1 + \cdots + c_nx_n \qquad \text{(1)}$$

So the dual objective function has a value that is always at least as large as that of the primal.

Proof: Multiply the m inequalities in (17.2.1) by the nonnegative numbers $u_1, \ldots, u_m$, then add. Also, multiply the n inequalities in (17.2.2) by the nonnegative numbers $x_1, \ldots, x_n$, then add. These two operations yield the two inequalities

$$(a_{11}x_1 + \cdots + a_{1n}x_n)u_1 + \cdots + (a_{m1}x_1 + \cdots + a_{mn}x_n)u_m \leq b_1u_1 + \cdots + b_mu_m$$
$$(a_{11}u_1 + \cdots + a_{m1}u_m)x_1 + \cdots + (a_{1n}u_1 + \cdots + a_{mn}u_m)x_n \geq c_1x_1 + \cdots + c_nx_n$$

By rearranging the terms on the left-hand side of each inequality, we see that each is equal to the double sum $\sum_{i=1}^{m} \sum_{j=1}^{n} a_{ij}u_ix_j$. Then (1) follows immediately. ∎

From Theorem 17.3.1 we can derive another interesting result:

THEOREM 17.3.2

Suppose that $(x_1^*, \ldots, x_n^*)$ and $(u_1^*, \ldots, u_m^*)$ are feasible in problems (17.2.1) and (17.2.2), respectively, and that

$$c_1x_1^* + \cdots + c_nx_n^* = b_1u_1^* + \cdots + b_mu_m^* \tag{2}$$

Then $(x_1^*, \ldots, x_n^*)$ solves the primal problem (17.2.1) and $(u_1^*, \ldots, u_m^*)$ solves dual problem (17.2.2).

Proof: Let $(x_1, \ldots, x_n)$ be an arbitrary feasible n-vector for problem (17.2.1). Using (1) with $u_1 = u_1^*, \ldots, u_m = u_m^*$, as well as (2), yields

$$c_1x_1 + \cdots + c_nx_n \leq b_1u_1^* + \cdots + b_mu_m^* = c_1x_1^* + \cdots + c_nx_n^*$$

This proves that $(x_1^*, \ldots, x_n^*)$ solves (17.2.1).

Suppose that $(u_1, \ldots, u_m)$ is feasible for problem (17.2.2). Then (1) and (2) together imply that

$$b_1u_1 + \cdots + b_mu_m \geq c_1x_1^* + \cdots + c_nx_n^* = b_1u_1^* + \cdots + b_mu_m^*$$

This proves that $(u_1^*, \ldots, u_m^*)$ solves (17.2.2). ∎

Theorem 17.3.2 shows that if we are able to find *feasible* solutions for problems (17.2.1) and (17.2.2) that give the same value to the relevant objective function in each of the two problems, then these feasible solutions are, in fact, *optimal* solutions.

The most important result in duality theory is the following:

THEOREM 17.3.3 (THE DUALITY THEOREM)

Suppose the primal problem (17.2.1) has a (finite) optimal solution. Then the dual problem (17.2.2) also has a (finite) optimal solution, and the corresponding values of the objective functions are equal. If the primal has no bounded optimum, then the dual has no feasible solution.

The proofs of Theorems 17.3.1 and 17.3.2 were very simple. It is much more difficult to prove the first statement in Theorem 17.3.3 concerning the existence of a solution to the dual, and we shall not attempt to provide a proof here. The last statement in Theorem 17.3.3, however, follows readily from inequality (1). For if $(u_1, \ldots, u_m)$ is any feasible solution to the dual problem, then $b_1 u_1 + \cdots + b_m u_m$ is a finite number greater than or equal to *any* number $c_1 x_1 + \cdots + c_n x_n$ when $(x_1, \ldots, x_n)$ is feasible in the primal. This puts an upper bound on the possible values of $c_1 x_1 + \cdots + c_n x_n$.

NOTE 1 An instructive exercise is to formulate and prove Theorems 17.3.1 and 17.3.2 using matrix algebra. Let us do so for Theorem 17.3.1. Suppose $\mathbf{x}$ is feasible in (17.2.5) and $\mathbf{u}$ is feasible in (17.2.6). Then $\mathbf{u}'\mathbf{b} \geq \mathbf{u}'(\mathbf{Ax}) = (\mathbf{u}'\mathbf{A})\mathbf{x} \geq \mathbf{c}'\mathbf{x}$. Note carefully how these inequalities correspond to those we established in the earlier proof of Theorem 17.3.1.

PROBLEMS FOR SECTION 17.3

1. (a) Solve the following problem by a graphical argument:

$$\max 2x + 7y \text{ subject to } \begin{cases} 4x + 5y \leq 20 \\ 3x + 7y \leq 21 \end{cases} \quad x \geq 0, \ y \geq 0$$

   (b) Write down the dual and solve it by a graphical argument.

   (c) Are the values of the objective functions equal? (If not, then according to Theorem 17.3.3, you have made a mistake.)

2. Write down the dual to the problem in Example 17.1.2 and solve it. Check that the optimal values of the objective functions are equal.

3. A firm produces small and medium television sets. The profit is 400 for each small and 500 for each medium television set. Each television has to be processed in three different divisions. Each small television requires respectively 2, 1, and 1 hour in divisions 1, 2, and 3. The corresponding numbers for the medium television sets are 1, 4, and 2. Suppose divisions 1 and 2 both have a capacity of at most 16 hours per day, and division 3 has a capacity of at most 11 hours per day. Let x_1 and x_2 denote the number of small and medium television sets that are produced per day.

   (a) Show that in order to maximize profits per day, one must solve the following problem:

$$\max 400x_1 + 500x_2 \text{ subject to } \begin{cases} 2x_1 + x_2 \leq 16 \\ x_1 + 4x_2 \leq 16 \\ x_1 + 2x_2 \leq 11 \end{cases} \quad x_1 \geq 0, \ x_2 \geq 0$$

   (b) Solve this problem graphically.

   (c) If the firm could increase its capacity by 1 hour a day in just one of the three divisions, which should have its capacity increased?

17.4   A General Economic Interpretation

This section gives a general economic interpretation of the LP problem (17.2.1) and its dual (17.2.2). Think of a firm that produces one or more different kinds of output using m different **resources** as inputs. There are n different **activities** (or processes) involved in the production process. A typical activity is characterized by the fact that running it at unit level requires a certain amount of each resource. If a_{ij} is the number of units of resource i that are needed to run activity j at unit level, the vector with components $a_{1j}, a_{2j}, \ldots, a_{mj}$ expresses the m different total resource requirements for running activity j at unit level. If we run the activities at levels $x_1, \ldots, x_n$, the total resource requirement can be expressed as the column vector

$$x_1 \begin{pmatrix} a_{11} \\ \vdots \\ a_{m1} \end{pmatrix} + \cdots + x_n \begin{pmatrix} a_{1n} \\ \vdots \\ a_{mn} \end{pmatrix}$$

If the available resources are $b_1, \ldots, b_m$, then the feasible activity levels are those that satisfy the m constraints in (17.2.1). The nonnegativity constraints reflect the fact that we cannot run the activities at negative levels.

Each activity brings a certain "reward." Let c_j denote the reward (or value) earned by running activity j at unit level. The total reward from running the n activities at levels $x_1, \ldots, x_n$ is then $c_1 x_1 + \cdots + c_n x_n$. So the firm faces the problem of solving the following LP problem: *Find those levels for the n activities that maximize the total reward, subject to the given resource constraints.*

The baker's problem in Example 17.1.1 provides an illustration. The two activities are baking the two different types of cake, and there are three resources—flour, sugar, and butter.

Let us turn to the dual problem (17.2.2). In order to remain in business, the firm has to use some resources. Each resource, therefore, has a value or price. Let u_j be the price associated with one unit of resource j. Rather than think of u_j as a market price for resource j, we should think of it as measuring the relative contribution that one unit of resource j makes to the total economic reward. Because these are not real market prices, they are often called **shadow prices**.

Because $a_{1j}, a_{2j}, \ldots, a_{mj}$ are the quantities of each of the m resources needed to run activity j at unit level, $a_{1j} u_1 + a_{2j} u_2 + \cdots + a_{mj} u_m$ is the total (shadow) cost of running activity j at unit level. Because c_j is the reward earned by running activity j at unit level, the difference

$$c_j - (a_{1j} u_1 + a_{2j} u_2 + \cdots + a_{mj} u_m)$$

can be regarded as the (shadow) *profit* from running activity j at unit level. Note that the jth constraint in the dual problem (17.2.2) says that the (shadow) profit from running activity j at unit level is ≤ 0.

The objective function $Z = b_1 u_1 + \cdots + b_m u_m$ in the dual LP problem measures the (shadow) value of the initial stock of all the resources. The dual problem is, therefore, the following: *Among all choices of nonnegative shadow prices $u_1, \ldots, u_m$ such that the profit from running each activity at unit level is ≤ 0, find those prices which together minimize the (shadow) value of the initial resources.*

The Optimal Dual Variables as Shadow Prices

Consider again the primal problem

$$\max c_1 x_1 + \cdots + c_n x_n \ \text{subject to} \begin{cases} a_{11} x_1 + \cdots + a_{1n} x_n \leq b_1 \\ \cdots\cdots\cdots\cdots\cdots\cdots\cdots \\ a_{m1} x_1 + \cdots + a_{mn} x_n \leq b_m \end{cases} \quad (1)$$

with $x_1 \geq 0, \ldots, x_n \geq 0$. What happens to the optimal value of the objective function if the numbers $b_1, \ldots, b_m$ change? If the changes $\triangle b_1, \ldots, \triangle b_m$ are positive, then the feasible set increases and the new optimal value of the objective function cannot be smaller. (Usually it increases.) The following analysis also applies when some or all the changes $\triangle b_1, \ldots, \triangle b_m$ are negative.

Suppose $(x_1^*, \ldots, x_n^*)$ and $(x_1^* + \triangle x_1, \ldots, x_n^* + \triangle x_n)$ are optimal solutions to the primal problem when the right-hand sides of the constraints in (1) are respectively $(b_1, \ldots, b_m)$ and $(b_1 + \triangle b_1, \ldots, b_m + \triangle b_m)$. Typically, if $\triangle b_1, \ldots, \triangle b_m$ are all sufficiently small, the duals of the two problems have the same optimal solution $u_1^*, \ldots, u_m^*$. Then, according to Theorem 17.3.3, one has

$$c_1 x_1^* + \cdots + c_n x_n^* = b_1 u_1^* + \cdots + b_m u_m^*$$
$$c_1 (x_1^* + \triangle x_1) + \cdots + c_n (x_n^* + \triangle x_n) = (b_1 + \triangle b_1) u_1^* + \cdots + (b_m + \triangle b_m) u_m^*$$

Hence, by subtraction,

$$c_1 \triangle x_1 + \cdots + c_n \triangle x_n = u_1^* \triangle b_1 + \cdots + u_m^* \triangle b_m$$

Here the left-hand side is the change we obtain in the objective function in (1) when $b_1, \ldots, b_m$ are changed by $\triangle b_1, \ldots, \triangle b_m$, respectively. Denoting this change in z by $\triangle z^*$, we obtain

$$\triangle z^* = u_1^* \triangle b_1 + \cdots + u_m^* \triangle b_m \quad (2)$$

NOTE 1 The assumption underlying (2) is that the numbers b_j do not change enough to cause the optimal dual variables to change. If $\triangle x_j = 1$, while all $\triangle x_i = 0$ for $i \neq j$, then $\triangle z^* = u_j^*$. This accords with the results in Example 17.2.1.

PROBLEMS FOR SECTION 17.4

1. Consider Problem 17.3.1,

$$\max 2x + 7y \ \text{subject to} \begin{cases} 4x + 5y \leq 20 \\ 3x + 7y \leq 21 \end{cases} \quad x \geq 0, \ y \geq 0$$

We found that the optimal solution of this problem was $x^* = 0$ and $y^* = 3$, with $z^* = 2x^* + 7y^* = 21$. The optimal solution of the dual was $u_1^* = 0$, and $u_2^* = 1$. Suppose we change 20 to 20.1 and 21 to 20.8. What is the corresponding change in the objective function?

17.5 Complementary Slackness

Consider again the baker's problem (∗) in Section 17.2 and its dual (∗∗). The solution to (∗) was $x_1^* = 5$ and $x_2^* = 22.5$, with the first and the third inequalities both satisfied with equality. The solution to the dual was $u_1^* = 10/3$, $u_2^* = 0$, and $u_3^* = 10$, with both inequalities in the dual satisfied with equality. Thus, in this example

$$x_1^* > 0, \ x_2^* > 0 \implies \left\{ \begin{array}{l} \text{the first and second inequalities} \\ \text{in the dual are satisfied with equality} \end{array} \right.$$

$$u_1^* > 0, \ u_3^* > 0 \implies \left\{ \begin{array}{l} \text{the first and third inequalities} \\ \text{in the primal are satisfied with equality} \end{array} \right.$$

We interpret the second implication this way: Because the shadow prices of flour and butter are positive, in the optimal solution, all the available flour and butter are used. We do not use all the available sugar, so its shadow price is zero—it is not a scarce resource. Results like this hold more generally.

Indeed, first, consider the problem

$$\max c_1 x_1 + c_2 x_2 \quad \text{subject to} \quad \left\{ \begin{array}{l} a_{11} x_1 + a_{12} x_2 \le b_1 \\ a_{21} x_1 + a_{22} x_2 \le b_2 \\ a_{31} x_1 + a_{32} x_2 \le b_3 \end{array} \right. \quad x_1 \ge 0, \ x_2 \ge 0 \qquad (*)$$

and its dual

$$\min b_1 u_1 + b_2 u_2 + b_3 u_3 \quad \text{subject to} \quad \left\{ \begin{array}{l} a_{11} u_1 + a_{21} u_2 + a_{31} u_3 \ge c_1 \\ a_{12} u_1 + a_{22} u_2 + a_{32} u_3 \ge c_2 \end{array} \right. \qquad (**)$$

with u_1, u_2, and $u_3 \ge 0$. Suppose (x_1^*, x_2^*) solves (∗) whereas (u_1^*, u_2^*, u_3^*) solves (∗∗). Then

$$\text{(a)} \quad \begin{array}{l} a_{11} x_1^* + a_{12} x_2^* \le b_1 \\ a_{21} x_1^* + a_{22} x_2^* \le b_2 \\ a_{31} x_1^* + a_{32} x_2^* \le b_3 \end{array} \qquad \text{(b)} \quad \begin{array}{l} a_{11} u_1^* + a_{21} u_2^* + a_{31} u_3^* \ge c_1 \\ a_{12} u_1^* + a_{22} u_2^* + a_{32} u_3^* \ge c_2 \end{array}$$

Multiply the three inequalities in (a) by the three nonnegative numbers u_1^*, u_2^*, and u_3^*, respectively. Then add the results. This yields the inequality

$$(a_{11} x_1^* + a_{12} x_2^*) u_1^* + (a_{21} x_1^* + a_{22} x_2^*) u_2^* + (a_{31} x_1^* + a_{32} x_2^*) u_3^* \le b_1 u_1^* + b_2 u_2^* + b_3 u_3^* \quad \text{(c)}$$

Multiply the two inequalities in (b) by x_1^* and x_2^*, respectively, and then add. This gives

$$(a_{11} u_1^* + a_{21} u_2^* + a_{31} u_3^*) x_1^* + (a_{12} u_1^* + a_{22} u_2^* + a_{32} u_3^*) x_2^* \ge c_1 x_1^* + c_2 x_2^* \qquad \text{(d)}$$

Looking closely at the left-hand sides of the two inequalities in (c) and (d) reveals that they are equal. Moreover, by the duality theorem of LP (Theorem 17.3.3), the right-hand sides of (c) and (d) are equal. Hence, both inequalities in (c) and (d) can be replaced by *equalities*. Thus, replacing ≤ by = in (c) and rearranging, we obtain

$$(a_{11} x_1^* + a_{12} x_2^* - b_1) u_1^* + (a_{21} x_1^* + a_{22} x_2^* - b_2) u_2^* + (a_{31} x_1^* + a_{32} x_2^* - b_3) u_3^* = 0$$

By (a), each term in the parentheses here is ≤ 0. So because (x_1^*, x_2^*) is feasible, all three terms terms in the sum are ≤ 0. If any were < 0, their sum would be < 0. Because their sum is 0, each of them must be 0. Thus,

$$(a_{j1}x_1^* + a_{j2}x_2^* - b_j)u_j^* = 0, \quad j = 1, 2, 3$$

We conclude that

$$a_{j1}x_1^* + a_{j2}x_2^* \leq b_j \ (a_{j1}x_1^* + a_{j2}x_2^* = b_j \text{ if } u_j^* > 0), \quad j = 1, 2, 3$$

Using the fact that $\geq$ in (d) can be replaced by =, and reasoning in exactly the same way as above, we also get

$$a_{1i}u_1^* + a_{2i}u_2^* + a_{3i}u_3^* \geq c_i \ (a_{1i}u_1^* + a_{2i}u_2^* + a_{3i}u_3^* = c_i \text{ if } x_i^* > 0), \quad i = 1, 2, 3$$

These last two sets of three inequalities (or equalities) are called *complementary slackness conditions*. The arguments used to show that these conditions are necessary extend in a straightforward way to the general case. Furthermore, the same complementary slackness conditions are also sufficient for optimality. Here is a general statement and proof:

THEOREM 17.5.1 (COMPLEMENTARY SLACKNESS)

Suppose that the primal problem (17.2.1) has an optimal solution $\mathbf{x}^* = (x_1^*, \ldots, x_n^*)$, whereas the dual (17.2.2) has an optimal solution $\mathbf{u}^* = (u_1^*, \ldots, u_m^*)$. Then for $i = 1, \ldots, n$, and $j = 1, \ldots, m$,

$$a_{1i}u_1^* + \cdots + a_{mi}u_m^* \geq c_i \ (a_{1i}u_1^* + \cdots + a_{mi}u_m^* = c_i \text{ if } x_i^* > 0) \qquad (1)$$

$$a_{j1}x_1^* + \cdots + a_{jn}x_n^* \leq b_j \ (a_{j1}x_1^* + \cdots + a_{jn}x_n^* = b_j \text{ if } u_j^* > 0) \qquad (2)$$

Conversely, if $\mathbf{x}^*$ and $\mathbf{u}^*$ have all their components nonnegative and satisfy (1) and (2), then $\mathbf{x}^*$ and $\mathbf{u}^*$ solve the primal problem (17.2.1) and the dual (17.2.2), respectively.

Proof: Suppose $\mathbf{x}^*$ solves (17.2.1) and $\mathbf{u}^*$ solves (17.2.2). Then, in particular (see (17.2.5) and (17.2.6)),

$$\mathbf{Ax}^* \leq \mathbf{b} \quad \text{and} \quad (\mathbf{u}^*)'\mathbf{A} \geq \mathbf{c}' \qquad (i)$$

Multiplying the first inequality in (i) on the left by $(\mathbf{u}^*)' \geq \mathbf{0}$ and the second inequality on the right by $\mathbf{x}^* \geq \mathbf{0}$ yields

$$(\mathbf{u}^*)'\mathbf{Ax}^* \leq (\mathbf{u}^*)'\mathbf{b} \quad \text{and} \quad (\mathbf{u}^*)'\mathbf{Ax}^* \geq \mathbf{c}'\mathbf{x}^* \qquad (ii)$$

According to Theorem 17.3.3, $(\mathbf{u}^*)'\mathbf{b} = \mathbf{c}'\mathbf{x}^*$. So both inequalities in (ii) must be equalities. They can be written as

$$(\mathbf{u}^*)'(\mathbf{Ax}^* - \mathbf{b}) = 0 \quad \text{and} \quad ((\mathbf{u}^*)'\mathbf{A} - \mathbf{c}')\mathbf{x}^* = 0 \qquad (iii)$$

But these two equations are equivalent to

$$\sum_{j=1}^{m} u_j^*(a_{j1}x_1^* + \cdots + a_{jn}x_n^* - b_j) = 0 \tag{iv}$$

and

$$\sum_{i=1}^{n} (a_{1i}u_1^* + \cdots + a_{mi}u_m^* - c_i)x_i^* = 0 \tag{v}$$

For $j = 1, \ldots, m$ one has both $u_j^* \geq 0$ and $a_{j1}x_1^* + \cdots + a_{jn}x_n^* - b_j \leq 0$. So each term in the sum (iv) is ≤ 0. The sum of all the terms is 0, so there can be no negative term, because there is no positive term to cancel it. Hence, each term in the sum (iv) must be 0. Therefore,

$$u_j^*(a_{j1}x_1^* + \cdots + a_{jn}x_n^* - b_j) = 0, \qquad j = 1, \ldots, m \tag{vi}$$

Now (2) follows immediately. Property (1) is proved in the same way by noting how (v) implies that

$$x_i^*(a_{1i}u_1^* + \cdots + a_{mi}u_m^* - c_i) = 0, \qquad i = 1, \ldots, n \tag{vii}$$

Suppose on the other hand that $\mathbf{x}^*$ and $\mathbf{u}^*$ have all their components nonnegative and satisfy (1) and (2) respectively. It follows immediately that (vi) and (vii) are satisfied. So summing over j and i, respectively, we obtain (iv) and (v). These equations imply that $\sum_{j=1}^{m} b_j u_j^* = \sum_{j=1}^{m} \sum_{i=1}^{n} a_{ji} x_i^* u_j^*$ and also $\sum_{i=1}^{n} c_i x_i^* = \sum_{i=1}^{n} \sum_{j=1}^{m} a_{ji} u_j^* x_i^*$. Because the two double sums are equal, $\sum_{j=1}^{m} b_j u_j^* = \sum_{i=1}^{n} c_i x_i^*$. So according to Theorem 17.3.2, $\mathbf{x}^*$ solves problem (1) and $\mathbf{u}^*$ solves the dual. ∎

NOTE 1 Using the general economic interpretations we gave in Section 17.4, conditions (1) and (2) can be interpreted as follows:

If the optimal solution of the primal problem implies that activity i is in operation ($x_i^* > 0$), then the (shadow) profit from running that activity at unit level is 0.

If the shadow price of resource j is positive ($u_j^* > 0$), then all the available stock of resource j must be used in any optimum.

How Complementary Slackness Can Help Solve LP Problems

If the solution to either the primal or the dual problem is known, then the complementary slackness conditions can help find the solution to the other problem by determining which constraints are slack. Let us look at an example.

EXAMPLE 1   Consider the problem

$$\max 3x_1 + 4x_2 + 6x_3 \text{ subject to } \begin{cases} 3x_1 + x_2 + x_3 \leq 2 \\ x_1 + 2x_2 + 6x_3 \leq 1 \end{cases} \tag{i}$$

with $x_1 \geq 0$, $x_2 \geq 0$, and $x_3 \geq 0$. Write down the dual problem and solve it by a graphical argument. Then use complementary slackness to solve (i).

Solution: The dual problem is

$$\min 2u_1 + u_2 \quad \text{subject to} \begin{cases} 3u_1 + u_2 \geq 3 \\ u_1 + 2u_2 \geq 4 \\ u_1 + 6u_2 \geq 6 \end{cases} \quad u_1, u_2 \geq 0 \qquad (ii)$$

Using the graphical solution technique shown in Example 17.1.2, we find the solution $u_1^* = 2/5$, and $u_2^* = 9/5$. Then $3u_1^* + u_2^* = 3$, and $u_1^* + 2u_2^* = 4$, and $u_1^* + 6u_2^* > 6$.

What do we know about the solution (x_1^*, x_2^*, x_3^*) to (i)? First, because $u_1^* + 6u_2^* > 6$, the complementary slackness condition (1) implies that $x_3^* = 0$. According to (2), because $u_1^* > 0$ and $u_2^* > 0$, both inequalities in (i) are satisfied with equality. So

$$3x_1^* + x_2^* + x_3^* = 2 \quad \text{and} \quad x_1^* + 2x_2^* + 6x_3^* = 1 \qquad (iii)$$

Letting $x_3^* = 0$ in (iii) and solving for x_1^* and x_2^* gives

$$x_1^* = 3/5, \qquad x_2^* = 1/5, \qquad x_3^* = 0$$

This is the solution to problem (i). Note that the optimal values of the objective functions in the two problems are indeed equal: $2u_1^* + u_2^* = 13/5$ and $3x_1^* + 4x_2^* + 6x_3^* = 13/5$, just as they should be according to the duality theorem.

The Kuhn–Tucker Theorem Applied to Linear Programs

Consider the general linear programming problem

$$\max c_1 x_1 + \cdots + c_n x_n \quad \text{s.t.} \begin{cases} a_{11} x_1 + \cdots + a_{1n} x_n \leq b_1 \\ \cdots\cdots\cdots\cdots\cdots \\ a_{m1} x_1 + \cdots + a_{mn} x_n \leq b_m \end{cases}, \quad x_1 \geq 0, \ldots, x_n \geq 0 \quad (3)$$

This problem is obviously a special case of the general nonlinear programming problem

$$\max f(x_1, \ldots, x_n) \quad \text{s.t.} \begin{cases} g_1(x_1, \ldots, x_n) \leq c_1 \\ \cdots\cdots\cdots\cdots \\ g_m(x_1, \ldots, x_n) \leq c_m \end{cases}, \quad x_1 \geq 0, \ldots, x_n \geq 0 \quad (4)$$

that was studied in Section 14.8. Note that the functions f and g_j in (3) are all linear, so are concave as well as convex. Thus, the Lagrangian is concave and the conditions in (14.8.4) and (14.8.5) are sufficient for optimality of a vector $\mathbf{x} = (x_1, x_2, \ldots, x_n)$ satisfying the constraints specified in (3). (The proof is a rather easy generalization of the proof of Theorem 14.7.1.) Let us see what form these conditions take in the linear case.

If we let $\lambda_j = u_j$ for $j = 1, \ldots, m$, conditions (14.8.4) and (14.8.5) become

$$c_i - (a_{1i} u_1 + \cdots + a_{mi} u_m) \leq 0 \ (= 0 \text{ if } x_i > 0), \quad i = 1, \ldots, n \qquad (5)$$

$$u_j \geq 0 \ (= 0 \text{ if } a_{j1} x_1 + \cdots + a_{jn} x_n < b_j), \quad j = 1, \ldots, m \qquad (6)$$

When combined with the requirement that **x** satisfy the constraints in problem (3), these conditions are precisely the complementary slackness conditions in Theorem 17.5.1.

Duality When Some Constraints are Equalities

Suppose that one of the m constraints in the primal problem is the equality

$$a_{i1}x_1 + \cdots + a_{in}x_n = b_i \qquad (*)$$

rather than the corresponding inequality in (17.2.1). In order to put the problem into the standard form, we can replace (*) by the two inequalities

$$a_{i1}x_1 + \cdots + a_{in}x_n \leq b_i, \qquad \text{and} \qquad -a_{i1}x_1 - \cdots - a_{in}x_n \leq -b_i \qquad (**)$$

Constraint (*) thus gives rise to two dual variables u_i' and u_i''. For each $j = 1, \ldots, n$ the term $a_{ij}u_i$ in the sum on the left-hand side of the constraint $\sum_{k=1}^{m} a_{kj}u_k \geq c_j$ in (17.2.2) gets replaced by $a_{ij}u_i' - a_{ij}u_i''$. Therefore, we can replace the two variables u_i' and u_i'' with the single variable $u_i = u_i' - u_i''$, but then there is no restriction on the sign of u_i. We see that *if the ith constraint in the primal is an equality, then the ith dual variable has an unrestricted sign*. This is consistent with the economic interpretation we have given. If we are forced to use all of resource i, then it is not surprising that the resource may command a negative shadow price—it may be something that is harmful in excess. For instance, if the baker of Example 17.1.1 was forced to include all the stock of sugar in the cakes, the best point in Fig. 17.1.2 would be C, not B. Some profit would be lost.

From the symmetry between the primal and the dual, we realize now that *if one of the variables in the primal has an unrestricted sign, then the corresponding constraint in the dual is an equality*.

PROBLEMS FOR SECTION 17.5

1. Consider Problem 17.3.1. The optimal solution of the primal was $x^* = 0$, and $y^* = 3$, whereas $u_1^* = 0$, $u_2^* = 1$ was the optimal solution of the dual. Verify that (1) and (2) are satisfied in this case.

2. (a) Solve the following problem graphically:

$$\min y_1 + 2y_2 \text{ s.t.} \begin{cases} y_1 + 6y_2 \geq 15 \\ y_1 + y_2 \geq 5 \\ -y_1 + y_2 \geq -5 \\ y_1 - 2y_2 \geq -20 \end{cases} \quad y_1 \geq 0, \ y_2 \geq 0$$

(b) Write down the dual problem and solve it.

(c) What happens to the optimal dual variables if the constraint $y_1 + 6y_2 \geq 15$ is changed to $y_1 + 6y_2 \geq 15.1$?

3. A firm produces two commodities A and B. The firm has three factories that jointly produce both commodities in the amounts per hour given in the following table:

	Factory 1	Factory 2	Factory 3
Commodity A	10	20	20
Commodity B	20	10	20

The firm receives an order for 300 units of A and 500 units of B. The costs per hour of running factories 1, 2, and 3 are respectively 10 000, 8 000, and 11 000.

(a) Let y_1, y_2, and y_3, respectively, denote the number of hours for which the three factories are used. Write down the linear programming problem of minimizing the costs of fulfilling the order.

(b) Show that the dual of the problem in part (a) is

$$\max 300x_1 + 500x_2 \text{ s.t. } \begin{cases} 10x_1 + 20x_2 \le 10\,000 \\ 20x_1 + 10x_2 \le 8\,000 \\ 20x_1 + 20x_2 \le 11\,000 \end{cases} \quad x_1 \ge 0,\ x_2 \ge 0$$

Solve this problem and then find the solution of the problem in part (a).

(c) By how much will the minimum cost of production increase if the cost per hour in factory 1 increases by 100?

HARDER PROBLEMS

4. Consider the LP problem

$$\max 3x_1 + 2x_2 \text{ s.t. } \begin{cases} x_1 + x_2 \le 3 \\ 2x_1 + x_2 - x_3 \le 1 \\ x_1 + 2x_2 - 2x_3 \le 1 \end{cases} \quad x_1 \ge 0,\ x_2 \ge 0,\ x_3 \ge 0$$

(a) Suppose x_3 is a fixed number. Solve the problem if $x_3 = 0$ and if $x_3 = 3$.

(b) Solve the problem for any fixed value of x_3 in $[0, \infty)$. The maximal value of $3x_1 + 2x_2$ becomes a function of x_3. Find this function and maximize it.

(c) Do the results in part (b) say anything about the solution to the original problem, in which x_3 can also be chosen?

1. A toy manufacturer makes two games: A and B. The per unit profit margins on A and B are $30 and $20 respectively. Producing one game A takes 6 hours of processing, 4 hours of assembly and 5 hours of packing. Producing one game B takes 3 hours of processing, 6 hours of assembly and 5 hours of packing. There are 54 hours available for processing, 48 hours for assembly, and 50 hours for packing.

   (a) Formulate and solve the linear programming problem of maximizing profit subject to the given constraints.

   (b) Formulate and solve the dual problem.

2. Consider the LP problem

$$\text{min } 16y_1 + 6y_2 - 8y_3 - 15y_4 \quad \text{s.t.} \quad \begin{cases} -y_1 + y_2 - 2y_3 - 4y_4 \geq -1 \\ 2y_1 - 2y_2 - y_3 - 5y_4 \geq 1 \end{cases}$$

   where $y_i \geq 0, i = 1, 2, 3, 4$.

   (a) Write down the dual problem and solve it.

   (b) Find the solution to the primal problem.

   (c) If the first constraint in the primal is changed to $-y_1 + y_2 - 2y_3 - 4y_4 \geq k$, for what values of k will the solution of the dual occur at the same point as for $k = -1$?

3. A firm produces x_1 cars and x_2 trucks per month. Suppose each car requires 0.04% of the capacity per month in the body division, 0.025% of the capacity per month in the motor division, and 0.05% of the capacity per month on the specialized car assembly line. The corresponding numbers for trucks are 0.03% in the body division, 0.05% in the motor division, and 0.08% on the specialized truck assembly line. The firm can therefore deliver x_1 cars and x_2 trucks per month provided the following inequalities are satisfied:

$$0.04x_1 + 0.03x_2 \leq 100$$
$$0.025x_1 + 0.05x_2 \leq 100$$
$$0.05x_1 \leq 100 \qquad (*)$$
$$0.08x_2 \leq 100$$

   with $x_1 \geq 0, x_2 \geq 0$. Suppose the profit per car is $500 - ax_1$, where a is a nonnegative constant, while the profit per truck is 250. The firm thus seeks to solve the problem

$$\text{max } (500 - ax_1)x_1 + 250x_2 \quad \text{subject to } (*)$$

   (a) Solve the problem graphically if $a = 0$.

   (b) Write down conditions (14.8.4) and (14.8.5) for the problem when $a \geq 0$.

   (c) Use the conditions obtained in (b) to examine for which values of $a \geq 0$ the solution is the same as for $a = 0$.

GEOMETRY

Let no one ignorant of geometry enter this door.
—Entrance to Plato's Academy

This appendix is to remind the reader about some simple formulas and results from geometry that are occasionally useful for economists, and sometimes used in this book.

Triangles

Area: $A = \frac{1}{2}gh$

Circles

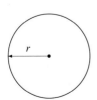

Area: $A = \pi r^2$

Circumference: $C = 2\pi r$

Area: $A = \frac{1}{2}xr$

Rectangular Box

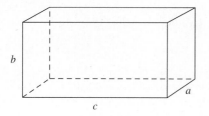

Volume: $V = abc$

Surface Area: $S = 2ab + 2ac + 2bc$

Sphere (Ball)

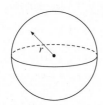

Volume: $V = \frac{4}{3}\pi r^3$

Surface Area: $S = 4\pi r^2$

Cone

Volume: $V = \frac{1}{3}\pi r^2 h$

Surface Area: $S = \pi r^2 + \pi r \sqrt{h^2 + r^2}$

Pyramid (or Tetrahedron)

Volume: $V = \frac{1}{3}a^2 h$

Surface Area: $S = a^2 + a\sqrt{a^2 + 4h^2}$

Angles

$$u = v$$

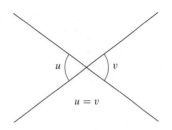

$$u = v$$

Proportions

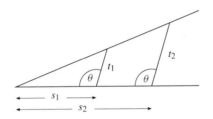

$$t_1/s_1 = t_2/s_2$$

Sum of Angles in a Triangle

$$u_1 + u_2 + u_3 = 180°$$

Pythagoras' Theorem

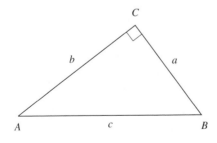

$$\angle C = 90° \iff a^2 + b^2 = c^2$$

The Greek Alphabet

A α	alpha	H η	eta	N ν	nu	T τ	tau
B β	beta	Θ θ ϑ	theta	Ξ ξ	xi	Υ υ	upsilon
Γ γ	gamma	I ι	iota	O o	omicron	Φ ϕ φ	phi
Δ δ	delta	K κ	kappa	Π π	pi	X χ	chi
E ϵ ε	epsilon	Λ λ	lambda	P ρ ϱ	rho	Ψ ψ	psi
Z ζ	zeta	M μ	mu	Σ σ	sigma	Ω ω	omega

ANSWERS TO SELECTED PROBLEMS

Chapter 1

Answers are given to all the problems in Chapter 1.

1.1

1. (a) True. (b) False. (c) False. (d) True. (e) False. (f) False. (Usually true, but not always: $\pi + (-\pi) = 0$.)
   (g) True. (h) True.

2. There is obviously no finite sequence of digits which repeats itself indefinitely, because one extra zero is added between each successive pair of ones: $1.0100100010000100001\ldots$

1.2

1. (a) $10^3 = 10 \cdot 10 \cdot 10 = 1000$ (b) $(-0.3)^2 = 0.09$ (c) $4^{-2} = 1/16$ (d) $(0.1)^{-1} = 1/0.1 = 10$

2. (a) $4 = 2^2$ (b) $1 = 2^0$ (c) $64 = 2^6$ (d) $1/16 = 2^{-4}$

3. (a) 15^3 (b) $\left(-\frac{1}{3}\right)^3$ (c) 10^{-1} (d) 10^{-7} (e) t^6 (f) $(a-b)^3$ (g) $a^2 b^4$ (h) $(-a)^3$

4. (a) $2^5 \cdot 2^5 = 2^{5+5} = 2^{10}$ (b) $3^8 \cdot 3^{-2} \cdot 3^{-3} = 3^{8-2-3} = 3^3$ (c) $(2x)^3 = 2^3 x^3 = 8x^3$
   (d) $(-3xy^2)^3 = (-3)^3 x^3 (y^2)^3 = -27x^3 y^6$

5. (a) $\dfrac{p^{24} p^3}{p^4 p} = p^{24+3-4-1} = p^{22}$ (b) $\dfrac{a^4 b^{-3}}{(a^2 b^{-3})^2} = \dfrac{a^4 b^{-3}}{a^4 b^{-6}} = a^{4-4} b^{-3-(-6)} = b^3$

   (c) $\dfrac{3^4 (3^2)^6}{(-3)^{15} 3^7} = \dfrac{3^4 3^{12}}{-3^{15} 3^7} = -3^{-6}$ (d) $\dfrac{p^\gamma (pq)^\sigma}{p^{2\gamma+\sigma} q^{\sigma-2}} = p^{-\gamma} q^2$

6. (a) $2^6 = 64$ (b) $64/27$ (c) $8/3$ (d) x^9 (e) y^{12} (f) $8x^3 y^3$ (g) $10^{-2} = 1/100$ (h) k^4 (i) $(x+1)^2$

7. Because $4\pi(3r)^2 = 4\pi 3^2 r^2 = 9(4\pi r^2)$, the surface area increases by the factor 9.

8. (a) False. $a^0 = 1$. (b) True. $c^{-n} = 1/c^n$ for all $c \neq 0$. (c) True. $a^m \cdot a^m = a^{m+m} = a^{2m}$.
   (d) False (unless $m = 0$ or $ab = 1$). $a^m b^m = (ab)^m$. (e) False (unless $m = 1$). For example, $(a+b)^2$ is equal to
   $a^2 + 2ab + b^2$. (f) False (unless $a^m b^n = 1$). For example, $a^2 b^3$ is not equal to $(ab)^{2+3} = (ab)^5 = a^5 b^5$.

9. (a) $x^3y^3 = (xy)^3 = 3^3 = 27$ (b) $(ab)^4 = (-2)^4 = 16$ (c) $(a^8)^0 = 1$ for all $a \neq 0$.
(d) $(-1)^{2n} = [(-1)^2]^n = 1^n = 1$

10. (a) $150 \cdot 0.13 = 19.5$ (b) $2400 \cdot 0.06 = 144$ (c) $200 \cdot 0.055 = 11$

11. 15% ($1.50 cheaper, which is 15% of $10.)

12. (a) Given a constant interest rate of 11% per year, then in 8 years, an initial investment of 50 dollars will be worth $50 \cdot (1.11)^8 \approx 115.23$ dollars.   (b) Given a constant interest rate of 12% per year, then in 20 years, an initial investment of 10 000 pounds will be worth $10\,000 \cdot (1.12)^{20} \approx 96\,462.93$ pounds.   (c) $5000 \cdot (1.07)^{-10} \approx 2541.75$ euros is what you should have invested 10 years ago in order to have 5000 euros today, given the constant interest rate of 7%.

13. (a) $12\,000 \cdot (1.04)^{15} \approx 21611.32$ (b) $50\,000 \cdot (1.06)^{-5} \approx 37362.91$

14. $p \approx 95.3\%$, because $(1.25)^3 = 1.953125$.

15. (a) The profit was higher in 1990. $((1 + 0.2)(1 - 0.17) = 1.2 \cdot 0.83 = 0.996$.)
(b) If the decrease in profits from 1991 to 1992 were $p\%$, then profits in 1990 and 1992 would be equal provided $1.2 \cdot (1 - p/100) = 1$, or $p = 100(1 - 1/1.2) = 100/6 \approx 16.67$.

1.3

1. (a) $x^2 + 4xy + 4y^2$ (b) $\dfrac{1}{x^2} - 2 + x^2$ (c) $9u^2 - 30uv + 25v^2$ (d) $4z^2 - 25w^2$

2. (a) $201^2 - 199^2 = (201 + 199)(201 - 199) = 400 \cdot 2 = 800$ (b) $u^2 - 4u + 4 = (u - 2)^2 = 1$ so $u - 2 = \pm 1$, and $u = 1$ or $u = 3$.

3. $1000^2/(252^2 - 248^2) = 1000^2/(252 + 248)(252 - 248) = 1000^2/500 \cdot 4 = 500$

4. (a) $(a + b)^3 = (a + b)^2(a + b) = (a^2 + 2ab + b^2)(a + b) = a^3 + 3a^2b + 3ab^2 + b^3$
(b) $(a - b)^3 = (a - b)^2(a - b) = (a^2 - 2ab + b^2)(a - b) = a^3 - 3a^2b + 3ab^2 - b^3$
(c) and (d): Expand the right-hand sides.

5. (a) 1   (b) 6   (c) -18 (d) -18 (e) $3x + 12$ (f) $45x - 27y$ (g) 3   (h) 0   (i) -1

6. (a) $3a^2 - 5b$ (b) $-2x^2 + 3x + 4y$ (c) t (d) $2r^3 - 6r^2s + 2s^3$

7. (a) $-3n^2 + 6n - 9$ (b) $x^5 + x^2$ (c) $4n^2 - 11n + 6$ (d) $-18a^3b^3 + 30a^3b^2$ (e) $a^3b - ab^3$
(f) $x^3 - 6x^2y + 11xy^2 - 6y^3$

8. (a) $acx^2 + (ad + bc)x + bd$ (b) $4 - t^4$ (c) $u^4 - 2u^2v^2 + v^4$

9. (a) $2t^3 - 5t^2 + 4t - 1$ (b) 4   (c) $x^2 + y^2 + z^2 + 2xy + 2xz + 2yz$ (d) $4xy + 4xz$

10. (a) $3 \cdot 7 \cdot xxyyy$ (b) $3(x - 3y + 9z)$ (c) $aa(a - b)$ (d) $2 \cdot 2 \cdot 2xy(xy - 2)$

11. (a) $2 \cdot 2 \cdot 7aabbb$ (b) $2 \cdot 2(x + 2y - 6z)$ (c) $2x(x - 3y)$ (d) $2aabb(3a + 2b)$ (e) $7x(x - 7y)$
(f) $5xyy(1 - 3x)(1 + 3x)$ (g) $(4 + b)(4 - b)$ (h) $3(x + 2)(x - 2)$

12. (a) $(x - 2)(x - 2)$ (b) $2 \cdot 2ts(t - 2s)$ (c) $2 \cdot 2(2a + b)(2a + b)$ (d) $5x(x + \sqrt{2}y)(x - \sqrt{2}y)$

13. (a) $(a + 2b)(a + 2b)$ (b) $KL(K - L)$ (c) $K^{-5}(K - L)$ (d) $(3z - 4w)(3z + 4w)$ (e) $-\frac{1}{5}(x - 5y)(x - 5y)$
(f) $(a^2 - b^2)(a^2 + b^2) = (a + b)(a - b)(a^2 + b^2)$

14. (a) $(5 + a)(x + y)$ (b) $(u - v + 3)(u + v)$ (c) $(P + Q)(P^2 + Q^2)$

15. (a) $KK(K - L)$ (b) $KL(L^2 + 1)$ (c) $(L + K)(L - K)$ (d) $(K - L)(K - L)$ (e) $KL(K - 2L)(K - 2L)$
(f) $K^{-6}(K^3 - 1) = K^{-6}(K - 1)(K^2 + K + 1)$ because of the answer to Problem 4(c).

1.4

1. (a) 2/7 (b) 13/12 (c) 5/24 (d) 2/25 (e) 9/5 (f) 1/2 (g) 1/2 (h) 11/27

2. (a) $3x/2$ (b) $3a/5$ (c) 1/5 (d) $\frac{1}{12}(-5x+11)$ (e) $-1/(6b)$ (f) $1/b$

3. (a) $\dfrac{5\cdot 5\cdot 13}{5\cdot 5\cdot 5\cdot 5}=\dfrac{13}{25}$ (b) $\dfrac{ab^2}{8c^2}$ (c) $\dfrac{2}{3}(a-b)$ (d) $\dfrac{P(P+Q)(P-Q)}{(P+Q)^2}=\dfrac{P(P-Q)}{P+Q}$

4. (a) 1/2 (b) 6 (c) 5/7 (d) 9/2

5. (a) $\dfrac{4}{x^2-4}$ (b) $\dfrac{21}{2(2x+1)}$ (c) $\dfrac{a}{a-3b}$ (d) $\dfrac{5a-2}{4ab(a^2-4)}$ (e) $\dfrac{-3t^2}{t+2}$ (f) $4(1-a)$

6. (a) $\dfrac{2-3x^2}{x(x+1)}$ (b) $\dfrac{-2t}{4t^2-1}$ (c) $\dfrac{7x^2+1}{x^2-4}$ (d) $x+y$ (e) $\dfrac{y^2-x^2}{y^2+x^2}$ (f) $\dfrac{y-x}{y+x}$

7. $\dfrac{-8x}{x^2+2xy-3y^2}$ **8.** (a) 400 (b) $\dfrac{-n}{n-1}$ (c) 1 (d) $\dfrac{1}{(x-1)^2}$ (e) $\dfrac{-2x-h}{x^2(x+h)^2}$ (f) $\dfrac{2x}{x-1}$

1.5

1. (a) 3 (b) 40 (c) 10 (d) 5 (e) 1/6 (f) 0.7 (g) 0.1 (h) 1/5

2. (a) = (Both expressions are equal to 20.) (b) $\neq$. In fact, $\sqrt{25+16}=\sqrt{41}\neq 9=\sqrt{25}+\sqrt{16}$. (c) $\neq$. (Put $a=b=1$.) (d) =. In fact, $(\sqrt{a+b})^{-1}=[(a+b)^{1/2}]^{-1}=(a+b)^{-1/2}$.

3. (a) 81 (b) 4 (c) 623 (d) 15 (e) -1 (f) $2^x-2^{x-1}=2^{x-1}(2-1)=2^{x-1}=4$ for $x=3$.

4. (a) $\frac{6}{7}\sqrt{7}$ (b) 4 (c) $\frac{1}{8}\sqrt{6}$ (d) 1 (e) $\frac{1}{6}\sqrt{6}$ (f) $\dfrac{2\sqrt{2y}}{y}$ (g) $\dfrac{\sqrt{2x}}{2}$ (h) $x+\sqrt{x}$

5. (a) $\frac{1}{2}(\sqrt{7}-\sqrt{5})$ (b) $4-\sqrt{15}$ (c) $-x(\sqrt{3}+2)$ (d) Multiply numerator and denominator by $x\sqrt{y}-y\sqrt{x}$:

$$\frac{x\sqrt{y}-y\sqrt{x}}{x\sqrt{y}+y\sqrt{x}}=\frac{(x\sqrt{y}-y\sqrt{x})^2}{(x\sqrt{y}+y\sqrt{x})(x\sqrt{y}-y\sqrt{x})}=\frac{x^2y-2x\sqrt{y}y\sqrt{x}+y^2x}{x^2y-y^2x}=\frac{(\sqrt{x}-\sqrt{y})^2}{x-y}$$

(e) $\sqrt{x+h}+\sqrt{x}$ (f) $\dfrac{1}{x}(2\sqrt{x+1}-x-2)$

6. (a) $\sqrt[3]{125}=5$ because $5^3=125$. (b) $(243)^{1/5}=3$ because $3^5=243$. (c) -2 (d) $\sqrt[3]{0.008}=0.2$

7. (a) $\sqrt[3]{55}\approx 3.80295$ (b) $(160)^{1/4}\approx 3.55656$ (c) $(2.71828)^{1/5}\approx 1.22140$ (d) $(1.0001)^{10000}\approx 2.718146$

8. $40(1+p/100)^{12}=60$ gives $(1+p/100)^{12}=1.5$, and therefore $1+p/100=(1.5)^{1/12}$. Solving this for p yields $p=100[(1.5)^{1/12}-1]\approx 3.44$.

9. (a) 9 (b) 1/4 (c) $16^{-2.25}=16^{-9/4}=(\sqrt[4]{16})^{-9}=2^{-9}=1/512$ (d) $(1/3^{-2})^{-2}=1/3^4=1/81$

10. (a) $3x^p y^{2q} z^{4r}$ (b) $(x+15)^{4/3-5/6}=(x+15)^{1/2}=\sqrt{x+15}$ (c) $-4x^{1/3}y^{-9/4}z^{-1}$

11. (a) $a^{1/5}$ (b) $a^{163/60}$ (c) $9a^7/2$ (d) $a^{1/4}$ **12.** (b) and (c) are valid; the others are not generally valid.

13. $x<4$ (If $x>0$, then $32x^{3/2}>4x^3$ provided $8x^{3/2}>x^3$, which is equivalent to $8>x^{3/2}$, and so $x<8^{2/3}=4$.)

1.6

1. (a), (b), (d), (f), and (h) are valid, (c), (e), and (g) are not valid.

2. (a) $x\geq -8$ (b) $x<-9$ (c) All x. (d) $x\leq 25/2$ (e) $x\leq 19/7$ (f) $t>-17/12$

3. (a) $-2 < x < 1$ (b) $x < -4$ or $x > 3$ (c) $-5 \le a \le 5$

4. (a) $-7 < x < -2$ (b) $n \ge 160$ or $n < 0$ (c) $0 \le g \le 2$ (d) $p \ge -1$ and $p \ne 2$ (e) $-4 < n < -10/3$
(f) $-1 < x < 0$ or $0 < x < 1$. (Hint: $x^4 - x^2 = x^2(x+1)(x-1)$.)

5. (a) $x > 1$ or $x < -4$ (b) $x > -4$ and $x \ne 1$ (c) $1 \le x \le 2$ (d) $x < 1$ and $x \ne 1/5$ (e) $1/5 < x < 1$
(f) $x < 0$ (g) $-3 < x < -2$ or $x > 0$ (h) $-5 \le x \le 1$ (Hint: $x^2 + 4x - 5 = (x+5)(x-1)$.)
(i) $-6 \le x \le 0$ or $x \ge 3$ (Hint: $-\frac{1}{3}x^3 - x^2 + 6x = -\frac{1}{3}x(x+6)(x-3)$.)

6. (a) $-41/6 < x \le 2/3$ (b) $x < -1/5$ (c) $-1 < x < 0$

7. (a) Yes (b) No, put $x = \frac{1}{2}$, for example. (c) No, not for $x \le 0$. (d) Yes, because the inequality is equivalent to $x^2 - 2xy + y^2 \ge 0$, or $(x-y)^2 \ge 0$, which *is* satisfied for all x and y.

8. (a) Between 39.2°F and 42.8°F. (b) Between 2.2°C and 4.4°C, approximately.

9. $\left(\sqrt{a} - \sqrt{b}\right)^2 = a - 2\sqrt{ab} + b \ge 0$ yields $a + b \ge 2\sqrt{ab}$; dividing by 2 gives $m_A \ge m_G$. Because $\left(\sqrt{a} - \sqrt{b}\right)^2 = 0$ is equivalent to $a = b$, one also has $m_A > m_G$ unless $a = b$. The inequality $m_G \ge m_H$ follows easily from the hint.

1.7

1. $|2 \cdot 0 - 3| = 3$, $|2 \cdot \frac{1}{2} - 3| = 2$, $|2 \cdot \frac{7}{2} - 3| = 4$

2. (a) $|5 - 3(-1)| = 8$, $|5 - 3 \cdot 2| = 1$, $|5 - 3 \cdot 4| = 7$ (b) $x = 5/3$ (c) $|5 - 3x| = 5 - 3x$ for $x \le 5/3$, $= 3x - 5$ for $x > 5/3$

3. (a) $x = -1$ and $x = 4$ (b) $-2 \le x \le 2$ (c) $1 \le x \le 3$ (d) $-1/4 \le x \le 1$ (e) $x > \sqrt{2}$ or $x < -\sqrt{2}$
(f) $1 \le x^2 \le 3$, i.e. $1 \le x \le \sqrt{3}$ or $-\sqrt{3} \le x \le -1$

4. (a) $4.999 < x < 5.001$ (b) $|x - 5| < 0.001$

Review Problems for Chapter 1

1. (a) $5^3 = 5 \cdot 5 \cdot 5 = 125$ (b) $10^{-3} = 1/10^3 = 1/1000$ (c) 27 (d) -1000 (e) 3 (f) 729 (g) -1 (h) -8

2. (a) 1 (b) Undefined. (c) 1 (d) 1   **3.** (a) $2^{-6} = 1/64$ (b) $\frac{3}{2} - \frac{3}{4} = \frac{3}{4}$ (c) $-45/4$ (d) 1

4. (a) $16x^4$ (b) 4 (c) $6xyz$ (d) $a^{27}b^9$ (e) a^3 (f) x^{-15} **5.** (a) $0.12 \cdot 300 = 36$ (b) 100 (c) 97.5

6. (a) Given a growth rate of 1% per year, then in 8 years, a population which was 100 million has grown to $100 \cdot (1.01)^8 \approx 108$ million. (b) Given an interest rate of 15% per year, then in 10 years, an initial investment of 50 000 yen will be worth $50\,000 \cdot (1.15)^{10} \approx 202\,277$ yen. (c) $6000 \cdot (1.03)^{-8} \approx 4736$ euros is what you should have deposited 8 years ago in order to have 6000 euros today, given the constant interest rate of 3%.

7. (a) $100\,000(1.08)^{10} \approx 215\,892$ (b) $25\,000(1.08)^{-6} \approx 15\,754$

8. (a) $a^2 - a$ (b) $x^2 + 4x - 21$ (c) $-3 + 3\sqrt{2}$ (d) $3 - 2\sqrt{2}$ (e) $x^3 - 3x^2 + 3x - 1$ (f) $1 - b^4$ (g) $1 - x^4$
(h) $x^4 + 4x^3 + 6x^2 + 4x + 1$

9. (a) $x^3y^3 = (x^{-1}y^{-1})^{-3} = 3^{-3} = 1/27$ (b) $(x^{-3})^6(x^2)^2 = x^{-18}x^4 = x^{-14} = (x^7)^{-2} = 2^{-2} = 1/4$
(c) $(z/xy)^6 = (xy/z)^{-6} = [(xy/z)^{-2}]^3 = 3^3 = 27$ (d) $(abc)^4 = (a^{-1}b^{-1}c^{-1})^{-4} = (1/4)^{-4} = 4^4 = 256$

10. (a) $5(5x - 1)$ (b) $xx(3 - xy)$ (c) $(\sqrt{50} - x)(\sqrt{50} + x)$ (d) $a(a - 2b)^2$

11. (a) $(5 + a)(x + 2y)$ (b) $(a + b)(c - d)$ (c) $(a + 2)(x + y)$ (d) $(2x - y)(x + 5z)$ (e) $(p - q)(p + q + 1)$
(f) $u^3 + v^3 - u^2v - v^2u = u^3 - u^2v + v^3 - v^2u = u^2(u - v) + v^2(v - u) = (u - v)(u^2 - v^2) = (u - v)(u - v)(u + v)$

12. (a) 2 (b) 1/3 (c) 5 (d) 1/8

13. (a) $8 = 2^3$, so $x = 3/2$ (b) $1/81 = 3^{-4}$, so $3x + 1 = -4$ or $x = -5/3$ (c) $x^2 - 2x + 2 = 2$, so $x = 0$ or $x = 2$.

14. (a) $5 + x = 3$, so $x = -2$.   (b) $3^x - 3^{x-2} = 3^{x-2}(3^2 - 1) = 3^{x-2} \cdot 8$, so $3^{x-2} = 3$, and thus $x = 3$.
(c) $3^x \cdot 3^{x-1} = 3^{2x-1} = 81 = 3^4$ provided $x = 2.5$.   (d) $3^5 + 3^5 + 3^5 = 3 \cdot 3^5 = 3^6$, so $x = 6$.
(e) $4^{-6} + 4^{-6} + 4^{-6} + 4^{-6} = 4 \cdot 4^{-6} = 4^{-5}$, so $x = -5$.   (f) $\dfrac{2^{26} - 2^{23}}{2^{26} + 2^{23}} = \dfrac{2^{23}(2^3 - 1)}{2^{23}(2^3 + 1)} = \dfrac{7}{9}$, so $x = 7$.

15. (a)$\dfrac{-2t}{4t^2 - 1}$ (b) $\dfrac{7x^2 + 1}{x^2 - 4}$ (c) $x + y$ **16.** (a) $\frac{1}{5}a^2b$ (b) $x - y$ (c) $\dfrac{2a - 3b}{2a + 3b}$ (d) $\dfrac{x(x + 2)}{2 - x}$

17. (a) $x < 13/2$ (b) $y \geq -3$ (c) Valid for all x (d) $x < 29/14$ (e) $-1 \leq x \leq 13/3$
(f) $-\sqrt{6} \leq x \leq -\sqrt{2}$ or $\sqrt{2} \leq x \leq \sqrt{6}$

18. (a) $30 + 0.16x$ (b) Smallest number of hours: 7.5. Largest number of hours: 10.

Chapter 2

Answers are given to all the problems in Chapter 2.

2.1

1. (a) $x = 5$ (b) $x = 3$ (c) $x = 6$ (d) Any x is a solution.   (e) $x = -12$ (f) $x = 1$
(g) $x = -5$. (*Hint:* $x^2 + 10x + 25 = (x + 5)^2$.)   (h) $x = -1$

2. (a) $x = 3$ (b) $x = -7$ (c) $x = -28/11$ (d) $x = 5/11$ (e) $x = 1$ (f) $x = 121$

3. (a) $x = 0$ (b) $x = -6$ (c) $x = 5$

4. (a) $2x + 5 = x - 3$. Solution: $x = -8$.   (b) With x as the smallest number, $x + (x + 1) + (x + 2) = 10 + 2x$,
so $x = 7$, and the numbers are 7, 8, and 9.   (c) If x is Jane's regular hourly wage, then $38x + (48 - 38)2x = 812$.
Solution: $x = 14$.   (d) $1500 + 12x/100 = 2100$. Solution: $x = 5000$.   (e) $\frac{2}{3}x + \frac{1}{4}x + 100\,000 = x$. Solution:
$x = 1\,200\,000$.

5. (a) $y = 17/23$ (b) $x = -4$ (c) $z = 4$ (d) $p = 15/16$

6. If x is the number of litres per minute from the slowest hose pipe, then the capacity of the pool is $60x$, while the
two other pipes deliver $2x$ and $3x$ litres per minute, respectively. The time needed to fill the pool if all hose pipes
are used is $60x/(x + 2x + 3x) = 60x/6x = 10$ minutes.

2.2

1. (i) $Y = 3000$ (ii) $Y = 7500$

2. (a) $x = \frac{1}{2}(\frac{1}{a} + \frac{1}{b})$ (b) $x = (dA - b)/(a - cA)$ (c) $x = p^2/4w^2$ (d) $x = -1/(1 + a)$ (e) $x = \pm b/a$
(f) $x = 0$

3. (a) $p = 20q/3 - 14/15$ (b) $P = (S - \alpha)/\beta$ (c) $g = 2A/h$ (d) $r = (3V/\pi)^{1/3}$ (e) $L = (Y_0 A^{-1} K^{-\alpha})^{1/\beta}$

4. (a) $x = (a - b)/(\alpha - \beta)$ (b) $p = (3q + 5)^2/q$ (c) $Y = 100$ (d) $K = (2wQ^4/r)^{1/3}$ (e) $L = rK/(2w)$
(f) $K = \frac{1}{32}p^4 r^{-3} w^{-1}$

5. (a) $s = \dfrac{tT}{T - t}$ (b) $M = \dfrac{(B + \alpha L)^2}{KL}$ (c) $z = \dfrac{4xy - x + 2y}{x + 4y}$ (d) $T = N\left(1 - \dfrac{V}{C}\right)$

2.3

1. (a) $x = 0$ and $x = 15$ (b) $p = \pm 4$ (c) $q = 3$ and $q = -4$ (d) No solution.   (e) $x = 0$ and $x = 3$
(f) $x = 2$. (Note that $x^2 - 4x + 4 = (x - 2)^2$.)

2. (a) $x^2 - 5x + 6 = (x - 2)(x - 3) = 0$ for $x = 2$ and $x = 3$ (From the equation we get $x^2 - 5x = -6$. Completing the square gives $x^2 - 5x + (5/2)^2 = (5/2)^2 - 6 = 25/4 - 6 = 1/4$, or $(x - 5/2)^2 = 1/4$. It follows that $(x - 5/2) = \pm 1/2$.)   (b) $y^2 - y - 12 = (y - 4)(y + 3) = 0$ for $y = 4$ and $y = -3$
(c) No solutions and no factorization.

(d) $-\frac{1}{4}x^2 + \frac{1}{2}x + \frac{1}{2} = -\frac{1}{4}\left[x - \left(1 + \sqrt{3}\right)\right]\left[x - \left(1 - \sqrt{3}\right)\right] = 0$ for $x = 1 \pm \sqrt{3}$

(e) $m^2 - 5m - 3 = \left[m - \frac{1}{2}\left(5 + \sqrt{37}\right)\right]\left[m - \frac{1}{2}\left(5 - \sqrt{37}\right)\right] = 0$ for $m = \frac{1}{2}\left(5 \pm \sqrt{37}\right)$

(f) $0.1p^2 + p - 2.4 = 0.1(p - 2)(p + 12) = 0$ for $p = 2$ and $p = -12$

3. (a) $r = -13, r = 2$ (b) $p = -16, p = 1$ (c) $K = 100, K = 200$ (d) $r = -\sqrt{3}, r = \sqrt{2}$
(e) $x = -0.5, x = 0.8$ (f) $p = -1/6, p = 1/4$

4. (a) $x = 1, x = 2$ (b) $t = \frac{1}{10}\left(1 \pm \sqrt{61}\right)$ (c) $x = \frac{1}{4}\left(3 \pm \sqrt{13}\right)$ (d) $x = \frac{1}{3}\left(-7 \pm \sqrt{5}\right)$ (e) $x = -300, x = 100$
(f) $x = \frac{1}{6}\left(5 \pm \sqrt{13}\right)$

5. (a) If the sides have length x and y, then $2x + 2y = 40$ and $xy = 75$. So x and y are the roots of $x^2 - 20x + 75 = 0$, which has the solutions $x = 5$ and $x = 15$.   (b) 2 and 3.   (c) The shorter side is 16 cm, the longer 30 cm.   (d) 50 km/h. (If the usual driving speed is x km/h and the usual time spent is t hours, then $xt = 80$ and $(x+10)(t-16/60) = 80$. From these equations we deduce $x^2 + 10x - 3000 = 0$, whose positive solution is $x = 50$.)

6. (a) $x = -2, \ x = 0, \ x = 2$. $(x(x^2 - 4) = 0$ or $x(x + 2)(x - 2) = 0$)   (b) $x = -2, \ x = -1, \ x = 1, \ x = 2$. (Let $x^2 = u$.)   (c) $z = -1/3, \ z = 1/5$. (Let $z^{-1} = u$.)

2.4

1. (a) $x = 8, \ y = 3$ (b) $x = 1/2, \ y = 1/3$ (c) $x = 1.1, \ y = -0.3$

2. (a) $x = 1, \ y = -1$ (b) $x = -4, \ y = 7$ (c) $x = -7/2, \ x = 10/3$

3. (a) $K = 2.8, \ L = 5.75$ (b) $p = 2, \ q = 3$ (c) $r = 2.1, \ s = 0.1$

4. (a) 39 and 13   (b) $120 for a table and $60 for a chair.   (c) 30 of quality A and 20 of quality B.
(d) $8000 at 7.2% and $2000 at 5% interest.

2.5

1. (a) $x = 0$ and $x = -3$ (b) $x = 0$ and $x = 1/2$ (c) $x = 1$ and $x = 3$ (d) $x = -5/2$ (e) No solutions.
(f) $x = 0$ and $x = -1$

2. (a) No solutions.   (b) $x = -1$ (c) $x = -3/2$ (d) $x = 0$ and $x = 1/2$

3. (a) $z = 0$ or $z = a/(1 - a - b)$ for $a + b \neq 1$. For $a + b = 1$ the only solution is $z = 0$.
(b) $\lambda = -1$ or $\mu = 0$ or $x = y$ (c) $\lambda = 0$ and $\mu \neq \pm 1$, or $\mu = 2$ (d) $a = 2$ or $b = 0$ or $\lambda = -1$

Review Problems for Chapter 2

1. (a) $x = 12$ (b) $x = 3$ (c) $x = -3/2$ (d) $x = -19$ (e) $x = 11/7$ (f) $x = 39$

2. (a) $x = 0$ (b) $x = -6$ (c) $x = 5$

3. (a) $y = \frac{3}{5}(x + 2)$ (b) $x = \dfrac{b + d}{a - c}$ (when $a \neq c$)   (c) $A^2 K^2 L = Y_0^2$, so $L = (Y_0/AK)^2$.

(d) $y = (m - px)/q$ (when $q \neq 0$)   (e) Put $s = 1/(1 + r)$. Then $s = (a + bc)/(1 - c)$, so $r = (1/s) - 1 = [(1 - a) - c(1 + b)]/(a + bc)$ (f) Multiplying by $(Px + Q)^{1/3}$ yields $Px + Px + Q = 0$, and so $x = -Q/2P$ $(P \neq 0)$.

4. (a) First insert $T = tY$ into the middle equation to get $C = b(Y - tY) = b(1 - t)Y$. Inserting this expression into the first equation yields $Y = b(1 - t)Y + \bar{I} + G$. Solving this equation for Y yields $Y = \dfrac{\bar{I} + G}{1 - b(1 - t)}$, and then $C = \dfrac{b(1 - t)(\bar{I} + G)}{1 - b(1 - t)}$.   (b) Note that $0 < b(1 - t) < 1$. When t increases, Y decreases, and so therefore must C.

5. (a) $K = 225L^{2/3}$ (b) $r = 100(2^{1/t} - 1)$ (c) $x_0 = (p/ab)^{1/(b-1)}$ (d) $(1 - \lambda)a^{-\rho} + \lambda b^{-\rho} = c^{-\rho}$ so $b = \lambda^{1/\rho}\left(c^{-\rho} - (1 - \lambda)a^{-\rho}\right)^{-1/\rho}$

6. (a) $z = 0$ or $z = 8$ (b) $x = -7$ or $x = 5$ (c) $p = -7$ or $p = 2$ (d) $p = 1/4$ or $p = 1/3$ (e) $y = 4 \pm \sqrt{31}$
(f) $x = -7$ or $x = 6$

7. (a) $x = \pm 2$ or $x = 5$ (b) $x = -4$. ($x^4 + 1$ is never 0.)   (c) $\lambda = 1$ or $x = y$

Chapter 3

3.1

1. (a) $1 + 2 + 3 + \cdots + 10 = 55$ (b) $(5 \cdot 3^0 - 2) + (5 \cdot 3^1 - 3) + (5 \cdot 3^2 - 4) + (5 \cdot 3^3 - 5) + (5 \cdot 3^4 - 6) = 585$
(c) $1 + 3 + 5 + 7 + 9 + 11 = 36$ (d) $2^{2^0} + 2^{2^1} + 2^{2^2} = 2^1 + 2^2 + 2^4 = 22$ (e) $2 \cdot 10 = 20$
(f) $2/1 + 3/2 + 4/3 + 5/4 = 73/12$

3. (a) $\displaystyle\sum_{k=1}^{n} 4k$ (b) $\displaystyle\sum_{k=1}^{n} k^3$ (c) $\displaystyle\sum_{k=0}^{n} (-1)^k \frac{1}{2k + 1}$ (d) $\displaystyle\sum_{k=1}^{n} a_{ik}b_{kj}$ (e) $\displaystyle\sum_{n=1}^{5} 3^n x^n$ (f) $\displaystyle\sum_{j=3}^{p} a_i^j b_{i+j}$ (g) $\displaystyle\sum_{k=0}^{p} a_{i+k}^{k+3} b_{i+k+3}$

(h) $\displaystyle\sum_{k=0}^{3} (81\,297 + 198k)$ **5.** (a) $\displaystyle\sum_{k=1}^{10} (k - 2)t^k = \sum_{m=-1}^{8} mt^{m+2}$ (b) $\displaystyle\sum_{n=0}^{N} 2^{n+5} = \sum_{j=1}^{N+1} 32 \cdot 2^{j-1}$

7. (a), (c), (d), and (e) are always true; (b) and (f) are generally not true. Concerning (b), note that it says that $(a_1 + a_2 + \cdots + a_n)^2 = a_1^2 + a_2^2 + \cdots + a_n^2$, which is generally false.

3.2

1. $\sum_{k=1}^{n}(k^2 + 3k + 2) = \sum_{k=1}^{n} k^2 + 3\sum_{k=1}^{n} k + \sum_{k=1}^{n} 2 = \frac{1}{6}n(n + 1)(2n + 1) + 3\left[\frac{1}{2}n(n + 1)\right] + 2n = \frac{1}{3}n(n^2 + 6n + 11)$

3. (a) In both sums, all terms cancel pairwise, except $-a_1$, the last term within the first parentheses, and a_9 (or, generally, a_n), the first term within the last parentheses.   (b) (i) $1 - (1/51) = 50/51$ (ii) $3^{13} - 3$ (iii) $ar(r^n - 1)$

5. $\sum_{i=0}^{n-1}(a + id) = \sum_{i=0}^{n-1} a + d\sum_{i=0}^{n-1} i = na + d\frac{1}{2}[1 + (n - 1)](n - 1) = na + \frac{1}{2}n(n - 1)d$. Using this formula, the sum Gauss (allegedly) computed is: $100 \cdot 81297 + \frac{1}{2}100 \cdot 99 \cdot 198 = 9\,109\,800$.

3.3

1. (a) $\displaystyle\sum_{i=1}^{3}\sum_{j=1}^{4} i \cdot 3^j = \sum_{i=1}^{3}(i \cdot 3 + i \cdot 9 + i \cdot 27 + i \cdot 81) = \sum_{i=1}^{3} 120i = 120\sum_{i=1}^{3} i = 120 \cdot 6 = 720$

(b) $\displaystyle\sum_{s=0}^{2}\sum_{r=2}^{4}\left(\frac{rs}{r + s}\right)^2 = \sum_{s=0}^{2}\left[\left(\frac{2s}{2 + s}\right)^2 + \left(\frac{3s}{3 + s}\right)^2 + \left(\frac{4s}{4 + s}\right)^2\right]$

$\qquad\qquad = \left(\frac{2}{3}\right)^2 + \left(\frac{3}{4}\right)^2 + \left(\frac{4}{5}\right)^2 + \left(\frac{4}{4}\right)^2 + \left(\frac{6}{5}\right)^2 + \left(\frac{8}{6}\right)^2 = 5 + \frac{3113}{3600}$

(c) $\frac{1}{2}m(m + 1) \cdot \frac{1}{6}n(n + 1)(2n + 1) = \frac{1}{12}m(m + 1)n(n + 1)(2n + 1)$

3. $\sum_{j=1}^{i} a_{ij}$ is the sum of all the i numbers in the ith row, so in the first double sum we sum all these m row sums. $\sum_{i=j}^{m} a_{ij}$ is the sum of all the $m - j + 1$ numbers in the jth column, so in the second double sum we sum all these m column sums.

3.4

1. (a) $2x - 4 = 2 \Longrightarrow x = 3$ (b) $x = 3 \Longrightarrow 2x - 4 = 2$ (c) $x = 1 \Longrightarrow x^2 - 2x + 1 = 0$ (d) $x^2 > 4 \Longleftrightarrow |x| > 2$

3. (a) $\Rightarrow$ true, $\Leftarrow$ false   (b) $\Rightarrow$ false, $\Leftarrow$ true   (c) $\Rightarrow$ true, $\Leftarrow$ false   (d) $\Rightarrow$ and $\Leftarrow$ both true
   (e) $\Rightarrow$ false $(0 \cdot 5 = 0 \cdot 4$, but $5 \neq 4)$, $\Leftarrow$ true   (f) $\Rightarrow$ true, $\Leftarrow$ false

5. (a) $x = 3$ (b) $x = 0$ or $x = -5$ (c) $x = -3$ or $x = 3$ (Solving the equivalent quadratic equation $|x|^2 - 2|x| - 3 = 0$ gives $|x| = 3$ or $|x| = -1$. Only $|x| = 3$ is possible.)

7. (a) Iff. (Note: $\sqrt{4}$ means 2, not ± 2.)   (b) Only if   (c) Only if   (d) Iff   (e) If   (f) Only if

9. (a) $x < 0$ or $y < 0$ (b) $x < a$ for at least one x.   (c) $x < 5$ or $y < 5$, or both. (Is it easier if the statement were: neither Ron nor Rita is less than 5 years old?) (d) There exists an $\varepsilon > 0$ such that B is not satisfied for any $\delta > 0$. (e) Someone may not like cats.   (f) Someone never loves anyone.

3.5

1. (b), (d), and (e) all express the same condition. (a) and (c) are different.

3. If x and y are *not* both odd, at least one of them must be even. If, for example, $x = 2n$, where n is an integer, then $xy = 2ny$ is also even.

3.6

1. (a) $5 \in C$, $D \subseteq C$, and $B = C$ are true. The three others are false.   (b) $A \cap B = \{2\}$, $A \cup B = \{2, 3, 4, 5, 6\}$, $A \setminus B = \{3, 4\}$, $B \setminus A = \{5, 6\}$, $(A \cup B) \setminus (A \cap B) = \{3, 4, 5, 6\}$, $A \cup B \cup C \cup D = \{2, 3, 4, 5, 6\}$, $A \cap B \cap C = \{2\}$, and $A \cap B \cap C \cap D = \emptyset$.

3. $50 - 35 = 15$ liked only coffee, $40 - 35 = 5$ liked only tea, 35 liked both, and 10 did not like either. In all there were $15 + 5 + 35 + 10 = 65$ who responded.

5. The $2^3 = 8$ subsets of $\{a, b, c\}$ are the set itself, the empty set, $\{a\}$, $\{b\}$, $\{c\}$, $\{a, b\}$, $\{a, c\}$, and $\{b, c\}$. The $2^4 = 16$ subsets of $\{a, b, c, d\}$ are the 8 preceding sets together with $\{d\}$, $\{a, d\}$, $\{b, d\}$, $\{c, d\}$, $\{a, b, d\}$, $\{a, c, d\}$, $\{b, c, d\}$, and $\{a, b, c, d\}$.

7. (a) Look at Fig. A3.6.7. $n(A \cup B)$ is the sum of the numbers of elements in (1), (2), and (3) respectively—that is, $n(A \setminus B) + n(A \cap B) + n(B \setminus A)$. But $n(A) + n(B)$ is the number of elements in (1) and (2) together, plus the number of elements in (2) and (3) together. Thus, the elements in (2) are counted twice. Hence, you must subtract $n(A \cap B)$, the number of elements in (2), to have equality.   (b) Look again at Fig. A3.6.7. $n(A \setminus B)$ is the number of elements in (1). $n(A) - n(A \cap B)$ is the number of elements in (1) and (2) together, minus the number of elements in (2). Hence, it is the number of elements in (1).

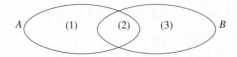

Figure A3.6.7

3.7

1. For $n = 1$, both sides are 1. Suppose ($*$) is true for $n = k$. Then $1+2+3+\cdots+k+(k+1) = \frac{1}{2}k(k+1)+(k+1) = \frac{1}{2}(k+1)(k+2)$, which is ($*$) for $n = k+1$. Thus, by induction, ($*$) is true for all n.

3. For $n = 1$, both sides are 1/2. Suppose ($*$) is true for $n = k$. Then
$$\frac{1}{1\cdot 2} + \frac{1}{2\cdot 3} + \frac{1}{3\cdot 4} + \cdots + \frac{1}{k(k+1)} + \frac{1}{(k+1)(k+2)} = \frac{k}{k+1} + \frac{1}{(k+1)(k+2)} = \frac{k(k+2)+1}{(k+1)(k+2)} =$$
$$\frac{(k+1)^2}{(k+1)(k+2)} = \frac{k+1}{k+2},$$ which is ($*$) for $n = k+1$. Thus, by induction, ($*$) is true for all n.

Review Problems for Chapter 3

1. (a) $\dfrac{1}{1\cdot 3} + \dfrac{1}{2\cdot 4} + \dfrac{1}{3\cdot 5} + \dfrac{1}{4\cdot 6} = \dfrac{17}{30}$ (b) $2^2 + 4^2 + 6^2 + 8^2 + 10^2 = 220$ (c) $\dfrac{0}{2} + \dfrac{1}{3} + \dfrac{2}{4} + \dfrac{3}{5} + \dfrac{4}{6} = \dfrac{21}{10} = 2.1$

3. (a) $\displaystyle\sum_{n=1}^{100}(2n+1)$ (b) $\displaystyle\sum_{k=1}^{96}\dfrac{k+1}{k}$

5. (a) Correct. Both sums are equal to $a_1 + a_2 + \cdots + a_n$.

   (b) Wrong, in general. $\displaystyle\sum_{i=1}^{n}(a_i + b_i)^2 = \sum_{i=1}^{n}(a_i^2 + 2a_ib_i + b_i^2) = \sum_{i=1}^{n}a_i^2 + \sum_{i=1}^{n}b_i^2 + 2\sum_{i=1}^{5}a_ib_i$.

   (c) Correct. Both sums are equal to $5a_{1,j} + 5a_{2,j} + \cdots + 5a_{n+1,j}$.

   (d) Wrong in general. $\displaystyle\sum_{i=1}^{3}\dfrac{a_i}{b_i} = \dfrac{a_1}{b_1} + \dfrac{a_2}{b_2} + \dfrac{a_3}{b_3}$, while $\dfrac{\sum_{i=1}^{3}a_i}{\sum_{i=1}^{3}b_i} = \dfrac{a_1 + a_2 + a_3}{b_1 + b_2 + b_3}$, and the two expressions are obviously not equal. (For example, put all a_i and b_i equal to 1.)

7. $A \cap B = \{1, 4\}$; $A \cup B = \{1, 3, 4, 6\}$; $A \setminus B = \{3\}$; $B \setminus A = \{6\}$; $(A \cup B) \setminus (A \cap B) = \{3, 6\}$; $A \cup B \cup C \cup D = \{1, 2, 3, 4, 5, 6\}$; $A \cap B \cap C = \{4\}$; and $A \cap B \cap C \cap D = \emptyset$.

9. (a) 100   (b) 670   (c) 95

Chapter 4

4.2

1. (a) $f(0) = 0^2 + 1 = 1$, $f(-1) = (-1)^2 + 1 = 2$, $f(1/2) = 5/4$, and $f(\sqrt{2}) = 3$ (b) (i) For all x.   (ii) When $(x+1)^2 + 1 = (x^2 + 1) + 2$, so when $x^2 + 2x + 2 = x^2 + 3$, or $2x + 2 = 3$, or $x = 1/2$.   (iii) $x = \pm\sqrt{1/2}$

3. (a) $f(0) = 0$, $f(a) = a^2$, $f(-a) = a^2 - (-a - a)^2 = -3a^2$, and $f(2a) = 0$
   (b) $3f(a) + f(-2a) = 3a^2 + [a^2 - (-2a - a)^2] = 3a^2 + a^2 - 9a^2 = -5a^2$

5. $F(0) = 2$, $F(-3) = \sqrt{19}$, $F(t+1) = \sqrt{t^2 + 3}$

7. (a) $D(8) = 4$, $D(10) = 3.4$, and $D(10.22) = 3.334$.   (b) $P = 10.9$

9. (a) $b(0) = 0$, $b(50) = 100/11$, $b(100) = 200$ (b) $b(50 + h) - b(50)$ is the additional cost of removing $h\%$ more than 50% of the impurities.

11. (a) $f(a + b) = A(a + b) = Aa + Ab = f(a) + f(b)$ (b) $f(a + b) = 10^{a+b} = 10^a \cdot 10^b = f(a) \cdot f(b)$

13. (a) $x \leq 5$ (b) $x \neq 0$ and $x \neq 1$ (c) $-3 < x \leq 1$ or $x > 2$

15. (a) $D_g = [-2, \infty)$, $R_g = (-\infty, 1]$. (The largest value of $g(x)$ is 1 for $x = -2$. As x increases from -2 to ∞, $g(x)$ decreases from 1 to $-\infty$.)

4.3

1. See Fig. A4.3.1.

Figure A4.3.1

Figure A4.3.3

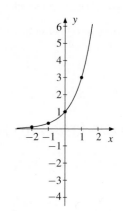

Figure A4.3.5

3.

x	0	1	2	3	4
$g(x) = -2x + 5$	5	3	1	−1	−3

See Fig. A4.3.3.

5.

x	−2	−1	0	1	2
$F(x) = 3^x$	1/9	1/3	1	3	9

See Fig. A4.3.5.

4.4

1. (a) Slope $= (8 - 3)/(5 - 2) = 5/3$ (b) $-2/3$ (c) $51/5$

3. $D = 300 - 10P$. (If $D = a + bP$, then $200 = a + 10b$, and $150 = a + 15b$. Solving for a and b yields $a = 300$ and $b = -10$.)

5. (a), (b), and (d) are all linear; (c) is not.

7. (a) L_1: $y - 3 = 2(x - 1)$ or $y = 2x + 1$ (b) L_2: $y - 2 = \dfrac{3 - 2}{3 - (-2)}[x - (-2)]$ or $y = x/5 + 12/5$
(c) L_3: $y = -x/2$ (d) L_4: $x/a + y/b = 1$, or $y = -bx/a + b$.

9. For (a), shown in Fig. A4.4.9a, the solution is $x = 3$, $y = -2$. For (b), shown in Fig. A4.4.9b, the solution is $x = 2$, $y = 0$. For (c), shown in Fig. A4.4.9c, there are no solutions, because the two lines are parallel.

Figure A4.4.9a

Figure A4.4.9b

Figure A4.4.9c

4.5

1. 0.78   **3.** The point–point formula gives $C - 200 = \dfrac{275 - 200}{150 - 100}(x - 100)$, or $C = \dfrac{3}{2}x + 50$.

5. (a) $P(t) = 20\,000 - 2000t$ (b) $W(t) = 500 - 50t$

4.6

1. (a)

x	-1	0	1	2	3	4	5
$f(x) = x^2 - 4x$	5	0	-3	-4	-3	0	5

(b) See Fig. A4.6.1.   (c) $f(x) = (x - 2)^2 - 4$. Minimum at $(2, -4)$.   (d) $x = 0$ and $x = 4$

Figure A4.6.1

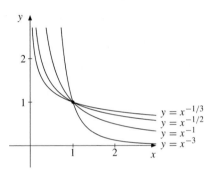

Figure A4.8.1

3. (a) $x^2 + 4x = (x + 2)^2 - 4$. Minimum -4 for $x = -2$.   (b) $x^2 + 6x + 18 = (x + 3)^2 + 9$. Minimum 9 for $x = -3$.
(c) $-3x^2 + 30x - 30 = -3(x - 5)^2 + 45$. Maximum 45 for $x = 5$.   (d) $9x^2 - 6x - 44 = 9(x - 1/3)^2 - 45$.
Minimum -45 for $x = 1/3$.   (e) $-x^2 - 200x + 30\,000 = -(x + 100)^2 + 40\,000$. Maximum 40 000 for $x = -100$.
(f) $x^2 + 100x - 20\,000 = (x + 50)^2 - 22\,500$. Minimum $-22\,500$ for $x = -50$.

5. (a) $x = 2p$ and $x = p$ (b) $x = p$ and $x = q$ (c) $x = -\frac{1}{2}p \pm \sqrt{\frac{1}{4}p^2 - q}$

7. (a) The areas when $x = 100, 250$, and 350 are $100 \cdot 400 = 40\,000$, $250 \cdot 250 = 62\,500$, and $350 \cdot 150 = 52\,500$,
respectively.   (b) The area is $A = (250 + x)(250 - x) = 62\,500 - x^2$, which obviously has its maximum for
$x = 0$. Then the rectangle is a square.

9. (a) (i) $289 \le 290$ (ii) $361 \le 377$ (b) If $B^2 - 4AC$ were > 0, then according to formula (3) the equation $f(x) = 0$
would have two distinct solutions, which is impossible when $f(x) \ge 0$ for all x. We find that $A = a_1^2 + a_2^2 + \cdots + a_n^2$,
$B = 2(a_1b_1 + a_2b_2 + \cdots + a_nb_n)$, and $C = b_1^2 + b_2^2 + \cdots + b_n^2$, so the conclusion follows easily.

4.7

1. (a) $-2, -1, 1, 3$ (b) $1, -6$ (c) none   (d) $1, 2, -2$

3. (a) $2x^2 + 2x + 4 + 3/(x - 1)$ (b) $x^2 + 1$ (c) $x^3 - 4x^2 + 3x + 1 - 4x/(x^2 + x + 1)$
(d) $3x^5 + 6x^3 - 3x^2 + 12x - 12 + (28x^2 - 36x + 13)/(x^3 - 2x + 1)$

5. (a) $x + 4$ (b) $x^2 + x + 1$ (c) $-3x^2 - 12x$ **7.** $E = \alpha\big(x - (\beta + \gamma)\big) + \dfrac{\alpha\beta(\gamma + \beta)}{x + \beta}$

4.8

1. See Fig. A4.8.1.   **3.** (a) 1.6325269   (b) 36.4621596

5. (a) $t = 3/7$ $(3^{5t}9^t = 3^{5t}(3^2)^t = 3^{5t+2t} = 3^{7t}$ and $27 = 3^3$, so $7t = 3$.)   (b) $t = -1/5$

4.9

1. The doubling time t^* is determined by $(1.0072)^{t^*} = 2$. Using a calculator, we find $t^* \approx 96.6$.

3. The amount of savings after t years: $100\,(1 + 12/100)^t = 100 \cdot (1.12)^t$.

t	1	2	5	10	20	30	50
$100 \cdot (1.12)^t$	112	125.44	176.23	310.58	964.63	2995.99	28 900.21

5. The graph is drawn in Fig. A4.9.5. We have the following table:

x	-2	-1	0	1	2
$y = \frac{1}{\sqrt{2\pi}} e^{-\frac{1}{2}x^2}$	0.05	0.24	0.40	0.24	0.05

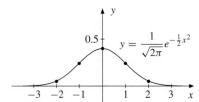

Figure A4.9.5

7. If the initial time is t, the doubling time t^* is given by the equation $Aa^{t+t^*} = 2Aa^t$, which implies $Aa^t a^{t^*} = 2Aa^t$, so $a^{t^*} = 2$, independent of t.

9. (a) $16(1.19)^5 \approx 38.18$ (b) $4.40(1.19)^{10} \approx 25.06$ (c) $250\,000(1.19)^4 \approx 501\,335$

4.10

1. (a) $\ln 9 = \ln 3^2 = 2\ln 3$ (b) $\frac{1}{2}\ln 3$ (c) $\ln \sqrt[5]{3^2} = \ln 3^{2/5} = \frac{2}{5}\ln 3$ (d) $\ln(1/81) = \ln 3^{-4} = -4\ln 3$

3. (a) $3^x 4^{x+2} = 8$ when $3^x 4^x 4^2 = 8$ or $(12)^x 4^2 = 8$, and so $12^x = 1/2$. Hence, $x = -\ln 2/\ln 12$.   (b) $\ln x^3 + \ln x^4 = 6$, or $\ln x^7 = 6$, so $7\ln x = 6$ and then $x = e^{6/7}$.   (c) $4^x(1 - 4^{-1}) = 3^x(3 - 1)$, so $(4/3)^x = 8/3$, implying that $x = \ln(8/3)/\ln(4/3)$. (Also $(4/3)^{x-1} = 2$, so an alternative correct answer is $x = 1 + \ln 2/\ln(4/3)$.)

5. (a) Wrong. (Put $A = B = C = 1$.)   (b) Correct by rule (2)(b).   (c) Correct. (Use (2)(b) twice.)   (d) Wrong. (If $A = e$ and $p = 2$, then the equality becomes $0 = \ln 2$.)   (e) Correct by (2)(c).   (f) Wrong. (Put $A = 2$, $B = C = 1$.)

7. (a) $x - x = 0$ (b) $4\ln x - x$ (c) x^2/y^2

Review Problems for Chapter 4

1. (a) $f(0) = 3$, $f(-1) = 30$, $f(1/3) = 2$, $f(\sqrt[3]{2}) = 3 - 27(2^{1/3})^3 = 3 - 27 \cdot 2 = -51$
  (b) $f(x) + f(-x) = 3 - 27x^3 + 3 - 27(-x)^3 = 3 - 27x^3 + 3 + 27x^3 = 6$.

3. $f(-x) = 3(-x) - (-x)^3 = -3x + x^3 = -(3x - x^3) = -f(x)$

5. (a) $C(0) = 100$, $C(100) = 24\,100$, $C(101) - C(100) = 24\,542 - 24\,100 = 442$.
  (b) $C(x + 1) - C(x) = 4x + 42$ is the additional cost of producing one more than x units.

7. (a) $y = -3x - 3$ (b) $y = 2x/5 + 31/5$ (c) $y = (2b/a)x - b$

9. (a) Assume $F = aC + b$. Then $32 = a \cdot 0 + b$ and $212 = a \cdot 100 + b$. Therefore $a = 180/100 = 9/5$ and $b = 32$, so $F = 9C/5 + 32$.   (b) If $X = 9X/5 + 32$, then $X = -40$.

11. (a) $\pi = \left(1000 - \frac{1}{3}Q\right)Q - \left(800 + \frac{1}{5}Q\right)Q - 100Q = 100Q - \frac{8}{15}Q^2$. Here $Q = 1500/16 = 93.75$ maximizes π.
(b) $\hat{\pi} = 100Q - \frac{8}{15}Q^2 - 10Q = 90Q - \frac{8}{15}Q^2$. So $\hat{Q} = 1350/16 = 84.375$ maximizes $\hat{\pi}$.

13. (a) $x = 160$ (b) $x = 140$ (c) $x = (p - \alpha - t)/2\beta$ if $p > \alpha + t$, $x = 0$ if $p \le \alpha + t$.

15. (a) $x^3 - x - 1$ is not 0 for $x = 1$, so the division leaves a remainder.   (b) $2x^3 - x - 1$ is 0 for $x = 1$, so the division leaves no remainder.   (c) $x^3 - ax^2 + bx - ab$ is 0 for $x = a$, so the division leaves no remainder.   (d) $x^{2n} - 1$ is 0 for $x = -1$, so the division leaves no remainder.

17. The other roots are $x = -3$ and $x = 5$.

19. The graph is drawn in Fig. A4.R.19.

x	-5	-4	-3	-2	-1	0	1
$y = x^2 e^x$	0.17	0.29	0.45	0.54	0.37	0	2.7

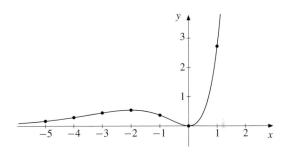

Figure A4.R.19

21. We show how to prove (c) and (d). For (c), when $x > 0$, one has $\ln(e^3 x^2) = \ln e^3 + \ln x^2 = 3 + 2\ln x$.   For (d), when $x > 0$, note that $\frac{1}{2}\ln x - \frac{3}{2}\ln(1/x) - \ln(x + 1) = \frac{1}{2}\ln x - \frac{3}{2}(-\ln x) - \ln(x + 1) = 2\ln x - \ln(x + 1) = \ln x^2 - \ln(x + 1) = \ln[x^2/(x + 1)]$.

Chapter 5

5.1

1. (a) $y = x^2 + 1$ has the graph of $y = x^2$ shifted up by 1. See Fig. A5.1.1a.   (b) $y = (x + 3)^2$ has the graph of $y = x^2$ shifted across by -3. See Fig. A5.1.1b.   (c) $y = 3 - (x + 1)^2$ has the graph of $y = x^2$ turned upside down, then with $(0, 0)$ shifted to $(-1, 3)$. See Fig. A5.1.1c.

Figure A5.1.1a

Figure A5.1.1b

Figure A5.1.1c

3. New equilibrium at $(\hat{P}^e, \hat{Q}^e) = (32, 74)$. See Fig. A5.1.3.

Figure A5.1.3

Figure A5.1.5

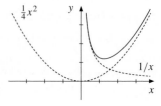

Figure A5.2.1

5. See Fig. A5.1.5.

5.2

1. See Fig. A5.2.1.

3. $(f + g)(x) = 3x$, $(f - g)(x) = 3x - 2x^3$, $(fg)(x) = 3x^4 - x^6$, $(f/g)(x) = 3/x^2 - 1$, $f(g(1)) = f(1) = 2$, and $g(f(1)) = g(2) = 8$

5. $\ln(\ln e) = \ln 1 = 0$, while $(\ln e)^2 = 1^2 = 1$.

5.3

1. $p = \frac{1}{3}(64 - 10D)$ **3.** (a) $x = -y/3$ (b) $x = 1/y$ (c) $x = y^{1/3}$ (d) $x = (y^2 + 2)^2$

5. $f(x) = x^2$ is not one-to-one over $(-\infty, \infty)$, and therefore has no inverse. Over $[0, \infty)$, f is strictly increasing and has therefore the inverse, $f^{-1}(x) = \sqrt{x}$.

7. $f^{-1}(C)$ determines the cost of C kilograms of carrots.

9. (a) $g(x) = (x^3 + 1)^{1/3}$ (b) $g(x) = \dfrac{2x + 1}{x - 1}$ (c) $g(x) = \left(1 - (x - 2)^5\right)^{1/3}$

11. We must solve $x = \frac{1}{2}(e^y - e^{-y})$ for y. Multiply the equation by e^y to get $\frac{1}{2}e^{2y} - \frac{1}{2} = xe^y$ or $e^{2y} - 2xe^y - 1 = 0$. Letting $e^y = z$ yields $z^2 - 2xz - 1 = 0$, with the solution $z = x \pm \sqrt{x^2 + 1}$. The minus sign would make z negative, so $z = e^y = x + \sqrt{x^2 + 1}$. This gives $y = \ln\left(x + \sqrt{x^2 + 1}\right)$ as the inverse function.

5.4

1. (a) Some solutions include $\left(0, \pm\sqrt{3}\right)$, $\left(\pm\sqrt{6}, 0\right)$, and $\left(\pm\sqrt{2}, \pm\sqrt{2}\right)$. See Fig. A5.4.1a.
(b) Some solutions include $(0, \pm 1)$, $\left(\pm 1, \pm\sqrt{2}\right)$, and $\left(\pm 3, \pm\sqrt{10}\right)$. See Fig. A5.4.1b.

Figure A5.4.1a

Figure A5.4.1b

Figure A5.4.3

3. The graph is in the positive quadrant, is symmetric about the line $y = x$, and includes the points $(25, 0)$, $(0, 25)$, and $(25/4, 25/4)$. See Fig. A5.4.3.

5.5

1. (a) $\sqrt{(2-1)^2 + (4-3)^2} = \sqrt{2}$ (b) $\sqrt{5}$ (c) $\frac{1}{2}\sqrt{205}$ (d) $\sqrt{x^2+9}$ (e) $2|a|$ (f) $2\sqrt{2}$

3. (a) 5.362 (b) $\sqrt{(2\pi)^2 + (2\pi - 1)^2} = \sqrt{8\pi^2 - 4\pi + 1} \approx 8.209$

5. (a) Completing the squares yield $(x+5)^2 + (y-3)^2 = 4$, so the circle has centre at $(-5, 3)$ and radius 2.
(b) $(x+3)^2 + (y-4)^2 = 12$, which has centre at $(-3, 4)$ and radius $\sqrt{12} = 2\sqrt{3}$.

7. $x^2 + y^2 + Ax + By + C = 0 \iff x^2 + Ax + y^2 + By + C = 0 \iff x^2 + Ax + \left(\frac{1}{2}A\right)^2 + y^2 + By + \left(\frac{1}{2}B\right)^2 = \frac{1}{4}(A^2 + B^2 - 4C) \iff \left(x + \frac{1}{2}A\right)^2 + \left(y + \frac{1}{2}B\right)^2 = \frac{1}{4}(A^2 + B^2 - 4C)$. The last is the equation of a circle centred at $\left(-\frac{1}{2}A, -\frac{1}{2}B\right)$ with radius $\frac{1}{2}\sqrt{A^2 + B^2 - 4C}$. If $A^2 + B^2 = 4C$, the graph consists only of the point $\left(-\frac{1}{2}A, -\frac{1}{2}B\right)$. For $A^2 + B^2 < 4C$, the solution set is empty.

5.6

1. Only (c) does not define a function. (Rectangles with different areas can have the same perimeter.)

Review Problems for Chapter 5

1. The shifts of $y = |x|$ are the same as those of $y = x^2$ in Problem 5.1.1. See Figs. A5.R.1(a)–(c).

Figure A5.R.1a

Figure A5.R.1b

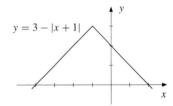

Figure A5.R.1c

3. (a) $P^* = 52$, $Q^* = 124$ (b) $S = 20 + 2(\hat{P} - 2) = 16 + 2\hat{P}$, so $S = D$ when $5\hat{P}/2 = 134$. Hence $\hat{P} = 53.6$, $\hat{Q} = 123.2$. (c) Before the tax, $R^* = P^* Q^* = 6448$. After the tax, $\hat{R} = (\hat{P} - 2)\hat{Q} = 51.6 \cdot 123.2 = 6357.12$.

5. $P = 24 - \frac{1}{5}D$ **7.** (a) $y = \ln(2 + e^{x-3})$, $x \in \mathbb{R}$. (b) $y = -\frac{1}{\lambda}\ln a - \frac{1}{\lambda}\ln\left(\frac{1}{x} - 1\right)$, $x \in (0, 1)$.

9. $(x-2)^2 + (y+3)^2 = 25$ (b) $(x+2)^2 + (y-2)^2 = 65$

11. The function cannot be one-to-one, because at least two persons out of any five must have the same blood group.

Chapter 6

6.1

1. The graph passes through $(3, 2)$, so $f(3) = 2$. The tangent passes through $(0, 3)$, so has slope $-1/3$. Thus, $f'(3) = -1/3$.

6.2

1. $f(5+h)-f(5) = 4(5+h)^2-4\cdot5^2 = 4(25+10h+h^2)-100 = 40h+4h^2$. So $[f(5+h)-f(5)]/h = 40+4h \to 40$ as $h \to 0$. Hence, $f'(5) = 40$. This accords with (6) when $a = 4$ and $b = c = 0$.

3. (a) $dD(P)/dP = -b$ (b) $C'(x) = 2qx$

5. (a) $f'(0) = 3$ (b) $f'(1) = 2$ (c) $f'(3) = -1/3$ (d) $f'(0) = -2$ (e) $f'(-1) = 0$ (f) $f'(1) = 4$

7. $f'(a) < 0$, $f'(b) = 0$, $f'(c) > 0$, $f'(d) < 0$

9. (a) $f(x+h) - f(x) = a(x+h)^3 + b(x+h)^2 + c(x+h) + d - (ax^3 + bx^2 + cx + d)$. Easy algebra then gives $[f(x+h) - f(x)]/h = 3ax^2 + 2bx + c + 3axh + ah^2 + bh$, which tends to $f'(x) = 3ax^2 + 2bx + c$ as $h \to 0$. (b) Put $a = 1$ and $b = c = d = 0$ to get the result in Example 2. Then put $a = 0$ to get a quadratic expression as in Problem 6(a).

6.3

1. $f'(x) = 2x - 4$, so $f(x)$ is increasing in $[2, \infty)$, decreasing in $(-\infty, 2]$.

3. If $x_2 > x_1$, then $x_2^3 - x_1^3 = (x_2 - x_1)\left[\left(x_1 + \frac{1}{2}x_2\right)^2 + \frac{3}{4}x_2^2\right] > 0$, since the bracket is positive. This shows that $f(x) = x^3$ is strictly increasing.

6.4

1. $C'(100) = 203$ and $C'(x) = 2x + 3$.   **3.** (a) $S'(Y) = b$ (b) $S'(Y) = 4Y + 10$

5. $\dot{x}(0) = -3$: During the first minute approximately 3 barrels are extracted.

7. (a) $R'(x) = a$, $C'(x) = 2a_1x + b_1$. $\pi'(x) = a - 2a_1x - b_1$. $\pi'(x) = 0$ when $x = (a - b_1)/(2a_1)$.
(b) $R'(x) = a - 2bx$, $C'(x) = a_1$. $\pi'(x) = a - 2bx - a_1$. $\pi'(x) = 0$ when $x = (a - a_1)/(2b)$.

6.5

1. (a) 3   (b) $-1/2$ (c) $13^3 = 2197$ (d) 40   (e) 1   (f) $-3/4$

3. (a)

x	0.9	0.99	0.999	1	1.001	1.01	1.1
$\dfrac{x^2 + 7x - 8}{x - 1}$	8.9	8.99	8.999	*	9.001	9.01	9.1

*not defined

(b) $x^2 + 7x - 8 = (x - 1)(x + 8)$, so $(x^2 + 7x - 8)/(x - 1) = x + 8 \to 9$ as $x \to 1$.

5. (a) For $h \neq 2$, $\dfrac{\frac{1}{3} - \frac{2}{3h}}{h - 2} = \dfrac{h - 2}{(h - 2)3h} = \dfrac{1}{3h}$, which tends to $1/6$ as $h \to 2$.   (b) $-\infty$ (does not exist)
(c) 2. (*Hint:* $t - 3$ is a common factor for $32t - 96$ and $t^2 - 2t - 3$.)   (d) $1/(2\sqrt{3}) = \sqrt{3}/6$. (*Hint:* Multiply numerator and denominator by $\sqrt{h+3} + \sqrt{3}$.)   (e) $-2/3$ (*Hint:* $t + 2$ is a common factor.)   (f) $1/4$ (*Hint:* $4 - x = (2 + \sqrt{x})(2 - \sqrt{x})$.)

7. (a) $x^3 - 8 = (x - 2)(x^2 + 2x + 4)$, so the limit is $1/6$.   (b) $\lim_{h\to0}[\sqrt[3]{27 + h} - 3]/h = \lim_{u\to3}(u - 3)/(u^3 - 27)$, and $u^3 - 27 = (u - 3)(u^2 + 3u + 9)$, so the limit is $1/27$.   (c) $x^n - 1 = (x - 1)(x^{n-1} + x^{n-2} + \cdots + x + 1)$, so the limit is n.

6.6

1. (a) 0   (b) $4x^3$ (c) $90x^9$ (d) 0 (Remember that π is a constant!)

3. (a) $6x^5$ (b) $33x^{10}$ (c) $50x^{49}$ (d) $28x^{-8}$ (e) x^{11} (f) $4x^{-3}$ (g) $-x^{-4/3}$ (h) $3x^{-5/2}$

5. In (1) of Section 6.2 (the definition of the derivative), choose $h = x - a$ so that $a + h$ is replaced by x, and $h \to 0$ implies $x \to a$. For $f(x) = x^2$ we get $f'(a) = 2a$.

7. (a) Let $f(x) = x^2$. Then $f'(x) = 2x$, and the limit is equal to $f'(5) = 2 \cdot 5 = 10$.
(b) Let $f(x) = x^5$. Then $f'(x) = 5x^4$, and the limit is equal to $f'(1) = 5 \cdot 1^4 = 5$.
(c) Let $f(x) = 5x^2 + 10$. Then $f'(x) = 10x$, and this is the value of the limit.

6.7

1. (a) 1 (b) $1 + 2x$ (c) $15x^4 + 8x^3$ (d) $32x^3 + x^{-1/2}$ (e) $\frac{1}{2} - 3x + 15x^2$ (f) $-21x^6$

3. (a) $-6x^{-7}$ (b) $\frac{3}{2}x^{1/2} - \frac{1}{2}x^{-3/2}$ (c) $-(3/2)x^{-5/2}$ (d) $-2/(x-1)^2$ (e) $-4x^{-5} - 5x^{-6}$ (f) $34/(2x+8)^2$
(g) $-33x^{-12}$ (h) $(-3x^2 + 2x + 4)/(x^2 + x + 1)^2$

5. $R'(P) = D(P) + PD'(P)$ **7.** (a) $y = -3x + 4$ (b) $y = x - 1$ (c) $y = (17x - 19)/4$ (d) $y = -(x-3)/9$

9. (a) $\dfrac{ad - bc}{(ct + d)^2}$ (b) $a(n + 1/2)t^{n-1/2} + nbt^{n-1}$ (c) $\dfrac{-(2at + b)}{(at^2 + bt + c)^2}$

11. If $f(x) = 1/x^n$, the quotient rule yields $f'(x) = (0 \cdot x^n - 1 \cdot nx^{n-1})/(x^n)^2 = -nx^{-n-1}$, which is the power rule.

6.8

1. (a) $dy/dx = (dy/du)(du/dx) = 20u^{4-1}\,du/dx = 20(1 + x^2)^3 2x = 40x(1 + x^2)^3$
(b) $dy/dx = (1 - 6u^5)\,(du/dx) = (-1/x^2)\big(1 - 6(1 + 1/x)^5\big)$

3. (a) $y' = -5(x^2 + x + 1)^{-6}(2x + 1)$ (b) $y' = \frac{1}{2}\big[x + (x + x^{1/2})^{1/2}\big]^{-1/2}\big(1 + \frac{1}{2}(x + x^{1/2})^{-1/2}(1 + \frac{1}{2}x^{-1/2})\big)$
(c) $y' = ax^{a-1}(px + q)^b + x^a bp(px + q)^{b-1} = x^{a-1}(px + q)^{b-1}[(a + b)px + aq]$

5. $dY/dt = F'\big(h(t)\big) \cdot h'(t)$ **7.** (i) $h'(x) = f'(x^2)2x$ (ii) $h'(x) = f'\big(x^n g(x)\big)\big(nx^{n-1}g(x) + x^n g'(x)\big)$

9. $dC/dx = q\big(25 - \frac{1}{2}x\big)^{-1/2}$

11. (a) (i) $g(5)$ is the amount accumulated if the interest rate is 5 % per year. (ii) $g'(5)$ is (very roughly) the increase in the accumulated value if the interest rate increases by 1%. ($g'(5) \approx [g(5.1) - g(5)]/0.1 \approx 154.8$ gives a better approximation.) (b) $g(p) = 1000(1 + p/100)^{10}$ is the final amount after 10 years if the interest rate was $p\%$ per year. $g(5) = 1000(1 + 5/100)^{10} \approx 1629$. Moreover, $g'(p) = 1000 \cdot 10(1 + p/100)^9 \cdot 1/100 = 100 \cdot (1 + p/100)^9$, so $g'(5) = 100 \cdot (1 + 5/100)^9 \approx 155$.

6.9

1. (a) $y'' = 20x^3 - 36x^2$ (b) $y'' = (-1/4)x^{-3/2}$ (c) $y'' = 20(1 + x^2)^8(1 + 19x^2)$

3. (a) $y'' = 18x$ (b) $Y''' = 36$ (c) $d^3z/dt^3 = -2$ (d) $f^{(4)}(1) = 84\,000$

5. $y'' = f''(x)g(x) + 2f'(x)g'(x) + f(x)g''(x), \quad y''' = f'''(x)g(x) + 3f''(x)g'(x) + 3f'(x)g''(x) + f(x)g'''(x)$

7. (a) $R = 1/2$ (b) $R = 3$ (c) $R = \rho$

9. The defence secretary: $P' < 0$. Gray: $P' \geq 0$ and $P'' < 0$.

6.10

1. (a) $y' = e^x + 2x$ (b) $y' = 5e^x - 9x^2$ (c) $y' = (1 \cdot e^x - xe^x)/e^{2x} = (1 - x)e^{-x}$
(d) $y' = [(1 + 2x)(e^x + 1) - (x + x^2)e^x]/(e^x + 1)^2 = [1 + 2x + e^x(1 + x - x^2)]/(e^x + 1)^2$
(e) $y' = -1 - e^x$ (f) $y' = x^2 e^x(3 + x)$ (g) $y' = e^x(x - 2)/x^3$ (h) $y' = 2(x + e^x)(1 + e^x)$

3. (a) $y' = -3e^{-3x}$, $y'' = 9e^{-3x}$ (b) $y' = 6x^2e^{x^3}$, $y'' = 6xe^{x^3}(3x^3 + 2)$ (c) $y' = -x^{-2}e^{1/x}$, $y'' = x^{-4}e^{1/x}(2x + 1)$
(d) $y' = 5(4x - 3)e^{2x^2 - 3x + 1}$, $y'' = 5e^{2x^2 - 3x + 1}(16x^2 - 24x + 13)$

5. (a) $y' = 2xe^{-2x}(1 - x)$. y is increasing in $[0, 1]$. (b) $y' = e^x(1 - 3e^{2x})$. y is increasing in $(-\infty, -\frac{1}{2}\ln 3]$.

(c) $y' = \dfrac{(2x + 3)e^{2x}}{(x + 2)^2}$. y is increasing in $[-3/2, \infty)$.

7. (a) $y' = 5^x \ln 5$ (b) $y' = 2^x + x2^x \ln 2 = 2^x(1 + x \ln 2)$ (c) $y' = 2x2^{x^2}(1 + x^2 \ln 2)$
(d) $y' = e^x 10^x + e^x 10^x \ln 10 = e^x 10^x(1 + \ln 10)$

6.11

1. (a) $y' = \dfrac{1}{x} + 3$, $y'' = \dfrac{-1}{x^2}$ (b) $y' = 2x - \dfrac{2}{x}$, $y'' = 2 + \dfrac{2}{x^2}$ (c) $y' = 3x^2 \ln x + x^2$, $y'' = x(6 \ln x + 5)$

(d) $y' = \dfrac{1 - \ln x}{x^2}$, $y'' = \dfrac{2 \ln x - 3}{x^3}$

3. (a) $1/(x \ln x)$ (b) $-x/(1 - x^2)$ (c) $e^x(\ln x + 1/x)$ (d) $e^{x^3}(3x^2 \ln x^2 + 2/x)$ (e) $e^x/(e^x + 1)$
(f) $(2x + 3)/(x^2 + 3x - 1)$

5. (a) $x > 1$ or $x < -1$ (that is, $|x| > 1$) (b) $x > 1$ (c) $x \neq e^e$ and $x > 1$

7. (a) (i) $y = x - 1$ (ii) $y = 2x - 1 - \ln 2$ (iii) $y = x/e$ (b) (i) $y = x$ (ii) $y = 2ex - e$ (iii) $y = -e^{-2}x - 4e^{-2}$

9. (a) $(2x)^x(1 + \ln 2 + \ln x)$ (b) $x^{\sqrt{x} - \frac{1}{2}}\left(\frac{1}{2}\ln x + 1\right)$ (c) $\frac{1}{2}\left(\sqrt{x}\right)^x(\ln x + 1)$

11. (a) Let $f(x) = e^x - (1 + x + \frac{1}{2}x^2)$. Then $f(0) = 0$ and $f'(x) = e^x - (1 + x) > 0$ for all $x > 0$, as shown in the problem. Hence $f(x) > 0$ for all $x > 0$, and the inequality follows. (b) Let $f(x) = \ln(1 + x) - \frac{1}{2}x$. Then $f(0) = 0$ and $f'(x) = 1/(x + 1) - \frac{1}{2} = (1 - x)/2(x + 1) > 0$ in $(0, 1)$, so $\ln(1 + x) > \frac{1}{2}x$ in $(0, 1)$. The other inequality is proved in the same way. (c) With $f(x) = 2(\sqrt{x} - 1) - \ln x$, $f(1) = 0$ and $f'(x) = 1/\sqrt{x} - 1/x = (\sqrt{x} - 1)/x > 0$ for $x > 1$.

Review Problems for Chapter 6

1. $[f(x + h) - f(x)]/h = [(x + h)^2 - (x + h) + 2 - x^2 + x - 2]/h = [2xh + h^2 - h]/h = 2x + h - 1 \to 2x - 1$ as $h \to 0$, so $f'(x) = 2x - 1$.

3. (a) $y' = 2$, $y'' = 0$ (b) $y' = 3x^8$, $y'' = 24x^7$ (c) $y' = -x^9$, $y'' = -9x^8$ (d) $y' = 21x^6$, $y'' = 126x^5$
(e) $y' = 1/10$, $y'' = 0$ (f) $y' = 5x^4 + 5x^{-6}$, $y'' = 20x^3 - 30x^{-7}$ (g) $y' = x^3 + x^2$, $y'' = 3x^2 + 2x$
(h) $y' = -x^{-2} - 3x^{-4}$, $y'' = 2x^{-3} + 12x^{-5}$

5. (a) $y = -6x + 3$ (b) $y = -(31/4)x + 17$ (c) $y = -(1/4)x + 1/4$

7. (a) $f'(x) = 3x^2 + 1$ (b) $g'(x) = -5w^{-6}$ (c) $h'(y) = 3y^2 - 1$ (d) $G'(x) = \dfrac{-2t^2 - 2t + 6}{(t^2 + 3)^2}$
(e) $\phi'(\xi) = (4 - 2\xi^2)/(\xi^2 + 2)^2$ (f) $F'(s) = -(s^2 + 2)/(s^2 + s - 2)^2$

9. (a) $y' = 20uu' = 20(5 - x^2)(-2x) = -40x(5 - x^2) = 40x^3 - 200x$

(b) $y' = \dfrac{1}{2\sqrt{u}} \cdot u' = \dfrac{1}{2\sqrt{1/x - 1}} \cdot \left(\dfrac{-1}{x^2}\right) = \dfrac{-1}{2x^2\sqrt{1/x - 1}}$

11. (a) $\dot{x}/x = 2\dot{a}/a + \dot{b}/b$ (b) $\dot{x}/x = \alpha\dot{a}/a + \beta\dot{b}/b$ (c) $\dot{x}/x = (\alpha + \beta)(\alpha a^{\alpha - 1}\dot{a} + \beta b^{\beta - 1}\dot{b})/(a^{\alpha} + b^{\beta})$

13. (a) $h'(L) = apL^{a-1}(L^a + b)^{p-1}$ (b) $C'(Q) = a + 2bQ$ (c) $P'(x) = ax^{1/q - 1}(ax^{1/q} + b)^{q-1}$

15. (a) Increases in $[1, \infty)$ (b) $x > 0$ (Show first that $y' = \dfrac{e^{-x}(e^{2x} - 1)}{e^x + e^{-x}}$.) (c) Increases in $(-\infty, 1]$ and in $[2, \infty)$.

Chapter 7

7.1

1. (a) Differentiating w.r.t. x yields (∗) $2xy + x^2 y' = 0$, so $y' = -2y/x = -2/x^3$. Differentiating (∗) w.r.t. x we have $2y + 2xy' + 2xy' + x^2 y'' = 0$. Inserting $y' = -2y/x$ and solving for y'' gives $y'' = 6y/x^2 = 6/x^4$.
(b) $y' = (1 + 3y)/(1 - 3x) = -5/(1 - 3x)^2$. $y'' = 6y'/(1 - 3x) = -30/(1 - 3x)^3$
(c) $y' = 6x^5/5y^4 = (6/5)x^{1/5}$, $y'' = 6x^4 y^{-4} - (144/25)x^{10}y^{-9} = (6/25)x^{-4/5}$

3. Differentiating w.r.t. x yields (∗) $4x + 6y + 6xy' + 2yy' = 0$, so $y' = -\dfrac{2x + 3y}{3x + y} = -\dfrac{8}{5}$ at $(1, 2)$. Differentiating (∗) w.r.t. x yields $4 + 6y' + 6y' + 6xy'' + 2(y')^2 + 2yy'' = 0$. Substituting $x = 1$, $y = 2$, and $y' = -8/5$ yields $y'' = 126/125$.

5. (a) $y' = \dfrac{x[a^2 - 2(x^2 + y^2)]}{y[2(x^2 + y^2) + a^2]}$ (b) From the figure, it is clear that y is not defined as a function of x near $(0, 0)$. $y' = 0$ when $x^2 + y^2 = \frac{1}{2}a^2$. Points on the curve satisfying this equality must also satisfy $x^2 - y^2 = \frac{1}{4}a^2$. Solving these equations simultaneously for x^2 and y^2 gives $x^2 = \frac{3}{8}a^2$ and $y^2 = \frac{1}{8}a^2$. Hence the points are $(\pm\frac{1}{4}a\sqrt{6}, \pm\frac{1}{4}a\sqrt{2})$, where all four sign combinations are allowed.

7.2

1. $dQ/dP = -19/P^{3/2}$

3. $D'_P < 0$ and $D'_r < 0$. Differentiating the equation w.r.t. r yields $D'_P(dP/dr) + D'_r = 0$, and so $dP/dr = -D'_r/D_P < 0$. So a rise in the interest rate depresses demand, and the price falls to compensate.

7.3

1. $f(1) = 1$ and $f'(x) = 2e^{2x-2} = 2$ for $x = 1$. So according to (3), $g'(1) = 1/f'(1) = 1/2$. The inverse function is $g(x) = 1 + \frac{1}{2}\ln x$, so $g'(x) = 1/2x = 1/2$ for $x = 1$.

3. (a) $f'(x) = e^{x-3}/(e^{x-3} + 2) > 0$ for all x, so f is strictly increasing. $f(x) \to \ln 2$ as $x \to -\infty$ and $f(x) \to \infty$ as $x \to \infty$, so the range of f is $(\ln 2, \infty)$.   (b) $g(x) = 3 + \ln(e^x - 2)$, defined on the range of f.
(c) $f'(3) = 1/g'(f(3)) = 1/3$

7.4

1. If $f(x) = \sqrt{1 + x}$, then $f'(x) = 1/(2\sqrt{1 + x})$, so $f(0) = 1$ and $f'(0) = 1/2$. Hence, (1) gives $\sqrt{1 + x} \approx 1 + \frac{1}{2}(x - 0) = 1 + \frac{1}{2}x$. See Fig. A7.4.1.

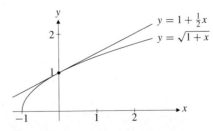

Figure A7.4.1

3. (a) $(1 + x)^{-1} \approx 1 - x$ (b) $(1 + x)^5 \approx 1 + 5x$ (c) $(1 - x)^{1/4} \approx 1 - \frac{1}{4}x$

5. (a) $30x^2\, dx$ (b) $15x^2\, dx - 10x\, dx + 5\, dx$ (c) $-3x^{-4}\, dx$ (d) $(1/x)\, dx$

7. If $f(x) = (1+x)^m$, then $f(0) = 1$ and $f'(0) = m$, so $1 + mx$ is the linear approximation to $f(x)$ about $x = 0$.
(a) $\sqrt[3]{1.1} = (1 + 1/10)^{1/3} \approx 1 + (1/3)(1/10) \approx 1.033$ (b) $\sqrt[5]{33} = 2(1 + 1/32)^{1/5} \approx 2(1 + 1/160) = 2.0125$
(c) $\sqrt[3]{9} = 2(1 + 1/8)^{1/3} \approx 2(1 + 1/24) \approx 2.083$ (d) $(0.98)^{25} = (1 - 0.02)^{25} = (1 - 1/50)^{25} \approx 1 - 1/2 = 1/2$
(e) $\sqrt{37} = (36 + 1)^{1/2} = 6(1 + 1/36)^{1/2} \approx 6(1 + 1/72) \approx 6.083$
(f) $(26.95)^{1/3} = (27 - 5/100)^{1/3} = 3(1 - 0.05/27)^{1/3} \approx 3 - 0.05/27 \approx 2.998$

9. (a) $y' = -3/2$ (Differentiation yields $3e^{xy^2} + 3xe^{xy^2}(y^2 + 2xyy') - 2y' = 6x + 2yy'$.)
(b) $y(x) \approx -\frac{3}{2}x + \frac{3}{2}$

11. $g(0) = A - 1$ and $g'(\mu) = (Aa/(1+b))(1+\mu)^{[a/(1+b)]-1}$, so $g'(0) = Aa/(1+b)$. Hence, $g(\mu) \approx g(0) + g'(0)\mu = A - 1 + \dfrac{aA}{1+b}\mu$.

7.5

1. (a) $(1+x)^5 \approx 1 + 5x + 10x^2$ (b) $AK^\alpha \approx A + \alpha A(K-1) + \frac{1}{2}\alpha(\alpha-1)A(K-1)^2$
(c) $(1 + \frac{3}{2}\varepsilon + \frac{1}{2}\varepsilon^2)^{1/2} \approx 1 + \frac{3}{4}\varepsilon - \frac{1}{32}\varepsilon^2$ (d) $(1-x)^{-1} \approx 1 + x + x^2$

3. $p(x) = -5 + \frac{5}{2}x - \frac{15}{8}x^2$

5. Implicit differentiation yields: (∗) $3x^2y + x^3y' + 1 = \frac{1}{2}y^{-1/2}y'$. Inserting $x = 0$ and $y = 1$ gives $1 = (\frac{1}{2})1^{-1/2}y'$, so $y' = 2$. Differentiating (∗) once more w.r.t. x yields $6xy + 3x^2y' + 3x^2y' + x^3y'' = -\frac{1}{4}y^{-3/2}(y')^2 + \frac{1}{2}y^{-1/2}y''$. Inserting $x = 0$, $y = 1$, and $y' = 2$ gives $y'' = 2$. Hence, $y(x) \approx 1 + 2x + x^2$.

7. Use (5) with $x = \sigma\sqrt{t/n}$, keeping only three terms on the right-hand side.

9. $h(1) = 0$ and $h'(1) = \frac{1}{2}(p-q)$, so $h(x) \approx \frac{1}{2}(p-q)(x-1)$

7.6

1. $\ln(1+x) = x - \frac{1}{2}x^2 + \frac{1}{3}x^3(1+c)^{-3}$ ($f'(x) = (1+x)^{-1}$, $f''(x) = -(1+x)^{-2}$, and $f'''(x) = 2(1+x)^{-3}$, so $f(0) = 0$, $f'(0) = 1$, $f''(0) = -1$, and $f'''(c) = 2(1+c)^{-3}$. Then use formula (3).)

3. $(1+1/8)^{1/3} = 1 + 1/24 - 1/576 + R_3(1/8)$, where $0 < R_3(1/8) < 5/(81 \cdot 8^3)$. Thus, $\sqrt[3]{9} = 2(1+1/8)^{1/3} \approx 2.080$, with three correct decimals.

7.7

1. (a) -3 (b) 100 (c) $1/2$ (d) $-3/2$

3. (a) A 10% increase in fares leads to a decrease in traffic of approximately 4%. (b) One reason could be that for long-distance travel, more people fly when rail fares go up. Another reason could be that many people may commute 60 km, whereas almost nobody commutes 300 km, and commuters' demand is likely to be less elastic.

5. $\text{El}_x(f(x))^p = \dfrac{x}{(f(x))^p}p(f(x))^{p-1}f'(x) = p\dfrac{x}{f(x)}f'(x) = p\,\text{El}_x f(x)$

7. $\ln m = -0.02 + 0.19\ln N$. When $N = 480\,000$, then $m \approx 11.77$.

9. $\text{El}_x Af(x) = \text{El}_x f(x)$, $\text{El}_x(A + f(x)) = \dfrac{f(x)\text{El}_x f(x)}{A + f(x)}$

11. (a) -5 (b) $\dfrac{1+2x}{1+x}$ (c) $\dfrac{30x^3}{x^3+1}$ (d) $\text{El}_x 5x^2 = 2$, so $\text{El}_x(\text{El}_x 5x^2) = 0$ (e) $\dfrac{2x^2}{1+x^2}$
(f) $\text{El}_x\left(\dfrac{x-1}{x^5+1}\right) = \text{El}_x(x-1) - \text{El}_x(x^5+1) = \dfrac{x\,\text{El}_x x}{x-1} - \dfrac{x^5\text{El}_x x^5}{x^5+1} = \dfrac{x}{x-1} - \dfrac{5x^5}{x^5+1}$

7.8

1. (b), (c), and (d) are continuous; only (a) is not.

3. (a) Continuous for all x.   (b) Continuous for all $x \neq 1$.   (c) Continuous for all $x < 2$.   (d) Continuous for all x.
(e) Continuous for all x where $x \neq \sqrt{3} - 1$ and $x \neq -\sqrt{3} - 1$.   (f) Continuous for all $x > 0$.

5. $a = 5$. (The straight line $y = ax - 1$ and the parabola $y = 3x^2 + 1$ must meet when $x = 1$, which is true if and only if $a = 5$.)

7.9

1. (a) -4 (b) 0 (c) 2 (d) $-\infty$ (e) ∞ (f) $-\infty$

3. $\lim_{x \to \infty} f_i(x) = \infty$ for $i = 1, 2, 3$; $\lim_{x \to \infty} f_4(x) = 0$. Then: (a) ∞ (b) 0 (c) $-\infty$ (d) 1 (e) 0 (f) ∞ (g) 1 (h) ∞

5. $y = Ax + A(b - c) + d$ is an asymptote as $x \to \infty$. ($x = -c$ is not an asymptote because $x \geq 0$.)

7.10

1. (a) Let $f(x) = x^7 - 5x^5 + x^3 - 1$. Then f is continuous, $f(-1) = 2$, and $f(1) = -4$, so according to Theorem 7.10.1, the equation $f(x) = 0$ has a solution in $(-1, 1)$. Parts (b), (c), and (d) can be shown using the same method of evaluating the sign of a suitable function at the end points of the appropriate interval.

3. Let $f(x) = x^3 - 17$. Then $f(x) = 0$ for $x = \sqrt[3]{17}$. Moreover, $f'(x) = 3x^2$. Put $x_0 = 2.5$. Then $f(x_0) = -1.375$ and $f'(x_0) = 18.75$. Formula (1) with $n = 0$ yields $x_1 = x_0 - f(x_0)/f'(x_0) = 2.5 - (-1.375)/18.75 \approx 2.573$.

5. Approximate solution: $x = 2$. Put $f(x) = (2x)^x - 15$. Then $f'(x) = (2x)^x[\ln(2x) + 1]$. Formula (1) with $n = 0$ yields $x_1 = x_0 - f(x_0)/f'(x_0) = 2 - f(2)/f'(2) = 2 - 1/[16(\ln 4 + 1)] \approx 1.9738$.

7.11

1. (a) $\alpha_n = \dfrac{(3/n) - 1}{2 - (1/n)} \to -\dfrac{1}{2}$ as $n \to \infty$ (b) $\beta_n = \dfrac{1 + (2/n) - (1/n^2)}{3 - (2/n^2)} \to \dfrac{1}{3}$ as $n \to \infty$ (c) $-1/6$ (d) $-1/6$

(e) $= -3/2$ (f) $\sqrt{(1/3) - (-1/2)} = \sqrt{5/6} = \sqrt{30}/6$

3. For a fixed number x, put $x/n = 1/m$. Then $n = mx$, and as $n \to \infty$, so $m \to \infty$. Hence $(1 + x/n)^n = (1 + 1/m)^{mx} = [(1 + 1/m)^m]^x \to e^x$ as $m \to \infty$.

7.12

1. (a) $\lim_{x \to 1} \dfrac{x - 1}{x^2 - 1} = \dfrac{\text{``0''}}{0} = \lim_{x \to 1} \dfrac{1}{2x} = \dfrac{1}{2}$

(b) $\lim_{x \to -2} \dfrac{x^3 + 3x^2 - 4}{x^3 + 5x^2 + 8x + 4} = \dfrac{\text{``0''}}{0} = \lim_{x \to -2} \dfrac{3x^2 + 6x}{3x^2 + 10x + 8} = \dfrac{\text{``0''}}{0} = \lim_{x \to -2} \dfrac{6x + 6}{6x + 10} = 3$

(c) 2 (l'Hôpital's rule is used twice.)

3. (a) 0 (Use l'Hôpital's rule.)   (b) 0 (Write $x \ln x = \dfrac{\ln x}{1/x}$, and then use l'Hôpital's rule.)

(c) $+\infty$ (Write $xe^{1/x} - x = x(e^{1/x} - 1) = (e^{1/x} - 1)/(1/x)$, and then use l'Hôpital's rule.)

5. $L = \lim_{v \to 0^+} \dfrac{1 - (1 + v^\beta)^{-\gamma}}{v} = \dfrac{\text{``0''}}{0} = \lim_{v \to 0^+} \dfrac{\gamma(1 + v^\beta)^{-\gamma - 1}\beta v^{\beta - 1}}{1}$. If $\beta = 1$, then $L = \gamma$.
If $\beta > 1$, then $L = 0$, and if $\beta < 1$, then $L = \infty$.

7. $L = \lim_{x \to a} \dfrac{f(x)}{g(x)} = \lim_{x \to a} \dfrac{1/g(x)}{1/f(x)} = \dfrac{\text{``0''}}{0} = \lim_{x \to a} \dfrac{-1/(g(x))^2}{-1/(f(x))^2} \cdot \dfrac{g'(x)}{f'(x)} = \lim_{x \to a} \dfrac{(f(x))^2}{(g(x))^2} \cdot \dfrac{g'(x)}{f'(x)} = L^2 \lim_{x \to a} \dfrac{g'(x)}{f'(x)} =$

$L^2 \lim_{x \to a} \dfrac{1}{f'(x)/g'(x)}$. Provided that $L \neq 0$, the conclusion follows. (Here, we have ignored problems with "division by 0" when either $f'(x)$ or $g'(x)$ tends to 0 as x tends to a.)

Review Problems for Chapter 7

1. (a) $y' = -5$, $y'' = 0$ (b) Differentiating w.r.t. x yields $y^3 + 3xy^2 y' = 0$, so $y' = -y/3x$. Differentiating $y' = -y/3x$ w.r.t. x yields $y'' = -[y'3x - 3y]/9x^2 = -[(-y/3x)3x - 3y]/9x^2 = 4y/9x^2$. Because $y = 5x^{-1/3}$, we get $y' = -(5/3)x^{-4/3}$ and $y'' = (20/9)x^{-7/3}$. The answers from differentiating $y = 5x^{-1/3}$ are the same. (c) $2y'e^{2y} = 3x^2$, so $y' = (3x^2/2)e^{-2y}$. Then $y'' = 3xe^{-2y} + \frac{1}{2}3x^2 e^{-2y}(-2y') = 3xe^{-2y} - \frac{1}{2}9x^4 e^{-4y}$. From the given equation we get $2y = \ln x^3 = 3\ln x$, so $y = \frac{3}{2}\ln x$, and then $y' = \frac{3}{2}x^{-1}$, $y'' = -\frac{3}{2}x^{-2}$.

3. Differentiating w.r.t. x yields $3x^2 + 3y^2 y' = 3y + 3xy'$. When $x = y = 3/2$, then $y' = -1$. See Fig. A7.R.3.

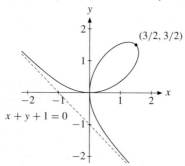

Figure A7.R.3

5. $(1/3)K^{-2/3}L^{1/3} + (1/3)K^{1/3}L^{-2/3}(dL/dK) = 0$, so $dL/dK = -L/K$.

7. (a) $D_f = (-1, 1)$, $R_f = (-\infty, \infty)$. (b) $f'(x) = 1/(1 - x^2) > 0$, so f is strictly increasing, and therefore has an inverse g. In fact, $g(y) = (e^{2y} - 1)/(e^{2y} + 1)$. Then $g'(\frac{1}{2}\ln 3) = 1/f'(\frac{1}{2}) = 3/4$ and $g'(y) = 4e^{2y}/(e^{2y} + 1)^2 = 3/4$ for $y = \frac{1}{2}\ln 3$.

9. (a) $f(x) \approx \ln 4 + \frac{1}{2}x$ (b) $g(x) \approx 1 - \frac{1}{2}x$ (c) $h(x) \approx x$

11. $df(x) = f'(x)\,dx = \dfrac{3x^2}{2\sqrt{1 + x^3}}\,dx$. Moreover, $\Delta f(2) \approx df(2) = \dfrac{3 \cdot 2^2}{2\sqrt{1 + 2^3}}(0.2) = 0.4$

13. (a) $f(x) \approx \ln 4 + \frac{1}{2}x - \frac{1}{8}x^2$ (b) $g(x) \approx 1 - \frac{1}{2}x + \frac{3}{8}x^2$ (c) $h(x) \approx x + 2x^2$

15. (a) For all $x \neq 0$. (b) Continuous for all $x > 0$. ($x^2 + 2x + 2$ is never 0.) (c) Continuous for all $x \in (-2, 2)$.

17. (a) 5 (b) 1/3 (c) $(5x^2 + 3)/(x^2 + 1)$ (d) $2x/(x^2 - 1)$

19. f is continuous, $f(1) = e - 3 < 0$ and $f(4) = e^2 - 3 > 0$. Thus, according to Theorem 7.10.1, there is a zero for f in $(1, 4)$. Because $f'(x) > 0$, the solution is unique. Formula (7.10.1) yields $x_1 = 1 - f(1)/f'(1) = 1 - (e - 3)/\frac{1}{2}e = -1 + 6/e \approx 1.21$.

21. (a) $-1/6$. (We need to use l'Hôpital's rule three times.) (b) 1/5 (Make a common denominator.) (c) 1/16

23. (a) $-1/2$ (b) 3/8 (c) $\lim_{x \to 1} \dfrac{x^x - x}{1 - x + \ln x} = \dfrac{\text{``0''}}{0} = \lim_{x \to 1} \dfrac{x^x(\ln x + 1) - 1}{-1 + 1/x} = \dfrac{\text{``0''}}{0} = \lim_{x \to 1} \dfrac{x^x(\ln x + 1)^2 + x^x(1/x)}{-1/x^2} =$

$\dfrac{1 + 1}{-1} = -2$ (using Example 6.11.4).

25. $\dfrac{1}{a - b}\ln\dfrac{a}{b}$

Chapter 8

8.1

1. (a) Maximum 2 at $x = 0$. No minimum. ($f(x) \to 0$ as $x \to \pm\infty$, but $f(x)$ is never *equal* to 0.) (b) Minimum -3 at $x = -2$. No maximum. (c) Maximum 1 at $x = 0$. Minimum 1/2 at $x = \pm 1$.

8.2

1. $y' = 1.06 - 0.08x$. So y has a maximum at $x = 1.06/0.08 = 13.25$. ($y' > 0$ for $x < 13.25$ and $y' < 0$ for $x > 13.25$.)

3. The plant is highest after 1 month, when it is 1/2 metre tall.

5. g has a minimum at $x = e^{-1/3}$, but has no maximum.

7. $y' = xe^{-x}(2 - x)$ is positive in $(0, 2)$ and negative in $(2, 4)$, so y has a maximum $4e^{-2} \approx 0.54$ at $x = 2$.

9. $d'(x) = 2(x - a_1) + 2(x - a_2) + \cdots + 2(x - a_n) = 2[nx - (a_1 + a_2 + \cdots + a_n)]$. So $d'(x) = 0$ for $x = \bar{x}$, where $\bar{x} = \frac{1}{n}(a_1 + a_2 + \cdots + a_n)$, the *arithmetic mean* of $a_1, a_2, \ldots, a_n$. Since $d''(x) = 2n > 0$, $\bar{x}$ minimizes $d(x)$. (Theorem 8.2.2.)

8.3

1. (a) The profit function is $\pi(L) = 160Q - 40L = 160 \cdot 2L^{1/2} - 40L = 320L^{1/2} - 40L$, $L \geq 0$. $\pi'(L) = 160L^{-1/2} - 40 = 0 \iff L^{1/2} = 4$. Hence $L = 16$. Because $\pi'(L) > 0$ for $0 \leq L < 16$ and $\pi'(L) < 0$ for $L > 16$, $L = 16$ maximizes profits. (b) The profit function is $\pi(L) = f(L) - wL$, so the first-order condition is $\pi'(L^*) = f'(L^*) - w = 0$. (c) The first-order condition in (b) defines L^* as a function of w. Differentiating w.r.t. w yields $f''(L^*)\dfrac{\partial L^*}{\partial w} - 1 = 0$, or $\dfrac{\partial L^*}{\partial w} = \dfrac{1}{f''(L^*)} < 0$. (If the price of labour increases, the optimal labour input decreases.)

3. See Figs. A8.3.1a and A8.3.1b. The volume in cm^3 is as given. $V'(x) = 12(x - 3)(x - 9)$. V has maximum 432 at $x = 3$. The box has maximum volume when the square cut out from each corner has sides of length 3 cm.

Figure A8.3.1a

Figure A8.3.1b

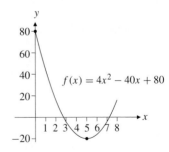

Figure A8.4.1

5. $\overline{T}'(W) = a(bW + c)^{p-1}(pbW - bW - c)/W^2$, which is 0 for $W^* = c/b(p - 1)$. This must be the minimum point because $\overline{T}'(W)$ is negative for $W < W^*$ and positive for $W > W^*$.

8.4

1. $f'(x) = 8x - 40 = 0$ for $x = 5$. $f(0) = 80$, $f(5) = -20$, and $f(8) = 16$. Maximum 80 for $x = 0$. Minimum -20 for $x = 5$. See Fig. A8.4.1.

3. (a) Total commission is, respectively, $\$4819$, $\$4900$, $\$4800$, and $C = \frac{1}{10}(60+x)(800-10x) = 4800 + 20x - x^2$, $x \in [0, 20]$.   (b) Maximum commission is with 70 travellers ($x = 10$).

5. (a) $f(x) = \ln x (\ln x - 1)^2$. $f(e^{1/3}) = 4/27$, $f(e^2) = 2$, $f(e^3) = 12$. Zeros: $x = 1$ and $x = e$.
(b) $f'(x) = (3/x)(\ln x - 1)(\ln x - 1/3)$. Minimum 0 at $x = 1$ and at $x = e$. Maximum 12 at $x = e^3$.
(c) $f'(x) > 0$ in $[e, e^3]$, so $f(x)$ has an inverse. $g'(2) = 1/f'(e^2) = e^2/5$.

7. There is at least one point where you must be heading in the direction of the straight line joining A to B (even if that straight line hits the shore).

9. f has a maximum at $x = 1$ and a minimum at all $x > 1$. (Draw your own graph.) Yet the function is discontinuous at $x = 1$, and its domain of definition is neither closed nor bounded.

8.5

1. $Q = 4000$ (Equation (**) yields $10 - 2Q/1000 = 2$.)

3. Profits: $\pi(x) = -0.003x^2 + 120x - 500\,000$, which is maximized at $x = 20\,000$.

5. (a) $\pi(Q) = QP(Q) - C(Q) = -0.01Q^2 + 14Q - 4500$, which is maximized at $Q = 700$.
(b) $\text{El}_Q\, P(Q) = (Q/P(Q))P'(Q) = Q/(Q - 3000) = -1$ for $Q^* = 1500$.
(c) $R(Q) = QP(Q) = 18Q - 0.006Q^2$, so $R'(Q) = 18 - 0.012Q = 0$ for $Q^* = 1500$.

8.6

1. $f'(x) = 3x^2 - 12 = 0$ at $x = \pm 2$. A sign diagram shows that $x = 2$ is a local minimum point and $x = -2$ is a local maximum point. Since $f''(x) = 6x$, this is confirmed by Theorem 8.6.2.

3. (a) $D_f = [-6, 0) \cup (0, \infty)$; $f(x) > 0$ in $(-6, -2) \cup (0, \infty)$.   (b) Local maximum $\frac{1}{2}\sqrt{2}$ at $x = -4$. Local minima $(8/3)\sqrt{3}$ at $x = 6$, and 0 at $x = -6$ (where $f'(x)$ is undefined).   (c) $f(x) \to -\infty$ as $x \to 0^-$, $f(x) \to \infty$ as $x \to 0^+$, $f(x) \to \infty$ as $x \to \infty$, and $f'(x) \to 0$ as $x \to \infty$. f attains neither a maximum nor a minimum.

5. (a) $a > 0$, $b = 0$ ($f'(0) = 0$ requires $b = 0$. $f''(0) \geq 0$ requires $a \geq 0$. If $a = 0$ and $b = 0$, then $f(x) = x^3 + c$, which does not have a local minimum at $x = 0$.)   (b) $a = -6$, $b = 9$

7. $f'(x) = 3x^2 + a$. In the case when $a \geq 0$, there are no local extreme points, and $f'(x) > 0$ for all $x \neq 0$. So $f(x) = 0$ can have at most one solution. Because $f(x) \to -\infty$ as $x \to -\infty$ and $f(x) \to +\infty$ as $x \to +\infty$, the intermediate-value theorem ensures that $f(x) = 0$ has exactly one solution. In the case when $a < 0$, then $x_1 = -\sqrt{-a/3} = -\sqrt{p}$ (where $p = -a/3$) is a local maximum point and $x_2 = \sqrt{p}$ is a local minimum point. There will be three different real roots of $f(x) = 0$ iff the local maximum value is positive and the local minimum value is negative. This occurs iff $|b| < 2p\sqrt{p}$ or iff $b^2 < 4p^3$ or iff $4a^3 + 27b^2 < 0$.

8.7

1. (a) Stationary points: $x = -2$ and $x = 1$. f increases in $(-\infty, -2]$ and in $[1, \infty)$.
(b) $x = -1/2$ is the only inflection point.

3. (a) $x = -1$ is a local (and global) maximum point, $x = 0$ is an inflection point.
(b) $x = 1$ is a local (and global) minimum point, $x = 2$ is an inflection point.
(c) $x = 3$ is a local maximum point, $x = 0$, $3 - \sqrt{3}$, and $3 + \sqrt{3}$ are inflection points.
(d) $x = \sqrt{e}$ is a local (and global) maximum point, $x = e^{5/6}$ is an inflection point.
(e) $x = 0$ is a local (and global) minimum point, $x = -\ln 2$ is an inflection point.
(f) $x = -\sqrt{2}$ is a local minimum point, $x = \sqrt{2}$ is a local maximum point, $x = 1 - \sqrt{3}$ and $x = 1 + \sqrt{3}$ are inflection points.

5. $x = -2$ and $x = 4$ are minimum points, whereas $x = 2$ is a (possibly local) maximum point. Moreover, $x = 0$, $x = 1$, $x = 3$, and $x = 5$ are inflection points.

7. $C''(x) = 6ax + 2b$, so $C(x)$ is concave in $[0, -b/3a]$, convex in $[-b/3a, \infty)$, and $x = -b/3a$ is the inflection point.

Review Problems for Chapter 8

1. (a) $f'(x) = \dfrac{4x}{(x^2+2)^2}$. Thus $f(x)$ decreases for $x \le 0$, increases for $x \ge 0$.   (b) $f''(x) = \dfrac{4(2-3x^2)}{(x^2+2)^3}$. Inflection points at $x = \pm\frac{1}{3}\sqrt{6}$. (c) $f(x) \to 1$ as $x \to \pm\infty$. See Fig. A8.R.1.

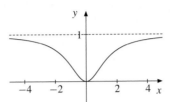

Figure A8.R.1

3. (a) $Q^* = 9000$ maximizes profits.   (b) $\mathrm{El}_Q\, C(Q) \approx 0.12$ means that if Q increases from 1000 by 1%, then costs will increase by about 0.12%.

5. (a) $D_f = (-1, \infty)$.   (b) f has a (global) maximum at $x = 1$. f has no minimum. $x = 0$ and $x = \frac{1}{2}(\sqrt{5}-1)$ are inflection points.   (c) $f(x) \to -\infty$ as $x \to (-1)^+$. See Figure A8.R.5.

7. (a) h is increasing in $(-\infty, \frac{1}{2}\ln 2\,]$ and decreasing in $[\,\frac{1}{2}\ln 2, \infty)$. Hence h has (global) maximum at $x = \frac{1}{2}\ln 2$. It has no minimum.   (b) h is strictly increasing in $(-\infty, 0]$ (with range $(0, 1/3]$), and therefore has an inverse. The inverse is $h^{-1}(y) = \ln(1 - \sqrt{1-8y^2}) - \ln(2y)$. (Solving $y = \dfrac{e^x}{2+e^{2x}}$ or $y(e^x)^2 - e^x + 2y = 0$ for e^x yields $e^x = (1/2y)(1 \pm \sqrt{1-8y^2}\,)$. The minus sign must be chosen to ensure that $x = 0$ when $y = 1/3$, as is necessary because $h(0) = 1/3$.)

9. $f'(x) = \dfrac{-6x^2(x^2-3)(x^2+2)}{(x^4+x^2+2)^2}$, so f is stationary when $x = 0$ and when $x = \pm\sqrt{3}$. $x = \sqrt{3}$ is a local (and global) maximum point, $x = -\sqrt{3}$ is a local (and global) minimum point, and $x = 0$ is neither. (It is an inflection point.) The graph of f is shown in Fig. A8.R.9.

Figure A8.R.5

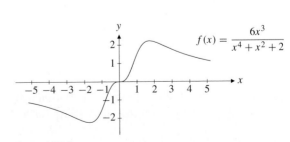

Figure A8.R.9

Chapter 9

9.1

1. (a) $\frac{1}{14}x^{14} + C$ (b) $\frac{2}{5}x^2\sqrt{x} + C$ (c) $2\sqrt{x} + C$ (d) $\frac{8}{15}x^{\frac{15}{8}} + C$. (*Hint:* $\sqrt{x\sqrt{x\sqrt{x}}} = x^{7/8}$.)

3. (a) $C(x) = \frac{3}{2}x^2 + 4x + 40$. ($C(x) = \int (3x + 4)\,dx = \frac{3}{2}x^2 + 4x + C$. $C(0) = 40$ gives $C = 40$.)
(b) $C(x) = \frac{1}{2}ax^2 + bx + C_0$

5. (a) $\frac{2}{5}y^2\sqrt{y} - \frac{8}{3}y\sqrt{y} + 8\sqrt{y} + C$ (b) $\frac{1}{3}x^3 - \frac{1}{2}x^2 + x - \ln|x + 1| + C$ (c) $\frac{1}{32}(1 + x^2)^{16} + C$

7. See Fig. A9.1.7. $f'(x) = A(x + 1)(x - 3)$ (because $f'(x)$ is 0 at $x = -1$ and at $x = 3$). Moreover, $f'(1) = -1$. This implies that $A = 1/4$, so that $f'(x) = \frac{1}{4}(x + 1)(x - 3) = \frac{1}{4}x^2 - \frac{1}{2}x - \frac{3}{4}$. Integration yields $f(x) = \frac{1}{12}x^3 - \frac{1}{4}x^2 - \frac{3}{4}x + C$. Since $f(0) = 2$, $C = 2$.

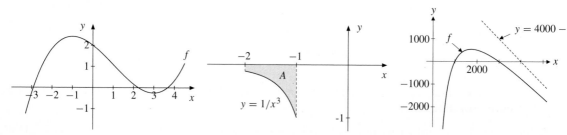

Figure A9.1.7   Figure A9.2.3   Figure A9.2.7

9. Differentiate the right-hand side.   **11.** (a) $F(x) = \frac{1}{2}e^x - x^2$ (b) $F(x) = \frac{1}{2}x^2 - \frac{1}{4}x^4 + \frac{1}{6}$

13. $f(x) = -\ln x + \frac{1}{20}x^5 + x^2 - x - \frac{1}{20}$

9.2

1. (a) $A = \int_0^1 x^3\,dx = |_0^1 \frac{1}{4}x^4 = \frac{1}{4}1^4 - \frac{1}{4}0^4 = \frac{1}{4}$. (b) $A = 1/11$

3. See Fig. A9.2.3. $A = -\int_{-2}^{-1} x^{-3}\,dx = -|_{-2}^{-1}(-\frac{1}{2})x^{-2} = -[-\frac{1}{2} - (-\frac{1}{8})] = \frac{3}{8}$

5. (a) $\int_0^1 x\,dx = |_0^1 \frac{1}{2}x^2 = \frac{1}{2}$ (b) $|_1^2(x^2 + \frac{1}{3}x^3) = 16/3$ (c) $|_{-2}^3(\frac{1}{6}x^3 - \frac{1}{12}x^4) = 5/12$ (d) $-12/5$ (e) $41/2$
(f) $\ln 2 + 5/2$

7. (a) $x = 1000\sqrt{3}$ maximizes profits. See Fig. A9.2.7.
(b) $I = \frac{1}{2000}|_{1000}^{3000}(4000x - \frac{1}{2}x^2 - 3000\,000\ln x) = 2000 - 1500\ln 3 \approx 352$

9.3

1. (a) $|_0^5(\frac{1}{2}x^2 + \frac{1}{3}x^3) = 325/6$ (b) 0 (c) $\ln 9$ (d) $e - 1$ (e) -136 (f) $687/64$

3. (a) $|_0^3[\frac{1}{9}e^{3t-2} + \ln(t + 2)] = \frac{1}{9}(e^7 - e^{-2}) + \ln(5/2)$ (b) $83/15$ (c) $2\sqrt{2} - 3/2$
(d) $A[b - 1 + (b - c)\ln[(b + c)/(1 + c)]] + d\ln b$

5. (a) t^2 (b) $-e^{-t^2}$ (c) $2/\sqrt{t^4 + 1}$

7. $W(T) = K(1 - e^{-\varrho T})/\varrho T$. Here $W(T) \to 0$ as $T \to \infty$, and using l'Hôpital's rule, $W(T) \to K$ as $T \to 0^+$. For $T > 0$, we find $W'(T) = Ke^{-\varrho T}(1 + \varrho T - e^{\varrho T})/\varrho T^2 < 0$ because $e^{\varrho T} > 1 + \varrho T$ (see Problem 6.11.11). We conclude that $W(T)$ is strictly decreasing and that $W(T) \in (0, K)$.

9.4

1. $x(t) = K - \int_0^t \bar{u}e^{-as}\,ds = K - \bar{u}(1 - e^{-at})/a$. Note that $x(t) \to K - \bar{u}/a$ as $t \to \infty$. If $K \geq \bar{u}/a$, the well will never be exhausted.

3. (a) $K(5) - K(0) = \int_0^5 (3t^2 + 2t + 5)\,dt = 175$ (b) $K(T) - K_0 = (T^3 - t_0^3) + (T^2 - t_0^2) + 5(T - t_0)$

5. The equilibrium quantity is $Q^* = 600$, where $P^* = 80$. Then, CS $= \int_0^{600}(120 - 0.2Q)\,dQ = 36\,000$, and PS $= \int_0^{600}(60 - 0.1Q)\,dQ = 18\,000$.

9.5

1. (a) Use (1) with $f(x) = x$ and $g'(x) = e^{-x}$: $\int xe^{-x}\,dx = x(-e^{-x}) - \int 1 \cdot (-e^{-x})\,dx = -xe^{-x} - e^{-x} + C$.
(b) $\frac{3}{4}xe^{4x} - \frac{3}{16}e^{4x} + C$ (c) $-x^2e^{-x} - 2xe^{-x} - 3e^{-x} + C$ (d) $\frac{1}{2}x^2 \ln x - \frac{1}{4}x^2 + C$.

3. The general formula follows from (1), and $\int \ln x\,dx = x \ln x - x + C$.

5. (a) $\dfrac{b}{r^2}\left[1 - (1 + rT)e^{-rT}\right]$ (b) $\dfrac{a}{r}(1 - e^{-rT}) + \dfrac{b}{r^2}\left[1 - (1 + rT)e^{-rT}\right]$

(c) $\dfrac{a}{r}(1 - e^{-rT}) - \dfrac{b}{r^2}\left[1 - (1 + rT)e^{-rT}\right] + \dfrac{c}{r^3}\left[2(1 - e^{-rT}) - 2rTe^{-rT} - r^2T^2e^{-rT}\right]$

9.6

1. (a) $\frac{1}{9}(x^2 + 1)^9 + C$ (Substitute $u = x^2 + 1$, $du = 2x\,dx$.)   (b) $\frac{1}{11}(x + 2)^{11} + C$ (Substitute $u = x + 2$.)
(c) $\ln|x^2 - x + 8| + C$ (Substitute $u = x^2 - x + 8$.)

3. (a) Substitute $u = \sqrt{1 + x^2}$. Then $u^2 = 1 + x^2$, so $u\,du = x\,dx$. If $x = 0$, then $u = 1$; if $x = 1$, then $u = \sqrt{2}$.
Hence, $\int_0^1 x\sqrt{1 + x^2}\,dx = \int_1^{\sqrt{2}} u\,u\,du = \int_1^{\sqrt{2}} u^2\,du = |_1^{\sqrt{2}}\frac{1}{3}u^3 = \frac{1}{3}(2\sqrt{2} - 1)$.   (b) $1/2$ (Let $u = \ln y$.)
(c) $\frac{1}{2}(e^2 - e^{2/3})$ (Let $u = 2/x$.)

5. Substitute $z = x(t)$. Then $dz = \dot{x}(t)dt$, and the result follows using (2).

7. (a) $\ln\left(\dfrac{1 + e^2}{1 + e}\right)^2$ (Introduce $z = 1 + e^{\sqrt{x}}$ as a new variable.)   (b) $\ln 2 - \ln(e^{-1/3} + 1)$

(c) $\displaystyle\int_{8.5}^{41} \frac{dx}{\sqrt{2x - 1} - \sqrt[4]{2x - 1}} = 2\int_2^3 \frac{z^2}{z - 1}\,dz = 2\int_2^3\left(z + 1 + \frac{1}{z - 1}\right)dz = 7 + 2\ln 2$

9.7

1. (a) $\int_1^b x^{-3}\,dx = |_1^b(-\frac{1}{2}x^{-2}) = \frac{1}{2} - \frac{1}{2}b^{-2} \to \frac{1}{2}$ as $b \to \infty$. So $\int_1^\infty(1/x^3)\,dx = \frac{1}{2}$.
(b) $\int_1^b x^{-1/2}\,dx = |_1^b 2x^{1/2} = 2b^{1/2} - 2 \to \infty$ as $b \to \infty$, so the integral diverges.
(c) 1   (d) $\displaystyle\int_0^a \frac{x\,dx}{\sqrt{a^2 - x^2}} = -\left|_0^a\sqrt{a^2 - x^2}\right. = a$

3. Using a simplified notation and the result in Example 1, we have:
(a) $\int_0^\infty x\lambda e^{-\lambda x}\,dt = -|_0^\infty xe^{-\lambda x} + \int_0^\infty e^{-\lambda x}\,dx = 1/\lambda$ (b) $1/\lambda^2$ (c) $2/\lambda^3$

5. (a) $f'(x) = 1/x^4 - 3\ln x/x^4 = 0$ at $x = e^{1/3}$. $f(x) \to -\infty$ as $x \to 0^+$ and $f(x) \to 0$ as $x \to \infty$. $f(e^{1/3}) = 1/3e > 0$. Hence, f has a maximum at $(e^{1/3}, 1/3e)$, but no minimum. (b) $\int_a^b x^{-3}\ln x\,dx = -|_a^b\frac{1}{2}x^{-2}\ln x + \int_a^b \frac{1}{2}x^{-3}\,dx = |_a^b(-\frac{1}{2}x^{-2}\ln x - \frac{1}{4}x^{-2})$. This diverges when $b = 1$ and $a \to 0$. But $\int_1^\infty x^{-3}\ln x\,dx = 1/4$.

7. $4\sqrt{5}$. (If both limits exist, the integral is the sum of the following two limits: $I_1 = \lim_{\varepsilon \to 0^+}\int_{-2+\varepsilon}^3\left(1/\sqrt{x + 2}\right)dx$
and $I_2 = \lim_{\varepsilon \to 0^+}\int_{-2}^{3-\varepsilon}\left(1/\sqrt{3 - x}\right)dx$. Here $I_1 = \lim_{\varepsilon \to 0^+}|_{-2+\varepsilon}^3\left(2\sqrt{x + 2}\right) = \lim_{\varepsilon \to 0^+}\left(2\sqrt{5} - 2\sqrt{\varepsilon}\right) = 2\sqrt{5}$,
and $I_2 = \lim_{\varepsilon \to 0^+}|_{-2}^{3-\varepsilon}\left(-2\sqrt{3 - x}\right) = \lim_{\varepsilon \to 0^+}\left(-2\sqrt{\varepsilon} + 2\sqrt{5}\right) = 2\sqrt{5}$.)

9. $\int x^{-2}dx = -x^{-1} + C$. So evaluating $\int_{-1}^{1} x^{-2}dx$ as $|_{-1}^{1} - x^{-1}$ gives the nonsensical answer -2. The error arises because x^{-2} diverges to $+\infty$ as $x \to 0$. (In fact $\int_{-1}^{1} x^{-2}dx$ diverges to $+\infty$.)

11. $\int_{1}^{A}[k/x - k^2/(1+kx)]\,dx = k\ln[1/(1/A+k)] - k\ln[1/(1+k)] \to k\ln(1/k) - k\ln[1/(1+k)] = \ln(1+1/k)^k$ as $A \to \infty$. So $I_k = \ln(1+1/k)^k$, which tends to $\ln e = 1$ as $k \to \infty$.

9.8

1. The functions in (c) and (d) are the only ones which have a constant relative rate of growth. This accords with (3). (Note that $2^t = e^{(\ln 2)t}$.)

3. $N(t) = P(1 - e^{-kt})$. Then $N(t) \to P$ as $t \to \infty$.

5. $k = 0.1\ln(705/641) \approx 0.0095$. $P(15) \approx 739$, $P(40) \approx 938$

7. (a) $x = Ae^{-0.5t}$ (b) $K = Ae^{0.02t}$ (c) $x = Ae^{-0.5t} + 10$ (d) $K = Ae^{0.2t} - 500$ (e) $x = \dfrac{0.1}{3 - Ae^{0.1t}}$

(f) $K = \dfrac{1}{2 - Ae^t}$

9. (a) 710   (b) A little more than 21 days.   (c) Yes, after about 35 days, 999 will have or have had influenza, and $N(t) \to 1000$ as $t \to \infty$.

Review Problems for Chapter 9

1. (a) $-16x + C$ (b) $5^5x + C$ (c) $3y - \frac{1}{2}y^2 + C$ (d) $\frac{1}{2}r^2 - \frac{16}{5}r^{5/4} + C$ (e) $\frac{1}{9}x^9 + C$ (f) $\frac{2}{7}x^{7/2} + C$
(g) $-\frac{1}{4}p^{-4} + C$ (h) $\frac{1}{4}x^4 + \frac{1}{2}x^2 + C$

3. (a) 600   (b) 2/3   (c) 24   (d) $2\ln 5$ (e) $3\ln(8/3)$ (f) 98/3

5. (a) $10 - 18\ln(14/9)$ (Substitute $z = 9 + \sqrt{x}$. Then $\int_0^{25} \frac{1}{9+\sqrt{x}}\,dx = 2\int_9^{14}(1 - 9/z)\,dz$.)
(b) 886/15 (Substitute $z = \sqrt{t+2}$.)   (c) 195/4 (Substitute $z = \sqrt[3]{19x^3+8}$.)

7. $C(Y) = 0.69Y + 1000$

9. $P^* = 70$, $Q^* = 600$, $CS = 9000$, $PS = 18\,000$.

11. (a) $f'(t) = 4\ln t(2 - \ln t)/t^2$, $f''(t) = 8[(\ln t)^2 - 3\ln t + 1]/t^3$.   (b) $(e^2, 16/e^2)$ is a local maximum point, $(1, 0)$ is a local (and global) minimum point. See Fig. A9.R.11.   (c) Area = 32/3 (*Hint:* $\int f(t)\,dt = \frac{4}{3}(\ln t)^3 + C$.)

Figure A9.R.11

$F(x) = \dfrac{a}{e^{-\lambda x} + a}$

$x_0 = -(\ln a)/\lambda$

Figure A9.R.15

13. (a) $V(x) = (V_0 + b/a)e^{-ax} - b/a$ (b) Given $V(x)$ as in (a), solve $V(x^*) = 0$ for $x^* = (1/a)\ln(1 + aV_0/b)$.
$0 = V(\hat{x}) = (V_m + b/a)e^{-a\hat{x}} - b/a$ yields $V_m = (b/a)(e^{a\hat{x}} - 1)$. When $a = 0.001$ and $b = 8$, then $x^* = (1/0.001)\ln(1 + 0.001 \cdot 12\,000/8) \approx 916$, and $V_m = (8/0.001)(e^{0.001 \cdot 1200} - 1) = 8000(e^{1.2} - 1) \approx 18561$.

15. (a) Verify that $F'(x) = f(x)$. Moreover, $\lim_{x \to \infty} F(x) = 1$ and $\lim_{x \to -\infty} F(x) = 0$.

(b) $\int_{-\infty}^{x} f(t)\, dt = \lim_{a \to -\infty} \int_{a}^{x} f(t)\, dt = \lim_{a \to -\infty} [F(x) - F(a)] = F(x)$, by (a). Since $F'(x) = f(x) > 0$ for all x, $F(x)$ is strictly increasing.

(c) $F''(x) = f'(x) = a\lambda^2 e^{-\lambda x}(e^{-\lambda x} - a)(e^{-\lambda x} + a)^{-3}$. Note that $F''(x) = 0$ for $e^{-\lambda x} = a$, i.e. for $x_0 = -\ln a/\lambda$. Because $F''(x)$ changes sign about $x_0 = -\ln a/\lambda$, this is an inflection point for $F(x)$. $F(x_0) = F(-\ln a/\lambda) = a/(a+a) = 1/2$. The graph is sketched in Fig. A9.R.15.

(d) $\int_{-\infty}^{\infty} f(x)\, dx = \lim_{a \to -\infty} \int_{a}^{0} f(x)\, dx + \lim_{b \to \infty} \int_{0}^{b} f(x)\, dx = \lim_{a \to -\infty} [F(0) - F(a)] + \lim_{b \to \infty} [F(b) - F(0)] = 1$, by (a).

Chapter 10

10.1

1. (a) (i) $8000(1 + 0.05/12)^{5 \cdot 12} \approx 10266.87$ (ii) $8000(1 + 0.05/365)^{5 \cdot 365} \approx 10272.03$
(b) $t = \ln 2/\ln(1 + 0.05/12) \approx 166.7$. It takes approx. $166.7/12 \approx 13.9$ years.

3. $p = 100[\sqrt[100]{100} - 1] \approx 4.7$

5. (i) $100[(1.085)^2 - 1] \approx 17.72\%$ (ii) $100[(1.0425)^4 - 1] \approx 18.11\%$ (iii) $100[(1 + 0.17/12)^{12} - 1] \approx 18.39\%$

7. (a) $12\,000 \cdot (1.04)^{15} \approx 21\,611.32$ (b) $50\,000 \cdot (1.05)^{-5} \approx 39\,176.31$ (c) $100[(1.02)^{12} - 1] \approx 26.82\%$

10.2

1. (a) $8000e^{0.05 \cdot 5} = 8000e^{0.25} = 10272.20$ (b) $8000e^{0.05t} = 16000$ which gives $e^{0.05t} = 2$. Hence $t = \ln 2/0.05 \approx 13.86$ years.

3. (a) $e^{0.1} - 1 \approx 0.105$, so the effective percentage rate is approximately 10.5.   (b) Same answer.

5. $e^{-0.06t^*} = 1/2$, so $t^* = \ln 2/0.06 \approx 11.55$ years.

10.3

1. (i) The present value is $350\,000 \cdot 1.08^{-10} \approx 162\,117.72$.   (ii) $350\,000 \cdot e^{-0.08 \cdot 10} \approx 157\,265.14$.

3. (a) $t = 35$ maximizes f with $f(35) \approx 278$. ($f'(t) = (t + 5)(1.75 - 0.05t)e^{-0.05t}$)   (b) $f(t) \to 0$ as $t \to \infty$. The graph is shown in Fig. A10.3.3.

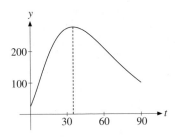

Figure A10.3.3

10.4

1. $s_n = \frac{3}{2}\left(1 - \left(\frac{1}{3}\right)^n\right) \to \frac{3}{2}$ as $n \to \infty$, so $\sum_{n=1}^{\infty} \frac{1}{3^{n-1}} = \frac{3}{2}$.

3. (a) Geometric series with quotient $1/8$. Its sum is $8/(1 - 1/8) = 64/7$.   (b) Geometric series with quotient -3. It diverges.   (c) Geometric, with sum $\dfrac{2^{1/3}}{1 - 2^{-1/3}}$.   (d) Not geometric. (Nevertheless, one can show that the series is convergent with sum $\ln 2$.)

5. Geometric series with quotient $(1 + p/100)^{-1}$. Its sum is $\dfrac{b}{1 - (1 + p/100)^{-1}} = b(1 + 100/p)$.

7. $1824 \cdot 1.02 + 1824 \cdot 1.02^2 + \cdots + 1824 \cdot 1.02^n = (1824/0.02)(1.02^{n+1} - 1.02)$ must equal 128 300. So $n \approx 43.77$. The resources will last until year 2037.

10.5

1. Use (2) with $n = 15$, $r = 0.12$, and $a = 3500$. This gives $P_{15} = \dfrac{3500}{0.12}\left(1 - \dfrac{1}{(1.12)^{15}}\right) \approx 23\,838$.

3. The future value after 10 years of (i) is obviously \$13 000, whereas according to (3), the corresponding value of (ii) is $F_{10} = \dfrac{1000}{0.06}(1.06^{10} - 1) \approx 13\,180.80$. So (ii) is worth more.

5. $\dfrac{1500}{0.08} = 18\,750$

7. This geometric series converges if $(1 + g)/(1 + r) < 1$ or $r > g$. The sum is equal to $D/(r - g)$.

10.6

1. Using formula (2) we find that the annual payments are: $a = 80\,000 \dfrac{0.07(1.07)^{10}}{1.07^{10} - 1} \approx 11\,390.20$.

3. (a) $\dfrac{8000}{0.07}[1.07^6 - 1] \approx 57\,226.33$. (Formula (3) in Section 10.5.) Four years after the last deposit you have $57\,226.33 \cdot 1.07^4 \approx 75012.05$. (b) With annual compounding: $r = 3^{1/20} - 1 \approx 0.0565$, so the rate of interest is about 5.65 %. With continuous compounding, $e^{20r} = 3$, so that $20r = \ln 3$, $r = \ln 3/20 \approx 0.0549$, so the rate of interest is about 5.49 %.

10.7

1. r must satisfy $-50\,000 + 30\,000/(1+r) + 30\,000/(1+r)^2 = 0$. With $s = 1/(1+r)$, this yields $s^2 + s - 5/3 = 0$, with positive solution $s = -1/2 + \sqrt{23/12} \approx 0.884$, so that $r \approx 0.13$.

3. By hypothesis, $f(0) = a_0 + a_1 + \cdots + a_n > 0$. Also, $f(r) \to a_0 < 0$ as $r \to \infty$. Moreover, $f'(r) = -a_1(1 + r)^{-2} - 2a_2(1 + r)^{-3} - \cdots - na_n(1 + r)^{-n-1} < 0$, so $f(r)$ is strictly decreasing. This guarantees that there is a unique internal rate of return, with $r > 0$.

5. After dividing all the amounts by \$ 10 000, the equation is $f(s) = s^{20} + s^{19} + \cdots + s^2 + s - 10 = 0$. Then $f(0) = -10$ and $f(1) = 10$, so by the intermediate-value theorem (Theorem 7.10.1), there exists a number s^* such that $f(s^*) = 0$. Here s^* is unique because $f'(s) > 0$. In fact $f(s) = -10 + (s - s^{21})/(1 - s)$, and $s = 0.928$ is an approximate root, which corresponds to an internal rate of return of about 7.8 %. (See Problem 7.R.26.)

Review Problems for Chapter 10

1. (a) $5000 \cdot 1.03^{10} \approx 6719.58$ (b) $5000(1.03)^{t^*} = 10\,000$, so $(1.03)^{t^*} = 2$, or $t^* = \ln 2/\ln 1.03 \approx 23.45$.

3. Because $(1 + 10/1200)^{12} \approx 1.1047 < 1 + 11/100 = 1.11$, paying interest monthly is cheaper.

5. (a) $8000e^{0.06 \cdot 3} \approx 9577.74$ (b) $t^* = \ln 2/0.06 \approx 11.6$

7. (a) $\int_0^T ae^{-rt}\, dt = (a/r)(1 - e^{-rT})$ (b) a/r, the same as (4) of Section 10.5.

9. (a) According to formula (10.6.2), the annual payment is: $500\,000 \dfrac{0.07(1.07)^{10}}{1.07^{10} - 1} \approx 71188.80$. The total amount is $10 \cdot 71188.80 = 711888$. (b) If the person has to pay twice a year, the biannual payment is $500\,000 \dfrac{0.035(1.035)^{20}}{1.035^{20} - 1} \approx 35180.50$. The total amount is then $20 \cdot 35180.50 = 703610.80$.

11. (a) $\int_0^{10}(1 + 0.4t)\, dt = 30$ (b) $\int_0^{10}(1 + 0.4t)e^{-0.05t}\, dt = 180 - 260e^{-0.5}$

Chapter 11

11.1

1. $f(0, 1) = 1 \cdot 0 + 2 \cdot 1 = 2$, $f(2, -1) = 0$, $f(a, a) = 3a$, and $f(a + h, b) - f(a, b) = h$

3. $f(1, 1) = 2$, $f(-2, 3) = 51$, $f(1/x, 1/y) = 3/x^2 - 2/xy + 1/y^3$, $p = 6x + 3h - 2y$, $q = -2x + 3y^2 + 3yk + k^2$

5. $F(1, 1) = 10$, $F(4, 27) = 60$, $F(9, 1/27) = 10$, $F(3, \sqrt{2}) = 10\sqrt{3} \cdot \sqrt[6]{2}$, $F(100, 1000) = 1000$, $F(2K, 2L) = 10 \cdot 2^{5/6} K^{1/2} L^{1/3} = 2^{5/6} F(K, L)$

7. (a) $e^{x+y} \neq 3$, that is $x + y \neq \ln 3$ (b) $x \neq a$ and $y \neq b$ (c) $x > a$ and $y > b$ (Note that $\ln(x - a)^2 = 2 \ln |x - a|$, which is equal to $2 \ln(x - a)$ only if $x > a$.)

11.2

1. (a) $\partial z/\partial x = 2$, $\partial z/\partial y = 3$ (b) $\partial z/\partial x = 2x$, $\partial z/\partial y = 3y^2$ (c) $\partial z/\partial x = 3x^2 y^4$, $\partial z/\partial y = 4x^3 y^3$
(d) $\partial z/\partial x = \partial z/\partial y = 2(x + y)$

3. (a) $f_1'(x, y) = 7x^6$, $f_2'(x, y) = -7y^6$, $f_{12}''(x, y) = 0$ (b) $f_1'(x, y) = 5x^4 \ln y$, $f_2'(x, y) = x^5/y$, $f_{12}''(x, y) = 5x^4/y$ (c) $f_1'(x, y) = 10x(x^2 - 2y^2)^4$, $f_2'(x, y) = -20y(x^2 - 2y^2)^4$, $f_{12}''(x, y) = -160xy(x^2 - 2y^2)^3$

5. (a) $z_x' = 2x$, $z_y' = 2e^{2y}$, $z_{xx}'' = 2$, $z_{yy}'' = 4e^{2y}$, $z_{xy}'' = z_{yx}'' = 0$ (b) $z_x' = y/x$, $z_y' = \ln x$, $z_{xx}'' = -y/x^2$, $z_{yy}'' = 0$, $z_{xy}'' = z_{yx}'' = 1/x$ (c) $z_x' = y^2 - ye^{xy}$, $z_y' = 2xy - xe^{xy}$, $z_{xx}'' = -y^2 e^{xy}$, $z_{yy}'' = 2x - x^2 e^{xy}$, $z_{xy}'' = z_{yx}'' = 2y - e^{xy} - xye^{xy}$ (d) $z_x' = yx^{y-1}$, $z_y' = x^y \ln x$, $z_{xx}'' = y(y - 1)x^{y-2}$, $z_{yy}'' = x^y (\ln x)^2$, $z_{xy}'' = z_{yx}'' = x^{y-1} + yx^{y-1} \ln x$

7. $xz_x' + yz_y' = x[2a(ax + by)] + y[2b(ax + by)] = (ax + by)2(ax + by) = 2(ax + by)^2 = 2z$

11.3

1. See Fig. A11.3.1.

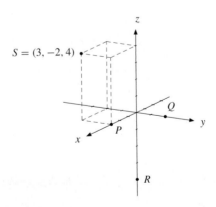

$S = (3, -2, 4)$

Figure A11.3.1

3. If $x^2 + y^2 = 6$, then $f(x, y) = \sqrt{6} - 4$, so $x^2 + y^2 = 6$ is a level curve of f at height $c = \sqrt{6} - 4$.

5. At the point of intersection f would have two different values, which is impossible when f is a function.

7. See Figs. A11.3.7a and b. (Note that only a portion of the graph is indicated in part (a).)

Figure A11.3.7a

Figure A11.3.7b

9. (a) $f'_x > 0$ and $f'_y < 0$ at P, whereas $f'_x < 0$ and $f'_y > 0$ at Q.   (b) (i) No solutions among points shown in the figure. (ii) $x \approx 2$ and $x \approx 6$ (c) 3

11.4

1. See Fig. A11.4.1.

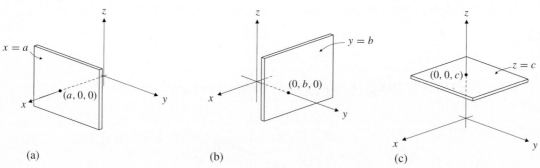

Figure A11.4.1

3. $d = \sqrt{(a+1-a)^2 + (b+1-b)^2 + (c+1-c)^2} = \sqrt{3}$ **5.** The sphere with centre at $(-3, 3, 4)$ and radius 5.

11.5

1. (a) $f(-1, 2, 3) = 1$, $f(-2, 4, 6) = 4$, and $f(a+1, b+1, c+1) - f(a, b, c) = 2a + 2b + 2c + 3$.
(b) $f(tx, ty, tz) = (tx)(ty) + (tx)(tz) + (ty)(tz) = t^2(xy + xz + yz) = t^2 f(x, y, z)$

3. (a) Because 1.053 is the sum of exponents, y would become $2^{1.053} \approx 2.07$ times as large.
(b) $\ln y = \ln 2.9 + 0.015 \ln x_1 + 0.25 \ln x_2 + 0.35 \ln x_3 + 0.408 \ln x_4 + 0.03 \ln x_5$

5. The following shows that $k = m$:

$$x(tv_1, \ldots, tv_n) = A\big(\delta_1(tv_1)^{-\varrho} + \delta_2(tv_2)^{-\varrho} + \cdots + \delta_n(tv_n)^{-\varrho}\big)^{-m/\varrho}$$

$$= A\big(t^{-\varrho}(\delta_1 v_1^{-\varrho} + \delta_2 v_2^{-\varrho} + \cdots + \delta_n v_n^{-\varrho})\big)^{-m/\varrho} = t^m A\big(\delta_1 v_1^{-\varrho} + \delta_2 v_2^{-\varrho} + \cdots + \delta_n v_n^{-\varrho}\big)^{-m/\varrho} = t^m x(v_1, \ldots, v_n)$$

11.6

1. $F_1'(x, y, z) = 2xe^{xz} + x^2 z e^{xz} + y^4 e^{xy}$, so $F_1'(1, 1, 1) = 4e$; $F_2'(x, y, z) = 3y^2 e^{xy} + xy^3 e^{xy}$, so $F_2'(1, 1, 1) = 4e$; $F_3'(x, y, z) = x^3 e^{xz}$, so $F_3'(1, 1, 1) = e$.

3. $\partial T/\partial x = ky/d^n$ and $\partial T/\partial y = kx/d^n$ are both positive, so that the number of travellers increases if the size of either city increases, which is reasonable. $\partial T/\partial d = -nkxy/d^{n+1}$ is negative, so that the number of travellers decreases if the distance between the cities increases, which is also reasonable.

5. $f_1' = p'(x)$, $f_2' = q'(y)$, $f_3' = r'(z)$

7. Put $w = u^h$, where $u = (x - y + z)/(x + y - z)$. Then $\partial w/\partial x = hu^{h-1}\partial u/\partial x$, $\partial w/\partial y = hu^{h-1}\partial u/\partial y$, and $\partial w/\partial z = hu^{h-1}\partial u/\partial z$. With $v = x+y-z$, we get $\partial u/\partial x = (2y-2z)/v^2$, $\partial u/\partial y = -2x/v^2$, and $\partial u/\partial z = 2x/v^2$. Hence

$$x\frac{\partial w}{\partial x} + y\frac{\partial w}{\partial y} + z\frac{\partial w}{\partial z} = hu^{h-1}v^{-2}[x(2y - 2z) + y(-2x) + z2x] = 0$$

(In the terminology of Section 12.7, the function w is homogeneous of degree 0. Euler's theorem 12.7.1 yields the result immediately.)

11.7

1. $\partial M/\partial Y = 0.14$ and $\partial M/\partial r = -0.84 \cdot 76.03(r - 2)^{-1.84} = -63.8652(r - 2)^{-1.84}$. So $\partial M/\partial Y$ is positive and $\partial M/\partial r$ is negative, which accords with standard economic intuition.

3. $D_p'(p, q) = -bq^{-\alpha}$, $D_q'(p, q) = bp\alpha q^{-\alpha-1}$. So $D_p'(p, q) < 0$, showing that demand decreases as price increases. And $D_q'(p, q) > 0$, showing that demand increases as the price of a competing product increases.

5. $\partial U/\partial x_i = e^{-x_i}$, for $i = 1, \ldots, n$

11.8

1. (a) $\text{El}_x z = 1$ and $\text{El}_y z = 1$ (b) $\text{El}_x z = 2$ and $\text{El}_y z = 5$ (c) $\text{El}_x z = n+x$ and $\text{El}_y z = n+y$ (d) $\text{El}_x z = x/(x+y)$ and $\text{El}_y z = y/(x + y)$

3. $\text{El}_i z = p + a_i x_i$ for $i = 1, \ldots, n$.

Review Problems for Chapter 11

1. $f(0, 1) = -5$, $f(2, -1) = 11$, $f(a, a) = -2a$, and $f(a + h, b) - f(a, b) = 3h$

3. $f(3, 4, 0) = 5$, $f(-2, 1, 3) = \sqrt{14}$, and $f(tx, ty, tz) = \sqrt{t^2x^2 + t^2y^2 + t^2z^2} = tf(x, y, z)$

5. (a) All (x, y) (b) For $xy \le 1$ (c) For $x^2 + y^2 < 2$

7. (a) $x + y > 1$ (b) $x^2 \ge y^2$ and $x^2 + y^2 \ge 1$. So $x^2 + y^2 \ge 1$ and $|x| \ge |y|$.   (c) $y \ge x^2$, $x \ge 0$, and $\sqrt{x} \ge y$. So $0 \le x \le 1$ and $\sqrt{x} \ge y \ge x^2$.

9. (a) $f(0, 0) = 36$, $f(-2, -3) = 0$, $f(a + 2, b - 3) = a^2 b^2$ (b) $f_x' = 2(x - 2)(y + 3)^2$, $f_y' = 2(x - 2)^2(y + 3)$

11. Because $g(-1, 5) = g(1, 1) = 30$, the two points are on the same level curve.

13. (a) $f_1'(x, y) = 4x^3 - 8xy$, $f_2'(x, y) = 4y - 4x^2 + 4$ (b) Stationary points: $(0, -1)$, $(\sqrt{2}, 1)$, and $(-\sqrt{2}, 1)$.

Chapter 12

12.1

1. (a) $dz/dt = F_1'(x, y)dx/dt + F_2'(x, y)dy/dt = 1 \cdot 2t + 2y \cdot 3t^2 = 2t + 6t^5$
(b) $dz/dt = px^{p-1}y^q a + qx^p y^{q-1}b = x^{p-1}y^{q-1}(apy + bqx) = a^p b^q(p+q)t^{p+q-1}$ (c) Easy verification.

3. (a) $dz/dt = F_1'(t, y) + F_2'(t, y)g'(t)$. If $F(t, y) = t^2 + ye^y$ and $g(t) = t^2$, then $F_1'(t, y) = 2t$, $F_2'(t, y) = e^y + ye^y$, and $g'(t) = 2t$. Hence $dz/dt = 2t(1 + e^{t^2} + t^2 e^{t^2})$.   (b) $dY/dL = F_K'(K, L)g'(L) + F_L'(K, L)$

5. The usual rules in Sections 6.7 and 6.8 for differentiating (a) a sum; (b) a difference; (c) a product; (d) a quotient; (e) a composite function of one variable.

7. Differentiating (1) w.r.t. t yields, $d^2z/dt^2 = (d/dt)[F_1'(x, y) \, dx/dt] + (d/dt)[F_2'(x, y) \, dy/dt]$. Here
$(d/dt)[F_1'(x, y) \, dx/dt] = [F_{11}''(x, y) \, dx/dt + F_{12}''(x, y) \, dy/dt]dx/dt + F_1'(x, y) \, d^2x/dt^2$,
$(d/dt)[F_2'(x, y) \, dy/dt] = [F_{21}''(x, y) \, dx/dt + F_{22}''(x, y) \, dy/dt]dy/dt + F_2'(x, y) \, d^2y/dt^2$. Assuming $F_{12}'' = F_{21}''$, the conclusion follows.

12.2

1. (a) $\partial z/\partial t = F_1'(x, y)\partial x/\partial t + F_2'(x, y)\partial y/\partial t = 1 \cdot 1 + 2ys = 1 + 2ts^2$ and
$\partial z/\partial s = (\partial z/\partial x)(\partial x/\partial s) + (\partial z/\partial y)(\partial y/\partial s) = 1 \cdot (-1) + 2yt = -1 + 2t^2 s$
(b) $\partial z/\partial t = 4x2t + 9y^2 = 8tx + 9y^2$ and $\partial z/\partial s = 4x(-1) + 9y^2 6s^2 = -4x + 54s^2 y^2$

3. (a) $\dfrac{\partial w}{\partial t} = \dfrac{\partial w}{\partial x}\dfrac{\partial x}{\partial t} + \dfrac{\partial w}{\partial y}\dfrac{\partial y}{\partial t} + \dfrac{\partial w}{\partial z}\dfrac{\partial z}{\partial t} = y^2 z^3 \cdot 2t + 2xyz^3 \cdot 0 + 3xy^2 z^2 \cdot 1 = 5s^2 t^4$

(b) $\dfrac{\partial w}{\partial t} = 2x\dfrac{\partial x}{\partial t} + 2y\dfrac{\partial y}{\partial t} + 2z\dfrac{\partial z}{\partial t} = \dfrac{x}{\sqrt{t+s}} + 2sye^{ts} = 1 + 2se^{2ts}$

5. (a) $\partial Z/\partial G = 1 + 2Y\partial Y/\partial G + 2r\partial r/\partial G$ (b) $\partial Z/\partial G = 1 + I_1'(Y, r)\partial Y/\partial G + I_2'(Y, r)\partial r/\partial G$

7. (a) Let $u = \ln v$, where $v = x^3 + y^3 + z^3 - 3xyz$. Then $\partial u/\partial x = (1/v)(\partial v/\partial x) = (3x^2 - 3yz)/v$. Similarly, $\partial u/\partial y = (3y^2 - 3xz)/v$, and $\partial u/\partial z = (3z^2 - 3xy)/v$. Hence,

$$x\frac{\partial u}{\partial x} + y\frac{\partial u}{\partial y} + z\frac{\partial u}{\partial z} = \frac{x}{v}(3x^2 - 3yz) + \frac{y}{v}(3y^2 - 3xz) + \frac{z}{v}(3z^2 - 3xy) = \frac{3v}{v} = 3$$

which proves (i). Equation (ii) is then proved by elementary algebra.
(b) $\partial z/\partial x = 2xyf'(x^2 y)$, $\partial z/\partial y = x^2 f'(x^2 y)$, so $x\partial z/\partial x = 2x^2 yf'(x^2 y) = 2y\partial z/\partial y$.

12.3

1. Formula (1) gives $y' = -F_1'/F_2' = -(4x + 6y)/(6x + 2y) = -(2x + 3y)/(3x + y)$.

3. (a) With $F(x, y) = 2x^2 + xy + y^2$, $y' = -F_1'/F_2' = -(4x + y)/(x + 2y) = -4$ at $(2, 0)$. Moreover, $y'' = -(28x^2 + 14y^2 + 14xy)/(x + 2y)^3 = -14$ at $(2, 0)$. The tangent has the equation $y = -4x + 8$.
(b) $y' = 0$ requires $y = -4x$. Inserting this into the original equation gives the two points $(a, -4a)$ and $(-a, 4a)$, where $a = 2\sqrt{7}/7$.

5. $\dfrac{dP}{dR} = \dfrac{f_R'(R, P)}{g'(P) - f_P'(R, P)}$. It is plausible that $f_R'(R, P) > 0$ (demand increases as the advertisement expenditure increases), and $g'(P) > 0$, $f_P'(R, P) < 0$, so $dP/dR > 0$.

12.4

1. (a) $\dfrac{\partial z}{\partial x} = 3$ (b) $\dfrac{\partial z}{\partial x} = -\dfrac{yz + z^3 - y^2 z^5}{xy + 3xz^2 - 5xy^2 z^4}$ (c) $\dfrac{\partial z}{\partial x} = -\dfrac{yze^{xyz} - 3yz}{xye^{xyz} - 3xy} = -\dfrac{z}{x}$

3. $P/2\sqrt{L^*} = w$ and thus $L^* = P^2/4w^2$. Then $\partial L^*/\partial P = P/2w^2 > 0$ and $\partial L^*/\partial w = -P^2/2w^3 < 0$.

5. Implicit differentiation gives $f_P'(R, P)P_w' = g_w'(w, P) + g_P'(w, P)P_w'$. Hence $P_w' = \dfrac{-g_w'(w, P)}{g_P'(w, P) - f_P'(R, P)} < 0$

because $g_w' > 0$, $g_P' > 0$, and $f_P' < 0$.

12.5

1. The marginal rate of substitution is $R_{yx} = 20x/30y$, so $y/x = (2/3)(R_{yx})^{-1}$ and $\sigma_{yx} = -1$.

3. With $F(K, L) = AK^a L^b$, $F_K' = aF/K$, $F_L' = bF/L$, $F_{KK}'' = a(a - 1)F/K^2$, $F_{KL}'' = abF/KL$, and $F_{LL}'' = b(b - 1)F/L^2$, we find that $-F_K' F_L'(KF_K' + LF_L') = -(aF/K)(bF/L)(a + b)F = -ab(a + b)F^3/KL$. Moreover, $KL[(F_L')^2 F_{KK}'' - 2F_K' F_2' F_{KL}'' + (F_K')^2 F_{LL}''] = -ab(a + b)F^3/KL$. It follows that $\sigma_{KL} = 1$.

12.6

1. $f(tx, ty) = (tx)^4 + (tx)^2(ty)^2 = t^4 x^4 + t^2 x^2 t^2 y^2 = t^4(x^4 + x^2 y^2) = t^4 f(x, y)$, so f is homogeneous of degree 4.

3. $f(tx, ty) = (tx)(ty)^2 + (tx)^3 = t^3(xy^2 + x^3) = t^3 f(x, y)$. f is homogeneous of degree 3.
(2): $xf_1'(x, y) + yf_2'(x, y) = x(y^2 + 3x^2) + y2xy = 3(x^3 + xy^2) = 3f(x, y)$
(3): It is easy to see that $f_1'(x, y) = y^2 + 3x^2$ and $f_2'(x, y) = 2xy$ are homogeneous of degree 2.
(4): $f(x, y) = x^3 + xy^2 = x^3[1 + (y/x)^2] = y^3[(x/y)^3 + x/y]$
(5): $x^2 f_{11}'' + 2xy f_{12}'' + y^2 f_{22}'' = x^2(6x) + 2xy(2y) + y^2(2x) = 6x^3 + 4xy^2 + 2xy^2 = 3 \cdot 2f(x, y)$

5. $Y/L = A[a(K/L)^{-\rho} + b]^{-1/\rho}$

7. From $(*)$, with $k = 1$, we get $f_{11}'' = (-y/x)f_{12}''$ and $f_{22}'' = (-x/y)f_{21}''$. With $f_{12}'' = f_{21}''$ we get $f_{11}'' f_{22}'' - (f_{12}'')^2 = (-y/x)f_{12}''(-x/y)f_{12}'' - (f_{12}'')^2 = 0$.

12.7

1. (a) Homogeneous of degree 1. (b) Not homogeneous. (c) Homogeneous of degree $-1/2$. (d) Homogeneous of degree 1. (e) Not homogeneous. (f) Homogeneous of degree n.

3. All are homogeneous of degree 1, as is easily checked by using (1).

5. (a) $h(t\mathbf{x}) = f((tx_1)^m, \ldots, (tx_n)^m) = f(t^m x_1^m, \ldots, t^m x_n^m) = (t^m)^r f(x_1^m, \ldots, x_n^m) = t^{mr} h(\mathbf{x})$, so h is homogeneous of degree mr. (b) Homogeneous of degree sp. (c) Homogeneous of degree r for $r = s$, not homogeneous for $r \neq s$. (d) Homogeneous of degree $r + s$. (e) Homogeneous of degree $r - s$.

12.8

1. (a) $f(x, y) \approx 1 + \frac{1}{2}x + \frac{1}{2}y$ (b) $f(x, y) \approx y$

3. $g^*(\mu, \varepsilon) = P^{\frac{1}{1-\beta}} - 1$, with $P = (1 + \mu)(1 + \varepsilon)^\alpha$, yields $\partial g^*/\partial \mu = [1/(1 - \beta)]P^{\frac{1}{1-\beta}-1} \partial P/\partial \mu$, $\partial g^*/\partial \varepsilon = [1/(1 - \beta)]P^{1/(1-\beta)-1} \partial P/\partial \varepsilon$. Here $\partial P/\partial \mu = (1 + \varepsilon)^\alpha$, $\partial P/\partial \varepsilon = (1 + \mu)\alpha(1 + \varepsilon)^{\alpha-1}$. Hence, for $(\mu, \varepsilon) = (0, 0)$, $\partial g^*/\partial \mu = 1/(1 - \beta)$ and $\partial g^*/\partial \varepsilon = \alpha/(1 - \beta)$. Because $g^*(0, 0) = 0$, we conclude that $g^*(\mu, \varepsilon) \approx \mu/(1 - \beta) + (\alpha \varepsilon)/(1 - \beta)$ if μ and ε are close to 0.

5. (a) $f(1.02, 1.99) = 1.1909$ (b) $f(1.02, 1.99) \approx f(1, 2) + (0.02) \cdot 8 + (-0.01) \cdot (-3) = 1.19$. The error is 0.0009.

7. (a) $z = 2x + 4y - 5$ (b) $z = -10x + 3y + 3$

9. The tangent plane (3) passes through $(x, y, z) = (0, 0, 0)$ iff $-f(x_0, y_0) = f_1'(x_0, y_0)(-x_0) + f_2'(x_0, y_0)(-y_0)$. This is satisfied for all (x_0, y_0) iff f is homogeneous of degree 1, according to Euler's theorem.

12.9

1. Both (a) and (b) give: $dz = (y^2 + 3x^2)dx + 2xy\,dy$.

3. (a) $dz = 2xu\,dx + x^2(u'_x\,dx + u'_y\,dy)$ (b) $dz = 2u(u'_x\,dx + u'_y\,dy)$

   (c) $dz = \dfrac{1}{xy + yu}\left[(y + yu'_x)dx + (x + u + yu'_y)dy\right]$

5. $dU = \dfrac{\sqrt{y}}{e^U + Ue^U}dx + \dfrac{x}{2\sqrt{y}(e^U + Ue^U)}\,dy$

7. (a) $dU = 2a_1u_1\,du_1 + \cdots + 2a_nu_n\,du_n$ (b) $dU = A(\delta_1 u_1^{-\varrho} + \cdots + \delta_n u_n^{-\varrho})^{-1-1/\varrho}(\delta_1 u_1^{-\varrho-1}du_1 + \cdots + \delta_n u_n^{-\varrho-1}du_n)$

9. (a) $d^2z = 2\,dx\,dy + 2(dy)^2$ (b) $dz/dt = 3t^2 + 4t^3$ and then $(d^2z/dt^2)(dt)^2 = (6t + 12t^2)(dt)^2$. On the other hand, the expression for d^2z derived from (a) is equal to $(4t + 8t^2)(dt)^2$.

12.10

1. (a) $4 - 2 = 2$ (b) $5 - 2 = 3$ (c) $4 - 3 = 1$

3. Let m denote the number of equations and n the number of unknowns.   (a) $m = 3, n = 2$; infinitely many solutions. (b) $m = n = 2$; no solutions.   (c) $m = n = 2$; infinitely many solutions.   (d) $m = 1, n = 100$; infinitely many solutions.   (e) $m = 1, n = 100$; no solutions.   We see that the counting rule fails dramatically.

12.11

1. Differentiating yields the two equations $a\,du + b\,dv = c\,dx + d\,dy$ and $e\,du + f\,dv = g\,dx + h\,dy$. Solving these for du and dv yields $du = [(cf - bg)\,dx + (df - bh)\,dy]/D$ and $dv = [(ag - ce)\,dx + (ah - de)\,dy]/D$, where $D = af - be$. The required partial derivatives are then easily read off.

3. By differentiation, $3\,dx_1 + 2x_2\,dx_2 - dy_1 - 9y_2^2\,dy_2 = 0$, $3x_1^2\,dx_1 - 2dx_2 + 6y_1^2\,dy_1 - dy_2 = 0$. Letting $dx_2 = 0$ and solving for dy_1 and dy_2 leads to $dy_1 = A\,dx_1$ and $dy_2 = B\,dx_1$, where $A = \partial y_1/\partial x_1 = J^{-1}(3 - 27x_1^2 y_2^2)$ and $B = \partial y_2/\partial x_1 = J^{-1}(3x_1^2 + 18y_1^2)$ with $J = 1 + 54y_1^2 y_2^2$.

5. Differentiation w.r.t. x yields $y + u'_x v + uv'_x = 0$, $u + xu'_x + yv'_x = 0$. Solving this system for u'_x and v'_x we get

$$u'_x = \frac{u^2 - y^2}{yv - xu} = \frac{u^2 - y^2}{2yv}, \quad v'_x = \frac{xy - uv}{yv - xu} = \frac{2xy - 1}{2yv}$$

where we substituted $xu = -yv$ and $uv = 1 - xy$. Differentiating u'_x w.r.t. x yields

$$u''_{xx} = \frac{\partial^2 u}{\partial x^2} = \frac{\partial}{\partial x}u'_x = \frac{2uu'_x 2yv - (u^2 - y^2)2yv'_x}{4y^2 v^2} = \frac{(u^2 - y^2)(4uv - 1)}{4y^2 v^3}$$

(The answers to this problem can be expressed in many different ways.)

7. (a) $6 - 3 = 3$ (b) Differentiating, then gathering all terms in dY, dr, and dI on the left-hand side, we obtain

$$(C'_Y - 1)\,dY + C'_r\,dr + dI = -d\alpha$$
$$F'_Y\,dY + F'_r\,dr - dI = -d\beta$$
$$L'_Y\,dY + L'_r\,dr \qquad\quad = dM$$

With $d\beta = dM = 0$ we get $dY = -(L'_r/D)\,d\alpha$, $dr = (L'_Y/D)\,d\alpha$, and $dI = [(F'_r L'_Y - F'_Y L'_r)/D]\,d\alpha$, where $D = L'_r(C'_Y + F'_Y - 1) - L'_Y(C'_r + F'_r)$.

9. (a) Differentiation yields $2uv\,du + u^2\,dv - du = 3x^2\,dx + 6y^2\,dy$, and $e^{ux}(u\,dx + x\,du) = v\,dy + y\,dv$. At P these equations become $3\,du + 4\,dv = 6\,dy$ and $dv = 2\,dx - dy$. Hence $du = 2\,dy - (4/3)dv = -(8/3)\,dx + (10/3)\,dy$. In particular, $dv = 2\,dx - dy$, so $\partial u/\partial y = 10/3$, $\partial v/\partial x = 2$.
(b) $\Delta u \approx du = -(8/3)0.1 + (10/3)(-0.2) = -14/15 \approx -0.93$, $\Delta v \approx dv = 2(0.1) - (-0.2) = 0.4$

Review Problems for Chapter 12

1. (a) $dz/dt = 6 \cdot 4t + 3y^2 9t^2 = 24t + 27t^2 y^2 = 24t + 243t^8$ (b) $dz/dt = px^{p-1}a + py^{p-1}b = pt^{p-1}(a^p + b^p)$
(c) Easy verification.

3. $\partial w/\partial t = 2x \cdot 1 + 3y^2 \cdot 1 + 4z^3 s = 2x + 3y^2 + 4sz^3$, $\partial w/\partial s = 2x - 3y^2 + 4tz^3$

5. (a) $\ln E = \ln A - a \ln p + b \ln m$, so $\dot E/E = -a(\dot p/p) + b(\dot m/m)$ (b) $\ln p = \ln p_0 + t \ln(1.06)$, so $\dot p/p = \ln 1.06$.
Likewise, $\dot m/m = \ln 1.08$. Then $\dot E/E = -a \ln 1.06 + b \ln 1.08 = \ln(1.08^b/1.06^a) = \ln Q$.

7. $R_{yx} = F'_x/F'_y = -x/10y$. Hence $y/x = -(1/10)R_{yx}^{-1}$, and so $\sigma_{yx} = \text{El}_{R_{yx}}(y/x) = -1$.

9. (a) -1 (b) $2ac$ (c) 4. (d) Not homogeneous. (If F were homogeneous, then by Euler's theorem, for some
constant k, we would have $x_1 e^{x_1+x_2+x_3} + x_2 e^{x_1+x_2+x_3} + x_3 e^{x_1+x_2+x_3} = ke^{x_1+x_2+x_3}$ for all x_1, x_2, x_3. This reduces
to $x_1 + x_2 + x_3 = k$ for all x_1, x_2, x_3, which is absurd.)

11. $\text{El}_x y = xy/(1 - 2y)$ (*Hint:* Take the elasticity w.r.t x of $y^2 e^x e^{1/y} = 3$.)

13. Since F is homogeneous of degree 1, according to (*) in Section 12.6, we have $KF''_{KK} + LF''_{KL} = 0$, so that
$F''_{KL} = -(K/L)F''_{KK} > 0$ since $F''_{KK} < 0$ and $K > 0, L > 0$.

15. $du + e^y dx + xe^y dy + dv = 0$ and $dx + e^{u+v^2} du + e^{u+v^2} 2v \, dv - dy = 0$. At the given point, these equations
reduce to $du + dv = -e \, dx - e \, dy$ and $du = -e \, dx + e \, dy$, implying that $u'_x = -e, u'_y = e, v'_x = 0$, and $v'_y = -2e$.

17. (a) Differentiation yields $\alpha u^{\alpha-1} du + \beta v^{\beta-1} dv = 2^\beta dx + 3y^2 dy$ and $\alpha u^{\alpha-1} v^\beta du + u^\alpha \beta v^{\beta-1} dv - \beta v^{\beta-1} dv = dx - dy$. At P we find $\partial u/\partial x = 2^{-\beta}/\alpha$, $\partial u/\partial y = -2^{-\beta}/\alpha$, $\partial v/\partial x = (2^\beta - 2^{-\beta})/\beta 2^{\beta-1}$,
$\partial v/\partial y = (2^{-\beta} + 3)/\beta 2^{\beta-1}$. (b) $u(0.99, 1.01) \approx u(1, 1) + \partial u(1, 1)/\partial x \cdot (-0.01) + \partial u(1, 1)/\partial y \cdot 0.01 = 1 - 2^{-\beta}/100\alpha - 2^{-\beta}/100\alpha = 1 - 2^{-\beta}/50\alpha$

Chapter 13

13.1

1. $x = 1, y = 2$ ($f'_1(x, y) = -4x + 4 = 0, f'_2(x, y) = -2y + 4 = 0$ for $x = 1, y = 2$.)

3. $F'_K = -2(K-3) - (L-6)$ and $F'_L = -4(L-6) - (K-3)$, so the first-order conditions yield $-2(K-3) - (L-6) = 0.65, -4(L-6) - (K-3) = 1.2$. The solution is $(K, L) = (2.8, 5.75)$.

13.2

1. (a) $\partial \pi^2/\partial x^2 = -0.08 \le 0$, $\partial^2 \pi/\partial y^2 = -0.02 \le 0$, and $(\partial^2 \pi/\partial x^2)(\partial^2 \pi/\partial y^2) - (\partial^2 \pi/\partial x \partial y)^2 = 0.0015 \ge 0$, so
the conditions in (a) in Theorem 13.2.1 are satisfied. (b) $f''_{11} = -4, f''_{12} = 0$, and $f''_{22} = -2$ for all (x, y), so the
conditions in (a) in Theorem 13.2.1 are satisfied. (c) With $\pi = F(K, L) - 0.65K - 1.2L, \pi''_{11} = -2, \pi''_{12} = -1$,
and $\pi''_{22} = -4$, so the conditions in (a) in Theorem 13.2.1 are satisfied.

3. P has maximum 3888 for $x = 36, y = 12$, and $z = 9$. (Note that $P = (108 - 3y - 4z)yz$. Then $\partial P/\partial y = 108z - 6yz - 4z^2 = 0$ and $\partial P/\partial z = 108y - 3y^2 - 8yz = 0$. Because y and z are assumed to be positive, these two
equations reduce to $6y + 4z = 108$ and $3y + 8z = 108$, with solution $y = 12$ and $z = 9$. Theorem 13.2.1 cannot
be used directly to prove optimality. However, it can be applied to the equivalent problem of maximizing $\ln z$. See
Theorem 13.6.3.)

5. The profit is $\pi(x, y) = px + qy - x^2 - xy - y^2 - x - y - 14$. Profit is maximized at $x^* = \frac{1}{3}(2p - q - 1)$ and
$y^* = \frac{1}{3}(-p + 2q - 1)$, provided $q \le 2p - 1$ and $q \ge \frac{1}{2}(p + 1)$. The sufficient conditions in Theorem 13.2.1 for
$x^* > 0, y^* > 0$ to maximize profits are easily seen to be satisfied.

7. Solve the constraint for z: $z = 4x + 2y - 5$. Then minimize $P(x, y) = x^2 + y^2 + (4x + 2y - 5)^2$ w.r.t. x and y
to get $x = 20/21, y = 10/21$. The minimum value is 525/441. The second-order conditions for a minimum are
easily seen to be satisfied.

13.3

1. (a) $f_1' = -2x + 6$, $f_2' = -4y + 8$, $f_{11}'' = -2$, $f_{12}'' = 0$, and $f_{22}'' = -4$ (b) (3, 2) is a local maximum point, because $A = -2 < 0$ and $AC - B^2 = 8 > 0$. Theorem 13.2.1 shows that (3, 2) is a (global) maximum point.

3. (a) $f_1' = 3x^2 + 2y - 5$, $f_2' = 2x - 2y$, $f_{11}'' = 6x$, $f_{12}'' = 2$, $f_{22}'' = -2$ (b) See the table.

(x, y)	A	B	C	$AC - B^2$	Type of point
$(1, 1)$	6	2	-2	-16	Saddle point
$(-5/3, -5/3)$	-10	2	-2	16	Local maximum

5. (a) (0, 0) saddle point, (1, 1) local minimum.   (b) $(-\frac{1}{2}\ln 2, \frac{1}{2}\ln 2)$ is a local minimum point. (Adding the equations $f_1' = e^{x+y} + e^{x-y} - 3/2 = 0$ and $f_2' = e^{x+y} - e^{x-y} - 1/2 = 0$ yields $e^{x+y} = 1$, and so $x + y = 0$, etc.)
(c) (0, 0) saddle point, $(a, 0)$ and $(-a, 0)$ local maxima where $a = \sqrt{3}/2$.   (d) (0, 0) saddle point, (1/2, 1/4) and $(-1/2, -1/4)$ local minima.

7. (a) We find $f_1'(x, y) = x - 1 + ay$, $f_2'(x, y) = a(x - 1) - y^2 + 2a^2y$, $f_{11}''(x, y) = 1$, $f_{12}''(x, y) = a$, and $f_{22}''(x, y) = -2y + 2a^2$. Stationary points require that $x - 1 = -ay$ and $a(x - 1) = y^2 - 2a^2y$. These two equations yield $-a^2y = y^2 - 2a^2y$, and so $a^2y = y^2$. Hence $y = 0$ or $y = a^2$. Since $x = 1 - ay$, the stationary points are (1, 0) and $(1 - a^3, a^2)$. The following table is used to classify the stationary points:

(x, y)	A	B	C	$AC - B^2$
$(1, 0)$	1	a	$2a^2$	a^2
$(1 - a^3, a^2)$	1	a	0	$-a^2$

We see that if $a \neq 0$, then (1, 0) is a local minimum point, while $(1 - a^3, a^2)$ is a saddle point. If $a = 0$, (1, 0) is the only stationary point, and the test gives no answer. However, note that $f(1, y) = -\frac{1}{2} - \frac{1}{3}y^3$, so $f(1, y) < f(1, 0)$ for all $y > 0$ and $f(1, y) > f(1, 0)$ for all $y < 0$. Thus (1, 0) is neither a local maximum point, nor a local minimum point. Hence it is a saddle point.
(b) $f(x, y)$ is convex $\iff$ $f_{11}''(x, y) \geq 0$, $f_{22}''(x, y) \geq 0$, and $f_{11}''(x, y)f_{22}''(x, y) - (f_{12}''(x, y))^2 \geq 0$. These conditions reduce to $-2y + 2a^2 \geq 0$ and $(-2y + 2a^2) - a^2 = -2y + a^2 \geq 0$, which is equivalent to $a^2 \geq y$ and $a^2 \geq 2y$. It follows that $f(x, y)$ is convex in that part of the xy-plane where $y \leq \frac{1}{2}a^2$.

9. (a) See Fig. A13.3.9. The domain where $f(x, y)$ is negative is shaded. The origin is easily seen to be the only stationary point, and $f(0, 0) = 0$. As the figure shows, $f(x, y)$ takes positive and negative values for points arbitrary close to (0, 0), so the origin is a saddle point.
(b) $g(t) = f(th, tk) = (tk - t^2h^2)(tk - 2t^2h^2) = 2h^4t^4 - 3h^2kt^3 + k^2t^2$, so $g'(t) = 8h^4t^3 - 9h^2kt^2 + 2k^2t$ and $g''(t) = 24h^4t^2 - 18h^2kt + 2k^2$. So $g'(0) = 0$ and $g''(0) = 2k^2$. Hence, $t = 0$ is a minimum point for $k \neq 0$. For $k = 0$, $g(t) = 2t^4h^4$, which has a minimum at $t = 0$.

13.4

1. (a) $Q_1^* = 45$, $Q_2^* = 20$, $P_1^* = 110$, $P_2^* = 100$, and $\pi^* = 5650$ (b) Let $P = P_1 = P_2$. Then $Q_1 = 100 - \frac{1}{2}P$, $Q_2 = 45 - \frac{1}{4}P$, so profit as a function of P is $\hat{\pi} = (P - 20)(Q_1 + Q_2) = (P - 20)(145 - \frac{3}{4}P) = -\frac{3}{4}P^2 + 160P - 2900$, which is maximized when $P = 320/3$. Corresponding profit: 16900/3. Loss of profits: $5650 - 16900/3 = 50/3$.
(c) New profit: $\tilde{\pi} = -2Q_1^2 - 4Q_2^2 + 175Q_1 + 160Q_2$, with maximum at $Q_1 = 43.75$, $Q_2 = 20$, with prices $P_1 = 112.50$ and $P_2 = 100$. Profit is 5428.125. The number of units sold in market 1 goes down, the price goes up and profits are lower. In market 2 the number of units sold and the price are unchanged.

Figure A13.3.9

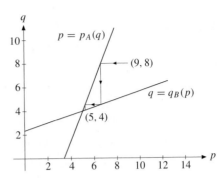

Figure A13.4.5

3. New profit function: $\hat{\pi} = (a_1 - \alpha - t)Q_1 + (a_2 - \alpha)Q_2 - b_1 Q_1^2 - b_2 Q_2^2$, which has a maximum at $\hat{Q}_1 = (a_1 - \alpha - t)/2b_1$, $\hat{Q}_2 = (a_2 - \alpha)/2b_2$. Tax revenues are maximized at $t = \frac{1}{2}(a_1 - \alpha)$.

5. (a) The firms choose p and q to maximize $px + qy - (5+x) - (3+2y) = 26p + 24q - 5p^2 - 6q^2 + 8pq - 69$. This is a concave function. The maximum is given by $p = 9$, $q = 8$, $x = 16$, $y = 4$. A's profit is 123, whereas B's is 21.   (b) $p_A(q) = (2q + 17)/5$, $q_B(p) = (p+7)/3$ (c) Equilibrium occurs where $p = p_A(q)$ and $q = q_B(p)$. So $5p = 2q + 17$ and $3q = p + 7$. These give $p = 5$, $q = 4$, $x = 20$, $y = 12$. A gets 75, B gets 21. (d) The process starts at $(9, 8)$ and converges to $(5, 4)$. See Fig. A13.4.5.

13.5

1. (a) $f_1'(x, y) = 4 - 4x$ and $f_2'(x, y) = -4y$. The only stationary point is $(1, 0)$, with $f(1, 0) = 2$.
(b) $f(x, y)$ has maximum 2 at $(1, 0)$ and minimum -70 at $(-5, 0)$. (A maximum and a minimum exist, by the extreme-value theorem. Along the boundary, the function value is $4x - 50$, with $x \in [-5, 5]$. So its maximum along the boundary is -30 at $x = 5$ and its minimum is -70 at $x = -5$.)

3. A maximum and a minimum exist by the extreme-value theorem. The maximum is 1 at $(2, 1/2)$. The minimum is 0 at $(x, 0)$, with x arbitrary, and at $(x, x - 1)$, with x arbitrary in $[1, 2]$.

5. (a) $(1, 2)$ is a local minimum; $(0, 0)$ and $(0, 4)$ are saddle points.   (b) Study $f(x, 1)$ as $x \to -\infty$, and $f(-1, y)$ as $y \to \infty$.   (c) f has a minimum $-4/e$ at $(1, 2)$, and maximum 0 at all $(x, 0)$ and $(x, 4)$ satisfying $x \in [0, 5]$, and at all $(0, y)$ satisfying $y \in [0, 4]$.   (d) $y' = -f_x'/f_y' = (x - 1)(y^2 - 4y)/x(2y - 4) = 0$ when $x = 1$ and $y = 4 - e$.

7. Let $g(x) = 1$ in $[0, 1)$, $g(x) = 2$ in $[1, 2]$. Then g is discontinuous at $x = 1$, and the set $\{x : g(x) \le 1\} = [0, 1)$ is not closed. (Draw your own graph of g.)

13.6

1. (a) $(1, 5, 0)$ (b) $(0, 0, 0)$

3. By the chain rule, $g_i'(\mathbf{x}) = F'(f(\mathbf{x})) f_i'(\mathbf{x})$ for $i = 1, 2, \ldots, n$. Because $F' \ne 0$ everywhere, the assertion follows.

5. (a) Because $F(u) = \frac{1}{2}(e^u - e^{-u})$ is strictly increasing, the problem is equivalent to: max $x^2 + y^2 - 2x$ subject to $(x, y) \in S$.   (b) The problem is equivalent to: max $\ln A + a_1 \ln x_1 + \cdots + a_n \ln x_n$ subject to $x_1 + \cdots + x_n = 1$.

13.7

1. (a) The profit is $\pi = px - ax - bx^2 - tx$, which has a maximum at $x^* = (p - a - t)/2b$, with $\pi^* = (p - a - t)^2/4b$.
(b) $\partial \pi^*/\partial p = 2(p - a - t)/4b = x^*$. If we increase p by 1 dollar, then the optimal profit increases by x^* dollars. (For each of the x^* units sold the revenue increases by 1 dollar.)

3. $\dfrac{\partial Q^*}{\partial r} = \dfrac{\partial}{\partial r}\left(\dfrac{\partial \hat{\pi}^*}{\partial p}\right) = \dfrac{\partial}{\partial p}\left(\dfrac{\partial \hat{\pi}^*}{\partial r}\right) = \dfrac{\partial}{\partial p}(-K^*) = -\dfrac{\partial K^*}{\partial p}$. The other equalities are proved in a similar way.

Review Problems for Chapter 13

1. $(x, y) = (2, -5)$. ($f_1'(x, y) = -4x + 2y + 18 = 0$, $f_2'(x, y) = 2x - 2y - 14 = 0$ at $(x, y) = (2, -5)$. Moreover, $f_{11}'' = -4$, $f_{12}'' = 2$, and $f_{22}'' = -2$, so $f_{11}'' f_{22}'' - (f_{12}'')^2 = 4$. The conditions in (a) in Theorem 13.2.1 are satisfied.)

3. (a) $\pi(Q_d, Q_w) = P_d Q_d + P_w Q_w - c(Q_d + Q_w)$ (b) The first-order conditions are: $P_d = c'(Q_d + Q_w)$, $P_w = c'(Q_d + Q_w)$. Thus the prices should be the same in the two markets and equal to the marginal cost. If the prices differ, the firm will sell only to the market in which it receives the higher price.

5. (a) $(x, y) = (230, 5)$ maximizes profit.   (b) When $x = 200 - y$, profit is maximized at $(x, y) = (195, 5)$.

7. (a) $f_1' = 2(2x+y+2)^{-1} - 2$, $f_2' = (2x+y+2)^{-1} - 1$, $f_{11}'' = -4(2x+y+2)^{-2}$, $f_{12}'' = f_{21}'' = -2(2x+y+2)^{-2}$, and $f_{22}'' = -(2x+y+2)^{-2}$. Stationary points are all points on the line $2x+y = -1$. We find that $f_{11}'' f_{22}'' - (f_{12}'')^2 = 0$ along $2x + y = -1$, so the second-derivative test of Theorem 13.2.1 fails to give an answer. Nevertheless, the function f is defined on the convex set S of all (x, y) where $2x + y > -2$. Because $f_{11}'' < 0$, $f_{22}'' < 0$, and $f_{11}'' f_{22}'' - (f_{12}'')^2 = 0$ for all (x, y) in S, Theorem 13.2.1 implies that these stationary points are all maxima. (Actually, f is concave on S.)   (b) See Fig. A13.R.7. There are no stationary points in the interior of S. The function attains its maximum value $\ln\left(2 - \frac{1}{2}\sqrt{2}\right) + \frac{1}{2}\sqrt{2}$ at the point $(-\frac{1}{2}\sqrt{2}, \frac{1}{2}\sqrt{2})$.

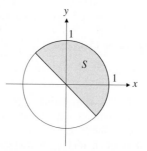

Figure A13.R.7

9. (a) $f_1' = e^{x+y} + e^{x-y} - \frac{3}{2}$, $f_2' = e^{x+y} - e^{x-y} - \frac{1}{2}$, $f_{11}'' = e^{x+y} + e^{x-y}$, $f_{12}'' = e^{x+y} - e^{x-y}$, $f_{22}'' = e^{x+y} + e^{x-y}$. It follows that $f_{11}'' \geq 0$, $f_{22}'' \geq 0$, and $f_{11}'' f_{22}'' - (f_{12}'')^2 = 4e^{2x} \geq 0$, so f is convex.

(b) At the stationary point, $e^{x+y} = 1$ and $e^{x-y} = \frac{1}{2}$, so $x + y = 0$ and $x - y = -\ln 2$. The stationary point is therefore $(x, y) = (-\frac{1}{2}\ln 2, \frac{1}{2}\ln 2)$, where $f(x, y) = \frac{1}{2}(1 + \ln 2)$. Because f is convex, this is the minimum.

Chapter 14

14.1

1. (a) $\mathcal{L}(x, y) = xy - \lambda(x + 3y - 24)$. The equations $\mathcal{L}_1' = y - \lambda = 0$, $\mathcal{L}_2' = x - 3\lambda = 0$ imply that $x = 3y$, which inserted into the constraint yields $3y + 3y = 24$, so $y = 4$, and then $x = 12$.   (b) Using (**) in Example 3 with $a = b = p = 1$, $q = 3$, and $m = 24$, we have $x = \frac{1}{2}(24/1) = 12$, $y = \frac{1}{2}(24/3) = 4$.

3. (a) $(2, 2)$, $(2, -2)$, $(-2, 2)$, and $(-2, -2)$ are the solution candidates. Here $f(2, 2) = f(-2, -2) = 12$ and $f(-2, 2) = f(2, -2) = -12$. So $(2, 2)$ and $(-2, -2)$ are the only possible solutions of the maximization problem, and $(-2, 2)$ and $(2, -2)$ are the only possible solutions of the minimization problem. (The extreme-value theorem ensures that we have found the solutions, because f is continuous and the constraint determines a circle which is a closed bounded set.)   (b) $(3, -1)$ and $(-3, 1)$ are the only possible solutions to the max/min problems, respectively.

5. (a) According to (**) in Example 3, $x = \frac{\frac{1}{2}}{\frac{1}{2}+\frac{1}{3}}\frac{1}{2}m = 3m/10$, and $y = \frac{\frac{1}{3}}{\frac{1}{2}+\frac{1}{3}}\frac{1}{4}m = m/10$.
(b) $x = 10$, $y = 6\,250\,000$ (c) $x = 8/3$, $y = 1$

14.2

1. The solution is $x^* = m/3$, $y^* = m/9$, with $\lambda = m^2/27$. The value function is $f^*(m) = (m/3)^2(m/9) = m^3/81$, so we see that $df^*(m)/dm = m^2/27 = \lambda$.

3. $m = \dfrac{aw}{a+b}T_0$, $l = \dfrac{b}{a+b}T_0$

5. $f(x, y) = x \int_0^y [-t^3 + (\alpha y^2 + y - 1)t^2 + (y - \alpha y^3)t]\,dt = x|_0^y[-\frac{1}{4}t^4 + (\alpha y^2 + y - 1)\frac{1}{3}t^3 + (y - \alpha y^3)\frac{1}{2}t^2] = -\frac{1}{6}\alpha xy^5 + \frac{1}{12}xy^4 + \frac{1}{6}xy^3$. In the same way, $g(x, y) = \frac{1}{6}xy^3$. The solution of $(*)$ is $x = 384\alpha^3 M$, $y = 1/4\alpha$, with $f^*(M) = M + M/16\alpha$. (The easiest way to solve the problem is to note that because $\frac{1}{6}xy^3 = M$, the problem reduces to that of maximizing $M + \frac{1}{2}My - \alpha My^2$ for $y \geq 0$. For $y = 0$, the expression is equal to M, and its maximum is attained for $y = 1/4\alpha$.) Alternatively, eliminating the Lagrange multiplier from the first-order conditions $f_1' = \lambda g_1'$ and $f_2' = \lambda g_2'$, we eventually obtain $y = 1/4\alpha$. The Lagrange multiplier is $\lambda = 1 + 1/16\alpha$. Clearly, $\partial f^*(M)/\partial M = \lambda$, which confirms (2).

14.3

1. $\mathcal{L}(x, y) = xy - \lambda(x + y - 2)$, so the first-order conditions are $y - \lambda = 0$, $x - \lambda = 0$, with the unique solution $x = y = \lambda = 1$ satisfying the constraint $x + y = 2$. Then, when $\lambda = 1$, one has $\mathcal{L}(2, 2) = 2 > \mathcal{L}(1, 1) = 1$. (In fact, $\mathcal{L}(x, y)$ has a saddle point at $(1, 1)$.)

3. (a) The Lagrangian is $\mathcal{L}(x, y) = 2x + 3y - \lambda(\sqrt{x} + \sqrt{y} - 5)$, and the first-order conditions are $\mathcal{L}_1'(x, y) = 2 - \lambda/2\sqrt{x} = 0$, $\mathcal{L}_2'(x, y) = 3 - \lambda/2\sqrt{y} = 0$. It follows that $y = 4x/9$. Inserting this equation into the constraint gives $x = 9$ and then $y = 4$.   (b) See Fig. A14.3.3. The solution is obtained by moving the straight line $2x + 3y = c$ as far as possible in the north-east direction. So the solution is at $(x, y) = (0, 25)$.   (c) $g(x, y)$ is continuously differentiable only on the set A of (x, y) such that $x > 0$ and $y > 0$, so the theorem does not apply at the point $(x, y) = (0, 25)$.

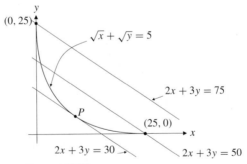

Figure A14.3.3

14.4

1. $\mathcal{L}(x, y) = 10x^{1/2}y^{1/3} - \lambda(2x + 4y - m)$ is concave in (x, y) (see Problem 13.2.8 and Note 13.2.2), so Theorem 14.4.1 applies.

3. $U_{11}''(x, y) = a(a-1)x^{a-2} \leq 0$, $U_{22}''(x, y) = a(a-1)y^{a-2} \leq 0$, and $U_{12}''(x, y) = 0$, so U is concave. The solution is $x = mp^{1/(a-1)}/R$, $y = mq^{1/(a-1)}/R$, where $R = p^{a/(a-1)} + q^{a/(a-1)}$.

14.5

1. (a) $\mathcal{L}(x, y, z) = x^2 + y^2 + z^2 - \lambda(x + y + z - 1)$. The only solution of the necessary conditions is $(1/3, 1/3, 1/3)$ with $\lambda = 2/3$.   (b) The problem is to find the shortest distance from the origin to a point in the plane $x + y + z = 1$. The corresponding maximization problem has no solution.

3. (a) $x^* = \alpha(wL + m)/p$, $y^* = \beta(wL + m)/q$, and $l^* = (\alpha + \beta)L - m(1 - \alpha - \beta)/w$. The condition given is equivalent to $l^* \geq 0$.   (b) The solution is $l^* = 0$, with $x^* = \alpha m/(\alpha + \beta)p$ and $y^* = \beta m/(\alpha + \beta)q$. (In this case, unearned income is so high that it is optimal for the individual not to work at all.)

5. Here $\mathcal{L} = a_1^2 x_1^2 + \cdots + a_n^2 x_n^2 - \lambda(x_1 + \cdots + x_n - 1)$. Necessary conditions are that $\mathcal{L}_j' = 2a_j^2 x_j - \lambda = 0$, $j = 1, \ldots, n$, and so $x_j = \lambda/2a_j^2$. Inserted into the constraint, this implies that $1 = \frac{1}{2}\lambda(1/a_1^2 + \cdots + 1/a_n^2)$. Thus, for $j = 1, \ldots, n$, we have

$$x_j = \frac{1}{a_j^2(1/a_1^2 + \cdots + 1/a_n^2)} = \frac{1}{a_j^2 \sum_{i=1}^{n}(1/a_i^2)}$$

If at least one a_i is 0, the minimum value is 0, which is attained by letting a corresponding x_i be 1, with the other x_j all equal to 0.

7. The Lagrangian is $\mathcal{L} = x + y - \lambda(x^2 + 2y^2 + z^2 - 1) - \mu(x + y + z - 1)$, which is stationary when:
(i) $\mathcal{L}_x' = 1 - 2\lambda x - \mu = 0$; (ii) $\mathcal{L}_y' = 1 - 4\lambda y - \mu = 0$; (iii) $\mathcal{L}_z' = -2\lambda z - \mu = 0$. From (i) and (ii), $2\lambda(x - 2y) = 0$. If $\lambda = 0$, then (ii) and (iii) yield $\mu = 1$ and $\mu = 0$. Therefore $x = 2y$ instead. Substituting this value for x into the constraints gives $6y^2 + z^2 = 1$, $3y + z = 1$. Thus $z = 1 - 3y$ and $1 = 6y^2 + (1 - 3y)^2 = 15y^2 - 6y + 1$. Hence $y = 0$ or $y = 2/5$, implying that $x = 0$ or $4/5$, and that $z = 1$ or $-1/5$. The only two solution candidates are $(x, y, z) = (0, 0, 1)$ with $\lambda = -1/2$, $\mu = 1$, and $(x, y, z) = (4/5, 2/5, -1/5)$ with $\lambda = 1/2$, $\mu = 1/5$. Because $x + y$ is 0 at $(0, 0, 1)$ and 6/5 at $(4/5, 2/5, -1/5)$, these are respectively the minimum and the maximum. (The constraints determine geometrically the curve which is the intersection of an ellipsoid (see Fig. 11.4.2) and a plane. The continuous function $x + y$ does attain a maximum and a minimum over this closed bounded set.)

9. (a) The two solution candidates are $(x, y, z) = (1, 1, 0)$ and $(x, y, z) = (-\frac{1}{2}, 1, \frac{3}{4})$. The corresponding values of (λ, μ) are $(4/3, -8/3)$ and $(-5/6, -5/6)$ respectively. Because $(y + z - 3)^2$ is 4 at $(1, 1, 0)$ and 25/16 at $(-1/2, 1, 3/4)$, the latter is the appropriate solution candidate. (The method used in Problem 4 can be applied to show that this gives the minimum.) (b) The other solution candidate, which is $(1, 1, 0)$, gives $f(1, 1, 0) = 4$. But $(-2, -2, 0)$, for example, satisfies both constraints, and gives $f(-2, -2, 0) = 25$.

14.6

1. The minimum point is $(x^*, y^*, z^*) = (a, 2a, 9a)$, where $a = -\sqrt{b}/6$, with $\lambda = -3/\sqrt{b}$. The value of the objective function is $f^*(b) = x^* + 4y^* + 3z^* = -6\sqrt{b}$, and $df^*(b)/db = -3/\sqrt{b} = \lambda$.

3. (a) $\left(\frac{1}{4}\sqrt{15}, 0, \frac{1}{8}\right)$ and $\left(-\frac{1}{4}\sqrt{15}, 0, \frac{1}{8}\right)$ (with $\lambda = 1$) both solve the maximization problem, while $\left(0, 0, -\frac{1}{2}\right)$ solves the minimization problem. (b) $\Delta f^* \approx \lambda \Delta c = 1 \cdot 0.02 = 0.02$

5. $\dfrac{\partial K^*}{\partial w} = \dfrac{\partial}{\partial w}\left(\dfrac{\partial C^*}{\partial r}\right) = \dfrac{\partial}{\partial r}\left(\dfrac{\partial C^*}{\partial w}\right) = \dfrac{\partial L^*}{\partial r}$, using the first and second equality in $(*)$.

14.7

1. (a) With the Lagrangian $\mathcal{L} = -x^2 - y^2 - \lambda(x - 3y + 10)$, the Kuhn-Tucker conditions are (i) $\mathcal{L}_x' = -2x - \lambda = 0$; (ii) $\mathcal{L}_y' = -2y + 3\lambda = 0$; (iii) $\lambda \geq 0$ ($\lambda = 0$ if $x - 3y < -10$). Suppose $\lambda = 0$. Then (i) and (ii) imply $x = y = 0$, contradicting $x - 3y \leq -10$. Thus $\lambda > 0$ and from (iii), $x - 3y = -10$. Furthermore, (i) and (ii) imply $\lambda = -2x = \frac{2}{3}y$, so $y = -3x$. Inserting this into $x - 3y = -10$ yields $x = -1$, and then $y = 3$. Since the Lagrangian is easily seen to be concave, the solution is $(x, y) = (-1, 3)$. (b) See Fig. A14.7.1. The solution is that point on the line $x - 3y = -10$ which is closest to the origin.

Figure A14.7.1

3. (a) The Kuhn-Tucker conditions are (i) $-2(x-1)-2\lambda x = 0$; (ii) $-2ye^{y^2}-2\lambda y = 0$; (iii) $\lambda \geq 0 (= 0 \text{ if } x^2+y^2 < a)$. So $x = (1+\lambda)^{-1}$ and $y = 0$. The constraint $x^2 + y^2 \leq a$ implies $(1+\lambda)^{-2} \leq a$, or $1+\lambda \geq a^{-1/2}$. For $0 < a < 1$, the solution is $x = \sqrt{a}$, $y = 0$, and $\lambda = a^{-1/2} - 1$; for $a \geq 1$, it is $x = 1$, $y = 0$, and $\lambda = 0$. Because the Lagrangian is concave, this is the optimal solution. (b) For $a \in (0, 1)$, we have $f^*(a) = 2\sqrt{a} - a$, and we see that $df^*(a)/da = \lambda$. If $a \geq 1$, then $f^*(a) = 2$, so $df^*(a)/da = \lambda = 0$.

5. With the Lagrangian $\mathcal{L} = aQ - bQ^2 - \alpha Q - \beta Q^2 + \lambda Q$, the Kuhn–Tucker necessary conditions for Q^* to solve the problem are: (i) $d\mathcal{L}/dQ = a - \alpha - 2(b + \beta)Q^* + \lambda = 0$; (ii) $\lambda \geq 0 (\lambda = 0 \text{ if } Q^* > 0)$. By Theorem 14.7.1, these conditions are also sufficient because the Lagrangian is concave. We find that $Q^* = (a - \alpha)/2(b + \beta)$ and $\lambda = 0$ if $a > \alpha$, whereas $Q^* = 0$ and $\lambda = \alpha - a$ if $a \leq \alpha$. (See also Example 4.6.4.)

14.8

1. (a) Writing the constraints as $g_1(x, y) = x + e^{-x} - y \leq 0$ and $g_2(x, y) = -x \leq 0$, the Lagrangian is $\mathcal{L} = \frac{1}{2}x - y - \lambda_1(x + e^{-x} - y) - \lambda_2(-x)$. The Kuhn–Tucker conditions are then: (i) $\frac{1}{2} - \lambda_1(1 - e^{-x}) + \lambda_2 = 0$; (ii) $-1 + \lambda_1 = 0$; (iii) $\lambda_1 \geq 0 (\lambda_1 = 0 \text{ if } x + e^{-x} < y)$; (iv) $\lambda_2 \geq 0 (\lambda_2 = 0 \text{ if } x > 0)$ (b) From (ii), $\lambda_1 = 1$, so from (iii), $x + e^{-x} = y$. Either $x = 0$ or $x > 0$. In the latter case, (iv) implies that $\lambda_2 = 0$. Then (i) implies $\frac{1}{2} - (1 - e^{-x}) = 0$, or $e^{-x} = \frac{1}{2}$. Hence $x = \ln 2$, and so $y = x + e^{-x} = \ln 2 + \frac{1}{2}$. If $x = 0$, then (i) implies $\lambda_2 = -\frac{1}{2}$, which contradicts $\lambda_2 \geq 0$. We conclude that $(x, y) = (\ln 2, \ln 2 + \frac{1}{2})$ is the only point satisfying the Kuhn–Tucker conditions, with $(\lambda_1, \lambda_2) = (1, 0)$. (By sketching the constraint set and studying the level curves $\frac{1}{2}x - y = c$, it is easy to see that the point we found solves the problem.)

3. (a) The feasible set and one of the level curves for $ax + y$ are shown in Fig. A14.8.3.

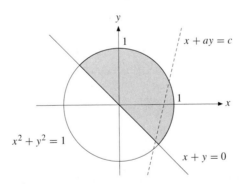

Figure A.14.8.3

Write the second constraint as $-x - y \leq 0$ and form the Lagrangian $\mathcal{L}(x, y) = x + ay - \lambda(x^2 + y^2 - 1) + \mu(x + y)$. The necessary conditions are: $1 - 2\lambda x + \mu = 0$; $a - 2\lambda y + \mu = 0$; $\lambda \geq 0 (\lambda = 0 \text{ if } x^2 + y^2 < 1)$; $\mu \geq 0 (\mu = 0 \text{ if } x + y > 0)$.

(b) The first equation gives $2\lambda x = 1 + \mu \geq 1 > 0$, so $\lambda > 0$, and then $x > 0$. Because $\lambda > 0$, it follows that $x^2 + y^2 = 1$, so possible solutions must lie on the circle.

Suppose $x + y = 0$. Then $y = -x$, and from $x^2 + y^2 = 1$, we get $x = \frac{1}{2}\sqrt{2}$ (because $x > 0$), and $y = -\frac{1}{2}\sqrt{2}$. Then the two first equations give $\lambda = (1 - a)/2\sqrt{2}$, $\mu = -(1 + a)/2$. The nonnegative restrictions on the multipliers require $a \leq -1$. For $x + y > 0$, we have $\mu = 0$, and we find $x = 1/\sqrt{1 + a^2}$ and $y = a/\sqrt{1 + a^2}$, with $\lambda = \frac{1}{2}\sqrt{1 + a^2}$. Because $x + y > 0$ in this case, we must have $1 + a > 0$, or $a > -1$. Finally, then,

$$(x^*, y^*) = \begin{cases} \left(\frac{1}{2}\sqrt{2}, -\frac{1}{2}\sqrt{2}\right) & \text{if } a \leq -1 \\ \left(1/\sqrt{1 + a^2}, a/\sqrt{1 + a^2}\right) & \text{if } a > -1 \end{cases}$$

5. A feasible triple (x_1^*, x_2^*, k^*) solves the problem iff there exist numbers λ and μ such that (i) $1 - 2x_1^* - \lambda \leq 0$ $(= 0$ if $x_1^* > 0)$; (ii) $3 - 2x_2^* - \mu \leq 0$ $(= 0$ if $x_2^* > 0)$; (iii) $-2k^* + \lambda + \mu \leq 0$ $(= 0$ if $k^* > 0)$; (iv) $\lambda \geq 0$ $(\lambda = 0$ if $x_1^* < k^*)$; and (v) $\mu \geq 0$ $(\mu = 0$ if $x_2^* < k^*)$. If $k^* = 0$, then feasibility requires $x_1^* = 0$ and $x_2^* = 0$, and so (i) and (iii) imply that $\lambda \geq 1$ and $\mu \geq 3$, which contradicts (iii). Thus, $k^* > 0$. Next, if $\mu = 0$, then $x_2^* \geq 3/2$ and $\lambda = 2k^* > 0$. So $x_1^* = k^* = 1/4$, contradicting $x_2^* \leq k^*$. So $\mu > 0$, which implies that $x_2^* = k^*$. Now, if $x_1^* = 0 < k^*$, then $\lambda = 0$, which contradicts (i). So $0 < x_1^* = \frac{1}{2}(1 - \lambda)$. Next, if $\lambda > 0$, then $x_1^* = k^* = x_2^* = \frac{1}{2}(1 - \lambda) = \frac{1}{2}(3 - \mu) = \frac{1}{2}(\lambda + \mu)$. But the last two equalities are only satisfied when $\lambda = -1/3$ and $\mu = 5/3$, which contradicts $\lambda \geq 0$. So $\lambda = 0$ after all, with $x_2^* = k^* > 0$, $\mu > 0$, $x_1^* = \frac{1}{2}(1 - \lambda) = \frac{1}{2}$. Now, from (iii) it follows that $\mu = 2k^*$ and so, from (ii), that $3 = 2x_2^* + \mu = 4k^*$. The only possible solution is, therefore, $(x_1^*, x_2^*, k^*) = (1/2, 3/4, 3/4)$, with $\lambda = 0$ and $\mu = 3/2$.

Review Problems for Chapter 14

1. (a) $x = 9$, $y = 12$. (With λ as the Lagrange multiplier, the first-order conditions imply $3 - 2\lambda x = 0$ and $4 - 2\lambda y = 0$, so $3y = 4x$. Inserted into the constraint, this yields $x^2 = 81$, so $x = \pm 9$. The solution is at $x = 9$, $y = 12$, with $\lambda = 1/6$.) (b) Using (14.2.3), $f^*(225 - 1) - f^*(225) \approx \lambda(-1) = -1/6$.

3. (a) $x = -2\sqrt{b}$, $y = 0$ solves the maximization problem. $x = 4/3$, $y = \pm\sqrt{b - 4/9}$ solves the minimization problem. (The first-order conditions give the four candidates: $(\pm 2\sqrt{b}, 0)$ and $(4/3, \pm\sqrt{b - 4/9})$. Now, $f(4/3, \pm\sqrt{b - 4/9}) = b - 1/3$, $f(2\sqrt{b}, 0) = 4b - 4\sqrt{b} + 1$, and $f(-2\sqrt{b}, 0) = 4b + 4\sqrt{b} + 1$. Verify that for $b > 4/9$ one has $4b + 4\sqrt{b} + 1 > 4b - 4\sqrt{b} + 1 > b - 1/3$. (b) For $x = -2\sqrt{b}$, $y = 0$, $\lambda = 4 + 2/\sqrt{b}$. Moreover, $f^*(b) = 4b + 4\sqrt{b} + 1$, and the suggested equality is easily verified.

5. (a) With λ as the Lagrange multiplier, the first-order conditions imply that $2x - 2 = 2y - 2$, so $x = y$. Inserting this into the constraint equation and squaring, then simplifying, one obtains the second equation in $(*)$.
(b) $\partial x/\partial a = 1/2x(3x + b)$, $\partial^2 x/\partial a^2 = -\frac{1}{4}(6x + b)[x(3x + b)]^{-3}$, and $\partial x/\partial b = -x/2(3x + b)$.
(c) Put $g(x) = 2x^3 + bx^2 - a$, $x \geq 0$. Then $g(0) = -a < 0$, and $g(x) \to \infty$ as $x \to \infty$, so by the intermediate-value theorem $g(x) = 0$ has a positive solution. Because $g'(x) = 6x^2 + 2bx > 0$ for $x > 0$, the solution is unique.

7. (a) With λ as the Lagrange multiplier, the first-order conditions imply (i) $A/(x^* - a) = \lambda p$; (ii) $B/(y^* - b) = \lambda q$. It follows that $px^* = pa + A/\lambda$ and $qy^* = qb + B/\lambda$. Inserted into the budget constraint and using $A + B = 1$, these give $1/\lambda = R$. The proposed expressions for x^* and y^* follow easily.
(b) $U^* = A[\ln A + \ln R - \ln p] + B[\ln B + \ln R - \ln q]$. Then $\partial U^*/\partial m = A/R + B/R = 1/R = \lambda > 0$. Moreover, $\partial U^*/\partial p = -aA/R - A/p - aB/R = -a/R - A/p$, while $-x^*\partial U^*/\partial m = -(a + AR/p)(1/R) = -a/R - A/p$ gives the same result. The last equality is proved similarly.

9. With the Lagrangian $\mathcal{L} = R(Q) - C(Q) - \lambda(-Q)$, the first-order conditions for Q^* to solve the problem are: (i) $R'(Q^*) - C'(Q^*) + \lambda = 0$; (ii) $\lambda \geq 0$ $(\lambda = 0$ if $Q^* > 0)$. (These conditions are also sufficient for optimality because the Lagrangian is concave in Q.) A sufficient (and necessary) condition for $Q^* = 0$ to be optimal is that $\pi'(0) \leq 0$, or equivalently, $R'(0) \leq C'(0)$. (Draw a figure.)

11. (a) The maximization problem is: $\max(-rK - wL)$ subject to $\sqrt{KL} \leq Q$. With the Lagrangian function $\mathcal{L} = -rK - wL - \lambda(\sqrt{KL} - Q)$, the Kuhn–Tucker conditions for (K^*, L^*) to solve the problem are: (i) $\mathcal{L}'_K = -r - \lambda(\sqrt{L^*}/2\sqrt{K^*}) = 0$; (ii) $\mathcal{L}'_L = -w - \lambda(\sqrt{K^*}/2\sqrt{L^*}) = 0$; (iii) $\lambda \geq 0$ $(\lambda = 0$ if $\sqrt{K^*L^*} < Q)$. Obviously $\lambda = 0$ would contradict (i) and (ii), so $\lambda > 0$ and (iv) $\sqrt{K^*L^*} = Q$. Eliminating λ from (i) and (ii), we find $L^* = rK^*/w$. Then (iv) yields $K^* = Q\sqrt{w/r}$ and $L^* = Q\sqrt{r/w}$.
(b) $c^*(r, w, Q) = rK^* + wL^* = 2Q\sqrt{rw}$, so $\partial c^*/\partial r = Q\sqrt{w/r} = K^*$. If the price of capital r increases by 1, then the minimum cost will increase by about K^*, the optimal choice of capital input. The equation $\partial c^*/\partial w = Q\sqrt{r/w} = L^*$ has a similar interpretation.

Chapter 15

15.1

1. (a), (c), (d), and (f) are linear, (b) and (e) are nonlinear.

3. If $a_{ij} = 1$ for all $i \neq j$ and $a_{ii} = 0$ for $i = 1, 2, 3, 4$, then the system is

$$
\begin{aligned}
x_2 + x_3 + x_4 &= b_1 \\
x_1 \qquad\;\; + x_3 + x_4 &= b_2 \\
x_1 + x_2 \qquad\;\; + x_4 &= b_3 \\
x_1 + x_2 + x_3 \qquad\;\; &= b_4
\end{aligned}
$$

Adding the 4 equations gives $x_1 + x_2 + x_3 + x_4 = \frac{1}{3}(b_1 + b_2 + b_3 + b_4)$, after dividing by 3. From this equation, subtracting each original equation in turn gives $x_1 = -\frac{2}{3}b_1 + \frac{1}{3}(b_2 + b_3 + b_4)$, $x_2 = -\frac{2}{3}b_2 + \frac{1}{3}(b_1 + b_3 + b_4)$, $x_3 = -\frac{2}{3}b_3 + \frac{1}{3}(b_1 + b_2 + b_4)$, $x_4 = -\frac{2}{3}b_4 + \frac{1}{3}(b_1 + b_2 + b_3)$.

5. $x_1 = \frac{1}{4}x_2 + 100$, $x_2 = 2x_3 + 80$, $x_3 = \frac{1}{2}x_1$. Solution: $x_1 = 160$, $x_2 = 240$, $x_3 = 80$.

7. The equation system is:

$$
\begin{aligned}
0.712y \quad - \quad\quad c &= -95.05 \\
0.158x \quad\quad - s + 0.158c &= 34.30 \\
x - \quad y - s + \quad c &= 0 \\
x \quad\quad\quad\quad &= 93.53
\end{aligned}
$$

Solution : $x = 93.53$, $y \approx 482.11$, $s \approx 49.73$, $c \approx 438.31$

15.2

1. $\mathbf{A} = \begin{pmatrix} 1 & 0 & 0 \\ 0 & 1 & 0 \\ 0 & 0 & 1 \end{pmatrix}$ **3.** $\mathbf{A} + \mathbf{B} = \begin{pmatrix} 1 & 0 \\ 7 & 5 \end{pmatrix}$, $3\mathbf{A} = \begin{pmatrix} 0 & 3 \\ 6 & 9 \end{pmatrix}$

15.3

1. (a) $\mathbf{AB} = \begin{pmatrix} -2 & -10 \\ -2 & 17 \end{pmatrix}$ and $\mathbf{BA} = \begin{pmatrix} 12 & 6 \\ 15 & 3 \end{pmatrix}$ (b) $\mathbf{AB} = \begin{pmatrix} 26 & 3 \\ 6 & -22 \end{pmatrix}$ and $\mathbf{BA} = \begin{pmatrix} 14 & 6 & -12 \\ 35 & 12 & 4 \\ 3 & 3 & -22 \end{pmatrix}$

(c) $\mathbf{AB} = \begin{pmatrix} 0 & 0 & 0 \\ 0 & 4 & -6 \\ 0 & -8 & 12 \end{pmatrix}$ and $\mathbf{BA} = (16)$, a 1×1 matrix.   (d) $\mathbf{AB}$ is not defined. $\mathbf{BA} = \begin{pmatrix} -1 & 4 \\ 3 & 4 \\ 4 & 8 \end{pmatrix}$

3. $\mathbf{A} + \mathbf{B} = \begin{pmatrix} 4 & 1 & -1 \\ 9 & 2 & 7 \\ 3 & -1 & 4 \end{pmatrix}$, $\mathbf{A} - \mathbf{B} = \begin{pmatrix} -2 & 3 & -5 \\ 1 & -2 & -3 \\ -1 & -1 & -2 \end{pmatrix}$, $\mathbf{AB} = \begin{pmatrix} 5 & 3 & 3 \\ 19 & -5 & 16 \\ 1 & -3 & 0 \end{pmatrix}$, $\mathbf{BA} = \begin{pmatrix} 0 & 4 & -9 \\ 19 & 3 & -3 \\ 5 & 1 & -3 \end{pmatrix}$,

$(\mathbf{AB})\mathbf{C} = \mathbf{A}(\mathbf{BC}) = \begin{pmatrix} 23 & 8 & 25 \\ 92 & -28 & 76 \\ 4 & -8 & -4 \end{pmatrix}$

5. (a) The product $\mathbf{AB}$ is only defined if $\mathbf{B}$ has n rows. And $\mathbf{BA}$ is only defined if $\mathbf{B}$ has m columns. So $\mathbf{B}$ must be an $n \times m$ matrix.   (b) $\mathbf{B} = \begin{pmatrix} w - y & y \\ y & w \end{pmatrix}$, for arbitrary y, w. (*Hint:* Let $\mathbf{B} = \begin{pmatrix} x & y \\ z & w \end{pmatrix}$. Then $\mathbf{AB} = \mathbf{BA}$ iff (i) $x + 2y = x + 2z$; (ii) $2x + 3y = y + 2w$; (iii) $z + 2w = 2x + 3z$; and (iv) $2z + 3w = 2y + 3w$. Now (i) and (iv) are true iff $z = y$. So (ii) and (iii) are true as well iff $x = w - y$.)

15.4

1. $A(B + C) = AB + AC = \begin{pmatrix} 3 & 2 & 6 & 2 \\ 7 & 4 & 14 & 6 \end{pmatrix}$

3. It is straightforward to show that $(AB)C$ and $A(BC)$ are both equal to the 2×2 matrix $D = (d_{ij})_{2 \times 2}$ with
$d_{ij} = a_{i1}b_{11}c_{1j} + a_{i1}b_{12}c_{2j} + a_{i2}b_{21}c_{1j} + a_{i2}b_{22}c_{2j}$ for $i = 1, 2$ and $j = 1, 2$.

5. (a) $\begin{pmatrix} 5 & 3 & 1 \\ 2 & 0 & 9 \\ 1 & 3 & 3 \end{pmatrix}$ (b) $(1, 2, -3)$

7. (a) Direct verification yields (i) $A^2 = (a + d)A - (ad - bc)I_2 = \begin{pmatrix} a^2 + bc & ab + bd \\ ac + cd & bc + d^2 \end{pmatrix}$

(b) For the matrix A in (a), $A^2 = 0$ if $a + d = 0$ and $ad = bc$, so one example with $A \neq 0$ is $A = \begin{pmatrix} 1 & 1 \\ -1 & -1 \end{pmatrix}$.

(c) Multiplying (i) in (a) by A and using $A^3 = 0$ yields (ii) $(a + d)A^2 = (ad - bc)A$. Multiplying by A once more gives $(ad - bc)A^2 = 0$. If $ad - bc \neq 0$, then $A^2 = 0$. If $ad - bc = 0$, (ii) yields $(a + d)A^2 = 0$, and if $a + d \neq 0$, again $A^2 = 0$. Finally, if $ad - bc = a + d = 0$, then (i) implies $A^2 = 0$.

15.5

1. $A' = \begin{pmatrix} 3 & -1 \\ 5 & 2 \\ 8 & 6 \\ 3 & 2 \end{pmatrix}$, $B' = (0, 1, -1, 2)$, $C' = \begin{pmatrix} 1 \\ 5 \\ 0 \\ -1 \end{pmatrix}$ **3.** Equation (1) implies that $A = A'$ and $B = B'$.

5. No! For example: $\begin{pmatrix} 0 & 0 \\ 0 & 1 \end{pmatrix} \begin{pmatrix} 1 & 1 \\ 1 & 1 \end{pmatrix} = \begin{pmatrix} 0 & 0 \\ 1 & 1 \end{pmatrix}$.

7. (a) Direct verification. (b) $\begin{pmatrix} p & q \\ -q & p \end{pmatrix} \begin{pmatrix} p & -q \\ q & p \end{pmatrix} = \begin{pmatrix} p^2 + q^2 & 0 \\ 0 & p^2 + q^2 \end{pmatrix} = \begin{pmatrix} 1 & 0 \\ 0 & 1 \end{pmatrix}$ iff $p^2 + q^2 = 1$.

(c) If $P'P = Q'Q = I_n$, then $(PQ)'(PQ) = (Q'P')(PQ) = Q'(P'P)Q = Q'I_nQ = Q'Q = I_n$.

15.6

1. (a) Gaussian elimination yields

$$\begin{pmatrix} 1 & 1 & 3 \\ 3 & 5 & 5 \end{pmatrix} \begin{smallmatrix} -3 \\ \hookleftarrow \end{smallmatrix} \sim \begin{pmatrix} 1 & 1 & 3 \\ 0 & 2 & -4 \end{pmatrix} {}_{1/2} \sim \begin{pmatrix} 1 & 1 & 3 \\ 0 & 1 & -2 \end{pmatrix} \begin{smallmatrix} \hookleftarrow \\ -1 \end{smallmatrix} \sim \begin{pmatrix} 1 & 0 & 5 \\ 0 & 1 & -2 \end{pmatrix}$$

The solution is therefore $x_1 = 5$, $x_2 = -2$.

(b) Gaussian elimination yields

$$\begin{pmatrix} 1 & 2 & 1 & 4 \\ 1 & -1 & 1 & 5 \\ 2 & 3 & -1 & 1 \end{pmatrix} \begin{smallmatrix} -1 & -2 \\ \hookleftarrow \\ \hookleftarrow \end{smallmatrix} \sim \begin{pmatrix} 1 & 2 & 1 & 4 \\ 0 & -3 & 0 & 1 \\ 0 & -1 & -3 & -7 \end{pmatrix} {}_{-1/3} \sim \begin{pmatrix} 1 & 2 & 1 & 4 \\ 0 & 1 & 0 & -1/3 \\ 0 & -1 & -3 & -7 \end{pmatrix} \begin{smallmatrix} \hookleftarrow \\ 1 & -2 \\ \hookleftarrow \end{smallmatrix}$$

$$\sim \begin{pmatrix} 1 & 0 & 1 & 14/3 \\ 0 & 1 & 0 & -1/3 \\ 0 & 0 & -3 & -22/3 \end{pmatrix} {}_{-1/3} \sim \begin{pmatrix} 1 & 0 & 1 & 14/3 \\ 0 & 1 & 0 & -1/3 \\ 0 & 0 & 1 & 22/9 \end{pmatrix} \begin{smallmatrix} \hookleftarrow \\ \\ -1 \end{smallmatrix} \sim \begin{pmatrix} 1 & 0 & 0 & 20/9 \\ 0 & 1 & 0 & -1/3 \\ 0 & 0 & 1 & 22/9 \end{pmatrix}$$

The solution is therefore: $x_1 = 20/9$, $x_2 = -1/3$, $x_3 = 22/9$ (c) Solution: $x_1 = (2/5)s$, $x_2 = (3/5)s$, $x_3 = s$, with s an arbitrary real number.

3. For $c = 1$ and for $c = -2/5$ the solution is $x = 2c^2 - 1 + t$, $y = s$, $z = t$, $w = 1 - c^2 - 2s - 2t$, for arbitrary s and t. For other values of c there are no solutions.

15.7

1. $\mathbf{a} + \mathbf{b} = \begin{pmatrix} 5 \\ 3 \end{pmatrix}$, $\mathbf{a} - \mathbf{b} = \begin{pmatrix} -1 \\ -5 \end{pmatrix}$, $2\mathbf{a} + 3\mathbf{b} = \begin{pmatrix} 13 \\ 10 \end{pmatrix}$, and $-5\mathbf{a} + 2\mathbf{b} = \begin{pmatrix} -4 \\ 13 \end{pmatrix}$

3. $x = 3$, $y = -3$, $z = -4$　　**5.** $(4, -11) = 3(2, -1) - 2(1, 4)$

7. $\mathbf{a} \cdot \mathbf{a} = 5$, $\mathbf{a} \cdot \mathbf{b} = 2$, and $\mathbf{a} \cdot (\mathbf{a} + \mathbf{b}) = 7$. We see that $\mathbf{a} \cdot \mathbf{a} + \mathbf{a} \cdot \mathbf{b} = \mathbf{a} \cdot (\mathbf{a} + \mathbf{b})$.

9. $\mathbf{x} = (5, 7, 12)$, $\mathbf{u} = (20, 18, 25)$, $\mathbf{u} \cdot \mathbf{x} = 526$

11. (a) Input vector $= \begin{pmatrix} 0 \\ 1 \end{pmatrix}$　　(b) Output vector $= \begin{pmatrix} 2 \\ 0 \end{pmatrix}$　　(c) Cost $= (1, 3) \begin{pmatrix} 0 \\ 1 \end{pmatrix} = 3$　　(d) Revenue $= (1, 3) \begin{pmatrix} 2 \\ 0 \end{pmatrix} = 2$

(e) Value of net output $= (1, 3) \begin{pmatrix} 2 \\ -1 \end{pmatrix} = 2 - 3 = -1$.　　(f) Loss $=$ cost $-$ revenue $= 3 - 2 = 1$.

15.8

1. $\mathbf{a} + \mathbf{b} = (3, 3)$ and $-\frac{1}{2}\mathbf{a} = (-2.5, 0.5)$. See Fig. A15.8.1.

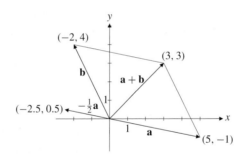

Figure A15.8.1

3. $\|\mathbf{a}\| = 3$, $\|\mathbf{b}\| = 3$, $\|\mathbf{c}\| = \sqrt{29}$. Also, $|\mathbf{a} \cdot \mathbf{b}| = 6 \le \|\mathbf{a}\| \cdot \|\mathbf{b}\| = 9$

5. The pairs of vectors in (a) and (c) are orthogonal.

7. If $\mathbf{P}$ is orthogonal and $\mathbf{c}_i$ and $\mathbf{c}_j$ are two different columns of $\mathbf{P}$, then $\mathbf{c}_i' \mathbf{c}_j$ is the element in row i and column j of $\mathbf{P}'\mathbf{P} = \mathbf{I}$, so $\mathbf{c}_i' \mathbf{c}_j = 0$. If $\mathbf{r}_i$ and $\mathbf{r}_j$ are two different rows of $\mathbf{P}$, then $\mathbf{r}_i \mathbf{r}_j'$ is the element in row i and column j of $\mathbf{P}\mathbf{P}' = \mathbf{I}' = \mathbf{I}$, so again $\mathbf{r}_i \mathbf{r}_j' = 0$.

15.9

1. (a) $x_1 = 3 + 7t$, $x_2 = -2 + 4t$, and $x_3 = 2 - t$　(b) $x_1 = 1$, $x_2 = 3 - t$, and $x_3 = 2 + t$

3. $x_1 - 3x_2 - 2x_3 = -3$. (One method: $(5, 2, 1) - (3, 4, -3) = (2, -2, 4)$ and $(2, -1, 4) - (3, 4, -3) = (-1, -5, 7)$ are two vectors in the plane. The normal (p_1, p_2, p_3) must be orthogonal to both these vectors, so $(2, -2, 4) \cdot (p_1, p_2, p_3) = 2p_1 - 2p_2 + 4p_3 = 0$ and $(-1, -5, 7) \cdot (p_1, p_2, p_3) = -p_1 - 5p_2 + 7p_3 = 0$. One solution of these two equations is $(p_1, p_2, p_3) = (1, -3, -2)$. Then using formula (4) with $(a_1, a_2, a_3) = (2, -1, 4)$ yields $(1, -3, -2) \cdot (x_1 - 2, x_2 + 1, x_3 - 4) = 0$, or $x_1 - 3x_2 - 2x_3 = -3$.)

5. $2x + 3y + 5z \le m$, with $m \ge 75$.

Review Problems for Chapter 15

1. (a) $\mathbf{A} = \begin{pmatrix} 2 & 3 & 4 \\ 3 & 4 & 5 \end{pmatrix}$ (b) $\mathbf{A} = \begin{pmatrix} 1 & -1 & 1 \\ -1 & 1 & -1 \end{pmatrix}$

3. (a) $2\mathbf{A} - 3\mathbf{B} = \begin{pmatrix} 7 & -6 \\ -5 & 5 \end{pmatrix}$ (b) $(\mathbf{A} - \mathbf{B})' = \begin{pmatrix} 3 & -2 \\ -2 & 2 \end{pmatrix}$ (c) and (d): $(\mathbf{C}'\mathbf{A}')\mathbf{B}' = \mathbf{C}'(\mathbf{A}'\mathbf{B}') = \begin{pmatrix} -6 & 5 \\ -4 & 5 \end{pmatrix}$

(e) Not defined.   (f) $\mathbf{D}'\mathbf{D} = \begin{pmatrix} 2 & 4 & 5 \\ 4 & 10 & 13 \\ 5 & 13 & 17 \end{pmatrix}$

5. $\mathbf{A} + \mathbf{B} = \begin{pmatrix} 0 & -4 & 1 \\ 8 & 6 & 4 \\ -10 & 9 & 15 \end{pmatrix}$, $\mathbf{A} - \mathbf{B} = \begin{pmatrix} 0 & 6 & -5 \\ -2 & 2 & 6 \\ -2 & 5 & 15 \end{pmatrix}$, $\mathbf{AB} = \begin{pmatrix} 13 & -2 & -1 \\ 0 & 3 & 5 \\ -25 & 74 & -25 \end{pmatrix}$,

$\mathbf{BA} = \begin{pmatrix} -33 & 1 & 20 \\ 12 & 6 & -15 \\ 6 & 4 & 18 \end{pmatrix}$, $(\mathbf{AB})\mathbf{C} = \mathbf{A}(\mathbf{BC}) = \begin{pmatrix} 74 & -31 & -48 \\ 6 & 25 & 38 \\ -2 & -75 & -26 \end{pmatrix}$

7. (a) $\mathbf{A}^2 = \begin{pmatrix} a^2 - b^2 & 2ab & b^2 \\ -2ab & a^2 - 2b^2 & 2ab \\ b^2 & -2ab & a^2 - b^2 \end{pmatrix}$ (b) $(\mathbf{C}'\mathbf{BC})' = \mathbf{C}'\mathbf{B}'(\mathbf{C}')' = \mathbf{C}'(-\mathbf{B})\mathbf{C} = -\mathbf{C}'\mathbf{BC}$. $\mathbf{A}$ is skew-symmetric if and only if $a = 0$.   (c) $\mathbf{A}'_1 = \frac{1}{2}(\mathbf{A}' + \mathbf{A}'') = \frac{1}{2}(\mathbf{A}' + \mathbf{A}) = \mathbf{A}_1$, so $\mathbf{A}_1$ is symmetric. The rest is equally easy. $\mathbf{A} = \mathbf{A}_1 + \mathbf{A}_2$ shows that any square matrix is the sum of a symmetric and a skew-symmetric matrix.

9. We represent the system of equations by its extended matrix, then perform elementary row operations as required by the Gaussian method:

$$\begin{pmatrix} 1 & a & 2 & 0 \\ -2 & -a & 1 & 4 \\ 2a & 3a^2 & 9 & 4 \end{pmatrix} \begin{smallmatrix} 2 & -2a \\ \hookleftarrow \\ \hookleftarrow \end{smallmatrix} \sim \begin{pmatrix} 1 & a & 2 & 0 \\ 0 & a & 5 & 4 \\ 0 & a^2 & 9-4a & 4 \end{pmatrix} {}_{-a} \sim \begin{pmatrix} 1 & a & 2 & 0 \\ 0 & a & 5 & 4 \\ 0 & 0 & 9-9a & 4-4a \end{pmatrix} \hookleftarrow$$

The last matrix represents the system

$$x + ay + 2z = 0$$
$$ay + 5z = 4 \qquad\qquad (*)$$
$$(9 - 9a)z = 4 - 4a$$

For $a = 1$, this has the solution $x = 3t - 4$, $y = -5t + 4$, $z = t$, with t arbitrary. If $a \neq 1$, then the last equation in (∗) gives $(9 - 9a)z = 4 - 4a$, so $z = 4/9$. The two other equations then become $x + ay = -8/9$ and $ay = 16/9$. If $a = 0$, there is no solution. If $a \neq 0$, the solution is $x = -8/3$, $y = 16/9a$, and $z = 4/9$.

11. (a) To produce $\mathbf{a}$, put $\lambda = 1/2$. To produce $\mathbf{b}$ would require $6\lambda + 2 = 7$, $-2\lambda + 6 = 5$, and $-6\lambda + 10 = 5$, but these equations have no solution.

(b) In (a) we saw that $\mathbf{a}$ can be produced even without throwing away outputs. For $\mathbf{b}$ to be possible if we are allowed to throw away output, there must exist a $\lambda \in [0, 1]$ such that $6\lambda + 2 \geq 7$, $-2\lambda + 6 \geq 5$, and $-6\lambda + 10 \geq 5$. These inequalities reduce to $\lambda \geq 5/6$, $\lambda \leq 1/2$, $\lambda \leq 5/6$, which are incompatible.

(c) Revenue $= R(\lambda) = p_1 x_1 + p_2 x_2 + p_3 x_3 = (6p_1 - 2p_2 - 6p_3)\lambda + 2p_1 + 6p_2 + 10p_3$. If the constant slope $6p_1 - 2p_2 - 6p_3$ is > 0, then $R(\lambda)$ is maximized at $\lambda = 1$; if $6p_1 - 2p_2 - 6p_3$ is < 0, then $R(\lambda)$ is maximized at $\lambda = 0$. Only in the special case where $6p_1 - 2p_2 - 6p_3 = 0$ can the two plants both remain in use.

Chapter 16

16.1

1. (a) $3 \cdot 6 - 2 \cdot 0 = 18$ (b) $ab - ba = 0$ (c) $(a+b)^2 - (a-b)^2 = 4ab$ (d) $3^t 2^{t-1} - 3^{t-1} 2^t = 3^{t-1} 2^{t-1}(3-2) = 6^{t-1}$

3. (a) $x = 11/5$ and $y = -7/5$ (b) $x = 4$ and $y = -1$ (c) $x = \dfrac{a + 2b}{a^2 + b^2}$, $y = \dfrac{2a - b}{a^2 + b^2}$, $(a^2 + b^2 \neq 0)$

5. If $A = B = \begin{pmatrix} 1 & 0 \\ 0 & 1 \end{pmatrix}$, then $|A + B| = 4$, whereas $|A| + |B| = 2$. (A and B can be chosen almost arbitrarily.)

7. (a) $X_1 = M_2$ because nation 1's exports are nation 2's imports. Similarly, $X_2 = M_1$.   (b) Substituting for X_1, X_2, M_1, M_2, C_1, and C_2 gives: (i) $Y_1(1 - c_1 + m_1) - m_2 Y_2 = A_1$;   (ii) $Y_2(1 - c_2 + m_2) - m_1 Y_1 = A_2$
Using Cramer's rule with $D = (1 - c_2 + m_2)(1 - c_1 + m_1) - m_1 m_2$ yields

$$Y_1 = \frac{1}{D}[A_2 m_2 + A_1(1 - c_2 + m_2)], \qquad Y_2 = \frac{1}{D}[A_1 m_1 + A_2(1 - c_1 + m_1)]$$

Because c_1 is the proportion of income consumed, we can assume that $0 \le c_1 \le 1$. Likewise, $0 \le c_2 \le 1$. Because $m_1 \ge 0$ and $m_2 \ge 0$, we see that $D > 0$ (excluding the case $c_1 = c_2 = 1$).
(c) Y_2 depends linearly on A_1. Increasing A_1 by one unit changes Y_2 by the factor $m_1/D \ge 0$, so Y_2 increases when A_1 increases. Here is an economic explanation: An increase in A_1 increases nation 1's income, Y_1. This in turn increases nation 1's imports, M_1. However, nation 1's imports are nation 2's exports, so this causes nation 2's income, Y_2, to increase, and so on.

16.2

1. (a) -2 (b) -2 (c) adf (d) $e(ad - bc)$

3. (a) $x_1 = 1$, $x_2 = 2$, and $x_3 = 3$ (b) $x_1 = x_2 = x_3 = 0$ (c) $x = 1$, $y = 2$, and $z = 3$

5. (a) $|A_t| = 2t^2 - 2t + 1 = 2(t - \frac{1}{2})^2 + \frac{1}{2} > 0$ for all t.   (b) $A_t^3 = \begin{pmatrix} 1 & 2t - 2t^2 & t - t^2 \\ 4t - 4 & 5t - 4 & -t^2 + 4t - 3 \\ 2 - 2t & t^2 - 4t + 3 & t^3 - 2t + 2 \end{pmatrix}$.
We find that $A_t^3 = I_3$ for $t = 1$.

16.3

1. (a) $1 \cdot 2 \cdot 3 \cdot 4 = 24$ (b) $d - a$ (c) $1 \cdot 1 \cdot 1 \cdot 11 - 1 \cdot 1 \cdot 4 \cdot 4 - 1 \cdot (-3) \cdot 1 \cdot 3 - 2 \cdot 1 \cdot 1 \cdot 2 = 0$

3. $-a_{15} a_{24} a_{32} a_{43} a_{51}$. (There are nine lines which rise to the right.)

16.4

1. (a) $AB = \begin{pmatrix} 13 & 16 \\ 29 & 36 \end{pmatrix}$, $BA = \begin{pmatrix} 15 & 22 \\ 23 & 34 \end{pmatrix}$, $A'B' = \begin{pmatrix} 15 & 23 \\ 22 & 34 \end{pmatrix}$, $B'A' = \begin{pmatrix} 13 & 29 \\ 16 & 36 \end{pmatrix}$

(b) $|A| = |A'| = -2$ and $|B| = |B'| = -2$. So $|AB| = 4 = |A| \cdot |B|$ and $|A'B'| = |A'| \cdot |B'| = 4$.

3. (a) 0 (one column has only zeros).   (b) 0 (rows 1 and 4 are proportional).   (c) $(a_1 - x)(-x)^3 = x^4 - a_1 x^3$ (Use definition (16.3.3) and observe that at most one term is nonzero.)

5. $A^2 = \begin{pmatrix} a^2 + 6 & a + 1 & a^2 + 4a - 12 \\ a^2 + 2a + 2 & 3 & 8 - 2a^2 \\ a - 3 & 1 & 13 \end{pmatrix}$ and $|A| = a^2 - 3a + 2$.

7. $X'X = \begin{pmatrix} 4 & 3 & 2 \\ 3 & 5 & 1 \\ 2 & 1 & 2 \end{pmatrix}$ and $|X'X| = 10$

9. Because $P'P = I_n$, it follows from rule G in Theorem 16.4.1 and (16.3.4) that $|P'||P| = |I_n| = 1$. But $|P'| = |P|$ by rule B in Theorem 16.4.1, so $|P|^2 = 1$. Hence, $|P| = \pm 1$.

11. Let $A = \begin{pmatrix} 0 & c & b \\ c & 0 & a \\ b & a & 0 \end{pmatrix}$. Then compute A^2 and recall G in Theorem 16.4.1.

16.5

1. (a) 2. (Subtract row 1 from both row 2 and row 3 to get a determinant whose first column has elements 1, 0, 0. Then expand by the first column.)   (b) 30   (c) 0.   (Columns 2 and 4 are proportional.)

16.6

1. $\begin{pmatrix} 3 & 0 \\ 2 & -1 \end{pmatrix} \cdot \begin{pmatrix} 1/3 & 0 \\ 2/3 & -1 \end{pmatrix} = \begin{pmatrix} 1 & 0 \\ 0 & 1 \end{pmatrix}$

3. $\mathbf{AB} = \begin{pmatrix} 1 & 0 & 0 \\ a+b & 2a+1/4+3b & 4a+3/2+2b \\ 0 & 0 & 1 \end{pmatrix} = \mathbf{I}$ iff $a+b = 4a+3/2+2b = 0$ and $2a+1/4+3b = 1$.
This is true iff $a = -3/4$ and $b = 3/4$.

5. $\mathbf{A}^{-1} = \mathbf{A}^2 = \frac{1}{2}\begin{pmatrix} -1 & \sqrt{3} \\ -\sqrt{3} & -1 \end{pmatrix}$

7. (a) $\mathbf{AA}' = \begin{pmatrix} 21 & 11 \\ 11 & 10 \end{pmatrix}$, $|\mathbf{AA}'| = 89$, and $(\mathbf{AA}')^{-1} = \frac{1}{89}\begin{pmatrix} 10 & -11 \\ -11 & 21 \end{pmatrix}$.   (b) No, $\mathbf{AA}'$ is always symmetric by
Example 15.5.3. Then $(\mathbf{AA}')^{-1}$ is symmetric by Note 2.

9. $\mathbf{B}^2 + \mathbf{B} = \mathbf{I}$, from which it follows that $\mathbf{B}^3 - 2\mathbf{B} + \mathbf{I} = \mathbf{B}(\mathbf{I} - \mathbf{B}) - 2\mathbf{B} + \mathbf{I} = \mathbf{0}$. From $\mathbf{B}^2 + \mathbf{B} = \mathbf{I}$, we get
$\mathbf{B}(\mathbf{B} + \mathbf{I}) = \mathbf{I}$, so $\mathbf{B}^{-1} = \mathbf{B} + \mathbf{I} = \begin{pmatrix} 1/2 & 5 \\ 1/4 & 1/2 \end{pmatrix}$.

11. (a) Let $\mathbf{B} = \mathbf{X}(\mathbf{X}'\mathbf{X})^{-1}\mathbf{X}'$. Then $\mathbf{A}^2 = (\mathbf{I}_m - \mathbf{B})(\mathbf{I}_m - \mathbf{B}) = \mathbf{I}_m - \mathbf{B} - \mathbf{B} + \mathbf{B}^2$. Here $\mathbf{B}^2 = (\mathbf{X}(\mathbf{X}'\mathbf{X})^{-1}\mathbf{X}')(\mathbf{X}(\mathbf{X}'\mathbf{X})^{-1}\mathbf{X}') = \mathbf{X}(\mathbf{X}'\mathbf{X})^{-1}(\mathbf{X}'\mathbf{X})(\mathbf{X}'\mathbf{X})^{-1}\mathbf{X}' = \mathbf{X}(\mathbf{X}'\mathbf{X})^{-1}\mathbf{X}' = \mathbf{B}$. Thus, $\mathbf{A}^2 = \mathbf{I}_m - \mathbf{B} - \mathbf{B} + \mathbf{B} = \mathbf{I}_m - \mathbf{B} = \mathbf{A}$.   (b) Direct
verification.

13. $\mathbf{D}^3 = \mathbf{D}^2\mathbf{D} = (2\mathbf{D} + 3\mathbf{I})\mathbf{D} = 2\mathbf{D}^2 + 3\mathbf{D} = 2(2\mathbf{D} + 3\mathbf{I}) + 3\mathbf{D} = 7\mathbf{D} + 6\mathbf{I}$. Moreover, tedious computations yield
$\mathbf{D}^6 = \mathbf{D}^3\mathbf{D}^3 = 182\mathbf{D} + 183\mathbf{I}$. To find $\mathbf{D}^{-1}$, note that from $\mathbf{D}^2 = 2\mathbf{D} + 3\mathbf{I}$, we obtain $\mathbf{D}(\mathbf{D} - 2\mathbf{I}) = 3\mathbf{I}$, and so
$\mathbf{D}\frac{1}{3}(\mathbf{D} - 2\mathbf{I}) = \mathbf{I}$. Thus, $\mathbf{D}^{-1} = \frac{1}{3}\mathbf{D} - \frac{2}{3}\mathbf{I}$.

16.7

1. (a) $\begin{pmatrix} -5/2 & 3/2 \\ 2 & -1 \end{pmatrix}$ (b) $\frac{1}{9}\begin{pmatrix} 1 & 4 & 2 \\ 2 & -1 & 4 \\ 4 & -2 & -1 \end{pmatrix}$ (c) The matrix has no inverse.

3. $(\mathbf{I} - \mathbf{A})^{-1} = \frac{5}{62}\begin{pmatrix} 18 & 16 & 10 \\ 2 & 19 & 8 \\ 4 & 7 & 16 \end{pmatrix}$

5. (a) $\mathbf{A}^{-1} = \begin{pmatrix} -2 & 1 \\ 3/2 & -1/2 \end{pmatrix}$ (b) $\begin{pmatrix} 1 & -3 & 2 \\ -3 & 3 & -1 \\ 2 & -1 & 0 \end{pmatrix}$ (c) There is no inverse.

16.8

1. (a) $x = 1$, $y = -2$, and $z = 2$ (b) $x = -3$, $y = 6$, $z = 5$, and $u = -5$

3. Show that the determinant of the coefficient matrix is equal to $-(a^3 + b^3 + c^3 - 3abc)$, and use Theorem 16.8.2.

16.9

1. (a) Let x and y denote total production in industries A and I, respectively. Then $x = \frac{1}{6}x + \frac{1}{4}y + 60$ and $y = \frac{1}{4}x + \frac{1}{4}y + 60$. So $\frac{5}{6}x - \frac{1}{4}y = 60$ and $-\frac{1}{4}x + \frac{3}{4}y = 60$.   (b) The solution is $x = 320/3$ and $y = 1040/9$.

3. $0.8x_1 - 0.3x_2 = 120$ and $-0.4x_1 + 0.9x_2 = 90$, with solution $x_1 = 225$ and $x_2 = 200$.

5. The input matrix is $\mathbf{A} = \begin{pmatrix} 0 & \beta & 0 \\ 0 & 0 & \gamma \\ \alpha & 0 & 0 \end{pmatrix}$. The sums of the elements in each column are less than 1 provided $\alpha < 1$, $\beta < 1$, and $\gamma < 1$, respectively. Then, in particular, the product $\alpha\beta\gamma < 1$.

Review Problems for Chapter 16

1. (a) $5(-2) - (-2)3 = -4$ (b) $1 - a^2$ (c) $6a^2b + 2b^3$ (d) $\lambda^2 - 5\lambda$

3. For $a \neq b$ the solutions are $x_1 = \frac{1}{2}(a + b)$ and $x_2 = -\frac{1}{2}(a + b)$. If $a = b$, the determinant is 0 for all values of x.

5. $|\mathbf{A}| = (p + 1)(q - 2)$, $|\mathbf{A} + \mathbf{E}| = 2(p - 1)(q - 2)$. $\mathbf{A} + \mathbf{E}$ has an inverse for $p \neq 1$ and $q \neq 2$. Obviously, $|\mathbf{E}| = 0$. Hence $|\mathbf{BE}| = |\mathbf{B}||\mathbf{E}| = 0$, so $\mathbf{BE}$ has no inverse.

7. We see that $(\mathbf{I} - \mathbf{A})(\mathbf{I} + \mathbf{A} + \mathbf{A}^2 + \mathbf{A}^3) = \mathbf{I} + \mathbf{A} + \mathbf{A}^2 + \mathbf{A}^3 - \mathbf{A} - \mathbf{A}^2 - \mathbf{A}^3 - \mathbf{A}^4 = \mathbf{I} - \mathbf{A}^4 = \mathbf{I}$.

9. From the first equation, $\mathbf{Y} = \mathbf{B} - \mathbf{AX}$. Inserting this into the second equation and solving for $\mathbf{X}$, yields $\mathbf{X} = 2\mathbf{A}^{-1}\mathbf{B} - \mathbf{C}$. Moreover, $\mathbf{Y} = \mathbf{AC} - \mathbf{B}$.

11. $|\mathbf{B}^3| = |\mathbf{B}|^3$. Because $\mathbf{B}$ is a 3×3-matrix, we have $|-\mathbf{B}| = (-1)^3|\mathbf{B}| = -|\mathbf{B}|$. Since $\mathbf{B}^3 = -\mathbf{B}$, it follows that $|\mathbf{B}|^3 = -|\mathbf{B}|$, and so $|\mathbf{B}|(|\mathbf{B}|^2 + 1) = 0$. The last equation implies $|\mathbf{B}| = 0$, and thus $\mathbf{B}$ can have no inverse.

13. Note first that if $\mathbf{A}'\mathbf{A} = \mathbf{I}_n$, then rule (16.6.5) implies that $\mathbf{A}' = \mathbf{A}^{-1}$, so $\mathbf{AA}' = \mathbf{I}_n$. But then $(\mathbf{A}'\mathbf{B}^{-1}\mathbf{A})(\mathbf{A}'\mathbf{BA}) = \mathbf{A}'\mathbf{B}^{-1}(\mathbf{AA}')\mathbf{BA} = \mathbf{A}'\mathbf{B}^{-1}\mathbf{I}_n\mathbf{BA} = \mathbf{A}'(\mathbf{B}^{-1}\mathbf{B})\mathbf{A} = \mathbf{A}'\mathbf{I}_n\mathbf{A} = \mathbf{A}'\mathbf{A} = \mathbf{I}_n$. By rule (16.6.5) again, it follows that $(\mathbf{A}'\mathbf{BA})^{-1} = \mathbf{A}'\mathbf{B}^{-1}\mathbf{A}$.

Chapter 17

17.1

1. (a) From Fig. A17.1.1(a) we see that the solution is at the intersection of the two lines $3x_1 + 2x_2 = 6$ and $x_1 + 4x_2 = 4$. Solution: max = 36/5 for $(x_1, x_2) = (8/5, 3/5)$.   (b) From Fig. A17.1.1(b) we see that the solution is at the intersection of the two lines $u_1 + 3u_2 = 11$ and $2u_1 + 5u_2 = 20$. Solution: min = 104 for $(u_1, u_2) = (5, 2)$.

Figure A17.1.1(a)

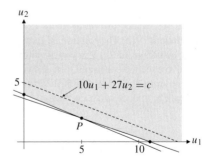

Figure A17.1.1(b)

3. (a) max = 18/5 for $(x_1, x_2) = (4/5, 18/5)$.   (b) max = 8 for $(x_1, x_2) = (8, 0)$.
(c) max = 24 for $(x_1, x_2) = (8, 0)$.   (d) min = −28/5 for $(x_1, x_2) = (4/5, 18/5)$.
(e) max = 16 for all (x_1, x_2) of the form $(x_1, 4 - \frac{1}{2}x_1)$ where $x_1 \in [4/5, 8]$.
(f) min= −24 for $(x_1, x_2) = (8, 0)$ (follows from the answer to (c)).

5. The slope of the line $20x_1 + tx_2 = c$ must lie between −1/2 (the slope of the flour border) and −1 (the slope of the butter border). For $t = 0$, the line is vertical and the solution is the point D in Fig. 2 in the text. For $t \neq 0$, the slope of the line is $-20/t$. Thus, $-1 \leq -20/t \leq -1/2$, which implies that $t \in [20, 40]$.

17.2

1. (a) $(x_1, x_2) = (2, 1/2)$ and $u_1^* = 4/5$ (b) $(x_1, x_2) = (7/5, 9/10)$ and $u_2^* = 3/5$
(c) Multiplying the two $\leq$ constraints by $4/5$ and $3/5$, respectively, then adding, we obtain
$(4/5)(3x_1 + 2x_2) + (3/5)(x_1 + 4x_2) \leq 6 \cdot (4/5) + 4 \cdot (3/5)$, which reduces to $3x_1 + 4x_2 \leq 36/5$.

3. (a) min $6u_1 + 4u_2$ subject to $\begin{cases} 3u_1 + u_2 \geq 3 \\ 2u_1 + 4u_2 \geq 4 \end{cases}$, $u_1 \geq 0, u_2 \geq 0$

(b) max $11x_1 + 20x_2$ subject to $\begin{cases} x_1 + 2x_2 \leq 10 \\ 3x_1 + 5x_2 \leq 27 \end{cases}$, $x_1 \geq 0, x_2 \geq 0$

17.3

1. (a) $x = 0$ and $y = 3$ gives max $= 21$. See Fig. A17.3.1(a), where the optimum is at P.
(b) min $20u_1 + 21u_2$ subject to $\begin{cases} 4u_1 + 3u_2 \geq 2 \\ 5u_1 + 7u_2 \geq 7 \end{cases}$, $u_1 \geq 0, u_2 \geq 0$
has the solution $u_1 = 0$ and $u_2 = 1$, which gives min $= 21$. See Fig. A17.3.1(b).   (c) Yes.

Figure A17.3.1(a)

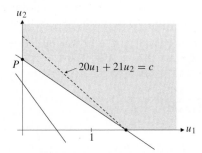

Figure A17.3.1(b)

3. (a) The profit from selling x_1 small and x_2 medium television sets is $400x_1 + 500x_2$. The first constraint, $2x_1 + x_2 \leq 16$, says that we cannot use more hours in division 1 than the hours available. The other constraints have similar interpretations.   (b) The solution is: max $= 3800$ for $x_1 = 7$ and $x_2 = 2$. (Supply your own graph.)   (c) Relaxing the first constraint to $2x_1 + x_2 \leq 17$ allows the new solution $x_1 = 23/3$, $x_2 = 5/3$, with an extra profit of 100. Relaxing the second constraint to $x_1 + 4x_2 \leq 17$ makes no difference, because some capacity in division 2 remained unused anyway. Relaxing the third constraint to $x_1 + 2x_2 \leq 12$ allows the solution $x_1 = 20/3$, $x_2 = 8/3$, with an extra profit of 200. So division 3 should have its capacity increased.

17.4

1. According to formula (2), $\Delta z^* = u_1^* \Delta b_1 + u_2^* \Delta b_2 = 0 \cdot 0.1 + 1 \cdot (-0.2) = -0.2$.

17.5

1. $4u_1^* + 3u_2^* = 3 > 2$ and $x^* = 0$; $5u_1^* + 7u_2^* = 7$ and $y^* = 3 > 0$. Also $4x^* + 5y^* = 15 < 20$ and $u_1^* = 0$; $3x^* + 7y^* = 21$ and $u_2^* = 1 > 0$. So we see that (1) and (2) are satisfied.

3. (a) min $10\,000y_1 + 8\,000y_2 + 11\,000y_3$ subject to $\begin{cases} 10y_1 + 20y_2 + 20y_3 \geq 300 \\ 20y_1 + 10y_2 + 20y_3 \geq 500 \end{cases}$, $y_1 \geq 0, y_2 \geq 0, y_3 \geq 0$
(b) Solution of the dual: max $= 255\,000$ for $x_1 = 100$ and $x_2 = 450$. Solution of the primal: min $= 255\,000$ for $(y_1, y_2, y_3) = (20, 0, 5)$.   (c) The minimum cost will increase by 2000.

Review Problems for Chapter 17

1. (a) Let x_1 and x_2 denote the number of A games and B games to be produced, respectively. Then the problem is:

$$\max 30x_1 + 20x_2 \text{ subject to } \begin{cases} 6x_1 + 3x_2 \le 54 \\ 4x_1 + 6x_2 \le 48 \\ 5x_1 + 5x_2 \le 50 \end{cases}, \quad x_1 \ge 0, \, x_2 \ge 0$$

Solution: $x_1 = 8$, $x_2 = 2$.

(b) The dual problem is:

$$\min 54u_1 + 48u_2 + 50u_3 \text{ subject to } \begin{cases} 6u_1 + 4u_2 + 5u_3 \ge 30 \\ 3u_1 + 6u_2 + 5u_3 \ge 20 \end{cases}, \quad u_1 \ge 0, u_2 \ge 0, u_3 \ge 0$$

Solution: $u_1 = 10/3$, $u_2 = 0$, $u_3 = 2$.

3. (a) For $a = 0$ the problem is an LP problem with solution at P, where $(x_1, x_2) = (2000, 2000/3)$; see Fig. A17.R.3.

(b) With the Lagrangian $\mathcal{L}(x_1, x_2) = (500 - ax_1)x_1 + 250x_2 - \lambda_1(0.04x_1 + 0.03x_2) - \lambda_2(0.025x_1 + 0.05x_2) - \lambda_3(0.05x_1) - \lambda_4(0.08x_2)$, the Kuhn–Tucker conditions are: There exist numbers $\lambda_1 \ge 0$, $\lambda_2 \ge 0$, $\lambda_3 \ge 0$, and $\lambda_4 \ge 0$ such that

$$500 - 2ax_1 - 0.04\lambda_1 - 0.025\lambda_2 - 0.05\lambda_3 \le 0 \quad (= 0 \text{ if } x_1 > 0)$$

$$250 - 0.03\lambda_1 - 0.05\lambda_2 - 0.08\lambda_4 \le 0 \quad (= 0 \text{ if } x_2 > 0)$$

$$\lambda_1 \ge 0 \ (\lambda_1 = 0 \quad \text{if} \quad 0.04x_1 + 0.03x_2 < 100)$$

$$\lambda_2 \ge 0 \ (\lambda_2 = 0 \quad \text{if} \quad 0.025x_1 + 0.05x_2 < 100)$$

$$\lambda_3 \ge 0 \ (\lambda_3 = 0 \quad \text{if} \quad 0.05x_1 < 100)$$

$$\lambda_4 \ge 0 \ (\lambda_4 = 0 \quad \text{if} \quad 0.08x_2 < 100)$$

(c) Same solution as in (a) for $a \le 1/24$. (At $(x_1, x_2) = (2000, 2000/3)$ the 2nd and 4th constraints are satisfied with strict inequality, so $\lambda_2 = \lambda_4 = 0$. Moreover, since x_1 and x_2 are positive, the first two constraints in (b) are satisfied with equality. Thus, $500 - 4000a - 0.04\lambda_1 = 0.05\lambda_3$ and $250 - 0.03\lambda_1 = 0$. It follows that $\lambda_1 = 25000/3$ and $0.05\lambda_3 = 500/3 - 4000a$ is nonnegative iff $a \le 1/24$. Since it is easily seen that the Lagrangian is concave and $(2000, 2000/3)$ satisfies all the Kuhn–Tucker conditions for all $a \le 1/24$, the conclusion follows.)

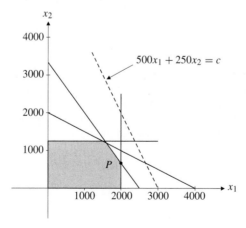

Figure A17.R.3

INDEX